THE CATHEDRAL LIBRARIES CATALOGUE

Books printed before 1701
in the libraries of
the Anglican Cathedrals of England and Wales

VOLUME ONE

Books printed in the British Isles and British America
and English books printed elsewhere

By Margaret S.G. McLeod (née Hands)
and others

Edited and completed by
Karen I. James
and
David J. Shaw
(Editor-in-Chief)

THE BRITISH LIBRARY

THE BIBLIOGRAPHICAL SOCIETY

© 1984 The Bibliographical Society

Published by
The British Library
Reference Division Publications
Great Russell Street
London WC1B 3DG

in association with the Bibliographical Society

 British Library Cataloguing in Publication Data

McLeod, Margaret S.G.
    The cathedral libraries catalogue.
    Vol. 1 : Books printed in the British Isles
    and British America and English books
    printed elsewhere
    1. Bibliography — Early printed books —
    Catalogs
    I. Title   II. James, Karen I.
    III. Shaw, David J.
    001'.44   Z1012

    ISBN 0-7123-0038-4

Computer-typeset by David Shaw at the
University of Kent at Canterbury,
with output generated on a Monotype
Lasercomp at Oxford University Computing
Service

Printed on acid-free paper in an edition of 500 copies

Printed and bound in England by Redwood Burn Ltd, Trowbridge

£30. — 00.

THE CATHEDRAL LIBRARIES CATALOGUE

VOLUME ONE

Contents

Foreword   vii

Introduction   ix

List of Cathedrals catalogued   xix

Abbreviations   xxi

Locations of English books to 1640
as enumerated in Pollard and Redgrave's *Short-Title Catalogue*

Volume One   1

Volume Two   83

Locations of English books 1641—1700
as enumerated in Wing's *Short-Title Catalogue*

Volume One   136

Volume Two   240

Volume Three   324

English books to 1640 not in Pollard and Redgrave's
Short-Title Catalogue   415

English books 1641—1700 not in Wing's *Short-Title Catalogue*   416

Locations of periodicals published 1641—1700   432

Locations of statutes published 1641—1700   438

FOREWORD

In the Preface to his *Notes on the Cathedral Libraries of England* published in 1849, Beriah Botfield wrote that whereas 'the History and Antiquities of the Cathedral Churches of England have been so often described and so profusely illustrated ... little or no mention occurs of the literary treasures contained within its precincts'. What Botfield sought to remedy, Miss Hands developed in detail. I have the honour and pleasure, on behalf of cathedral deans, chapters and librarians, to voice gratitude to all who have made possible the completion of the invaluable pioneering labours of Miss Hands. The collections of books in cathedral libraries have a special relationship with the place where they are and tell a story distinctive of the continuing community of each cathedral over the centuries. For many years to come, scholars will value the great assistance that they find for their researches from this Catalogue.

SYDNEY EVANS

Chairman of the Cathedral
Librarians' Conference

Salisbury
31st January 1984

Dean of Salisbury

INTRODUCTION

History of the Catalogue

The Cathedral Libraries Catalogue has been a long time in the making. In an article published in *The Library* (5, ii, 1947, pp. 1 – 13), Miss M.S.G. Hands, the Catalogue's creator, decribes the project's origins in the Oxford Inter-Collegiate Catalogue under Strickland Gibson in the thirties. In October 1943 the Bibliographical Society and the Pilgrim Trust were asked to support the creation of a Cathedral Libraries Catalogue. The Bibliographical Society's sponsorship of the project has been vital throughout, through the enthusiasm firstly of Sir Frank Francis during his time as the Society's Hon. Secretary and then of his successor, Mr R.J. Roberts.

The Pilgrim Trust provided finance for the project and in March 1944 Miss Hands started work at Worcester Cathedral where she worked until August of that year, cataloguing 3230 books printed before 1701. It was originally intended that all entries should be made in duplicate so that a copy could be left for each cathedral. This proved to be too time-consuming, though as late as 1956 Miss Hands was still trying to devise a way of providing such a record. The Society can now make good this debt through publication of the Catalogue, something which was only tentatively considered at the beginning of the project.

Miss Hands estimated that there were approximately 20,000 – 25,000 books to be catalogued and that the work could be completed in six years. In fact, this estimate must be doubled (at least) — this first volume contains about the same number of entries simply for the English books and the number of individual copies is far in excess of this. Consequently, when the grant from the Pilgrim Trust finally ran out after twelve years in 1956, Miss Hands had catalogued the early printed books of twenty-eight cathedrals. Several of the remaining libraries were known to be very large and the Society was for many years perplexed as to what steps it should take to see the catalogue completed.

The catalogue boxes were made available to scholars in the North Library at the British Museum Library, while the Society made frequent efforts to renew the impetus. Miss Hands had married (becoming Mrs McLeod) and a sick husband prevented her giving much time to the catalogue. In 1966 after his death she returned (at the age of 79) to deal with Carlisle Cathedral. Thereafter she still managed to continue with editorial work on the catalogue in the North Library. She died quite recently, in June 1979 (obituary in *The Library*, 6, ii, 1980, p.86). Present workers on the Catalogue would like to record their admiration for her astonishing achievement, the fruits of which they have inherited.

Before she died, Mrs McLeod was able to learn that the Society had at last managed to obtain a new source of subsidy for the project. The newly established British Library had been empowered to make grants to historical cataloguing projects and in 1976 the Society was successful in obtaining a grant to catalogue Salisbury and Wells. This work was undertaken by Miss Suzanne Eward (now Librarian at Salisbury) whose initial work at Salisbury in 1977 had been financed from the Society's own funds supplemented by a donation from the late Dr N.R. Ker and a grant from the British Academy. Some work at York was also undertaken as part of the British Library grant.

At the same time, the Dean and Chapter of Canterbury Cathedral obtained a British Library grant to catalogue the pre-1801 books at Canterbury, with a condition that cataloguing information should be supplied to the Cathedral Libraries Catalogue. Work at Canterbury was started in 1978 under the direction of Mr W.J. Simpson, the University Librarian, and Dr D.J. Shaw, a lecturer in French at the University and a member of the Bibliographical Society's Council. Mrs M. Brown and Miss K. James worked on the Canterbury material until mid 1980, preparing a MARC catalogue (MAchine Readable Catalogue) which is stored on the University computer at Canterbury.

Durham Cathedral also successfully asked the British Library for a cataloguing grant for the pre-1801 books, to be supervised by Dr A.I. Doyle, Keeper of Rare Books at Durham University Library, who was at that time Chairman of the Bibliographical Society's Cathedral Libraries Committee with Dr Shaw as his Secretary. The grant was again made conditional on submission of data for incorporation into the Union Catalogue. The work at Durham was done mainly by Miss S. Strongman (now Mrs Hingley), Mr R. Kornicki and Mr D. Pearson (who had previously given some voluntary help at Canterbury), directed by Miss E.M. Rainey.

By 1980, it was clear that completion of the Catalogue was sufficiently certain for thought to be given to publication. The outstanding tasks were to complete the cataloguing of the York material and to incorporate this and the Canterbury and Durham material into the catalogue boxes which Miss Eward had inherited at Salisbury and Wells. It was realised that the material would also require considerable editing, since it had its origin in several independent catalogue projects.

The Bibliographical Society once again applied to the British Library and was awarded a grant to edit the Catalogue and publish it in two volumes — a finding list of STC and Wing books (the English material), and a short-title catalogue of the continental material. The project was offered accommodation in the University Library at Canterbury and was to be processed on the University computer using the programs which Dr Shaw had developed for the Canterbury Cathedral project. Dr Shaw was asked to be Editor-in-Chief and Miss James transferred from the Canterbury Cathedral catalogue to work on the project as Editorial Assistant. The catalogue boxes were moved to Canterbury and work started on the English material in early 1981. The problem of the York material was soon resolved. The Bibliographical Society found monies from its own funds to have a list (rather than a catalogue) prepared for the pre-1701 English material for Volume One of the Catalogue. This work was done by David Pearson before he moved to Durham.

This account brings us to the publication (jointly by the Bibliographical Society and the British Library) of the first part of the Catalogue. There had been an earlier intention to produce a microfiche catalogue of Miss Hands's hand-written slips, but the addition of the Canterbury, Durham and York material, all on slips of different physical size and layout, made this impracticable. We hope that the present solution of splitting the catalogue into English and continental sections and using computer methods to store and print the catalogue will offer scholars a usable end-product at an acceptable price.

Scope of the Catalogue

At its simplest, the scope of this volume of the Catalogue is the English books printed before 1701 in the English and Welsh Anglican cathedral libraries. It covers the same ground as (and acts as a supplement to) the Bibliographical Society's *Short-title Catalogue of books printed in England Scotland & Ireland and of English books printed abroad, 1475 – 1640* (STC), now being issued in a second, enlarged and revised edition, and Donald Wing's similar *Short-title Catalogue* for the period 1641 – 1700, also currently undergoing revision at Yale. Our Catalogue additionally lists periodical material for the whole period (included by STC but excluded by Wing), and Statutes for the Wing period. The following Anglican libraries, often mentioned in conjunction with the cathedrals, have not been included in the Catalogue: Christ Church Cathedral, Oxford (which is included as a college library in the Oxford Inter-Collegiate Catalogue); Lambeth Palace Library; St George's Chapel, Windsor (of which a printed catalogue was published in 1976); Westminster Abbey; and some modern foundations without a library of the traditional type.

So far as completeness is concerned, a number of qualifications must be made, mostly resulting from the particular nature of the cathedral libraries and especially from their frequent lack of permanent specialised staff. An entry in this catalogue cannot guarantee the presence of the book in a particular library today. The book will have been seen in that library by Miss Hands or one of her successors at some time between 1944 and early 1984, but it could have been lost, mislaid or otherwise disposed of since. The local catalogues of individual cathedrals are of very variable quality and several have radically changed their shelving arrangements since their books were entered in the Cathedral Libraries Catalogue. It could well be that a particular book is still in its library but cannot for the moment be located, especially in the case of pamphlet material (which is abundantly represented in this volume). Only recently, Canterbury received a request for information about a binding which was specified by pre-war shelfmark but not by author or title. As the whole library had been rebuilt and reshelved as a result of wartime bombing, it will not prove easy to trace the item. For the most part, of course, these problems will not arise, but scholars wishing to consult books in cathedral libraries should not be unaware of the potential difficulties.

We have attempted to make enquiries about possible dispersals. Fortunately, it seems that there have been very few in the post-war period for the early printed books. The one serious case is the regrettable sale of much of the Ely Cathedral Library. Here, we have checked the lists of that portion of the Ely books which was, happily, acquired by Cambridge University Library but have listed the Ely books in full as Miss Hands recorded them in 1945, since this does help to give a record of the contents of a now defunct library. In the case of deposits of books elsewhere, we also continue to record them under the name of the cathedral in question. For example, Peterborough (deposited at Cambridge) is still recorded as Peterborough.

As to the comprehensiveness of our records, we cannot pretend to have every book which should have been included. Given the frequent inadequacy of local catalogues, work has always been done directly from the shelves and always with the goodwill and advice of the local Canon Librarian or his staff. However, books are not always on their shelves at the right time; they may have been borrowed by one of the canons or otherwise be away from the library. In any cathedral library there is always the possibility that some odd corner has been used by a previous librarian to store books, which is unknown to the present incumbent. Some printed material can often be found in the cathedral archives: it is our feeling that it has rarely been possible to find time to search such a source. Finally, there must remain the fear that occasional catalogue slips might have been lost during the catalogue's long peripatetic existence or during its time of rest at the British Library. The second edition of STC lists cathedral locations which we cannot find in Miss Hands's records. Where it has not been possible to verify these in the time available, we have omitted them from this catalogue.

While the main cathedral collections have always been recorded, the treatment of deposited smaller collections may not have been consistent during the long period of work on the Catalogue. Our impression is that deposits of parish libraries, for example, have been included where they are considered to have become a permanent part of the cathedral library but that other less closely associated collections will have been excluded.

One further question is that of accuracy. Our basic data come from a variety of sources (mainly Miss Hands's and Miss Eward's work and the entries supplied by Canterbury, Durham and York). Every entry has been checked against STC or Wing for the allocation of the appropriate identifying number and at this stage we have sometimes been able to raise queries with individual libraries. It has clearly not been practicable to query every single variant. In view of the frequency of variation in early printing, we generally assume that our cataloguing information is correct and record variation as we find it. Particularly with Wing, where the level of detail is less than with STC, we would recommend caution in assuming that a record of variation always means a genuine new or variant edition. We suspect that the variation may sometimes be due to inadequate transcription on one part or the other.

We remain confident that deficiencies due to these various causes are small and that this volume and its successor overwhelmingly represent the true holdings of the cathedral libraries.

Using Volume One of the Catalogue

Most of the Catalogue takes the form of references to STC and to Wing and it is expected that it will be used in conjunction with them. There are two main sections, for STC books and for Wing books, subdivided by volume. These show, in the form of finding lists, the cathedrals' holdings of known STC and Wing items. Most of the Catalogue's new material is also to be found in these two main sections, where new editions or variant issues of known STC or Wing items are recorded. We have brought into separate sections the totally new material; that is, titles previously not recorded at all. These have been given a much fuller form of entry, under a heading corresponding to the style used in STC or Wing. This completely new material consists mostly of Wing items, since the revisers of the second edition of STC have drawn on the Catalogue and new material has also been communicated to them by a number of cathedrals. This has also happened with Wing material, but to a lesser extent.

Since STC lists Newsbooks, etc. whereas Wing does not, we have provided a separate section of periodical material for 1641 – 1700. In doing this we have been much helped by Dr M. Seccombe of the Wing Revision team who is himself working on a catalogue of Wing periodical material. We have been able to draw on pre-publication material from his *Short-Title Catalogue of British Serials, 1641 – 1700* for reference numbers and for cross-references to alternative headings. We have also brought together in a separate section the Wing period Statutes so as to give fuller information about this material which is not dealt with very consistently by Wing.

The following notes explain our method of recording entries.

NUMBER

The first item of each entry, given in bold type, is the STC or Wing number. In the case of STC, this is taken from the second edition of volume two and from the proofs of the second edition of volume one (for letters A – G) or from the typescript (for letter H). For Wing entries, we have used the second edition of volume two. We have not used the second edition of volume one, since its numbering system is inconsistent with that of the first edition and general preference has been to retain the numbers of the first edition. However, entries new to the first edition of Wing and present in the second edition have been inserted in their appropriate position in the first edition numbering sequence, with a reference to the second edition, where the detailed entry will be found. The Wing Revision Project intends to reissue volume one in a revised form following the practices it has adopted for volumes two and three.

After the number may be found one of the following symbols:

+ and - are used to indicated the relative position of new items with respect to the existing STC and Wing numbers. The section of entries for Wing S2043 – 60 shows a typical example (John Scott's *The Christian life*) where we have added a number of new or variant entries into Wing's sequence. We have not wanted to devise our own new numbers since this would lead to confusion if different numbers had to be adopted when the items came to be incorporated into new editions of STC or Wing. All of our numbers are in fact unique as we allow sequences of + or -. For example, a sequence such as 123 - - - 123 - - 123 - 123 123 + 123 + + 123 + + + is theoretically possible.

? is used (mainly in Wing entries) to indicate that although there are discrepancies between our entries and Wing, we think it likely that the number should be allocated to the book and that the differences are due to error on Wing's part. A note of the discrepancies is given. Where there is clear evidence of an error in Wing, we have assigned the number without a query and again have listed the discrepancies.

When numbers are quoted for the new material in this catalogue, we should like them to be preceded by the abbreviation CLC.

HEADING

We have given for each entry a brief heading, taken (sometimes abbreviated or modified) from STC or Wing as appropriate. We hope that this will improve the readability of the Catalogue and also that, together with the date, it will help to act as a check on any remaining misprints in the numbers, by showing an item which is not in its correct place. We have generally retained the wording and spelling, etc. of the form of heading found in STC and Wing, even when this results in inconsistencies between the sections or in forms of heading which we would not ideally choose.

DATE

As with the heading, the date is generally as given in STC and Wing, including inferred dates in square brackets. For new material, we have tried to follow STC practice of giving colophon dates in parentheses.

NOTES

Where necessary, we give brief notes to indicate the nature of variations from the STC or Wing entry to which we are relating the item. These notes are not necessarily intended to be comprehensible without reference to the detailed wording of the original entry. Information noted includes pagination, format, edition statement, and variant title or imprint information. Variants are often noted as a single word; its significance should be clear on reference to the original entry. We have tried to distinguish title variants from imprint variants by enclosing the former in single quotes and by citing the latter without quotation marks.

The different practices of STC and of Wing have been followed in the respective sections of the Catalogue. In notes concerning titles, we indicate where STC Volume One in the first edition has silently omitted words within the opening five words of the title; for the rest of the title, we indicate only errors of spelling, etc. Wing's practice of making no silent omissions of title information has been followed for Wing entries. In notes concerning imprints, for STC we follow STC's practice of abbreviation, but for Wing imprints we follow Wing in giving full Christian names, etc. Wing has given all edition statements (in whatever language or form) in a standardised English form. It is assumed that users of Wing are familiar with this practice. Accordingly, the edition statement as given in the book is only noted where Wing has omitted it; for new entries; or to emphasise the presence of an edition statement on the title-page where Wing has given it in quotation marks.

HOLDINGS

The cathedrals recorded as holding a copy of the book are listed in alphabetical order. The abbreviations used are explained at the end of the Introduction. For each cathedral, there may be a note in parentheses giving details of imperfections, e.g. Ex (tpw), or the number of copies held, e.g. Cant (4), or a combination of both, e.g. Linc (2 − 1 imp), or other details, usually relating to the Notes section. These notes should be self-explanatory. The asterisk * is used where it has proved impossible to assign a book to a particular number. This may be because the book is imperfect or because of insufficient evidence in the bibliography in question or because STC now makes a distinction between numbers which the information in our catalogue entries does not enable us to make.

Production of the Catalogue

It might be of interest to give a brief, non-technical account of the way this volume of the Catalogue has been produced. The data are stored on the University of Kent's ICL 2960 computer. A set of programs was prepared to handle a simple database in which each record consisted of five fields: reference number, heading, date, notes (optional), and locations. The first program guides the keyboarder when typing in the data from the catalogue slips which have been checked and marked up and also produces printout for initial proofing. An interactive editor for the database allows corrections, changes and additions to be made as required. For example, this editor has made it a simple matter to add new locations to existing entries in the database as we have received them from collaborators. The order of preparation of material is of no consequence to the computer as it can sort the database into numerical order of STC or Wing number whenever necessary. This has enabled us to proceed with straightforward material and to leave queries and difficult items until later: we did not at first enter any of the material requiring greek type, preferring to handle these entries in a single block and merge them into their correct place.

The next stage of proof-reading was done using a small laser printer made available in the Computing Laboratory at Canterbury which produced roman, italic and bold type in several sizes and also some of the additional special characters needed. A program was written which combined the material from the database with commands to make the laser printer take appropriate actions (change fount, change point size, flush to a new line, indent, print an accented character, print a superior character, etc.) This output enabled us to make a final check for literals and for typographical presentation.

The final form of the Catalogue was produced on a Monotype Lasercomp photo-typesetter at the University of Oxford Computing Centre. Once again, a program was prepared to read the database and generate a mixture of data and typesetting commands to drive the Lasercomp. This time, the program had to produce the correct column widths and depths, three columns to the page, with running titles, without breaking entries over the column ends. The film-set output was then dispatched to the printer.

On the whole this seems to have worked successfully. If the reader notices any small imperfections due to this method of automated production, he should blame the Editor-in-Chief, not the computer, but he should also consider the considerable savings of cost which have been achieved over more conventional methods and the unlikelihood of the Catalogue appearing in any other form at all.

Most of the programs were written by the Editor-in-Chief in the programming language BCPL running under the EMAS operating system on the University Computer. Specialised software to drive the photo-typesetters was made available by colleagues in the Electronic Publishing Research Unit at Canterbury and by the Lasercomp Service at the Oxford University Computing Centre.

Statistics

For those who like such things, we are able to offer some statistics on the survival of the STC and Wing material in the cathedral libraries. These figures have been produced automatically by the computer from the database for the material in the main STC and Wing sections. The other sections (Periodicals and Statutes) were not stored in the same way and so are not included in the counts.

Globally, there are 8,017 entries for STC and 17,837 for Wing, a total of 25,854 entries, representing (more or less) the number of editions in the catalogue. Of these entries, 1,637 are new ones (whose numbers have a + or −), there being 38 for STC and 1,599 for Wing. The number of separate copies recorded is 15,260 for STC (an average of 1.9 per edition) and 37,645 for Wing (an average of 2.1). The total number of copies in the catalogue is 52,905.

As the statistics of survival for early printed books are of some interest to historians of printing and to social historians, we provide a fuller analysis of the two sets of data, showing the number of editions surviving in 1, 2, 3, ... copies.

	STC	Wing		STC	Wing
1	4,836	10,059	19	3	11
2	1,636	3,566	20	1	4
3	684	1,671	21	2	2
4	328	955	22	0	1
5	188	554	23	0	1
6	121	357	24	0	0
7	64	178	25	0	1
8	41	133	26	0	3
9	35	94	27	0	1
10	32	73	28	0	0
11	16	44	29	0	0
12	10	42	30	0	0
13	4	32	31	0	0
14	6	19	32	0	2
15	5	10	33	0	1
16	2	13	34	0	0
17	1	5	35	0	1
18	2	4			

Not surprisingly, by far the largest single group is the group of editions surviving (in this catalogue) in only one copy: 60 per cent of the STC items, and 56 per cent of the Wing items. The missing category in these data is for editions surviving in no copies. We invite statisticians to investigate the distributions shown in the table and to try to estimate the size of this zero category. (Would this figure, added to the figure for the total cathedral holdings, represent an estimate of the output of the English booktrade to 1700?)

A further satisfaction for the curious is provided by asking the computer to identify the most popular books in the catalogue. The survival figures given (as in the table above) do not always indicate the number of cathedrals owning the book, as there are many examples of multiple copies (in some cases as many as five or more copies in one cathedral).

For STC, the list of best-sellers is:

1 =	14629a	John, *Chrysostom, Saint*, Τα ευρισκομενα, 1613. (21 copies).
1 =	15298	William Laud, *A relation of the conference betweene William Lawd, and Mr Fisher the Jesuite*, 1639. (21 copies).
3	25382	Francis White, *A replie to jesuit Fishers answere*, 1624. (20 copies).
4 =	602	Lancelot Andrewes, *Opuscula quædam posthuma*, 1629. (19 copies).
4 =	18033	Richard Montague, *Apparatus ad origines ecclesiasticas*, 1635. (19 copies).
4 =	23066	Sir Henry Spelman, *Concilia, decreta, leges, constitutiones, in re ecclesiarum orbis Britannici*, 1639. (19 copies).
7 =	17598	Francis Mason, *Vindiciæ ecclesiæ Anglicanæ*, 1625. (18 copies).
7 =	25223	John Weever, *Ancient funerall monuments*, 1631. (18 copies).
9	18037	Richard Montagu, *Diatribæ upon the first part of of the late history of tithes*, 1621. (17 copies).
10 =	3534	Thomas Bradwardine, *De causa Dei, contra Pelagium, et de virtute causarum, libri tres*, 1618. (16 copies).
10 =	5821	Richard Cosin, *An apologie for sundrie proceedings*, 1593. (16 copies).

For Wing, the corresponding figures are:

1	B2797	Bible, *Biblia sacra polyglotta*, 1657. (35 copies).
2	B3622	Book, *Book of Common Prayer*, By His Ma:^{ties} printers, 1662. (33 copies).
3 =	C1224+	Edmund Castell, *Lexicon heptaglotton*, 1669. (32 copies).
3 =	P2853+	Matthew Poole, *Synopsis criticorum*, 5 vols, fol., 1669−76. (32 copies).
5	F2416	Thomas Fuller, *The church-history of Britain*, 1655. (27 copies).
6 =	B2115	William Beveridge, Συνοδικον *sive pandectae*, 1672. (26 copies).
6 =	L3565	William Lyndwood, *Provinciale*, 1679, fol. (26 copies).
6 =	O607	John Overall, *Bishop Overall's convocation-book*, 1690. (26 copies).
9	W1560	Henry Wharton, *Anglia sacra*, 1691. (25 copies).
10	C7711	St Cyprian, *Opera*, 1682. (23 copies).

Access to Cathedral Libraries

It is likely that the publication of this Catalogue will increase the demands made on the resources of the cathedral libraries. We would ask those who need to access to early printed books in person or who request postal information to remember that the cathedral libraries are not public libraries. Only a few of them have full-time professional staff. Some have no staff at all and any requests made must be dealt with by the Canon Librarian who will have many other claims on his time. A query of some bibliographical complexity is likely to be very taxing for an untrained volunteer. Requests about individual books should include full details of author, title, imprint, etc. (and not simply STC or Wing number) since many libraries simply do not own copies of the standard reference works.

Equally, the cathedrals (contrary to popular belief) do not enjoy vast revenues. The courtesy of a stamped addressed envelope for a reply would always be appreciated.

Several cathedrals do have professional staff, in some cases provided by a local university library. Here, a wider range of technical help might be expected. At the time of writing, the cathedrals with resident specialist staff include Canterbury, Chichester, Durham, Hereford, Lincoln, Salisbury, St Paul's and York, and of course those specialist libraries where some cathedral collections are deposited. Exeter, Lichfield, Ripon, Rochester, Winchester, and Worcester have access to occasional specialist help.

Acknowledgments

The Bibliographical Society would like to thank the several bodies which have made grants to the Cathedral Libraries Catalogue: the Pilgrim Trust which financed the first twelve years of work, the British Academy which helped to prime the pump when a new drive to complete the Catalogue was being attempted, and the British Library which has not only financed the editorial work on the Catalogue but also through its separate grants to Canterbury and Durham cathedrals enabled these two libraries to contribute entries. Thanks are also due to the Canon Librarians and their staff who have assisted the project during the last forty years.

Within the Bibliographical Society, mention should be made of the many officers who have given of their time to try to keep the project alive when it seemed in difficulties or who gave of their time when the project was prospering and required discussion, negotiations and decisions. The past and present chairmen of the Ecclesiastical Libraries Committee, Ian Doyle and Anthony Hobson, have both been of especial help to the Editor in Chief.

At the British Library, Miss Doris Crews and Dr Richard Christophers deserve the thanks of the bibliographical community for the support and encouragement they have offered the Catalogue and cathedral libraries in general while administering the Library's funds for external cataloguing projects.

The Bibliographical Society is indebted to the University of Kent at Canterbury on several grounds. The University Librarian, Mr Will Simpson, has provided the project with office space for the past three years and has constantly helped and supported us. The Finance Office in the University Registry has administered the project's funds on behalf of the Bibliographical Society. The Director of the Computing Laboratory, Professor Brian Spratt, has made invaluable computing resources available for the project and given us his support. Several members of his staff, in particular Mr Bob Eager, have offered encouragement in general and practical help at times of need. Members of the French Board of Studies deserve thanks for tolerating the activities of a colleague whose enthusiasms for early printing and for computing must sometimes seem to take him a long way from the line of duty.

The Editor-in-Chief would personally like to thank those who have worked with him on Volume One, especially his full-time editorial assistant, Karen James, on whose diligence and skills the success of the project has constantly depended.

David Shaw

Canterbury
1 September 1984

List of Cathedrals catalogued

The following list shows the abbreviations used for each library whose books are included in the Catalogue and indicates the date and cataloguer, the number of STC books and Wing books, and notes on modern published catalogues, sales, deposits, etc.

Ban Bangor. 1949, Miss Hands. 74 STC, 847 Wing. Deposited at University College of Wales, Bangor. Published catalogue, 1961.

Brec Brecon. 1947, Miss Hands. 5 STC, 8 Wing.

Bris Bristol. 1947, 1948, Miss Hands. 32 STC, 160 Wing. Some books sold in 1961.

Bur Bury St Edmunds. 1945, Miss Hands. 291 STC, 355 Wing. In Suffolk parochial libraries catalogue, published 1977.

Cant Canterbury. 1978 – 82, Mrs M. Brown and Miss K. James, with contributions from Dr D.J. Shaw, Mr D. Pearson, Mr A.D. Whiting and others, as part of a catalogue project funded by the British Library. 1,228 STC, 3,401 Wing.

Carl Carlisle. 1966, Mrs McLeod (Miss Hands). 393 STC, 2,767 Wing.

Chelm Chelmsford. 1953, Miss Hands. 80 STC, 407 Wing.

Ches Chester. 1949, Miss Hands. 178 STC, 604 Wing.

Chi Chichester. 1954, Miss Hands. 111 STC, 308 Wing.

Derb Derby. Miss Hands?, date unknown. 5 STC, 0 Wing.

Dur Durham. 1978 – 1982, Mr R. Kornicki, Miss E.M. Rainey, Miss S. Strongman (Mrs Hingley), Mr D. Pearson, as part of catalogue project funded by the British Library. 314 STC, 2,023 Wing.

Ely Ely. 1945, Miss Hands. 187 STC, 1,044 Wing. The library was sold in 1972, after many of the early printed books had been selected by Cambridge University Library. The Ely references have all been retained in the Catalogue.

Ex Exeter. 1947 – 49, Miss Hands. 558 STC, 2,586 Wing.

Glo Gloucester. 1953, Miss Hands. 227 STC, 438 Wing. Published catalogue (1972) prepared by Miss S. Eward, 1968 – 72.

Her Hereford. 1947 – 48, Miss Hands. 412 STC, 848 Wing.

IoM Isle of Man (Peel). 1953, Miss Hands. 9 STC, 31 Wing.

Lich Lichfield. 1954, Miss Hands. 171 STC, 579 Wing.

Linc Lincoln. 1944 – 46, Miss Hands. 1,608 STC, 2,700 Wing. Published catalogue (1983) prepared by Mr C. Hurst as part of catalogue project funded by the British Library.

Liv Liverpool. 1956, Miss Hands. 157 STC, 232 Wing. Published catalogue, 1968. Deposited in the University Library.

Llan Llandaff. 1949, Miss Hands. 28 STC, 358 Wing. Deposited in the National Library of Wales.

New Newcastle. 1951 – 52, Miss Hands. 53 STC, 83 Wing. Mostly deposited in the University Library.

Nor   Norwich.   1955, Miss Hands. 160 STC, 984 Wing.

Pet   Peterborough.   1950–52, Miss Hands. 2,440 STC, 2,112 Wing. Deposited in Cambridge University Library.

Rip   Ripon.   1952, Miss Hands. 199 STC, 132 Wing.

Roch   Rochester.   1952, Miss Hands. 80 STC, 156 Wing. Currently being recatalogued by Mr A. Wellard as part of a catalogue project funded by the British Library.

S Alb   St Albans.   1947, Miss Hands. 15 STC, 36 Wing.

S Asa   St Asaph.   1949, Miss Hands. 138 STC, 993 Wing. Deposited at the National Library of Wales.

S Dv   St David's.   1947, Miss Hands. 34 STC, 153 Wing.

S Pl   St Paul's, London. 1953–55, Miss Hands. 756 STC, 1,602 Wing.

Sal   Salisbury.   1977–79, Miss S. Eward. 544 STC, 1,358 Wing.

Swar   Southwark.   1945, Miss Hands. 9 STC, 5 Wing.

Swel   Southwell.   1946, Miss Hands. 74 STC, 265 Wing.

Tru   Truro.   1948, Miss Hands. 39 STC, 41 Wing.

Wel   Wells.   1980, Miss S. Eward. 187 STC, 1,412 Wing.

Win   Winchester.   1952, Miss Hands. 248 STC, 1,308 Wing. Currently being recatalogued by Mr R. Osmond as part of a catalogue project funded by the British Library.

Wor   Worcester.   1944, Miss Hands. 701 STC, 774 Wing.

Yk   York.   1981, Mr D. Pearson; 1982–83, Dr D.J. Shaw and Mrs C. Fieldhouse; previous work done by Miss J. Williams and Mr C.B.L. Barr. 2,288 STC, 4,097 Wing.

Abbreviations

addit.	additional	fol.	folio
anr ed.	another edition	frag.	fragment
B.L.	black letter	imp.	imperfect
BL	British Library	impr.	imprint
BM	British Museum	n.d.	no date
	General Catalogue of Printed Books	n.pl	no place
brs.	broadside	pr.	printed
cap.	caption title	rom.	roman
col.	column	sep.	separate
d.	died	s.sh.	single sheet
ed.	editor, edited, edition	suppl.	supplement
engr.	engraved	tp	title-page
fl.	floruit	tpw	title-page wanting

Aldis	Harry G. Aldis, *A list of books printed in Scotland before 1700*. Edinburgh, 1970.
Allison & Rogers	A.F. Allison and D.M. Rogers, *A catalogue of Catholic books in English printed abroad or secretly in England, 1558—1640*. London, 1964.
Almack	Edward Almack, *A bibliography of The King's Book or Eikon Basilike*. London, 1896.
Evans	C. Evans, *American bibliography*. Chicago, 1903.
Greg	W.W. Greg, *A bibliography of the English printed drama to the Restoration*. London, 1939—1959, 4 vols.
Macdonald & Hargreaves	H.Macdonald and M. Hargreaves, *Thomas Hobbes, a bibliography*. London, 1952.
Madan, *Milton*	F.F. Madan, 'Milton, Salmasius, and Dugard', *The Library*, 4th series, iv, 1923—24
Madan	*Oxford books, a bibliography of printed works relating to the University and City of Oxford or printed or published there*. Oxford, 1895—1931, 3 vols.
NUC	*National Union Catalogue: pre-1956 imprints*. [London], 1968--80.
STC	*A Short-Title Catalogue of books printed in England, Scotland, & Ireland and of English books printed abroad, 1475—1640*, first compiled by A.W.Pollard & G.R. Redgrave; second edition, revised and enlarged begun by W.A. Jackson & F.S. Ferguson, completed by Katharine F. Panzer. Vol. 1: London, 1976; vol. 2: in proof.
Tuer	A.W. Tuer, *History of the horn book*. London, 1896.
Wing	*Short-Title Catalogue of books printed in England, Scotland, Ireland, Wales, and British America and of English books printed in other countries, 1641—1700*, compiled by Donald Wing. New York, 1945-1951, 3 vols; vol. 2, revised and edited by Timothy J. Crist (and others), New York, 1982.

Locations of English books to 1640
as enumerated in Pollard and Redgrave's *Short-Title Catalogue*
Volume One

1 A., [1593]
'The passoinate [*sic*] morrice' (heading B1[r]).
Pet (tpw).

4 A., J., 1631
Bur. Linc. Wor. Yk.

13 A., O., 1624
8°.
Pet (imp).

14 A., R., 1600
Harison.
Linc.

21.5 A.B.C., [c.1620]
[*Hornbook*. The A.B.C. with the Lord's Prayer] s.sh. 8°; A. Tuer, *History of the Horn-book*, no.140.
S Asa.

22.3 A.B.C., 1571
Formerly STC 18793; Title and impr. in Irish.
Linc.

27 Abbot, George, *Abp*, 1608
Pet.

30 Abbot, George, *Abp*, 1624
The sixt edition; f. J. Marriot.
Linc.

31.5 Abbot, George, *Abp*, 1635
[Anr ed.] 12°; f. W. Sheares.
Yk.

34 Abbot, George, *Abp*, 1600
Pet.

34.5 Abbot, George, *Abp*, 1600
[Variant] R. Field.
Pet. Yk.

35 Abbot, George, *Abp*, 1613
Carl. Linc. New. Yk.

36 Abbot, George, *Abp*, 1598
Chelm. Dur. Pet. Wor. Yk.

37 Abbot, George, *Abp*, 1604
'The reasons which ...'
Pet. Wor. Yk.

38 Abbot, George, *Abp*, 1608
'A sermon preached at Westminster May 26. 1608. At the funerall ...';
A3[r] catchword: 'it'
Pet (imp).

38.5 Abbot, George, *Abp*, 1608
[Anr issue] A3[r] catchword: 'ted'
Pet (imp).

39 Abbot, George, *Abp*, 1624
Milbourne's address in impr.
Linc*.

39.3 Abbot, George, *Abp*, 1624
[Variant] Without Milbourne's address; Preface ends A4[r].
Pet. Win.

40 Abbot, George, *Abp*, 1624
Yk.

41 Abbot, George, *Religious writer*, 1640
'booke'
Yk.

42 Abbot, John, 1623
Yk.

43 Abbot, Robert, *Bp*, 1603
R. Barkerus.
Dur. Yk.

44 Abbot, Robert, *Bp*, 1608
R. Barkerus.
Sal. Win.

45 Abbot, Robert, *Bp*, 1613
'Antilogia adversus apologiam ...'
Dur. Pet. Sal. Wor. Yk.

46 Abbot, Robert, *Bp*, 1618
Cant. Dur (imp). Ex. Linc.
S Pl. Sal (2). Win. Yk.

47 Abbot, Robert, *Bp*, 1619
Win. Wor. Yk.

48 Abbot, Robert, *Bp*, 1606
'The first part'; 4°.
Her. Linc. Pet. Yk.

48.5 Abbot, Robert, *Bp*, 1611
[Anr ed. of pt 1] 4°; Imp. T. Adams.
Cant. Dur. Nor.

49 Abbot, Robert, *Bp*, 1607
Her. Linc (2). Pet. Sal.

50 Abbot, Robert, *Bp*, 1611
[Anr ed. of pt 2].
Cant. Dur. Nor. Yk.

50.5 Abbot, Robert, *Bp*, 1609
'The third part of the defence ...'; 4°;
Imp. G. Bishop.
Cant. Dur. Her. Linc. Nor.
Yk.

51 Abbot, Robert, *Bp*, 1601
Yk.

52 Abbot, Robert, *Bp*, 1594
Yk.

53 Abbot, Robert, *Bp*, 1610
Pet. Yk.

54 Abbot, Robert, *Bp*, 1611
Cant. Dur. Her. Yk (2).

55 Abbot, Robert, *Bp*, 1608
Pet. Yk.

56 Abbot, Robert, *Minister*, 1626
Pet (tp imp). Yk.

58 Abbot, Robert, *Minister*, 1639
Pet. Yk.

59 Abbot, Robert, *Minister*, 1623
Ex (imp).

59.7 Abbot, Robert, *Minister*, 1640
'The holinesse of Christian churches ...'; 12°; T. Paine f. P. Stephens a. C. Meredith; Collates F−G[12].
Carl.

60 Abbot, Robert, *Minister*, 1639
T. Payne f. P. Stephens a. C. Meredith.
Cant. Ex. Nor. Yk.

60.3 Abbot, Robert, *Minister*, 1636
'The young mans warning-peece ...'; 12°; R.B. f. P. Stephens a. C. Meredeth.
Yk.

64.5 Aberdeen University, 1638
Formerly STC 67.
Pet (2 −1 tpw*). S Pl. Yk.

65 Aberdeen, 1638
[R. Young], his majesties printer for Scotland.
Linc. S Pl. Win.

66 Aberdeen, 1638
(R. Young), his majesties printer for
Scotland.
Cant. Sal (2).

67 *See:* 64.5

68.5 Aberdeen, 1638
[Anr ed., with additions] 4°;
[Edinburgh?].
Yk.

69 Aberdeen, 1638
S Pl.

70 Aberdeen, 1638
Carl. Linc. S Pl.

71.23 Aberdeen University, 1637
Formerly STC 15356.
Yk.

72 Abernethie, Thomas, 1638
S Pl. Yk.

74 Abernethy, John, 1622
Yk.

75 Abernethy, John, 1630
Her. Linc. Pet.

80 Abraham, 1597
Pet. Sal.

81 *See:* 12357.7

89 Achilles Tatius, [1589?]
'Achillis Statii Alexandrini de
Clitophontis & Leucippes amorib. ...';
8°; Legat.
Pet.

92 Acontius, Jacobus, [1579?]
Ex.

93 Acontius, Jacobus, 1631
Pet (tpw)*.

94 Acosta, Joseph de, 1604
Yk.

99 Acworth, George, 1573
Lich*. Pet. Yk (imp).

99.5 Acworth, George, 1573
[Anr issue, with cancel tp] As STC 99
(which is anon.), but with author's
name on tp.
Linc. Pet*.

104 Adams, Thomas, 1629
'The workes of Tho: Adams'
Cant. Carl. Her.

106 Adams, Thomas, 1623
B1r catchword: 'the'
Chelm*. Pet.

106.5 Adams, Thomas, 1623
[Anr ed.] As STC 106, but B1r
catchword: 'on'
Pet.

107 Adams, Thomas, 1615
Cant (imp). Pet. Yk.

108 Adams, Thomas, 1633
'A commentary or, exposition upon
...'; 2 vols; 2°; R. Badger [a.] (F.
Kyngston) f. J. Bloome.
Glo. Linc. Pet. S Asa. Sal.
Win. Wor.

110.5 Adams, Thomas, 1614
[Anr issue] 'The devills banket.
Described in foure sermons'; T.
Snodham f. R. Mab.
Linc. Yk.

111 Adams, Thomas, 1616
Ex. Pet (tpw).

114 Adams, Thomas, 1615
... a. R. Mab.
Yk.

117 Adams, Thomas, 1612
S Pl.

119 Adams, Thomas, 1616
Pet.

120 Adams, Thomas, 1618
'happines'
Pet. S Pl. Yk.

122 Adams, Thomas, 1613
Cant (imp).

124 Adams, Thomas, 1615
Purslowe.
Cant. Pet (imp).

127 Adams, Thomas, 1617
Nor. Pet.

128 *See:* Pt 3 of 107

129 Adams, Thomas, 1624
Ex. S Pl.

130 Adams, Thomas, 1625
'The sermons preached'; A.
Matthewes a. J. Norton.
Linc (imp). Pet (imp).

131 Adams, Thomas, 1613
Pet.

131a Adams, Thomas, 1613
S Pl.

132 Adams, Thomas, 1614
Pet (tpw).

134 Adams, Thomas, 1621
Pet.

143 Adamson, John, 1623
Linc.

148.5 Adamson, Patrick, 1619
[Anr issue of STC 148, which has
verso of tp blank] 'Reverendissimi ...
Patricii Adamsoni ... Poëmata ...';
Ap. J. Billium; Royal arms on tp
verso.
Linc*.

152 Adrichem, Christiaan van, 1595
Yk (imp).

159 Aelfric, [1566?]
Preface unfoliated.
Cant. Nor.

159.5 Aelfric, [1566?]
[Anr ed.] As STC 159 but preface
foliated.
Cant (imp). Linc. Pet. Sal.

160 Aelfric, 1623
Cant. Chi. Linc. Wor. Yk
(imp).

160.5 Aelfric, 1638
Formerly STC 15705.
Cant. Ex. S Pl.

161 Aelianus, *Tacticus*, [1616]
'... Englished & illustrated ...';
'Contents' begin p. 5.
Ex*.

161.5 Aelianus, *Tacticus*, [1616]
[Anr issue] As STC 161, but
'Contents' begin on p. 6.
Cant.

163 Aelianus, *Tacticus*, 1631
Ex.

165.5 Aepinus, Joannes, [1548?]
[Anr issue of STC 166] 4°; [N.pl.].
Sal.

166 Aepinus, Joannes, 1549
Linc. Pet.

166.5 Aepinus, Joannes, [1548?]
Formerly STC 10429; '... fruitful &
godly ...'; (J. Daye).
Yk.

173.7 Aesop, 1633
[Anr ed.] 8°; Cantabrigiae ex acad.
typog.
Ex.

190 Affinati d'Acuto, Jacopo, 1605
Yk.

194 Agard, Arthur, 1631
'... records: remaining ... at ...'; Line
7 of title ends: 'Remembrancers'
Sal.

194.1 Agard, Arthur, 1631
[Anr issue, sig. A repr.] Line 7 of title
ends: 'Remembran-'
Linc*. Pet*.

205 Agrippa, Henricus Cornelius,
1575
Pet.

206 Ahmad I, *Sultan*, 1613
'The great Turkes defiance: or his
letter to ...'; 4°.
Yk.

210 Ainsworth, Henry, 1616
Sal. Yk.

211 Ainsworth, Henry, 1621
Cant. Pet.

212 Ainsworth, Henry, 1617
Pet. Sal.

213 Ainsworth, Henry, 1622
Cant.

214 Ainsworth, Henry, 1618
Cant. Pet.

215 Ainsworth, Henry, 1619
Cant. Pet. Sal.

216 Ainsworth, Henry, 1619
Cant. Pet.

218 Ainsworth, Henry, 1622
Cant. Wor.

219 Ainsworth, Henry, 1627
(M. Flesher [a.] J. Haviland) f. J.
Bellamie.
Cant (2 −1 tpw). Chelm. Ches.
Dur. Linc. Pet (2). S Asa. Win.

220 Ainsworth, Henry, 1639
Cant (imp). Carl. Ches. Ex (2).
Her. Lich. Nor. Sal. Swel (imp).
Wel. Yk.

222 Ainsworth, Henry, 1624
Yk.

231 Ainsworth, Henry, 1628
Her.

232 Ainsworth, Henry, 1640
Pet.

234 Ainsworth, Henry, 1608
Sal. Yk.

235 Ainsworth, Henry, 1609
Yk.

236 Ainsworth, Henry, 1620
Yk.

238 Ainsworth, Henry & Johnson,
Francis, 1604
Yk.

240 Ainsworth, John, [1615]
Pet. Wor. Yk.

245 Airay, Henry, 1618
Carl (imp). Chi. Ex (2 −1 imp).
Linc.

246 Alabaster, William, 1633
Win.

250 Alabaster, William, 1632
Linc.

251 Alabaster, William, [1633]
Linc. Pet.

274 Albin de Valsergues, Jean d',
1575
Formerly also STC 21058; '...
discourse, plainelye and truely
discussing ...'
Pet (imp).

281 Alcock, John, (1501)
(W. de worde).
Pet (tpw).

285 Alcock, John, [c.1497]
(Westmynstre, W. de worde).
Pet (tpw).

286 Alcock, John, [1497?]
'... Spoussage of a virgyn ...';
(Westmynstre, W. de worde).
Wel (frag.).

289 Aleman, Mateo, 1623
G.E. only on pt 2 tp.
Wel.

291 Aleman, Mateo, 1634 (1633,
1631)
'The rogue: or the life of Guzman de
Alfarache. To which ...'; Pt 2: (J.B.,
sold by R. Allot).
Yk.

291.5 Aleman, Mateo, 1634 (1633)
[Anr issue of pt 1, with cancel tp
omitting mention of Calisto] R.
Badger f. R. Allot.
Cant (tpw).

292 Alesius, Alexander, [1544?]
S Pl (imp).

293 Alessio, *Piemontese, pseud.*,
1558
'Piemount'
Pet.

295 Alessio, *Piemontese, pseud.*,
1559
(H. Sutton).
Linc.

296 Alessio, *Piemontese, pseud.*,
1562
England.
Pet.

301 Alessio, *Piemontese, pseud.*,
1563
Pet.

314 Alexander, *ab Alexandria*,
(1481)
(In alma ...).
Dur (2 −1 imp, 1 frag.). Linc
(imp).

332 Alexander [Farnese], [1591]
'A breefe ... battailes, ... triumphes,
atchiued by the D. of Parma'
Pet.

336 Alexander [Farnese], 1590
'The things ... since the 20. of
Nouembre, till the 27'; Wolfe.
Pet.

338 Alexander, William, 1614
Linc.

354 Ali Abencufian, 1627
Linc. Yk.

357.5 Alleine, Richard, 1630
[Anr ed. of STC 358] 8°; G. Miller f.
E. Blackmore.
Pet.

358.5 Allen, Edmond, (1548)
[Anr ed. of STC 359] 8°; (E.
Whitchurche).
Linc (tpw).

362 Allen, Robert, 1596
Yk.

363 Allen, Robert, 1612
Yk.

366 Allen, Robert, 1600
8°.
Yk.

367 Allen, Robert, 1600
Yk.

369 Allen, William, 1581
Her. Yk (2).

371 Allen, William, 1565
'purgatory'
Pet. Wor. Yk.

372 Allen, William, 1567
'defence'
Pet.

375 Alley, William, (1571)
Bur. Linc. Pet. Tru.

407.16 Almanacks −Allestree, 1633
8°; W.S. f. the Co. of Statrs.
Yk.

415 Almanacks −Bomelius, 1567
Linc.

421.1 Almanacks −Browne, [1616]
'A new almanacke & prognostication
for 1616 ...'; 12°; f. the Co. of Statrs.
Yk.

430.2 Almanacks −Clark, 1633
1633. 8°; Prs to the Univ. of
Cambridge.
Yk.

435.22 Almanacks −Dade, William,
1633
1633. 8°; J. Dawson f. the Co. of
Statrs; Formerly included in STC 434.
Yk.

444.1 Almanacks −Frende, 1587
1587. 8°.
Cant (imp).

444.3 Almanacks −Frende, [1588]
1588. 8°; R. Watkins a. J. Robertes.
Cant.

444.4 Almanacks −Frende, [1589]
1589. 8°; R. Watkins a. J. Robertes.
Cant.

444.6 Almanacks — Frende, 1590
1590. 8°; (R. Watkins a. J. Robertes).
Cant.

444.7 Almanacks — Frende, 1591
1591. 8°; R. Watkins a. J. Robertes.
Cant (imp).

444.9 Almanacks — Frende, 1592
1592. 8°; (R. Watkins a. J. Robertes).
Cant (imp).

469.2 Almanacks — Kidman, 1633
1633. 8°; Prs. to the Univ. of
Cambridge.
Yk.

472 *See*: 474.7

474.7 Almanacks — Laet, G., *the
Younger*, 1543
Formerly STC 472; s.sh.fol.
Her (imp).

476 Almanacks — Laet, G., *the
Younger*, 1544
Ex (frag.). S Pl (frag.).

489.18 Almanacks — Neve, Jeffery,
1618
1618. s.sh.fol.; f. the Co. of Statrs.
Nor (imp).

490.9 Almanacks — Neve, John,
1633
1633. 8°; f. the Co. of Statrs.
Yk.

495.8 Almanacks — Perkins, 1633
1633. 8°; f. the Co. of Statrs.
Yk.

501.7 Almanacks — Pond, 1607
1607. 8°; f. the Co. of Statrs.
Ex (frag.).

501.23 Almanacks — Pond, 1633
1633. 8°; Prs to the Univ. of
Cambridge.
Yk.

505.7 Almanacks — Rivers, P., 1633
1633. 8°; Prs to the Univ. of
Cambridge.
Yk.

515.16 Almanacks — Sofford, 1633
1633. 8°; f. the Co. of Statrs.
Yk.

517.1 Almanacks — Swallow, 1633
1633. 8°; Prs to the Univ. of
Cambridge.
Yk.

517.9 Almanacks — Tanner, 1584
1584. 8°.
Dur (frag.).

518 Almanacks — Turner, 1633
1633. 8°; Prs to the Univ. of
Cambridge.
Yk.

522.13 Almanacks — Vaux, 1633
1633. 8°; f. the Co. of Statrs.
Yk.

525 Almanacks — Watson, 1595
1595. 8°; R. Watkins a. J. Robertes.
Linc (frag.)*.

525.6 Almanacks — Watson, 1601
1601. 16°; f. E. White, the assigne of
J. Roberts.
Linc (cropped).

530 Almanacks — Winter, 1633
1633. 8°; Prs to the Univ. of
Cambridge.
Yk.

533 Almansa y Mendoza, Andrés de,
1623
Yk.

539 Alting, Henricus, 1615
S Pl.

540 Alvarez de Toledo, Fernando,
[1573?]
'An answer to a certain letter lately
sent by the Duke of Alba ... to those
...'; 8°.
Linc.

548 Ambrose, *St*, 1637
Sal.

549.5 Ambrose, Isaac, (1640)
'Prima & ultima the first & last
thinges'; 4°; J. Okes f. S. Broun.
Yk (tpw).

550 Ames, William, 1629
Chelm. S Asa (imp). Wel.

550.5 Ames, William, 1629
[Variant] Oxoniae, G. Turner.
Bur. Linc. S Pl. Wor.

551 Ames, William, 1633
... [a.] (H. Robinson).
Ely.

553 Ames, William, 1630
12°; Kingstonus.
Wel.

554 Ames, William, 1632
Allotti.
Her. Yk.

555 Ames, William, 1633
Carl. Win. Yk.

563.5 Anabaptists, 1620
'A most humble supplication of many
... loyall subiects'; 8°; [London].
Pet.

569 Anderson, Anthony, 1581
Pet.

570 Anderson, Anthony, 1581
Pet. Yk.

571 Anderson, Anthony, [1586]
'A sermon profitably preached ...'
Linc. Pet.

572 Anderson, Anthony, 1581
Linc. Pet. S Pl.

574 *See*: Wing A3099

576 Anderton, Lawrence, 1640
'Miscellania'
Linc.

579 Anderton, Lawrence, 1633
2°, with horizontal chain lines.
Her. Pet.

585 Andrewes, Bartimaeus, 1583
Linc.

588 Andrewes, John, 1631
Pet.

589.5 Andrewes, John, 1631
'Andrewes repentance, sounding
alarum'; 8°; f. I. Wright.
Pet.

591 Andrewes, John, 1621
... sold by E. Wright.
Pet (tpw). S Pl.

594 Andrewes, John, 1614
Ely. Yk.

596 Andrewes, Lancelot, 1610
Yk.

597 Andrewes, Lancelot, 1604
Ends F2^V.
Chelm (tp imp)*. Yk*.

598 Andrewes, Lancelot, [1610?]
A – E⁴ F².
Ely. S Pl (2).

598.5 Andrewes, Lancelot, [1610?]
[Anr ed.] As STC 598 but A – E⁴.
Yk.

602 Andrewes, Lancelot, 1629
STC 625 is pt of this.
Bur. Cant (2). Carl. Dur (2 – 1
imp). Ely. Ex. Lich. Linc. Liv.
Pet. S Asa. S Pl. Sal. Swar.
Wel. Win. Yk.

603.5 Andrewes, Lancelot, 1630
[Anr ed.] As STC 603 but p. 1 line 3
'we have', line 5 ends: 'be-'
S Asa.

604 Andrewes, Lancelot, 1610
Carl. Ex. Liv. Rip. Roch. Sal.
Swel. Wor. Yk.

605 Andrewes, Lancelot, 1611
Her (imp).

605.5 Andrewes, Lancelot, 1612
[Anr issue] As STC 605 apart from
date.
Yk.

606 Andrewes, Lancelot, 1629
IoM. Linc. Sal. Wel (2). Yk.

607 Andrewes, Lancelot, 1631
Bur. Win. Yk.

607.5 Andrewes, Lancelot, 1632
[Variant] As STC 607, apart from
date.
Ban (2 −1 imp). Bris. Ex. Wor.

609 Andrewes, Lancelot, 1635
(1634)
Cant. Carl. Ely. Ex (imp). Her.
Liv. S Asa. Sal (tpw)*. Swar.
Win. Yk.

611 Andrewes, Lancelot, 1620
Bur.

612 Andrewes, Lancelot, 1610
A3ᵛ line 7: 'We'
S Pl. Yk*.

614 Andrewes, Lancelot, [1611?]
Yk.

615 Andrewes, Lancelot, 1606
Bur. Ely. Lich. Pet (2 −1 imp).
S Pl. Yk (2).

616 Andrewes, Lancelot, [1610?]
Yk.

617 Andrewes, Lancelot, 1608
Pet.

619 Andrewes, Lancelot, [1610?]
Yk.

620 Andrewes, Lancelot, 1611
S Asa. S Pl.

621 Andrewes, Lancelot, 1611
Yk.

622 Andrewes, Lancelot, 1614
Nor. Pet. S Pl. Yk.

623 Andrewes, Lancelot, 1618
Cant. Chelm (imp). Nor.

624 Andrewes, Lancelot, 1618
Nor. Yk.

624.5 Andrewes, Lancelot, (1618)
[Sermons without gen. tp; 1st tp
begins:] 'The copie of the sermon …
Good-Friday 1604'; 4 pts; 4°; R.
Barker.
Chi (sermons 2 and 3 only). Pet.

625 *See*: Pt 2 of 602

626 Andrewes, Lancelot, 1609
Errata on Eee2ʳ.
Bur*. Carl. Chi. Linc*. Liv*.
Roch. S Pl (2)*. Swel*. Wel*.
Yk*.

626.5 Andrewes, Lancelot, 1609
Eee2 blank; B2ʳ line 11 ends: 'agi-'
Cant. Carl (2). Chi. Dur. Sal
(2 −1 with mixed sheets, has Eee2
of STC 626). Wor.

628 Andrewes, Lancelot, 1610
S Asa. S Pl.

635 Angelos, Christopher, 1619
'… (An encomion …)'; Gr. & Eng.
Linc (frag.). Pet. Yk.

636 Angelos, Christopher, 1619
Carl. Pet. Sal. Wor.

637 Angelos, Christopher, 1624
Pt 2: Londini.
Chelm. Wor.

638 Angelos, Christopher, 1617
Lichfeild.
Pet.

641 Angelos, Christopher, 1618 [*i.e.*
1620?]
4°; Oxford, [*i.e.* London] J. Lichfield
a. J. Short; Orn with cupid on tp.
Wor.

643 Angelos, Christopher, [1618?]
½ sh.fol.; Line 1 ends: 'beene'
Pet.

651 Anglerius, Petrus Martyr,
[1625?]
'The historie of the West-Indies'
Cant.

652 Anglerius, Petrus Martyr, 1628
Lich.

658 Answer, [1557]
Pet (imp). Yk.

665 Answers, [1638]
'Answeres to the particulars proponed
by His Majesties Commissionar';
Catchword of 1st page:
'Commissionar' *or* 'Commission'
S Pl*. Yk*.

667 Anthonie, Francis, 1616
'potabili'
Pet (imp). Yk.

668 Anthonie, Francis, 1610
Yk.

669 *See*: 11199

679 Antidote, 1636
Linc. Pet. S Asa. Sal. Wor.

684 Anti-Spaniard, 1590
Tp line 3 ends: 'made'
Yk.

684.5 Anti-Spaniard, 1590
[Anr ed.] As STC 684, but tp line 3
ends: 'Anti-Spaniard'
Pet.

691 Antwerp, (1586)
Pet.

692 Antwerp, [1580]
Linc.

697 Anyan, Thomas, 1612
'A sermon preached at S. Maries
church … Being the Act Sunday'
Yk.

698 Anyan, Thomas, [1615]
'Saint Marie'
Yk.

700.3 Aphthonius, 1575
[Anr ed.] 8°; T. Marsh.
Pet.

700.7 Aphthonius, 1580
[Anr ed.] 8°; T. Marsh.
Pet. Rip.

703 Aphthonius, 1611
Yk (imp)*.

704 Aphthonius, 1616
Imp. Soc. Stat.
Yk.

711 *See*: 11617.2

713.5 Appian, 1578
[Anr issue] R. Newberrie a. H.
Bynniman.
Pet (imp).

716 Ap-Robert, J., 1624
Linc.

719a.5 Apuleius, Lucius, 1582
[Variant of STC 719a which is: 8°; (T.
East) f. A. Veale] T. East f. A. Veale.
Pet (tp imp).

723 Arcaeus, Franciscus, 1588
'A most excellent and compendious
method …'
Cant.

738 Argall, John, 1604
Pet. Yk.

745 Ariosto, Lodovico, 1611
Linc. Pet.

747 Ariosto, Ludovico, 1607
(R. Field f. …).
Cant. Pet (imp).

755 Aristotle, 1634
Cantabrigiae, ap. T. & J. Buck, ac R.
Daniel.
Ban.

760 Aristotle, 1598
Cant (imp). Lich. Pet.

766 Aristotle, 1619
Ches. Linc. Nor. Pet. Sal.
Wor. Yk (2).

779 Arnauld, Antoine, 1594
Pet. Yk.

791 Art, [1503]
(parys, 30 May).
Linc (imp).

792 Art, (1505)
'The crafte to lyue well and to dye well'; (W. de worde).
S Pl (imp).

799 Arthington, Henry, [1592]
Yk (tp imp).

818 Articles, 1539
Pet.

823 Arundel Marbles, 1628
Ches. Lich. Linc. Wel.

824 Arundel Marbles, 1629
S Pl (2).

825 Ascham, Roger, 1577
(Ex typog. H. Middletoni) pro F. Coldocko.
Pet. S Pl (date altered in MS to 1578).

826 Ascham, Roger, [1576]
Coldocki.
Ches. Pet. Yk (2).

828 Ascham, Roger, 1581
(Ex off. H. Bynneman) pro ...
Rip.

829 Ascham, Roger, 1590
Pet (2). S Pl. Yk (2).

830 Ascham, Roger, [1570?]
Yk.

832 Ascham, Roger, (1570)
Yk.

834 Ascham, Roger, (1571)
Pet.

836 Ascham, Roger, 1589
Pet.

837 Ascham, Roger, (1545)
(In aed. E. Whytchurch).
Pet (tpw).

838 Ascham, Roger, 1571
Cant.

839 Ascham, Roger, 1589
Linc (tpw). Sal.

841 Ashe, Thomas, 1614
Nor (vol. 2 only)*.

848 Askew, Anne, (1546)
(Marpurg ...).
Linc (tpw).

850 Askew, Anne, (1547)
(Marpurg in the lande of Hessen).
Linc (imp).

855 Askew, Egeon, 1605
Linc. Pet (imp). Yk.

887 Atkins, John, 1624
'The Christians race: teaching us all. ...'
Cant.

889.5 Attersoll, William, 1614
'The new covenant, or a treatise of the sacraments'; The second edition; 4°; W. Iaggard, solde by N. Bourne.
Pet.

891 Attersoll, William, 1633
The second edition; Sparke.
Wor.

893 Attersoll, William, 1618
Bris. Ex. Her. Wor.

895 *See*: 900

900 Attersoll, William, 1632
Pt 1 formerly also STC 895; Pt 3: E.A. f. M.Sparke, the yonger.
Pet (pt 3 only). Yk (pt 1 only).

908 Augsburg Confession, (1536)
(R. Redman).
Linc. Pet.

909 Augsburg Confession, [1539?]
(R. Redman).
S Pl (imp).

916 Augustine, *St*, 1610
Cant (imp). Lich. Linc. Nor. Yk.

917 Augustine, *St*, 1620
This second edition.
Cant. Llan. Pet. Wel (imp).

920 Augustine, *St*, 1550
(wydowe of J. Herforde f. G. Lynne).
Pet (imp).

923.5 Augustine, *St*, (1557)
'Certaine sermons'; 8°; (J. Cawoode).
Pet.

928 Augustine, *St*, 1586
Wolfe.
Cant (imp). Pet.

937 Augustine, *St*, [1580?]
'litle'
Pet.

938 Augustine, *St*, 1581
Pet.

944 Augustine, *St*, 1581
... (the assigne of W. Seres).
Pet.

947 Augustine, *St*, 1616
Swar.

947.5 Augustine, *St*, 1621
[Anr ed.] 12°; f. the Co. of Statrs.
Cant.

950 Augustine, *St*, 1581
Pet.

959 Aungervile, Ricardus d', 1599
Dur. Yk.

960 Aurelius, Abraham, 1613
Yk.

962 Aurelius Antoninus, Marcus, 1634
Carl. Ex. Linc. Nor. Pet. S Pl.

963 Aurelius Antoninus, Marcus, 1635
The second edition.
Cant. Sal.

964 Aurellio, Giovanni Battista, 1587
Ex. Yk.

972 Austin, William, 1635
Cant. Wor.

973 Austin, William, 1637
(J. Legat) f. R. Meighen a. J. Legatt.
Ex.

974 Austin, William, 1637
... sold by C. Greene.
Pet.

981 Averell, William, 1588
'A meruailous ... Malignantlie striuing ...'
Linc.

983 Avila, Juan de, 1620
Cant.

985 Avila, Juan de, 1631
Roüen, widdow of Nicolas Courant.
S Pl*.

986 Avila, Juan de, 1632
Pet.

988 Avity, Pierre d', 1615
'... empires & principallities ...'
Ex (2). Her. Win.

997.5 Aylesbury, Thomas, 1624
'Christus redivivus'; 8°; G.E. f. L. Becket.
Her (imp).

998 Aylesbury, Thomas, 1624
S Pl.

999 Aylesbury, Thomas, 1626
Linc.

1000 Aylesbury, Thomas, 1623
Her. S Pl.

1013? Ayrault, Pierre, 1616
2°.
Yk (tp imp).

1019 B., A., 1639
Cant. Yk.

1023 B., A.D., 1620
Sal.

1029 *See*: 4179.5

1030.7 B., G., *M.A.*, [1591?]
'Newes out of France'; 4°; f. J. Kid.
Pet (tp imp).

1038 B., I., 1589
'freind'
Pet.

1039 B., I., 1581
Pet.

1064 B., R., *Esquire*, 1585
'betwene'
Pet.

1073 B., W., 1601
Yk.

1074 B., W., 1601
Pet. Yk.

1074.5 B., W., 1602
'The confession and publike
recantation of thirteene …
personages'; 4°; f. G.P.
Rip. Yk.

1077 Babington, Gervase, 1615
[a.] (T. Charde).
Wor.

1078 Babington, Gervase, 1615
Cant (imp). Rip (tp imp).

1079 Babington, Gervase, 1622
Ches. Chi. Glo. Lich.

1080 Babington, Gervase, 1637
Cant. Dur. Ex. Her. Linc.
Win.

1086 Babington, Gervase, 1592
Rip.

1088 Babington, Gervase, 1604
Rip.

1090 Babington, Gervase, 1588
Pet.

1091 Babington, Gervase, 1596
Pet (imp).

1092 Babington, Gervase, [1591]
S Pl.

1093 Babington, Gervase, 1599
S Pl.

1094 Babington, Gervase, 1591
Linc.

1096 Babington, Gervase, 1586
Linc.

1099 Babington, John, 1635
'… discourse of …'
Cant.

1100 Babington, John, 1635
Cant.

1106.5 Bachiler, Samuel, 1629
[Anr issue] 'The campe royal';
Amsterdam, R.P.
Ex.

1107 Bachiler, Samuel, 1629
Pet.

1108 Bacon, Francis, 1623
Win.

1109 Bacon, Francis, 1638
'Francisci Baconi, … operum …'
Yk.

1110 Bacon, Francis, 1638
Ex. Lich. S Pl.

1114 Bacon, Francis, 1605
Yk.

1118.5 Bacon, Francis, 1604
[Variant] T.P. f. Henrie Tomes.
Yk.

1120 Bacon, Francis, [after 1620]
Cant. Linc.

1122 Bacon, Francis, 1640
Bur. Pet. Sal (2). Win.

1123 Bacon, Francis, 1640
Yk.

1124 Bacon, Francis, 1629
Linc. Win. Yk.

1125 Bacon, Francis, 1614
Dur. S Pl.

1126 Bacon, Francis, 1629
Dur. Win. Wor.

1127 Bacon, Francis, 1609
Linc.

1128 Bacon, Francis, 1617
Carl.

1133 Bacon, Francis, 1601
Carl. Linc. Pet (imp). Yk.

1134 Bacon, Francis, 1630
Linc (pt 2 only). Yk.

1135 Bacon, Francis, 1636 (1635)
Cant. Glo. Linc (pt 1 only).
Pet. Yk.

1136 Bacon, Francis, 1639
Sal.

1140 *See*: 1141.5

1141.5 Bacon, Francis, 1612
Formerly STC 1140.
Yk (tpw).

1147 Bacon, Francis, 1625
'civill'
Carl. Linc (tp imp). Sal.

1150 Bacon, Francis, 1632
Ban. S Alb.

1151 Bacon, Francis, 1639
Cant.

1154 Bacon, Francis, 1618
'Saggi morali … con …'
Ex. Yk.

1155 Bacon, Francis, 1622
Sal.

1156 Bacon, Francis, 1623
Linc.

1159 Bacon, Francis, 1622
p. 3, line 12 has: 'Souldiers'
Cant (2 −1 imp). Linc*. Wel
(imp)*.

1160 Bacon, Francis, 1622
p. 3, line 12: '*Souldiours*'
Sal (imp).

1161 Bacon, Francis, 1629
Lich. S Asa. Swel.

1163 Bacon, Francis, 1620
Bur. Sal. Win. Yk.

1165 Bacon, Francis, 1629
Wor.

1167.3 Bacon, Francis, 1640
[Anr issue of STC 1167, which has
colophon dated 1639] As STC 1167,
but engr. tp only, and colophon dated
1640.
Cant. Her. Lich. Linc. Sal.
Wel. Yk.

1169 Bacon, Francis, 1627
Linc.

1170 Bacon, Francis, 1628
The second edition.
Cant. Ely.

1171 Bacon, Francis, 1631
The third edition.
S Alb. Yk.

1173 Bacon, Francis, 1639
The fifth edition.
Cant. Carl. S Asa. Sal. Wel.
Wor.

1181 Bacon, Roger, 1590
'retardandis'
Pet.

1182 Bacon, Roger, 1597
(T. Creede) f. R. Oliue.
Pet (tpw).

1185 Baddeley, Richard, 1622
Carl. Linc. Pet. Yk.

1187 Bagnall, Robert, 1622
Pet (imp).

1188 Bagshaw, Christopher, 1601
Linc. Pet (2). Yk (2).

1189 *See*: 3242

1190 *See*: 3244

1196 Bailey, Walter, 1616
… J. Barnes.
Pet.

1202 Baillie, Alexander, 1628
'offspring'
Yk.

1204 *See*: Pt 2 of 25382

1205 Baillie, Robert, 1640
Tp line 9: 'postscript … Personat'
Yk (tpw)*.

1208 Bainbridge, John, 1619
Linc. S Pl.

1211.5 Baker, Humphrey, [1582?]
[Anr ed.] 8°; (T. Purfoote).
Pet (tpw).

1216 Baker, Humphrey, 1612
Cant (imp).

1219 Baker, John, (1581)
Ex (imp).

1220 Baker, John, (1583)
Pet (pt 2 only).

1221 Baker, John, (1584)
Her. Linc. Wor (tpw).

1222 Baker, John, 1613
Wel (imp).

1223.5 Baker, *Sir* Richard, 1637
[Anr ed.] 4°; A. Griffin sold by A.
Bouler.
Sal.

1224 Baker, *Sir* Richard, 1637
The second edition; Bouler.
Wor.

1225 Baker, *Sir* Richard, 1638
Bur. Cant. Pet.

1226 Baker, *Sir* Richard, 1640
Carl.

1229 Baker, *Sir* Richard, 1638
Bur. Pet. Sal. Wor.

1231 Baker, *Sir* Richard, 1638
'... and disquisitions upon the one and
fiftieth ...'
Bur. Pet. Sal. Wor.

1233 Balbani, Niccolò, 1608
Yk.

1237 Balcanquhall, Walter, 1633
Carl. Linc. Pet. S Pl. Yk.

1238 Balcanquhall, Walter, 1634
Bur. Dur. Her (imp). Yk.

1239 Balcanquhall, Walter, 1626
Linc.

1240 Balcanquhall, Walter, 1623
Pet.

1241 Balcanquhall, Walter, 1634
Allott.
Bur. Lich. S Asa. Yk.

1242 Baldwin, 1521
[J. Siberch] ...
Linc (imp). Pet.

1246 Baldwin, William, [1554?]
Pet (tp only).

1248 Baldwin, William, [1563]
Pet.

1254 Baldwin, William, (1550)
(E. Whitchurche).
Pet.

1256 Baldwin, William, [1556]
(J. Waylande).
Pet (imp).

1259 Baldwin, William, (1567)
(R. Tottill).
Carl (imp)*.

1270 Bale, John, (1546)
(Wesel).
S Pl.

1271 Bale, John, (1548)
'The actes ...'; (T. Raynalde); Gen.
prelims and pt 2 now = STC 1273.5;
Collates A – K⁸ L⁴.
Pet.

1273 Bale, John, (1551)
'The fyrste part ...'; (A. Vele);
Collates A – K⁸.
Linc. Pet.

1273.5 Bale, John, (1551)
Gen. prelims and pt 2: 'The first two
partes ...'; 8°; (f. J. Bale); Formerly
pt of STC 1271; Collates *⁴; A – P⁸ Q⁴.
Linc. Pet.

1274 Bale, John, (1560)
(J. Tysdale).
Cant. Dur. Linc.

1275 Bale, John, [1550?]
(J. Day).
Cant. Linc.

1289 Bale, John, (1561)
(J. Tysdall f. F. Coldocke).
Cant. Linc. Pet. Sal. Win
(imp).

1291 Bale, John, [1544?]
Tp line 1 ends: 'ex-'
Pet.

1292 Bale, John, [1548?]
Linc.

1295 Bale, John, (1548)
(Gippeswici, per J. Ouerton).
Dur. Pet (no colophon). Win.
Yk.

1296 Bale, John, 1549
... (Gippeswici ...).
Her.

1297 Bale, John, [1548?]
(R. Jugge).
Pet. Yk.

1298 Bale, John, [c.1550]
(J. Daye a. W. Seres).
Cant (2 − 1 imp). Linc (pt 3 only).

1299 Bale, John, (1550)
(J. Wyer).
Linc. S Pl.

1301 Bale, John, [c.1570]
Wor.

1303 Bale, John, 1545
Linc.

1307 Bale, John, (1553)
(In Rome ...).
Linc (tpw).

1309 Bale, John, (1543)
(At Zurik ...).
Linc.

1313 Ball, John, 1640
Carl. Pet. Sal. Wor.

1318 Ball, John, 1635
Pet.

1336 Balmford, James, 1623
'A modest reply to ... Mr. Gataker';
8°; (sub. tp as STC1).
Pet.

1340 Balnaves, *Sir* Henry, 1584
Linc. S Pl. Yk.

1344.5 Bancroft, Richard, 1593
[Anr ed.] As STC 1344, but ends on
Aa4.
Cant. Ely*. Ex. Linc. Pet. Sal.
Win.

1345 Bancroft, Richard, 1640
Carl. Dur. Pet. S Pl. Yk.

1346 Bancroft, Richard, 1588
Linc. Yk.

1347 Bancroft, Richard, 1588
Pet. S Pl.

1349 Bancroft, Richard, 1636
Ex. Liv.

1352 Bancroft, Richard, 1593
Bur. Cant. Carl. Ches. Ely.
Glo. Lich. Linc. Liv. Pet. Rip.
S Pl (2). Win. Yk.

1358 Banister, John, 1589
Pet.

1364 Bankes, Thomas, 1611
Linc (tp imp). Pet.

1365 Bankes, Thomas, 1586
Pet.

1381 Barckley, *Sir* Richard, 1598
Her. Pet.

1382 Barckley, *Sir* Richard, 1603
Yk.

1387 Barclay, John, 1615
Linc.

1389 Barclay, John, 1636
Oxonii ...
Ely.

1390 Barclay, John, 1622
Linc. Pet. Yk.

1392 Barclay, John, 1625
Cant.

1392.5 Barclay, John, 1636
Formerly STC 1395.
Pet. S Dv.

1400 Barclay, John, 1633
Linc.

1404 Barclay, William, *M.D.*, 1620
Linc.

1408 Barclay, William, *Prof.*, 1609
Bur. Dur. Ely. Her. Linc. Pet.
S Pl. Yk.

1408.3 Barclay, William, *Prof.*,
1609
[Anr issue] Mussiponti, ap. F. du Bois
& J. Garnich.
Liv.

1411 Baret, John, (1580)
(H. Denhamus, G. Seresii vnicus
assignatus).
Ches. Her. Pet. Yk (imp).

1414 Bargrave, Isaac, 1627
Cant. Yk.

1415 Bargrave, Isaac, 1624
Spencer.
Cant (imp). Ely. Pet.

1415.5 Bargrave, Isaac, 1624
[Anr ed.] 4°; G.P. f. J. Bartlet a. J.
Spencer.
Linc. S Pl.

1423 Barker, Laurence, 1599
S Pl.

1425 Barker, Peter, 1624
'commandements'
Bur.

1426 Barker, Peter, 1633
'commandements'; The second
edition; Harison.
Win.

1430 Barlaamus, 1592
Linc. Liv.

1434- Barlow, John, 1624
[Anr ed.] 4°; J.D. f. J. Bellamie.
Yk.

1435 Barlow, John, 1632
Cant (frag.)*. Ches. Ex.

1436 Barlow, John, 1618
Nor.

1440 Barlow, John, 1619
Her.

1446 Barlow, William, *Bp of
Rochester and of Lincoln*, 1609
B1ʳ line 13 ends: 'ad-'
Bur. Carl. Ches*. Linc*. Pet.
Wor. Yk*.

1446.5 Barlow, William, *Bp of
Rochester and of Lincoln*, 1609
[Anr ed.] As STC 1446, but B1ʳ line
13 ends: 'aduerse'
Ex. Pet (2).

1447 Barlow, William, *Bp of
Rochester and of Lincoln*, 1607
Ches. Lich. Wel. Yk.

1449 Barlow, William, *Bp of
Rochester and of Lincoln*, 1601
Linc. Pet. Sal. Yk.

1450 Barlow, William, *Bp of
Rochester and of Lincoln*, 1609
Pet.

1451 Barlow, William, *Bp of
Rochester and of Lincoln*, 1606
Pet. Wor.

1452.5 Barlow, William, *Bp of
Rochester and of Lincoln*, 1607
[Anr ed.] As STC 1452 which has title
'The first of the foure sermons', but
line 10 of tp has: 'Bishops'
Cant. Lich. Linc. Yk (2).

1454 Barlow, William, *Bp of
Rochester and of Lincoln*, 1601
Ches. Linc (2 − 1 imp). Pet (imp).
S Pl (imp). Yk.

1455 Barlow, William, *Bp of
Rochester and of Lincoln*, 1606
Yk.

1455.5 Barlow, William, *Bp of
Rochester and of Lincoln*, 1606
[Anr ed.] 4°; f. M. Lawe.
Cant (imp). Ches. Ex. S Pl.

1456 Barlow, William, *Bp of
Rochester and of Lincoln*, 1604
'… which it pleased …'; Impr.:
'Powles'
Ches*. Linc*. S Pl*. Yk (2 −
both imp)*.

1456.5 Barlow, William, *Bp of
Rochester and of Lincoln*, 1604
[Anr ed.] As STC 1456, but: 'Paules'
Pet.

1457 Barlow, William, *Bp of
Rochester and of Lincoln*, 1605
Dur (imp).

1458 Barlow, William, *Bp of
Rochester and of Lincoln*, 1625
Ches. Yk.

1459 Barlow, William, *Bp of
Rochester and of Lincoln*, 1638
Cant. Carl. Ches (2). Her.
Linc. Sal.

1460 Barlow, William, *Bp of
Rochester and of Lincoln*, 1598
Yk.

1463 Barnaud, Nicolas, 1574
Formerly also STC 10577.
Linc. Pet. Yk.

1467 Barnes, Barnabe, 1595
Yk.

1468 Barnes, Barnabe, 1606
Ex (tp only). Win. Yk.

1472 Barnes, Robert, *Dr*, [c.1550]
(H. Syngelton).
Linc. Pet.

1476 Barnes, Thomas, 1622
Linc. Pet.

1477 Barnes, Thomas, 1624
Yk.

1478 Barnes, Thomas, 1626
'alarum'
Cant.

1489 Baro, Peter, 1580
Carl. Pet. S Pl. Yk.

1491 Baro, Peter, [1587?]
Ex. Pet. Sal.

1492 Baro, Peter, 1579
Bur. Carl. Ex. Pet. Yk.

1493 Baron, Robert, 1631
Dur. Wor.

1495 Baron, Robert, 1633
Win.

1498 Barrell, Robert, 1624
'spirituall'
Her. Yk.

1501 Barret, William, 1612
Wor (imp). Yk.

1513 Barrough, Philip, 1617
Linc.

1516 Barrough, Philip, 1639
Pet.

1518.5 Barrow, Henry, 1590
Formerly STC 5555.
Linc (imp).

1521 Barrow, Henry, [1591]
Pet. Yk (3).

1524 Barrow, Henry, [1606?]
Dur. Linc. Pet. Sal. Yk.

1528 Barry, Gerrat, 1634
Wor.

1529 *See*: 13926a

1535 Bartholinus, Casparus, 1633
Oxonii …
Carl.

1535.5 Bartholinus, Casparus, 1633
'Enchiridion ethicum'; 12°; Ap. G.
Turner.
Ely. Ex (2).

1536 Bartholomaeus, *Anglicus,*
[1495]
2°.
Cant (frag.). Her (v. imp).

1537 Bartholomaeus, *Anglicus,*
[1535]
Yk.

1538 Bartholomaeus, *Anglicus,*
(1582)
Dur. Her.

1544 Basle, *Preachers at,* [1548]
'Bancrafte'
S Pl.

1555 Basse, William, 1602
Linc.

1564 Bastingius, Jeremias, 1589
'catechisme'
Pet.

1565 Bastingius, Jeremias, [1591?]
Pet (2).

1566 Bastingius, Jeremias, 1595
Yk.

1568 Bastwick, John, 1637
Dur. Yk.

1570 Bastwick, John, 1638
'A briefe relation ...'
Yk.

1570.5 Bastwick, John, 1638
[Anr ed.] 'A breife ...'; 4°.
S Pl.

1571 Bastwick, John, 1627
Linc. S Pl. Sal. Wor.

1572 Bastwick, John, 1637
Yk.

1573 Bastwick, John, 1637
S Pl. Yk.

1574 Bastwick, John, 1637
Yk (2).

1575 Bastwick, John, 1637
Yk.

1576 Bastwick, John, 1636
Ches. Yk.

1577.5 Bate, John, *Mechanician,*
1634
[Variant] f. R. Mab, sold by J.
Jackson a. F. Church.
Cant.

1581 Bateman, Stephen, 1569
Pet (imp).

1586 Bateson, Thomas, 1604
Pet (Quintus only).

1592 Bauderon, Brice, 1639
S Pl. Sal.

1593 Baudier, Michel, 1635
Pet.

1594 Baughe, Thomas, 1614
S Pl.

1596 Baxter, J., 1600
Wor.

1600 Bayley, Thomas, 1626
'Thomae Baylaei ... De merito ...'
Bur. Ex (frag.).

1601 Bayly, John, 1630
S Pl.

1607 Bayly, Lewis, 1626
Bur.

1609.2 Bayly, Lewis, 1630
26. edition; 12°; f. R. Allot.
Ex.

1614 Bayly, Lewis, 1635
35. edition.
Ex.

1615 Bayly, Lewis, [c.1635?]
'... The last ... edition. Newly
overseene'; 24°; A4^r line 2 from
bottom: '*31. time*'
Cant (imp).

1622 Bayly, Lewis, 1640
A4^v line 6: '49. time'
Ely*.

1626 Baynes, Paul, 1618
Ely.

1628 Baynes, Paul, 1618
Ex. Yk.

1634 Baynes, Paul, 1618
Ex.

1638 Baynes, Paul, 1618
Pet.

1641 Baynes, Paul, 1619
Chelm.

1643.5 Baynes, Paul, 1635
[Variant] The third edition; R.Y. f. E.
Brewster at Fleet-bridge.
Pet.

1646 Baynes, Paul, 1619
Yk.

1648 Baynes, Paul, 1618
Ex.

1653 Beacon, Richard, 1594
Yk.

1657 Beard, Thomas, 1625
Yk (tp imp).

1657.5 Beard, Thomas, 1616
[Anr issue of STC 1658] W. Stansby.
Yk (imp).

1659 Beard, Thomas, 1597
4°.
Pet. Yk.

1660 Beard, Thomas, 1612
4°.
Linc. Wor.

1661 Beard, Thomas, 1631
Cant. Ely. Pet.

1662 Beatniffe, John, 1590
Linc.

1669 Beaumont, Francis & Fletcher,
John, 1635
Carl.

1675 Beaumont, Francis, &
Fletcher, John, 1635
Carl.

1685.5 Beaumont, Francis, &
Fletcher, John, 1639
[Anr issue] The fourth impression; E.
Griffin f. W. Leak ... neere the Rowles.
Carl.

1694 Beaumont, *Sir* John, 1629
Sal.

1698 Beauvais, Charles de, 1636
Carl.

1700 Becanus, Martinus, 1612
Pet.

1702 Becanus, Martinus, 1612
'concerning'
Yk.

1703 Becanus, Martinus, 1513 [*i.e.*
1613]
'concilij'; 2 pts; Pt 2 formerly STC
19205.
Pet (pt 2 only). Sal (pt 1 only).
Yk (pt 1 only).

1704 Becanus, Martinus, 1613
Continuous signatures.
Pet. Wor.

1705 Becanus, Martinus, 1622
Carl. Linc. Sal. Yk.

1706 Becanus, Martinus, 1622
Bur.

1707 Becanus, Martinus, 1619
S Pl. Yk (imp).

1708 Becanus, Martinus, 1610
Yk.

1710 Becon, Thomas, 1564 (1560,
1563)
Cant (frag.). Pet (vol. 1 only).
S Pl.

1730 Becon, Thomas, 1554
Formerly also STC 10384 & 23435.
Cant.

1736 Becon, Thomas, 1566
Pet. Rip (imp).

1737 Becon, Thomas, 1567
Pet. Yk (imp).

1754 Becon, Thomas, [c.1560]
Linc.

1755 Becon, Thomas, [1563]
Cant (imp). Yk.

1761 Becon, Thomas, (1574)
(J. Daye).
Cant (imp).

1762 Becon, Thomas, 1577
Pet.

1764.5 Becon, Thomas, 1587
[Anr ed.] 8°; By the assignes of R.
Daie.
Ex (tpw).

1777 Bede, 1592
Yk.

1778 Bede, 1565
Her. Pet.

1781 Bede, Jean, 1619
Pet.

1783 Bedel, Henry, (1572)
Linc.

1786 Bedel, William, 1628
'recusansie'
Linc.

1787 Bedford, Thomas, 1624
Carl. Linc.

1788 Bedford, Thomas, 1621
S Pl.

1790 Bedford, Thomas, 1639
S Asa.

1791.3 Bedford, Thomas, 1635
[Variant] A. Griffin f. W. Russell in
Plimmouth.
Pet.

1792 Bedingfield, Robert, 1625
S Pl.

1801 Bekinsau, Joannes, 1546
(In aed ...).
Pet.

1814 Bell, Thomas, 1603
Yk.

1815 Bell, Thomas, 1610
Yk.

1816 Bell, Thomas, 1609
Pet. Yk.

1818.5 Bell, Thomas, 1604
Formerly STC 1817.
Pet (tp imp). Yk.

1822 Bell, Thomas, 1603
Yk.

1824 Bell, Thomas, 1608
Yk.

1825 Bell, Thomas, 1605
Pet. Win. Yk.

1826 Bell, Thomas, 1606
Nor (imp).

1827 Bell, Thomas, 1606
Win. Yk.

1829 Bell, Thomas, 1596
Pet. Rip. Yk.

1830 Bell, Thomas, 1593
Dur. Pet. Rip. Sal (imp)*. Yk.

1831 Bell, Thomas, 1605
Pet.

1832 Bell, Thomas, 1608
Yk.

1833 Bell, Thomas, 1605
Yk.

1840 Bellarmino, Roberto, 1616
Ely. Yk.

1846 Bellehachius, Ogerius, 1583
Linc.

1848 Bellewe, Richard, (1585)
... (R. Robinson, T. Dunne, Th.
Hauylande, Ja. Bowring, and Th.
Moris); Date in title.
Pet (imp).

1853 Bellot, Jacques, 1588
Rip.

1861 Benefield, Sebastian, 1613
Oxford, Joseph Barnes, sold by John
Barnes.
Linc.

1862 Benefield, Sebastian, 1629
Bur. Wor.

1863 Benefield, Sebastian, 1620
Bur. Wor.

1865 Benefield, Sebastian, 1629
Bur.

1867 Benefield, Sebastian, 1610
Wor. Yk.

1868 Benefield, Sebastian, 1614
Cant.

1872 Benefield, Sebastian, 1615
Wor.

1880 Benlowes, Edward, [1636]
Linc. Pet.

1881.5 Bennet, Henry, *Rector*, 1640
'The pastors plea for peace'; 12°; J.
Okes f. C. Duncan.
Bur.

1884 Bennett, John, 1601
Linc. Yk.

1885 Bense, Petrus, 1637
Oxoniae, G. Turner, imp. authoris.
Glo. Linc. Pet.

1886 Benson, George, 1609
S Pl. Wor. Yk.

1888 *See:* 1889

1889 Bentham, Joseph, [1630?]
Formerly also STC 1888.
Bur. Pet (tpw)*.

1891 Bentham, Thomas, [1583?]
Pet.

1895 Benvenuto, Italiano, 1612
Cant (2). Pet (imp)*.

1909 Bernard, *St*, 1616
'Ex vetusto codice descripta'; Ex off.
G. Purslow, sumpt. L. Becket; STC1
gives addit. English tp; Pt 2 formerly
STC 6019.
Linc (lacks pt 2).

1938 Bernard, Richard, 1619
Carl. Sal.

1940 Bernard, Richard, 1609
Ex.

1941 Bernard, Richard, 1621
Pet (tp imp). Yk.

1944 Bernard, Richard, 1629
Pet. Yk.

1949 Bernard, Richard, 1630
Pet.

1951 Bernard, Richard, 1635
Yk.

1952 Bernard, Richard, 1640
Linc.

1952.5 Bernard, Richard, 1609
[Anr ed. of STC 1953] J. Legatt, pr.
to the Univ. of Cambridge, sold by S.
Waterson [London].
Yk (impr. not confirmed).

1955 Bernard, Richard, 1617
Yk.

1956 Bernard, Richard, 1623
'... answere ... before Luthers ...'; B1ʳ
line 2 ends: 'in an'
Cant (imp)*. Wor. Yk*.

1956.3 Bernard, Richard, 1623
[Anr ed.] As STC 1956, but B1ʳ line 2
ends: 'in an in-'
Pet.

1957 Bernard, Richard, 1624
Cant (imp). Ex. Pet.

1958 Bernard, Richard, 1610
Wor.

1962 Bernard, Richard, 1628
Yk.

1964 Bernard, Richard, 1613
Pet.

1977 Bethune, Philippe de, *Comte
de Selles et de Charost*, 1634
Pet.

1979.5 Betti, Francesco, 1589
'Lettera di F. Betti ... all' illustriss.
Marchese di Pescara'; Stampato la
seconda volta; 8°; G. Wolfio.
Linc.

1982.5 Beurhusius, Fridericus, 1585
[Anr ed.] 8°; H. Midletonus, imp. G.
Bishop.
Yk.

1983 Beurhusius, Fridericus, 1582
Rip. Yk.

1983.5 Beurhusius, Fridericus, 1583
'Ad P. Rami Dialecticam ... inductio.
Pars tertia ...'; Editio secunda; 8°;
(Ex off. T. Dawson) imp. G. Bishop.
Yk.

2006.5 Bèze, Théodore de, 1581
[Anr ed.] As STC 2006, apart from
date.
Yk.

2006.7 Bèze, Théodore de, 1563
[A trans.] 'A briefe ...'; 8°; R. Hall.
Pet.

2012 Bèze, Théodore de, 1585
Linc. Pet.

2014 Bèze, Théodore de, [1582?]
Pet.

2018 Bèze, Théodore de, [1578?]
Yk.

2019 Bèze, Théodore de, 1589
Pet (2 −1 tp imp).

2020 Bèze, Théodore de, [1589?]
(Cambridge) J. Legatt, pr. to the
Univ. of Cambridge, sold in London;
Pt 2 formerly STC 2764.
Cant. Pet.

2025 Bèze, Théodore de, 1587
Pet (2 −1 imp).

2032 Bèze, Théodore de, 1580
Formerly also STC 2357.
Cant.

2034 Bèze, Théodore de, 1581
Formerly also STC 2398.
Linc (imp).

2035 Bèze, Théodore de, 1590
... f. the assignes of W. Seres.
Pet (pt 2 only).

2046 Bèze, Théodore de, 1580
Pet (2).

2050 Bèze, Théodore de, 1581
Bur.

2053 Bèze, Théodore de, 1591
Pet. Yk.

2056 Bible. Latin, 1580 (1579)
N.T. formerly also STC 2807; Copies
may have mixed imprints.
S Asa. Tru.

2058 Bible. Latin, 1581
H. Middletonus, imp. W.N.
Chi. Rip.

2058a Bible. Latin, 1581
H. Middletonus, imp. G.B.
Bur. Linc (N.T. imp).

2059 Bible. Latin, 1585
N.T. in both Bèze's and Tremellius's
versions.
New. Sal (Bèze's N.T. only)*.

2060 Bible. Latin, 1585
Ex.

2060.3 Bible. Latin, 1585
[Variant] H. Midletonus, imp. C.B.
Chelm.

2060.5 Bible. Latin, 1585
[Variant] H. Midletonus, imp. J.H.
Ex (imp). Pet (imp). Yk.

2061 Bible. Latin, 1593 (1592)
N.T. formerly also STC 2810a.
Ban. Ely. Her. New. Nor
(tpw)*. Yk (2 −1 tpw*).

2061.5 Bible. Latin, 1593 (1592)
[Variant] G.B., R.N. & R.B.
Chi (2). Glo. Linc. S Asa.
Wor.

2062 Bible. Latin, 1597
S Pl.

2062.5 Bible. Latin, 1640
[Anr ed.] 12°; Typis M. Flesher & R.
Young.
Bur. S Alb. Yk.

2063 Bible. English, (1535)
Cant (4 −all imp)*. Dur (imp)*.
Ex (frag.)*. Roch (tpw)*.

2063.5 Bible. English, (1535)
[Variant] Date in title 'M.D.XXXVI.'
Glo.

2064 Bible. English, [1537]
Date in title.
Linc (imp).

2066 Bible. English, (1537)
Cant (2 −both imp). Linc (imp).
S Pl (imp).

2067 Bible. English, 1539
Cant (2 −both imp). Pet (imp)*.
Sal (imp)*.

2068 Bible. English, 1539
Cant (2 −both imp). Roch. S Pl.

2069 Bible. English, 1540
Cant (imp). S Pl (tpw).

2070 Bible. English, 1540
E. whytchurche *or* R. Grafton.
Bris (imp; Withchurch; tp has
'archebyshop'). Cant (3 −2
'whytchurche' (imp); 1 'Grafton').
Lich (whytchurche; tp has
'archbyshop'). S Pl (imp;
whitchurch; tp has 'archbyshop').

2071 Bible. English, 1540
Cant (imp). Linc (imp; text
mainly STC 2071, with prelims
from 2070).

2072 Bible. English, 1541 (1540)
Cant (2 −both imp). Dur (imp).
Linc (imp). Wel (imp)*.

2075 Bible. English, 1541
E. Whitchurch *or* R. Grafton.
Cant (2 −both imp). S Pl (3 −2
imp).

2076 Bible. English, 1540 (1541)
R. Grafton *or* E. Whitchurch.
Cant (imp).

2077 Bible. English, 1549
Cant (3 − all imp). Chi. Glo
(imp). Linc (imp). Liv (imp).
Tru (imp)*.

2078 Bible. English, 1549
Dur (imp). Linc (imp). Nor
(imp)*. Yk (imp).

2079 Bible. English, 1549
Cant (imp). Liv (imp).

2080 Bible. English, (1550)
Cant (2 −both imp). Dur (imp).
S Pl (imp).

2081 Bible. English, 1550
S Pl (2 −both imp).

2083 Bible. English, 1551
(N. Hyl f.) R. Toye.
Cant (2 −both imp; 1 may be any
of STC 2083−2086.5).

2084 Bible. English, 1551
(N. Hyl f.) T. Petyt.
S Pl. Sal (imp)*.

2085 Bible. English, 1551
(N. Hyl f.) J. Wyghte.
Cant.

2087.2 Bible. English, 1549
'The second parte of the byble,
containyng Josua ... Hiob'; 8°; (J.
Day a. W. Seres).
Pet (imp).

2087.4 Bible. English, 1550
'The boke of the Prophetes'; 8°; (J.
Daye a. W. Seres).
S Pl (imp).

2088 Bible. English, 1551
Cant (2 −both imp). S Pl (N.T. only). Wel (imp).

2089 Bible. English, (1552)
N. Hyll (f. A. Veale); Includes the B.C.P., part of which was formerly also STC 16442.
Cant (3 −1 imp; 1 frag.).

2090 Bible. English, 1553 (1550)
Cant (imp). Carl. S Pl (2 −both imp).

2091 Bible. English, (1553)
Pet (imp)*. S Pl (imp).

2092 Bible. English, 1553
(R. Grafton).
Cant (2 −both imp). New (imp).
S Pl (2 −1 tpw, 1 imp).

2096 Bible. English, 1562
Cant (imp). Dur (imp). Her.
Rip (imp). S Pl (3 −all imp).

2098 Bible. English, 1566
Rouen (C. Hamillon), at the coste …
Cant (2 −both imp). Linc (imp).
Liv (imp). S Pl (tpw). Tru (imp).

2099 Bible. English, [1568]
(R. Jugge).
Cant (imp)*. Carl (imp)*. Glo.
Llan (imp)*. Nor (imp)*. Roch.
Yk (imp)*.

2100 *See*: 2102.5

2102.5 Bible. English, (1569)
Formerly STC 2100; 4°; (J. Cawood).
Cant (imp).

2103 Bible. English, [1569?]
Pt 2 tp, line 2: 'contayninge'; Pt 3 tp, line 2: 'Byble contay-'
Roch (imp)*.

2106 Bible. English, 1569 *or* 1570
'The Bible and holy scriptures. … added in this second edition certeine tables'
Cant (2 −both imp). Swel (2 −1 tpw).

2107 Bible. English, (1572)
(R. Jugge).
Cant. Ches (imp). Dur (2 states −both imp). Nor. Yk (imp).

2108 Bible. English, (1573)
(R. Jugge).
Cant (N.T. only). Glo (tpw).
S Pl.

2110 Bible. English, (1575)
W. Norton (R. Jugge).
Cant (imp)*. Yk (imp)*.

2114 Bible. English, 1575
(R. Jugge).
Cant (imp). Tru (tpw).

2117 Bible. English, 1576
Cant (imp). Nor.

2118 Bible. English, 1576
Liv.

2119 Bible. English, 1577
Dur (imp)*.

2122 Bible. English, (1577)
(R. Jugge).
Cant (imp). S Pl (imp).

2123 Bible. English, (1578)
Cant (2 −1 imp). Carl (imp). Ex (tpw). Glo. Linc. Pet. Swel (tpw).

2124 Bible. English, 1578
Glo (imp).

2125 Bible. English, 1579 (1576)
Edinbrugh, …
Cant (imp). Glo (imp).

2126 Bible. English, 1579
With B.C.P. with text collating A − B⁸
C⁴; A − C⁸ D⁴.
Pet (N.T. only, imp)*. Rip (imp)*. Wor (imp)*.

2129 Bible. English, 1580
70 lines to a column.
Ex (imp)*.

2131 Bible. English, 1581
Wor (imp).

2133 Bible. English, 1582
Bris. Roch.

2134 Bible. English, 1582
Linc (imp).

2136 Bible. English, 1583
Chelm. S Dv. Sal (imp). Swel (imp). Wel. Yk (imp).

2136.5 Bible. English, 1583
[Anr ed.] 4°; C. Barker.
New (imp)*. Roch (2 −1 tpw).

2141 Bible. English, 1584
Roch (2 −1 imp).

2143 Bible. English, 1585
Cant (3 −all imp). Derb (imp).
IoM (imp). Win (imp). Yk.

2146 Bible. English, 1587
Carl (imp). Roch (tpw, one dated 1599 substituted)*.

2148 Bible. English, 1588
Cant (imp). Dur (imp).

2150 Bible. English, 1589
Roch (tpw). S Pl (O.T. only)*.
Tru*.

2153 Bible. English, 1590
Cant (imp). Sal (tpw).

2158 Bible. English, 1592
S Pl (N.T. only).

2160 Bible. English, (1594, 1593)
Linc.

2161 Bible. English, 1594 (1495
[*sic*])
Brec (N.T. only)*. Chi. Glo.

2165 Bible. English, 1595
Nor (tpw). Pet.

2167 Bible. English, 1595
Cant (imp). Dur (imp).

2168 Bible. English, 1597
Deputies …
Cant (imp). Her (N.T. only).
Linc. S Asa.

2171 Bible. English, 1598 (1597)
Cant (tpw). Liv. S Asa (imp).
Sal. Tru. Win. Yk.

2172 Bible. English, 1598 (1597)
Chi (N.T. tp only).

2174 Bible. English, 1599 [*i.e.* after 1640?]
Carl (2 −1 tpw)*. Llan (tpw)*.
Roch (imp). Tru (2)*.

2175 Bible. English, 1599 [*i.e.* after 1640?]
Cant (imp). Roch (2).

2177 Bible. English, 1599 [*i.e.* 1633]
Cant (imp). New.

2179 Bible. English, 1599 [*i.e.* c.1639]
Bris. Rip. S Asa (imp).

2180 Bible. English, 1599 [*i.e.* after 1617?]
Cant (imp; issue with colophon).

2181 Bible. English, 1600
S Asa.

2182 Bible. English, 1600
Chi (tpw). Liv (N.T. only). Rip.

2183 Bible. English, 1601
Cant (imp). Chi. Linc (imp; O.T. has tp of STC 2166, N.T. that of STC 2172, substituted).

2185 Bible. English, 1602
Her (lacks N.T.). Roch (tpw).
Wel (imp). Yk.

2188 Bible. English, 1602
Cant (imp). Yk.

2189 Bible. English, 1603
Swel*.

2190 Bible. English, 1603
S Asa. Swel.

2192 Bible. English, 1603
Cant (tpw).

2194 Bible. English, 1605
S Dv.

2197 Bible. English, 1606
Nor.

2198 Bible. English, 1606
8°.
Win.

2199 Bible. English, (1607)
Ely. Her. Yk.

2200 Bible. English, 1607
Cant.

2201 Bible. English, 1607
Bris.

2202 Bible. English, 1608
Dur (imp; N.T. dated 1610). Ex.
Linc.

2203 Bible. English, 1608
Gen.i.3.: 'Then sayd God'
Cant. Liv (imp). Yk.

2204 Bible. English, 1608
Cant (imp). S Alb (tpw).

2207 Bible. English, 1609 (1610)
Cant (3). New (Genesis —Job
only). Sal. Tru. Wel. Wor (2).
Yk.

2210 Bible. English, 1610
Swel (tpw).

2211 Bible. English, 1610
Her (imp)*.

2213 Bible. English, 1610 (1611)
Her. Yk (N.T. only).

2215 Bible. English, 1611
Linc. Tru (tpw). Yk.

2216 Bible. English, 1611
Bur. Ches (tpw). Ely (2 —1 tpw).
Glo (tpw). Her. Rip (imp).
S Asa. Swel (2 —1 imp*). Win.
Yk (4 —all imp).

2217 Bible. English, 1611
Ches (imp)*. Ex. Roch (imp)*.
Sal (imp). Win.

2218 Bible. English, (1611
[colophon:]1612)
Her (imp). Sal. Swel.

2219 Bible. English, 1612
Her.

2224 Bible. English, 1613 (1611)
Cant (4 —all imp). Chelm. Her
(imp)*. Swel (tp imp).

2225 Bible. English, 1613 (1612)
Derb. Liv.

2226 Bible. English, 1613
Derb. Nor. Rip. Sal (imp). Yk.

2227 Bible. English, 1613
Roch. S Pl (imp). Tru.

2232 Bible. English, 1614 (1613)
Brec. Cant. S Asa.

2233 Bible. English, 1614 (1613)
Linc.

2234 Bible. English, 1614 (1615)
Rip. Roch (tpw)*.

2236 Bible. English, 1614
Carl.

2239 Bible. English, 1615
Cant (2 —1 imp). Swar (imp)*.
Tru (imp).

2241 Bible. English, 1615
Linc. Rip. Roch (tpw). Sal.
Wel.

2242 Bible. English, 1615
Glo.

2243 Bible. English, 1616 (1615)
Cant (imp). Roch.

2244 Bible. English, 1616
Cant. Linc (imp). Yk.

2245 Bible. English, 1616
Cant. Dur. Rip. Win.

2247 Bible. English, 1617
Win (N.T. only).

2252 Bible. English, 1618
Cant (imp).

2254 Bible. English, 1619
Carl.

2256 Bible. English, 1619
Liv.

2258 Bible. English, 1619 (1620)
S Asa (tpw).

2258a *See:* 2262

2262 Bible. English, 1620 (1621)
Formerly also STC 2258a.
Ches. Ex (tpw). S Alb. Win
(tpw).

2263 Bible. English, 1621
Win.

2265 Bible. English, 1622 (1623)
Dur. S Alb.

2270 Bible. English, 1625 (1624)
Cant. Her.

2271 Bible. English, 1625
Liv (imp). Roch.

2279 Bible. English, 1627
Lich (tpw). Sal.

2280 Bible. English, 1627
Cant.

2281 Bible. English, 1628
Roch. Yk.

2284 Bible. English, 1629
Ex. Her (tpw). Nor. Wel (imp).

2285 Bible. English, (1629)
T. a. J. Buck, prs to the Univ. of
Cambridge.
Wor (tpw)*.

2285.5 Bible. English, (1629
[c.1635])
[Anr issue] T. Buck & R. Daniel, prs
to the Univ. of Cambridge.
Pet.

2286 Bible. English, 1629
Tru.

2288 Bible. English, 1629
Tru.

2289 Bible. English, 1630
Ches (tpw)*.

2289.5 Bible. English, 1630
[Anr issue] R. Barker a. J. Bill; N.T.
and colophon retain impr. as in STC
2289.
Pet. S Pl (frag.)*.

2290 Bible. English, 1630
B.L., Wisd. xix. 22: 'neither diddest'
Her*. Liv*. Sal.

2294 Bible. English, (1630)
Cant. Roch (imp).

2297 Bible. English, 1631
Z1ʳ headline: '... in the creature'; Job
xl. 8: 'iudgement ... mee'
Sal*.

2298.5 Bible. English, 1632
[Anr ed.] 2°; R. Barker a. assignes of
J. Bill.
Roch (N.T. only). Swel (tpw).
Wel (date altered in MS to 1633).
Yk (date altered in MS to 1633).

2300 Bible. English, 1632 (1631)
Bris. Cant (frag.)*. Swel (imp).

2302 Bible. English, 1632
1 Chron. xxix. 30, last line begins:
'uer all the kingdomes'; Orn. before 2
Chron.: crown.
Lich*.

2306 Bible. English, 1633 (1634)
Cant (imp). Sal (imp)*. Win.
Yk.

2310 Bible. English, (1633)
Chi. S Asa.

2313 Bible. English, 1634
Linc (imp). Liv (tpw)*. Nor.

2313a Bible. English, 1634
p. 3 headline: 'Adams genealogie'
Ex*. Swel*.

2313b Bible. English, 1634
Gen. tp: 're-/vised, By'
Cant (with gen. tp of STC 2313).

2313b.5 Bible. English, 1634 (1636) [Anr ed., Roy.] R. Barker a. assignes of J. Bill.
Derb.

2320 Bible. English, (1635)
Cant (tpw). Wel.

2321 Bible. English, 1635 'authentical'; (Rouen), J. Cousturier. Her (vol. 1 only). Roch. S Asa (vol. 1 only).

2323 Bible. English, 1637 (1638)
Roch.

2326 Bible. English, 1637
Cant. Linc (imp). Roch.

2327 Bible. English, 1637
S Pl. Yk.

2328.3 Bible. English, 1637 (1631) [Anr ed.] 8°; Edinburgh, R. Young; Ends Kkk8.
Cant.

2329 Bible. English, 1638 Orn. before Ezra: church.
Sal*.

2329.2 Bible. English, 1638 [Anr ed.] As STC 2329; Orn. before Ezra: lion and unicorn.
Cant (2 − 1 imp).

2329.6 Bible. English, 1638 [Anr ed.] 12°; R. Barker a. assignes of J. Bill; A3ʳ, col. 1, line 3: 'the earth'
Glo (tpw).

2331 Bible. English, (1638)
Brec (2). Cant (3 − 2 imp). Chi (2). Ex (O.T. only, tpw). Lich. Win (3). Yk (imp).

2335 Bible. English, 1639 (1638)
Lich. Roch (2 − 1 lacks N.T.).

2337 Bible. English, 1639 R. Barker a. assignes of J. Bill; N.T. tp: 'Tetsament [sic]'
Cant (N.T. only).

2337.3 Bible. English, 1639 [Anr ed.] As STC 2337, but N.T. tp: 'Testament'
Cant.

2338 Bible. English, 1639 T. Buck a. R. Daniel, prs to the Univ. of Cambridge.
Swel.

2339 Bible. English, 1640 (1639)
Cant. Dur. Ex. Glo (imp). Pet. S Pl. Win (2 − 1 imp).

2340 Bible. English, 1640 (1641, 1642)
Formerly also STC 2341.
Dur (imp).

2341 *See:* 2340

2342 Bible. English, 1640 (1639)
S Alb*.

2343 Bible. English, 1640
S Asa.

2344 Bible. English, 1640 'The Bible ...'
Chi (tpw; tp of 1672 subst.). S Alb*.

2346 Bible. English, 1640 (1639)
Tru (imp).

2347 Bible. Welsh, 1588
Ban (imp). S Asa (imp).

2348 Bible. Welsh, 1620
Ban (3 − 2 imp, 1 tpw). Linc. S Asa (5 − 1 imp, 1 tpw). S Dv (imp).

2349.5 Bible. Welsh, 1630 [Anr issue] R. Barker a chan assignes J. Bill; Heading to Genesis begins: 'Llyfr'
Ban (imp)*. Cant. S Asa (4 − 2 imp, 1 tpw)*.

2351 Bible. O.T. Pentateuch, 1534 No impr. on tp.
S Pl.

2352 Bible. O.T. Psalms. Greek, 1590
S Pl.

2353.5 Bible. O.T. Psalms. Greek & Latin, [1611] 'Davidis regii prophetae votum'; 4°; Etonae, J. Norton.
Yk.

2356 Bible. O.T. Psalms. Latin, 1575 16°; T. Vautrollerius.
Ely. Pet.

2357 *See:* 2032

2361 Bible. O.T. Psalms. Latin, 1581 '... Eobanum Hessum ...'; 16°.
Pet.

2367 Bible. O.T. Psalms. Latin, 1640
Yk.

2368 Bible. O.T. Psalms. Latin & English, 1540
S Pl (imp).

2369 Bible. O.T. Psalms. Latin & Anglo-Saxon, 1640
Bur (tpw). Cant. Carl. Dur. Ex. Linc. S Pl (2). Wor.

2372.4 Bible. O.T. Psalms. English. Prose, 1535 [Anr ed. of STC 2372.6, which was formerly 14620] 16°; No impr.
Linc (imp).

2374 Bible. O.T. Psalms. English. Prose, [1544?] (E. Whytchurch).
Linc. S Pl.

2377 Bible. O.T. Psalms. English. Prose, 1549 (R. Grafton).
Linc (pt 2 only).

2383.6 Bible. O.T. Psalms. English. Prose, 1557 'The Psalmes of Dauid'; 16°; No impr.; a − z⁸ A − F⁸.
Pet (imp).

2386.2 Bible. O.T. Psalms. English. Prose, 1567 [Anr ed.] 4°; In off. G. Seres.
S Pl (frag.).

2389 *See:* 4395

2398 *See:* 2034

2399.3 Bible. O.T. Psalms. English. Prose, 1584 [Anr ed.] 8°; R. Warde.
Wor (frag.).

2399.7 Bible. O.T. Psalms. English. Prose, (1587) [Anr ed.] 4°; (H. Denham) the assigne of W. Seres.
S Pl (imp). Win (imp).

2407 Bible. O.T. Psalms. English. Prose, 1612 'psalmes'
Linc. Swel.

2411 Bible. O.T. Psalms. English. Prose, 1617 (1618)
Pet.

2413.5 Bible. O.T. Psalms. English. Prose, 1622 'The psalter or psalmes of David'; 8°; f. the Co. of Statrs.
S Pl (imp).

2413 *See:* 16353

2415.2 Bible. O.T. Psalms. English. Prose, 1629 [Variant] Amstelredam, printed by J.F. Stam.
Wor.

2417.3 Bible. O.T. Psalms. English, 1635 [Anr ed.] 16°; f. the Co. of Statrs.
Linc (pt 2 only, imp).

2424.1 Bible. O.T. Psalms. English. Metrical, (1552) [Anr ed.] 'All suche psalmes of Dauid ...'; 8°; 1 col., B.L., A − G⁸ H⁴; A2ʳ line 5 of heading begins: 'the church'; Cl ʳ begins: 'that I slepe'
Cant.

2428 Bible. O.T. Psalms. English.
Metrical, 1561
S Pl.

2435 Bible. O.T. Psalms. English.
Metrical, 1565
S Asa (imp).

2439.5 Bible. O.T. Psalms. English.
Metrical, (1569)
[Anr ed.] 4°; J. Daye, cum priuilegio
per decennium.
Rip (proof (?) sheets of tp only)*.

2439 *See: 2729*

2444 Bible. O.T. Psalms. English.
Metrical, 1574
Cant (imp).

2446 Bible. O.T. Psalms. English.
Metrical, 1576
Liv.

2450 Bible. O.T. Psalms. English.
Metrical, 1578
Rip (imp).

2452 Bible. O.T. Psalms. English.
Metrical, 1579
1 col., B.L.
Linc (imp)*.

2452.7 Bible. O.T. Psalms. English.
Metrical, 1579
[Anr ed.] 4°; J. Daye; 2 cols, B.L.,
A – H^8 I^2.
S Pl (imp).

2454 Bible. O.T. Psalms. English.
Metrical, 1580
Formerly also STC 2455.
S Pl (imp).

2455 *See: 2454*

2457 Bible. O.T. Psalms. English.
Metrical, 1581
Yk.

2458 Bible. O.T. Psalms. English.
Metrical, 1581
2 cols, B.L., A^4 B – H^8; 'A' of sig. A2
under 'p' of 'playnt'
New*. Wor (imp).

2460 Bible. O.T. Psalms. English.
Metrical, 1582 (1583)
J. Daye.
S Pl (imp).

2462 Bible. O.T. Psalms. English.
Metrical, 1583
Bris.

2463 Bible. O.T. Psalms. English.
Metrical, 1583
Dur.

2466 Bible. O.T. Psalms. English.
Metrical, 1583
Cant. Liv. Pet (imp)*.

2467 Bible. O.T. Psalms. English.
Metrical, 1584
1 col., B.L., A^4 B – Y^8 Aa – Ff^8 Gg^4.
Glo (imp).

2472.5 Bible. O.T. Psalms. English.
Metrical, 1586
As STC 2472, but: A – M^8.
Win (imp).

2486 Bible. O.T. Psalms. English.
Metrical, 1594
Linc (imp).

2490.3 Bible. O.T. Psalms. English.
Metrical, 1595
[Anr ed.] As STC 2490; 2 cols, B.L.,
A – M^8.
Wor (imp).

2492 Bible. O.T. Psalms. English.
Metrical, 1597 (1595)
Glo (imp).

2494 Bible. O.T. Psalms. English.
Metrical, 1598
S Asa. Tru. Win.

2494a Bible. O.T. Psalms. English.
Metrical, 1598
Dur.

2497.3 Bible. O.T. Psalms. English.
Metrical, 1599
[Anr ed. of STC 2498, with same
impr.] 2°.
Cant (imp). Dur. Nor.

2497.5 Bible. O.T. Psalms. English.
Metrical, 1599
[Anr ed. of STC 2498] 4°; J. Windet
f. the assignes of R. Daye.
Chi.

2499 Bible. O.T. Psalms. English.
Metrical, [after 1640?]
[Anr ed.] 4°; No impr.; 2 cols, rom.
A – G^8, 'C' of sig. C1 under 'e' of
'heard'
Llan*. Roch (imp).

2499.2 Bible. O.T. Psalms. English.
Metrical, [after 1640?]
[Anr ed.] As STC 2499; 'C' of sig. C1
under space after 'our'
Roch (2 – 1 imp).

2499.6 Bible. O.T. Psalms. English.
Metrical, [c.1639]
[Anr ed.] 4°; 2 cols, rom., A – G^8; 'C'
of sig. C1 under 'ar' of 'heard'
S Asa.

2500.5 Bible. O.T. Psalms. English.
Metrical, 1600
[Anr ed.] 8°; J. Windet f. the assignes
of R. Day.
S Asa.

2502 Bible. O.T. Psalms. English.
Metrical, 1601
Cant (imp). Linc (imp).

2503 Bible. O.T. Psalms. English.
Metrical, 1601
Day; 2 cols, rom., A – G^8.
New*.

2503.5 Bible. O.T. Psalms. English.
Metrical, 1601
[Anr ed.] 8°; J. Windet f. the assignes
of R. Day; 1 col., B.L.
Cant.

2508 Bible. O.T. Psalms. English.
Metrical, 1603
... Day.
Yk.

2512 Bible. O.T. Psalms. English.
Metrical, 1604
Cant.

2512a Bible. O.T. Psalms. English.
Metrical, 1604
Carl.

2513 Bible. O.T. Psalms. English.
Metrical, 1604
Swel.

2517 Bible. O.T. Psalms. English.
Metrical, 1605
S Dv (imp).

2518 Bible. O.T. Psalms. English.
Metrical, 1605
Linc.

2518+ Bible. O.T. Psalms. English.
Metrical, 1605
'The whole booke of psalmes ...'; 8°;
f. the Co. of Statrs.
S Pl.

2519 Bible. O.T. Psalms. English.
Metrical, 1606
Lich.

2521.3 Bible. O.T. Psalms. English.
Metrical, 1606
[Anr ed.] 2 cols, rom., A – G^8, as STC
2521, but tp has border of type orns.
Ely. Ex. Win.

2523 Bible. O.T. Psalms. English.
Metrical, 1607
2 cols, B.L., A – G^8; Tp line 4:
'meeter'
Bris*. Cant (imp).

2526 Bible. O.T. Psalms. English.
Metrical, 1608
2 cols, B.L., A – G^8.
Cant (imp)*.

2526.6 Bible. O.T. Psalms. English.
Metrical, 1608
[Anr ed.] 8°; f. the Co. of Statrs.
S Pl.

2528 Bible. O.T. Psalms. English. Metrical, 1609
A2ʳ heading: 'MEETRE'
Her*.

2529 Bible. O.T. Psalms. English. Metrical, 1609
2 cols, B.L., A–G⁸; 'B' of sig. B1 under 'r' of 'snares'
S Alb*.

2529.3 Bible. O.T. Psalms. English. Metrical, 1609
[Anr ed.] 4°; f. the Co. of Statrs; 2 cols, B.L., A–G⁸; 'B' of sig. B1 under 'l' of 'subtile'
Linc (imp)*. Liv*. Rip (imp).

2533 Bible. O.T. Psalms. English. Metrical, 1610
2 cols, rom., A–G⁸.
Glo (imp)*. Yk (imp)*.

2534 Bible. O.T. Psalms. English. Metrical, 1610
2 cols, rom., A–G⁸; pp. '110' [i.e. 100].
Her*.

2539 Bible. O.T. Psalms. English. Metrical, 1612
Cant. Dur. Rip. Sal. Swel.

2540 Bible. O.T. Psalms. English. Metrical, 1612
A–G⁸.
Linc (imp).

2548 Bible. O.T. Psalms. English. Metrical, 1614
Brec*. Derb. S Asa (imp).

2549 Bible. O.T. Psalms. English. Metrical, 1614
S Pl (imp).

2551 Bible. O.T. Psalms. English. Metrical, 1615
2 cols, rom., A–G⁸.
Cant (2 –both imp). Chelm*. Linc (imp)*. Rip*.

2551.3 Bible. O.T. Psalms. English. Metrical, 1615
[Anr ed.] As STC 2551, but 2 cols, B.L., A–G⁸.
Cant.

2556 Bible. O.T. Psalms. English. Metrical, 1616
2 cols, rom., A–G⁸.
Carl.

2557 Bible. O.T. Psalms. English. Metrical, 1617
2 cols, rom., A–G⁸.
Rip*.

2558 Bible. O.T. Psalms. English. Metrical, 1617
Cant.

2560 Bible. O.T. Psalms. English. Metrical, 1618
2 cols, rom., A–I⁶ K⁸.
Ex*. Yk*.

2560a Bible. O.T. Psalms. English. Metrical, 1618
2 cols, B.L., A–G⁸.
Cant (imp). Lich (imp)*. Swar*.

2563 Bible. O.T. Psalms. English. Metrical, 1619
Dur (imp). Sal (imp).

2565 Bible. O.T. Psalms. English. Metrical, 1619
Cant.

2569.7 Bible. O.T. Psalms. English. Metrical, (1620)
[Anr ed.] 4°; (f. the Co. of Statrs).
Win (tpw).

2571.5 Bible. O.T. Psalms. English. Metrical, 1620
[Anr ed.] 12°; f. the Co. of Statrs.
Yk.

2572 Bible. O.T. Psalms. English. Metrical, 1621 (1620)
2 cols, B.L., A–G⁸.
S Alb (imp)*.

2575.3 Bible. O.T. Psalms. English. Metrical, 1621
[Anr issue with prelims altered and additional tp and preface] f. Co. of Statrs; Tp A2ʳ line 12 ends: 'Efficacie'; Additional tp line 12 ends: 'Efficacie, and Vertue'
Dur*. S Pl (2 –1 imp)*.

2575a Bible. O.T. Psalms. English. Metrical, 1622
S Alb. S Asa (imp). Wor (imp).

2576.7 Bible. O.T. Psalms. English. Metrical, 1622
[Anr ed.] 8°; f. the Co. of Statrs.; 1 col., B.L., A–Aa⁸.
S Pl (imp).

2581 Bible. O.T. Psalms. English. Metrical, 1623
Her.

2582 Bible. O.T. Psalms. English. Metrical, 1623
Her.

2584 Bible. O.T. Psalms. English. Metrical, 1623
Ex.

2585 Bible. O.T. Psalms. English. Metrical, 1624
Carl.

2590 Bible. O.T. Psalms. English. Metrical, 1625
Cant (imp).

2591 Bible. O.T. Psalms. English. Metrical, 1625
1 col., B.L., A–Aa⁸.
S Asa.

2592 Bible. O.T. Psalms. English. Metrical, 1625
2 cols, rom., A–G⁸.
S Asa.

2594 Bible. O.T. Psalms. English. Metrical, 1626
Liv (imp).

2599 Bible. O.T. Psalms. English. Metrical, 1627
Cant. Linc. Pet.

2599.5 Bible. O.T. Psalms. English. Metrical, 1627
[Anr ed.] 4°; f. the Co. of Statrs.
Chi.

2600 Bible. O.T. Psalms. English. Metrical, 1627
Cant.

2604.5 Bible. O.T. Psalms. English. Metrical, 1628
[Anr ed.] 4°; f. the Co. of Statrs; 2 cols, rom., A–H⁸.
Cant (imp). Sal.

2606 Bible. O.T. Psalms. English. Metrical, 1628
Win.

2608 Bible. O.T. Psalms. English. Metrical, 1628
Chi.

2612 Bible. O.T. Psalms. English. Metrical, 1629 (1630)
2 cols, rom., A–H⁶ I⁴.
Her*.

2612.5 Bible. O.T. Psalms. English. Metrical, 1629
[Anr ed.] 2°; f. the Co. of Statrs; 1 col., B.L., A–P⁶ Q⁴.
Cant. Ex. Nor. Roch. Wel.

2613 *See*: 2617.7

2614 Bible. O.T. Psalms. English. Metrical, 1629
Roch. S Pl (imp).

2617.7 Bible. O.T. Psalms. English. Metrical, 1629
[Anr ed.] 2°; T. a. J. Buck, prs to the Univ. of Cambridge; Formerly STC 2613.
Nor (2). Wor.

2619 Bible. O.T. Psalms. English. Metrical, 1630
2 cols, rom., A – H⁸.
Sal (imp)*.

2625 Bible. O.T. Psalms. English. Metrical, 1631
Cant.

2629 Bible. O.T. Psalms. English. Metrical, 1631
Cant.

2633 Bible. O.T. Psalms. English. Metrical, 1632
Yk (2).

2634 Bible. O.T. Psalms. English. Metrical, 1632
Bris (imp). Swel (imp).

2635 Bible. O.T. Psalms. English. Metrical, 1632
Cant. Tru.

2637 Bible. O.T. Psalms. English. Metrical, 1632
2 cols, rom., A – F⁸.
Bur (imp)*. Tru*.

2637.4 Bible. O.T. Psalms. English. Metrical, 1632
[Anr ed.] 12°; f. the Co. of Statrs.
Bur. S Alb. Tru.

2640 Bible. O.T. Psalms. English. Metrical, 1633
Sal (imp). Win.

2642 Bible. O.T. Psalms. English. Metrical, 1633
Lich. Sal. Yk.

2647 Bible. O.T. Psalms. English. Metrical, 1633
Dur (imp). Roch (imp)*.

2648 Bible. O.T. Psalms. English. Metrical, 1633
Ex.

2649 Bible. O.T. Psalms. English. Metrical, 1634
W.S. f. the Co. of Statrs.
Sal.

2650 Bible. O.T. Psalms. English. Metrical, 1634
Cant.

2654 Bible. O.T. Psalms. English. Metrical, 1634
Wor.

2655 Bible. O.T. Psalms. English. Metrical, 1635
Wor.

2656 Bible. O.T. Psalms. English. Metrical, 1635
Cant. Nor. Swel (imp).

2656.5 Bible. O.T. Psalms. English. Metrical, 1635
[Anr ed.] 4°; T.P. f. the Co. of Statrs.
Yk.

2663 Bible. O.T. Psalms. English. Metrical, 1636
Wel. Yk.

2664 Bible. O.T. Psalms. English. Metrical, 1636
S Asa.

2668 Bible. O.T. Psalms. English. Metrical, 1637
Linc (imp). Wel. Yk.

2670 Bible. O.T. Psalms. English. Metrical, 1637
Her.

2671.5 Bible. O.T. Psalms. English. Metrical, 1637
[Anr ed.] As STC 2671, which has orns on A2ʳ: rose, thistle, fleur-de-lis; this has: rose, fleur-de-lis, rose.
Cant. Glo*. Yk*.

2674 Bible. O.T. Psalms. English. Metrical, 1637
Yk.

2675 Bible. O.T. Psalms. English. Metrical, 1637
Cant (imp). Linc (tpw).

2676 Bible. O.T. Psalms. English. Metrical, 1638
Roch.

2677 Bible. O.T. Psalms. English. Metrical, 1638
Her.

2678 Bible. O.T. Psalms. English. Metrical, 1638
2 cols, rom., A – F⁸ G⁴; Tp has 5 pairs of acorns.
Ex*. Sal*.

2678.2 Bible. O.T. Psalms. English. Metrical, 1638
[Anr ed.] 8°; G.M. f. the Co. of Statrs; 2 cols, rom., A – F⁸ G⁴; Tp has 7 pairs of acorns.
Yk*.

2682 Bible. O.T. Psalms. English. Metrical, 1638
Brec. Chi. Win. Yk.

2683 Bible. O.T. Psalms. English. Metrical, 1638
Lich (imp).

2685 Bible. O.T. Psalms. English. Metrical, 1639
S Pl.

2686 Bible. O.T. Psalms. English. Metrical, 1639
2 cols, rom., A – F⁸.
Cant. Ex*. Lich*.

2686.2 Bible. O.T. Psalms. English. Metrical, 1639
[Anr ed.] As STC 2686, but A – F⁸ G⁴, no rule between columns.
Cant (2 – both imp).

2693 Bible. O.T. Psalms. English. Metrical, 1640
Linc. Liv. S Dv.

2694 Bible. O.T. Psalms. English. Metrical, 1640
(J.Okes) f. the Co. of Statrs.
Cant. Pet.

2696 Bible. O.T. Psalms. English. Metrical, 1640
B8ʳ catchword: 'Judica'
S Asa.

2697+ Bible. O.T. Psalms. English. Metrical, 1640
16°; E.G. for the Co. of Statrs.
Yk.

2698 Bible. O.T. Psalms. English. Metrical, 1640
1 col., rom., A – O¹²; B1ʳ line 7 from bottom: 'jealous'
Linc*.

2708 Bible. O.T. Psalms. English. Metrical, 1615
Liv.

2717 Bible. O.T. Psalms. English. Metrical, 1632
Bris.

2729 Bible. O.T. Psalms. English. Metrical, [1567?]
Formerly also STC 2439.
Cant. Linc.

2731 Bible. O.T. Psalms. English. Metrical, 1620
'Al the psalmes of David: with certaine songes & canticles ...'
Chi. Wor.

2732 Bible. O.T. Psalms. English. Metrical, (1631)
'The Psalmes of King David ...'; (Oxford ...); Formerly also STC 14389.
Chi (tpw). Dur. Linc.

2733 *See*: 2736.5

2734 Bible. O.T. Psalms. English. Metrical, 1632
'All the French psalm tunes with English words ...'; ... with permission of the Co. of Statrs.
Chi. Linc.

2735 Bible. O.T. Psalms. English.
Metrical, 1632
Cant.

2736 Bible. O.T. Psalms. English.
Metrical, 1636
'The psalmes of King David ...'
Cant. Ches. Ex. Lich. New.
Yk (2).

2736.5 Bible. O.T. Psalms. English.
Metrical, [1637?]
[Anr ed. with prose in the margin] 8°;
[T.Harper]; Formerly STC 2733 &
2736b.
Chi. Ex (tpw)*.

2736b *See*: 2736.5

2740 Bible. O.T. Psalms. Dutch,
1566
S Pl.

2744 Bible. O.T. Psalms. Welsh,
1603
Formerly also STC 17915.
S Asa (tpw).

2745 Bible. O.T. Psalms. Welsh,
1621
S Asa (2 −1 imp). Wel.

2746 Bible. O.T. Psalms. Welsh,
1630
Cant. S Asa (2).

2747 Bible. O.T. Psalms. Welsh,
1638
Ban (imp). Linc.

2749 Bible. O.T. Psalms, 1613
Pet.

2752.5 Bible. O.T. Books of
Solomon, 1537
'The bokes of Salomō'; 8°;
Southwarke, J. Nicolson.
S Pl.

2753 Bible. O.T. Books of Solomon,
1540
(R. Redmā).
S Pl (imp).

2754 Bible. O.T. Books of Solomon,
[c.1545]
(E. Whytchurch).
Linc.

2759.5 Bible. O.T. Books of
Solomon, 1601
'The schoole of wisedome. ...
Gathered ... by T. Timme'; 8°; E.
Allde.
Pet.

2761 Bible. O.T. Ecclesiastes, 1579
Pet. Rip. Yk.

2761.5 Bible. O.T. Ecclesiastes,
[1551]
'The knoledge of good and iuyle,
other wyse calyd Ecclesiastes'; 8°; R.
Crowleye f. J. Case.
Linc.

2764 *See*: 2020

2769 Bible. O.T. Song of Solomon,
1587
S Pl.

2772 Bible. O.T. Song of Solomon,
1603
'partes'
Pet (2 −1 has pt 1 only). Yk.

2775 Bible. O.T. Song of Solomon,
1623
Wor.

2779.5 Bible. O.T. Lamentations,
[1587?]
'The Lamentations and holy
mourninges of ... Jeremiah, ...'; 12°;
J. Windet f. H. Bate.
Pet (imp).

2780 Bible. O.T. Lamentations,
1606
Chi. Rip. Wor.

2785 Bible. O.T. Daniel, 1596
Chi. Linc (A^4 only, as Yk). Rip.
Yk (1 copy, plus A^4 of an
incomplete and different version
of pt of the prelims headed 'The
graces of Daniel').

2787 Bible. O.T. Daniel, 1607
Ex.

2787.7 Bible. O.T. Obadiah, 1601
'Prophetia Hhobadyah, ... Shelomo
Yarchi, ... Gulielmum Bedwellum';
4°; Ex off. R. Field.
Wor.

2790 Bible. O.T. Haggai, 1586
'prophet'
Yk.

2792.5 Bible. N.T. Polyglot, with
English, 1599 (1600)
'Nouum testamentum ... Studio &
labore E. Hutteri'; 2 vols; 2°;
Noribergae.
Ex. Glo (tpw). Linc. Pet. Roch.
Win.

2794 Bible. N.T. Greek, 1592
Cant (cropped). Lich.

2795 Bible. N.T. Greek, 1622
Ely (tpw)*. Linc. Yk.

2796 Bible. N.T. Greek, 1632
Cant (2). Chi. Ex (imp)*. Rip.
S Asa. S Pl. Tru*. Yk (2).

2798 Bible. N.T. Greek, 1633
*4^v last line: 'spiciat. Vale.'
Ex*. Her. Lich (2)*. Llan*.
S Pl (2)*. Tru*. Yk (3)*.

2798.5 Bible. N.T. Greek, 1633
[Anr ed.] As STC 2798, but this has:
'*tem opportunitatis* ... Vale.'
Bris. Cant (2).

2799 Bible. N.T. Latin, 1540
Linc. S Pl (imp). Yk.

2803 Bible. N.T. Latin, 1574
Ex. Rip (imp).

2807 *See*: 2056

2810a *See*: 2061

2815 Bible. N.T. Latin & English,
(1538)
Cant (imp). Linc (imp). S Pl
(imp). Wor.

2816 Bible. N.T. Latin & English,
[1538]
Date in title; E8^r lines 13−14: 'before/
the cock synge'
Liv (imp). Pet (imp).

2816.7 Bible. N.T. Latin & English,
[1538]
Formerly STC 2818; 'The newe
testament ...'; Date in title.
Cant (imp)*. S Pl (imp).

2817 Bible. N.T. Latin & English,
1538
Cant (imp). S Pl. Yk (imp).

2818 *See*: 2816.7

2819 Bible. N.T. Latin & English,
1548 (1547)
'The newe testament ...'; (W. Powell);
Also found with colophon dated 1548.
Cant (tpw; colophon: 1547).

2820 Bible. N.T. Latin & English,
1549
(W. Powell).
S Pl (tpw).

2821 Bible. N.T. Latin & English,
1550
Cant (2 −1 imp). S Pl (tpw). Sal
(imp).

2824 Bible. N.T. English, [1526?]
8°.
S Pl (imp).

2826 Bible. N.T. English, (1534)
(Anwerp, ...).
S Pl (imp).

2830 Bible. N.T. English, 1535
(1534)
'The newe testament ...'; Foliated;
Matt. begins on A2^r.
S Pl (frag.)*.

2831 Bible. N.T. English, 1536
Cant (imp). S Pl (imp).

2835 Bible. N.T. English, 1536
First page of Acts, line 1 of text:
'I[7]N'
S Pl (imp).

2835.4 Bible. N.T. English, [1536?]
[Anr ed.] As STC 2835, but: 'I[6]N
the'; and line 5 from bottom ends:
'yᵉ'
S Pl (imp).

2836 Bible. N.T. English, 1538
'The new testament ...'; (Antwerpe,
M. Crom).
S Pl (imp).

2841 Bible. N.T. English, 1538
'The newe testament ...'
Cant (tp imp).

2842 Bible. N.T. English, 1539
(Antwerpe, M. Crom).
S Pl (2 −both imp).

2844 Bible. N.T. English, 1539
(T. Petyt f. ...).
S Pl.

2854 Bible. N.T. English, 1548
'... newe testamente'; Tome 2 now at
STC 2854.6 and STC 2854.7.
Bur (3 −2 imp)*. Chelm*. Glo
(imp)*. Her (imp)*. Lich*. Pet*.
S Asa (imp)*. Tru (imp)*. Wel*.
Wor*.

2854.5 Bible. N.T. English, 1548
[Anr ed.] 2°; E. Whitchurche; Preface,
B1ʳ catchword: 'a manne'
Cant.

2854.6 Bible. N.T. English, 1549
'The second tome ...'; 2°; E.
Whitchurche; Romans, A1ʳ heading:
'The paraphrase'
Bur (3 −2 imp)*. Cant. Glo
(imp)*. Her*. Lich (tpw)*. Pet*.
Wel*.

2854.7 Bible. N.T. English, 1549
[Anr issue] As STC 2854.6, but:
'paraprase' [sic].
Cant.

2856 Bible. N.T. English, 1549
'The newe testament ...'
Cant (imp). Wor (tpw)*.

2857 Bible. N.T. English, 1549
(W. Copland).
Nor (imp)*.

2859 Bible. N.T. English, 1550
(R. Wolfe).
Cant.

2862.5 Bible. N.T. English, [1550?]
[Anr ed.] 4°; (Worcester, J. Oswen,
they be also to sell at Shrewesbury).
S Pl (Ss⁸ only).

2866 Bible. N.T. English, 1551
(1552)
(E. Whitchurche).
Cant (vol. 1 only; imp). Liv (vol.
1 only, tpw). Pet (imp). Roch
(tpw). Sal (2 −1 tpw). Swar.

2867 Bible. N.T. English, [1552]
(R. Jugge).
S Pl (2 −both imp).

2869 Bible. N.T. English, [1553]
(R. Jugge).
Cant (2 −1 tpw; 1 imp). Sal
(imp)*.

2871 Bible. N.T. English, 1557
Cant (2).

2872c.5 Bible. N.T. English, [after
1561?]
[Anr ed.] 16°; (R. Jugge); Headlines
in rom.
S Pl (imp).

2873 Bible. N.T. English, [1566?]
(R. Jugge).
Pet (tpw). S Pl (2 −both imp).

2878 Bible. N.T. English, 1576
'The new testament ... Greeke'
Cant.

2879 Bible. N.T. English, 1577
Cant (imp).

2881.5 Bible. N.T. English, [c.1580]
[Anr ed.] 16°; [C. Barker].
S Asa.

2884 Bible. N.T. English, 1582
Cant. Carl. Rip. Sal (imp).
Wor (2 −1 tp imp; 1 imp).

2885 Bible. N.T. English, (1583)
'newe'
Cant. Chi (imp). Liv. Pet (imp).

2888 Bible. N.T. English, 1589
Cant (2). Pet. Wor.

2894 Bible. N.T. English, 1596
Linc. S Pl. Swel.

2898 Bible. N.T. English, 1600
'authentical'
Cant (3 −1 imp). Dur. Ely. Glo.
Nor. Sal. Wel. Wor.

2900 Bible. N.T. English, 1601
'The text of the new testament ...
translated by the papists ...'; R.
Barker.
Ban (imp). Cant (2). Dur. Ely.
Glo (imp). Linc. Liv. Wor. Yk.

2900.3 Bible. N.T. English, 1601
[Anr issue] Imp. G.B.
Cant (imp). Swel.

2904 Bible. N.T. English, 1605
S Pl.

2906 Bible. N.T. English, 1608
S Pl (imp)*.

2908 Bible. N.T. English, 1610
S Pl (imp)*.

2910 Bible. N.T. English, 1612
Liv.

2912 Bible. N.T. English, 1613
Wor (tp only)*.

2917 Bible. N.T. English, 1617
'The text of the new testament ...'; Tp
varies: 'Fvke' or 'Fvlke'
Bur. Cant. Chelm. Ely (tpw).
Her. Sal. Wor.

2918 Bible. N.T. English, 1617
Bris. Ex. IoM. Lich. New.
Nor. Wel. Win.

2918+ Bible. N.T. English, 1617
[Variant?] 2°; Deputies of C. Barker.
Ches.

2920 Bible. N.T. English, 1619
12° or 24°?
Yk.

2923 Bible. N.T. English, 1621
'The new testament ... translated ...'
Cant. Ches.

2938 Bible. N.T. English, 1631
Cant. S Asa. Tru.

2947 Bible. N.T. English, 1633
'The text of the new testament ...'; ...
on [sic] of the assignes of H. Ogden.
Cant. Carl. Her. Linc. Liv.
S Asa.

2955 *See*: 2956

2956 Bible. N.T. English, 1640
Formerly also STC 2955; 1st 3 words
of title occupy 2 lines.
Cant.

2959 Bible. N.T. Spanish, 1596
Cant (imp). Ely. Her.

2960 Bible. N.T. Welsh, 1567
(H. Denham at the costes of H. Toy).
Ban (imp). Her. Linc. S Asa
(imp). Wel (v. imp).

2961 Bible. N.T. Gospels, 1571
Cant (2). Linc. Roch.

2963 Bible. N.T. Gospels, 1610
(T. Dawson,) imp. ...
Ches. Ely. Her.

2964.5 Bible. N.T. Liturgical
Epistles & Gospels, [1537?]
'Here be-/gynneth the pystles and/
gospels ...'; 4°; (Robert Redman).
Linc.

2965 Bible. N.T. Liturgical Epistles
& Gospels, 1538
(Paris).
Cant.

2967.7 Bible. N.T. Liturgical
Epistles & Gospels, [1545?]
[Anr ed.] 'The epi-/stles and gospelles
wyth a brief/ postil ...'; 4°; (R.
Bankes,/ and are to be solde in Powles
churche yarde/ by Thomas Petyt).
Linc.

2968 Bible. N.T. Liturgical Epistles
& Gospels, [1540?]
'The epi-/stles and gospelles with a
brief po-/stil ... from after Easter/ tyll
Aduent ...'; 4°; (R. Bankes); Tp verso
has 5-line 'F'
Cant (imp). Ches*. S Pl*.

2968.5 Bible. N.T. Liturgical
Epistles & Gospels, [1545?]
[Anr ed.] 4°; (R. Bankes); Tp verso
has 3-line 'F'
Linc. Pet.

2968.7 Bible. N.T. Liturgical
Epistles & Gospels, [1547?]
[Anr ed.] 4°; (R. Bankes); Tp verso
has 2-line 'F'
Pet (1 leaf only, bound with STC
2968.5).

2969 Bible. N.T. Liturgical Epistles
& Gospels, [1540?]
'The epi-/stles and gospelles with a
brief postyll/ ... from Trinitie sonday
tyll/ Aduent ...'; 4°; (R. Bankes, solde
by A. Clerke); ff. lxvij–clxxxvi.
Cant. Ches*. S Pl*.

2969.5 Bible. N.T. Liturgical
Epistles & Gospels, [1546?]
[Anr ed.] As STC 2969, but: ff. lxvii–
clxxxvi.
Linc*. Pet.

2973 Bible. N.T. Liturgical Epistles
& Gospels, [c.1545]
(J. Herforde).
Cant (imp).

2975.5 Bible. N.T. Liturgical
Epistles & Gospels, [1549?]
'Here/ begineth the/ pystles and
gos-/pels of euery/ ...'; 8°; [N.pl.].
Linc.

2975.7 Bible. N.T. Liturgical
Epistles & Gospels, (1550)
'The/ epystles & gospels, of/ euery
Sondaye, ...'; 8°; (T. Raynalde).
S Pl.

2979 Bible. N.T. Liturgical Epistles
& Gospels, [c.1555?]
'pistles'; (A. Vele).
Liv.

2980 Bible. N.T. Liturgical Epistles
& Gospels, [c.1555?]
(W. Powell).
Cant (imp).

2980.2+ Bible. N.T. Liturgical
Epistles & Gospels, 1559
'The epistles/ and gospels, of euery/
Sondaye, and holy day/ ...'; 8°; [W.
Seres]; A–N⁸ +?
Cant (imp).

2987.5 Bible. N.T. Epistles of John,
1536
'In secundam et tertiam, epistolam
Joannis expositio'; 8°; Per J. Byddel.
Sal.

2988 Bible. N.T. Revelation, 1592
'Apocalypsis. A briefe ...'
Cant.

2990 Bible. N.T. Revelation, 1596
Legate.
Pet.

2995 Bible. Selections. Latin, 1544
(In off. ...).
Yk.

2998 Bible. Selections. English,
1621
Linc (imp).

3003.5 Bible. Selections. English,
1545 [1547–53]
[Anr ed.] 8°; (In the house of T.
Berthelet).
Linc (tpw).

3006.5 Bible. Selections. English,
1556
[Anr ed.] 8°; No impr.
S Pl.

3014 Bible. Selections. English,
1535 (1536)
(Andwarpe, ...).
S Pl (tpw).

3040 Bible. Appendix, (1548)
(W. Hill).
Cant. Linc. Pet (3).

3046 Bible. Appendix, 1535
(T. Gybson).
S Pl (imp).

3047 Bibliander, Theodore, (1542)
(Basill, ...).
Pet (2).

3049 Bicknoll, Edmond, 1579
[Anr ed., as STC 3048] F7ᵛ–8ᵛ blank.
Pet (imp).

3064 Bilson, Thomas, 1599
Cant (2). Dur. Ex (tp imp).
Her. Linc. Liv. Pet. Rip. S Pl.
Win. Wor. Yk (2).

3065 Bilson, Thomas, 1593
Carl. Dur. Her. Linc. Pet.
S Asa. Sal. Win (2). Yk.

3066 Bilson, Thomas, 1610
Bur. Cant. Ely. Ex. Her. S Pl.
Yk.

3067 Bilson, Thomas, 1611
Chi. Her. S Pl. Yk.

3068 Bilson, Thomas, 1603
Cant. Win. Yk.

3069 Bilson, Thomas, 1604
T.E. f. ...
Linc.

3070 Bilson, Thomas, 1604
Dur. Ex. Her. Linc. Pet.
S Asa. S Pl. Win. Yk (2).

3071 Bilson, Thomas, 1585
Ban. Cant (Xx1ʳ line 3 ends:
'Car-'). Carl. Ex. Linc. Pet.
S Pl. Sal. Win. Yk.

3072 Bilson, Thomas, 1586
Bur. Ely. Ex. Pet. Sal. Swel.
Win. Wor. Yk.

3083 Birckbek, Simon, 1635
Bur. Cant (imp). Dur. Ex.
Wor. Yk (2).

3087 Bird, Samuel, 1598
Yk.

3092 Bishop, John, 1598
Pet.

3096 Bishop, William, 1604
Her. Yk.

3097 Bishop, William, 1607
Cant (without the main text).
Pet. Yk.

3098 Bishop, William, 1608
Cant. Her. Yk.

3100 Bisse, James, 1585
Linc (imp). S Pl (tp imp?, or
another undated ed.?)*.

3101 Blackfriars, 1623
S Pl.

3102 Blackwell, George, 1601
Linc. Pet. Yk.

3103 Blackwell, George, 1609
Pet.

3104 Blackwell, George, 1607
'Blakwell'
Ely. Liv. Pet (2). Yk.

3105 Blackwell, George, 1607
Liv. Wel. Wor.

3106 Blackwell, George, [1601?]
Pet. Yk (2).

3115.3 Blage, Thomas, 1603
'A sermon preached at the
Charterhouse ... tenth of May. 1603';
8°; S. Stafford.
Linc.

3116 Blagrave, John, 1609
Wel (imp).

3119 Blagrave, John, [1585]
'The mathematical iewel'; (T. Dawson
f.) W. Venge.
Pet.

3121 *See*: 3115.3

3129 Blaxton, John, 1634
'Church of England'
Cant (cropped). Wor.

3129a Blaxton, John, 1634
J. Norton, sold by F. Bowman in
Oxford.
Ex. Pet.

3133 Blenkow, John, 1640
Carl. S Pl.

3150 Blundeville, Thomas, 1622
(1621)
Cant (tp imp).

3151 Blundeville, Thomas, 1636
Wor. Yk.

3151a.5 Blundeville, Thomas, 1638
[Anr issue] R. Bishop sold by T.
Nichols.
Sal.

3160 Blundeville, Thomas, 1602
Pet. Wor.

3162 Bluom, Joannes, 1608
Cant.

3168 Boaistuau, Pierre, [1566?]
Pet.

3169 Boaistuau, Pierre, 1574
Pet (tpw). Sal (tpw). Yk.

3171.3 Boanerges, 1624
[Anr ed.] 4°; Edinburgh (STC 3171
has Edenburgh).
Yk.

3177 Boccaccio, Giovanni, (1554)
Dur (imp). Her (imp).

3178 Boccaccio, Giovanni, [1554?]
Pet.

3185 Boccalini, Trajano, 1626
Wel. Wor. Yk.

3186 Boccus, *King*, [1537?]
(London, T. Godfray, at the coste of
dan R. Saltwode mōke at Cantorbury).
Linc (tpw). Pet.

3193 Bodin, Jean, 1606
(A. Islip) imp. G. Bishop.
Bur. Dur. Lich.

3194 Bodley, *Sir* Thomas, 1613
Yk.

3199 Boethius, Anicius Manlius
Torquatus Severinus, [1481?]
[Westminster, W. Caxton].
Rip.

3201 Boethius, Anicius Manlius
Torquatus Severinus, 1556
(J. Cawoode).
Pet.

3206 Bohemia, 1620
Yk.

3208 Bohemia, 1620
'newes'
Yk.

3209 *See*: 11356

3210 Bohemia, 1620
Yk.

3211 Bohemia, 1619
'Newes ...'
Yk.

3221 Bolton, Edmund, 1624
T.S. f. T. Walkley.
Yk.

3222 Bolton, Edmund, 1627
Her (imp).

3227 Bolton, Robert, 1640
Linc. Pet.

3228 Bolton, Robert, 1611
S Pl. Yk.

3229 Bolton, Robert, 1612
Carl.

3232 Bolton, Robert, 1631
Her. S Pl.

3233 Bolton, Robert, 1636
Cant.

3233a Bolton, Robert, 1637
Pet.

3234 Bolton, Robert, 1638
Ban. S Pl.

3236 Bolton, Robert, 1633
Pet.

3237 Bolton, Robert, 1637
Linc. Pet.

3238 Bolton, Robert, 1631
Her.

3239 Bolton, Robert, 1635
Ban. S Pl.

3240 Bolton, Robert, 1640
Pet.

3241 *See*: 3245

3242 Bolton, Robert, 1632
'... foure last things ...'; STC 1189 is
pt of this.
Bur. Glo. Llan.

3244 Bolton, Robert, 1635
STC 1190 is pt of this.
Cant. Chelm. Ex. Linc.

3245 Bolton, Robert, 1639
4 pts; Pt 3 formerly STC 3241.
Linc. Pet. S Pl.

3250 Bolton, Robert, 1625
Sal.

3251 Bolton, Robert, 1626
Linc.

3252 Bolton, Robert, 1630
Glo. Wor.

3253 Bolton, Robert, 1634
Chelm.

3254 Bolton, Robert, 1638
Ban. Pet.

3255 Bolton, Robert, 1634
E. Purslow (A. Griffin, [a.] J.
Haviland) f. R. Harford; Formerly
also STC 3248, 3246 and 3247.
Glo. Linc. Pet. S Pl.

3256 Bolton, Robert, 1635
Cant. Ex. Linc. S Pl. Wor.

3262 Bonaventura, *St*, [1494]
(R. Pynson); 36 lines to a page.
Cant (imp).

3269.5 Bonaventura, *St*, [1511 – 14]
Linc.

3277 Bonde, William, (1526)
(R. Pynson); Pt 2 formerly STC 14571.
Nor.

3278 Bonde, William, (1531)
(W. de Worde).
Cant (pt 2 only)*. Pet.

3282 Bonner, Edmund, (1555)
(In aed. I. Cawodi).
Pet (2). Sal*.

3283 Bonner, Edmund, [1555]
(In aed. I. Cawodi); Title: 'doctrine ...
homelyes ... enformation'
Ches. S Pl. Sal*.

3283.7 Bonner, Edmund, [1555]
[Anr ed.] '... doctrine ... homelies ...
reuerēd'; 4°; (In aed. I. Cawodi).
Cant.

3285.2 Bonner, Edmund, 1555
'Homelies sette forth ...'; 4°; (I.
Cawodde); 'Domine saluos fac regem'
on T1ᵛ, colophon on T2ʳ.
Ches*. Linc (imp)*. Pet (imp).
S Pl (imp)*. Sal*.

3285.9 Bonner, Edmund, 1555
'Homelies sette fourth ...'; 4°; (I.
Cawoode or I. Cawodde or I. Cawodi).
Sal (Cawodde)*. Wor (Cawodi)*.

3305 Book, [1491]
Formerly also STC 13827; '... (The
xij. proffites ...; A compendious
abstracte ...)'; (westmynstre, ...).
Dur (imp).

3309 Book, (1496)
(Westmestre, w. the worde).
Nor (imp).

3327 Book, [1543]
'... newe ... euydence'; (In ed. E.
Whytchurche be to sell by W.
Tylotson).
Pet.

3332.7 Book, (1559)
[Anr ed.] 8°; (R. Tottyll).
Ely.

3341.3 Book, (1579)
[Anr ed.] 8°; In aed. R. Tottelli.
Pet.

3342.3 Book, [1583]
[Anr ed., as STC 3342] M2ʳ line 1
ends: 'presē'
Yk (imp).

3343 Book, (1584)
Glo. Sal.

3349 Book, 1631
Yk.

3357 Book, (1532)
(R. wyer).
Linc.

3371 Boquinus, Petrus, [1581]
Pet (tpw). S Pl.

3376 Borde, Andrew, [1575]
Pet (imp).

3382 Borde, Andrew, 1576
Pet.

3393 Bossewell, John, 1572
Linc. Pet.

3394 Bossewell, John, 1597
Wor. Yk.

3396 Botero, Giovanni, 1635
Pet.

3404 Botero, Giovanni, 1630
Carl. Yk.

3407 Boughan, Edward, 1620
Pet.

3408 Boughan, Edward, 1635
Cant. S Pl.

3409.5 Boughan, Edward, 1635
[Variant w. impr.:] R.B.
Cant (2 −1 pt 1 only).

3416 Bourne, Immanuel, 1623
Yk.

3417 Bourne, Immanuel, 1620
Cant (imp).

3418 Bourne, Immanuel, 1617
S Pl. Yk.

3419 Bourne, Immanuel, 1622
Ex. S Pl (imp). Sal. Yk.

3421 Bourne, William, [1590?]
Pet (tp imp).

3427 Bourne, William, (1592)
Pet (pt 1 only).

3428 Bourne, William, 1596
Pet (pt 2 only).

3430 Bourne, William, 1620
Linc.

3434.5 Bowle, John, 1621
'Concio ad reverendissimos patres et
presbyteros totius provinciae
Cantuariensis ...'; 4°; Ap. J. Billium.
S Pl (tp imp).

3435.5 Bowle, John, 1616
'A sermon preached at
Mapple-Durham'; 4°; T.S. f. I.
Hodgets.
Pet. S Pl. Wor.

3435.7 Bownd, Nathaniel, 1615
'Saint Pauls trumpet, sounding an
alarme ...'; 2 pts; 8°; E. Griffin f. R.
Mabbe [a.] (G. Gibbes).
Linc.

3437 Bownd, Nicholas, 1606
Linc. Yk.

3452 Boys, John, 1622
(J. Haviland) f. ... .
Chi. Dur. Her (tpw). Linc
(tpw). New (imp).

3453 Boys, John, 1629 (1630)
(G. Miller) f. ...
Cant (2 −1 tpw). Carl. Nor
(tpw). Pet. Wor.

3454 Boys, John, 1629 (1638)
STC 3461 is pt of this; (R. Badger) f.
...
Cant (3 −2 imp). Linc. S Asa
(tpw). Sal. Win.

3455 Boys, John, 1609
'An exposition of al ...'; ... sold by
W. Aspley.
Wor.

3456 Boys, John, 1610
Tp line 4 begins: "
Cant. Her (tpw)*.

3456.4 Boys, John, 1610
[Anr ed.] As STC 3456, but, tp line 4
begins: 'PAL'; In impr.:
'KINGSTON'
Glo (tpw)*.

3456.7 Boys, John, 1610
[Anr ed.] As STC 3456.4, but impr.
has: "
Ches. Rip.

3458 Boys, John, 1610
'An exposition of the dominical
epistles and gospels ... winter ...'; 4°;
F. Kyngston f. W. Aspley.
Ches. Rip.

3458.5 Boys, John, 1615
'An exposition of the dominical
epistles and gospels ... winter ...'; 4°;
F. Kyngston f. W. Aspley.
Her.

3459 Boys, John, 1610
'... spring ...'; 4°; F. Kyngston f. W.
Aspley; B1ʳ catchword: 'ans'; errata
on R3ᵛ.
Rip*.

3459.7 Boys, John, 1615
[Anr ed.] 4°; E. Griffin f. W. Aspley.
Her.

3460 Boys, John, 1611
'... summer ...'; 4°; F. Kyngston f.
W. Aspley; D2ʳ line 2 ends: 'the';
errata on R4ʳ.
Ex.

3460.3 Boys, John, 1616
[Anr ed.] 4°; F. Kyngston f. W.
Aspley.
Her.

3460.7 Boys, John, 1615
'... autumne ...'; 4°; E. Griffin f. W.
Aspley.
Her.

3461 See: 3454

3462.3 Boys, John, 1615
'An exposition of the festivall epistles
and gospels. The first part ...'; 4°; E.
Griffin f. W. Aspley.
Cant. Glo. Her.

3462.7 Boys, John, 1614
'... the second part ...'; f. W. Aspley.
Cant. Glo (tpw). Her.

3463 Boys, John, 1615
'... the third part ...'; 4°; F. Kyngston
f. W. Aspley.
Cant. Glo. Her.

3465 Boys, John, 1615
Cant (imp). Glo. Her. S Pl.

3466a Boys, John, 1616
'... The first part'
Her.

3467 Boys, John, 1617
'... The second part'
Her.

3468 Boys, John, 1631
Aug: Math: f. ...
Carl. Chelm.

3475 Bracton, Henricus de, 1569
Ex. Pet. Wel.

3476 Bracton, Henricus de, 1640
... assign: J. More.
Cant. Dur. Yk.

3491 Bradford, John, *Prebendary*,
1614
Cant.

3492 Bradford, John, *Prebendary*,
1622
Bur.

3500 Bradford, John, *Prebendary*,
1574
'... sermons ... the one ...'
Cant.

3501 Bradford, John, *Prebendary*,
1581
Pet.

3505 Bradley, Francis, 1600
Linc.

3506 Bradshaw, Henry, (1521)
(R. Pynson).
Yk (imp).

3515.3 Bradshaw, William, 1636
The 10. edition. (The 9. edition); 12°;
J. B(eale) f. S.M.
Yk*.

3516 Bradshaw, William, 1605
'containening [*sic*]'
Yk.

3517 Bradshaw, William, 1640
Yk.

3518 Bradshaw, William, 1601
Formerly also STC 6873 and 6875;
A1ᵛ last line: 'effects'
Linc*. S Pl*.

3518.3 Bradshaw, William, 1601
[Anr ed.] As STC 3518, but A1ᵛ last
line: 'effectes'
Yk.

3519 Bradshaw, William, 1603
Linc. Yk.

3521 Bradshaw, William, 1621
Nor.

3522 Bradshaw, William, 1606
Yk.

3523 Bradshaw, William, 1620
Yk.

3525 Bradshaw, William, 1605
'protestation'
Yk.

3528 Bradshaw, William, 1604
Yk.

3530 Bradshaw, William, 1605
Wor. Yk.

3531 Bradshaw, William, 1605
Yk.

3533 Bradshaw, William, 1640
Carl. Yk.

3534 Bradwardine, Thomas, 1618
Bris. Bur. Chi. Dur. Ex. Her
(2). Lich. Nor. Pet. S Pl. Sal.
Swel. Win. Wor. Yk.

3538.5 Brahe, Tycho, 1632
[A variant] Nealand's name not in
colophon.
Pet (2).

3545 Brant, Sebastian, (1509)
(R. Pynson).
Linc.

3546 Brant, Sebastian, [1570]
(J. Cawood).
Cant (imp). Nor (imp?). Pet.
Yk.

3548 Brasbridge, Thomas, 1574
Wor.

3550 Brasbridge, Thomas, 1579
(T. Dawson) f. ...
Pet.

3551.5 Brasbridge, Thomas, 1580
[Anr ed.] 8°; (T. East) f. G. Byshop.
Pet.

3563 Brathwait, Richard, 1630
Cant.

3565 Brathwait, Richard, 1631
'doe'
Cant.

3581 Brathwait, Richard, 1638
'paraphras'd'
Chi. Linc. Pet.

3593 Bravonius, Florentius, 1592
Wor. Yk (2).

3598.5 Bredwell, Stephen, 1586
[A variant] J. Wolfe.
Pet.

3599 Bredwell, Stephen, 1588
Liv (date cropped?). Yk (tpw).

3603 Brentz, Johann, (1550)
(J. Daie ...).
Cant.

3604 Brereley, John, 1604
Pet.

3604.5 Brereley, John, 1608
[Anr ed., enlarged] 'The Protestants
apologie for the roman church'; 4°;
Allison & Rogers 132.
Yk (imp).

3605 Brereley, John, *pseud.*, 1608
Allison & Rogers 133.
Her (2)*. Yk.

3606 Brereley, John, 1624
Yk.

3607 Brereley, John, *pseud.* [*i.e.*
Lawrence Anderton?], 1620
'lyturgie'
Yk.

3608 Brereley, John, 1620
8°.
Bur. Pet.

3612 Brerewood, Edward, 1614
Cant. Ches. Chi.

3614 Brerewood, Edward, 1615
12°; Ap. J. Billium.
S Pl*.

3615 Brerewood, Edward, 1619
Linc.

3616 Brerewood, Edward, 1621
12°.
Yk.

3618 Brerewood, Edward, 1614
Ches. Dur. Liv. Win. Wor.

3619 Brerewood, Edward, 1622
Ban. Bris. Cant. Ex (2). Sal.
Yk.

3621 Brerewood, Edward, 1635
Bur. Cant (2). Ely (2). Ex.

3622 Brerewood, Edward, 1630
Huggins.
Cant. Linc (2). Win. Wor. Yk.

3623 Brerewood, Edward, 1631
Ban. Bur. Cant. Ely (tpw). Pet.
Yk.

3624 Brerewood, Edward, 1632
Ban. Bur. Cant. Pet (imp).
Win.

3627 Brerewood, Edward, 1640
Win.

3628 Brerewood, Edward, 1628
Sal.

3702.5 Breton, Nicholas, 1622
Formerly STC 3704; 'Strange newes
...'; ... G. Fayerbeard.
Yk.

3704 *See*: 3702.5

3712.3 Breton, Nicholas, 1640
[Anr ed.] 4°; B. Alsop, a. T. Fawcet,
f. G. Hurlock.
Linc.

3716 Brett, Richard, 1603
Pet.

3734 Bridges, John, 1587
Her (imp). Wor. Yk.

3735 Bridges, John, 1604
Pet. Yk.

3736 Bridges, John, [1571]
... f. H. Toy.
Pet. S Pl.

3737 Bridges, John, 1573
Rip.

3739 Briggs, Henry, 1624
Sal. Wor.

3740 Briggs, Henry, 1631
'arithmetike'
Wor.

3743 Bright, Timothy, 1588
'secrete'; 12°; ... the assigne of Tim.
Bright.
Sal.

3744 Bright, Timothy, [1582]
Linc.

3746 Bright, Timothy, 1583
Linc.

3747 Bright, Timothy, 1586
Linc. Yk.

3752 Bright, Thomas, 1615
Yk.

3755 Brightman, Thomas, 1615
Bur. Lich. Nor. Yk.

3756 Brightman, Thomas, 1616
Ches.

3759.5 Brinkelow, Henry, [1542?]
[Anr ed. of STC 3760] 8°; '...
complaynt ... certen'; (Sauoy, per F.
de Turona).
Pet.

3761 Brinkelow, Henry, [1548?]
Linc.

3767 Brinsley, John, the Elder, 1622
Linc.

3782 Brinsley, John, the Elder, 1619
Carl.

3783 Brinsley, John, the Elder, 1626
The tenth edition.
Cant (imp). S Pl.

3786 Brinsley, John, the Elder, 1622
Pet.

3787 Brinsley, John, the Elder, 1623
Cant. Carl (2).

3788 Brinsley, John, the Elder, 1624
Carl.

3789 Brinsley, John, the Younger,
1631
Pet.

3790 Brinsley, John, the Younger,
1631
f. R. Bird.
Carl. Ex. Lich. S Asa.

3790.5 Brinsley, John, the Younger,
1631
[Variant] f. R. Bird, sold by T. Carre
in Norwich.
Yk.

3800 Bristow, Richard, 1599
Cant. Liv. Pet. Yk.

3800.5 Bristow, Richard, (1576)
[Anr ed. of STC 3801] 12°;
(Antuerpiae, J. Foulero Anglo, excud.
L. de Winde).
Yk.

3802 Bristow, Richard, 1580
Louvaine ...
Yk.

3804 Britton, John, 1640
Cant. Dur. Wel.

3806 Broad, Thomas, 1621
Ex.

3810 Brocardo, Giacopo, 1582
Pet.

3816 Broke, Thomas, Esquire, 1548
'Certeyn meditations ...'; (J. Day ...).
Cant.

3828 Brook, Sir Robert, 1576
Dur. Yk.

3830 Brooke, Christopher, 1614
Pet.

3831 Brooke, Christopher, 1613
Yk.

3832 Brooke, Ralph, 1619
Dur (imp). Linc.

3833 Brooke, Ralph, 1622
Glo. Wor.

3834 Brooke, Ralph, [1599]
Her. Yk.

3836 Brookes, Matthew, 1627
Pet.

3843 Broughton, Hugh, 1604
Linc. Yk.

3844 Broughton, Hugh, 1605
Ex.

3845 Broughton, Hugh, 1592
Yk.

3845.5 Broughton, Hugh, [1597?]
[Heading A1ʳ:] 'An apologie to my
lorde treasorer'; 4°; [Middelburg].
Linc. Yk.

3847 Broughton, Hugh, [1611?]
Linc.

3848 Broughton, Hugh, 1605
Linc.

3849 Broughton, Hugh, 1605
'Princf [sic] Henri'
Cant. Chi*. Linc (tpw)*. Rip*.
Yk.

3850 Broughton, Hugh, [1588–90]
(f. G. Simson ...).
Cant (2 – both imp). Pet (2 – 1
imp). Rip (imp). Yk.

3851 Broughton, Hugh, [1590?]
Ex (imp). Linc. S Pl. Sal (imp)*.

3855 Broughton, Hugh, 1603
Dur. Linc. Yk (2).

3857 Broughton, Hugh, 1611
Yk.

3859 Broughton, Hugh, [1595?]
Linc.

3861 Broughton, Hugh, [1594?]
[Epistles to Queen Elizabeth et al;
heading:] 'To the most high and
mightie prince Elizabet'; 4°; Formerly
also STC 3871.
Linc (frag.). Pet. Yk.

3862 Broughton, Hugh, 1597
Linc. Yk.

3862a.3 Broughton, Hugh, 1599
'Epistolae variae, ...'; 4°; Basileae,
ap. C. Waldkirch.
Linc.

3862a.5 Broughton, Hugh, 1599
[Anr ed. of STC 3863] 4°.
Liv. Yk.

3863 Broughton, Hugh, 1605
Linc.

3864 Broughton, Hugh, 1599
Yk.

3867 Broughton, Hugh, [1613?]
Wor.

3867.9 Broughton, Hugh, [1612?]
[Heading:] 'The holy genealogie of
Jesus Christ'; 4°.
Yk.

3868 Broughton, Hugh, 1610
Chi.

3869 Broughton, Hugh, 1590
Ex. Pet. Wor. Yk.

3870 Broughton, Hugh, 1612
Linc. Yk.

3871 See: 3861

3874 Broughton, Hugh, 1612
Linc.

3875 Broughton, Hugh, 1608
Cant. Linc.

3878 Broughton, Hugh, 1608
Linc. Yk.

3879.5 Broughton, Hugh, 1609
[Anr ed. of STC 3880] 4°; A – D⁴E².
Linc. Yk.

3881 Broughton, Hugh, 1605
No imprint.
Yk.

3882 Broughton, Hugh, 1611
Linc (2). Yk (2).

3883 Broughton, Hugh, 1610
Ends on E2.
Chi*. Linc (imp). Wor*.

3884 Broughton, Hugh, 1610
A – Vu⁴Xx².
Yk.

3885 Broughton, Hugh, 1594
Linc. Pet (2).

3887 Broughton, Hugh, [1594?]
No impr. on gen. tp.
Ex. Linc (frag.). Pet.

3888 Broughton, Hugh, 1591
Yk.

3890 Broughton, Hugh, 1591
Pet (imp)*. Yk.

3891 Broughton, Hugh, 1606
'Britanie'
Linc. Yk.

3892 Broughton, Hugh, 1604
Tp line 6 ends: 'heathen'
Dur*.

3892.5 Broughton, Hugh, 1604
[Anr ed.] 4°; Tp l.6 ends: 'Hea-'
Linc. Yk.

3893 Broughton, Richard, 1601
Antwerp, (A. Coninx).
S Pl.

3894 Broughton, Richard, 1633
Cant. Her. Wor.

3897 Broughton, Richard, 1603
Yk.

3899 Broughton, Richard, 1618
8°.
Ely.

3906 Browne, Abraham, 1623
'A sermon preached at the assises ...'
Yk.

3909 Browne, Robert, [1585?]
'churches'
Glo (imp). Yk.

3910 Browne, Robert, 1582
Collates A – B⁴ C² D – H⁴; A – O⁴
Pet*.

3912 Browne, Thomas, 1634
Bur. Linc.

3912.5 Browne, Thomas, 1634
[Variant] ... sold by W. Webbe.
Wor.

3915 Browne, William, *Poet*,
[1616?]
[Bk 1] f. G. Norton.
Cant. Sal.

3915.5 Browne, William, *Poet*, 1616
[Bk 2] 2°; T. Snodham f. G. Norton.
Cant. Sal.

3919 Browning, John, 1636
Ely. S Asa. Yk (2).

3921.5 Bruce, Robert, 1614
[Anr issue] 'The mystery ...'; H.L. f.
T. Man.
Yk.

3924 Bruce, Robert, [1591?]
Yk.

3926 Bruch, Richard, 1627
Linc.

3927 Bruch, Richard, 1615
Pet (imp). S Asa.

3930 Bruele, Gualterus, 1639
Sal.

3930.3 Bruen, Robert, 1621
'The pilgrimes practice'; 12°; F.K. f.
I. Budge.
Ely.

3933 Bruni, Leonardo, 1563
Pet.

3939 Bruno, Giordano, [1583?]
Pet.

3951.5 Bruyn, Ambrosius de, 1619
[Variant] Apud J.W.
Pet.

3957 Brydges, Grey, *5th Lord
Chandos*, 1620
Cant.

3958 Bryskett, Lodowick, 1606
Pet.

3962 *See*: 10387

3964 Bucer, Martin, 1566
Pet.

3967 Buchanan, George, 1571
'mantinaris'
Pet (imp). Yk.

3974 Buchanan, George, 1579
Pet.

3977 Buchanan, George, 1581
S Pl.

3978 Buchanan, George, [1571]
Linc. Yk.

3981 Buchanan, George, [1571]
Pet.

3986 Buchanan, George, 1611
8°.
Liv.

3988 Buchanan, George, 1640
Apud E. Griffinum.
Dur. Sal.

3991 Buchanan, George, 1582
Dur. Her (imp). Lich. Rip
(tpw). S Asa*. Win.

3992 *See*: CLC foreign books – not
an STC book

3996 Buck, *Sir* George, 1605
Yk.

3997.5 Buck, James, 1637
[Variant of STC 3998] (B.A. a. T.F.)
f. J. Clark (a. W. Cooke).
Her.

3998 Buck, James, 1637
(B.A. a. T.F. f. J. Clark a.) f. W.
Cooke.
Carl (imp)*. S Asa.

4002 Buckeridge, John, 1614
Dur. Lich (tp imp). Rip. Win.
Wor. Yk.

4002.5 Buckeridge, John, [1606]
[Anr ed. of STC 4003] 4°; R. Barker;
Unpaged.
Ex. Pet. Yk.

4003 Buckeridge, John, 1606
42p.
Lich. Pet. Wor. Yk.

4005 Buckeridge, John, 1618
Formerly also STC 24039.
Bur. Ex. Linc. New. S Pl. Sal.
Win. Wor. Yk.

4012 Budden, John, 1602
Linc.

4014 Buddle, George, 1609
Dur (tpw). Linc. Pet.

4017 Buenting, Heinrich, 1619
Linc (imp). Win. Yk.

4018 Buenting, Heinrich, 1623
Cant (2).

4019 Buenting, Heinrich, 1629
A. Islip, sould by ...
Yk (imp).

4020 Buenting, Heinrich, 1636
Her. S Asa.

4022 Buggs, Samuel, 1622
Pet.

4023 Buggs, Samuel, 1622
Formerly also STC 13593.
Ex. Yk.

4024 Bulkeley, Edward, 1588
'downe'
Pet. Sal. Yk.

4025 Bulkeley, Edward, 1602
'Certaine'
Yk.

4026 Bulkeley, Edward, 1608
Sal.

4032 Bull, Henry, 1596
Pet (imp).

4033 Bullein, William, [1562]
Pet.

4043 Bullinger, Heinrich, 1571
Linc. Pet. Sal.

4045 Bullinger, Heinrich, [1541]
Cant. Pet.

4054 Bullinger, Heinrich, (1538)
'Thessaloniãs'; (Southwarke, ...).
Pet.

4056 Bullinger, Heinrich, 1577
Newberrie.
Chelm. Her. Llan (imp).

4057 Bullinger, Heinrich, 1584
Chelm.

4058 Bullinger, Heinrich, 1587
Her. Pet. S Dv.

4059 Bullinger, Heinrich, (1548)
(H. Powell).
Pet.

4061 Bullinger, Heinrich, [1561]
(J. Day).
Pet.

4062 Bullinger, Heinrich, 1573
Pet. Wel (imp). Wor.

4070 Bullinger, Heinrich, [1580?]
Pet (2 − 1 imp).

4073 Bullinger, Heinrich, 1624
Formerly also STC 5893.
Linc. Wor.

4076 Bullinger, Heinrich, [1587]
Midletonus.
Her.

4080 Bullinger, Heinrich, 1548
Linc.

4088 Bunny, Edmund, 1589
Pet. Yk.

4089 Bunny, Edmund, 1585
'Certaine prayers and other godly
exercises, for the seuenteenth of
Nouember'; Dedication to the Abp of
Canterbury.
Sal (imp)*.

4089.5 Bunny, Edmund, 1585
[Anr issue] As STC 4089, but has
dedication to the Abp of York.
Linc (dates altered to 1586,
possibly by hand-stamping; this
copy apparently also entered at
16481 in STC).

4090 Bunny, Edmund, [1588]
'... wee have set ...'
Wor.

4090.5 Bunny, Edmund, 1588
'A necessarie admonition out of the
prophet Joël ...'; 8°; R. Robinson f.
T. Man a. T. Gubbins.
Yk.

4091 Bunny, Edmund, 1610
'... adulterie, and marrying ...'
Her (frag.)*. Wor. Yk.

4093 Bunny, Edmund, 1611
Her. Yk.

4094 Bunny, Edmund, 1584
Pet (2 − 1 tp imp). Wor.

4096 Bunny, Edmund, 1576
Harison.
Pet (tpw).

4098 Bunny, Francis, 1595
Dur. Linc.

4099 Bunny, Francis, 1616
Yk.

4101 Bunny, Francis, 1595
Dur (2). Linc.

4102 Bunny, Francis, 1595
Jacson.
Dur. Pet. Yk.

4109 Burges, Cornelius, 1629
'Church of England'
Her. S Pl. Wor.

4110 Burges, Cornelius, 1622
12°.
Wor.

4111 Burges, Cornelius, 1625
... (f. W. Sheffard).
Wor (engr. tpw?). Yk (engr.
tpw).

4112 Burges, Cornelius, 1625
Pet. Wor.

4113 Burges, John, 1631
Bur. Carl. Ches. Her. Liv. Pet.
S Pl. Sal. Win. Yk.

4114 Burges, John, 1631
Bur. Her. Liv. Pet. S Pl. Sal.
Win. Yk.

4115 Burgo, Joannes de, (1510)
4°; (In alma Parisiorum academia
opera W. hopylii,) imp. W. bretton,
[London]. Uenūdatur London.
Cant. Liv. New. Yk.

4117 Burhill, Robert, 1613
Linc.

4118 Burhill, Robert, 1611
Pet.

4119 Buridanus, Joannes, 1637
Curtayne.
Ex.

4120 Buridanus, Joannes, 1640
Sal. Wel.

4123.5 Burlz, Thomas, [1580]
'An excellent and comfortable
treatise'; 8°; J. Charlewood.
Linc.

4124 Burne, Nicol, 1581
Linc. Pet. Rip. Yk.

4126 Burrell, Percival, 1629
'English'
S Asa.

4126.5 Burrell, Percival, [1629]
[Variant] As STC 4126, apart from
date.
Ex.

4129 Burroughs, Jeremiah, 1640
Ex.

4131 Burt, Thomas, 1607
Linc.

4134 Burton, Henry, 1636
[Amsterdam]; D4ᵛ line 2 from
bottom: 'throane'
S Pl*.

4135 Burton, Henry, 1636
[London]; D4ᵛ line 2 from bottom:
'throne'
Yk (2)*.

4136 Burton, Henry, 1629
Carl. Sal (2). Yk.

4137 Burton, Henry, 1627
Her (tpw)*. S Pl*. Yk (2 − 1
frag., 1 tp imp)*.

4137.7 Burton, Henry, [1635?]
[Anr ed. of STC 4137.9] 'A brief
answer to a late treatise of the
Sabbath day'; 4°.
Pet (imp).

4137.9 Burton, Henry, 1636
Formerly STC 20468.
Ex (2).

4139 Burton, Henry, 1624
Carl. Her (imp). Yk (2).

4140.7 Burton, Henry, 1636
Formerly STC 20459; Examples given
out of order, beginning with no. 19.
Yk.

4141 Burton, Henry, 1636
Collates A²b²A − X⁴.
Yk (2).

4142 Burton, Henry, 1636
[Anr ed.] As STC 4141, but collates
(a)⁴A − X⁴.
S Pl.

4146 *See*: 4147.5

4147 Burton, Henry, 1628
Ex. Linc (imp). S Pl.

4147.5 Burton, Henry, 1628
Formerly STC 4146.
Carl. Ex. Her. Pet. S Asa. Sal.
Wor. Yk.

4151 Burton, Henry, 1631
Linc. Pet. Yk (2).

4153 Burton, Henry, 1626
Errata on A4^r and N3^r.
Her*. Pet*. Yk*.

4153.3 Burton, Henry, 1626
[Anr ed.] As STC 4153, but errata
corrected in the text.
Carl.

4154 Burton, Henry, 1640
Formerly also STC 10913.
Bur. Yk.

4155 Burton, Henry, 1628
Her (imp). Pet.

4156 Burton, Henry, 1629
Yk.

4157 Burton, Henry, 1628
Carl*. Her*. Yk.

4158 *See:* 13269

4160 Burton, Robert, 1624
Pet.

4161 Burton, Robert, 1628
Oxford, (J. Lichfield) f. H. Cripps.
Ex. Wel.

4162 Burton, Robert, 1632
Oxford (J. Lichfield) f. ...
Ex.

4163 Burton, Robert, 1638
Lich. Linc. Yk.

4164 Burton, Samuel, 1620
Cant.

4166 Burton, William, *Minister*,
1593
'suerties'; ... f. T. Cooke.
Pet.

4167 Burton, William, *Minister*,
1591
Pet.

4168.5 Burton, William, *Minister*,
1594
[Variant of STC 4169] 8°; A. Islip f.
T. Cooke.
Pet (imp).

4171 Burton, William, *Minister*,
1596
Pet.

4172 Burton, William, *Minister*,
1598
... f. I. B.
Pet (imp).

4173 Burton, William, *Minister*,
1602
Ely (tp imp).

4174 Burton, William, *Minister*,
1594
Pet (imp).

4174.5 Burton, William, *Minister*,
1596
'God wooing his church'; 8°; V.S. f.
I. Hardie.
Pet (cropped).

4176.5 Burton, William, *Minister*,
1598
[Anr ed.] 8°; F. Kingston f. T. Man.
Pet.

4177 Burton, William, *Minister*,
1634
R. Raworth f. J. Man, sold by T.
Paine a. M. Simmons.
Yk.

4179 Burton, William, *Topographer*,
[1622]
Cant (imp). Dur (tpw). Linc.
Nor. S Pl. Yk.

4179.5 Bury, George, 1607
Formerly STC 1029; 'judgement'
S Pl.

4180 Bury, John, 1631
Ex.

4182 Busche, Alexander van den,
1596
Pet. S Pl (imp).

4183 Bush, Edward, 1576
8°.
Linc. S Pl.

4187 Bushell, Thomas, 1628
Wor.

4190 Butler, Charles, 1633
... f. the authour.
Wor. Yk (imp).

4193 Butler, Charles, 1623
Cant (imp).

4194 Butler, Charles, 1634
Cant (tpw).

4194.5 Butler, Charles, 1629
[Anr issue of STC 4195] As 4195,
apart from date.
Yk.

4196 Butler, Charles, 1636
Wel.

4200 Butler, Charles, 1629
... imp. authoris.
Yk.

4201 Butler, Charles, 1625
Carl. Linc.

4205 Butterfield, Robert, 1629
Pet.

4212 Byfield, Nicholas, 1637 (1636)
... (pt 1: f. N. Butter).
Ex (tp imp). IoM. Pet.

4216 Byfield, Nicholas, 1615
Linc. Sal.

4218 Byfield, Nicholas, 1627
Ex. Wor. Yk (tpw)*.

4231 Byfield, Nicholas, 1637
Yk.

4233 Byfield, Nicholas, 1626
Bur.

4233.3 Byfield, Nicholas, 1626
[Anr issue] G.M. f. (R.R.,) P.
Stephens a. C. Meredith.
Linc.

4235 Byfield, Nicholas, 1626
Pet.

4238 Byfield, Richard, 1631
Linc. Wor.

4239 Byfield, Richard, 1630
12°.
Cant (imp).

4240.5 Bygod, *Sir* Francis, [1535?]
[Anr ed.] No imprint; B3^r l.1 of text
beg. 'gregatyon'
Pet (imp).

4242 Byrd, Josias, 1613
Ely (frag.).

4243.5 Byrd, William, 1605
[Anr issue of STC 4244] T. Este.
Yk.

4244 Byrd, William, 1610
Linc.

4245 Byrd, William, 1610
Linc.

4247 Byrd, William, 1589
Linc. Yk (Superius only?).

4248 Byrd, William, 1591
Linc (lacks Sextus). Yk (lacks
Sextus).

4250 Byrd, William, [1593?]
Linc.

4251 Byrd, William, [1595?]
Linc.

4253 Byrd, William, 1588
Errors uncorrected, errata list.
Pet (Contratenor only, imp)*.
Yk (Medius, Tenor, Bassus only).

4253.7 Byrd, William, 1588
[Anr ed.] As STC 4253, but no errata
list.
Linc (Medius; also Superius and
Bassus mixed with STC 4254).
Yk (Contratenor only).

4254 Byrd, William, [1599?]
5 pts.
Linc (Contratenor, Tenor; also
Superius and Bassus, mixed with
STC 4253.7).

4255 Byrd, William, 1611
Linc. Pet (Contratenor only).
Yk (lacks Tenor).

4256.5 Byrd, William, 1589 [1595?]
[Anr ed.] T. Este, the assigne of W.
Byrd.
Linc (Medius and Bassus only).

4257 See: 4258

4258 Byrd, William, 1610
6 pts; Formerly also STC 4257.
Linc (Superius, Contratenor and
Tenor only).

4259 Bythner, Victorinus, 1638
... imp. authoris.
Carl. Glo. Sal. Wor.

4284 C., J., Student, 1620
Win.

4293 C., N., 1636 [o.s.]
Carl (tpw)*. Yk.

4303 C., T., 1603
Linc.

4321 C., W., 1603
Pet. Rip. Yk (imp).

4323.6 C., W., Bachelor of the Civil
Law, 1633
Formerly STC 6012.
Cant. S Asa.

4323.8 C., W., Bachelor of the Civil
Law, 1635
Formerly STC 6013.
Cant. Linc. S Asa. Yk.

4324 See: 6017.5

4327 Cade, Anthony, 1630
Ely. Yk.

4328 Cade, Anthony, 1618
Pet (imp). Wor.

4329a Cade, Anthony, 1636
Pet.

4332 Caesar, Caius Julius, 1585
16°.
Pet (imp).

4333 Caesar, Caius Julius, 1590
Sal.

4336 Caesar, Caius Julius, 1590
Rip (tp imp).

4342 Caesar, Philippus, 1578
(J. Kyngston) ...
Pet.

4344 Caius, Joannes, 1568
Liv. Pet. Yk.

4345 Caius, Joannes, 1574
Cant.

4346 Caius, Joannes, 1570
Linc.

4349 Caius, Joannes, 1574
Cant. Ex.

4360 Calderwood, David, 1619
'... proofe of the nullitie ...'
Her (tpw). Yk.

4361 See: CLC foreign books – not
an STC book

4362 Calderwood, David, 1638
Linc.

4364 Calderwood, David, 1619
Yk.

4367 Caldwell, John, 1577
Linc (tpw). Pet (imp).

4368 Calfhill, James, 1565
Rip (imp). Sal. Yk.

4393 Calvin, Jean, 1578
(H. Middleton) f. ...
Cant (imp). Linc.

4395 Calvin, Jean, 1571
(T. East a. ...); Formerly also STC
2389.
Cant. Chi (tpw). New. Pet.

4396 Calvin, Jean, 1609
Kyngston.
Ban. Ex. Her. Yk.

4397 Calvin, Jean, 1570
Linc (imp). Pet.

4398 Calvin, Jean, 1585
(T. Dawson) imp. ...
Carl. Pet.

4399 Calvin, Jean, 1583
(T. Dawson) f. ...
Pet.

4401 Calvin, Jean, 1581
'Galathians'
Ex. Pet (tpw).

4402 Calvin, Jean, 1584
Cant. Ex.

4403 Calvin, Jean, [1581]
Ex. Pet.

4404.5 Calvin, Jean, [c.1580]
[Anr ed.] 8°; J. Kyngstone f. J.
Harrison the yonger; A–P⁸ Q⁴ B–D⁸
E².
Pet.

4412 Calvin, Jean, [1548?]
(J. Day a. ...).
Pet (2).

4414 Calvin, Jean, 1576
Ches.

4417 Calvin, Jean, 1574
Her.

4418 Calvin, Jean, 1578
Pet.

4421 Calvin, Jean, 1582
Cant (tp imp). IoM. Sal.

4422 Calvin, Jean, 1587
Liv.

4423 Calvin, Jean, 1599
Carl. Pet.

4424 Calvin, Jean, 1611
Llan. Yk.

4425 Calvin, Jean, 1634
Ex. Her.

4426 Calvin, Jean, 1597
Wor.

4426.4 Calvin, Jean, 1576
[Abridgement] 'Institutionis
christianae religionis, ...'; 8°; Imp. G.
Byshop & T. Vautrollerij.
Pet. Yk.

4428 Calvin, Jean, 1584
Pet. Rip.

4429 Calvin, Jean, 1585 [1586?]
Cant. Linc. Pet.

4431 Calvin, Jean, 1587
Pet.

4435 Calvin, Jean, [1548]
'The mynde of the godly and excellent
Ihon Caluyne, ...'; Date in title;
(Ippyswiche, J. Oswen).
Pet (lacks colophon)*.

4439 Calvin, Jean, 1579
(T. Dawson) f. ...
Pet.

4439.5 Calvin, Jean, 1581
'A sermon of the famous and godly
learned man'; 8°; R. Waldegraue f. E.
White.
Pet (tpw).

4441 Calvin, Jean, 1579
Woodcoke.
Bur. Pet.

4443.5 Calvin, Jean, 1583
[Variant] H. Middleton, f. T.
Woodcocke.
Bur. Cant. Ex.

4444 Calvin, Jean, (1574)
'Sermons ... vpon ...'; (H. Binneman
f.) L. Harison a. G. Byshop.
Ex (tpw)*. Glo. Pet*.

4446a Calvin, Jean, 1580
(T. Dawson) f. G. Byshop a. T.
Woodcocke.
Cant. Nor. Pet.

4447 Calvin, Jean, 1584
(T. Dawson f. G. Byshop a. T.
Woodcocke,) imp. T. Woodcocke.
Wor (tpw)*.

4448 Calvin, Jean, 1577
'... of M. Iohn Caluin ...'
Bur. Cant.

4449 Calvin, Jean, 1574
(H. Bynneman f.) ...
Ex (tp imp). Pet.

4457 Calvin, Jean, 1579
(T. Dawson f.) ...
Pet. Yk.

4460 Calvin, Jean, 1580
4°; (T. Dawson) f. ...
Pet.

4463 Calvin, Jean, [1549]
'... for to arme ... agaynst ...'; (J. Daye ...).
Cant.

4464 Calvin, Jean, 1580
Wor.

4468 *See*: 5160.3

4471 Cambium, 1628
Linc.

4473 Cambridge University, 1587
Pet. Yk.

4475 Cambridge University, 1632
Linc. Pet. Yk.

4477 Cambridge University, 1625
Yk (2).

4478 Cambridge University, 1625
Linc. Pet.

4479 Cambridge University, 1635
Linc (2 − 1 tpw). Pet. Yk.

4480 Cambridge University, 1633
Linc (2). Yk.

4481 Cambridge University, 1612
'... in obitum ... Henrici ...'
Linc. Pet (imp).

4482 Cambridge University, 1612
Cant. Yk.

4483 *See*: 13518

4484 Cambridge University, 1625
Linc. Pet. S Asa. Yk.

4486 Cambridge University, 1631
Ches. Linc. Yk.

4487 Cambridge University, 1623
Linc. Yk.

4488 Cambridge University, 1623
Ely. Pet (2). S Asa.

4489 Cambridge University, 1619
Linc. Pet. Yk.

4491 Cambridge University, 1633
Linc. Pet. Yk.

4492 Cambridge University, 1637
Linc. Pet. Yk.

4493 Cambridge University, 1603
Linc. Yk.

4494 Cambridge University, 1623
Pet (tp imp).

4495 Cambridge University, 1640
Linc. Pet. Yk.

4496 Camden, William, 1615
Bks 1 − 3.
Cant. Ches. Dur. Lich. Linc (2 − 1 imp). S Asa (imp). S Pl. Win. Wor.

4496.5 Camden, William, 1627
Bk 4; 2°; Impr. as STC 4496.
Cant. Ches. Dur. Lich. Linc (2). S Pl. Win. Wor.

4497 Camden, William, 1625
'royall'
Ex (2 − 1 tpw*). Swel (tpw).

4500 Camden, William, 1630
Her.

4501 Camden, William, 1635
Nor.

4503 Camden, William, 1586
Pet. S Asa (imp).

4505 Camden, William, 1590
Pet.

4506 Camden, William, 1594
Ban (tpw). Ex. Pet.

4507 Camden, William, 1600
Pet. S Dv. Wel. Yk.

4508 Camden, William, 1607
Dur. Lich. Linc. S Pl. Sal. Wel. Win. Wor. Yk (2 − 1 frag.).

4509 Camden, William, 1610
Cant. Her (2). Pet. S Asa (imp)*. Sal (imp). Yk (imp).

4510 Camden, William, 1637
Bris. Carl. Linc. Wor.

4513.4 Camden, William, 1613
[Anr ed.] 8°; Typis B. Norton.
Linc.

4514 Camden, William, 1617
Wor (imp).

4518 Camden, William, 1600
Pet (2).

4520 Camden, William, 1606
Liv.

4521 Camden, William, 1605
Linc. Nor. Pet. S Asa. Yk.

4522 Camden, William, 1614
Ex (2).

4524 Camden, William, 1629
Cant.

4526 Camden, William, 1637
Carl. Nor.

4529 Camerarius, Philippus, !621
Ex. Glo. Sal.

4531 Cameron, John, 1626
Yk*.

4531.5 Cameron, John, 1626
[Anr issue] As STC 4531, but with dedication, signed W.P.
Carl.

4532 Cameron, John, 1628
Carl. Pet.

4541 Campion, Thomas, 1619
S Asa.

4552 Camus, Jean Pierre, 1632
Linc.

4561 Cancellar, James, (1576)
Pet.

4562.3 Cancellar, James, (1601)
[Anr ed.] 16°; (P. Short, by [sic] the assignes of W. Seres).
S Pl (imp).

4564 Cancellar, James, [1554?]
(J. Waylande).
Linc.

4566 Caninius, Angelus, 1613
Linc. Sal.

4567 Caninius, Angelus, 1624
Apud J. Billium.
Yk.

4574 Canne, John, 1634
Win. Yk.

4576 Cannon, Nathanael, 1613
S Pl.

4577 Cannon, Nathanael, 1616
Linc.

4583 Canterbury, *Province of*, [1584]
Rip. Yk.

4585 Canterbury, *Province of*, 1605
Ex. S Asa. Yk.

4586 Canterbury, *Province of*, 1640
R. Barker a. assignes of J. Bill.
Cant (3 − 1 tp imp).

4587 Canterbury, *Province of*, [1586]
Formerly also STC 16513a; Arms on A4ᵛ.
Sal. Yk (2)*.

4600 Capell, Moses, 1632
Pet.

4601 Capgrave, John, (1516)
(ī domo ...).
Dur (imp). Linc. Wor (imp).

4606 Caradoc, (1584)
(R. Newberie ...).
Cant. Her. Pet. S Dv. S Pl. Yk.

4607 Cardano, Girolamo, 1573
Pet.

4608 Cardano, Girolamo, 1576
Pet.

4615 Carew, Richard, 1602
Dur (2 − 1 tp imp). Linc (imp).

4617 Carew, Thomas, 1605
Linc (tpw).

4626 Carion, Johann, (1550)
(f. Gwalter Lynne).
Pet.

4629 Carleton, Dudley, *Viscount Dorchester*, 1618
'Sir Dudley Carlton'
Linc.

4630 Carleton, George, 1624
Wor.

4631 Carleton, George, 1613
Linc. Yk.

4632 Carleton, George, 1615
Pet.

4633 Carleton, George, 1626
Glo. Pet. S Pl. Yk.

4634 Carleton, George, 1626
Chi. Linc. Pet. Wor. Yk.

4636 Carleton, George, 1603
Lich. Yk.

4637 Carleton, George, 1610
Chi (2). Ex. Pet. S Pl. Sal. Yk.

4638 Carleton, George, 1619
Rounthwait.
Cant (imp).

4640 Carleton, George, 1624
Chi (tpw). Ely (tp imp).

4641 Carleton, George, 1625
Yk.

4642 Carleton, George, 1627
Lich.

4644 Carleton, George, 1606
Ex (2). Linc. S Asa.

4645 Carleton, George, 1611
Bur. Sal. Yk.

4646 Carleton, George, 1628
'Bernardi'
Linc (2). Yk.

4647 Carleton, George, 1629
'Bernard'
Ex. Wor. Yk.

4648 Carleton, George, 1636
Dur. Yk.

4654 Carlile, Christopher, 1582
Yk.

4657 Carlile, Christopher, (1582)
Wor. Yk.

4660 Carmichael, James, 1587
Cantebrigiae, ex off. T. Thomasii.
Yk.

4663 Carpenter, John, *Minister*, 1607
Wor (2).

4664 Carpenter, John, *Minister*, 1597
Pet (imp).

4666 Carpenter, John, *Minister*, 1606
Pet (2). Wor. Yk.

4667 Carpenter, John, *Minister*, 1599
Linc.

4669 Carpenter, Nathanael, 1629
Carl. Pet. Yk.

4670 Carpenter, Nathanael, 1633
Wor.

4673 Carpenter, Nathanael, 1633
Wor.

4676 Carpenter, Nathanael, 1625
Ex. Her. Linc.

4677 Carpenter, Nathanael, 1635
Ban. Cant. Wor (2).

4678 Carpenter, Nathanael, 1622
Ban.

4679 Carpenter, Nathanael, 1636
Linc. Yk.

4681 Carpenter, Richard, 1623
Ex.

4682 Carpenter, Richard, 1616
'pastoral'
Yk (tp imp).

4683.5 Carpenter, Richard, 1617
'Three profitable sermons'; 8°; E. Griffin f. F. Constable.
Linc (date altered in MS to 1620).

4691 Cartari, Vincenzo, 1599
Pet (2 − 1 imp).

4692 Carter, Bezaleel, 1621
Yk.

4695 Carter, John, *of Belstead*, 1627
Ex.

4697 Carter, Oliver, 1579
'An answere made by Oliuer Carter, vnto ...'; (T. Dawson) f. ...
Pet.

4706 Cartwright, Thomas, 1596
'A briefe apologie of Thomas Cartwright against ... Mr Sutcliffe ...'
Yk.

4707.5 Cartwright, Thomas, 1611
Formerly STC 5186.
Linc.

4707.7 Cartwright, Thomas, 1616
Formerly STC 4313.
Wor. Yk.

4707 *See*: 13721

4708 Cartwright, Thomas, 1612
Ex. Yk.

4709 Cartwright, Thomas, 1618
Cant. Chelm (tp imp). Dur. Glo. Her. Linc. Nor. S Asa (imp). Win. Wor. Yk.

4710 Cartwright, Thomas, 1604
Pet. Wor. Yk.

4711 Cartwright, Thomas, [1573]
'Whitgift'
Yk.

4712 Cartwright, Thomas, [1573]
Ex. Pet. Wor. Yk.

4714 Cartwright, Thomas, 1575
'... of Thomas Cartwright: agaynst ...'
Cant. Wor (imp). Yk (2).

4715 Cartwright, Thomas, 1577
Cant. Pet. Wor (2). Yk.

4716 Cartwright, Thomas, 1602
S Pl. Yk.

4717 Cartwright, William, 1639
Linc.

4719 Cary, Richard, 1601
In aed. Thomae Wight.
Pet.

4731 Cary, Walter, *of High Wycombe*, 1587
Pet.

4737 Casa, Giovanni della, 1630
'Jo. Casae V. Cl. Galateus ...'
Carl.

4740 Casaubon, Isaac, 1612
'Isaaci ...'
Ban. Chi. Linc.

4741 Casaubon, Isaac, 1612
'... Isaac ...'
Yk.

4742 Casaubon, Isaac, 1611
'Isaaci ...'
Cant. Ely. Linc. Sal. Yk.

4745 Casaubon, Isaac, 1614
'Isaaci ...'
Ban. Cant. Chi. Her (2). Lich. S Pl. Win. Wor. Yk.

4747 Casaubon, Isaac, 1624
4°.
Cant (imp). Wor. Yk.

4748 Casaubon, Isaac, 1630
Ex (imp). Yk.

4749 Casaubon, Méric, 1621
'Merici Casauboni Is F pietas ...'
Carl. Yk.

4750 Casaubon, Méric, 1624
'Merici Casauboni ... Vindicatio ...
idololatriae ...'
Cant.

4751 Casaubon, Méric, 1624
'The vindication or defence of ...'
Yk.

4753 Casaubon, Méric, 1638
Cant. Carl. Ex. Linc.

4754 Case, John, 1599
Sal.

4756 Case, John, [1599]
Sal.

4759 Case, John, 1585
Pet.

4761 Case, John, 1588
'Sphaera'
Linc.

4764 Case, John, 1598
Pet.

4765 Case, John, 1597
... & veneunt Londini.
Ex.

4770.9 Castalio, Sebastian, 1576
Ap. Thomam Marsh; 8°.
Glo.

4778 Castiglione, Baldassare, 1561
Yk.

4779 Castiglione, Baldassare, 1577
Yk.

4780 Castiglione, Baldassare, 1603
Cant (tpw).

4781 Castiglione, Baldassare, 1588
'Baldessar'
Glo.

4782 Castiglione, Baldassare, 1571
'Balthasaris Castilionis comitis :..'
Glo. Pet (2).

4783 Castiglione, Baldassare, 1577
Roch.

4784 Castiglione, Baldassare, 1585
Carl. Pet. S Pl.

4803.4 Catechism, [1575?]
'A short catechisme collected by a
Christian vnlearned'; 8°; (J. Allde).
Linc.

4810 Catechismus, 1553
(Ap. Reginaldum Wolfium).
Linc. Sal.

4813.4 Catharine, [de Medici],
[1562]
'The verye trueth of the conference
betwixt the queene mother, and the
prince of Conde'; 8°; [W. Seres?].
Pet (imp).

4813.6 Catharine, *of Alexandria, St,*
[1505?]
'The life of saincte katheryne'; 4°; [R.
Pynson].
Rip (frag.)*.

4815 Catharine, *of Siena,* (1519)
'orcharde ... the whiche ...'; (Wynken
de Worde).
Pet (imp).

4823 Catharine [Parr], [c.1550]
(In the house of Thomas Berthelet).
Linc.

4835 Catholics, 1604
'Catholikes'
Cant. Pet.

4858- Cato, Dionysius, 1577
[Anr ed. of STC 4858] 8°; f. A.
Maunsell.
Yk.

4868 Caumont, Jean de, 1591
Pet (imp). Yk (imp).

4873 Caussin, Nicolas, 1631
'Second tome'
Bur. Sal.

4874 Caussin, Nicolas, 1634
"
Bur. Wel (tpw). Wor.

4875 Caussin, Nicolas, 1638
Copies found with or without the
following variations from STC 1 in
different combinations: 'fourth tome';
'commaund'; J. Cousturier.
S Dv.

4880 Cavendish, Richard, [1571?]
Pet.

4881 Cawdrey, Daniel, 1624
'... liverie; ... in two ...'
Cant. Pet (2).

4887 Cawdrey, Robert, 1600
Pet.

4888 Cawdrey, Robert, 1609
Ex. S Asa.

4892 Cecil, Edward, *Viscount
Wimbledon,* 1626
'... action which Edward Lord Cecyl,
...'
Linc.

4895 Cecil, Robert, *Earl of
Salisbury,* 1606
Bur. Pet (2). Yk.

4902 Cecil, William, *Baron Burghley,*
1583
'maintenaunce'
Yk.

4904 Cecil, William, *Baron Burghley,*
1584
1st 2 words of title in roman type.
Linc*. Pet*. Rip*.

4906 Cecil, William, *Baron Burghley,*
[1584]
[T. Vautrollier].
Yk.

4907 Cecil, William, *Baron Burghley,*
1584
Linc.

4909 Cecil, William, *Baron Ros,*
1617
'entertainement'
Yk.

4911 Celestina, 1631
Yk.

4924 Chaderton, Laurence, [1578?]
A3[r]line 1 ends: 'flesh'
Cant. Linc*.

4925 Chaderton, Laurence, 1580
Pet.

4930.5 Chadwich, John, 1614
[Anr issue w. additions] 'A sermon
preached at Snarford at the funerals
...'; W. Stansby f. W. Barret.
Linc.

4934 Chaloner, Edward, 1625
Linc*. Pet (tpw)*. Wor*. Yk*.

4934.3 Chaloner, Edward, 1625
[Anr issue] W. Stansby sold in Pauls
Church-yard at the signe of the
Gray-Hound.
Cant.

4935 Chaloner, Edward, 1638
Carl. Her. Pet.

4936 Chaloner, Edward, 1623
Linc.

4937 Chaloner, Edward, 1629
Carl. Ex. S Pl.

4938 Chaloner, *Sir* Thomas, *the
Elder,* 1579
Dur. Linc. Pet. Rip.

4939 Chaloner, *Sir* Thomas, *the
Elder,* [1560]
'... octaui, regis ... carmen ...'
Pet.

4941 Chamber, John, 1601
Carl.

4946.6 Chamberlaine, Bartholomew,
1584
Formerly STC 4951.
Pet.

4952 Chamberlaine, Bartholomew,
1591
Pet.

4957 *See:* 10910.4

4958 Champny, Anthony, 1614
Pet.

4959 Champny, Anthony, 1620
'Parallela'
Yk.

4960 Champny, Anthony, 1616
Pet.

4961 Chapman, Alexander, 1610
Bur. Carl. S Pl. Wel. Yk (imp).

4974 Chapman, George, 1612
Pet.

4998 Chapman, Richard, 1635
Yk.

5000 Chardon, John, 1595
'... Exeter, the sixth day of ...'
Bur. Linc (tpw).

5001 Chardon, John, 1580
Pet.

5002 Chardon, John, 1586
'... ninth ... in Oxford'
Linc.

5003 Chardon, John, 1587
Linc. Pet.

5005 Charke, William, 1580
Pt 2 formerly also STC 11325.
Yk (pt 2 only).

5007 Charke, William, 1581
'answers'
Pet.

5008 Charke, William, 1583
'... that foule Defence ...'
Pet. Sal (tpw).

5009 Charke, William, 1586
T. Thomas, pr. to Univ. of
Cambridge; Found dated or undated.
Her (pt 2 only). Pet. Rip. Wor
(2 − 1 tpw).

5014 Charles V, *Emperor*, [1543]
'... vnto the letters conuocatorye of ...
cõcell'
Pet.

5020 *See:* 20521.2

5023 Charles I, *King of England*,
1633
Pet. Yk.

5025 Charles I, *King of England*,
1623
Yk.

5030 Charles I, *King of England*,
1625
'mariage'
Linc (tpw).

5031 Charles I, *King of England*,
1623
Yk.

5032 Charles I, *King of England*,
1623
Yk.

5033 Charles I, *King of England*,
1623
Yk (imp).

5034 Charles IX, *King of France*,
[1562]
... f. Edwarde Sutton.
Pet.

5042? Charles IX, *King of France*,
[1562]
'The requestes presented (the fourthe
of Maye 1562) vnto the Frenche kinge
... With an aunswere ...'; 12°; W.
S[eres].
Pet.

5045.5 Charles Emmanuel I, *Duke
of Savoy*, 1590
'A true discourse. Of the most
horrible and barbarous murthers ...';
4°; J. Wolfe.
Pet.

5046 Charles Louis, *Elector Palatine*,
1637
'... of the most illustrious, prince ...'
Carl. Ex. Linc. S Pl. Sal.

5050 Charles Louis, *Elector Palatine*,
1637
'A protestation of ... Prince Charles
Lodowicke'; A3ʳ last line ends: 'our'
Dur.

5051 Charron, Pierre, [1608?]
Cant. Pet (imp). Sal.

5052 Charron, Pierre, [1615?]
Ely.

5053 Charron, Pierre, [1620?]
Nor.

5054 Charron, Pierre, (1630)
Lich. Yk (imp).

5055 Charron, Pierre, (1640)
S Asa.

5056 Charterhouse, 1614
Linc.

5065 Chastising, [1493]
Linc.

5071 Chaucer, Geoffrey, [1550?]
(W. Bonham).
Pet (imp)*.

5074 Chaucer, Geoffrey, [1550?]
(R. Toye).
Chi. Swel.

5075 Chaucer, Geoffrey, (1561)
(J. Kyngston f. J. Wight).
Pet (imp)*.

5077 Chaucer, Geoffrey, 1598
Ex. Yk (imp)*.

5079 Chaucer, Geoffrey, 1598
... at the charges of T. Wight.
Cant.

5080 Chaucer, Geoffrey, 1602
Cant. Carl. Ely. Her. Linc.
S Pl.

5081 Chaucer, Geoffrey, 1602
Glo (imp).

5084 Chaucer, Geoffrey, [1492?]
[R. Pynson].
Ex (frag.)*.

5097 Chaucer, Geoffrey, 1635
Ban. Ex. Wor.

5102 *See:* 5103.5

5103.5 Chauncie, William, 1587
[Anr ed.] Formerly STC 5102; 'tyme'
Yk.

5105 Cheaste, Thomas, 1613
'... Crosse, the last of ...'
Pet. S Pl.

5106 Cheaste, Thomas, 1609
Pet. S Pl.

5106.5 Chedsay, William, (1545)
'Two notable sermons'; 8°; (J.
Herford, at the costes of R. Toye).
Pet.

5110 Cheke, *Sir* John, 1569
Yk.

5112 Cheke, *Sir* John, 1610
Linc.

5113 Chelidonius, 1571
Pet (imp).

5127.5 Chetwind, Edward, 1632
The second edition; 12°; By John
Beale.
Pet.

5128 Chetwind, Edward, [1612]
'... lachrymae. A vow of ... losse of
... Henry. In ...'
Linc (tpw).

5134 Chibald, William, 1622
Pet.

5138 Chillingworth, William, 1638
Cant. Her. Linc. Sal. Wel. Yk.

5138.2 Chillingworth, William,
1638
2°; Oxford, by Leonard Lichfield.
S Pl.

5139 Chillingworth, William, 1638
Cant. Linc. Pet. Rip.

5144 Cholmley, Hugh, 1629
Pet. Yk.

5146 Chouneus, Thomas, 1636
Editio secunda.
Win.

5151a *See*: 11199

5155 Christian & Reformed
Churches, 1586
Thomas Thomas, pr. to the
Uniuersitie of Cambridge.
Ely. Pet. Yk.

5158 Christian Discourse, 1578
Pet.

5160.3 Christian Faith, 1553
Formerly STC 4468.
Pet.

5162 *See*: 10450.3

5164 Christian Man, (1537)
(In aed. T. Bertheleti); a⁴A – Z⁴Aa⁶;
Main text in 95mm. textura type.
S Pl (imp). Sal.

5165 Christian Man, (1537)
(In aed. T. Bertheleti); a⁴A – Z⁴Aa⁶;
85mm bastard type.
Pet (imp). Yk (tpw).

5166 Christian Man, (1537)
(In aed. T. Bertheleti, Oct.); a⁴A – P⁸.
Cant.

5167 Christian Man, (1537)
(In aed. T. Bertheleti); No month in
colophon.
Ches (imp)*.

5168 Christian Man, (1543)
(T. Barthelet); A⁴A – Y⁴Z⁶.
Yk (imp).

5168.7 Christian Man, (1543)
Formerly STC 5170a; (T. Barthelet);
A – Z⁴a – d⁴e⁶.
Ches (imp).

5169 Christian Man, (1543)
(T. Barthelet); Collation as STC
5168.7.
Liv. Yk (imp)*.

5170 Christian Man, (1543)
(T. Barthelet); Collation as STC
5168.7; A1 & A2 as STC 1; N4ᵛ
catchword: 'welth'; Z2ʳ line 2 ends
'resistynge ther-'
S Pl (imp)*. Wor*.

5170a *See*: 5168.7

5171 Christian Man, (1543)
(Thomas Berthelet).
Yk.

5172 *See*: 5171

5175 Christian Man, 1543
(J. Mayler).
Dur (imp).

5178 Christian Man, 1544
Dur. Sal.

5189 *See*: 11617.8 .

5199 Christians, (1506)
(Wynkyn de worde).
Linc. Yk.

5200 Christians, (1548)
... W. Seares.
Linc (imp).

5207 Christopherson, John, (1554)
'... hede and beware of ...'; (John
Cawood).
Pet.

5216 Church, Henry, 1636
Carl.

5217 Church, Henry, 1637
Carl.

5219 Churchson, John, [1556]
12°; (Jhon Cawod).
Linc.

5263 Chytraeus, David, 1570
Liv.

5264 Chytraeus, David, 1577
Harryson.
Bur. Dur. Linc. Pet (2).

5266.5 Cicero, Marcus Tullius,
1587
[Anr ed.] 8°; Ex typ. viduae Georgii
Robinsoni.
Sal.

5281 Cicero, Marcus Tullius, 1556
(Richard Tottel).
Pet.

5284 Cicero, Marcus Tullius, 1574
(1575)
(Rycharde Tottell).
Pet (imp)*. Rip (imp).

5285 Cicero, Marcus Tullius, 1583
(R. Tottell).
Pet (imp).

5286 Cicero, Marcus Tullius, 1596
Pet.

5296 Cicero, Marcus Tullius, 1574
Yk.

5298.8 Cicero, Marcus Tullius,
1584
[Anr ed.] 8°; G. Dewes & H. Marsh,
ex assignatione T. Marsh.
Rip.

5300.4 Cicero, Marcus Tullius,
1595
[Anr ed.] 8°; R. Robinsonus, imp. R.
D[exter].
S Pl. Wor.

5305 Cicero, Marcus Tullius, [1620]
Yk.

5310.2 Cicero, Marcus Tullius,
1616
'Vol. primum'; 16°; R. Field.
Sal.

5314.5 Cicero, Marcus Tullius,
1574
'Marci Tullii Ciceronis quaestiones
Tusculanae'; 8°; Ap. J. Kyngstonem.
Pet.

5317 Cicero, Marcus Tullius, [1561]
'Marke Tullye'
Pet.

5319 Cicero, Marcus Tullius, 1584
16°.
S Pl. Yk.

5322 Cicero, Marcus Tullius, 1630
Ely.

5323 Cicero, Marcus Tullius, 1583
Rip.

5332 Clapham, Henoch, 1596
'... drawne first into English poësy'
Yk.

5336 Clapham, Henoch, 1609
Sal (tp imp).

5336.5 Clapham, Henoch, 1601
'A description of new Ierushalem'; 8°;
V. Simmes.
Pet.

5339 Clapham, Henoch, 1603
'... present pestilence'
Sal (tpw).

5340 Clapham, Henoch, 1603
'... some additions'
Sal.

5343 Clapham, Henoch, 1604
'Henoch ...'
Sal.

5345 Clapham, Henoch, 1598
Yk.

5345.4 Clapham, Henoch, 1596
'The sinners sleepe wherein Christ
willing her to arise ...'; 8°; Edinburgh,
R. Walde-graue.
Yk.

5345.7 Clapham, Henoch, 1595
'Sommons to doomes daie'; 8°;
Edinburgh, R. Walde-graue.
Pet. Yk.

5346.5 Clapham, Henoch, 1602
'A tract of prayer'; 8°; W. White.
Pet.

5347 Clapham, John, 1602
Ex. Linc (imp).

5348 Clapham, John, 1606
Ex. Pet. Yk (imp).

5353 Clarke, John, *Apothecary?*, 1602
8°.
Yk.

5355 Clarke, John, *B.D.*, 1632
(A.M.) imp. R. Mylbourn.
Carl. Llan (imp).

5359 Clarke, John, *B.D.*, 1630
Dur. S Asa. S Pl. Sal. Wel.

5364 Clarke, Thomas, *of Sutton Coldfield*, 1621
Chelm (imp).

5367 Claudianus, Claudius, 1617
Linc (imp)*.

5378 Cleaver, Robert, 1615
'booke'; F. Kyngston ...
Ex (imp)*.

5379 Cleaver, Robert, 1625
A.M. a. I.N. f. ...
Wor.

5386 Cleaver, Robert, 1612
Pet.

5387 Cleaver, Robert, 1614
... sold by A. Johnson.
Yk.

5389 Cleaver, Robert, 1624
4°; Hunscot.
Her. S Asa.

5396 Cleland, James, 1624
'... death and funerals of ... late duke ...'
Linc.

5397 Clemangiis, Nicolaus de, 1606
'pontificiae'
Dur. Linc. Yk.

5398 Clement I, *St*, 1633
Carl. Ches (2). Dur. Ely. Her. Linc. S Asa. S Pl. Sal (2). Wor.

5401 Clenardus, Nicolaus, [1588?]
'N. Clenardi Graecae ...';
assignationem.
Wel.

5407 Clerke, Bartholomew, 1573
Linc. Pet. Yk (2 −1 imp).

5409 Clerke, John, (1547)
[Anr ed. w. additions] 'De mortuorum resurrectione'; (J. Herforde f. R. Toye).
Linc.

5410 Clerke, Richard, 1637
'Sermons preached by ... Clerke. ... published ...'
Bris. Cant (2). Carl. Ex (2 − both imp). Linc. Wor.

5411 Clerke, William, 1594
Rip.

5412 Clever, William, *Writer*, 1590
Pet.

5436.7 Closet, 1627
[Anr ed.] 12°; J. Haviland.
Linc.

5469 Cocus, Robertus, 1614
'... sanctorum ... citari ...'
Bur. Chi (2). Lich. S Pl. Sal.
Yk.

5470 Cocus, Robertus, 1623
Carl. Ches (2). Linc. Pet (2). S Pl (3). Wor.

5471 Codomannus, Laurentius, 1590
Pet.

5471a Codomannus, Laurentius, 1590
The second edition corrected and augmented.
Pet. S Pl.

5476 Coffin, Edward, 1622
Linc.

5480 Cogan, Thomas, 1589
Pet.

5486 Coignet, Matthieu, 1586
'discourses'
Pet.

5489 Coke, *Sir* Edward, 1635
Linc.

5491 Coke, *Sir* Edward, 1607
'The Lord ...'
Yk.

5493.4 Coke, *Sir* Edward, [1601?]
[Anr ed.] 2°; In aed. T. Wight.
Dur. Wel.

5494 Coke, *Sir* Edward, 1609
Cant.

5494.8 Coke, *Sir* Edward, 1636
[Anr ed.] 2°; Per assignationem J. More armigeri.
Wor.

5495 Coke, *Sir* Edward, 1602
Dur (imp).

5496 Coke, *Sir* Edward, [1604?]
Wel.

5497 Coke, *Sir* Edward, 1610
Cant.

5498.5 Coke, *Sir* Edward, 1635
[Anr ed.] 2°; Per assignatos J. More armigeri.
Wor.

5499 Coke, *Sir* Edward, 1602
Tp line 4 ends: 'GE-'
Dur (imp).

5499.2 Coke, *Sir* Edward, 1602
[Anr ed.] 2°; In aed. T. Wight; Tp line 4 ends: 'LATTORNEY'
Wel*.

5500 Coke, *Sir* Edward, 1610
Cant (imp).

5501.5 Coke, *Sir* Edward, 1635
[Anr ed.] 2°; By the assignes of J. More.
Wor.

5502.3 Coke, *Sir* Edward, 1604
[Anr ed.] 2°; In aed. T. Wight; Tp line 4 has: 'L'attorney'
Wel*. Yk*.

5503 Coke, *Sir* Edward, 1610
Cant.

5503.7 Coke, *Sir* Edward, 1635
[Anr ed.] 2°; Per assignationem J. More armigeri.
Dur. Wor.

5504 Coke, *Sir* Edward, 1605
'... pars ... The ...'
Cant. Wel. Yk (2 −1 imp).

5505 Coke, *Sir* Edward, 1606
(1607)
2 pts; Pt 2 formerly also STC 5506.
Cant (imp).

5506 *See*: 5505

5507 Coke, *Sir* Edward, 1612
Dur.

5508 Coke, *Sir* Edward, 1624
Wor.

5509 Coke, *Sir* Edward, 1607
A1r catchword: 'haeredes'
Cant. Dur.

5509.5 Coke, *Sir* Edward, 1607
[Anr ed.] 2°; f. the Soc. of Statrs; A1r catchword: 'heredes'
Wel*.

5510 Coke, *Sir* Edward, 1621
Wor.

5511 Coke, *Sir* Edward, 1608
e1r line 1 begins: 'by naturall'
Rip*. Wel*. Yk (imp)*.

5511.2 Coke, *Sir* Edward, 1608
[Anr ed.] As STC 5511, but e1r line 1 begins: 'oportet quod'
Cant. Dur.

5512 Coke, *Sir* Edward, 1629
Wor.

5513 Coke, *Sir* Edward, 1611
Tp line 5 in rom.
Wel*.

5513.2 Coke, *Sir* Edward, 1611
[Anr ed.] As STC 5513, but tp line 5 is in italic, line 6 has: 'Iuges'
Cant. Dur.

5514 Coke, *Sir* Edward, 1626
Wor.

5515 Coke, *Sir* Edward, 1613
Wel. Yk.

5516 Coke, *Sir* Edward, 1615
Cant.

5517 Coke, *Sir* Edward, 1627
Dur. Wor.

5518 Coke, *Sir* Edward, 1614
Wel.

5519 Coke, *Sir* Edward, 1618
Cant.

5520 Coke, *Sir* Edward, 1629
Wor.

5521 Coke, *Sir* Edward, 1615
Cant. Wel. Yk (2 −1 v. imp; 1
imp*).

5524 Coke, *Sir* Edward, 1631
By the assignes ...; 'B' of sig. B1 is
under 'n' of 'in'
Dur. Wor*.

5526 Coke, *Sir* Edward, 1618
Wel.

5527 Coke, *Sir* Edward, 1640
Linc.

5534 Cole, Nathanael, 1624
S Pl.

5535 Cole, Nathanael, 1625
Pet (imp).

5542 Colet, John, 1527
'Ioannis Coleti ... aeditio ...';
(Vaenundantur Londini).
Pet.

5542.6 Colet, John, 1534
[Anr ed.] 8°; A⁴B−F⁸G⁴.
Chi.

5545 Colet, John, [1512?]
'Oratio habita a D. Joanne Colet ad
clerum ... Anno. M.D.xj.'; 4°; Tp has
Pynson's device, with his name .
Pet.

5550 Colet, John, [1530?]
'Conuocacion'; (T. Berthelet).
S Pl (imp).

5557 Colleton, John, 1602
Cant. Pet (2). Wor. Yk (imp).

5561 Collins, Samuel, 1617
C. Legge, pr. to the Univ. of
Cambridge.
Carl. Pet. Sal. Yk.

5562 Collins, Samuel, 1628
Pet.

5563 Collins, Samuel, 1612
Bur (tp imp). Carl. Linc. Pet
(2). Yk.

5565 Collins, Samuel, 1608
Linc (2 −1 imp). S Pl.

5571 Colmore, Matthaeus, 1613
'... obitum clarissimi viri Georgii ...'
Pet. Yk.

5575.2 Colom, Jacob Aertsz, 1633
'The fierie sea-columne'; 2°;
Amsterdam, J. Columne.
Wel.

5580 Colonne, Guido delle, 1555
(T. Marshe).
Pet.

5584 Colson, William, 1612
'... tresury, a perpetual repertory, ...
of accounts ...'; ... at the expences of
the author.
Cant. Linc.

5588 Colville, John, 1604
8°; ... solde by W. Burre [London].
Yk.

5589 Colville, John, 1602
'... Io. Coluille ...'
Yk.

5590 Colynet, Antony, 1591
(T. Orwin) f. ...
Pet. Yk.

5601 *See*: 11273

5602 Comines, Philippe de, 1596
Pet. Yk.

5603 Comines, Philippe de, 1601
Cant. Dur. Nor.

5604 Comines, Philippe de, 1614
Linc.

5615 Conceits, 1584
Formerly also STC 10925.
Pet (tpw).

5622 Concini, Concino, 1617
Pet.

5624 Conestaggio, Girolamo
Franchi di, 1600
Linc. Pet.

5636.2 Constable, Henry, 1623
Formerly STC 6377; '... moderator:
or a moderate examination ... First
written ...'
Yk.

5636.4 Constable, Henry, 1623
'The catholike moderator'; Formerly
STC 6378.
Cant. Linc.

5636.6 Constable, Henry, 1623
Formerly STC 6379.
Cant. Pet. Wel.

5642 Contarini, Gasparo, 1599
Cant. Pet.

5650 Conversion, 1604
'... conversion and severall
recantations of foure ...'; ... W. Jones
solde by W. Aspley.
Ex. Linc (date altered in MS to
1606).

5658 Cooke, Alexander, 1625
Bur. Linc. Yk.

5659 Cooke, Alexander, 1610
Linc. Pet. Yk (2 −1 imp).

5660 Cooke, Alexander, 1625
Nor. Yk (2 −1 tpw).

5661 Cooke, Alexander, 1625
Yk.

5662 Cooke, Alexander, 1617
Liv.

5663 Cooke, Alexander, 1621
Tp line 7 ends: '& *smite*'
Yk (2)*.

5663a Cooke, Alexander, 1622
Ex (tpw).

5664 Cooke, Alexander, 1622
Ex. Yk (2).

5665 Cooke, Alexander, 1628
Linc. Wor. Yk.

5666.5 Cooke, Alexander, 1630
[Variant] The third edition; W. Jones,
sold by S. Albyn.
Pet.

5671 Cooke, James, 1608
Chi (imp).

5676 Cooke, Richard, 1629
S Pl.

5680 Cooper, John, 1638
... f. N. Vavasour.
Linc.

5683 Cooper, Thomas, *Bp*, 1589
4°.
Pet (2).

5684 Cooper, Thomas, *Bp*, (1573)
H. D(enham) ...
Carl. Linc. S Pl. Yk.

5685 Cooper, Thomas, *Bp*, 1580
Pet (2). Yk.

5686 Cooper, Thomas, *Bp*, 1565
Carl. Dur (imp). Sal (tpw)*.

5687 Cooper, Thomas, *Bp*, 1573
Ely. Ex. Glo. Lich. Wel. Win.
Wor.

5688 Cooper, Thomas, *Bp*, 1578
Cant. Liv. Llan. S Pl. Yk.

5689 Cooper, Thomas, *Bp*, 1584
(In aed. ...).
Her. S Asa (imp). Yk.

5691 Cooper, Thomas, *Bp*, [1575]
8°; ... f. R. Newberie.
Pet. Yk.

5692 Cooper, Thomas, *Preacher*,
1615
Yk.

5693.5 Cooper, Thomas, *Preacher*,
1606
Formerly STC 5705.
Yk.

5696 Cooper, Thomas, *Preacher*,
1609
'... deliuerance, contayning
meditations ...'
Pet.

5702 Cooper, Thomas, *Preacher*,
1607
Pet. Yk.

5705 *See*: 5693.5

5706 Cooper, Thomas, *Preacher*,
1619
12°; B. Alsop, sold by T. Jones.
Cant.

5717 Cope, *Sir* Anthony, 1547
Wor (tpw).

5723 Cope, Michael, 1580
(T. Dawson) f. ...
Her. Linc. Pet. Yk.

5724 Copies, 1601
Pet. Yk.

5735 Copley, Anthony, 1601
Pet. Yk.

5736 Copley, Anthony, 1602
Pet (2).

5742 Copley, John, 1612
Ely. Pet. Wor. Yk.

5742.9 Copy, 1584
'The copie of a leter, wryten by a
master of arte of Cambrige ...'; 8°;
[France]; Formerly STC 19399.
Yk.

5751 Corbet, John, 1640
A – L⁴.
Win. Yk (2)*.

5751.5 Corbet, John, 1640
[Anr ed.] As STC 5751, but: A – K⁴;
E3ʳ line 2 has: 'Laws,'
Ban*. Ely*. Linc*. S Pl*.

5752 Corbet, John, 1640
[Anr ed.] As STC 5751, but: A – K⁴;
E3ʳ line 2 has: 'Lawes'
Carl.

5754 Corbet, John, 1639
Pet (with E⁴ of STC 5755). Win.

5755 Corbet, John, 1639
Linc. Pet (E⁴ only).

5756.5 Corderoy, Jeremy, 1615
Edit. 3.; 12°; Oxford, J. Barnes.
Carl.

5759 Cordiale, [1496?]
[a1ʳ:] 'Memorare ...'; [a4ʳ:] 'Here
after foloweth the prologue ...';
(westmystre).
Dur (imp).

5759.2 Cordier, Mathurin, 1592
[Anr ed. of STC 5760] 8°; Imp. T.
Newman.
Rip.

5762 Cordier, Mathurin, 1614
Her (imp).

5775 Cornwallis, *Sir* William, 1600
(1601)
'... Sir William ...'
Pet (pt 2 only).

5776 Cornwallis, *Sir* William, 1606
S Asa.

5777 Cornwallis, *Sir* William, 1610
'Essayes ... Newly ...'
Linc (tpw). Sal.

5778 Cornwallis, *Sir* William, 1616
Cant. Linc (imp).

5779 Cornwallis, *Sir* William, 1616
Linc.

5780 Cornwallis, *Sir* William, 1617
(1616)
Cant.

5781 Cornwallis, *Sir* William, 1632
(1631)
'Essayes, ... Newlie ...'
Pet.

5782.5 Cornwallis, *Sir* William,
1604
[Anr ed.] As STC 5782, but last line
of text on E4ʳ has: 'ued it.'
Yk (2).

5784 Corro, Antonio de, 1574
Sal.

5785 Corro, Antonio de, 1581
[A different work:] 'Epistola beati
Pauli apostoli ad Romanos, ... in
dialogi formam redacta'
Yk.

5800 Cortes, Martin, (1579)
Date in title; '... prynted by R.
Jugge'; (widowe of R. Jugge).
Pet (lacks map).

5801 Cortes, Martin, (1584)
Date in title; '... printed by Johan
Jugge wydowe'; (widowe of R. Jugge).
Pet.

5806 Corvinus, Antonius, 1550
Formerly also STC 20131; (R. Wolfe).
Cant. Lich. Pet. Wor (2 – 1
imp).

5810 Coryate, Thomas, 1611
Ban (imp).

5815.5 Cosin, John, 1627
Formerly STC 5817.
Linc (imp). Yk.

5815 *See*: 5819.5

5819.5 Cosin, Richard, 1584
Formerly STC 5815; '... certeine acts
of Parlement ...'
Cant. Carl. Linc. New. S Pl.
Yk (4 – 1 pt 2 only).

5819.7 Cosin, Richard, 1584
[Anr issue] f. T. Chard.
Dur*.

5821 Cosin, Richard, 1593
Cant (2). Carl. Dur. Ely. Ex.
Lich. Linc (imp)*. New. Pet.
S Pl (2). Sal. Wel. Yk (2).

5822 Cosin, Richard, [1593]
Bur. Carl. Dur (2 – 1 pt 3 only).
Win. Yk.

5823 Cosin, Richard, 1592
Linc. Yk (imp).

5825 Cosin, Richard, 1634
Obl. ½ sheets.
Cant. Linc. Yk.

5830 Cotgrave, Randle, 1611
Cant. Glo.

5831 Cotgrave, Randle, 1632
Dur. Lich. Linc. Sal. Wel.
Win.

5836 Cotta, John, 1616
Ex. Linc. S Pl.

5843 Cotton, Clement, 1627
'bookes'
Wor. Yk.

5845 Cotton, Clement, 1631
'Downs'
Chelm. Yk.

5845.5 Cotton, Clement, 1631
[Variant:] f. T. D[ownes] a. R.
Y[oung], sold by H. Overton.
Sal.

5846 Cotton, Clement, 1635
Dur. Linc. S Pl. Swel. Win.

5846.4 Cotton, Clement, 1635
[Anr ed. of STC 5844] 4°;
[Amsterdam, successors of G. Thorp].
S Dv (imp). Wel.

5847 Cotton, Clement, 1616
'wherein'
Yk.

5854 Cotton, John, 1630
... solde at the three Golden Lyons by the Royall Exchange.
Sal (tp imp)*.

5858 Cotton, Pierre, 1614
Wor. Yk.

5859 Cotton, Pierre, 1615
Pet.

5861 Cotton, Pierre, 1611
A – M⁴.
Liv. Pet*. Yk*.

5863 Cotton, *Sir* Robert Bruce, 1628
'kingdome'; A2ʳ line 2 ends: 'it'
Pet.

5863.2 Cotton, *Sir* Robert Bruce, 1628
[Anr ed.] As STC 5863, but A2ʳ line 2 ends: 'selfe'
Wel*.

5864.4 Cotton, *Sir* Robert Bruce, 1627
[Anr ed.] 4°; [London]; a2ᵛ lines 1–2: 'against ... *Norfolke*'; e3ᵛ last line: 'therefore', line 2: 'To'
Pet.

5865 Cotton, Roger, 1596
Pet.

5867 Cotton, Roger, 1592
Yk.

5867.3 Cotton, Roger, (1592)
[Anr ed.] 4°; f. G. Simson a. W. White, solde by W. Barley.
Linc.

5869 Cotton, Roger, 1596
'conteining'
Pet.

5870.5 Coucheman, Giles, 1551
'An exhortatyon or warnynge'; 8°; (T. Raynalde).
Pet (imp).

5880 Covell, William, 1606
Cant. Pet. S Asa.

5881 Covell, William, 1603
Cant. S Asa. Sal. Yk.

5882 Covell, William, 1604
Ex. Linc. Pet. Yk (imp)*.

5883 Covell, William, 1595
'... means lawfull and vnlawfull, to judge ...'
Pet.

5886 Coverdale, Miles, 1564
'... godly, fruitful, and comfortable letters ...'
Glo. Linc. Pet (2). Rip.

5888 Coverdale, Miles, [1541?]
Cant. Linc.

5893 *See:* 4073

5898 Cowell, John, 1593
Chi. Pet. Sal (imp). Win. Yk.

5899 Cowell, John, 1605
Linc. Rip. Yk.

5900 Cowell, John, 1607
Cant. Yk.

5901 Cowell, John, 1637
Bur. Carl*. Ches*. Ex. Linc. Pet. Wel. Yk*.

5902 Cowell, John, 1637
Formerly also STC 5903.
Sal.

5903 *See:* 5902

5907 Cowley, Abraham, 1636
Yk.

5909 Cowper, William, 1623
'Williã'
Glo. Her (tpw)*. Roch (tpw)*. Wor.

5911 Cowper, William, 1629 (1628)
Carl. Ex (tpw). S Dv (tpw).

5912 Cowper, William, 1611
Nor. Wor.

5913 Cowper, William, 1613
Yk.

5915 Cowper, William, 1614
Sal. Yk.

5921.2 Cowper, William, 1613
[Variant:] T. Snodham f. T. Archer.
Sal.

5922 Cowper, William, 1616
Cant (tp imp). Yk.

5925 Cowper, William, 1632
Yk.

5926 Cowper, William, 1613
'Psalme'
Wor. Yk.

5926.5 Cowper, William, 1607
'Jacobs wrestling with God'; 8°; V.S. f. J. Budge.
Linc.

5931 Cowper, William, 1619
'Saint John'
Yk.

5932 Cowper, William, 1616
'... or a most heavenly and fruitfull sermon ...'
Linc. Yk.

5933 Cowper, William, 1607
'A preparatiue ... passeouer'
Linc.

5936 Cowper, William, 1612
'Three heavenly treatises, concerning Christ ...'
Yk.

5942 Cowper, William, 1639 (1636)
... sold by J. Emry.
Yk.

5944 Cowper, William, 1618
'... the Kings majesty'
Yk (imp).

5945 Cowper, William, 1619
'... death of ... William Cowper ...'
Wor.

5962 Craig, John, 1581
Yk.

5964.5 Craig, John, 1587
[Anr ed.] 8°; R. Waldegraue f. T. Man a. W. Broome.
Pet.

5973 Crakanthorp, Richard, 1623
Carl. Linc. Pet.

5974 Crakanthorp, Richard, 1621
Cant. Carl. Ely. Linc. Pet. S Asa. S Pl. Win. Wor. Yk.

5975 Crakanthorp, Richard, 1625
Ban. Cant. Carl. Dur. Ely. Ex. Linc. S Pl. Win. Yk.

5976 Crakanthorp, Richard, 1619
Chelm. Linc. Pet. Rip. Sal.

5977 Crakanthorp, Richard, 1616
Cant. Linc. Yk.

5978 Crakanthorp, Richard, 1622
Ex off. J. Legati, imp. J. Teage.
Chelm. Linc.

5979 Crakanthorp, Richard, 1609
Carl. Ex. Linc. Pet (imp). S Pl. Yk.

5980 Crakanthorp, Richard, 1620
Linc. Pet (imp). Yk.

5981 Crakanthorp, Richard, 1623
Carl.

5982 Crakanthorp, Richard, 1608
Linc. Yk.

5983 Crakanthorp, Richard, 1631
Bur. Her. Linc (2 – 1 tp only). New. S Pl. Yk.

5984 Crakanthorp, Richard, 1634
Ely. Nor. S Pl.

5985 Crakanthorp, Richard, 1637
Pet.

5991 Cranmer, Thomas, 1551
'An answer of ... vnto ...'
Dur. Ely. Liv. Pet. S Pl. Sal. Yk.

5992 Cranmer, Thomas, 1580
Carl. Pet. S Pl. Sal (tp imp). Wor (tpw).

5993 Cranmer, Thomas, 1548
(N. Hyll f.) ...; ff. ccxliii.
Cant (imp).

5994 Cranmer, Thomas, 1548
Linc.

5996 Cranmer, Thomas, [1556?]
Pet.

6000 Cranmer, Thomas, (1550)
(R. Wolfe); B4^{r}catchword: 'me'; S1^r
catchword: 'but'
Cant (mixed sheets − with B4 (at
least) of STC 6001). Yk*.

6002 Cranmer, Thomas, (1550)
(R. Wolfe); B4^{r}catchword: 'des'; S1^r
catchword: 'before'
Glo. Pet.

6004 Cranmer, Thomas, 1553
Pet (imp).

6005 *See*: CLC foreign books − not
an STC book

6006 Cranmer, Thomas, 1571
Cant. Dur. Ex. Linc. Liv.
S Pl. Yk.

6007 Cranmer, Thomas, 1640
Ban. Liv. S Pl (2). Sal. Win.
Wor. Yk.

6008 Cranmer, Thomas, 1640
Cant. Ches. Dur. Ex. Glo.
Pet. Sal.

6009 Crashaw, Richard, 1634
Pet (2 − 1 tpw).

6010 Crashaw, William, 1624
'Ad Severinum Binnium Lovaniensem
theologum, epistola ... ipso nuper
adornata'
Wor.

6012 *See*: 4323.6

6013 *See*: 4323.8

6014 Crashaw, William, 1606
'Tomi primi liber primus'; (R. Field),
imp. ...
Linc. New. Pet. Rip. S Pl
(tpw). Yk.

6015 Crashaw, William, 1623
'... vesper, or a true relation of that
accident in the Black-Friers'
Linc.

6016 Crashaw, William, 1610
Linc. Pet. Sal. Yk.

6017.5 Crashaw, William, 1625
'Londons lamentations ...'; Formerly
STC 4324; 8°.
Yk (tp imp).

6019 *See*: 1909

6023 Crashaw, William, 1625
Ex. Yk.

6024 Crashaw, William, 1618
Yk.

6027 Crashaw, William, 1608
'The sermon ... Feb. xiiij. ...'
S Pl (2).

6028 Crashaw, William, 1609
Carl. Yk.

6031 Craven, Isaac, 1631
Cant (cropped). S Pl.

6032 Crawfurd, Patrick, 1627
'... Mr. Patrik ...'
Yk.

6033 Crawshey, John, 1636
'... instructor. Or, a briefe method ...'
Yk.

6037 Crespin, Jean, 1581
'Lexicon Graecolatinum Joannis
Crispini ... repurgatum ... operâ &
studio E. G.'
Cant. Rip.

6038 Creswell, George, 1607
STC1 date incorrect.
Linc (tpw).

6039 Crewe, Thomas, 1580
Pet.

6044a.5 Croke, Richard, (1520)
'Richardi Croci Britanni
introductiones in rudimenta graeca';
4°; (Coloniae, in aed. E. Ceruicorni,
exp. J. Lair de Siborch).
Linc.

6052 Crompton, Richard, 1586
Dur. Pet.

6054 Crompton, Richard, 1599
Pet.

6056 Crompton, Richard, 1630
'... belong to the cognizance of that
Court ...'
Ely. Ex. Glo. Linc. Sal (imp).

6058 Crompton, William, 1630
S Asa.

6059 Crompton, William, 1624
Cant.

6060 Crompton, William, 1625
Pet. Sal. Yk.

6062.2 Crooke, Helkiah, 1616
[Anr. issue:] W. Jaggard.
Wor.

6063 Crooke, Helkiah, 1631
Cant (imp). Sal.

6066 Crooke, Samuel, 1613
Yk.

6069 Crooke, Samuel, 1615
Linc (tpw).

6075 Crowley, Robert, 1581
Pet (2).

6077 Crowley, Robert, 1566
Pet.

6080 Crowley, Robert, [1578]
Pet.

6081 Crowley, Robert, 1581
Linc.

6082 Crowley, Robert, [1548]
(J. Day a. W. Seres).
Linc (imp).

6083 Crowley, Robert, [1548]
Pet (imp).

6084 Crowley, Robert, 1588
Pet. Rip (imp).

6091 Crowley, Robert, [1586]
Charlewoode.
Linc. Pet.

6093 Crowley, Robert, 1569
Pet.

6097 Crowne, William, 1637
'... Thomas Lord Howard'
S Pl.

6098 Croy, François de, 1620
Cant. Dur. Wor.

6103 Cuffe, Henry, 1607
Yk.

6104 Cuffe, Henry, 1633
Lich.

6105 Cuffe, Henry, 1640
Pet.

6106 Cuique, (1635)
(Cantabrigiae ...).
Linc.

6108 Culpeper, *Sir* Thomas, 1621
Pagination: 3, 6, 7, 6-21.
Wor*.

6108.5 Culpeper, *Sir* Thomas, 1624
The second edition; 4°; J. H[aviland?]
f. N. Vavasour.
Linc.

6129 Curio, Caelius Augustinus,
1575
'historie'
Pet. Sal.

6130 Curio, Caelius Secundus,
[1566?]
Linc (imp). Pet.

6134 Curteys, Richard, 1600
Yk.

6137 Curteys, Richard, 1579
Pet.

6138 Curteys, Richard, 1586
Linc.

6139 Curteys, Richard, (1575)
Pet (2).

6140 Curteys, Richard, 1576
'... preached by the bishop of
Chichester, the ... Crosse. ... And the
second ...'
S Pl.

6141 Curteys, Richard, 1584
T. Man ...
S Pl.

6142 Curtius Rufus, Quintus, 1553
Pet.

6143 Curtius Rufus, Quintus, 1561
In aed. R. Tottell.
Pet (tp imp).

6145 Curtius Rufus, Quintus, 1584
Pet (tpw).

6146 Curtius Rufus, Quintus, 1592
Pet (imp).

6147 Curtius Rufus, Quintus, 1602
Yk.

6156 Cyprian, *St*, (1539)
'A sermon of S. Cyprian ...'; (In aed.
...).
Pet. Yk.

6158 Cyprian, *St*, 1539
(In aed. ...).
Pet. Yk.

6166 D., G., 1588
Yk.

6189 *See*: 11199

6192 Dalechamp, Caleb, 1632
Carl. Linc. Pet. Sal (tpw). Wor.
Yk.

6193 Dalechamp, Caleb, 1624
'... usum in theologia legitimum: ...
ostendit'
Pet.

6194 Dalechamp, Caleb, 1636
Linc. Pet.

6195 Dalechamp, Caleb, 1622
'... lapsu statuque aeterno regis ...'
Linc. Pet. S Pl.

6196 Dalechamp, Caleb, 1624
'... patris-familias, ... delineatum'
Pet.

6197 Dallington, *Sir* Robert, 1613
Cant (imp). Ex. Lich. Linc.

6198 Dallington, *Sir* Robert, 1629
Dur.

6200 Dallington, *Sir* Robert, 1605
Linc.

6203 Dallington, *Sir* Robert,
[1605?]
Linc. Wel.

6204a Dalton, Edward, 1623
'... Londons laurell'
S Pl (tp imp).

6208 Dalton, Michael, 1626
S Asa.

6209 Dalton, Michael, 1630
Cant.

6211 Dalton, Michael, 1635
Now the sixth time published.
Glo.

6217 Damman, Hadrianus, 1590
'Schediasmata Hadr. Dammanis ...'
Linc.

6228 Daneau, Lambert, [1590?]
Yk.

6230 Daneau, Lambert, 1586
Pet.

6231 Daneau, Lambert, 1578
Pet.

6233 Danes, John, 1638
Ely. Wor.

6234 Danett, Thomas, 1600
Linc.

6238 Daniel, Samuel, 1623
'... Samuel Daniel ...'; Waterson.
Linc.

6247 Daniel, Samuel, 1613
Pet.

6248 Daniel, Samuel, [1618]
Pet. S Pl. Swel.

6249 Daniel, Samuel, 1621
Her. Wel. Win.

6251 Daniel, Samuel, 1626
Ex. Sal. Yk.

6252 Daniel, Samuel, 1634
Lich. Linc (tpw). Pet (imp).
S Asa.

6260 Daniel, Samuel, 1603
Linc.

6266 Daniel Ben Alexander, 1621
Linc (frag.).

6267 Dansie, John, 1627
Cant (imp).

6275 Dariot, Claude, [1583?]
'A breefe and most easie introduction
...'
Pet.

6276 Dariot, Claude, 1598
Cant (imp).

6283 Darrell, John, 1600
Linc. Pet (2). Rip.

6284 Darrell, John, 1602
'... John Darrell ...'
Pet.

6285 Darrell, John, 1602
Pet.

6286 Darrell, John, 1617
Sal.

6290 Daunce, Edward, 1590
Linc.

6291 Daunce, Edward, 1590
Linc.

6293 Davenant, John, 1640
... R. Danielis.
Bur. Carl. Sal. Yk.

6294 Davenant, John, 1634
Ches. Her. Lich. Linc (2).
S Asa. S Pl.

6295 Davenant, John, 1639
Cant. Carl. Chelm. Dur. Ely.
Her. S Pl. Tru. Win. Wor.

6296 Davenant, John, 1627
'... epistolae D. Pauli ad Colossenses'
Bur. Her. Linc. Sal (2).

6297 Davenant, John, 1630
Bur (imp). Ex. Her. Nor.
S Asa. S Pl. Sal. Wor.

6298 Davenant, John, 1639
Cant. Carl. Chelm. Dur. Ely.
S Asa.

6299 Davenant, John, 1628
Carl. Linc.

6300 Davenant, John, 1628
Cant (cropped).

6301 Davenant, John, 1631
... (ap. T. Buck).
Bur (imp). Cant. Carl. Chi.
Dur. Ely. Ex (3). Her. S Pl.
Sal. Swel. Wel (tpw). Wor.

6301.5 Davenant, John, 1634
[Anr issue:] 'Quibus iam accesserunt
Determinationes'; 2 pts; Cantabrigiae,
ap. T. & J. Buck, ac R. Daniel.
Linc.

6308 Davenant, *Sir* William, 1635
Linc.

6313 Davenport, John, 1629
Ex.

6316 David, *King of Israel*, 1638
'remembred'; ... sold by D. Frere.
Pet.

6322 Davidson, John, *Minister*,
1590
8°.
Yk.

6333 Davies, John, *of Hereford*,
1603
Pet.

6334 Davies, John, *of Hereford*,
1605
Oxford, Jos. Barnes, solde by John
Barnes [London].
Pet.

6336 Davies, John, *of Hereford*, 1602
Pet.

6337 Davies, John, *of Hereford*, 1607
Linc.

6346 Davies, John, *of Mallwyd*, 1621
'Antiquae linguae Britannicae ... rudimenta'
Cant. Dur. Linc.

6347 Davies, John, *of Mallwyd*, 1632
'Antiquae linguae Britannicae ... et linguae ...'
Ban. Cant. Dur. Her. Linc. S Asa (imp)*. Wor.

6348 Davies, *Sir* John, 1612
Wor.

6349 Davies, *Sir* John, 1613
Cant.

6352 *See*: 6358

6358 Davies, *Sir* John, 1619 (1618)
STC 6352 is pt of this.
Linc.

6361 Davies, *Sir* John, 1615
Cant.

6362 Davies, *Sir* John, 1628
Dur.

6377 *See*: 5636.2

6378 *See*: 5636.4

6379 *See*: 5636.6

6382 Davy du Perron, Jacques, 1601
Yk.

6383 Davy du Perron, Jacques, 1612
Pet.

6385 Davy du Perron, Jacques, 1630
'The reply of the most illustrious Cardinall ...'
S Asa. Wor.

6388 Dawes, Lancelot, 1609
8°.
S Pl.

6402 Day, Angel, 1592
[T. Orwin f.] R. Jones.
Pet. Rip.

6405 Day, Angel, 1607
Pet.

6417 Day, John, *Dramatist*, 1607
Cant (without the dedication; Greg 248 [AI]).

6421 Day, John, *Rector*, 1615
Oxoniae, excud. J. Barnesius.
Wor.

6422 Day, John, *Rector*, 1612
Linc.

6423 Day, John, *Rector*, 1615
Wor.

6424 Day, John, *Rector*, 1620
'psalmes'
Carl. Ex.

6425 Day, John, *Rector*, 1614
Ex. Wor.

6426 Day, John, *Rector*, 1615
Ex. Wor.

6427 Day, Martin, 1636
4°.
Ex. Wor.

6428 Day, Richard, 1569
S Pl (imp).

6429 Day, Richard, 1578
'tyme'
Lich. S Pl (imp). Win.

6430 Day, Richard, 1581
Cant (tpw; tp of STC 6432 substituted).

6431 Day, Richard, 1590
Cant (3 − 1 imp). Her (imp). Liv. Pet (imp). Wor (imp).

6432 Day, Richard, 1608
Carl.

6435 Daye, Lionel, 1632
Chi. Pet.

6437 Deacon, John, [1587?]
Pet.

6439 Deacon, John & Walker, J., 1601
S Pl.

6441 Deane, Edmund, 1626
Yk (2).

6453 Declaration, 1636
'A briefe declaration ...'; Text begins on B1ʳ.
Ex*. Linc*.

6460 Dee, John, (1599)
(P. Short).
Yk.

6461 Dee, John, (1603 [1604?])
(E. Short).
Linc.

6462 Dee, John, 1573
Linc. Pet. Sal.

6463 Dee, John, (1558)
'... Joannis Dee Londinensis, de praestantioribus ...'; (H. Suttonus).
Yk.

6465 Dee, John, [1604?]
s.sh. 4°.
Linc.

6466 Dee, John, [1604?]
½ sh.obl.fol.
Linc.

6468 Defence, 1602
Linc (p. 65-66 only).

6498 Dekker, Thomas, 1606
Yk.

6510 Dekker, Thomas, 1604
T.C. f. T. Man the yonger.
Yk.

6539 Dekker, Thomas & Webster, J., 1607
S Pl.

6540 Dekker, Thomas & Webster, J., 1607
S Pl.

6545.5 Delamothe, G., 1592
'The French alphabeth'; 8°; R. Field, sold by H. Jackson.
Pet.

6549 Delamothe, G., 1633
Pet.

6572.5 Demands, 1605
'Certaine demandes ... propounded unto Richard Archbishop of Canterbury'; 4°; [Middelburg].
Ex. Liv. Pet. S Asa. Yk.

6574 Demands, 1609
Yk.

6577 Demosthenes, 1571
'Demosthenis, Graecorum oratorum principis Olynthiacae ...'
Pet. Rip. Yk.

6578 Demosthenes, 1570
'The three orations of Demosthenes ... in favour ...'
Pet (2 − 1 imp).

6582 Denakol, *pseud.*, 1609
Her.

6586 Denison, John, 1621
Yk.

6587 Denison, John, 1620
8°; STC 6593 is pt of this.
Yk (tp imp).

6589 Denison, John, 1631
Yk.

6591 Denison, John, 1611
S Pl.

6593 *See*: 6587

6597.7 Denison, John, 1630
The fifth edition; 12°; R. Badger for N. Bourne.
Wor.

6598 Denison, Stephen, [1626]
Linc.

6601 Denison, Stephen, 1621
Yk.

6603 Denison, Stephen, 1622
Ex (tpw). Yk.

6603.7 Denison, Stephen, 1620
[Anr ed. of STC 6604] The second
impression; 8°; R. Field.
Cant.

6605 Denison, Stephen, 1622
S Pl (pt 2 only).

6606 Denison, Stephen, 1631
Cant. Yk.

6607.5 Denison, Stephen, 1627
[Variant of STC 6608] G. Miller; E3ʳ
catchword: 'pared'
S Pl.

6608.7 Denison, Stephen, 1627
[Anr ed.] The second impression (on
L2ᵛ); 4°; G. Miller; E3ʳcatchword:
'next'
Yk.

6613.5 Dent, Arthur, 1608
The second edition; 8°; G. E[ld] f. J.
Wright.
Pet.

6616 Dent, Arthur, 1614
8°.
Pet (imp).

6626 Dent, Arthur, 1601
Pet.

6630.7 Dent, Arthur, 1616
The fifteenth impression; 8°; I. Legatt
f. E. Bishop.
Cant.

6634.5 Dent, Arthur, 1633
The two and twentieth edition; 8°; R.
Y[oung] f. G. Lathum.
Cant (tp imp). Sal.

6640 Dent, Arthur, 1603
Linc. Pet.

6645 Dent, Arthur, 1631
Wor.

6652.5 Dent, Arthur, 1583
'very godly'; 8°; f. J. Harison.
Pet.

6659 Dent, Arthur, 1606
Linc.

6666 Dent, Arthur, 1630
Pet.

6673 Dent, Daniel, 1628
Prs. to the Univ. of Cambridge.
Pet.

6673.2 Dent, Daniel, [1628]
[Variant:] Prs. to the Univ. of
Cambridge.
Pet.

6676 Dering, Edward, [1590?]
3 *or* 4 pts; Only the half-title now at
this number, the following are
generally bound with it; In 3 pts:
6733, 6730, 6680.5; In 4 pts: 6732,
6730.5, 6680.7, 6682.5.
Linc (4 pts). Pet (3 pts).

6678 Dering, Edward, 1614
Only the gen. prelims now at this
number, the following are generally
bound with it: 6683.3, 6731.5, 6682.3.
Carl. Yk.

6679.3 Dering, Edward, 1573
[Anr ed. of the catechism only?] 'A
briefe & necessary catechisme'; 8°; J.
Awdely.
Pet.

6679.4 Dering, Edward, 1574
[Anr ed. with preface] 8°; J. Awdely.
S Pl (imp).

6680.5 Dering, Edward, 1590
'A briefe and necessarie catachisme …
'; 8°; [Middelburg].
Pet.

6680.7 Dering, Edward, [1590?]
[Anr issue].
Linc.

6682.3 Dering, Edward, 1614
[Anr ed. of STC 6681] 4°; W. Jaggard.
Carl. Yk.

6682.5 Dering, Edward, [1590?]
[Anr ed. of STC 6683] 8°; [N.pl.].
Linc.

6683.3 Dering, Edward, [1614]
[Anr ed.] 4°; A1ʳline 2 of heading
ends: 'vn-'
Carl. Yk.

6684.5 Dering, Edward, 1574
[Anr ed. of STC 6685] 'Godlye
priuate praiers for housholders in their
families'; 8°; J. Awdely; A – G⁴.
Pet.

6684.7 Dering, Edward, 1574
[Anr ed. of STC 6685] 'Godlye
priuate praiers for housholders to
meditate vpon, and to say in their
families'; 8°; J. Awdely; A – C⁸.
S Pl.

6692 Dering, Edward, 1574
S Pl.

6699 Dering, Edward, [1569?]
Linc.

6710.5 Dering, Edward, 1580
[Anr ed. of STC 6711] 8°; J.
Charlewood.
Pet.

6725 Dering, Edward, [1568]
Chelm (tpw). Pet.

6726 Dering, Edward, 1576
Dur (imp). Pet (mixed sheets).

6729 Dering, Edward, 1583
4°; f. T. Woodcoke.
Cant.

6730 Dering, Edward, 1590
Pet.

6730.5 Dering, Edward, [1590]
[Anr issue].
Linc.

6731.5 Dering, Edward, 1614
[Anr ed.] 4°; E. Griffin f. E. Blount.
Carl. Yk.

6732 Dering, Edward, [1590]
Linc.

6733 Dering, Edward, 1590
Pet.

6736.5 Desainliens, Claude, 1580
[Anr ed.] As STC 6736, but collates:
*⁴A – H⁸(2 bks) I – L⁸(Oratio).
Linc. Pet.

6737 Desainliens, Claude, 1593
Rip.

6743 Desainliens, Claude, 1597
Pet.

6747 Desainliens, Claude, 1630
G. Miller, sold by N. Fussell a. H.
Mosely.
Ex.

6755 Desainliens, Claude, 1631
Cant (imp).

6760 Desainliens, Claude, 1608
Ches.

6762 Desainliens, Claude, 1580
Pet (2).

6773 Discription, 1620
Pet (cropped).

6787 Dethick, Henry, 1577
Yk.

6788 Devereux, Robert, *2nd Earl of
Essex*, 1603
Linc (tp imp).

6789 Devereux, Robert, *2nd Earl of
Essex*, 1633
Carl.

6790 Devereux, Robert, *2nd Earl of
Essex*, 1589
Linc.

6801 Dialogue, 1584
'churche'
Pet. Yk.

6814 Dialogue, 1605
Cant. Liv. Pet. Yk.

6821 Dickinson, William, 1619
'The kings right, briefly set downe in
a sermon ...'
Yk.

6823 Dickson, Alexander, 1583
'Alexandri Dicsoni Arelii de vmbra
...'
Ex. Yk.

6825 Dickson, David, 1637
Pet.

6832 Dictionary, (1570)
'... French and English'; (H.
Bynneman f. L. Harrison).
Carl.

6842 Digby, Everard, [1590]
'Euerard Digbie ...'
Bur.

6843 Digby, Everard, 1579
Pet. Rip.

6844 Digby, George, *Earl of Bristol*,
1640 [o.s.]
= Wing B4775.
Cant. Linc. Pet. Yk (2 – both
imp).

6845 Digges, *Sir* Dudley, 1615
Sal.

6848 Digges, Leonard, 1579
Pet.

6849 Digges, Leonard, 1590
Yk.

6853 Digges, Leonard, 1614
Linc.

6858 Digges, Leonard, 1571
Pet.

6859 Digges, Leonard, 1591
Wor.

6871 Digges, Thomas, 1573
ap. T. Marsh.
Linc. Pet. Sal.

6873 *See*: 3518

6874 Digges, Thomas, 1634
Linc.

6875 *See*: 3518

6878 Diguières, *Monsieur de* [*i.e.*
Bonne, François de], 1591
'... perfourmed ... armie ...'; J. Wolfe.
Pet.

6889 Dillingham, Francis, 1603
Ex. Yk.

6891 Dillingham, Francis, 1605
'Spicilegium de Antichristo, in quo
protestantium argumenta contra ...';
Ex off. J. Legat.
Linc. Pet.

6892 Dillingham, Francis, 1603
'Tractatus brevis, in quo ex
praecipuorum ... multa ...'; Ex off. J.
Legat.
Yk.

6935 Dod, John, 1614
Pet (tpw). Wor.

6939 Dod, John, 1635
Tp varies: with or without 'The
second edition'
Wel (The second edition).

6941 Dod, John, 1610
Pet (imp).

6944 Dod, John, 1614
'fruitfull'
Ex.

6953 Dod, John, 1618
Ex.

6954.5 Dod, John & Cleaver, R.,
1606
[Anr ed. revised] 4°; H. Lownes f. T.
Man.
Wor.

6956 Dod, John & Cleaver, R.,
1612
Ex. Wor.

6958 Dod, John & Cleaver, R.,
1608
Wor (2).

6959 Dod, John & Cleaver, R.,
1612
Ex.

6959.5 Dod, John & Cleaver, R.,
1608
[1st ed. of 6960] 4°; R. B[radock] f.
R. Jackson.
Pet. Wor.

6960 Dod, John & Cleaver, R.,
1609
Ex.

6964 Dod, John & Cleaver, R.,
1611
Ex. Wor.

6966 Dod, John & Cleaver, R.,
1611
For R. Jackson.
Ex. Wor.

6968 Dod, John & Cleaver, R.,
1604
'commandements'
Yk.

6970 Dod, John & Cleaver, R.,
1607
Yk.

6971.5 Dod, John & Cleaver, R.,
1612
[Anr ed., revised] 4°; F. Kyngston f.
T. Man.
Wor.

6971.7 Dod, John & Cleaver, R.,
1614
[Anr ed.] 4°; F. Kyngston f. T. Man.
S Pl. Wor.

6975 Dod, John & Cleaver, R.,
1622
The fifteenth edition.
Linc.

6978 Dod, John & Cleaver, R.,
1632
Bur.

6979 Dod, John & Cleaver, R.,
1635
Wel.

6980 Doddridge, *Sir* John, 1630
Cant. Glo. Tru. Yk (2).

6981 Doddridge, *Sir* John, 1631
Cant. Dur.

6983 Doddridge, *Sir* John, 1629
'... light: ... annexed The use of the
law'
Linc.

6984 Dodoens, Rembert, 1578
(Antwerpe, H. Loë, solde) at London
by G. Dewes.
Bur (imp). Pet (tpw)*. S Dv
(imp). Win (imp).

6990 Dodson, Thomas, 1608
'A sermon preached in the cathedrall
church of Yorke ...'
Carl.

6994 Dominis, Marco Antonio,
1617
Pt 2 now = STC 6995.5.
Ban. Cant. Chi. Dur. Ex. Her.
Lich. Linc. Liv. Nor. Pet.
S Pl. Wor. Yk.

6995.5 Dominis, Marco Antonio,
1620
Formerly pt 2 of STC 6994; Impr. as
6994.
Cant. Chi. Dur. Linc. Pet.
S Pl. Wel. Wor. Yk.

6996 Dominis, Marco Antonio,
1616
'Marcus Antonius de Dominis ... suae
profectionis ...'
Linc. Pet. S Pl (2). Yk (2).

6998 Dominis, Marco Antonio, 1616
'Archbishop of Spalato'
Chi. S Pl (2 −1 'Decretum' only; 1 imp).

6999 Dominis, Marco Antonio, 1617
Cant.

7001 Dominis, Marco Antonio, 1623
'... of Marcus Antonius de Dominis ...'
Linc. Pet.

7002 Dominis, Marco Antonio, 1617
Wor. Yk.

7003 Dominis, Marco Antonio, 1617
'Predico fatta da Monsr. Marc' Antonio de Dominis la prima domenica dell' auuento ...'
Yk.

7004 Dominis, Marco Antonio, 1617
Chelm. Pet (2).

7005 Dominis, Marco Antonio, 1618
Ban. Yk.

7006 Dominis, Marco Antonio, 1624
'... M. Ant. de Dominis ...'
Yk.

7007 Dominis, Marco Antonio, 1624
Linc (2 −1 imp).

7008 *See*: 11116

7021 Donne, Daniel, 1623
'Grismand'
Linc. S Pl.

7026 Donne, John, [1611]
'Conclaue Ignati; ... accessit ...'; 12°.
Yk.

7029 Donne, John, 1634
Bur. Pet.

7030 Donne, John, 1635
12°; ... sold by W. Sheares.
Carl. Pet. S Pl. Yk.

7031 Donne, John, 1632
Chelm (imp)*. Her. Linc. S Pl. Yk (tp cropped).

7032 Donne, John, 1633
Ends G4^r.
S Pl.

7032a Donne, John, 1633
Ends F3^r.
Ex.

7033 Donne, John, 1624
Pet.

7034 Donne, John, 1624
S Pl.

7035 Donne, John, 1626 (1627)
Linc.

7035a Donne, John, 1627
Ex (imp).

7038 Donne, John, 1640
Cant (imp). Carl. Dur. Ex. Glo. Her. Lich. Linc. Pet (engr. tpw). S Dv (engr. tpw). S Pl. Sal (2 −both engr. tpw). Win. Wor.

7039 Donne, John, 1623
Yk.

7040 Donne, John, 1625
S Pl. Yk.

7043 Donne, John, 1633
Linc. S Pl. Win.

7044 Donne, John, 1633
S Pl.

7045 Donne, John, 1633
'Poems, by J.D. With ...'
Linc. Wel. Win.

7047 Donne, John, 1639
Mariot.
Cant (tp imp). Carl.

7048 Donne, John, 1610
'... Wherein out of certaine propositions and gradations, this conclusion ...'
Carl. Ex. Her. Pet. S Pl (2). Sal. Yk (3).

7050 Donne, John, 1626
Ex. S Pl.

7052 Donne, John, 1624
Ex.

7053 Donne, John, 1622
A4^v has 5 errata; C4^r line 6 begins: 'haue had do'; H3^v line 12 begins: 'Say'
Bur*. Carl. Pet (2 − both imp). S Pl.

7054 Donne, John, 1622
S Pl.

7055 *See*: 7056

7056 Donne, John, 1634
... [London]; STC 7055 is pt of this.
Linc. S Pl.

7058 Donne, John, 1634
S Pl.

7060 Dorislaus, Isaac, 1640
Ban.

7061 Dorman, Thomas, 1565
Sal. Wor (2). Yk.

7062 Dorman, Thomas, 1564
Her. Rip. Wor. Yk.

7063 Dorman, Thomas, 1567
Linc. Wor.

7066 Dort, *Synod of*, 1619
Ends Q4.
Glo.

7066.5 Dort, *Synod of*, 1619
[Anr ed.] As STC 7066, but ends N2.
Cant.

7068 Dort, *Synod of*, 1627
Bur. Dur.

7069 Dort, *Synod of*, 1633
12°.
Carl. S Pl.

7070 Dort, *Synod of*, 1629
'The collegiat suffrage of the divines of Great Britaine'; 4°.
Cant (tp imp). Carl. Dur. Lich (imp). Yk (2).

7072 Doughty, John, 1628
Carl. Wel.

7072.2 Doughty, Thomas, 1621
Formerly STC 13985; 'crafte & pollicie'
Yk.

7072.3 Doughty, Thomas, 1620
Formerly STC 13986.
Yk.

7072.4 Doughty, Thomas, 1637 (1638)
Formerly STC 21540.
Nor.

7072.6 Doughty, Thomas, 1619
'IHS. Maria Ioseph. The practise how to finde ease, ... The second part ...'; 12°; Roan, J. Foüet.
Cant (imp).

7077 Dove, John, 1610
Yk.

7078 Dove, John, 1605
Pet.

7080 Dove, John, 1613
Linc.

7081 Dove, John, 1606
Bur (tpw)*. Liv.

7082 Dove, John, 1607
T. C[reede] f. H. Rockit, sold by J. Hodgets.
Pet.

7083 Dove, John, 1601
Linc. Yk (imp).

7085 Dove, John, 1603
Linc. Yk.

7086.5 Dove, John, [1594?]
The second time imprinted; 8°; V.
S[immes] f. W. Jaggard.
Yk.

7088 Dow, Christopher, 1636
Ban. Bur. Cant (2). Ches. Ex.
Linc (2). Pet. Wor. Yk.

7089 Dow, Christopher, 1636
Pet. Sal.

7090 Dow, Christopher, 1637
Bur. Cant. Ex. Linc. Nor. Sal.
Yk.

7094 Dowland, John, 1613
Linc.

7095 Dowland, John, 1600
Linc.

7096 Dowland, John, 1603
... by the assignement of a patent
granted to T. Morley.
Linc (tpw).

7097 Dowland, John, [1604]
... solde at the authors house in
Fetter-lane.
Linc.

7098 Dowland, John, 1612
'musicall'
Linc (tpw).

7101 Dowle, John, 1630
Pet.

7103 Downame, George, 1607
H. L[ownes] soulde by A. Johnson.
Linc.

7104 Downame, George, 1620
Carl.

7105 Downame, George, 1625
Ely.

7109 Downame, George, 1620
Yk.

7113 Downame, George, 1604
Cant. S Pl. Yk.

7115 Downame, George, 1611
Tp varies: 'L. Bishop' or 'Bishop'
Bur. Cant (tpw). Ex (2 − 1 imp).
Pet (2 − 1 pt 4 only). S Pl. Yk.

7116 Downame, George, 1607
'A funerall sermon preached at
Walton ... at the ...'
Linc.

7117 Downame, George, 1640
'Bourn'
Chelm. Linc. Pet. S Pl.

7118 Downame, George, 1604
Carl. Linc. S Pl (2 − 1 with
variant tp, adding: 'Whereunto
are annexed ...'). Yk.

7119 Downame, George, 1620
Ex. Her. S Pl. Sal.

7120 Downame, George, 1603
'... Antichrist, divided into two
bookes, the former, ...'
Ex. Pet (2). S Pl. Win. Yk.

7121 Downame, George, 1633
Chelm. Lich. S Pl. Sal. Wel.
Wor.

7123 Downame, George, 1639
E. Purslow, for N. Bourne, and part
of the impression ... for the ...
children of J. Minshew.
Carl. Ex. Her. Yk.

7124 Downame, George, 1609
S Pl. Yk.

7125 Downame, George, 1608
Ex (tpw). Linc. S Pl (2). Yk.

7125.5 Downame, John, 1630
[Anr ed. of STC 7126] 4°; the assignes
of C. Cotton.
Her.

7128 Downame, John, 1632
'A concordance to the Bible'
Cant (imp).

7128.5 Downame, John, [1633?]
'A concordance ...'; 4°; the assignes
of C. Cotton; Formerly STC 7131.
Roch. Yk.

7130 Downame, John, [1635?]
'A briefe concordance'
Cant. Sal.

7131 *See*: 7128.5

7133 Downame, John, 1604
Kyngston.
Yk (imp)*.

7134 Downame, John, 1608
Kyngston.
Wor.

7136 Downame, John, 1612
[Pt 1] 4°.
S Alb.

7137 Downame, John, 1634 (1633)
Cant. Carl.

7138.5 Downame, John, 1619
[Anr ed.] 4°; T. Snodham.
Linc. Wel (imp).

7139 Downame, John, 1618
[Pt 4] 'betweene'
Yk.

7140 Downame, John, 1613
[Pt 3].
Linc.

7141 Downame, John, 1609
'disswade'
Yk.

7142 Downame, John, 1613
... M. Baker.
S Asa. Yk.

7143 Downame, John, (1622)
Weuer; Pt 2 formerly also STC 7151.
Ban. Win (tpw)*. Yk (pt 2 only).

7144 Downame, John, 1629
Her. S Dv. Yk.

7146 Downame, John, 1616
Yk.

7148.3 Downame, John, [1630?]
[Anr issue, with impr. on engr. tp
altered:] W. Stansby; 4°.
Chelm (tpw)*.

7149 Downame, John, 1636
Carl. Yk.

7151 *See*: 7143

7152 Downe, John, 1633
'Certaine treatises of the late Mr John
Downe. Published ...'
Ban. Cant (imp). Carl (imp?).
Chelm. Ex. Linc. S Pl. Yk.

7153 Downe, John, 1635
Wor. Yk.

7154 Downes, Andrew, 1621
Ex. S Pl (imp). Sal.

7156 Downing, Calybute, 1632
Dur. Wor.

7157 Downing, Calybute, 1633
Carl. Linc. Liv. Yk.

7158 Downing, Calybute, 1634
Cant. Ex.

7164 Drant, Thomas, *of Shaston*,
1637
'... lanthorne: or, a sermon ...'
Ex. Linc. Pet (2 − 1 imp).

7166 Drant, Thomas, *Poet*, [1572]
Linc.

7169 Drant, Thomas, *Poet*, [1576?]
Pet.

7172 Drant, Thomas, *Poet*, [1570?]
J. Daye; [*]²B − L⁸; orn on L8ʳ.
Pet.

7175 Draxe, Thomas, 1633
Her. Linc.

7182 Draxe, Thomas, 1611
Cant.

7184 Draxe, Thomas, 1613
S Pl.

7187 Draxe, Thomas, 1608
Yk.

7190 Drayton, Michael, 1627
'... Agincourt. Fought by Henry the
fift. The miseries ...'
Lich.

7210 Drayton, Michael, 1630
Cant.

7216 Drayton, Michael, 1605
'Michaell'
Pet (imp).

7222 Drayton, Michael, (1619)
... J. Swethwicke [sic].
Nor (tpw)*.

7226 Drayton, Michael, [1612]
'Poly-Olbion By Michaell Drayton
esqu:'; Engr. tp only.
Wel (imp).

7227 Drayton, Michael, 1613
Cant. Glo. S Pl (2 − 1 lacks
letterpress tp*).

7228 Drayton, Michael, 1622
Cant.

7229 Drayton, Michael, 1622
Cant. S Pl.

7231 Drayton, Michael, 1603
'... rites and ceremonies ...'
Linc.

7244 Drum, Jack, 1616
'Newly corrected'
S Pl.

7262 Duarenus, Franciscus, 1585
Carl. Dur (pt 1 only). Linc.
New. Rip (imp). S Pl. Sal. Wel.
Yk.

7263 Du Bec-Crespin, Jean, 1597
Cant.

7278 Duck, Arthur, 1617
'Henrici'
Cant. Ex.

7285.2 Dudley, Robert, *Earl of
Leicester*, 1587
[Anr ed.] 4°; A. Hatfield f. G. Seton;
End of text signed T.D.
Pet.

7294 Dugrès, Gabriel, 1636
Carl. Linc.

7298 Du Jon, François, *the Elder*,
1602
Pet.

7298.5 Du Jon, François, *the Elder*,
1602
'A christian letter'; 4°; f. R. Dexter.
Cant.

7299 Du Jon, François, *the Elder*,
1595
'Francisci Junii de peccato ...'
Bur.

7300 Du Jon, François, *the Elder*,
[1588]
'... tres: id est, comparatio locorum
scripturae sacrae, ... Editio ...'
Bur. Her. Linc. Pet.

7301 Du Jon, François, *the Elder*,
[1591]
Chelm.

7303 Du Laurens, André, 1599
'Andreae Laurentii ... de morbis ...'
Linc.

7304 Du Laurens, André, 1599
Linc. Pet.

7306 Du Moulin, Pierre, *the Elder*,
1613
Pet (tpw). Yk.

7308 Du Moulin, Pierre, *the Elder*,
1620
Wor. Yk.

7309 Du Moulin, Pierre, *the Elder*,
1626
Yk.

7310 Du Moulin, Pierre, *the Elder*,
1635
Wor.

7312 Du Moulin, Pierre, *the Elder*,
1612
Pet. S Asa. Sal. Wor. Yk.

7313 Du Moulin, Pierre, *the Elder*,
1620
Her (2). Llan. Pet. Yk.

7314 Du Moulin, Pierre, *the Elder*,
1623
Ban. Wor. Yk.

7315 Du Moulin, Pierre, *the Elder*,
1631
Pet.

7318 Du Moulin, Pierre, *the Elder*,
1623
(T. S[nodham]) f. T. Pavier [pt 3:] (J.
Haviland f. T. Pavier).
Yk (2 − 1 pt 2 only).

7319 Du Moulin, Pierre, *the Elder*,
1615
Pet (2).

7320 Du Moulin, Pierre, *the Elder*,
1624
'Petri Molinaei de ...'; Ap. J. Billium.
Sal.

7322 Du Moulin, Pierre, *the Elder*,
1610
Cant. Pet. Roch. Wor. Yk.

7328 Du Moulin, Pierre, *the Elder*,
1624
Cant. Yk.

7330 Du Moulin, Pierre, *the Elder*,
1632
Yk.

7333 Du Moulin, Pierre, *the Elder*,
1610
Pet. Yk.

7335 Du Moulin, Pierre, *the Elder*,
1614
'Petri'
Ely. S Pl. Sal. Yk.

7343 Du Moulin, Pierre, *the Elder*,
1612
Sal. Yk.

7345 Du Moulin, Pierre, *the
Younger*, 1640
Cant. Linc. Pet (2).

7346 Dunbar, John, 1616
'Epigrammaton Joannis Dunbari
Megalo-Britanni centuriae ...'
Linc.

7354 Dunster, John, 1610
Linc.

7359 Du Plessis, Armand Jean,
1635
Carl.

7361 Du Plessis, Armand Jean,
1635
Pet.

7365 Duport, James, 1637
S Pl. Sal.

7365.5 Duport, John, 1591
'A sermon preached at Pauls Crosse
on the 17. day of Nouember 1590';
8°; J. Wolfe f. E. Aggas.
S Pl (imp).

7367.5 Durie, John, 1639
'Motives to induce the protestant
princes'; 4°; [Amsterdam].
Yk.

7373.5 Du Vair, Guillaume, 1609
'A most heavenly and plentifull
treasure'; 12°; H.L. f. H. Fetherstone.
Ely.

7374 Du Vair, Guillaume, 1598
Yk.

7385 Dyer, *Sir* James, [c.1595?]
Tp + A − H^8.
Pet.

7386 Dyer, *Sir* James, 1602
Glo.

7388 Dyer, *Sir* James, 1585
Pet.

7391 Dyer, *Sir* James, [1588]
Pet.

7393.5 Dyer, Robert, 1633
'The christian's theorico-practicon: or, his whole duty ...'; 8°; G.M. f. W. Hammond, sold by H. Hammond in Salisbury.
Pet (imp).

7393.5+ Dyer, Robert, 1633
[Anr ed.(?)] 8°; G.M. f. W. Hammond.
Cant.

7394.5 Dyke, Daniel, 1633
'The second and last part of the workes'; The second edition; 2 pts; 4°; A. M(ath.) f. R. Milbourne; Formerly vol. 2 of STC 7394.
Chelm. Her.

7397 Dyke, Daniel, 1635
Pet. Sal.

7399 Dyke, Daniel, 1615
Yk (tp imp).

7400 Dyke, Daniel, 1615
Cant.

7405 Dyke, Daniel, 1633
Carl.

7406 Dyke, Daniel, 1634
Linc. Win.

7407 Dyke, Daniel, 1617
Carl.

7408.5 Dyke, Daniel, 1618
The third impression; 4°; E. Griffin f. J. Bloome.
Carl.

7409 Dyke, Daniel, 1631
Ely. Yk.

7409a Dyke, Daniel, 1635
Sal.

7410 Dyke, Daniel, 1618
'... The one, a most fruitfull exposition upon ... schoole ...'
Carl.

7411 Dyke, Jeremiah, 1619
Pet. Yk (tpw).

7412 Dyke, Jeremiah, 1619
'covetousnes'
Pet (imp).

7414.5 Dyke, Jeremiah, 1640
[Variant, w. impr:] T. Paine, sold by J. Rothwell.
Ely.

7420 Dyke, Jeremiah, 1632
Carl.

7423 Dyke, Jeremiah, 1623
Pet. Yk.

7424 Dyke, Jeremiah, ·1628
Pet.

7432 Dyos, John, 1579
Linc.

7438 Eadmer, 1623
Cant. Carl. Dur. Ex. Pet. S Pl (2). Wor. Yk.

7438.2 Eadmer, 1623
[Variant, w. impr.:] Typis & impensis G. Stanesbeij.
Chi. Linc. Nor. Sal.

7443 Earle, John, 1630
Cant.

7445 Earle, John, 1638
Win.

7450a East India Company, 1632
[Pt 2 tp:] 'An authentick copy of the acts'
Linc.

7451 East India Company, 1624
Newberry.
Cant.

7452 East India Company, 1624
'Newberry'
Dur.

7460 East, Michael, 1604
Yk (Quintus only).

7467.5 East, Thomas, [1575? – 1608?]
[Blank ruled music paper, sometimes signed 'T.E.'] Various formats.
Yk.

7468 Eaton, Richard, 1616
'Thomas Dutton'
Pet (imp).

7469 Eburne, Richard, 1609
Bur. Sal. Wor (2). Yk.

7470 Eburne, Richard, 1609
Cant. Ex. Linc. Pet.

7472 Eburne, Richard, 1616
Yk.

7474 Eburne, Richard, 1613
Yk.

7479 Echlin, David, 1626
'Perjurium officiosum: ad vere nobilem, ... Robertum Aytonum'
Yk (imp?).

7482 Edgeworth, Roger, 1557
Wor.

7486 Edinburgh University, 1633
Linc. Pet (imp).

7487 Edinburgh University, 1617
'... In serenissimi, potentissimi et invictissimi Jacobi regis ...'
Yk (2).

7491 Edmondes, Sir Clement, 1609
Lich.

7525 Edwards, Thomas, 1595
'Cephalus & Procris. ...'
Pet.

7526 Eedes, Richard, 1604
Wor.

7527 Eedes, Richard, 1627
'Three sermons ... Now published ...'
Ex.

7528.5 Egerton, Stephen, 1612
The ninteenth [sic] edition; 8°; F. K[ingston] f. H. Fetherstone.
Yk.

7539 Egerton, Stephen, (1603)
Pet (imp).

7540 Egerton, Thomas, *Viscount Brackley*, 1609
'Eschequer'; No errata on tp verso.
Carl*. Linc*. Sal*.

7551 Elborow, John, 1637
'zelots'
Yk.

7573 Elidad, [1574?]
Pet.

7575 Eliot, John, 1592
Pet.

7579 Elizabeth I, *Queen of England*, [c.1628, etc.]
At least 4 undated eds.
Linc. Pet.

7585 Elizabeth I, *Queen of England*, 1588
Yk.

7605.5 Elizabeth, *St, Abbess of Schönau*, [1557?]
'Liber viarum Dei'; 8°; [N.pl.].
Yk.

7612 Elton, Edward, 1615
Ex.

7613 Elton, Edward, 1620
Her (2 – 1 tpw). IoM. Linc. Rip. Yk.

7621 Elton, Edward, 1623
Tp varies: Milbourne, Mylburne or Mylbourne.
Ex (Mylbourne).

7628 Ely, Humphrey, [1602]
Pet.

7629 Elyot, George, 1581
Linc (D1 – 2 only).

7636 Elyot, Sir Thomas, (1537)
(T. Berthelet).
Cant. Pet.

7639 Elyot, Sir Thomas, 1553
(In the house of T. Berthelet).
Pet.

7640 Elyot, *Sir* Thomas, 1557
Pet.

7642 Elyot, *Sir* Thomas, 1580
Pet.

7642.7 Elyot, *Sir* Thomas, 1539
[Anr ed. of STC 7643] 4°; (In aed. T.
Bertheleti).
Cant.

7644 Elyot, *Sir* Thomas, [1541]
(In aed. T. Bertheleti).
Pet.

7651 Elyot, *Sir* Thomas, [1561?]
(T. Marshe); Date in title.
Pet.

7653 Elyot, *Sir* Thomas, 1580
Pet.

7660 Elyot, *Sir* Thomas, 1545
(1542)
'Bibliotheca Eliotae ...'
Pet.

.7666 Elyot, *Sir* Thomas, 1549
(In the house of T. Berthelette).
Pet (imp).

7667 Elyot, *Sir* Thomas, 1556
(W. Seres).
Cant. Pet.

7674 Elyot, *Sir* Thomas, 1545
(T. Berthelet).
S Pl (imp).

7675 Em, *Fair*, [1591?]
Cant (imp).

7689 England. Customs, 1582
(1567)
Sal.

7691 England. Customs, [1608]
'set downe'
Yk.

7695 England. Customs, 1635
Sal (tpw).

7713 England. Local Courts, 1536
(In aed. ...).
Pet.

7736 England. Parliament, 1606
'arguments'
Sal. Yk.

7739 England. Parliament, [1585]
Cant.

7746.6 England. Parliament, 1640
'A catalogue of the Lords spirituall
and temporall'; 8°; J.D. f. T. Walkley.
Linc.

7746.7 England. Parliament, 1640
'A catalogue of the names of the
knights for this Parliament. Begun the
13. of Aprill, 1640'; 8°; f. T. Walkley.
Linc.

7746.9 England. Parliament, 1640
'A catalogue of the dukes,
marquesses, ...'; 8°; f. T. Walkley;
p.7, line 23: 'Iohn Bancroft Bishop of
Oxford'; Formerly STC 24980.
Linc.

7746.10 England. Parliament, 1640
Formerly STC 24981; As STC 7746.9,
but p.7, line 23 has blank left for
bishop's name.
Linc.

7746.13 England. Parliament, 1640
'A catalogue of the names of the
knights for this Parliament. Begun the
3. of November, 1640'; 8°; f. T.
Walkley.
Linc.

7747 England. Parliament, 1640
Last word of impr.: 'streete'
Linc*.

7749 England. Parliament, 1628
Wor.

7750 England. Parliament, 1640
Linc.

7754 England. Privy Council, 1590
Rip. Yk (3).

7755 England. Privy Council, *Star
Chamber*, 1633
'A decree lately made in the high
court ...'
Yk.

7757 England. Privy Council. *Star
Chamber*, 1637
Royal arms on tp.
Ely*. Linc. Sal*.

7759 England. Proclamations,
[1610]
Yk.

7803 England. Proclamations,
[1544]
Cant.

7910.7 England. Proclamations,
(1559) [o.s.]
[A trans.] ['Proclamation contenant la
declaration ... sur lobseruation de la
paix'] 8°; (R. Jugge & J. Cawood).
Pet (tpw).

8048 England. Proclamations,
[c.1590?]
Cant.

8062 England. Proclamations,
[1573]
Cant.

8077 England. Proclamations, 1576
'The seuerall rates ... for wages, ...
Canterburie'
Cant.

8106 *See:* 8178

8113 England. Proclamations, 1579
'By the queene. A proclamation
against ...'
Cant.

8137 England. Proclamations,
[1582]
'By the queene. A proclamation for
adiournment ...'
Cant.

8166 England. Proclamations,
[1587]
Last complete line of text ends: 'pub-'
Cant.

8178 England. Proclamations,
[1588]
Formerly also STC 8106; 'By the
queene. A proclamation for ...'
Cant.

8179 England. Proclamations,
[1589]
Formerly also STC 8180; 'By the
queene. A proclamation concerning
the souldiours'
Cant (2).

8180 *See:* 8179

8202 England. Proclamations,
[1591]
'By the queene. A proclamation to ...'
Cant.

8224 England. Proclamations,
[1592]
'By the queene. A proclamation for ...
'
Cant.

8237 England. Proclamations,
[1594]
'The seuerall rates ... for wages, for
Canterburie'; [2 May].
Cant.

8238 England. Proclamations,
[c.1618]
'By the queene. A proclamation
against ...'
Cant.

8240 England. Proclamations, 1594
'By the queene. A proclamation
against ...'
Cant (2).

8257 England. Proclamations, 1597
Cant (imp).

8258 England. Proclamations, 1597
Cant.

8261 England. Proclamations, 1597
'By the queene. A proclamation
publishing ...'
Cant.

8274 England. Proclamations, 1600
'By the queene. A proclamation inhibiting ...'
Cant.

8309 England. Proclamations, 1603
Sheet 1, last indented line to right of initial begins: 'be'
Cant.

8384 England. Proclamations, 1605
Formerly also STC 8385.
Cant.

8385 *See*: 8384

8389 England. Proclamations, 1605
[o.s.]
Cant.

8392 England. Proclamations, 1606
'By the King. Such is the zeale and inward affection ...'
Cant.

8448 England. Proclamations, 1511 [1611]
'A proclamation published under the name of James. ...'
Yk.

8464 *See*: 9240.5, another ed. of 9240.3 which was formerly 8464

8498 England. Proclamations, 1613
[o.s.]
Sal*. Yk (2 – both imp)*.

8520 England. Proclamations, [1615]
'By the king. A proclamation touching ...'
Cant.

8540 England. Proclamations, 1616
'By the king. A proclamation against ...'
Cant.

8566 *See*: 9238.9

8678 England. Proclamations, 1621
[o.s.]
Line 3 of tp impr. ends: 'Excellent'
Pet (2). Yk.

8723 England. Proclamations, 1623
[o.s.]
'By the king. A proclamation for ambassadours'
Cant.

8725 England. Proclamations, 1624
'By the king. A proclamation for the restraint ...'; Arms without rose and thistle.
Cant.

8738 England. Proclamations, 1624
'By the king. A proclamation concerning ...'; Sheet 4, last complete line ends: 'diligent'
Cant.

8742 England. Proclamations, 1624
'By the king. A proclamation for ...'
Cant.

8747 England. Proclamations, 1624
[o.s.]
'By the king. A proclamation for restraint ...'; Sheet 1 has last indented line to right of initial beginning: 'daies' and arms with 'I R' at top.
Cant.

8750 England. Proclamations, 1624
[o.s.]
'By the king. A proclamation touching ...'
Cant.

8783 England. Proclamations, 1625
'By the king. A proclamation for the continuing of our farthing ...'; fol.
Cant.

8785 England. Proclamations, 1625
'By the king. A proclamation for the adjournement ...'
Cant.

8908 England. Proclamations, 1628
'By the king. A proclamation ... touching the English souldiers ...'
Cant.

8909 England. Proclamations, 1628
'By the king. A proclamation ... to confirme ...'
Cant.

8910 England. Proclamations, 1628
Cant.

8911 England. Proclamations, 1628
'By the king. A proclamation for ...'
Cant.

8928 England. Proclamations, 1629
'By the king. A proclamation for the better ordering of those who [come] for cure of the kings evill'
Cant.

8929 England. Proclamations, 1629
'By the king. A proclamation concerning ...'; Sheet 2, line 1 ends: 'to'
Cant.

8931 England. Proclamations, 1629
'By the king. A proclamation touching ...'
Cant.

8934 England. Proclamations, 1629
'By the king. A proclamation for preventing ...'
Cant.

8942 England. Proclamations, 1630
'By the king. A proclamation for the ... kings evill'
Cant.

8943 England. Proclamations, 1630
'By the king. A proclamation for the preventing of the ...'
Cant.

8946 England. Proclamations, 1630
'By the king. A proclamation for the restraining of the importation ...'; Arms with 1 leaf (not 2) under lion's leg.
Cant.

8950 England. Proclamations, 1630
'By the king. A proclamation ... to confirme ...'
Cant.

8951 England. Proclamations, 1630
Cant.

8956 England. Proclamations, 1630
'By the king. A proclamation for the ease of subjects ... for not receiving ...'; ... assignes ...; Arms without 'C R' at top.
Cant.

8960 England. Proclamations, 1630
'By the king. A proclamation prohibiting ...'; ... assignes ...
Cant.

8961 England. Proclamations, 1630
'By the king. A proclamation against ...'; ... assignes ...
Cant.

8964 England. Proclamations, 1630
'By the king. ...'; ... assignes ...
Cant.

8970 England. Proclamations, 1630
... assignes ...
Cant.

8971 England. Proclamations, 1630
[o.s.]
... assignes ...
Cant.

8973 England. Proclamations, 1631
'By the king. A proclamation for the ... kings evill'; ... assignes ...
Cant.

8975 England. Proclamations, 1631
'By the king. A proclamation for ...'; ... assignes ...
Cant.

8976 England. Proclamations, 1631
'By the king. A proclamation for ...'; ... assignes ...
Cant.

8979 England. Proclamations, 1631
'By the king. A proclamation for revoking the commission ...'; ... assignes ...
Cant.

8980 England. Proclamations, 1631
'By the king. A proclamation for the
... kings evill'; ... assignes ...
Cant.

8982 England. Proclamations, 1631
'By the king. A proclamation
inhibiting the resort ...'; ... assignes ...
Cant.

8984 England. Proclamations, 1631
[o.s.]
'By the king. A proclamation ...
against eating ... flesh in Lent'; ...
assignes ...
Cant.

8986 England. Proclamations, 1631
[o.s.]
... assignes ...
Cant.

8987 England. Proclamations, 1632
'By the king. A proclamation for ...';
... assignes ...
Cant.

8988 England. Proclamations, 1632
'By the king. A proclamation
inhibiting the resort ... for cure of the
kings evill'; ... assignes ...
Cant.

8989 England. Proclamations, 1632
'By the king. A proclamation
commanding ...'; ... assignes ...
Cant.

8999 England. Proclamations, 1633
'By the king. A proclamation against
frauds ...'; ... assignes ...
Cant.

9006 England. Proclamations, 1633
[o.s.]
'By the king. A proclamation for ...';
... assignes ...
Cant.

9008 England. Proclamations, 1633
[o.s.]
'By the king. A proclamation
concerning ...'; ... assignes ...
Cant.

9014 England. Proclamations, 1634
'By the king. A proclamation
appointing the flags'; ... assignes ...
Cant.

9018 England. Proclamations, 1634
'By the king. A proclamation
concerning ...'; ... assignes ...
Cant.

9019 England. Proclamations, 1634
'By the king. A proclamation
concerning the well-ordering the trade
of soape'; ... assignes ...
Cant.

9023 England. Proclamations, 1634
'By the king. A proclamation for
reforming and preventing frauds ... in
butter-casks ...'; ... assignes ...
Cant.

9032 England. Proclamations, 1634
[o.s.]
'By the king. A proclamation for ...
the manufacture of soape'; ... assignes
...
Cant.

9041 England. Proclamations, 1635
'By the King. A proclamation for the
setling of the letter office'; ... assignes
...
Linc.

9050 England. Proclamations, 1635
'By the king. A proclamation for
restraint ...'; ... assignes ...
Cant.

9052 England. Proclamations, 1635
[o.s.]
'By the king. A proclamation for the
restraint ...'; ... assignes ...
Cant.

9060 England. Proclamations, 1636
'By the king. A proclamation to
forbid importing ... Mare Clausum';
... assignes ...; Arms with 2 leaves
under lion's leg.
Cant.

9062 England. Proclamations, 1636
'By the king. A proclamation
prohibiting the wearing ... of
counterfeit jewels'; ... assignes ...
Cant.

9063 England. Proclamations, 1636
'By the king. A proclamation ...
touching orders ... for prevention ...';
... assignes ...
Cant.

9064 England. Proclamations, 1636
'By the king. A proclamation touching
bookes first printed here and after
reprinted ...'; ... assignes ...
Cant.

9065 England. Proclamations, 1636
'By the king. A proclamation for
restraint ...'; ... assignes ...
Cant.

9077 England. Proclamations, 1636
'By the king. A proclamation for the
revocation and repeale of certaine
letters patents ...'; ... assignes ...
Cant.

9083 England. Proclamations, 1636
[o.s.]
'By the king. A proclamation for
putting ...'; ... assignes ...
Cant.

9086 England. Proclamations, 1637
'By the king. A proclamation against
the disorderly transporting ...'; ...
assignes ...
Cant.

9088 England. Proclamations, 1637
'By the king. A proclamation touching
the manufactures of ...'; ... assignes
...
Cant.

9093 England. Proclamations, 1637
... assignes ...
Linc.

9098 England. Proclamations, 1637
'By the King. A proclamation
restraining the withdrawing his
majesties subjects from ...'; ...
assignes ...
Linc.

9134 England. Proclamations, 1638
[o.s.]
'By the king. A proclamation ...'; 2°;
... assignes ...
Pet (frag.)*.

9135 England. Proclamations, 1638
[o.s.]
'By the King. A proclamation and
declaration ... of the seditious ...'; ...
assignes ...
Linc.

9140 England. Proclamations, 1639
'... A proclamation ... touching ...';
... assignes ...; Sheet 2, last complete
line of text ends: 'whereof'
Linc*.

9149 England. Proclamations, 1639
'By the king. A proclamation
prohibiting ...'; ... assignes ...
Cant.

9153 England. Proclamations, 1639
[o.s.]
'By the king. A proclamation
commanding the due execution of the
laws ... against eating ...'; ... assignes
...
Cant.

9156 England. Proclamations, 1640
'By the King. A proclamation
commanding all ...'; ... assignes ...
Linc.

9157 England. Proclamations, 1640
'By the King. A proclamation for the
repressing ... of the ... assemblies'; ...
assignes ...
Linc.

9159 England. Proclamations, 1640
'By the King. A proclamation for a ...
'; ... assignes ...
Linc.

9161 England. Proclamations, 1640
'By the king. A proclamation for
apprehending and punishing of
souldiers ...'; ... assignes ...
Cant.

9162 England. Proclamations, 1640
'By the king. A proclamation
declaring his ... pardon ...'; ...
assignes ...
Cant.

9163 England. Proclamations, 1640
'By the king. A proclamation
concerning ...'; ... assignes ...
Cant.

9164 England. Proclamations, 1640
'By the king. A proclamation for the
apprehending ...'; ... assignes ...
Cant.

9165 England. Proclamations, 1640
'By the king. A proclamation
concerning the sequestration of the
office ...'; ... assignes ...
Cant.

9166 England. Proclamations, 1640
'By the King. A proclamation
declaring ...'; ... assignes ...
Linc.

9167 England. Proclamations, 1640
'By the King. A proclamation for the
levying ...'; ... assignes ...
Linc.

9168 England. Proclamations, 1640
'By the King. A proclamation to
summon ...'; ... assignes ...
Linc.

9169 England. Proclamations, 1640
'By the King. A proclamation
commanding ...'; ... assignes ...
Cant. Linc.

9170 England. Proclamations, 1640
'By the King. A proclamation for ...';
... assignes ...
Cant. Linc.

9171 England. Proclamations, 1640
'By the king. A proclamation
commanding ...'; ... assignes ...; Line
1 of text ends: 'extraordinary'
Cant. Linc*.

9173 England. Proclamations, 1640
'By the king. A proclamation for ...';
... assignes ...
Cant.

9178 England. Public documents,
(1534)
(In aed. T. Bertheleti).
Linc.

9183.5 England. Public documents,
(1560)
Pet.

9189 England. Public documents,
(1585)
A3^r line 11 of text ends: 'ha-'
Linc.

9196 England. Public documents,
1589
Linc.

9211 England. Public documents,
1605
'Articles of peace, entercourse, and
commerce, ... In a treatie ... the 18.
day of August ... 1604'
Dur.

9214 England. Public documents,
[1608]
'... xxi of March 1607'
Sal*.

9230 England. Public documents,
1612
Dur. Pet.

9232 England. Public documents,
1612
'Declaratio serenissimi Magnae ...'
Pet.

9233 England. Public documents,
1612
Yk.

9237 England. Public documents,
1615
Sal.

9238.9 England. Public documents,
1618
Formerly STC 8566; 'The kings
majesties declaration to his subjects,
concerning lawfull sports'
Linc. Yk.

9240.5 England. Public documents,
1619
'A declaration of his Maiesties royall
pleasure [how] to enlarge himselfe in
matter of bountie'; 4°; B. Norton a.
J. Bill; A3^v line 1: 'any such'
Yk.

9241 England. Public documents,
1621 [o.s.]
Pet (2). Yk (2 − 1 cropped).

9244.3 England. Public documents,
1625
[Anr ed.] As STC 9244, but tp line 7
has: 'bee heerafter'
Linc.

9245 England. Public documents,
1625
A1^v has arms without garter.
Dur*.

9246 England. Public documents,
1626
Pet. Yk.

9247 England. Public documents,
1626
Linc.

9249 England. Public documents,
1628 [o.s.]
'... declaration to all his loving
subjects, of the causes ...'
Ex. Linc.

9250.5 England. Public documents,
1630
Formerly STC 9253; '... appointed by
his majestie for ...'; Ends D4.
Dur*. Linc*. Wor*.

9251 England. Public documents,
1630
'Articles of peace, entercourse, and
commerce ... In a treaty ...'; ...
assignes ...; B2^v last line begins:
'friendly'
Linc*. Wor*.

9252 England. Public documents,
1630 [o.s.]
'... directions, together with a
commission for ...'; A − G^4 H^2; D3^r
line 1 has: 'C[swash]ommand'
Linc*. S Pl*.

9253 See: 9250.5

9254 England. Public documents,
1631
'... commission giving power to
enquire ...'
Linc. Pet. S Pl.

9254.7 England. Public documents,
1633
Formerly STC 9257.
Cant. Linc. Pet. Yk.

9256 England. Public documents,
1633
Dur.

9257 See: 9254.7

9258 England. Public documents,
1634
Ely.

9260 England. Public documents,
1640
Formerly also STC 22006.
Cant. Ex. Linc. Pet.

9262 England. Public documents,
1640
Cant. Linc. Pet. Sal.

9268 England. Statutes, (1519)
Pet (imp).

9273 England. Statutes, 1529
Pet.

9274 England. Statutes, 1540
Pet.

9276 England. Statutes, (1542)
Pet.

9277 England. Statutes, 1556
Glo. Pet.

9278 England. Statutes, (1556)
[c.1560?]
(In aed. ...); Tp pt 1: '12. Inn [sic].
1556.'
Cant. Pet.

9280 England. Statutes, 1576
Pet (tpw).

9282 England. Statutes, 1587
Linc. Pet.

9283 England. Statutes, 1602
Pet.

9284 England. Statutes, 1608
Yk.

9291 England. Statutes, 1542
Pet (imp).

9294 England. Statutes, 1570
Glo.

9300 England. Statutes, 1625
Yk.

9301 England. Statutes, (1543)
(In off. T. Bertheleti); Tp line 9:
'soueraine'
Yk (imp).

9301.3 England. Statutes, (1543)
[c.1550?]
[Anr ed.] 2°; (In off. T. Berleti [sic];
Tp line 9: 'soueraigne'
Yk.

9302 *See*: 9303.6

9303.6 England. Statutes, 1551
[Vol. 2] Formerly STC 9302; Tp line 7
has: 'Eyght'
Win. Yk*.

9303.7 England. Statutes, 1551
[Vol. 2] 2°; In aed. T. Bertheleti; Tp
line 7 has: 'Eight'
Yk (tpw)*.

9303.9 England. Statutes, 1563
[Vol. 2] 2°; T. Powell.
Bur.

9304 England. Statutes, 1575
Pet.

9305.3 England. Statutes, 1587
[Hen. III – 29 Eliz. I] Formerly STC
9316.
Liv.

9305.7 England. Statutes, 1618
'The statutes at large'; Formerly STC
9326.
Cant. Ex (2 – 1 vol. 2 only).
Glo. Linc (vol. 1 only).

9307 England. Statutes, 1559
Pet (tpw).

9308 England. Statutes, 1565
Glo.

9309 England. Statutes, 1568
Ban.

9312 England. Statutes, 1574
Pet.

9314 England. Statutes, 1579
Yk.

9315 England. Statutes, (1583)
Dated colophon on f. 559^v.
Ches (tp imp). Ex (imp)*.

9315.5 England. Statutes, [1583?]
[Anr ed.] As STC 9315, but has
undated colophon on f. 559^v.
S Pl.

9316 *See*: 9305.3

9319 England. Statutes, 1594
Ban (imp). Rip.

9320 England. Statutes, 1595
Pet.

9324 England. Statutes, 1611
Carl. Yk.

9325 England. Statutes, 1615
Cant (imp).

9326 *See*: 9305.7

9329 England. Statutes, 1632
Her. Pet.

9330 England. Statutes, 1636 (1635)
Ely. Lich. Swel. Yk (imp).

9331 England. Statutes, 1640
Carl. Ches (tp imp).

9335 England. Statutes, 1639
Tp line 3 ends: 'of'
Cant. Linc*.

9336 England. Statutes, 1640
Linc.

9339+ England. Statutes, [1556?]
[Anr ed.?] 'The king and the quenes
moost excellent Maiesties ...'; 2°; (In
aed. I. Cawodi).
Yk.

9351a.4 England. Statutes, [1515?]
Pet (lacks a1).

9358.7 England. Statutes, [1521?]
Pet.

9361.3 England. Statutes, [1522?]
[Anr ed.] As STC 9361, but cut of
enthroned king on tp verso.
Pet.

9362.3 England. Statutes, [1515]
[5 Hen. VIII] 'Anno regni regis
Henrici .viii. quinto.' 2°; [R. Pynson].
Pet.

9362.3A England. Statutes, [1514]
[5 Hen. VIII. An act of subsidy] 2°;
[R. Pynson].
Her (B^4 only).

9362.4 England. Statutes, [1515]
[6 Hen. VIII] 'Anno sexto. Henrici
.viii.'; 2°; (R. Pynson); A–B^6 C–D^4.
Pet.

9362.6 England. Statutes, [1516?]
[7 Hen. VIII] 'Anno septimo Henrici
.viii.'; 2°; (R. Pynson); A^6 B^4 C^6.
Pet.

9362.8 England. Statutes, [1516?]
[7 Hen. VIII] 'The acte of the kynges
reuenues'; 2°; (R. Pynson).
Pet.

9362.9 England. Statutes, [1523?]
[14 & 15 Hen. VIII] 'Anno .xiiii. et
anno .xv. Henrici. .viii.'; 2°; (R.
Pynson); Tp + a^4 b–c^6.
Pet.

9407 England. Statutes, 1543
Tp line 5: 'parlyament'
Cant.

9417 *See*: 9421.3

9418 *See*: 9421.6

9421 England. Statutes, (1548)
[1549]
(In aed. ...); In title: 'Parliamente'
Yk*.

9421.3 England. Statutes, (1548)
[1553?]
Formerly STC 9417; 2°; (In aed. R.
Graftoni).
Yk.

9421.6 England. Statutes, (1548)
[c.1570?]
Formerly STC 9418; (In aed. R.
Graftoni); Tp line 5 ends: 'daye'
Pet.

9423 England. Statutes, (1549)
(In aed. ...).
Yk.

9424 England. Statutes, (1552)
[1557?]
(R. Graftonus).
Yk.

9425 England. Statutes, (1552) [i.e.
1565?]
(R. Graftonus); In title:
'EDOVARDI'
Pet.

9429 England. Statutes, (1549)
[o.s.]
(R. Grafton); A2^r line 4: 'of ...
accordynge'
Yk*.

9432 England. Statutes, 1553
[1576?]
Pet. Yk*.

9435 *See*: 9437.7

9437.7 England. Statutes, 1552
[1576?]
Formerly STC 9435; (R. Graftonus).
Pet. Yk*.

9438 *See*: 9440.2

9439 England. Statutes, (1553)
(In aed. ...).
Yk.

9440 England. Statutes, (1553)
(In aed. R. Graftoni).
Yk.

9440.2 England. Statutes, 1553
[c.1570]
Formerly STC 9438; (In aed. R.
Graftoni).
Pet.

9440.8 England. Statutes, (1554)
'Anno Mariae primo ...'; (In aed. J.
Cawodi); A2^r catchword: 'by'
Yk*.

9440.10 England. Statutes, (1554)
Formerly STC 9445; (In aed. J.
Cawodi); Tp: 'be-/gonne'; A2^r
catchword: 'or'
Yk (2)*.

9440.16 England. Statutes, 1554
[1577?]
[Anr ed.] 2°; (In aed. J. Cawoodi);
Border McKerrow & Ferguson 126.
Pet.

9444 England. Statutes, (1554)
[1556?]
(In aed. J. Cawodi).
Yk.

9444.8 England. Statutes, 1554
[1577?]
[Anr ed.] 2°; (In ed. J. Cawodi); Not
foliated; Border McKerrow &
Ferguson 126.
Pet.

9445 *See*: 9440.10

9448 England. Statutes, (1555)
[1558?]
(In aed. J. Cawodi); Tp line 6:
'Nouember'
Yk*.

9449 England. Statutes, (1555)
[1570?]
(In aed. ...); ff. xxxiiij; B2^r catchword:
'Prouided'
Yk*.

9450 England. Statutes, 1555
[1575?]
Pet.

9450.3 England. Statutes, (1555)
Formerly STC 9453; (In aed. ...); A2^r
line 5: 'Counties'
Yk*.

9453 *See*: 9450.3

9454 England. Statutes, (1555)
[1573?]
(In aed. J. Cawodi); Tp line 6: 'yere'
Yk*.

9454.5 England. Statutes, 1555
[1577?]
[Anr ed.] 'Anno secundo & tertio'; 2°;
(In aed. J. Cawodi); Tp line 6: 'yeere'
Pet.

9455 England. Statutes, 1555
[1574?]
Pet.

9457 England. Statutes, (1558)
(In aed. J. Cawodi); Tp line 6 has:
'fourth' and line 3 has an orn.
Yk (2)*.

9458 *See*: 9459.5

9459.5 England. Statutes, 1559
Formerly STC 9458; (R. Jugge a. J.
Cawood); Tp line 6: 'Januarye ...
fyrste'
Yk (2)*.

9461.5 England. Statutes, 1559
[1577]
[Anr ed.] 2°; (R. Jugge); Tp line 5:
'reigne'
Cant.

9464 England. Statutes, 1563
[1564?]
(R. Jugge a. I. Cawood); ff. '72'; Tp
line 3 ends: 'THE'; 'D' of D1 under
and to right of 'r' of 'other'
Cant. Yk*.

9468.3 England. Statutes, 1566
[o.s.]
[Anr ed.] 2°; (R. Jugge a. J.
Cawood); ff. 28.
Yk*.

9471.2 England. Statutes, 1567
[Anr state of STC 9468.4, formerly
STC 9470] 2°; (R. Jugge).
Cant.

9471.4 England. Statutes, 1571
[Anr ed. of STC 9472] 2°; (R. Jugge
a. J. Cawood); Formerly STC 9476;
Last line as STC1 or 'trary thereof'
Cant. Yk*.

9476 *See*: 9471.4

9477a.5 England. Statutes, 1572
[Anr ed. of STC 9478] 2°; (R. Iugge).
Cant. Yk*.

9481 England. Statutes, 1575 [o.s.]
(R. Jugge).
Yk.

9482 England. Statutes, 1575 [o.s.]
(R. Jugge).
Cant.

9484.5 England. Statutes, 1581
[Anr ed.] 2°; C. Barker; 16 acts in
table, and in text.
Cant. Yk*.

9485 England. Statutes, 1585
Cant. Yk.

9487.5 England. Statutes, 1587
[Anr ed.] 2°; C. Barker; B2^r last line:
'Prayer,'
Cant. Yk*.

9488 England. Statutes, 1589
Tp line 7: 'Ladie'; C2^r line 1:
'Pallantine'
Cant. Yk*.

9489 England. Statutes, 1593
Cant. Yk.

9494 England. Statutes, [1598]
Aa—Bb^6 have the regnal year
misprinted 'xl.'
Yk*.

9497 England. Statutes, (1601)
Yk.

9500 England. Statutes, 1604
B8^r line 18: 'lowed', line 1: 'own'
Yk*.

9502 England. Statutes, 1606
B1^r line 1 of text ends: 'Almightie'
Yk*.

9505 England. Statutes, 1607
Yk.

9506 England. Statutes, 1610
A4^r line 3: 'aforesaid'
Yk*.

9507 England. Statutes, 1624
'... regis ... 21°.'; B2^r line 7 ends:
'Manours'
Linc*. Yk (2)*.

9508 England. Statutes, 1625
Linc. Yk.

9509 England. Statutes, 1630 (1629)
Dur. Yk.

9510 England. Statutes, 1628
'... regis ... tertio'
Dur. Linc. Yk (2).

9511 England. Statutes, 1640
[1641?]
'... Caroli regis ... decimo sexto';
Formerly also STC 9512.
Linc.

9512 *See*: 9511

9517.5 England. Statutes, (1517)
[*i.e.* 1527]
[Enlarged ed. of STC 9516] 'Le
bregemēt de toutes estatutes'; 8°; Per
R. Redmā.
Glo.

9519 England. Statutes, (1528)
(R. Redman).
Yk (imp).

9520 England. Statutes, (1528)
'... ad annum .xv. ...'; (J. Rastel
imprimi me fecit).
Pet (tp imp).

9521 England. Statutes, [1531?]
Formerly also STC 9521a; '... vntyll
.xxii. Henry the .viii'
Pet.

9521a *See*: 9521

9522 England. Statutes, [1538?]
'... abbrydgement ... vntyll ...'; (R.
Redman).
Pet.

9530 England. Statutes, 1586
Pet.

9545 England. Statutes, 1553
Yk.

9546 England. Statutes, [1570]
Pet.

9548 England. Statutes, 1608
Ex.

9549 England. Statutes, 1612
Glo.

9551 England. Yearbooks, (1562)
(R. Tottyll).
Ches. Pet. Yk.

9552 England. Yearbooks, [1596]
Date in title; In aed. J. Yetsweirt
relictae Caroli Yetsweirt.
Dur. Pet.

9554 England. Yearbooks, 1619
Dur. Yk.

9556 England. Yearbooks, [1561?]
Ches (imp).

9557 England. Yearbooks, [1584?]
Pet.

9559 England. Yearbooks, [1561?]
Ches.

9560 England. Yearbooks, [1584?]
Pet.

9563 England. Yearbooks, (1561)
(R. Tottyll).
Ches.

9564 England. Yearbooks, (1584)
(R. Tottyll).
Pet.

9566 England. Yearbooks, (1567)
(R. Tottel); STC 9568, 9569a are pts
of this.
Ches.

9567 England. Yearbooks, (1585)
(R. Tottyl).
Pet.

9568 *See*: 9566

9569a *See*: 9566

9571 England. Yearbooks, (1561)
(R. Tottyll).
Ches.

9572 England. Yearbooks, (1585)
(R. Tottyl).
Pet.

9574 England. Yearbooks, (1561)
(R. Tottyll).
Ches.

9575 England. Yearbooks, (1585)
(R. Tottell).
Pet.

9577 England. Yearbooks, (1561)
(R. Tottyll).
Ches.

9578 England. Yearbooks, (1585)
(R. Tottel).
Pet.

9580 England. Yearbooks, (1561)
(R. Tottyll).
Ches (imp).

9581 England. Yearbooks, (1585)
(R. Tottill).
Pet.

9583 England. Yearbooks, 1565
In aed. R. Tottelli.
Yk.

9584 England. Yearbooks, 1576
Pet.

9585 England. Yearbooks, 1600
Dur. Yk.

9601 England. Yearbooks, 1580
Pet.

9602 England. Yearbooks, 1606
Dur. Yk.

9605 England. Yearbooks, 1555
R. Tottle.
Pet.

9609 England. Yearbooks, 1575
Imp. R. Tottelli.
Ches. Pet.

9610 England. Yearbooks, 1605
Dur.

9615 England. Yearbooks, 1563
In aed. R. Tottelli.
Ches.

9615.4 England. Yearbooks, 1587
[Anr ed.] 3pts; 2°; In aed. R. Tottelli.
Pet.

9616 England. Yearbooks, 1609
Dur. Yk (tpw).

9623 England. Yearbooks, (1584)
(R. Tottyl).
Ches. Pet.

9630 England. Yearbooks, (1584)
(R. Tottyl).
Ches. Pet.

9636 England. Yearbooks, (1582)
(R. Tottell).
Ches. Pet.

9641 England. Yearbooks, (1582)
(R. Tottell).
Ches. Pet.

9647 England. Yearbooks, (1584)
(R. Tottyl).
Ches. Pet.

9654 England. Yearbooks, (1562)
(R. Tottell).
Pet.

9657 England. Yearbooks, [1585?]
Ches.

9658 England. Yearbooks, [1525?]
(Per R. Pynsonum).
Linc (Diii only)*.

9663 England. Yearbooks, (1587)
(R. Tottyll).
Ches. Pet.

9667 England. Yearbooks, (1567)
(R. Tottill).
Ches.

9668 England. Yearbooks, (1582)
(R. Tottel).
Pet.

9672 England. Yearbooks, (1574)
(R. Tottel).
Pet.

9679 England. Yearbooks, (1574)
(R. Tottel).
Pet (with A1,4 of STC 9680).

9680 England. Yearbooks, [1586?]
A – E⁴ F⁶; ff. 'xxi' [26].
Ches.

9684 England. Yearbooks, [1582?]
(R. Tottel).
Ches. Pet.

9689 England. Yearbooks, (1567)
[1582?]
(R. Tottel).
Ches. Pet.

9696 England. Yearbooks, [1586?]
Ches. Pet.

9697 England. Yearbooks, 1601
Pt 2 also issued separately as STC 1479.
Dur. Yk.

9700 England. Yearbooks, [1556?]
(R. Tottill).
Ches.

9701 England. Yearbooks, (1567)
(R. Tottill).
Pet.

9702 England. Yearbooks, (1575)
(R. Tottell).
Wor.

9706 England. Yearbooks, [1556?]
(R. Tottill).
Ches.

9707 England. Yearbooks, (1567)
(R. Tottill).
Pet.

9708 England. Yearbooks, (1575)
(R. Tottel).
Wor.

9713 England. Yearbooks, (1562)
(R. Tottell).
Ches.

9714 England. Yearbooks, (1567)
(R. Tottill).
Pet.

9715 England. Yearbooks, (1575)
(R. Tottel).
Wor.

9718 England. Yearbooks, (1556)
(R. Tottle).
Ches.

9719 England. Yearbooks, (1567)
(R. Tottel).
Pet.

9720 England. Yearbooks, (1575)
(R. Tottel).
Wor.

9723 England. Yearbooks, (1556)
(R. Tottel).
Ches.

9724 England. Yearbooks, (1567)
(R. Tottel).
Pet (2).

9725 England. Yearbooks, (1575)
(R. Tottel).
Wor.

9728 England. Yearbooks, (1556)
(R. Tottel).
Ches.

9729 England. Yearbooks, (1566)
(R. Tottel).
Pet.

9730 England. Yearbooks, (1576)
(R. Tottel).
Wor.

9734 England. Yearbooks, (1556)
(R. Tottel).
Ches.

9735 England. Yearbooks, (1556)
(R. Tottell).
Pet.

9736 England. Yearbooks, (1575)
(R. Tottell).
Wor.

9739 England. Yearbooks, (1556)
(R. Tottel).
Ches.

9740 England. Yearbooks, (1556)
(R. Tottel).
Pet.

9741 England. Yearbooks, (1575)
(R. Tottel).
Wor.

9746 England. Yearbooks, (1556)
(R. Tottel).
Ches.

9747 England. Yearbooks, (1556)
(R. Tottell).
Pet.

9748 England. Yearbooks, (1575)
(R. Tottel).
Wor.

9752 England. Yearbooks, (1557)
(R. Tottle).
Ches.

9753 England. Yearbooks, (1567)
(R. Tottel).
Pet.

9754 England. Yearbooks, (1575)
(R. Tottel).
Wor.

9757 England. Yearbooks, [1557?]
(R. Tottill).
Ches.

9758 England. Yearbooks, (1567)
(R. Tottill).
Pet.

9761 England. Yearbooks, (1556)
(R. Tottel).
Ches.

9762 England. Yearbooks, (1566)
(R. Tottel).
Pet.

9763 England. Yearbooks, (1575)
(R. Tottel).
Wor.

9766 England. Yearbooks, (1557)
(R. Tottle).
Ches.

9767 England. Yearbooks, (1567)
(R. Tottill).
Pet.

9768 England. Yearbooks, (1575)
(R. Tottel).
Wor.

9769 England. Yearbooks, 1599
Glo (imp).

9769.5 England. Yearbooks, 1640
[Anr ed.] Formerly STC 9805.
Dur. Yk.

9774 England. Yearbooks, (1556)
(R. Tottel).
Wor (2)*.

9776 England. Yearbooks, (1556)
[1571?]
(R. Tottill).
Ches.

9778 England. Yearbooks, (1582)
(R. Tottel).
Pet.

9782 England. Yearbooks, (1566)
(R. Tottell).
Ches. Wor.

9783 England. Yearbooks, (1572)
(R. Tottel).
Wor.

9783.5 England. Yearbooks, (1584)
[Anr ed.] 2°; (R. Tottel).
Pet.

9787 England. Yearbooks, (1566)
(R. Tottell).
Wor.

9788 England. Yearbooks, (1566)
[1572?]
(R. Tottill).
Ches. Wor.

9789 England. Yearbooks, (1583)
(R. Tottel).
Pet.

9792 England. Yearbooks, (1558)
[1566?]
(R. Tottell).
Wor.

9794 England. Yearbooks, (1558)
[1572?]
(R. Tottill).
Ches. Wor.

9795 England. Yearbooks, (1583)
(R. Tottel).
Pet.

9800 England. Yearbooks, (1566)
(R. Tottell).
Wor.

9801 England. Yearbooks, (1566)
[1573?]
(R. Tottill).
Ches. Wor.

9802 England. Yearbooks, (1584)
R. Tottel.
Pet.

9804 England. Yearbooks, 1638
Dur.

9805 *See:* 9769.5

9808 England. Yearbooks, (1556)
[1583?]
(R. Tottell).
Pet.

9809 England. Yearbooks, (1557)
[1566?]
(R. Tottell).
Wor.

9811 England. Yearbooks, (1572)
(R. Tottel).
Ches. Wor.

9817 England. Yearbooks, (1567)
[1573?]
(R. Tottill).
Ches. Wor (2).

9818 England. Yearbooks, (1584)
(R. Tottel).
Pet.

9823 England. Yearbooks, (1556)
(R. Tottel).
Wor.

9824 England. Yearbooks, (1556)
[1572?]
(R. Tottill).
Ches. Wor.

9824.5 England. Yearbooks, (1582)
[Anr ed.] 2°; (R. Tottell).
Pet.

9829 England. Yearbooks, (1556)
[1566?]
(R. Tottell).
Wor.

9830 England. Yearbooks, (1572)
(R. Tottel).
Ches.

9831 England. Yearbooks, (1582)
(R. Tottel).
Pet. Wor.

9834 England. Yearbooks, (1566)
(R. Tottell).
Wor.

9835 England. Yearbooks, (1566)
[1573?]
(R. Tottill).
Ches. Wor (years X & XI only)*.

9835.5 England. Yearbooks, (1584)
[10 – 12 Edw. IV; Anr ed.] 2°; (R.
Tottyl).
Pet.

9842 England. Yearbooks, (1566)
(R. Tottill).
Ches. Wor (2).

9844 England. Yearbooks, (1582)
(R. Tottel).
Pet.

9848.5 England. Yearbooks, [1565?]
Formerly STC 9847; (R. Tottell).
Wor.

9849 England. Yearbooks, (1572)
(R. Tottel).
Ches.

9850 England. Yearbooks, (1582)
(R. Tottel).
Pet. Wor.

9853 England. Yearbooks, (1556)
(R. Tottel).
Wor*.

9854 England. Yearbooks, (1572)
(R. Tottel).
Ches.

9855 England. Yearbooks, (1582)
(R. Tottel).
Pet. Wor.

9857 England. Yearbooks, (1556)
[1566?]
(R. Tottell).
Wor.

9858 England. Yearbooks, (1556)
[1573?]
(R. Tottill).
Ches. Wor.

9860 England. Yearbooks, (1583)
(R. Tottel).
Pet.

9863 England. Yearbooks, (1557)
(R. Tottel).
Wor*.

9864 England. Yearbooks, (1572)
(R. Tottel).
Ches. Wor.

9864.5 England. Yearbooks, (1583)
[Anr ed.] 2°; (R. Tottel).
Pet.

9868.5 England. Yearbooks, [1565?]
Formerly STC 9867; (R. Tottell).
Wor.

9869 England. Yearbooks, (1572)
(R. Tottel).
Ches. Wor.

9870 England. Yearbooks, (1582)
(R. Tottell).
Pet.

9874.5 England. Yearbooks, (1556)
[1565?]
[Anr ed.] Formerly STC 9873; (R.
Tottel).
Wor.

9875 England. Yearbooks, (1556)
[1572?]
(R. Tottill).
Ches. Wor (imp?)*.

9875.5 England. Yearbooks, (1556)
[1582?]
[Anr ed.] 2°; (R. Tottell).
Pet.

9880 England. Yearbooks, (1556)
[1572?]
(R. Tottill).
Ches. Wor.

9881 England. Yearbooks, [1565?]
(R. Tottell).
Wor.

9882 England. Yearbooks, (1582)
(R. Tottyll).
Pet.

9886 England. Yearbooks, (1566)
(R. Tottell).
Wor.

9887 England. Yearbooks, (1566)
[1573?]
(R. Tottill).
Ches. Wor.

9887.5 England. Yearbooks, (1584)
[Anr ed.] 2°; (R. Tottel).
Pet.

9891 *See:* 9892.5

9892.5 England. Yearbooks, (1556)
[1564?]
[Anr ed.] Formerly STC 9891; (R.
Tottell).
Wor.

9893 England. Yearbooks, (1572)
(R. Tottle).
Ches.

9894 England. Yearbooks, (1578)
(R. Tottel).
Pet. Wor.

9896.5 England. Yearbooks, (1555)
[Anr ed.] 2°; (R. Tottel).
Ches.

9901 England. Yearbooks, (1579)
(R. Tottyll).
Pet.

9902 England. Yearbooks, (1585)
(R. Tottyl).
Pet (2).

9904 England. Yearbooks, 1620 (1619)
Pts 2 and 3 formerly also STC 9927 and 9944.
Dur. Yk.

9906+ England. Yearbooks, 1543
[Anr ed.] 2°; (Per me Henricum Smyth).
Wor.

9910 England. Yearbooks, (1574)
(R. Tottel).
Pet.

9911 England. Yearbooks, (1581)
(R. Tottel).
Pet.

9912 England. Yearbooks, [1587?]
Pet.

9913+ England. Yearbooks, 1543
[Anr ed.] 2°; (Per me Henricum Smyth).
Wor.

9914 England. Yearbooks, [1555?]
(R. Tottel).
Ches.

9918 England. Yearbooks, (1574)
(R. Tottel).
Pet.

9919 England. Yearbooks, (1581)
(R. Tottel).
Pet.

9919.5 England. Yearbooks, (1587)
[Anr ed.] 2°; (R. Tottyll).
Pet.

9922 England. Yearbooks, (1555)
(R. Tottel).
Ches.

9925 England. Yearbooks, 1580
Pet (2 − 1 has mixed sheets).

9926 England. Yearbooks, 1585 (1583)
Pet (with sheets from STC 9925).

9927 *See*: 9904

9929.3 England. Yearbooks, 1543
[Anr ed.] 2°; H. Smythe.
Swel.

9929.5 England. Yearbooks, 1547
[Anr ed.] 2°; W. Myddylton.
Wor.

9930.3 England. Yearbooks, [1544?]
[Anr ed.] 2°; (H. Smyth).
Swel. Wor.

9931.3 England. Yearbooks, [1544?]
[Anr ed.] 2°; (H. Smyth).
Swel. Wor.

9932.5 England. Yearbooks, [1545?]
[Anr ed.] 2°; (In aed. H. Smyth).
Swel.

9932.7 England. Yearbooks, [1550?]
[Anr ed.] 2°; (W. Powell).
Wor.

9933.5 England. Yearbooks, [1545?]
[Anr ed.] 2°; (In aed. H. Smyth).
Swel. Wor.

9934.3 England. Yearbooks, [1544?]
[Anr ed.] 2°; (H. Smith).
Swel. Wor.

9935.7 England. Yearbooks, [1542?]
[Anr ed.] 2°; (J. Byddell).
Swel.

9936 England. Yearbooks, (1548)
(W. Powell).
Wor.

9936.5 England. Yearbooks, [1553?]
[Anr ed.] 2°; (R. Tottel).
Ches.

9937 England. Yearbooks, (1556) [1583?]
(R. Tottel).
Pet.

9942 England. Yearbooks, (1579)
(R. Tottel).
Pet.

9943 England. Yearbooks, 1591
Pet.

9944 *See*: 9904

9946.3 England. Yearbooks, [1544?]
[Anr ed.] 2°; (H. Smyth).
Swel. Wor.

9946.5 England. Yearbooks, [1553?]
[Anr ed.] 2°; (R. Tottel).
Ches.

9946.9 England. Yearbooks, [1544?]
[18 Hen. VIII] 2°; (H. Smyth).
Swel.

9947.4 England. Yearbooks, [1548?]
[Anr ed.] 2°; (W. Powell).
Wor.

9947.7 England. Yearbooks, [1553?]
[Anr ed.] 2°; (R. Tottel).
Ches.

9948 England. Yearbooks, (1556) [1583?]
(R. Tottel).
Pet.

9952 England. Yearbooks, (1579)
(R. Tottel).
Pet.

9954.7 England. Yearbooks, [1544?]
[Anr ed. of STC 9955] 2°; (H. Smyth).
Swel.

9955.3 England. Yearbooks, [1550?]
[Anr ed.] 2°; (W. Powell).
Wor.

9955.7 England. Yearbooks, (1556)
[Anr ed.] 2°; (R. Tottel).
Ches.

9957 England. Yearbooks, (1556) [1583?]
(R. Tottel).
Pet.

9961 England. Yearbooks, (1579)
(R. Tottel).
Pet.

9961.7 England. Yearbooks, [1544?]
[Anr ed. of STC 9962] 2°; (H. Smyth).
Swel.

9962 England. Yearbooks, [1545?]
'De termino Pasche ...'; (W. Myddylton); A1ʳ catchword: 'le person'
Wor (imp)*.

9966 England. Yearbooks, (1569)
(R. Tottel); Line 1 of colophon ends: 'Lon-'
Ches (imp)*.

9966.5 England. Yearbooks, (1579)
[Anr ed.] 2°; (R. Tottel).
Pet.

9967 England. Yearbooks, (1583)
(R. Tottel).
Pet.

9991 England. Appendix, (1480)
(westmynstre, ...).
Liv (l3 only).

9999 England. Appendix, (1510)
[Begins Aa2ʳ:] 'Here begynneth a shorte & a breue/ table'; (R. Pynson).
Pet (imp).

10001 England. Appendix, (1520)
[Begins Aa1ᵛ:] 'Here begynneth a shorte and a breue/ table'; (w. de worde).
Ely (imp).

10002 England. Appendix, (1528)
'The cronycles of Englonde'; (W. de Worde).
Wor (imp?).

10005 England. Appendix, 1592
Formerly also STC 19400.
Yk.

10008 England. Appendix, 1640
Ex. Pet. Yk.

10009 England. Appendix, 1640
[o.s.]
Pet.

10013 England. Appendix, 1640
Pet.

10023 *See*: 11905

10032.3 England, Church of.
Advertisements, 1584
[Anr ed.] 4°; T. Dawson; Tp line 6:
'apparel', line 7: 'Ecclesiasticall'
Chi.

10034 England, Church of. *Articles*,
1553
'... Synode ... M.D.LII. ...'; (R.
Graftonus).
Linc.

10036 England, Church of. *Articles*,
1571
Formerly also STC 10036a, pt 2 now
= STC 10037.5.
New.

10036a *See:* 10036

10037 England, Church of. *Articles*,
1575
Swel (imp?). Yk.

10037.5 England, Church of.
Articles, [1571]
[Pt 2] 'Liber quorundam canonum
disciplinae ecclesiae Anglicanae';
Formerly pt of STC 10036, etc.; E–
G⁴, 23p.
Dur. New. Yk.

10038 England, Church of. *Articles*,
1636
Ely. S Asa. Wor.

10039 England, Church of. *Articles*,
(1571)
(R. Jugge a. J. Cawood); A2ʳ line 2 of
heading: 'fayth'; line 6 of text:
'wisedome'
Dur (imp)*. Rip*. Sal (imp)*.

10045 England, Church of. *Articles*,
(1593)
(Deputies ...).
Cant.

10046 England, Church of. *Articles*,
(1593)
(Deputies of C. Barker).
Yk.

10047 England, Church of. *Articles*,
1605
Tp has orn. with squirrels.
Yk*.

10051 England, Church of. *Articles*,
1628
Cant. Yk.

10054 England, Church of. *Articles*,
1630 [*i.e.* c.1663]
Yk.

10058 England, Church of. *Articles*,
1633
4°.
Ban. Ely.

10060 England, Church of. *Articles*,
1638
Ex (tp imp)*.

10062.5 England, Church of.
Constitutions & Canons, [1571]
[Anr issue of STC 10063] A2ʳ
headline: 'Of Bishoppes.'; A2ᵛ line 4:
'before the Kalendes'
Dur. New*. Sal (imp)*. Wel*.

10066 England, Church of.
Constitutions & Canons, 1597
New*. Yk (2).

10068 England, Church of.
Constitutions & Canons, 1604
New. Pet. Sal.

10069.3 England, Church of.
Constitutions & Canons, 1604
Formerly STC 10071; A–Y⁴.
Ban. Cant (imp). Ex.

10069 *See:* 10070.5 & 10070.7

10070 England, Church of.
Constitutions & Canons, 1604
D1ʳ catchword: 'cars', last line of
heading: 'Ecclesiasticall'
Liv (imp)*. Yk*.

10070.5 England, Church of.
Constitutions & Canons, 1604
[Anr ed.] 4°; R. Barker; D1ʳ
catchword: 'Ecclesiasticall', line 4 of
head-title ends: 'and'
Linc (imp)*.

10071.5 England, Church of.
Constitutions & Canons, 1604
[c.1608?]
[Anr ed.] 4°; R. Barker; A–P⁴; D1ʳ
catchword: 'Reuerence'
Wor.

10071 *See:* 10069.3

10072.5 England, Church of.
Constitutions & Canons, 1612
[Anr ed.] 4°; R. Barker; Tp line 4
ends: 'Lon-', line 9 ends: 'Sy-'
Linc (imp)*.

10073 England, Church of.
Constitutions & Canons, 1616
Sal.

10076 England, Church of.
Constitutions & Canons, 1633
Ely*.

10077 England, Church of.
Constitutions & Canons, 1633
[c.1640?]
Linc. Pet.

10078 England, Church of.
Constitutions & Canons, 1633 [after
1640?]
S Pl.

10080 England, Church of.
Constitutions & Canons, 1640
Dur. Linc (2). Pet. S Pl. Yk
(3).

10087.5 England, Church of.
Injunctions, [1547]
Formerly STC 10092; 'Iniunccions ...
'; (R. Grafton).
Win.

10088 England, Church of.
Injunctions, (1547)
Formerly also STC 10093; (R.
Grafton).
Pet. Win.

10090.3 England, Church of.
Injunctions, (1547)
[Anr ed.] Title as in STC 10089; 4°;
(R. Grafton); b4ʳ catchword:
'stament' and line 6 from bottom
ends: 'thei'
Nor*.

10092 *See:* 10087.5

10093 *See:* 10088

10100 England, Church of.
Injunctions, [1559?]
A2ʳ line 1 of text: 'all', last line:
'any', line 3 from bottom ends: 'mens'
Ches*.

10104.4 England, Church of.
Injunctions, [1583]
[Anr ed.] 4°; [C. Barker]; D4ᵛ last
line of text: 'iunctiōs'
New (tpw).

10108 England, Church of.
Injunctions, [1595]
Linc (2).

10109 *See:* 10110

10110 England, Church of.
Injunctions, [1600]
Formerly also STC 10109.
Yk.

10112 *See:* 10115.5

10115.5 England, Church of.
Visitation articles, General, [1547?]
Formerly STC 10112; (R. Grafton).
Nor.

10127 England, Church of.
Visitation Articles, General, [1583]
(C. Barkar).
New.

10130 England, Church of.
Visitation articles, General, [1591]
(Deputies of C. Barker).
Liv.

10131 England, Church of.
Visitation articles, General, (1595)
(Deputies of C. Barker).
Linc (2).

10133 England, Church of.
Visitation articles, General, (1600)
(By the assignement of R. Barker).
Yk (date erased).

10137.2 England, Church of.
Visitation articles, Bath & Wells,
1594
4°; [f.] J. Wolfe.
Win.

10158 England, Church of.
Visitation articles, Canterbury,
Province, 1605
Linc.

10188.3 England, Church of.
Visitation articles, Colchester
Archdeaconry, 1600
4°; E. Allde.
Yk.

10192.7c England, Church of.
Visitation articles, Durham, 1627
4°; R. Young.
Yk.

10192.7E England, Church of.
Visitation articles, Durham, 1629
4°; J. Haviland.
Cant.

10192 *See:* 10227.7

10227.2 England, Church of.
Visitation articles, Lichfield &
Coventry, 1629
4°; J. Bill.
Yk.

10227.5 England, Church of.
Visitation articles, Lichfield &
Coventry, [1633]
4°; A. Mathewes.
Yk.

10227.6 England, Church of.
Visitation articles, Lichfield &
Coventry, 1636
4°; f. H. Robinson.
Yk.

10227.7 England, Church of.
Visitation articles, Lichfield &
Coventry, 1639
Formerly STC 10192.
Yk.

10245 England, Church of.
Visitation articles, Lincoln, 1638
S Pl.

10249 England, Church of.
Visitation articles, London, (1555)
(J. Cawood).
S Pl.

10267 England, Church of.
Visitation articles, London, 1640
S Pl. Win. Yk.

10280.7 England, Church of.
Visitation articles, Norfolk,
Archdeaconry, [1636]
4°; A1^r blank; Date on A2^r.
Pet.

10292 England, Church of.
Visitation articles, Norwich, 1619
S Pl.

10298 England, Church of.
Visitation articles, Norwich, 1636
A2^r catchword: 'tering'
S Pl*

10299.5 England, Church of.
Visitation articles, Norwich, 1638
[Anr ed.] As STC 10299, but B1^r line
4 ends: 'lower' .
Pet.

10300 England, Church of.
Visitation articles, Norwich, [1638]
Pet.

10306.5 England, Church of.
Visitation articles, Oxford, [1575]
4°; J. Charlewoode f. Dionis Emily.
Cant.

10318 England, Church of.
Visitation articles, Peterborough,
1634
Yk.

10320 England, Church of.
Visitation articles, Peterborough,
1639
Pet.

10363 England, Church of.
Visitation articles, Winchester,
[1633]
Yk.

10363.7 England, Church of.
Visitation articles, Winchester,
163[3?]
4°; R. Badger.
Her (date completed in MS as
1635).

10372.6 England, Church of.
Visitation articles, Worcester,
Archdeaconry, 1625
4°; Oxford, J. Lichfield & W. Turner.
Yk.

10372.7 England, Church of.
Visitation articles, Worcester,
Archdeaconry, [1634?]
4°; f. J. Grismond.
Yk (dated 1634 in MS).

10383 England, Church of.
Appendix, 1554
'ceremonyes'
Linc.

10384 *See:* 1730

10387 England, Church of.
Appendix, [1566]
'... examination for the tyme, of ...';
(R. Jugge); Formerly also STC 3962.
Bur (imp). Pet.

10388 England, Church of.
Appendix, [1566]
Yk (imp).

10391.5 England, Church of.
Appendix, [1570?]
Formerly STC 22572.
Pet. Wor.

10392 England, Church of.
Appendix, [1572]
'brethren'
Yk.

10393 England, Church of.
Appendix, 1574
'... defaced by T. C[artwright] in ...'
Linc. Pet (tp imp).

10394 England, Church of.
Appendix, [1583]
Bur. Dur. Linc. New. Pet.
S Pl. Yk.

10395 England, Church of.
Appendix, 1584
Ely. Pet.

10400 England, Church of.
Appendix, [1593?]
Liv.

10403 England, Church of.
Appendix, 1616
Douay ...
Wor.

10406 England, Church of.
Appendix, 1640
Ex. Pet. Yk (2).

10414 English Protestants, 1617
Ches.

10423 Epictetus, 1567
Pet.

10425 Epictetus, 1610
S Pl.

10428 *See:* 20521.4

10429 *See:* 166.5

10450.3 Erasmus, Desiderius, (1520)
[Anr ed. of STC 10450.2, which was formerly STC 5162] 4°; (Per H. Pepwell).
S Alb (frag.).

10475 Erasmus, Desiderius, (1533)
(In aed. ...).
Pet (imp).

10480 Erasmus, Desiderius, (1534)
(w. de worde ...).
Pet (imp).

10484 Erasmus, Desiderius, (1544)
(at the sygne ...).
Pet (imp)*.

10488 Erasmus, Desiderius, (1545)
(Ausborch, Adam Anonimus).
Pet.

10492 Erasmus, Desiderius, [1536?]
'... epystle, ... in laude ...'; 8°; (R. Redman).
Yk.

10493 Erasmus, Desiderius, (1529)
(Malborow in the londe of Hesse. By my Hans Luft).
Pet.

10500 Erasmus, Desiderius, (1569)
[i.e. 1549]
(In the house of T. Berthelet); In title: 'latine'
Glo (imp)*. Pet*. Yk*.

10504 Erasmus, Desiderius, [1534]
(R. Redman).
Pet.

10511 Erastus, Thomas, 1589
'Explicatio grauissimae quaestionis vtrùm ...'
Dur. Her. Linc. Yk.

10531 Espagne, Jean d', 1632
T. Harper f. B. Fisher.
Linc.

10535 Est, William, 1611
'mirrour'; Pt 2 now = STC 10536.5.
Yk.

10536.5 Est, William, 1611
Formerly pt 2 of STC 10535: 'Sathans sowing season'; 8°; N. Okes f. R. Bonian.
Yk.

10537 Est, William, 1609
'... expulsion and returne ...'; 8°;... Dauson.
Linc.

10538 Est, William, 1613
'... teares, or the summons to repentance'
Yk.

10539 Est, William, 1614
Yk (1st sermon only).

10541.4 Estella, Diego de, 1604
[Anr ed.] 8°; Doway, L. Kellam.
Yk.

10542 Estella, Diego de, 1586
Pet.

10547 Estienne, Charles & Liebault, Jean, 1600
Pet.

10549 Estienne, Charles & Liebault, Jean, 1616
Cant. Her.

10550 Estienne, Henri, 1575
Linc (imp).

10553 Estienne, Henri, 1607
Linc. S Pl. Wor.

10556 Estwick, Nicolas, 1633
Ex.

10557 Estwick, Nicolas, 1635
Cant.

10559 Euclid, 1620
Linc. Win. Wor.

10560 Euclid, (1570)
Cant. Linc.

10562 Eudes, Morton, 1610
Wor. Yk.

10570 Europe, 1625
Wor.

10572 Eusebius, *Pamphili*, 1577
Carl.

10573 Eusebius, *Pamphili*, 1585
Pet. Yk.

10574 Eusebius, *Pamphili*, 1607
Her. Linc.

10575 Eusebius, *Pamphili*, 1619
Her.

10576 Eusebius, *Pamphili*, 1636
Her. Lich. Nor. Sal.

10577 *See*: 1463

10578 Eustachius, *a Sancto Paulo*, 1640
... Danielis.
Sal.

10584.5 Evans, Edward, 1623
[Anr issue] f. R. Bulmer.
Yk (imp).

10591 Evans, Lewis, [1570]
(T. Purfoote).
Pet.

10593 Evans, Lewis, [1569]
(T. Purfoote).
Pet.

10597 Evans, William, *of Oxford*, 1633
Pet.

10598 Everard, John, 1618
E. G. f. ...
Carl. Linc. Pet.

10600 Everardus, Joannes, 1611
Linc.

10607 Ewich, Johann, 1583
'Of the duetie of a faithfull and wise magistrate, ...'
Pet.

10621 Exhortation, (1544)
(T. Berthelet).
Linc (imp).

10648 F., I., 1603
8°.
Carl. Chi. Linc. Pet (2).

10659 Fabyan, Robert, (1516)
(R. Pynson).
Lich (imp)*.

10660 Fabyan, Robert, 1533
Her (imp).

10661 Fabyan, Robert, [1542]
'... printed, & in many ...'
Chi.

10662 Fabyan, Robert, [1542]
Yk (imp)*.

10664 Fabyan, Robert, 1559
J. Kyngston.
Cant (tpw). Her. Pet. Wor.

10667 Fage, Mary, 1637
Ex.

10668 Fairlambe, Peter, 1606
Yk.

10673 Falckenburgius, Jacobus, 1579
Pt 2 = STC 10674.3.
Linc.

10674 Falckenburgius, Jacobus, 1578
'Jacobi à Falckenburgk, Saxonis Brandeburgi, Britannia ...'
Linc. Yk.

10674.3 Falckenburgius, Jacobus, 1579
Formerly pt 2 of STC 10673; 'Casimirus'; 8°; Typis R. Graphei.
Linc.

10675 Falconer, John, 1618
'... of John Traskes ...'
Pet.

10679.3 Fale, Thomas, 1626
[Anr issue] F. Kyngston, sold by R. Allott.
Linc.

10683 Family of Love, 1606
[London, H. Lownes, f.] J. Legate pr.
to the Univ. of Cambridge.
Yk.

10693 Farley, Robert, 1638
Yk.

10694 Farley, Robert, 1638
'morall'
Yk.

10699 Farmer, Richard, 1629
Cant. Pet (tp imp). S Asa. S Pl.

10701 Farnaby, Thomas, 1629
F. Kyngstonius.
Linc.

10702 Farnaby, Thomas, 1634
12°.
Sal.

10708 Farnaby, Thomas, 1638
Editio septima; F. Kingstonius.
Yk.

10716 Favour, John, 1619
Sal. Yk (3).

10717 Favyn, André, 1623
Ex (imp). Her. Swel (tpw).

10719 Fawkner, Antony, 1630
'pedegree'
Yk.

10722 Fawkner, Antony, 1630
Impr. and format as STC 10721,
which is a ghost.
Yk.

10723 Fawkner, Antony, 1634
Yk.

10724 Fawkner, Antony, 1635
'... petition, delivered in a sermon ...'
Chelm. Yk.

10730 Featley, Daniel, 1636
Ban. Bur. Ches. Ex (2). Llan.
Nor. S Dv. Wor. Yk.

10731 Featley, Daniel, 1629
Bur. Linc. Pet (2). Yk.

10732 Featley, Daniel, 1623
A2ʳ line 2 of text begins: 'yeares'
Cant*. Carl*. Ex*. Pet. Wor*.

10732.3 Featley, Daniel, 1623
[Anr ed.] As STC 10732, but: 'yeare'
Pet.

10733 Featley, Daniel, 1630
Bur. Ex. Pet (2 – 1 imp).

10734 Featley, Daniel, 1626
Cant. Pet (2). Yk (3).

10735 Featley, Daniel, 1626
Most copies: 'new-old'; some have
'newe-old'
Cant ('new-old'). Pet ('new-old').
Yk (2 – both 'new-old').

10736 Featley, Daniel, 1626
Pet (2). Yk.

10737 Featley, Daniel, 1626
Pet (2). Yk.

10738 Featley, Daniel, 1624
Yk*.

10738.3 Featley, Daniel, 1624
[Anr issue] As STC 10738, but H*1 –
L*1 cancelled and replaced by single
leaf L1.
Cant.

10740 Featley, Daniel, 1638
Bur. Cant (imp).

10742 Featley, John, 1636
Ex.

10744 Feckenham, John, 1555
S Pl.

10747 Feguernekinus, Isaacus, 1588
'... theologicorum, rerum,
exemplorum, ...'
Ban. Linc. Pet. Wel. Yk.

10752 Felicius, Constantius, (1557)
'... Catiline, written by ...'; (J. Waley).
Pet.

10753 Felippe, Bartolome, 1589
Pet.

10754 Fell, Samuel, 1627
Linc.

10759 Feltham, Owen, 1631
Cant. Ely. S Asa. Yk.

10760 Feltham, Owen, 1634 (1633)
(E. Purslow) ...
Cant.

10760a *See*: 10761

10761 Feltham, Owen, 1636
Formerly also STC 10760a; (E.P.) f.
...
Cant. Sal.

10764.3 Fenner, Dudley, 1583
[Anr issue] As STC 10764, but with
A1 cancelled and replaced by tp, and
dedication to the Earl of Leicester.
Pet. Rip*. Yk*.

10765 Fenner, Dudley, 1602
S Pl.

10765.5 Fenner, Dudley, 1584
[Anr ed. of STC 10766] Pt 1 tp has
Schilders' device with his name, rather
than a block of type orns.
Pet.

10770 Fenner, Dudley, [1584]
Pet. S Pl. Yk.

10771 Fenner, Dudley, 1587
Ex. Pet. Rip. Sal. Win. Yk.

10772 Fenner, Dudley, 1586
S Pl.

10775 *See*: 10872.7

10793a Fenton, *Sir* Geoffrey, 1574
Middelton.
Pet.

10794 Fenton, *Sir* Geoffrey, 1575
Cant (imp).

10795 Fenton, *Sir* Geoffrey, 1577
Linc. Pet. Yk.

10799 Fenton, Roger, 1599
'... to William Alablaster ...'
Liv (tp imp).

10805 Fenton, Roger, 1617
Ex.

10806 Fenton, Roger, 1611
Wor.

10807 Fenton, Roger, 1612
Ex. Pet.

10809 Ferdinand II, *Emperor*, 1620
Date of declaration not on tp.
Yk.

10812 Ferdinand II, *Emperor*, 1620
Yk.

10816 Ferdinand II, *Emperor*, 1620
Linc.

10818 Ferebe, George, 1615
'Lifes farewell. Or a funerall sermon.
...'
Pet.

10824 Ferne, *Sir* John, 1586
Linc. Pet.

10825 Ferne, *Sir* John, 1586
Yk.

10829 Ferrand, Jacques, 1640
Carl. Dur. Linc.

10831 Ferrarius, Joannes, 1559
'A woorke of Joannes Ferrarius ...'
Rip (imp).

10833 Ferrier, Auger, 1593
Pet (tpw)*.

10843 Fidelitas, [1574?]
Pet.

10844 Field, John, [1581]
Pet (tpw).

10848 Field, John & Wilcox,
Thomas, [1572]
Preface begins on A1ʳ.
Linc (tpw).

10855 Field, Richard, 1604
Linc. Pet.

10857 Field, Richard, 1606
Carl. Chelm. Her. Pet. Yk.

10857.5 Field, Richard, 1606
[1614?]
[Anr ed.] 4°; f. S. Waterson.
Cant.

10857.7 Field, Richard, 1610
Formerly pt of STC 10856/7; 'The fifth booke ...'; N. Okes f. S. Waterson.
Cant. Roch.

10858 Field, Richard, 1628
'... five bookes ...'
Bur. Ex. Her. Linc. Sal. Wel. Win.

10859 Field, Richard, 1635
Cant. Dur. Ely. Glo. Llan. Nor. S Asa. S Pl. Wel. Yk.

10861.5 Field, Theophilus, 1624
'The earths encrease. ...'; 8°; M. Flesher f. N. Feild.
Linc (imp).

10862 Field, Theophilus, 1625
M.F. f. N. Feild.
Linc.

10871 Finch, *Sir* Henry, 1627
Cant.

10872.7 Finch, *Sir* Henry, 1613
Formerly STC 10775; Found with impr.: Foelix Kyngstone *or* Felix Kyngston.
Chelm (imp). Pet (2 – 1 imp).

10874 Finch, *Sir* Henry, 1621
Wor.

10876 Finch, John, *Baron*, 1640
Linc. Yk.

10877.5 Finch, Richard, 1590
[Anr ed. of STC 10878] 'The epiphanie of the church. ...'; 4°; R. Ward.
Pet.

10885 Fisher, Ambrose, 1630
Ex (2). Linc. Liv. S Asa. Sal (tpw). Wor. Yk.

10891 Fisher, John, *St*, [1509]
(W. de Worde).
Linc.

10899 Fisher, John, *St*, [1578?]
'A spirituall consolation, written by John Fyssher ...'
Linc.

10902 Fisher, John, *St*, (1508)
(w. de worde).
Chi. S Pl.

10903a Fisher, John, *St*, (1509) [1514?]
(W. de Worde); Catch title: 'vii. [or vij.] psal.' on all signed leaves.
Pet (imp).

10906 Fisher, John, *St*, (1525)
(w. de worde).
Linc.

10908 Fisher, John, *St*, 1555
(T. Marshe).
Pet. S Pl. Yk (imp).

10910.4 Fisher, John, [*i.e.* John Percy], 1623
Formerly STC 4957.
Carl. Yk.

10911 Fisher, John, [*i.e.* John Percy], 1626
Her. Wor.

10912 Fisher, John, [*i.e.* John Percy], 1614
'catholike'
Pet.

10913 *See*: 4154

10914 Fisher, John, [*i.e.* John Percy], 1612
'... Mr. Anthony Wotton and Mr. John White ...'
Yk.

10915.5 Fisher, John, [*i.e.* John Percy], 1605
[Anr ed. of STC 10916] 8°; [N.pl.].
Yk.

10915 *See*: 10916.5

10916 Fisher, John, [*i.e.* John Percy], 1614
Pet.

10916.5 Fisher, John, [*i.e.* John Percy], 1626
Formerly STC 23530; 'between'; 3 pts; Pt 3 formerly STC 10915.
Carl. Yk.

10925 *See*: 5615

10926 Fitch, William, 1619
Yk (imp).

10934 Fitz-Geffrey, Charles, 1601
'Caroli Fitzgeofridi affaniae: ...'
Pet.

10935 Fitz-Geffrey, Charles, 1634
Pet (imp).

10936 Fitz-Geffrey, Charles, 1636
Win (frag.).

10937 Fitz-Geffrey, Charles, 1637
Pet.

10938 Fitz-Geffrey, Charles, 1631
Pet. Sal.

10942 Fitz-Geffrey, Charles, 1622
'Elisha his lamentation, for his owne ... losse ... A sermon ...'
Ex. Pet.

10956.5 Fitzherbert, *Sir* Anthony, 1565
Formerly pt of STC 10956; 'La table côteynant ...'; 2°; In aed. R. Tottell.
Pet (2).

10962 Fitzherbert, *Sir* Anthony, 1581
Pet.

10964 Fitzherbert, *Sir* Anthony, 1598
Dur (imp). Pet.

10964.5 Fitzherbert, *Sir* Anthony, 1609
[Anr ed.] 8°; f. the Co. of Statrs.
Glo. Yk.

10976 Fitzherbert, *Sir* Anthony, (1560)
(R. Tottyll).
Pet.

10978 Fitzherbert, *Sir* Anthony, [1583]
4°.
Pet.

11013.6 Fitzherbert, John, [c.1560]
Formerly STC 11015: 'The boke of surueying and improuementes, newly corrected ...'
Pet.

11015 *See*: 11013.6

11016 Fitzherbert, Thomas, 1602
Yk (2).

11017 Fitzherbert, Thomas, 1606
Cant.

11018 Fitzherbert, Thomas, 1615
Yk.

11019 Fitzherbert, Thomas, 1610
Cant.

11019.5 Fitzherbert, Thomas, 1615
[Anr issue] Douay, J. Heigham.
Yk.

11020 Fitzherbert, Thomas, 1621
Yk.

11021 Fitzherbert, Thomas, 1613
'judgment'
Pet. Yk.

11022 Fitzherbert, Thomas, 1613
'... Robert Persons ...'
Her. Pet. Yk.

11023 Fitzherbert, Thomas, 1614
Her.

11025 Fitzsimon, Henry, 1608
'... John Riders ...'
Cant. Her.

11026 Fitzsimon, Henry, 1611
Pet. S Pl.

11031 Flavel, John, 1619
'... methodicus & polemicus ...'; Oxoniae, J. Lichfield & J. Short.
Chelm.

11031.5 Flavel, John, 1624
[Anr issue] Oxoniae, J. Lichfield & J. Short.
Pet.

11034 Fleetwood, William, 1579
'Annalium tam regum Edwardi ...'; In aed. R. Tottelli.
Pet.

11035 Fleetwood, William, 1597
Linc. Pet.

11036 Fleetwood, William, [1571]
Pet. Rip (imp). Yk.

11049 Fleming, Abraham, 1576
Pet.

11051a *See*: 18413.7

11052 Fleming, Giles, 1634
'... Saint Pauls ...'; ... Alchorn.
Linc.

11056 Fletcher, Giles, *the Elder*, 1591
... Charde.
Yk.

11058 Fletcher, Giles, *the Younger*, 1610
Ex. Linc.

11065 Fletcher, John, 1640
Carl.

11071 Fletcher, John, 1639
Carl.

11072 Fletcher, John, 1640
Carl.

11073 Fletcher, John, 1640
Carl.

11080 Fletcher, Phineas, 1632
Ely.

11081 Fletcher, Phineas, 1627
'... Apollyonists'; ... (prs. to the Univ. of Cambridge).
Ban (pt 1 only). Linc.

11082 Fletcher, Phineas, 1633
Pet.

11082.5 Fletcher, Phineas, 1633
[Anr issue] As STC 11082, but on large paper with added engravings.
Sal.

11085 Fletcher, Phineas, 1632
Linc. S Pl.

11096 Florio, John, [1578]
'... fruites: ... Also a perfect ...'
Rip (imp).

11097 Florio, John, 1591
Pt 2 formerly also STC 11100.
Pet.

11098 Florio, John, 1598
Cant. Pet. Yk.

11099 Florio, John, 1611
Lich. Linc. Sal. Yk.

11100 *See*: 11097

11101 Florus, Lucius Annaeus, 1631
Cant.

11110 Floyd, John, 1638
Formerly also STC 25776.
Ex. Pet.

11111 Floyd, John, 1612
Wor.

11112 Floyd, John, 1631
Yk.

11116 Floyd, John, 1617
Formerly also STC 7008; '... of Marcus Antonius de Dominis ... by Fidelis Annosus ... *tr.* by A.M. ...'
Yk.

11117 Floyd, John, 1639
Ex. Pet.

11120 Fludd, Robert, 1631
Linc. Sal.

11121 Foliot, Gilbert, 1638
'Gilberti Foliot episcopi Londinensis, expositio ...'; ... [R. Barker ...].
Linc. S Asa (imp). S Pl. Win. Wor.

11126 Fonseca, Christoval de, 1629
'Devout contemplations expressed in two and fortie sermons ...'
Cant. Carl. Chelm. Her. S Asa. Wor.

11136 Forbes, John, *Minister*, 1616
Pet. Yk.

11139 Forbes, John, *of Corse*, 1629
S Pl. Yk.

11141 Forbes, John, *of Corse*, 1636
Carl. Ely. Pet. S Asa.

11143 Forbes, John, *of Corse*, 1638
Yk.

11146 Forbes, Patrick, 1614
Linc. Pet.

11150 Forbes, Patrick, 1614
'... Saint John ...'; 2 pts.
Pet (imp). Yk.

11151 Forbes, Patrick, 1635
'Funerals of ... Patrick Forbes of Corse, bishop of ...'
S Asa.

11176 Forde, William, 1616
Wor.

11178 *See*: 18507.249 & 18507.251

11181 Form, 1576
Formerly also STC 24625; Antuerpiae, ap. J. Foulerum.
S Pl.

11183.5 Form, 1581
[Anr ed.] 'The maner and forme of examination ...'; 8°; T. Marsh.
Linc.

11185 Forman, Simon, 1591
Sal.

11193 Fortescue, *Sir* John, [1543?]
'... militis, cognomento Forescu [*sic*] ...'; ... Whitechurche ...
Pet (imp).

11195 Fortescue, *Sir* John, (1573)
(R. Tottell).
Carl. Pet.

11196 Fortescue, *Sir* John, 1599
Pet. Sal.

11197 Fortescue, *Sir* John, 1616
'... Angliae ... Hereto ...'
Cant. Linc. Wor.

11199 Fosbroke, John, 1633
'... delivered in the lecture at Kettering ... and other places'; Pts also formerly STC 669, 22903, 6189, 5151a, 12601.
Pet.

11201 Foster, Samuel, 1638
Wor.

11202 Foster, Thomas, 1631
'... the scourge of covetousnesse. A sermon at the assises'
Cant (imp). Linc.

11203 Foster, William, 1631
Linc. Pet. Sal.

11204 Foster, William, 1629
S Asa.

11205 Fotherby, Martin, 1622
Cant. Chi. Dur. Linc. Sal. Wor. Yk.

11206 Fotherby, Martin, 1608
S Pl. Wor. Yk.

11207 Fougasses, Thomas de, 1612
'The generall historie of the magnificent state of Venice. ...'
Cant. Ex. Glo. Her. Lich. Wel.

11216 Fowns, Richard, 1618
Yk.

11217 Fowns, Richard, 1619
H. Lownes f. M. Lownes.
Linc.

11218 Fox, Edward, 1534
Linc. Sal. Yk.

11219 Fox, Edward, (1538)
(In aed. ...).
Nor. Yk.

11220 Fox, Edward, [1548]
'Stafforde'; (W. Coplād).
Linc. Yk.

11221 Fox, Luke, 1635
Cant.

11222 Foxe, John, (1563)
Cant (imp). Pet (imp).

11223 Foxe, John, 1570
'ecclesiasticall'
Bur (tpw). Her (v. imp)*. Yk.

11224 Foxe, John, (1576)
Wor (2 — 1 imp, 1 v. imp)*.

11225 Foxe, John, 1583
Fourth time published; (J. Daye).
Wel.

11226 Foxe, John, 1596
... by the assigne of R. Day.
Cant (3 — 2 imp, 1 frag.). Roch
(vol. 2 only). S Asa (vol. 1 only,
imp). Wor.

11226a Foxe, John, 1597
Cant (imp). S Asa (imp).

11227 Foxe, John, 1610
Ches (vol. 1 only, imp). Her.
Liv. Yk (vol. 1 only).

11228 Foxe, John, 1632 (1631)
Kingston.
Cant. Dur (2 — 1 lacks vol. 3).
New (vol. 1 only). Sal (lacks vol.
1). Yk (vol. 2 only).

11229 Foxe, John, 1589
'An abridgement of the booke of Acts
and monumentes ...'; ... assignment
...
Cant. Pet. Yk.

11231 Foxe, John, 1579
'... triumphant. A fruitefull treatise ...
From Latin ...'
Pet.

11234 Foxe, John, 1583
Pet. Wor. Yk.

11236 Foxe, John, 1578
Ex off. C. Barkeri.
Linc. Pet.

11237 Foxe, John, 1587
... Byshop.
Bur (tpw). Carl. Ex (2). Pet.
Rip. Wor (tpw). Yk.

11239 Foxe, John, 1572
J. Dayus.
Rip.

11240 Foxe, John, 1580
Pet (2).

11241 Foxe, John, 1580
Pet. Yk.

11242.3 Foxe, John, 1570
[Anr ed.] Newly recognised by the
author; 4°; J. Daye; Text within rules;
A2ʳ line 1 of heading ends: 'bee'
S Pl (2)*. Yk*.

11244 Foxe, John, 1577
Pet.

11245 Foxe, John, 1585
Linc. Pet. S Pl.

11247 Foxe, John, 1571
Trans. of STC 11242, etc.
Ex. Pet.

11248 Foxe, John, 1578
Pet (tpw). Yk.

11256 France, 1589
'... nobilitie & commons ... against
theeues ...'
Yk.

11260 France, 1592
'The chiefe occurrences ... eight of
Aprill, till the seuenteenth ...'; J.
Wolfe.
Pet.

11265 France, 1590
'reportes'; J. Wolfe, solde by W.
Wright.
Pet.

11270 France, 1592
J. Wolfe.
Pet.

11273 France, 1639
Formerly also STC 5601.
Yk.

11274 France, 1624
Pet.

11275 France, 1598
'historicall'
Pet. Wor.

11277.5 France, 1592
Formerly STC 14818; '... wherein is
truely sette ...'
Pet.

11277 *See:* 12507

11280 *See:* 11282.5

11282.5 France, [1591]
Formerly STC 11280; 'Newes from
France. Where monsieur de Signiers
...'
Pet.

11285 France, 1592
'Newes'; J. Wolfe, ...
Pet.

11288 France, 1593
'... & others ...'
Yk.

11289 France, 1589
Cant. Yk.

11290 France, [1591]
'... armie ... in Prouince ...'; T.
Purfoot.
Pet.

11291 France, 1589
'Aumalle'
Pet. Yk.

11294 *See:* 11742

11296 France, Reformed Churches,
[1624]
Wor.

11308 Franchis, Giovanni Maria de,
1613
'... nuptiis. Illustrissimi Principis ...'
Pet.

11315 Francis, *of Borja, St,* 1620
'practise'
Bur.

11323 Francis, *of Sales, St,* 1630
Wel.

11325 *See:* 5005

11326 Francklin, Richard, 1630
Chelm. Glo. Linc.

11327 Francklin, Richard, 1633
S Asa.

11328.1 Frankfurt Fair, [1617]
Pts of STC 11328—11331 now assigned
separate numbers; [Autumn] 1617; Ex
off. Nortoniana, ap. J. Billium.
Pet. Yk.

11328.2 Frankfurt Fair, [1618]
[Spring] 1618; Impr. as STC 11328.1.
Yk.

11328.3 Frankfurt Fair, [1618]
[Autumn] 1618; Impr. as STC 11328.1.
Yk.

11328.4 Frankfurt Fair, [1619]
[Spring] 1619; Impr. as STC 11328.1.
Yk.

11328.6 Frankfurt Fair, [1619]
[Autumn] 1619; Impr. as STC 11328.1.
Yk.

11328.8 Frankfurt Fair, [1620]
[Spring] 1620; Ap. J. Billium.
Yk.

11328.10 Frankfurt Fair, [1620]
[Autumn] 1620; Impr. as STC 11328.1.
Yk.

11329.7 Frankfurt Fair, 1622
[Spring] 1622; Francofurti.
Yk.

11330 Frankfurt Fair, 1623
[Autumn] 1623; Francofurti.
Yk.

11333 Frarinus, Petrus, 1566
Antuerpiae, ...
Yk.

11335 Fraser, John, 1605
'Great Britanie'
Pet.

11339 Fraunce, Abraham, 1591
Linc.

11340 Fraunce, Abraham, 1591
Linc.

11341 Fraunce, Abraham, 1592
Linc.

11342 Fraunce, Abraham, 1588
'Abrahami Fransi, insignium,
armorum, emblematum,
hieroglyphicorum, ... explicatio'
Linc. Rip.

11344 Fraunce, Abraham, 1588
Linc. Pet. Yk.

11346 Freake, William, 1630
Cant.

11346.3 Freake, William, 1632
[Anr issue with new tp] Formerly STC
14538.
Yk.

11349 Frederick I, *King of Bohemia*,
1620
Yk.

11351 Frederick I, *King of Bohemia*,
1620
'crowne'; Middleburg, ...; 23p.
Sal*.

11354 *See*: 18507.40

11356 Frederick I, *King of Bohemia*,
1620
Formerly also STC 3209.
Yk.

11371 Frégeville, Jean de, 1593
Bur (tpw). Pet. Wor (imp). Yk.

11372 Frégeville, Jean de, 1589
'politicke'
Pet. Yk.

11382 Frith, John, 1546
S Pl.

11383 Frith, John, (1548)
Cant.

11394 Frith, John, (1529)
(Malborow ...).
Linc.

11396 Froissart, Jean, (1523)
'... Sir Johan Froyssart ...'; (R.
Pynson).
Linc.

11397 Froissart, Jean, (1525)
[Vol. 2] (R. Pynson).
Linc (imp).

11397a Froissart, Jean, (1525)
[c.1563]
(R. Pinson).
Pet (imp).

11399 Froissart, Jean, 1608
'... Frossard: or, a summarie
collection ... Compiled ...'
Yk.

11400 Froissart, Jean, 1611
Linc.

11401 Fromondus, Libertus, 1639
'Liberti Fromondi ...
Meteorologicorum ...'
Carl. Roch.

11402 Frontinus, Sextus Julius,
1539
(In aed. ...).
Pet.

11410 Fulbecke, William, 1600
Cant.

11411 Fulbecke, William, 1620
Pet.

11412 Fulbecke, William, 1601
Linc. Pet. Sal.

11414 Fulbecke, William, 1602
Cant. Linc. S Pl.

11415 Fulbecke, William, 1601
Cant. Linc. Pet. S Pl.

11415a Fulbecke, William, 1602
Cant. Linc.

11417 Fulke, William, 1578
'Gulielmi Fulconis Angli, ad epistolam
...'
Linc.

11418 Fulke, William, 1579
'Ad Thomae Stapletoni ...
côtrouersiarum ...'; (Typis T.
Dawson) imp. ...
Rip.

11421 Fulke, William, 1581
(T. Dawson) f. ...
Pet (2). Yk.

11422 Fulke, William, 1574
S Pl.

11423 Fulke, William, 1578
J. Charlwood.
Cant (cropped).

11425 Fulke, William, 1611
Ex. Linc.

11426 Fulke, William, 1571
Undated copies now = STC 11426.2.
Linc (imp)*. Pet (imp).

11426.7 Fulke, William, [1572?]
[Anr issue] 'An answere to a popishe
and slaunderous libell ...'; W. Jones.
Pet.

11427 Fulke, William, 1573
S Pl.

11429 Fulke, William, 1584
Pet. Rip. Yk.

11430 Fulke, William, 1583
'... sincere and true ...'
Bur. Linc. Pet. Rip. Yk.

11430.5 Fulke, William, 1583
[Variant] H. Bynneman.
S Pl.

11431 Fulke, William, 1617
Bur. Cant. Ely. Lich. Sal.
Wor.

11431a Fulke, William, 1617
Ches. Wel.

11432 Fulke, William, 1633
... one of the assignes of Hester
Ogden.
Cant. Her. Linc. Liv. S Asa.

11433 Fulke, William, 1579
Pet. Rip.

11434.5 Fulke, William, [1580?]
[Anr ed.] As STC 11434, but A3^v line
1 begins 'much' *not* 'of'
Pet.

11441 Fulke, William, 1640
As STC 11440, apart from date.
Pet.

11442 Fulke, William, 1573
'Apocalypsim'
Ex. Pet. Yk.

11443 Fulke, William, 1573
'... vpon the sacred and holy
Reuelation of S. John'; 4°.
Pet (tpw).

11444.5 Fulke, William, [1578]
[Variant] As STC 11444 but no date.
Linc.

11445.5 Fulke, William, 1572
[Variant] Per T. Eastum & H.
Middeltonum, imp. Guil. Jones.
Linc.

11448 Fulke, William, 1581
Carl. Pet. Yk (tpw).

11449 Fulke, William, 1580
Rip. Yk.

11449.5 Fulke, William, (1570)
[Anr ed. of STC 11450] 8°; J. Awdely.
Pet.

11451 Fulke, William, (1572)
Linc.

11452 Fulke, William, 1574
J. Awdely.
Pet.

11454 Fulke, William, (1577)
'... preached on Sundaye, being the
.17. of March 1577 at ...'
Wor.

11455 Fulke, William, 1581
'... preached vpon Sunday, beeing the
twelfth of March ... 1581, within ...'
Pet.

11456 Fulke, William, 1580
'... Martiall (two popish heretikes)
confuted'
Rip. Yk (2 – 1 tp imp).

11458 Fulke, William, 1577
Pet. Yk.

11460 Fuller, Nicholas, *of Gray's
Inn*, 1607
'The argument of master Nicholas
Fuller, ...'
Carl. Win.

11461 Fuller, Nicholas, *Prebendary*,
1616
'... theologicorum ... libri tres ...'
Cant. Chi (2). Dur. S Pl (3).
Wel.

11462 Fuller, Nicholas, *Prebendary*,
1617
Her. Linc.

11463 Fuller, Thomas, *D.D.*, 1631
Linc.

11464 Fuller, Thomas, *D.D.*, 1639
T. Buck, one of the prs. to the Univ.
of Cambridge; Engr. tp: T. Buck, sold
by J. Williams [London].
Brec. Cant. Chi. Sal.

11465 Fuller, Thomas, *D.D.*, 1640
... sold by J. Williams [London].
Bris. Cant (engr. tpw). Ches.
Her. Swel. Win.

11466 Fuller, Thomas, *D.D.*, 1640
Ban. Ex. Win.

11468 Fuller, William, 1628
'... Libanon. A sermon ... In
commemoration of ... Lady Frances
Clifton, ...'
Cant (imp).

11469 Fuller, William, 1625
Pet.

11470 Fullonius, Gulielmus, 1540
'Joannis Palsgraui ...'; (In aed. ...).
Glo (imp). Rip (frag.).

11482 Fulwood, William, 1598
Pet.

11487 Fumée, Martin, 1600
Her. Lich.

11492 G., C., 1596
J. Legat, pr. to the Univ. of
Cambridge.
Pet (2).

11503.3 G., R., 1584
[Anr ed.] 8°; (J. Windet a. T. Judson)
f. N. Lyng.
Pet.

11505 G., R., [1571]
A3ʳ line 16 ends: 'euil'; A3ᵛ line 1
has: 'vn knowen'
Rip*.

11506 G., R., [1571]
Text begins A1ʳ, line 16 has: 'euill'
Yk.

11507 *See*: 12101

11513 Gaebelkhover, Oswald, 1599
Dorte, by Isaack Caen.
Cant. Pet.

11516 Gager, William, 1592
Yk.

11520 Gainsford, Thomas, 1622
Yk (imp).

11529 Gale, Thomas, (1563)
R. Hall (f. T. Gale).
Pet (with extra quire *⁸ with
colophon: H. Denham f. T. Gale,
1564).

11530 Galen, 1640
'... in linguam Latinam ...'
Wor.

11539 Galliardi *or* Gagliardi,
Achilles, 1625
'... of Christian perfection ...'; The
second edition.
Ely.

11547 Gamon, Hannibal, 1629
Pet (imp).

11554.5 Garden, (1569)
[Anr ed. of STC 11555] 'A godlie
gardeine ...'; 16°; (W. Griffith).
Linc.

11568 Gardiner, Richard, *of Oxford*,
1622
Cant (imp). Chelm.

11570 Gardiner, Richard, *of Oxford*,
1638
'preach'd'; 4°.
Her (tpw).

11572 Gardiner, Samuel, 1606
Yk.

11575 Gardiner, Samuel, 1605
R. Braddock ...
Pet. Yk.

11581 Gardiner, Samuel, 1605
'A sermon preached at ...'; f. E.
White.
S Pl.

11583 Gardiner, Stephen, [1553]
Pet.

11585 Gardiner, Stephen, 1553
'obediencia'
Linc. Pet (tpw).

11587 Gardiner, Stephen, 1553
Pet.

11588 Gardiner, Stephen, (1546)
(J. Herford, at the costes and charges
of R. Toye).
Linc.

11589 Gardiner, Stephen, 1546
(J. Herforde, at the costes and charges
of R. Toye).
Sal.

11590 *See*: 11591.3

11591 Gardiner, Stephen, 1546
(J. Herforde, ...); Colophon on S4ʳ.
Rip (imp). Sal (imp). Yk (imp)*.

11591.3 Gardiner, Stephen, 1546
Formerly STC 11590; As STC 11591,
but colophon on T4ʳ.
Linc.

11592 Gardiner, Stephen, [1551]
Pet.

11593 Gardiner, Stephen, 1553
'An admonishion ...'
Pet.

11597 Garey, Samuel, 1618
Yk (imp).

11598 Garey, Samuel, 1623
... sold by E. Casson at Norwich.
Yk (2).

11601 Garlandia, Joannes de,
(1496)
(R. pynson).
Pet (tpw).

11609 Garlandia, Joannes de,
(1496)
(per R. Pynson).
Pet.

11617.2 Garnet, Henry, [1593]
Formerly STC 711.
Pet. Rip. Yk.

11617.8 Garnet, Henry, [1593]
Formerly STC 5189; Pt 2 formerly
STC 24264.
Pet.

11618 Garnet, Henry, 1606
Wel.

11619 Garnet, Henry, 1606
Line 5 of title ends: 'Iesuite'
Carl*. Linc*. Liv. Pet*. S Asa
(2)*. S Pl*.

11619a Garnet, Henry, 1606
R. Barker.
Ex. Yk.

11620 Garnet, Henry, 1607
'... in Henricum Garnetum ... Omnia ...'
Yk.

11621 Garnier, Jean, [1562]
'A briefe and plaine confession of the Christian faithe'; J. Kingston.
Linc.

11624 Garrard, Edmund, 1624
Yk.

11625 Garrard, William, 1591
Pet.

11633 Garthwait, Henry, 1634
'evangelicall'
Wel.

11637 Gascoigne, George, [1575]
Lich.

11639 Gascoigne, George, 1587
A. Jeffes.
Pet (imp?).

11647 Gataker, Thomas, 1627
'... A meditation on Genesis 25.8. Delivered at the funerall ...'
Pet. Yk.

11648 Gataker, Thomas, 1626
Yk.

11649 See: 11652 & 11652a

11650 Gataker, Thomas, 1638
'Thomae Gatakeri ... partim Guilielmi Amesii ...'
Pet.

11651 See: 11679

11652 Gataker, Thomas, 1637
Carl. Roch. S Asa. S Dv. S Pl (frag.). Wor.

11652a Gataker, Thomas, 1637
Dur. Her. Pet.

11653 Gataker, Thomas, 1624
Yk.

11654 Gataker, Thomas, 1624
S Asa. Yk.

11655a See: 11652 & 11652a

11657 Gataker, Thomas, 1624
Yk.

11657.5 Gataker, Thomas, 1640
'Francisci Gomari disputationis elencticae, ...'; 8°; B.A. & T.F. pro P. Cole.
Bur.

11661 See: 11652 & 11652a

11662 Gataker, Thomas, 1624
Ex. S Asa. Yk.

11664 See: 11652 & 11652a

11665 Gataker, Thomas, 1623
Ex.

11666 Gataker, Thomas, 1623
'... certaine passages ...'
Ban. Linc.

11667 Gataker, Thomas, 1620
Cant.

11668 See: 11652 & 11652a

11669 Gataker, Thomas, 1624
Yk.

11670 Gataker, Thomas, 1619
'... nature and use ...'; ... sold by W. Bladen.
Cant. Chelm. Ex. Linc.

11671 Gataker, Thomas, 1627
Bur. Cant. Ely. Wor. Yk.

11672 See: 11679

11673 Gataker, Thomas, 1638
Pet. S Dv. Wor.

11674 Gataker, Thomas, 1638
Ex.

11678 Gataker, Thomas, 1620
Yk.

11679 Gataker, Thomas, 1620
'funeral'; STC 11651, 11672 are pt of this.
Linc.

11681.3 Gataker, Thomas, 1623
[Variant] J. Haviland.
Ex. S Asa.

11683 Gates, Geoffrey, 1579
Rip.

11685 Gatti, Alessandro, 1619
'La caccia d'Alessandro Gatti, poema heroico ...'
Linc.

11688 Gaule, John, 1630
Ex.

11689 Gaule, John, 1629
Cant.

11690 Gaule, John, 1630
'entertainment'
Ex.

11691 Gaule, John, 1629 (1628)
Ex (2 – 1 imp). S Pl.

11700 Gee, Edward, 1620
Ex.

11701 Gee, John, 1624
'The foot ...'
Pet. Wor.

11703 Gee, John, 1624
Cant (imp). Yk.

11704 Gee, John, 1624
H. L(ownes) f. ...
S Pl. Yk.

11705 Gee, John, 1624
Bur. S Pl (2).

11706 Gee, John, 1624
Linc. Pet. S Pl. Wor. Yk.

11709? Gelli, Giovanni Battista, 1557
Date on tp, both eds of STC have [1558-59]; (J Cawood).
Linc. Pet.

11713 Gellius, Joannes, 1617
'Ad augustissimum monarcham, Jacobum .I. ...'; Edinburgi, T. Finlason.
Yk (tp imp).

11719 Geminus, Papyrius, (1522)
'Papyrii Gemini ...'; ... (Per me J. Siberch).
Linc.

11722 Genesius de Sepulveda, Joannes, 1553
'Joannis Genesii Sepuluedae ... de ritu ...'
Pet.

11725 Geneva, 1562
R. Hall (a. T. Hacket).
Pet (imp). Yk.

11728.4 Gennadios II, *Patriarch of Constantinople* [Georgios Scholarios], [1625-26]
'... τὸ σύνταγμα'; 4°; [W. Jones].
S Pl (3).

11728.8 Gentili, Scipione, 1586
'Annotationi di Scipio Gentili sopra La Gierusalemme liberata di Torquato Tasso'; 8°; Leida [*i.e.* London, J. Wolfe].
Yk.

11732 Gentilis, Albericus, 1593
'Alberici Gentilis ... ad tit. C. de maleficis ...'
Yk.

11734 Gentilis, Albericus, 1590
'Alberici Gentilis ... de ...'
Pet.

11735 Gentilis, Albericus, 1589
'Alberici Gentilis ... de iure belli commentationes duae'; 2 pts; Lugduni Batauorum, ap. J. de la Croy [*i.e.* London, J. Wolfe].
Yk (imp).

11736 Gentilis, Albericus, 1582
'Alberici Gentilis de ...'; 4°.
Yk (imp).

11737 Gentilis, Albericus, 1585
'Alberici Gentilis de ...'
Yk.

11739 Gentilis, Albericus, 1583 (1584)
'Alberici Gentilis lectionum ...'; J. Wolfius.
Linc. Yk (bk 1 only).

11740 Gentilis, Albericus, 1585
'Alberici Gentilis. Legalium
Comitiorum Oxoniensium ...'; J.
Wolfius.
Linc.

11741 Gentilis, Albericus, 1605
'Alberici Gentilis ... regales ...'
Yk.

11742 Gentillet, Innocent, 1579
Formerly also STC 11294.
Linc.

11743 Gentillet, Innocent, 1602
'Machiavell'
Pet.

11744 Gentillet, Innocent, 1608
Cant (imp).

11746 Georgievits, Bartholomeus,
[1569?]
Pet.

11750 Gerard, John, *Surgeon*, 1597
(E. Bollifant f. B. a.) ...
Cant (tp imp). Linc (imp).

11751 Gerard, John, *Surgeon*, 1633
Cant (imp). Linc. Yk.

11752 Gerard, John, *Surgeon*, 1636
Ex. Lich. Liv. S Dv.

11753 *See*: 11754

11754 Gerard, Pierre, 1598
Formerly also STC 11753.
Yk.

11755 Gerardus, Andreas, *Hyperius*,
1579
Pet.

11758.5 Gerardus, Andreas,
Hyperius, 1577
[Variant] As STC 11758, but 'The
practise ...'
Pet (2 – 1 imp).

11760 Gerardus, Andreas, *Hyperius*,
[1588?]
Pet.

11765 Gerhard, Johann, 1615
[Anr ed., revised] 'The soules watch
...'; The second edition.
Cant.

11767.5 Gerhard, Johann, 1614
[1st ed. of STC 11768] 12°; T.S. f. R.
Jackson.
Cant.

11770 Gerhard, Johann, 1633
'Joh: Gerhardi ...'
Wel.

11775 Gerhard, Johann, 1635
Ely. Ex (acc. STC – not
confirmed).

11778 Gerhard, Johann, 1638
12°; T. Buck a. R. Daniel, prs. to the
Univ. of Cambridge.
Carl.

11784 *See*: 23525.7

11790 *See*: 23525.5

11794 Germany, 1612
... W. Bladon.
Yk (impr. not confirmed).

11795.5 Germany, 1591
'A true recitall of the armie levied by
the princes of Germanie'; 4°; f. T.
Nelson.
Pet.

11798 Gesner, Conrad, 1576
Linc.

11799 Gesner, Conrad, 1599
Pet (imp).

11800 Gesner, Conrad, [1559]
Pet.

11801 Gesner, Conrad, (1565)
Pet.

11802 Gest, Edmund, 1548
Pet.

11806.5 Geveren, Sheltco à, 1583
[Anr ed.] As STC 11806, apart from
date.
Pet.

11814 Gibbens, Nicholas, 1601
Linc. Pet. Yk (tp imp)*.

11817 Gibbon *or* Gybbon, Charles,
1604
J. Legat, pr. to the Univ. of
Cambridge, sold by S. Waterson
[London].
Linc.

11826 Gibbons, Orlando, 1612
Yk.

11828 Gibson, Abraham, 1619
'Christiana-polemica, or a preparative
to warre. A sermon ...'
Linc.

11830 Gibson, Abraham, 1613
Linc.

11830a Gibson, Abraham, 1614
... W. Erondel.
Linc.

11837 Gibson, Samuel, 1616
'walke'
Linc (imp).

11838 Gibson, Samuel, 1620
Pet. Yk.

11839 Gibson, Thomas, *M.A.*, 1584
Formerly also STC 11840a.
Pet. Yk*.

11840a *See*: 11839

11841 Gibson, Thomas, *Minister*,
1614
Pet.

11842 Gibson, Thomas, *Minister*,
1607
'... hundred and sixteene psalme'
Pet (2).

11848 Gifford, George, 1583
Pet. Sal (imp).

11853 Gifford, George, 1589
'Eight sermons, vpon the first foure
chapters, and part of the fift, of
Ecclesiastes'
Pet.

11858.5 Gifford, George, 1584
[Anr ed.] 8°; (J. Windet a. T. Judson
f.) T. Cooke.
Pet.

11859 Gifford, George, 1598
... f. T. Cooke a. R. Walker.
Pet (imp). Yk (impr. not
confirmed).

11862 Gifford, George, 1590
Pet. Yk.

11862.3 Gifford, George, 1591
'A sermon preached at Pauls Crosse
the thirtie day of May. 1591'; 8°; J.
Windet f. T. Cooke.
Pet. Yk.

11863.7 Gifford, George, [1583]
[Anr issue] R. Walde-graue f. T.
Cooke; Formerly STC 11865.
Yk (impr. not confirmed).

11865 *See*: 11863.7

11866.5 Gifford, George, 1599
[Anr ed.] 4°; f. T. Man.
Pet.

11867 Gifford, George, 1599
Yk.

11868 Gifford, George, 1591
'... reply vnto the last printed books
of ...'
Yk.

11869 Gifford, George, 1590
(J. Windet) f. ...
Pet. Sal (tp imp).

11874 Gil, Alexander, *the Elder*,
1621
Cant. Yk.

11875 *See*: 11879.4

11877 *See*: 11879.9

11878 Gil, Alexander, *the Elder*,
1635
Dur. Linc. Roch. S Pl. Sal.
Yk.

11879.4 Gil, Alexander, *the Younger*, 1632
Formerly STC 11875.
Pet. Yk.

11879.9 Gil, Alexander, *the Younger*, 1632
Formerly STC 11877.
Chi. Linc.

11883 Gilbert, William, *M.D.*, 1600
'Guilielmi Gilberti ... de magnete'
Linc. Pet. Sal.

11884 Gilby, Anthony, [1548?]
'deuillish'
Cant (imp). Linc. Pet (tpw).

11887 Gilby, Anthony, [1551?]
(J. Daye); Date in title.
Pet.

11888 Gilby, Anthony, 1581
Pet (tpw).

11894 Gildas, 1568
Linc. Pet.

11897.5 Gilpin, Bernard, [1581]
[Variant] As STC 11897, but no date.
Linc.

11898 Gilpin, Bernard, 1630
Cant. Dur. Linc. Pet. S Asa.

11899 Giovio, Paolo, (1546)
(E. Whitchurche).
Pet (tpw).

11900 Giovio, Paolo, 1585
Cant. Pet (2).

11904 Glanvill, *Sir* John, [1628]
Pet (2).

11905 Glanvilla, Ranulphus de, [1554?]
Formerly also STC 10023; (In aed. R. Totteli).
Pet. Sal (imp).

11906 Glanvilla, Ranulphus de, 1604
Linc.

11916 Glasgow University, 1633
'... ad augustissimum monarcham Carolum'; Edinburgi ...
Linc.

11916.5 Glasier, Hugh, 1555
'A notable and very fruictefull sermon made at Paules Crosse, the XXV. day of August'; 8°; R. Caly.
S Pl.

11919.5 Glass, (1532)
[Trans.] 'Le myrouer de verite'; 8°; (T. Berthelet).
Linc.

11922 Glover, Robert, 1608
'... politica vel civilis ...'
S Pl. Wor.

11923 Goad, Thomas, 1623
Cant (imp). Pet. S Pl.

11924 Goad, Thomas, 1606
Imp. M. Clerk.
Dur. Pet. Yk.

11926.5 God, 1606
'Gods mercie and justice'; 12°; G.S. f. Roger Jackson.
Yk.

11935 Godskall, James, 1604
S Pl.

11937 Godwin, Francis, 1601
Cant. Her. Pet. S Asa. Sal (2). Wel (2 − 1 imp). Yk.

11938 Godwin, Francis, 1615
Cant. Ely. Ex (tpw)*. Linc. Liv (tpw). Llan. S Asa. S Pl. Sal (frag.)*. Wor (imp)*. Yk.

11939 Godwin, Francis, [1625?]
Linc.

11941 Godwin, Francis, 1616
Bur. Dur. Ex. Her. Linc. Pet. S Asa. S Pl. Tru. Wel. Wor. Yk.

11945 Godwin, Francis, 1616
Cant. Linc. S Asa. Wor. Yk.

11946 Godwin, Francis, 1628
Dur. Ex. Pet.

11947 Godwin, Francis, 1630
Cant. Ex. Lich.

11951 Godwin, Thomas, 1625
'Hebrewes'
Ban. Linc.

11952 Godwin, Thomas, 1626
Bur (2). Glo.

11953 Godwin, Thomas, 1628
Ex. Sal.

11954 Godwin, Thomas, 1631
Cant. Yk.

11955 Godwin, Thomas, 1634
Cant. Carl. Chelm.

11957 Godwin, Thomas, 1616
Dur.

11958 Godwin, Thomas, 1620
Sal.

11959 Godwin, Thomas, 1623
Ban.

11960 Godwin, Thomas, 1625
Bur.

11961 Godwin, Thomas, 1628
Ex. Yk.

11962 Godwin, Thomas, 1631
Cant. Yk.

11963 Godwin, Thomas, 1633
Cant (imp). Ex.

11964 Godwin, Thomas, 1638
Carl.

11965 Godwin, Thomas, 1616
Dur.

11972 Goeurot, Jehan, (1560)
(E. Whitchurche); Formerly also STC 11973.
Pet (2 − 1 tpw).

11973 *See*: 11972

11976 Goeurot, Jehan, 1596
Pet.

11979 Goffe, Thomas, 1620
Yk.

11982 Goffe, Thomas, 1633
Yk.

11994 Gomersall, Robert, 1634
S Pl.

11997 Gonsalvius Montanus, Reginaldus, 1569
Pet (lacks cut).

11998 Gonsalvius Montanus, Reginaldus, 1625
4°.
Wor.

11999 Gonsalvius Montanus, Reginaldus, 1625
[Anr issue with cancel tp:] 'A full, ample and punctuall discovery ...'; 4°.
Yk (retains tp of STC 11998).

12003 González de Mendoza, Juan, 1588
Pet (imp). Rip.

12004 González de Mendoza, Juan, 1587
Yk.

12020 Goodman, Christopher, 1558
Pet. Yk.

12021 Goodman, Godfrey, 1622
F. Kingston.
Pet.

12022.7 Goodman, Godfrey, 1616
[Anr issue of STC 12023] F. Kyngston f. Joseph Browne.
Roch (tp imp).

12029 Goodwin, George, 1620
Cant. S Pl.

12033.5 Goodwin, Thomas, 1637
[Variant] M. Flesher f. R. Dawlman a. J. Rothwell.
Ex.

12037 Goodwin, Thomas, 1636
158, 95p.
Glo.

12037.5 Goodwin, Thomas, 1636
[Anr ed.] 4°; M.F. f. R. Dawlman a.
L. Fawne; 255p.
S Dv. Yk (imp).

12040 Goodwin, Thomas, 1636
Glo. S Dv.

12045 Goodwin, William, 1614
Linc. Yk.

12053 Gordon, George, *2nd
Marquess of Huntly*, 1640
London, R. Young, his Majesties
printer for Scotland.
Linc.

12054 Gordon, John, *Dean of
Salisbury*, 1610
Pet. Yk.

12056 Gordon, John, *Dean*, 1612
Pet (imp)*.

12059 Gordon, John, *Dean of
Salisbury*, 1604
Cant. Pet. Yk.

12060 Gordon, John, *Dean of
Salisbury*, 1611
Wor.

12060a Gordon, John, *Dean of
Salisbury*, 1161 [*i.e.* 1611]
Linc.

12071 Gore, John, 1636
7 pts.
S Pl.

12072 Gore, John, 1638
S Pl.

12074 Gore, John, 1636
Alchorne.
S Pl.

12078 Gore, John, 1635
4°.
S Pl.

12081 Gore, John, 1635
S Pl.

12084 Gore, John, 1634
R. Badger f. T. Alchorn.
S Asa. S Pl.

12088 Gore, John, 1635
S Pl.

12092 Gosselin, Peter, 1623
Yk.

12094 Gosson, Stephen, 1586
Pet (2 − 1 imp).

12099 Gosson, Stephen, [1598]
Linc. S Pl.

12100 Gostwyke, Roger, 1616
Yk.

12101 Gostwyke, Roger, 1618
Formerly also STC 11507.
Bur. Sal. Wor. Yk.

12109a Gouge, William, 1627
Grismond.
Ban. Her.

12111 Gouge, William, 1626
Linc (imp)*.

12116 Gouge, William, 1631
'arrowes'; No ed. statement.
Ex.

12117 Gouge, William, 1626
Pet. Yk.

12119 Gouge, William, 1622
Pet.

12120 *See*: 12109a

12122 Gouge, William, 1616
Carl.

12136 Goulart, Simon, 1621
Linc.

12142 Gower, John, *the Poet*, 1493
[*i.e.* 1483]
(westmestre, w. Caxton).
Her. Sal (frag.).

12144 Gower, John, *the Poet*, 1554
Dur. Ex (imp). Linc. Pet (imp).
S Pl.

12147 Grafton, Richard, (1569)
'... large ... vnto the first yere of
queene Elizabeth'; 2 vols; Impr. from
colophon.
Cant (imp). Linc (vol.1 only,
tpw). Nor (imp).

12151 Grafton, Richard, (1570)
Pet.

12175 Granger, Thomas, 1616
Yk.

12177 Granger, Thomas, 1616
'foode'
Yk.

12179 Granger, Thomas, 1616
Yk.

12182 Granger, Thomas, 1616
Yk.

12184 Granger, Thomas, 1620
Pet.

12188 Grant, Edward, 1575
Yk.

12192 Gratarolus, Gulielmus,
[1573]
Pet.

12193 *See*: 12193a

12193a Gratarolus, Gulielmus, 1574
Formerly also STC 12193.
Pet.

12194 Grave, [1586?]
'... out of the Dutch copye printed at
Middleborough'; [London?].
Linc.

12198 Grave, Jean de, 1633
Sal.

12209 Greaves, Thomas, *of Oxford*,
1639
Linc.

12211 Greek Poets, 1635
Sal. Wel. Yk.

12314 Greenham, Richard, 1599
S Asa.

12314.7 Greenham, Richard, 1600
'The second part of the workes ...';
4°; F. Kyngston f. R. Jacson.
S Asa.

12317 Greenham, Richard, 1605
S Dv. Yk.

12318 Greenham, Richard, 1612
(1611)
(T. Creede) f. ...
Carl. Ex.

12323 Greenham, Richard, 1597
Pet.

12324.5 Greenham, Richard, 1604
'Three very fruitfull and comfortable
sermons'; 8°; T.E. f. T. Man.
Linc.

12331 Greenwood, Henry, 1628
The eleventh impression.
Yk (imp).

12333 Greenwood, Henry, 1620
Pet.

12333.5 Greenwood, Henry, 1616
'A joyfull tractate of the most blessed
baptisme'; 8°; G. Purslowe f. H. Bell.
Linc (tpw).

12333.5+ Greenwood, Henry, 1618
[Anr ed.] The third edition; 8°; G.
Purslow, f. H. Bell.
Pet.

12335.5 Greenwood, Henry, 1613
'The race celestiall'; The second
impression; 8°; N.O. f. H. Bell.
Linc.

12336+ Greenwood, Henry, 1628
[Anr ed.] 8°; I.H. f. Henry Bell.
S Pl.

12337 Greenwood, Henry, 1606
'A treatise of the great and generall
daye ...'
Linc. Pet (imp).

12340 Greenwood, John, *Puritan*,
1590
[*i.e.* Amsterdam?, 1603].
Yk.

12342 Greenwood, John, *Puritan*,
[1589]
Pet.

12343.5 Gregory [Palamas], *Abp of
Thessalonica*, [1625–26]
'... λόγοι ἀποδεικτικοὶ δύο'; 4°;
[W. Jones].
S Pl (2).

12346 Gregory, *of Nazianzus*, 1610
Ban. Ches. Chi (tp imp). Dur.
Ely. Ex. Lich. Linc. Nor. S Pl
(2). Wor. Yk.

12347 Gregory, *of Nazianzus*, 1615
Liv.

12348 Gregory I, *Pope*, 1629
'B. Gregorii magni ... De cura
pastorali ...'; ... T. Harper ...
Chi. S Pl. Yk.

12349 Gregory I, *Pope*, 1608
Cant.

12357 Gregory XV, *Pope*, 1623
Yk (imp).

12357.7 Gregory, Arthur, 1599
Formerly STC 81; 'L'abridgment ...';
8°.
Glo.

12359 Grenoble, 1591
'... yeelding ...'; J. Wolfe.
Pet.

12361 Greville, Fulke, *Baron
Brooke*, 1633
Ex. Lich. Linc. Sal. Wor. Yk.

12362 Greville, Fulke, *Baron
Brooke*, 1609
Cant (imp).

12368 Griffith, Matthew, 1633
Sal. Wor.

12370a Griffith, Matthew, 1634
Engr. tp only, found with some copies
of STC 12368 etc.
Sal. Wor.

12372 Grimaldus Goslicius,
Laurentius, 1598
Pet.

12374 Grimeston, Edward, 1608
Her (tpw)*.

12375 Grimeston, Edward, 1609
Ely.

12376 Grimeston, Edward, 1627
The second impression.
Cant. Wor.

12377 Grindal, Edmund, (1564)
Pet.

12390 Grisons, 1619
Linc (tp imp). Sal.

12396 *See*: Wing G2077

12398 Grotius, Hugo, 1640
Yk.

12401 Grotius, Hugo, 1636
Bur. Carl. Ely. Win. Yk.

12402 Grotius, Hugo, 1639
'Hugonis Grotii poemata ...'
Linc.

12402a Grotius, Hugo, 1639
Her.

12408 Grymeston, Elizabeth,
[1608?]
Formerly also STC 12409.
Yk.

12409 *See*: 12408

12418 Guarna, Andreas, 1635
... imp. Joh: Spenceri.
Linc.

12422 Guazzo, Stefano, 1581
Glo.

12423 Guazzo, Stefano, 1586
Pet.

12426 Guevara, Antonio de, 1577
Pet.

12427 Guevara, Antonio de, 1557
Pet.

12428 Guevara, Antonio de, 1568
Pet.

12429 Guevara, Antonio de, 1582
4°.
Pet.

12430 Guevara, Antonio de, 1619
Her.

12433 Guevara, Antonio de, [1575?]
Cant. Pet (imp).

12434 Guevara, Antonio de, 1577
Ex (imp). Linc (imp). Yk.

12445a Guevara, Antonio de, 1566
Linc.

12446 Guevara, Antonio de, 1573
Pet (imp).

12448.5 Guevara, Antonio de, 1594
[Anr issue of STC 12449] 'The
mysteries of mount Calvary'; 4°; By
A. Islip f. E. White.
Pet (imp).

12450 Guevara, Antonio de, 1618
Her.

12451 Guevara, Antonio de, 1597
Her. Pet.

12452 Guez, Jean Louis, *Sieur de
Balzac*, 1634
Dur. Wel (tpw).

12453 Guez, Jean Louis, *Sieur de
Balzac*, 1638
... W. Edmonds a. I. Colby.
Cant. Wel.

12455 Guez, Jean Louis, *Sieur de
Balzac*, 1639
Nor.

12457 Guibert, Philibert, 1639
... W. Sheeres.
Pet.

12458 Guicciardini, Francesco,
1579
Pet (imp). Rip.

12458a Guicciardini, Francesco,
1579
Wor.

12460 Guicciardini, Francesco,
1618
Her. Lich. S Dv. S Pl. Wor.

12463 Guicciardini, Ludovico, 1593
Pet.

12469 Guido, *de Cauliaco*, (1579)
Pet.

12474 Guido, *de Monte Rocherii*,
(1508)
(Per R. Pynson).
S Pl.

12476 Guido, *Huguenot Writer*,
1577
S Pl.

12485 Guild, William, 1620
Linc.

12487 Guild, William, 1626
Carl.

12490 Guild, William, 1627
S Asa.

12495 Guillemard, Jean, 1621
Yk.

12503 Guillim, John, 1638
Cant (imp). Carl. Linc.

12503.5 Guillim, John, 1640
'A most exact alphabeticall table ...';
2°; J. Raworth f. L. Blaikelock;
Usually bound with STC 12503.
Carl.

12506 Guise, *House of*, 1589
Yk.

12507 Guise, *House of*, 1562
Formerly also STC 11277; 'whiche'
Pet.

12512.5 Gulielmus, *Parisiensis*,
(1516)
'Guillermus parisiensis de septem
sacramentis'; Long 12°; (Exp. R.
Pynson).
Pet.

12513 Gulielmus, *Parisiensis*, (1509)
Pet.

12514 Gumbleden, John, 1628
S Pl.

12515 Gumbleden, John, 1626
London, A. Mathewes ...
Chelm.

12516 Gunter, Edmund, 1620
Sal.

12518 Gunter, Edmund, 1620
Linc (imp?).

12523+ Gunter, Edmund, 1636
The 2^d edition; 4°; By W.G.
Her.

12526 Gunter, Peter, 1615
Yk.

12528 Gurnay, Edmund, 1630
Linc. Win.

12529 Gurnay, Edmund, 1631
Linc.

12531 Gurnay, Edmund, 1639
T. Buck, one of the prs. to the Univ.
of Cambridge.
Carl.

12534 Gustavus II Adolphus, 1633
Pet. Sal. Yk.

12535 Gustavus II Adolphus, 1630
'... which the most illustrious
Gustavus ...'; [Delft].
Sal.

12543 Guy, Nicholas, 1626
Linc.

12551 Gwinne, Matthew, 1603
Ex.

12555.5 Gwinne, Matthew, 1607
[Variant] ... Blount (STC 12555 has
Blunt).
Ex.

12560 Gwynneth, John, 1557
'... John Frithes ...'; (T. Powell).
Wor.

12563 H., E., 1592
Linc.

12567 H., I., 1610
Liv.

12581 H., W., 1634
Linc.

12586 Habington, William, 1640
Carl. Lich (imp). Linc. Nor.
Wel. Wor.

12593 Haddon, Walter, 1577
'Contra Hieron. Osorium ...'
Glo. Her. Rip. S Pl. Yk (2).

12594 Haddon, Walter, 1581
Cant.

12596 Haddon, Walter, 1567
'G. Haddoni ... lucubrationes passim
collectae, ...'
Dur. Lich. Linc. Pet (2). S Pl.
Wor. Yk.

12598 Haddon, Walter, [1565?]
(W. Seres).
Pet (2 — 1 imp).

12601 *See*: 11199

12604 Hagthorpe, John, 1623
Yk (imp).

12610 Hakewill, George, 1616
Carl. Pet (2 — 1 imp). Wor. Yk.

12611 Hakewill, George, 1627
'An apologie of the power ...'
Glo. Lich. Linc. S Asa. Sal.
Wor.

12612 Hakewill, George, 1630
'An apologie or declaration of the
power ...'; Impr. as STC 12613.
Cant. Pet.

12613 Hakewill, George, 1635
'An apologie or declaration of the
power ...'
Ches. Ely. Lich. Linc. Yk.

12614 Hakewill, George, 1613
Liv. Wor. Yk.

12615 Hakewill, George, 1626
Carl. Pet.

12616 Hakewill, George, 1621
Linc.

12617 Hakewill, George, 1622
Impr. as STC 12616.
Pet. Yk (date altered, apparently
in MS, from 1621 = STC 12616?).

12618 Hakewill, George, 1612
Wor.

12619 Hakewill, George, 1613
Linc. Yk.

12620 Hakewill, George, 1632
Cant. Ex. Liv.

12623 Hakewill, George, 1633
Carl.

12626 Hakluyt, Richard, 1598
(1599, 1600)
Glo (vol. 3 only). Linc (vol. 1
[tpw*] & 2 only). Pet (vol. 1
[tpw*] & 2 only). S Asa (vol. 1
[imp*] & 2 only). Yk (vol. 1
[tpw*] & vol. 2 [pts 1 & 2] only).

12626a Hakluyt, Richard, 1599
(1599, 1600)
[Anr issue].
Her (lacks vol. 3).

12628 Hales, John, 1617
Ely. Wel. Yk.

12635 Hall, Joseph, 1625
Tome 1.
Ex. Her. Linc. Wor (imp).

12635.5 Hall, Joseph, 1625
[Variant] M. Flesher f. R. Meighen.
Cant.

12635a Hall, Joseph, 1625
Nor.

12636.3 Hall, Joseph, 1628
[Variant] Vol.1; M. Flesher f. N.
Butter.
Sal.

12636.7 Hall, Joseph, 1628
[Variant] Vol.1; J. Haviland.
Glo. Nor. S Dv.

12637 Hall, Joseph, 1628
Vol.1.
Ches.

12639.3 Hall, Joseph, 1634
[Variant] Vol.1; M. Flesher.
Rip. Sal. Yk.

12639.5 Hall, Joseph, 1634
[Variant] Vol. 1; f. N. Butter.
Ex.

12639.7 Hall, Joseph, 1634
[Variant] Vol.1; f. E. Brewster.
Yk.

12640 Hall, Joseph, 1634
Vol.1.
Ex. Wor.

12640.5 Hall, Joseph, 1634 (1633)
'The second tome'; 2°; M. Flesher f.
N. Butter; Formerly pt of STC 12636.
Cant. Nor (tp imp). S Pl. Sal
(imp)*. Wor (2).

12640.7 Hall, Joseph, 1634
[Variant of STC 12640.5] 'The
contemplations ... The second tome';
M. Flesher f. N. Butter.
Chelm. Ely. Ex. Lich. Nor.
Roch. Sal. Win.

12644.5 Hall, Joseph, 1609
[Anr ed.] 12°; f. S. Macham a. L.
Lyle.
Yk.

12645 Hall, Joseph, 1635
Nor. Wel.

12646 Hall, Joseph, 1623
Linc.

12646b Hall, Joseph, 1639
'Certaine irrefragable propositions
worthy of serious consideration'
Carl. Pet. Yk.

12647 Hall, Joseph, 1635
Linc.

12648a.5 Hall, Joseph, 1608
[Anr ed.] 8°; M. Bradwood f. E. Edgar a. S. Macham; Tp: 'By IOSEPH HALL'
Cant.

12648c Hall, Joseph, 1624
Linc. S Pl.

12649 Hall, Joseph, 1610
Pet (tpw)*.

12649a Hall, Joseph, 1610
Yk.

12651 *See:* 12707

12653 *See:* 12707

12655 *See:* 12707

12661 Hall, Joseph, 1640
Separately paged in 3 sections.
Bur. Ex. Linc.

12661.5 Hall, Joseph, 1640
[Anr ed.] As STC 12661, but paged continuously.
Bur. Glo. S Asa. Sal. Yk.

12662.5 Hall, Joseph, 1608
[Variant of STC 12662, which is now vol. 1 only] 8°; A.H. f. S. Macham & E. Edgar.
Cant.

12663.2 Hall, Joseph, 1608
'The second volume'; 8°; A.H. f. E. Edgar & S. Macham.
Cant.

12664 *See:* 12702

12665.3 Hall, Joseph, 1623
[Variant] J. Haviland for H. Fetherstone.
Linc (imp). Yk.

12666 Hall, Joseph, 1606
'... peace, and tranquillitie of minde. ...'
Cant (lacks table).

12669 Hall, Joseph, 1607
H. Lownes f. J. Porter.
Yk.

12671 Hall, Joseph, 1607
Yk.

12673 Hall, Joseph, 1613
Pet.

12674 Hall, Joseph, 1620
'maintayned'
Her.

12674a Hall, Joseph, 1620
Yk.

12675 Hall, Joseph, 1640 [o.s.]
Ex (3). Yk.

12676 Hall, Joseph, 1640 [o.s.]
Carl. Win.

12677 Hall, Joseph, 1630
Linc (tpw).

12680 Hall, Joseph, 1606
Third century now = STC 12680.5 etc.; A3^r catchword: 'enough'
Cant.

12680.5 Hall, Joseph, 1606
'A third century'; 12°; H. Lownes f. J. Porter; B1^r line 3 begins: 'we'
Cant.

12681 Hall, Joseph, 1607
Yk.

12685 Hall, Joseph, [1605?]
Rectos in all quires have catchwords.
Cant. Carl*. Ex (2)*. Linc*. Wor*.

12690.5 Hall, Joseph, 1628
The second edition; 8°; f. N. Butter a. R. Hawkins.
Pet (tpw). Yk.

12692 Hall, Joseph, 1628
Linc.

12693.7 Hall, Joseph, 1609
[Anr ed. of STC 12694] Formerly STC 12695; ... and S. Macham.
S Pl (2).

12694 Hall, Joseph, 1609
'... preached at Paules-Crosse ...'
Cant. S Pl.

12695 *See:* 12693.7

12697 Hall, Joseph, 1609
Pet. Yk.

12698 *See:* 12715

12699 Hall, Joseph, 1608
Ex.

12701 Hall, Joseph, 1609
Cant. S Pl.

12702 Hall, Joseph, 1633
Formerly also STC 12664.
Ches. Dur. Ely. Pet. Wel. Yk.

12703 Hall, Joseph, 1611
Linc (2 − 1 tpw*). Yk.

12704 Hall, Joseph, 1633
Linc.

12706 Hall, Joseph, 1614
'nowe'; (H. Lownes) f. S. Macham, (A. Johnson, a. L. Lisle).
Ex.

12707 Hall, Joseph, 1617
(E. Griffin, W. Stansby) f. ...; STC 12651, 12653, 12655 are pts of this.
Glo. Her (tp imp?).

12708 Hall, Joseph, 1621
(F. Kyngston, E. Griffin, W.S.) f. H. Fetherstone.
Bur. Cant.

12709a Hall, Joseph, 1629
Linc.

12710.9 Hall, Joseph, 1618
[Anr issue of STC 12711] E. Griffin f. N. Butter.
Linc.

12712 Hall, Joseph, 1609
'... arts, of 1. ethickes, 2. politickes, ... Drawne out of his Proverbs & Ecclesiastes. ...'
Cant.

12713 Hall, Joseph, 1626
Linc (imp). Yk.

12714 Hall, Joseph, 1624
Linc.

12714.5 Hall, Joseph, 1622
'A sermon preached before his majestie ... Sept. 15. 1622'; 8°; J. Haviland f. N. Butter.
Linc.

12715 Hall, Joseph, 1624
Formerly also STC 12698.
Linc.

12718 Hall, Joseph, 1602
Pet.

12719 Hall, Joseph, 1599
Pet.

12727 *See:* 22001

12728 Hamilton, James, *1st Duke*, 1638
Pet. S Pl. Yk.

12729 Hamilton, John, 1581
Yk.

12731 Hamilton, John, *Abp*, 1552
Formerly also STC 22056; 'The catechisme, that is to say, ane instruction set furth be Johne Aschbischop [sic] ...'; (sanct Androus).
Linc.

12735 Hamond, Walter, 1640
Linc.

12737.5 Hampton, Christopher, 1622
'An inquisition of the true church ...'; 4°; Dublin, Soc. of Statrs.
Yk.

12742 Hanapus, Nicolaus, 1561
(J. Tisdale).
Pet.

12744 Hanmer, Meredith, [1586?]
Linc (2 − 1 tpw).

12745.5 Hanmer, Meredith, 1581
[Anr ed.] As STC 1245, but 26 *not* 27 ff.
Linc. Yk*.

12756 Harding, John, *Friar*, 1620
Pet.

12758 Harding, Thomas, 1564
Yk (imp).

12759.5 Harding, Thomas, [1565]
'A briefe answere ... touching ...
vntruthes with which ... Iohn Iuell
charged him'; 8°; Antuerpiae, Aegid.
Diest.
Wor.

12760 Harding, Thomas, 1566
Antuerpiae ...
Pet. Rip (imp).

12761 Harding, Thomas, 1567
Pet. Sal. Yk.

12762 Harding, Thomas, 1565
'... booke ...'; Antwerpe ...
Pet. Rip (imp). Yk.

12763 Harding, Thomas, 1568
Louanii ...
S Pl.

12766 Hardwick, William, 1638
'... piety requisite in Gods service ...'
Ex. Yk (2).

12766.7 Hardyng, John, 1543
Formerly STC 12768; '... of Jhon
Hardyng in metre ...'
Linc (imp). Pet (imp). Wor
(frag.).

12767 Hardyng, John, 1543
'... of Jhon Hardyng ...'
Cant. Chi (tp imp). Her.

12768 *See*: 12766.7

12780 Harington, *Sir* John, 1596
A2ʳ last line ends: 'dyd'; I2ᵛ last line
ends: '*priuy faults*' or '*priuie faults*'
Linc.

12784 Hariot, Thomas, 1631
Sal.

12806 Harris, John, *Preacher*,
[1629]
Date in title; Lathum.
Cant.

12807 Harris, Matthew, 1639
Pet.

12808 Harris, Paul, 1633
'... sive Edmundus Vrsulanus ...
dejectus'; [Dublin, Soc. of Statrs.].
Linc. S Pl.

12808.3 Harris, Paul, 1627
Formerly STC 12813; 'A briefe
confutation of certaine ... James
Usher ...'; S. Omers, f. J. Heigham.
Linc.

12809 Harris, Paul, 1632
'... L. Archbishop of Dublin ...'
Wor.

12813 *See*: 12808.3

12814 Harris, Richard, 1612
Yk.

12815 Harris, Richard, 1614
Pet. Yk.

12816 Harris, Robert, 1635 (1634)
'The workes ...'
Carl. S Asa.

12817 Harris, Robert, 1610
'... funerall: preached at Banbyrie'
Carl (tpw)*.

12820 Harris, Robert, 1622
S Asa.

12823 *See*: 12816

12828 Harris, Robert, 1622
Yk.

12831 Harris, Robert, 1622
S Pl.

12832 Harris, Robert, 1624
Yk.

12833 Harris, Robert, 1626
S Pl.

12834 Harris, Robert, 1631
Linc. S Pl.

12835 *See*: 12816

12836 Harris, Robert, 1626
Pet. Yk.

12837 Harris, Robert, 1626
Cant.

12838 Harris, Robert, 1630
Pet.

12839 *See*: 12816

12840 Harris, Robert, 1624
Ex.

12841 Harris, Robert, 1626
The fourth edition.
S Asa. Yk.

12849 Harris, Robert, 1622
Yk.

12850 Harris, Robert, 1626
Ex.

12851.5 Harris, Robert, 1628
[Anr ed. of STC 12852] 'Six sermons
never heretofore published ...'; 4 pts;
4°; f. J. Bartlet.
Yk.

12856 *See*: 12816

12870 Harrison, William, 1614
'... hearers. Or an exposition ...'; T.C.
for A. Johnson.
Ches. Pet.

12872 Harry, George Owen, 1604
'The genealogy of ... James, ...'
Yk.

12875+ Harsnet, Adam, 1640
'... generall ...'; 12°; John Dawson,
sold by Francis Eglesfield.
Yk.

12878 Harsnet, Adam, 1633
Linc.

12883 Harsnet, Samuel, 1599
Linc. Pet.

12888 Hart, James, 1633
Linc.

12895 Hartgyll, George, 1594
... imp. A. Maunselli.
Sal.

12897.5 Harvey, Christopher, *the
Elder*, 1636
'The conditions of Christianity'; 12°;
R.B. f. P. Stephens a. C. Meredith.
Pet.

12899 Harvey, Gabriel, 1577
'Gabrielis Harueii Ciceronianus ...'
Pet.

12904.5 Harvey, Gabriel, 1577
Issue 2 of STC1 12904; 'Gabrielis
Harueii Rhetor ...'; Ex off. typ. H.
Binneman.
Pet.

12905 Harvey, Gabriel, 1578 (1577)
'Gabrielis Harueii Valdinatis; Smithus;
...'
Pet.

12915 Harvey, Richard, 1590
Chi. Pet.

12923.5 Harward, Simon, 1599
'Three sermons vpon some portions of
the former lessons'; 8°; R. Bradocke
f. R. Iohns.
Linc. Pet.

12924 Harward, Simon, 1582
Linc. Pet.

12927 Hastings, *Sir* Francis, 1598
Linc. Yk.

12927.5 Hastings, *Sir* Francis, 1598
[Anr ed.] 8°; F. Kingston f. R. Jacson.
Pet.

12928 Hastings, *Sir* Francis, 1600
... R. Jacson.
Yk.

12937 Hausted, Peter, 1636
Bur. Chelm. Yk.

12939 Haward, Nicholas, 1569
Rip (imp).

12942 Hawes, Richard, 1634
Pet.

12956 Hawkesworth, Walter, 1636
H. Robinson.
Sal (frags).

12960 Hawkins, John, *of Crawley,*
1595
... soulde ...
Linc.

12964 Hawkins, William, 1634
Pet.

12966 Hawkins, William, 1631
Ban.

12969 Hay, John, *Jesuit,* 1580
Yk.

12972 Hay, Peter, 1616
Yk.

12975 Hayne, Thomas, 1614
Formerly also STC 12982; 'A briefe
...'
Carl. Yk (tpw).

12976 Hayne, Thomas, 1632
Pet.

12979 Hayne, Thomas, 1639
Yk.

12981.5 Hayne, Thomas, 1607
[Variant] f. R. Ockould.
Yk.

12982 *See:* 12975

12983 Hayne, Thomas, 1640
Wor.

12984 Hayward, John, 1603
Linc.

12984.5 Hayward, John, 1602
'A sermon of the stewards danger';
8°; f. H. Lownes.
S Pl (imp).

12988 Hayward, *Sir* John, 1603
Bur. Linc. Wor. Yk (2).

12992 Hayward, *Sir* John, 1623
Colophon dated 1623; In most (all?)
copies date on engr. tp altered to 1623.
Cant. Pet. Wor. Yk.

12997 Hayward, *Sir* John, 1599
[*i.e.* 1629?]
Square of type orns on tp; A2^r line 22
as STC1.
Swel.

12997a Hayward, *Sir* John, 1599
[*i.e.* 1638?]
Square of type orns on tp; A2^r line
22: 'Teucer'
Pet. Yk.

12998 Hayward, *Sir* John, 1630
Carl. Linc. Pet. Swel.

13000 Hayward, *Sir* John, 1613
Carl. Linc. Nor. Swel.

13001 Hayward, *Sir* John, 1606
4° with vertical chainlines.
Pet. Yk.

13002 Hayward, *Sir* John, 1607
... sold by J. Flasket.
Pet.

13003 Hayward, *Sir* John, 1624
Linc. Wor. Yk.

13004 Hayward, *Sir* John, 1604
2 pts.
Yk.

13007 Hayward, *Sir* John, 1620
Cant (tp imp).

13009 Hayward, *Sir* John, 1631
Yk.

13011 Hayward, *Sir* John, 1604
Linc.

13020 Hedlambe, John, 1579
Pet.

13021 Hegendorff, Christopher,
1548
(Ippiswich, ...).
Pet.

13025 Heidelberg Catechism, 1623
Aberdoniae, E. Rabanus, imp. D.
Melvil.
Linc.

13025.4 Heidelberg Catechism, 1623
[Anr ed.] 12°; G.E. imp. H.
Fetherstone.
Ex.

13030 Heidelberg Catechism, 1588
8°.
Pet.

13032 Heigham, John *or* Roger,
1614
Yk.

13040 Heinsius, Daniel, 1640
'Danielis Heinsii ...'
Ban. Glo. Her. Pet. Sal. Win.
Wor.

13043 Heliodorus, 1587
Pet.

13045 Heliodorus, 1606
Yk.

13046 Heliodorus, 1622
Sal.

13047.5 Heliodorus, 1631
[Variant] J. Haviland, at the authors
charge, sold [by J. Smethwick?,
London] and by St. Maries in both
universities.
Cant.

13053.5 Helwys, Thomas, 1611
'A declaration of faith'; 8°;
[Amsterdam].
Yk.

13055 Helwys, Thomas, 1611
'... off anye mans sinne ...'
Linc. Pet.

13057 Hemmingsen, Niels, 1580
Yk.

13057.5 Hemmingsen, Niels, 1576
[Original of STC 13058]
'Commentarius in epistolam Pauli ad
Ephesios'; 8°; T. Vautrollerius.
Pet.

13058.7 Hemmingsen, Niels, 1577
'Commentarius in Epistolam Pauli ad
Romanos'; 8°; ap. T. Vautrollerium
imp. G. Norton.
Pet.

13059.4 Hemmingsen, Niels, 1580
'A godlie and learned exposition vpon
the XXV. Psalme'; 8°; T. Vautroullier.
Pet.

13060 Hemmingsen, Niels, 1577
'A learned and fruitefull ...'
Pet.

13061 Hemmingsen, Niels, (1569)
Tp line 12 ends: 'the'
Bur. Dur*. Liv*. Wor (imp)*.

13063 Hemmingsen, Niels, (1574)
Pet (tpw).

13063.5 Hemmingsen, Niels, [1577?]
[Anr ed.] 4°; f. L. Harison a. G.
Byshop.
Dur. Pet.

13066.5 Hemmingsen, Niels, 1579
'The proffessions of the true church ...
'; 8°; (T. Dawson) f. A. Maunsell.
Yk.

13069 *See:* 13538.5

13083 Henry VIII, *King of England,*
(1521)
Pt 2 (reissue of STC 13078) colophon:
In aed Pysonianis.
Sal.

13085 Henry VIII, *King of England,*
(1527)
(In aed. ...).
Pet.

13092.5 Henry III, *King of France,*
1585
'Edict du roy'; Roan, M. Mesgissier,
London, R. Ihones; Pt 2 formerly
STC 13107.
Pet (pt 2 [English] only).

13094 *See:* 13098.2

13095 *See:* 13098.8

13096 Henry III, *King of France,*
1589
Pet.

13097 *See:* 13098.5

13098 Henry III, *King of France,*
1589
'... Burdeaux, touching ...'
Pet.

13098.2 Henry III, *King of France,*
1589
Formerly STC 13094.
Pet.

13098.5 Henry III, *King of France,*
1589
Formerly STC 13097; '... kinges ...'
Pet.

13098.8 Henry III, *King of France,*
1589
Formerly STC 13095.
Pet.

13101 Henry III, *King of France,*
1589
'... discourse most excellent for this
time present: composed ...'
Dur (tpw).

13104 Henry IV, *King of France,*
[1570]
Linc.

13106 Henry IV, *King of France,*
1585
'The declaration ... slaunders ...'
Pet.

13107 *See:* 13092.5

13113 Henry IV, *King of France,*
[1590]
Pet.

13113.5 Henry IV, *King of France,*
1590
'A letter sent ... vnto Monsieur de la
Verune'; 4°; I. Wolfe f. W. Wright.
Pet.

13114 Henry IV, *King of France,*
1590
'... Henrie the fourth ...'; ... f. J.B. ...
Pet.

13115 *See:* 13116.5

13116 Henry IV, *King of France,*
1591
Pet.

13116.5 Henry IV, *King of France,*
[1591]
Formerly STC 13115; '... accountes ...
'
Pet.

13126 Henry IV, *King of France —
Appendix,* 1590
Pet.

13128 Henry IV, *King of France —
Appendix,* 1590
'A briefe ... yeelding vp of Saint
Denis ...'; J. Wolfe, solde by ...
Pet.

13130 Henry IV, *King of France —
Appendix,* [1592]
J. Wolfe a. E. White.
Pet.

13131 Henry IV, *King of France —
Appendix,* 1590
... f. R. Oliffe.
Pet.

13132 *See:* 13131

13133 Henry IV, *King of France —
Appendix,* 1592
'A discourse of the great ouerthrow ...
vnto the Leaguers in Poictiers'
Pet.

13139 Henry IV, *King of France —
Appendix,* 1590
Pet.

13142.5 Henry IV, *King of France —
Appendix,* [1591]
'A true declaration of the ... victorie
... of Noyan'; 4°; T. Scarlet f. T.
Nelson.
Pet. Yk.

13143 Henry IV, *King of France —
Appendix,* 1589
Pet.

13145 Henry IV, *King of France —
Appendix,* 1590
'... victorie, obteined ...'
Pet.

13146 Henry IV, *King of France —
Appendix,* 1590
'True newes ... towne ...'
Pet.

13147 Henry IV, *King of France —
Appendix,* 1592
Pet.

13156 Henry, *Prince de Dombes,*
1591
Pet.

13157 Henry, *Prince of Wales,* 1613
'... funerals ...'; ... J. Budgde [sic].
Pet.

13175.19 Herbal, [1561]
'A litle herball of the properties of
herbes'; 8°; (I. kynge).
Pet.

13180 Herbert, Edward, *Baron,*
1633
Linc. S Pl.

13181 Herbert, George, 1623
'Oratio quâ ... principis ...'
Ely. Linc. Pet (2). S Asa.

13184.5 Herbert, George, 1633
[Variant of STC 13185] T. Buck a. R.
Daniel, prs. to the Univ. of
Cambridge.
Cant.

13185 Herbert, George, 1633
T. Buck a. R. Daniel, prs. to the
Univ. of Cambridge, sold by F. Green.
Sal (imp). Yk.

13186 Herbert, George, 1634
Impr. as STC 13185.
Cant.

13188 Herbert, George, 1638
12°; Impr. as STC 13185.
Carl. Yk.

13190 Herbert, *Sir* Thomas, 1634
Pet. Win. Yk.

13191 Herbert, *Sir* Thomas, 1638
R. Bi[sho]p. f. ...
Yk (2).

13198 Heresbach, Conrad, 1586
Pet. S Pl (imp).

13199 Heresbach, Conrad, 1596
... f. T. Wight.
Pet.

13203.5 Hering, Theodore, 1624
'Panacea Christiana'; 8°; I. Iaggard, f.
R. Bird.
Linc (imp).

13204 Hering, Theodore, 1625
Ely. Ex. S Pl.

13205 Herle, Charles, 1631
Carl.

13207 Herman IV, *Abp of Cologne,*
(1566)
... for T. Hacket; Found with
colophon dated or undated.
Pet (colophon dated).

13213 Herman V, *Abp of Cologne,*
1547
J. D(aye).
Cant. Liv.

13214 Herman V, *Abp of Cologne,*
[1548]
Date in title.
Linc. Pet. Rip. Sal. Yk (imp).

13220 Herodian, 1639 (1638)
'... Herodiani historiae ...'
Pet.

13221 Herodian, [1550?]
Pet (imp).

13228b.7 Herrey, Robert F., [1588]
A – K⁸L²; 'B' of sig. B4 under 'tat' of 'habitation'
Bur*. Dur*.

13228b.14 Herrey, Robert F., [1598]
[Anr ed.] 4°; Deputies of C. Barker; A – K⁸L²; 'B' of sig. B4 under 'ab' of 'habitation'
Cant. Sal (bound with 1598 Bible)*.

13230 Herrey, Robert F., 1606
Nor.

13231 Herrey, Robert F., 1607
Cant.

13232 Herrey, Robert F., 1608
Cant (2 − 1 tpw). S Alb (2).

13232.5 Herrey, Robert F., 1611
[Anr ed.] 4°; R. Barker.
Yk.

13233 Herrey, Robert F., 1613
Cant.

13234 Herrey, Robert F., 1615
Cant (tp imp). Roch. Sal. Wel.

13235 Herrey, Robert F., 1619 (1620)
S Alb. S Asa.

13238 Herrey, Robert F., 1622 (1621)
Her. Win (imp).

13250 Heskyns, Thomas, 1566
Formerly also STC 13842; 2°.
Cant. Her. S Pl. Sal. Wor. Yk.

13259 Hewes, John, 1633
'Florilegium phrasicωn ... Latine ...'
S Asa.

13261 Hewes, John, 1632
Glo.

13264.8 Hexam, Henry, 1623
Formerly STC 22090; '... English souldiers ...'
Linc.

13266 Heydon, *Sir* Christopher, 1603
Pet. Sal (tpw).

13267 Heylyn, Peter, 1637
Bur. Cant. Linc (2). Liv. Nor. S Pl. Sal. Win (2). Yk (2).

13267.5 Heylyn, Peter, 1637
The second edition; 4°; f. J. Clark.
Ex. Sal. Yk.

13269 Heylyn, Peter, 1637
2 issues; 'A briefe and moderate ...'; Formerly also STC 4158.
Bur. Cant. Carl. Linc. Pet (2). S Pl. Yk (2 − 1 tpw).

13270 Heylyn, Peter, 1636
B2ʳcatchword: 'the'; H1ʳcatchword: 'fied:'
Cant (mixed sheets, with B2 (at least) of STC 13270.5). Lich*. Linc. Win*. Yk (2)*.

13271 Heylyn, Peter, 1637
Bur. Nor. S Pl. Yk.

13272 Heylyn, Peter, 1631
'The historie of ... St. George ...'; (B.A. a. T.F.) f. H. Seyle.
Dur (imp). Ex. Linc. Yk.

13273 Heylyn, Peter, 1633
Her. Pet. Yk.

13274 Heylyn, Peter, 1636
(T. Harper) f. H. Seile.
Cant. Ely. Her. Linc. Pet. Wor. Yk.

13275 Heylyn, Peter, 1636
Bur. Her. S Asa. S Pl.

13276 Heylyn, Peter, 1621
Sal.

13277 Heylyn, Peter, 1625
Linc.

13279 Heylyn, Peter, 1629
Lich. Yk.

13280 Heylyn, Peter, 1631
Cant.

13281 Heylyn, Peter, 1633
Cant.

13311 Heywood, Thomas, 1636
Cant (imp).

13316 Heywood, Thomas, 1640
Cant.

13327 Heywood, Thomas, 1635
Glo.

13377.5 Hieron, Samuel, [1620?]
[Engr. tp only:] 'The workes ...'; ½ sh.fol.; W. Stansby, sold by J. Parker.
Her.

13377.7 Hieron, Samuel, [1628?]
[Engr. tp only:] 'The workes ...'; ½ sh.fol.; W. Stansby.
Wor.

13378 Hieron, Samuel, 1614 (1613)
'... Samuel Hieron...'; Vol. 1 of his works; Includes STC 13387, 13390, 13400, 13408, 13421, 13425.
Ex. Lich.

13379 Hieron, Samuel, 1620 (1619)
... (J. Beale, T. Snodham).
Her. Yk.

13381 Hieron, Samuel, 1624 (1625)
J. Legatt, (J. Beale, J.D.); Vol. 2 now = STC 13384.3.
Wor.

13383 *See*: 13384.5

13384.5 Hieron, Samuel, (1628, 1629)
[Vol. 2, no letterpress gen. tp] 2°; (W. Stansby); Formerly STC 13383 and pt of 13382 .
Wor.

13385 Hieron, Samuel, 1623
'... a-sounding. In a sermon ...'
Pet (2 − 1 tpw).

13388 Hieron, Samuel, 1604
Yk.

13392.3 Hieron, Samuel, 1607
'Certaine sermons ...'; 8°; T.C. f. T. Man.
Yk.

13394a Hieron, Samuel, 1617
4°; C. Legge, pr. to the Univ. of Cambridge.
Yk.

13395 Hieron, Samuel, 1607 (1608)
Ex (pt 1 only). Linc (pt 3 only). Sal (pt 2 only). Yk (3 − 1 pt 2 only; 1 pt 3 only).

13407 Hieron, Samuel, 1612
Linc (imp).

13409 Hieron, Samuel, 1614
The sixt edition; 12°; H.L. f. S. Macham.
Ely.

13416? Hieron, Samuel, 1636
... sold by Henry Taunton.
Carl.

13417 Hieron, Samuel, 1612
Yk.

13419 Hieron, Samuel, 1604
Yk.

13423 Hieron, Samuel, 1618
Cant (imp).

13424 Hieron, Samuel, 1611
Pet.

13426 Hieron, Samuel, 1607
Yk.

13433 Hieronymus, *von Braunschweig*, 1561
'... excellent and perfecte homish ...'
Cant. Pet. Wel. Yk.

13435 Hieronymus, *von Braunschweig*, (1527)
'... distyllacyon ...'; (L. Andrewe).
Cant.

13440 Higden, Ranulphus, (1527)
'Polycronycon'; (Southwerke, P. Treueris at ye expences of J. Reynes).
Ches (imp). Chi (imp). Her. Linc. Pet (imp). Rip (imp). Yk.

13446   Higgins, John, *Poet*, 1610
(1609)
'A mirour ...'
Cant. Lich (imp).

13454   Higgons, Theophilus, 1609
Her. Pet. Yk (2 −1 pt 2 only).

13455   Higgons, Theophilus, 1624
New. Yk.

13455.7   Higgons, Theophilus, 1611
[Anr ed. of STC 13456] 4°; F.
Kyngston f. W. Aspley.
Cant. Ches. Linc. S Pl.

13459   Hildersam, Arthur, 1633
Ely. Her. Pet (2 −1 imp).

13461   Hildersam, Arthur, 1629
Her (tpw). Wor.

13462   Hildersam, Arthur, 1632
Dur. S Asa (tpw).

13463   Hildersam, Arthur, 1635
Wor.

13464   *See*: 14663.5

13466   Hill, Adam, 1592
Pet. Yk.

13467   Hill, Augustine, 1640
S Pl.

13468   Hill, Augustine, 1640
Ex.

13470.3   Hill, Edmund Thomas,
1600
[Anr issue] Tp has cut with IHS,
rather than a representation of the
crucifixion.
Pet (imp).

13476   Hill, Robert, 1617
Wor.

13477   Hill, Robert, 1629
Title: 'The path-way to pietie'
Wor (imp)*.

13477.5   Hill, Robert, 1629
[Variant] J. Haviland, sold by J.
Grismond.
Pet.

13478   Hill, Robert, 1596
Pet (pt 1 only).

13480   *See*: 14040.7

13482   Hill, Thomas, *Londoner*,
(1571)
(W. Seres); Formerly also STC 17787.
Pet.

13485   Hill, Thomas, *Londoner*,
1577
Yk (pt 1 only, imp)*.

13506   Hill, William, *D.D.*, 1605
Pet. Yk.

13514   Hinde, William, 1623
Bris (tpw)*. Ex (2). Pet (imp)*.

13518   Hippocrates, 1633
Pt 2 formerly also STC 4483.
Dur. Ex. Linc. Pet. S Pl.

13519   Hippocrates, 1631
Linc.

13532   Hiud, Johan, 1632
Ely. Sal.

13533   Hoard, Samuel, 1637
Bur. Carl. Ex. Linc. Pet (3 −1
tpw). S Asa. Yk (2).

13534   Hoard, Samuel, 1633
A1^r line 8 of text has: 'ronscience'
[*sic*].
Bur. Dur (imp)*. Linc*.
S Asa*. Sal*.

13534.5   Hoard, Samuel, 1633
[Anr ed.] As STC 13534, but: A1^r line
8: 'conscience'; N3^v catchword:
'soule'
Cant.

13536   Hoard, Samuel, 1636
'... miserie and recoverie ...'
Ban. Bur.

13538   Hobbs, Stephen, 1610
Glo.

13538.5   Hobson, Robert, 1631
Formerly STC 13069.
Cant (with addit. engr. tp, 1632).
Linc (with addit. engr. tp, 1632).
Pet (with addit. engr. tp, 1632).
Yk.

13539a   Hoby, *Sir* Edward, 1613
Yk.

13540.5   Hoby, *Sir* Edward, 1615
[Anr issue, adding:] (Appendix de
jesuitica batrachologia); W. Stansby f.
N. Butter.
Yk*.

13541   Hoby, *Sir* Edward, 1609
Linc. Pet (tpw). Yk.

13551   Hodson, Phineas, 1628
Yk.

13552   Hodson, Phineas, 1625
Linc. Yk.

13552.5   Hodson, William, 1633
[Anr ed. of STC 13553] 12°; E.P. f.
N. Bourne.
Sal.

13554   Hodson, William, 1640
'... cosmographer; or, a brief survey
of the whole world ... in a tractate ...'
Linc.

13555   Hodson, William, 1639
Linc.

13557   Hogarde, Miles, 1556
Anon.; In aed. R. Caly.
Pet.

13558   Hogarde, Miles, (1556)
Newly imprinted and augmented; (R.
Caly).
Linc.

13564   Holbrooke, William, [1610?]
S Pl.

13568   Holinshed, Raphael, [1577]
Tp found with: Harrison *or* Harison;
Vol. 1 sub tpp often name a different
publisher from the one on the gen. tp.
Ban (vol. 2 only, tpw). Her (vol.
2 only, tpw)*. Pet (imp)*.

13568.5   Holinshed, Raphael, [1577]
[Variant, with impr. on gen. tpp:] f.
L. Harrison *or* Harison.
Nor (lacks vol. 2 tp).

13568a   Holinshed, Raphael, [1577]
[Variant, with impr. on gen. tpp:] f.
G. Bishop.
Lich.

13568b   Holinshed, Raphael, [1577]
[Variant, with impr. on gen. tpp:] f. J.
Hunne.
Cant (imp). Linc.

13569   Holinshed, Raphael, (1587)
Bur (vols 1−2, tpw). Cant (lacks
vol. 3). Chi. Dur (with vol. 3 of
13569.5). Her. Linc (2 −1 tpw,
that of vol. 3 of 13569.5
substituted). Liv. Nor (tpw).
Wel (imp). Yk.

13569.5   Holinshed, Raphael, (1587)
[Anr issue, with cancel tpp:] 'The
whole volume of chronicles ...' ('The
chronicles of England ...').
Dur (vol. 3 only as part of
13569).

13580   Holland, Abraham, 1622
Linc (tpw).

13582   Holland, Henry, *Bookseller*,
[1620]
... calcographus ...
Linc.

13583   Holland, Henry, *Bookseller*,
[1614]
S Pl.

13584   Holland, Henry, *Bookseller*,
1633
'untill'
S Pl.

13586   Holland, Henry, *Vicar of St
Bride's*, 1596
Pet.

13587 Holland, Henry, *Vicar of St Bride's*, 1606
Yk.

13593 *See:* 4023

13596 Holland, Thomas, 1599
Oxoniae, J. Barnesius.
Dur. Ex (from STC, not confirmed).

13597 Holland, Thomas, 1601
S Pl. Yk.

13600 Hollingworth, Rodolphus, 1640
Dublinii, ex off. Societatis Bibliopolarum.
Linc. Sal.

13613 Holy Roman Empire, 1623
'acts'
Pet.

13614 Holyday, Barten, 1633
Ex. Linc. Sal.

13615 Holyday, Barten, 1626
'August the 5.'
Pet. S Pl.

13616 Holyday, Barten, 1626
'March the 24.'
Cant. Linc. S Pl.

13617 Holyday, Barten, 1618
Pet.

13618 Holyday, Barten, 1630
Linc.

13619 Holyday, Barten, 1626
Cant. Linc.

13619.5 Holyoke, Francis, 1627
[Anr ed. of STC 13620] 4°; Oxford, W. Turner.
Wor (tpw).

13622 Holyoke, Francis, 1610
Oxford, Jos. Barnes.
Pet.

13624 Homer, [1616?]
In recto headlines: 'HOMERS'
Chelm (tpw)*. Glo*.

13633 Homer, [1609?]
Linc.

13634 Homer, [1611]
Cant. Her (tpw).

13637 Homer, [1615?]
Her. Linc (tpw).

13639.5 Homilies, 1547
[Anr ed.] 'Homelies, ... Vicares,'; 4°;
(R. Grafton); Ends Z4; C3ᵛ line 6 has: 'forgeuenes'
Liv. Nor.

13640.5 Homilies, 1547
[Anr ed.] 'Homelies, ... Vicars,'; 4°;
(R. Grafton); Ends Z4; C3ᵛ lines 6 – 7: 'righteou-/nes [*sic*]'
Linc.

13641.3 Homilies, 1547
[Anr ed.] 4°; (E. Whitchurche); Ends U2; A1ʳ line 2 of heading ends: 'Christen faith'
Pet (imp).

13649 Homilies, 1560
(R. Jugge a. J. Cawood); Tp has border of 4 lace panels, with 'R.I.' in circle at bottom.
Linc (tpw)*.

13649.5 Homilies, 1560
[Anr ed.] 4°; (R. Jugge a. J. Cawood); Tp has border with Cawood's monogram in sill.
Pet (imp).

13650.7 Homilies, 1562
[Anr ed.] 4°; (R. Jugge a. J. Cawood); Tp has border with lions in sill.
Chi (imp)*. Linc (imp).

13651 Homilies, 1563
(R. Jugge a. J. Cawood).
Cant. New.

13652 Homilies, 1569
(R. Jugge a. J. Cawood).
Yk.

13654 Homilies, 1574
(R. Jugge).
Liv.

13657 Homilies, 1587
Tru (imp).

13658 Homilies, 1595
Sal.

13659 Homilies, 1623
Bur. Cant (2). Glo. Her. New.

13660 Homilies, 1633
Tp line 5 begins: 'appoynted'
Carl*. Dur*. Lich*. Llan*. Pet*.

13661 Homilies, 1635
Cant. Linc. Liv. S Pl. Swel. Wel. Win.

13662 Homilies, 1640
[Anr ed. of bks I and II, continuous signatures] Bk II formerly STC 13677; Ends 2N8.
Cant*. Ex. Linc. Llan (imp). Tru (imp). Wel (tpw)*.

13663.3 Homilies, 1563
[Anr ed.] 4°; (R. Jugge a. J. Cawood); Ends 3P6.
S Pl*.

13665 Homilies, 1563
(R. Jugge a. J. Cawood); 3P6ʳ line 9: 'inheritance'
Cant. New*.

13667 Homilies, 1563 (1567)
(R. Jugge a. J. Cawood).
Pet (imp).

13668 Homilies, 1570
(R. Jugge a. J. Cawood).
Yk.

13670 Homilies, 1574
(R. Jugge).
Liv (imp).

13673 Homilies, 1587
Tru (imp).

13674 Homilies, 1595
Pet (imp). Sal.

13675 Homilies, 1623
Bur. Cant (2). Her (imp).

13676 Homilies, 1633
Bur. Carl. Dur (imp). Lich. Llan. Pet.

13676a Homilies, 1635 (1633)
Bur. Cant (imp). Linc. Liv. S Pl. Swel. Wel. Win.

13677 *See:* 13662

13678 Homilies, 1606
'... i'w darllein ...'
S Asa (imp).

13681 Homilies, 1596
Linc (tp imp). Yk.

13683 Hommius, Festus, 1630
'... theologicae ... Editio secunda'; ... imp. G. Turner.
Bur. Carl.

13696.5 Hood, Thomas, 1592
[Engr. map of west coast of Europe and Africa]; brs; [N.pl.].
Pet.

13697 Hood, Thomas, 1590
'... in plano ...'; (J. Windet) f. ...
Wor.

13704 Hooke, Henry, 1604
'A sermon preached before the King ... eight of May. 1604 ... Jerusalems peace'
Linc.

13706 Hooker, Richard, 1612
'... Mr. Richard Hooker ...'
Ex. Pet (2). S Pl. Wor (tp only). Yk.

13707 Hooker, Richard, 1612
S Pl. Yk.

13708 Hooker, Richard, 1612
Pet. Yk.

13709 Hooker, Richard, 1613
S Pl.

13710 *See*: 13718

13711 Hooker, Richard, 1612
S Pl. Yk (2).

13712 Hooker, Richard, [1593]
Pt 2 now = STC 13712.5.
Cant. Her. S Pl. Tru. Win.

13712.5 Hooker, Richard, 1597
'... The fift booke'; 2°; J. Windet;
Formerly pt 2 of STC 13712.
Cant (2). Ches. Tru (2). Win.

13713 Hooker, Richard, 1604
Bks 1−4.
Cant. Ches. Her.

13714 Hooker, Richard, (1611)
... (sold by M. Lownes).
Cant. Ches. Linc. Yk.

13715 *See*: 13716

13716 Hooker, Richard, 1617
(1616, 1618)
Formerly also STC 13715.
Cant (tp imp). Chelm. Ches (pt
2 only). Lich. Linc. Wel.

13716a Hooker, Richard, 1617
(1622)
Mixed copies of STC 13716 and 13717.
Cant (2). Glo. Her (with pt of
13718). Roch.

13717 Hooker, Richard, (1622)
W. Stansbye.
Ches (tpw). Linc. S Pl.

13718 Hooker, Richard, (1632,
1631)
No ed. statement; W. Stansbye, sold
by G. Lathum; STC 13710 is pt of
this.
Bur (tpw?). Cant (2 −1 imp, 1
tpw). Her. Llan. S Asa. Wel.

13719 Hooker, Richard, (1632,
1635, 1636)
No ed. statement; W. Stansbye, sold
by G. Lathum.
Her. Rip.

13719b Hooker, Richard, (1635−39)
Mixed copies of STC 13719 and 13720.
Cant. Chelm. Glo.

13720 Hooker, Richard, (1639)
Lathum; Formerly also STC 13720a.
Ban.

13720a *See*: 13720

13721 Hooker, Richard, 1599
Formerly also STC 4707.
Cant. Pet. Win. Yk (imp).

13722 Hooker, Richard, 1612
S Pl. Yk.

13723 Hooker, Richard, 1614
'Two sermons upon part of S. Judes
epistle'; ... Jos. Barnes.
Ely. S Pl.

13727 Hooker, Thomas, 1638
Her.

13729 Hooker, Thomas, 1638
Bur. Llan (imp).

13733 Hooker, Thomas, 1637
Her. Win.

13739 Hooker, Thomas, 1638
Bur. Yk.

13743 Hooper, John, 1580
Linc. Pet. S Pl (imp).

13745 Hooper, John, (1547)
(Zurych, ...).
Glo. Rip. Yk (tp imp).

13745.5 Hooper, John, [1582?]
[Anr ed. with title:] 'A godlie and
profitable treatise ...'; 12°; f. J. Perrin.
Glo (imp).

13746 Hooper, John, 1548 [1549?]
Glo. S Pl (2). Sal.

13747 *See*: 13750.5

13748 *See*: 13750

13750 Hooper, John, 1550
Formerly also STC 13748; (R. Jugge).
Cant (imp). Glo. Pet.

13750.5 Hooper, John, 1550
Formerly STC 13747; (R. Jugge).
Ely. Linc.

13751 Hooper, John, [1588]
Glo. Pet. S Pl.

13753 Hooper, John, (1549)
'... day of January ...'; (E.
Whitechurch).
Glo (imp).

13756 Hooper, John, 1551
'... too the Romaynes'; (Worceter, ...).
Pet.

13757 Hooper, John, [1551?]
(J. Daye); A−H⁴.
Linc (tpw).

13759 Hooper, John, [1553]
(Worceter, ...); Some copies have
(Worcester, ...).
Linc (Worceter).

13763 Hooper, John, [1550]
(J. Daye a. ...); Date in title.
Pet. Win.

13764 Hooper, John, [1550]
(J. Daye a. ...); Date in title.
Glo.

13765 Hooper, John, [1560]
Date in title.
S Pl. Yk.

13767.5 Hopkins, John, 1604
[Anr ed.] 8°; H. Lownes f. T. Man.
Pet.

13768 Hopkins, John, 1609
'... queenes majestie ... 16. day of
October'
Linc (tp imp).

13773 Hopkins, Thomas, 1623
S Pl.

13780 Hopton, Arthur, 1616
Linc.

13792 Horatius Flaccus, Quintus,
1611
Cant.

13797 Horatius Flaccus, Quintus,
1567
'... pistles, and satyrs ...'
Pet (2 −both imp).

13799 Horatius Flaccus, Quintus,
1621
Yk (2).

13801 Horatius Flaccus, Quintus,
[1631]
Date in title.
Linc.

13811 Horman, William, 1519
(R. Pynson).
Linc (tpw). Pet (tpw). Yk.

13812 Horman, William, 1530
(W. de Worde).
Pet. Sal (tpw).

13818 Horne, Robert, *Bp*, 1566
'... Rob. Bishoppe of Wynchester, ...
suche scruples ...'
Bur. Sal.

13823 Horne, Robert, *of Ludlow*,
1619
Pet (imp)*.

13825 Horne, Robert, *of Ludlow*,
1625
Ex.

13827 *See*: 3305

13829.7 Hortus, [1506−09?]
[Anr ed.] 2°; [York]; 45 lines per
column.
Cant (1 leaf only).

13833.5 Hortus, 1517
[Anr ed.] 4°; Rothomagi, per E.
Hardy, imp. J. Caillard librarii
Rothomagi et J. Gachet Herfordensis.
Her (frag.).

13841 Hoskins, John, 1615
Cant (2). Linc. S Pl (2 −1 lacks
pt 2).

13842 *See*: 13250

13843.5 Hotman, François, 1586
Formerly STC 22589.
Pet.

13846 Hotman, François, 1573
Pet. Rip.

13848 Hotman, Jean, 1603
Linc.

13855 How, Samuel, 1640
Linc.

13858 Howard, Henry, *Earl of Northampton*, 1583
'A defensatiue against ...'
Pet. Wor.

13859 Howard, Henry, *Earl of Northampton*, 1620
J. Charlewood, 1583. And reprinted
...
Cant (imp). Her. Linc.

13869 Howard, Thomas, *Duke of Norfolk*, [1571?]
Yk.

13870 Howard, Thomas, *Duke of Norfolk*, [1571?]
Linc. Pet.

13871 Howard, William, 1634
Wor. Yk.

13872 Howell, James, 1640
Glo. Her. Linc. Wel.

13879 Howson, John, 1622
Bur. Ex (2). Pet. Win. Wor.
Yk (2).

13881 Howson, John, 1597
S Pl.

13882 Howson, John, 1597
Pet. Wor. Yk.

13883 Howson, John, 1598
Pet. S Pl. Wor. Yk.

13885 Howson, John, 1603
Yk (2).

13886 Howson, John, 1602
Pt 2 formerly STC 19015 and 20525;
Text begins on A1.
Linc*. S Pl*.

13887 Howson, John, 1606
... & veneunt Londini ap. S.
Watersonum.
Linc. Win. Yk.

13888 Hozyusz, Stanislaus, 1565
Yk.

13889 Hozyusz, Stanislaus, 1567
Wor.

13894 Huarte Navarro, Juan de
Dios, 1604
Linc. Pet.

13895 Huarte Navarro, Juan de
Dios, 1616
Her. Wel.

13896 *See*: 13898.5

13898 Hubbocke, William, 1595
Pet.

13898.5 Hubbocke, William, 1606
Formerly STC 13896.
Pet.

13899 Hubbocke, William, 1604
'... gratulatory to ... James ...'
Yk.

13904 Hudson, John, 1584
Pet. Yk.

13906 Hues, Robertus, 1594
'... globis et eorum vsu'
Carl. Rip.

13909 Hugget, Anthony, 1615
S Pl.

13917 Hughes, Lewis, 1640
Linc.

13924 Hugo, *de Sancto Victore*, 1577
Cant (cropped).

13926 Hugo, Hermanus, 1627
Printer's name in colophon, not on tp;
some copies found without printer.
Ex (without printer's name).

13926a Hugo, Hermanus, 1627 (1628)
Formerly also STC 1529; 'The seige of
Breda'; Louanii, ex off. Hastenii; 2°.
Linc.

13927 Huish, Alexander, 1626
London, sold by W. Turner in Oxford.
Yk.

13931 Hull, John, 1618
Pet. Yk.

13933a Hull, John, 1611
Linc.

13934 Hull, John, 1602
Pet.

13935 Hull, John, 1602
Linc.

13937 Hull, William, 1612
S Pl.

13946 Hume, Alexander,
Schoolmaster, 1612
... T. Finlason.
Yk.

13948 Hume, Alexander,
Schoolmaster, [1594?]
Pet.

13950 Hume, David, 1605
'Davidis Humii Theagrii ...'
Yk.

13951 Hume, David, 1605
'Britannicae'
Yk.

13953 Hume, David, 1617
Yk.

13954 Hume, John, 1628
Ely. Pet (imp).

13959 Humphrey, Laurence, 1572
'Ad illustrissimam R. Elizabetham,
L.H. Vice-can. Oxon. oratio ...'; A –
C⁴.
Win*. Yk*.

13961 Humphrey, Laurence, 1582
Pet (imp). Sal. Yk.

13961.5 Humphrey, Laurence, 1582
Editio secunda; 8°; H. Middletonus,
imp. G. Byshop.
Cant. Carl. Wel. Wor (2).

13962 Humphrey, Laurence, 1584
Carl. Pet. Wel. Win. Wor. Yk.

13963 Humphrey, Laurence, 1573
'Ioannis Iuelli Angli Episcopi ...'
Cant. Carl. Dur. Linc. Pet.
S Pl. Win. Wor. Yk (2).

13964 Humphrey, Laurence, 1563
Pet.

13966 Humphrey, Laurence, 1588
Oxford, Jos. Barnes.
Linc. Pet. Yk.

13967 Humphreys, Richard, 1607
Linc.

13968 Humphreys, Richard, 1624
Yk.

13969 Humston, Robert, 1589
'... preached at Reyfham ... 22. of
September ...'; J. Wolfe ...
Linc.

13970 Hun, Richard, [1536?]
S Pl (imp).

13985 *See*: 7072.2

13990 Hunt, Nicholas, 1631
Linc.

13998 Huntley, James Gordon, 1618
Yk (tp imp).

14000 Hurault, Jacques, *Sieur de Veul*, 1595
'... moral, and martial ...'
Chelm. Glo (tpw). Pet.

14001a Hurault, Michel, *Sieur du Fay*, 1590
Pet.

14002 Hurault, Michel, *Sieur du Fay*, 1590
Pet.

14020 Hutchinson, Roger, 1160
[=1560]
Cant.

14022 Hutchinson, Roger, 1580
Cant.

14023 Hutten, Leonard, 1605
... sold by S. Waterson [London].
Yk.

14025 Hutten, Ulrich von, 1536
Pet.

14027 Hutten, Ulrich von, 1540
Pet.

14034 Hutton, Matthew, 1579
(T. Dawson) f. ...
Linc. Yk.

14035 Hutton, Thomas, 1605
... S. Waterson.
S Asa. Yk.

14036 Hutton, Thomas, 1606
'The second and last ...'
Cant. Pet. S Asa. Yk.

14037 Hutton, Thomas, 1606
Yk (2).

14038 Hyatt, James, 1625
'... president, or the master and
scholler. In a sermon ...'
Carl. Yk.

14040.7 Hylles, Thomas, 1600
Formerly STC 13480.
Pet.

14042 Hylton, Walter, (1494)
Linc (imp).

Locations of English books to 1640
as enumerated in Pollard and Redgrave's *Short-Title Catalogue*
Volume Two

14050 I., E., 1620
Pet.

14057 I., S., 1595
Pet. Yk.

14058.7 I., S., 1631
Sal.

14059 I., S. A., 1577
Pet.

14060.5 I., S. A., 1583
Linc. Pet. Rip.

14073 Ince, William, 1640
Bur.

14075 Indagine, Joannes ab, 1558
Pet.

14077 Indagine, Joannes ab, 1598
Pet.

14077c.49 Indulgences, [c.1510]
Linc.

14077c.117A Indulgences, [c.1512]
Yk (imp).

14077c.130 Indulgences, [1511]
Glo (frag.).

14077c.147A Indulgences, 1556
Yk (imp).

14084 Informations, 1608
Yk.

14087 Ingmethorp, Thomas, 1609
Wel.

14088 Ingmethorp, Thomas, 1619
Yk.

14097 Innocent VIII, *Pope*, [1494]
Rip (2).

14099 Innocent VIII, *Pope*, [1497]
Cant (imp).

14104 Institution, 1555
Pet.

14117 Intrationes, 1546
Pet. Wor.

14130 Ireland, 1621
Yk.

14135 Ireland, 1634
Yk.

14136 Ireland, 1635
Yk.

14136.3 Ireland, 1635
Yk.

14136.7 Ireland, 1635
Yk (2).

14262 Ireland, Church of, 1629
S Pl. Yk.

14265 Ireland, Church of, 1635
Linc.

14267 Ireland, Thomas, 1610
Yk.

14268 Ironside, Gilbert, 1637
Bur (2). Cant (2 – 1 imp). Carl.
Pet. S Asa. Sal (2). Yk.

14269 Isaacson, Henry, 1633
Cant (3). Carl. Chelm. Ely. Ex.
Glo. New. Pet. Sal. Win. Wor.
Yk.

14270 Isidore, *St*, 1534
Pet.

14270.5 Isidore, *St*, 1539
Yk (imp).

14286 Italy and France, (1530)
Pet. S Pl (2). Yk (imp).

14287 Italy and France, (1531)
Linc. Yk.

14297 Jackson, John, 1628
Carl. S Pl. Yk.

14297a Jackson, John, 1640
Pet.

14298 Jackson, Thomas, *Canon*,
1609
Pet (tpw). S Pl.

14299 Jackson, Thomas, *Canon*,
1603
Linc.

14300 Jackson, Thomas, *Canon*,
1624
Carl.

14303 Jackson, Thomas, *Canon*,
1609
Pet (2). S Pl.

14304 Jackson, Thomas, *Canon*,
1612
S Pl.

14305a Jackson, Thomas, *Canon*,
1614
Linc.

14306 Jackson, Thomas, *Dean*,
1625
Cant (2). Dur. Linc. S Pl.

14307 Jackson, Thomas, *Dean*,
1637
Linc.

14308 Jackson, Thomas, *Dean*,
1613
Her. Linc. Yk (err. on Zz4^v).

14309 Jackson, Thomas, *Dean*,
1635
S Pl.

14311 Jackson, Thomas, *Dean*,
1615
Her.

14312 Jackson, Thomas, *Dean*,
1631
Chi. Ely.

14313 Jackson, Thomas, *Dean*,
1634
New. S Pl.

14314 Jackson, Thomas, *Dean*,
1617
Cant. Pet. Yk.

14315 Jackson, Thomas, *Dean*,
1614
Her.

14316 Jackson, Thomas, *Dean*,
1625
Linc. S Pl. Yk.

14317 Jackson, Thomas, *Dean*,
1638
Glo.

14318 Jackson, Thomas, *Dean*,
1628 (1629)
New. Yk (pt 1 only).

14319 Jackson, Thomas, *Dean*, 1627
Only bk 1 published in this ed.
Cant. Chelm. Dur. Linc. Yk.

14321 Jackson, William, 1616
Wor.

14328 Jacob, Henry, 1613
Yk.

14329 Jacob, Henry, 1606
Yk.

14333 Jacob, Henry, 1600
Pet (2). Yk.

14335 Jacob, Henry, 1599
Yk.

14338 Jacob, Henry, 1604
Pet (2). Yk (2).

14339 Jacob, Henry, 1609
Dur. Liv. Pet. Yk.

14340 Jacob, Henry, 1598
Pet. Yk.

14344 James I, *King of England*, 1616
Carl. Dur. Glo. Her. Nor (imp). S Asa. Sal. Wor.

14345 James I, *King of England*, 1616
Cant. Her. Linc. Win. Yk.

14346 James I, *King of England*, 1619
Ex. Win. Yk.

14346.3 James I, *King of England*, 1619
Nor. Pet.

14350 James I, *King of England*, 1603
Pet. Yk (tp imp).

14354 James I, *King of England*, 1603
Yk.

14366 James I, *King of England*, 1603
S Pl.

14367.5 James I, *King of England*, 1615
Ches*. Yk.

14368 James I, *King of England*, 1616
Cant. Sal. Yk.

14371 James I, *King of England*, 1619
Pet (frag.). Sal (2). Yk (imp)*.

14373 James I, *King of England*, 1584
Wel (imp)*.

14381 James I, *King of England*, 1603
Yk.

14384 James I, *King of England*, 1619
Cant.

14385 James I, *King of England*, 1619
Yk.

14387 James I, *King of England*, 1618
Yk (2 − both sigs C−E only).

14388 James I, *King of England*, 1619
Yk (3 − 2 with sigs C−E of STC 14387).

14388.7 James I, *King of England*, 1621
Sal (tp only).

14390 James I, *King of England*, 1604
Pet.

14392 James I, *King of England*, 1605
Pet (2). Yk.

14393 James I, *King of England*, 1605
Carl (imp). Ely. Yk.

14394 James I, *King of England*, 1606
Yk.

14395 James I, *King of England*, [1607]
Dur. Pet. Yk.

14396 James I, *King of England*, [1609]
Yk*.

14396.7 James I, *King of England*, [1609]
Pet.

14397.3 James I, *King of England*, [1616]
Yk.

14397.7 James I, *King of England*, [1616]
Pet. Yk.

14399 James I, *King of England*, 1621
Cant. Pet. Yk.

14400 James I, *King of England*, 1607
Pet. Yk.

14401 James I, *King of England*, 1609
Cant (pt 2 only). Ely (tpw)*. S Pl*.

14402 James I, *King of England*, 1609
Ban. Ex. Pet. Roch. Sal. Wor. Yk.

14403 James I, *King of England*, 1607
Yk.

14405 James I, *King of England*, 1609
Carl. Chi. Pet. Roch. Yk.

14410.5 James I, *King of England*, 1603
Yk.

14415 James I, *King of England*, 1615
Yk.

14416 James I, *King of England*, 1615
Carl.

14417 James I, *King of England*, 1615
Pet.

14419 James I, *King of England*, 1615
Cant. Ex. Yk.

14426 James I, *King of England*, 1607
Yk.

14427 James I, *King of England*, 1604
Yk.

14428 James I, *King of England*, 1622
Linc (2).

14429.5 James I, *King of England*, 1604
Liv. Yk (3).

14430 James I, *King of England*, 1604
Yk.

14432 James I, *King of England*, 1604
Cant. Liv (imp). Pet (imp). Yk.

14437 James, Richard, 1625
Pet.

14439 James, Richard, 1633
Pet.

14441 James, Richard, 1629
Pet.

14442 James, Richard, 1632
Pet.

14443 James, Richard, 1630
Pet.

14444 James, Thomas, *Captain*,
1633
Cant (imp).

14445 James, Thomas, *D.D.*, 1608
Carl (imp). Linc. Yk (2).

14447 James, Thomas, *D.D.*, 1600
Ex*. Linc.

14447.5 James, Thomas, *D.D.*,
1600
Yk (2).

14448 James, Thomas, *D.D.*, 1635
S Asa.

14450 James, Thomas, *D.D.*, 1620
Cant. Linc. Wor. Yk.

14451 James, Thomas, *D.D.*, 1635
Yk.

14452 James, Thomas, *D.D.*, 1607
Yk.

14453 James, Thomas, *D.D.*, 1600
Cant. Ex. Linc. Pet. Wor. Yk.

14454 James, Thomas, *D.D.*, 1625
Linc. Wel.

14457 James, Thomas, *D.D.*, 1627
Carl.

14458? James, Thomas, *D.D.*, 1624
In off. ...
Yk.

14459 James, Thomas, *D.D.*, 1612
Cant. Linc. Wor (2). Yk.

14460 James, Thomas, *D.D.*, 1625
Ban. Ex. Wel. Wor. Yk.

14461 James, Thomas, *D.D.*, 1626
Carl.

14462 James, Thomas, *D.D.*, 1611
Chi. Dur. S Pl (2). Win. Wor.
Yk.

14463 James, Thomas, *D.D.*, 1612
Bur. Carl. Linc. Rip.

14464 James, William, 1590
Pet (imp). S Pl.

14465 James, William, 1578
Pet.

14466 Janua, 1615
Ex (tp imp).

14467.5 Janua, 1617
Pet.

14472 Janua, 1634
Yk.

14475 Japan, 1624
Pet. Yk.

14479.3 Jay, George, 1632
Pet.

14480 Jeanes, Henry, 1640
Carl. Nor (tpw).

14497 Jenney, George, 1626
Ex.

14500 Jermin, Michael, 1639
Cant (imp).

14500.5 Jermin, Michael, 1639
Her.

14501 Jermin, Michael, 1638
Ches. Ex.

14502 Jerome, *St*, 1630
Pet (tpw).

14505.5 Jerome, *St*, [c.1510]
Pet (imp).

14507 Jerome, *St*, (1495)
Dur (imp). Linc.

14510 Jerome, Stephen, 1628
Ex.

14510+ Jerome, Stephen, 1639
[Anr issue, w. title:]'The diversion of
Gods iudgments'; f. Henry Hood.
Yk.

14511.5 Jerome, Stephen, 1625
Pet (imp).

14513 Jerome, Stephen, 1619
Yk.

14520 Jessop, Edmund, 1623
Linc (tpw).

14529 Jesuits, 1619
Linc.

14541 Jesus Christ, 1640
Pet. S Pl.

14579 Jewel, John, 1609
Cant. Chi. Dur (imp). Ely
(tpw)*. Ex. Her. Linc. Nor.
Pet. S Pl. Sal (frag.)*.

14580 Jewel, John, 1611 (1609)
Ches. Her. Lich. New. S Asa.
Wel. Wor. Yk.

14580.5 Jewel, John, 1611
Bur. Chelm (frag.). S Pl. Wel
(imp). Yk (imp).

14581 Jewel, John, 1562
Pet.

14582 Jewel, John, 1581
Cant. Ely. Liv. Pet.

14585 Jewel, John, 1599
S Pl. Wel.

14586 Jewel, John, 1606
S Pl.

14588 Jewel, John, 1637
Bur.

14589 Jewel, John, 1639
Carl. Ches. Sal (2 − 1 imp). Yk.

14590 Jewel, John, 1562
Pet.

14591 Jewel, John, 1564
Pet (imp). S Pl.

14593 Jewel, John, 1635
Sal (no date on tp).

14596 Jewel, John, 1583
Pet (imp). S Pl.

14597 Jewel, John, 1583
Pet.

14599 Jewel, John, 1603
Linc. Yk.

14600 Jewel, John, 1567
Cant. Her. New (imp)*. Rip*.
Roch*. Sal (2). Swel*. Yk.

14600.5 Jewel, John, 1567
Glo. Pet. Win.

14601 Jewel, John, 1570
Ex (imp)*. Linc. Wel. Yk.

14602 Jewel, John, 1571
Carl. Pet. S Pl.

14603 Jewel, John, 1583
Pet (2). Wor (imp). Yk.

14604 Jewel, John, 1584
Ex. Linc.

14606 Jewel, John, 1565
Bur. Linc (tpw). Sal (2). Yk.

14606.5 Jewel, John, 1565
Pet.

14607 Jewel, John, 1566
Cant. Carl. Pet. S Pl. Sal.
Win. Yk.

14608 Jewel, John, 1578
Her (imp)*. Pet. Rip.

14612 Jewel, John, [1560]
Ex. Pet. S Pl.

14613.5 Jewel, John, 1582
S Pl.

14615 Jewel, John, 1562
Bur.

14622 Joannes, *Metropolitanus
Euchaitensis*, 1610
Linc.

14628 Johann Justus, 1610
Pet.

14629a John, *Chrysostom, St*, 1613
Cant (imp). Ches. Chi. Dur.
Ely. Ex (lacks vol. 1). Glo. Her.
Linc. Liv. Llan (imp). Pet. Rip.
Roch. S Pl (vols 3, 5 − 8 only).
Sal. Swar (vol. 3 only, tpw). Wel.
Win. Wor (vols 1 − 3 only). Yk.

14630 John, *Chrysostom, St*, 1545
Carl.

14633 John, *Chrysostom, St,* 1597
Yk.

14636 John, *Chrysostom, St,* 1590
Pet. Rip.

14651 John, *of the Cross,* 1623
Pet. Wor. Yk.

14654 John XXI, *Pope,* 1585
Pet.

14658 Johnson, Francis, 1600
Pet. Yk.

14659 Johnson, Francis, 1609
Linc.

14660 Johnson, Francis, 1608
Pet. Yk.

14661 Johnson, Francis, 1617
Win.

14662 Johnson, Francis, 1606
Dur.

14663.5 Johnson, Francis, [1595]
Pet (imp). Yk (2).

14664 Johnson, George, 1603
Linc (imp).

14665 Johnson, Jacobus, 1615
Linc.

14682 Johnson, Richard, [1626]
Linc (pt 1 tp imp).

14689.3 Johnson, Richard, [1634?]
Liv (imp).

14691.1 Johnson, Richard, *Moralist,*
1598
Sal.

14692 Johnson, Robert, *B.D.,* 1633
Wor.

14693 Johnson, Robert, *B.D.,* 1624
Her.

14694 Johnson, Robert, *Chaplain,*
1609
S Pl.

14694.5 Johnson, Robert, *Chaplain,*
1628
Pet.

14715 Johnston, Thomas, 1630
Ex.

14715.5 Johnston, William, 1635
Linc.

14720 Jones, John, *B.D.,* 1615
Linc.

14721.5 Jones, John, *M.A.,* 1639
Ex.

14722 Jones, John, *M.A.,* 1633
Pet. S Pl.

14724a.3 Jones, John, *M.D.,* (1572)
Pet.

14724a.7 Jones, John, *M.D.,* [1572]
Pet.

14728 Jones, Philip, 1588
Yk.

14739.5 Jones, William, *of Suffolk,*
1635
Ex. Wor.

14739.8 Jones, William, *of Suffolk,*
1636
Wel.

14741 Jones, William, *of Wight,*
1631
Ex.

14744.5 Jones, William, *of Wight,*
1633
Ex.

14753 Jonson, Benjamin, 1640
Nor. Yk.

14754 Jonson, Benjamin, 1640
(1631, 1641)
Linc (imp). Nor (vol. 3 only).
Sal (vol. 3 only).

14754a Jonson, Benjamin, 1640
(1641)
Cant.

14756 Jonson, Benjamin, 1604
Ex (frag.). Linc.

14780 Jonson, Benjamin, 1631
Cant.

14786 Jonston, John, 1603
Linc.

14787 Jonston, John, 1602
Linc.

14792 Jorden, Edward, 1632
Carl (imp). Ex (tpw).

14798 Joseph, *ben Gorion, pseud.,*
1575
Cant. Pet.

14805 Joseph, *ben Gorion, pseud.,*
1615
Carl.

14809 Josephus, Flavius, 1602
Linc (imp).

14810 Josephus, Flavius, 1609
Cant (imp). Her.

14813a Josephus, Flavius, 1640
Glo.

14814 Josephus, Flavius, 1590
Pet.

14815 Josiah, [1590?]
Pet. Yk.

14823 Joye, George, (1545)
Pet. Wor.

14824 Joye, George, (1550)
Pet. S Pl.

14825 Joye, George, (1550)
Pet (imp).

14826 Joye, George, (1543)
Pet.

14828 Joye, George, (1544)
Linc.

14828.5 Joye, George, 1546
Rip.

14841.5 Julius II, *Pope,* [1534?]
Yk.

14860 Junius, Adrian, 1585
Cant. Liv. Pet. Yk.

14861 Junius, Adrian, 1554
Linc.

14873 Justices (Justice) of Peace,
[1535 – 37?]
Pet.

14882 Justices (Justice) of Peace,
(1559)
Pet (2).

14893.5 Juvencus, Caius Vettius
Aquilinus, [1534]
Dur.

14894.8 Keale *or* Kayll, Robert,
1615
Sal.

14895 Keckermann, Bartholomaeus,
1606
Sal.

14901 Keilwey, Robert, 1602
Cant. Yk.

14903 Kellet, Edward, 1633
Ex. Wel.

14904 Kellet, Edward, 1635
Linc.

14905 Kellet, Edward, 1628
S Asa.

14911 Kellison, Matthew, 1621
Pet.

14912 Kellison, Matthew, 1603
Yk.

14913 Kellison, Matthew, 1605
Pet (2).

14914 Kellison, Matthew, 1629
Linc.

14920 Keltridge, John, 1578
Pet.

14921 Keltridge, John, [1581]
Pet.

14943 Kethe, William, [1571?]
S Pl (frag.).

14944.5 Kett, Francis, 1585
Pet.

14946 Key, 1599
Pet.

14948 Kichener, Nathaniel, 1616
Linc (tpw).

14951 Kilby, Richard, *of Derby*, 1614
Yk.

14954.7- Kilby, Richard, *of Derby*, 1614
[Anr ed. of STC 14954.7] 8°;
Cambridge, C. Legge, sold by M. Law.
Yk.

14959.5 Kimedoncius, Jacobus, 1598
Pet. Sal.

14960 Kimedoncius, Jacobus, 1598
Cant. Sal.

14964 King, Edward, 1638
Linc.

14965 King, Henry, 1628
Bur (tpw). S Pl.

14967 King, Henry, 1634
Chi. Linc. Sal.

14968 King, Henry, 1626
Ely (tpw).

14969 King, Henry, 1621
Cant (imp). Ex (2). S Pl.

14969.5 King, Henry, 1621
Yk (2).

14970 King, Henry, 1640
Cant (imp). S Pl (2).

14971 King, Henry, 1627
Cant. Yk (tp imp).

14972 King, Henry, 1625
Roch. Wel. Yk (pt 2 only).

14974 King, John, *Bp*, 1606
Wor.

14975 King, John, *Bp*, 1607
Bur. Lich. Pet (2). Yk (3).

14976 King, John, *Bp*, 1597
Bur. Lich (tpw). Pet.

14977 King, John, *Bp*, 1599
Her (tp imp). Pet (imp). Swel. Wor. Yk (ı ag.).

14978 King, John, *Bp*, 1600
Carl. Linc. Yk.

14979 King, John, *Bp*, 1611
Cant. Chelm. Liv. Nor. S Asa. Win. Yk (imp?).

14981 King, John, *Bp*, 1618
Chi. Dur. Ex. Sal. Yk (imp?).

14982 King, John, *Bp*, 1620
Linc. Pet. S Pl.

14983 King, John, *Bp*, 1619
Yk (imp)*.

14984 King, John, *Bp*, 1619
Cant. Linc. S Pl*. Wel*. Yk (2 − 1 imp).

14984.5 King, John, *Bp*, 1619
Linc (tp imp). Nor.

14985 King, John, *Bp*, 1607
Pet.

14986 King, John, *Bp*, 1608
Ex. S Pl. Yk.

14987 King, John, *Bp*, 1608
Pet (2 − both imp).

14989.5 King, John, *Bp*, 1614
Linc. Nor.

14990 King, John, *Bp*, 1614
Pet (imp). Yk.

14992 King, John, *Public Orator*, 1625
Pet. Yk.

15006 Kingsmill, Thomas, 1605
Yk.

15011 Kirchmeyer, Thomas, 1570
Pet.

15018 Kitchen, John, 1581
Rip.

15022 Kitchen, John, 1598
Glo. Pet.

15024 Kitchen, John, 1613
Glo. Pet. Wor.

15033.3 Knell, Thomas, 1581
S Pl (imp).

15037.5 Knewstub, John, 1579
Yk.

15040 Knewstub, John, 1579
Cant. Pet (2 − 1 imp). S Pl. Yk (2).

15042 Knewstub, John, 1577
Rip (tp imp).

15043 Knewstub, John, 1578
Rip (imp).

15044 Knewstub, John, 1579
Cant. Pet.

15045 Knewstub, John, 1584
Pet.

15049 Knight, William, 1610
Her. Sal.

15051 Knolles, Richard, 1603
Bur. Pet.

15052 Knolles, Richard, 1610
Bur. Lich (tpw).

15053 Knolles, Richard, 1621 (1620)
Glo.

15054 Knolles, Richard, 1631
Glo. Linc.

15055 Knolles, Richard, 1638
Cant. Ely. Ex. Wel (2). Yk.

15060 Knox, John, 1560
Linc. Pet. Yk.

15063 Knox, John, 1558
Yk.

15067 Knox, John, 1558
Yk.

15071 Knox, John, [1587]
Linc (2 − 1 imp). S Pl (imp). Yk.

15075 Knox, John, 1566
Pet.

15077 Komenský, Jan Amos, 1637
S Pl.

15082 Komenský, Jan Amos, 1639
Her.

15083 Korydaleus, Theophilos, 1625
S Pl.

15087 Kyd, Thomas, 1594
Cant (does not match Greg's running-titles)*.

15099 Kynaston, *Sir* Francis, 1636
Dur.

15102 L., A., 1589
Pet.

15109.3 L., R., 1549
Linc.

15111.5 L., T., 1610
Sal.

15117 Lacey, William, *pseud.*, 1639
New Halkett & Laing attrib. to William Wolfe.
Sal.

15134 Lake, Arthur, 1629
Bur (2). Ex. Llan (tpw). Pet. S Asa. S Pl. Wel. Wor.

15135 Lake, Arthur, 1640
Carl. Linc.

15136 Lake, Osmund, 1612
S Pl.

15137 L'Allouette, Edmond de, [1585−86]
Pet.

15139 La Marche, Olivier de, 1594
Pet.

15142 Lambard, William, 1568
Cant. Chi. Ex (2). Pet. Yk.

15143 Lambard, William, 1635
'commentary'
Cant (imp). Carl (imp).

15144 Lambard, William, 1635
Linc.

15157 Lambard, William, 1606
Cant (2).

15158.5 Lambard, William, 1612
Pet.

15159 Lambard, William, 1614
Nor.

15160 Lambard, William, 1619
Yk.

15161 Lambard, William, 1624
Pet.

15163 Lambard, William, 1581
Pet (2).

15169 Lambard, William, 1599
Pet.

15171 Lambard, William, 1607
Cant (2).

15172 Lambard, William, 1610
Nor (date imp)*.

15174 Lambard, William, 1619
Yk.

15175 Lambard, William, 1576
Cant (2 − both imp). Glo. Lich.
Pet.

15176 Lambard, William, 1596
Cant (2 − 1 tpw). Linc. Nor.
S Asa. S Pl.

15179 Lambert, François, 1536
Glo. Pet.

15188 Lancaster, Thomas, [1550?]
Yk.

15192 Lanfrancus, *Mediolanensis*,
1565
Pet (2 − 1 imp).

15195 Langham, William, 1579
[=1597]
Pet.

15198.5 Langhorne, Launcelot,
1624
Linc (imp).

15206 Langton, Robert, (1522)
Linc.

15206.5 Languedoc, Reformed
Churches, 1574
Rip (imp).

15207.5 Languet, Hubert, 1581
Linc.

15211 Languet, Hubert, 1579
Pet. Wor.

15215 La Noue, François de, 1587
(1588)
Linc. Pet.

15217.5 Lanquet, Thomas, (1559)
Linc. Yk.

15218 Lanquet, Thomas, 1560
Cant (without the cancels). Her.

15220 Lanquet, Thomas, 1565
Pet.

15225 Lantern, [1535?]
Pet.

15228.5 La Perrière, Guillaume de,
1598
Pet.

15230.5 La Place, Pierre de, 1578
Pet.

15231 La Place, Pierre de, 1576
Pet.

15233 La Primaudaye, Pierre de,
1586
Pet. Yk.

15234 La Primaudaye, Pierre de,
1589
Pet. Yk.

15236 La Primaudaye, Pierre de,
1602
Lich.

15238 La Primaudaye, Pierre de,
1594
Her (imp).

15241 La Primaudaye, Pierre de,
1618
Her. Wor.

15241.7 La Ramée, Pierre de, 1574
Pet.

15242 La Ramée, Pierre de, 1576
Rip.

15243 La Ramée, Pierre de, 1584
Carl. Pet. Wor.

15244 La Ramée, Pierre de, 1589
Yk.

15251 La Ramée, Pierre de, 1636
Wor.

15255 La Roche de Chandieu,
Antoine, 1584
Cant. Her (2). Pet.

15257 La Roche de Chandieu,
Antoine, 1583
Pet.

15259 Lasco, Joannes à, 1552
Rip (imp). Sal.

15267.3 Latham, Simon, 1615
Cant.

15268.3 Latham, Simon, 1618
Cant.

15272 Latimer, Hugh, [1549]
Cant.

15272.5 Latimer, Hugh, [1549]
Pet.

15274.3 Latimer, Hugh, [1549]
Cant.

15274.7 Latimer, Hugh, [1549]
Pet.

15276 Latimer, Hugh, 1562
Linc.

15277 Latimer, Hugh, (1572, 1571)
Linc (imp). Nor.

15279 Latimer, Hugh, (1578)
Lich. Pet (imp?).

15280 Latimer, Hugh, 1584
Cant. S Pl (imp)*.

15281 Latimer, Hugh, 1596
Tru.

15282 Latimer, Hugh, 1607
New. Nor.

15283 Latimer, Hugh, 1635
Bur. Cant (2). Carl. Llan. Pet.
Roch. Yk (2).

15290 Latimer, Hugh, [1553?]
Pet.

15291 Latimer, Hugh, [1548]
Pet.

15293 Latimer, Hugh, [1550]
Pet.

15297 Latteburius, Joannes, (1482)
Linc.

15298 Laud, William, 1639
Bris. Bur (2). Carl. Ches (2).
Dur. Ely (imp). Ex. Glo. Her
(2). IoM. Linc. Liv. S Dv.
S Pl. Wel. Win. Yk (2).

15299 Laud, William, 1639
Bur. Cant (2). Pet.

15300 Laud, William, 1622
Cant (2 − 1 imp). Linc. Yk.

15301 Laud, William, 1621
Cant (imp). Linc. Yk.

15302 Laud, William, 1625
Cant. Pet.

15303 Laud, William, 1626
Cant. Yk.

15304 Laud, William, 1625
Yk.

15305 Laud, William, 1628
Yk.

15305.5 Laud, William, 1628
Cant. Wor.

15306 Laud, William, 1637
Ex. Linc. Nor. S Asa. S Pl.
Sal.

15307 Laud, William, 1637
Bur. Cant (2 − 1 imp). Carl. Ex
(2). S Pl. Yk (2).

15309 Laud, William, 1638
Linc (imp). Yk.

15310.3 Laud, William, 1640
Cant. Nor (tpw).

15310.8 Laud, William, 1640
Linc.

15311 Lauder, George, 1623
Yk.

15317 Lauzière, Pons, *Marquis de Thémines*, 1593
Pet.

15318 La Vardin, Jacques de, 1596
Cant. Her. Pet.

15322 Lavater, Ludwig, 1596
Pet (tpw).

15324 Lawne, Christopher, 1612
Wor. Yk (2).

15325 Lawrence, John, 1624
Yk.

15326 Lawrence, Thomas, 1637
Ex (imp)*. Yk.

15326.5 Lawrence, Thomas, 1637
Ex. Linc.

15327 Lawrence, Thomas, 1637
Carl. Pet.

15328 Lawrence, Thomas, 1635
Ex.

15333 Layfielde, Edmund, 1630
Carl. Ex (2).

15334 Layfielde, Edmund, 1632
Ex (tpw).

15342 Leake, Richard, 1599
Pet.

15349 Lechmere, Edmund, 1632
Wor.

15354 Lee, Richard, 1625
Linc. S Pl.

15362 Leech, Humfrey, 1609
Pet.

15362.5 Leech, Humfrey, 1609
Yk.

15363 Leech, Humfrey, 1609
Pet (imp). Yk.

15363.7 Leech, Jeremy, 1607
Linc.

15364 Leech, Jeremy, 1619
Linc. Pet.

15374.3 Leech, John, *Schoolmaster*,
[c.1590?]
Pet.

15374.7 Leech, John, *Schoolmaster*,
1618
Cant.

15391 Legh, Gerard, (1591)
Dur (imp). Linc.

15392 Legh, Gerard, (1597)
Pet. Wor (tpw).

15393 Legh, Gerard, 1612
Yk (2 − 1 imp).

15411 Leigh, Edward, 1633
Sal.

15412 Leigh, Richard, 1588
Pet. S Asa.

15417 Leigh, Valentine, 1578
Rip.

15422 Leigh, William, 1605
Linc.

15423 Leigh, William, 1613
Linc.

15423.3 Leigh, William, 1615
Linc.

15423.5 Leigh, William, 1610
Linc.

15425 Leigh, William, 1606
Yk (2).

15428.5 Leighton, Alexander,
[1629]
Win (tpw).

15429 Leighton, Alexander, [1629?]
Yk.

15439 Leius, Matthias, 1623
Linc.

15440 Leland, John, 1544
Her. Linc. S Pl.

15442 Leland, John, 1546
Her. Linc. S Pl.

15443 Leland, John, 1543
Her. S Pl. Sal.

15444.5 Leland, John, 1545
Cant. Ex. Her. Linc. S Pl.

15446 Leland, John, 1542
S Pl.

15447 Leland, John, 1589
Linc.

15448 Le Loyer, Pierre, 1605
Yk.

15451 Le Maçon, Robert, 1600
Pet.

15454 Lemnius, Levinus, 1587
Pet.

15456 Lemnius, Levinus, 1576
Pet.

15462 Lenthall, William, 1640
Pet.

15469 Lentulo, Scipio, 1575
Linc (imp).

15470 Lentulo, Scipio, 1587
Ex.

15481 Leo, John, *Africanus*, 1600
Her. Lich.

15485 Le Petit, Jean François, 1609
Pet.

15488 Le Roy, Louis, 1594
Pet.

15492 Lescarbot, Marc, [after 1625]
Yk (imp).

15494 Leslie, Henry, 1625
Pet. Wor.

15495 Leslie, Henry, 1627
Pet. S Asa.

15496 Leslie, Henry, 1639
Win.

15497 Leslie, Henry, 1639
Dur.

15499 Leslie, Henry, 1637
Yk.

15502 Leslie, Henry, 1625
Pet.

15507 Leslie, John, 1584
Yk.

15511a L'Espine, Jean de, 1587
Yk.

15516 L'Espine, Jean de, 1592
Rip.

15537 Lever, Christopher, 1627
Pet. Wel. Yk.

15541 Lever, Ralph, 1573
Linc.

15543.5 Lever, Thomas, 1550
S Pl.

15546 Lever, Thomas, [1551]
S Pl.

15547 Lever, Thomas, (1550)
S Pl.

15551 Lever, Thomas, 1572
Linc.

15551.5 Lever, Thomas, 1571
Pet.

15556 Lewes, Richard, 1594
Linc.

15558 Lewis, John, 1620
Linc.

15559 Lewis, John, 1624
Her.

15564 Lewkenor, *Sir* Lewis, 1595
Linc. Pet (2).

15565 Lewkenor, *Sir* Lewis, 1596
Yk.

15566 Lewkenor, Samuel, 1600
Cant.

15583.7 Libellus, [1535?]
Pet.

15593 Lightfoot, John, 1629
Linc. S Pl. Yk.

15597 Lilburne, John, [1640]
Yk.

15613 Lily, William, 1557
Rip (pt 2 only, imp)*.

15627.6 Lily, William, 1628
Ely.

15628 Lily, William, 1630 (1631)
Wel (pt 2 only).

15634 Linacre, Thomas, (1524)
Cant. Pet (tp imp).

15646 Lincoln, *Diocese of*, 1605
Ex. S Asa. Yk (2).

15648 Lincoln, *Diocese of*, 1638
Linc.

15653 Lindanus, Willelmus, 1565
Pet (imp).

15657 Lindsay, David, *Bp*, 1621
Ex. Linc. Pet. Win. Yk.

15662 Lindsay, *Sir* David, 1582
Pet (tpw).

15664 Lindsay, *Sir* David, 1597
Dur (imp).

15674.5 Lindsay, *Sir* David, 1558
Pet.

15676 Lindsay, *Sir* David, 1566
Pet.

15681.5 Lindsay, *Sir* David, 1602
Linc (imp)*.

15684 Lindsay, David, *Minister*, 1625
Cant.

15694 Lipsius, Justus, 1586
S Pl.

15697 Lipsius, Justus, 1586
Pet. S Pl.

15698 Lipsius, Justus, 1590
S Pl.

15700.7 Lipsius, Justus, 1590
S Pl.

15701 Lipsius, Justus, 1594
Ex (imp). Linc (imp). Pet. Yk.

15704 Lisbon, 1591
Linc.

15712 Lithgow, William, 1623
Ely (tpw)*. Linc.

15731.5 Littleton, *Sir* Thomas, 1539
Pet.

15733 Littleton, *Sir* Thomas, 1545
Glo.

15740 Littleton, *Sir* Thomas, 1569
Pet.

15743 Littleton, *Sir* Thomas, 1577
Pet.

15744 Littleton, *Sir* Thomas, 1579
Pet.

15747 Littleton, *Sir* Thomas, 1585
Rip.

15759? Littleton, *Sir* Thomas, 1639
12°.
Glo.

15763 Littleton, *Sir* Thomas, (1544)
Pet.

15767 Littleton, *Sir* Thomas, (1556)
Cant. Pet.

15773 Littleton, *Sir* Thomas, (1586)
Rip.

15780 Littleton, *Sir* Thomas, 1612
Pet.

15783 Littleton, *Sir* Thomas, 1627
Yk.

15784 Littleton, *Sir* Thomas, 16?8
Cant. Linc. Sal (2).

15786 Littleton, *Sir* Thomas, 1633
Pet. Wor (tpw).

15787 Littleton, *Sir* Thomas, 1639
Cant (imp).

15789 Littleton, *Sir* Thomas, 1630
Linc. Sal.

15790a Liturgies. Antiphoners, (1520)
Liv.

15793 Liturgies. Breviaries, 1505
Wor (imp).

15816 Liturgies. Breviaries, (1519)
Wor (P.E. only).

15818 Liturgies. Breviaries, (1524)
Yk.

15822 Liturgies. Breviaries, 1525 (1526)
Wor (P.H. only).

15829+ Liturgies. Breviaries, 1530
'Portiforiũ seu Breuiariũ ad vsum ecclesie Sarisburiẽsis'; 8°; Parisijs, in ed. J. kaerbriand necnõ Joannis petit impensis.
Ex.

15830 Liturgies. Breviaries, 1531
Liv (imp).

15832 Liturgies. Breviaries, 1533
Cant (P.H. only).

15833 Liturgies. Breviaries, (1535)
Cant (P.H. only, tpw). Tru (P.E. only, tpw). Yk (P.E. only).

15836 Liturgies. Breviaries, 1554 (1555)
Linc (tpw)*. S Pl (2 − 1 tpw*).

15837 Liturgies. Breviaries, 1555
Bur.

15839 Liturgies. Breviaries, 1555
Liv (P.E. only, imp). Yk (P.H. only).

15840 Liturgies. Breviaries, 1555
Pet (P.H. only). Yk (P.E. only, imp).

15842 Liturgies. Breviaries, 1556
Her (P.H. only). S Pl. Sal.

15844 Liturgies. Breviaries, 1556
Ely (P.E. only, imp).

15846 Liturgies. Breviaries, 1556
Cant (P.E. only). S Pl (P.E. only).

15847 Liturgies. Breviaries, 1556 (1557)
Cant (frag.). Ex (P.H. only). Liv. Yk (2 − both P.H. only).

15847.3 Liturgies. Breviaries, [1490]
Her (frag.).

15858 Liturgies. Breviaries, 1526
Yk (2 − both P.H. only).

15861+ Liturgies. Officium Novum, [c.1514]
[Supplement to the Sanctorale] 8°; (Ebor nouiter impresse per Ursyñ Mylner).
Her (frag.).

15864 Liturgies. Graduals, 1528
Liv (imp). Sal.

15869 Liturgies. Hours & Primers, [1485]
Linc (frag.).

15901.5 Liturgies. Hours & Primers, [c.1503]
Linc (imp).

15909 Liturgies. Hours & Primers, (1510)
S Pl (imp).

15913.5 Liturgies. Hours & Primers, [1512]
Win.

15915 Liturgies. Hours & Primers, [1513?]
Yk (imp).

15934 Liturgies. Hours & Primers, (1523)
Sal (imp).

15937 Liturgies. Hours & Primers, (1524)
Liv (imp). S Pl (imp).

15944 Liturgies. Hours & Primers, (1526)
Liv.

15957 Liturgies. Hours & Primers, 1528
Liv.

15973 Liturgies. Hours & Primers, 1531
Yk.

15979 Liturgies. Hours & Primers, 1533
Linc (imp).

15983 Liturgies. Hours & Primers, [1533?]
S Pl (tpw).

15991 Liturgies. Hours & Primers, (1536)
S Pl (imp).

15993 Liturgies. Hours & Primers, (1536)
Carl (imp)*.

15997 Liturgies. Hours & Primers, [1537?]
Cant (imp).

15998 Liturgies. Hours & Primers, [1538?]
Linc (imp).

16003 Liturgies. Hours & Primers, 1538
S Pl (imp).

16008.5 Liturgies. Hours & Primers, (1538)
Cant.

16012 Liturgies. Hours & Primers, [1539?]
Yk (tpw).

16017.5 Liturgies. Hours & Primers, [c.1540]
S Pl (imp).

16026 Liturgies. Hours & Primers, 1542
Linc (frag.). S Pl (imp).

16028.5 Liturgies. Hours & Primers, (1543)
Ex.

16029 Liturgies. Hours & Primers, (1543)
Cant. S Pl (imp)*.

16039 Liturgies. Hours & Primers, (1545)
Linc (imp; mixed sheets?).

16040 Liturgies. Hours & Primers, 1545
Cant (tpw). Dur (imp). Pet. Yk (imp).

16042 Liturgies. Hours & Primers, 1546
Linc.

16044 Liturgies. Hours & Primers, 1546
Nor. Tru. Yk.

16048 Liturgies. Hours & Primers, (1547)
Linc.

16057 Liturgies. Hours & Primers, 1552
Cant.

16058 Liturgies. Hours & Primers, 1554
Cant.

16059 Liturgies. Hours & Primers, 1554
S Pl (imp)*.

16060 Liturgies. Hours & Primers, 1555
Liv.

16063 Liturgies. Hours & Primers, 1555
Pet (imp).

16064 Liturgies. Hours & Primers, 1555
S Pl (imp).

16065 Liturgies. Hours & Primers, 1555
Cant.

16073.5 Liturgies. Hours & Primers, [1556?]
Linc (imp).

16081 Liturgies. Hours & Primers, 1557
Cant (imp).

16083 Liturgies. Hours & Primers, 1558
Linc (imp).

16084 Liturgies. Hours & Primers, 1558
Pet.

16085 Liturgies. Hours & Primers, 1558
Yk (imp).

16089 Liturgies. Hours & Primers, 1560
Liv. S Pl. Yk (tpw).

16094 Liturgies. Hours & Primers, 1599
S Pl (tpw)*.

16095 Liturgies. Hours & Primers, 1604
Cant. Yk.

16101.6 Liturgies. Hours & Primers, 1633
'rubrikes'
Liv (v. imp). Yk.

16103 Liturgies. Hours & Primers, [1516?]
Yk (imp).

16104.5 Liturgies. Hours & Primers, (1520)
Yk (imp).

16105 Liturgies. Hours & Primers, [1532?]
Yk (tpw).

16106 Liturgies. Hours & Primers, (1536)
Linc (imp).

16107 Liturgies. Hours & Primers, 1555
Yk.

16109 Liturgies. Hours & Primers, [1557?]
Yk (frag.).

16109.5 Liturgies. Hours & Primers, [1557?]
Yk (frag.).

16110 Liturgies. Hymns, [1496]
Linc. Pet (pt 2 only).

16111 Liturgies. Hymns, [1496]
Linc.

16122 Liturgies. Hymns, (1510)
S Pl.

16129.3 Liturgies. Hymns, (1518)
Liv.

16131 Liturgies. Hymns, (1525)
S Pl.

16137 Liturgies. Legenda, (1518)
Liv (imp).

16141.5 Liturgies. Manuals, (1515)
Liv (imp).

16148.2 Liturgies. Manuals, 1530
Linc.

16148.6 Liturgies. Manuals, 1537
Glo (imp).

16151 Liturgies. Manuals, 1554
S Pl (imp).

16152 Liturgies. Manuals, 1554
Her (imp). Yk.

16153 Liturgies. Manuals, 1554
Pet (frag.)*.

16155 Liturgies. Manuals, 1554
Glo. Liv.

16158 Liturgies. Manuals, 1604
Liv. Sal.

16159 Liturgies. Manuals, 1610
Ely.

16163 Liturgies. Missals, 1502
Glo (imp).

16174 Liturgies. Missals, (1500)
Win.

16175 Liturgies. Missals, 1500
Date is probably 1502.
Ely.

16179 Liturgies. Missals, (1504)
Win (frag.).

16186 Liturgies. Missals, (1509)
Yk (frag.).

16188 Liturgies. Missals, 1510
(1511)
Win (imp). Yk.

16193 Liturgies. Missals, (1514)
Liv.

16195 Liturgies. Missals, 1515
Yk (imp).

16197 Liturgies Missals, 1516
Wor (imp).

16201 Liturgies. Missals, (1519)
Sal (imp).

16205 Liturgies. Missals, 1526
Tru (imp). Wel (imp). Yk (tpw).

16205+ Liturgies. Missals, 1526
(1527)
'Missale ad vsum insiginis [sic] ...';
4°; In alma Parisiorum acad., (per F. regnault).
Yk.

16206 Liturgies. Missals, (1527)
Sal.

16208 Liturgies. Missals, 1527
Liv (imp).

16212 Liturgies. Missals, 1532
Her.

16213 Liturgies. Missals, 1533
Linc. Pet.

16214 Liturgies. Missals, 1534
Chi. Roch. S Pl.

16217 Liturgies. Missals, 1555
Cant. Ches (imp). Liv (imp).
Wor (imp).

16218 Liturgies. Missals, 1555
Ely. S Pl (imp).

16219 Liturgies. Missals, 1557
Liv.

16221 Liturgies. Missals, 1516
Yk (imp).

16222 Liturgies. Missals, 1517
Linc.

16224 Liturgies. Missals, 1533
Liv (imp).

16224.7 Liturgies. Missals, [1555?]
Tru.

16227 Liturgies. Missals, 1626
Ex. Liv (imp). Sal. Yk.

16232.4 Liturgies. Ordinals, (1509)
Yk (imp).

16237 Liturgies. Processionals, 1528
S Pl.

16242 Liturgies. Processionals, 1544
Wel. Yk.

16243 Liturgies. Processionals, 1545
Yk.

16244 Liturgies. Processionals, 1554
Her (imp)*. Liv.

16246 Liturgies. Processionals, 1555
Her (imp). Linc (imp).

16247 Liturgies. Processionals, 1555
Wor.

16251 Liturgies. Processionals, 1530
Linc (imp).

16259.3 Liturgies. Psalters, [c.1517]
Yk (imp).

16260 Liturgies. Psalters, (1522)
Yk (imp).

16265 Liturgies. Psalters, [1555]
Yk.

16266 Liturgies. Psalters, 1555
Linc. Liv.

16267 Liturgies. Book of Common
Prayer, 1549
S Asa (imp)*.

16269 Liturgies. Book of Common
Prayer, 1549
Cant (imp). Wor. Yk (imp).

16270 Liturgies. Book of Common
Prayer, 1549
Glo (imp)*.

16270a Liturgies. Book of Common
Prayer, 1549
Liv (imp). S Asa (imp)*.

16271 Liturgies. Book of Common
Prayer, 1549
Cant (imp).

16272 Liturgies. Book of Common
Prayer, 1549
S Asa (with tp of STC 16269?)*.

16273 Liturgies. Book of Common
Prayer, 1549
Cant. Rip. Win. Yk (imp).

16279 Liturgies. Book of Common
Prayer, 1552
Ex*. Liv (imp)*.

16281 Liturgies. Book of Common
Prayer, 1552
Cant (2 − 1: imp; Act 2, rubric
insert 2a, errata 1 subst. for
BB12; 2: imp; Act 2, rubric insert
2a). Linc (imp)*.

16281.5 Liturgies. Book of
Common Prayer, 1552
Cant (rubric insert 2b; imp).

16285 Liturgies. Book of Common
Prayer, 1552
Wel (tpw). Win*.

16285.7 Liturgies. Book of
Common Prayer, 1552
Yk (imp).

16285a Liturgies. Book of Common
Prayer, 1552
Cant (imp; 'C' of sig. C2 under
'ak' of 'awake')*.

16287 Liturgies. Book of Common
Prayer, 1552
Wor (imp).

16288a Liturgies. Book of Common
Prayer, [1553?]
S Pl (imp).

16292 Liturgies. Book of Common
Prayer, 1559
Linc (imp).

16292a Liturgies. Book of Common
Prayer, 1559 [1561?]
Yk (imp; variant no. 4.).

16296 Liturgies. Book of Common
Prayer, (1564)
Cant (Psalter only)*.

16296.5 Liturgies. Book of
Common Prayer, (1565)
New (v. imp)*. S Asa (imp).

16304.5 Liturgies. Book of
Common Prayer, (1574)
Win (imp).

16304.6 Liturgies. Book of
Common Prayer, 1574
Impr. and date on tp; Last printed
leaf is Dd7.
Cant (lacks Psalter).

16304.7 Liturgies. Book of
Common Prayer, (1575)
Cant (lacks Psalter)*.

16306.5 Liturgies. Book of
Common Prayer, (1577)
Linc (imp).

16309.8 Liturgies. Book of
Common Prayer, [1584?]
Glo (imp).

16311.3 Liturgies. Book of
Common Prayer, 1586
Liv.

16311.7 Liturgies. Book of
Common Prayer, 1587
Dur.

16311.9 Liturgies. Book of
Common Prayer, [1587?]
Cant (imp).

16314 Liturgies. Book of Common
Prayer, 1589
Cant (imp)*.

16321.5 Liturgies. Book of
Common Prayer, 1596
S Asa (tpw).

16321a Liturgies. Book of Common
Prayer, 1596
Linc.

16322 Liturgies. Book of Common
Prayer, 1596 (1597)
Nor (tpw).

16323 Liturgies. Book of Common
Prayer, 1599
Cant (sigs C−E only). S Asa.

16323.5 Liturgies. Book of
Common Prayer, 1600
Cant (imp). Dur (imp).

16324.3+ Liturgies. Book of
Common Prayer, 1600 (1601)
[Anr ed.] 8°; R. Barker; 1 col., B.L.,
A−Z⁸ Aa−Nn⁸.
Cant.

16326.5 Liturgies. Book of
Common Prayer, 1603 [o.s.]
Linc (tpw).

16327 Liturgies. Book of Common
Prayer, 1604
Carl (tpw).

16328.5 Liturgies. Book of
Common Prayer, 1604
Swel.

16328a Liturgies. Book of Common
Prayer, 1604
Linc.

16329 Liturgies. Book of Common
Prayer, 1605
Cant.

16330.3 Liturgies. Book of
Common Prayer, 1606
Cant (imp)*.

16332 Liturgies. Book of Common
Prayer, 1607
Ely. Her.

16332.8 Liturgies. Book of
Common Prayer, 1608
Cant (imp)*.

16336 Liturgies. Book of Common
Prayer, 1611
Lich.

16337 Liturgies. Book of Common
Prayer, 1611
Yk (imp).

16338.3 Liturgies. Book of
Common Prayer, 1613
S Asa.

16341.5 Liturgies. Book of
Common Prayer, 1614
Cant (imp). Linc. S Alb*.
S Asa (frag.).

16343 Liturgies. Book of Common
Prayer, 1615
Dur (imp).

16344 Liturgies. Book of Common
Prayer, 1615
Lich*.

16344.5 Liturgies. Book of
Common Prayer, 1615
Cant (tpw)*.

16345.5 Liturgies. Book of
Common Prayer, 1615
Carl (imp)*.

16347 Liturgies. Book of Common
Prayer, 1616
Cant. Dur (imp)*. Linc (imp).

16347a Liturgies. Book of Common
Prayer, 1616
Sal.

16349 Liturgies. Book of Common
Prayer, 1617
Dur (Psalter only). Sal.

16349.7 Liturgies. Book of
Common Prayer, 1618
Win (imp)*.

16350 Liturgies. Book of Common
Prayer, 1618
Cant.

16353 Liturgies. Book of Common
Prayer, 1619
Sal (tpw). Yk.

16354 Liturgies. Book of Common
Prayer, 1620
Ex.

16357 Liturgies. Book of Common
Prayer, 1621
S Alb*.

16357.3 Liturgies. Book of
Common Prayer, 1621
Win.

16357.7 Liturgies. Book of
Common Prayer, 1621
Cant (imp).

16364 Liturgies. Book of Common
Prayer, 1625
Linc.

16365 Liturgies. Book of Common
Prayer, 1625
S Asa.

16366 Liturgies. Book of Common
Prayer, 1626
Liv (imp).

16368 Liturgies. Book of Common
Prayer, 1627
Cant. Chi (tpw). Linc (imp).

16369.3 Liturgies. Book of
Common Prayer, 1627
Pet (imp).

16369.7 Liturgies. Book of
Common Prayer, 1627
Cant (tpw). Sal (tpw).

16370 Liturgies. Book of Common
Prayer, 1627
Cant.

16370.5 Liturgies. Book of
Common Prayer, 1627
Ely.

16372 Liturgies. Book of Common
Prayer, [1628?]
Roch (imp)*.

16374 Liturgies. Book of Common
Prayer, 1629
Ex. Her. Roch.

16375 Liturgies. Book of Common
Prayer, 1629
Liv. Nor. Wor.

16376 Liturgies. Book of Common
Prayer, 1629
Sal (imp)*.

16378 Liturgies. Book of Common
Prayer, 1630
Cant. Ely.

16380 Liturgies. Book of Common
Prayer, 1630
Ely.

16380.9 Liturgies. Book of
Common Prayer, 1630
Linc (imp).

16383 Liturgies. Book of Common
Prayer, 1631
Yk.

16385 Liturgies. Book of Common
Prayer, 1631
Sal.

16385.7 Liturgies. Book of
Common Prayer, 1632
Tru (imp)*.

16387 Liturgies. Book of Common
Prayer, 1632
Tru (2)*.

16390 Liturgies. Book of Common
Prayer, 1633 (1632)
Yk.

16391 Liturgies. Book of Common
Prayer, 1633 (1632)
Sal (imp)*. Win (imp). Yk (tpw).

16392 Liturgies. Book of Common
Prayer, 1633
Lich.

16393 Liturgies. Book of Common
Prayer, 1633
Chi*.

16393.5 Liturgies. Book of
Common Prayer, 1633
Yk.

16397.3 Liturgies. Book of
Common Prayer, 1634
Glo. Wor. Yk.

16397.7 Liturgies. Book of
Common Prayer, 1634
Bris (imp)*. Nor (tpw). Sal.

16398 Liturgies. Book of Common
Prayer, 1634
Cant.

16399.5 Liturgies. Book of
Common Prayer, 1634
Cant.

16401 Liturgies. Book of Common
Prayer, 1635
Liv. Tru.

16403 Liturgies. Book of Common
Prayer, 1636
Cant (tpw). Pet.

16404.4 Liturgies. Book of
Common Prayer, 1636
Wel. Wor.

16405 Liturgies. Book of Common
Prayer, 1637
Yk (2 – 1 imp*).

16406 Liturgies. Book of Common
Prayer, 1637
Cant. Linc (imp). Wel (tpw)*.

16408 Liturgies. Book of Common
Prayer, 1637
Ex. Lich.

16409 Liturgies. Book of Common
Prayer, 1638
Her.

16410 Liturgies. Book of Common
Prayer, 1638
Cant. Chi. Win. Yk (imp).

16411 Liturgies. Book of Common
Prayer, 1638
Her.

16412 Liturgies. Book of Common
Prayer, 1638
Lich.

16413 Liturgies. Book of Common
Prayer, 1638
Yk.

16413.3 Liturgies. Book of
Common Prayer, 1638
Cant (imp).

16413.5 Liturgies. Book of
Common Prayer, 1638
Sal (tpw).

16414.3 Liturgies. Book of
Common Prayer, 1638
Yk.

16415 Liturgies. Book of Common
Prayer, 1638 (1639)
Roch.

16416 Liturgies. Book of Common
Prayer, 1639
Liv (tpw)*.

16417 Liturgies. Book of Common
Prayer, 1639
Cant. Chi. Lich. Linc. Pet
(imp).

16417.2 Liturgies. Book of
Common Prayer, 1639
Dur. S Asa.

16417.3 Liturgies. Book of
Common Prayer, 1639
S Pl.

16417.5 Liturgies. Book of
Common Prayer, 1639
Linc (tp imp).

16418a Liturgies. Book of Common
Prayer, 1639
Cant. Sal. Yk.

16421 Liturgies. Book of Common
Prayer, 1640
S Asa.

16421.5 Liturgies. Book of
Common Prayer, 1640
Yk (imp)*.

16422 Liturgies. Book of Common
Prayer, 1640
Yk (imp)*.

16424 Liturgies. Book of Common
Prayer, [1560]
Liv. Nor (imp).

16424a Liturgies. Book of Common
Prayer, [1560]
S Asa.

16426 Liturgies. Book of Common
Prayer, (1571, 1572)
Linc.

16427 Liturgies. Book of Common
Prayer, (1574)
Cant. Ches. Ex. S Pl (tpw).
Win (2). Yk (2 – 1 imp).

16428 Liturgies. Book of Common
Prayer, 1594
S Pl. Sal (tpw)*. Win.

16429 Liturgies. Book of Common
Prayer, 1604
Linc.

16429.5 Liturgies. Book of
Common Prayer, 1569
Linc.

16430 Liturgies. Book of Common
Prayer, 1553
Liv.

16431 Liturgies. Book of Common
Prayer, 1616
Linc. Liv. S Pl. Wor. Yk.

16432 Liturgies. Book of Common
Prayer, 1638
Ex (2). Linc. Tru (pt 2 only).
Win. Yk.

16433 Liturgies. Book of Common
Prayer, 1608
Linc (imp). Wor (imp).

16434 Liturgies. Book of Common
Prayer, [1623]
Ches. Her. S Pl.

16437 Liturgies. Book of Common
Prayer, 1599
S Asa (imp).

16438 Liturgies. Book of Common
Prayer, 1621
S Asa (tpw). Wel.

16439 Liturgies. Book of Common Prayer, 1630
S Asa (tpw).

16440 Liturgies. Book of Common Prayer, 1634
Ban (imp). Linc. Liv (imp).
S Asa (imp).

16447 Liturgies. Book of Common Prayer, 1615
Linc.

16448.7 Liturgies. Book of Common Prayer, [c.1640]
S Asa.

16450 Liturgies. Book of Common Prayer, 1606
Linc. Wor.

16451 Liturgies. Book of Common Prayer, 1610
Yk (imp).

16452 Liturgies. Book of Common Prayer, 1637
Win.

16457 Liturgies. Communion, (1548)
S Pl.

16461 Liturgies. Catechism, 1633
Yk.

16462.5 Liturgies. Ordinal, 1549
Linc. New*. S Pl*.

16466.5 Liturgies. Ordinal, 1596
Nor.

16468 Liturgies. Ordinal, 1618
Linc.

16469 Liturgies. Ordinal, 1627
Cant. Linc.

16470 Liturgies. Ordinal, 1629
Cant.

16474 Liturgies. Ordinal, 1634
Yk.

16475 Liturgies. Ordinal, 1636
Cant.

16478 Liturgies. Ordinal, 1639
Liv.

16481 *See*: 4089.5

16483 Liturgies. State Services, [1604]
Win. Yk.

16484 Liturgies. State Services, [1620]
Linc.

16485 Liturgies. State Services, 1626
Cant. Linc.

16489 Liturgies. State Services, 1603
Win.

16492 Liturgies. State Services, 1623
Linc.

16494 Liturgies. State Services, [1606?]
Dur. Yk.

16496.5 Liturgies. State Services, 1623
Linc.

16501 Liturgies. State Services, 1638
Pet.

16502 Liturgies. State Services, 1640
Rip.

16504+ Liturgies. Special Forms of Prayer, [1562?]
'A prayer for the present estate'; 8°;
(R. Iugge and I. Cawood).
Her (frag.; proof sheets?).

16505 Liturgies. Special Forms of Prayer, [1563]
Yk.

16506 Liturgies. Special Forms of Prayer, [1563]
New*.

16506.3 Liturgies. Special Forms of Prayer, [1563]
Linc (imp). S Pl. Sal (imp)*.

16508.7 Liturgies. Special Forms of Prayer, [1565]
Sal.

16509 Liturgies. Special Forms of Prayer, (1565)
Sal.

16510 Liturgies. Special Forms of Prayer, [1566]
'realme'
Linc. Sal.

16511 Liturgies. Special Forms of Prayer, [1572]
Sal (imp).

16513 Liturgies. Special Forms of Prayer, (1580)
Sal (frag.)*. Yk.

16515 Liturgies. Special Forms of Prayer, 1585
Cant.

16516 Liturgies. Special Forms of Prayer, [1585]
Sal.

16517 Liturgies. Special Forms of Prayer, 1586
Sal.

16519 Liturgies. Special Forms of Prayer, 1588
Linc.

16524 Liturgies. Special Forms of Prayer, [1593]
Yk.

16525 Liturgies. Special Forms of Prayer, 1594
Yk.

16531 Liturgies. Special Forms of Prayer, 1600
Yk.

16532 Liturgies. Special Forms of Prayer, 1603
Linc.

16533 Liturgies. Special Forms of Prayer, 1604
Sal.

16540 Liturgies. Special Forms of Prayer, 1625
Yk.

16541 Liturgies. Special Forms of Prayer, 1625
Linc. Sal.

16542 Liturgies. Special Forms of Prayer, 1625
Linc. Sal.

16543 Liturgies. Special Forms of Prayer, 1626
Linc. Sal.

16546 Liturgies. Special Forms of Prayer, [1628]
Linc.

16547 Liturgies. Special Forms of Prayer, 1628
Win. Yk.

16547.5 Liturgies. Special Forms of Prayer, 1628
Linc. Sal.

16553a Liturgies. Special Forms of Prayer, 1636
Cant. Dur (imp). Pet.

16556 Liturgies. Special Forms of Prayer, 1639
Linc.

16557 Liturgies. Special Forms of Prayer, 1640
Cant. Linc. Pet. Yk.

16559 Liturgies. Special Forms of Prayer, 1640
Sal.

16561.5 Liturgies. Common Prayer used abroad, (1557)
Pet (imp).

16563 Liturgies. Common Prayer used abroad, 1561
S Pl.

16565 Liturgies. Common Prayer used abroad, 1556
S Pl. Yk.

16567 Liturgies. Common Prayer used abroad, [1585?]
'... common prayers ...'
Cant.

16568 Liturgies. Common Prayer used abroad, 1586
Linc (tpw). S Pl.

16574 Liturgies. Common Prayers used in London, 1556
Cant. Linc.

16577a Liturgies. Book of Common Order, 1565
Liv (imp).

16578 Liturgies. Book of Common Order, 1566
Pet (imp).

16579.5 Liturgies. Book of Common Order, 1575
S Pl (imp?).

16585.5 Liturgies. Book of Common Order, 1596
Linc.

16597 Liturgies. Book of Common Order, 1633
Chi.

16599 Liturgies. Book of Common Order, 1635
Ches. Ex. Liv (imp). New.

16606 Liturgies. Book of Common Prayer, 1637 (1636)
Cant (3). Ches. Ex (imp). Lich. Linc. Liv. New. S Asa. Wel. Wor. Yk (2 − 1 imp).

16607 Liturgies. Book of Common Prayer, 1636
Cant (2). Ches. Ex. Yk (2).

16608 Lively, Edward, 1587
Pet. Rip. Yk.

16609 Lively, Edward, 1597
Ches. Linc. Pet. Sal.

16611.5 Livius, Titus, 1589
Pet.

16612 Livius, Titus, 1589
Pet.

16612a Livius, Titus, 1589
Wor.

16616 Lloyd, Lodowick, 1602
Yk.

16618 Lloyd, Lodowick, 1607
Cant (imp).

16619 Lloyd, Lodowick, 1590
Her. Pet.

16621 Lloyd, Lodowick, 1590
Linc. Pet. Rip.

16628 Lloyd, Lodowick, [1600?]
Yk.

16629 Lloyd, Lodowick, 1602
Lich. Pet.

16630 Lloyd, Lodowick, 1602
Ex.

16631 Lloyd, Lodowick, 1607
Bur (tp imp).

16641.7 Loarte, Gaspare, 1584
Yk.

16644 Loarte, Gaspare, 1610
Wor (tp imp).

16676 Lodge, Thomas, 1603
Linc.

16683 Loe, William, *the Elder*, 1614
Glo.

16685 Loe, William, *the Elder*, 1609
S Pl. Yk.

16689 Loe, William, *the Elder*, 1619
Cant (imp).

16692 Loeus, Robertus, 1605
Pet. Wel (imp). Yk.

16693 Logici, [1483?]
Rip (frag.).

16694 Logie, Andrew, 1624
Pet. Wor.

16695 Lohetus, Daniel, 1618
Rip (tpw). Yk.

16696 Lok, Henry, 1597
Pet.

16703 London, 1596
S Asa.

16747 London, 1584
Pet.

16755 London, 1630
S Pl.

16769 London, College of Physicians, 1636
Cant. Carl.

16769.5 London, College of Physicians, 1636
Pet.

16788 Longinus, Dionysius Cassius, 1636
Carl. Nor (tpw)*. Wel (imp)*.

16789 Longinus, Dionysius Cassius, 1638
Ely. Ex.

16790 Longland, John, [1527?]
Yk (tpw).

16791 Longland, John, [1527?]
Linc. Yk.

16791.5 Longland, John, (1532)
Linc. Yk.

16793 Longland, John, [1527?]
Linc. S Pl. Yk (2).

16793.5 Longland, John, [1527?]
Linc. S Pl. Yk (2).

16795.5 Longland, John, [1535]
Pet.

16797 Longland, John, [1527?]
Linc. S Pl. Yk (2).

16798 Longueval, Charles Bonaventure de, *Comte de Bucquot*, 1621
Pet.

16805 Lopes, Duarte, 1597
Linc.

16806 Lopes de Castanheda, Fernam, 1582
Pet.

16812 Loque, Bertrand de, 1581
Pet.

16825 Lord, Henry, 1630
Linc (engr. tpw).

16828.5 Lougher, Robert, 1624
Yk.

16833 Louis XIII, *King of France*, 1616
Pet.

16835 Louis XIII, *King of France*, 1617
Pet.

16849.7 Louis I, *Prince de Condé*, 1562
Pet.

16852 Louis I, *Prince de Condé*, 1562
Pet.

16854 Loukaris, Cyril, *Patriarch*, 1629
Yk.

16869.5 Lowe, Peter, 1597
Pet (2 − 1 imp).

16871 Lowe, Peter, 1634
Sal.

16880 Lubin, Eilhard, 1629
Ex (imp).

16883 Lucanus, Marcus Annaeus, 1618
Ely. Yk.

16885a Lucanus, Marcus Annaeus, 1614
Lich.

16887 Lucanus, Marcus Annaeus, 1627
Lich.

16888 Lucanus, Marcus Annaeus, 1631
Linc. Nor.

16889 Lucanus, Marcus Annaeus, 1635
Cant (engr. tpw).

16890 Lucar, Cyprian, 1590
Pet.

16892.7 Lucian, 1636
Yk.

16893 Lucian, 1634
Wor.

16897 Lucinge, René de, 1606
Pet.

16899 Lugo, Peregrinus de, [1508?]
Linc.

16902 Luis, *de Granada*, 1598
Pet.

16903 Luis, *de Granada*, 1586
Pet. Yk.

16904 Luis, *de Granada*, 1599
Pet.

16908 Luis, *de Granada*, 1584
Yk.

16915 Luis, *de Granada*, 1633
Carl.

16918 Luis, *de Granada*, 1598
Pet (2 − 1 imp). Yk.

16922 Luis, *de Granada*, 1599
Yk.

16923 Luminalia, 1637
Linc.

16932 Lupset, Thomas, 1546
Pet.

16933 Lupset, Thomas, 1560
Pet.

16935 Lupset, Thomas, (1541)
Yk (tpw).

16937 Lupset, Thomas, (1538)
Yk.

16941 Lupset, Thomas, (1539)
Yk (tpw).

16943 Lupton, Donald, 1640
Cant. S Asa. Wor (tp imp). Yk.

16944 Lupton, Donald, 1632
S Pl.

16946 Lupton, Thomas, 1582
Yk.

16954.5 Lupton, Thomas, 1581
Pet.

16959 Lupton, Thomas, 1601
Pet.

16965 Luther, Martin, 1575
Bur. Cant (imp). Ex.

16966 Luther, Martin, 1577
Her (tpw)*. Yk.

16967 Luther, Martin, 1580
Cant (tpw). Win.

16968 Luther, Martin, 1588
Liv. Pet.

16973 Luther, Martin, 1616
Cant. Lich.

16975 Luther, Martin, 1577
Ex. Pet.

16975.5 Luther, Martin, 1577
Her (tpw). Rip.

16979 Luther, Martin, 1573
Pet.

16993 Luther, Martin, 1578
Cant (Fox). Pet (2 − 1 tpw).

16994? Luther, Martin, 1581
T. Voutroullier [*sic*].
Cant. Pet.

16996 Luther, Martin, 1579
Pet.

16998 Luther, Martin, (1578)
Yk (imp).

17004 Lycosthenes, Conrad, 1635
Wel.

17040 Lydiat, Thomas, 1607
Cant (imp). Rip. Wel.

17041 Lydiat, Thomas, 1609
Cant (imp). Linc. Win.

17043 Lydiat, Thomas, 1605
Ex. Wel.

17047 Lydiat, Thomas, 1605
Ex. Glo. Wel.

17064 Lyly, John, 1617
Nor (tpw).

17065 Lyly, John, (1623)
Cant. Pet.

17066 Lyly, John, 1631
Pet.

17089 Lyly, John, 1632
S Pl.

17095 Lynde, *Sir* Humphrey, 1630
Pet.

17096 Lynde, *Sir* Humphrey, 1632
Bur. Cant. Yk.

17098 Lynde, *Sir* Humphrey, 1629
Ely.

17099 Lynde, *Sir* Humphrey, 1629
Lich. Pet. Yk.

17100 Lynde, *Sir* Humphrey, 1630
Cant (tpw). Yk (imp).

17101 Lynde, *Sir* Humphrey, 1638
Bur. Cant. Ex (2). Her (pt 2 only). Linc. Pet (2 − 1 imp). Sal. Yk.

17102 Lyndewode, William, [1483]
Bur (imp). Dur. Her.

17107 Lyndewode, William, (1501)
Ches. Dur. S Pl. Sal. Yk.

17108 Lyndewode, William, (1504)
Cant. Ely. Lich. Linc (2 − 1 tpw). S Pl (2). Wel. Yk.

17109 Lyndewode, William, (1505)
Carl. Chelm. Dur (pt 2 only, imp). Ex (imp). Glo (tpw). Lich. Linc. New (imp). Pet. Rip. S Dv. Win.

17110 Lyndewode, William, (1517)
Pet.

17111 Lyndewode, William, (1525)
Lich. Linc. Pet. S Pl (2 − 1 imp*). Wor.

17112.5 Lyndewode, William, 1557
Linc. Swel.

17117 Lynne, Walter, 1550
S Pl.

17118 Lynne, Walter, 1563
Pet. S Pl.

17121 Lysias, 1593
Ches. Ex. Pet (2).

17123 Lyte, Henry, *the Younger*, 1619
Wor.

17130 M., Ch., 1635
Her.

17132 M., D.F.R. de, 1589
Linc. Pet.

17141 M., J., 1634
Ex.

17149.5 M., R., 1609
Yk.

17151 M., T., 1603
Pet.

17156.7 Mabb, John, 1609
Pet.

17160 Macchiavelli, Niccolò, 1636
Cant (B1 cancelled; italic).

17161 Macchiavelli, Niccolò, 1587
Yk (tp imp).

17162 Macchiavelli, Niccolò, 1595
Pet. Yk.

17166 Macchiavelli, Niccolò, 1588
Pet.

17167 Macchiavelli, Niccolò, 1584
Yk.

17173.5 Macey, George, 1601
Linc (tpw).

17176.4 Macropedius, Georgius,
1600
Pet.

17176.6 Macropedius, Georgius,
1609
Yk.

17176.7 Macropedius, Georgius,
1614
Wor.

17178 Maddison, *Sir* Ralph, 1640
Linc. Yk.

17179 Maden, Richard, 1637
Carl (tpw). Linc.

17183.5 Magirus, John, 1619
Her. Sal.

17197.5 Maihew, Edward, 1608
Pet. Yk.

17200 Mainardi, A., 1556
Linc. Sal.

17218 Malvezzi, Virgilio, 1637
Cant. Linc.

17219 Malvezzi, Virgilio, 1637
Cant. Carl.

17221 Malynes, Gerard de, 1623
Yk.

17224 Malynes, Gerard de, 1636
Glo.

17239.7 Mancinus, Dominicus,
1613
Wor.

17242.5 Mancinus, Dominicus,
[1520?]
Linc.

17274 Manual, 1613
Yk.

17277.7 Manual, 1637
Yk (tp imp).

17283.5 Manuzio, Aldo, 1630
Ely.

17286.5 Manuzio, Paolo, 1573
Her.

17287.3 Manuzio, Paolo, 1581
Wor.

17289 Manuzio, Paolo, 1603
Ches.

17291 Manwood, John, 1598
Pet.

17292 Manwood, John, 1615
Cant. Wor.

17296 Maplet, John, (1567)
Pet.

17299 Marbecke, John, 1581
Cant (imp). Pet (imp).

17300 Marbecke, John, 1550
Cant (2 − 1 tp imp). S Pl.

17303 Marbecke, John, 1574
Pet. Yk.

17305 Marbury, Francis, 1602
Linc. Yk.

17307 Marbury, Francis, 1602
S Pl. Yk.

17308 Marcelline, George, 1625
Pet.

17309 Marcelline, George, 1610
Yk.

17311 Marcellinus, Ammianus,
1609
Cant. Her.

17317 Mardeley, John, [1548]
Linc.

17320 Margaret, *of Angoulême*,
(1548)
Linc.

17331 Markham, Francis, 1625
Glo. Win.

17332 Markham, Francis, 1622
Glo.

17336 Markham, Gervase, 1614
Pet.

17378 Markham, Gervase, 1631
Yk.

17379 Markham, Gervase, 1636
Ex.

17397 Markham, Gervase, 1638
Carl.

17404 Marlorat, Augustine, 1570
Chelm (tpw). Pet.

17405 Marlorat, Augustine, 1583
Pet (2 − 1 imp).

17406 Marlorat, Augustine, 1575
Chelm. Her. Lich. Pet. Wel.

17408 Marlorat, Augustine, (1574)
Her.

17409 Marlorat, Augustine, 1574
Dur. Linc. Wor.

17444a Marmion, Shakerley, 1638
Pet.

17445.5 Marnix van Sant
Aldegonde, Philips van, 1579
Pet.

17446 Marnix van Sant Aldegonde,
Philips van, 1580
Pet.

17447 Marnix van Sant Aldegonde,
Philips van, 1598
Yk.

17448 Marnix van Sant Aldegonde,
Philips van, 1623
Cant. Linc.

17448.5 Marnix van Sant
Aldegonde, Philips van, 1636
Nor (imp).

17450.3 Marnix van Sant
Aldegonde, Philips van, [1583]
Yk.

17450.7 Marnix van Sant
Aldegonde, Philips van, 1583
Pet.

17453 Marprelate, Martin, *pseud.*,
[1588]
Yk.

17470 Marshe, Richard, 1625
Pet. Yk.

17475 Marston, John, 1605
Cant (imp).

17490 Marten, Anthony, 1590
Sal.

17491 Marten, Anthony, 1589
Pet (2). Yk.

17492 Martialis, Marcus Valerius,
1615
Ches. Linc.

17493 Martialis, Marcus Valerius,
1633
Secunda cura longè emendatior.
Ex. Yk.

17494 Martialis, Marcus Valerius,
1629
Cant (imp).

17496 Martiall, John, 1564
Bur. Linc. Rip (imp). Sal. Yk.

17497 Martiall, John, 1566
Pet. Wor. Yk.

17503 Martin, Gregory, 1582
Nor. Pet. S Pl. Wor. Yk (2).

17509 Martin, James, 1615
Linc.

17515 Martin, Robert, 1640
Pet.

17517 Martin, Thomas, 1554
Linc. Pet. Rip.

17518 Martin, Thomas, [1567?]
Yk (imp).

17519 Martin, Thomas, [1567?]
Rip.

17523 Martinius, Petrus, 1593
Ely. Yk.

17524 Martinus, Jacobus, 1584
Pet. Rip.

17526 Martyn, William, 1615
Bur (tpw)*. Linc.

17527 Martyn, William, 1615
Glo.

17528 Martyn, William, 1628
Wor.

17529 Martyn, William, 1638
Cant (2 − 1 imp). Dur (imp).
S Asa (tpw). Sal.

17530+ Martyn, William, 1612
[Anr ed.?] 4°; J. Beale f. R. Redmer.
Sal.

17532 Martyrology, (1526)
Linc (imp). Liv.

17542 Mary, *the Blessed Virgin,*
(1530)
Pet (imp).

17553 Mary, *de' Medici,* 1638
Pet.

17554 Mary, *de' Medici,* 1639
Dur. Sal.

17556 Mary, *de' Medici,* 1601
Yk (imp).

17558 Mary, *Queen Consort of
Louis XII,* [1509]
Her (frag.).

17565 Mary, *Queen of Scotland,*
[1572]
Pet.

17588 Mascall, Leonard, 1633
S Asa (tpw).

17594 Mason, Edmund, 1622
Yk.

17595 Mason, Francis, 1607
Linc. Liv. Pet (2).

17596 Mason, Francis, 1634
Bur (2). Carl. Ely. Ex (2). Pet.
Wor. Yk.

17597 Mason, Francis, 1613
Cant (2). Dur (imp). Her. Roch.
S Pl. Sal. Wor. Yk.

17598 Mason, Francis, 1625
Ban (tpw)*. Bris. Bur. Cant.
Dur. Her. Lich. Linc. New
(tpw)*. Nor. Roch. S Asa.
S Dv. S Pl. Wel (tpw)*. Win.
Wor. Yk.

17599 Mason, Francis, 1638
Cant. Chi. Ely. Ex. Lich.
Linc. Llan. S Asa. Sal. Swel.
Yk.

17600 Mason, Francis, 1621
Bur. Linc.

17603 Mason, Henry, 1627
Carl. Wor.

17605 Mason, Henry, 1627
Linc.

17605a Mason, Henry, 1628
Wor.

17608 Mason, Henry, 1626
Ban. Carl. Pet.

17610 Mason, Henry, 1624
Wor. Yk.

17611 Mason, Henry, 1634
Yk.

17612 Mason, Henry, 1634
Yk.

17613 Mason, Henry, 1626
Linc. Wor.

17622 Mason, Thomas, 1615
Linc (imp). Pet. Wor.

17624 Mason, William, 1621
Pet.

17648.7 Masterson, Thomas, 1595
Pet.

17652 Matthaeus,
Westmonasteriensis, 1567
Glo.

17653a Matthaeus,
Westmonasteriensis, 1570
Carl*. Rip*. Wel. Wor. Yk.

17653a.3 Matthaeus,
Westmonasteriensis, 1570
Ex. Win (imp).

17654 Matthew, Roger, 1634
Ex.

17661 Matthieu, Pierre, 1612
Cant. Ex (imp). Yk.

17662 Matthieu, Pierre, 1614
Bur. Ex. Her.

17665 Matthieu, Pierre, 1628
Linc.

17667 Matthieu, Pierre, 1639
Cant (imp).

17668 Matthieu, Pierre, 1638
Carl.

17669 Maunsell, Andrew, 1595
Linc.

17670 Maupas, Charles, 1634
Pet.

17672 Maurice, *Prince of Orange,*
1621
Sal.

17676 Maurice, *Prince of Orange,*
1613
Lich. Linc. Wel.

17677 Maurice, *Prince of Orange,*
1620
Ex.

17683a Mavericke, Radford, 1603
Linc.

17687 Maxey, Anthony, 1610
Cant (cancel tp). Pet (cancel tp).
Yk (cancel tp).

17690 Maxey, Anthony, 1606
Linc.

17691 Maxey, Anthony, 1610
Cant. Pet. Yk.

17697.3 Maximos, *Bp of Cythera,*
[1625−26]
S Pl (2).

17709 May, Edward, *Physician,*
1639
Pet.

17711 May, Thomas, 1630
Linc.

17715 May, Thomas, 1633
Linc.

17730+ Mayer, John, 1632
[Vol. 1] 'A commentarie upon the
whole New Testament'; 2°; T. Cotes
f. J. Bellamie.
Lich.

17730++ Mayer, John, 1632
[Vol. 1] 'A commentarie upon the
whole New Testament'; 2°; T. Cotes
f. J. Grismond.
Ches. Ex.

17730.5 Mayer, John, 1631
Ches. Ex.

17731 Mayer, John, 1627
Bur. Ex (tp imp). Lich.

17733 Mayer, John, 1622
Yk.

17734 Mayer, John, 1623
Carl.

17735 Mayer, John, 1630
Bur (tp imp). Ex. Sal.

17737 Mayer, John, 1634
New.

17738 Mayer, John, 1635
Lich. S Asa.

17743 Mayer, John, 1629
Ex. Her.

17744 Mayer, John, 1622
Linc.

17747 Mayerne Turquet, Louis de,
1612
Bris. Cant (2). Her. Sal (tp
imp).

17751 Maynwaring, Roger, 1627
Linc.

17751.5 Maynwaring, Roger, 1627
Yk.

17756 Mayo, John, 1630
Linc. Yk.

17758 Mean, 1614
Cant (imp). Linc.

17759.5 Mean, 1638
Tp verso has: 3a. editio.
Cant.

17762 Meara, Dermitius de, 1619
Linc.

17765 Mede, Joseph, 1638
Cant. Linc. Yk.

17766 Mede, Joseph, 1627
Wor.

17767 Mede, Joseph, 1632
Linc. Wel. Wor.

17768 Mede, Joseph, 1637
Bur*. Cant. Linc. Yk.

17769 Mede, Joseph, 1638
Linc. Yk.

17780 Meene, Joshua, 1638
Cant. Pet.

17793 Melanchthon, Philipp, 1543
S Pl.

17798 Melanchthon, Philipp, [1541]
Linc. Pet.

17801 Melbancke, Brian, 1583
Pet (imp).

17806 Melton, William de, [1510?]
Pet.

17810 Melville, Andrew, 1620
Linc.

17814 Melville, Elizabeth, 1620
Linc.

17815.5 Melville, James, 1597
Pet.

17817 Menandrinus, Marsilius,
(1535)
Pet. Yk.

17823.5 Merbury, Charles, 1581
Pet. Yk (imp)*.

17824 Mercator, Gerard, 1635
Ches. S Asa.

17825 Mercator, Gerard, 1637
Swel.

17826 Mercator, Gerard, 1639
Yk.

17827 Mercator, Gerard, &
Hondius, Jodocus, 1636
Pet (vol. 1 only). Tru (frag.)*.

17830 Meredeth, John, 1624
Bur. Cant. Yk.

17832 Meredeth, Richard, 1606
Yk.

17834 Meres, Francis, 1598
Pet.

17837 Meriton, George, 1614
Pet. Yk (3 — 1 frag.).

17838 Meriton, George, 1607
Pet. Yk (imp).

17839 Meriton, George, 1607
Yk (imp).

17840 Meriton, George, 1611
Yk.

17841.3 Merlin, (1529)
Linc (4 leaves only).

17843 Merlin, Pierre, 1599
Linc. S Asa.

17846 Meteren, Emanuel van, 1602
Linc.

17850 Mexia, Pedro, 1576
Pet.

17851 Mexia, Pedro, 1604
Linc. Sal (tp imp).

17852 Mexia, Pedro, 1623
Her. Sal. Yk (2).

17854a Michaelis, Sebastien, 1613
Pet. Yk (imp).

17889 Middleton, Thomas, 1640
S Pl.

17891 Middleton, Thomas, 1630
S Pl.

17893 Middleton, Thomas, 1630
S Pl (2).

17897 Middleton, Thomas, 1616
S Pl.

17917 Milborne, Richard, (1607)
Linc. Wor.

17919 Milbourne, William, 1639
Carl.

17926 Milles, Thomas, 1610
Ex. Lich. Linc. Sal. Yk (2 — 1
imp).

17936 Milles, Thomas, 1613
Ex. Yk.

17936.5 Milles, Thomas, 1619
Her.

17942 Milwarde, John, 1610
S Pl.

17943 Minadoi, Giovanni Tommaso,
1595
Pet.

17944 Minsheu, John, 1617
Cant. Dur. Her. Lich. Linc (2).
New (tp imp). Nor. Wor.

17944a Minsheu, John, [1617—20]
Cant (variant no. 10). Dur
(variant no. 9). Her (2 — variant
no. 8 & 10). Lich. Linc (variant
no. 9). New. Nor. Wor.

17945.5 Minsheu, John, 1625
S Asa.

17947 Minsheu, John, 1627
Bur. Cant. Ely. Nor. Pet. S Pl.
Win. Yk (2).

17950 Minucius Felix, Marcus,
1627
Ex.

17970 Mirk, John, [1506?]
Pet (imp).

17972 Mirk, John, (1515)
Yk (imp).

17992 Mocket, Richard, 1617
Ban. Pet. S Pl. Yk.

17993 Moffett, Thomas, 1634
Linc. Pet. Yk.

17993a Moffett, Thomas, 1634
Carl.

17995 Mohammed, *the Prophet*,
1615
Linc (tpw). Pet.

17997 Mohammedan History, 1600
Pet.

17999 Molina, Antonio de, 1623
S Pl.

18003 Molinier, Etienne, 1635
Cant.

18007 Monardes, Nicolas, 1596
Yk.

18011 Monginot, François, 1618
Pet.

18014a Monipennie, John, 1612
Linc.

18018 Monipennie, John, 1603
Linc.

18020 Monlas, John, 1633
Pet.

18022 Monro, Robert, 1637
Carl. Lich. Nor. Pet.

18026 Montagu, Henry, 1633
Cant (imp). S Asa.

18026.5 Montagu, Henry, 1635
Linc.

18028 Montagu, Henry, 1638
Bur. Pet.

18029 Montagu, Richard, [1622]
Ban. Cant (imp). Dur. S Pl.
Wor. Yk.

18030 Montagu, Richard, 1625
S Asa. Sal. Win. Wor. Yk (2).

18031 Montagu, Richard, 1625
Carl. Dur. Ex. Glo. Lich.
Linc. Pet. Sal. Yk.

18032 Montagu, Richard, [1625?]
Linc (imp). Yk (imp).

18033 Montagu, Richard, 1635
Cant. Carl. Chi (2). Dur. Ely.
Ex. Glo (2). Linc. New. Pet.
S Pl. Sal (2). Swel. Wel. Wor.
Yk.

18034 Montagu, Richard, 1636
Carl. Chi. Linc. S Pl. Sal (with
tp of STC 18035a inserted). Swel.
Yk.

18035 Montagu, Richard, 1640
Ex (tpw)*.

18035a Montagu, Richard, 1640
Cant. Carl. Chi. Dur. Glo.
Lich. New. Nor. S Pl. Sal.
Win. Wor. Yk.

18036- Montagu, Richard, 1639
[Anr ed. of STC 18036] 'Originum
ecclesiasticarum, tomi prioris, pars
posterior'; 2°; Typis R.O. & E.P.,
prostant apud H. Seile.
Yk.

18036 Montagu, Richard, 1640
Cant (imp)*. Carl. Chi. Dur.
Ex (tpw)*. Glo. Lich. Linc.
New. Nor. Sal (2). Win. Wor.

18036.5 Montagu, Richard, 1640
Yk.

18037 Montagu, Richard, 1621
Cant (2). Carl. Dur. Ex. Glo.
Linc (2 − 1 tpw). New. Pet.
S Asa. Sal (2). Win. Wor. Yk
(2).

18038 Montagu, Richard, 1624
Dur. Glo. Lich. Linc. New.
S Asa. S Pl. Sal (2). Wor. Yk
(2).

18039 Montagu, Richard, 1624
Carl. Ches. Glo. Lich. Linc.
S Asa. Sal (3). Win. Wor. Yk.

18041 Montaigne, Michel de, (1603)
Cant. Dur (imp). Sal.

18042 Montaigne, Michel de, 1613
Ely. Wor.

18043 Montaigne, Michel de, 1632
Cant (frag.). Pet. Wel.

18058 Moore, John, 1612
Linc (tpw).

18060 Moore, Philip, 1565
Pet.

18070 More, George, *Preacher*,
1600
Linc.

18071 More, *Sir* George, 1597
Pet (tpw)*. Yk.

18074 More, John, 1593
Linc. Pet.

18074.5 More, John, 1594
Pet.

18076 More, *Sir* Thomas, 1557
CLC copies vary in pp. 303-6.
Dur. Ex. Her (2 -1 imp). Linc.
Pet (imp). Win. Wor. Yk.

18077 More, *Sir* Thomas, (1534)
Linc (tpw).

18078 More, *Sir* Thomas, (1533)
Pet.

18079 More, *Sir* Thomas, 1532
Carl. Glo. Linc. Pet.

18080 More, *Sir* Thomas, 1533
Carl (tpw). Glo. Linc. Pet.

18082 More, *Sir* Thomas, (1553)
Rip (tpw).

18083 More, *Sir* Thomas, 1573
Pet. Yk.

18085 More, *Sir* Thomas, 1530
Glo.

18087 More, *Sir* Thomas, 1633
Linc. Pet.

18089 More, *Sir* Thomas, 1523
Chi. Ex. Sal.

18092 More, *Sir* Thomas, [1529]
Glo. Liv (imp).

18097 More, *Sir* Thomas, 1624
S Pl.

18098 More, *Sir* Thomas, 1639
Roch.

18099 Morel, Jean, 1589
Dur. Pet. Yk.

18101 Morelius, Gulielmus, 1583
Linc. Pet. Sal (tpw). Yk.

18102 Moresinus, Thomas, 1594
Pet.

18106 Morice, James, [1590?]
Linc (imp). Win. Yk.

18109 Morison, *Sir* Richard, (1537)
Yk.

18130.5 Morley, Thomas, 1601
Pet (Quintus only).

18133 Morley, Thomas, 1597
Dur. Yk.

18134 Morley, Thomas, 1608
Wor (imp).

18134.3 Mornay, Philippe de, 1600
Pt 3 of STC 23453.
Linc. Pet. Wor. Yk (2).

18142 Mornay, Philippe de, 1600
Glo. Pet. Wor. Yk.

18146 Mornay, Philippe de, 1599
Pet.

18147 Mornay, Philippe de, 1612
Her. Wor.

18149 Mornay, Philippe de, 1587
Wel (imp).

18150 Mornay, Philippe de, 1592
Her. Pet. Wel (imp).

18152 Mornay, Philippe de, 1617
Cant. Carl. Ex (imp). Sal. Yk.

18159 Mornay, Philippe de, 1579
Pet.

18160 Mornay, Philippe de, 1580
Pet.

18161.5 Mornay, Philippe de, 1581
Pet.

18162 Mornay, Philippe de, 1606
Linc. Yk.

18165 Morocco, 1637
Linc.

18172 Morton, Thomas, *Bp*, 1637
Ches. Linc. Pet (2). Yk.

18173.5 Morton, Thomas, *Bp*, 1605
Rip (imp).

18174 Morton, Thomas, *Bp*, 1605
Ches. Ely. Her. Pet. Yk.

18174a Morton, Thomas, *Bp*, 1605
Bur. Yk.

18175 Morton, Thomas, *Bp*, 1606
Ches. Linc. Pet. Wor.

18175.5 Morton, Thomas, *Bp*, 1606
Bur. Her. Pet. Win. Yk (2).

18176 Morton, Thomas, *Bp*, 1609
Bur. Ches. Dur. Nor. Pet. Yk.

18177 Morton, Thomas, *Bp*, 1610
Bur. Cant. Ches. Her. Lich.
Linc. S Pl. Sal. Wor. Yk.

18178 Morton, Thomas, *Bp*, 1620
Cant. Ches. Pet. Wor. Yk.

18179 Morton, Thomas, *Bp*, 1618
Dur. Ex. Pet (2). S Pl. Wor (2).
Yk.

18180 Morton, Thomas, *Bp*, 1619
Ches (3). Dur. Ex. Linc. Pet.
Yk.

18181 Morton, Thomas, *Bp*, 1609
Ches.

18182 Morton, Thomas, *Bp*, 1633
Ex. Linc. Pet. S Pl. Yk.

18183 Morton, Thomas, *Bp*, 1610
Ches. Pet (2). Sal. Wor. Yk
(2).

18184 Morton, Thomas, *Bp*, 1605
Bur (2)*. Ches*. Llan*. Yk.

18184.5 Morton, Thomas, *Bp*, 1605
Pet. Sal. Yk.

18185 Morton, Thomas, *Bp*, 1606
Ban (imp). Cant. Ches. Pet
(imp). Rip (imp). Sal. Yk.

18186 Morton, Thomas, *Bp*,
[1626?]
Ches (2). Chi. Ex. Glo. Lich.
Pet. Wor (2). Yk.

18187 Morton, Thomas, *Bp*, 1628
Ches (2). Yk.

18188 Morton, Thomas, *Bp*, [1606]
Cant. Pet (imp). Yk.

18189 Morton, Thomas, *Bp*, 1631
Bur (2). Ches. Ex. Her. Lich.
Linc. New. Roch. S Asa. S Pl.
Yk (2).

18190 Morton, Thomas, *Bp*, 1635
Ches. Lich (tp only). Nor. Pet.
Win. Wor. Yk.

18191 Morton, Thomas, *Bp*, 1608
Cant. Ches. Rip. Yk.

18193 Morton, Thomas, *Bp*, 1638
Yk.

18196a Morton, Thomas, *Bp*, 1639
Carl. Ches*. Dur (tp imp). Ex.
Nor. S Asa. Yk.

18197 Morton, Thomas, *Bp*, 1640
Bur. Ches (2). Lich. Linc. Pet.
S Pl. Wor.

18197.3 Morton, Thomas, *of
Berwick*, 1596
Linc. Pet. Yk.

18197.7 Morton, Thomas, *of
Berwick*, 1596
Linc. Pet (imp).

18198 Morton, Thomas, *of Berwick*,
1599
Pet.

18200 Morton, Thomas, *of Berwick*,
1629
Ely. Yk.

18200.5 Morton, Thomas, *of
Berwick*, 1597
Pet.

18205 Moryson, Fynes, 1617
Glo. Sal.

18206 Moses, *ben Maimon*, 1631
Linc. S Pl. Yk.

18209 Mosse, Miles, 1614
Pet. S Pl.

18210 Mosse, Miles, 1603
Pet.

18224 Moulton, Thomas, [1566]
Pet.

18245 Muffet, Peter, 1592
Pet.

18246 Muffet, Peter, 1596
Pet (tpw). Yk.

18250 Mulcaster, Richard, 1582
Pet.

18253a Mulcaster, Richard, 1581
Pet.

18255 Mun, Thomas, 1621
Linc.

18256 Mun, Thomas, 1621
Sal.

18272 Munday, Anthony, 1582
Yk.

18292 Muriell, Christopher, 1603
Yk (2 − 1 imp).

18292.7 Murmellius, Joannes,
[c.1521]
Pet (imp).

18305 Muschet, George, *Priest*,
1623
S Pl. Yk (2).

18306 Muschet, George, *Priest*,
1624
Linc. Pet (tpw). Wor.

18307.5 Musculus, Wolfgang,
[1566?]
S Pl (imp).

18308 Musculus, Wolfgang, 1563
Cant (imp; both cols 1563). Pet.
Wel.

18309 Musculus, Wolfgang, 1578
Pet.

18314 Musculus, Wolfgang, 1584
Yk.

18314.5 Muse, 1616
Pet.

18316 Musgrave, Christopher, 1621
Carl. Linc. Yk.

18320 Mynshul, Geffray, 1638
Cant.

18321 Myriell, Thomas, 1623
Pet. Yk.

18322 Myriell, Thomas, 1613
Linc.

18323 Myriell, Thomas, 1610
Linc.

18326 N., C., 1595
Linc (imp).

18334 N., R., 1613
Pet.

18348 Nannini, Remigio, 1601
Yk.

18349 Napier, John, 1614
Linc.

18349a Napier, John, 1614
Sal.

18354 Napier, John, 1593
Linc. Pet. Win (tpw). Wor. Yk.

18355 Napier, John, 1594
Sal.

18359 Narne, William, 1625
Ex. Linc.

18363 Narrationes, 1561
Pet.

18368 Nash, Thomas, 1613
Pet.

18382 Nash, Thomas, *Philopolites*,
1633
Glo. Linc.

18397.5 Natura Brevium, (1551)
Pet.

18400 Natura Brevium, 1572
Pet.

18402 Natura Brevium, 1584
Pet.

18408.5 Natura Brevium, (1553)
Pet.

18413.7 Nausea, Fridericus, 1618
Pet.

18421 Neile, Richard, 1624
Carl. Linc. Wor. Yk (2).

18428 Nenna, Giovanni Battista,
1595
Pet.

18432 Nesbit, E., 1601
Yk.

18440 Netherlands, 1571
Linc.

18445 Netherlands, 1578
Linc.

18450 Netherlands. States General, 1591
Linc.

18473 Nethersole, *Sir* Francis, 1612
Pet. S Asa. Yk.

18474 Nettles, Stephen, 1625
Cant. Ex (2 − 1 tp imp). Linc. Sal. Wor.

18478 Neville, Alexander, 1575
Pet. Rip*. S Pl*.

18478a.5 Neville, Alexander, 1575
Nor.

18481 Neville, Alexander, 1623
Nor (imp)*.

18485 New England, 1630
Linc.

18486 New England, 1630
Linc.

18490 New Year's Gift, (1576)
Win (imp).

18493 Newhouse, Thomas, 1614
Pet. Yk (tp imp).

18494 Newhouse, Thomas, 1612
Linc. Yk.

18507.8 Newsbooks, 1621
Cant.

18507.40? Newsbooks, 1622
No question mark in title.
Yk.

18507.47 Newsbooks, 1622
Yk (tp imp).

18507.56A Newsbooks, 1622
Yk.

18507.75 Newsbooks, 1622
Yk.

18507.80 Newsbooks, 1622
Yk.

18507.82 Newsbooks, 1622
Yk.

18507.84 Newsbooks, 1622
Yk (2).

18507.89 Newsbooks, 1622
Yk.

18507.97 Newsbooks, 1623
Yk.

18507.128 Newsbooks, 1623
Pet.

18507.144 Newsbooks, 1624
Yk.

18507.155 Newsbooks, 1624
Yk.

18507.160 Newsbooks, 1625
Yk.

18507.173 Newsbooks, 1625
Yk.

18507.177 Newsbooks, 1626
Yk.

18507.249 Newsbooks, 1632
Pet.

18507.251 Newsbooks, 1632
May 12 *not* May 21.
Linc (imp).

18507.349 Newsbooks, 1624
Yk.

18527 Nicetas, *Bp*, 1637
Cant (2). Carl. Dur. Ely. Ex. Linc. S Pl. Win. Wor.

18533 Nichols, John, 1581
Pet. Yk.

18534 Nichols, John, 1581
Pet (tpw). Yk.

18536 Nichols, John, 1581
Linc. Pet (tpw). Yk.

18537 Nichols, John, 1583
Pet.

18538 Nichols, Josias, 1602
Pet (tpw)*. Yk.

18541 Nichols, Josias, 1602
Linc. Wor. Yk.

18542 Nichols, Josias, 1602
Pet.

18550 Niclas, Hendrik, [1574?]
Pet.

18554 Niclas, Hendrik, [1574?]
Pet.

18555 Niclas, Hendrik, [1574?]
Linc.

18556 Niclas, Hendrik, [1575?]
Pet.

18557 Niclas, Hendrik, [1574?]
Linc.

18562 Niclas, Hendrik, 1574
Pet.

18564 Niclas, Hendrik, [1575?]
Pet.

18579 Nid, Gervase, 1616
Linc.

18581 Nîmes University, 1584
Pet. Wor.

18631? Norden, John, 1631
E.A. f. R. Allot.
Cant.

18635 Norden, John, 1593
Glo (imp). Linc (tpw). Pet.

18645 Norice, Edward, 1638
Linc.

18655 Norris, *Sir* John, 1591
Pet.

18657 Norris, Silvester, 1615
Yk.

18658 Norris, Silvester, 1622
Wor.

18658.5 Norris, Silvester, 1621
Wor (2).

18659 Norris, Silvester, 1621
Wor.

18663 Northbrooke, John, 1571
Pet.

18664 Northbrooke, John, 1582
Pet.

18668 Northbrooke, John, 1600
Pet (imp?).

18678 Norton, Thomas, [1570]
Pet. Yk.

18678a Norton, Thomas, [1570]
Pet.

18678a.5 Norton, Thomas, [1570]
Yk.

18679 Norton, Thomas, [1570]
Pet. Yk.

18682 Norton, Thomas, (1569)
Pet. Yk.

18686 Norton, Thomas, [1570?]
Pet. Yk*.

18690 Norwood, Richard, 1639
Yk.

18692 Norwood, Richard, 1631
Cant (R − &⁴ reset; errata on [*]1ᵛ).

18701 Nowell, Alexander, 1570
S Pl.

18703 Nowell, Alexander, 1572
Dur. Linc.

18704 Nowell, Alexander, 1574
Yk.

18706 Nowell, Alexander, 1580
Pet.

18707 Nowell, Alexander, 1573
S Pl. Yk.

18709 Nowell, Alexander, 1571
S Pl.

18710a Nowell, Alexander, 1575 (1576)
S Pl (imp).

18711a Nowell, Alexander, 1574
Pet.

18712 Nowell, Alexander, 1574
Yk (tpw)*.

18713.5 Nowell, Alexander, 1577
Pet.

18715.5 Nowell, Alexander, 1590
S Pl.

18722 Nowell, Alexander, 1626
Nor.

18725.5 Nowell, Alexander, 1639
Carl.

18726 Nowell, Alexander, 1575
S Pl (tpw).

18727 Nowell, Alexander, 1577
Ely. Pet.

18729 Nowell, Alexander, 1638
Ely. S Pl. Yk.

18733.3 Nowell, Alexander, 1584
Yk.

18739 Nowell, Alexander, 1567
Pet. Sal (2). Yk.

18740 Nowell, Alexander, 1565
Pet. S Pl. Wor. Yk.

18742 Nowell, Alexander, 1566
Pet. Sal.

18744 Nowell, Alexander, & Day,
William, 1583
Liv*. Pet. S Pl*. Wor (2).

18744.5 Nowell, Alexander, & Day,
William, 1583
Yk.

18754 O., E., 1602
Wor. Yk.

18766 Ochino, Bernardino, [1551?]
Pet (imp).

18768 Ochino, Bernardino, [1570?]
Linc (imp). Pet.

18769 Ochino, Bernardino, 1580
Pet.

18770 Ochino, Bernardino, 1549
Pet (tpw).

18772 Ockland, Christopher, 1580
Pet.

18773 Ockland, Christopher, 1582
Ely (pt 3 only)*. Yk.

18773.3 Ockland, Christopher, 1582
Linc (tpw).

18773.7 Ockland, Christopher, 1582
Nor. Sal. Yk (imp).

18775a Ockland, Christopher, 1582
Rip.

18776 Ockland, Christopher, 1589
Pet.

18782 Odingsells, Charles, 1637
Pet.

18783 Odingsells, Charles, 1620
Linc.

18800 Oldenbarneveld, Jan van,
1618
Pet. Yk.

18800+ Oldenbarneveld, Jan van,
1618
'Barnevelts apology ...'; 4°; f. T.
Thorp; Dedication signed: Robert
Houlders.
Linc.

18806 Oldmayne, Timothy, 1636
Pet.

18807.3 Olevian, Caspar, 1582
Cant.

18809 Oliver, Thomas, 1604
Linc.

18832 Optatus, St, 1631
Cant (with errata). Ches. Win.
Yk (with errata).

18834 Orange, Princess of, 1589
Pet. Yk.

18837 Oration, 1624
Sal. Yk (frag.).

18850 Ormerod, Oliver, 1606
Pet (2). Yk.

18851 Ormerod, Oliver, 1605
Yk (imp).

18852 Ormerod, Oliver, 1605
Cant. Yk.

18855 Ortelius, Abraham, 1606
Wel.

18862.5 Ortuñez de Calahorra,
Diego, 1585
Pet.

18880 Osiander, Lucas, 1606
Yk.

18884 Osorio da Fonseca, Jeronimo,
1580
Ex.

18886 Osorio da Fonseca, Jeronimo,
1576
Pet. Rip (imp).

18887 Osorio da Fonseca, Jeronimo,
1565
Yk (tpw).

18889 Osorio da Fonseca, Jeronimo,
1568
Pet.

18896 Otes, Samuel, 1633
Ex. Linc.

18897 Oudin, César, 1622
Ely.

18899a Oughtred, William, 1632
Ex (tpw)*. Yk.

18899c Oughtred, William, 1633
Ex.

18902 Outreman, Philippe d', 1622
12°.
Yk.

18909 Overbury, Sir Thomas, 1616
Yk (imp).

18918 Overbury, Sir Thomas, 1632
Cant.

18924 Overton, John, 1586
Pet.

18925 Overton, William, [1579?]
Pet. Yk.

18926 Overton, William, 1601
Yk.

18927 Ovidius Naso, Publius, 1583
Ex (tp imp).

18929.3 Ovidius Naso, Publius,
1602
Ex (imp).

18939 Ovidius Naso, Publius, 1640
Linc.

18943 Ovidius Naso, Publius,
[c.1584]
Liv (imp). Pet (imp)*.

18946 Ovidius Naso, Publius, 1639
Linc.

18947.5 Ovidius Naso, Publius,
1574
Rip.

18948 Ovidius Naso, Publius, 1640
Cant. Linc. Pet.

18956 Ovidius Naso, Publius, 1567
Lich. Pet (2 − 1 imp).

18964 Ovidius Naso, Publius, 1626
Sal.

18966 Ovidius Naso, Publius, 1632
Bris. Cant. Her. Wor.

18968 Ovidius Naso, Publius, 1640
Cant (imp).

18976.4 Ovidius Naso, Publius,
1574
Sal (imp)*.

18980 Ovidius Naso, Publius, 1637
Linc.

18982 Owen, David, 1622
Bur. Linc. Wor. Yk.

18983 Owen, David, 1610
Linc.

18983.5 Owen, David, 1610
Yk (imp).

18986 Owen, John, 1607
S Pl.

18987 Owen, John, 1612
Chi. Ex (tp only). S Pl. Yk.

18989 Owen, John, 1618
Chi. Yk.

18991 Owen, John, 1633
Ely.

18996 Owen, Lewis, 1626
Linc. Yk.

18998 Owen, Lewis, 1628
Ban (imp). Bur (tpw)*. Pet.

18999 Owen, Thomas, 1611
Yk.

19000 Owen, Thomas, 1610
Wor.

19006 Oxford University, 1635
S Asa.

19007 Oxford University, 1638
Cant (no chart). Dur. Ex. Linc.
Yk (no chart).

19012 Oxford University, 1603
Yk (2 − 1 imp*).

19012a Oxford University, [1603]
Linc.

19013 Oxford University, 1604
Cant. Pet. Yk.

19014 Oxford University, 1622
Linc.

19018 Oxford University, 1603
Linc. Pet. Yk.

19019 Oxford University, 1603
Wor. Yk.

19020 Oxford University, 1612
Yk.

19021 Oxford University, 1612
Yk.

19021.5 Oxford University, 1612
Linc.

19022 Oxford University, 1613
Linc.

19023 Oxford University, 1617
Linc.

19024 Oxford University, 1619
Pet. Yk.

19025 Oxford University, 1622
Pet. Yk.

19026 Oxford University, 1623
Yk.

19027 Oxford University, 1623
Carl. Linc.

19028 Oxford University, 1624
Pet (2). Yk.

19030 Oxford University, 1625
Linc. Yk.

19031 Oxford University, 1625
Linc. Pet. S Asa.

19032 Oxford University, 1630
Pet. Yk.

19033 Oxford University, 1633
Carl. Linc. Pet. Wor. Yk.

19034 Oxford University, 1633
Yk.

19035 Oxford University, 1633
Yk.

19035a Oxford University, 1633
Linc. Wor. Yk.

19036 Oxford University, 1636
Linc. Yk.

19037 Oxford University, [1637]
Linc. Yk.

19038 Oxford University, 1638
Yk.

19039 Oxford University, 1640
Carl. Pet.

19042 Oxford University, 1638
Pet.

19043 Oxford University, 1605
Yk.

19047 Oxford University, 1612
Linc.

19048 Oxford University, 1613
Linc. Pet.

19053 Oxley, Thomas, 1609
Yk.

19056 P., A., 1603
Yk (2).

19057.3 P., B., 1613
Pet.

19072 P., J., 1629
Sal.

19078.8 P., T., 1608
Yk.

19083 Pacius, Julius, 1597
Pet.

19088 Page, Samuel, 1616
Ex.

19091 Page, Samuel, 1616
Ex (2). Yk (imp).

19096 Page, William, 1631
Ex. Pet (imp). Wor. Yk.

19096a Page, William, 1631
Linc.

19098 Paget, John, 1618
Cant. Win. Wor (tpw). Yk.

19103 Pagit, Eusebius, [1584?]
Pet.

19110 Pagitt, Ephraim, 1635
Carl.

19111 Pagitt, Ephraim, 1636
Her. Linc. S Asa. Sal. Win.
Wor.

19112 Pagitt, Ephraim, 1640
Cant. Ex. Yk (2).

19115 Paglia, Antonio dalla,
[1575?]
S Pl.

19117 Paglia, Antonio dalla, 1633
Pet.

19126 Palatinate, 1624
Dur. Yk.

19130 Palatinate, 1614
Linc.

19131 Palatinate, 1637
Pet. Sal.

19138.5 Palingenius, Marcellus, [*i.e.*
P.A. Manzolli], 1569
Rip.

19140 Palingenius, Marcellus, [*i.e.*
P.A. Manzolli], 1574
Pet.

19143 Palingenius, Marcellus, [*i.e.*
P.A. Manzolli], 1592
Pet.

19149 Palingenius, Marcellus, [*i.e.*
P.A. Manzolli], 1561
Pet.

19152 Palingenius, Marcellus, [*i.e.*
P.A. Manzolli], 1588
Pet.

19166 Palsgrave, John, 1530
Cant (tpw). Wel (imp). Yk.

19168 Panacea, 1630
Pet.

19170 Panke, John, 1612
Wor.

19174 Papal Exchequer, 1617
Bur. Cant (imp). Dur. Wor.
Yk.

19174a Papal Exchequer, 1621
Ex. Yk.

19192 Paré, Ambroise, 1630
Pet.

19194 Pareus, David, 1631
Lich.

19195 Parfeius, Gulielmus, (1547)
Pet.

19197 Paris, 1590
Pet.

19203 Paris, 1634
Wor.

19204 Paris University, 1610
Dur. Sal. Yk.

19209 Paris, Matthaeus, 1571 (1570)
Her. Lich. Pet.

19209a Paris, Matthaeus, 1571 (1570)
Linc. Yk.

19210 Paris, Matthaeus, 1640
Ban. Cant. Carl. Ches. Linc. Nor. Pet. S Pl (2 − 1 imp). Win (imp). Wor.

19212 Parker, Henry, *D.D.*, (1493)
Yk (imp).

19213 Parker, Henry, *D.D.*, (1496)
Cant (imp).

19214 Parker, Henry, *D.D.*, (1536)
S Pl. Yk (imp).

19215 Parker, Henry, *of Lincoln's Inn*, 1640
Cant. Dur. Linc. Pet. Sal.

19216 Parker, Henry, *of Lincoln's Inn*, 1640
Ex.

19292a Parker, Matthew, 1574
Linc. S Pl.

19293 Parker, Matthew, [1551?]
Linc (imp). Pet.

19294 Parker, Robert, 1607
Glo. Sal. Yk.

19295 Parkes, Richard, 1607
Wor. Yk.

19296 Parkes, Richard, 1604
Linc. Wor. Yk.

19299 Parkhurst, John, 1573
Pet.

19302 Parkinson, John, 1640
Cant (2 − 1 addit. engr. tpw). Her (imp). Liv. Sal.

19311 Parr, Elnathan, 1632
Sal.

19320 Parr, Elnathan, 1620
Carl.

19342 Parry, William, *Doctor of Laws*, [1585]
Linc (imp).

19345 Parsons, Bartholomew, 1633
Pet.

19346 Parsons, Bartholomew, 1631
Pet.

19347 Parsons, Bartholomew, 1618
Cant.

19349 Parsons, Bartholomew, 1616
Yk.

19350 Parsons, Bartholomew, 1635
Pet.

19351 Parsons, Bartholomew, 1636
Pet.

19352 Parsons, Robert, 1606
Dur (cancel tp). Yk (2 − both original tp).

19353 Parsons, Robert, 1582
Pet (2 − 1 imp).

19354.1 Parsons, Robert, 1585
Carl. Ely. Linc. Pet. Yk.

19354.3 Parsons, Robert, 1598
Pet. Wor. Yk.

19354.5 Parsons, Robert, 1607
Win.

19354.7 Parsons, Robert, 1622
Linc.

19355 Parsons, Robert, 1584
Pet.

19356.5 Parsons, Robert, 1585
Ban.

19357 Parsons, Robert, 1585
Yk.

19358 Parsons, Robert, 1585
Pet.

19360.7 Parsons, Robert, 1585
Her.

19363 Parsons, Robert, 1586
Pet.

19367 Parsons, Robert, 1598
Yk.

19372 Parsons, Robert, 1609
Her.

19374 Parsons, Robert, 1615
Yk.

19375 Parsons, Robert, 1621
Yk.

19376.5 Parsons, Robert, 1630
Wor. Yk.

19381 Parsons, Robert, 1591
Her.

19383 Parsons, Robert, 1594
Pet. Yk.

19384 Parsons, Robert, 1598
Yk.

19386 Parsons, Robert, 1610
Pet.

19387 Parsons, Robert, 1615
Yk.

19388 Parsons, Robert, 1619
Her. Yk.

19388a Parsons, Robert, 1631
Yk.

19391.5 Parsons, Robert, [1601]
Pet (imp). Rip*.

19392 Parsons, Robert, [1601]
Yk.

19393 Parsons, Robert, 1581
Pet.

19394 Parsons, Robert, 1580
Pet.

19398 Parsons, Robert, 1594
Bur. Dur. Linc. Pet. Yk.

19401 Parsons, Robert, 1582
Pet.

19402 Parsons, Robert, [1581]
Yk.

19408 Parsons, Robert, 1608
Bur. Dur. Her (imp). Pet (2). Yk.

19409 Parsons, Robert, 1612
Pet (2). Yk.

19409.5 Parsons, Robert, 1620
Pet (tpw).

19410 Parsons, Robert, 1620
Yk.

19411 Parsons, Robert, 1602
Yk.

19412 Parsons, Robert, 1609
Yk.

19414 Parsons, Robert, 1604
Yk.

19415 Parsons, Robert, 1599
Pet. Yk.

19416 Parsons, Robert, 1603 (1604)
Cant (vol. 2 only). Ex. Linc. Pet (2 − 1 vol. 3 only, imp). Wel (vol. 3 only). Win. Wor (tpw). Yk (2 − 1 vol. 3 only).

19417 Parsons, Robert, 1607
Her. Pet. Yk (tpw).

19418 Parsons, Robert, 1602
Her. Linc. Pet. Sal. Yk.

19444 Pasor, George, 1621
Bur.

19445 Pasor, Matthias, 1627
Pet.

19449 Pasquier, Etienne, 1602
Ely. Pet. Wor.

19461 Paterson, William, 1620
Yk.

19465.5 Patriarchs, 1539
Pet.

19476 Patten, William, [1575]
Pet.

19476.5 Patten, William, (1548)
Linc.

19481 Pattenson, Matthew, 1623
Cant. Her. Pet. Yk.

19483 Paul V, [1620?]
Yk.

19484 Paule, *Sir* George, 1612
Cant. Linc. Win. Wor.

19487 Pavonius, Franciscus, 1633
Carl.

19488 Paybody, Thomas, 1629
Linc. Win. Yk.

19492 Paynell, Thomas, 1562
Pet.

19494 Paynell, Thomas, 1550
Liv.

19503 Peacham, Henry, *the Younger*, 1627
Cant.

19504 Peacham, Henry, *the Younger*, 1634
Yk (imp).

19512 Peacham, Henry, *the Younger*, 1615
Yk.

19517 Peacham, Henry, *the Younger*, 1638
Cant (imp).

19518.5 Peake, *Sir* Robert, [1637?]
Liv.

19556 Pelegromius, Simon, 1580
Pet.

19562 Pelegromius, Simon, 1619
Yk.

19563 Pelegromius, Simon, 1632
Yk.

19564 Pelegromius, Simon, 1639
Glo.

19566.5 Pellham, *Sir* William, 1625
Yk.

19569 Pemberton, William, 1613
S Pl.

19569a Pemberton, William, 1616
Linc.

19570 Pemble, William, 1635
Chi. Ex (2 — 1 lacks pt 3). Lich (tpw)*. Linc. Sal.

19573 Pemble, William, 1629
Carl.

19574 Pemble, William, 1629
Carl.

19575 Pemble, William, 1633
S Asa (imp).

19577 Pemble, William, 1629
Carl. Pet.

19578 Pemble, William, 1629
Cant (2). Pet. S Asa.

19579 Pemble, William, 1628
Cant.

19580.5 Pemble, William, 1633
Carl.

19587 Pemble, William, 1632
Cant.

19588 Pemble, William, 1631
Pet. Sal.

19589 Pemble, William, 1625
Cant. Carl. Wor.

19590 Pemble, William, 1629
Pet.

19591 Pemble, William, 1627
S Pl. Sal.

19592 Pemble, William, 1629
Pet.

19594 Peña, Juan Antonio de la, 1623
Yk.

19595 Peña, Petrus, & L'Obel, Matthias de, 1570
Linc (imp).

19595.5 Peña, Petrus, & L'Obel, Matthias de, 1605
Wor.

19602 Penry, John, 1589
Pet (imp).

19603 Penry, John, [1590]
Pet. Yk.

19604 Penry, John, [1588]
Pet (imp).

19612 Penry, John, 1590
Pet (2). Rip (imp). Wor (imp). Yk (2 — 1 tpw).

19613 Penry, John, [1589]
Pet (2 — 1 imp, 1 tpw).

19617 Percy, Henry, *Earl of Northumberland*, [1585]
Pet.

19619 Percyvall, Richard, 1591
Dur. Pet.

19621a Percyvall, Richard, 1623
Cant. Yk.

19624 Peretto, Francesco, 1616
Linc.

19624.5 Pérez, Antonio, [1594]
Win.

19625 Perez de Guzman, Alonso, 1588
Linc.

19626.5 Perez de Pineda, Juan, 1576
Pet (2).

19635.5 Perkins, John, (1567)
Pet.

19636 Perkins, John, (1576)
Glo.

19638 Perkins, John, (1586)
Pet.

19645 Perkins, John, 1639
Glo.

19646 Perkins, William, 1600
Nor.

19648 Perkins, William, 1605
Her. New (imp). Pet.

19649 Perkins, William, 1608 (1609)
Bris (lacks vol. 1). Carl (lacks vol. 3). Ex (2 — both lack vol. 1, 1 set v. imp). S Asa (lacks vol. 1). Wel (vol. 1 tpw).

19650 Perkins, William, 1612 (1613)
Carl (vol. 3 only). Glo (2 — both vol. 2 only). Linc. S Asa (vol. 1 only). Win (vol. 1 only). Wor. Yk.

19651 Perkins, William, 1616 (1618)
Cant (2 — 1 vol. 2 only). Ches (lacks vol. 2). Chi (vol. 2 only). Ex (vol. 1 only). Glo (lacks vol. 2). Her (lacks vol. 1).

19652 Perkins, William, 1626 (1623, 1626)
Cant (2 — 1 imp).

19653 Perkins, William, 1631
Dur. Win.

19653a Perkins, William, 1631
Dur.

19653b Perkins, William, 1631
Win.

19654 Perkins, William, 1635
Dur. Win.

19658 Perkins, William, [1591?]
Carl. Pet.

19661.5 Perkins, William, 1592
Yk.

19662 Perkins, William, 1595
Lich (tpw)*.

19667 Perkins, William, 1595
Lich.

19668 Perkins, William, 1604
Pet.

19672 Perkins, William, 1619
Sal.

19676 Perkins, William, 1636
Chelm.

19677.5 Perkins, William, 1607
S Pl.

19682 Perkins, William, 1598
Pet. Sal.

19687a Perkins, William, [c.1638]
Bur.

19694.5 Perkins, William, [c.1638]
Bur.

19696 Perkins, William, 1596
Pet.

19697 Perkins, William, 1608
Ely.

19699.5 Perkins, William, 1592
S Pl.

19702a Perkins, William, 1595
Lich.

19702a.5 Perkins, William, 1596
Linc.

19703 Perkins, William, 1595
Lich.

19704 Perkins, William, 1596
Pet.

19707 Perkins, William, 1606
Pet.

19707.5 Perkins, William, 1607
Bur.

19709 Perkins, William, 1590
S Pl (frag.)*.

19711 Perkins, William, 1595
Lich (tpw)*.

19713.5 Perkins, William, 1604
Yk.

19723 Perkins, William, 1611
Cant (imp).

19724.3 Perkins, William, 1606
Pet.

19727 Perkins, William, [c.1638]
Bur.

19728.5 Perkins, William, 1603
Bur.

19730.7 Perkins, William, [c.1638]
Bur.

19731 Perkins, William, 1604
Bris.

19732 Perkins, William, 1606
Her. New. Pet.

19733a Perkins, William, 1606
Pet.

19734 Perkins, William, 1604
Dur. S Asa. Sal.

19735 Perkins, William, 1592
Chi. Glo. Yk.

19735.8 Perkins, William, 1597
Cant (tp imp)*. Pet.

19736 Perkins, William, 1598
Cant ('discrip-'). Pet ('descrip-').

19740 Perkins, William, 1634
Bur. Her. S Asa.

19743.5 Perkins, William, 1603
Bur.

19747.3 Perkins, William, [c.1638]
Bur.

19749 Perkins, William, (1598)
Linc (imp). Wor.

19752.5 Perkins, William, [1590?]
Pet.

19754 Perkins, William, 1595
Lich (imp).

19766.7 Perneby, William, 1599
Pet.

19768.5 Perrin, Jean Paul, 1624
Lich.

19769 Perrin, Jean Paul, 1624
Glo. Wor. Yk.

19770 Perrot, Richard, 1627
Chi (imp). Linc. Pet. Yk.

19773 Perrott, *Sir* James, 1600
Pet (2).

19777 Persius Flaccus, Aulus, 1614
Linc.

19786 Peryn, William, [1546]
Pet (imp). Rip.

19789 Pestell, Thomas, 1615
Cant.

19790 Pestell, Thomas, 1615
Cant (2).

19794 Peter, *of Alcantara, St*, 1632
8°.
Yk.

19796.5 Peter, *St*, 1585
Pet (2 − 1 tpw).

19798.3 Peters, Hugh, 1631
Yk.

19799 Peters, Nicholaus, 1596
Pet.

19801 Petley, Elias, 1623
Cant. S Pl (2 − 1 tp imp).

19809 Petrarca, Francesco, 1579
Linc. Pet.

19813 Petrucci, Ludovico, 1619
Yk (imp?).

19814 Petrucci, Ludovico, 1613
Glo.

19826 Pflacher, Moses, 1587
Pet. Yk.

19830 Philalethes, Andreas, *pseud.*,
1602
Linc. Pet (2). Yk.

19838 Philip II, *of Spain*, 1598
Pet. Wor.

19840 *See*: 22992.5

19847 Philippson, Joannes,
Sleidanus, 1584
Linc. Rip.

19848 Philippson, Joannes,
Sleidanus, (1560)
Cant (imp)*. Pet.

19848a Philippson, Joannes,
Sleidanus, (1560)
Ex (imp). Her.

19849 Philippson, Joannes,
Sleidanus, 1563
Pet (2).

19853 Philips, Edward, 1605
Yk.

19854 Philips, Edward, 1607
Ex.

19856.7 Phillips, George, [1598?]
Linc (imp).

19858 Phillips, George, 1594
Linc.

19862 Phillips, Jerome, 1623
Ex. Yk.

19878 Phillips, John, *of Feversham*,
1625
Pet.

19879 Phillips, Thomas, 1639
Linc.

19881.5 Philodikaios, Irenicus,
pseud., [1599?]
Yk.

19885 Philopatris, John, 1592
Linc. Yk.

19892 Philpot, John, [1556?]
Pet.

19893a Philpot, John, (1559)
Glo (imp).

19899 Pie, Thomas, 1603
Pet (2).

19900 Pie, Thomas, 1597
Pet. Sal.

19901 Pie, Thomas, 1604
Sal. Yk.

19907 Piers, *Ploughman*, 1550
Pet (tpw).

19908 Piers, *Ploughman*, 1561
Yk (imp).

19910 Pierson, Thomas, 1636
Pet.

19910.5 Pietro, *Aretino*, 1635
Cant.

19911.5 Pietro, *Aretino*, 1584
Linc.

19926.3 Pilkington, James, 1560
Pet. S Pl. Yk (tp imp).

19929 Pilkington, James, 1585
Pet. Sal. Yk (imp).

19931 Pilkington, James, (1563)
Linc. Pet. Rip. S Pl. Yk.

19933 Pilkington, Richard, 1618
Pet. Yk (tp imp).

19944 Pinke, William, 1636
Bur. Ely.

19946? Pinner, Charles, 1597
'words'
Linc (imp).

19948 Piscator, Johann, 1594
Wor. Yk.

19949 Piscator, Johann, 1595
Wor.

19951 Piscator, Johann, 1598
Yk.

19952 Piscator, Johann, 1596
Pet. Wor.

19953 Piscator, Johann, 1591
Linc.

19954 Piscator, Johann, 1595
Wor. Yk.

19956 Piscator, Johann, 1591
Yk.

19957 Piscator, Johann, 1594
Linc. Wor.

19957.3 Piscator, Johann, 1608
Her. S Asa.

19958 Piscator, Johann, 1593
Linc. Wor.

19959 Piscator, Johann, 1597
Her. S Asa.

19960 Piscator, Johann, 1603
Pet (2). Wor.

19962 Piscator, Johann, 1583
Linc.

19963 Piscator, Johann, 1599
Yk (tpw).

19966 Pitiscus, Bartholomew, 1630
Yk.

19967 Pitiscus, Bartholomew,
(1614)
'Trigonometry'
Linc.

19968 Pitiscus, Bartholomew,
(1630)
Yk.

19974.2 Pius V, *Pope*, [1570]
Yk.

19983.7 Platt, *Sir* Hugh, 1628
Linc.

19993 Platt, *Sir* Hugh, 1600
Linc.

20001 Platus, Hieronymus, 1632
Her. Pet.

20003 Playfere, Thomas, 1623
Ely.

20004 Playfere, Thomas, 1633
S Pl ('The power of prayer',
only)*. Wor.

20008 Playfere, Thomas, 1606
Pet.

20010 Playfere, Thomas, 1603
Cant. S Pl.

20025 Playfere, Thomas, 1603
Cant.

20026 Playfere, Thomas, 1609
Cant (2). Ex.

20028 Playfere, Thomas, 1607
Pet.

20029 Plinius Secundus, Caius,
1601
Her. Linc.

20030 Plinius Secundus, Caius,
1634
Cant (imp). Win.

20037 Plowden, Edmund, [1598?]
Pet.

20040 Plowden, Edmund, (1571)
Dur.

20044 Plowden, Edmund, 1588
Glo.

20046.3 Plowden, Edmund, 1579
Dur.

20046.7 Plowden, Edmund, 1584
Pet.

20047 Plowden, Edmund, (1594)
Glo.

20050 Plummer, Timothy, 1622
Linc.

20051 Plumtre, Huntingdon, 1629
Ex.

20057.5 Plutarch, (1571)
Pet.

20063 Plutarch, 1603
Ely. Liv. Nor (tpw). Yk.

20066 Plutarch, 1579
Pet.

20067 Plutarch, 1595
Bur (tpw)*. Wel (tpw)*.

20068 Plutarch, 1603
Sal. Wel.

20068a Plutarch, 1603
Cant.

20069 Plutarch, 1612
Pet.

20075 Pocklington, John, 1637
Cant (imp). Her. Pet. S Pl (2).
Win. Yk.

20076 Pocklington, John, 1637
Bur. Linc. Yk (2).

20077 Pocklington, John, 1636
Cant. Ely. Ex. Linc (with tp of
2nd ed.). Sal. Yk.

20078 Pocklington, John, 1636
Ex. Linc.

20082 Pointz, Robert, 1566
Carl. Pet.

20083.3 Poland. Socinian Churches,
1609 [after 1635]
Carl*. Glo*. Linc. Win*.

20083.5 Polanus, Amandus, 1591
Pet (imp).

20086 Polanus, Amandus, 1599
Yk.

20088 Pole, Reginald, 1569
Yk.

20089 Polemon, John, [1578]
Pet.

20090 Polemon, John, 1587
Pet.

20099a Polybius, 1634
Glo. S Dv.

20100 Pont, Robert, 1599
Linc.

20104 Pont, Robert, 1599
Sal.

20109 Ponticus, Ludovicus Virunius,
1585
Lich. Linc. Pet.

20111 Pope, 1624
Pet.

20114 Popes, [1560]
Pet.

20118 Porta, Giovanni Battista
della, 1591
Pet. Wor.

20124 Porter, Jerome, 1632
Linc.

20130 Posselius, Johannes, 1640
Ely. Her. S Asa. Yk.

20133 Potter, Barnaby, 1613
Pet.

20134 Potter, Christopher, 1629
Linc. Yk.

20135 Potter, Christopher, 1633
Dur. Liv. Pet.

20135.3 Potter, Christopher, 1633
Yk.

20135.7 Potter, Christopher, 1633
Glo. S Asa. Sal.

20136 Potter, Christopher, 1634
Carl.

20136.3 Potter, Christopher, 1634
Cant. Linc. Liv. Nor. Win.

20138 Potts, Thomas, 1613 (1612)
Yk (imp).

20140 Powel, Edward, (1523)
Rip. Roch.

20141.3 Powel, Gabriel, 1603
Yk.

20141.5 Powel, Gabriel, 1603
Ely*. Linc. Pet.

20142 Powel, Gabriel, 1606
Yk.

20144 Powel, Gabriel, 1604
Linc. Liv. Yk.

20145 Powel, Gabriel, 1606
Linc. Yk (imp).

20146 Powel, Gabriel, 1607
Wor. Yk (imp).

20147 Powel, Gabriel, 1605
Cant. Pet. Rip. Sal. Wor
(imp?). Yk.

20149 Powel, Gabriel, 1605
Yk.

20151 Powel, Gabriel, 1602
Yk.

20154 Powel, Gabriel, 1623
Chelm (imp).

20163 Powell, Thomas,
Londino-Cambrensis, 1623
Wor.

20163.5 Powell, Thomas,
Londino-Cambrensis, 1623
S Asa.

20170 Powell, Thomas,
Londino-Cambrensis, 1603
Pet.

20172 Powell, Thomas, *of Brasenose
Coll.*, 1613
Ex.

20175 Poynet, John, (1555)
Pet. Sal (tpw).

20175a Poynet, John, (1556)
Yk.

20176 Poynet, John, (1549)
Pet.

20177 Poynet, John, (1550)
Pet.

20178 Poynet, John, 1556
Pet. Yk.

20184 Praise, 1586
Cant.

20201 Prelates, [1584?]
Cant. Pet (2 − 1 imp).

20210 Preston, John, 1631
Her.

20219 Preston, John, 1636
Linc. Yk.

20221.5 Preston, John, 1632
Glo.

20221.7 Preston, John, 1632
Glo (imp).

20223 Preston, John, 1636
Win.

20225 Preston, John, 1640
Ex (imp).

20227 Preston, John, 1638
Ex (2 − 1 imp). Win (tpw).

20232 Preston, John, 1631
Cant. Carl. Wor.

20233 Preston, John, 1632
Linc.

20235 Preston, John, 1633
Ex.

20238 Preston, John, 1638
Cant (imp).

20240.3 Preston, John, 1640
Ex (imp).

20241 Preston, John, 1629
Glo (imp)*.

20242 Preston, John, 1630
Bur (tpw)*.

20244 Preston, John, 1631
Linc.

20253 Preston, John, 1629
Ex. Wor.

20254 Preston, John, 1630
Bur.

20257 Preston, John, 1632
Ex.

20259 Preston, John, 1634
Yk.

20265.5 Preston, John, 1637
Ex.

20275 Preston, John, 1633
Glo (tpw)*.

20278.5 Preston, John, 1630
Pet.

20280.3 Preston, John, 1631
Cant (tpw)*.

20281 Preston, John, 1631
Glo.

20282.3 Preston, John, *of East
Ogwell*, 1619
Linc (imp). Wor.

20285 Preston, Richard, 1622
Ex.

20285+ Preston, Richard, 1622
[Anr ed.?] 4°; I.D. f. J. Bellamie.
Yk.

20286.7 Preston, Thomas, & Green,
Thomas, 1621
Yk.

20290 Price, Daniel, 1610
S Pl. Wor.

20291 Price, Daniel, 1613
Linc.

20292 Price, Daniel, 1610
Yk.

20294 Price, Daniel, 1613
Linc.

20295 Price, Daniel, 1613
Cant. Pet. Yk.

20296 Price, Daniel, 1608
Linc.

20297 Price, Daniel, 1617
Ex (2). Linc. S Pl.

20298 Price, Daniel, 1608
Ely. Linc.

20299 Price, Daniel, 1613
Cant. Yk.

20301 Price, Daniel, 1608
Cant (imp). Ex.

20302 Price, Daniel, 1609
Cant. Linc. S Pl.

20304 Price, Daniel, 1613
Linc. Yk (imp)*.

20305 Price, Daniel, 1609
Linc.

20306 Price, Gabriel, 1616
Linc. S Pl.

20308 Price, John, 1640
Ches.

20309 Price, *Sir* John, 1573
Cant. Her. Linc. Pet. Sal. Yk.

20329 Price, Sampson, 1617
Wor.

20330 Price, Sampson, 1616
Cant (2). Ex. S Pl.

20331 Price, Sampson, 1614
Cant (imp).

20332 Price, Sampson, 1626
Wor (imp).

20333 Price, Sampson, 1613
Cant. Pet. S Pl. Sal (imp).

20334 Price, Sampson, 1624
Pet.

20342 Pricket, Robert, 1606
Yk.

20343 Pricket, Robert, 1603
Pet (imp). Yk.

20344 Prideaux, John, 1614
Ban. Linc. Wor (2). Yk.

20345- Prideaux, John, 1636
[Anr ed.?] 'Two decads of sermons';
4°; Oxford, L. Lichfield, sold by H.
Crypps and H. Curteyne.
Wor.

20345 Prideaux, John, 1637 (1636)
Carl (imp). Her (imp). S Pl (10
sermons).

20347 Prideaux, John, 1626
Bur. Her. Wor.

20348 Prideaux, John, 1634
Wor.

20349 Prideaux, John, 1634
Bur. Ex. Linc (2). Pet. Yk.

20350 Prideaux, John, 1635
Bur. Ely. Linc.

20351 Prideaux, John, 1621
Cant. Roch. Wor.

20356 Prideaux, John, 1625
Yk.

20357 Prideaux, John, 1626
Bur. Her. Linc (2). Roch.
S Asa. S Pl. Swel. Wor.

20358 Prideaux, John, 1626
Bur. Linc (2). Nor (tpw). Roch.
Wor.

20359 Prideaux, John, 1625
Cant (2). Roch. Wor.

20361 Prideaux, John, 1625
Cant (2). Roch. Wor.

20369 Prime, John, 1587
Pet. Yk.

20370 Prime, John, 1583
Pet.

20371.5 Prime, John, 1585
Pet.

20379 Primer, 1568
S Pl.

20380 Primer, 1573
Ely. Her. Linc. Pet. Yk.

20382 Primerosius, Jacobus, 1631
Sal. Yk.

20384 Primerosius, Jacobus, 1638
Ely.

20385 Primerosius, Jacobus, 1630
Sal.

20387 Primrose, David, *Minister*,
1636
Bur. Cant. Glo. Linc. Sal (2).
Win.

20393 Primrose, W., [1612]
Linc.

20398 Proclus, Diadochus, 1620
Glo.

20403 Procter, Thomas, *Poet*, 1578
Pet. Wel.

20405 Procter, William, 1625
Cant. Pet. S Pl.

20407 Proctor, John, 1554
Pet.

20409 Proctor, Thomas, 1621
Linc.

20410 Proctor, Thomas, 1621
Linc.

20411 Proctor, Thomas, 1621
Sal.

20439.7 Properties, [1565?]
Linc.

20447 Protestants, 1638
Yk.

20447.5 Protestants, 1638
Bur.

20448 Protestants, 1607
Cant.

20450 Protestants, 1615
Her (imp)*.

20454 Prynne, William, 1637
Carl. Pet. S Pl. Yk.

20454.5 Prynne, William, [1637]
Pet.

20455a Prynne, William, 1628
Dur. Sal. Yk.

20456 Prynne, William, 1636
Ex.

20457 Prynne, William, 1629
Yk.

20458 Prynne, William, 1630
Bris. Bur. Cant. Yk (2 — 1 imp).

20460 Prynne, William, 1629
Yk.

20461 Prynne, William, 1630
Bris. Bur. Cant (retains
cancelled tp). Yk (2 — 1 with a*1
apparently replaced by 1 leaf only
= tp).

20462 Prynne, William, 1628
Yk.

20463 Prynne, William, 1628
Dur. Pet.

20464a Prynne, William, 1633
Bur. Ex. Sal (tp imp). Wor.

20467 Prynne, William, 1640
Cant (pt 1 only). Ex. Pet. Yk
(2).

20469 Prynne, William, [1636?]
S Pl.

20469.7 Prynne, William, 1636
Sal.

20471 Prynne, William, 1626
Bur. Yk.

20472 Prynne, William, 1627
S Pl. Yk.

20474 Prynne, William, 1637
Chelm (imp). Sal. Yk.

20475 Prynne, William, 1637
Cant. Yk.

20476.5 Prynne, William, 1636
Bur*. Cant (imp). Ex. Yk*.

20477 Prynne, William, 1628
Bur*. Dur.

20477.5 Prynne, William, 1628
Yk.

20486 Puente, Luis de la, 1619
Her (imp).

20492 Puget de la Serre, Jean, 1632
Linc.

20493 Pullein, Thomas, 1608
Yk (2).

20497 Pulton, Ferdinand, 1615
Glo.

20502 Purchas, Samuel, 1623
S Pl.

20503 Purchas, Samuel, 1619
Cant. Linc. Yk (imp).

20505 Purchas, Samuel, 1613
Ex. Linc.

20506 Purchas, Samuel, 1614
Cant. Liv. Yk (imp).

20507 Purchas, Samuel, 1617
Bur. Sal. Wor. Yk.

20508 Purchas, Samuel, 1626
Lich. Llan (imp)*.

20508.5 Purchas, Samuel, 1626
Cant. Glo.

20509 Purchas, Samuel, 1625
Cant. Glo. Her (vols 3, 4 only).
Lich (vol. 3 only). Wor.

20516 Puteanus, Erycius, 1634
Ex. Linc. Pet. S Pl.

20517 Puteanus, Erycius, 1634
Ex. S Pl.

20518 Puteanus, Erycius, 1640
Glo.

20520 Puttock, Roger, 1632
Bur. Yk.

20521.2 Pyne, John, [1626]
Yk.

20521.4 Pyne, John, [1626]
Yk.

20527.5 Quarles, Francis, 1632
Carl (date erased).

20530 Quarles, Francis, 1633
Cant.

20555 Quelch, William, 1636
Pet. Wor.

20556 Querimonia, 1592
Cant. Pet. Wor.

20575.5 R., I. *or* J., 1605
Yk.

20577 R., I. *or* J., 1628
Yk.

20594 R., W., 1629
Linc.

20600 Racster, John, 1605
Linc (tp imp).

20601 Racster, John, 1598
Linc (imp). Liv.

20602 Radford, John, 1605
Pet. S Asa (imp).

20603 Rainbow, Edward, 1635
Cant (imp). Carl. Ex (2). Pet.
S Pl. Yk.

20605 Rainolds, John, 1609
Ex (3).

20606 Rainolds, John, 1596
Bur. Dur. Her. Linc. Pet. S Pl.
Win. Wor. Yk.

20607 Rainolds, John, 1609
Bur. Pet.

20608 Rainolds, John, 1610
Carl. Linc.

20609 Rainolds, John, 1614
Cant.

20611+ Rainolds, John, 1613
[Anr ed.] 4°; J. Beale f. J. Man.
Linc.

20612 Rainolds, John, 1587
Pet. Yk.

20612.5 Rainolds, John, 1613
Chi.

20614 Rainolds, John, 1619
Pet.

20615 Rainolds, John, 1628
S Pl (tp imp).

20615.5 Rainolds, John, 1628
Yk.

20618 Rainolds, John, 1629
Sal.

20620 Rainolds, John, 1613 (1614)
Sal (pt 2 only). Yk.

20621.5 Rainolds, John, 1586
Linc. Pet.

20623.5 Rainolds, John, (1586)
Pet.

20624 Rainolds, John, 1580
Pet. Yk.

20625 Rainolds, John, 1602
Bur (2). Linc. Pet. Wor. Yk.

20626 Rainolds, John, 1584
Cant ('He [*sic*] summe ...'). Carl.
Chi. Ex. Linc. Rip. S Asa.

20627 Rainolds, John, 1588
Dur. Pet. S Pl. Swel. Wor.

20628 Rainolds, John, 1598
Bur. Pet. Sal. Yk.

20629 Rainolds, John, 1609
Bur. Dur. Ely. Her. Lich.
Nor. Pet. Win.

20630 Rainolds, John, 1610
Chi. Her. S Pl. Wor. Yk.

20632 Rainolds, William, 1583
Pet. Rip. Wor. Yk.

20633 Rainolds, William, 1593
Pet (2 − 1 imp).

20637 Raleigh, *Sir* Walter, 1614
Her (imp). Sal. Swel (imp).
Wor (imp?). Yk (tpw).

20639 Raleigh, *Sir* Walter, (1621)
Bur. Cant. S Asa (imp). Win.
Yk.

20640 Raleigh, *Sir* Walter, (1628)
Cant.

20641 Raleigh, *Sir* Walter, (1634)
Ex. Glo. Pet. Yk.

20649.3 Raleigh, *Sir* Walter, 1628
Linc.

20649.5 Raleigh, *Sir* Walter, 1628
Yk.

20649.7 Raleigh, *Sir* Walter, 1628
S Pl*.

20649.9 Raleigh, *Sir* Walter, 1640
Carl.

20650 Raleigh, *Sir* Walter, 1640
Pet.

20652.5 Raleigh, *Sir* Walter, 1618
Carl. Yk*.

20657 Ramsay, Andrew, 1638
S Pl. Yk.

20660 Ramsden, Henry, 1639
Yk.

20667 Ranchin, Guillaume, 1638
Bur (2). Carl. Dur. Ex. Linc.
Pet. S Pl. Swel. Wor. Yk.

20673 Randall, John, 1630
Yk.

20680 Randall, John, 1629
Yk.

20684 Randol, John, 1633
Pet.

20694 Randolph, Thomas, 1638
Glo (imp).

20695 Randolph, Thomas, 1640
Yk (pt 3 only, bound with Wing
R240 & R241).

20706 Rastell, John, *Barrister*, 1575
Yk.

20706.5 Rastell, John, *Barrister*,
1579
Pet.

20708 Rastell, John, *Barrister*, 1592
Glo (tpw).

20709 Rastell, John, *Barrister*, 1595
Yk.

20715a Rastell, John, *Barrister*,
1618
Linc.

20719 Rastell, John, *Barrister*,
(1530)
Glo (imp)*.

20725 Rastell, John, *Jesuit*, 1567
Pet. Wor.

20726 Rastell, John, *Jesuit*, 1564
Wor.

20727 Rastell, John, *Jesuit*, 1565
Wor.

20728 Rastell, John, *Jesuit*, 1565
Pet. Sal. Wor. Yk.

20728.5 Rastell, John, *Jesuit*, 1566
Sal (tpw).

20729 Rastell, John, *Jesuit*, 1566
Sal. Wor.

20730 Rastell, William, 1566
Ex. Pet.

20735.5 Rastell, William, 1563
Pet.

20740 Rastell, William, 1598
Pet.

20755 Ravaillac, François, 1610
Linc (frag.).

20772 Rawlinson, John, 1609
Ely. Pet (imp). Yk.

20773 Rawlinson, John, 1606
Cant.

20773a Rawlinson, John, 1612
Ex. S Pl.

20774 Rawlinson, John, 1625
Cant.

20775 Rawlinson, John, 1611
Linc.

20776 Rawlinson, John, 1616
Cant. Ex.

20777 Rawlinson, John, 1619
Cant. S Pl (tp imp). Wor.

20784 Read, Alexander, *M.D.*,
1638
Wel.

20789 Reading, John, 1621
Pet (3).

20790 Reading, John, 1624
Pet (imp).

20791? Reading, John, 1626
4°.
Cant (imp). Her. Pet.

20792 Reading, John, 1621
Pet.

20796 Record, Robert, (1556)
Pet.

20797 Record, Robert, 1596
Pet.

20803 Record, Robert, 1590
Yk.

20808 Record, Robert, 1623
Wor.

20810 Record, Robert, 1636
Cant.

20812 Record, Robert, (1551)
Pet.

20813 Record, Robert, 1574
Wor (imp).

20818 Record, Robert, 1567
Pet (2).

20820 Record, Robert, (1557)
Pet.

20829 Reeve, Edmund, 1631
Bur. Lich. Yk (2).

20831 Reeve, Edmund, 1636
Pet (tp imp). Wor.

20832a Reeve, Thomas, 1624
Carl. Linc.

20836 Registrum, 1531
Dur (imp). Pet. Wel (tpw).
Wor.

20837 Registrum, 1553
Linc.

20838 Registrum, [1595]
Pet.

20839 Registrum, [1634]
Cant. Dur. Sal.

20842 Regius, Urbanus, (1548)
Pet.

20846 Regius, Urbanus, 1593
Pet.

20850 Regius, Urbanus, 1578
Bur (imp). Pet.

20855 Regnier de la Planche, Louis,
1577
Linc (tpw). Pet.

20881 Remonstrance, 1590
Pet. Rip. Wor. Yk (2).

20886 Reniger, Michel, 1582
Linc. Yk.

20887 Reniger, Michel, 1604
Yk.

20899.5 Retorna, [1537−40?]
Pet.

20906 Reuchlin, Johann, 1570
Pet.

20910 Reuter, Adam, 1612
Pet.

20911 Reuter, Adam, 1626
Sal (imp).

20914 Reuter, Adam, 1609
Pet.

20925a.5 Reynoldes, Richard,
[1563]
Pet.

20926 Reynoldes, Richard, 1571
Pet. Wor.

20927 Reynolds, Edward, 1632
Chelm. Wor. Yk.

20928 Reynolds, Edward, 1635
Her.

20929 Reynolds, Edward, 1638
Yk (tpw)*.

20929a Reynolds, Edward, 1638
Chelm. Linc (2).

20930 Reynolds, Edward, 1639
Yk.

20931 Reynolds, Edward, 1638
Cant. Linc. Pet (2).

20931.5 Reynolds, Edward, 1638
Carl.

20932 Reynolds, Edward, 1636
Cant. Carl. Pet (2). Win.

20935 Reynolds, Edward, 1632
Chelm.

20938 Reynolds, Edward, 1640
Chelm. Linc. Pet. S Asa. Sal.

20942 Reynolds, John, *Merchant*,
1621
Yk.

20946 Reynolds, John, *Merchant*,
1640
Yk.

20946.3 Reynolds, John, *Merchant*,
1624
Sal. Yk (tp imp).

20946.4 Reynolds, John, *Merchant*,
1624
Pet (imp)*.

20946.6 Reynolds, John, *Merchant*,
1624
Yk.

20946.7 Reynolds, John, *Merchant*,
1624
Sal.

20966 Rhys, John David, 1592
Ban (3 − 1 imp). Glo. Wor.

20978 Rich, Barnaby, 1578
Pet.

20990 Rich, Barnaby, 1619
Cant.

21002a Rich, Barnaby, 1584
Pet.

21012 Richardson, Alexander, 1629
Win. Yk.

21013.5 Richardson, Charles, 1621
Yk.

21015 Richardson, Charles, 1617
Linc.

21017 Richardson, Charles, 1615
S Pl. Yk.

21018 Richardson, Charles, 1616
Ex. S Pl.

21019 Richardson, Charles, 1616
Cant. Pet.

21020 Richardson, Gabriel, 1627
Bur. Ex. Her. Lich. S Asa.
Sal.

21022 Richeome, Louis, 1619
Her. Pet.

21024 Richer, Edmond, 1612
Yk (2).

21032 Rider, John, 1606
Pet.

21036a.3 Rider, John, 1640
Cant.

21038 Ridley, Lancelot, [1540]
Pet.

21038.5 Ridley, Lancelot, [1540]
S Pl.

21039 Ridley, Lancelot, (1548)
Linc. Pet.

21042 Ridley, Lancelot, [1538]
S Pl (imp).

21043 Ridley, Lancelot, [1549?]
S Pl.

21045 Ridley, Mark, 1613
Linc.

21046 Ridley, Nicholas, 1555
'declaration'
Yk (imp).

21047 Ridley, Nicholas, 1586
S Pl.

21048 Ridley, Nicholas, [1556]
Linc (imp).

21050 Ridley, Nicholas, 1574
Cant.

21052 Ridley, Nicholas, (1566)
Yk.

21054 Ridley, *Sir* Thomas, 1607
Cant. S Pl. Tru.

21055 Ridley, *Sir* Thomas, 1634
Linc.

21055.5 Ridley, *Sir* Thomas, 1634
Carl. Ches. Dur. Ex. Pet. S Pl.

21057.5 Ripon, [1596]
Rip.

21059 Rive, Edmund, 1621
Linc.

21068 Robartes, Foulke, 1639
Linc. Pet. Yk.

21069 Robartes, Foulke, 1613
Bur. Ex. Linc. Pet (2). Sal.
Yk (2).

21072a Roberti, Antonius, 1638
Chelm.

21073 Roberts, Alexander, 1610
Nor.

21074 Roberts, Alexander, 1614
Sal.

21075 Roberts, Alexander, 1616
Linc.

21084 Roberts, Henry, [1585]
Linc.

21094 Roberts, Lewis, 1638
Carl.

21098.7 Robertson, Bartholomew,
1621
Ely.

21109 Robinson, John, *of Leyden*,
1610
Yk.

21112a Robinson, John, *of Leyden*,
1628
Yk.

21114 Robinson, John, *of Leyden*,
1638
Yk.

21123 Robinson, Thomas, 1622
Wel.

21125 Robinson, Thomas, 1630
Linc.

21141 Rodoginus, Irenaeus, *pseud.*,
1625
Bur.

21145 Rodriguez, Alonso, 1631
Cant (imp).

21148 Rodriguez, Alonso, 1627
Pet.

21151 Roe, Nathaniel, 1633
Yk.

21152 Roe, William, 1615
Linc. Sal.

21153 Roesslin, Eucharius, (1540)
Pet.

21155 Roesslin, Eucharius, 1552
Pet.

21156 Roesslin, Eucharius, 1560
Pet.

21166 Rogers, Daniel, 1632
Glo. Pet (imp).

21173 Rogers, Daniel, 1640
Wor.

21174 Rogers, Francis, 1613
Cant.

21175 Rogers, Francis, 1633
Cant.

21176 Rogers, Francis, 1633
Cant. Yk.

21177 Rogers, Henry, *of
Herefordshire*, 1623
Cant. Wor.

21179 Rogers, Hugh, 1640
Carl.

21180 Rogers, John, *Author*, 1579
Pet.

21181.5 Rogers, John, *Author*,
[1578]
Pet.

21186 Rogers, John, *of Chacombe*,
1618
Carl. Linc (imp).

21194 Rogers, Nehemiah, 1621
Yk.

21196 Rogers, Nehemiah, 1640
Chelm. Ely (pt 2 only).

21198 Rogers, Nehemiah, 1632
Sal.

21199 Rogers, Nehemiah, 1623
Yk.

21202 Rogers, Nehemiah, 1632
Linc. Nor. Sal.

21204 Rogers, Richard, 1615
Cant (imp). Carl. Wor.

21208 Rogers, Richard, 1620
Wor.

21214 Rogers, Richard, 1620
Yk.

21215 Rogers, Richard, 1603
Bur. Pet. Yk (2 − 1 imp).

21216a Rogers, Richard, 1605
Glo. Her.

21221 Rogers, Richard, 1618
Bur.

21223 Rogers, Richard, 1629
Yk.

21223.7 Rogers, Richard, 1635
Carl.

21226 Rogers, Thomas, *M.A.*, 1585
S Pl (tpw)*. Wor.

21226.5 Rogers, Thomas, *M.A.*,
1585
Yk (tp imp).

21227 Rogers, Thomas, *M.A.*, 1587
Cant. Wor. Yk (2 − 1 imp).

21228 Rogers, Thomas, *M.A.*, 1607
Ex (2). Yk.

21229 Rogers, Thomas, *M.A.*, 1621
Bur.

21230 Rogers, Thomas, *M.A.*, 1625
Roch.

21230a Rogers, Thomas, *M.A.*,
1625
Linc.

21231 Rogers, Thomas, *M.A.*, 1629
Cant.

21232 Rogers, Thomas, *M.A.*, 1633
Ely. Linc.

21233 Rogers, Thomas, *M.A.*, 1639
Pet. S Asa. S Pl. Swel.

21236 Rogers, Thomas, *M.A.*, 1587
Ely.

21237 Rogers, Thomas, *M.A.*, 1589
Yk.

21239 Rogers, Thomas, *M.A.*, 1576
Pet (imp).

21241 Rogers, Thomas, *M.A.*, 1608
Yk.

21244 Rogers, Timothy, 1619
Cant (imp)*.

21250 Rogers, Timothy, 1621
Bur. Dur (tpw).

21253 Rohan, Henri, *duc de*, 1640
Linc.

21265 Rollenson, Francis, 1612
Yk.

21266 Rollock, Hercules, 1589
Linc (tpw).

21268 Rollock, Robert, 1594
Pet. Swel.

21270 Rollock, Robert, 1605
Ely.

21274 Rollock, Robert, 1600
Pet.

21278 Rollock, Robert, 1590
Pet.

21279 Rollock, Robert, 1598
Swel.

21280 Rollock, Robert, 1591
Carl. Pet. Yk.

21281 Rollock, Robert, 1606
Rip (pt 2 only).

21286 Rollock, Robert, 1603
Wor.

21291 Rome, 1600
Ex.

21293 Rome, 1590
Pet.

21294 Rome, 1595
Yk.

21317 Rosa, Thomas, 1608
Linc. Rip (tp imp). Yk.

21327 Ross, Alexander, 1627
Linc.

21334 Rote, [1496]
Dur (imp).

21340a Rous, Francis, *the Elder*,
1622
Pet.

21342 Rous, Francis, *the Elder*,
1616
Pet.

21344 Rous, Francis, *the Elder*,
1623
Pet (imp).

21347 Rous, Francis, *the Elder*,
1626
Glo. Wor. Yk (2).

21347.7 Rous, Francis, *the Elder*,
1633
Bur.

21350 Rous, Francis, *the Younger*,
1637
Carl (2 variants: tp with Leonard
or Leonakd [*sic*] Lichfield in
impr.).

21354 Rouspeau, Yves, 1584
Yk.

21361 Rowlands *or* Verstegan,
Richard, 1605
Cant. Ex. Yk.

21362 Rowlands *or* Verstegan,
Richard, 1628
Cant. Nor. S Pl.

21363 Rowlands *or* Verstegan,
Richard, 1634
Cant. Ely. S Asa. Yk.

21415 Rowlandson, James, 1623
Carl.

21415.5 Rowlandson, James, 1627
Carl. S Pl.

21430 Royal Book, [1507]
Yk (imp)*.

21432 Rudd, Anthony, 1603
Cant. Yk.

21433 Rudd, Anthony, 1603
Bur. Pet. Yk.

21435- Rudd, Anthony, 1605
[Anr ed. of STC 21435?] 'A sermon
preached before his maiestie at
White-hall upon the ninth of
Februarie 1605'; 4°; H. Lownes f. C.
Knight.
Carl.

21435.7 Rudierd, *Sir* Benjamin,
[1628]
Cant. Ex. Pet.

21446 Ruggle, George, 1630
Cant. Carl. Linc.

21454 Rushworth, William, 1640
Carl.

21456 Russell, *Lady* Elizabeth, 1605
Yk.

21460 Russell, John, *of Magd.
Coll., Cambridge*, 1634
Pet.

21466.7 Ruthven, John, 1603
Linc.

21474 Ryves, *Sir* Thomas, 1629
Pet.

21477 Ryves, *Sir* Thomas, 1626
S Pl.

21478 Ryves, *Sir* Thomas, 1620
Cant. Carl. Ex. Linc. Pet.
Wor. Yk (2).

21479 Ryves, *Sir* Thomas, 1624
Pet (tp imp).

21482 S., C., 1590
Yk.

21483.5 S., D., [1584?]
Pet.

21492 S., G., 1625
Wor.

21499 S., I. *or* J., 1597
Pet (imp).

21533.7 S., W., *Gentleman*, 1577
Pet.

21542 Sadler, John, 1640
Linc.

21555.8 Saint Andrew's University,
1602
Pet.

21559 Saint German, Christopher,
(1528)
Linc. Pet.

21560 Saint German, Christopher,
1604
Linc.

21562 Saint German, Christopher,
[1531]
Pet.

21563.5 Saint German, Christopher,
(1531)
Pet.

21566 Saint German, Christopher,
(1531)
Pet.

21571 Saint German, Christopher,
1554 [*i.e.* 1556?]
Pet.

21572 Saint German, Christopher,
(1569)
Pet.

21573 Saint German, Christopher,
(1575)
Yk.

21574.5 Saint German, Christopher,
1580
Tru.

21575 Saint German, Christopher,
1593
Pet.

21578 Saint German, Christopher,
1607
Cant. Linc.

21581 Saint German, Christopher,
1623
Wor.

21582.5 Saint German, Christopher, 1638
Pet. Yk.

21583 Saint German, Christopher, 1630
Ex.

21589 Saint John, Oliver, 1640 [o.s.]
Carl. Ex (2). Pet.

21589.3 Saint John, Oliver, 1640 [o.s.]
Pet.

21589.7 Saint John, Oliver, 1640 [o.s.]
Cant. Sal. Yk.

21598 Salerno, (1535)
Cant.

21599 Salerno, (1541)
Linc. Pet.

21601 Salerno, [1575]
Pet.

21621 Salkeld, John, 1613
Ex. Nor.

21625 Sallustius Crispus, Caius, 1608
Linc.

21635 Saltern, George, 1605
Yk.

21637 Saltmarsh, John, 1640
Yk.

21639 Saltmarsh, John, 1639
Carl.

21650 Saluste du Bartas, Guillaume de, (1608)
Liv (tpw).

21651 Saluste du Bartas, Guillaume de, (1611)
S Dv (with engr. tp of STC 21652).

21652 Saluste du Bartas, Guillaume de, 1613
Glo.

21653 Saluste du Bartas, Guillaume de, (1620, 1621)
Her (tpw). Lich.

21657 Saluste du Bartas, Guillaume de, 1600
Linc. Yk.

21663 Saluste du Bartas, Guillaume de, 1625
Cant.

21666 Saluste du Bartas, Guillaume de, 1621
Cant (imp)*.

21672 Saluste du Bartas, Guillaume de, 1592
Her (frag.).

21675 Salvianus, 1633
Bur. Carl. Ely. Linc. Wel.

21676 Salvianus, 1618
S Pl.

21677 Salvianus, 1580
Pet.

21679 Sampson, Richard, (1539)
Pet. S Pl.

21682 Sampson, Thomas, *Dean*, 1581
Pet.

21684 Sampson, Thomas, *Dean*, 1593
S Pl (frag.). Swel (frag.).

21692 Sanders, Nicholas, 1567
Swar.

21695 Sanders, Nicholas, 1566
Her. Rip. Wor.

21696 Sanders, Nicholas, 1567
Pet.

21697 Sanders, Nicholas, 1624
Yk.

21702 Sanderson, Robert, 1618
S Pl.

21703 Sanderson, Robert, 1631
Bur. Her.

21705 Sanderson, Robert, 1627
Linc. S Asa.

21706 Sanderson, Robert, 1632
Ely. Yk (2).

21707 Sanderson, Robert, 1637
Bur. Cant (imp). Wel.

21709 Sanderson, Robert, 1628
S Pl.

21710 Sanderson, Robert, 1635
Pet. S Pl.

21711 Sanderson, Thomas, 1611
Carl. Yk.

21713 Sandys, Edwin, *Abp*, 1585
Bur. S Pl. Yk (2).

21714 Sandys, Edwin, *Abp*, 1616
Pet. Swel. Wor. Yk (3).

21717 Sandys, *Sir* Edwin, 1605
Ex. Yk.

21717.5 Sandys, *Sir* Edwin, 1605 [*i.e.* 1622?]
Linc. Yk.

21718 Sandys, *Sir* Edwin, 1629
Glo. Pet. Wel. Yk.

21719 Sandys, *Sir* Edwin, 1632
Cant. Carl.

21720 Sandys, *Sir* Edwin, 1632
Ely (pt 1 only). Pet (2 – 1 pt 1 only). Wel. Yk.

21721 Sandys, *Sir* Edwin, 1637
Cant. S Asa.

21722 Sandys, *Sir* Edwin, 1638
Cant. Nor.

21723 Sandys, *Sir* Edwin, 1615
Chi.

21724 Sandys, George, 1636
Cant. Chi (tpw). Yk (2).

21725 Sandys, George, 1638 (1637)
Chi. Ex. Lich. S Pl. Win. Yk.

21726 Sandys, George, 1615
Cant (imp; 1st variant setting in C, 2nd in D).

21727 Sandys, George, 1621
Carl. Her. Linc.

21728 Sandys, George, 1627
Yk (imp).

21729 Sandys, George, 1632
Cant. Nor. Pet.

21732 Sandys, *Sir* Miles, (1634)
Cant (without the cancellations & additions). Linc (as Cant). Yk (as Cant).

21736 Sanford, John, 1604
S Pl.

21738 Sanford, John, 1611
Pet.

21744 Sansovino, Francesco, 1590
Pet.

21746 Saravia, Hadrianus, 1590
Her. Pet. Rip.

21747 Saravia, Hadrianus, 1593
Cant. Her. Linc. Rip.

21748 Saravia, Hadrianus, 1594
Glo. Linc (tp imp). Sal.

21750 Saravia, Hadrianus, 1592
Pet.

21751 Saravia, Hadrianus, 1611 (1610)
Cant. Chi. Dur. Ely. Ex. Liv. S Pl. Sal. Win. Wor. Yk.

21752 Saravia, Hadrianus, 1629
Cant. S Pl.

21752.5 Sarcerius, Erasmus, (1538)
Linc (tpw).

21753 Sarcerius, Erasmus, (1538)
S Pl.

21757a Sarpi, Paolo, 1628
Linc. Yk.

21759 Sarpi, Paolo, 1606
Liv.

21760 Sarpi, Paolo, 1619
Linc.

21761 Sarpi, Paolo, 1620
Cant. Carl. Ches. Chi. Her.
Lich. Linc (imp, pt of STC 21762
substituted). Pet. Wor.

21762 Sarpi, Paolo, 1629
Bur (2). Cant ('Second edition'
in lower case). Chelm. Ches.
Dur. Linc (frag.). Llan. Rip.
Wel.

21763 Sarpi, Paolo, 1640
Ches. Ex. S Dv. Swel.

21764 Sarpi, Paolo, 1620
Bris. Glo. Her. Nor. Pet. S Pl.

21765 Sarpi, Paolo, 1639
Dur. Nor. Yk (2).

21766 Sarpi, Paolo, 1626
Cant. Ex. Her. Sal.

21767 Sarpi, Paolo, 1626
Dur. Linc. Pet (2). S Pl.

21768 Sarpi, Paolo, 1630
Ban. Dur. Linc. Pet.

21782 Savile, *Sir* Henry, 1621
Ches. Yk.

21783 Savile, *Sir* Henry, 1596
Cant (2). Dur (imp). Ex. Glo.
Her. Linc. Nor. S Pl. Wel.
Wor. Yk.

21787 Savile, Thomas, 1606
Yk.

21788 Saviolo, Vincentio, 1595
(1594)
Pet.

21791 Savonarola, Girolamo,
(1538)
Cant. S Pl (imp).

21794 Savonarola, Girolamo,
[1542?]
Cant.

21805.1 Saxton, Christopher, [1579]
Lich (imp)*.

21806 Scapula, Joannes, 1637
Cant. Ex. Linc. Nor. Sal.
Swel. Wor. Yk.

21816.5 Schickard, Wilhelmus, 1639
Sal.

21817 Schilander, Cornelius, 1596
Pet.

21817.5 Schindler, Valentin, 1635
Sal.

21819 Schloer, Friedrich, 1633
Pet.

21821.2 Schonaeus, Cornelius, 1601
Pet.

21824 Schonaeus, Cornelius, 1635
S Pl.

21830 Sclater, William, *the Elder*,
1627
Bur. Her.

21832 Sclater, William, *the Elder*,
1632
Ex. Nor. Sal. Swel.

21835 Sclater, William, *the Elder*,
1627
Bur. Her.

21836 Sclater, William, *the Elder*,
1630
Ex. Nor. Sal.

21837 Sclater, William, *the Elder*,
1638
Swel.

21840 Sclater, William, *the Elder*,
1629
Sal.

21842 Sclater, William, *the Elder*,
1623
Bur. Ex. S Pl. Sal.

21843 Sclater, William, *the Elder*,
1616
Yk.

21844 Sclater, William, *the Elder*,
1638
Bur. Ex (2).

21846 Sclater, William, *the Elder*,
1629
Linc (imp). Nor (tpw).

21847 Sclater, William, *the Elder*,
1610
S Pl.

21848 Sclater, William, *the Elder*,
1633
Bur. Ex. Her. Sal.

21850 Sclater, William, *the Younger*,
[1639]
Ex (2). Linc (tpw).

21857 Scot, Patrick, 1622
Yk.

21860 Scot, Patrick, 1621
Yk (tp imp).

21863 Scot, Patrick, 1625
Sal.

21864 Scot, Reginald, 1584
Wor (imp).

21873.5 Scot, Thomas, *of Ipswich*,
1623
Linc.

21874 Scot, William, 1622
Yk (2).

21875 Scotland, (1566)
Sal.

21877 Scotland, 1597
Cant (letter-press tp).

21902 Scotland, 1633
Linc.

21903 Scotland, 1638
Yk.

21903.3 Scotland, 1638
S Pl*.

21904.3 Scotland, 1638
S Pl. Yk (mixed sheets with STC
21904).

21904.5 Scotland, 1639
S Pl.

21905 Scotland, 1639
Yk.

21906 Scotland, 1639
Ban. Cant. Carl. Dur. Ely. Ex.
Linc. Liv. Pet. S Asa (imp).
Win. Wor. Yk (2).

21907 Scotland, 1639
S Pl. Yk.

21915 Scotland, 1640
Linc. Sal.

21924 Scotland, 1640
Pet.

21926 Scotland, 1640
Yk.

21928 Scotland, 1640
Pet.

21929 Scotland, 1640
Pet.

21961 Scotland, 1606
Linc. Pet.

21996 Scotland, [1638]
S Pl.

21997+ Scotland, [1638]
[Anr ed.?] s.sh.fol.; Variant of both
STC 21996 & 21997.
Yk.

21998 Scotland, 1638
S Pl*. Yk.

21998.5 Scotland, 1638
Linc.

21999 Scotland, 1638
Yk (date cropped?).

22000 Scotland, 1638
S Pl. Yk.

22001 Scotland, 1639
Sal.

22001.5 Scotland, 1639
Cant (imp). Ex. Pet. Sal. Yk*.

22007.5 Scotland, 1640
Pet.

22015 Scotland, Church of, 1621
New.

22017 Scotland, Church of, 1561
Linc.

22023 Scotland, Church of, 1590
Yk.

22024.3 Scotland, Church of, 1603
Her (frag.).

22026 Scotland, Church of, [1638]
S Pl.

22026.4 Scotland, Church of, [1638]
Sal. Yk.

22026.6 Scotland, Church of, 1638
Linc.

22027 Scotland, Church of, 1638
S Pl.

22030.3 Scotland, Church of, 1638
S Pl.

22032 Scotland, Church of, [1638]
S Pl.

22037 Scotland, Church of, (1638)
S Pl.

22038 Scotland, Church of, (1638)
Dur. Sal.

22039 Scotland, Church of, 1638
S Pl. Yk.

22041 Scotland, Church of, 1566
Linc (tp imp).

22047 Scotland, Church of, 1638
S Pl.

22047.5 Scotland, Church of, 1638
Yk.

22048a Scotland, Church of, [1639]
S Pl. Yk.

22051 Scotland, Church of, 1639
S Pl. Sal. Yk.

22054.5 Scotland, Church of, 1638
Linc. S Pl*. Yk.

22058 Scotland, Episcopal Church
of, 1639
Bur. Cant (2). Ex (imp). Linc.
Llan. Sal (2).

22060 Scotland, Episcopal Church
of, 1639
Cant (D1ʳ catchword:
Commissi-). S Pl. Yk.

22070 Scott, Thomas, *B.D.*, 1623
Linc (tpw). Pet.

22072 Scott, Thomas, *B.D.*, 1624
Yk.

22073.4 Scott, Thomas, *B.D.*, 1624
Yk*.

22074 Scott, Thomas, *B.D.*, 1616
Pet (imp).

22075 Scott, Thomas, *B.D.*, [1623]
Ex.

22077 Scott, Thomas, *B.D.*, 1623
Yk (imp).

22077.3 Scott, Thomas, *B.D.*, 1623
Pet.

22077.5 Scott, Thomas, *B.D.*, 1623
Yk.

22079 Scott, Thomas, *B.D.*, 1623
Pet. Yk.

22081 Scott, Thomas, *B.D.*, 1623
Cant. Yk.

22085 Scott, Thomas, *B.D.*, 1626
Yk.

22086 Scott, Thomas, *B.D.*, 1624
Yk.

22086.5 Scott, Thomas, *B.D.*,
[1621]
Yk.

22088 Scott, Thomas, *B.D.*, 1624
Yk.

22089 Scott, Thomas, *B.D.*, [1624]
Yk.

22097a Scott, Thomas, *B.D.*,
[1623?]
Linc. Yk.

22098 Scott, Thomas, *B.D.*, 1620
Sal. Yk.

22100 Scott, Thomas, *B.D.*, 1620
Yk (imp).

22100.8 Scott, Thomas, *B.D.*, 1620
Yk.

22102 Scott, Thomas, *B.D.*, [1624]
Yk.

22103.3 Scott, Thomas, *B.D.*, 1624
Yk (tp imp).

22110 Scribonius, Gulielmus
Adolphus, 1583
Yk.

22114 Scribonius, Gulielmus
Adolphus, 1583
Yk.

22123 Scull, John, 1624
Yk.

22124 Scultetus, Abraham, 1618
Ex. Pet.

22126 Scultetus, Abraham, 1620
Cant.

22150 Sedgwick, John, 1624
Linc.

22161 Seeing, (1562)
Pet.

22163 Segar, *Sir* William, 1590
Cant. Linc.

22164 Segar, *Sir* William, 1602
Dur. Yk.

22166 Selden, John, 1640
Linc.

22167 Selden, John, 1617
Cant. Linc. Wel. Win. Yk.

22168 Selden, John, 1640
Carl. Ex. Lich. S Pl. Win.
Wor. Yk.

22170 Selden, John, 1636
Ex. S Asa. S Pl. Win. Wor.
Yk.

22171 Selden, John, 1610
Carl. Linc. Sal.

22172 Selden, John, 1618
Ches*. Ely*. Ex (2 – 1 has
'first-borne'). Glo (2)*. Lich.
S Asa. S Dv*.

22172.3 Selden, John, 1618
Linc (2). Sal. Yk.

22172.5 Selden, John, 1618
Cant. Pet.

22172.7 Selden, John, 1618
Dur. Win.

22173 Selden, John, 1618 [*i.e.* 1680]
Carl. Linc. S Pl. Win.

22174 Selden, John, 1610
Ely. Linc.

22175 Selden, John, 1635
Ex. Pet. S Pl. Swel. Wor. Yk.

22176 Selden, John, 1636
Cant.

22177 Selden, John, 1614
Linc. S Asa.

22178 Selden, John, 1631
Cant. Carl. Chi. Dur. Ely. Ex.
S Pl. Swel. Wel.

22185 Seminary Priests, 1592
Pet.

22186 Sempill, *Sir* James, 1619
Dur. Ex. Linc (tp imp). Pet.
S Asa (2). Wor. Yk (2).

22213 Seneca, Lucius Annaeus,
1614
Chelm. Lich. Yk (3).

22214 Seneca, Lucius Annaeus,
(1620)
Bris. Glo. Pet.

22218 Seneca, Lucius Annaeus, 1613
Linc.

22220 Seneca, Lucius Annaeus, 1634
S Pl.

22221 Seneca, Lucius Annaeus, 1581
Pet (imp?).

22230 Senhouse, Richard, 1627
Cant. Linc (tpw). Pet. Yk.

22232 Sennertus, Daniel, 1637
Sal.

22237 Sermon, 1585
Pet (2 − 1 tpw). Yk.

22242 Serres, Jean de, 1574
Dur.

22243 Serres, Jean de, 1576
Dur.

22244 Serres, Jean de, 1607
Lich. Wor.

22245 Serres, Jean de, 1611
Bur. Ex. Her.

22246 Serres, Jean de, 1624
Cant. Glo.

22247 Serres, Jean de, 1585
Pet.

22249.5 Seton, Alexander, [1542?]
Rip (frag.).

22250.2 Seton, John, (1560)
Yk.

22250.6 Seton, John, 1568
Rip.

22252 Seton, John, 1574
Pet.

22253.7 Seton, John, 1582
Ex (imp).

22254 Seton, John, 1584
Pet.

22254.3 Seton, John, 1599
Glo. Yk (imp).

22256 Seton, John, 1617
Ely. Sal.

22257 Seton, John, 1631
Yk.

22274 Shakespeare, William, 1632
Cant (imp)*. Nor (imp)*.

22274a Shakespeare, William, 1632
Ex (imp).

22341 Shakespeare, William, 1619
Yk.

22369 Sharp, Patrick, 1599
Pet.

22372 Sharpe, Leonell, 1616
Carl.

22374 Sharpe, Leonell, 1612
Pet (imp). Yk.

22375 Sharpe, Leonell, 1612
Linc. Pet (2). Yk.

22376 Sharpe, Leonell, 1603
Pet.

22390 Shaw, John, *Divine*, 1623
Yk.

22391.8 Sheafe, Thomas, 1639
Yk.

22393 Sheldon, Richard, 1611
Linc. Roch. Yk (2).

22394 Sheldon, Richard, 1622
Pet.

22395 Sheldon, Richard, 1612
Yk.

22396 Sheldon, Richard, 1634
Linc. Pet. Yk.

22397 Sheldon, Richard, 1612
Pet. Wor. Yk (2 − 1 imp).

22398 Sheldon, Richard, 1625
S Pl.

22399 Sheldon, Richard, 1616
Glo. Yk.

22400 Shelford, Robert, 1635
Bur. Carl. Linc. Pet. Sal. Yk.

22406 Shepery, John, 1586
Yk.

22415 Shepherds' Kalendar, [1570?]
Pet (tpw).

22428 Sherry, Richard, [1550]
Pet.

22429 Sherry, Richard, (1555)
Pet.

22429.5 Sherwood, Robert, 1625
Yk.

22440 Shirley, James, 1640
Carl.

22465.5 Shute, John, 1587
Sal.

22466 Shute, Nathaniel, 1626
Her. Wor.

22475 Sibbes, Richard, 1639 (1638)
Lich (imp). Yk (imp).

22476 Sibbes, Richard, 1639
Her.

22477 Sibbes, Richard, 1639
Win.

22481 Sibbes, Richard, 1631
Dur.

22487 Sibbes, Richard, 1638
Win.

22488 Sibbes, Richard, 1639
Win.

22491 Sibbes, Richard, 1640 (1639)
Her. Win.

22492 Sibbes, Richard, 1639
Win.

22493 Sibbes, Richard, 1639
Glo.

22497.5 Sibbes, Richard, 1638
Pet.

22498 Sibbes, Richard, 1638
Her.

22503 Sibbes, Richard, (1629)
Cant. Linc.

22504 Sibbes, Richard, 1637
Ex. Her. Wor. Yk.

22508 Sibbes, Richard, 1635
Her. Llan.

22508.5 Sibbes, Richard, 1635
Her.

22514 Sibbes, Richard, 1638
Win.

22515 Sibbes, Richard, 1636
Pet.

22521 Sibbes, Richard, 1638
Win.

22523 Sibthorp, *Sir* Christopher, 1623
Rip.

22525.5 Sibthorpe, Robert, 1627
Bur. Yk.

22525.7 Sibthorpe, Robert, 1627
Linc.

22526a Sibthorpe, Robert, 1627
Cant.

22527a Sibthorpe, Robert, 1618
Ex.

22534 Sidney, *Sir* Philip, 1595
Linc (imp).

22543a Sidney, *Sir* Philip, 1605
Glo.

22552 Sidney, *Sir* Philip, 1587
Yk.

22568 Simson, Archibald, 1623
Linc.

22571 Simson, Edward, 1636
Sal.

22571.5 Simson, Leonard, 1585
Yk.

22574 Singleton, Isaac, 1615
Pet. Yk.

22575 Singleton, Robert, [1536]
Linc.

22620 Skelton, John, 1589
Linc.

22624 Skene, *Sir* John, 1609
Cant. Dur. Linc.

22626 Skene, *Sir* John, 1609
Linc.

22628 Skinner, Robert, 1634
Carl. Linc. Pet. Wor. Yk
(imp).

22629 Skory, Edmund, 1610
Sal.

22634 Slatyer, William, (1621)
Cant (without colophon). Linc
(without colophon).

22635 Slatyer, William, [1631]
Linc (2 − 1 imp).

22636 Slatyer, William, 1619
Pet.

22640 Smart, Peter, 1628
Dur. Ex. Yk.

22640.3 Smart, Peter, 1628
Cant. Dur (imp). Pet.

22641 Smart, Peter, 1640
Carl. Dur. Pet.

22641.5 Smart, Peter, 1640
Chelm*. Linc. Yk*.

22648 Smetius, Heinrich, 1628
Yk.

22651 Smeton, Thomas, 1579
Linc. Pet. Yk.

22652 Smiglecki, Marcin, 1634
Her.

22666 Smith, Henry, *Minister*, 1593
Yk (imp)*.

22668 Smith, Henry, *Minister*, 1609
Ex.

22670 Smith, Henry, *Minister*, 1614
Yk.

22671 Smith, Henry, *Minister*, 1617
S Asa.

22677 Smith, Henry, *Minister*, 1595
Yk.

22698 Smith, Henry, *Minister*, 1594
Pet.

22699 Smith, Henry, *Minister*, 1594
Yk.

22701 Smith, Henry, *Minister*, 1594
Pet.

22701.3 Smith, Henry, *Minister*,
1594
Pet.

22702 Smith, Henry, *Minister*, 1594
Pet.

22702.3 Smith, Henry, *Minister*,
1594
Pet.

22704 Smith, Henry, *Minister*, 1592
Yk.

22711.7 Smith, Henry, *Minister*,
1632
Pet (imp).

22719 Smith, Henry, *Minister*, 1593
Pet (frag.).

22721 Smith, Henry, *Minister*, 1594
(1595)
Cant (imp).

22727 Smith, Henry, *Minister*, 1609
Ex (imp)*. S Dv.

22729 Smith, Henry, *Minister*, 1614
Yk.

22731.5 Smith, Henry, *Minister*,
1628
S Asa.

22738 Smith, Henry, *Minister*, 1607
S Dv.

22739 Smith, Henry, *Minister*, 1609
Ex.

22744 Smith, Henry, *Minister*, 1624
Ex.

22745 Smith, Henry, *Minister*, 1628
S Asa.

22755 Smith, Henry, *Minister*, 1609
Ex (frag.).

22757 Smith, Henry, *Minister*, 1614
Ex. Yk.

22768 Smith, Henry, *Minister*, 1610
Ex.

22779 Smith, Henry, *Minister*, 1596
Cant (imp).

22781 Smith, Henry, *Minister*, 1629
S Asa.

22790d Smith, John, *Governor*,
1632
Ely.

22791 Smith, John, *Governor*, 1612
Sal.

22794 Smith, John, *Governor*, 1627
Linc.

22797 Smith, John, *Minister*, 1595
Ex. Linc. Yk.

22798 Smith, John, *of Clavering*,
1629
Cant (tpw). Chi.

22800.5 Smith, John, *of Clavering*,
1637
Nor.

22801 Smith, John, *of Clavering*,
1632
Cant.

22807 Smith, Miles, 1602
Cant. Linc.

22808 Smith, Miles, 1632
Her.

22809 Smith, Richard, *Bp*, 1605
Her.

22809a Smith, Richard, *Bp*, 1606
Yk.

22810 Smith, Richard, *Bp*, 1631
Her.

22812 Smith, Richard, *Bp*, 1621
Wor.

22813 Smith, Richard, *Bp*, 1609
Sal. Yk.

22815 Smith, Richard, *Dean*, 1546
Pet. Sal.

22816 Smith, Richard, *Dean*, [1554]
Pet.

22817.5 Smith, Richard, *Dean*,
1555
Pet.

22820a Smith, Richard, *Dean*, 1546
Cant. Ex (tpw)*. Wor.

22823 Smith, Richard, *Dean*, (1548)
Pet.

22828 Smith, Samuel, *A.M.*, 1618
Yk.

22831.7 Smith, Samuel, *A.M.*, 1634
Linc (imp).

22832 Smith, Samuel, *A.M.*, 1634
S Pl.

22833 Smith, Samuel, *A.M.*, 1639
Pet.

22847.3 Smith, Samuel, *Minister*,
1616
Chelm.

22852 Smith, Samuel, *Minister*,
1620
Linc.

22856.5 Smith, *Sir* Thomas, *Doctor*,
1568 (1567)
Cant. Linc.

22857 Smith, *Sir* Thomas, *Doctor*,
1583
Linc. Pet. Rip (imp).

22858 Smith, *Sir* Thomas, *Doctor*,
1584
Pet. S Asa.

22862 Smith, *Sir* Thomas, *Doctor*, 1609
Pet.

22863 Smith, *Sir* Thomas, *Doctor*, 1612
Dur (tp imp).

22866 Smith, *Sir* Thomas, *Doctor*, 1635
Carl.

22868 Smith, *Sir* Thomas, *Doctor*, [1610]
Cant. Win.

22875 Smyth, John, 1609
Linc.

22877.1 Smyth, John, 1605
Yk.

22877.2 Smyth, John, 1624
Pet.

22877.3 Smyth, John, 1607
Yk (2).

22877.4 Smyth, John, [1613?]
Yk (tpw).

22880.9 Smyth, William, 1606
Linc.

22881 Smyth, William, 1606
Pet. S Pl.

22882 Smyth, William, 1598
Pet.

22883 Smythe, *Sir* John, 1590
Linc.

22885 Smythe, *Sir* John, 1595
Linc. Pet.

22895 Soliman, (1599)
Cant (imp)*.

22897 Solme, Thomas, [1540?]
Linc (imp).

22906 Some, Robert, 1582
Pet.

22906.5 Some, Robert, 1583
Pet.

22908 Some, Robert, 1588
Ex (2). Pet. Yk.

22909 Some, Robert, 1588
Pet. Yk.

22910 Some, Robert, 1582
Pet.

22912 Some, Robert, 1589
Yk (2).

22918 Somner, William, 1640
Cant (5 — 2 imp). Carl. Linc. S Alb. S Pl. Sal. Wel.

22927 Sonnibank, Charles, 1617
S Pl.

22931 Soranzo, Lazzaro, 1603
Yk.

22946 Southwell, Robert, [1587?]
Pet. Yk.

22947 Southwell, Robert, 1605
Pet.

22965 Southwell, Robert, 1620
f. W. Barrett.
Cant.

22978 Spagnuoli, Baptista, (1523)
Nor (imp).

22992.5 Spain, 1604
Dur.

22992.9 Spain, [1623]
Wor.

22997 Spain, 1594
Yk.

23002 Spangenberg, Johann, 1570
Ely. Rip. Yk.

23019 Sparke, Thomas, 1591
Pet. Rip. Yk.

23019.5 Sparke, Thomas, 1607
Pet.

23020 Sparke, Thomas, 1607
Carl. Yk.

23021.5 Sparke, Thomas, [1585]
Linc.

23026 Sparke, William, 1628
Pet (tpw).

23027 Sparke, William, 1629
Linc.

23029 Sparrow, Anthony, 1637
Bur*. Linc. Wor.

23029.5 Sparrow, Anthony, 1637
Carl. Ex. Yk.

23030.7 Speculum, (1510)
Pet (imp). Rip. Sal. Wor.

23031 Speed, John, 1616
Pet. Yk.

23032 Speed, John, (1620)
Cant.

23035 Speed, John, 1627
Ban*. Ex*.

23039.2 Speed, John, [1612?]
Cant (map cropped).

23039.2A Speed, John, [1613?]
Cant (imp).

23039.3 Speed, John, [1613?]
Sal.

23039.4 Speed, John, [1617?]
Cant (imp).

23039a Speed, John, [1612?]
Sal.

23039a.2 Speed, John, [1618?]
Cant (imp).

23039a.4 Speed, John, [1632?]
Yk (2).

23039d Speed, John, [1611 – 12]
Cant (imp)*. Her (2 – 1 has Ie, IIj, IVa1, IVb2, Ve). Linc. Roch (v. imp)*. Sal (tpw)*. Yk*.

23039d.2 Speed, John, [1613 – 14]
Linc.

23039d.3 Speed, John, [1615?]
Cant (imp). Wel.

23039d.6 Speed, John, [1618?]
Cant.

23039d.7 Speed, John, [1619 – 21?]
Yk.

23039d.9 Speed, John, [1624 – 25]
Cant (2 — both with Ve).

23039d.10 Speed, John, [1626 – 27?]
Roch.

23039d.11 Speed, John, [1628 – 29?]
Roch (imp). Sal.

23039d.12 Speed, John, [1630?]
Cant (imp). Roch (imp)*.

23039d.14 Speed, John, [1632 – 35?]
Bris (imp). Cant. Sal. Wel.

23039d.15 Speed, John, [1636?]
Cant.

23039e.3 Speed, John, [1612?]
Cant (with IVb6 & Vb; imp). Carl*.

23039e.6 Speed, John, [1626 – 27?]
Cant.

23039e.11 Speed, John, 1633
Sal.

23039e.14 Speed, John, 1636
Yk (tp only).

23039e.16 Speed, John, 1638
Cant (3 — 1 imp). Sal.

23039e.17 Speed, John, 1640
Liv. S Asa.

23039g.7 Speed, John, 1627
Cant.

23041 Speed, John, 1611 (1612)
Ex (imp). Glo (imp).

23042 Speed, John, 1627
Cant.

23045 Speed, John, 1611
Chi (tpw)*. Glo. Lich.

23046 Speed, John, 1614
Linc. Wel.

23046.3 Speed, John, 1623
Book is small only in comparison to
STC 23046.7; pp. 1–1258.
Bur. Cant (2). Chi. Glo (imp).
Pet.

23048 Speed, John, 1627
Ban. Cant. Dur (imp).

23049 Speed, John, 1632
Cant. Ex (2). Nor (imp). Swar.
Swel (imp). Wor. Yk.

23056 Speght, James, 1615
Linc.

23063.5 Speidell, John, [1622]
Yk.

23065 Spelman, *Sir* Henry, 1626
Ex. Glo (imp)*. Pet. S Asa.

23065.5 Spelman, *Sir* Henry, 1626
Chi. Yk.

23066 Spelman, *Sir* Henry, 1639
Bur. Carl. Chi (3). Dur. Ely.
Ex. IoM. Linc. Liv. Llan. Pet.
S Asa. S Pl. Sal. Wel. Win.
Yk.

23067.4 Spelman, *Sir* Henry, 1613
Cant (tp conjugate; cancel B7).

23067.8 Spelman, *Sir* Henry, 1616
Linc. Pet.

23073 Spencer, Thomas, [1629]
Sal.

23074 Spenser, Benjamin, 1625
Carl.

23080 Spenser, Edmund, 1590
Yk (tpw)*.

23082 Spenser, Edmund, 1596
Linc.

23083 Spenser, Edmund, 1609
Cant.

23084 Spenser, Edmund, 1611
[1615?]
Glo (tpw). Sal.

23085 Spenser, Edmund, 1617
Wel.

23091 Spenser, Edmund, 1586
Yk (imp).

23095 Spenser, Edmund, 1580
Pet.

23096 Spenser, John, 1615
S Pl.

23100a Spicer, Alexander, 1617
Linc (2).

23101 Spicer, John, 1611
Pet.

23104 Spotiswood, John, 1615
Yk.

23108 Sprint, John, *Vicar*, 1618
Cant. Her (imp). Linc. Liv.
Pet (2). Roch. S Pl. Win. Wor.
Yk.

23108.4 Sprint, John, *Vicar*, 1628
Pet.

23109 Sprint, John, *Vicar*, 1607
Pet.

23110 Sprint, John, *Vicar*, 1635
Win.

23114 Squire, John, *Minister*, 1630
Lich. Pet.

23115 Squire, John, *Minister*, 1624
Ex. S Pl.

23115.5 Squire, John, *Minister*,
1617
Pet.

23119 Squire, John, *Minister*, 1637
S Pl.

23119.5 Squire, John, *Minister*,
1637
S Pl. Wor.

23120 Squire, John, *Minister*, 1637
Cant. Chelm (imp). S Pl.

23124.5 Stafford, Anthony, 1634
Pet.

23130 Stafford, Anthony, 1611
Cant (imp). Linc.

23132 Stafford, Thomas, 1633
Cant. Pet. Win.

23132a Stafford, Thomas, 1633
Glo.

23134 Stafford, William, 1581
Pet (2).

23137 Stafforde, Robert, 1634
Wor.

23150.3 Stanbridge, John, [1530?]
Pet (tpw).

23160.7 Stanbridge, John, [1529?]
Pet.

23174.3 Stanbridge, John, (1529)
Pet.

23210 Standish, John, (1540)
Linc.

23214 Stanford, *Sir* William, (1568)
Rip (tpw). Yk.

23215 Stanford, *Sir* William, (1573)
Cant (imp). Pet (2).

23216 Stanford, *Sir* William, (1577)
Yk.

23218 Stanford, *Sir* William, 1607
Wel.

23219 Stanford, *Sir* William, (1557)
Cant.

23220 Stanford, *Sir* William, (1560)
Lich. Linc. Pet. Yk.

23221 Stanford, *Sir* William, (1567)
Yk.

23224 Stanford, *Sir* William, 1607
Wel.

23225 Stanhope, John, 1624
Linc. Pet (imp).

23226 Stanhope, Michael, 1632
Yk (2).

23229 Stanyhurst, Richard, 1570
Glo.

23230 Staphylus, Fridericus, 1565
Ely. Her (imp). Wor. Yk.

23231 Stapleton, Thomas, 1567
Pet (2 – 1 imp). Sal (2).

23232 Stapleton, Thomas, 1565
Her. Pet.

23234 Stapleton, Thomas, 1566
Her. Pet. Sal (2).

23245 Stella, Joannes, 1637
Pet (tpw).

23248 Stephens, John, 1613
Pet.

23250 Stephens, John, 1615
Pet.

23259 Sterrie, D., [1586]
Wor.

23270 Stint, Thomas, 1621
Pet.

23273.5 Stock, Richard, 1614
Linc.

23274 Stock, Richard, 1614
Ex.

23278 Stockwood, John, 1598
Pet.

23278.7 Stockwood, John, 1607
Chelm.

23279 Stockwood, John, 1619
Wel.

23279.5 Stockwood, John, 1634
Yk.

23280 Stockwood, John, 1590
Pet.

23284 Stockwood, John, [1578]
Pet. Wor.

23285? Stockwood, John, 1579
T. Dawson f. G. Bishop.
Wor.

23288 Stone, William, 1623
Pet.

23289 Stoneham, Matthew, 1610
Linc. Wor (imp).

23299 Stoughton, John, 1640
Cant.

23300 Stoughton, John, 1640
Cant.

23302 Stoughton, John, 1640
Cant. S Pl (sermon 2 only).

23303 Stoughton, John, 1640
Cant.

23304 Stoughton, John, 1640
Cant. Wor.

23305 Stoughton, John, 1640
Linc.

23306 Stoughton, John, 1640
Ex (2). Linc. Pet (2 — 1 frag.).
Wor (imp).

23307 Stoughton, John, 1640
Linc.

23309 Stoughton, John, 1640
Dur. Linc. Yk.

23310 Stoughton, John, 1640
Dur. Linc. Pet.

23311 Stoughton, John, 1640
Cant. Linc. Nor. Wor.

23312 Stoughton, John, 1640
Cant.

23313 Stoughton, John, 1640
Carl.

23316 Stoughton, Thomas, 1598
Pet.

23318 Stoughton, William, 1604
Cant. Pet. Wor. Yk.

23322? Stow, John, [1570]
'Englande'
Cant (cropped).

23325.6 Stow, John, [1573]
Bur (tpw).

23328 Stow, John, 1598
Pet.

23329 Stow, John, 1604
S Pl.

23330 Stow, John, [1607]
Pet. Win.

23333 Stow, John, [1580]
Cant (imp).

23334 Stow, John, [1592]
Cant. Pet.

23338 Stow, John, 1615
Cant. Linc (imp). Yk (2 — 1
imp).

23340 Stow, John, 1631 (1632)
Cant. Glo. Linc. Nor. S Pl.
Yk.

23341 Stow, John, 1598
Pet.

23342 Stow, John, 1599
Carl. Pet.

23343 Stow, John, 1603
Ex.

23344 Stow, John, 1618
Cant ('1618'). Linc ('1618').

23345 Stow, John, 1633
Cant (3 — 2 imp). Chi. Ely (imp).
Glo (imp). Linc. S Pl (2 — 1
imp). Swar. Wor. Yk.

23351 Strada, Famianus, 1631
Carl. Pet. Yk.

23358 Strigelius, Victorinus, 1582
Cant.

23360 Strigelius, Victorinus, 1593
Pet.

23362 Strigelius, Victorinus, 1596
Pet (2 — 1 imp).

23363 Strigelius, Victorinus, 1598
Pet (imp).

23368 Struther, William, 1629
Ely. Yk.

23368.5 Struther, William, 1629
Ely.

23369 Struther, William, 1632
Yk.

23371 Struther, William, 1633
Ex. Pet.

23374 Stubbe, Edmund, 1632
Sal. Yk.

23376.5 Stubbes, Philip, 1583
Pet.

23390 Stubbes, Philip, 1626
Yk.

23400 Stubbs, John, 1579
Yk.

23401 Stuckley, *Sir* Lewis, (1618)
Pet (tpw).

23403 Studley, Peter, 1634
Pet.

23404 Studley, Peter, 1635
Pet.

23419.5 Suckling, Edmund, [1590]
Linc (tpw).

23422 Suetonius Tranquillus, Caius,
1606
Her. Liv.

23423 Suetonius Tranquillus, Caius,
1606
Sal.

23424 Suetonius Tranquillus, Caius,
1606
Yk.

23427a.3 Sulpitius, Joannes, (1511)
Glo.

23429a.5 Sulpitius, Joannes, [1530?]
Pet.

23433 Sum, 1563
Pet (tp imp).

23440.7 Susenbrotus, Joannes, 1616
Sal.

23447 Sutcliffe, Alice, 1634
Pet.

23448 Sutcliffe, Matthew, 1606
Wor. Yk.

23449 Sutcliffe, Matthew, 1599
Her. Pet. Yk.

23450 Sutcliffe, Matthew, 1592
Pet (2 — 1 imp). Yk (2).

23451 Sutcliffe, Matthew, 1595
Yk.

23452 Sutcliffe, Matthew, 1606
Yk.

23452a Sutcliffe, Matthew, 1606
Yk (tpw)*.

23453 Sutcliffe, Matthew, 1600
Pt 3 = STC 18134.3.
Linc. Pet. Wor. Yk.

23454 Sutcliffe, Matthew, 1602
Ex. Pet. Rip (imp). Wor. Yk.

23455 Sutcliffe, Matthew, 1592
Linc. Pet. S Pl. Sal. Yk.

23456 Sutcliffe, Matthew, 1603
Her (imp). Linc. Pet. Wor. Yk.

23457 Sutcliffe, Matthew, 1599
Carl. Her. Pet. Yk.

23458 Sutcliffe, Matthew, 1591
Her. Pet. Yk (imp?).

23459 Sutcliffe, Matthew, 1602
Ex. Pet.

23460 Sutcliffe, Matthew, 1599
Her (pt 2 only). Linc. Pet (2).
Yk.

23461 Sutcliffe, Matthew, 1604
Yk.

23462 Sutcliffe, Matthew, 1600
Her. Pet. Win. Wor. Yk.

23463 Sutcliffe, Matthew, 1596
Wor. Yk.

23464 Sutcliffe, Matthew, 1606
Bur. Cant. Wor. Yk.

23465 Sutcliffe, Matthew, 1604
Yk.

23468 Sutcliffe, Matthew, 1593
Cant. Yk.

23469 Sutcliffe, Matthew, 1606
Ex. Linc. Wor.

23470 Sutcliffe, Matthew, 1606
Linc. Yk.

23471 Sutcliffe, Matthew, 1590
Yk.

23472 Sutcliffe, Matthew, 1591
Pet. Yk.

23473 Sutcliffe, Matthew, 1626
Wor.

23491 Sutton, Christopher, 1601
Yk (imp).

23493 Sutton, Christopher, 1616
Cant.

23496 Sutton, Edward, 1624
Yk.

23500 Sutton, Thomas, 1613
S Pl.

23502 Sutton, Thomas, 1616
Pet. S Pl. Yk (imp).

23503 Sutton, Thomas, 1633
Yk.

23512 Swale, Christopher, 1621
Yk.

23513 Swan, John, *of Trinity College, Cambridge, Senior*, 1639
Yk.

23514 Swan, John, *of Trinity College, Cambridge, Senior*, 1640
Wor.

23515 Swan, John, *of Trinity College, Cambridge, Senior*, 1639
Pet. Yk.

23516 Swan, John, *of Trinity College, Cambridge, Junior*, 1635
Cant (imp).

23520 Swedish Discipline, 1632
Yk.

23523 Swedish Intelligencer, 1632
Yk.

23524a(i) Swedish Intelligencer, 1632
Yk.

23525 Swedish Intelligencer, 1633
Carl.

23525.5 Swedish Intelligencer, 1634
Glo.

23525.7 Swedish Intelligencer, 1634
Glo.

23526 Sweeper, Walter, 1622
Pet.

23528 Sweet, John, 1624
Pet (2). Win.

23529 Sweet, John, 1617
Cant. Pet. Yk.

23534 Swetnam, Joseph, 1615
Sal.

23547 Swinburne, Henry, 1590 (1591)
Dur. Pet. Rip. Yk.

23548 Swinburne, Henry, 1611
Cant. Yk.

23550 Swinburne, Henry, 1635
Dur. Linc. Llan.

23551 Swinburne, Henry, 1640
Sal. Yk.

23563 Sydenham, Humphrey, 1626 (1627)
Ex (imp). S Pl (frag.).

23564 Sydenham, Humphrey, 1627
Ely (tpw). Pet (4th sermon only). Wor.

23564.5 Sydenham, Humphrey, 1627
Chelm. Yk.

23565 Sydenham, Humphrey, 1636
S Pl (tp imp).

23569 Sydenham, Humphrey, 1626
Chelm.

23572 Sydenham, Humphrey, 1630
Linc. S Pl. Yk (imp).

23574 Sydenham, Humphrey, 1630
S Pl.

23576 Sylvester, Joshua, (1612)
Glo.

23584 Syme, John, 1637
Chelm.

23588 Symmer, Archibald, 1629
Linc. Pet.

23588.5 Symmes, Thomas, 1584
Ex (frag.).

23591 Symonds, William, 1606
Yk.

23593 Symonds, William, 1606
Pet. Wor.

23598 Symson, Patrick, 1624
Sal.

23598.5 Symson, Patrick, 1634
Chelm. Ex. Her. Lich. Nor. Rip (tpw). S Asa. Wor. Yk.

23599 Symson, Patrick, 1625
Bur. Linc. Yk.

23601 Symson, Patrick, 1613
Yk (vol. 1 only).

23602 Symson, William, [1617]
Wor.

23604 Synge, George, 1632
Bur (2). Linc. Wor. Yk.

23610 T., A., 1630
Pet.

23621 T., I. *or* J., 1597
Pet.

23625 T., R., 1638
Cant. Ex. Lich.

23632 T., W., 1603
Sal (4°?)*.

23638 Tables, 1628
Cant. Linc.

23642 Tacitus, Publius Cornelius, 1591
Ex. Pet (2).

23643 Tacitus, Publius Cornelius, 1598
Cant.

23644 Tacitus, Publius Cornelius, 1598
Cant.

23646 Tacitus, Publius Cornelius, 1612
Linc (pt 1 only).

23647 Tacitus, Publius Cornelius, 1622
Cant (imp). Glo. Her. Linc (pt 2 only). Nor.

23648 Tacitus, Publius Cornelius, 1640
Lich. Sal.

23650 Taffin, Jean, 1595
Yk.

23656.5 Taffin, Jean, 1625
12°.
Ely.

23666 Tallis, Thomas, & Byrd, William, 1575
Yk (imp).

23670.5 Tanner, John, 1597
Pet.

23697a Tasso, Torquato, [1594]
Linc.

23698 Tasso, Torquato, 1600
Yk.

23700 Tasso, Torquato, 1584
Yk.

23705 Tatius, Titus, 1604
Dur. Yk (2).

23717 Tayler, Francis, *B.D.*, 1633
Pet.

23724 Taylor, Jeremy, 1638
Linc (2). Pet. S Asa. S Pl. Wel.

23725 Taylor, John, 1630
Glo.

23740 Taylor, John, 1637
Linc.

23789.7 Taylor, John, 1623
Yk (imp).

23800 Taylor, John, 1621
Linc (mixed with sheets from
STC 23800.5).

23818 Taylor, Stephen, [1637?]
Linc (tp imp).

23819 Taylor, Theophilus, 1629
Ex.

23821 Taylor, Thomas, 1635
Her. Linc (imp).

23822a.5 Taylor, Thomas, 1618
Linc.

23823 Taylor, Thomas, 1633
Ex. Her.

23824 Taylor, Thomas, 1631
Yk.

23825a Taylor, Thomas, 1612
Pet. Wel. Yk.

23826 Taylor, Thomas, 1619
Ex. Her. Sal.

23827 Taylor, Thomas, 1617
'happinesse'
Linc.

23830.3 Taylor, Thomas, 1612
Bur.

23831 Taylor, Thomas, 1620
S Pl.

23837 Taylor, Thomas, 1619
Wel. Yk.

23841 Taylor, Thomas, 1623
Cant (imp). Wor.

23842 Taylor, Thomas, 1634
Chelm.

23857.5 Taylour, Nathaniel, 1627
Pet.

23858 Tedder, Richard, 1637
Pet. Yk (2).

23858.7 Tedder, William, 1588
Pet. Rip.

23861 Teelinck, Willem, 1621
Cant. Ex.

23862 Teelinck, Willem, 1622
Cant.

23864 Teixeira, José, 1601
Linc. Yk.

23867 Telin, Guillaume, 1592
Pet.

23869 Temple, Robert, 1592
S Pl. Yk.

23870 Temple, *Sir* William, 1605
Linc. Pet (imp). Rip (imp).

23873 Temple, *Sir* William, 1582
Linc. Rip.

23874 Temple, *Sir* William, 1581
Pet.

23876 Ten Commandments, (1510)
Cant.

23877 Ten Commandments, (1521)
Wor.

23883 Tenures, 1538
Pet.

23884.5 Tenures, [c.1560]
Pet.

23890 Terentius, Publius, *Afer*,
1598
Pet.

23891 Terentius, Publius, *Afer*,
1607
S Asa. Yk.

23895 Terentius, Publius, *Afer*,
1588
Linc.

23901 Terentius, Publius, *Afer*,
1560
Pet.

23916.5 Tesauro, Emmanuele, 1637
Carl.

23917 Tesauro, Emmanuele, 1637
Cant.

23920 Texeda, Fernando de, 1623
Pet. Yk.

23921 Texeda, Fernando de, 1625
Linc.

23922 Texeda, Fernando de, 1624
Sal.

23923 Texeda, Fernando de, 1623
Yk.

23934 Theloall, Simon, 1579
Pet (imp).

23934.9+ Themylthorp, Nicholas,
1633
The twentie and third time imprinted;
12°; I. Dawson f. A.V., sold by A.
Ritherdon.
Win.

23948 Theophylact, *Abp of Akhrida*,
1636
Bur. Cant. Chi. Dur. Ely. Ex.
Glo. Her. Linc. New. S Pl. Sal.
Wel. Win. Wor.

23961 Thomas, *à Kempis*, [1531?]
Yk (imp).

23967 Thomas, *à Kempis*, 1556
Pet.

23968 Thomas, *à Kempis*, 1585
Yk (tp imp).

23980 Thomas, *à Kempis*, 1596
Yk.

24013 Thomas, Thomas, 1606
Cant. S Pl. Yk.

24014 Thomas, Thomas, 1610
Cant.

24019 Thomas, William, (1561)
Cant (A1ᵛ: 'enough'). Pet. Rip
(imp). Yk.

24020 Thomas, William, 1550
Pet.

24021 Thomas, William, 1562
Cant. Pet. Rip.

24022 Thomas, William, 1567
Yk.

24025 Thompson, Thomas, 1618
Pet. S Pl. Wor.

24025+ Thompson, Thomas,
[1618?]
[Anr ed.?] 'The pope arraigned'; 4°; f.
R.M.
Sal.

24026 Thompson, Thomas, 1612
Pet.

24028 Thompson, Thomas, 1616
S Pl.

24031 Thomson, George, 1606
Linc. Rip. Yk.

24032 Thomson, Richard, 1611
Linc.

24033 Thorius, Raphael, 1626
Linc.

24036 Thornborough, John, [1605?]
Yk.

24037 Thornborough, John, 1630
Linc. Yk.

24041 Thorne, William, 1603
Cant.

24044 Thornton, Richard, 1635
Wor.

24046 Thou, Jacques Auguste de,
1640
Glo. Her. S Pl.

24048 Threnoikos, 1640
Linc (2 − 1 imp). S Asa.

24049+ Threnoikos, 1640
[Anr issue?] 2°; J. Dawson f. R.M.,
sold by M. Sparke.
Yk.

24050 Throckmorton, Francis, 1584
Yk.

24056 Thucydides, 1550
Her (tpw). Pet (tp imp).

24058 Thucydides, 1629
Sal. Win. Yk.

24059 Thucydides, 1634
Bris. Cant. Glo.

24067 Tilenus, Daniel, 1622
Linc.

24070 Tilenus, Daniel, 1620
Linc.

24071 Tilenus, Daniel, 1606
Pet. Yk (tp imp).

24072 Tilenus, Daniel, 1605
Yk.

24073 Tillesley, Richard, 1619
Bur. Ex. Linc. S Asa. Yk.

24074 Tillesley, Richard, 1621
Cant (2). Ex. Lich. Roch. Sal.

24104 Tomkis, Thomas, 1607
Cant.

24113 Tomson, Laurence, [1570]
Pet.

24114 Tomson, William, 1583
Pet.

24118 Tooker, William, 1597
Glo. Linc.

24119 Tooker, William, 1611
Bur. Chi. Yk.

24120 Tooker, William, 1604
Linc. Pet.

24123 Topsell, Edward, 1607
Glo (tpw). Her. Lich.

24124 Topsell, Edward, 1608
Her. Lich.

24128 Topsell, Edward, 1597
Pet.

24130 Topsell, Edward, 1613
Pet.

24131 Topsell, Edward, 1599
Pet.

24134 Torporley, Nathanael, 1602
Pet. Sal.

24137 Torriano, Giovanni, 1640
Ches.

24137.5 Torriano, Giovanni, 1640
Yk.

24142 Torshell, Samuel, 1633
Linc.

24143 Torshell, Samuel, 1632
Carl.

24144 Tossanus, Daniel, 1583
Pet (2 — 1 imp).

24151 Tourneur, Cyril, 1613
Yk (imp).

24161.5 Tozer, Henry, 1640
Carl.

24163 Tracy, Richard, 1548
Cant. Pet.

24168.5 Traheron, Bartholomew, 1557
Linc.

24169 Traheron, Bartholomew, 1558
'manie'
Yk.

24172 Traheron, Bartholomew, (1577)
Linc (tpw).

24178 Traske, John, 1620
Pet. Wor.

24180 Travers, Robert, 1579
Linc.

24180.7 Travers, Walter, [1583]
Pet.

24181 Travers, Walter, 1583
Pet. Yk.

24183 Travers, Walter, 1588
Pet (2). Sal. Wor. Yk (tpw).

24184 Travers, Walter, 1574
Pet (2 — 1 imp). S Pl. Yk (imp).

24185 Travers, Walter, 1580
Pet.

24187 Travers, Walter, 1612
Ex. Pet (3). Yk.

24188 Travers, Walter, 1630
Bris. Bur. S Asa (tp imp).

24190.3 Traversanus, Laurentius
Gulielmus, [1480?]
Rip (now at Leeds Univ. acc.
STC).

24197.5 Treasure, 1601
S Pl (imp).

24217 Treatise, (1541)
Pet.

24218.5 Treatise, 1585
Pet.

24233 Treatise, 1612
Linc.

24234 Treatise, [1493]
Linc (imp).

24262 Trelcatius, Lucas, 1604
Yk.

24265 Trent, *Council of*, 1564
Pet. Sal. Yk (tpw).

24265.5 Trent, *Council of*, 1564
Linc (tp imp).

24268 Treswell, Robert, 1605
Yk.

24270 Trial, 1612
Wor. Yk.

24274 Trial, 1591
Yk.

24281a Trigge, Francis, 1600
Pet. Yk.

24282.5 Trigge, Francis, 1613
Yk.

24288 Trogus Pompeius, 1593
Linc.

24291 Trogus Pompeius, 1570
Pet.

24292 Trogus Pompeius, 1578
Rip (imp).

24294 Truman, Richard, 1629
Wor.

24297 Trussell, John, 1636
Chi. Linc. Swel.

24308a Tuke, Thomas, 1610
Linc.

24311 Tuke, Thomas, [1617]
Yk.

24317 Tuke, Thomas, 1607
Pet.

24318 Tunstall, Cuthbert, (1558)
S Pl.

24319 Tunstall, Cuthbert, (1522)
Dur. Wel (imp).

24322 Tunstall, Cuthbert, (1539)
Pet.

24323 Tunstall, Cuthbert, 1633
Yk.

24335 Turkey, 1597
Pet.

24339 Turnbull, Richard, 1591
Pet (imp). S Pl (2 — both imp).

24339.5 Turnbull, Richard, 1592
S Pl (2 — 1 imp).

24340 Turnbull, Richard, 1592
Pet.

24341 Turnbull, Richard, 1606
Yk.

24348 Turner, Roger, 1634
Ex. Wor.

24349 Turner, Thomas, 1635
Bur. Carl. Ex. Her (imp). Pet.
Yk (2).

24355 Turner, William, (1545)
Linc.

24356 Turner, William, [1555?]
Linc. Wel.

24357 Turner, William, [1565]
Carl.

24360 Turner, William, 1568
Pet.

24361 Turner, William, 1555
Wel.

24365 Turner, William, 1551
Cant.

24366 Turner, William, 1562
Cant (without the extra errata slip).

24367 Turner, William, 1568
Pet. Wel. Yk.

24371 Turvell, Thomas, 1616
Yk.

24375 Tusser, Thomas, 1573
Pet.

24378.5 Tusser, Thomas, 1576
Linc.

24383 Tusser, Thomas, [1590]
Pet.

24387 Tusser, Thomas, [1604]
Pet.

24388 Tusser, Thomas, [1610]
Yk.

24394 Tuvil *or* Toutevile, Daniel, 1614
Yk.

24396 Tuvil *or* Toutevile, Daniel, 1608
Ex. Linc.

24402 Twisse, William, 1631
Lich.

24403 Twisse, William, [1631?]
Chelm. Yk (imp).

24404 Twittee, Thomas, 1640
Carl.

24405 Twyne, Brian, 1608
Cant. Linc. Roch. S Pl. Wor. Yk.

24407 Twyne, John, 1590
Cant. Ex. Glo. Linc.

24414.5 Tye, William, 1608
Pet (imp).

24418 Tymme, Thomas, 1592
Pet.

24422 Tymme, Thomas, 1606
Yk.

24426 Tymme, Thomas, 1616
Wor.

24436 Tyndale, William, 1573
(1572)
Bur. Cant (2). Glo. Her (tpw). New (tpw). Pet. Win. Wor.

24441a Tyndale, William, [1548]
Linc (tpw).

24442 Tyndale, William, [1549?]
Cant. Linc. S Pl.

24444 Tyndale, William, [1538]
Pet. S Pl (tpw).

24445 Tyndale, William, [1548?]
Linc. Pet.

24446 Tyndale, William, (1528)
Pet (tpw).

24447 Tyndale, William, 1535
Cant.

24448? Tyndale, William, [1548]
'chrysten'
Glo. Pet (imp).

24450 Tyndale, William, [1548?]
Cant. Yk.

24453 Tyndale, William, (1561)
Ex (imp?)*. Pet.

24458 Tyndale, William, [1548]
Glo. Pet.

24459 Tyndale, William, 1549
Cant.

24461 Tyndale, William, [1561?]
Pet.

24472 Tynley, Robert, 1609
Bur.

24473 Typing, William, 1633
Bur*.

24475.5 Tyrer, Ralph, 1602
S Pl.

24480 Ubaldini, Petruccio, 1588
Glo.

24483 Ubaldini, Petruccio, 1596
Linc.

24486 Ubaldini, Petruccio, 1581
Yk.

24487 Ubaldini, Petruccio, 1599
Linc (tpw).

24487.5 Ubaldini, Petruccio, 1591
Linc.

24490 Udall, John, 1588
Yk.

24491 Udall, John, 1596
Pet. Yk.

24493 Udall, John, 1589
Yk.

24494 Udall, John, 1593
Bur. Pet. Yk (imp).

24498.5 Udall, John, 1637
Yk (imp).

24499 Udall, John, [1588]
Yk.

24502 Udall, John, 1588
Yk.

24503.3 Udall, John, 158[5?]
Pet (imp).

24504 Udall, John, [1587?]
Yk.

24506a Udall, John, [1588]
Yk.

24507 Udall, John, [1588]
Yk.

24508.5 Udall, Thomas, 1606
Pet.

24509 Udall, William, 1624
Wor.

24510 Udall, William, 1636
Linc. Wel.

24512 Udny, Alexander, 1625
Cant. S Asa.

24513a Udny, Alexander, 1628
Pet.

24526 Ursinus, Joachimus, *pseud.*, 1609
New Halkett & Laing identifies as Joachim Béringer.
Pet.

24529 Ursinus, Zacharias, 1585
Chelm.

24530 Ursinus, Zacharias, 1586
Glo.

24532 Ursinus, Zacharias, 1587
Ex.

24534 Ursinus, Zacharias, 1591
Linc.

24535 Ursinus, Zacharias, 1595
Pet.

24536 Ursinus, Zacharias, 1601
Cant (imp). Pet.

24537 Ursinus, Zacharias, 1611
Ely. Her. Sal. Yk.

24538 Ursinus, Zacharias, 1617
Carl. Her (imp).

24539.3 Ursinus, Zacharias, 1633
Her.

24539.7 Ursinus, Zacharias, 1633
S Dv.

24542 Ussher, James, 1624
Dur (imp). Linc. Sal. Yk.

24543 Ussher, James, 1625
Cant (imp). Carl (lacks gen. tp?). S Asa. S Pl (lacks gen. tp?). Yk (lacks gen. tp?).

24544 Ussher, James, 1631
Ban. Bur. Ely. Nor. Pet. Rip. S Dv. S Pl (tpw). Wel. Wor.

24544.5 Ussher, James, 1631
Llan.

24545 Ussher, James, [1624]
Carl. Linc. Pet.

24546 Ussher, James, 1625
Pet.

24548 Ussher, James, 1631
Bur.

24548a Ussher, James, 1639
Bur. Cant. Carl. Dur. Linc.
Nor. S Pl (2). Win.

24549 Ussher, James, 1631
Bur. Wor.

24550 Ussher, James, 1631
Bur (2). Cant. Ex. Linc. Liv.
Pet. S Pl. Wel. Yk (2).

24551 Ussher, James, 1613
Bur. Ches. Ex. Lich. Liv. S Pl.
Win. Yk (2).

24553 Ussher, James, 1638
Carl. Nor.

24553.5 Ussher, James, 1621
Linc. Nor. Pet. S Asa. S Pl (2).

24554a Ussher, James, 1631
Bur. Wor.

24555 Ussher, James, 1631
Bur. Wor.

24557 Ussher, James, 1632
Bur (2). Linc. Liv. S Pl. Wor.
Yk.

24568 Valdes, Alfonso de, 1586
Linc.

24570 Valdes, Francisco de, 1590
Sal.

24571 Valdes, Juan de, 1638
Ely. Yk.

24574 Valentine, Henry, 1635
Chelm. Linc. Pet (2). Yk.

24575 Valentine, Henry, 1639
Cant. Carl (tp imp). Linc. Pet.
S Pl. Wel (tp imp).

24576 Valentine, Henry, 1627
Pet (2).

24580 Valera, Cipriano de, 1599
Pet (2 — 1 imp).

24581 Valera, Cipriano de, 1600
Pet. S Pl.

24594 Vase, Robert, 1625
Cant. S Pl.

24599 Vaughan, Edward, 1594
Pet (2 — 1 imp).

24622.5 Vaughan, William, 1611
Pet.

24626.7 Vaux, Laurence, 1583
Sal.

24627 Vaux, Laurence, 1583
Yk.

24627a Vaux, Laurence, 1590
Linc.

24627a.2 Vaux, Laurence, 1599
Pet.

24631 Vegetius Renatus, Flavius,
[1572]
Pet. Rip.

24633 Velleius Paterculus, Caius,
1632
Yk.

24645 Venner, Tobias, 1628
Carl (pt 1 only?). Linc (pt 1
only).

24646 Venner, Tobias, 1637
Pet.

24647 Venner, Tobias, 1638
Carl (2). Wel.

24652 Vere, *Sir* Francis, 1591
Linc.

24656 Vergilius, Polydorus, 1546
Pet.

24658 Vergilius, Polydorus, [c.1560]
Cant. Pet (2 — 1 imp). Rip.

24665 Vermigli, Pietro Martire,
[1550]
Pet. Yk.

24666 Vermigli, Pietro Martire,
(1550)
Pet (imp).

24667 Vermigli, Pietro Martire,
1576
Carl (2). Dur. Lich. Pet. Rip.

24668 Vermigli, Pietro Martire,
1583
Cant (imp). Glo. Her. Linc.
S Pl. Wel. Yk (2).

24669 Vermigli, Pietro Martire,
(1583)
Ban (imp). Bur. Her (2 — 1 imp).
Lich. Linc. Pet. Swel (imp).

24670 Vermigli, Pietro Martire,
(1564)
Her. Pet.

24672 Vermigli, Pietro Martire,
(1568)
Pet.

24673 Vermigli, Pietro Martire,
[1549]
Pet.

24673.5 Vermigli, Pietro Martire,
[1555]
Yk.

24680 Veron, Jean, [1561]
Pet (2 — 1 imp, 1 frag.). Sal
(imp).

24681 Veron, Jean, (1561)
Pet. Rip.

24683 Veron, Jean, (1561)
Pet. Yk.

24684 Veron, Jean, [1561]
Pet (2). Sal.

24685 Veron, Jean, (1561)
Pet (2 — 1 imp).

24686 Veron, Jean, (1562)
Pet (imp).

24691 Vertue, Henry, 1637
S Pl.

24696 Vicars, John, *Linguist*, 1639
Cant (engr. tpw). Ex. Her. Lich.
Linc. Rip. Sal (2). Win. Wor
(imp?).

24710 Vicary, Thomas, 1613
Cant.

24719 Vignier, Nicolas, 1607
Pet (imp).

24722 Vigo, Joannes de, 1571
Pet.

24723 Vigo, Joannes de, 1586
Pet.

24726.5 Vigor, Simon, [1571]
Pet (imp).

24727 Vigor, Simon, 1602
Pet.

24730 Villegas, Alfonso de, [1609]
Yk.

24731a Villegas, Alfonso de, 1615
S Pl.

24731b Villegas, Alfonso de, 1621
Her (imp).

24733 Villegas, Alfonso de, 1628
Cant (imp)*. Yk (imp).

24734 Villegas, Alfonso de, 1630
S Pl.

24735 Villegas, Alfonso de, 1634
Carl.

24749 Vincent, *of Lerins, St*, 1631
Bur. Carl. S Asa. S Pl (2).
Win.

24753 Vincent, *of Lerins, St*, 1611
Cant.

24754 Vincent, *of Lerins, St*, (1554)
Pet.

24756 Vincent, Augustine, 1622
Yk.

24767 Viques, *Captain*, 1591
Pet.

24768 Virel, Matthieu, 1594
Pet.

24768.5 Virel, Matthieu, 1595
Pet.

24769a Virel, Matthieu, 1603
Yk.

24771 Virel, Matthieu, 1612
Yk.

24775 Viret, Pierre, 1584
Linc. Pet. Yk.

24776 Viret, Pierre, 1579
Pet.

24777 Viret, Pierre, [1565]
Pet.

24778 Viret, Pierre, 1573
Pet.

24779 Viret, Pierre, 1582
Pet.

24780 Viret, Pierre, 1582
Pet.

24781 Viret, Pierre, [1548]
Linc (imp).

24782 Viret, Pierre, 1579
Pet.

24784 Viret, Pierre, [1548?]
Pet (2 − 1 imp).

24786 Viret, Pierre, 1583
Pet.

24786.5 Viret, Pierre, 1583
Pet.

24797 Virgilius Maro, Publius, 1553
Linc.

24800 Virgilius Maro, Publius, 1562
Glo. Pet (2).

24801 Virgilius Maro, Publius, 1573
Pet (imp).

24802 Virgilius Maro, Publius, 1584
Pet.

24805a Virgilius Maro, Publius, 1620
Ely. Pet.

24827 Virgilius Maro, Publius, 1638
Linc.

24852 Vives, Joannes Ludovicus, 1612
Carl. Ex. Wor.

24855 Vives, Joannes Ludovicus, [1555?]
Pet.

24861 Vives, Joannes Ludovicus, 1557 [*i.e.* 1567?]
Cant. Lich. Liv.

24863 Vives, Joannes Ludovicus, 1592
Ex (imp). Yk.

24869 Vocabulary, 1639
Linc.

24872 Volusianus, *Bp*, 1569
Rip. Yk.

24873 Voragine, Jacobus de, [1483]
Her (imp).

24874 Voragine, Jacobus de, [1487?]
Linc (imp).

24875 Voragine, Jacobus de, (1493)
Cant (imp). Linc (imp). Sal (imp).

24876 Voragine, Jacobus de, (1498)
Cant (T6 only).

24879 Voragine, Jacobus de, (1512)
Pet (imp).

24882.3 Vossius, Gerardus, 1640
Yk.

24882.7 Vossius, Gerardus, 1628
Linc. S Pl. Yk.

24883 Vossius, Gerardus, 1628
Cant (imp). Carl. Pet.

24884 Vossius, Gerardus, 1631
Her.

24890 Voyon, Simon de, 1598
Pet.

24891 Voyon, Simon de, [1585?]
Pet. Yk (imp)*.

24899 W., A., 1592
Linc (date cropped).

24904 W., G., 1600
Yk (imp).

24905 W., H., (1631)
Linc.

24912 W., R., 1621
Cant.

24925 Wadsworth, James, *the Elder*, 1624
Yk.

24925a Wadsworth, James, *the Elder*, 1624
Carl. Pet. Win.

24926 Wadsworth, James, *the Younger*, 1629
Yk.

24926a Wadsworth, James, *the Younger*, 1630
Yk.

24927 Wadsworth, James, *the Younger*, 1630
Linc. Sal.

24928 Wadsworth, James, *the Younger*, 1630
Sal.

24929 Wadsworth, James, *the Younger*, 1630
Sal (tpw)*.

24929a Wadsworth, James, *the Younger*, 1630
Yk.

24930 Waferer, Myrth, 1634
Carl. Pet (2 − 1 imp). Yk.

24939 Wake, *Sir* Isaac, 1607
Linc. Yk (2 − 1 tp imp).

24939.5 Wake, *Sir* Isaac, 1607
Pet. Sal. Wor.

24940 Wake, *Sir* Isaac, 1615
Pet.

24941 Wake, *Sir* Isaac, 1627
Sal.

24942 Wake, *Sir* Isaac, 1635
Win.

24943 Wakefield, Robert, [1533?]
Dur (imp).

24944 Wakefield, Robert, [1528?]
Linc. S Pl.

24947 Wakeman, Robert, 1605
Pet (2).

24947.7 Wakeman, Robert, 1603
Pet.

24948 Wakeman, Robert, 1606
Pet. S Pl.

24949 Wakeman, Robert, 1612
S Pl.

24950 Wakeman, Robert, 1610
Linc.

24951 Wakeman, Robert, 1607
Linc. Pet (2 − 1 tpw).

24952 Wakeman, Robert, 1605
Pet (2).

24953 Wakeman, Robert, 1620
Linc.

24957 Walker, George, 1638
Pet.

24958 Walker, George, 1639
Ex.

24959.5 Walker, George, 1640
Cant.

24960 Walker, George, 1624
Wor.

24964 Walker, William, 1614
S Pl.

24966 Walkington, Thomas, 1609
Author is, in fact, Thomas Wilson, of
Canterbury.
Cant. S Pl.

24967 Walkington, Thomas, 1607
Cant.

24970 Walkington, Thomas, 1620
Pet. S Pl.

24976 Walkley, Thomas, 1634
Linc.

24984 Wall, George, 1635
Linc.

24985 Wall, John, 1627
Linc.

24988 Wall, John, 1626
Bur. Linc.

24989 Wall, John, 1628
S Pl.

24991 Wall, John, 1625
Linc. S Pl.

24993 Walpole, Michael, 1613
Pet. Yk.

24994.5 Walpole, Richard, 1603
Wor. Yk.

24995 Walsall, John, [1578]
S Pl. Wor.

24998 Walsall, Samuel, 1622
Linc.

25002 Walsingham, Francis, 1609
Yk (2 — both imp).

25003 Walsingham, Francis, 1615
Yk.

25012 Walther, Rudolph, 1582
Pet.

25013 Walther, Rudolph, 1572
Her (imp).

25020 Warburton, George, 1623
Yk.

25023.5 Ward, Nathaniel, 1638
Ely.

25024 Ward, Richard, 1640
Ban. IoM.

25026 Ward, Samuel, *of Cambridge*,
1626
Ex. Glo.

25027 Ward, Samuel, *of Cambridge*,
1627
Bur (2 — 1 imp). Dur.

25028 Ward, Samuel, *of Cambridge*,
1637
Linc. Sal (imp)*.

25031 Ward, Samuel, *of Ipswich*,
1627 (1628)
Yk (frag.)*.

25033a Ward, Samuel, *of Ipswich*,
(1622)
Yk (tpw).

25035 Ward, Samuel, *of Ipswich*,
1617
S Pl.

25036 Ward, Samuel, *of Ipswich*,
1618
S Pl.

25037 Ward, Samuel, *of Ipswich*,
1622
Yk.

25042 Ward, Samuel, *of Ipswich*,
1622
Yk.

25045 Ward, Samuel, *of Ipswich*,
1622
Carl. Yk.

25046 Ward, Samuel, *of Ipswich*,
1618
S Pl.

25048 Ward, Samuel, *of Ipswich*,
1623
Yk.

25050 Ward, Samuel, *of Ipswich*,
1622
Yk.

25052 Ward, Samuel, *of Ipswich*,
1622
Yk.

25055 Ward, Samuel, *of Ipswich*,
1622
Yk.

25058 Ward, William, 1627
Yk.

25066 Ware, *Sir* James, 1639
Dur. Linc. Pet (tpw). S Pl.

25068 Warford, William, 1604
Ely (tpw). Pet. Yk.

25076 Warmington, William, 1612
Pet. Wor.

25082 Warner, William, 1596
Cant (tpw)*.

25083 Warner, William, 1602
Pet.

25084 Warner, William, 1612
Yk.

25085 Warner, William, 1606
Yk.

25090a? Warre, James, 1624
Second impression not on tp;
Matthewes.
Yk (imp?).

25092? Warre, James, 1634
Fourth impression not on tp.
Yk.

25109 Wats, James, 1621
Ches.

25112 Watson, Thomas, *Bp*, 1558
Wor. Yk (imp).

25112.5 Watson, Thomas, *Bp*, 1558
Linc. Pet. Yk (imp).

25113 Watson, Thomas, *Bp*, 1558
Pet.

25114 Watson, Thomas, *Bp*, 1558
Yk (imp).

25115.3 Watson, Thomas, *Bp*,
(1554)
Sal.

25115.5 Watson, Thomas, *Bp*,
(1554)
Pet.

25117 Watson, Thomas, *Poet*, 1592
Linc. Pet.

25123 Watson, William, 1602
Linc. Pet. S Pl. Wor. Yk.

25124 Watson, William, 1601
Pet.

25124.5 Watson, William, 1601
Rip. Yk (imp).

25125 Watson, William, 1601
Linc. Pet. Yk.

25126 Watson, William, 1601
Pet (2). Yk (imp).

25127 Watt, Joachim von, (1534)
Linc.

25129 Watts, William, 1637
Carl. S Pl.

25139 Way, [1640?]
Chi*. Pet.

25150 Web, Richard, 1610
Yk (tpw)*.

25160.7 Webbe, George, 1624
Pet. Wor (2).

25162 Webbe, George, 1609
Pet.

25163 Webbe, George, 1612
Linc.

25165 Webbe, George, 1615
Yk.

25169 Webbe, Joseph, 1622
Cant. Linc.

25170 Webbe, Joseph, 1623 [o.s.]
Linc.

25171 Webbe, Joseph, 1626
Sal.

25191 Wedderburn, David, 1617
Yk.

25195 Wedding, 1597
Pet.

25196.5 Wedlocke, Walter, [1558?]
'... the Image ... Bawdyn Bacheler ...'
Linc.

25207 Weemes, John, 1633
Dur. Her. Win. Yk.

25207.3 Weemes, John, 1632
Dur. Her. Linc. Nor. Win.
Yk.

25207.5 Weemes, John, 1632
Dur. Ex. Glo. Her. Linc. Yk.

25208 Weemes, John, 1636
Bur. Sal.

25208.3 Weemes, John, 1636
Ex. S Pl. Sal.

25208.5 Weemes, John, 1636
Bur (2). S Pl. Sal.

25209 Weemes, John, 1637
Ex. S Pl.

25211 Weemes, John, 1630
Bur. Roch. Win. Yk.

25211.3 Weemes, John, 1633
Her.

25212 Weemes, John, 1632
Glo. Her. Linc. Yk.

25212.5 Weemes, John, 1634
Bur. Dur.

25217 Weemes, John, 1627
Linc. Pet.

25218 Weemes, John, 1636
Bur. Dur. Ex. S Pl. Win.

25223 Weever, John, 1631
Cant (3 – 2 imp). Carl. Ches.
Chi (tpw). Dur (imp). Ex. Linc
(2 – 1 imp). Nor. Pet (imp).
Roch. S Alb. S Pl (imp). Swel
(imp). Wor. Yk (imp).

25229.3 Weldon, John, 1588
Pet.

25234 Wells, John, 1635
Wor.

25234.5 Wells, John, 1637
Yk (with the tables).

25235 Welsch, John, 1602
Yk.

25241 Welwood, William, 1622
Cant.

25245 Wentworth, Peter,
Parliamentarian, 1598
Linc. Pet. Yk.

25248.3 Wentworth, Thomas, Earl
of Strafford, 1640 [o.s.]
Linc. Yk (2 eds)*.

25251 Werdmueller, Otto, [1555?]
Carl.

25255 Werdmueller, Otto, (1550)
Pet (imp).

25256 Werdmueller, Otto, [1555?]
Carl.

25261 Wescombe, Martin, 1639
Linc. Sal (imp).

25268 West, William, 1594
Pet.

25268.5 West, William, 1597
Yk.

25269 West, William, 1598
Cant (imp). Pet.

25275 West, William, 1622
Yk.

25276.7 West, William, 1594
Pet.

25278 West, William, 1601
Cant.

25279.5 West, William, 1618
Yk.

25280 Westerman, William, 1608
Ex. Linc.

25281 Westerman, William, 1613
Linc.

25282 Westerman, William, 1600
Linc.

25284 Westerne, Thomas, 1624
Linc (2).

25285 Westfaling, Herbert, 1582
Pet (2). S Pl. Yk.

25290 Weston, Edward, 1614
Cant (imp).

25291.5 Weston, Hugh, [1555]
Pet.

25294 Whalley, John, 1616
S Pl.

25298 Whately, William, 1623
Bur (tpw).

25299 Whately, William, 1624
(1623)
Bur.

25300 Whately, William, 1609
Yk.

25302 Whately, William, 1616
S Pl.

25305 Whately, William, 1619
Pet.

25306 Whately, William, 1622
Bur. Yk.

25309 Whately, William, 1619
Yk (imp; in 4's)*.

25309.7 Whately, William, 1622
Bur.

25317 Whately, William, 1640
Wor.

25317.5 Whately, William, 1640
Ex.

25319 Whately, William, 1607
Linc.

25319.5 Whately, William, 1609
Yk.

25320 Whately, William, 1619
Bur.

25321 Whately, William, 1634
Ex.

25322a Whately, William, 1628
Cant.

25324 Whately, William, 1630
Pet.

25325 Whear, Diggory, 1623
Wor.

25326 Whear, Diggory, 1625
Wor.

25328 Whear, Diggory, 1637
Carl. Yk.

25332 Whetenhall, Thomas, 1606
Pet. Yk.

25340 Whetstone, George, 1586
Pet.

25357 Whitaker, William, 1583
Glo. Lich. Linc. Pet. Rip. Sal.

25358 Whitaker, William, 1581
Carl (imp). Linc.

25360 Whitaker, William, 1606
Yk.

25362 Whitaker, William, 1583
Dur (imp). Her. Linc. Pet. Rip.
Sal. Wor (imp).

25363 Whitaker, William, 1594
Bur. Pet. Rip. S Pl. Yk.

25364a Whitaker, William, 1585
Rip. Yk (retains cancelled tp).

25364b Whitaker, William, 1585
Pet.

25366 Whitaker, William, 1588
Pet. Rip. Wor.

25367 Whitaker, William, 1600
Carl. Pet.

25368 Whitaker, William, 1599
Carl. Linc. Pet. Sal. Wor.

25370 Whitaker, William, 1600
Pet.

25371 Whitbie, Oliver, 1637
Pet. S Pl.

25376 White, Anthony, 1628
Carl. S Asa.

25378 White, Christopher, 1622
Wor.

25379 White, Francis, *Bp*, 1637
Cant. Dur.

25379a White, Francis, *Bp*, 1637
Bur (2). Ex (2). Pet (2). Sal.
Yk.

25380 White, Francis, *Bp*, 1617
Ely. Linc. Roch. S Pl. Sal.

25382 White, Francis, *Bp*, 1624
Cant (2 – 1 imp). Carl. Dur.
Ely. Ex (2). Her (2). Nor. Pet
(2). S Asa (2). S Pl. Sal (2 – 1
imp). Win. Wor (imp?). Yk.

25383 White, Francis, *Bp*, 1635
Cant (2). Ex. Linc (2). Win.
Wor. Yk.

25384 White, Francis, *Bp*, 1635
Bur. Cant. Ely. Her. Linc.
S Asa. Sal (2). Yk (2).

25385 White, Francis, *Bp*, 1636
Bur.

25386 White, Francis, *M.A.*, 1619
S Pl.

25387 White, Harim, 1618
Linc.

25388 White, John, *Bp*, 1553
Cant (imp).

25389 White, John, *D.D.*, 1624
Pet (tpw).

25389.5 White, John, *D.D.*, 1624
Carl. Nor. S Asa. Win. Yk.

25389a White, John, *D.D.*, 1624
Dur. Her. S Pl. Yk (imp).

25390 White, John, *D.D.*, 1614
Ex. Wor.

25392 White, John, *D.D.*, 1615
Carl. Pet (imp). S Pl.

25394 White, John, *D.D.*, 1608
Cant (2). Yk.

25395 White, John, *D.D.*, 1610
Ex (tpw)*. Pet. S Pl.

25397 White, John, *D.D.*, 1616
Glo. Sal.

25399 White, John, *of Dorchester*,
1630
Sal.

25401 White, Peter, (1582)
Pet (2).

25402 White, Peter, 1581
Linc. Pet.

25405 White, Thomas, *Founder of
Sion College*, 1578
Linc. S Pl.

25408 White, Thomas, *Writer*, 1605
Yk.

25413.7 Whitford, Richard, [1534?]
Linc (imp).

25427 Whitgift, John, 1572
Pet (3 – 1 imp). S Pl. Wor. Yk.

25428 Whitgift, John, 1572
Pet (imp).

25429 Whitgift, John, 1573
Bur. Pet. Win. Yk.

25430 Whitgift, John, 1574
Chi. Dur. Glo*. Linc. Pet.
Rip (imp)*. S Pl (2 – 1 imp)*.
Wel*. Wor. Yk (mixed sheets?:
A1ʳ catchword 'fence'; orn on
b8ʳ)*.

25430.5 Whitgift, John, 1574
Cant. Carl. Ex. Nor. Sal. Yk
(2).

25433 Whitgift, John, 1575
16°.
Yk.

25438 Whitney, Geffrey, 1586
Pet (imp).

25441 Whittell, Robert, 1620
Wor.

25443 Whittingham, William, 1575
Carl. Ches. Linc. Liv (imp).
Pet. Wor.

25453 Whittinton, Robert, (1525)
Pet.

25461 Whittinton, Robert, (1519)
Pet (imp).

25464.5 Whittinton, Robert, (1522)
Yk (imp).

25469 Whittinton, Robert, (1526)
Pet (imp).

25483.5 Whittinton, Robert, (1522)
Pet (imp).

25489 Whittinton, Robert, (1527)
Pet.

25515a Whittinton, Robert, (1521)
Pet.

25520 Whittinton, Robert, (1526)
Pet.

25531 Whittinton, Robert, (1522)
Pet.

25535 Whittinton, Robert, (1527)
Pet.

25552.5 Whittinton, Robert, (1525)
Pet.

25560.3 Whittinton, Robert, (1522)
Pet.

25564.2 Whittinton, Robert, (1527)
Pet (tpw).

25586 Wiburn, Perceval, 1581
Bur. Carl. Yk.

25587 Wickins, Nathaniel, 1638
Yk.

25587.5 Wiclif, John, (1540)
Linc (imp).

25589 Wiclif, John, 1608
Carl. Linc. Yk (2).

25592 Wiclif, John, 1612
Carl. Ex (2). Pet (frag.). Win.
Yk.

25593 Widdowes, Giles, 1631
Yk.

25594 Widdowes, Giles, 1630
Cant (imp). Wor. Yk.

25596 Widdrington, Roger, *pseud.*
[*i.e.* Thomas Preston], 1611
Cant. Linc. Pet. S Pl*. Yk.

25597 Widdrington, Roger, *pseud.*
[*i.e.* Thomas Preston], 1612
Yk.

25599 Widdrington, Roger, *pseud.*
[*i.e.* Thomas Preston], 1619
Glo. Pet. Yk.

25600 Widdrington, Roger, *pseud.*
[*i.e.* Thomas Preston], 1633
Win.

25601 Widdrington, Roger, *pseud.*
[*i.e.* Thomas Preston], 1618
Wor. Yk.

25602 Widdrington, Roger, *pseud.*
[*i.e.* Thomas Preston], 1613
Her (imp). Yk.

25604 Widdrington, Roger, *pseud.*
[*i.e.* Thomas Preston], 1616
Win.

25605 Widdrington, Roger, *pseud.*
[*i.e.* Thomas Preston], 1616
Yk.

25606 Widdrington, Roger, *pseud.*
[*i.e.* Thomas Preston], 1614
Wor.

25612 Wigand, Johann, 1562
Pet. Rip (imp)*.

25615 Wigmore, Michael, 1620
S Pl.

25616 Wigmore, Michael, 1619
Pet (2).

25617 Wigmore, Michael, 1633
Yk.

25620 Wilcox, Thomas, 1624
Her.

25621 Wilcox, Thomas, 1598
Pet (2).

25622 Wilcox, Thomas, 1585
Pet.

25625 Wilcox, Thomas, 1586
Pet.

25626 Wilcox, Thomas, 1591
Lich.

25627 Wilcox, Thomas, [1589]
Pet. Yk.

25630 Wilcox, Thomas, 1597
Linc.

25633 Wilkes, William, 1605
Linc (imp)*.

25634 Wilkes, William, 1608
Yk.

25640 Wilkins, John, 1638
Ches*.

25641 Wilkins, John, 1640
Ches (tpw). Ex. Linc (tpw).

25646 Wilkinson, Henry, 1625
Linc (tpw).

25652 Wilkinson, Robert, 1617
Yk.

25652.5 Wilkinson, Robert, 1593
Yk.

25656 Wilkinson, Robert, 1607
S Pl.

25657 Wilkinson, Robert, 1607
Pet. Yk.

25658.5 Wilkinson, Robert, 1607
Carl.

25659.5 Wilkinson, Robert, 1613
Chelm. Pet.

25661 Wilkinson, Robert, 1614
Yk.

25662 Wilkinson, Robert, 1607
Yk.

25664 Wilkinson, Robert, 1617
Carl.

25665 Wilkinson, William, 1579
Pet (2). Yk.

25670 Willan, Robert, 1630
Pet.

25671 Willes, Richard, 1573
Pet. Yk (imp).

25672 Willet, Andrew, 1603
Yk.

25673 Willet, Andrew, 1602
Yk.

25674 Willet, Andrew, 1585
Linc. Pet. Yk.

25675 Willet, Andrew, 1590
Linc.

25677 Willet, Andrew, 1614
Ely. Rip. Win.

25678 Willet, Andrew, 1607
Pet. Wor. Yk.

25679 Willet, Andrew, 1614
Carl.

25679.5 Willet, Andrew, 1614
Ely. Rip.

25680 Willet, Andrew, 1614
Ely. Rip.

25682 Willet, Andrew, 1605
Carl. Ex (tpw). Linc. Wor. Yk.

25683 Willet, Andrew, 1608
Her.

25683a Willet, Andrew, 1608
Dur. Her.

25684 Willet, Andrew, 1632 (1633)
Cant. Rip (tpw).

25686 Willet, Andrew, 1608
Dur. Ex. Her. Linc. Wor. Yk.

25687 Willet, Andrew, 1633
Cant. Rip.

25688 Willet, Andrew, 1631
Ex. Linc. Rip. Wor.

25689 Willet, Andrew, 1610
Carl. Wor. Yk.

25689.3 Willet, Andrew, 1610
Carl. Dur. Ex.

25689.7 Willet, Andrew, 1611
Carl. Dur. Linc.

25690 Willet, Andrew, 1611
Ex. Her. Wor.

25691 Willet, Andrew, 1620
Cant (imp). Ely.

25691.5 Willet, Andrew, 1620
Her.

25693 Willet, Andrew, 1607
Wor. Yk (2).

25696 Willet, Andrew, 1592
Bur. Chelm.

25697 Willet, Andrew, 1594
Ex. Rip.

25698 Willet, Andrew, 1600
Cant. Her. Linc. Nor. Sal. Yk.

25699 Willet, Andrew, 1613
Ches.

25699a Willet, Andrew, 1614
Cant. Carl. Lich. Yk.

25700a Willet, Andrew, 1634
Ely.

25700a.3 Willet, Andrew, 1634
Ex.

25700a.5 Willet, Andrew, 1634
Bur. Wor.

25701 Willet, Andrew, 1593
Yk.

25703 Willet, Andrew, 1599
Linc. Pet.

25705 Willet, Andrew, 1612 [o.s.]
Yk (2).

25712 William I, *Prince of Orange*,
(1575)
Pet.

25718 Williams, Griffith, 1636
Ban (imp).

25719 Williams, Griffith, [1624]
Cant. Carl. Pet.

25720.5 Williams, Griffith, [1627]
'candlestickes'
Bur.

25721 Williams, Griffith, 1629
Ban. Llan.

25723 Williams, John, *Abp*, 1625
Cant. Nor. Pet. Yk (2).

25723a Williams, John, *Abp*, 1625
Linc. Pet. S Asa.

25724 Williams, John, *Abp*, 1637
Bur. Carl. Linc. Nor. S Pl.

25725 Williams, John, *Abp*, 1637
Cant. S Pl*. Yk (2).

25725.2 Williams, John, *Abp*, 1637
Win.

25725.4 Williams, John, *Abp*, 1637
Pet (2). Sal.

25727 Williams, John, *Abp*, 1628
Bur. Cant. Linc. Yk (4).

25728 Williams, John, *Abp*, 1620
Bur. Yk.

25728.5 Williams, John, *Abp*, 1620
Carl.

25729 Williams, John, *Abp*, 1628
Cant. Yk (2).

25731 Williams, *Sir* Roger, 1618
Cant. Linc. Yk.

25734 Williams, *Sir* Roger, 1591
Pet.

25738 Williamson, Thomas, 1630
Linc. Pet.

25759 Willoughbie, John, 1603
Yk.

25760 Willymat, William, 1604
Ex (tpw)*.

25767 Wilson, Christopher,
Preacher, 1625
Cant.

25771 Wilson, John, *Priest*, 1608
Wel.

25774 Wilson, Matthew, 1630
Carl.

25775 Wilson, Matthew, 1638
Carl. Linc. Pet.

25778 Wilson, Matthew, 1634
Her.

25780 Wilson, Matthew, 1638
Linc. Pet.

25786 Wilson, Thomas, *Divine*,
1612
Cant (pt 1 only, imp).

25787 Wilson, Thomas, *Divine*,
1616
Ely. Her.

25788 Wilson, Thomas, *Divine*,
1622
Cant (with misprint).

25789 Wilson, Thomas, *Divine*,
[c.1635]
Cant.

25790 Wilson, Thomas, *Divine*,
1614
Linc.

25791 Wilson, Thomas, *Divine*,
1614
Her (2 − 1 imp).

25793 Wilson, Thomas, *Divine*,
1627
Cant. Her.

25795 Wilson, Thomas, *Divine*,
1611
Cant (final sermon only). Pet.

25797 Wilson, Thomas, *Divine*,
1610
Linc (imp).

25800 Wilson, Thomas, *Secretary of
State*, 1560
Pet.

25803 Wilson, Thomas, *Secretary of
State*, 1567
Pet.

25807 Wilson, Thomas, *Secretary of
State*, 1572
Cant. Pet.

25808 Wilson, Thomas, *Secretary of
State*, 1584
Pet (imp).

25809 Wilson, Thomas, *Secretary of
State*, 1551
Pet.

25810 Wilson, Thomas, *Secretary of
State*, (1552)
Carl.

25811 Wilson, Thomas, *Secretary of
State*, 1553
Pet (imp).

25812 Wilson, Thomas, *Secretary of
State*, 1563
Pet.

25813 Wilson, Thomas, *Secretary of
State*, 1567
Pet.

25814 Wilson, Thomas, *Secretary of
State*, 1567 [1584?]
Lich.

25818 Wily, 1606
Cant (imp).

25825.3 Wimbledon, Richard,
[1561?]
Yk.

25825.7 Wimbledon, Richard, 1572
S Pl.

25827 Wimbledon, Richard, 1575
S Pl.

25828 Wimbledon, Richard, 1578
(1579)
Cant (imp).

25830 Wimbledon, Richard, 1582
S Pl (imp).

25831 Wimbledon, Richard, 1584
S Pl.

25834.5 Wimbledon, Richard, 1603
S Pl.

25835 Wimbledon, Richard, 1617
Cant (imp). S Pl.

25838 Wimbledon, Richard, 1634
S Pl.

25841 Windsor, Miles, 1590
Linc (tpw)*.

25847 Wing, John, 1623
Pet (tpw).

25848 Wing, John, 1624
Pet.

25849 Wingate, Edmund, 1630
Glo. Linc.

25855 Winslow, Edward, 1624
Linc (2 − 1 frag.).

25862 Wirsung, Christoph, 1598
Pet (imp).

25889 Wither, George, *Archdeacon*,
[1588]
Bur. Pet.

25897 Wither, George, *Poet*, 1617
Chi (imp).

25899 Wither, George, *Poet*, 1628
Wor.

25899.5 Wither, George, *Poet*,
[1623?]
S Pl.

25902 Wither, George, *Poet*, 1620
Yk.

25903a Wither, George, *Poet*, 1622
Cant.

25910a.3 Wither, George, *Poet*,
1623
Pet.

25911 Wither, George, *Poet*, 1622
Cant.

25914 Wither, George, *Poet*, (1619)
Pet.

25919 Wither, George, *Poet*, [1624]
Pet (imp).

25928.5 Wither, George, *Poet*, 1621
Cant (sheet F from STC
25928.7?).

25931 Witt, Richard, 1613
Linc.

25935 Witzell, Georg, 1625
Carl.

25942 Wolcomb, Robert, 1606
Pet.

25956 Wood, William, *of Middleton
Cheney*, 1581
Linc (tpw).

25963 Woodall, John, 1639
Cant.

25965 Woodcoke, Richard, 1608
Sal. Yk.

25972.4 Woodward, Philip, 1607
Yk.

25975 Woolton, John, (1577)
Pet.

25993 Worship, William, 1615
Linc.

25994 Worship, William, 1614
Yk.

25995 Worship, William, 1616
Pet. S Pl.

25999 Worthington, Robert, 1620
Linc. Pet.

26000 Worthington, Thomas, 1618
Yk.

26000.3 Worthington, Thomas, 1620
Wor.

26001 Worthington, Thomas, 1615
Wor.

26002 Wotton, Anthony, 1605
Pet. Yk.

26003 Wotton, Anthony, 1626
Ex. Linc. Pet (2). Yk (2).

26004 Wotton, Anthony, 1606
Chelm. Glo. Linc. Pet. Wor. Yk.

26005 Wotton, Anthony, 1624
Pet. Yk.

26009 Wotton, Anthony, 1608
Pet. Wor. Yk.

26009.5 Wotton, *Sir* Henry, [1612]
Linc.

26010 Wotton, *Sir* Henry, 1633
Ex. Linc. S Pl. Yk.

26011 Wotton, *Sir* Henry, 1624
Yk.

26013 Wouwerus, Joannes à, 1636
Ely.

26015 Wren, Matthew, 1627
Linc. Nor. Wor. Yk (2 — both imp).

26017a Wright, Abraham, 1637
Chi.

26031 Wright, Leonard, 1589
Pet.

26032 Wright, Leonard, 1591
Sal.

26034.3 Wright, Leonard, 1589
Pet.

26034.7 Wright, Leonard, 1589
Pet.

26035 Wright, Leonard, 1596
Pet (tpw). Yk.

26036.5 Wright, Leonard, 1637
Ex (tp imp).

26037 Wright, Robert, 1625
S Asa.

26038.5 Wright, Thomas, *Priest*, 1600
Wor.

26038.8 Wright, Thomas, *Priest*, 1596
Pet. Yk.

26040 Wright, Thomas, *Priest*, 1604
Her. Pet. Yk.

26042 Wright, Thomas, *Priest*, 1621
Pet.

26043 Wright, Thomas, *Priest*, 1630
Her. Linc.

26045 Wright, William, 1614
Yk.

26049 Wright, William, 1616
Pet (2).

26055 Wybarne, Joseph, 1609
Wor.

26058 Wylshman, Walter, 1616
Linc.

26065 Xenophon, 1613
Ex. Linc. Yk.

26066 Xenophon, [1552?]
Rip.

26081 Yates, John, 1615
Bur. Linc.

26083 Yates, John, 1626
Glo. Linc. Pet (2). Sal. Wor. Yk (2).

26085 Yates, John, 1622
Yk.

26089 Yates, John, 1637
Ex (imp). Linc.

26090 Yaxlee, Henry, 1630
Yk.

26098.7 York, *Diocese of*, [1554?]
Yk.

26099 York, *House of*, 1594
Creed.
Cant (sigs A – C only).

26102.5 Yorke, James, 1640
Cant (imp)*. Linc (2 – 1 imp*). Yk.

26103 Yorke, James, 1640
Linc.

26110.5 Young, John, *Bp of Rochester*, [1576?]
Pet.

26119.5 Zanchius, Hieronymus, 1592
Pet.

26120 Zanchius, Hieronymus, 1599
Pet.

26121a.7 Zanchius, Hieronymus, 1614
Bur. Pet (tpw).

26122 Zarain, 1639
Cant ('our Omni Potent'; A1 blank).

26129 Zouch, Richard, 1640
Carl.

26131a Zouch, Richard, 1629
Her.

26132 Zouch, Richard, 1636
Cant. S Asa (2). S Pl. Yk.

26134 Zutphen, 1591
Linc.

26139 Zwingli, Ulrich, 1548
S Pl (imp).

26140 Zwingli, Ulrich, 1555
Pet.

Location of English books 1641−1700
as enumerated in Wing's *Short-Title Catalogue*
Volume One

A1A A., 1680
Yk.

A2A A., A., 1689
S Asa.

A3 A., D., 1684
For D. Brown ...
Ex.

A11+ A., J., 1700
=Wing2 A11A.
Dur.

A17? A., M., 1672
... sold by William Hinchman; 8°.
Ex.

A18 A., M., 1680
Win.

A19 A., M., 1680
Lich. Yk.

A26 A., P., 1685
'... death of ... King Charles II'
Ban.

A32 A., T., 1681
Ex. S Pl.

A43 Aaron's, 1680
Sal.

A55 Abbadie, Jacques, 1676
Ex.

A58 Abbadie, Jacques, 1694
Nor. Rip.

A59 Abbadie, Jacques, 1698
Nor.

A63 Abbot, George, *Abp*, 1641
Chelm (2 − 1 sig. A only). Linc.
Pet. S Pl (2).

A64 Abbot, George, *Abp*, 1641
Sal.

A66 Abbot, George, *Religious
writer*, 1641
Cant. Yk.

A69 Abbot, Robert, 1646
Yk.

A71 Abdicated, 1690
S Asa.

A95 Abernethie, Thomas, 1941 [*i.e.*
1641]
Pet.

A97 Abolishing, 1641
Linc.

A103+ Abridgment, 1678
=Wing2 A102B?; By John Bill,
Christopher Barker, Thomas
Newcomb and Henry Hills.
S Asa.

A108 Abridgment, 1688
Ban. Ches. Ex. Lich. Nor.
S Pl. Sal. Swel. Wel.

A109 Absalom's, 1680
Linc.

A115 Abstract, 1642
Linc.

A115+ Abstract, 1642
As A115, but impr. dated Iuly the
fifth.
Linc. Yk.

A124 Abstract, 1642
Linc.

A124+ Abstract, 1650
See: CLC1.
Linc.

A131 Abstract, [1679?]
Linc.

A132- Abstract, 1688
=Wing2 A131B, but: 12°.
Yk.

A151+ Abu Bakr Ibn A Tufail,
1686
For Richard Chiswell; 8°.
Pet (date altered in MS to 1687).

A152 Abu Bakr Ibn A Tufail, 1671
Oxonii, excudebat ...
Cant. S Pl. Sal. Wel. Win. Yk.

A154 Abudacnus, Josephus, 1675
Cant.

A156 Abudacnus, Josephus, 1693
Yk (tpw).

A169? Account, 1649
For T.R. & E.M.
Chelm.

A171 Account, 1690
Carl.

A189+ Account, [1691]
=Wing2 A189A?; '... now a second
time with additions offered ...'
Cant.

A209 Account, 1672
Carl.

A210 Account, [1642]
Linc.

A250 Accompt, 1678
Yk.

A275 Account, 1689
Impr. & date from colophon; cap.; 4°.
S Pl (cropped).

A276 Account, 1678
Carl. Linc.

A280 Account, 1700
Dur. Wel.

A310 Account, 1692
Dur.

A315 Account, 1688
S Pl (2).

A318 Account, 1653
Yk.

A320 Account, 1684
'The account ...'
Ely.

A327? Account, 1685
Colophon: For W.C.; cap.
Ex.

A344 Account, 1689
S Pl (tpw).

A357 Account, [1679]
Linc.

A382 Account, 1700
Wel.

A409 Account, 1690
Cant.

A425 Account, 1679
Linc (2).

A427 Account, 1695[6]
In the Savoy, printed by Edward
Jones; Date as Wing2.
Dur.

A439+ Achard, John, 1697
=Wing2 A440; Author as Wing2.
Yk.

A439A Ahitophel's, 1683
Carl. Yk.

A442 Acontius, Jacob, 1651
Ex.

A443 Acontius, Jacob, 1648
Carl. Pet.

A446? Act, 1670
4°.
Win (imp).

A456A Acts, 1690
Cant.

A458? Acts, 1685
8p. & 43p.
Ex (2).

A458+ Acts, 1685
As A458, but: 8p. & 52p.
Carl. Ex.

A479 Adams, John, *of the Inner
Temple*, 1680
S Pl. Wel (tpw, or anr ed.
without impr.?; 404p.).

A480 Adams, John, *of the Inner
Temple*, 1690
Cant (imp). Dur. Ex. S Alb
(imp). Sal.

A480+ Adams, John, *of the Inner
Temple*, 1690
For T. Sawbridge, M. Gillyflower, W.
Hensman and P. Lea; 2°.
Swel.

A481 Adams, John, *of the Inner
Temple*, 1700
Impr. as Wing2.
Yk.

A483 Adams, John, *Provost*, 1700
Dur. Ely. New.

A484 Adams, John, *Provost*, 1695
Ely.

A485 Adams, John, *Provost*, 1695
Dur. Wor.

A486 Adams, John, *Provost*, 1696
Ban. Cant. Carl.

A487 Adams, John, *Provost*, 1700
'preach'd'
S Pl.

A496 Adams, *Sir* Thomas, 1648
Yk.

A500 Adamson, John, 1698
Her.

A512 Addison, Lancelot, 1698
S Pl.

A516 Addison, Lancelot, 1696
Dur.

A518 Addison, Lancelot, 1679
Carl.

A521? Addison, Lancelot, 1682
Crooke; 12°.
Carl.

A524 Addison, Lancelot, 1677
Carl. S Pl.

A526 Addison, Lancelot, 1675
Cant. Ex. Lich. S Asa. Win.

A527 Addison, Lancelot, 1676
Carl. Nor.

A530 Addison, Lancelot, 1674
Carl. Yk.

A537 Address, 1689
S Pl.

A542 Address, 1690
'given in to'
Nor.

A545 Addresse, 1658
Dur. Pet.

A561 Address, [1689]
Half-title only, no tp.
Cant.

A562A Address, 1688
Cant. Her. S Pl.

A594A Admonition, 1646
Dur.

A601 *See*: D828-

A623 Advertisement, 1642
Pet.

A627 Advertisements, 1642
'... and Beverly, July the 20th 1642'
Ex. Linc. Yk.

A627+ Advertisements, 1642
As A627, but: '... July the 28th'
Yk (details not confirmed).

A633 Advice, 1688
Ban.

A648+ Advice, 1688
=Wing2 A648B; Printed and sold by
...
Wel.

A653 Advice, 1687
Ex. Wel.

A656 Advice, 1681
Linc.

A659 Advice, 1681
Linc.

A660 Advice, [1679]
Dur. Linc.

A664 Advice, 1678
Carl.

A665+ Advice, 1697
Another ed.(?) of Wing2 A665A;
'Advice to those who never receiv'd
the sacrament'; Printed, sold by E.
Whitlock; 8°.
Dur.

A678 Aelfric, 1687
Ban. Dur.

A682 Aeschines, [1696]
8°.
Ches. Ex. Glo.

A684 Aeschylus, 1663
S Pl.

A685 Aeschylus, 1664
Impr. as Wing2.
Dur. Ely. Glo.

A685+ Aeschylus, 1664
Typis Jacobi Flesher, prostant apud
Richardum Davis, Oxoniae; 2°.
S Pl.

A689 Aesop, 1651
'paraphras'd'
Lich. Linc. Yk.

A693 Aesop, 1665
1 pt only.
Cant. Linc.

A697 Aesop, 1668
... for the author.
Ex.

A706 Aesop, 1692
Cant. Glo.

A707 Aesop, 1694
1 vol. only.
Pet.

A715 Aesop, 1657
Ex.

A719 Aesop, 1668
'Aesopi Fabulae Anglo-Latinae';
Impr. as Wing2.
Cant (tp imp).

A729 Aesop, 1698
Ely. Win.

A732A? Aesop, 1684
... impensis authoris; 12°.
Nor.

A747+ Afbeeldingen, [1700?]
See: CLC2.
Nor (imp).

A758A Agas, Benjamin, 1655
S Pl.

A763 Agitator, 1648
Cant.

A766 Aglionby, William, 1669
For John Starkey.
Carl. Ex.

A767 Aglionby, William, 1671
Carl.

A774 Agreement, 1656
Impr. as Wing2?
Yk.

A775 Agreement, 1658
Dur. Yk.

A776 Agreement, 1658
S Pl.

A778 Agreement, 1659
Pet. S Pl (imp).

A783 Agreement, 1649
Pet. Yk.

A791 Agrippa, Henricus Cornelius, 1684
Impr. as Wing2.
Bris.

A792 Agrippa, Henricus Cornelius, 1694
Cant.

A802 Ailesbury, Thomas, 1657
Ex. Linc. Pet.

A803 Ailmer, John, 1652
Ely. Sal.

A807 Ainsworth, Henry, 1641
12°.
Linc. Yk.

A811 Ainsworth, Henry, 1641[2]
S Asa. Yk.

A812 Ainsworth, Henry, 1644
Ex.

A818 Ainsworth, William, 1652
Yk.

A826 Alarum, 1642
Impr. as Wing2.
Yk.

A834 Alarum, [1647]
Pet.

A835 Alarum, [1660]
Yk.

A840 Albemarle, George Monck, *Duke of*, 1660
Yk.

A848 Albemarle, George Monck, *Duke of*, 1659
Sal.

A854+ Albemarle, George Monck, *Duke of*, 1660
As A854, but no date in title.
Ex. Sal.

A864 Albemarle, George Monck, *Duke of*, 1671
'... military & political ...'; ... Henry Mortlocke ...
Ex (imp). Linc. S Asa (imp).

A865 Albemarle, George Monck, *Duke of*, 1660
Yk.

A874? Albemarle, George Monck, *Duke of*, 1653
By Tho. Newcomb.
Glo.

A881 Albizzi, Bartholomaeus, 1679
Cant.

A885 Alchorne, William, 1674
Cant.

A886 Alcinous, 1667
Ex. S Pl.

A888 Alcofarado, Francisco, 1675
Yk (tpw).

A894B Aldam, Thomas, [1652]
Second entry.
Yk.

A894C Aldam, Thomas, 1655
Yk.

A899 Aldrich, Henry, 1687
Cant. Carl. Ex (2). Lich. Nor.
S Pl (2). Sal. Wel.

A901 Aldrich, Henry, [1688]
Part of another work, pp. 47–91.
Ex.

A912+ Alexander, Benjamin, 1659
See: CLC3.
Pet.

A920 Aleyn, John, 1681
Wor.

A921? Alford, Joseph, 1649
12°.
Cant (imp).

A925? Algood, *Major*, 1684
'... George Ritschel ...'
Carl.

A943 All, 1680
Linc. Win.

A961+ Alleine, Joseph, 1672
=Wing2 A961A.
Yk.

A978 Alleine, Joseph, 1689
Cant (imp).

A984 Alleine, Richard, 1661
Cant. Dur.

A996 Alleine, Richard, 1668
Pet (imp).

A1003 Alleine, Richard, 1663
Carl.

A1009 Alleine, Richard, 1668
Cant.

A1012 Alleine, Theodosia, 1672
S Asa.

A1014 Alleine, Theodosia, 1673
Simons.
Liv.

A1017 Ἀλληλοκρισια, 1675
Pet.

A1034 Allen, John, *of Trinity Coll., Cambridge*, 1682
S Asa.

A1042 Allen, Richard, *of Henfield*, 1674
Pet.

A1044 Allen, Richard, *of Henfield*, 1675
Win.

A1048 Allen, Thomas, *Minister*, 1659
Yk.

A1054? Allen, William, *Controversial writer*, 1676
'... Mr. Robert Ferguson's ...'
Ban. Ely. Ex. Pet. S Pl.

A1055 Allen, William, *Controversial writer*, 1683
Ban. Carl. Ely. S Pl.

A1056? Allen, William, *Controversial writer*, 1699
By S. Hawes.
Llan.

A1057 Allen, William, *Controversial writer*, 1678
Ban. Ely. Pet. S Pl. Win.

A1058 Allen, William, *Controversial writer*, 1674
Bur. Ely.

A1059 Allen, William, *Controversial writer*, 1679
S Pl. Win.

A1060? Allen, William, *Controversial writer*, 1693
8°.
Ban. Ely. Llan.

A1061 Allen, William, *Controversial writer*, 1673
Ban. Ex. Pet. S Pl.

A1062 Allen, William, *Controversial writer*, 1689
Ely.

A1064 Allen, William, *Controversial writer*, 1679
Win.

A1066 Allen, William, *Controversial writer*, 1675
Ban. Carl. Ely. S Pl.

A1067 Allen, William, *Controversial writer*, 1684
Ban. Ely. S Pl. Yk.

A1069 Allen, William, *Controversial writer*, 1680
Ban. Ely. Pet (2).

A1070 Allen, William, *Controversial writer*, 1681
Ely. S Pl.

A1072 Allen, William, *Controversial writer*, 1676
Carl. Win.

A1073? Allen, William, *Controversial writer*, 1693
Second ed. not on tp.
Ely.

A1078 Allen, William, *Vicar of Bridgewater*, 1697
... Yeavill.
Cant. Llan.

A1080 Allestree, Charles, 1694/5
Ches.

A1082 Allestree, Richard, 1684
Ban. Chelm. Ches. Glo. Her.
S Dv (imp). Yk.

A1083 Allestree, Richard, 1687
Bris. Bur. Glo. Roch.

A1084 Allestree, Richard, 1695
S Dv.

A1085 Allestree, Richard, 1675
... Theater ...
Cant (2 − 1 imp). Carl. Pet. Yk.

A1088? Allestree, Richard, 1676
The third impression; ... and to be sold in his shop; 12°.
Cant.

A1089 Allestree, Richard, 1677
Fourth ed. not on tp.
Her.

A1095 Allestree, Richard, 1684
For W. Cademan.
Carl.

A1097 Allestree, Richard, 1667
452p.
Ban. Carl*. Ely*. Win*. Yk.

A1097+ Allestree, Richard, 1667
As A1097, but: 439p.
Bur. Yk.

A1099 Allestree, Richard, 1669
Her (2).

A1100 Allestree, Richard, 1671
Yk (tpw).

A1100+ Allestree, Richard, 1671
As A1101, apart from date.
S Pl.

A1101 Allestree, Richard, 1672
Cant. Ches (imp). Linc. Pet.

A1102 Allestree, Richard, 1674
Bur. Wel (tp imp: 1 of the eds with this impr. and format; 449p.)*.

A1104 Allestree, Richard, 1677
Dur. S Pl.

A1105 Allestree, Richard, 1679
Cant.

A1108 Allestree, Richard, 1694
New.

A1111 Allestree, Richard, 1677
... Enoch Wyer.
Ely. Pet. Win.

A1111+ Allestree, Richard, 1678
=Wing2 A1111A?; Printed and sold by Hen. Bonwicke.
Dur.

A1112 Allestree, Richard, 1673
Carl. Dur. Her. Wor.

A1113 Allestree, Richard, 1669
Carl. Ely. Ex. Yk (2).

A1114 Allestree, Richard, 1684
Cant. Chi. Ex. Her. Lich.
Nor. S Asa.

A1114+ Allestree, Richard, 1684
As A1114, but: ... T. Sawbridge, R. Bentley and Abel Swall.
S Dv.

A1117? Allestree, Richard, 1662
Second ed. not on tp.
Yk.

A1119 Allestree, Richard, 1667
Dur. Ely. Ex. Yk.

A1121 Allestree, Richard, 1670
S Pl (tpw).

A1121+ Allestree, Richard, 1671
=Wing2 A1121A.
Yk.

A1122 Allestree, Richard, 1672
Cant. Ches. Pet.

A1123 Allestree, Richard, 1673
Bur. Ely.

A1125 Allestree, Richard, 1676
Ex.

A1128 Allestree, Richard, 1682
Impr. as A1122.
Sal.

A1129 Allestree, Richard, 1687
Cant. Glo. IoM.

A1130 Allestree, Richard, 1696
Sal.

A1133 Allestree, Richard, 1674
8°.
Yk.

A1134 Allestree, Richard, 1674
8°.
Bur. Cant. Linc. Wel.

A1135 Allestree, Richard, 1675
Ban. Carl. Pet. Yk.

A1138 Allestree, Richard, 1667
[1677]
The fifth impression.
Her.

A1139 Allestree, Richard, 1693
The fifth impression.
Cant.

A1140 Allestree, Richard, 1672
Ban. S Asa.

A1141 Allestree, Richard, 1673
Madan 2960.
Yk.

A1141+ Allestree, Richard, 1673
As A1141, but: 12°; Madan 2961.
Cant.

A1141++ Allestree, Richard, 1673
As A1141, but: ... Theatre; Madan 2962.
Win.

A1142 Allestree, Richard, 1673
Bur. Ely. Pet.

A1143 Allestree, Richard, 1675
Cant. Ex.

A1143+ Allestree, Richard, 1675
Edinburgh, printed by Thomas Brown, to be sold at his shop; 12°.
Cant.

A1144? Allestree, Richard, 1676
8°.
Cant (imp?).

A1145 Allestree, Richard, 1677
Cant. Ex. Sal.

A1148 Allestree, Richard, 1700
Yk.

A1149 Allestree, Richard, 1678
8°.
Ches. Linc. Win. Yk.

A1150 Allestree, Richard, 1678
Second ed. not on tp.
Dur.

A1151? Allestree, Richard, 1678
Second ed. not on tp; ... and are to be sold by Peter Parker, London.
Cant.

A1152 Allestree, Richard, 1679
Cant.

A1155 Allestree, Richard, 1696
Her.

A1156 Allestree, Richard, 1680
Dur. Wel.

A1157 Allestree, Richard, 1693
Pro Edvardo Pawlet.
Cant. Chi.

A1161 Allestree, Richard, 1660
Carl. S Pl.

A1163 Allestree, Richard, 1660
Carl. Win.

A1164 Allestree, Richard, 1662
Cant. Carl.

A1165 Allestree, Richard, 1663
Win.

A1166? Allestree, Richard, 1666
… James Allestree and Richard Davis.
Carl. Yk.

A1167 Allestree, Richard, 1667
Carl. Her. Win.

A1168? Allestree, Richard, 1684
For John Kidgell.
Cant. Carl. Win.

A1169 Allestree, Richard, [1658]
Carl.

A1171 Allestree, Richard, 1661
Her. Linc.

A1172 Allestree, Richard, 1663
Cant (imp). Pet.

A1176+ Allestree, Richard, 1671
=Wing2 A1176B.
Yk.

A1177 Allestree, Richard, 1673
Ely.

A1182 Allestree, Richard, 1678
Cant.

A1185 Allestree, Richard, 1680
Impr. as Wing2.
Yk.

A1185+ Allestree, Richard, 1682
=Wing2 A1185B.
New.

A1186+ Allestree, Richard, 1686
No ed. statement; By R. Norton for
George Pawlet; 12°.
Nor.

A1188+ Allestree, Richard, 1690
=Wing2 A1188A.
Cant. Liv.

A1193+ Allestree, Richard, 1685
'Part II'; The second edition; By
Francis Clark, for H. Sawbridge and
Tho. Simmons; 8°.
Ban.

A1196 Allestree, Thomas, 1671
Dur. Yk.

A1197 Allestree, Thomas, 1671
Dur. Yk.

A1206 Allington, John, 1649
Ex.

A1207 Allington, John, [1660]
Linc. Sal.

A1208+ Allington, John, 1654
=Wing2 A1209A.
Linc. Pet. Yk.

A1209 Allington, John, 1654
Bur. Carl.

A1210 Allington, John, 1655
Impr. as A1209.
Cant.

A1211? Allington, John, 1657
Fifth ed. not on tp.
Sal. Wor.

A1212 Allington, John, 1663
'… of the grand conspiracy …'; By J.
Grismond.
Ely.

A1213 Allington, John, 1678
Pt 2 = 'A review of a brief apology'
Carl. Dur. Liv (pt 2 only). Pet.

A1214 Allington, John, 1672
Carl. Linc.

A1218 Allix, Pierre, 1695
Carl. S Asa.

A1219 Allix, Pierre, 1691
Cant. Carl. Wel.

A1220 Allix, Pierre, 1688
Ban. Ches. Ex. Nor. Sal. Swel.

A1221 Allix, Pierre, 1688
Ban. Cant (imp). Ex. Nor.
Swel.

A1222 Allix, Pierre, 1689
Bur.

A1223 Allix, Pierre, 1688
Liv. Sal. Wel.

A1224 Allix, Pierre, 1699
S Asa. Win.

A1225 Allix, Pierre, 1693
Yk.

A1227 Allix, Pierre, 1688
Dur. Ely. Nor. Roch. S Pl (2).

A1228 Allix, Pierre, 1687
S Pl. Yk.

A1230 Allix, Pierre, 1692
Chi. Ely. Linc. S Asa. S Pl.
Swel. Win.

A1231 Allix, Pierre, 1690
Chi. Dur. Ely. Ex. S Asa.
S Pl. Sal. Swel. Win.

A1288 Almanacs — Andrews, 1692
Dur.

A1290 Almanacs — Andrews, 1694
Dur.

A1291 Almanacs — Andrews, 1695
Dur.

A1292 Almanacs — Andrews, 1696
Dur (2).

A1293 Almanacs — Andrews, 1697
Dur.

A1294 Almanacs — Andrews, 1698
Dur.

A1295 Almanacs — Andrews, 1699
Dur.

A1296 Almanacs — Andrews, 1700
Dur.

A1305 Almanacs — Atkinson, 1670
Yk.

A1306 Almanacs — Atkinson, 1671
Yk.

A1309+ Almanacs — B., G., [1667]
=Wing2 A1309A?; 'Kalendarium
Julianum … M.DC.LXVII'
Carl.

A1321+ Almanacs — Blount, 1662
'1662'; 12°.
Carl.

A1322- Almanacs — Blount, 1666
'1666'; 12°.
Linc.

A1353 Almanacs — Booker, [1667]
Impr. as Wing A1352.
Carl.

A1389 Almanacs — Catholic, 1688
'Catholic'
Dur.

A1394 Almanacs — Chapmans, 1694
Dur.

A1395 Almanacs — Chapmans, 1695
Dur.

A1409 Almanacs — City, 1692
Dur.

A1443 Almanacs — Coley, 1692
The one and twentieth impression.
Dur.

A1445 Almanacs — Coley, 1694
Dur.

A1446 Almanacs — Coley, 1695
Dur (tp imp).

A1447 Almanacs — Coley, 1696
Dur (2).

A1448 Almanacs — Coley, 1697
Dur.

A1449 Almanacs — Coley, 1698
Dur.

A1450 Almanacs — Coley, 1699
Dur.

A1451 Almanacs – Coley, 1700
Dur.

A1468 Almanacs – Cookson, 1699
Dur.

A1469 Almanacs – Cookson, 1700
'MDCC'
Dur.

A1515 Almanacs – Culpeper,
Nathaniel, 1695
Dur.

A1536? Almanacs – Dade, 1695
Impr. date as title date.
Dur.

A1637 Almanacs – Dove, 1692
Dur (imp).

A1639 Almanacs – Dove, 1694
Dur. Yk.

A1640 Almanacs – Dove, 1695
Dur.

A1641 Almanacs – Dove, 1696
Dur (2).

A1642 Almanacs – Dove, 1697
Dur.

A1643 Almanacs – Dove, 1698
Dur.

A1644 Almanacs – Dove, 1699
Dur.

A1645 Almanacs – Dove, 1700
Dur.

A1648+ Almanacs – Eagle, 1666
'Eagle. 1666. A new almanack ... for
... 1666'; York, by Stephen Bulkley,
for Francis Mawbarne; 8°.
Yk.

A1652 Almanacs – English, 1697
Dur.

A1653 Almanacs – English, 1698
Dur.

A1654? Almanacs – English, 1698
Impr. has different date from Wing.
Dur.

A1698 Almanacs – Fly, 1695
Dur.

A1728 Almanacs – Fowle, 1695
Dur.

A1747 Almanacs – Gadbury, [1668]
Carl.

A1771 Almanacs – Gadbury, 1692
Dur.

A1773 Almanacs – Gadbury, 1694
Dur.

A1774 Almanacs – Gadbury, 1695
Dur.

A1775 Almanacs – Gadbury, 1696
Dur (2).

A1776 Almanacs – Gadbury, 1697
Dur.

A1777 Almanacs – Gadbury, 1698
Dur.

A1778 Almanacs – Gadbury, 1699
Dur.

A1779 Almanacs – Gadbury, 1700
Dur.

A1793+ Almanacs – Goldsmith,
1681
'Goldsmith, 1681 ...'; By Mary Clark
for the company of stationers; 12°.
Dur.

A1825 Almanacs – Hobbs, 1695
Dur.

A1855 Almanacs – Kendal, 1700
Dur.

A1919 Almanacs – Lilly, 1644
4°.
Sal.

A1946 Almanacs – Moore, 1699
Dur.

A2007 Almanacs – Parker, 1692
Dur.

A2009 Almanacs – Parker, 1694
Dur.

A2010 Almanacs – Parker, 1695
Dur.

A2011 Almanacs – Parker, 1696
Dur (2).

A2012 Almanacs – Parker, 1697
Dur.

A2013 Almanacs – Parker, 1698
Dur.

A2034 Almanacs – Partridge, J.,
[1692]
Dur.

A2036 Almanacs – Partridge, J.,
[1694]
Dur.

A2037 Almanacs – Partridge, J.,
[1695]
Dur.

A2038 Almanacs – Partridge, J.,
[1696]
Dur (2).

A2039 Almanacs – Partridge, J.,
[1697]
Dur.

A2040 Almanacs – Partridge, J.,
1698
Dur.

A2041 Almanacs – Partridge, J.,
[1699]
Dur (imp).

A2042 Almanacs – Partridge, J.,
[1700]
Dur.

A2080? Almanacs – Perkins, F.,
1669
By J.C. for the Company of Stationers.
Carl.

A2096 Almanacs – Perkins, F.,
1695
Dur.

A2147A Almanacs – Pond, 1667
Linc.

A2172 Almanacs – Pond, 1692
Dur.

A2174 Almanacs – Pond, 1694
Dur.

A2175 Almanacs – Pond, 1695
Dur.

A2176 Almanacs – Pond, 1696
Dur (2).

A2177 Almanacs – Pond, 1697
Dur.

A2178 Almanacs – Pond, 1698
Dur.

A2179 Almanacs – Pond, 1699
Dur.

A2180 Almanacs – Pond, 1700
Dur.

A2190 Almanacs – Poor, 1671
Carl.

A2191 Almanacs – Poor, 1672
Carl.

A2211 Almanacs – Poor, 1692
Dur.

A2213 Almanacs – Poor, 1694
The two and thirtieth ...; Impr. as the
others.
Dur.

A2215 Almanacs – Poor, 1696
Dur (2).

A2216 Almanacs – Poor, 1697
'1697'
Dur.

A2218 Almanacs – Poor, 1699
Dur.

A2232 Almanacs – Protestant, 1692
Dur.

A2234 Almanacs – Protestant, 1694
Dur.

A2235 Almanacs – Protestant, 1695
Dur.

A2236 Almanacs – Protestant, 1696
Dur (2).

A2237 Almanacs — Protestant, 1697
Dur.

A2238 Almanacs — Protestant, 1698
Dur.

A2239 Almanacs — Protestant, 1699
Dur.

A2240 Almanacs — Protestant, 1700
Dur.

A2301 Almanacs — Rose, 1695
By Thomas Hodgkin ...
Dur.

A2316 Almanacs — Salmon, 1692
Dur.

A2318 Almanacs — Salmon, 1694
Cant.

A2319 Almanacs — Salmon, 1695
Dur.

A2320 Almanacs — Salmon, 1696
Dur (2).

A2321 Almanacs — Salmon, 1697
Dur.

A2322 Almanacs — Salmon, 1698
Dur (2).

A2323 Almanacs — Salmon, 1699
Dur.

A2324 Almanacs — Salmon, 1700
Dur.

A2362 Almanacs — Saunders, 1692
Dur.

A2364 Almanacs — Saunders, 1694
Dur.

A2365 Almanacs — Saunders, 1695
Dur.

A2366 Almanacs — Saunders, 1696
Dur (2).

A2367 Almanacs — Saunders, 1697
Dur.

A2368 Almanacs — Saunders, 1698
Dur.

A2369 Almanacs — Saunders, 1699
Dur.

A2370 Almanacs — Saunders, 1700
Dur.

A2459? Almanacs — Swallow, 1695
Cambridge, by John Hayes.
Dur.

A2529 Almanacs — Tanner, 1692
Dur.

A2531 Almanacs — Tanner, 1694
Dur.

A2532 Almanacs — Tanner, 1695
Dur.

A2533 Almanacs — Tanner, 1696
Dur (2).

A2535 Almanacs — Tanner, 1698
Dur.

A2536 Almanacs — Tanner, 1699
Dur.

A2537 Almanacs — Tanner, 1700
Dur.

A2576 Almanacs — Trigge, 1695
Dur.

A2603 Almanacs — Turner, 1695
Dur.

A2639 Almanacs — Welsh-mans, 1643
Linc.

A2655 Almanacs — Wharton, 1664
Carl.

A2656 Almanacs — Wharton, 1665
Carl. Dur.

A2657 Almanacs — Wharton, 1666
Carl.

A2658- Almanacs — Wharton, 1657
=Wing2 A2657A.
Carl. Yk.

A2658 Almanacs — Wharton, 1658
Impr. as Wing2.
Carl.

A2659 Almanacs — Wharton, 1659
By J. Grismond.
Carl.

A2662 Almanacs — Wharton, 1655
8°.
Carl.

A2663 Almanacs — Wharton, 1656
8°.
Carl.

A2668 Almanacs — Wharton, 1653
Carl.

A2669 Almanacs — Wharton, 1654
Carl.

A2733 Almanacs — White, T., 1695
Dur.

A2783 Almanacs — Wing, J., 1692
Dur.

A2785 Almanacs — Wing, J., 1694
Dur.

A2786 Almanacs — Wing, J., 1695
Dur.

A2787 Almanacs — Wing, J., 1696
Dur (2).

A2788 Almanacs — Wing, J., 1697
Dur.

A2789 Almanacs — Wing, J., 1698
Dur.

A2790 Almanacs — Wing, J., 1699
Dur.

A2799A Almanacs — Wing, V., 1652
Sal.

A2804 Almanacs — Wing, V., 1655
Yk (sig. C only).

A2813 Almanacs — Wing, V., [1664]
By W. Leybourn ...
Carl.

A2816 Almanacs — Wing, V., [1667]
Carl.

A2816+ Almanacs — Wing, V., 1667
=Wing2 A2816A.
Carl.

A2873 Almanacs — Woodhouse, 1695
Dur.

A2881 Almanacs — Woodward, [1692]
Dur.

A2883 Almanacs — Woodward, 1694
Dur.

A2884 Almanacs — Woodward, 1695
Dur.

A2885 Almanacs — Woodward, 1696
Dur (2).

A2887 Almanacs — Woodward, 1698
Dur.

A2902 Alsop, George, 1669
Impr. as Wing2.
Cant.

A2904 Alsop, Nathaniel, 1682
Cant. Carl. Wor.

A2905 Alsop, Vincent, 1675
Carl. Chelm (imp). S Pl.

A2911 Alsop, Vincent, 1696
Cant.

A2912 Alsop, Vincent, 1687
Cant.

A2914 Alsop, Vincent, 1678
S Asa. Wel.

A2915 Alsop, Vincent, 1679
Carl.

A2917 Alsop, Vincent, 1680
Carl. Dur. Pet.

A2918 Alsop, Vincent, 1680
Nor.

A2919 Alsop, Vincent, 1681
S Pl.

A2924 Alsted, Johann Heinrich, 1643
Yk.

A2931 Altham, Michael, 1688
Ex. Wel.

A2932 Altham, Michael, 1687
Bur. Ex.

A2933+ Altham, Michael, 1687
The third edition; For Luke Meredith; 12°.
Carl. Pet.

A2934 Altham, Michael, 1686
39p.
Llan. S Asa. Sal.

A2934+ Altham, Michael, 1686
As A2934, but: 41p.
Ex.

A2935 Altham, Michael, 1687
Bur.

A2936? Altham, Michael, 1687
38p.
Ban. Cant. Chi. Dur. Nor.
S Pl. Sal. Wel. Yk (3).

A2936+ Altham, Michael, 1687
As A2936, but: 30p.
Dur.

A2936++ Altham, Michael, 1687
As A2936, but: 40p.
Bur.

A2937 Altham, Michael, 1687
Ban. Chi. Dur. Ex. Nor (2).
S Pl. Sal. Wel. Yk (3).

A2939A Alured, Matthew, 1659
Ex (tp imp). Yk.

A2952 Ambrose, Isaac, 1674
Her.

A2956A Ambrose, Isaac, 1674
Her. Yk.

A2966? Ambrose, Isaac, 1674
Reynolds.
Her. Yk.

A2968 Ambrose, Isaac, 1658
Chelm.

A2969 Ambrose, Isaac, 1674
Her. Yk.

A2974 Amelot de la Houssaye, Abraham Nicolas, 1677
Carl. S Asa. Win.

A2994 Ames, William, 1641
'analyticall'
Carl. Yk.

A2995A Ames, William, 1643
Impr. as Wing2.
Yk.

A2996 Ames, William, 1659
Dur.

A2999 Ames, William, 1647
Chelm.

A3000+ Ames, William, 1642
Impr. as A3000; 4°.
Yk.

A3009 Ames, William, *of Wrentham*, 1652
Ex. S Pl.

A3030 Amurath, [1643]
'blasphemous'
Linc.

A3031- Amy, S., 1680
=Wing2 A3030A.
Bris (tp imp). Nor.

A3033 Amydenus, Theodorus, 1687
8°.
Ban. Ches.

A3034 Amyraut, Moses, 1676
Carl. Pet.

A3037 Amyraut, Moses, 1660
Cant. Carl. Chelm.

A3045 Anacreon, 1695
S Asa.

A3048 Ananias, 1679
Carl. Chi. Dur (2). Linc. Win.

A3051 Anastasius, *Sinaita*, 1682
Ex. Her. S Pl. Wor.

A3055 Anatomy, 1660
'The anatomy ...'
Dur.

A3059 Anatomy, 1700
By W. Bowyer for Charles Brome; 12°.
Nor.

A3080 Anderdon, John, 1670
Linc.

A3085 Anderson, *Sir* Edmund, 1664—5
'principals'
Dur.

A3086 Anderson, *Sir* Edmund, 1665
Dur.

A3088 Anderson, Francis, 1643[4]
Sal.

A3092 Anderson, Henry, 1684
Win.

A3093 Anderson, Henry, 1681
Carl.

A3094 Anderson, Henry, *M.P.*, 1648
Yk.

A3099 Anderson, Patrick, [1680]
Linc.

A3110 Anderton, Thomas, 1671
Ex.

A3121 Andrewes, John, 1682
Carl.

A3125 Andrewes, Lancelot, 1657
Carl. Ely. IoM (imp). Lich.
Win. Wor. Yk.

A3126 Andrewes, Lancelot, 1659
24°.
S Asa. Wel.

A3130-- Andrewes, Lancelot, 1655
=Wing2 A3129.
Yk.

A3130- Andrewes, Lancelot, 1675
=Wing2 A3129B?; The sixth edition; 12°.
Carl.

A3135 Andrewes, Lancelot, 1648
24°.
Win.

A3138 Andrewes, Lancelot, 1682
Ex. Wel.

A3140 Andrewes, Lancelot, 1642
2°.
Cant. Dur. Ely (imp). Ex. Liv.
S Asa. S Pl. Wel. Wor.

A3141 Andrewes, Lancelot, 1641
... Roger Daniel.
Cant. Sal.

A3142 Andrewes, Lancelot, 1641
Impr. as Wing2.
Cant (2). Ches. Dur. Lich.
Linc. Pet. Roch. S Asa (imp).
S Pl. Sal. Wel. Wor.

A3142+ Andrewes, Lancelot, 1661
=Wing2 A3142A.
Bris. Glo. Win.

A3142++ Andrewes, Lancelot, 1661
=Wing2 A3142B; The fifth edition.
Chi. Nor. Rip.

A3142+++ Andrewes, Lancelot, 1661
The fifth edition; 2°.
Glo. Win. Yk.

A3143 Andrewes, Lancelot, 1647
Cant. Ex. Sal. Yk (2).

A3144 Andrewes, Lancelot, 1647
Sal.

A3145 Andrewes, Lancelot, 1641
Sal.

A3146 Andrewes, Lancelot, 1641
... Wil. Garret.
New.

A3146+ Andrewes, Lancelot, 1641
=Wing2 A3146A.
Ex. Sal.

A3147? Andrewes, Lancelot, 1650
Second ed. not on tp.
Cant (2). Carl. Chi. Her. Lich.
Linc. Nor. S Pl. Sal (imp).

A3147+ Andrewes, Lancelot, 1655
No ed. statement; 12°.
Yk.

A3148? Andrewes, Lancelot, 1675
For M.G. sold by George Swinnock.
Ban. Ely. Linc. Wor.

A3149 Andrewes, Lancelot, 1675
Ely. S Asa. Tru. Win. Yk.

A3151 Andrewes, Lancelot, 1646
'Sacrilege a snare'
Carl. Sal (2). Yk.

A3153 Andrewes, Lancelot, 1641
... Leon. Lichfield; Pt of C1687A.
Carl. Ex (2). Linc. Pet. Sal.
Yk (2).

A3153+ Andrewes, Lancelot, 1647
=Wing2 A3153; 4°; Consists of
A3143, A3144 & A3151.
Sal.

A3155 *See*: C2758

A3167 Anglesey, Arthur Annesley,
Earl of, 1659
Carl. S Pl.

A3168 Anglesey, Arthur Annesley,
Earl of, 1659
Dur. Pet. Yk (2).

A3169 Anglesey, Arthur Annesley,
Earl of, 1688
Ban. Wel.

A3172 Anglesey, Arthur Annesley,
Earl of, 1682
Wor.

A3175 Anglesey, Arthur Annesley,
Earl of, 1693
Carl.

A3176 Anglesey, Arthur Annesley,
Earl of, 1676
Carl. Chelm.

A3177 Anglesey, Arthur Annesley,
Earl of, 1667 [*i.e.* 1676]
Carl.

A3177+ Anglesey, Arthur Annesley,
Earl of, 1676
Printed; 4°.
Chelm (tp imp).

A3178 Anglia, 1651
Sal (imp; matches A3437,
cancelled in Wing2 as a duplicate
of A3178).

A3185 Anglo-Saxon Chronicle,
1692
Ban. Cant. Carl. Dur. Ex.
Glo. Nor. S Pl. Swel. Wel.
Wor. Yk.

A3189 Animadversions, 1691
Carl.

A3191 Animadversions, 1697
Impr. as Wing2.
Carl.

A3192 Animadversions, [1695?]
Wel.

A3193+ Animadversions, 1654
See: CLC4.
Cant.

A3193A *See*: A11+

A3201 Animadversions, 1647
Yk.

A3204? Animadversions, 1688
By George Larkin.
Wel.

A3206 Animadversions, 1681
Win.

A3209 Animadversions, 1642
Linc.

A3218 Annand, William, 1661
Win.

A3218+ Annand, William, 1661
For Edward Brewster; 4°.
Ex.

A3221 Annand, William, 1661
Carl.

A3222 Annand, William, 1661
Ex.

A3223 Annand, William, 1670
Win.

A3225? Annesley, Samuel, 1690
By James Atwood ...
Llan.

A3227 Annesley, Samuel, 1655
S Pl.

A3228 Annesley, Samuel, 1683
Ex. Llan.

A3229 Annesley, Samuel, 1655
Cant (imp). Pet.

A3233? Annesley, Samuel, 1664
Second ed. not on tp.
Ex.

A3234? Annesley, Samuel, 1671
By T. Milbourn, for Joshua Johnson,
sold by Edw. Brewster, Nevil
Simmons, Tho. Parkhurst and Robert
Boulter.
Llan.

A3237 Annesley, Samuel, 1673
Her.

A3239 Annesley, Samuel, 1674
Llan (tpw).

A3245 Annotations, 1641
Pet. Yk.

A3254 *See*: R1033A

A3270 Another, 1643
Linc. Yk.

A3278 Answer, 1687
Title as Wing2.
Wel.

A3283+ Answer, [1689]
=Wing2 A3283A.
Yk.

A3284? Answer, 1689
For Ri. Chiswell.
Carl. Wel.

A3286? Answer, 1667
By A. Maxwell.
Ban. Pet.

A3304 Answer, 1644
Ex.

A3309 Answer, 1687
S Asa. S Pl.

A3313 Answer, [1679?]
Linc (3).

A3317? Answer, [1679]
Colophon: For John Blythe at Mr.
Playford's shop; cap.
Dur. Linc.

A3319 Answer, 1687
Cant. Dur (cropped). Yk.

A3320 Answer, [1679]
Title as Wing2.
Linc.

A3323 Answer, 1681
Linc.

A3339 *See*: S5101

A3350 Answer, 1642[3]
Cant.

A3351 Answer, 1643
Linc.

A3365 Answer, 1688
Impr. as Wing2.
Carl.

A3367 Answer, 1696
Dur.

A3368 Answer, [1679]
Yk.

A3372 Answer, [1681?]
Dur.

A3381 Answer, [1679]
Linc.

A3386? Answer, 1691
... and sold by John Harris.
Cant.

A3387 Answer, [1689]
Yk.

A3388 Answer, 1689
Carl. S Asa. Wel.

A3390 Answer, 1689
Carl.

A3392 Answer, 1642
Linc.

A3398 Answer, 1648
Sal.

A3399A Answer, [1688?]
Impr. as Wing2.
Wel (tp imp).

A3400? Answer, 1688
cap.; 4°.
Pet.

A3403+ Ansuere, 1652
As A3403 but 'ansuere'
Sal.

A3406 Answer, 1698
'... dragon & ...'
S Pl.

A3407 Answer, [1680?]
Linc.

A3413 Answer, 1643
Carl (imp). Yk.

A3416+ Answer, 1687
=Wing2 A3416A.
Wel.

A3420 Answer, 1641
Linc.

A3421 Answer, 1642
Cant. Carl. Sal.

A3427 Answer, 1641
Cant. Ex. Linc. Sal.

A3430 Answer, 1641
Cant. Dur. Pet. Yk.

A3436 Answer, 1694
Title as Wing2.
Carl. Yk.

A3437 *See*: A3178

A3446 Answer, 1652
Carl.

A3446A Answer, 1652
Ex.

A3448 Answer, 1660
Sal.

A3454 Answer, 1661
Linc. S Asa. Win (2).

A3455 *See*: S3264+

A3456+ Answer, 1658
=Wing2 A3456; 4°.
Ex.

A3476? Ἀνθολογία, 1684
... Cantabrigiensium.
Ex. Nor. Yk.

A3485 Antichristian, 1679
Ex. Yk.

A3486 Anti-confederacie, 1644
Yk.

A3487 Anti-confederacy, 1644
Linc. Win. Yk.

A3489 Anti-covenant, 1643
Cant.

A3490 Anti-covenant, 1643
Linc.

A3496 Antidote, 1679
Linc. Sal.

A3499 Antidotes, 1642
Carl.

A3506 Anti-Quaker, 1676
Sal.

A3512 Anti-remonstrance, 1641
Cant. Linc.

A3515 Anti-toleration, 1646
Pet.

A3524+ Antrobus, Richard, 1675
For Henry Twyford; 8°.
Cant.

A3536 Apollonius, *Pergaeus*, 1675
Impr. as Wing2 A3534.
Yk.

A3537 Apologetick, [1649]
Yk.

A3538 Apologeticall, 1641
Pet.

A3539A Apologeticall, 1649
Printed in the yeer.
Yk.

A3540A Apology, 1674
'... advice for some ...'
Carl.

A3554 Apology, 1681
Cant. Carl. Her. Win. Yk.

A3555A Apology, 1683
Dur. Nor. S Pl.

A3556? Apology, 1689
Chiswel.
Dur. Wel.

A3560 Apology, 1643
Linc.

A3561A Apostolick, 1673
Carl.

A3565 Appeale, 1656
Title as Wing2.
Ex (2). Linc (tp imp).

A3566 Appeale, 1641
Ely.

A3567 Appeal, 1700
Wel.

A3569 Appeale, [1642]
Dur. Linc.

A3575 Appendix, [1697?]
Nor (tpw or cap.?).

A3583 Apprehending, 1641
Linc.

A3596 Aratus, 1672
Carl. Ches. Ely. Linc. Sal.
Win.

A3605 Ἀρχαιονομία, 1644
Usually found in B1662.
Cant (2 − 1 is the separate issue).
Dur. Linc. Nor (anr state issued
separately). S Dv. S Pl. Sal.
Win. Wor.

A3609 Archer, John, *M.D.*, 1673
Ex.

A3615 Archer, John, *Preacher*,
1642
... Benjamin Allen.
Pet.

A3617? Archer, John, *Preacher*,
1642
54p.
S Pl. Yk.

A3621 Archimedes, 1675
Yk.

A3622 Archimedes, 1676
Carl. Pet. Yk.

A3625 Arderne, James, *Dean*, 1677
Ches (2). Ex. Nor.

A3629 Aretius, Benedictus, 1696
Ex. S Pl. Yk.

A3632? Argument, 1697
'The argument ...'
Nor. S Pl.

A3649? Arguments, 1649
'The arguments ...'; 4°.
Pet.

A3654 Argyll, Archibald Campbell,
Marquis of, 1641
Cant.

A3657? Argyle, Archibald
Campbell, *Marquis of*, 1661
By T. Young for John Latham.
Carl.

A3672? Argyle, Archibald
Campbell, *Marquis of*, 1641
'A true ...'
Ex.

A3683 Aristeas, 1692
Ex. Sal.

A3684 Aristophanes, 1695
'... Plutus & Nubes ...'
Bur. Linc. S Asa. S Dv. Sal.

A3686? Aristophanes, 1659
8°.
Pet.

A3688 Aristotle, 1679
Ban. Ely (2). S Asa. Wel.

A3690 Aristotle, 1696
Title as Wing2
Ches. Ex. Linc. Nor. S Asa.

A3695 Aristotle, 1686
Cant.

A3697 Aristotle, 1696
Typis Ben. Griffini, impensis Edvard
Hall, Cantabr'.
Ex.

A3697+ Aristotle, 1696
Typis Ben. Griffini impensis Edvard
Hall, & Eliz. Dickinson, Cantabr'.
Cant. S Asa.

A3700 Arminius, Jacobus, 1657
Pet (tp imp).

A3702 Armitage, Timothy, 1678
Nor.

A3712A Army's, 1660
Linc.

A3716 Army's, 1659
Dur (imp). Pet. S Pl. Yk.

A3720 *See:* L307A

A3721 *See:* L307B

A3723- Arnauld, Antoine, 1679
=Wing2 A3720, but: 'The king-killing
doctrine'; For W. Crooke and T.
Dring.
Cant. Carl.

A3724+ Arnauld, Antoine, 1693
The second edition; By T.B. sold by
Randal Taylor; 12°.
S Pl.

A3724A? Arnauld, Antoine, 1696
... for J. Taylor.
Nor.

A3725 Arnauld, Antoine, 1674
Entry as Wing2 A3724.
Bur. Carl. Ex.

A3726- Arnauld, Antoine, 1682
No ed. statement; Impensis R.
Littlebury, R. Scot, G. Wells, & J.
Green, Cantabrigiensis; 8°.
Ely. Nor.

A3727+ Arnauld, Antoine, 1687
=Wing2 A3728, but no ed. statement.
Cant.

A3729 Arnauld, Antoine, 1664
Carl. Pet. Sal (tp imp). Win.

A3730 Arnauld, Antoine, 1662
'Jesuits'
Carl.

A3737 Arnway, John, 1649
Linc.

A3739 Arnway, John, 1661
S Asa.

A3744 Arraignment, 1648
Ex. Win.

A3746 Arraignment, 1681
Linc. Nor. Wor.

A3748+ Arraignment, 1696
=Wing2 A3748A.
Ely.

A3751? Arraigement, 1641
'arraigement'
S Pl.

A3754 Arraignment, 1684
Ely. S Pl. Wor.

A3755 Arraignment, 1696
Ely.

A3757 Arraignment, 1696
Ely.

A3760 Arraignment, 1696
Ely.

A3761 Arraignment, 1681
Ely. Glo. S Pl.

A3765+ Arraignment, 1691
=Wing2 A3765A.
Win.

A3767 Arraignments, 1696
Ely.

A3768 Arraignment, 1691
Ely. Win.

A3772 Arrowsmith, John, 1659
Bur. Carl. Chelm. Ex.

A3773 Arrowsmith, John, 1643
Cant (2). Carl.

A3775 Arrowsmith, John, 1645
Carl. Ex. Her. Pet (2).

A3776 Arrowsmith, John, 1647
Pet.

A3777 Arrowsmith, John, 1657
Carl. Chelm. Ely. Ex. Lich.
Linc. Nor. Sal.

A3786 Art, 1691
Ex. S Pl.

A3787 Art, 1692
Yk.

A3798 Artaxerxes, 1661
Yk.

A3803+ Articles, 1645
=Wing2 A3803A; 'betweene'
Yk.

A3809 Articles, 1641
Ches.

A3811 Articles, 1673
S Asa.

A3815 Articles, 1646
Win.

A3817 Articles, 1646
Pet.

A3823 Articles, 1641
Pet.

A3825 Articles, 1646
Yk.

A3827 Articles, 1645[6]
Linc.

A3828 *See:* C4009+

A3832 Articles, 1642
Dur. Yk.

A3838 *See:* C4009A

A3844 Articles, 1660
Yk.

A3847 Articles, 1641[2]
Bill.
Ex.

A3853 Articles, 1642
Dur.

A3873 Articles, 1654
... at London.
Dur.

A3874 Articles, 1650
Glo.

A3875 Articles, 1651
Glo.

A3888 Articles, 1661
Yk.

A3890? Articuli, 1651
'Lambethani'; 12°.
Carl. Linc (imp). S Pl.

A3890+ Articuli, 1651
=Wing2 A3891.
Nor. Sal.

A3891 *See:* E581

A3893 *See:* E581

A3901 Arwaker, Edmund, *the Elder*,
1695
Ex.

A3910 Arwaker, Edmund, *the
Younger*, 1695
Nor.

A3920 Ascham, Anthony, 1648
Cant (imp). Carl. Linc (imp).
Yk.

A3921 Ascham, Anthony, 1649
Pet.

A3922 Ascham, Anthony, 1649
Ches.

A3923 Ascham, Anthony, 1650
Impr. as Wing2.
Carl. Dur.

A3924 Ascham, Anthony, 1689
Bur. Pet. S Asa. Wel.

A3926 Asgill, John, 1700
8°.
Dur (2).

A3933 Ash, St George, 1694
'January the 9th, 1693/4'; ... William
Norman.
Her.

A3940 Ashby, Richard, 1699
Dur.

A3945 Ashe, John, 1642
Dur. Linc.

A3949 Ashe, Simeon, 1642
Ex.

A3951 Ashe, Simeon, 1645
Pet.

A3953 Ashe, Simeon, 1654
Sawbridge.
Carl. Pet (tpw).

A3954 Ashe, Simeon, 1659
Yk.

A3956+ Ashe, Simeon, 1642
=Wing2 A3956A.
S Asa.

A3959 Ashe, Simeon, 1655
Impr. as Wing2.
Cant (2 – both imp). Carl.

A3961 Ashe, Simeon, 1654
Yk (2 – 1 imp?*).

A3962 Ashe, Simeon, 1654
Pet (2).

A3963 Ashe, Simeon, 1656
Cant. Yk.

A3964 Ashe, Simeon, 1645
Pet. S Pl.

A3967 Ashe, Simeon, 1642
Pet.

A3970 Ashe, Thomas, 1653
Third ed. not on tp.
Linc.

A3971? Ashe, Thomas, 1672
Fourth ed. not on tp; ... Richard
Atkins and Edward Atkins ...
Wor.

A3976 Ashhurst, William, 1648
Pet.

A3980 Ashley, Thomas, 1642
Linc.

A3983 Ashmole, Elias, 1672
'institution'
Chi. Dur. Ex. Lich. Linc.
Win. Wor.

A3988 Ashmole, Elias, 1658
Cant. Pet.

A3995 Ashwell, George, 1680
Dur. Win. Yk.

A3997 Ashwell, George, 1653
Carl. Ely. Sal. Win.

A3998 Ashwell, George, 1663
Carl. Yk.

A4002 Asinus, 1642
Sal.

A4003 Aspin, William, 1684
Llan. Pet.

A4003A Aspinwall, William, 1657
Ex.

A4019 Assenters, 1681
Yk.

A4021A *See*: G1981B

A4022? Assheton, William, 1685
2°.
Ex.

A4023 Assheton, William, 1674
Impr. as Wing2.
Carl. Chelm. Linc. Win.

A4027? Assheton, William, 1673
For R. Royston.
Her. S Asa.

A4032 Assheton, William, 1696
Ely.

A4033 Assheton, William, 1663
Cant. Carl. Linc. Win.

A4034 Assheton, William, 1682
Pet.

A4038 Assheton, William, 1684
Carl. Ex.

A4040 Assheton, William, 1676
Cant (imp). Carl. Dur. Ex.
S Asa. Win. Yk.

A4045 Assheton, William, 1690
Yk.

A4046 Assheton, William, 1696
Carl. Dur. Ely.

A4048 Assheton, William, 1670
Win.

A4052 Association, 1643[4]
Yk.

A4058 Astell, Mary, 1696
Yk.

A4072 Aston, *Sir* Thomas, 1642
43p.
Dur. Linc. S Pl. Yk*.

A4072+ Aston, *Sir* Thomas, 1642
As A4072, but: 67p.
Ex. Pet.

A4075 Aston, *Sir* Thomas, 1642
Cant.

A4076 Aston, *Sir* Thomas, 1681
Win.

A4077+ Aston, *Sir* Thomas, 1641
[N.pl.]; brs.
Linc.

A4078 Aston, *Sir* Thomas, 1641
Cant. Ex. Linc. Pet.

A4105 Atfield, Ambrose, 1685
Per Edvardum Millingtonum; 4°.
Carl. Wor.

A4111 Athenagoras, 1682
12°.
Ex. Win. Yk (2 – 1 tpw).

A4136 Atkyns, *Sir* Robert, 1689
Title as Wing2.
S Pl.

A4138 Atkyns, *Sir* Robert, 1689
Ban. Wel.

A4141 Atkyns, *Sir* Robert, 1689
Ban. Wel.

A4146? Atterbury, Francis, 1687
4°.
Ex (2). Lich. S Pl (2).

A4147 Atterbury, Francis, 1694
Cant (2). Carl. Ely.

A4148 Atterbury, Francis, 1698
'occasion'd'
Her.

A4149 Atterbury, Francis, 1698
'occasion'd'
Carl. Dur.

A4150 Atterbury, Francis, 1694
Cant (2).

A4151 Atterbury, Francis, 1700
Ban. Bur (2). Cant. Carl. Ches.
Ely (2). Ex. Nor. S Pl. Wel.

A4152 Atterbury, Francis, 1694
Cant. Ely. Linc. Sal.

A4153 Atterbury, Francis, 1692
Cant (2). Dur. Sal.

A4154 Atterbury, Lewis, *the Elder*,
1691
Cant (tpw). Her. Wor.

A4157- Atterbury, Lewis, *the Younger*, 1687
=Wing2 A4156A.
Bris. Wor.

A4157 Atterbury, Lewis, *the Younger*, 1699
Carl. Linc. S Pl.

A4160 Attestation, 1648
Ex.

A4163 Atwell, George, 1658
'surveyour'; Rowls.
Cant.

A4172 Atwood, William, 1698
Pet.

A4174 Atwood, William, 1680
Linc.

A4182? Atwood, William, 1683
'Catholick'
Cant.

A4184 Aubery du Maurier, Louis, 1693
Ex.

A4190A Aucher, John, [1650]
Chelm.

A4203 Audley, John, 1647
Pet.

A4210 Augustine, *St*, 1670
Win.

A4212+ Augustine, *St*, 1686
=Wing2 A4212A.
Win.

A4218A Aulnoy, Marie Catherine La Mothe, *Comtesse*, 1692
Ex.

A4223+ Aulnoy, Marie Catherine La Mothe, *Comtesse*, 1692
=Wing2 A4223A.
Ely.

A4224 Aurelius Antoninus, Marcus, 1643
S Pl. Win. Yk.

A4225 Aurelius Antoninus, Marcus, 1652
'... de rebus suis ...'
Carl. Ely. Linc. Pet. S Asa.
S Pl. Wel. Wor. Yk.

A4226 Aurelius Antoninus, Marcus, 1680
Ches. Sal.

A4227 Aurelius Antoninus, Marcus, 1697
Secundae editioni; Impensis Edv. Millingtoni.
Ban. Cant (2). Ches. Dur. Ely. Lich. Linc. Nor. Pet. S Pl. Swel.

A4229 Aurelius Antoninus, Marcus, 1673
'Marcus Aurelius ...'; Printed for, and sold by ...
Cant. S Asa.

A4230 Aurelius Antoninus, Marcus, 1692
S Pl.

A4232 Aurora, 1648
Yk (2).

A4238 Austen, Ralph, 1653
Carl. Ex.

A4239 Austen, Ralph, 1657
Yk (imp).

A4243+ Austin, John, 1651
[N.pl.]; 4°.
Carl. Pet.

A4244 Austin, John, 1652
Cant.

A4245 Austin, John, 1652
8°.
Linc.

A4247 Austin, John, 1652
Cant.

A4248 Austin, John, 1653
Cant.

A4249 Austin, John, 1672
12°.
Carl. Yk.

A4250A Austin, John, 1685
Pet.

A4253 Austin, Robert, 1644
Pet. Yk.

A4265- Authors, 1661
See: CLC5.
Ex.

A4275 Avril, Philip, 1693
For Tim. Goodwin.
Glo. Wel.

A4282 Aylesbury, Thomas, 1659
Carl.

A4289- Ayloffe, James, (1696)
See: CLC6.
Ely.

A4289 Ayloffe, Thomas, 1696
Ely.

A4301 Ayres, John, 1695
Cant.

B13 B., A., 1648
Cant. Linc. Pet.

B14 B., A., [1679]
Date as Wing2; cap.
Dur. Linc.

B21 B., A., 1650
S Asa.

B22 B., A., 1698
Ex (2). Yk.

B24 B., A., 1681
Ches.

B26 B., A., 1679
S Asa. Win.

B35 B., A. J., 1642
Dur. Linc.

B46 B., C., 1690
Yk.

B53+ B., E., 1643
See: CLC7.
Cant.

B77 B., H., [1679]
Linc (2).

B80 B., H., 1680
Ches.

B81 B., H., [1679?]
Linc (2).

B87 B., I., [1642]
Linc.

B98 B., J., 1679
... Henry Million.
Carl. Dur. Linc.

B111 B., J., [1679]
Linc (2).

B117 *See*: B3581+

B120 B., J., 1680
Linc.

B123? B., J., 1652
'A sermon or the survey of man'
Sal.

B124 B., J., 1641
'Severall petitions ... honorable ...'
Linc.

B127 B., J., [1679]
Linc (2).

B143+ B., N., 1646
=Wing2 B144, but: 'Elisha succeeding Eliah [sic]'
Yk.

B162 B., R., 1648[9]
Cant.

B176 B., S., 1680
Ex.

B185 B., T., 1686
Dur.

B194+ B., T., 1642
'... dog, called Boy'; [N.pl.]; 4°.
Linc.

B204+ B., Thomas, [1679?]
See: CLC8.
Linc (imp).

B212 B., W., 1642
Ex.

B219+ B., W., [c.1642?]
[N.pl.]; brs.
Linc.

B220 B., W., 1691
Ex.

B223 B., W., 1660
Carl. Yk.

B227 B., W., 1679
Linc. Sal. Wel.

B248 Babington, Zachary, 1677
S Pl.

B267? Bacon, *Sir* Francis, 1642
'certaine'
Carl.

B269 Bacon, *Sir* Francis, 1679
By J.D. ...
Carl. Ely. Ex.

B272 Bacon, *Sir* Francis, 1641
Pet. Yk.

B274- Bacon, *Sir* Francis, 1642
'Certaine considerations'; [N.pl.], for
William Sheares; 4°.
Carl.

B277 Bacon, *Sir* Francis, 1676
Linc. Yk.

B279A Bacon, *Sir* Francis, 1641
Linc.

B282 Bacon, *Sir* Francis, 1642
Linc.

B288 Bacon, *Sir* Francis, 1680
Ban.

B298 Bacon, *Sir* Francis, 1641
Third ed. not on tp; ... R. Meighen.
Ban. Carl. Nor. Win (2).

B300 Bacon, *Sir* Francis, 1676
Yk.

B301 Bacon, *Sir* Francis, 1642
Pet.

B302 Bacon, *Sir* Francis, 1661
Bris. Carl. Sal. Yk.

B312 Bacon, *Sir* Francis, 1674
Nor. Pet. S Asa.

B314? Bacon, *Sir* Francis, 1658
'posthuma'; Excudebat R. Daniel,
impensis Octaviani Pulleyn.
Carl. Sal.

B315 *See*: B314

B318 Bacon, *Sir* Francis, 1648
Linc (imp). Yk (imp).

B319 Bacon, *Sir* Francis, 1657
Carl. Lich. S Asa.

B320 Bacon, *Sir* Francis, 1661
Ex. Linc. Pet. Win. Yk.

B321 Bacon, *Sir* Francis, 1671
Wel.

B322 Bacon, *Sir* Francis, 1670
Other locations on B320 may also
have this.
Win.

B326 Bacon, *Sir* Francis, 1641
Cant (imp).

B327 Bacon, *Sir* Francis, 1651
Ex.

B330 Bacon, *Sir* Francis, 1664
Lich.

B331? Bacon, *Sir* Francis, 1670
... Lee, sold by George Sawbridg,
Francis Tyton and other booksellers.
Pet. Wel.

B332 Bacon, *Sir* Francis, 1676
Win.

B337 Bacon, *Sir* Francis, 1641
Ely.

B343 Bacon, *Sir* Francis, 1641
Cant (2). Carl. Ex (2). Linc.
Pet (2).

B351 Bacon, Nathaniel, 1664
'life & actions'; ... Eccleston.
Carl. Ex.

B352 Bacon, Nathaniel, 1669
S Asa.

B358 Bacon, Nathaniel, 1653
Carl.

B363 Bacon, Nathaniel, 1681
12°.
Ex.

B365 Bacon, Nathaniel, 1688
Pet.

B367 Bacon, *Sir* Nicholas, 1641
Linc.

B369 Bacon, Robert, 1649
Yk.

B382+ Baddeley, Richard, 1669
=Wing2 B382B; Formerly B387.
Carl. Ches. Dur. Yk (2).

B387 *See*: B382+

B393 Bagshaw, Edward, *the Elder*,
1659
Carl.

B394 Bagshaw, Edward, *the Elder*,
1641
Cant. Linc.

B395 Bagshaw, Edward, *the Elder*,
1641
'Novemb.'
Cant.

B396 Bagshaw, Edward, *the Elder*,
1660
Yk.

B398 Bagshaw, Edward, *the Elder*,
1648
Win.

B399 Bagshaw, Edward, *the Elder*,
1641
Yk.

B400 Bagshaw, Edward, *the Elder*,
1642
Linc.

B401 Bagshaw, Edward, *the Elder*,
1641
Ex. Pet. Yk.

B402 Bagshaw, Edward, *the Elder*,
1641[2]
Cant. Dur. Yk.

B403 Bagshaw, Edward, *the
Younger*, 1670
Win (2). Yk.

B404 Bagshaw, Edward, *the
Younger*, 1662
Cant. Carl. Ex. Pet (3).

B405 Bagshaw, Edward, *the
Younger*, 1662
Carl. Pet. Win.

B407? Bagshaw, Edward, *the
Younger*, 1671
4°.
Win. Yk.

B408 Bagshaw, Edward, *the
Younger*, 1661
Cant (2 – 1 imp). Carl. Llan.
Pet.

B410 Bagshaw, Edward, *the
Younger*, 1662
Carl. Pet.

B411 Bagshaw, Edward, *the
Younger*, 1669
Cant. Win.

B412 Bagshaw, Edward, *the
Younger*, 1661
Cant. Pet.

B413 Bagshaw, Edward, *the
Younger*, 1660
Dur.

B413+ Bagshaw, Edward, *the
Younger*, 1660
=Wing2 B413A.
Cant.

B414 Bagshaw, Edward, *the
Younger*, 1660
Cant (2). Liv. Pet.

B415 Bagshaw, Edward, *the
Younger*, 1659
Carl.

B416 Bagshaw, Edward, *the Younger*, 1662
Carl. Linc. Llan. Pet.

B417 Bagshaw, Edward, *the Younger*, 1662
12p.
Carl. Pet (2).

B417+ Bagshaw, Edward, *the Younger*, 1662
As B417, but: 'honour & quality';
13p.
Chelm. Pet.

B419 Bagshaw, Edward, *the Younger*, 1662
Cant. Liv. Pet (2).

B420 Bagshaw, Edward, *the Younger*, 1659
Carl. Ex. Pet.

B421 Bagshaw, Edward, *the Younger*, 1671
Win. Yk.

B422 Bagshaw, Edward, *the Younger*, 1660
'soveraignty'
Carl.

B423 Bagshaw, Edward, *the Younger*, 1662
Cant. Carl. Linc. Pet.

B424 Bagshaw, Edward, *the Younger*, 1661
Cant (2 − 1 imp). Liv. Pet.

B425 Bagshaw, Edward, *the Younger*, 1662
Nor. Pet (2).

B426 Bagshaw, Edward, *the Younger*, 1659
Carl. Ex.

B429 Bagshaw, Henry, 1680
Impr. as Wing2.
Cant. Dur. S Pl. Yk.

B430 Bagshaw, Henry, 1673
Cant.

B431 Bagshaw, Henry, 1667
Her. Win.

B432 Bagshaw, Henry, 1676
Ban. Cant. Llan. Sal. Yk (2).

B437 Bagwell, William, 1645
Pet (imp).

B453 Baillie, Robert, 1647
'Anabaptism the true fountaine ... unsealed'
Linc. Win.

B455? Baillie, Robert, 1654
16°.
Ely.

B456? Baillie, Robert, 1645
252p.; Anr ed. with this impr. & date has 242p.
Pet. Win.

B457 Baillie, Robert, 1646
Second ed. not on tp.
Ex.

B459 Baillie, Robert, 1645
Pet.

B460 Baillie, Robert, 1646
Win.

B461 Baillie, Robert, 1641
Carl. Linc. Pet. Sal. Yk.

B462 Baillie, Robert, 1641
Carl. Linc. Liv. Pet. Sal. Yk (2).

B463 Baillie, Robert, 1643
Yk.

B464 Baillie, Robert, 1661
Win.

B465 Baillie, Robert, 1641
Pet (2 − 1 imp). Sal (2). Yk (2 − 1 tpw).

B466 Baillie, Robert, 1649
Linc.

B467 Baillie, Robert, 1649
Impr. as Wing2.
Carl. Ex. Pet.

B468 Baillie, Robert, 1643[4]
Yk.

B473 Bainbridge, Thomas, 1687
Ban. Ex. Nor. Wel. Yk.

B474 Bainbridge, Thomas, 1689/90
Wel.

B480 Baker, Augustine, 1657
Carl. Ely. S Asa. Win.

B501 Baker, *Sir* Richard, 1643
Ely. Sal.

B505 Baker, *Sir* Richard, 1665
Nor. Wel. Wor.

B506 Baker, *Sir* Richard, 1670
Ex. Glo.

B507 Baker, *Sir* Richard, 1674
Bris (imp). Cant. Glo (imp). Pet. S Dv. Swel.

B508 Baker, *Sir* Richard, 1679
Cant. Lich. Win.

B509 Baker, *Sir* Richard, 1684
Ban. Rip.

B510 Baker, *Sir* Richard, 1696
Cant. Yk.

B517 Baker, Thomas, 1684
Dur. Sal.

B518 Baker, Thomas, 1681
Dur (imp).

B519 Baker, Thomas, 1699
S Pl.

B520 Baker, Thomas, 1700
Bur (imp). Dur. Glo.

B521 Baker, Thomas, 1700
Yk.

B526 Bakewell, Thomas, 1646
Dur. Yk (2).

B526+ Bakewell, Thomas, 1646
=Wing2 B526A.
Dur.

B533 Bakewell, Thomas, 1644
Sal.

B534 Bakewell, Thomas, 1646
Impr. as Wing2.
Chelm. Win.

B537 Bakewell, Thomas, 1643
Pet. Sal.

B541 Ballance, 1646[7]
Linc.

B549 Bales, Peter, 1650
'conformity'
Pet (imp).

B550 Bales, Peter, 1643
Wor.

B558 Ball, John, 1642
Bur. Ex. Sal. Wor.

B570+ Ball, John, 1655
Anr ed. of Wing2 B570A; London, printed, sold by William Churchils in Dorchester; 8°.
Pet.

B571- Ball, John, 1646
=Wing2 B570B, but: 'contayning'
Yk.

B574+ Ball, John, 1656
The fifteenth impression; For John Wright; 8°.
Carl. Pet.

B579 Ball, John, 1645
Chelm. Her.

B584 Ball, Thomas, 1656
Carl. Chelm. Yk.

B587 Ball, William, 1642
Linc. Pet.

B588 Ball, William, 1646
Pet.

B595 Ball, William, 1655
Carl.

B596 Ball, William, 1641
Pet (tpw).

B611 Baltimore, George Calvert, *Baron*, 1642[3]
Carl (cropped). Pet.

B612 Balzac, Jean Louis Guez, *Sieur de*, 1659
Pet.

B615 Balzac, Jean Louis Guez, *Sieur de*, 1648
Pet.

B616 Balzac, Jean Louis Guez, *Sieur de*, 1658
Pet.

B619 Bamfield, Francis, 1677
Ex.

B628 Bamfield, Francis, 1677
Ex.

B629 Bampfield, Thomas, 1692
Ex.

B632 Banckes, Matthew, 1677
Dur. Win. Yk (3).

B638 Bancroft, Richard, 1663
... Hodgkinson.
Dur. Nor.

B639 Bancroft, Richard, 1663
Impr. as Wing2.
Dur.

B669 Banks, Jonathan, 1688
Pet. Yk.

B671 Banks, Richard, 1688
Ely. Yk.

B678 Barba, Alvaro Alonso, 1674
Carl.

B703 Barbon, John, 1662
'... a most divine ...'
Carl (date altered to 1663). Pet (tp imp).

B704 Barbon, Nicholas, 1685
Wel.

B706 Barbon, Nicholas, 1696
Yk.

B715 Barclay, John, 1688
Ban. Wel.

B736? Barclay, Robert, 1676
Typis excusa pro Jacob Claus, Amstelodami. Veneunt praeterea Londini apud ...; Wing2 B736A is a ghost?
S Pl.

B749 Barebon, Praisegod, 1645
S Asa.

B752 Barebon, Praisegod, 1660
Linc.

B755 Barebon, Praisegod, 1643
Pet.

B757 Barecroft, Charles, 1688
Ex. Nor. Wel.

B766 Barker, Edmund, 1661
Impr. as Wing2.
Her.

B767 Barker, Edmund, 1660
Ex. Pet (2).

B768 Barker, George, 1697
Yk (2).

B776 Barker, Matthew, 1651
Ex. S Pl.

B777A Barker, Ralph, 1691
Ban. Cant. Her. Pet.

B786 Barker, Thomas, *of Bracemeale*, 1659
Carl.

B788 Barker, Thomas, *Poet*, 1700
Ely.

B794+ Barksdale, Clement, 1654
=Wing2 B794A?; The second edition; Hyet.
Pet.

B795 Barksdale, Clement, 1660
Carl. Wor.

B800 Barksdale, Clement, 1661
Linc.

B806 Barksdale, Clement, 1670
Carl. Ex. Linc. Llan.

B808 Barksdale, Clement, 1680
Her.

B816 Barkstead, John, 1662
Linc. Pet.

B819 Barlee, William, 1656
Ban. Carl.

B824 Barlow, Thomas, 1699
Ex. Glo.

B825 Barlow, Thomas, 1700
Second ed. not on tp.
Yk.

B825+ Barlow, Thomas, 1700
Oxford, by L. Lichfield, sold by T. Leigh and D. Midwinter in London; 4°.
Dur.

B826 Barlow, Thomas, 1681
... for Robert Clavell.
Dur. Ex. Lich. Linc. S Pl. Win.

B827 Barlow, Thomas, 1681
Ban. Ches.

B828 Barlow, Thomas, 1682
Carl. Dur. Yk.

B829 Barlow, Thomas, 1679
Dur. Linc. Win.

B830 Barlow, Thomas, 1658
Editio secunda.
Lich. Win.

B831 Barlow, Thomas, 1688
Carl. Dur. Ex (3). S Pl. Wel (3).

B832 Barlow, Thomas, 1693
Carl. Ches. Ex (2 − 1 tpw). Linc. Nor. S Asa.

B833 Barlow, Thomas, 1679
58, 263p.
Ban. Carl. Dur. Linc. Nor. Wel.

B833+ Barlow, Thomas, 1679
As B833, but: 58, 72, 191p.
Cant.

B834 Barlow, Thomas, 1679
Ban. Cant. Carl. Ex. Llan. Wel.

B836- Barlow, Thomas, 1680
Prostant venales apud Jacobum Collins; 8°.
Sal.

B837 Barlow, Thomas, 1682
Ban. S Pl. Sal.

B839 Barlow, Thomas, 1679
Carl. S Pl. Win.

B840 Barlow, Thomas, 1679
Lich. Llan (2). Nor. Sal. Wel. Win (tp imp).

B841 Barlow, Thomas, 1679
Ex. Linc.

B843 Barlow, Thomas, 1692
Ex. Linc. Nor. Rip. Win. Yk.

B845 Barlow, Thomas, 1680
Linc.

B849? Barnabas, *St*, 1685
'[Greek] Barnabae apostoli, epistola catholica. Accessit S. Hermae ... Pastor ...'
Cant. Ches. Ex. S Pl. Yk.

B853 Barnard, John, 1641
By Edward Griffin.
Glo (1 pt only − imp). Lich (7 pts only). Wor (4 pts only − 1 tpw).

B854 Barnard, John, 1683
Yk.

B854A Barnard, John, 1683
8°.
Carl.

B857 Barne, Miles, 1682
Ban. Carl.

B858 Barne, Miles, 1682
Her. Llan.

B859 Barne, Miles, 1675
Carl. Her. S Asa. Wor.

B860 Barne, Miles, 1670
... sold by Edw. Story.
Carl. S Asa. Yk (tpw).

B862 Barne, Miles, 1683
Wor.

B863+ Barne, Miles, 1683
As B863, but different ed. from BL
copy.
Cant (imp).

B865 Barnes, John, 1680
Carl. Ex. S Pl.

B868+ Barnes, Joshua, 1679
Typis M.C. impensis authoris; 8°.
S Pl. Yk.

B871 Barnes, Joshua, 1688
Cant. Dur. Nor. Pet. Win.
Yk.

B875A Barnett, Andrew, 1695
Ches.

B879 Baron, John, 1699
'preach'd'
Dur.

B880 Baron, Robert, *of Aberdeen,*
1657
Ex. S Asa (tpw). Sal. Win.

B881 Baron, Robert, *of Aberdeen,*
1658
Ex. Pet. Sal. Wor.

B882 Baron, Robert, *of Aberdeen,*
[1657?]
S Pl. Yk.

B883 Baron, Robert, *of Aberdeen,*
1658
Carl. Dur.

B884? Baron, Robert, *of Aberdeen,*
[1669?]
Impr. as B883; 12°.
Sal.

B885 Baron, Robert, *of Aberdeen,*
1685
... Londini.
Cant. Yk.

B886 Baron, Robert, *of Aberdeen,*
1641
... impensis Guliel: Davis ...
Ex. S Asa. Win.

B888 Baron, Robert, *of Gray's Inn,*
1649
Pet.

B895 Baron, William, 1698
Cant.

B897 Baron, William, 1699
Carl. Yk.

B898 Baron, William, 1700
Ex.

B901? Barozzi, Giacomo, 1669
For Rowland Reynolds and William
Sherwin.
Dur.

B910 Barret, John, 1680
S Pl.

B910+ Barret, John, 1680
=Wing2 B910A?; ... by Samuel
Richards ...
Win.

B915 Barrett, William, 1679
Pet.

B921 Barrough, Philip, 1652
4°.
Chelm.

B925 Barrow, Isaac, 1683—87
Ban (4v.; anr copy vol. 2). Brec.
Bur (vol. 4). Cant. Carl. Ches
(vol. 2). Chi (vol. 1—2). Ex (vol.
2—3). Her. Linc. Pet. Rip (vol.
2 only, tpw)*. S Asa (vol. 2—4).
S Dv (vol. 1, 3). S Pl (vol. 1—2,
4). Sal (vol. 1—3). Wel (vol. 3).
Win.

B926? Barrow, Isaac, 1687—92
Vol. 1 = 1687; Vol. 2 = 1686; Vol. 3
= 1692; Vol. 4 = 1687; No ed.
statement in vol. 3—4.
Dur. Ely (lacks vol. 4). Nor.
Rip (vol. 2). S Asa (vol. 1—2).
S Dv (vol. 2). Wel (vol. 2, 4).
Win (lacks vol. 4).

B927? Barrow, Isaac, 1700
Vol. 1: no ed. statement; Vol. 2: 2nd
ed.; Vol. 3: 3rd ed.
Ban. New (lacks vol. 3). Wel
(vol. 1). Yk.

B928 Barrow, Isaac, 1681
Bur. Llan. S Pl. Win.

B929 Barrow, Isaac, 1697
Dur. Ely.

B931 Barrow, Isaac, 1697
S Asa.

B933 Barrow, Isaac, 1671
Bur. Ex. Liv. Pet. Yk (tpw).

B934 Barrow, Isaac, 1677
Yk.

B936 Barrow, Isaac, 1678
Typis J. Redmayne, prostant apud J.
Williams.
Linc.

B938 Barrow, Isaac, 1669
Pet. Sal. Win.

B940 Barrow, Isaac, 1670
Win.

B940+ Barrow, Isaac, 1670
=Wing2 B940.
Sal.

B946 Barrow, Isaac, 1685
Cant.

B949 Barrow, Isaac, 1680
Impr. as Wing2.
Dur.

B953 Barrow, Isaac, 1679
Chi. Wor.

B954 Barrow, Isaac, 1677
Cant (2 − 1 imp). Carl. Wel
(tpw).

B957 Barrow, Isaac, 1678
Title as Wing2.
Dur. Glo (imp). S Asa.

B958 Barrow, Isaac, 1679
Bur.

B959 Barrow, Isaac, 1678
Bur. Dur. Ex. Llan. Yk.

B961 Barrow, Isaac, 1680
Ban (imp). Bur. Llan. Rip.
S Asa (imp). S Dv. Wel. Win.
Yk (2).

B962+ Barrow, Isaac, 1687
By M. Flesher and J. Heptinstall, for
Brabazon Aylmer; 2°.
New.

B966 Barrow, John, 1683
Cant. Ches.

B973 Barry, John, 1642
Yk.

B974 Bartholin, Caspar, 1698
Her.

B979 Bartholomew, William, 1660
Carl.

B989 Barton, David, 1670
Ex.

B989+ Barton, John, *of
Birmingham,* 1652
See: CLC9.
Cant.

B990 Barton, Samuel, 1689
Cant.

B993 Barton, Samuel, 1696
Cant. Wor.

B998 Barton, Thomas, 1649
Impr. as Wing2.
Nor. Yk.

B999 Barton, Thomas, 1643
Wel (imp).

B1001 Barton, William, 1668
S Pl.

B1008 Barwick, John, 1660
Cant (2 − 1 imp). Carl. Ches (2
− 1 imp). Dur (2 − 1 imp). Linc.
New. Pet. S Asa (imp). S Pl.
Win.

B1009 Barwick, John, 1646
Ex. Linc. Liv. Pet. Yk.

B1010 Barwick, John, 1647
Carl*.

B1011 Barzia y Zambrana, Joseph
de, 1685
Dur.

B1018 Basil Valentine, 1671
Sal.

B1025 Basill, William, 1650
Pet.

B1029 Basire, Isaac, 1661
Carl. Ely. Ex. Pet. Yk.

B1031 Basire, Isaac, 1673
Cant (imp). Carl. Dur (3). Linc.
Win. Yk.

B1032 Basire, Isaac, 1646
Cant. Ex. Liv. Yk.

B1033 Basire, Isaac, 1668
Cant. Carl. Dur. Ex (2). Pet.
Sal. Win. Yk.

B1042 Basset, Joshua, 1687
Bur. Sal. Wel.

B1043? Basset, Thomas, 1671
12°.
Ex. Linc.

B1044? Basset, Thomas, 1682
[London], collected by Thomas
Bassett and are to be sold at his shop.
S Pl.

B1049 Basset, William, 1693
Ban. S Pl.

B1051 Basset, William, 1670
For Tho. Basset.
Llan. Wor.

B1052 Basset, William, 1684
S Pl.

B1053 Basset, William, 1679
Llan. Pet.

B1054 Basset, William, 1683
Llan (2).

B1058 Bastwick, John, 1645
Ex. Yk.

B1062 Bastwick, John, 1641
Typis Edwardi Griffini ...
Ches. Yk.

B1063 Bastwick, John, 1645
Ex. Sal. Win. Yk.

B1065 Bastwick, John, 1645
Yk.

B1069 Bastwick, John, 1645
Ex. Win. Yk.

B1071 Bastwick, John, 1647
London, by T.W. ...
Yk.

B1072 Bastwick, John, 1646
Ex (tpw). Wor. Yk.

B1078 Bate, George, 1661 [−63]
2 pt.
Cant (pt 2 only). Carl. Dur.
S Pl. Sal. Win.

B1079- Bate, George, 1649
Lutetiae Parisiorum [i.e. London], pro
R.R.; 12°.
Cant. Ex. Lich. Pet.

B1081 Bate, George, 1663
2 pt; Pt 2 = Editio nova.
Ely. Linc (pt 2 only). Wor (pt 2
only). Yk.

B1082 Bate, George, 1676
2 pt.
Cant (imp). Linc. S Asa (tpw).
Yk.

B1083- Bate, George, 1685
For Abel Swalle, sold by Samuel
Eddowes; 8°.
Pet.

B1086 Bate, George, 1691
Impensis Sam. Smith.
Nor.

B1087 Bate, George, 1700
Cant. S Pl.

B1088 Bate, George, 1694
'... Bate's dispensatory'; For S. Smith
and B. Walford.
Cant.

B1089 Bate, George, 1700
'... Bate's dispensatory'; For S. Smith
and B. Walford; 8°.
S Pl.

B1090 Bate, George, 1648
Ex. Linc. Win.

B1094 Bateman, George, [1653]
Dur.

B1100 Bates, William, 1700
Impr. as Wing2.
Lich.

B1101 Bates, William, 1676
Carl. Ex.

B1107 Bates, William, 1692
8°.
Ex (2 − 1 imp). Pet. Yk.

B1108 Bates, William, 1692
8°.
S Pl.

B1109 Bates, William, 1678
... for Brabazon Aylmer.
Cant. Carl. Ex.

B1110 Bates, William, 1678
S Pl.

B1113 Bates, William, 1674
S Pl. Win.

B1115 Bates, William, 1688
Impr. as Wing2.
Bur. Dur. Llan.

B1116 Bates, William, 1697
Ex.

B1117 Bates, William, 1662
Yk.

B1118 Bates, William, 1695
4°.
Ches.

B1121 Bates, William, 1695
Carl. Her.

B1123 Bates, William, 1683
Carl.

B1125 Bates, William, 1687
S Pl.

B1126 Bates, William, 1680
Carl.

B1128 Bates, William, 1699
Llan.

B1129 Bates, William, 1689
Ex.

B1130 Bates, William, 1681
Ban. Carl. Chi (2). Ely. Ex.
S Pl (2). Wel. Wor. Yk.

B1132 Bath, Henry Bourchier, *Earl
of*, [1642]
Dur. Linc.

B1133- Bathe, Henry de, 1647
By Tho. Paine, for John Parker; 8°.
Pet.

B1133? Bathe, Henry de, 1686
By S.R. for Samuel Keble.
Cant.

B1140 *See*: B526+

B1149 Battell, Ralph, 1694
'church-musick'
Dur.

B1150 Battell, Ralph, 1683
Ban. Ely. Ex.

B1151 Battely, John, 1694
Cant. Wor.

B1159 Battie, William, 1680
Bur. Cant (2 − 1 imp). Lich.

B1160 Battie, William, 1678
'November the 18th'
Dur. Llan.

B1163 Bauderon, Brice, 1657
'phisician'
Cant (imp).

B1176 Baxter, Richard, 1661
Bur. Cant. Lich. Liv. Yk
(imp).

B1177 Baxter, Richard, 1661
Cant (2 − 1 imp). Win. Yk (2).

B1178 Baxter, Richard, 1657
Yk.

B1179 Baxter, Richard, 1662
Yk (2).

B1181 Baxter, Richard, 1654
Pet. Yk (2).

B1182 Baxter, Richard, 1691
Yk.

B1183 Baxter, Richard, 1680
100p.
Dur. Nor.

B1183+ Baxter, Richard, 1680
As B1183, but: 107p.
Yk.

B1184 Baxter, Richard, 1682
Pet. Yk.

B1185 Baxter, Richard, 1649
Carl.

B1186 Baxter, Richard, 1655
Ex. Yk.

B1187 Baxter, Richard, 1654
Ex. Pet. Yk (2 - 1 pt 2 only).

B1189 Baxter, Richard, 1681
Win.

B1189+ Baxter, Richard, 1681
=Wing2 B1189A.
Liv. Yk.

B1190 Baxter, Richard, 1674
Yk.

B1194 Baxter, Richard, 1681
Win (imp). Yk.

B1195 Baxter, Richard, 1689
Yk.

B1202+ Baxter, Richard, 1680
The one and twentieth edition; For
Tho. Parkhurst, Tho. Cockeril, &
Tho. Simonds; 12°.
Cant (imp; not 1658, 1663,
1682)*. Ex.

B1204+ Baxter, Richard, 1694
The five and twentieth edition; For
Richard Baldwin and Richard Wilde;
12°.
Yk.

B1205 Baxter, Richard, 1683
Sal. Yk (2).

B1206 Baxter, Richard, 1684
Pet. Yk (2).

B1208? Baxter, Richard, 1684
'... Richard Baxter ...'
Yk (2 − 1 imp).

B1209 Baxter, Richard, 1675
Carl. Chelm. Ex. Pet.

B1210? Baxter, Richard, 1660
12°.
Pet. Yk.

B1211 Baxter, Richard, 1657
Chelm. Her. Yk (2).

B1212 Baxter, Richard, 1658
Pet. Win.

B1213 Baxter, Richard, 1672
Her.

B1218 Baxter, Richard, 1653
4°.
Chelm. Dur. S Pl. Yk (3 − 1
imp).

B1219 Baxter, Richard, 1673
Cant. Ches. Ex. Pet. Rip.
S Dv. Wor.

B1220 Baxter, Richard, 1678
Ban. Ches. Roch. Yk.

B1221 *See*: B1444: apparently
B1221 is an addit. tp in this work

B1223 Baxter, Richard, 1691
Yk.

B1224A+ Baxter, Richard, 1680
By B. Griffin for Thomas Simmons;
4°.
Ban.

B1225 Baxter, Richard, 1681
Yk.

B1226 Baxter, Richard, 1672
Yk (cropped).

B1231? Baxter, Richard, 1655
... Tho. Vnderhil ...
Bur. Pet. Win. Yk.

B1232 Baxter, Richard, 1658
Carl. Chelm. Pet. Win. Yk (2
− 1 imp).

B1233 Baxter, Richard, 1658
Carl. Pet. Yk (2).

B1234 Baxter, Richard, 1670
Ex. Pet. Win. Wor. Yk.

B1238 Baxter, Richard, 1680
Yk.

B1239 Baxter, Richard, 1671
Carl. Ex. Win. Yk.

B1241 Baxter, Richard, 1671
Yk.

B1244+ Baxter, Richard, 1658
By A.M. for Nevil Simmons in
Kederminster sold by Tho. Brewster
and John Starkey; 8°.
Pet.

B1245- Baxter, Richard, 1658
By A.M. for Joseph Cranford, sold by
Richard Scot in Carlisle; 8°.
Carl.

B1248+ Baxter, Richard, 1683
The fourth edition; For John Dunton;
12°.
Yk.

B1253 Baxter, Richard, 1671
Yk.

B1254 Baxter, Richard, 1664
Lich. Yk.

B1255 Baxter, Richard, 1671
Yk (2).

B1256 Baxter, Richard, 1683
Ex. Win. Wor (frag.)*. Yk.

B1258 Baxter, Richard, 1691
Yk.

B1259 Baxter, Richard, 1689
Carl. Glo. S Pl. Yk.

B1263 Baxter, Richard, 1663
cf. F104 & W3548.
Cant. Chelm.

B1264 *See*: F104

B1265 Baxter, Richard, 1681
Yk.

B1266 Baxter, Richard, 1683
Carl.

B1267- Baxter, Richard, 1659
By R.W. for Nevil Simmons; 4°.
Wor.

B1267? Baxter, Richard, 1659
... Simmons, in Kederminster, sold by
him there, and by ...
Ban. Carl. Chelm. Ex. Pet.
Yk.

B1272 Baxter, Richard, 1674
Carl. Ex.

B1274 Baxter, Richard, 1656
Ban.

B1275 Baxter, Richard, 1656
... Nevil Simmons, at Kederminster ...
Ex. Pet. S Asa. Yk.

B1276 Baxter, Richard, 1657
The second edition.
Carl.

B1277 Baxter, Richard, 1691
Yk.

B1278 Baxter, Richard, 1671
Cant. Carl.

B1278A Baxter, Richard, 1661
Bur. Cant (2 − 1 imp). Carl.
Chelm. Ches. Dur. Pet (2).
Win. Yk.

B1280 Baxter, Richard, 1658
Ex. Linc. Pet. S Pl. Wor. Yk.

B1281 Baxter, Richard, 1659
Glo. Win. Yk (tp imp).

B1282? Baxter, Richard, 1671
Simons.
Yk.

B1283 Baxter, Richard, 1682
Her. Yk (2).

B1284 Baxter, Richard, 1655
Carl. Yk (2).

B1285 Baxter, Richard, 1652
Chelm (tp imp). S Pl.

B1288 Baxter, Richard, 1658
Carl. Yk (2).

B1292- Baxter, Richard, 1676
[N.pl.]; 4°.
Win. Yk.

B1293 Baxter, Richard, 1676
Cant. Yk.

B1295 Baxter, Richard, 1659
... Nevil Simmons, in Kederminster,
and are to be sold by him there, and
by Thomas Johnson, [London].
Ban. Carl. Ex. Pet. S Asa.
Win. Wor. Yk.

B1298 Baxter, Richard, 1682
Yk.

B1299 Baxter, Richard, 1660
... at Kederminster; 4°.
Cant (2). Carl. Her (imp)*. Pet.

B1300 Baxter, Richard, 1660
Yk (2).

B1301 Baxter, Richard, 1670
Glo (imp). Pet. Win. Wor (pt 1
only)*. Yk.

B1306 Baxter, Richard, 1691
The second edition.
Cant.

B1308 Baxter, Richard, 1681
Cant. Carl. Ex. Lich (imp).
Pet. Wor. Yk.

B1309 Baxter, Richard, 1662
Carl. Yk.

B1311 Baxter, Richard, 1680
Win. Yk (3).

B1312 Baxter, Richard, 1675
'infants'
Ex. Yk.

B1313 Baxter, Richard, 1672
Carl. Yk.

B1315 Baxter, Richard, 1677
Yk (2).

B1319 Baxter, Richard, 1679
Ex. Yk.

B1320+ Baxter, Richard, 1662
=Wing2 B1320A, but: ... and Nevil
Simmons in Kedermister.
Yk.

B1322 Baxter, Richard, 1671
Ex.

B1327 Baxter, Richard, 1683
Yk.

B1328 Baxter, Richard, 1658
Pet.

B1329 Baxter, Richard, 1691
Yk.

B1330+ Baxter, Richard, 1658
=Wing2 B1330A; ... Nevil Simmons
in Kederminster ...
Carl. Yk.

B1331? Baxter, Richard, 1682
8°.
Yk.

B1334 Baxter, Richard, 1657
... in Kederminster.
Carl. Yk.

B1335 Baxter, Richard, 1657
... in Kederminster.
Carl. Yk.

B1336 *See*: B1446+

B1337 Baxter, Richard, [1661]
Cant (2). Win. Yk (2).

B1338? Baxter, Richard, 1685
... and Tho. Simmons.
Ex. Lich.

B1338+ Baxter, Richard, 1685
For B. Simmons, and Tho. Simmons,
and sold by Nevil Simmons in
Sheffield; 4°.
Cant.

B1339 Baxter, Richard, 1695
Bur.

B1341 Baxter, Richard, 1691
Yk (3).

B1342 Baxter, Richard, 1661
Yk (3 − 1 imp*).

B1343 Baxter, Richard, 1661
At least 2 eds .
Cant (2 eds: p. 1, line 3 ends
'and the' *or* 'and'). Carl*. Linc
(imp). Liv. Pet (3 − 1*). S Pl (2).
Sal (imp). Win (3 − 1 tpw). Wor.
Yk (2 − 1 imp).

B1343+ Baxter, Richard, 1661
As B1343, but: 102p.
Chelm.

B1344 Baxter, Richard, 1651
Chelm. Ex. Pet. Yk.

B1345 Baxter, Richard, 1653
Bur. Ex. Her.

B1346 Baxter, Richard, 1656
Pet. Win. Yk.

B1349 Baxter, Richard, 1681
Yk.

B1352 Baxter, Richard, 1674
Yk.

B1354+ Baxter, Richard, 1677
The third edition; By R.W. for Nevill
Simmons, sold by William Bromwich;
8°.
Yk.

B1357 Baxter, Richard, 1697
Yk.

B1359 Baxter, Richard, 1692
Yk.

B1362 Baxter, Richard, 1655
Pet (2). Yk (2).

B1364 Baxter, Richard, 1656
Yk.

B1366 Baxter, Richard, 1682
Part of B1438.
Ban. Yk (2).

B1367 Baxter, Richard, 1667
Bur. Cant (2 issues). Carl. Her.
Linc. Pet. Roch. Yk.

B1368 *See*: T1838

B1370 Baxter, Richard, 1696
Cant. Ex. Linc (2). Yk.

B1371 Baxter, Richard, 1691
Yk.

B1372 Baxter, Richard, 1676
Yk.

B1373A? Baxter, Richard, 1653
For T. Underhil, F. Tyton, and W.
Raybould.
Carl. Pet (tp imp).

B1375 Baxter, Richard, 1657
Carl. Win. Yk (2).

B1377 Baxter, Richard, 1660
... Jane Underhil.
Carl. S Pl. Sal. Yk.

B1378 Baxter, Richard, 1676
Yk (2).

B1380 Baxter, Richard, 1672
Pet. Win.

B1381 Baxter, Richard, 1657
S Asa (tp imp). Yk.

B1382 Baxter, Richard, 1662
... at Kederminster.
Chi. Ex. Yk.

B1383 Baxter, Richard, 1650
Ely. Roch. Yk.

B1384 Baxter, Richard, 1651
Wor.

B1385 Baxter, Richard, 1652
Cant. Carl. Glo. Yk.

B1386 Baxter, Richard, 1653
Pet.

B1389 Baxter, Richard, 1658
Win.

B1390 Baxter, Richard, 1659
Ex.

B1391 Baxter, Richard, 1662
Cant.

B1392+ Baxter, Richard, 1669
=Wing2 B1392A; The tenth edition.
Cant. Her.

B1394 Baxter, Richard, 1677
The eleventh edition.
Dur. Sal.

B1395 Baxter, Richard, 1688
Ex. Swar.

B1396 Baxter, Richard, 1684
4°.
Yk.

B1399? Baxter, Richard, 1681
For Nevill Simmons.
Yk.

B1400 Baxter, Richard, 1671
Carl.

B1401 Baxter, Richard, 1684
Yk.

B1402 Baxter, Richard, 1680
Win. Yk (2).

B1403 Baxter, Richard, 1665
Pt 2 of B1441.
Yk.

B1404 Baxter, Richard, 1657
... in Kederminster.
Carl. Yk.

B1405 Baxter, Richard, 1681
Win. Yk.

B1407 Baxter, Richard, 1689
cap.
Yk.

B1408 Baxter, Richard, 1655
'judgement'
S Pl (tpw).

B1411? Baxter, Richard, 1668
By R.W. for W. Whitwood.
S Pl.

B1413 Baxter, Richard, 1660
Cant. Lich (imp).

B1414 Baxter, Richard, 1660
Yk.

B1415 Baxter, Richard, 1662
Yk.

B1416 Baxter, Richard, [1680]
Chelm. Her. Yk.

B1418 Baxter, Richard, 1660
... Simmons in Kederminster ...
Yk.

B1419 Baxter, Richard, 1681
Yk.

B1420 Baxter, Richard, 1656
Carl (tp imp).

B1421 Baxter, Richard, 1658
... Nevil Simmons, in Kederminster,
and by ...; 8°.
Ex. Yk.

B1423 Baxter, Richard, 1657
Yk.

B1424 Baxter, Richard, 1658
Carl. Ex. IoM. Pet. Yk.

B1425 Baxter, Richard, 1660
Yk.

B1427 Baxter, Richard, 1681
Yk (2).

B1428 Baxter, Richard, 1676
For Nevil Simons ...
Bur (imp). Win.

B1429 Baxter, Richard, 1689
Yk.

B1430 Baxter, Richard, 1660
Carl. Lich. Pet. Yk (2).

B1431 Baxter, Richard, 1675
Second ed. not on tp.
Ex. Yk.

B1432 Baxter, Richard, 1680
Ex. Sal.

B1433 Baxter, Richard, 1680
4°.
Yk.

B1435 Baxter, Richard, 1660
Pet. Yk.

B1438 Baxter, Richard, 1682
Includes B1366 & C4571.
Ban. Yk (2 – 1 imp).

B1439 Baxter, Richard, 1675
Yk.

B1440 Baxter, Richard, 1661
Cant (3). Carl. S Pl. Sal.

B1441 Baxter, Richard, 1665
Yk.

B1442? Baxter, Richard, 1672
'Two treatises: the first of death'; 8°.
Ex.

B1444 Baxter, Richard, 1660
... in Kederminster.
Yk.

B1445 Baxter, Richard, 1694
Roch. Yk.

B1446 Baxter, Richard, 1655
Ex. Yk.

B1446+ Baxter, Richard, 1685
'Vnum necessarium'; For J.
Salusbury; 12°; B1336 with cancel tp?
Yk.

B1448 Baxter, Richard, 1660
Yk.

B1449 Baxter, Richard, 1682
For Walter Kettilby.
Lich. Yk.

B1452 Baxter, Richard, 1684
Yk.

B1454 Baxter, Richard, 1657
Carl. Yk.

B1455 Baxter, Richard, 1653
Chelm. S Pl. Yk (tp imp).

B1458 Bayard, Nicholas, 1693
Cant.

B1474 Bayly, Francis, 1660
Carl. Ex. Her.

B1502 Bayly, Lewis, 1695
Forty-second ed. not on tp.
Glo.

B1506+ Bayly, Thomas, 1649
[London], by H. Hills, sold by George
Whittington; 8°.
Cant (tpw).

B1506++ Bayly, Thomas, 1649
As B1506+, but: ... sold by John
Williams.
Ex.

B1507? Bayly, Thomas, 1651
Preface signed C.C.
S Asa. Sal.

B1507+ Bayly, Thomas, 1651
As B1507, but preface signed Chr.
Cartwright.
Carl.

B1508 Bayly, Thomas, 1652
Yk (2).

B1510 Bayly, Thomas, 1654
Carl. Chelm.

B1511 Bayly, Thomas, 1650
Yk.

B1513 Bayly, Thomas, 1655
'life and death'
Cant. Yk.

B1514 Bayly, Thomas, 1649
Chi. Dur. Ex.

B1514+ Bayly, Thomas, 1656
=Wing2 B1514A.
Yk.

B1515 Bayly, Thomas, 1682
Wor.

B1546- Baynes, Paul, 1641
See: CLC10.
Ex.

B1546 Baynes, Paul, 1621 [*i.e.*
1641]
Win.

B1547 Baynes, Paul, 1641
'trial'
Ex. Pet.

B1548 Baynes, Paul, 1644
'tryall'
Pet.

B1559 Beale, Thomas, 1641
Linc.

B1561 Beane, Richard, 1681
Linc. Wel.

B1563 Bear, Edmond, 1647
Wrongly cancelled in Wing2?, cf
W2168.
Yk.

B1564- Bear, Nicolas, 1679
=Wing2 B1563.
Cant.

B1564 Bear, Nicolas, 1700
S Pl.

B1565 Beard, Thomas, 1648
Liv. S Asa. Yk.

B1567 Beaton, John, 1647
Wel.

B1572 Beaulieu, Luke de, 1687
Chi. Ex. Nor. Sal. Wel. Yk.

B1574 Beaulieu, Luke de, 1681
Carl.

B1575+ Beaulieu, Luke de, 1688
=Wing2 B1575A.
Liv (imp).

B1578 Beaulieu, Luke de, 1675
Win.

B1581 Beaumont, Francis, 1647
Swel.

B1582 Beaumont, Francis, 1679
By J. Macock, for John Martyn, ...
Dur. Ely.

B1586 Beaumont, Francis, 1651
The second edition.
Carl.

B1594 Beaumont, Francis, 1641
Carl.

B1609+ Beaumont, Francis, 1651
'scornefull'; The sixt edition; For
Humphrey Moseley; 4°.
Carl.

B1621 Beaumont, John, 1693
Wel.

B1627 Beaumont, Joseph, 1690
Entry as Wing2.
Lich.

B1628 Beaumont, Joseph, 1665
'... apologie of Dr. Henry More ...'
Carl. Ely. Linc. Pet. Win.

B1640 Beauty, 1641[2]
Linc. S Pl.

B1640+ Beauvais, Charles de, 1665
=Wing2 B1640B; 'Exercitations ...'
Win.

B1641 Beccadelli, Lodovico, 1690
Dur. S Pl.

B1641+ Beccadelli, Lodovico, 1696
=Wing2 B1641A.
Ex.

B1653 Beckham, Edward, 1700
Pet (imp).

B1656 Beconsall, Thomas, 1697
Cant. Wor.

B1657? Beconsall, Thomas, 1698
'discovered'
Ely.

B1658 Bede, *the Venerable*, 1693
Dur. S Pl (2).

B1660? Bede, *the Venerable*, 1664
Dublinii, typis Johannis Crook,
sumptibus Sam. Dancer & sociorum.
S Pl.

B1661 Bede, *the Venerable*, 1643
Ban (imp). Ex. Pet. S Alb.

B1662 Bede, *the Venerable*, 1644
Cant. Dur. Linc. S Dv. S Pl.
Sal. Win. Wor.

B1668 Bedford, Thomas, 1647
Ex.

B1669 Bedford, Thomas, 1649
Cant (imp).

B1670 Bedford, Thomas, 1650
Win.

B1675 Bedle, Joseph, 1679
Llan.

B1676 Bedloe, William, 1679
Ely.

B1677 Bedloe, William, 1679
Carl. Dur. Ely. Linc. Yk.

B1680 Beech, William, 1645
Yk.

B1692+ Beesley, Henry, 1660
=Wing2 B1692A.
Yk.

B1708+ Behaviour, [1679]
=Wing2 B1708A.
Linc.

B1708++ Behaviour, [1679]
=Wing2 B1708B?; 'The behaviour,
last words, non-confession, ...'
Yk.

B1776 Behn, Aphra, 1683
Ex.

B1783+ Belcher, William, (1680)
See: CLC11.
Ely.

B1787 Belief, 1688
Wel.

B1788 Belief, [1693]
Cant.

B1796 Bell, Henry, 1650
Ex (tp imp).

B1809 Bell, William, 1661
S Pl.

B1812 Bell, William, 1650
Printed by F. N. for Tho: Vnderhill.
Yk.

B1818 Bellamie, John, 1646
Pet (2).

B1823 *See*: N1392

B1824 *See*: U144

B1827 Bellers, Fulk, 1652
S Pl.

B1860 Bellum, 1665
Ban.

B1864 Belwood, Thomas, 1642
For John Thomas ...; Date not on tp?
Linc. Yk.

B1865+ Benbrigge, John, 1646
As B1865, apart from date.
Yk.

B1866 Benbrigge, John, 1646
Pet.

B1871 Benloe, William, 1661
Cant.

B1883A Bennet, Isaac, 1643
Linc.

B1884 Bennet, John, 1683
8°.
Ex.

B1887 Bennet, Robert, 1657
S Pl.

B1889 Bennet, Thomas, 1700
The second edition.
Dur. Linc. Sal.

B1898 Benoit, Élie, 1694
Dur.

B1900 Benson, Gervase, 1656
=Wing2 F1780.
Dur. Yk.

B1909 Bentham, Joseph, 1669
Pet.

B1911 Bentivoglio, Guido, 1652
Pet. Sal. Wor.

B1912- Bentivoglio, Guido, 1654
For Humphrey Moseley; 2°.
Carl. Ex. Lich.

B1915 Bentley, Richard, 1692
Cant. Ely. Ex. Llan. Nor. Rip.

B1916 Bentley, Richard, 1694
Cant.

B1917 Bentley, Richard, 1693
Cant. Ely. Ex. Llan. Nor. Rip.
Wor.

B1917+ Bentley, Richard, 1693
By J.H. for Henry Mortlock; 4°.
Cant.

B1918 Bentley, Richard, 1693
Cant. Ely. Ex. Llan. Nor. Rip.

B1919 Bentley, Richard, 1692
Cant. Ely. Ex. Llan. Nor. Rip.

B1921 Bentley, Richard, 1693
Cant.

B1922 Bentley, Richard, 1692
Cant. Ely. Ex. Llan. Nor. Rip.

B1923 Bentley, Richard, 1693
Cant.

B1925 Bentley, Richard, 1692
Cant. Ely. Ex. Llan. Nor. Rip.

B1929 Bentley, Richard, 1699
Dur. Nor. Pet.

B1930 Bentley, Richard, 1693
8 pts; 4°.
Cant (2 − 1: pts 1, 3−8 = 1st ed.,
pt 2 = 2nd ed.; 2: pt 1 = 4th ed.,
pts 2, 3, 5 = 3rd ed., pts 4, 6 =
2nd ed., pts 7−8 = 1st ed.). Ely.
Ex. Llan. Nor. Rip.

B1931 Bentley, Richard, 1699
Chi. Roch. S Pl (2).

B1932 Bentley, Richard, 1692
Cant. Ely. Ex. Llan. Nor. Rip.

B1936 Bentley, Richard, 1692
Ely. Ex. Her. Llan. Nor. Rip.

B1937 Bentley, Richard, 1692
Cant. Wor.

B1940 Bentley, Richard, 1694
Cant.

B1941 Bentley, Richard, 1696
Ely.

B1942 Bentley, Richard, 1696
Cant. Her. Nor. S Asa. S Pl.

B1947- Bérault, Pierre, 1684
=Wing2 B1947?; 12°.
Yk.

B1949 Bérault, Pierre, 1681
Date as Wing2.
Ex.

B1957+ Berchet, Toussaint, 1648
=Wing2 B1957A; '... Elementaria ...'
Carl.

B1960 Bergius, Johannes, 1655
'pearle'; By T.C. for ...
Sal.

B1960+ Beridge, John, 1662
See: CLC12.
Pet.

B1963? Berkeley, George Berkeley,
Earl of, 1666
24°.
Linc.

B1976? Berkeley, *Sir* William, 1651
'The speech of ... to the burgesses';
Hagh, by Samuell Broun.
Linc. Sal.

B1978 Berkshire, Charles Howard,
Earl of, 1641
Cant.

B1979 Berkshire, Charles Howard,
Earl of, 1641
Linc.

B1980 Berlu, John Jacob, 1690
Cant (imp).

B1987 Bernard, Edward, 1688
Editio altera; ... Theatro Seldonio [*sic*].
Ex. Glo. Yk.

B1992 Bernard, Francis, *M.D.*,
1698
Wor.

B1994 Bernard, Jacques, 1698
Entry as Wing2, but Clavel *not* Clavell.
Nor.

B1997 Bernard, John, [1641]
Yk.

B1998 Bernard, John, [1641]
Or B2000.
Pet (3 − 1 tpw)*.

B2005 Bernard, John, *Capt.*, 1650
Ex.

B2006 Bernard, Nathaniel, 1644
Wel.

B2007 Bernard, Nicholas, 1661
Hodgkinson.
S Asa.

B2007+ Bernard, Nicholas, 1661
As B2007 but: ... Hodgkinson [*sic*] ...
Carl. Liv. Yk.

B2007++ Bernard, Nicholas, 1661
By Richard Hodgkinson; 4°.
S Pl.

B2008 Bernard, Nicholas, 1660
Yk.

B2012 Bernard, Nicholas, 1656
Cant (2 − both imp). Carl. Chi.
Ex. Linc. Pet. Win. Yk.

B2015 Bernard, Nicholas, 1642
The second edition.
Cant. Ex. Linc.

B2016 Bernard, Nicholas, 1651
Carl.

B2022 Bernard, Richard, 1641
Pet.

B2023 Bernard, Richard, 1642
'epitome'
Ex. Her. Linc (2). Wel (2).

B2028 Bernard, Richard, 1668
Cant.

B2030? Bernard, Richard, 1677
The fifteenth edition; By R.E. for J.
Wright and T. Sawbridge.
Ex.

B2032 Bernard, Richard, 1641
Pet. Yk.

B2033 Bernard, Richard, 1641
Sal (2). Yk.

B2035 Bernard, Richard, 1644
Ex. Her. Linc (2). Wel.

B2035+ Bernard, Richard, 1644
By Felix Kingston for Andrew
Crooke; 2°.
Wel.

B2036 Bernard, Richard, 1661
Bur. Chelm. Sal.

B2037 Bernard, Richard, 1641
Yk.

B2040 *See*: A4223+

B2042 Bernier, François, 1672
Wel.

B2044 Bernier, François, 1676
Wel.

B2046 Berry, Richard, 1672
Win.

B2049B? Bertramus, 1686
As B2050, apart from date.
Linc.

B2049B+ Bertramus, 1686
=Wing2 B2049BA?; The third edition.
Linc.

B2049B++ Bertramus, 1686
=Wing2 B2049C?; 8°.
Wel.

B2049B + + + Bertramus, 1686
= Wing2 B2049D.
S Pl.

B2051 Bertramus, 1688
'Bertram or Ratram ...'; The second
edition.
Ches. Ely.

B2052A - Besogne, Nicolas, 1671
= Wing2 B2052A.
Linc.

B2057 Best, 1686
Lich.

B2060 Betham, John, 1686
Cant (2).

B2061 Bethel, Hugh, 1648
Yk.

B2064 Bethel, Slingsby, 1680
Pet.

B2066 Bethel, Slingsby, 1689
Yk.

B2072 Bethel, Slingsby, 1671
Win.

B2080 Bethel, [1681]
Linc.

B2087 Betts, John, 1669
Entry as Wing2.
Lich (tpw).

B2090 Beveridge, William, 1678
Chi (2). Dur. Ely. Ex. Glo.
Her. Linc. New. Nor. S Asa
(2). S Pl. Sal (2). Win. Yk.

B2091 Beveridge, William, 1689
Cant (2 − 1 tpw). Ex. Her. Yk.

B2092 Beveridge, William, 1658
S Pl.

B2092A Beveridge, William, 1664
Ches. Wor.

B2093 Beveridge, William, 1658
Pulleyn.
Ches.

B2095? Beveridge, William, 1669
... Thomae Roycroft ... Gualterium
Kettilby.
S Asa. S Pl.

B2095 + Beveridge, William, 1669
= Wing2 B2096.
Cant. Ches. S Pl. Sal. Wor.
Yk.

B2095 + + Beveridge, William, 1669
Typis Thomae Roycroft; 4°.
New.

B2097 Beveridge, William, 1695
Her.

B2100 Beveridge, William, 1682
Bur (tpw)*. S Pl (tpw)*. Yk.

B2101 Beveridge, William, 1682
Cant. Carl. Ex. Llan (2).

B2102 Beveridge, William, 1682
Yk (2).

B2104 Beveridge, William, 1683
Llan. Pet. S Asa.

B2105 Beveridge, William, 1684
Chi. S Pl.

B2106 Beveridge, William, 1687
Sal.

B2113 Beveridge, William, 1689
Her.

B2114 Beveridge, William, 1690
Cant. S Asa.

B2115 Beveridge, William, 1672
2v.
Ban. Cant. Carl. Chi. Dur.
Ely. Ex (2). Glo (2 − 1 vol. 2
only). Her. Lich. Linc. New.
Nor. Roch. S Asa. S Pl (2).
Swel. Tru. Wel. Win. Wor. Yk
(2).

B2132 Beverley, Thomas, 1688
Wel.

B2137 Beverley, Thomas, 1668
Carl.

B2147? Beverley, Thomas, 1670
By J. Redmayne ...
Ex. Llan. Yk.

B2154 Beverley, Thomas, 1676
Carl.

B2159 Beverley, Thomas, 1689
Carl.

B2177 Beverley, Thomas, 1695
Ches (imp)*.

B2191 Bewick, John, 1660
Ex.

B2198 - Bible. Anglo-Saxon. O.T.,
1696
Oxoniae, e Theatro Sheldoniano; 8°.
Linc.

B2198 Bible. Anglo-Saxon. O.T.,
1698
8°.
Cant. Carl. Dur. Ex. Nor. Sal.
Wor.

B2200 Bible. English, 1641
Tru.

B2206 Bible. English, 1644
Roch.

B2211 + Bible. English, 1645
Amsterdam, by Joachim Nosche; 12°.
Roch (imp).

B2212 Bible. English, 1646
Cant. Glo.

B2217 Bible. English, 1647
... assignes ...
Her.

B2219 Bible. English, 1647
Cant.

B2222 Bible. English, 1648
Carl.

B2225 Bible. English, 1648
Linc.

B2225 + Bible. English, 1648
By Ioh. Field; 4°.
New.

B2226 + Bible. English, 1648
Cambridge, by Roger Daniel; 12°.
Roch (2 variants).

B2226 + + Bible. English, 1648
By Roger Dainel [sic] printer to the
Universitie of Cambridge; 18°; D. &
M. 612 or 616.
Cant. Roch (... Roger Daniel
...).

B2226 + + + Bible. English, 1648
By Roger Daniel, printer to the
Universitie of Cambridge; 18°; D. &
M. 614.
Cant.

B2228 Bible. English, 1649
Ex. Liv. Rip.

B2230 Bible. English, 1649 [N.T.
1648]
8°.
Cant (2 − 1 imp).

B2235 + Bible. English, 1652 [N.T.
1653]
By the Companie of Stationers; 12°.
Roch.

B2238 Bible. English, 1653
Roch. Yk (O.T. only).

B2239? Bible. English, 1653
24°.
Linc.

B2241 Bible. English, 1654
Linc.

B2242 Bible. English, 1654
Yk.

B2242 + Bible. English, 1654
As B2242, but: 24°.
Cant.

B2248? Bible. English, 1657 [N.T.
1656]
By Iohn Feild [sic].
Cant.

B2251 Bible. English, 1657
Cant.

B2252 Bible. English, 1657
Cant (D. & M. 656). Roch.

B2253 Bible. English, 1658
Llan. Roch. Yk (2 — 1: D. &
M. 663; 2: D. & M. 664).

B2255 *See*: B2258: this no. should
be dated 1659 only

B2256 Bible. English, 1660
Cant (2). Liv (N.T. only, imp)*.

B2256A Bible. English, 1660
Roch.

B2257 Bible. English, 1660
Roch.

B2258 Bible. English, 1660 [N.T.
1659]
2v.
Cant (vol. 2 tpw). Ches (imp).
Chi (tpw). Glo. Her (2). Lich (4
— 1 tpw, 1 imp). Linc (tpw). Liv.
Pet (imp). S Pl (imp). Wel (imp).
Yk.

B2263? Bible. English, 1661 [N.T.
1660]
By Iohn Feild.
Roch.

B2265 Bible. English, 1661
Liv (O.T. only).

B2265+ Bible. English, 1661 [N.T.
1662]
As B2265, apart from date; D. & M.
679.
Sal (tpw)*.

B2268 Bible. English, 1663
Cant (imp). Dur (2 — both imp).

B2269 Bible. English, 1663 [N.T.
1662]
Roch. Yk.

B2275 *See*: B2277

B2277 Bible. English, 1668 [N.T.
1666]
Cant (N.T. only). Ely (2 — 1
lacks O.T.). Her. Roch. Wel.

B2278 Bible. English, 1669
S Alb.

B2281 Bible. English, 1670
Sal (Apocrypha only)*.

B2282 Bible. English, 1671 [N.T.
1669]
Cant (2 — 1 N.T. only). Dur.
Liv. Yk.

B2284 Bible. English, 1672
For Stephen Swart.
Swel.

B2285 Bible. English, 1672
Cant. Yk.

B2287? Bible. English, 1673
... assignes ...
Roch.

B2290+ Bible. English, 1674
N.T.: By the assigns of John Bill and
Christopher Barker; 12°.
Roch (tpw).

B2294 Bible. English, 1675
Ely (with N.T. of B2303?).

B2295 Bible. English, 1675
4°.
Cant (colophon: 1673). Tru.
Wor.

B2298 Bible. English, 1676
Roch.

B2300 Bible. English, 1676
Cant.

B2303 Bible. English, 1677
Cant. Ely (N.T. only, bound
with B2294)*. Yk (2 — 1 imp).

B2304 Bible. English, 1678
4°.
Roch.

B2307 Bible. English, 1679
Lich.

B2309 Bible. English, 1679
4°; D. & M. 744.
Cant (2 — both imp). Liv*.

B2309+ Bible. English, 1679
As B2309; D. & M. 745.
Cant (3 — 2 imp).

B2309++ Bible. English, 1679
As B2309; D. & M. 746.
Cant (frag.).

B2314 Bible. English, 1680
Ex (lacks colophon?). Glo (tpw,
replaced by tp of B2341).

B2319 Bible. English, 1682
Cant.

B2320 Bible. English, 1682
Cant.

B2324 Bible. English, 1682
Cant (2 — both imp).

B2325 Bible. English, 1682
4°.
Cant (Apocrypha only).

B2325+ Bible. English, 1682
Oxford at the Theater, sold by Moses
Pitt, London; 2°.
Nor.

B2327+ Bible. English, 1682
As B2325+, but: 4°.
Yk.

B2328 Bible. English, [1682]
Oxford, printed for Tho: Guy at
Lond.; D. & M. 774.
Cant (2 — 1 tpw).

B2328+ Bible. English, [1682]
As B2328; D. & M. 775.
Cant (3 — 2 tpw).

B2333 Bible. English, 1683
Date altered from 1682.
Cant (lacks N.T.). Chelm. Dur.
Glo (O.T. only, with B2667). Pet.

B2334? Bible. English, 1683
... sold by Thomas Guy at London;
N.T. tp as D. & M. 784.
Cant (2 — 1 tpw, 1 imp).

B2335 Bible. English, 1684
Linc. Roch.

B2338 Bible. English, 1684
Cant (2).

B2339 Bible. English, 1685
4°.
Glo (tpw).

B2341 Bible. English, 1685
... by P. Parker and Thomas Guy.
Cant (N.T. tpw). Pet.

B2342+ Bible. English, 1685
As B2342; Not in D. & M.; Guy on
both tps.
Cant.

B2342++ Bible. English, 1685
[N.T. 1686]
As B2342; D. & M. 801.
Cant.

B2342+++ Bible. English, 1685
[N.T. 1686]
As B2342; Not in D. & M.; N.T. tp:
At the Theatre, for Peter Parker,
London.
Cant (imp).

B2342++++ Bible. English, 1685
[N.T. 1686]
Printed at the Theater in Oxford, and
are to be sold by Peter Parker,
London; 12°.
Cant.

B2345+ Bible. English, 1686
As B2342, apart from date.
Cant.

B2348 Bible. English, 1687
Printed at the Theater in Oxford, to
be sold by Thomas Guy, London.
Cant.

B2348+ Bible. English, 1687
[Oxford], sold by Thomas Guy in
London; 4°.
Cant.

B2350 Bible. English, 1688
Cant (imp).

B2351 Bible. English, 1688
Cant.

B2353 Bible. English, 1689
Cant.

B2353+ Bible. English, 1689
As B2353, but: ... by Peter Parker ...
Yk (imp).

B2354 Bible. English, 1690
Cant.

B2355 Bible. English, 1690
By Charles Bill and Thomas
Newcomb.
Roch.

B2357 Bible. English, 1691
Cant.

B2357+ Bible. English, 1691
Printed at the Theater in Oxford, and
are to be sold by Peter Parker,
London; 12°.
Cant (lacks N.T.).

B2361- Bible. English, 1693
By Charles Bill and Thomas
Newcomb; 12°.
Yk.

B2366 Bible. English, 1695
Roch.

B2372 Bible. English, 1697
4°.
Cant.

B2374? Bible. English, 1698
24°.
Roch.

B2374+ Bible. English, 1698
As B2373, but: 4°.
Roch (O.T. only).

B2374++ Bible. English, 1698
[N.T. 1699]
As B2373, but: 18°.
Roch.

B2375 Bible. English, 1699
Linc.

B2379 Bible. English. O.T., 1690
Ban.

B2381 Bible. English. Psalms, 1641
8°.
Cant. S Alb. S Pl. Yk (2).

B2391+ Bible. English. Psalms,
1642
=Wing2 B2391B?; 16°.
Yk.

B2393+ Bible. English. Psalms,
1642
'The booke of Psalmes in English
metre'; [N.pl.]; 8°.
Chi.

B2394A Bible. English. Psalms,
1643
Companie.
S Pl.

B2395 Bible. English. Psalms, 1643
16°.
S Pl.

B2397 Bible. English. Psalms, 1643
Cant (imp).

B2400 Bible. English. Psalms, 1644
S Alb.

B2405 Bible. English. Psalms, 1644
Yk.

B2407? Bible. English. Psalms, 1645
By G.M., sold by S. Gellibrand, I.
Kirton, T. Underhill and Stephen
Bowtell.
Ex.

B2415 Bible. English. Psalms, 1646
... Companie ...
Cant. S Pl.

B2416 Bible. English. Psalms, 1646
Bur.

B2418 Bible. English. Psalms, 1646
Chi.

B2422 Bible. English. Psalms, 1647
Cant. Carl. S Pl.

B2430 Bible. English. Psalms, 1648
New (imp).

B2431 Bible. English. Psalms, 1648
Bris. Glo.

B2432? Bible. English. Psalms, 1648
... Daniel, printer to the University of
Cambridge; 12°.
Roch.

B2435 Bible. English. Psalms, 1649
Entry as Wing2.
Liv.

B2436+ Bible. English. Psalms,
1649
=Wing2 B2436A?; 12°.
Cant (imp).

B2438 Bible. English. Psalms, 1649
Her.

B2443 Bible. English. Psalms, 1650
Roch.

B2445 Bible. English. Psalms, 1651
Dur.

B2445+ Bible. English. Psalms,
1651
By W. Bentley; 24°.
Sal (tp imp).

B2453 Bible. English. Psalms, 1653
Linc.

B2457+ Bible. English. Psalms,
1654
'The whole book of Psalms'; By the
Companie of Stationers; 12°.
S Pl.

B2459 Bible. English. Psalms, 1655
'Psalmes'; 8°.
Cant.

B2459+ Bible. English. Psalms,
1655
By the Companie of Stationers; 12°.
Cant.

B2464 Bible. English. Psalms, 1656
Yk.

B2470 Bible. English. Psalms, 1658
Roch. Yk.

B2475 Bible. English. Psalms, 1661
Carl.

B2476 Bible. English. Psalms, 1661
Yk.

B2477A Bible. English. Psalms,
1661
Cant. Pet.

B2483 Bible. English. Psalms, 1663
[Cambridge], by John Field; 4°.
Cant.

B2484 Bible. English. Psalms, 1664
Lich.

B2485? Bible. English. Psalms, 1664
For T. Garthwait.
S Asa.

B2486 Bible. English. Psalms, 1664
Sal.

B2486+ Bible. English. Psalms,
1664
As B2486, but: 8°.
Liv. Yk.

B2490 Bible. English. Psalms, 1666
... Field, printer to the University of
Cambridge.
Cant. Glo. Roch. Wel.

B2491 Bible. English. Psalms, 1667
Pet.

B2494 Bible. English. Psalms, 1668
Cant. Carl. Ely. Linc. New (2
– both engr. tpw?). Pet. Sal
(addit. engr. tpw). Yk.

B2495+ Bible. English. Psalms,
1668
Entry as B2492, apart from date.
Wor.

B2496 Bible. English. Psalms, 1669
Wel.

B2497 Bible. English. Psalms, 1669
Dur. S Alb.

B2498+ Bible. English. Psalms,
1669
By J.M. for the Company of
Stationers; 12°.
Yk.

B2503? Bible. English. Psalms, 1670
... Hayes, printer to the Universitie of Cambridge; 4°.
Sal.

B2504 Bible. English. Psalms, 1671
Cant (imp). Liv. Yk (2).

B2506 Bible. English. Psalms, 1671
The second edition.
Chi.

B2509 Bible. English. Psalms, 1672
Yk.

B2511+ Bible. English. Psalms, 1673
=Wing2 B2511A?; 'Psalmes'; ... assignes ...; 12°.
Roch.

B2513+ Bible. English. Psalms, 1673
By T.N. for the Company of Stationers; 2°.
Win.

B2514 Bible. English. Psalms, 1674
Roch.

B2518 Bible. English. Psalms, 1675
Cant. Tru. Wor.

B2519 Bible. English. Psalms, 1675
Cant.

B2520 Bible. English. Psalms, 1676
Cant.

B2521A Bible. English. Psalms, 1676
Wel.

B2523 Bible. English. Psalms, 1676
... Hayes, printer to the University of Cambridge.
Cant. Ely.

B2526 Bible. English. Psalms, 1677
8°.
S Asa.

B2527+ Bible. English. Psalms, 1677
=Wing2 B2527A?; By William Godbid and Andrew Clark, ...
Ban.

B2529 Bible. English. Psalms, 1678
Ex. Win.

B2533 Bible. English. Psalms, 1679
4°.
Cant (3 − 1 imp). Liv.

B2534 Bible. English. Psalms, 1679
... Hayes, printer to the University of Cambridge.
Pet. Yk.

B2536 Bible. English. Psalms, 1679
By J.M. ...
Ely. Win. Yk.

B2537 Bible. English. Psalms, 1680
Cant (2 eds − 1: tp 'corrupting of/ youth'; 2: tp 'corrupt-/ing of youth').

B2538 Bible. English. Psalms, 1680
2v.; Impr. as Wing2.
Ban. Dur. Llan (vol. 2. only). Pet (vol. 1. only). S Pl.

B2545 Bible. English. Psalms, 1682
Nor.

B2546B Bible. English. Psalms, 1682
Chi.

B2547 Bible. English. Psalms, 1682
'The whole book of Psalms'
Cant (2). Nor.

B2547+ Bible. English. Psalms, 1682
As B2547, but: 4°.
Yk.

B2548 Bible. English. Psalms, 1682
'The whole book of Psalms'
Cant (2 − 1 imp).

B2551+ Bible. English. Psalms, 1683
=Wing2 B2551B.
Yk (tpw)*.

B2552A+ Bible. English. Psalms, 1683
Cambridge, by John Hayes; 4°.
Chelm.

B2552B Bible. English. Psalms, 1684
Dur. Ex. Roch*.

B2552B+ Bible. English. Psalms, 1684
Colophon: Printed at the Theater in Oxford; cap.; 12°.
Cant.

B2553 Bible. English. Psalms, 1684
12°.
Chi.

B2554 Bible. English. Psalms, 1684
Lichfield.
Chi. Glo.

B2555+ Bible. English. Psalms, 1685
Oxford, at the Theatre; and are to be sold by Thomas Guy, London; 2°.
Cant (imp).

B2555++ Bible. English. Psalms, [1685?]
[Oxford, at the Theatre?]; 2°; 44p.
Cant (imp).

B2556+ Bible. English. Psalms, 1685
The third edition; For Robert Clavel; 8°.
Chi. Glo.

B2557+ Bible. English. Psalms, 1685
Entry as Wing1 B2557; '... James 5. ...'
Cant.

B2557++ Bible. English. Psalms, 1685
As B2557+, but: '... James 5. 13. ...'
Cant.

B2562 Bible. English. Psalms, 1687
Cant.

B2565+ Bible. English. Psalms, 1688
=Wing2 B2565A?; ... S. Keeble.
Chi.

B2567 Bible. English. Psalms, 1688
Liv.

B2568 Bible. English. Psalms, 1688
Cant.

B2568+ Bible. English. Psalms, 1688
=Wing2 B2568B; 12°.
Cant.

B2569 Bible. English. Psalms, 1688
Chi.

B2569+ Bible. English. Psalms, 1688
'The Psalms of David in metre'; Edinburgh, printed by the heir of Andrew Anderson; 4°.
Dur.

B2577 Bible. English. Psalms, 1691
Cant (pt 2 only). Ches. Chi.

B2580+ Bible. English. Psalms, 1692
For Richard Baldwin; 12°.
Yk.

B2585 Bible. English. Psalms, 1693
'The Psalms of David in meeter'; ... and are to be sold at his shop.
Cant.

B2598 Bible. English. Psalms, 1696
12°.
Cant. Chi. Dur.

B2599 Bible. English. Psalms, 1696
Cant.

B2602+ Bible. English. Psalms, 1696
'The Psalter of David'; The twelfth edition; By J. L. for L. Meredith; 12°.
S Pl.

B2607 Bible. English. Psalms, 1698
The second edition.
S Pl.

B2609 Bible. English. Psalms, 1698
Chi (tpw).

B2611 Bible. English. Psalms, 1698
By Roger Daniel, printer to the
Universitie of Cambridge.
Cant.

B2616+ Bible. English. Psalms,
[1698]
=Wing2 B2616A; ... Peter Laurence.
Chi.

B2617? Bible. English. Psalms, 1699
... sold by Samuel Sprint and Henry
Playford.
Yk.

B2617A Bible. English. Psalms,
1699
Linc.

B2618A Bible. English. Psalms,
1699
Dur.

B2623 Bible. English. Psalms, 1700
Wor.

B2624? Bible. English. Psalms, 1700
By J. Heptinstall, and sold by D.
Brown and J. Wild; 12°.
Dur.

B2625 Bible. English. Psalms, 1700
Bur.

B2629B+ Bible. O.T., apart from
Psalms, 1642
=Wing2 B2629C.
Yk.

B2632A Bible. O.T., apart from
Psalms, 1679
Ban.

B2633A Bible. O.T., apart from
Psalms, 1682
By H.H. for Henry Faithorne ...; 8°.
Win.

B2635 Bible. O.T., apart from
Psalms, 1683
Ban. Carl.

B2639? Bible. O.T., apart from
Psalms, 1679
By E. Flesher for ...
Ban. Bur.

B2639+ Bible. O.T., apart from
Psalms, 1685
=Wing2 B2639A.
Cant. Her.

B2642 Bible. O.T., apart from
Psalms, 1685
'... Ecclesiastes and the Song of
Solomon ...'
Ban. Cant. Ches. Pet.

B2667 Bible. English. N.T., 1666
Glo. Roch.

B2680 Bible. English. N.T., 1679
Cant.

B2686+ Bible. English. N.T., 1682
By the assigns of John Bill deceas'd,
and by Henry Hills and Thomas
Newcomb; 8°.
Sal.

B2688 Bible. English. N.T., 1683
Ban. Carl.

B2707A Bible. French, 1687
Cant (imp).

B2707A+ Bible. French, 1688
=Wing2 B2707B.
Ches.

B2710+ Bible. French, 1700
'Le nouveau testament'; A
Amsterdam au dépens d'Estienne
Roger, et se vend. à Londres, chez
François Vaillant. Colophon: A
Amsterdam, de l'imprimerie de Daniel
Boulesteys de la Contie; 8°.
Cant.

B2715 Bible. Gaelic, 1681
Wor (tpw).

B2718 Bible. Greek, 1653
Cant (imp). Dur. Ely. Lich.
Linc (imp). Rip (imp). S Asa.

B2718+ Bible. Greek, 1653
As B2718, but: 4°.
Chi. Ex. Linc. S Pl. Sal (imp).
Wel.

B2719 Bible. Greek, 1665
Bur (imp). Cant (3 − 1 imp).
Ches (2). Ely. Ex (2). Liv (2 eds
− 1: D. & M. 4701; 2: D. & M.
4702). Yk (2 − 1 imp).

B2719A Bible. Greek, 1652
S Pl (tpw).

B2719B Bible. Greek, [1652?]
Cant.

B2720? Bible. Greek, 1664
... παρ' Ἰωαννου του Φιελδου.
Bur. Ches. Dur. Ely. Liv. Rip.
Yk.

B2720+ Bible. Greek, 1664
As B2720, but: 12° .
Cant (4 − 1 imp). Ches (2). Linc
(3). Liv. Nor (2). S Pl (2). Sal
(2). Swel. Tru. Yk.

B2723 *See*: D2648

B2724 *See*: D2649

B2725 Bible. Greek, 1678
[Gk & Latin].
Cant (tp imp).

B2729 *See*: B2801 & B2801+

B2730 Bible. Greek, 1652
Cant. S Pl.

B2731 Bible. Greek, 1653
Cant.

B2731+ Bible. Greek, 1653
=Wing2 B2731A; ... Josuae Kerton ...
Rip.

B2733 Bible. Greek, 1665
... παρ' Ἰωαννου Φιελδου; Dated in
Greek.
Bur. Cant. Ches. Sal. Yk.

B2737 Bible. Greek, 1675
12°.
Ches. Ely. Llan. Roch. Win.

B2742 Bible. Hebrew, 1656
[Psalms & Lamentations].
Glo. Yk (2).

B2742+ Bible. Hebrew, 1656
As B2742, but: '[Hebrew] The Hebrew
text ... revised'; ... L. Fawn, J.
Kirton, and S. Thomson ...
Cant. Wel.

B2742++ Bible. Hebrew, 1656
As B2742+, but: '... published'; 12°.
Yk (2).

B2743 Bible. Hebrew, 1685
... Johan. Hayes, ... Londini.
Linc. S Asa. Yk.

B2746 Bible. Hebrew, 1661
Title as Wing2; Typis Thomae
Roycroft, venales prostant apud
plerosq; bibliopolas Londinenses.
Wel.

B2750 Bible. Algonquin, 1663
Evans 72 '3rd variety'
Cant. Ex (imp)*. Win*.

B2755 Bible. Algonquin, 1663
4°.
Linc (imp).

B2757 Bible. Algonquin, 1661
Cant (imp).

B2758 Bible. Algonquin, 1661
Pt 2 of B2750.
Cant (imp).

B2761 Bible. Latin, 1656
Yk.

B2761+ Bible. Latin, 1556 [*i.e.*
1656?]
E.T. [*or* E.G.?] et R.W. sumpt.
Societ.; 12°.
S Dv.

B2763 Bible. Latin, 1680
… prostat venalia …
Sal.

B2764A Bible. Latin, 1649
[Pentateuch].
Cant. Sal (2).

B2765 Bible. Latin, 1648
Cant.

B2775+ Bible. Latin, 1651
'[Hebrew] sive Jeremiae vatis
Lamentationes'; Impensis Johannis
Ridley; 4°; Wrongly placed at T281.
Cant.

B2776 Bible. Latin, 1655
'Esteram'
Cant.

B2789 Bible. Latin, 1677
Impr. as Wing2?
Cant (tpw)*.

B2796 Bible. Malay, 1677
Wor.

B2797 Bible. Polyglot, 1657
'… Brianus Waltonus'
Bris (2 − 1 imp). Bur (2 − 1 vol.
3 only). Cant. Carl. Chelm.
Ches. Chi (vols 1, 3, 5). Dur.
Ely. Ex (2). Glo. Her. Lich.
Linc. Llan. New (imp). Nor.
Pet. Rip. Roch (2). S Asa. S Pl
(2). Sal (2). Swar. Swel. Wel.
Win. Wor. Yk.

B2798 Bible. Polyglot, 1643
'… W.S.'
Linc.

B2800+ Bible. Polyglot, 1653
As D2657, but: … Guilielmum …
Dur.

B2801 Bible. Polyglot, 1642
Cantabrigiae, ex officina Rogeri
Danielis; Gk & Lat.
Chelm. Ely. Her. Lich. S Pl.
Swel. Tru (2).

B2801+ Bible. Polyglot, 1642
As B2801, but: … Danielis, et Londini
venales prostant.
Dur. Ex. Her (imp). Lich.

B2811 Bible. Shorthand, [1673]
32°.
Linc.

B2813A Bible. Welsh, 1654
Gan James Flesher ac a werthir gan
Thomas Brewster.
S Asa (imp).

B2814 Bible. Welsh, 1677 [N.T.
1678]
… gan John Hancock.
Ban. S Asa (imp).

B2815? Bible. Welsh, 1678
… Thomas Newcomb … gan John
Hancock.
Ban.

B2815A Bible. Welsh, 1689 [N.T.
1690]
Impr. as Wing2.
Glo. Roch (imp). S Asa.

B2816 Bible. Welsh, 1690
Rhydychain …
Her. S Asa (2).

B2831 *See*: B5726

B2841 Bibliotheca, 1659
S Pl.

B2858 Bibliotheca, 1685
'… octavo die Septembris 1685. Per
Edwardum Millingtonum bibliopolam
Lond.'
Wor.

B2866 Biddle, Hester, 1660
Yk.

B2868 Biddle, John, 1653
Carl. S Pl.

B2868+ Biddle, John, 1691
[London]; 4°; Pt of F258B.
Cant.

B2869 Biddle, John, 1653
Dur. S Pl.

B2876 *See*: F258B

B2877 Biddle, John, [1653]
S Pl.

B2878 Biddle, John, 1648
Dur.

B2881 Biddle, John, 1655
Carl.

B2882 Biddle, John, 1654
Carl (pt 2 only). S Pl.

B2891- Bill, 1679
= Wing2 B2891; Should be under
'England'
Linc.

B2891 *See*: E2532

B2892 *See*: E2533

B2894 Bill, [1680]
2°.
Linc.

B2909 Billingsley, John, 1656
Linc.

B2915 Binet, Étienne, 1663
8°.
Carl.

B2921 Bingley, William, 1683
Yk (2).

B2936 Biondi, Giovanni Francesco,
1641
2°.
Cant (engr. tpw).

B2936+ Biondi, Giovanni
Francesco, 1646
= Wing2 B2936A.
Cant (tpw).

B2937 Birch, Peter, 1700
Cant.

B2938 Birch, Peter, 1689
Bur. Cant. Her (2). Wor.

B2939 Birch, Peter, 1694
Cant. Her (2). Nor. Wor.

B2940 Birchall, John, 1644
Yk (2).

B2941 Birchen, 1694
Carl. Her. Pet.

B2945- Birckbeck, Simon, 1657
No ed. statement; By John Streater,
sold by Edward Brewster and the rest
of the booksellers; 2°.
Lich.

B2945 Birckbeck, Simon, 1657
Ex. Pet. Yk (2).

B2946 Birckbeck, Simon, 1655
Yk.

B2952 Bird, John, *at Cheddington*,
1663
Sal.

B2960 Birkenhead, *Sir* John, [1646]
cap.
Pet.

B2961 Birkenhead, *Sir* John, 1662/3
Pet (2). Yk.

B2964 Birkenhead, *Sir* John, 1653
Yk.

B2965 Birkenhead, *Sir* John, 1663
Second ed. not on tp.
Linc.

B2970 Birkenhead, *Sir* John,
[1651/2]
Linc. S Pl (2).

B2971 Birkenhead, *Sir* John, 1644
Cant.

B2973 Birkenhead, *Sir* John, [1653]
8°.
S Pl.

B2978 Birkhead, Henry, 1656
Pet.

B2980 Bisbie, Nathaniel, 1691
Yk.

B2981 Bisbie, Nathaniel, 1686
Cant.

B2982 Bisbie, Nathaniel, 1683
Cant. Dur.

B2983 Bisbie, Nathaniel, 1682
Cant. Carl. Her. Llan.

B2984 Bisbie, Nathaniel, 1684
Cant. Llan. Yk.

B2985 Bisbie, Nathaniel, 1692
Wel. Yk (2).

B2990 Bishop, George, 1656
Yk.

B3007 Bishop, George, 1660
Pet. Yk.

B3010 Bishop, George, [c.1660]
Yk*.

B3011A Bishop, George, 1663
S Pl.

B3029 Bishops, 1641
Lich. Yk.

B3034 Bispham, Thomas, [1660]
Ban (tpw).

B3047 Blackall, Offspring, 1700
Cant. S Asa.

B3050 Blackall, Offspring, 1700
Nor. Sal.

B3051 Blackall, Offspring, 1694
Cant. Carl. Her. Nor.

B3053 Blackall, Offspring, 1699
Her (2). S Asa (2). Yk.

B3054 Blackall, Offspring, 1700
Cant. Linc. S Asa. Wor.

B3057 Blackall, Offspring, 1700
Cant. Linc. S Asa.

B3058 Blackall, Offspring, 1700
Cant. Linc. S Asa.

B3059 Blackall, Offspring, 1700
Cant. Linc. S Asa.

B3060 Blackall, Offspring, 1700
Cant. S Asa.

B3067 Blackburne, Lancelot, 1697
Cant.

B3068 Blackburne, Lancelot, 1694
Cant. Dur. Wor.

B3077 Blackmore, *Sir* Richard,
1697
Churchil.
Carl. Glo. Nor.

B3080 Blackmore, *Sir* Richard,
1695
Ex. Glo.

B3081 Blackmore, *Sir* Richard,
1695
Bris. Dur. Yk.

B3088 Blackmore, *Sir* Richard,
1699
Ban.

B3088+ Blackmore, *Sir* Richard,
1699
The second edition; For Jacob
Tonson; 4°.
Nor.

B3090 Blackwell, Elidad, 1645
Pet.

B3103 Blackwood, Christopher,
1644
Win.

B3106 Bladen, William, 1641[2]
For William Bladen ...
Dur.

B3108+ Blaeu, Willem Janszoon,
1665
=Wing2 B3108A?; ... Joh. Forrest.
Ex.

B3110 Blagrave, Jonathan, 1693
Cant.

B3110+ Blagrave, Jonathan, 1693
For John Southby; 4°.
Ban.

B3111 Blagrave, Jonathan, 1691
Cant.

B3121 Blagrave, Joseph, 1674
Cant (tpw).

B3123- Blagrave, Obadiah, [1677?]
See: CLC13.
Cant.

B3133? Blake, Martin, 1661
... to be sold by Christopher Hunt in
Barnstaple.
Sal.

B3134 Blake, Martin, 1645
Pet. Sal.

B3137 Blake, *Sir* Richard, 1641
Dur (imp).

B3138 Blake, Robert, 1653
Dur.

B3141 Blake, Thomas, *Puritan
divine*, 1646
Her. Win.

B3143 Blake, Thomas, *Puritan
divine*, 1644
Ex. Her. Pet. Win.

B3144 Blake, Thomas, *Puritan
divine*, 1655
Chelm. Pet. S Asa. Yk.

B3146 Blake, Thomas, *Puritan
divine*, 1645
Chelm. S Asa. Win.

B3147 Blake, Thomas, *Puritan
divine*, 1656
S Asa.

B3149 Blake, Thomas, *Puritan
divine*, 1653
Bur. S Asa.

B3152 Blake, William, *House-keeper*,
[1670]
cap.
Yk.

B3156? Bland, Francis, 1647
... Yorke; Pt 2 of B3156+.
Pet. Yk (details not confirmed).

B3156+ Bland, Francis, 1647
'The souldiers search for salvation:
also The souldiers march to salvation';
Pt 1: [N.pl.]; Pt 2: Printed at Yorke;
4°.
Pet. Yk (details not confirmed).

B3160 Bland, Peter, 1643
Pet. S Pl.

B3161 Bland, Peter, [1643]
Yk.

B3162 Bland, Peter, 1642
Dur. Yk (2).

B3163 Bland, Peter, 1642
Linc. Sal.

B3164+ Blankaart, Stephen, 1684
By J.D. and are to be sold by Samuel
Crouch and John Gellibrand; 8°.
Yk.

B3177+ Blaxton, John, 1642
... sold by John Long in Dorchester;
4°.
Linc.

B3184 Blechynden, Richard, 1698
Pet.

B3196 Blith, Walter, 1653
The third impression.
Carl. Ex. Pet.

B3197 Blithe, Nathaniel, 1674
Carl.

B3207 Blome, Richard, 1673
Brec (frag.). Cant (2 − 1 frag.).
Pet. S Asa.

B3209 Blome, Richard, 1678
Win.

B3212 Blome, Richard, 1660
Yk.

B3213 Blome, Richard, 1686
Wel.

B3220 Blondel, David, 1661
Ex. Nor. Wor.

B3227? Bloody, 1659
'discoverd'
Win.

B3254 Bloody, 1653
'... neighbour. Or ... two murthers ...'
Pet.

B3287+ Bloudy, 1641
=Wing2 B3287A?; '....protestants in Ireland'
Linc.

B3296 Blount, Charles, 1695
Ely. Ex. Linc. Pet.

B3300+ Blount, Charles, [1679]
=Wing2 B3300A.
Ches.

B3300A Blount, Charles, 1679
Linc.

B3310 Blount, Charles, 1683
Ex.

B3316 Blount, *Sir* Henry, 1650
Cant (tp imp).

B3327 Blount, Thomas, 1672
Cant. Carl. Lich. Wel.

B3329 Blount, Thomas, 1660
Cant (imp). Carl. Linc.

B3331 Blount, Thomas, 1680
'Boscobel: or the compleat history ...'
Linc. Nor.

B3333 Blount, Thomas, 1679
Cant. Linc.

B3334 Blount, Thomas, 1656
Impr. as Wing2.
Cant. Carl. Dur.

B3337 Blount, Thomas, 1674
Linc.

B3338 Blount, Thomas, 1681
Carl. Ches. Ely.

B3340 Blount, Thomas, 1670
Cant. Carl. Rip. Sal.

B3341 Blount, Thomas, 1691
Ex.

B3346 Blount, *Sir* Thomas Pope, 1690
Impensis Richardi Chiswel.
Dur. Ex. Liv. Nor. Wel. Yk.

B3347 Blount, *Sir* Thomas Pope, 1694
Yk.

B3353 Blow, John, 1700
Lich.

B3358 Blow, 1650
Cant. Ex (imp). Pet (3).

B3368 Boate, Arnold, 1644
Carl. Dur. Roch.

B3369 Boate, Arnold, 1651
12°.
Pet.

B3370 Boate, Arnold, 1649
Impr. as Wing2.
Carl.

B3372 Boate, Gerard, 1652
Carl.

B3374 Boate, Gerard, 1641
Dublinij.
Carl.

B3376? Bobart, Jakob, 1648
... Oxoniensis.
Cant. Carl. Sal. Yk.

B3380 Boccalini, Trajano, 1656
Cant. Lich.

B3381? Boccalini, Trajano, 1657
For Humphrey Moseley.
Ban.

B3383 Boccalini, Trajano, 1674
Ex.

B3386 Bochart, Samuel, 1663
Cant. Carl. Dur. Glo. Her.
S Pl. Sal. Win. Wor. Yk.

B3387 Bockett, John, 1696
Her.

B3390 Boden, Joseph, 1644
Pet.

B3390+ Bodington, John, 1662
=Wing2 B3391?: For William Grantham; 12°.
Carl.

B3392 Bodley, *Sir* Thomas, 1647
S Asa.

B3397 Böhme, Jacob, 1656
Dur (imp). Her.

B3404 Böhme, Jacob, 1649
4°.
Yk.

B3409 Böhme, Jacob, 1649
Cant.

B3411 Böhme, Jacob, 1654
Chi (tpw).

B3415 Böhme, Jacob, 1662
Cant (tpw). Linc.

B3417 Böhme, Jacob, 1648
Her.

B3421 Böhme, Jacob, 1691
Cant (imp). Yk.

B3429 Boethius, Anicius Manlius Torquatus Severinus, 1698
... sumtibus editoris, typis Junianis; 8°.
Cant. Dur (imp). Ex (tp imp).
Lich.

B3433 Boethius, Anicius Manlius Torquatus Severinus, 1695
'Anicius ...'; ... Hildyard in York.
Dur. Ely. Ex (imp). Yk (2).

B3434 Boethius, Anicius Manlius Torquatus Severinus, 1674
Bur. Carl.

B3435 *See*: C1551+

B3440 Bogan, Zachary, 1658
Cant. Ex.

B3442 Bogan, Zachary, 1653
... R. Davis.
Ban. Carl. Chelm.

B3445+ Bohun, Edmund, 1683
=Wing2 B3445A.
Cant. Lich. Nor. Wel. Yk.

B3445++ Bohun, Edmund, 1683
'An address to the freemen and freeholders of the Nation. In three parts ...'; For George Wells; 4°;
Includes B3445+, B3460, B3461, & B3459.
Cant. Lich. Nor. Yk (lacks pt 4).

B3446 Bohun, Edmund, 1689
'An answer ...'
S Pl.

B3447 Bohun, Edmund, 1685
Cant.

B3448 Bohun, Edmund, 1693
Carl.

B3451 Bohun, Edmund, 1689
Wel.

B3452 Bohun, Edmund, 1688
Glo.

B3453 Bohun, Edmund, 1691
Wel.

B3454 Bohun, Edmund, 1693
Third ed. not on tp.
Carl. Ex. Swel. Yk.

B3455 Bohun, Edmund, 1695
For Charles Brome.
Chi. Pet.

B3456 Bohun, Edmund, 1689
Cant (imp). Carl. Wel.

B3457 Bohun, Edmund, 1689
S Asa.

B3458- Bohun, Edmund, 1684
=Wing2 B3457A.
Carl.

B3459 Bohun, Edmund, 1683
Cant. Lich. Nor.

B3460 Bohun, Edmund, 1682
Cant. Lich. Nor. Wel. Yk.

B3461 Bohun, Edmund, 1683
Cant. Lich. Nor. Wel. Yk.

B3464 Boileau-Despréaux, Nicolas, 1683
Ex.

B3477 Bolde, Samuel, 1688
Ban. Dur. Ex. Nor.

B3477+ Bolde, Samuel, 1696
=Wing2 B3477A.
S Pl.

B3477++ Bolde, Samuel, 1697
=Wing2 B3477B?; Printed by W.
Onley, for A. Bosvile.
Cant. Dur.

B3479 Bolde, Samuel, 1690
Cant. Yk.

B3480 Bolde, Samuel, 1689
Her.

B3483 Bolde, Samuel, 1698
Cant. Liv.

B3484 Bolde, Samuel, 1682
Cant. Nor.

B3486 Bolde, Samuel, 1697
Cant. Liv.

B3488 Bolde, Samuel, 1682
Her.

B3489 Bolde, Samuel, 1682
Yk.

B3489+ Bolde, Samuel, 1682
The second edition; For A. Churchill;
4°.
Pet.

B3493 Bolde, Samuel, 1697
Cant. Liv. Pet.

B3494 Bolde, Samuel, 1699
Liv.

B3495 Bolde, Samuel, 1697
Cant. Liv. Pet.

B3496 Bolde, Thomas, 1660
Bur. Carl. Yk.

B3499 Bolron, Robert, 1680
Win.

B3501 Bolron, Robert, 1680
... and Jacob Sampson.
Glo. Linc. Yk (imp).

B3502? Bolron, Robert, 1680
Author's name on tp.
Linc. Nor. Win. Yk.

B3512 Bolton, Robert, 1641
Reissue, with added gen. tp, of
various tracts printed 1638–40;
Contents vary.
Dur (7 pts only). Pet (2 pts only).

B3513 Bolton, Robert, 1644
Sal.

B3516 Bolton, Samuel, 1646
Pet (imp). Yk.

B3518 Bolton, Samuel, 1657
Rip.

B3519 Bolton, Samuel, 1647
Yk.

B3520 Bolton, Samuel, 1644
Cant.

B3547 Bona, Giovanni, 1693
Ely.

B3551 Bona, Giovanni, 1672
Cant. Carl.

B3557 Bond, Cimelgus, 1660
Ex.

B3558 Bond, Edward, 1642
Dur (tp imp).

B3564 Bond, Henry, 1676
Linc. Sal.

B3569 Bond, John, *Master of the
Savoy*, 1641
... for Iohn Bartlet.
Chelm.

B3570 Bond, John, *Master of the
Savoy*, 1648
... for Samuell Gellibrand.
Chelm.

B3572 Bond, John, *Master of the
Savoy*, 1645
Pet.

B3573+ Bond, John, *Master of the
Savoy*, 1645
As B3573, but title begins 'Oriens ab
Occidente'
Her.

B3574 Bond, John, *Master of the
Savoy*, 1644
Ex. Yk.

B3581+ Bond, John, *of St. John's,
Cambridge*, [1642]
=Wing2 B3582.
Linc.

B3591 Bonet, Théophile, 1684
Cant. Ex.

B3593 Bonhome, Joshua, 1679
Ban. Win.

B3594 Bonhome, Joshua, 1675
Nor.

B3612 Book, 1641
Linc. New (imp)*. Yk.

B3612+ Book, 1641
As B3612, but: 8°.
S Alb. S Pl.

B3613 Book, 1642
... assignes ...
Bris. Her.

B3615 Book, 1660
Linc. Liv (Psalter & Ordinal
only)*.

B3616 Book, 1660
Carl. S Dv.

B3617+ Book, 1660
As B3617, but: 2°; Impr. from Psalter.
Wor (imp).

B3619 Book, 1660
Her. Liv. Wel.

B3620 Book, 1661
By John Bill.
Dur. Ely. Wel (imp)*. Win.

B3622 Book, 1662
Cant (2). Ches (2). Chi (2). Ex
(3). Glo. Her (2). Lich. Linc
(2). Nor (2). Pet. Rip. Roch (2).
S Asa. S Pl. Sal (2). Tru. Wel.
Win (2). Wor. Yk (3 – 1 imp).

B3623 Book, 1662
2°.
Chi. Linc (imp). Liv (lacks
Psalter). Yk (3 – 1 imp).

B3624 Book, 1662
Cant (imp). Yk (imp)*.

B3625 Book, 1662
Dur. Yk (2).

B3626+ Book, 1663
=Wing2 B3626A.
Sal.

B3628 Book, 1664
Yk.

B3629 Book, 1664
Entry as Wing2.
Ban (2). Dur. S Asa (2 – 1 imp).
Yk.

B3630 Book, 1665
S Alb.

B3632 Book, 1665
Greek as Wing2, but impr. has: ...
Ἰωάννου ...
Cant (4). Ches (2). Linc (3).
Liv. Nor (2). S Pl (2). Sal (2).
Swel. Tru. Yk.

B3632+ Book, 1665
As B3632, but: 8°.
Bur. Ches. Dur. Ely. Liv. Rip.
Yk.

B3633 Book, 1666
... Field, printer to the University of
...
Cant. Ely (tpw)*. Glo. Her.
Liv. Wel.

B3633+ Book, 1666
=Wing2 B3633A.
Cant. Pet (tp imp).

B3633++ Book, 1667
In the Savoy, by the assignes of John
Bill and Christopher Barker; 8°.
Yk.

B3635 Book, 1669
Cant. Ex (2). Lich. Linc.
S Alb. Wel (2). Win. Yk.

B3635+ Book, [1669?]
By John Bill & Christopher Barker;
2°; Psalter dated 1669.
Carl*. Ex. Wel (v. imp).

B3637 Book, 1670
Sal.

B3638 Book, 1671
Liv.

B3638+ Book, 1672
Impr. of Psalter, as B3638; 2°.
Yk (tpw).

B3641+ Book, 1674
Impr. as B3639; 8°.
Yk.

B3641A Book, 1674
Impr. as Wing2, but: ... Academiae;
8°.
S Pl. Sal. Wel. Yk.

B3642 Book, 1675
Chi (tpw)*.

B3644 Book, 1675
Cant. Tru. Wor.

B3646 Book, 1676
S Asa.

B3649 Book, 1677
Ex (imp)*.

B3650+ Book, 1678
Impr. of Psalter as B3650; 2°.
Ban (imp). Ches (tpw).

B3651 Book, 1678
S Pl.

B3652 Book, 1678
Entry as Wing2, but impr. should
read: Printiedig yn Llundain gan ...
Ban. S Asa (imp).

B3654 Book, 1679
Cant.

B3656 Book, 1679
Pet. S Pl. Yk.

B3657 Book, 1679
Cant (2).

B3658 Book, 1680
Glo. Yk.

B3658+ Book, 1680
Impr. as B3658; 8°.
Lich.

B3660 Book, 1680
Cant.

B3662+ Book, [1680?]
Oxford: at the Theater for Moses Pitt,
Thomas Guy, Peter Parker, William
Leak, London; 2°.
Linc.

B3666? Book, 1682
Date on tp.
Yk.

B3668+ Book, 1682
Impr. as B3668 but: ... sold by
Thomas Guy, London; 8°.
Cant.

B3669 Book, 1683
Cant (with the cancels of James
II). Wel (2 − 1 as Cant).

B3670 Book, 1683
Chelm. Yk.

B3672 Book, 1683
Theater.
Cant (imp). Chelm.

B3674 Book, 1684
Cant (imp).

B3676+ Book, [1685−88]
[N.pl.], sold by Thomas Guy in
London; 4°; State prayers for James
II.
Bris (tpw)*. Cant.

B3677+ Book, 1686
Oxford at the Theater; and sold by
Peter Parker, London; 8°.
Dur. Ex (imp)*.

B3678 Book, 1686
Impr. as Wing2.
Ely.

B3678+ Book, 1686
Printed at the Theater in Oxford, and
are to be sold by Thomas Guy,
London; 12°.
Cant (cropped).

B3678++ Book, [1686?]
At yᵉ Theatre in Oxford, sold by P.
Parker [London]; 2°.
Cant (tpw). Ex. Sal.

B3679 Book, 1687
By Charles Bill ...
Cant. Lich. Rip. Yk.

B3680 Book, 1687
Cant.

B3682 Book, 1688
Impr. as Wing2.
Chi (imp).

B3683+ Book, 1691
=Wing2 B3683B.
Glo. S Pl.

B3684+ Book, 1691
By Charles Bill, and Thomas
Newcomb; 12°.
Yk.

B3686 Book, 1692
Liv.

B3688+ Book, 1693
Impr. as B3685; 8°.
Cant.

B3689 Book, 1693
Chi (imp). Sal.

B3701 Book, 1699
Dur.

B3702 Book, 1700
Her. Swel (imp).

B3704+ Book, 1700
'Llyfr gweddi gyffredin, ...';
Argraphwŷd dros Thomas Jones yn y
Flwŷddŷn; 4°.
Ban.

B3713? Booke, 1641
'A booke of presidents ...'
Ex.

B3717 Book, 1657
Linc.

B3720 Book, 1680
Yk.

B3720+ Book, 1680
Entry as Wing2 B3720.
Cant. S Dv. S Pl. Yk.

B3741 Booth, William, 1642
Dur (tpw). Linc.

B3757 Boreman, Robert, 1652
Cant (cropped). Ex. Pet.

B3758 Boreman, Robert, 1669
Ex.

B3761? Boreman, Robert, 1663
'patern'
Cant.

B3762 Boreman, Robert, 1654
Ex. Pet (2).

B3763 Borfet, Abiel, 1696
Cant.

B3764 Borfet, Abiel, 1696
Cant.

B3767+ Borlase, Edmund, 1680
For Henry Brome, and Richard
Chiswell; 2°.
Dur.

B3768 Borlase, Edmund, 1680
For Robert Clavel.
Wor.

B3769 Borlase, Edmund, 1670
S Asa.

B3774 *See*: B6129

B3779+ Bosse, Abraham, 1659
=Wing2 B3779A.
Pet.

B3780 Bossuet, Jacques Bénigne,
1687
Ban. Bur. Ex. Wel.

B3781 Bossuet, Jacques Bénigne, 1686
Carl. Ex.

B3783 Bossuet, Jacques Bénigne, 1685
Chi (imp). Dur (imp). Ex. S Pl. Sal. Swel. Wel (imp).

B3784 Bossuet, Jacques Bénigne, 1686
Second ed. not on tp.
Ban. Bur. Lich. Pet.

B3784+ Bossuet, Jacques Bénigne, 1686
=Wing2 B3784A; The second edition.
Carl. Ely. Nor.

B3786 Bossuet, Jacques Bénigne, 1699
Cant.

B3787 Bossuet, Jacques Bénigne, 1686
Bur. Swel.

B3788 Bossuet, Jacques Bénigne, 1686
Yk.

B3790 Bossuet, Jacques Bénigne, 1684
Carl.

B3791 Bossuet, Jacques Bénigne, 1684
... F.C. for H.R. (?) ...
Carl.

B3792 Bossuet, Jacques Bénigne, 1685
Ex.

B3793 Bossuet, Jacques Bénigne, 1687
'... both kinds'
Bur. Ex. Swel. Wel.

B3795+ Bostock, Robin, 1663
=Wing2 B3795A.
Yk.

B3801 Boteler, Edward, 1662
Pet.

B3803+ Boteler, Edward, 1669
=Wing2 B3803B.
Linc.

B3812 Boughen, Edward, 1653
S Pl.

B3813 Boughen, Edward, 1648
Win. Yk (imp)*.

B3815 Boughen, Edward, 1645
Ex. Linc.

B3815A Boughen, Edward, [1645?]
Cant.

B3819 Boughen, Edward, 1671
Llan (tpw)*.

B3820 Boughen, Edward, 1673
Linc.

B3825 Bouhours, Dominique, 1688
Linc.

B3826 Bouhours, Dominique, 1686
Dur. S Alb. S Asa. Yk.

B3827 Bouhours, Dominique, 1679
Carl.

B3834+ Bounds, 1694
=Wing2 B3834A?; For R. Baldwin.
Carl.

B3838 Bourchier, *Sir* John, 1642
brs.
Linc.

B3839 Bourchier, *Sir* John, [1642]
Cant. Yk (2).

B3843 Bourk, Hubert, [1680]
For Randolph Taylor.
Yk.

B3844 Bourne, Benjamin, 1646
Cant.

B3851 Bourne, Immanuel, 1659
Pet.

B3866 Bowber, Thomas, 1695
Ches. Wor.

B3871 Bowles, Edward, 1655
Pet. Yk (3).

B3872 Bowles, Edward, 1648
Pet. S Pl.

B3874 Bowles, Edward, 1646
Yk (2).

B3877 Bowles, Edward, 1643
4°.
Pet. Sal. Win. Yk.

B3877+ Bowles, Edward, 1647
See: CLC14.
Carl.

B3877++ Bowles, Edward, 1659
See: CLC15.
Cant.

B3878 Bowles, Edward, 1643
Linc. Pet. Sal. Yk.

B3880 Bowles, Oliver, 1649
Carl. Linc. Pet. Wor.

B3882 Bowles, Oliver, 1655
Rip. Sal. Yk.

B3884 Bowles, Oliver, 1643
Linc.

B3902 Boyce, Thomas, 1675
Yk.

B3917 Boyer, Abel, 1699
Chi.

B3919 Boyer, Pierre, 1692
12°.
Cant.

B3921 Boyle, Robert, 1699–1700
Chi. Lich (vol. 1 only). Pet (vols 1, 3 only). S Dv (vol. 2 only).

B3922 Boyle, Robert, 1700
'The works ...'; Impr. as Wing2.
Chi.

B3929 Boyle, Robert, 1661
Carl (frag.). Pet (tp imp).

B3931 Boyle, Robert, 1690
Llan. Nor.

B3932 Boyle, Robert, 1662
Ex.

B3941 Boyle, Robert, 1662
... in Oxon; 4°.
Carl. Wel. Win. Yk.

B3944 Boyle, Robert, 1681
Carl*. Ex*.

B3946 Boyle, Robert, 1688
Ex.

B3947 Boyle, Robert, 1672
Ex. Wel.

B3950 Boyle, Robert, 1690
Ex.

B3951 Boyle, Robert, 1673
'... subtilty great efficacy determinate nature of ...'; Fulton 105.
Carl. Ex.

B3951+ Boyle, Robert, 1673
As B3951, but: '... subtilty determinate nature great efficacy of ...'; Fulton 106.
Dur.

B3955 Boyle, Robert, 1674
Carl. Ex. S Pl. Wel.

B3959 Boyle, Robert, 1691
Ex.

B3967 Boyle, Robert, 1664
Carl. Ex. Pet.

B3972 Boyle, Robert, 1680
... Ric. Davis.
Ex.

B3979 Boyle, Robert, 1685/6
Carl. Ex.

B3980 Boyle, Robert, 1692
Cant.

B3981 Boyle, Robert, 1692
Ex.

B3983 Boyle, Robert, 1691
By Edward Jones ...
Llan. Nor.

B3985 Boyle, Robert, 1666
Carl. Yk.

B3987 Boyle, Robert, 1687
Bur.

B3990- Boyle, Robert, 1692
As B3990, apart from date.
Carl.

B3994 Boyle, Robert, 1684
Carl. Ex.

B3995 Boyle, Robert, 1681/2
Ex.

B3996 Boyle, Robert, 1665
Carl.

B3997 Boyle, Robert, 1683
Second ed. not on tp; ... in Oxford.
Ex.

B3998 Boyle, Robert, 1660
Carl.

B3999 Boyle, Robert, 1662
Ex. Wel. Win. Yk.

B4000A Boyle, Robert, 1673
Carl. Dur. Ex.

B4005 Boyle, Robert, 1665
... for Henry Herringman; 8°.
Carl. Ex. Linc. Pet. Win.

B4006 Boyle, Robert, 1669
S Asa.

B4009 Boyle, Robert, 1685
Carl.

B4013 Boyle, Robert, 1685
Ex. S Asa.

B4014 Boyle, Robert, 1666
Carl.

B4016 Boyle, Robert, 1669
Impr. as Wing2.
Yk.

B4018 Boyle, Robert, 1687
Bur. Cant. Ex (2). Lich. Nor.
Sal. Swel. Yk.

B4019 Boyle, Robert, 1690
Llan. Nor.

B4021 Boyle, Robert, 1661
Sal.

B4022 Boyle, Robert, 1680
Ex.

B4023 Boyle, Robert, 1684/5
Cant. Ex.

B4024 Boyle, Robert, 1675
Carl. Ely. Ex.

B4025 Boyle, Robert, 1661
Carl. Chi. Linc. Sal.

B4026 Boyle, Robert, 1663
Second ed. not on tp; 8°.
Ex. Nor. Pet.

B4027 Boyle, Robert, 1668
Ely. Wel. Win.

B4029 Boyle, Robert, 1663
Win.

B4030? Boyle, Robert, 1664
... Ric: Davis.
Ex.

B4031 Boyle, Robert, 1671
Ex.

B4034 Boyle, Robert, 1663
Ex. S Pl.

B4035 Boyle, Robert, 1665
Pet.

B4038 Boyle, Robert, 1678
S Asa.

B4041 Boyle, Robert, 1700
Chi. Linc.

B4042 Boyle, Robert, 1675
=Pt 2 of B4024.
Carl. Ely. Ex.

B4050 Boyle, Robert, 1672
Yk.

B4051 Boyle, Robert, 1676
Linc. Yk.

B4052- Boyle, Robert, 1670
=Wing2 B4052.
Yk.

B4053- Boyle, Robert, 1673
As B4053, apart from date.
Wel.

B4053 Boyle, Robert, 1674
... in Oxford.
Wel.

B4054 Boyle, Robert, 1674
Pet. Sal.

B4056 Boyle, Robert, 1670
Yk (imp)*.

B4057 Boyle, Robert, 1671
Carl. Ex. Wel.

B4059 Boyle, Robert, 1671
Bris. Wel.

B4061 Boyle, Robert, 1673
Pet.

B4065 Boys, Edward, 1672
Nor.

B4066- Boys, John, *of Hode Court*,
1662
See: CLC16.
Cant.

B4066 Boys, John, *Prebendary of
Ely*, 1655
Impr. as Wing2.
Ches. Her. Linc. Nor. S Pl.

B4066+ Boys, John, *Prebendary of
Ely*, 1655
=Wing2 B4066A.
Ely. Ex.

B4067 Boys, William, 1680
Glo.

B4072 Boyse, Joseph, 1694
Carl. Pet.

B4083? Boyse, Joseph, 1688
'Calvinisticae'; ... sold by the
booksellers of London and
Westminster.
Nor.

B4084 Boyse, Joseph, 1690
S Asa.

B4087 *See*: B4152+

B4091 Brabourne, Theophilus, 1660
Win.

B4093+ Brabourne, Theophilus,
1653
See: CLC17.
Cant.

B4097 Brabourne, Theophilus, 1661
Carl.

B4097A Brachet de la Militière,
Théophile, 1653
Carl. Linc. Sal. Win.

B4097B Brachet de la Militière,
Théophile, 1654
Second ed. not on tp.
Bur. Yk.

B4107 Bradford, Samuel, 1699
Ban. Bur. Cant. Nor. S Asa.

B4108 Bradford, Samuel, 1700
Contains B4107, B4110-4116, B4118,
with added gen. tp.
Ban. S Asa.

B4109 Bradford, Samuel, 1700
... sold by John Nutt.
Wor.

B4110 Bradford, Samuel, 1699
Ban. Cant. Nor. S Asa.

B4111 Bradford, Samuel, 1699
Ban. Cant. Nor. S Asa.

B4112 Bradford, Samuel, 1699
Ban. Cant. Nor. S Asa. Wor.

B4113 Bradford, Samuel, 1699
'... April the 3d. 1699'
Ban. Cant. Nor. S Asa.

B4114 Bradford, Samuel, 1699
'... May the 1st, 1699'
Ban. Cant. Nor. S Asa.

B4115 Bradford, Samuel, 1700
Ban. Cant. Nor. S Asa.

B4116 Bradford, Samuel, 1699
Ban. Cant. Nor. S Asa.

B4117 Bradford, Samuel, 1698
Cant.

B4118 Bradford, Samuel, 1699
Ban. Cant. Nor. S Asa.

B4119 Bradford, Samuel, 1697
Bur. Cant.

B4121 Bradford, Samuel, 1699
Ban. Her. Wor.

B4122 Bradford, Samuel, 1700
Wor.

B4124 Bradley, Christopher, 1666
Yk (2 − 1 imp).

B4125 Bradley, John, 1699
Dur.

B4129 Bradley, Thomas, 1663
'Caesars due'
Yk.

B4129+ Bradley, Thomas, 1663
'Caesars due'; York, by Alice Broade;
4°.
Yk (2).

B4131 Bradley, Thomas, 1670
Dur. Yk.

B4131+ Bradley, Thomas, 1672
The second impression; York, by
Stephen Bulkley and to be sold at the
Cross Swords in Stonegate; 4°.
Yk.

B4132 Bradley, Thomas, 1669
Yk.

B4133+ Bradley, Thomas, 1672
The second impression; York, by
Stephen Bulkley at the Cross Swords
in Stonegate; 4°.
Yk.

B4134 Bradley, Thomas, 1668
Yk (tpw).

B4136 Bradley, Thomas, 1668
4°.
Yk.

B4137 Bradley, Thomas, 1663
Carl. Yk (2).

B4137A Bradley, Thomas, 1661
Yk.

B4138 Bradley, Thomas, 1663
Yk (2).

B4140 Bradshaw, Ellis, 1656
... Lodowike Lloyd.
Sal.

B4152- Bradshaw, John, 1660
=Wing2 B4151B?; 'Brittain'; Rothwel.
Wor.

B4152+ Bradshaw, John, 1679
=Wing2 B4152B.
Linc.

B4154+ Bradshaw, John, 1663
As B4154, but dated 1663.
S Asa.

B4157 Bradshaw, William, 1658
Sal.

B4158 Bradshaw, William, 1641
Yk.

B4161 Bradshaw, William, 1660
Cant. Carl. Pet. Win. Wor.

B4162 Bradshaw, William, 1660
Cant. Yk.

B4169 Brady, Nicholas, 1697
Ex. Her.

B4175 Brady, Nicholas, 1693
S Asa.

B4176 Brady, Nicholas, 1693
Her.

B4177 Brady, Nicholas, 1694
Ely. Her. Nor (2).

B4178 Brady, Nicholas, 1695
Ches. Ex.

B4179 Brady, Nicholas, 1695
S Asa. Wor.

B4180? Brady, Nicholas, 1696
4°.
Cant.

B4181 Brady, Nicholas, 1696
Cant.

B4186 Brady, Robert, 1685
Cant. Dur. Ex. Glo. Nor.
Swel. Wel. Win.

B4187+ Brady, Robert, 1700
=Wing2 B4187A; Churchil.
Dur. Ex. Nor.

B4192 Brady, Robert, 1690
Cant.

B4193 Brady, Robert, [1690?]
Wel.

B4194 Brady, Robert, 1684
Ban. Cant. Dur. Glo. Nor.
Sal. Wel. Win. Wor. Yk.

B4195 Brady, Robert, 1681
Carl.

B4199 Bragge, Francis, 1699
Yk.

B4203 Bragge, Robert, 1676
Impr. as Wing2.
Her.

B4204? Bragge, Robert, 1677
4°.
Cant.

B4210 Bramhall, John, 1676
... Majesties ...
Ex. Nor.

B4211 Bramhall, John, 1677
Second ed. not on tp; 1050p.
Cant (2). Chi*. Dur. Ely*. Glo.
Lich*. Pet*. S Asa*. S Dv*.
S Pl*. Sal*. Wel. Win*. Wor*.
Yk*.

B4211+ Bramhall, John, 1677
As B4211, but: 1053p.
Ban. Bur.

B4214 Bramhall, John, 1657
Carl.

B4215 Bramhall, John, 1658
Bur. Linc. Yk.

B4216 Bramhall, John, 1658
Carl. Lich (2). Linc (2). Yk.

B4218 Bramhall, John, 1655
Bur. Carl. Ely. Linc. Yk.

B4220 Bramhall, John, [1661]
Dur. Yk.

B4221 Bramhall, John, [1649?]
Linc.

B4222 Bramhall, John, 1649
Carl. Ex. Pet. S Pl.

B4223 Bramhall, John, 1649
Pet. Yk.

B4223+ Bramhall, John, 1649
As B4223, but: 'faire'
Linc.

B4226 Bramhall, John, 1654
Carl. Lich. Linc. Pet. S Pl.
Sal.

B4227 Bramhall, John, 1661
Sal.

B4228 Bramhall, John, 1656
Carl. Linc. Pet. S Pl. Sal. Yk.

B4230 Bramhall, John, 1659
Carl. Lich (2). Yk.

B4232 Bramhall, John, 1658
'garded'
Carl. Lich (2). Linc. Sal. Yk
(2).

B4233 Bramhall, John, 1643
Dur. Yk.

B4234? Bramhall, John, 1643[4]
... Yorke ...
Carl.

B4236 Bramhall, John, 1643
Carl. Yk.

B4236+ Bramhall, John, 1643
=Wing2 B4236A; York, by Stephen
Bulkley.
Yk.

B4237 Bramhall, John, 1672
8°.
Carl. Linc. S Pl. Sal (imp). Yk.

B4238 Bramhall, William, 1668
Yk (imp).

B4243 Bramston, William, 1697
Cant. S Asa.

B4251 Brandon, John, *of Finchampsted*, 1678
Dur. Win. Yk.

B4256 Brathwaite, Richard, 1641
Yk.

B4260B Brathwaite, Richard, 1665
Wing has wrong date.
Linc.

B4262 Brathwaite, Richard, 1641
The third edition.
Ex.

B4281 Brave, 1642
Yk.

B4283 Bray, Thomas, 1700
Carl.

B4285 Bray, Thomas, 1698
Cant.

B4286 Bray, Thomas, 1699
Second ed. not on tp.
Nor.

B4287 Bray, Thomas, 1700
Third ed. not on tp.
Dur. New.

B4290 Bray, Thomas, 1697
... for Robert Clavel.
Cant. Ely. Ex. S Asa.

B4292 Bray, Thomas, 1696
... Litchfield, for the author.
Ban. Ex. Lich. S Pl.

B4292A Bray, Thomas, 1697
Entry as Wing2.
Chi.

B4292A+ Bray, Thomas, 1699
The third edition; Amsterdam, printed in the year; 8°.
Yk.

B4294 Bray, Thomas, 1700
Carl.

B4297 Bray, Thomas, 1697
Ely.

B4299 Bray, Thomas, 1699
Ban.

B4299+ Bray, Thomas, 1700
=Wing2 B4299A; The second edition.
Her.

B4304 Bray, William, *Captain*, 1649
Cant. Pet.

B4312 Bray, William, *Captain*, 1649
'honourable'
Ex. Pet.

B4316 Bray, William, *D.D.*, 1641
Ex (2). Linc (2 – 1 imp). Wor.

B4335+ Breach, 1648
=Wing2 B4335; By Tho. Paine, for Edward Blackmore.
Pet.

B4338 Break-neck, 1644
Yk.

B4341 Breedon, Zachariah, 1649
Boler.
Yk.

B4374 Brerewood, Edward, 1649
Pet.

B4375 Brerewood, Edward, 1657
S Pl.

B4376 Brerewood, Edward, 1668
Ches. Yk.

B4378 Brerewood, Edward, 1674
8°.
Wel.

B4379 Brerewood, Edward, 1674
8°.
Bur (2). Lich. Linc. Yk.

B4379+ Brerewood, Edward, 1659
See: CLC18.
Cant.

B4380 Brerewood, Edward, 1659
... excudebat Hen: Hall, impensis Johan: Adams.
Cant.

B4381 Brès, Guy de, 1668
Yk.

B4382 Brethren, 1690
Ex (imp).

B4401 Bréval, François Durant de, 1670
Cant. S Asa. Win.

B4402 Bréval, François Durant de, 1670
Carl. S Asa.

B4405 Bréval, François Durant de, 1671
Win.

B4409 Breviate, [1689?]
Wel.

B4416 Breviate, [1648]
Ex.

B4417 Brevint, Daniel, 1673
S Asa. Win.

B4418 Brevint, Daniel, 1673
12°.
Cant. Yk.

B4419? Brevint, Daniel, 1679
12°.
Dur.

B4420 Brevint, Daniel, 1672
Carl. Chelm. Dur. Ex (2). Linc. New. S Pl. Yk.

B4421 Brevint, Daniel, 1673
Pet. Win.

B4421+ Brevint, Daniel, 1673
=Wing2 B4421A.
Cant (2 – 1 imp). Carl.

B4422 Brevint, Daniel, 1686
Impr. as Wing2.
Cant.

B4423 Brevint, Daniel, 1674
Cant. Carl. Ches. Dur. Ely. Ex (2). Lich. Linc. Nor. S Asa. S Pl. Wel. Win. Wor. Yk.

B4424 Brevis, 1674
Carl.

B4440 Brice, Germain, 1687
Ex.

B4448 Bridge, William, 1641
Ex.

B4451 Bridge, William, 1648
Pet.

B4454 Bridge, William, 1671
Carl.

B4461 Bridge, William, 1647
Ex. Yk.

B4464 Bridge, William, 1642
Ex.

B4466 Bridge, William, 1642[3]
Cant (2). Chelm. Pet.

B4467 Bridge, William, 1643
Cant (imp).

B4470 Bridge, William, 1642
Ex.

B4476 Bridge, William, 1642
Cant (2). Chelm.

B4483A Bridges, W., 1643
Cant (2 eds: 'counsell, and' *or* 'counsell and'). Chelm. Nor.

B4487 Bridgman, *Sir* John, 1659
Dur.

B4494 Bridgman, Robert, 1700
Wel.

B4495 Bridoul, Toussaint, 1687
Bur. Ex (2 – 1 tpw). Lich. Nor. Sal. Swel. Wel. Yk (2).

B4496 Bridoul, Toussaint, 1687
For Randal Taylor.
Cant (imp).

B4512 Brief, 1689
Carl.

B4516 Brief, 1682
Win.

B4520 Brief, 1679
Ban. Linc.

B4533 Brief, 1690
Cant (imp).

B4538 Brief, 1650
Yk.

B4540 Briefe, 1642[3]
Cant.

B4548 Brief, 1653
'apology'
Chelm.

B4552 Brief, 1664
Carl.

B4558 Brief, [1680]
Ches.

B4565 Brief, 1647
brs.; Madan 1919.
Carl.

B4567- Brief, 1652
=Wing2 B4567; ... Timothie
Garthwait.
S Asa.

B4582 Brief, 1654
Ex.

B4583 Brief, 1648
Yk.

B4597 Brief, 1689
Wel.

B4599 Brief, 1690
Carl.

B4607 Briefe, 1643
Impr. as Wing2.
Pet.

B4612 Brief, 1663
Dur.

B4614 Brief, 1643
Linc. Pet.

B4622 Briefe, 1642[3]
Date wrongly entered in Wing.
Linc.

B4629 Brief, 1662
S Pl.

B4629+ Brief, 1664
=Wing2 B4629A; 'Tangier'; By T.
Mabb.
Sal.

B4642 Brief, 1658
Carl. Chelm.

B4644 Briefe, 1650
4°.
Pet.

B4644+ Brief, 1661
=Wing2 B4645.
Cant.

B4656 Brief, 1689
Wel. Yk.

B4656+ Brief, 1670
=Wing2 B4656A.
Win.

B4659 Brierley, Roger, 1677
Yk (2).

B4662 Briggs, Joseph, 1696
Yk.

B4668 Briggs, William, 1676
... Joan. Hayes, ... Jon. Hart; 8°.
Ex.

B4672 Bright, George, 1682
Carl. Pet.

B4677 Bright, George, 1678
Ely. Pet.

B4679 Brightman, Thomas, 1644
Sal.

B4691 Brightman, Thomas, 1647
Ex.

B4692 Brightman, Thomas, 1644
Bur. Carl.

B4693 Brightman, Thomas, 1644
The fourth edition.
Ex.

B4705+ Brinsley, John, *the Younger*,
[1650]
As B4705, but no date.
Ex.

B4707 Brinsley, John, *the Younger*,
1646
'arraignment'
Ex. Yk (2).

B4709 Brinsley, John, *the Younger*,
1648
Pet.

B4711 Brinsley, John, *the Younger*,
1643
Ex.

B4712 Brinsley, John, *the Younger*,
1645
Ex. Pet.

B4714 Brinsley, John, *the Younger*,
1658
Dur.

B4715 Brinsley, John, *the Younger*,
1659
Chelm.

B4716 Brinsley, John, *the Younger*,
1642
Ex (2 – 1 imp). Yk.

B4719 Brinsley, John, *the Younger*,
1653
Maxey.
Ex.

B4721 Brinsley, John, *the Younger*,
1652
Maxey.
Chelm.

B4722 Brinsley, John, *the Younger*,
1643
Pet.

B4725 Brinsley, John, *the Younger*,
1645
Yk (tpw).

B4730 Brinsley, John, *the Younger*,
1647
Ex. Pet. Yk.

B4737 Brinsley, John, *the Younger*,
1651
Maxey.
Chelm.

B4761 Bristol, George Digby, *Earl
of*, 1642[3]
Carl. Pet.

B4762 Bristol, George Digby, *Earl
of*, 1642[3]
Linc (2).

B4763 Bristol, George Digby, *Earl
of*, 1646
... March 26. ...
Ex. Yk.

B4767 Bristol, George Digby, *Earl
of*, 1641
Cant (imp).

B4768 Bristol, George Digby, *Earl
of*, 1651
Carl. Ex. Yk (March 39, 1639).

B4771? Bristol, George Digby, *Earl
of*, 1641
'21 of April'; 10p.
Carl. Linc. Yk*.

B4771+ Bristol, George Digby, *Earl
of*, 1641
'21 of April'; 5 [*i.e.* 12]p.
Cant.

B4774 Bristol, George Digby, *Earl
of*, 1641
Walkely.
Linc. Sal. Yk.

B4774+ Bristol, George Digby, *Earl
of*, 1641
As B4774, but: Walkley.
Cant.

B4775 Bristol, George Digby, *Earl
of*, 1640[1]
=STC 6844.
Cant. Linc. Pet. Yk (2 – both
imp).

B4777 Bristol, George Digby, *Earl
of*, 1643
Sal.

B4779 Bristol, George Digby, *Earl
of*, 1642
Linc.

B4781 Bristol, George Digby, *Earl of*, 1642
Yk.

B4783 Bristol, George Digby, *Earl of*, 1642
Linc. Yk.

B4784 Bristol, George Digby, *Earl of*, 1642
Ex.

B4786 Bristol, George Digby, *Earl of*, 1674
Linc.

B4788 Bristol, John Digby, *Earl of*, 1656
S Pl.

B4789 Bristol, John Digby, *Earl of*, 1657
Carl.

B4792 *See*: T1042A

B4794 Bristol, John Digby, *Earl of*, 1642
Cant. Ex. Yk (tp imp)*.

B4798 Bristol, John Digby, *Earl of*, 1642
Cant.

B4804 Britaine, William de, 1672
Linc.

B4808 Britaine, William de, 1672
Pet.

B4815+ Britania, 1698
=Wing2 B4815?; 'Britania ...'
Cant.

B4817 Britannia, 1654
Carl.

B4833 Brocardo, Francisco, 1679
Cant. Dur. S Asa.

B4840+ Broeckhuysen, Benjamin, 1684
'Catalogus librorum ... quorum auctio habenda est Londini ... Decembris 1. 1684. per Guilielmum Cooper'; [London?]; 4°.
Wor.

B4841 Brograve, Robert, 1689
Cant. S Asa.

B4844 Brokesby, Francis, 1680
Yk.

B4851 Brome, Alexander, 1662
8°.
Ex.

B4853 Brome, Alexander, 1664
Ex.

B4899 Brooke, Fulke Greville, *Baron*, 1652
Carl. Liv.

B4900 Brooke, Fulke Greville, *Baron*, 1670
Ex. Win.

B4907 Brooke, Nathaniel, 1660
Impr. as Wing2.
Cant (imp). Linc. Sal (imp).

B4911 Brooke, Robert Greville, *Baron*, 1641
Cant. Linc. Sal.

B4912 Brooke, Robert Greville, *Baron*, 1642
Cant. Her. S Asa. Yk.

B4913 Brooke, Robert Greville, *Baron*, 1641
Linc.

B4914 Brooke, Robert Greville, *Baron*, 1642
Cant.

B4914+ Brooke, Robert Greville, *Baron*, 1642
Printed for Thomas Bates and Iohn Ball; 4°.
Cant.

B4916 Brooke, Samuel, [1680/1]
Pet.

B4920 Brookes, Thomas, 1657
In this second impression [follows contents list].
S Asa (imp).

B4938 Brookes, Thomas, 1653
Pet.

B4940 Brookes, Thomas, 1648
Cant.

B4983+ Brossard, Davy, 1651
=Wing2 B4983A?; 'The country-mans new art of planting'; By I. Bell ...
Yk.

B4987 Brough, William, 1657
Carl. Nor. S Asa. Yk.

B4991 Brough, William, 1650
Glo.

B4992 Brough, William, 1652
Yk.

B4992A? Brough, William, 1656
By T.N. for John Clark.
Yk.

B4997 Broughton, Hugh, 1662
Win.

B4999 Broughton, John, 1698
Ely.

B5001 Broughton, Richard, 1650
Ex. Yk.

B5002+ Broughton, William, (1678)
See: CLC19.
Ely.

B5003 Brousson, Claude, 1699
Ban.

B5003+ Browene, Richard, 1642
=Wing2 B5004.
Yk.

B5016A? Brown, Edward, 1699
'Novemb. the 16th'
Yk.

B5020 Brown, Humfrey, 1649[50]
Cant.

B5022 Brown, Ignatius, 1675
S Asa.

B5031 Brown, John, *of Wamphray*, 1695
Yk.

B5033 Brown, John, *of Wamphray*, 1678
Yk.

B5041 Brown, John, *Philomath*, 1671
'trianguler'
Cant (imp).

B5042 Brown, John, *Philomath*, 1671
Cant (sig. A only).

B5047+ Brown, Robert, 1658
Anr ed. of Wing2 B5047A; [N.pl.], for Giles Calvert and Dan. White; 8°.
Carl.

B5050 Brown, Robert, 1649
Chelm (imp). Nor. Pet (3 – 2 imp). S Asa (imp). Sal. Yk (2).

B5050+ Brown, Robert, 1649
Hage, by Samuel Broun; 8°.
Linc.

B5060? Brown, Thomas, 1688
Second ed. not in book; cap.
Pet.

B5067 Brown, Thomas, 1691
... assigns ...
Cant. Ely.

B5069 Brown, Thomas, 1688
Wel.

B5073 Brown, Thomas, 1691
Ban.

B5077 Brown, Thomas, 1691
Linc.

B5077+ Brown, Thomas, 1691
As B5077, but: 'Weesils ...'
Cant.

B5080+ Brown, William, 1695
=Wing2 B5080A?; The second edition; ... Joseph Raven.
Cant.

B5104 Browne, Edward, *Clerk*, [1642]
Pet.

B5108 Browne, Edward, *Compiler*, 1642
Ex.

B5109 Browne, Edward, *M.D.*, 1677
Sal.

B5110 Browne, Edward, *M.D.*, 1673
Cant. Linc. Sal.

B5115- Browne, Humphry, 1650
See: CLC20.
Pet.

B5121 Browne, John, *Quaker*, 1681
Yk.

B5122 Browne, John, *Surgeon*, 1684
Yk.

B5123 *See*: B5122

B5135 Browne, Peter, 1697
S Pl.

B5139 Browne, Philip, 1682
Pet.

B5150 Browne, *Sir* Thomas, 1686
Cant (3). Ex. Lich. Nor. S Asa. S Dv. Wel. Wor.

B5151 Browne, *Sir* Thomas, 1683
Cant.

B5152 Browne, *Sir* Thomas, 1684
Ely (imp)*. Nor.

B5154 Browne, *Sir* Thomas, 1658
Cant (variant of Keynes 93, no comma after 'Hydriotaphia').
Carl.

B5155- Browne, *Sir* Thomas, 1668
As B5155, apart from date; Pt of B5164.
Ex. Yk.

B5159 Browne, *Sir* Thomas, 1646
Cant. Glo. Lich. Linc. Yk.

B5160 Browne, *Sir* Thomas, 1650
Cant. Carl. Pet. Yk.

B5161 Browne, *Sir* Thomas, 1658
Cant (tpw).

B5162 Browne, *Sir* Thomas, 1658
Dur. Ely. Nor.

B5163 Browne, *Sir* Thomas, 1659
Cant. Linc.

B5164 Browne, *Sir* Thomas, 1669
Ex. Yk.

B5165 Browne, *Sir* Thomas, 1672
Cant (imp).

B5165+ Browne, *Sir* Thomas, 1686
The seventh and last edition; For Richard Chiswell, and Thomas Sawbridge; 2°.
Cant (3). Ex. Lich. Nor. S Asa. S Dv. Wel. Wor.

B5166 Browne, *Sir* Thomas, 1642
Ely*. Linc (imp).

B5169 Browne, *Sir* Thomas, 1643
Liv. Nor. Wel (tpw).

B5172 Browne, *Sir* Thomas, 1656
8°.
Carl.

B5173 Browne, *Sir* Thomas, [1659?]
Pt of B5163.
Cant. Linc.

B5175 Browne, *Sir* Thomas, 1669
Pet. Wel.

B5176 Browne, *Sir* Thomas, 1672
Cant. Carl*.

B5177 Browne, *Sir* Thomas, 1678
The seventh edition; 8°.
Cant. Win. Yk.

B5178 Browne, *Sir* Thomas, 1682
Yk.

B5181A Browne, Thomas, *Canon* , 1645
Carl. Win.

B5182 Browne, Thomas, *Fellow of St John's* , 1691
Llan.

B5184 Browne, Thomas, *Fellow of St John's*, 1688
Ex. Her. Win. Yk.

B5184A+ Browne, Thomas, *Fellow of St John's*, 1683
=Wing2 B5184A.
Ely (tpw). Ex.

B5184A *See*: B5184

B5185B- Browne, Thomas, *of London*, 1669
=Wing2 B5185AB; By Will. Godbid, to be sold at the Writing-School in Christ's-Hospital, and by Nathaniel Brooke .
Sal.

B5201? Brownlow, Richard, 1652
... and Henry Twyford.
Cant.

B5204 Brownrig, Ralph, 1661
Ban. Carl. Chi. Ex. Her. Linc. Nor. Sal (imp). Wor.

B5207 Brownrig, Ralph, 1685
Cant (imp).

B5207+ Brownrig, Ralph, 1685
Title reads 'Twenty five sermons', although it is another ed. of B5204; Impr. as Wing2 B5207.
Dur.

B5211 Brownrig, Ralph, 1674
Vol. 2 = B5213.
Bur (imp). Chi. Glo. Lich. Win.

B5211+ Brownrig, Ralph, 1686
By R.E., sold by John Salisbury; 2°; Vol. 2 = B5214.
Pet.

B5212 Brownrig, Ralph, 1664
Carl. Ex. Her. Nor. Wel. Win. Wor.

B5213 Brownrig, Ralph, 1674
Bur. Chi. Glo. Lich. Win.

B5214 Brownrig, Ralph, 1685
Cant. Dur. Pet.

B5221 Bruce, Titus, 1682
Date as Wing2.
Llan.

B5231 Bruning, Benjamin, 1660
Bur. Cant. Chi (tpw).

B5233 Brunsell, Samuel, 1660
Carl. Linc.

B5247 Bryan, Matthew, 1686
Her.

B5248 Bryan, Matthew, 1692
Wel.

B5253 Brydall, John, 1676
S Pl.

B5255 Brydall, John, 1679
Carl. Win.

B5264 Brydall, John, 1682
Entry as Wing2.
S Asa.

B5270 Bucer, Martin, 1644
Carl. S Pl.

B5274 Buchanan, David, 1645
Linc.

B5276 Buchanan, George, 1689
Pet.

B5292 Buchanan, George, 1686
Nor. S Pl.

B5298 Buchanan, George, 1642[3]
Pet. Yk.

B5300 Buchler, Johann, 1642
Ex.

B5306 Buck, *Sir* George, 1646
Ban. Chelm. Yk.

B5307 Buck, *Sir* George, 1647
Second ed. not on tp; Impr. as B5306.
Chi (imp). Linc.

B5308 Buck, James, 1660
Carl. Pet.

B5310 Buckingham, George Villiers, *Duke of,* 1648
Yk.

B5312 Buckingham, George Villiers, *Duke of,* 1672
Dur.

B5313 Buckingham, George Villiers, *Duke of,* 1672
Win.

B5329 Buckingham, George Villiers, *Duke of,* 1685
Carl. Dur (imp). Ex. Her. S Pl.

B5330 Buckingham, George Villiers, *Duke of,* 1685
Carl. Wel.

B5333? Buckingham, George Villiers, *Duke of,* 1677
'1676' in title.
Cant.

B5347 Buckler, Edward, 1647
Carl.

B5351 Buckler, Edward, [1658]
Win.

B5352 Buckley, Francis, 1660
Pet.

B5362 Budgell, Gilbert, 1690
Cant.

B5366 Bugg, Francis, 1690/1
S Pl (2).

B5368 Bugg, Francis, 1700
S Pl.

B5369 Bugg, Francis, 1699
S Pl (2).

B5371 Bugg, Francis, [1684]
cap.
S Pl (2).

B5372 Bugg, Francis, [1699]
8° and 12°.
S Pl (2).

B5374 Bugg, Francis, 1690
S Pl (2).

B5374A+ Bugg, Francis, 1689
As B5374A, but: The second edition; Also attrib. to J. Pennyman.
Wel.

B5375? Bugg, Francis, 1700
... Ch. Broome ...
S Pl (2).

B5376? Bugg, Francis, 1693
... J. Guillim.
S Pl.

B5377 Bugg, Francis, 1694
S Pl. Swel.

B5378 Bugg, Francis, 1692
S Pl (2).

B5379 Bugg, Francis, 1691
S Pl (2).

B5380 Bugg, Francis, 1683
S Pl (2).

B5381 Bugg, Francis, 1697
Ely. S Pl.

B5382 Bugg, Francis, 1698
Ely. S Pl. Swel. Yk.

B5383 Bugg, Francis, 1700
S Pl.

B5384 Bugg, Francis, [1694]
'anatomiz'd'
S Pl (3). Swel.

B5385 Bugg, Francis, 1699
56p., followed by B5372.
S Pl.

B5385+ Bugg, Francis, 1699
As B5385, but: 64p.; pp. 57–64 = a shorter version of B5372.
S Pl.

B5386 Bugg, Francis, 1694
S Pl (3).

B5387 Bugg, Francis, 1686
S Pl (2).

B5388 Bugg, Francis, 1696
S Pl. Swel. Wel.

B5389 Bugg, Francis, 1696
S Pl.

B5391 Bugg, Francis, 1695
'The Quakers ...'
S Pl. Swel.

B5392? Bugg, Francis, 1695
... John Guillam.
S Pl (2). Swel.

B5393 Bugg, Francis, 1698
Swel.

B5394 Bugg, Francis, [1697/8]
S Pl (2).

B5395? Bugg, Francis, 1693
... and Richard Baldwin.
S Pl.

B5397 Bugg, Francis, [1693]
S Pl.

B5399 Bugg, Francis, [1700]
S Pl.

B5403 Bulkley, Peter, 1646
Yk.

B5404+ Bulkley, Peter, 1651
The second edition; By Matthew Simmons; 4°.
Carl. Chelm.

B5406 Bulkley, Richard, 1685
Wor.

B5409 Bull, Digby, 1695
Wel.

B5410 Bull, Digby, 1695
Ex. Wel.

B5412 Bull, Digby, 1695
Pet. Wel.

B5413 Bull, Digby, 1695
Wel.

B5414 Bull, George, 1685
Ban. Ely. Ex. Glo. S Pl. Sal. Wel. Wor.

B5416 Bull, George, 1676
... Oxoniensem.
Carl. Ely. Ex. Her. Llan.

B5417 Bull, George, 1670
Ely. Ex. Her. Llan. Wel. Wor.

B5418 Bull, George, 1694
Ex. Llan. Wel.

B5424 Bullingham, Nicolas, 1665
Ex.

B5429 Bullokar, John, 1641
Third ed. not on tp.
Cant.

B5452 Bulteel, John, *the Elder,* 1645
Cant (imp). Pet.

B5460 Bulwer, John, 1650
12°.
Cant (imp). Carl (tp imp).

B5462 Bulwer, John, 1644
Carl.

B5468 Bulwer, John, 1649
Carl.

B5469 Bulwer, John, 1648
'dumbe'
Cant. Carl. Linc.

B5473A *See*: P569+

B5482 Bunyan, John, 1698
Cant (imp).

B5483 Bunyan, John, 1688
Yk.

B5488 Bunyan, John, 1698
London, by R. Janeway, jun., for Jonathan Robinson; 12°.
Yk.

B5498 Bunyan, John, 1686
The third edition; Found with 'Jesus Christ' in roman *or* B.L. type.
Cant (imp; 'Jesus Christ' in B.L.).

B5512 Bunyan, John, 1685
For Jo. Harris.
Dur.

B5547 Bunyan, John, 1697
The third edition.
Yk.

B5553? Bunyan, John, 1696
... Nath. Ponder.
Yk.

B5570 Bunyan, John, 1684
The ninth edition; For Nathanael
Ponder.
Cant (imp).

B5580 Bunyan, John, 1690
Cant.

B5583 Bunyan, John, 1693
Not by Bunyan.
Cant (imp).

B5611 Burbury, John, 1671
Linc.

B5616 Burd, Richard, 1684
'May 29.'
Llan. S Pl.

B5629 Burgersdijck, Franco, 1667
Dur.

B5630? Burgersdijck, Franco, 1644
Cantabrigiae ...
Her. Linc.

B5631 Burgersdijck, Franco, 1647
Yk.

B5632 Burgersdijck, Franco, 1651
Carl. Ex.

B5633 Burgersdijck, Franco, 1660
Yk.

B5634 Burgersdijck, Franco, 1666
S Pl.

B5636 Burgersdijck, Franco, 1680
Ches. S Asa. Yk.

B5637 *See*: B5634

B5638 Burgersdijck, Franco, 1653
Carl.

B5643 Burgess, Anthony, 1643
Title as Wing2.
Ex.

B5646 Burgess, Anthony, 1659
Her. Swel.

B5651 Burgess, Anthony, 1656
Carl.

B5651+ Burgess, Anthony, 1663
London; 2°.
Carl. Ex.

B5655 Burgess, Anthony, 1645
Her. Pet.

B5656 Burgess, Anthony, 1659
Ex.

B5657 Burgess, Anthony, 1652
Cant (imp). Chi. Ex. Yk.

B5658- Burgess, Anthony, 1654
=Wing2 B5657A?; By A.M. ...
Carl. Ex.

B5658+ Burgess, Anthony, 1654
=Wing2 B5658A?; By T.U., sold by
Thomas Newberry; 4°.
Carl.

B5663 Burgess, Anthony, 1651
'... asserted and vindicated, from the
errours of Papists ...'
Ex. Glo.

B5664 Burgess, Anthony, 1654
'... asserted & vindicated from the
errours of many ...'
Chelm. Glo. Pet.

B5665 Burgess, Anthony, 1655
'... justification, in two parts'; Pt 1:
The third edition; Pt 2 = B5664.
Chelm. Pet.

B5666 Burgess, Anthony, 1646
Ex.

B5667 Burgess, Anthony, 1647
Pet.

B5668 Burgess, Cornelius, 1641
Cant. Ex (2). Nor. Pet (2).
Wel. Yk.

B5669 Burgess, Cornelius, 1642
Yk.

B5670 Burgess, Cornelius, 1659
Carl. Yk (2).

B5671 Burgess, Cornelius, 1641
Found with, or without colophon: By
T.B. ...
Carl. Her (with colophon). Pet
(2 − 1 with colophon, 1 without).
S Pl (without colophon).

B5672 Burgess, Cornelius, 1641
Pet.

B5673 Burgess, Cornelius, 1645
Pet. Yk.

B5675 Burgess, Cornelius, 1659
Impr. as Wing2.
Carl.

B5676 Burgess, Cornelius, 1660
Dur. Yk.

B5678 Burgess, Cornelius, 1660
Carl. Ely. Yk (2).

B5679 Burgess, Cornelius, 1660
Pet (tp imp). S Pl (imp).

B5683 Burgess, Cornelius, 1641
Linc. Nor. S Asa.

B5684 Burgess, Cornelius, 1641
Ex (2).

B5686 Burgess, Cornelius, [1660]
cap.
Dur. Linc.

B5687 Burgess, Cornelius, 1641
Carl.

B5689 Burgess, Cornelius, 1645
... for Christopher Meredith.
S Pl.

B5690 Burgess, Cornelius, 1648
Dur (tp imp).

B5692 Burgess, Cornelius, 1641
Cant (tp imp).

B5693 Burgess, Daniel, 1675
Cant.

B5694 Burgess, Daniel, 1690
S Asa.

B5720 Burgess, John, 1642
Pet.

B5726 Burghley, William Cecil,
Baron, 1687
Wrongly moved to A801A in Wing2.
Wor.

B5732 Burghope, George, 1695
Carl (2).

B5737 Burkitt, William, 1680
By M.W. ...
Her.

B5754 Burnet, Gilbert, 1682
S Dv.

B5755+ Burnet, Gilbert, 1682
By J.D. for Richard Chiswell, sold by
John Lawrence.
Liv.

B5756 Burnet, Gilbert, 1683
Cant (imp?). Liv. Nor. S Asa.
Yk.

B5757 Burnet, Gilbert, 1688
Cant (imp).

B5759 Burnet, Gilbert, [1687]
Pet.

B5761 Burnet, Gilbert, 1682
Ban. Cant. Wel.

B5762 Burnet, Gilbert, [1688]
Cant (2 eds: 'Church of England'
in B.L. *or* roman). Carl. Pet.

B5766 Burnet, Gilbert, 1700
Wor (imp). Yk.

B5768 Burnet, Gilbert, 1689
Cant. Carl. Ex. Wel.

B5770 Burnet, Gilbert, 1685
Llan. Wel.

B5771+ Burnet, Gilbert, [1688]
=Wing2 B5771A; 'Enquiry'
Dur.

B5772 Burnet, Gilbert, 1680
Cant. Carl. Pet.

B5774 Burnet, Gilbert, 1687
12°.
Ex. Nor.

B5775 Burnet, Gilbert, 1688
Ex. Wel.

B5776 Burnet, Gilbert, 1692
8°.
Bur. Ches. Chi. Dur. Ex. Linc.
Llan. Nor. S Asa. S Pl. Sal (2).
Swel. Wel.

B5777 Burnet, Gilbert, 1692
Second ed. not on tp; For Richard
Chiswell; 4°.
Sal.

B5779 Burnet, Gilbert, 1688
Cant (imp). Ex (2). S Dv. S Pl.
Yk.

B5780 Burnet, Gilbert, 1688
Bris. Wel.

B5783 Burnet, Gilbert, 1695
For Ric. Chiswell.
Cant (3 − 1 imp). Carl. Llan.

B5786 Burnet, Gilbert, 1696
The second edition.
Pet.

B5787 Burnet, Gilbert, 1681
Cant (2). Carl. Wor.

B5791 Burnet, Gilbert, 1699
2°.
Ban. Cant. Carl. Chi. Ely.
Linc. Pet. Rip. S Asa. S Pl.
Sal.

B5792 Burnet, Gilbert, 1700
Bur (2). Chi. Dur. Ely. Lich.
New. Nor. Pet. S Asa. Sal.
Swel (2). Wel. Wor.

B5793 Burnet, Gilbert, 1694
Cant. Ches. Dur. Ely. Her.
Llan. Nor. S Asa (2). S Pl.
Swel.

B5794 Burnet, Gilbert, 1689
S Pl.

B5795? Burnet, Gilbert, 1683−85
Impr. as Wing2, but: Chiswell.
S Pl.

B5796 Burnet, Gilbert, 1688
4°.
Dur. Lich. S Pl.

B5797 Burnet, Gilbert, 1679
Pt 1.
Cant (2). Carl. Ches. Dur.
Linc. Pet. Swel. Wel. Win. Yk.

B5798 Burnet, Gilbert, 1681
Pt 1.
Bur. Chi (2). Glo (2). Her (2).
IoM. Lich. Nor. S Dv. Sal (3).
Wor. Yk.

B5799- Burnet, Gilbert, 1681
=Wing2 B5798A.
Cant. Carl. Chelm. Dur. Glo
(3). Her. Pet. Sal. Swel. Wel.
Win. Wor. Yk.

B5799 Burnet, Gilbert, 1683
The second edition.
Bur. Ches. Chi. Her. Lich.
Nor. S Dv. Sal (2).

B5801 Burnet, Gilbert, 1682
8°.
Cant. Carl. Chi. Ely. Ex.
S Asa. S Pl. Sal. Wel.

B5802 Burnet, Gilbert, 1688
S Pl.

B5804 Burnet, Gilbert, 1685
8°.
Ex. Nor.

B5805 Burnet, Gilbert, 1680
Bris. Carl. Sal. Yk.

B5808 Burnet, Gilbert, [1688]
Cant. Dur. Lich.

B5810 Burnet, Gilbert, 1693
Yk.

B5811 Burnet, Gilbert, 1689
Ban (2). S Asa. Wel. Yk.

B5813 Burnet, Gilbert, [1688]
Dur. Wel.

B5815 Burnet, Gilbert, [1689]
Pet.

B5816 Burnet, Gilbert, [1686]
Pet*.

B5818 Burnet, Gilbert, 1685
Cant.

B5823 Burnet, Gilbert, 1689
Carl. Ex. Wel.

B5824 Burnet, Gilbert, 1693
'... of Cov. ...'
Cant. Dur. Yk.

B5825 Burnet, Gilbert, 1678
Carl. Dur. Wel. Win.

B5828 Burnet, Gilbert, 1682
Second ed. not on tp.
Ban. Carl. Ely. Ex. S Asa. Yk.

B5828A Burnet, Gilbert, 1682
Cant (imp).

B5828A+ Burnet, Gilbert, 1696
=Wing2 B5828B; 8°.
Linc.

B5830 Burnet, Gilbert, 1685
Cant (imp). Carl. Ely. Ex (2).
Liv (pt 2 only). S Pl (2). Wel.
Yk (tpw).

B5831 Burnet, Gilbert, 1692
Second ed. not on tp.
Ches. Liv. Yk.

B5832 Burnet, Gilbert, 1677
Cant. Carl. Chi. Ely. Linc.
Swel (2 − both imp). Win (imp).

B5833 Burnet, Gilbert, 1669
Carl.

B5835 Burnet, Gilbert, 1676
Bur. Carl. Chelm. Linc. Wel.
Win.

B5836 Burnet, Gilbert, 1676
Carl.

B5838 Burnet, Gilbert, 1673
Bur. Ex. Linc. Win.

B5839 Burnet, Gilbert, 1682
Cant. Carl. Wel. Win.

B5840 Burnet, Gilbert, 1673
8°.
Carl. Ely. Ex. Nor. Wel.

B5841 Burnet, Gilbert, 1698
S Asa. Wor.

B5842 Burnet, Gilbert, 1689
Ban. Bris. Bur. Cant (2 − 1
imp). Carl. Her. Pet. Sal (2).
Yk (2).

B5845 Burnet, Gilbert, 1685
Ban. Bur. Chi. Ex (2). Nor.
Wel.

B5846 Burnet, Gilbert, 1675
Ex. Linc.

B5847 Burnet, Gilbert, 1687
Pet.

B5848 Burnet, Gilbert, 1700
Ban. Cant (imp). Ex. S Asa.
Yk.

B5849+ Burnet, Gilbert, [1688?]
'Reflections on a pamphlet ...';
[N.pl.]; cap.; 4°.
Dur.

B5850 Burnet, Gilbert, 1689
S Asa. S Pl.

B5852 Burnet, Gilbert, 1686
Carl. Yk.

B5852+ Burnet, Gilbert, 1686
=Wing2 B5852A.
Linc. Sal.

B5854 Burnet, Gilbert, 1688
Ban. Llan. S Pl. Sal. Wel.

B5856 Burnet, Gilbert, 1688
Ex.

B5857 Burnet, Gilbert, 1688
Cant. Carl.

B5860 Burnet, Gilbert, 1696
8°.
Cant. Carl. Ex. Pet. Wel.

B5861 Burnet, Gilbert, 1676
Bur. Cant. Chi. Ex. Linc.
S Asa. S Pl. Sal. Win.

B5863 Burnet, Gilbert, 1687
Cant. Ex. Sal. Wor.

B5868 Burnet, Gilbert, 1673
Carl. Linc.

B5869 Burnet, Gilbert, 1675
Consists of B5870- & B5928.
S Asa.

B5870- Burnet, Gilbert, 1675
For R. Royston; 4°.
S Asa. Sal.

B5870 Burnet, Gilbert, 1689
Cant (with half-title as B5869).
Her. Llan. New.

B5871- Burnet, Gilbert, 1689
See: CLC21.
Cant. Yk.

B5872 Burnet, Gilbert, 1680
Llan (2). New. Wor.

B5873 Burnet, Gilbert, 1681
Chiswel.
Cant. Carl. Her. S Pl.

B5874 Burnet, Gilbert, 1681
Ban. Cant (2 – 1 imp). Carl.
S Dv (imp). Wor.

B5875 Burnet, Gilbert, 1681
Cant (2 – 1 imp). Chi. Llan.
New. Wor.

B5876 Burnet, Gilbert, 1681
Chiswel.
Carl. Sal.

B5878 Burnet, Gilbert, 1682
Chiswel.
Cant (2). Chi. Her. Llan.

B5879 Burnet, Gilbert, 1684
Ex. Wor.

B5881 Burnet, Gilbert, 1689
Ban. Cant (2 – 1 imp). Wor.
Yk.

B5884 Burnet, Gilbert, 1689
The second edition.
Nor.

B5885 Burnet, Gilbert, 1689
Impr. not misprinted.
Ban. Her. Nor. Pet. Sal. Wor.
Yk (3).

B5888 Burnet, Gilbert, 1689
Ban. Cant (3 [tp in 2 states] – 1
imp). Carl. Dur (imp). Ely. Ex
(2). New. Nor. Pet. S Asa. Sal.
Wor. Yk (2).

B5889 Burnet, Gilbert, 1689
Chiswel.
Cant. Ex. Her (2). Sal. Yk (2).

B5890 Burnet, Gilbert, MDCLXC
[*i.e.* 1690]
Cant. Sal. Wel. Yk.

B5891 Burnet, Gilbert, 1690
S Pl. Sal. Wel. Wor.

B5892 Burnet, Gilbert, 1690
Wor.

B5893 Burnet, Gilbert, 1690
Dur. Ely. Wel. Wor.

B5896 Burnet, Gilbert, 1691
Ban. Ex.

B5897 Burnet, Gilbert, 1691
Ban. Her. Nor. Wor.

B5899 Burnet, Gilbert, 1692
'A sermon preached at the funeral of
... Robert Boyle; ... January 7.
1691/2'
Cant (3). Chelm. Ely. Her (2).
S Dv. Sal. Wor. Yk.

B5900 Burnet, Gilbert, 1694
Cant. Carl. Her.

B5902 Burnet, Gilbert, 1694
Cant (2). Chelm. Ches. Ex.
Her (3). Llan. Pet. S Dv. Wor.

B5904 Burnet, Gilbert, 1695
Ban. Cant. Carl. S Asa. Wor.

B5905 Burnet, Gilbert, 1697
Cant. Carl. Her. Wor.

B5906 Burnet, Gilbert, 1697
Cant.

B5906+ Burnet, Gilbert, 1698
As B5906, apart from date?
Bur.

B5907 Burnet, Gilbert, 1698
Bur. Her (2). Sal.

B5909 Burnet, Gilbert, 1698
The second edition.
Wor.

B5912 Burnet, Gilbert, 1687
Ban. Cant. Dur.

B5913 Burnet, Gilbert, 1689
S Asa. S Pl. Yk.

B5914 Burnet, Gilbert, 1686
Linc. Sal.

B5915 Burnet, Gilbert, 1686
Cant.

B5916 Burnet, Gilbert, 1686
Impr. as B5915.
Sal. Yk.

B5917 Burnet, Gilbert, 1687
Ex.

B5918 Burnet, Gilbert, 1687
The second edition.
Ely.

B5922 Burnet, Gilbert, 1680
Carl. Ely. Ex. Nor. Sal.

B5923? Burnet, Gilbert, 1681
Dublin, reprinted by Joseph Ray, for
William Winter, and Eliphal Dobson;
4°.
Cant.

B5925? Burnet, Gilbert, 1700
For Richard Chiswell.
Cant. IoM.

B5926 Burnet, Gilbert, [1687]
Pet.

B5927 Burnet, Gilbert, 1689
Yk.

B5928 Burnet, Gilbert, 1675
Carl. S Asa. Sal.

B5929 Burnet, Gilbert, 1689
Her. New.

B5931 Burnet, Gilbert, 1688
Dur.

B5932 Burnet, Gilbert, 1688
Ban. Carl. S Asa (imp). Yk.

B5933 Burnet, Gilbert, 1689
12°.
Wel.

B5934 Burnet, Gilbert, 1687
Carl.

B5935 Burnet, Gilbert, 1678
Bris. Carl. Dur. Ex. Wel.

B5938 Burnet, Gilbert, 1673
Carl. Ely. Ex. Nor. Wel.

B5939 Burnet, Gilbert, 1677
Ban. Carl. Ex. Linc. S Asa (2).
S Pl. Sal. Wel. Win.

B5940 Burnet, Gilbert, 1688
For Ric. Chiswell.
Cant. Ex. Liv.

B5943 Burnet, Thomas, *at
Charterhouse*, 1692
Ches. S Pl.

B5944 Burnet, Thomas, *at
Charterhouse*, 1697
Dur. Nor. Yk.

B5946 Burnet, Thomas, *at
Charterhouse*, 1697
Nor. Yk.

B5947 Burnet, Thomas, *at
Charterhouse*, 1691
Nor.

B5948 Burnet, Thomas, *at
Charterhouse*, 1681
Roch. S Asa.

B5948+ Burnet, Thomas, *at Charterhouse*, 1689
=Wing2 B5948A.
Ex. Sal.

B5949 Burnet, Thomas, *at Charterhouse*, 1689
Ex. Roch. S Asa. Sal. Wel.

B5950 Burnet, Thomas, *at Charterhouse*, 1684
Lich. S Dv. Tru. Wel. Yk.

B5952 Burnet, Thomas, *at Charterhouse*, 1691
Carl.

B5953 Burnet, Thomas, *at Charterhouse*, 1697
Ely. Glo. S Pl.

B5954 Burnet, Thomas, *at Charterhouse*, 1690
Lich.

B5955 Burnet, Thomas, *at Charterhouse*, 1699
Ely. Yk.

B5962 Burnett, Andrew, 1696
Cant.

B5964 Burney, Richard, [1660]
Cant.

B5965 Burning, 1673
Impr. as Wing2.
Yk.

B5974 Burrell, John, 1683
Her.

B5975 Burridge, Ezekiel, 1697
Glo.

B6017 Burrough, Edward, 1660
Yk.

B6030 Burrough, Edward, 1658
Yk.

B6054 Burrough, Edward, 1660
Yk.

B6067 Burroughes, Jeremiah, 1662
Ex.

B6068 Burroughes, Jeremiah, 1643
Ex.

B6070 Burroughes, Jeremiah, 1650
Ex.

B6072 Burroughes, Jeremiah, 1659
Ex.

B6074? Burroughes, Jeremiah, 1643
Not anon.; 4°; 146p.
Ex (imp). Linc (2 − 1 imp).
S Asa. Win.

B6074+ Burroughes, Jeremiah, 1643
As B6074, but 2 pts: 128p. & 14p.
Ex (2 issues). Pet.

B6080 Burroughes, Jeremiah, 1657
Chelm.

B6086 Burroughes, Jeremiah, 1658
Chelm.

B6097 Burroughes, Jeremiah, 1641
Ex (2).

B6100 Burroughes, Jeremiah, 1655
Carl.

B6117 Burroughes, Jeremiah, 1646
Ex. Pet. Yk.

B6118 Burroughes, Jeremiah, 1646
Ex.

B6119+ Burroughes, Jeremiah, 1641
By T.P. and M.S. for R. Dawlman; 4°.
Ex (2). Pet (2 issues).

B6125+ Burroughes, Jeremiah, 1652
=Wing2 B6125A.
Carl. Pet.

B6125++ Burroughes, Jeremiah, 1656
=Wing2 B6125B.
Ex.

B6129 Burroughs, *Sir* John, 1651
For Humphrey Moseley.
Linc.

B6131 Burroughs, Thomas, 1657
'kindes'
Ex.

B6132 Burroughs, Thomas, 1662
'kindes'
Pet.

B6136 Burscough, Robert, 1699
Dur. Ex.

B6137 Burscough, Robert, 1692
Ex.

B6146 Burt, William, 1659
Pet.

B6149 Burthogge, Richard, 1675
Ches. S Asa. Win.

B6150 Burthogge, Richard, 1694
Lich. Pet.

B6154 Burthogge, Richard, 1678
'... vetus & novum ...'
Ex.

B6157 Burthogge, Richard, 1672
Sal. Win.

B6160 Burton, Henry, 1646
Pet (imp). Yk (2).

B6161 Burton, Henry, 1641
Yk.

B6162 Burton, Henry, 1641
Pet. S Pl. Yk.

B6163 Burton, Henry, [1644/5]
Yk.

B6164 Burton, Henry, 1641
Linc.

B6165 Burton, Henry, 1641
Printed, sold by ...
S Pl. Yk.

B6166 Burton, Henry, 1660
Pet.

B6169 Burton, Henry, 1643
S Pl.

B6169A? Burton, Henry, 1643
'A narrative ...'
Yk.

B6170 Burton, Henry, 1646
Dur.

B6171A Burton, Henry, 1641
Linc.

B6172 Burton, Henry, 1641
Yk.

B6173 Burton, Henry, 1645
S Pl. Yk (2).

B6174 Burton, Henry, 1645
S Pl. Yk (2).

B6175 Burton, Henry, 1644
Pet. S Pl. Sal. Yk (2).

B6176 Burton, Henry, 1644
S Pl. Yk.

B6177 Burton, Henry, 1645
S Pl. Yk.

B6178+ Burton, Hezekiah, 1685
For Richard Chiswell; 8°.
Bur. Ely. Ex.

B6179 Burton, Hezekiah, 1684
S Dv.

B6179+ Burton, Hezekiah, 1684
For Richard Chiswell; 8°.
Ban. Ely. S Pl.

B6180 Burton, John, 1661
Bur (tpw).

B6182 Burton, Robert, 1652
The sixt edition; Printed & are ...;
Colophon as B6181.
Cant. Dur.

B6183 Burton, Robert, 1660
Carl. Nor (imp). S Pl (imp).

B6184 Burton, Robert, 1676
Colophon: By R.W. ...
Cant (2). S Asa.

B6185 Burton, William, 1658
Cant (2 − both imp). Ches. Dur.
S Pl. Win. Yk.

B6186 Burton, William, 1657
Cant. S Pl.

B6189 Bury, Arthur, 1662
Carl. Ex. Pet.

B6190 Bury, Arthur, 1691
Cant. Carl. S Pl.

B6191 Bury, Arthur, 1681
Carl. Ex.

B6192 Bury, Arthur, 1683
Cant. S Pl.

B6193 Bury, Arthur, 1692
Carl.

B6195 Bury, Arthur, 1694
Carl. Wel.

B6196 Bury, Arthur, 1696
S Asa.

B6197+ Bury, Arthur, 1697
Impensis Sam. Buckley; 12°; Different
ed. from British Library copy, which
is also 12°.
Cant.

B6199 Bury, Arthur, 1690
Cant (2 eds: with or without type
orns on tp). Dur. Ex. Wel.

B6202 Bury, Arthur, 1691
Wel.

B6207 Bury, Edward, 1677
Cant.

B6215 Bury, John, 1679
Carl. Dur. Ely. Yk.

B6217 Busbeq, Ogier Ghislain de,
1660
Glo. S Pl.

B6218 Busbeq, Ogier Ghislain de,
1660
… excudebat …
Glo. Llan.

B6220- Busby, Richard, 1694
=Wing2 B6219A; 'compendiaria'; 8°.
Wel.

B6222 Busby, Richard, 1663
Impr. as Wing2.
S Pl.

B6222+ Busby, Richard, 1671
=Wing2 B6222A.
Cant. Ches.

B6223 Busby, Richard, 1683
Nor.

B6223+ Busby, Richard, 1689
=Wing2 B6223A.
Ely. Her.

B6224 Busby, Richard, 1693
Impr. as B6223.
Cant.

B6231+ Bush, Rice, 1649[50]
=Wing2 B6231A.
Pet.

B6236? Bushell, Seth, 1678
Sawbridg.
Her.

B6238 Bushell, Seth, 1673
Her.

B6241+ Bushell, Thomas, 1652
Printed in the year; 4°.
Yk.

B6251 Busher, Leonard, 1646
Pet.

B6258 Bussières, Jean de, 1663
Oxoniae, excudebat …
Ex.

B6267+ Butler, Charles, 1667
=Wing2 B6267A; Ex officina J.M. pro
Andraeo Crook; 12°.
Ely. Yk.

B6268 Butler, John, *B.D.*, 1680
Win (date misprinted).

B6277 Butler, John, *Canon*, 1678
Cant. Carl. Wor.

B6278A Butler, Lilly, 1691
Her.

B6279 Butler, Lilly, 1694
Her.

B6280 Butler, Lilly, 1696
Wor.

B6281 Butler, Lilly, 1696
Cant. Sal.

B6283 Butler, Lilly, 1697
Bur.

B6284? Butler, Lilly, 1698
'January the 31st.'; By J.H. for B.
Aylmer.
Her. Wor.

B6288+ Butler, Nathaniel, *Captain*,
1672
=Wing2 B6288B+; For Peter Parker;
8°.
Pet.

B6290 Butler, Samuel, 1659
S Pl.

B6292- Butler, Samuel, 1674
=Wing2 B6291B.
Linc.

B6298 Butler, Samuel, 1663
Ex.

B6300 Butler, Samuel, 1663
Win*.

B6309 Butler, Samuel, 1664
Carl*. Linc*. Win*.

B6311 Butler, Samuel, 1674
Bris. Bur. Cant. Yk.

B6312 Butler, Samuel, 1678
Yk.

B6313 Butler, Samuel, 1678
Bris*. Bur. Win*. Yk.

B6314? Butler, Samuel, 1678
Second ed. not in book.
Wel.

B6315 Butler, Samuel, 1679
Yk.

B6320? Butler, Samuel, 1689
4°.
Chelm.

B6322+ Butler, Samuel, 1700
=Wing2 B6322A; 8°.
Cant.

B6323 Butler, Samuel, 1643
Yk (2 − 1 imp).

B6324 Butler, Samuel, 1643
'Mercurius'
Cant. Yk.

B6325 Butler, Samuel, 1682
Dur (imp). Yk.

B6325+ Butler, Samuel, 1659
=Wing2 B6325A.
Pet (date misprinted).

B6329 Butler, Samuel, 1662[3]
'proposall'; 10p.
Linc. Pet.

B6330+ Butler, Samuel, 1663
As B6329, but: 'proposal'; 4°; 16p.
Pet.

B6343? Buxtorf, Johann, 1646
… ex officina Rogeri Daniel.
Chelm.

B6345 Buxtorf, Johann, 1666
Linc.

B6348 Buxtorf, Johann, 1646
Editio sexta.
Bur. Lich. Linc. Sal. Wor. Yk.

B6350- By, [1672?]
See: CLC22.
Linc.

B6357 By, [1642]
Dur.

B6363 By, 1653
Dur (cropped).

B6364+ By, 1641
=Wing2 B6365.
Pet.

B6375 Byam, Henry, 1675
Dur. Sal.

B6378 Byfield, Adoniram, 1645
Win.

B6384 Byfield, Nicholas, 1649
Impr. as Wing2.
Chelm. Yk.

B6394 Byfield, Richard, 1645
Pet.

B6395 Byfield, Richard, 1645
Nor.

B6403 Bynns, Richard, 1693
Cant. Sal.

B6408 Byrom, John, 1681
Took.
Llan.

B6412 Bythner, Victorinus, 1648
Nor.

B6414 Bythner, Victorinus, 1650
Entry as Wing2.
Roch.

B6416 Bythner, Victorinus, 1675
Typis T. Roycroft, & venales prostat
...
Ches. Ely. Wel.

B6418 Bythner, Victorinus, 1650
Ely. Ex. Glo (2). Linc. Roch.
S Pl. Yk.

B6419 Bythner, Victorinus, 1653
Swel. Yk.

B6421 Bythner, Victorinus, 1664
Bris. Cant. Dur. Linc. Liv.
Rip. S Pl. Sal. Wel.

B6422 Bythner, Victorinus, 1664
Ches. Wel.

B6423? Bythner, Victorinus, 1679
Impr. as B6422, but begins: Typis
Eliz. Flesher ...
Ely. Her. Pet. S Asa. S Dv
(tpw).

C1 C., [1679]
Yk.

C1A C., 1689
Ban. Bur. Cant. Carl. Pet.
Wel.

C7 C., A., 1645
Ely.

C19 C., C., 1680
Wel.

C23 C., E., 1680
Linc.

C29 C., E., 1653
Carl.

C35 C., G.B., 1642
Yk.

C66 C., J., 1657
Sal.

C73 C., J., [1662?]
'epidemical'
S Pl.

C79+ C., J. B., 1648
'A Venice ...'; Formerly H3126.
Carl. Lich.

C90 C., O., 1664
Linc.

C91? C., P., 1691
'prophesies'
Cant. Dur. S Asa.

C101 C., R., 1689
Wel.

C113A C., R., 1698
Printed and sold ...
Her.

C114 C., R., 1663
Carl. Ex. S Asa. Wel. Win.

C119 *See:* D2686+

C127? C., T. , [1642]
[London] ...
Linc.

C131+ C., T., 1698
See: CLC23.
Sal.

C135 C., T., 1698
Sal.

C142 C., T., 1650
Yk.

C142A C., T., 1642
Dur. Linc.

C146 C., W., 1700
For John Nutt; 12°.
Yk.

C154 C., W., 1662
Yk.

C160 C., W., 1696
'... contradicting Mr. Geo. Keith ...'
Dur.

C181 Cabal, 1679
Dur. Linc (tp imp). Nor. Yk.

C183 Cabala, 1654
Carl. Linc. Wel. Yk.

C184 Cabala, 1654
Bedel.
Sal. Yk.

C185 Cabala, 1663
Dur. Lich. Swel. Wor. Yk.

C186 Cabala, 1691
Impr. as Wing2 but: ... Mat. Wootton
...
Cant. Chelm. Chi. Ex.

C189 Cabinet, 1679
Dur.

C194 Cade, William, 1678
Cant (imp?). Carl. Llan.

C198 Caesar, Caius Julius, 1693
Ex. Wel.

C199 Caesar, Caius Julius, 1655
'The commentaries ...'
Carl. Glo. S Pl.

C200 Caesar, Caius Julius, 1677
Win.

C201 Caesar, Caius Julius, 1695
Cant.

C202A *See:* S4666

C207+ Caillières, Jacques de, 1675
=Wing2 C207B; By J.C. for Richard
Tonson.
Carl. Ex.

C212 Calamy, Benjamin, 1683
Carl. Wor.

C214 Calamy, Benjamin, 1673
Carl.

C215 Calamy, Benjamin, 1682
Wor.

C216 Calamy, Benjamin, 1682
Llan.

C217 Calamy, Benjamin, 1683
Cant. Carl. Her. Nor.

C218 Calamy, Benjamin, 1683
Bur. Cant. Carl. Ches (imp)*.
Lich.

C219 Calamy, Benjamin, 1685
Cant. Dur (cropped).

C220 Calamy, Benjamin, 1685
Cant. S Asa.

C221 Calamy, Benjamin, 1687
Ban. Ches.

C222? Calamy, Benjamin, 1690
Impr. ends at Green.
Nor.

C223 Calamy, Benjamin, 1700
Llan.

C224 Calamy, Benjamin, 1683
S Pl.

C226 Calamy, Edmund, *the Elder*,
1642
Linc.

C228 Calamy, Edmund, *the Elder*,
1657
S Pl.

C229 Calamy, Edmund, *the Elder*,
1655
Carl.

C230 Calamy, Edmund, *the Elder*,
1645
S Pl. Yk (2).

C231 Calamy, Edmund, *the Elder*,
1662
4°.
Pet.

C231+ Calamy, Edmund, *the Elder*,
1662
London; 4°.
Ex (2).

C232 Calamy, Edmund, *the Elder*, 1663
Carl. Linc. S Asa (2 leaves only).

C233 Calamy, Edmund, *the Elder*, 1645
Her. Yk.

C234 Calamy, Edmund, *the Elder*, 1652
Carl. S Pl.

C236? Calamy, Edmund, *the Elder*, 1642
39p.
Carl. S Asa. S Pl.

C237? Calamy, Edmund, *the Elder*, 1642
62p.
Ex. Pet.

C238? Calamy, Edmund, *the Elder*, 1642
... sold by Stationers.
Her. Linc.

C239? Calamy, Edmund, *the Elder*, 1642
... sold by Stationers.
Pet (2).

C243 Calamy, Edmund, *the Elder*, 1663
Lich.

C247 Calamy, Edmund, *the Elder*, 1657
Carl.

C253? Calamy, Edmund, *the Elder*, 1642
51p.
Chelm. Pet. S Asa.

C253+ Calamy, Edmund, *the Elder*, 1642
As C253, but: 50p.
Carl. Ex. Pet (2 − 1 imp). S Pl.

C254 Calamy, Edmund, *the Elder*, 1646
Carl. S Pl.

C256- Calamy, Edmund, *the Elder*, 1642
For Christopher Meredith; 4°.
Carl.

C256 Calamy, Edmund, *the Elder*, 1645
Pet (2). S Pl.

C257 Calamy, Edmund, *the Elder*, 1646
Carl. S Pl.

C259 Calamy, Edmund, *the Elder*, 1655
Pet. S Pl.

C261 Calamy, Edmund, *the Elder*, 1643
Cant. Carl. Ex. Pet.

C262 Calamy, Edmund, *the Elder*, 1658
Carl.

C265 Calamy, Edmund, *the Elder*, 1655
Cant (gathering A only).

C269 Calamy, Edmund, *the Younger*, 1699
Dur.

C271 Calamy, Edmund, *the Younger*, 1694
Carl.

C274 Calamy, Edmund, *the Younger*, 1697
Ches.

C279 Calderwood, David, 1678
Dur. Ex (2). Linc.

C292 Calfine, Giles, 1642
Linc.

C293 Calfine, Giles, 1660
Cant. Dur.

C301 *See*: C207+

C305 Callis, Robert, 1685
4°.
Cant. Linc.

C311 Calthrop, *Sir* Henry, 1670
Sal.

C316 Calver, Edward, 1641
4°.
Yk.

C319 Calvert, James, 1672
... Londini.
Chelm. Her. Yk (2).

C321 Calvert, Thomas, 1648
8°.
Yk (3).

C323+ Calvert, Thomas, 1675
=Wing2 C324?; By F.L. for Tho. Passenger, and William Thorpe in Yorke.
Yk (2).

C326+ Calvert, Thomas, 1657
=Wing2 C326A; '... caeli ...'
Yk (2 − 1 imp).

C333 Cambridge University, 1660
Chelm. Lich. Linc. Yk.

C334 Cambridge University, 1671
Linc.

C335 Cambridge University, 1662
Linc (2 − 1 tpw). Pet (imp).

C336 Cambridge University, 1677
Linc.

C337 Cambridge University, [1697]
Ely. Sal (2).

C338 Cambridge University, 1683
Dur. Yk.

C339 Cambridge University, 1688
Nor. Sal.

C340 Cambridge University, 1641
Lich. Linc. Yk.

C341 Cambridge University, 1670
Linc. Yk.

C342 Cambridge University, 1694/5
Yk.

C343 Cambridge University, 1684/5
Yk.

C344 Cambridge University, 1689
'Cantabrigienses'
Nor. Yk.

C345 Cambridge University, 1658
Chelm.

C347 Cambridge University, 1670
Cant (imp). Linc. Sal.

C353 Cambridge University, 1684
S Asa. Yk.

C354 Cambridge University, 1661
Ches. Nor. Pet.

C355 Cambridge University, 1669
'Cantabrigienses'
Linc. Win.

C357 Cambridge University, 1700
2°.
Ely. Nor. Sal.

C358 Cambridge University, [1643]
Linc.

C359 Camden, William, 1695
... A. & J. Churchil.
Ban (imp). Cant (2 − 1 frag.).
Chelm. Chi. Dur. Ely. Ex. Glo.
Her. IoM. Lich. Linc. Pet.
Sal. Swel. Wel. Wor.

C361 Camden, William, 1691
Ban. Ches (imp). Dur. Ex.
Lich. Pet. S Asa. S Pl. Yk.

C362 Camden, William, 1675
... for Charles Harper and John Amery.
Cant (imp). Rip.

C363A Camden, William, 1688
The fourth edition.
Ex. Yk.

C368 Camden, William, 1662
Excudit Rogerus Nortonus; 8°.
Ex.

C372 Camden, William, 1692
Excudit Rogerus Nortonus; 8°.
Nor.

C372A+ Camden, William, 1697
=Wing2 C372C; Excudit Rogerus
Nortonus.
S Pl.

C374A Camden, William, 1657
The sixth impression.
Lich. S Pl.

C375 Camden, William, 1674
S Dv. Yk.

C377 Camfield, Benjamin, 1680
Cant (2). Carl. Linc. Pet. Sal.

C381 Camfield, Benjamin, 1682
Ban. Yk.

C382 Camfield, Benjamin, 1684
Chiswell.
Carl. S Pl. Yk.

C383 Camfield, Benjamin, 1668
Nor.

C384? Camfield, Benjamin, 1669
Impr. as C383.
Ely (retains the tp of C383).

C385 Camfield, Benjamin, 1678
Carl. Pet.

C386 Camfield, Benjamin, 1685
Her. S Asa.

C388 Camfield, Benjamin, 1678
Carl. Win. Yk.

C388A Camiltons, 1641
Pet.

C398 Camp, [1642]
Linc.

C401 Campanella, Tommaso, 1654
Glo. Pet.

C405 Campion, Abraham, 1700
Nor.

C407 Campion, Edmund, 1687
Wel.

C411 *See:* Pt 2 of S3803

C412 Camus, Jean Pierre, 1641
'Diotrephe. Or, an historie ...'
Ely.

C417+ Camus, Jean Pierre, 1654
As C417, apart from date.
Ex.

C426 Canes, John Baptist Vincent,
1672
S Pl.

C427 Canes, John Baptist Vincent,
1665
Carl.

C428 Canes, John Baptist Vincent,
1663
Carl.

C429 Canes, John Baptist Vincent,
1661
8°.
Win.

C430 Canes, John Baptist Vincent,
1662
Pet. Sal. Wor.

C432+ Canes, John Baptist Vincent,
[1662]
=Wing2 C432A.
Carl.

C433 Canes, John Baptist Vincent,
1672
Ex (includes tp of C426).

C435 Canes, John Baptist Vincent,
1655
Carl. Pet.

C438 Canne, John, 1649
Ex. Yk.

C439 Canne, John, 1650
Ex. Yk.

C442A Canne, John, 1653
Yk.

C443 Canne, John, 1657
Yk.

C443B Canne, John, 1653
Yk.

C446 Canons, 1687
Ex. Sal (2).

C447 *See:* L1538

C458 Canterburies, 1641
Yk.

C460 Canterburies, 1641
'potion'
S Pl.

C469 Capel, Arthur Capel, *Baron*,
1683
Ely.

C473 Capel, Richard, 1655
Carl.

C476 Capel, Richard, 1655
Ex.

C479 Capitall, 1643
Linc.

C496 Cardenas, Alonso de, 1643
Carl.

C499+ Cardonnel, Philip de, 1674
=Wing2 C501, but: '... of money';
For Nath. Brooke.
Linc.

C500 Cardonnel, Philip de, 1662
Ex. Win.

C503 Care, George, 1689
Bris.

C505 Care, Henry, 1687
Carl. Wel.

C506 Care, Henry, 1688
S Pl.

C507 Care, Henry, 1688
Pet.

C508 Care, Henry, 1678
Cant. Linc. Yk.

C512 Care, Henry, 1688
S Asa. Yk.

C516 Care, Henry, [1680?]
Cant (cropped).

C520 Care, Henry, 1673
Carl.

C522 Care, Henry, 1680
Dur.

C527 Care, Henry, 1688
Carl. S Pl (2). Wel.

C529 Care, Henry, 1687
Ban. Bur. Ex. Linc. Nor. Sal.
Swel. Wel. Yk.

C535 Care, Henry, 1682
Bur. Ex. Lich. Sal.

C536 Care, Henry, 1688
Ban. Carl. Chi. Ely. Nor. S Pl.
Wel. Yk.

C555+ Carew, *Sir* George, 1665
=Wing1 C557 and Wing2 C556; 8°.
Linc.

C557 *See:* C555+

C565 Carew, Thomas, *Poet*, 1651
Cant.

C566 Carew, Thomas, *Poet*, 1670
Ex (tpw)*.

C572 Carier, Benjamin, 1649
Carl. Sal.

C605 Carolan, Neal, 1688
'conversion'; ... Eliphal Dobson.
Wel.

C610 Caron, Raymond, 1665
Win.

C612 Carpender, William, 1661
Carl. Ex (2). Yk (2).

C618 Carpenter, Richard, [1653]
Chelm.

C621 Carpenter, Richard, 1642
Chi.

C626 Carpenter, Richard, 1663
Carl.

C629 Carr, Richard, 1691
Impensis Stafford Anson.
Nor.

C643 Carrington, S., 1659
Cant.

C649 Carswell, Francis, 1689
Her. Wor.

C650 Carswell, Francis, 1689
Yk.

C654 Carter, John, [1647]
Cant.

C659 Carter, Matthew, 1660
Second ed. not on tp.
Yk.

C661 Carter, Matthew, 1673
For Hen. Herringman.
Cant. Linc. S Asa.

C662 Carter, Matthew, 1650
8°.
Linc.

C668 Carter, Thomas, 1643
Cant. Ex. Pet.

C673 Carter, William, *Clothier*,
1669
Llan.

C675 Carter, William, *Clothier*,
1671
Win.

C679A+ Carter, William, *Minister*,
1642
As C679A, but: ... Meredith.
Ex. Pet (2 − 1 imp*).

C685 *See*: B1508

C687 Cartwright, Christopher, 1650
Yk (2).

C688 Cartwright, Christopher, 1648
Carl. Linc. S Asa. S Pl.

C689 Cartwright, Christopher, 1653
Linc. Win.

C690 Cartwright, Christopher, 1658
Yk (2).

C691 Cartwright, Christopher, 1675
Yk (2).

C692 Cartwright, Christopher, 1647
Yk.

C693 Cartwright, Christopher, 1658
Yk.

C696 Cartwright, Thomas, 1687
Cant. Carl. Ches.

C698 Cartwright, Thomas, 1659
'arraignment'
Ches. S Pl.

C699 Cartwright, Thomas, 1659
Wor.

C700 Cartwright, Thomas, 1648
Pet. Yk.

C701 Cartwright, Thomas, 1673
Pet. Yk.

C701+ Cartwright, Thomas, 1688
=Wing2 C701A.
Wel.

C702 Cartwright, Thomas, 1675/6
Ches. Her. Pet. Wor. Yk.

C703 Cartwright, Thomas, 1676
Carl. Ches. Yk.

C703+ Cartwright, Thomas, 1676
=Wing2 C703A.
Yk (imp).

C704 Cartwright, Thomas, 1682
Yk.

C704A Cartwright, Thomas, 1682
Ches.

C705 Cartwright, Thomas, 1684
Carl. Ches. Yk (2).

C706 Cartwright, Thomas, 1686
Cant. Dur. S Asa. Wor. Yk
(3).

C707 Cartwright, Thomas, 1686
Yk.

C708? Cartwright, Thomas, 1686
By J. Leake, re-printed at Edinburgh.
Ches.

C713 Cartwright, William,
Playwright, 1652
Carl.

C718 Carver, Marmaduke, 1666
Not anon.
Yk (2).

C719 Carver, Marmaduke, 1666
By James Flesher; Dedication signed
M.C.
S Asa. Win.

C719+ Carver, Marmaduke, 1661
=Wing2 C719A; 'restor'd'
Yk.

C721 Carwell, Thomas, 1658
Cant. Carl. Her.

C724 Cary, John, 1700
Impr. as Wing2.
Dur.

C725 Cary, John, 1696
Bris.

C735 Carey, John, 1700
Glo.

C743 Cary, Robert, 1677
Bris. Bur. Cant. Ches. Ex.
Linc. Pet. S Asa. Win. Wor.

C743+ Cary, Thomas, 1691
See: CLC24.
Wor.

C749 Caryll, Joseph, 1645
Pet.

C751? Caryll, Joseph, 1646
... and Giles Calvert.
Ex (imp).

C752 Caryll, Joseph, 1646
Her. Yk.

C755+ Caryll, Joseph, 1647
=Wing2 C755A, but no printer in
impr.
Carl. S Asa.

C755++ Caryll, Joseph, 1651
=Wing2 C755B.
Bur.

C756+ Caryll, Joseph, 1669
Impr. as C756; 4°.
Sal.

C758? Caryll, Joseph, 1676−77
'An exposition ... upon the Book of
Job'; 2v.
Her. Nor. Roch.

C760 Caryll, Joseph, 1648
Bur. Carl. Rip. S Asa.

C760A+ Caryll, Joseph, 1671
=Wing2 C760B.
Sal.

C762 Caryll, Joseph, 1649
Bur. Carl. Rip.

C762A Caryll, Joseph, 1669
Sal.

C763- Caryll, Joseph, 1649
=Wing2 C762B.
Carl. Rip.

C763 Caryll, Joseph, 1652
Fawn.
Bur. Sal.

C765 Caryll, Joseph, 1650
Carl.

C765A+ Caryll, Joseph, 1654
By Matthew Simmons, sould by John
Allen; 4°.
Bur (impr. and format not
confirmed).

C766 Caryll, Joseph, 1671
Sal.

C767 Caryll, Joseph, 1653
... sould at his house.
Bur. Carl.

C767+ Caryll, Joseph, 1653
=Wing2 C767; ... sould by Giles
Calvert; 4°.
Rip.

C768 Caryll, Joseph, 1658
Sal.

C769 Caryll, Joseph, 1655
Bur (tpw). Rip.

C769+ Caryll, Joseph, 1655
By M. Simmons, sould at her house;
4°.
Carl.

C770 Caryll, Joseph, 1659
Sal.

C771 Caryll, Joseph, 1657
Carl.

C772 Caryll, Joseph, 1670
Sal.

C773 Caryll, Joseph, 1659
Carl. Sal.

C774+ Caryll, Joseph, 1661
For M. Simmons, sould at her house;
4°.
Carl.

C775 Caryll, Joseph, 1669
Sal.

C776 Caryll, Joseph, 1664
... sold at her house.
Carl. Sal.

C777 Caryll, Joseph, 1666
Carl. Sal.

C779 Caryll, Joseph, 1646
Yk.

C783 Caryll, Joseph, [1651]
'oppressor'; By J.B.
S Pl.

C785 Caryll, Joseph, 1680
Linc.

C786 Caryll, Joseph, 1646
S Pl.

C787 Caryll, Joseph, 1644
Ex (2). Yk (2).

C790 Caryll, Joseph, 1642
Ex. Pet. Win.

C791 Casa, Giovanni della, 1665
Win.

C792? Casa, Giovanni della, 1670
The second edition; 8°.
Dur.

C795 Casa, Giovanni della, 1679
Carl.

C798 Casas, Bartholome de las,
1689
Nor.

C799 Casas, Bartholome de las,
1656
Carl.

C800 Casaubon, Méric, 1659
... Joh. Shirley.
Win (2).

C801 Casaubon, Méric, 1650
8°.
Cant. Carl. Ex. Linc. Roch.
S Pl. Yk.

C802 Casaubon, Méric, 1647
Impr. as Wing2.
Cant. Carl. Dur (imp). Linc.
Nor. S Pl (2). Yk.

C803 Casaubon, Méric, 1646
Ex. Linc. Win. Yk.

C805 Casaubon, Méric, 1669
Bris.

C806 Casaubon, Méric, 1670
Ex. Liv. Wel.

C807 Casaubon, Méric, 1668
Cant. Carl. Llan. Win. Yk.

C808 Casaubon, Méric, 1664
Cant. Carl. Llan. Pet. Yk (2).

C809 Casaubon, Méric, 1645
Ex. Yk.

C810 Casaubon, Méric, 1663
Cant. Carl. Dur (cropped).
S Asa. Yk (2).

C812 Casaubon, Méric, 1655
Carl. Pet (2 – 1 tp imp). Yk.

C813 Casaubon, Méric, 1656
Cant (imp). Carl. Ely. Ex.
Llan. S Dv. Wel.

C815 Casaubon, Méric, 1672
Ex.

C817 Casaubon, Méric, 1660
Carl. Yk.

C827 Case, Thomas, 1646
Pet. Yk.

C831 Case, Thomas, 1642
Ex (3 – 1 imp).

C833 Case, Thomas, 1646
Ches. Her.

C835 Case, Thomas, 1660
S Asa. Sal. Win.

C836 Case, Thomas, 1676
Llan.

C837 Case, Thomas, 1670
Ex. Her.

C838 Case, Thomas, 1644
'quarrell'
Pet.

C840 Case, Thomas, 1659
Yk.

C842 Case, Thomas, 1645
Her.

C845 Case, Thomas, 1641
Cant.

C848 Case, 1682
Rip.

C867 Case, 1648
Yk.

C883 Case, 1679
Linc.

C898 Case, 1684
Carl. S Pl.

C967 Case, 1682
Win.

C971 Case, [1689]
Wel.

C1099 Case, 1647
Yk.

C1181 Case, 1680
Win. Yk.

C1204 Case, 1652
4°.
Ex.

C1205+ Case, [c.1660?]
See: CLC25.
Ex.

C1218 See: S2166+

C1219 See: S2166++

C1220 See: S2166+++

C1224+ Castell, Edmund, 1669
=Wing2 C1225.
Bris. Bur. Cant (2). Carl.
Chelm (vol. 1 only). Ches. Chi.
Dur. Ely. Ex (2 – 1 imp). Glo
(imp). Her. Lich. Linc. Llan.
New (tpw)*. Nor. Pet. Roch
(vol. 1 only, imp)*. S Asa (imp).
S Pl (2). Sal (2 – 1 vol. 1 only).
Swar (imp). Swel (imp). Wel.
Win. Wor. Yk.

C1226? Castell, Edmund, 1686
Imprimebat Thomas Roycroft,
sumptibus Roberti Scott.
Rip.

C1227 Castell, Edmund, 1667
Cant. Pet.

C1229 Castell, William, 1642
Linc.

C1230 Castell, William, 1641
Linc (imp).

C1231A Castigatio, 1660
Carl.

C1235 Castlehaven, James Touchet,
Earl of, 1681
Yk.

C1239 Castlemaine, Roger Palmer,
Earl of, 1666
Carl. Ex.

C1240 Castlemaine, Roger Palmer, *Earl of*, 1674
Ban. Glo.

C1241 Castlemaine, Roger Palmer, *Earl of*, 1679
Cant.

C1243 Castlemaine, Roger Palmer, *Earl of*, 1673
Cant. Wel.

C1245 Castlemaine, Roger Palmer, *Earl of*, 1681
Sal.

C1246 Castlemaine, Roger Palmer, *Earl of*, 1668
Carl. Chelm.

C1247 Castlemaine, Roger Palmer, *Earl of*, 1671
Carl. Ex. Linc.

C1253 Catalogi, 1697
Also entered at B1986 in Wing2.
Cant (2). Chi. Dur. Ely. Ex (2). Her. Lich. S Pl (3). Swel. Wel. Wor. Yk.

C1363 *See*: W462A+

C1368? Catalogue, 1667
8°.
Carl. Ex. Sal.

C1371 Catalogue, 1664
Win.

C1372 Catalogue, 1642
Linc.

C1385? Catalogue, 1642
'... severall counties ...'
Linc.

C1385+ Catalogue, 1655
=Wing2 C1385A?; 8°.
Pet (tpw)*.

C1391 Catalogue, 1642
S Pl.

C1395+ Catalogue, 1641
As C1395, apart from date.
Linc.

C1398 Catalogue, [1642]
Dur.

C1404 Catalogue, 1679
Linc.

C1409 Catalogue, 1661
Linc.

C1410+ Catalogue, 1642
=Wing2 C1410A.
Yk.

C1412 Catalogue, [1680]
Linc.

C1463+ Κατηχησεις, 1655
Excudebat Rogerus Daniel, venales autem prostant apud Samuelem Thomson; 12°.
Ely. S Pl.

C1472 Catechism, 1687
Cant. Chi. Yk (2).

C1478+ Catechisme, 1664
See: CLC26.
Cant.

C1492 *See*: C4592

C1498 Catholicon, 1674
Sal.

C1499 Catholikes, 1644
Yk.

C1526 Catullus, 1684
'Vossii'
Ches. S Pl.

C1527 Caus, Isaac de, 1659
Ex. Sal.

C1531 Causae, 1685
Editio altera; Trinobantûm.
Cant. Wel (imp).

C1533 Cause, 1659
Ex (imp). S Pl.

C1537 Causes, 1675
Dur.

C1546+ Caussin, Nicolas, 1687
=Wing2 C1546C; For John Williams ... sold by Matth. Turner.
Cant.

C1547 Caussin, Nicolas, 1650
Ely.

C1548+ Caussin, Nicolas, 1663
=Wing2 C1548A.
Ex.

C1550 Caussin, Nicolas, 1678
Nor. Yk (imp).

C1551+ Caussin, Nicolas, 1681
=Wing2 C1551C; Formerly B3435.
Yk.

C1571 Cavaleers, 1661
Ches.

C1576 Cavaleers, 1661
Ches.

C1580 Cave, John, 1685
Her.

C1583 Cave, John, 1681
Carl. Dur. S Asa.

C1585 Cave, John, 1679
Her.

C1586 Cave, John, 1679
Carl. Dur.

C1587- Cave, William, 1675
=Wing2 C1586A.
Glo. Linc. Nor. S Pl. Sal. Win.

C1587+ Cave, William, 1676
=Wing2 C1587A.
Carl. Lich. Swel.

C1588 Cave, William, 1677
Bur. Cant (2). Ches. Chi. Ex. Nor. Roch. Wel. Wor. Yk.

C1588A? Cave, William, 1678
Fourth ed. not on tp.
Chelm. S Asa (possibly has fourth ed. on tp). Wor.

C1589 Cave, William, 1684
Cant. Ches. Ely. Ex. Her. Swel.

C1589+ Cave, William, 1684
As C1589, but no ed. statement; Pt of T288.
Brec. Dur. S Dv. Swel. Win.

C1589++ Cave, William, 1686
By R. Norton for R. Royston; 2°.
Carl.

C1589A Cave, William, 1694
Chi. Her. S Alb. S Asa.

C1590 Cave, William, 1677
Ban. Cant (2). Carl. Chelm. Ches. Chi. Ex (2). Her. Lich. Linc. Liv (2). New. Roch. S Dv. Tru. Win.

C1591 Cave, William, 1682
Chiswel.
Bur. Cant. Chi. Ely. Glo. Wel. Wor. Yk.

C1592 Cave, William, 1687
Ban. Carl. Chi. Swel.

C1593 Cave, William, 1685
Bris. Ches. Ex. Roch. S Asa. S Pl (2). Yk (2).

C1594 Cave, William, 1684
Ban. Cant. Carl. Chi. Ex. S Pl (2). Sal. Swel. Wel.

C1595 Cave, William, 1683
Bur. Dur. Linc. S Asa.

C1596 Cave, William, 1683
Chiswel.
Ban (2). Bur. Cant. Carl (2). Chelm. Ches. Ely. Ex. Her. Linc. Liv. Nor. Roch. S Asa. Swel. Wel. Win. Wor. Yk.

C1597 Cave, William, 1700
Impr. as Wing2.
Cant. Ely. Ex. S Asa. S Pl. Wel.

C1598 Cave, William, 1673
Carl. Ches. Ely. Ex (engr. tpw).
Llan. Pet. S Pl (2 — 1 engr. tpw).
Yk.

C1599 Cave, William, 1675
Nor. Win.

C1600? Cave, William, 1676
By J.G. for R. Chiswell.
S Dv. Yk.

C1601 Cave, William, 1682
Cant (2). Roch. S Asa. Wel.

C1601+ Cave, William, 1698
=Wing2 C1601A?; Chiswel.
Llan.

C1602 Cave, William, 1688—98
Date as Wing2.
Ban. Bris. Ches. Dur. Ely. Ex.
Her (2 — 1 pt 1 only). Linc. Pet.
S Asa. S Dv. S Pl (2 — 1 pt 2
only). Swel (pt 1 only). Wel.
Win. Wor. Yk (vol. 1 only).

C1603 Cave, William, 1683
Ex. S Pl. Yk.

C1605 Cave, William, 1676
Ban. Bur. Cant (2).

C1606 Cave, William, 1680
'... November MDCLXXX'
Ban. Carl. Chi. Her.

C1607 Cave, William, 1685
Cant.

C1619 Cavendish, George, 1641
Yk.

C1621 Cawdrey, Daniel, 1658
Carl.

C1623 Cawdrey, Daniel, 1661
Chelm.

C1624 Cawdrey, Daniel, 1657
Carl.

C1628 Cawdrey, Daniel, 1643[4]
Yk.

C1629 Cawdrey, Daniel, 1651
Sal.

C1630 Cawdrey, Daniel, 1657
8°.
Carl. Chelm. Sal.

C1631 Cawdrey, Daniel, 1658
Carl. Chelm. Her.

C1637 Cawdrey, Daniel, 1641
Linc. Pet. Yk.

C1637+ Cawdrey, Daniel, 1641
=Wing2 C1637A?; Whaley.
Linc.

C1638 Cawdrey, Daniel, 1641
Ex. Linc. Pet.

C1640 Cawdrey, Daniel, 1645
Ex. Pet.

C1646 Cawdrey, Zachary, 1675
Cant. Dur. Linc. Yk.

C1648 Cawdrey, Zachary, 1681
Nor.

C1650 Cawley, John, 1689
Carl. Linc. Wel.

C1653 Cawton, Thomas, 1662
Carl.

C1661 Cellier, Elizabeth, 1680
Ely. Linc. Nor (imp).

C1662+ Cellier, Elizabeth, [1680?]
[N.pl.]; cap.; 2°.
Linc.

C1664 Censorinus, 1695
Ches. Ely. Ex. S Pl.

C1667 *See*: E2791+

C1673- Cerdan, Jean Paul de, 1681
=Wing2 C1672B.
Ely. Nor. Pet.

C1673 Cerdan, Jean Paul de, 1681
Nor. Win.

C1675 Ceremonies, 1686
12°; See also C1677+.
Yk.

C1677+ Ceremonies, 1686
'The ceremonies us'd in the time of
King Henry VII. for ... the kings evil';
By Henry Hills; 4°; See also C1675.
S Pl.

C1677 *See*: L1330C

C1679 Ceriziers, René, 1654
... William Lee.
Cant (imp).

C1687A Certain, 1641
Carl. Ex (3). Linc. Pet. Sal.
Yk (2).

C1690 Certain, 1646
Cant.

C1695 Certain, 1674
Nor.

C1696A Certaine, [1643]
Yk.

C1697 Certaine, 1648
Win. Yk.

C1700A Certain, 1644
Carl.

C1706 Certaine, 1641
Dur.

C1708 Certain, 1665
Impr. as Wing2.
Chelm. Linc. S Asa. S Pl (2 — 1
tpw).

C1713 Certaine, 1642
Pet.

C1714? Certain, 1643[4]
... Rich. Harsell.
Carl. Win. Yk.

C1723 Certaine, 1641
Dur (tp imp).

C1724 Certain, 1657
Yk.

C1734 Certaine, 1642
Linc (2).

C1736 Certaine, 1643
Cant.

C1740 Certain, 1643
Pet.

C1741 Certaine, 1641
Pet (2).

C1745 Certain, 1663
Ex. Linc. Pet. S Asa.

C1751 Certaine, 1641
Yk.

C1766 Certificate, 1641
Ely. Ex. Linc. Pet.

C1787 Chadwell, William, 1659
Her.

C1793 Chalfont, Richard, 1644
Carl. Wel.

C1800 Chaloner, Richard, 1643
Cant.

C1801 Chaloner, Thomas, 1646
Pet.

C1818 Chamberlayne, Edward,
1671
Linc.

C1820 Chamberlayne, Edward,
1669
'Angliae ...'
Linc. Yk.

C1823 Chamberlayne, Edward,
1671
'Angliae ...'
Carl.

C1824 Chamberlayne, Edward,
1672
'Angliae ...'
Cant.

C1825 Chamberlayne, Edward,
1673
'Angliae ...'
Yk.

C1828 Chamberlayne, Edward,
1677
'Angliae ...'; ... J. Martin.
Win. Yk.

C1829 Chamberlayne, Edward, 1679
'Angliae ...'; ... J. Martin.
Yk.

C1830 Chamberlayne, Edward, 1682
'Angliae ...'
Ex.

C1840 Chamberlayne, Edward, 1668
Carl. Wel.

C1841 Chamberlayne, Edward, 1685
Carl. Yk.

C1843 Chamberlayne, Edward, 1660
Pet.

C1845 Chamberlayne, Edward, 1647
Linc.

C1847? Chamberlayne, Edward, 1671
'Angliae notitia ... the second part'
Yk.

C1848 Chamberlayne, Edward, 1671
Cant. Carl. Linc.

C1850 Chamberlayne, Edward, 1673
Yk.

C1853 Chamberlayne, Edward, 1677
... J. Martin.
Win. Yk.

C1854 Chamberlayne, Edward, 1679
... J. Martin.
Yk.

C1855 Chamberlayne, Edward, 1682
Ex.

C1890 Chamberlen, Hugh, [1682?]
Ban.

C1896 Chamberlen, Peter, 1659
Yk.

C1915 Chambers, Humfry, 1643
Ex. Pet (imp). Sal.

C1916 Chambers, Humfry, 1649
S Pl.

C1926 Chandler, Henry, 1699
'biggotry'; Lawrence.
Bur.

C1954? Chapman, John, 1684
'September'; 28p.
Dur.

C1954+ Chapman, John, 1684
As C1954, but: 26p.
Carl.

C1956 Chappell, William, 1648
Carl. Ely. Pet. Sal. Yk.

C1957 Chappell, William, 1656
Cant (imp).

C1960 Character, [1680]
Linc.

C1972 Character, 1675
Sal.

C1983A Character, 1660
Yk.

C2002 Character, 1690
Ban.

C2017 Character, 1660
Win.

C2023 Character, [1681]
Dur. Linc.

C2043 Chardin, Jean, 1686
Ex. Nor (tpw). Pet. Wel.

C2050 Charge, 1647
Cant.

C2052 Charge, 1682
... Richard Janeway.
S Pl.

C2060 Charge, 1641
Ex. Linc. Yk.

C2061 Charge, 1641
Dur ('Lieutenant'). Pet ('Livetenant'). Sal ('Lievetenant').
Yk (2).

C2062 *See*: E2537

C2065 *See*: I28A

C2071 Charles I, [1649]
Ban (imp)*. Lich (imp). S Dv. S Pl.

C2072? Charles I, 1650
12°.
Llan.

C2073 Charles I, 1651
Ban. Cant. Liv. Yk.

C2074 Charles I, 1657
Cant (tpw). Ely. Yk.

C2075 Charles I, 1662
'workes'
Cant. Chi. Dur. Ex. IoM. Nor. Pet. Win. Wor.

C2076 Charles I, 1687
Ban (3 — 2 imp). Cant. Carl. Ches (imp). Ely. Glo. Her (2 — 1 engr. tpw). Lich. Liv. Llan. Pet. Sal (engr. tpw). Yk.

C2087 *See*: A826

C2090 Charles I, 1642
Cant. Yk.

C2090A Charles I, 1642
Yk (2).

C2092 Charles I, 1642
Cant. Dur. Pet.

C2093 Charles I, 1642
Yk.

C2094 Charles I, 1642
Cant.

C2095 Charles I, 1642
Cant. Linc. Yk (2).

C2096? Charles I, 1642
Cambridge, by Roger Daniel.
Sal.

C2101 Charles I, 1641[2]
Yk.

C2103 Charles I, 1642
Cant (2). Ex.

C2103A? Charles I, 1642
York, by Robert Barker and the assignes of John Bill.
Yk.

C2105 Charles I, 1642
Yk (2).

C2106 Charles I, 1642
Imprinted at Yorke ...
Dur. Linc. Yk (3).

C2107 Charles I, 1642
Linc. Pet. Yk (2).

C2108 Charles I, 1642
Yk.

C2109 Charles I, 1642
Yk.

C2110 Charles I, 1647[8]
Pet.

C2112? Charles I, 1642
'... to the declaration of both Houses ...'
Linc. Yk (2 eds).

C2113? Charles I, 1642
Yorke ...
Cant (cropped). Yk (3).

C2114 Charles I, 1642
Sal. Yk (2).

C2115 Charles I, 1642
Yk.

C2116 Charles I, 1642
Linc. Pet. Sal.

C2118 Charles I, 1642
Yk.

C2119 Charles I, [1642]
Dur (cropped). Linc.

C2122 Charles I, 1642
Cant. Dur (imp). Linc. Pet.
Sal. Yk.

C2123 Charles I, 1642
Cant. Yk.

C2124 Charles I, 1642
Cant.

C2125 Charles I, 1648
... October ...
Carl. Dur.

C2126 Charles I, 1660
Yk.

C2127 Charles I, 1642
Yk.

C2128 Charles I, 1642
Yk.

C2131A? Charles I, 1642
First printed at York, and new
re-printed at London for Charles
Greene.
Dur.

C2132+ Charles I, 1641[2]
=Wing2 C2132A; For Iohn Thomas.
Cant.

C2137 Charles I, 1642
Cant. Dur. Linc. Pet. Yk (2
issues: 'His Majesties' in small
caps or lower-case).

C2137B+ Charles I, 1642
'... Aprill 18.1642'; Printed by Tho.
Fawcet; 4°.
Dur.

C2138 Charles I, 1641
Cant.

C2142 Charles I, 1643
Linc.

C2146 Charles I, 1647
Yk.

C2147 Charles I, 1642
Sal.

C2149 Charles I, 1642
Pet.

C2151 Charles I, 1659
Ban. Carl. Ex. Lich. Pet. Yk.

C2153A+ Charles I, 1642
=Wing2 C2153B.
Dur.

C2154? Charles I, 1649
'Majestie'; Haghe, by Samuel Broun;
8°.
Linc. Sal.

C2156 Charles I, 1642
Cant. Linc.

C2157+ Charles I, 1662
=Wing2 C2157.
Nor. Win.

C2159 Charles I, 1642
Ex. Pet.

C2164 Charles I, 1642
Dur. Linc.

C2164+ Charles I, 1642
For Thomas Walton, July 5; brs.
Linc (on verso of E1669+).

C2168 Charles I, 1642
Linc.

C2168A Charles I, 1642
Yk.

C2187 Charles I, 1642
Yk.

C2190 Charles I, 1642
Pet. Sal. Yk.

C2191 Charles I, 1642
Cant.

C2192 Charles I, 1642
Linc.

C2194 Charles I, 1647
Yk.

C2196 Charles I, 1648
Her.

C2204 Charles I, 1648
Pet.

C2208 Charles I, 1642
Dur.

C2209 Charles I, 1643
First printed ...
Linc.

C2211 Charles I, [1642]
Cant (imp). Dur. Linc. Yk.

C2214 Charles I, 1645[6]
Cant. Dur. Pet.

C2223 Charles I, 1642
Linc.

C2224 Charles I, 1642
Printed at Oxford [London] by
Leonard Lichfield.
Dur.

C2225 Charles I, 1643
Cant.

C2226 Charles I, 1643
Yk (2).

C2233 Charles I, 1643
London counterfeit.
Cant. Linc.

C2237 Charles I, 1642
Cant. Dur. Ex. Linc. Pet. Yk.

C2238 Charles I, 1642
Yk.

C2238A Charles I, 1642
Linc. Sal.

C2241 Charles I, 1642
Yk.

C2242 Charles I, 1642
Dur. Sal. Yk.

C2246+ Charles I, 1642
Impr. as C2246, but is a London
counterfeit (Madan 1083).
Linc.

C2247- Charles I, 1642
Impr. as C2246, but is a London
counterfeit (Madan 1084).
Dur.

C2248 Charles I, 1642
... assignes ...
Linc. Yk.

C2249 Charles I, 1642
... Yorke ...
Pet. Yk.

C2249A Charles I, 1641
Ex. Sal.

C2251 Charles I, 1641[2]
Cant. Linc. Pet.

C2255 Charles I, 1642
Pet.

C2256 Charles I, 1642
Second ed. not on tp.
Cant (2). Linc.

C2256A Charles I, 1642
Third ed. not on tp.
Cant.

C2259 Charles I, 1642
London counterfeit (Madan 1046).
Cant. Dur. Linc. Pet.

C2261 Charles I, 1642
Cant.

C2263+ Charles I, 1643
As C2263, but: 'kingdome'; January.
Yk.

C2264 Charles I, 1648
6p.
Pet.

C2264+ Charles I, 1648
8p.
Linc.

C2265 Charles I, 1647
Yk*.

C2266 Charles I, 1642
Yk (3).

C2268 Charles I, 1641[2]
... assignes ...
Cant. Dur (imp). Linc.

C2269 Charles I, 1641[2]
Yk.

C2272A Charles I, 1642
Linc.

C2277 Charles I, 1643
Linc.

C2283+ Charles I, 1642
For Thomas Bates; 4°.
Yk.

C2284 Charles I, 1642
Yk.

C2286 Charles I, 1642
Linc.

C2287 Charles I, 1642
Cant. Dur. Yk.

C2290 Charles I, 1642
Title as Wing2.
Sal.

C2291 Charles I, [1642]
Linc.

C2300 Charles I, 1647
Yk.

C2302 Charles I, 1661
12°.
Liv.

C2306 Charles I, 1648
Cant. Carl. Dur. Win.

C2307 Charles I, 1660
4°.
Cant. Yk.

C2313 Charles I, 1641
Linc.

C2320? Charles I, 1643
'... message sent from ... London'
Linc.

C2321 Charles I, 1641[2]
Dur.

C2326 Charles I, 1643
Linc. Pet.

C2327- Charles I, 1642
=Wing2 C2326A?; 'gratious'; Oxford,
by Leonard Lichfield.
Linc.

C2327+ Charles I, 1642
[N.pl.], Decemb. 21. Prrinted [sic] for
J. Bladen; 4°.
Linc.

C2333 Charles I, 1642
Linc.

C2334 Charles I, 1642
Cant.

C2334+ Charles I, 1642
Impr. as C2334; brs.
Linc.

C2334A- Charles I, 1642
Printed for Iohn Wright, August 29;
4°.
Dur.

C2334A Charles I, 1642
Linc.

C2349 Charles I, 1642
Linc. Yk.

C2351 Charles I, 1642
Linc.

C2356 Charles I, 1642
Yk.

C2358 Charles I, 1645
4°.
Ex (2). Linc. Pet. Sal. Yk (3).

C2368 Charles I, 1645[6]
Pet.

C2370 Charles I, 1642
Cant. Dur. Linc.

C2372 Charles I, 1648
Cant.

C2375 Charles I, 1648
Cant. Yk (tp imp).

C2378 Charles I, [1643]
Cant.

C2385+ Charles I, 1642[3]
As C2385, but differs slightly from
Madan's 4 eds.
Cant.

C2387 Charles I, 1643[4]
Cant.

C2390 Charles I, [1642]
Dur (cropped)*. Linc.

C2392? Charles I, 1642
... February 7.
Carl. Linc.

C2396 Charles I, [1642]
Linc.

C2396+ Charles I, [1642]
=Wing2 C2396A, which has wrong
date.
Dur (cropped).

C2397 Charles I, 1643
Cant.

C2398+ Charles I, 1641[2]
For Joseph Hunscott; brs.
Linc.

C2400? Charles I, 1642
... Richard Watson.
Pet.

C2405? Charles I, 1641[2]
For J. Franke and J. Wright.
Linc.

C2406? Charles I, 1642
'Feb. 28.'; For John Franke.
Dur.

C2407 Charles I, 1641[2]
'Feb. 28'
Linc.

C2408 Charles I, 1642
Pet.

C2409 Charles I, [1642]
'... eighth of June ...'
Linc. Yk.

C2413 Charles I, 1642[3]
Cant.

C2414+ Charles I, [1642]
As C2414, but no bookseller in impr.
Yk (2).

C2419 Charles I, 1646
Pet.

C2425 Charles I, 1641
Linc.

C2426 Charles I, 1641
'His Majesties manifestation
concerning ...'
Linc.

C2431 Charles I, 1641
Dur. Linc.

C2436 Charles I, 1642
Yk.

C2438 Charles I, 1643
Linc.

C2444 Charles I, 1642
Yk.

C2447 Charles I, 1642
... assignes ...
Cant.

C2448A Charles I, 1642
Linc.

C2449 Charles I, 1641[2]
Linc.

C2450 Charles I, 1641
Impr. as Wing2.
Cant. Linc. Sal.

C2453? Charles I, 1642
'... April 28, 1642. Concerning ...'
Dur.

C2453+ Charles I, 1642
Printed; 4°.
Yk.

C2454 Charles I, 1642
Yk (2).

C2456 Charles I, 1642
Cant. Dur. Ex. Linc. Yk (2).

C2466 Charles I, 1648
'Isle'
Cant.

C2468 Charles I, [1642]
Linc.

C2473? Charles I, 1641[2]
... assignes ...
Dur (cropped). Linc.

C2475 Charles I, 1641[2]
'The Kings Maiesties ...'
Dur.

C2478 Charles I, 1642
Cant. Dur.

C2479 Charles I, 1642
Linc.

C2480 Charles I, 1642
Yk (2).

C2481? Charles I, 1642
'Aprill'; ... Robert Barker, and ...
Linc.

C2482 Charles I, 1642
Yk.

C2485 Charles I, 1646
Cant. Pet.

C2488 Charles I, 1642
Linc.

C2490 Charles I, 1642
For Hugh Perry, September the 8th.
Dur.

C2493 Charles I, 1643
Lich. Linc. Yk.

C2494 - Charles I, 1642
Printed at York by Stephen Bulkley;
4°.
Yk.

C2495 Charles I, 1642[3]
Yk.

C2500 Charles I, 1648
Yk.

C2501 Charles I, [1642]
'His Majesties most gratious ...'
Linc.

C2503 Charles I, 1648
Yk*.

C2505 Charles I, 1648
Pet.

C2506 Charles I, 1647
Pet.

C2511 Charles I, 1647
Yk.

C2517 Charles I, 1647
Yk.

C2521 Charles I, 1641
Yk.

C2522 Charles I, 1641
'Maiesties'
Cant.

C2532 + Charles I, 1642
=Wing2 C2532; By R. Barker (?) ...
Yk (impr. not confirmed).

C2532 *See*: E1788

C2533 Charles I, 1648
Dur. Yk.

C2535? Charles I, 1649
'... Mr Al: Henderson'
Ex. Pet. Yk (3)*.

C2535 + Charles I, 1649
As C2535, but: '... Mr. Alex:
Henderson'
Ely.

C2537 Charles I, 1646
Win.

C2548 Charles I, 1642
Yk (2).

C2553 Charles I, 1641
... assignes ...
Cant.

C2553? Charles I, 1641
... assignes ...
Linc.

C2563 Charles I, 1645
Ex. Yk.

C2571 *See*: C2829 +

C2574 + Charles I, [1642]
=Wing2 C2574A; cap.; Impr. from
colophon.
Linc.

C2575 Charles I, 1642
Dur.

C2580 Charles I, 1642
Yk.

C2587 Charles I, 1641
... assignes ...
Cant (imp).

C2588 Charles I, 1641
Cant.

C2596 Charles I, 1642
Linc.

C2600 Charles I, 1641
... assignes ...
Cant.

C2606 Charles I, [1642]
Linc.

C2613 Charles I, [1642]
'clothes'
Linc (2).

C2636 Charles I, 1642
Linc.

C2650A? Charles I, 1642
... assignes ...; 2°.
Linc.

C2652 Charles I, 1642
Cant. Dur. Pet. Yk.

C2693 Charles I, [1642]
Linc.

C2709 Charles I, [1642]
Linc.

C2722 - Charles I, 1648
=Wing2 C2721; '... (for ... comming
...)'
Yk.

C2727 Charles I, 1642
Fowler.
Dur.

C2730 Charles I, [1642]
Yk.

C2736 Charles I, 1646[7]
Linc.

C2738 Charles I, 1648
'Episcopall'
Cant. Carl.

C2739 Charles I, 1660[1]
Yk.

C2743 Charles I, 1642
Dur. Pet.

C2744 Charles I, 1641
Yk.

C2744A Charles I, 1641
Sal.

C2744B Charles I, 1642
Yk.

C2746 Charles I, 1642
Yk.

.C2748? Charles I, 1642
'Earl of Warwicke'; ... J. Smith ...
Sal.

C2749 Charles I, 1642
Yk.

C2751 Charles I, 1642
Ex. Yk.

C2753 Charles I, 1641
Linc.

C2756 Charles I, 1642
Yk.

C2758? Charles I, 1642
'... setting up of his standard ...
York'; ... I. Tompson ...
Cant. Dur. Yk (2).

C2760 *See*: S572

C2764 Charles I, 1649
Yk.

C2765 Charles I, 1641
Linc.

C2766 Charles I, 1642
Yk.

C2768 Charles I, 1642
Yk.

C2769 Charles I, 1642
Dur (cropped; 1st 3 lines of text
end 'an', 'received', 're =')*. Yk
(2).

C2776 + Charles I, 1642
Printed by Robert Barker and by the
assignes of John Bill; 4°.
Cant. Dur. Linc.

C2778 Charles I, 1642
Cant. Dur. Linc.

C2780 Charles I, 1642
Linc.

C2781? Charles I, 1642
Imprinted at York by Robert Barker
and by the assignes of John Bill.
Linc.

C2782 Charles I, 1642
brs.
Linc.

C2783 Charles I, 1643
London counterfeit.
Cant. Linc.

C2784 Charles I, 1643[4]
Yk.

C2784+ Charles I, 1643[4]
As C2784; Madan 1521; London
counterfeit.
Cant.

C2786 Charles I, 1641
Cant.

C2788 Charles I, 1641[2]
Cant (2 eds: A3 line 7 ends 'for
this' or 'this oc-').

C2792 Charles I, 1649
Cant. Dur. Her. Pet. Yk.

C2793 Charles I, 1641
Dur. Yk.

C2797A Charles I, 1641
Cant.

C2798 Charles I, 1641
Cant (2).

C2800 Charles I, 1641[2]
For Iohn Wright ...
Cant.

C2801 Charles I, 1641[2]
Linc.

C2802 Charles I, 1642
Cant.

C2803 Charles I, 1642
Linc. Yk (3).

C2803+ Charles I, 1642
Printed at York, and re-printed at
London, by A. Norton; 4°.
Dur. Linc.

C2804 Charles I, 1642
Yk.

C2805 Charles I, 1642
Yk (2).

C2808 Charles I, 1642
Cant.

C2810 Charles I, 1642
Cant. Dur. Linc (2).

C2813 Charles I, 1644
[N.pl.], by Leonard Lichfield; London
counterfeit.
Cant.

C2814? Charles I, 1642
'The Kings Maiesties ...'
Ex.

C2819 Charles I, 1641
Cant. Linc.

C2824? Charles I, 1642
... July, the nineth.
Linc. Pet. Yk.

C2825 Charles I, [1642]
Cant. Dur. Pet.

C2829+ Charles I, 1642
=Wing2 C2829A.
Yk*.

C2829++ Charles I, 1642
As C2829, but: ... London for J.B.
Dur. Yk.

C2832? Charles I, 1642
... assignes ...
Linc.

C2837 Charles I, 1642
Dur. Linc.

C2853 Charles I, 1642
Dur. Linc.

C2854 Charles I, 1642
For Iohn Wright.
Linc. Yk.

C2855 Charles I, 1642[3]
Cant. Linc.

C2855+ Charles I, 1642
'Two messages of His Maiesties ...';
For Francis Cowles; 4°; Anr ed. of
C2854.
Yk (2).

C2857 Charles I, 1642
... re-imprinted at London ...
Dur. Linc. Pet. Yk (2).

C2858 Charles I, 1642
... Yorke ...
Linc (2). Yk (2).

C2859? Charles I, 1641
... new reprinted ...
Linc (date altered in MS to 1642).

C2863 Charles I, [1642]
Cant. Linc.

C2864 Charles I, 1642
Yk.

C2866 Charles I, 1642
Ex. Yk.

C2873 Charles I, 1648
Linc.

C2879 Charles I, [1642]
'county'
Linc.

C2880 Charles I, 1642
Yk.

C2882+ Charles I, 1642
Printed at London for T. Bates; brs.
Yk.

C2886? Charles II, [1678]
'patent'
Linc.

C2888+ Charles II, 1648
=Wing2 C2890D?; 'The answere of
His Highnes'; Dated.
Linc.

C2894 *See:* C2897

C2895 *See:* C2897

C2896 Charles II, 1662
Sal.

C2897 Charles II, 1667
=C2898, C2895, C2894 & C2913.
Sal.

C2898 Charles II, 1667
Impr. as C2897.
Pet. Sal.

C2905 Charles II, 1673/4
Pet.

C2907 Charles II, 1664
Sal. Win.

C2909 Charles II, 1677
Win (imp).

C2910? Charles II, 1667
... assignes ...
Linc.

C2911 Charles II, 1667
Linc. Sal.

C2913 *See:* C2897

C2917 Charles II, 1662
Sal.

C2919 *See:* E2887

C2927B *See:* E809

C2927F *See:* E820

C2927G *See:* E846

C2932 Charles II, [1681]
Linc.

C2937 Charles II, 1660
Sal.

C2938 Charles II, 1663
Linc. Win.

C2942 Charles II, [1685]
Wel.

C2943 Charles II, 1686
Yk (cropped).

C2943+ Charles II, [1686?]
'Copies of two paper [*sic*] written by ...'; 4 leaves; 2°.
Liv.

C2944 Charles II, 1686
Bur.

C2952 Charles II, 1666
... Christopher Barker.
Lich. Linc (tpw). S Pl.

C2953 Charles II, 1671/2
Lich. Linc.

C2961 Charles II, 1648
Cant.

C2964+ Charles II, 1664
As C2964; 8p.; 2°.
Lich.

C2965 Charles II, 1674/5
Lich.

C2967 Charles II, 1679
Win.

C2970 Charles II, 1648[9]
Cant (imp). Yk.

C2972 Charles II, 1648
'... Charles ... concerning the grounds
and ends of his present ...'
Cant (imp). Yk.

C2980 Charles II, 1649
Linc.

C2988 Charles II, 1662
Lich.

C2990? Charles II, 1671/2
'March 15th'
Lich. Linc.

C2997 Charles II, 1660
Lich. Linc. Win.

C2998 Charles II, 1683
Bris. Cant. Carl. Dur (2). Nor.
S Pl. Win. Wor. Yk.

C3000 Charles II, 1681
Carl. Dur. Linc. Wor.

C3007 Charles II, 1664[5]
Lich. Linc.

C3009 Charles II, 1660
Pet.

C3010 Charles II, 1660
Linc.

C3011 Charles II, 1672
Lich.

C3013 Charles II, 1660
Lich.

C3015 Charles II, 1660
S Pl. Win.

C3021 Charles II, 1669
Linc.

C3025 Charles II, 1681
Linc.

C3026 Charles II, 1681
'The King's Majesties gracious ...'
Ches.

C3029 Charles II, 1678
Linc.

C3032 Charles II, 1661
Lich. Linc.

C3036 Charles II, 1680/81
Linc.

C3038 Charles II, 1660
Dur (imp). Lich.

C3039 Charles II, 1677
Linc.

C3042 Charles II, 1660
Yk.

C3043 Charles II, 1661
Lich. Linc.

C3044 Charles II, 1661
Lich. Linc.

C3045? Charles II, 1661
'November 20.'
Lich.

C3048 Charles II, 1662[3]
Lich. Linc. Win.

C3049 Charles II, 1664
'April 5.'
Lich. Linc.

C3051 Charles II, 1664
'November 24.'
Lich. Win.

C3052 Charles II, 1665
Lich.

C3055 Charles II, 1673
Lich. Linc.

C3056 Charles II, 1673/4
Lich. Linc.

C3064 Charles II, 1679/80
Linc.

C3066 Charles II, 1680
'... to both Houses ...'
Ches. Linc. Win.

C3069? Charles II, 1661[2]
'March 1.'
Linc.

C3070 Charles II, 1660
Lich.

C3071 Charles II, 1661
49p.; pp. 31−49 = T3365.
Lich (pp. 31−49 only). Linc (as
Lich).

C3071+ Charles II, 1661
As C3071, but: 26p.
Lich.

C3074 Charles II, 1660[1]
Lich.

C3075 Charles II, 1673/4
'January 7.'
Lich. Linc.

C3078 Charles II, 1675
Lich.

C3084 Charles II, 1676/7
Linc. Win (2).

C3085 Charles II, 1678
Linc. Win.

C3096 Charles II, 1660
Dur (imp). Her.

C3097A Charles II, 1660
Ban. Win.

C3104 Charles II, 1669
'October 19'
Linc.

C3109 Charles II, 1651
Glo.

C3111 *See*: C3097A

C3113 Charles II, 1681
Linc.

C3121 Charles II, 1648
Carl.

C3123- Charles II, 1648
=Wing2 C3123A?; 'A message from
His Highnesse the Prince of Wales,
delivered to ... the Lord Baron of
Inchiquin'
Linc.

C3129? Charles II, 1680
For Richard Tonson.
Linc.

C3133 Charles II, 1664
Linc (imp).

C3134 Charles II, 1660
Linc.

C3136 Charles II, 1663
·Linc.

C3139 Charles II, 1666
Lich.

C3140 Charles II, 1666[7]
'Majesties'
Lich. Linc.

C3142 Charles II, 1666[7]
'8th of February'
Lich. Linc.

C3145 Charles II, 1667
Lich.

C3147 Charles II, 1667[8]
'10th of February'
Lich.

C3148 Charles II, 1669
Lich.

C3151 Charles II, 1669/70
Impr. as Wing2.
Dur (imp). Lich. Linc.

C3153A Charles II, 1672/3
Lich (2).

C3159 Charles II, 1680
Ches. Linc.

C3169 Charles II, 1660
Lich. Linc.

C3170 Charles II, 1662
Lich. Linc.

C3172 Charles II, 1672/3
Lich. Linc.

C3177 Charles II, 1673
Lich. Linc.

C3182 Charles II, 1678
'21th of October'
Linc. Win.

C3184A Charles II, 1678/9
Linc. Wel.

C3187+ Charles II, [1660]
See: CLC28.
Linc.

C3201 Charles II, 1665
Lich. Linc.

C3202+ Charles II, 1670/1
23 March 1671; In the Savoye: printed
by the assigns of Jo: Bill, and Chris.
Barker; obl.fol.
Linc.

C3209 Charles II, 1679
... the heir of Andrew Anderson ...
Linc.

C3225 *See*: S1615

C3235 Charles II, 1663
Linc.

C3252 Charles II, 1661
Linc.

C3278 Charles II, [1679]
Edinburgh, by the heir of Andrew
Anderson, 1679, re-printed at London.
Linc.

C3282 Charles II, 1662
Lich.

C3287? Charles II, 1660
brs.
Linc.

C3295A Charles II, 1674
Lich.

C3299 Charles II, 1661[2]
Carl. Linc.

C3301 Charles II, 1665
Carl (cropped). Linc.

C3301+ Charles II, 1665
=Wing2 C3301A; Impr. from
colophon.
Rip.

C3303? Charles II, 1666
obl.fol.
Linc (2).

C3306 Charles II, 1673/4
Linc.

C3308 Charles II, 1678
Linc. Pet.

C3309 Charles II, 1679
Last line of text begins: 'inflict upon
all'
Linc.

C3309+ Charles II, 1679
As C3309, but last line of text begins:
'upon all such'
Linc. Pet.

C3310 Charles II, 1680
Linc.

C3322 Charles II, 1660
Cant. Carl.

C3330 Charles II, 1661
Linc.

C3348 Charles II, 1672
Linc.

C3349 Charles II, 1660[1]
brs.
Carl.

C3351 Charles II, 1675/6
Re-printed by ...
Linc (2).

C3354 Charles II, 1673/4
Linc.

C3364 Charles II, 1669/70
Linc.

C3378 Charles II, 1675
Lich.

C3392 Charles II, 1673/4
Linc.

C3401 Charles II, 1667
Linc.

C3414 Charles II, 1674
Lich.

C3418 Charles II, 1660
Cant.

C3426? Charles II, 1660
'... fifth day of June'; brs.
Carl.

C3429 Charles II, 1673
Linc.

C3435? Charles II, 1678
brs.
Linc.

C3461 Charles II, 1678
Linc.

C3469 Charles II, 1674
Linc.

C3497 Charles II, 1663
3 leaves pasted together to form brs.
Win (imp).

C3513 Charles II, 1660
Linc.

C3527 Charles II, 1674
Linc.

C3566 Charles II, 1666
Linc.

C3583 Charles II, 1674
Linc.

C3584 Charles II, 1660
'A proclamation ...'
Cant.

C3597+ Charles II, 1667
As C3597, but: 2°.
Lich (cropped).

C3606 Charles II, 1675
Yk.

C3613- Charles II, 1662
'To the most reverend father in God,
accepted, ... Archbishop of York'; As
C3613.
Linc.

C3613 Charles II, 1662
Impr. from colophon; cap.
Lich. Win.

C3617 Charles II, 1677
Linc. Win.

C3624 Charles II, 1660
Lich.

C3625? Charles II, 1670
By Thomas Milbourn.
Linc.

C3631 Charles II, 1678
Linc.

C3647- Charles II, [1661]
'... informed, as well by the humble
petition ... that the ... Church of
Rippon, ... on the eighth day of
December last ...'; By W.G. for the
assignes of J. Bodington; brs.
Rip. Yk.

C3647+ Charles II, [1660]
See: CLC27.
Linc.

C3649+ Charles V, 1670
=Wing2 C3651.
Carl.

C3655+ Charles X, 1659
=Wing2 C3656.
Ex.

C3659 Charles Louis, 1657
Ex.

C3666 Charleton, Walter, 1663
Lich. S Pl. Wel.

C3668 Charleton, Walter, 1652
'darknes'
Cant (imp). Carl. Pet.

C3672 Charleton, Walter, 1677
Editio secunda.
Linc.

C3674 Charleton, Walter, 1682
Carl.

C3675 Charleton, Walter, 1657
Carl.

C3678 Charleton, Walter, 1680
Ex.

C3679 Charleton, Walter, 1697
For J. Conyers.
Ex.

C3684 Charleton, Walter, 1659
Pet (2).

C3684+ Charleton, Walter, 1674
=Wing2 C3684A; ... James Magnes.
Carl. Wel.

C3685 Charleton, Walter, 1659
Bur.

C3685+ Charleton, Walter, 1660
As C3685, apart from date.
Cant.

C3686 Charleton, Walter, 1666
Ex officina Rogeri Danielis.
Dur.

C3687 Charleton, Walter, 1669
Sal.

C3690 Charleton, Walter, 1680
Cant.

C3691 Charleton, Walter, 1654
'Charltoniana'
Bris. Cant. Carl.

C3694 Charleton, Walter, 1669
Cant (imp).

C3695 Charleton, Walter, 1675
Ex.

C3703 Charnock, Stephen, 1684
Her.

C3704 Charnock, Stephen, 1699
Chi. Dur.

C3705 Charnock, Stephen, 1684
Ex. Her (2). Roch.

C3706 Charnock, Stephen, 1699
Chi. Dur.

C3708 Charnock, Stephen, 1684
Impr. as Wing2.
Cant.

C3708+ Charnock, Stephen, 1685
For John Harris; 8°.
Wel.

C3710+ Charnock, Stephen, 1680
By Thomas Milbourn; 4°.
Carl.

C3711 Charnock, Stephen, 1682
Ex. Her.

C3712 Charnock, Stephen, 1680
Carl.

C3717? Charron, Pierre, 1651
Sixth ed. not on tp.
Ex.

C3718 Charron, Pierre, 1658
Roch.

C3728 Chassepol, François de,
1677
'visiers'
Carl.

C3729 Chasteigner de la
Roche-Pozay, Henri Louis, 1657
... impensis Jos. Godwin ...
Pet.

C3731 Châteillon, Sébastien, 1679
Carl.

C3732 Châteillon, Sébastien, 1651
Ely.

C3734+ Chateillon, Sebastien, 1700
=Wing2 C3734B.
Wel (imp)*.

C3736 Chaucer, Geoffrey, 1687
Cant. Nor (tpw). Swel. Win.

C3753A Chauncy, Isaac, 1690
Cant (imp).

C3757+ Chauncy, Isaac, 1684
'The second part of the Theological
dialogue'; For E. Reyner; 4°; Pt 2 of
Wing2 C3757A.
Ex.

C3771 Cheesman, Ab., 1663
Cant.

C3775+ Cheeseman, Thomas, 1663
=Wing2 C3775A.
Pet.

C3778 Cheke, *Sir* John, 1641
Carl. Linc. Liv. Yk.

C3779+ Chemin, 1654
=Wing2 C3779A.
Linc.

C3781 Cheshire, Thomas, 1642
Yk.

C3782 Cheshire, Thomas, 1641
'... at St. Pauls the tenth day ...'
Carl. Pet (2). Yk.

C3782+ Cheshire, Thomas, 1641
'... at Saint Pauls the tenth day ...';
London, printed; 4°.
Carl. S Pl.

C3783 Cheshire, 1642
Impr. as Wing2.
Dur. Linc.

C3785 Chestlin, ?, 1648
Yk (2).

C3786 Chestlin, ?, 1681
2°.
S Dv.

C3788 Chetham, James, 1681
Yk.

C3792 Chetwind, Charles, 1679
Impr. as Wing2.
Dur. Ely. Linc. Yk.

C3793 Chetwind, John, 1674
Cant. Ex.

C3795 Chetwind, John, 1653[4]
Yk.

C3797 Chetwind, John, 1682
Carl.

C3803 Chevreau, Urbain, 1656
Carl.

C3804 Chewney, Nicholas, 1656
Pet.

C3806 Cheynell, Francis, 1647
Dur. Win. Yk.

C3810 Cheynell, Francis, 1644
Lich. Sal. Yk.

C3812 Cheynell, Francis, 1645
Pet. Win.

C3813 *See:* E3234+

C3814 Cheynell, Francis, 1646
Yk.

C3815 Cheynell, Francis, 1643
Cant. Carl. Ex. Yk.

C3816 Cheynell, Francis, 1643
Cant (2). Pet (imp).

C3817 Cheynell, Francis, 1647
Pet.

C3819 Cheyney, John, 1677
Pet.

C3820? Cheyney, John, 1680
By J.M. for J. Robinson.
Win. Yk.

C3821 Cheyney, John, 1680
Impr. as Wing2.
S Pl.

C3827 Cheyney, John, 1676
Lich.

C3841 Chidley, Samuel, 1653
Dur.

C3847+ Chilcot, William, 1697
= Wing2 C3847A.
S Asa.

C3852 Child, *Sir* Josiah, 1668
Wel. Win.

C3860 Child, *Sir* Josiah, 1693
Yk.

C3866 Child, *Sir* Josiah, 1681
Wel.

C3869A Childrens, 1669
Ex.

C3871 Childrey, Joshua, 1661
Cant.

C3880 Chillingworth, ?, 1642[3]
Pet. Sal (2).

C3882 Chillingworth, ?, 1642
Yk.

C3885 Chillingworth, William, 1687
Ban. Ely. S Pl. Wel.

C3887+ Chillingworth, William,
[1692]
= Wing2 C3887A.
Cant.

C3888 Chillingworth, William, 1662
Carl. Ex.

C3890 Chillingworth, William, 1664
Ban. Carl. Chelm. Ches. Dur.
Her. Roch. Swel.

C3890+ Chillingworth, William,
1664
This third impression; By E. Cotes for
Thomas Thornicroft; 2°.
Sal.

C3891 Chillingworth, William, 1674
Bur. Carl. Her. Liv. Win.
Wor.

C3892 Chillingworth, William, 1684
Ban. Chi. Nor. Pet. Yk.

C3895 Chillingworth, William, 1644
Carl. Sal. Wel.

C3899 Chisenhale, Edward, 1653
Entry as Wing2.
Pet.

C3901? Chishull, Edmund, 1698
'preach'd'
Her.

C3903 Chishull, John, 1657
Yk.

C3908- Chiswell, Richard, [1686]
See: CLC29.
Cant.

C3922 Cholgius, 1650
Pet.

C3924 Cholmley, *Sir* Hugh, *the
Elder*, 1643
Yk.

C3928 Chorlton, John, 1695
Ban. Cant.

C3932 Christal, 1641[2]
Pet.

C3937 Christian, Edward, 1679
Linc.

C3941 *See*: B3477+

C3942 *See*: B1218

C3967 Christs, 1649
Chelm. Dur.

C3988 Church, Josiah, 1652
Pet (tp imp).

C3994A- Church, 1699
= Wing2 C3994A.
Nor.

C3999 Church of England, 1642
S Asa.

C4000+ Church of England, 1630
[*i.e.* c.1663]
= STC 10054.
Yk.

C4000++ Church of England, 1669
= Wing2 C4000A; Impr. as C4001.
Wel.

C4000+++ Church of England,
1673
= Wing2 C4000B?; Impr. as C4001.
Yk.

C4004 Church of England, 1681
Nor.

C4005 Church of England, 1684
Fourth ed. not on tp.
Cant. Yk.

C4009+ Church of England, 1662
'Articles given ...'; Wrongly placed at
A3828.
Win. Yk.

C4009A Church of England, 1648
Cant.

C4018? Church of England, 1662
'ministred'
Win (2). Yk.

C4024? Church of England, 1678
For H. Brome.
Carl.

C4026 Church of England, 1662
Win. Yk.

C4030 Church of England, 1690
Dur (tp only).

C4030+ Church of England, 1686
'Articles to be enquired of ...
Cleaveland'; York; 4°.
Yk.

C4030++ Church of England, 1687
'Articles of inquiry ... Cleveland';
York; 4°.
Yk.

C4030+++ Church of England,
1688
'Articles of inquiry ... Cleaveland';
York; 4°.
Yk.

C4031 Church of England, 1662
Impr. as Wing2.
Win. Yk.

C4033 Church of England, 1662
Win (2). Yk.

C4033A Church of England, 1684
Dur.

C4034 Church of England, 1662
Cant. Win. Yk.

C4037 Church of England, 1679
Yk.

C4038 Church of England, 1662
Win. Yk.

C4038+ Church of England, 1662
= Wing2 C4038A?; '... commissariship
of Essex ...'
Win. Yk.

C4041 Church of England, 1662
Win. Yk.

C4044 Church of England, [1661]
Win.

C4048 Church of England, 1662
Win. Yk.

C4051 Church of England, 1662
Win. Yk.

C4051+ Church of England, 1683
'Articles of enquiry ... Lewes'; For
Obadiah Blagrave; 4°.
Yk.

C4052 Church of England, 1662
Win (2). Yk.

C4053 Church of England, 1641
Yk.

C4054 Church of England, 1662
Win. Yk.

C4055 Church of England, 1662
Win. Yk.

C4059 Church of England, 1668
Linc.

C4060 Church of England, 1671
Win. Yk.

C4061+ Church of England, 1677
'Articles of Visitation and enquiry ... Lincoln'; 4°.
Linc.

C4066 Church of England, 1662
Win. Yk.

C4067 Church of England, 1664
Win.

C4069? Church of England, 1662
For Timothy Garthwait.
Win. Yk.

C4070 Church of England, 1662
Win. Yk.

C4070+ Church of England, 1666
=Wing2 C4070B.
Cant.

C4072 Church of England, 1662
Win. Yk.

C4077 Church of England, 1662
Win. Yk.

C4079+ Church of England, 1680
'Articles of visitation and enquiry, ... Richmond'; York, by John Bulkley; 4°.
Dur.

C4079++ Church of England, 1662
=Wing2 C4079C.
Yk.

C4080 Church of England, 1662
Win. Yk.

C4081 Church of England, 1662
Win. Yk.

C4081+ Church of England, 1682
'Articles of inquiry ... St. Asaph'; By M. Clarke; 4°.
S Asa.

C4081++ Church of England, 1685
'Articlau o ymweliad ... Llanelwy [St Asaph]'; Printiedig yn y Theater yn Rhydychen; 4°.
S Asa.

C4082 Church of England, 1662
Win. Yk.

C4083+ Church of England, 1690
'Articles of instruction for enquiry, ... S. Maries in Salop'; 4°.
Nor.

C4084 Church of England, 1662
Win. Yk.

C4084A- Church of England, 1674
=Wing2 C4084C?; For Ja. Collins.
Dur.

C4086 Church of England, 1662
Win. Yk.

C4087 Church of England, 1662
Win. Yk.

C4087+ Church of England, 1665
=Wing2 C4087A.
Win (2).

C4090 Church of England, 1662
Win. Yk.

C4091A-- Church of England, 1662
=Wing2 C4091E; 'Yorke'; York, by Alice Broade.
Yk.

C4091A- Church of England, 1692
As C4091A, apart from date.
Yk ('York' added in MS).

C4091A Church of England, 1698
'inquired'
Yk.

C4091C Church of England, 1645
Sal.

C4091D Church of England, 1648
Carl.

C4091E Church of England, 1673
Her. Sal. Wor. Yk.

C4091F Church of England, 1676
Ban. Cant (imp). Ex. S Asa. Wel.

C4091G Church of England, 1683
Bur. Cant. Pet.

C4091H? Church of England, 1683
2°.
Cant (2 – both lack N2–3). Chi. Yk.

C4091H+ Church of England, 1683
=Wing2 C4091O.
Ely. Linc.

C4091H++ Church of England, 1683
=Wing2 C4091P, but: ... Peter Parker.
Nor. S Alb (2). Wel.

C4091I Church of England, 1687
Ely. S Alb. Yk (2).

C4092 *See:* S4825

C4093 Church of England, 1699
Lich. Liv. Nor. S Pl. Swel. Yk (2 – 1 imp).

C4094 *See:* S4824

C4094A Church of England, 1643
Carl. Yk.

C4094B Church of England, [1643]
Her.

C4094E *See:* C5624+

C4095- Church of England, 1633
[after 1640?]
=STC 10078.
S Pl.

C4096? Church of England, 1662
By A. Warren, for Joshua Kirton.
Cant. Yk (imp)*.

C4097? Church of England, 1665
For A. Crook, J. Kirton and T. Garthwait; 4°.
Linc (2). Nor (tp imp). Rip. Wel. Yk.

C4099 Church of England, 1673
Dur (imp).

C4100 Church of England, 1676
Ex. Her.

C4101 Church of England, 1678
Cant.

C4102 Church of England, 1678
Linc.

C4103+ Church of England, 1684
As C4103, apart from date.
Nor.

C4103A Church of England, 1641
Cant (tpw).

C4103B Church of England, 1641
7p.
Linc. Yk.

C4103C Church of England, 1641
10p.
Cant. Dur. Linc. Pet.

C4103E Church of England, 1660
Cant. Carl.

C4108 Church of England, 1678
Cant (2). Linc. Yk.

C4110? Church of England, 1643
'moneth'
Sal.

C4111 Church of England, 1643
76p.
Carl. Linc. Yk*.

C4111+ Church of England, 1643
As C4111, but: 45p.; Madan 1470.
Linc.

C4112 Church of England, 1644[5]
Carl. Linc.

C4113 Church of England, 1661
Carl.

C4114 Church of England, 1661
Cant. Carl. Dur. Pet. Rip. Yk.

C4115 Church of England, 1665
Carl. Linc. Rip. Yk.

C4116 Church of England, 1666
Cant. Dur (2). Linc. Rip. Sal. Win. Yk (2 – 1 tp imp).

C4117 Church of England, 1672
Cant. Carl. Sal. Win (tpw). Yk.

C4118 Church of England, 1673/4
Cant. Pet. Sal. Win. Yk (tpw).

C4119 Church of England, 1665
Cant. Carl. Linc. Pet (imp).
Sal. Yk.

C4119+ Church of England, 1665
York, by Stephen Bulkley; 4°.
Rip.

C4120 Church of England, 1665
'twentieth'
Cant (2). Carl. Pet. Sal. Win.
Yk.

C4121 Church of England, 1666
'... London, ... 14th of August; and
through all England, ... 23ᵈ of
August'
Cant (2). Linc. Pet. Rip. Yk.

C4121+ Church of England, 1690
=Wing2 C4121B?; 'A form of prayer
and humiliation'
Lich.

C4122 Church of England, 1685
'... the twenty sixth of this instant
July'
Cant. Linc.

C4123 Church of England, 1690
Dur. Linc.

C4123+ Church of England, 1690
'A form of prayer and solemn
thanksgiving ... nineteenth of ...
October'; By Charles Bill and Thomas
Newcomb; 4°.
Dur. Linc.

C4125 Church of England, 1688
Dur. Linc. Win (2).

C4125+ Church of England, 1690
=Wing2 C4125B; ... assignee ...
Cant.

C4126 Church of England, 1691
'... six and twenty ...'
Carl. Linc.

C4127- Church of England, 1692
As C4127, but no date in title,
'October 7th 1692' on tp verso.
Cant.

C4128 Church of England, 1692
Ches (imp). Win (imp).

C4128+ Church of England, 1692
=Wing2 C4128A.
Cant.

C4129 Church of England, 1693
'... 12th day ...'
Cant. Carl. Dur (imp).

C4130 Church of England, 1693
Cant.

C4131 Church of England, 1694
Cant. Carl. Linc. Liv. Win.

C4132 Church of England, 1695
Cant. Dur. Linc. Liv. Win (tp
only, imp).

C4133 Church of England, 1695
Impr. as C4132.
Cant (imp). Carl. Linc.

C4133+ Church of England, 1695
'... eighth day of ... October'; Dublin,
by Andrew Crook; 4°.
Cant.

C4133++ Church of England, 1695
'... to be used ... till the feast of St.
Simon'; Impr. as C4132; 4°.
Cant.

C4134? Church of England, 1696
No date in title, 'September the 28th'
on tp verso; Impr. as C4132; 4°.
Cant.

C4135? Church of England, 1697
'... second of December'; Impr. as
C4132; 4°.
Cant. Ches. Dur. Linc. Liv.
Win.

C4139 Church of England, 1692
Cant.

C4141 Church of England, 1696
Cant. Linc.

C4141A? Church of England, 1697
'... next after the General
Thanksgiving'
Cant.

C4141A+ Church of England, 1697
As C4141A, but: '... next after the
Prayer in the time of war'
Cant.

C4142 Church of England, 1661
Cant. Carl. Linc. Yk.

C4143 Church of England, 1661
Yk.

C4145 Church of England, 1678
Dur (2). Linc. Pet. Win. Yk.

C4146 Church of England, 1679
Dur. Linc. Pet. Sal. Win. Yk.

C4148 Church of England, 1680
Dur (2). Linc. Win. Yk.

C4150 Church of England, 1689
Carl. Dur. Linc.

C4151 Church of England, 1689
'... fifth day ...'
Carl. Dur. Linc. S Pl. Win.

C4153 Church of England, 1691
Cant. Carl. Dur (imp). Linc.

C4153+ Church of England, 1691
=Wing2 C4153A.
Cant (imp).

C4154 Church of England, 1692
Cant. Linc.

C4155 Church of England, 1692
Cant.

C4156 Church of England, 1693
Carl. Liv.

C4157 Church of England, 1694
Cant (imp). Carl. Dur (2). Lich.

C4158 Church of England, 1695
Cant (2 - 1 imp). Carl. Dur.
Win. Yk.

C4159 Church of England, 1695
Cant. Dur. Linc. Win.

C4160 Church of England, 1696
Cant. Carl. Ches. Linc.

C4162 Church of England, 1697
Cant. Carl (2 issues). Ches.
Dur. Linc. S Asa. Win.

C4163 Church of England, 1699
Cant. Carl. Dur (2).

C4164 Church of England, 1700
Cant. Carl. Dur (2). Linc.

C4165 Church of England, 1648
Cant. Carl. Win.

C4166 Church of England, 1650
Sal (tp imp). Win.

C4167 Church of England, 1685
Cant (2 - 1 imp). Carl. Dur (2
states: catchword A4 blackletter
or Roman). Win.

C4168 Church of England, 1688
Dur. Linc (2 eds: final page line
2 begins 'his' *or* 'with'). S Pl.

C4170 Church of England, 1660
Carl. Win.

C4171 Church of England, 1661
Carl. Linc. Yk.

C4171+ Church of England, 1662
=Wing2 C4171A.
Cant. Pet (tpw). Rip.

C4172 Church of England, 1683
4°.
Bris. Cant. Carl. Dur (2 states).
Win. Wor. Yk.

C4173 Church of England, 1685
Cant. Carl.

C4174- Church of England, 1685
=Wing2 C4174.
Carl. Win.

C4175? Church of England, [1685]
Part of another work?; 8°.
Yk.

C4177 - Church of England, 1686
'... thanksgiving ... for ... the
restauration ...'; [May 29]; Impr. as
C4177; 4°.
Dur.

C4177 + Church of England, 1688
=Wing2 C4177.
Yk.

C4178 Church of England, 1690
Cant.

C4179 + Church of England, 1643
'A forme of publique thankesgiving ...
14. day of July'; At York, by Stephen
Bulkley; 4°.
Dur.

C4181 Church of England, 1693
Cant.

C4181 + Church of England, 1694
'... thanksgiving to Almighty God ...';
Impr. as C4181; 4°.
Cant.

C4182 Church of England, 1687
Carl. Dur. Linc. Yk.

C4183 Church of England, 1689
Linc. S Pl.

C4184? Church of England, [1700]
'Forma sive descriptio Convocationis
celebrandae'; [London]; 4°.
Cant (4).

C4185 Church of England, 1649
'Highnesse'
S Pl.

C4187 *See:* W1443

C4188 Church of England, 1685
Ban. Ex. Glo. S Pl.

C4188A Church of England, 1670
Dur (2 issues: impr. occupies 4 or
5 lines). Liv. Nor (tpw)*. S Pl.
Yk.

C4188C + Church of England, 1690
=Wing2 C4188CB.
S Alb.

C4188D - Church of England, 1691
Impensis Abelis Swalle & Tim. Childe;
12°.
Nor.

C4188D Church of England, 1696
Impr. as Wing2.
Cant. Ex. S Pl (2). Yk.

C4188E *See:* D2690

C4188F Church of England, 1690
Cant.

C4188I - Church of England, 1688
As C4188I, but: ... by Edward Jones
...
Cant. S Pl. Win (2).

C4188I Church of England, 1688[9]
'A prayer for His Highness the ...'
Dur.

C4188I + Church of England,
[1697]
=Wing2 C4188IB; 'A prayer to be
used at the opening the Cathedral
Church of St. Paul, December 2,
1697'
Cant.

C4188I + + Church of England,
1663
Anr ed. of Wing2 C4188IC; By John
Bill and Christopher Barker; 2°.
Yk.

C4188I + + + Church of England,
1685
=Wing2 C4188IC.
Linc (tpw)*.

C4196 Church, 1679
Ex.

C4196B? Church of Scotland, 1641
Edinburg ...
Linc.

C4202C Church of Scotland, 1641
Linc.

C4206 Church of Scotland, 1648
'General'
Yk.

C4207 Church of Scotland, 1649
Date not in title.
Sal.

C4217 Church of Scotland, 1648
Dur.

C4220? Church of Scotland, 1650
'General'
Ex.

C4223 Church of Scotland, 1647
Sal.

C4224 Church of Scotland, 1641
Linc. Sal (tp imp).

C4225 Church of Scotland, 1662
Ex.

C4227 + Church of Scotland, 1680
=Wing2 C4227D.
Yk (tpw).

C4229A + Church of Scotland, 1648
'The humble representation of the
Generall Assembly'; Printed at York
by T. Broad; 4°; Anr ed. of Wing2
C4229D, which has error in title.
Yk.

C4231B Church of Scotland, 1646
Cant.

C4231B + Church of Scotland, 1641
=Wing2 C4231BB.
Ex.

C4245 Church of Scotland, 1691
S Pl.

C4246 Church of Scotland, 1692
4°.
Dur.

C4247 Church of Scotland, 1694
S Pl.

C4247A Church of Scotland, 1695
S Pl.

C4248A Church of Scotland, 1697
2°.
S Pl.

C4249 Church of Scotland, 1698
S Pl.

C4250 Church of Scotland, 1699
S Pl.

C4251 Church of Scotland, 1700
S Pl.

C4251A *See:* S1304

C4251B Church of Scotland, [1650]
cap.; 4°.
Cant.

C4257 Church of Scotland, 1652
'A remonstrance ...'
Pet.

C4260 *See:* S4441 & following, for
C4260 & following

C4270 Church of Scotland, 1642[3]
Cant.

C4271 Church of Scotland, 1642[3]
Linc.

C4271 + Church of Scotland,
1642[3]
As C4271, but: [2], 6, [8]p.; Not in
Madan.
Pet (pt 2 only).

C4272 Church of Scotland, 1682
Liv.

C4275 Churchill, *Sir* Winston, 1675
Chi. Ex. Linc. Yk.

C4276 - Churchwardens, [1683]
See: CLC30.
Yk.

C4286 Cicero, Marcus Tullius, 1681
Title as Wing2.
Ely. S Asa. Sal (2). Wor.

C4288 Cicero, Marcus Tullius, 1648
Linc.

C4297 Cicero, Marcus Tullius, 1695
8°.
Ex.

C4307 Cicero, Marcus Tullius, 1683
Rip.

C4309 Cicero, Marcus Tullius, 1680
Cant. Carl.

C4311 Cicero, Marcus Tullius, 1684
Yk.

C4313 Cicero, Marcus Tullius, 1699
Cant.

C4314 Cicero, Marcus Tullius, 1689
Wel.

C4315 Cicero, Marcus Tullius, 1692
Cant. Nor. S Asa.

C4315+ Cicero, Marcus Tullius,
1692
Cantabrigiae, ex officina Johann.
Hayes; 8°.
Ches.

C4316A? Cicero, Marcus Tullius,
1675
Impr. ends: ... J. Wright, et R.
Chiswel.
Yk.

C4317? Cicero, Marcus Tullius,
1679
Impr. as Wing2; 12°.
Yk.

C4318 Cicero, Marcus Tullius, 1686
Her.

C4322 Cicero, Marcus Tullius, 1699
Yk.

C4323 Cicero, Marcus Tullius, 1683
12°.
Wel.

C4330 Cities, 1661
Yk.

C4338 Citizens, 1673
S Pl.

C4343 Citizens, 1641
Dur. Linc.

C4346? City, 1645
34p.
Chelm. Sal.

C4346+ City, 1645
As C4346, but: 32p.
Ex.

C4353 City-law, 1647
Ex.

C4360 City, 1682
Carl. S Pl.

C4361 City, 1682
Carl. S Pl. Win.

C4370 Clagett, Nicholas, 1685
Cant (2 − 1 imp). Chi. S Pl (2).
Swel. Wel.

C4371 Clagett, Nicholas, 1683
Cant. Yk.

C4372 Clagett, Nicholas, 1686
Sal (imp).

C4373 Clagett, William, 1683
=Wing2 C4374A.
S Pl (2). Yk (date altered in MS
to 1687).

C4376 Clagett, William, 1688
Ban. Nor. S Pl. Swel. Wel.

C4377 Clagett, William, 1683
Carl. Lich. S Pl. Sal. Wel.

C4378 Clagett, William, 1686
Ban. Chi. S Pl. Swel.

C4379 Clagett, William, 1678
Impr. as Wing2.
Carl. Ex. Her. S Pl. Win.

C4381 Clagett, William, 1680
Carl. Ex. S Pl. Win.

C4383 Clagett, William, 1687
Ban. Ches. Chi. Ex (3). Linc.
Nor. Swel. Wel.

C4384 Clagett, William, 1686
Bur. Ex (2). Nor. S Pl.

C4384+ Clagett, William, 1686
For Tho. Bassett and Tho.
Newborough; 4°.
Ex. Lich. S Pl. Wel.

C4385 Clagett, William, 1693
Ely. S Asa.

C4386? Clagett, William, 1699
For W. Rogers.
Dur.

C4387 Clagett, William, 1687
Yk.

C4388 Clagett, William, 1686
Ban. Bur. Dur. Ex. Nor. Sal.
Wel.

C4390 Clagett, William, 1687
Ban. Carl. Chi. Ex (2). S Pl.
Sal. Wel.

C4391 Clagett, William, 1688
Cant.

C4395 Clagett, William, 1688
Ex.

C4396 Clagett, William, 1689
Ban. Ely. S Asa. S Dv. Wel.

C4397 Clagett, William, 1694
Glo.

C4398 Clagett, William, 1699
Dur.

C4399 Clagett, William, 1688
Impr. as Wing2.
Ex (3). Wel.

C4400 Clagett, William, 1688
Ban. Bris. Chi. Ex. Liv. Nor
(2). Sal. Wel.

C4402 Clagett, William, 1687
Ban. Bur. Carl. Dur. Ex (2).
Nor. S Pl. Sal. Swel. Wel.

C4404 Clamor, 1680
Linc.

C4407 Clapham, Jonathan, 1656
Yk.

C4414 Clarendon, Edward Hyde,
Earl of, 1673
Cant. Carl. Chelm. Ches. Ely.
Ex. Linc. S Asa. Yk.

C4415 Clarendon, Edward Hyde,
Earl of, 1674
Liv. Sal.

C4419 Clarendon, Edward Hyde,
Earl of, 1641
Cant. Linc. Sal. Yk (5).

C4420 Clarendon, Edward Hyde,
Earl of , 1676
Bris. Cant. Her. Sal. Win.
Wor.

C4421 Clarendon, Edward Hyde,
Earl of, 1676
Ely. Nor. Yk.

C4423 Clarendon, Edward Hyde,
Earl of, 1648
Linc. Yk.

C4424 Clarendon, Edward Hyde,
Earl of, 1656
Carl. Linc. Yk.

C4425+ Clarendon, Edward Hyde,
Earl of, [1689?]
cap.; 4°.
Yk (imp).

C4426 Clarendon, Edward Hyde,
Earl of, 1641
Cant. Linc.

C4429 Clarendon, Edward Hyde,
Earl of, [1680?]
Dur. Linc. Wor.

C4437+ Clark, Edward, 1680
By T.B., to be sold by Enoch Prossor;
12°.
Cant (imp).

C4440 Clark, Francis, 1666
Cant (2). Carl. Roch. S Pl.

C4441 Clark, Francis, 1667
Impr. as Wing2.
Cant. Carl.

C4443 Clark, Francis, 1684
Editio secunda.
Bris. Yk.

C4445- Clarke, George, 1677
=Wing2 C4444B.
Win.

C4466 Clark, James, 1690
'... Auldhamstocks, September ...'
Cant.

C4468A-- Clark, John, 1647
= Wing2 C4468B.
Lich.

C4468A- Clark, John, 1653
= Wing2 C4468C.
Ex.

C4472 Clark, John, 1646
Pet (2 − 1 imp).

C4478 Clark, John, 1684
Cant. Llan.

C4479 Clark, Joshua, 1691
Cant. Carl (imp). Ex. Pet.
Wor.

C4480 Clark, Joshua, 1698
Yk.

C4490 Clarke, Samuel, *Minister of Grendon-Underwood*, 1699
Ex.

C4494+ Clarke, Samuel, *Minister of Grendon-Underwood*, 1696
= Wing2 C4494A; 'Neck and all'; For Samuel Manship; 4°; Date as given.
Cant.

C4499 Clarke, Samuel, *Minister of Grendon-Underwood*, 1693
... for Jonathan Robinson.
Dur.

C4500 Clarke, Samuel, *of Oxford*, 1661
Wel. Yk.

C4502 Clarke, Samuel, *Minister of St Bennet Fink*, 1664
Carl.

C4504 Clarke, Samuel, *Minister of St Bennet Fink*, 1659
Carl. Pet.

C4506 Clarke, Samuel, *Minister of St Bennet Fink*, 1662
Cant.

C4508 Clarke, Samuel, *Minister of St Bennet Fink*, 1643
Yk.

C4512+ Clarke, Samuel, *Minister of St Bennet Fink*, 1679
= Wing2 C4512A, no number assigned in Wing1; 12°.
Ex.

C4513 Clarke, Samuel, *Minister of St Bennet Fink*, 1651
... Thomas Underhill and John Rothwell.
Glo.

C4514 Clarke, Samuel, *Minister of St Bennet Fink*, 1660
Wel.

C4515 Clarke, Samuel, *Minister of St Bennet Fink*, 1677
Cant. Ex.

C4520 *See:* H2094B

C4522 *See:* H2094D

C4525 Clarke, Samuel, *Minister of St Bennet Fink*, 1653
Cant. Carl. Ex.

C4533 Clarke, Samuel, *Minister of St Bennet Fink*, 1671
'The life & death ...'
Llan.

C4539 Clarke, Samuel, *Minister of St Bennet Fink*, 1677
The third edition.
Cant.

C4544 Clarke, Samuel, *Minister of St Bennet Fink*, 1654
Lich.

C4545 Clarke, Samuel, *Minister of St Bennet Fink*, 1675
Ches. Dur. Ex. Liv (tpw).

C4546 Clarke, Samuel, *Minister of St Bennet Fink*, 1652
Glo. Linc.

C4547 Clarke, Samuel, *Minister of St Bennet Fink*, 1659
Ratcliff.
Her.

C4552 Clarke, Samuel, *Minister of St Bennet Fink*, 1671
Dur.

C4556 Clarke, Samuel, *Minister of St Bennet Fink*, 1650
Sal.

C4556A Clarke, Samuel, *Minister of St Bennet Fink*, 1650
4°.
Sal.

C4560 Clarke, Samuel, *Minister of St Bennet Fink*, 1664
For William Miller.
Yk.

C4561 Clarke, Samuel, *of St James, Westminster*, 1699
Bur. Chi. Ely. Ex. S Pl.

C4566 Clarke, William, *of North Crawley*, 1656
Ex.

C4567 *See:* F2368A

C4569 Clarkson, David, 1681
Cant. Linc. Nor (imp). Win.

C4571 Clarkson, David, 1682
Part of B1438.
Ban. Yk.

C4573 Clarkson, David, 1688
Linc.

C4574 Clarkson, David, 1681
S Pl (imp).

C4575 Clarkson, David, 1676
Ban. Bur. Carl. Ex. Her. S Pl.

C4576 Clarkson, David, 1688
Nor. Yk.

C4577 Clarkson, David, 1689
... Jonathon Robinson; 8°.
Yk.

C4581? Clarkson, Lawrence, 1660
... sold by William Learner; 4°.
Pet.

C4582? Clarkson, Lawrence, 1659
... Wil. Learner.
Pet.

C4588 Claude, Jean, 1686
Carl. Wel.

C4589 Claude, Jean, 1686
Wel.

C4591 Claude, Jean, 1687
Ban. Ex. Sal. Wel.

C4592 Claude, Jean, 1684
Date as Wing2.
Bris. Lich. Pet. S Asa.

C4593 Claude, Jean, 1683
Dur.

C4595? Claude, Jean, 1688
'... Mr. Claude's answer to Monsieur de Meaux's book ...'
Sal.

C4597? Claude, Jean, 1683
12°.
Win.

C4600 Clavell, Robert, 1675
Second ed. not on tp.
S Pl. Sal.

C4601? Clavell, Robert, 1680
'... MDCLXXX'; Third ed. not on tp; ... Robert Clavell.
Pet. Yk.

C4604+ Clavell, Roger, 1669
= Wing2 C4604B; The second impression.
Yk.

C4610 Clayton, John, 1651
Yk (2).

C4617 Cleere, 1647
Yk (2).

C4618 Cleare, 1648
Dur. Yk.

C4621 Cleere, 1645
Yk.

C4625 Cleeve, Charles, 1685
· Cant. Ex.

C4628 Clement, *of Alexandria*, 1683
Ex. S Pl. Win. Yk.

C4629 Clement I, 1647
Carl. Ches. Linc (2). Pet.

C4631 Clement I, 1669
... excudebat A. & L. Lichfield; 12°.
Carl (tp imp). Ches. Dur. Linc.
S Pl. Win.

C4632 Clement I, 1677
Nor. Yk.

C4633 Clement I, 1687
Dur. S Asa. S Pl. Wel. Yk.

C4635? Clement I, 1695
Impensis Jacobi Adamson.
Ches.

C4640 Clenche, William, 1686
Bur.

C4641 Clendon, Thomas, 1653
Bris.

C4641+ Clendon, Thomas, 1674
=Wing2 C4641A.
Ex.

C4643 Clerambault, Philippe de,
1677
Author as Wing2.
Carl.

C4644 Clergyes, 1643
Pet. Yk.

C4654 Cleveland, John, 1687
8°.
S Pl.

C4661 Cleveland, John, 1644[5]
6p.
Linc.

C4662? Cleveland, John, 1647
Third ed. not on tp; 50p.; Morris,
John Cleveland, 1967: no. D1.
Pet.

C4666− Cleveland, John, 1647
Optima & novissima editio; [N.pl.];
56p.; 4°; Morris, no. D5.
Pet.

C4673 Cleveland, John, 1654
8°; 154p.
Cant. Linc.

C4676 Cleveland, John, 1662
Cant.

C4679 Cleveland, John, 1649
Ely. Sal. Yk.

C4681 Cleveland, John, 1649
Pet. Yk.

C4696 Cleveland, John, 1662
Sixteenth ed. not on tp.
Cant.

C4704 Clifford, James, 1664
Linc. Pet. S Pl. Yk.

C4706 Clifford, Martin, 1687
Yk.

C4708? Clifford, Martin, 1675
For Henry Brome.
Bur. Cant (imp). Ely. Wel.
Win.

C4709+ Clifford, Thomas, [1672]
=Wing2 C4709A?; 2°.
Linc.

C4710 Clifford, William, 1659
Cant (imp).

C4714 Clifford, William, 1682
Yk.

C4714+ Clifford, William, 1687
The fourth edition; London; 12°.
Yk (impr. not confirmed).

C4719 Cloak, 1679
S Asa.

C4741+ Clüver, Philip, 1697
=Wing2 C4741A?; Amstelaedami:
typis Joannis Wolters, prostant apud
...; 4°.
Glo (imp).

C4746 Coachman, Robert, 1642
S Asa.

C4769 Cob, Christopher, 1651
Ely.

C4776 Cobbet, Thomas, 1653
Chelm. Yk.

C4778 Cobbet, Thomas, 1648
Chelm.

C4781 Cobbet, Thomas, 1657
Yk.

C4789 Cock, Charles George, 1651
Pet.

C4804 Cockburn, John, 1698
Ely (Narrative I only, tpw)*.

C4804+ Cockburn, John, 1698
=Wing2 C4805.
Wel (Narrative I only).

C4805 Cockburn, John, 1691
Yk.

C4809 Cockburn, John , 1691
Yk.

C4809+ Cockburn, John , 1691
=Wing2 C4809A.
Wel.

C4814 Cockburn, John, 1698
Ely. Sal.

C4824 Cocker, Edward, 1691
Cant.

C4862A Cocker, Edward, 1689
Printed for, and sold by Thomas
Basset and George Pawlet.
S Pl.

C4874 Cocks, Roger, 1642
Linc. Pet.

C4877 Codrington, Robert, 1646
Pet.

C4879A? Codrington, Thomas,
1687
'November the 28th'; By Nathaniel
Thompson.
Cant.

C4881 Coe, Richard, 1644
Impr. as Wing2.
Cant.

C4901 Cokayn, George, 1658
Impr. as Wing2.
Yk.

C4906 Coke, *Sir* Edward, 1651
This second impression.
Cant.

C4907+ Coke, *Sir* Edward, 1682
=Wing2 C4907A; Author is in fact
Edward Cooke, of the Middle Temple.
Carl. Dur.

C4909 Coke, *Sir* Edward, 1659
Cant. Linc.

C4912 Coke, *Sir* Edward, 1641
Dur (imp). Yk.

C4914 Coke, *Sir* Edward, 1650
S Asa.

C4917 Coke, *Sir* Edward, 1659
Linc.

C4921 Coke, *Sir* Edward, 1657
Cant (imp).

C4922 Coke, *Sir* Edward, 1670
Cant.

C4924 Coke, *Sir* Edward, 1656
Dur.

C4926 Coke, *Sir* Edward, 1670
Impr. as Wing2.
Wel.

C4928 Coke, *Sir* Edward, 1684
Nor.

C4929 Coke, *Sir* Edward, 1644
Cant.

C4930 Coke, *Sir* Edward, 1648
Second ed. not on tp.
Dur. S Asa.

C4931 Coke, *Sir* Edward, 1669
Impr. as Wing2.
S Pl. Sal (imp).

C4933 Coke, *Sir* Edward, 1681
Nor.

C4936 *See*: A3971

C4938 Coke, *Sir* Edward, 1650
Pet.

C4944 Coke, *Sir* Edward, 1658
Linc.

C4948 Coke, *Sir* Edward, 1642
Cant. Pet. Wor.

C4949 Coke, *Sir* Edward, 1662
Second ed. not on tp.
Dur.

C4950? Coke, *Sir* Edward, 1669
... W. Leake, A. Roper, F. Tyton, T.
Dring [& others].
Llan (imp)*. S Pl.

C4953 Coke, *Sir* Edward, 1681
Impr. as Wing2.
Ex. Nor.

C4960 Coke, *Sir* Edward, 1644
Cant.

C4962 Coke, *Sir* Edward, 1660
Third ed. not on tp.
Dur.

C4963 Coke, *Sir* Edward, 1669
Impr. as Wing2.
S Pl.

C4966 Coke, *Sir* Edward, 1680
Ex. Nor.

C4970 Coke, *Sir* Edward, 1658
Cant. Linc.

C4973 Coke, Roger, 1694
Ex (vol. 1 only).

C4974 Coke, Roger, 1696
Nor.

C4979 Coke, Roger, 1660
Sal. Win.

C4984+ Coke, Roger, 1671
By J.C. for Henry Brome; 4°.
Llan. Win.

C4991 Colbatch, John, 1700
Dur.

C4997 Colbatch, John, 1698
The second edition; By J.D. for
Daniel Brown.
Ely.

C5016 *See*: C6601-

C5022 *See*: C6683A

C5028 Cole, Robert, 1642
Linc.

C5029A - Cole, Thomas, 1688
As C5029A, apart from date.
Yk.

C5032 Cole, Thomas, 1676
Pet (2).

C5036 Cole, William, *a lover of his
country*, 1645[6]
Yk (2).

C5037 Cole, William, *a lover of his
country*, 1661
Win.

C5045 *See*: W1268A-

C5045A *See*: W1268A

C5046 Coleman, Edward, 1678
Yk.

C5049 Coleman, Thomas, 1646
Win.

C5051 Coleman, Thomas, 1644
Her. Yk.

C5052 Coleman, Thomas, 1643
By I.L. for ...
Ex. Linc. Pet.

C5053 Coleman, Thomas, 1645
Win.

C5055 Coleman, Thomas, 1644
Yk (2).

C5056 Coleman, Thomas, 1646
Pet. Win.

C5058 Colepeper, John, *Baron*,
1641
Cant (2).

C5063 Coleraine, Henry Hare,
Baron, 1681
Cant.

C5069+ Coles, Elisha, *the Younger*,
1679
=Wing2 C5069A?; The second edition;
... George Sawbridg, ... John Wright,
Richard Chiswell; 4°.
Ex.

C5069++ Coles, Elisha, *the
Younger*, 1692
The third edition; By R.E. for Peter
Parker; 8°.
Wel.

C5084 Coles, Gilbert, 1688
Ban. Ex. Wel.

C5085 Coles, Gilbert, 1674
Sal. Win.

C5092 Colet, John, 1674
S Pl.

C5093 Colet, John, 1684
Ex.

C5095 Colet, John, 1700
S Pl.

C5096 Colet, John, 1661
By J. Field (printer to the Universitie
of Cambridge) for William Morden.
Cant (imp). Ely. Linc. Pet.
S Pl.

C5102+ Collard, Thomas, 1678
=Wing2 C5102A?; By T.D. for
Thomas Basset.
Carl.

C5105? Collection, 1693
'A collection of all the acts ... relating
to the clergy'; For Jo. Hindmarsh; 8°.
Cant.

C5107+ Collection, 1679
=Wing2 C5107; 'pass'd'
Carl.

C5112 Collection, 1643
London counterfeit ed.
Cant.

C5114 Collection, 1685
'... discourses lately written to recover
...'
Ban. Ely. Ex. Lich. Roch.
Win (tpw).

C5115 Collection, 1685
Ban. Ely. Ex. Lich. Roch.

C5116+ Collection, 1694
The second edition; For Thomas
Basset and Benj. Tooke; 2°.
Ches. S Pl.

C5117 Collection, 1698
Cant (2). Her. Nor. S Asa.
Wor.

C5118 Collection, 1679
Dur. Linc. Wel.

C5145+ Collection, 1662
=Wing2 C5145A.
Cant (2 issues: preachers
numbered or not numbered on tp).

C5146 Collection, 1678
'Dutchess'
Linc. Swel.

C5169A Collection, 1688
Ban. Ely. Pet. S Asa. Wel.

C5192A Collection, 1675
For Richard Royston.
Bur. Dur. Glo. Win.

C5192B Collection, 1688
... Randall Taylor.
Sal.

C5196? Collection, 1652
8°.
Cant.

C5202+ Collection, 1662
'A collection of the farewel-sermons';
8°; Anr ed. of C5638.
Pet.

C5207? Collection, 1642
For Laurence Chapman.
Linc. Pet.

C5216 Collections, 1649
Ex.

C5223 College, Stephen, 1681
Ches.

C5224 College, Stephen, 1681
Ches.

C5229 College, Stephen, 1681
Ches.

C5231 College, Stephen, 1681
Ches.

C5241 Collier, Jeremy, [1689]
Ban.

C5242 Collier, Jeremy, [1696]
S Asa.

C5247? Collier, Jeremy, [1696]
'Sir William Perkins'
Carl. S Asa.

C5248 Collier, Jeremy, 1699
Bur. Cant. Yk.

C5249 Collier, Jeremy, [1689]
Cant.

C5251 Collier, Jeremy, 1686
Pet. S Asa.

C5252 Collier, Jeremy, 1691
S Asa. Wel.

C5254 Collier, Jeremy, 1698
Dur. Ely. Llan.

C5255 Collier, Jeremy, 1700
Bur. Cant. Chi. S Pl.

C5258 Collier, Jeremy, 1688
Lich. S Pl.

C5259 Collier, Jeremy, 1693
Nor.

C5260 Collier, Jeremy, 1695
Cant. Her. S Asa.

C5261 Collier, Jeremy, [1696]
S Asa.

C5262 Collier, Jeremy, 1700
Cant (2). Ches.

C5263 Collier, Jeremy, 1698
Cant. Ches. Ely. Linc. Nor.
Rip.

C5264 Collier, Jeremy, 1698
Yk.

C5265 Collier, Jeremy, 1698
Bur.

C5266 Collier, Jeremy, 1699
Cant (2).

C5267 Collier, Jeremy, 1689
'... juris regii. ...'
S Asa. Wel.

C5267A Collier, Thomas, 1652
Yk.

C5272 Collier, Thomas, [1649?]
8°.
Yk.

C5276 Collier, Thomas, 1659
Yk.

C5279 Collier, Thomas, 1649
8°.
Yk.

C5282 Collier, Thomas, 1647
8°.
Yk.

C5283 Collier, Thomas, 1647
8°.
Yk.

C5287 Collier, Thomas, 1649
8°.
Yk.

C5288 Collier, Thomas, 1647–49
Nor (vol. 1 only). Yk.

C5292 Collier, Thomas, 1650
8°.
Yk.

C5293 Collier, Thomas, 1651
London, for Giles Calvert; 8°.
Yk.

C5295 Collier, Thomas, 1651
Chelm. Liv. Yk.

C5297 Collier, Thomas, 1649
Yk.

C5298 Collier, Thomas, 1649
8°.
Yk.

C5299 Collier, Thomas, 1649
8°.
Yk.

C5306 Collinges, John, 1652
Carl.

C5307 Collinges, John, 1657
Ex.

C5309 Collinges, John, 1650
Carl.

C5310 Collinges, John, 1659
Ex.

C5311 Collinges, John, 1652
Carl. Ex.

C5313 Collinges, John, 1657
New.

C5313+ Collinges, John, 1657
=Wing2 C5313A.
Nor. Yk.

C5315 Collinges, John, 1680
Sal.

C5316 Collinges, John, 1669
Yk.

C5317 Collinges, John, 1650
Wel (pts 3–5 only).

C5322 Collinges, John, 1654[5]
Yk.

C5323? Collinges, John, 1676
Maxwel.
Cant (imp). Ex.

C5324 Collinges, John, 1683
Cant. Ex.

C5326 Collinges, John, 1647
Frankling.
Glo.

C5328 Collinges, John, 1654
Yk.

C5331 Collinges, John, 1652
Dur. Ex. Yk.

C5332 Collinges, John, 1653
Yk.

C5333 Collinges, John, [1655]
Chelm.

C5335+ Collinges, John, 1678
For Tho. Parkhurst; 4°.
Ex.

C5336 Collinges, John, 1680
Carl. Pet.

C5341 Collinges, John, 1647
Ex.

C5342 Collinges, John, 1676
Wor.

C5346 Collinges, John, 1651
Chelm. Dur. Ex. Yk.

C5348 Collinges, John, 1658
Dur.

C5370- Collins, John, 1688
See: CLC31.
Dur.

C5371 Collins, John, 1658
Sal.

C5372 Collins, John, 1685
Pet.

C5375? Collins, John, 1664
... for Thomas Clark.
Sal.

C5381 Collins, John, 1658
Sal.

C5382 Collins, John, 1659
Chelm. Pet.

C5385 Collins, Samuel, 1671
Nor (imp).

C5387 Collins, Samuel, 1685
... Thomas Newcomb.
Dur. Pet.

C5393 Collop, John, 1661
Cant. Carl. Linc. Pet. Win.

C5401- Colom, Jacob Aertsz, 1668
See: CLC32.
Pet.

C5401+ Colom, Jacob Aertsz, 1671
'The fyrie sea-colomne'; Amsterdam,
printed by him selfe; 2°.
Lich.

C5404 Colomiès, Paul, 1686
'Guilielmi'
Bris. S Asa. S Pl. Yk (2).

C5405 Colomiès, Paul, 1687
Ex.

C5406+ Colomiès, Paul, 1688
=Wing2 C5406A.
S Pl.

C5414 Colquitt, Anthony, 1682
Ex.

C5425 Colvill, Samuel, 1673
Ex.

C5425+ Colvill, Samuel, 1673
As C5425, but title is: 'The true grand
impostor ...'
Carl.

C5441 Comber, Thomas, 1678
Win. Yk (3).

C5444+ Comber, Thomas, 1681
=Wing2 C5444A.
Ex. Yk.

C5445- Comber, Thomas, 1682
As C5445, apart from date.
Cant.

C5446? Comber, Thomas, 1686
By M.C. for Robert Clavell & Charles
Brome.
Yk.

C5446+ Comber, Thomas, 1686
By M.C. for Robert Clavel; 8°.
Ely.

C5447 Comber, Thomas, 1695
Dur. Ely. Her. S Pl. Sal. Win.
Yk.

C5450 Comber, Thomas, 1675
Carl. Ches. Yk (2).

C5450+ Comber, Thomas, 1678
=Wing2 C5450A; By John Macock,
for ...
Swel. Wel.

C5451- Comber, Thomas, 1681
=Wing2 C5450B.
Ban. Chi. Ely. Yk.

C5451 Comber, Thomas, 1685
Bur. Llan. Yk.

C5452 Comber, Thomas, 1672
Ches. Linc. Yk.

C5453 Comber, Thomas, 1676
Ches. New. Yk.

C5454 Comber, Thomas, 1679
Ban. Carl. Ely. Her (imp). Yk
(2).

C5455? Comber, Thomas, 1684
... Joan. Brome ...
Dur (imp). New. S Dv.

C5455+ Comber, Thomas, 1684
=Wing2 C5455A.
Her. IoM. Nor. Yk.

C5456- Comber, Thomas, 1684
No ed. statement; By Samuel
Roycroft for Robert Clavell; 2°.
Chi. S Alb. Tru. Win.

C5456 Comber, Thomas, 1688
The third edition.
Ban. Cant. Chelm. Chi. Linc.
Swel (imp?). Wel.

C5456+ Comber, Thomas, 1688
The third edition; By Miles Flesher,
for Robert Clavell; 2°.
Dur. Yk.

C5456++ Comber, Thomas, 1688
The third edition; For R. Clavell, R.
Chiswell, T. Sawbridge, G. Wells, R.
Lambert and R. Bentley; 2°.
Her.

C5456+++ Comber, Thomas, 1688
The third edition; For R. Chiswell, T.
Sawbridge, G. Wells, R. Lambert and
R. Bentley; 2°.
Ex.

C5457 Comber, Thomas, 1676
Carl. Ches. Llan. Yk.

C5458 Comber, Thomas, 1679
Ban. Ely. Her (imp). New.
Wel. Yk (3).

C5459 Comber, Thomas, [1684]
Dur. S Asa. S Dv. S Pl. Yk.

C5461 Comber, Thomas, 1688
Ban. Dur. Swel. Yk.

C5462 Comber, Thomas, 1687
Ban. Carl. Dur (2). S Asa.
S Dv. Yk (2).

C5463 Comber, Thomas, 1696
Ban. Ches. Dur. Ely. S Pl. Yk
(2).

C5464 Comber, Thomas, 1699
Ban. Carl. Ches. Dur (2 states).
Ely. Ex. Lich. Llan. S Asa.
Tru. Yk.

C5465 Comber, Thomas, 1691
Dur (2). Ex. Nor. Yk.

C5466 Comber, Thomas, 1687
Dur. Ely. S Asa.

C5467+ Comber, Thomas, 1675
=Wing2 C5467A.
Carl.

C5468? Comber, Thomas, 1677
12°.
Ely. S Pl.

C5469 Comber, Thomas, 1685
Yk.

C5470 Comber, Thomas, 1686
The fourth edition.
Nor. Yk.

C5472 Comber, Thomas, 1682
4°.
Carl. Ex. Sal. Win. Yk.

C5473 Comber, Thomas, 1685
4°.
Dur. S Asa (2). Swel. Yk.

C5474 Comber, Thomas, 1685
Clavell.
Dur. Ex (tpw). S Asa (2). S Dv.
S Pl. Yk.

C5476 Comber, Thomas, 1689
Ban. Bris. Carl. Ex. Wel (2).

C5477 Comber, Thomas, 1689
Ban. Her. Yk.

C5478 Comber, Thomas, 1689
Bur. Cant.

C5479? Comber, Thomas, 1682
... in York.
Chi. Dur.

C5479+ Comber, Thomas, 1682
By Samuel Roycroft, for Robert
Clavell; 4°.
Yk (2).

C5480 Comber, Thomas, 1679
Ban. Cant. Carl. Ches. Ely.
S Pl. Wel. Yk (3).

C5481 Comber, Thomas, 1686
Cant. Ex. Pet. S Pl. Yk.

C5482+ Comber, Thomas, 1687
=Wing2 C5482A; 'The plausible
arguments of a Romish priest from
antiquity, answered'
Cant. Dur. Ex.

C5483? Comber, Thomas, 1688
For R. Clavell.
Dur.

C5484 Comber, Thomas, 1692/3
Carl (tpw). Yk.

C5485 Comber, Thomas, 1694
Carl. Dur. Her (2). Wor.

C5486 Comber, Thomas, 1681
Cant. Carl. Dur. Sal. Yk.

C5487 Comber, Thomas, 1683
Yk.

C5488 Comber, Thomas, 1677
8°.
Dur (imp). S Pl. Yk.

C5489 Comber, Thomas, 1680
8°.
Dur. S Pl. Win. Yk.

C5490 Comber, Thomas, 1689
Ban. Ches. Dur (2). Ely. Ex.
Her. Lich. Yk.

C5492 Comber, Thomas, 1690
Ban (imp). Bur. Ches (pt 1
only). Dur. Ely (imp?). Ex. Glo.
S Asa. Wel (pt 1 only). Yk.

C5493 Comber, Thomas, 1697
Dur. Her. Wor. Yk.

C5494 Comber, Thomas, 1684
Carl. Yk.

C5495 Comber, Thomas, 1688
Dur. Llan. New. Yk.

C5496 Comber, Thomas, [1688]
Cant. Yk.

C5506 Comenius, Johann Amos,
[1648]
Cant (cropped).

C5508 Comenius, Johann Amos,
1650
8°.
Pet (imp).

C5509 Comenius, Johann Amos,
1670
Cant.

C5511 Comenius, Johann Amos,
1641
Ex.

C5512? Comenius, Johann Amos,
1643
By James Young, for Thomas Slater.
Yk.

C5515? Comenius, Johann Amos,
1652
... to be sold by the Company of
Stationers.
Wel.

C5518 Comenius, Johann Amos,
1662
S Asa (tpw).

C5520 Comenius, Johann Amos,
1685
Impr. as Wing2.
Ches. Glo. Nor.

C5521 Comenius, Johann Amos,
1656
By William Du-Gard; ...
Cant.

C5523 Comenius, Johann Amos,
1659
'Joh. Amos Commenii Orbis
sensualium pictus ... visible world'
Linc.

C5542 Comines, Philippe de, 1674
Ban. Carl. S Asa.

C5545 *See:* S4400A

C5573? Common, 1660
'... unmasked. Wherein is declared the
unlawfulnesse ... by divers ministers
...'
Carl (2). Dur.

C5602 Company of Scotland,
[1700]
Dur.

C5607 Compendious, 1641
Ex. Pet. Yk.

C5620 Complaint, 1642
Linc. Sal*.

C5621 Complaint, 1642
Cant. Linc (2).

C5623 Complaint, 1642[3]
Yk*.

C5624+ Complaints, 1641
=Wing2 C5625.
S Pl. Yk.

C5636+ Compleat, 1677
'The compleat clerk'; Formerly H43.
Cant.

C5636++ Compleat, 1683
'The compleat clerk'; Formerly H44.
Yk.

C5638 Compleat, 1663
See also C5202+.
Cant (2 eds − 1 imp). Yk.

C5638+ Compleat, 1663
As C5638, but: 'farewell'; 8°.
Yk.

C5638A Compleat, 1689
S Asa. S Pl.

C5638A+ Compleat, 1689
Impr. as C5638A, but: Richard *not*
R.; 4°.
Ely.

C5644 Compleat, 1661
Ed. statement on addit. engr. tp.
Dur (imp).

C5645+ Compleat, 1668
Printed; 12°.
Cant.

C5648 Compleat, 1687
Impr. as Wing2.
Cant.

C5671 Compton, Henry, 1699
Cant.

C5680 Comyne, Eustace, 1680
Linc. Yk.

C5684 Conant, John, 1693
Ely.

C5685? Conant, John, 1699
For Ri. Chiswell ...
Bur. Dur.

C5686? Conant, John, 1697
For Richard Chiswell ...
Bur. Ely.

C5687 Conant, John, 1699
Dur.

C5688 Conant, John, 1698
Bur. Dur. Ely.

C5691 Conant, Malachi, 1669
Carl. Chi. Ex. S Asa.

C5692 Concavum, 1682
Carl.

C5696 Concerning, 1644
Carl.

C5714 Concubinage, 1698
Ely.

C5737 Confessio, 1656
Ex. Pet.

C5738 Confessio, 1659
Dur. Her. Yk.

C5762 Confession, 1651
Entry as Wing2.
Dur. Ely.

C5767? Confession, 1656
12°.
S Pl.

C5780 Confession, 1646
Dur. Win.

C5788+ Confession, 1653
The fifth impression; By Henry Hills;
4°.
Wel. Win.

C5789 Confession, 1644
Carl.

C5791? Confession, 1684
For Samuel Walsall.
Cant.

C5794+ Confession, 1677
For Benjamin Harris; 8°.
S Pl.

C5795 Confession, 1688
Yk.

C5796 Confession, 1658
'Catechismes'; Copies vary.
Ban. Ches. Ex. Lich. Nor.

C5798? Confession, 1688
For the Company of Stationers, to be
sold by Tho. Parkhurst, and Dorman
Newman.
Sal.

C5803- Confessions, 1678/9
See: CLC33.
Ex.

C5813 Confutation, 1643
Yk.

C5844 Congreve, William, 1698
Cant (D6 is a cancel).

C5882? Connection, 1681
'The connection ...'
Carl.

C5886? Connor, Bernard, 1697
... Henrici Nelme, & Samuelis Briscoe.
Yk.

C5889 Connor, Bernard, 1698
Ex.

C5891? Conold, Robert, 1676
... Rose in Norwich, to be sold by
them there and ... [in London].
Pet.

C5892? Conold, Robert, 1677
By R.W. for William Oliver in
Norwich, sold by him there, and R.
Chiswell.
Carl. Pet. Yk.

C5899 Conscience, 1650
Dur. Yk.

C5901 Conset, Henry, 1685
Wel.

C5902? Conset, Henry, 1700
Deeve.
Cant.

C5903 - Conset, John, 1660
=Wing2 C5902A.
Yk.

C5906 Considerations, 1690
Ex.

C5909 Considerations, [1642]
Linc.

C5920 Considerations, 1645
Win.

C5923 Considerations, 1698
Ban.

C5932? Conspiracie, 1641
'A conspiracie discovered: or the
report of a committee to the House of
Commons'
Dur. Linc.

C5948 - Constantine, Henry, 1683
=Wing2 C5947A?; ... Isaac Cleave.
Wor.

C5948 Constantine, William, 1642
Blaicklocke.
Ex.

C5981 - Conversion, 1663
As C5981, apart from date.
Cant.

C5994 Conyers, Tobias, 1660
Carl. S Pl. Yk.

C5998 Cooke, Edward, *of the Inner Temple*, 1681
Carl.

C6003 Cooke, Edward, *of the Middle Temple*, 1680
Linc.

C6018 Cooke, John, *of Cuckstone*, 1676
Cant. Llan.

C6021? Cooke, John, *of Ireland*, 1652
... sold at London, ...
Dur.

C6025 Cooke, John, *Solicitor General*, 1649
Yk.

C6029 Cooke, John, *Solicitor General*, 1646
Ely (imp)*.

C6033 Cooke, Moses, 1679
Glo (tpw).

C6037 Cooke, Shadrach, 1689
Cant. Her.

C6039 Cooke, Thomas, 1641
Ex (2). Pet.

C6045 Coole, [1644]
Date from BM.
Yk.

C6048 Cooper, Andrew, 1642
Linc.

C6052? Cooper, Christopher, 1685
'tripartita' not on tp; Impr. as Wing2.
Ely. Yk.

C6064 Cooper, William, *of St. Olave's*, 1649
Pet.

C6067 + Coote, Edmund, 1655
The 26 time imprinted; By R. & W.
Leybourn for the Company of
Stationers; 4°.
Pet.

C6079 Copies, 1648
Cant. Yk.

C6081 *See:* E1284 +

C6083 Copleston, John, 1661
S Pl.

C6085 Copley, Lionel, 1642
Cant.

C6087 Coppe, Abiezar, 1649[50]
Ex.

C6087 + Coppe, Abiezar, 1649
'Fiery flying roule'; [N.pl.]; 4°.
Ex.

C6112 Copie, 1650[1]
S Asa.

C6119? Copie, 1642
'4. Jul.'
Linc.

C6125 Copie, 1644
Yk.

C6132 Copy, 1642
Dur.

C6133 Copy, [1647]
Cant.

C6137 Coppy, 1641
'coppy'
Linc.

C6139 Copie, 1642
Linc. Pet.

C6140 Copie, 1642
Linc.

C6142 Copie, 1642
Yk.

C6151 Copie, 1642
Yk.

C6163 Coppy, 1660
Yk.

C6174 Copy, 1643
Yk.

C6175 Copy, 1643
Linc.

C6176 + Coppy, 1641
=Wing2 C6176A, but: ... Thomas
Walkley.
Linc. Sal.

C6196 Coppy, 1641
Dur. Linc. Pet.

C6206 *See:* E2543 +

C6210 Copie, 1644
Carl.

C6241 Corbet, Edward, 1642[3]
Cant. Carl. Pet (tpw).

C6243 Corbet, Jeffery, 1654
Ex.

C6247 Corbet, John, *1603—41*, 1684
... for Tho. Fickus.
S Pl.

C6250 Corbet, John, *1603—41*, 1646
Pet.

C6252 Corbet, John, *1620—80*, 1667
Cant. Carl. Chelm. Ex. Her.
Win.

C6252A Corbet, John, *1620—80*, 1668
Carl.

C6254 Corbet, John, *1620—80*, 1682
Win.

C6255 Corbet, John, *1620—80*, 1660
Cant (imp). Ex.

C6256 Corbet, John, *1620—80*, 1661
Carl. Pet.

C6263 Corbet, John, *1620—80*, 1668
Win.

C6270 Corbet, Richard, 1647
Pet.

C6281 Cordemoy, Géraud de, 1670
Yk.

C6282 Cordemoy, Géraud de, 1668
Carl.

C6299? Cork, Richard Boyle, *1st Earl of*, 1642
'of the'
Linc.

C6306 Corker, James, 1681
'memoires'; N. pl.
Yk.

C6329 Cornwallis, *Sir* Charles, 1641
Linc. Pet.

C6342 Coronelli, Vincenzo Maria, 1687
Nor.

C6345 Corraro, Angelo, 1664
Carl.

C6346+ Corraro, Angelo, 1668
For Thomas Raimer; 8°.
Linc.

C6352 Cosin, John, 1655
Cant (2 – 1 imp). Win. Yk.

C6354+ Cosin, John, 1672
=Wing2 C6354A; Sixth ed. not on tp.
Cant (imp).

C6355 Cosin, John, 1676
Cant. Yk (2).

C6357 Cosin, John, 1693
S Asa.

C6358 Cosin, John, 1675
Cant (imp). Carl. Dur. Ely.
Lich. Linc. S Pl (2). Sal (imp).
Yk.

C6359 Cosin, John, 1676
Ban. Ely. Pet (imp). S Asa.

C6359A Cosin, John, 1679
For Henry Brome.
Yk.

C6359A+ Cosin, John, 1687
Anr ed. of Wing2 C6360; For Charles Brome; 8°.
S Pl.

C6361 Cosin, John, 1657
Cant (2). Carl. Dur. Lich.
Linc. New. S Asa. S Pl. Sal.
Wel. Yk.

C6362 Cosin, John, 1672
Second ed. not on tp.
Cant. Ely. Ex. Glo. Her. Liv.
Nor. Roch. Sal. Tru. Wor (2).
Yk (2).

C6363 Cosin, John, 1683
Fourth ed. not on tp.
Ban. Her.

C6373 Cotgrave, Randle, 1679
Cant.

C6374 Cotgrave, Randle, 1650
Ban. Carl.

C6377+ Cotgrave, Randle, 1650
=Wing2 C6377C.
Ex.

C6378 Cotgrave, Randle, 1660
Ely. Pet. Sal.

C6379 Cotgrave, Randle, 1673
Wor.

C6380A Cotton, Charles, 1675
Ex.

C6389 Cotton, Charles, 1689
Dur.

C6392? Cotton, Charles, 1665
'Scarronnides ...'
Ex. Linc (tpw)*.

C6401 Cotton, Charles, 1683
Yk.

C6404 *See*: N929

C6408 Cotton, John, *1585—1652*, 1641
Linc. Yk.

C6411 Cotton, John, *1585—1652*, 1648
S Asa.

C6413 Cotton, John, *1585—1652*, 1654
'briefe'
Carl. Dur.

C6419 Cotton, John, *1585—1652*, 1642
S Asa.

C6420 Cotton, John, *1585—1652*, 1646
Yk.

C6421 Cotton, John, *1585—1652*, 1649
Ex (2).

C6422 Cotton, John, *1585—1652*, 1641
Linc.

C6427 Cotton, John, *1585—1652*, 1658
Carl.

C6433 Cotton, John, *1585—1652*, 1641
Cant. Yk.

C6436 Cotton, John, *1585—1652*, 1647
Her.

C6448 Cotton, John, *1585—1652*, 1650
... for Hanna Allen.
Pet.

C6450 Cotton, John, *1585—1652*, 1645
Carl.

C6451 Cotton, John, *1585—1652*, 1656
Carl.

C6456 Cotton, John, *1585—1652*, 1647
Chelm. Her.

C6457 Cotton, John, *1585—1652*, 1650
Pet. Yk.

C6468 Cotton, John, *1585—1652*, 1642
S Asa.

C6471 Cotton, John, *1585—1652*, 1645
Pet.

C6476 Cotton, *Sir* Robert Bruce, [1642]
Carl.

C6478 Cotton, *Sir* Robert Bruce, 1655
Ex. Linc.

C6480 Cotton, *Sir* Robert Bruce, 1675
Carl.

C6482 Cotton, *Sir* Robert Bruce, 1680
Win.

C6483 *See*: S4233

C6484 *See*: S2083

C6485 Cotton, *Sir* Robert Bruce, 1651
Carl. Ely. Lich.

C6486 Cotton, *Sir* Robert Bruce, 1672
Linc. Nor.

C6487 Cotton, *Sir* Robert Bruce, 1679
Cant. Ex. Wel. Yk.

C6489 Cotton, *Sir* Robert Bruce, 1657
Linc. S Asa. Sal. Win.

C6491 Cotton, *Sir* Robert Bruce, 1689
Cant.

C6492 Cotton, *Sir* Robert Bruce, 1642
'governement'
Linc. Pet.

C6494 Cotton, *Sir* Robert Bruce, 1642
Cant (imp). Carl.

C6497 Cotton, *Sir* Robert Bruce, 1641
Linc. Sal. Yk.

C6502 Cotton, *Sir* Robert Bruce, 1641
Carl.

C6503 Cotton, *Sir* Robert Bruce, 1641
Yk.

C6504 Cotton, *Sir* Robert Bruce, 1642
Linc.

C6514+ Coult, Nicholas, [1645]
See: CLC34.
Yk.

C6514++ Coulton, Richard, 1685
=Wing2 C6514A.
Yk.

C6522 Counter-plot, 1680
Wel. Yk.

C6561 Countrey-minister's, [1688]
cap; 'allowed to be published 1688'
S Asa.

C6566 Country-parson's, 1680
Llan.

C6572 Countreys, 1647
Ex.

C6573 Countries vindication, [1679?]
Dur. Linc.

C6583A Courcelles, Etienne de, 1684
Nor. S Asa.

C6589A Court, 1679
Her.

C6591 Court, 1654
Carl.

C6597+ Courtilz de Sandras, Gatien de, 1684
By H. Hills, for William Cademan; 8°.
Carl.

C6598 Courtilz de Sandras, Gatien de, 1686
Ex. S Pl.

C6599 Courtilz de Sandras, Gatien de, 1695
Title as Wing2.
Ex.

C6600 Courtilz de Sandras, Gatien de, 1696
Ex. Nor.

C6601- Courtilz de Sandras, Gatien de, 1695
=Wing2 C6600B.
Nor. Wel.

C6602 Courtin, Antoine de, 1671
Cant.

C6605 Courtin, Antoine de, 1685
Ex.

C6621 Covenant, 1643
Ex.

C6623 Covenanters, 1647
Sal.

C6624 *See*: D350-

C6631 Coventry, *Sir* William, 1685
Cant (tp imp).

C6643 Cowell, John, *LL.D.*, 1676
Impr. as Wing2; 8°.
Ely.

C6645? Cowell, John, *LL.D.*, 1672
Fourth ed. not on tp.
Ely.

C6646? Cowell, John, *LL.D.*, 1684
The second edition.
Cant. Ex.

C6649 Cowley, Abraham, 1668
Linc. Pet. Roch.

C6651 Cowley, Abraham, 1672
Ex.

C6652 Cowley, Abraham, 1674
Sal.

C6653 Cowley, Abraham, 1678
Ex. Glo.

C6654 Cowley, Abraham, 1680
2°.
Ban (imp). Dur. Ely. Lich (imp).

C6655 Cowley, Abraham, 1681
Cant. S Pl (tp imp). Wel.

C6657 Cowley, Abraham, 1684
The eighth edition; ... Abel Swalle.
Chelm. Glo. Nor. Yk (2).

C6663 Cowley, Abraham, 1681
S Pl (tp imp).

C6665 Cowley, Abraham, 1689
Cant.

C6678 Cowley, Abraham, 1662
Pet.

C6680 Cowley, Abraham, 1668
Ches (imp). Ely. Lich (imp). Linc. Nor (imp). S Asa (imp). S Pl. Win.

C6680+ Cowley, Abraham, 1678
Typis T. Roycroft, impensis J. Martyn; 8°.
Ex.

C6683 Cowley, Abraham, 1656
Cant. Carl.

C6683A Cowley, Abraham, 1642
Pet. S Pl (imp).

C6695 Cowley, Abraham, 1661
Carl. Linc.

C6697 Cowley, Abraham, 1682
Carl.

C6712 Coxe, Benjamin, 1646
'after-reckoning'
Pet.

C6720 Coxe, *Sir* Richard, 1689
Wel.

C6722 Coxe, *Sir* Richard, 1689-90
Dur. Ex. Pet.

C6727+ Coxe, Thomas, 1669
=Wing2 C6728.
Her. Win.

C6739 Crackanthorp, Richard, 1641
Her. Sal.

C6740 Crackanthorp, Richard, 1670
Lich.

C6741 Crackanthorp, Richard, 1677
Oxoniae, typis L. Lichfield ... impensis Iohannis Williams.
Liv.

C6743 Cradock, Francis, 1661
Yk.

C6744 Cradock, Samuel, 1672
Ely. Ex. Her. Linc.

C6748 Cradock, Samuel, 1668
Carl. Ely. Glo. Pet.

C6750 Cradock, Samuel, 1683
Ely.

C6752+ Cradock, Samuel, 1665
For William Grantham, Henry Mortlock and William Miller; 4°.
Carl.

C6754 Cradock, Samuel, 1673
4°.
Ban. Ex.

C6756 Cradock, Samuel, 1679
Impr. as Wing2.
Ban. Carl. Ex.

C6760? Cradock, Walter, 1651
4°.
Pet.

C6765 Cradock, Walter, 1646
Ex.

C6766 Cradock, Zachary, 1678
Cant. Ches. Llan. Wor.

C6766+ Cradock, Zachary, 1678
As C6766, but: '... February 10th 1677'
Sal.

C6767 Cradock, Zachary, 1678
Ban. Cant. Carl. Her. Yk.

C6769 Cradock, Zachary, 1693
Ely.

C6770 Cradock, Zachary, 1695
Her. Nor.

C6782 Cragg, John, 1656
Dur. Pet. S Asa.

C6783 Cragg, John, 1657
Pet.

C6787 Cragg, John, 1654
Pet (tp imp).

C6798 Craig, John, 1699
Glo.

C6806 Crandon, John, 1654
Sal.

C6809 Crane, Richard, 1662
S Pl.

C6818 Crane, Thomas, 1672
S Asa.

C6819 Crane, Thomas, 1690
Cant. Ches. Her.

C6821 *See*: C6852-

C6822A *See*: F1666

C6823 Cranford, James, 1646
Pet. S Pl.

C6826 Cranmer, George, 1642
Cant. Carl. Ex.

C6827 Cranmer, Thomas, 1689
Ex. Roch. Wel.

C6828 Cranmer, Thomas, 1641
4°.
Bur. Ches. Ely. Llan.

C6828+ Cranmer, Thomas, 1661
Iuxta exemplar Londinense 1571, & venales habentur apud T. Garthwait;
4°.
Bris. Win.

C6834 Crashaw, Richard, 1670
Ely. Yk.

C6837 Crashaw, Richard, 1648
Carl.

C6839 Crashaw, Richard, 1670
The 2nd edition.
Ex.

C6841 Crashaw, William, 1641[2]
Pet. Yk.

C6844 Crashaw, William, 1662
Carl. Yk.

C6845 Crashaw, William, 1665
4°.
Linc. S Pl.

C6848 Crashaw, William, 1676
S Pl (imp).

C6849 Crashaw, William, 1683
Dur.

C6852- Crauford, James, 1643
=Wing2 C6851B.
Pet. Yk.

C6853 Crauford, James, 1681
Impr. as Wing2.
Ely.

C6867 Creamer, Charles, 1675
Win.

C6873 Creed, William, [1660]
Carl. Pet.

C6874? Creed, William, 1660
'allegeance'
Carl.

C6875 Creed, William, 1660
Pet. Yk (imp).

C6876 Creighton, Robert, 1682
Cant.

C6877 Crell, Johann, 1646
Cant (2). Ex. Linc. S Asa.

C6878 Crell, Johann, 1650
Carl. Ex. Linc. Pet.

C6879 Crell, Johann, 1646
Pet.

C6885 Cressener, A., 1687
Ex. Llan. Yk.

C6886 Cressener, Drue, 1690
Bur. Ely (2). Pet.

C6887 Cressener, Drue, 1689
Ely. Swel.

C6890-- Cressy, Edmund, 1675
As Wing2 C6889B, apart from date.
S Asa.

C6890- Cressy, Edmund, 1676
=Wing2 C6889B.
S Pl. Yk.

C6890 Cressy, Hugh Paulin, 1668
Impr. as Wing2.
Dur. Ely. Ex. Glo. Lich. Linc. Sal. Yk (tpw).

C6890+ Cressy, Hugh Paulin, 1672
[N.pl.]; 2°.
Wor.

C6891 Cressy, Hugh Paulin, 1672
Consists of C6892, C6898, W3454, W3455.
Glo. Linc. Win.

C6892 Cressy, Hugh Paulin, 1671
Ex. Glo. Linc. Win.

C6893 Cressy, Hugh Paulin, 1674
'An epistle ...'
Carl. Linc. Win.

C6894 Cressy, Hugh Paulin, 1647
Cant. Carl. Lich. Yk.

C6895 Cressy, Hugh Paulin, 1653
Wel.

C6898 Cressy, Hugh Paulin, 1672
Glo. Linc. Win.

C6899 Cressy, Hugh Paulin, 1662
Title as Wing2.
Carl. Win.

C6901+ Cressy, Hugh Paulin, 1661
=Wing2 C6901.
Win.

C6902 Cressy, Hugh Paulin, 1663
Why [*sic*]?
Carl. Pet. Sal. Win.

C6903 *See*: W2070+

C6918 Crisp, Samuel, 1691
Bur.

C6926 Crisp, Stephen, 1688
Wel.

C6941+ Crisp, Stephen, 1694
=Wing2 C6941A.
Carl.

C6947 Crisp, Thomas, 1694
Swel.

C6949 Crisp, Thomas, 1695
Wel.

C6950 Crisp, Thomas, 1695
Swel. Wel.

C6951? Crisp, Thomas, 1682
... Enoch Prosser.
Swel.

C6952 Crisp, Thomas, 1697
S Pl.

C6953+ Crisp, Thomas, [168-]
=Wing2 C6953A.
Swel.

C6956 Crisp, Tobias, 1644
Sal (vol. 1 only).

C6957 Crisp, Tobias, 1690
Ex (imp).

C6959 - Crisp, Tobias, 1646
As C6959, apart from date.
Lich.

C6960 Crispianism, 1693
Carl (tpw).

C6961 Crockat, Gilbert, 1692
S Asa (imp). Yk.

C6962 Crockat, Gilbert, 1693
Cant. Linc. Yk.

C6964 Crodacott, John, 1655
Yk.

C6965 Croese, Gerard, 1696
Dur. Ex.

C6966 Croft, Herbert, 1679
Cant (2). Carl. Dur. Ex. Her.
S Dv (imp). Yk.

C6967 Croft, Herbert, 1679
Dur.

C6968 Croft, Herbert, 1674
Cant.

C6969 Croft, Herbert, 1679
Carl.

C6970 Croft, Herbert, 1675
Bris. Bur. Cant (imp). Linc.
Llan. Pet. Sal.

C6972 Croft, Herbert, 1689
Cant. S Pl. Wel.

C6973 Croft, Herbert, 1678
Cant. Carl. Dur. Her. Linc.
Wor.

C6974 Croft, Herbert, 1674
Her (2). Linc. Wor (tp imp).
Yk (tp imp).

C6975? Croft, Herbert, 1676
'A sermon preached before the King
...'
Bur. Cant. Carl. Dur. Her*.

C6975+ Croft, Herbert, 1676
As C6975, but: 'A sermon preached in
Lent before the King ...'
Pet.

C6976 Croft, Herbert, 1688
Cant.

C6976+ Croft, Herbert, 1688
For Charles Harper; 4°.
S Pl.

C6977 Croft, Herbert, 1679
Linc. Wel.

C6979 Croft, Herbert, 1685
Lich. S Pl.

C6981 Crofton, Zachary, 1661
Dur.

C6988 Crofton, Zachary, 1661
Pet.

C6995 Crofton, Zachary, 1662
Wor.

C6996 Crofton, Zachary, 1657
Impr. as Wing2.
Yk.

C6997 Crofton, Zachary, 1657
New.

C6998 Crofton, Zachary, 1657
Yk.

C7000 Crofton, Zachary, 1662
Lich (imp).

C7001 Crofton, Zachary, 1671
Sal (imp). Win.

C7003 Crofton, Zachary, [1661]
Cant. Yk (tp imp)*.

C7003+ Crofton, Zachary, 1660/61
As C7003, apart from date.
Wor.

C7003++ Crofton, Zachary, 1663
As Wing2 C7003A, apart from date.
Pet.

C7011 Croke, *Sir* George, 1661
Dur. Wor.

C7012 Croke, *Sir* George, 1669
Win.

C7015 Croke, *Sir* George, 1657
Entry as Wing2; ... Leak ...
Dur.

C7016 Croke, *Sir* George, 1659
Dur. Wor.

C7017 Croke, *Sir* George, 1669
Win.

C7019 - Croke, *Sir* George, 1669
As C7019, apart from date and no ed.
statement.
Wor.

C7019 Croke, *Sir* George, 1669
Win.

C7030 Crompton, Richard, 1641
Title as Wing2.
Ely.

C7031 Crompton, Thomas, 1642[3]
Yk.

C7044 Cromwell, Oliver, 1658[9]
S Pl.

C7045 *See:* E1271

C7054 Cromwell, Oliver, 1656
Yk.

C7057 Cromwell, Oliver, 1653
Pet.

C7060 Cromwell, Oliver, 1653
Linc.

C7075 Cromwell, Oliver, 1655
Linc.

C7080 Cromwell, Oliver, 1654
Dur.

C7081? Cromwell, Oliver, 1655
4°; pp. [113] – 142.
Linc.

C7081+ Cromwell, Oliver, 1653
See: CLC35.
Pet.

C7082 Cromwell, Oliver, 1655
Linc. Win.

C7092 Cromwell, Oliver, 1648
Yk.

C7094 Cromwell, Oliver, 1650
Glo.

C7095 Cromwell, Oliver, 1651
Glo.

C7096 Cromwell, Oliver, 1651
Glo.

C7097 Cromwell, Oliver, 1650
Cant. Pet.

C7098? Cromwell, Oliver, 1649
'... Lenthall ... giving an account ...'
Pet.

C7105 Cromwell, Oliver, 1651
Glo.

C7111 Cromwell, Oliver, 1648
Yk.

C7114 Cromwell, Oliver, 1645
Cant. Pet.

C7116 Cromwell, Oliver, 1648
Yk.

C7134A Cromwell, Oliver, 1653[4]
Dur (no impr., cropped?)*.

C7141? Cromwell, Oliver, 1655
2 leaves, obl.fol.
Linc.

C7142 Cromwell, Oliver, 1656
Linc (imp).

C7143 - Cromwell, Oliver, 1654
'A proclamation ... concerning a
cessation of ... hostility between ...
England, and ... the United
Provinces'; Colophon: By Will.
Du-Guard and Hen. Hills; pp. 185
[*i.e.* 285] – 288; cap.; 2°.
Dur.

C7149+ Cromwell, Oliver, 1653
As C7149; Steele 3024.
Dur.

C7152? Cromwell, Oliver, 1655
2 leaves, obl.fol.
Linc.

C7159+ Cromwell, Oliver, 1654
By Will. du-Gard and Hen. Hills; brs.
Dur.

C7171 Cromwell, Oliver, 1654[5]
Dur (imp). Ex. Linc. Pet.

C7173 Cromwell, Oliver, 1655
Printed at London, and re-printed in
Edinburgh.
Sal.

C7175 Cromwell, Oliver, 1654
Ex. Pet.

C7178 Cromwell, Oliver, 1654
Dur (cropped).

C7191 Cromwell, Richard, [1659]
Ex (2). S Asa. Sal.

C7227 - Crook, Samuel, 1643
See: CLC36.
Pet.

C7228A Crooke, Banks, 1698
Title as Wing2 C7229.
Her. Wor.

C7229 Crooke, Banks, 1695
Her.

C7249 Cross, John, *alias More*,
1687
'An apology ...'; By Nath.
Thompson; 8°.
Wel.

C7256 Crosse, Robert, 1655
... impensis Th. Robinson.
Carl. Ex. Yk.

C7266 + Crosse, William, (1678)
See: CLC37.
Ely.

C7267 Crosses, 1642
... T.V.
Pet.

C7268A Crossman, Samuel, 1682
Carl.

C7270 Crossman, Samuel, 1676
Wor.

C7270 + Crossman, Samuel, 1680
=Wing2 C7270A?; '... preached upon
April xxiii. MDCLXXX. ...'
Cant.

C7291 + Crouch, John, 1663
=Wing2 C7291A?; By H. Brugis for
the author.
Pet.

C7292 + Crouch, John, 1662
See: CLC38.
Linc.

C7310 + Crouch, Nathaniel, [1689]
See: CLC39.
Cant.

C7322 + Crouch, Nathaniel, 1698
The fifth edition; For N. Crouch; 12°.
Cant (imp).

C7329 Crouch, Nathaniel, 1681
Yk (imp).

C7350 Crouch, Nathaniel, 1685
12°.
Cant (tp imp).

C7363 - Crouch, Nathaniel, [before
1691?]
12°; 94p.; Possibly 18th cent.
Cant (tpw, not 3rd or 12th ed.).

C7367 Crowe, William, 1668
Entry as Wing2.
Ban. Cant. Ely. Her. Liv (imp).
S Asa. S Dv. S Pl (2). Sal.

C7368 Crowe, William, 1672
... Mosen Pitts.
Dur. Ex. S Pl. Wor. Yk.

C7369 Crowe, William, 1663
Cant. Carl. Ex. Linc.

C7372 Crown, S., 1660
Linc.

C7378 Crowne, John, 1683
Ex.

C7408A Crowshey, John, 1651
Yk.

C7408A + Crowshey, John, 1646
[*i.e.* 1656]
=Wing2 C7408AA?; ... Francis
Mawbury ...
Yk (date corrected in MS).

C7408C + Crowshey, John, 1683
The eleventh edition; York; 8°.
Yk (impr. not confirmed).

C7416 Cruell, 1642
Dur.

C7426 Crull, Jodocus, 1694
Carl.

C7431 + Crusius, Thomas
Theodorus, 1684
=Wing2 C7431A?; For Walter
Kettilby; Wing has wrong date.
S Asa.

C7432 Cruso, John, 1642
Cant. Sal. Yk.

C7435 Cruso, Timothy, 1689
Sal.

C7438 Cruso, Timothy, 1689
Sal.

C7440 Cruso, Timothy, 1689
Sal. Wor.

C7441 Cruso, Timothy, 1693
Cant.

C7446 Cruso, Timothy, 1689
Sal.

C7449 *See*: B2990

C7450 Cry, 1664
Yk.

C7452? Crymes, Thomas, 1654
'carmina'; ... venundat L. Chapman.
Ex.

C7464 Cudworth, John, 1688
Sal. Yk.

C7466 Cudworth, Ralph, 1642
Carl. Pet.

C7467 Cudworth, Ralph, 1670
Cant. Ches. Pet. S Asa. S Pl.
Win.

C7468 Cudworth, Ralph, 1676
Carl. Dur. Sal.

C7469 Cudworth, Ralph, 1647
Carl. Chelm. Pet.

C7470? Cudworth, Ralph, 1664
'Honourable'
Wor.

C7471 Cudworth, Ralph, 1678
Ban (2). Cant (2). Chi. Dur.
Ely. Glo. Lich (2). Linc. S Asa.
S Pl (2). Sal (2 − 1 imp). Swel.
Win. Wor. Yk.

C7472 Cudworth, Ralph, 1642
Carl.

C7477 + Culman, Leonard, 1697(?)
Excudebat J.R. pro Societatis
Stationariorum; 8°.
Wel (v. imp).

C7478 Culmer, Richard, 1644
Cant (2).

C7479 Culmer, Richard, 1649
Cant (cropped). S Pl.

C7480 Culmer, Richard, 1655
Cant (2).

C7485 Culpeper, Nicholas, 1652
Yk (imp).

C7514 + Culpeper, Nicholas, 1698
=Wing2 C7514A.
Cant.

C7530 Culpeper, Nicholas, 1659
This sixt edition.
Linc.

C7541? Culpeper, Nicholas, 1650
By Peter Cole, and are to be sold at
his shop.
Cant (imp).

C7542 Culpeper, Nicholas, 1651
Pet (imp).

C7555 Culpeper, *Sir* Thomas, *the
Younger*, 1668
Yk..

C7563 Culpeper, *Sir* Thomas, *the Younger*, 1668
Llan.

C7566 Culverwell, Ezekiel, 1646
Sal.

C7567 Culverwell, Ezekiel, 1648
Sal.

C7568 Culverwell, Ezekiel, 1646
12°.
Sal.

C7569 Culverwell, Nathaniel, 1652
Carl. Chelm.

C7570 Culverwell, Nathaniel, 1654
Rothwel.
Bur.

C7572? Culverwell, Nathaniel, 1669
Dymock.
Sal.

C7573? Culverwell, Nathaniel, 1651
Cambridge, by ...
Ex.

C7573+ Culverwell, Nathaniel, 1654
=Wing2 C7573A.
Yk.

C7576 Cumberland, Henry Clifford, *Earl of*, 1642
Yk (2).

C7577 Cumberland, Henry Clifford, *Earl of*, 1642
Linc. Yk.

C7578 Cumberland, Henry Clifford, *Earl of*, 1642
Yk.

C7579 Cumberland, Henry Clifford, *Earl of*, 1642
Yk.

C7580 Cumberland, Richard, 1672
Ely. Ex. Linc. Nor. Pet.
S Asa. S Pl. Sal. Win. Wor.

C7581 Cumberland, Richard, 1686
Ban. Ches. Dur. Ely. S Asa.

C7582 Cumberland, Richard, 1699
Pet.

C7583+ Cumming, John, 1695
=Wing2 C7583A; 'A sermon ...'; ...
Brown at Shepton Mallet.
Ches. Her.

C7586 Cunning, 1643[4]
Sal.

C7590 Cunningham, Alexander, 1689
Ban (sig. A only).

C7592 Cunningham, Alexander, 1690
Cant. Ex. Wel.

C7617 Curates, 1641
Yk.

C7620 Curb, 1641
Linc.

C7622A Curio, Caelius Secundus, 1689
Ex. Wel.

C7678 Curious, 1688
Ban. Wel.

C7681 Curriehill, *Sir* John Skene, *Lord*, 1641
Lich. Linc.

C7687 Cursory, 1699
Nor.

C7697 Curtius Rufus, Quintus, 1670
Liv.

C7697B Curtius Rufus, Quintus, 1674
Linc.

C7700 Curtois, John, 1685
Wel.

C7702? Curtois, John, 1684
... Joseph Lawson of Lincoln ...
Carl. Linc.

C7706 Cutlore, Joseph, 1682
Cant. Llan.

C7711 Cyprian, 1682
Ban. Cant. Carl. Ches. Chi.
Dur. Ely. Glo (imp). Her (2).
Linc. Nor. Rip. S Asa. S Pl (2).
Sal (2). Wel. Win. Wor. Yk (2).

C7712 Cyprian, 1700
Roch. S Alb.

C7712+ Cyprian, 1700
Editio tertia; Oxonii, et veneunt
Parisiis apud Joannem Boudot; 2°.
Roch.

C7714 Cyprian, 1681
Cant. Glo. Yk.

D7 D., C., 1646
=Pt 2 of L1883 – not really separate
item?
Pet. Yk.

D25 D., I., 1653
Win.

D35 D., J., 1641
'judgement'
Pet.

D46 D., J., 1679
Linc.

D48 D., J., [1679]
4p.
Linc.

D50 D., J. D., 1663
For John Crook.
Cant.

D53 D., L., 1661
For the author; Signed C.D.
Carl.

D53+ D., L., [1661?]
As D53, but no date.
Pet.

D63 D., M., 1679
Nor (imp).

D68 D., N., 1679
Dur. Linc.

D87- D., T., 1696
=Wing2 D86A?; ... Will. Bonny ...
Bris.

D92 D., T., [1681/2]
Linc (2).

D99 D., W., 1688
Wel.

D113 Daillé, Jean, 1653
Carl. Pet.

D114 Daillé, Jean, 1672
Cant. Ex (2). Her. Pet.

D116 Daillé, Jean, 1680
Also issued as pt 1 of L2593A.
Ban. Cant. Carl. Linc.

D117 Daillé, Jean, 1671
Cant. Ex (2). Her. Pet.

D118 Daillé, Jean, 1651
Carl. Dur. Ely. Ex. Glo. Llan.
New. S Asa. S Pl.

D119 Daillé, Jean, 1675
Second ed. not on tp.
Liv. Sal. Yk.

D126 Dale, Samuel, 1693
Impr. as Wing2.
Ex (2).

D128 Dalgarno, George, 1661
Pet.

D131+ Dalhusie, John Herman, 1692
Impr. as D131; 8°.
Carl.

D132 Dalhusie, John Herman, 1689
Cant. Carl. Nor. Wel (2).

D135 Dalicourt, Pierre, 1669
Ex.

D138 Dallison, Charles, 1648
Dur. Yk.

D139 Dallison, Charles, 1642
Entry as Wing2; brs.
Dur.

D139+ Dallison, Charles, 1642
'A speech delivered ...'; First printed
at Yorke, and now re-printed at
London for T.J., Agust [sic] 3; 4°.
Linc.

D145 Dalton, Michael, 1661
Yk.

D146 Dalton, Michael, 1666
Dur. Wel. Wor.

D147 Dalton, Michael, 1677
Ches. Dur. Sal. Yk.

D157 Damnable, 1641
Linc.

D161 Dampier, William, 1697
Ex.

D164 Dampier, William, 1699
Dur.

D165 Dampier, William, 1699
Ex.

D166 Dampier, William, 1700
Dur.

D183 Dangerfield, Thomas, 1680
Ely. Linc. Win.

D187 Dangerfield, Thomas, 1680
Ches. Ely. Glo. Linc. Win.
Yk (imp).

D190 Dangerfield, Thomas, 1685
S Pl.

D192 Dangerfield, Thomas, 1679
Ely. Linc. Yk.

D193 Dangerfield, Thomas, 1680
Linc. Win. Yk.

D195 Dangerous, 1652
Glo.

D201 Daniel, Gabriel, 1692
Wel.

D206 Daniel, Samuel, 1642
Ches.

D207 Daniel, Samuel, 1650
... John Williams.
Carl.

D208 Daniel, Samuel, 1685
Impr. as Wing2.
Ban. Nor. S Asa.

D213 Danson, Thomas, 1676
Linc.

D234 D'Anvers, Henry, 1674
For Fran. Smith.
S Pl. Sal.

D236 D'Anvers, Henry, 1674
S Pl. Sal.

D242 Dapper, Olfert, 1671
Ex. Win.

D251 Darell, John, 1652
Sal.

D262+ Darling, John, 1694
=Wing2 D262A.
Cant.

D266 Darrell, William, 1687
S Asa.

D268 Darrell, William, 1687
Wel.

D269+ Darrell, William, 1688
=Wing2 D269A; '... human respects'
Cant.

D270 Darrell, William, 1688
Wel.

D273 Darton, Nicholas, 1641
Linc. Sal.

D277? Dary, Michael, 1677
... William Fisher; 8°.
Linc.

D281 D'Assigny, Marius, 1699
Ex. S Asa.

D289 Dauncey, John, 1661
Carl.

D290 Dauncey, John, 1660
Bris.

D291 Dauncey, John, 1660
Linc. Yk.

D298 D'Auvergne, Edward, 1694
Cant.

D299 D'Auvergne, Edward, 1693
Cant. Wel (imp).

D300 D'Auvergne, Edward, 1693
Cant.

D304 Davenant, Charles, 1700
Glo.

D305 Davenant, Charles, 1700
For James Knapton.
S Pl. Swel. Yk.

D306 Davenant, Charles, 1698
Glo. Swel.

D308 Davenant, Charles, [1697]
For J.K.
Glo.

D309 Davenant, Charles, 1699
For James Knapton.
Swel. Yk.

D310 Davenant, Charles, 1700
For James Knapton.
Glo.

D312 Davenant, Charles, 1695
Glo. Swel.

D314 Davenant, John, 1641
Pet.

D315 Davenant, John, 1641
Ban. Bur. Cant. Carl. Her.
Linc. Sal (tpw)*. Wor.

D315+ Davenant, John, 1641
Cambridge, by Roger Daniel, sold by
Andrew Crooke [London]; 8°.
S Pl.

D317 Davenant, John, 1650
Dur. Ex. Her. S Asa. Swel.
Wor.

D318 Davenant, John, 1641
Pet. Sal.

D319 Davenant, John, 1641
Carl. Pet. Sal. Win. Yk (2).

D320 Davenant, Sir William, 1673
Ely. Glo. Nor.

D326 Davenant, Sir William, 1651
Lich. Linc.

D333? Davenant, Sir William, 1663
Herringman.
Linc.

D334A? Davenant, Sir William,
1650
... Matthieu Guillemot.
Ches.

D350- Davenport, Christopher,
1654
=Wing2 D350, but: 'An enchyridion
...'; 12°.
Carl.

D361 Davenport, John, 1653
Pet.

D364 Davenport, John, 1642
Linc. S Asa (tp imp). Yk.

D371 Davenport, Robert, 1662
Pet (date pr. as 662).

D373+ Davenport, Thomas,
[1675?]
See: CLC40.
Dur.

D385 Davies, Athanasius, 1656
Carl.

D392 Davies, John, of Kidwelly,
1672
Carl. Dur (2). Linc. S Pl. Yk.

D393 Davies, John, of Kidwelly,
1661
S Asa.

D397 Davies, Sir John, 1674
Glo. Lich.

D398 Davies, Sir John, 1677
Dur.

D401 Davies, Sir John, 1664
Second ed. not on tp.
Carl.

D407 Davies, *Sir* John, 1656
By S.G. for Henry Twyford and Rich:
Marriot.
Pet.

D408 Davies, *Sir* John, 1674
Carl. Dur (imp).

D410? Davies, *Sir* John, 1658
... Thomas Jenner.
Cant.

D412A Davila, Enrico Caterino,
1648
'civill'
Wor.

D413 Davila, Enrico Caterino, 1647
Ban. Bur. Carl. Ely. Ex. Glo.
Pet (imp). Wor.

D414 Davila, Enrico Caterino, 1678
In the Savoy ...
Bur. Dur. Nor. Wel (2). Yk.

D417 Davis, Hugh, 1669
2°.
Carl. Chi. Sal. Win. Yk.

D434 Davis, Richard, 1693
Wor.

D440? Davison, Thomas, 1684
... sold by Joseph Hall, New-castle.
Carl. Win.

D441 Davison, Thomas, 1688
Wor. Yk (3).

D443 Davy, John, 1651
Yk.

D449? Dawbeny, Henry, 1661
114p.
Cant. Nor. Pet. Win. Wor.
Yk (2 − 1 tp imp).

D449+ Dawbeny, Henry, 1661
As D449, but: 110p.
Dur.

D450- Dawes, Lancelot, 1652
As D450, apart from date.
Carl.

D450 Dawes, Lancelot, 1653
Ex.

D451 Dawes, Thomas, 1695
Ches.

D453 Dawes, *Sir* William, 1694
Ches.

D454 *See*: Wing vol. 2, 2nd ed.,
'Concordance of vol. 1 numbers':
date = 1707

D455 Dawes, *Sir* William, 1700
Ches. Yk (imp).

D456 Dawes, *Sir* William, 1696
Cant. Yk.

D456+ Dawes, *Sir* William, 1696
The second edition; For Thomas
Speed; 4°.
Yk.

D457 Dawes, *Sir* William, 1697
Bur. Cant. Ex. Yk.

D458 Dawkins, William, 1679
Linc.

D459 Dawson, George, 1694
For Richard Chiswell.
Dur. Glo. Pet. S Asa. Sal. Yk.

D459+ Dawson, Richard, 1661
= Wing2 D459B.
Pet.

D463 Day, Henry, 1696
Cant.

D470 Day, Richard, 1652
Pet.

D471 Day, Robert, 1700
Pet.

D472 Day, William, 1654
Ex. S Asa.

D473 Day, William, 1666
S Asa. Win. Yk.

D478 De, 1654
Dur.

D484 Deacon, John, *Polemical
writer*, 1656
Yk.

D490 Deageant de Saint-Martin,
Guichard, 1690
Ex (tp imp).

D491 Dean, Edmund, 1649
... by Tho. Broad.
Yk.

D499 Deane, Thomas, 1688
S Pl.

D506 Debate, 1695
... sold by the booksellers of London
and Westminster.
S Asa.

D511 Debes, Lucas Jacobson, 1676
Ex. Pet (imp). Win.

D512 Decay, 1641
Linc.

D548 Declaration, 1647
Yk.

D550 Declaration, 1647
'Northerne'
Yk.

D559 Declaration, 1660
Linc.

D562 Declaration, 1645
Yk.

D570 Declaration, 1642
Linc.

D579 Declaration, 1647
Yk (2).

D581+ Declaration, 1647
= Wing2 D581A?; '... his excellence Sir
Thomas Fairfax ... at Putney, ...
September 16, 1647 ...'; For George
Whittington.
Yk.

D582 Declaration, [1648]
Pet. Yk (2).

D583 Declaration, 1647[8]
Yk.

D584 Declaration, 1649
Yk.

D585 Declaration, 1648
Yk (2).

D586 Declaration, 1648
Cant.

D593 Declaration, 1648[9]
Yk.

D604 Declaration, 1642
Dur.

D610+ Declaration, 1648
'... Generall Fairfax and his Generall
Councell of officers ... shewing the
grounds'; For John Partridge; 4°.
Dur.

D625 Declaration, 1648
Ex. Yk.

D642 Declaration, 1646[7]
Yk (2).

D646 Declaration, 1642
Linc.

D660 Declaration, 1648
Yk.

D664 Declaration, 1647
Yk*.

D665 Declaration, [1659]
BM: [1650].
Ex.

D667 Declaration, 1659
Ex.

D670 Declaration, [1655]
Linc (2).

D673 Declaration, 1659
Pet. Yk.

D683 Declaration, [1642]
Yk.

D686 Declaration, 1642
Yk.

D691 Declaration, 1643[4]
Cant. Pet. Sal.

D695 Declaration, 1642[3]
Linc.

D701 Declaration, 1653
Dur.

D704 Declaration, 1647
Pet.

D709 Declaration, 1643
Linc.

D712 Declaration, 1642
Yk.

D722? Declaration, 1642
'Earle'
Linc.

D729 Declaration, 1648
Yk*.

D734 Declaration, 1649
Yk.

D742 Declaration, 1647
'pointes'; 12°.
Carl.

D743 Declaration, 1649
Yk.

D746+ Declaration, 1654
As D746, but: '... Highness the Lord
Protecto [sic] ...'; No impr.?
Dur (impr. cropped?).

D747 Declaration, 1648
Yk.

D760 Declaration, [1679]
Linc.

D760+ Declaration, [1679]
As D760, but: brs.
Linc.

D785 Declaration, 1642
For Tho. Lewes.
Linc.

D787 Declaration, 1648
Yk (2).

D788 Declaration, 1659
Yk.

D792 Declaration, 1642
'Earle'
Dur.

D793 Declaration, 1651
'Barbados'
Linc.

D795? Declaration, 1641
4 leaves.
Linc.

D795+ Declaration, 1641
As D795, but: 6 leaves.
Sal.

D804 Decoy, 1642
Yk.

D809 Deduction, 1667
Entry as Wing2.
Carl.

D811 Dee, John, 1659
Cant (imp). Lich. Pet. Win.
Wor.

D817 Defence, 1661
Yk.

D818 Defence, 1698
Cant (imp).

D823A Defensive, 1641
Linc. Pet.

D828- Defoe, Daniel, 1689
=Wing2 D827B.
Wel.

D829 Defoe, Daniel, 1698
Impr. as Wing2.
Cant. S Pl.

D833 *See*: H2995A

D836 Defoe, Daniel, 1698
Ban. Cant.

D837+ Defoe, Daniel, 1698
=Wing2 D837A.
Cant.

D844 Defoe, Daniel, 1689
Carl. S Asa.

D847 Defoe, Daniel, 1697
Ban.

D848 Defoe, Daniel, 1697
S Pl.

D852 Degge, *Sir* Simon, 1676
Linc.

D853 Degge, *Sir* Simon, 1677
Linc. S Asa. Yk.

D854 Degge, *Sir* Simon, 1681
S Pl.

D855 Degge, *Sir* Simon, 1685
Impr. ends: ... Twyford.
Ban. Cant. Dur. S Pl. Swel.
Wor.

D856 Degge, *Sir* Simon, 1695
... Atkyns ... Jos: Hindmarsh.
Cant. Dur.

D868 De La March, John, 1641
Pet (tp imp). Yk (tpw).

D872 Delamere, George Booth,
Baron, 1659
Pet.

D877 Delamere, Henry Booth, *Earl
of*, 1692
S Pl.

D881 Delamere, Henry Booth, *Earl
of*, 1681
Ches.

D894 Delaune, Thomas, 1681
Impr. as Wing2.
Cant.

D896- Delaune, Thomas, 1681
As D896, apart from date.
Glo.

D896 Delaune, Thomas, 1682
2v.
Carl.

D918 Dell, William, 1646
Yk.

D918+ Dell, William, 1647
=Wing2 D918A.
Yk.

D921 Dell, William, [1652]
Chelm.

D926- Dell, William, 1646
Impr. as D926; 31p.; 4°.
Pet.

D926 Dell, William, 1646
Win.

D926+ Dell, William, 1646
Impr. as D926; 41p.; p. 31 catchword:
Mr.; 4°.
Pet.

D927- Dell, William, 1646
Impr. as D926; 41p.; p. 31 catchword:
Mr. Love; 4°.
Pet.

D929 Dell, William, 1652
Sal.

D930 Dell, William, 1653
Carl. Chelm.

D942 Dellon, Claude, 1688
Author as Wing2?
Bris. Wel.

D975 Demands, 1641[2]
Dur.

D978 Democritus, 1659
Ex (date cropped).

D983 Demosthenes, 1686
12°.
Bur.

D995 Denham, Sir John, 1650
Ban. Pet.

D997 Denham, Sir John, 1676
Cant (tp imp).

D998 *See*: M869B

D1001 Denham, Sir John, 1668
Ban.

D1002 Denham, Sir John, 1673
For R. Vaughan.
Cant.

D1013A+ Denison, Stephen, 1641
See: CLC41.
S Pl.

D1015? Denne, Henry, 1646
... and are to be sold among the
Stationers.
Cant.

D1031 Dennis, John, 1700
Cant.

D1040 Dennis, John, 1696
Dur. Ex. Wel.

D1046 Dennis, John, 1698
'usefulness'
Cant.

D1047+ Denniston, Walter, 1700
= Wing2 D1047; 8°.
Dur.

D1055 Dent, Arthur, 1664
12°.
Linc (tpw).

D1064 Denton, William, 1675
Sal.

D1065 Denton, William, 1664
Wel.

D1068+ Denton, William, 1679
= Wing2 D1068A.
Yk.

D1086 Derby, Charles Stanley, *Earl
of*, 1669
Yk.

D1089+ Derby, Charles Stanley,
Earl of, 1669
= Wing2 D1089A.
S Asa.

D1090 Derby, Charles Stanley, *Earl
of*, 1671
Ed. statement from preface.
Linc. Liv.

D1090+ Derby, Charles Stanley,
Earl of, 1671
As D1090, but: Third edition, in
preface.
Dur.

D1090B Derby, Charles Stanley,
Earl of, 1671
Yk.

D1091 Derby, James Stanley, *Earl
of*, 1649
Cant.

D1097 Derham, Robert, 1647
8°.
Chi.

D1099 Derham, William, 1696
8°.
Cant.

D1103 Dering, *Sir* Edward, 1642
Cant. Ex.

D1104 Dering, *Sir* Edward, 1642
Cant (imp). Pet. Yk.

D1106 Dering, *Sir* Edward, 1641
Cant.

D1107 Dering, *Sir* Edward, 1641
Dur. S Pl.

D1109 Dering, *Sir* Edward, 1641
Linc. Yk.

D1111 Dering, *Sir* Edward, 1641
Chi.

D1112 Dering, *Sir* Edward, 1641
Cant. Ex.

D1113 Dering, *Sir* Edward, 1642
Cant. Lich.

D1115 Dering, *Sir* Edward, 1644
Yk.

D1116 Dering, *Sir* Edward, 1641
Cant (imp).

D1118? Dering, *Sir* Edward, 1641
For John Stafford.
Ex.

D1119 Dering, Richard, 1662
Dur. Yk (Cantus primus, bassus,
bassus continuus).

D1120 Dering, Richard, 1674
Dur.

D1121 Derodon, David, 1673
S Pl.

D1122? Derodon, David, 1677
By T.H. for Andrew Clark, to be sold
by Randal Taylor.
Wel.

D1123+ Derodon, David, 1685
= Wing2 D1123C.
Yk.

D1127 *See*: B3779+

D1129 Descartes, René, 1649
Carl.

D1130 Descartes, René, 1668
'Renati Descartes ...'; ... Octaviani
Pulleyn.
Dur. Llan. Pet.

D1132 Descartes, René, 1653
Dur.

D1133A Descartes, René, 1664
Ban.

D1134 Descartes, René, 1650
Pet.

D1135 Descartes, René, 1664
Ex. Sal.

D1138 Descriptio, 1643
Yk.

D1147? Description, 1670
... William Crook.
Linc.

D1151? Description, 1664
2°.
Carl.

D1157 Description, 1641
Sal.

D1193? Desjardins, Marie Catherine
Hortense, 1679
'unfortunate'; ... Henry Herringman.
Cant.

D1212 Detestable, 1689
Ex. Wel.

D1212A? Devarius, Matthaeus,
1657
[London], typis Du-Gardianis excusus,
venit apud Robertum Beaumont.
Ches. Linc. Nor.

D1233 Devonshire, William
Cavendish, *1st Duke of*, 1681
Impr. as Wing2.
Linc (imp).

D1246 D'Ewes, *Sir* Simonds,
1641[2]
Linc.

D1247? D'Ewes, *Sir* Simonds, 1693
For Jonathan Robinson, Jacob
Tonson, A. & J. Churchil and John
Wyat.
Bur. Cant. S Asa.

D1249 D'Ewes, *Sir* Simonds, 1641
Cant. Linc.

D1250 D'Ewes, *Sir* Simonds, 1682
Nor. Wel.

D1251 D'Ewes, *Sir* Simonds, 1645
'practise'
Ex (2). Sal.

D1253 D'Ewes, *Sir* Simonds, 1641
Cant (imp).

D1256 D'Ewes, *Sir* Simonds, 1642
Cant.

D1258 Dewsbury, William, 1656
Yk (2).

D1266 Dewsbury, William, 1655
Yk.

D1267 Dewsbury, William, [1689]
Yk.

D1272 Dewsbury, William, 1654
Yk.

D1276 Dewsbury, William, 1661
Yk.

D1285 Dewsbury, William, 1664
Yk.

D1288 Dey, Richard, 1641
Ex. Yk.

D1295 Dialogue, 1660
Impr. as Wing2.
S Pl.

D1297 Dialogue, 1686
Sal. Wel.

D1309 Dialogue, [1679?]
Linc.

D1316 Dialogue, 1681
Linc.

D1319 Dialogue, 1681
Yk.

D1326+ Dialogue, 1641
=Wing2 D1326A; 'Canterbury'
Yk.

D1333 Dialogue, 1680
Ban. Yk.

D1334 Dialogue, 1681
Linc.

D1336 Dialogue, 1689
Wel.

D1346 Dialogue, [1642]
Pet.

D1353 Dialogue, 1681
Cant.

D1358 Dialogue, 1641
Cant.

D1362 Dialogue, 1667
Carl. Linc. Pet.

D1368 Dialogue, 1641
Carl.

D1370 Dialogue, 1681
Linc.

D1372 *See*: W1156+

D1383 Dickenson, Henry, 1642
Linc. Yk.

D1385 Dickinson, Edmund, 1655
Heading corrected.
Carl. Pet. S Pl.

D1390? Dickinson, Jonathan, 1700
Second ed. not on tp; 8°.
Cant (imp).

D1392 Dickson, David, 1655
Chelm.

D1393 Dickson, David, 1654
Chelm (tp imp)*.

D1396 Dickson, David, 1653
Yk.

D1397 Dickson, David, 1655
Chelm.

D1399 Dickson, David, 1647
Ex.

D1401 Dickson, David, 1645
Pet.

D1402? Dickson, David, 1647
Second ed. not on tp.
Her.

D1403 Dickson, David, 1659
Ex (tpw)*. Sal.

D1404 Dickson, David, 1649
Carl. Ex.

D1406 Dickson, David, 1656
Dur.

D1407 Dickson, David, 1656
Chelm.

D1418? Difference, 1657
'lawful'
Ex.

D1419 Differences, 1648
Pet (imp).

D1440 Digby, *Sir* Kenelm, 1644
Cant.

D1442 Digby, *Sir* Kenelm, 1643
Carl. Linc. Liv.

D1443 Digby, *Sir* Kenelm, 1644
Cant (imp).

D1445 Digby, *Sir* Kenelm, 1669
4°.
Yk.

D1447 Digby, *Sir* Kenelm, 1648
Pet.

D1448 Digby, *Sir* Kenelm, 1644
Carl. Dur.

D1449 Digby, *Sir* Kenelm, 1645
Cant.

D1450 Digby, *Sir* Kenelm, 1658
Lich. Pet. Yk.

D1453 Digges, Dudley, *the Elder*, 1655
Bedell.
Cant. Carl. Chi. Linc. Nor.
S Pl. Sal (engr. tpw).

D1455 Digges, Dudley, *the Younger*, 1642
Linc. Pet.

D1455+ Digges, Dudley, *the Younger*, 1642
As D1454; London counterfeit;
Madan 1080.
Cant.

D1459 Digges, Dudley, *the Younger*, 1643
29p.
Linc. Pet.

D1459+ Digges, Dudley, *the Younger*, 1643
As D1459, but: 21p.; A London
counterfeit; Madan 1314.
Cant.

D1460 Digges, Dudley, *the Younger*, 1643
Yk.

D1461 Digges, Dudley, *the Younger*, 1643
Cant.

D1462 Digges, Dudley, *the Younger*, 1643[4]
Cant. Carl.

D1464 Digges, Dudley, *the Younger*, 1644
Linc. S Pl. Wel. Win.

D1465 Digges, Dudley, *the Younger*, 1647
Bur. Cant. Pet.

D1467 Digges, Dudley, *the Younger*, 1664
Pet.

D1467A Digges, Dudley, *the Younger*, 1679
Cant (imp).

D1469 Digges, Leonard, 1656
Wor.

D1471 Digges, Thomas, 1680
Linc. Win.

D1482 Dillingham, William, 1680
Cant.

D1484 Dillingham, William, 1678
Linc. Liv.

D1485 Dillingham, William, 1689
Ely. Wel.

D1486 Dillingham, William, 1656
Cant. Pet (3).

D1487 Dillingham, William, 1678
Her. Wor.

D1488? Dillingham, William, 1700
'Chadertoni'; Cantabrigii, typis
Academicis, prostant venales apud
Tho. Dawson, bibliop. Cantab.,
necnon Sam. Smith & Benj. Walford
bipliopolas Londin.
Ex.

D1504 Diodati, Giovanni, 1646
16p.
Linc (2).

D1504+ Diodati, Giovanni, 1646
'acclesiasticall [*sic*]'; Genevah [*sic*]; 4°;
12p.
Dur.

D1505 Diodati, Giovanni, 1647
Carl.

D1506 Diodati, Giovanni, 1648
4°.
Rip.

D1506+ Diodati, Giovanni, 1648
The second edition; By M. Flesher for
N. Fussel, sold by H. Moseley; 4°.
S Pl. Wor.

D1507 Diodati, Giovanni, 1651
Ban. Bur. Cant. Carl. Ely. Ex.
Lich. S Asa. Wel.

D1508 Diodati, Giovanni, 1664
By Tho. Roycroft for Nicholas
Fussell; 2°.
Ex. Her (2). Pet. S Asa. S Dv.

D1510 Diodati, Giovanni, 1643
By T.B. for …
S Asa. Yk.

D1512 Diodorus Siculus, 1700
… Churchil and Edw. Castle.
Ex.

D1513 Diodorus Siculus, 1653
Sal.

D1515 Diogenes Laertius, 1664
Impr. as Wing2.
Cant. Ely. Ex. Linc. Sal.

D1519 Dionysius, *Periegetes*, 1658
… Humphredi Robinson.
S Pl. Yk.

D1521 Dionysius, *Periegetes*, 1679
Rip. S Dv.

D1522 Dionysius, *Periegetes*, 1688
Impr. as Wing2.
Nor. S Asa.

D1527 Direction, 1643
4°.
Ex (imp).

D1529 Directions, 1685
Impr. from colophon; cap.
S Asa. Yk.

D1539 Directions, 1695
S Pl.

D1544 Directory, 1644[5]
Cant. Ches (2). Dur. Liv (2).
Rip. S Pl. Sal. Wel. Yk (3).

D1545 Directory, 1644[5]
Ex (2).

D1545+ Directory, [1644/5?]
[York, Thomas Broad?]; 4°; 44p.
Yk.

D1547 Directory, 1645
Sal.

D1548 Directory, 1645
Bris.

D1550 Directory, 1646
Cant. Liv. Yk (2).

D1551 Directory, 1646
Linc. Yk.

D1551A? Directory, 1651
12°.
Dur. Ely.

D1553? Directory, 1656
12°.
S Pl.

D1563 Disconsolate, 1647
Yk.

D1568 Discourse, 1684
Carl. Ex. Her (2).

D1580? Discourse, 1697
12°; Author was P. Nelson.
Dur.

D1588 Discourse, 1689
Wel.

D1592 Discourse, 1645
Yk.

D1593 Discourse, 1687
Carl. S Pl. Wel.

D1593+ Discourse, 1665
=Wing2 D1593A.
Carl.

D1598 Discourse, 1690
'humane'
Wel.

D1601 Discourse, 1641[2]
Carl.

D1602 Discourse, 1690
S Pl. Sal.

D1603 Discourse, 1674
… for William Crook.
Sal.

D1608 Discourse, 1679
Impr. as Wing2.
Carl. Win.

D1610+ Discourse, 1675
=Wing2 D1610.
Cant.

D1617+ Discourse, 1641
=Wing2 D1617.
Pet. Sal.

D1621 *See*: S3057

D1622 Discourse, 1682
Carl.

D1628? Discourse, [1642]
16p.
Linc. Pet.

D1628+ Discourse, [1642]
As D1628, but: 19p.
Linc.

D1630 Discourses, 1680
Linc.

D1636 Discovery, 1641
Dur (cropped). Pet.

D1640 Discovery, 1642
Pet.

D1642 Discovery, 1641
'roberies'
Dur (cropped).

D1645? Discoverie, 1641
'A discoverie … preachers, in
Middlesex, …'
S Pl.

D1657 Discovery, 1643
4 leaves.
Linc.

D1662+ Discovery, 1641
'A discovery …'; 4°.
Dur. Linc.

D1670? Disloyal, 1680
cap.
Linc.

D1677 Disputation, 1679
Sal.

D1685? Dissenters, 1689
'… about the five hundred pounds
forfeiture'; By H.C. and sold by R.
Baldwine.
Cant.

D1690 Dissolution, 1641
Linc.

D1698A Distractions, 1643
Pet.

D1707 *See*: Periodicals

D1710 Divers, 1641[2]
For Ioseph Hunscott, March 1.
Dur. Linc.

D1712? Divers, 1648
'… present great action …'
Win.

D1713 Divers, 1643
Linc.

D1715 Divine, 1693
Cant.

D1716? Divine, 1686
By J.R. for Nath. Crouch; 12°.
Cant.

D1720 Divine, 1641
Linc.

D1747 Dixon, Robert, 1668
Ex. Yk.

D1748 Dixon, Robert, 1676
Roch. Yk.

D1753 Dobson, John, [1663]
Cant.

D1755 Dobson, John, [1663]
Linc. Pet. S Asa. Win.

D1755+ Dobson, John, [1663]
=Wing2 D1755.
Chelm. Nor.

D1756 Dobson, John, 1670
Her (2). Wor.

D1767 Dr. Sherlock's, 1691
Llan. Wel.

D1768+ Doctors, 1641
=Wing2 D1768A?; 'wil'
Yk.

D1771 *See*: O366A

D1773+ Doctrine, [1673?]
[For Edward Brewster?]; 12°.
Cant (tpw, advt for Brewster
dated 1673).

D1774 Doctrine, 1697
Cant.

D1792 Doddridge, *Sir* John, 1641
Ely.

D1793 Doddridge, *Sir* John, 1652
Carl.

D1796 Doddridge, *Sir* John, 1658
Chi. S Pl.

D1802A Dodwell, Henry, 1698
Ex. Sal.

D1803- Dodwell, Henry, 1676
For Benj. Tooke; 12°.
Cant. Ex (2). S Asa. S Pl. Win.

D1803? Dodwell, Henry, 1688
Took.
Ex. Yk.

D1804 Dodwell, Henry, [1689]
Wel.

D1805 Dodwell, Henry, 1695
Wel.

D1806 Dodwell, Henry, 1681
Ban. Dur. Liv. S Asa. S Pl.
Wel.

D1807 Dodwell, Henry, 1691
Ches. Glo. Liv.

D1808 Dodwell, Henry, 1683
Ban. Cant (2 – both imp). Carl.
Ex. S Asa.

D1809 Dodwell, Henry, [1682]
S Pl. Yk.

D1810 Dodwell, Henry, 1684
Ban. Cant. Ely. Ex. S Pl. Tru.
Wel. Wor.

D1812 Dodwell, Henry, 1689
Ches. Ely. S Dv. S Pl. Wel.

D1815 Dodwell, Henry, 1692
Ex. Linc. S Pl. Wel. Wor.

D1816 Dodwell, Henry, 1698
Entry as Wing2.
Cant. Wel.

D1817 Dodwell, Henry, 1681
Ban. Carl. Dur. Ex. Sal (2).
Win.

D1818 Dodwell, Henry, 1679
Ban. Carl. Ely. Ex (2). Linc.
S Pl. Sal. Wel. Win.

D1819 Dodwell, Henry, 1675
Ban. Carl. Pet. Win.

D1820? Dodwell, Henry, 1700
'musick'
Her.

D1821 Dodwell, Henry, 1700
Chi. Dur (2). Ex. S Asa.

D1822 Dodwell, Henry, 1672
... by Benjamin Tooke ...
Cant. Linc. S Pl. Win. Yk.

D1823 Dodwell, Henry, 1680
Ban. Dur. Liv. S Asa. S Pl.
Wel.

D1824 Dodwell, Henry, 1691
Bur. Ches (tpw). Glo. Liv.

D1825? Dodwell, Henry, 1676
12°.
Cant (imp). Ex (2). S Asa. S Pl.
Win.

D1826 Dodwell, Henry, 1688
Ex. Yk.

D1827 Dodwell, Henry, 1692
Carl. Ex. Wel. Yk.

D1830+ Dolaeus, Johan, 1686
=Wing2 D1830A; 'Systema
medicinale'
Cant.

D1831 Dolben, John, 1665
Cant. Carl. S Asa. Yk.

D1832 Dolben, John, 1665
Carl. S Asa. Yk.

D1833 Dolben, John, 1666
Carl. Her. S Pl. Yk.

D1837 Dolefull, 1641
Dur. Linc. S Pl.

D1844? Don Henriquez, [1686]
'Henriquez'
Cant.

D1858 Donne, John, [1644]
Pet. Win.

D1859 Donne, John, 1648
Linc. S Pl.

D1862 Donne, John, 1649
Carl. Dur. Ex. Lich. S Pl.
Win. Wor.

D1864 Donne, John, 1651
Sal.

D1869+ Donne, John, 1650
No ed. statement; By M.F. for John
Marriot and sold by Richard Marriot;
8°.
Cant.

D1872 Donne, John, 1660/1
S Pl (imp). Win. Wor. Yk.

D1874 Donne, John, 1661
Carl.

D1880A Doolittle, Thomas, 1674
Yk.

D1884 Doolittle, Thomas, [1688]
cap.
Cant.

D1890 Doolittle, Thomas, 1699
Bris. Cant.

D1891+ Doolittle, Thomas, 1679
See: CLC42.
Llan.

D1895? Doolittle, Thomas, 1666
... and R. Boulter.
Her. Pet.

D1899A+ Doolittle, Thomas, 1674
The eighth edition; By E. Crowch, for
G. Calvert and S. Sprint; 12°.
Cant.

D1919+ Dorchester, Henry
Pierrepont, *Marquis of*, 1642
=Wing2 D1919A.
Cant. Dur.

D1921 Dorchester, Henry
Pierrepont, *Marquis of*, 1641
Cant. Ex. Linc. Sal (tpw).

D1926 Dormer, John, 1688
Cant.

D1928 Dormer, John, 1687
Sal.

D1937 Dorrington, Theophilus,
1700
Cant.

D1942 Dorrington, Theophilus,
1696
Cant. Wor.

D1944 Dorrington, Theophilus,
1699
'... state of religion ...'
Ex.

D1945 Dorrington, Theophilus,
1686
Carl.

D1947 Dorrington, Theophilus,
1693
Ely.

D1956 *See*: L1246A

D1958+ Douch, John, 1660
For R. Royston; 4°.
Pet. Wor.

D1959 Doughty, John, 1658
... apud quem prostant venales.
Bur. Ely. Ex. Linc. Win. Yk.

D1960 Doughty, John, 1660
Ely. Lich. Win.

D1961 Doughty, John, 1644
Pet.

D1963 Doughty, John, 1651
Impr. as Wing2.
Dur.

D1964 Doughty, John, 1652
Pet. Yk.

D2027 Douglas, Robert, 1651
Carl*. Yk (imp).

D2028 Douglas, Robert, 1651
Dur. Yk (tpw)*.

D2030+ Douglas, Robert, 1660
No number assigned in Wing1;
=Wing2 D2030B.
Chelm.

D2032 Douglas, Robert, 1660
Printed.
Yk.

D2037 Douglas, Robert, 1661
Carl.

D2039 Douglas, Thomas, 1664
Entry as Wing2.
Win.

D2040 Douglas, Thomas, 1661
Entry as Wing2.
Pet.

D2041 *See*: P2980

D2048 Dove, Henry, 1680
Cant. Dur (2 issues). Her. Llan
(tpw). Pet (2 − 1 imp). Wor.

D2049 Dove, Henry, 1682
Cant. Llan. Nor (imp).

D2050 Dove, Henry, 1685
Ches.

D2051 Dove, Henry, 1687
S Asa.

D2052 Dove, Henry, 1691
Cant. Ches. Her.

D2056+ Dowell, John, 1683
Oxon, by L. Lichfield, sold by Tho.
Simmons, London; 12°.
Ex. Pet.

D2059 Downame, George, 1647
12°.
Pet.

D2061 *See*: D2096+

D2062 Downame, John, 1645
IoM. Yk.

D2063 Downame, John, 1651
Bur. Cant. Chelm. Ex. Glo.
Her. Lich. Nor (2). Rip (tpw).
Sal.

D2064 Downame, John, 1657
Carl. Dur. Ely. Her. Pet. Sal
(vol. 1 only).

D2065 Downame, John, 1642
S Pl.

D2066 Downame, John, 1646
Impr. as Wing2; 8°.
Cant (tp imp).

D2069 Downame, John, 1659
Cant.

D2070 Downame, John, 1663
S Pl.

D2074 Downame, John, 1646
Cant. Yk.

D2080 Downes, Henry, 1697
Cant. Dur. Her. Nor.

D2083 Downes, Theophilus, 1691
Lich. Wel.

D2084 Downe-fall, 1643
Linc. S Pl.

D2086 Downfall, 1641
Yk.

D2089 Downfall, 1661
Linc.

D2096+ Downham, George, 1643
=Wing2 D2096A, which has wrong
date.
Pet.

D2100 Downing, Calybute, 1641
Linc. Pet.

D2102 Downing, Calybute, 1641
Sal.

D2103 Downing, Calybute, 1641
Carl.

D2104 Downing, Calybute, 1641
Sal.

D2105 Downing, Calybute, 1641
Carl. Linc.

D2106 Downing, *Sir* George, 1664
Linc.

D2108 Downing, *Sir* George, 1672
Carl. Win.

D2109 Downing, *Sir* George, 1665
Pet.

D2110? Downing, *Sir* George, 1651
'Parlaments'
Glo.

D2123 Drake, James, 1699
Bur.

D2126 Drake, Nathaniel, 1695
Cant. Sal. Yk (3 − 1 imp).

D2127 Drake, Nathaniel, 1697
Yk (imp).

D2128 Drake, Roger, 1656
Yk.

D2130 Drake, Roger, 1653
Cant.

D2134 Drake, Samuel, 1670
Yk.

D2136 Drake, *Sir* William, 1661
Cant.

D2137 Drake, *Sir* William, 1661
Win. Yk (2).

D2138 Drake, *Sir* William, 1641
Cant. Dur. Linc.

D2147 Drayton, Thomas, 1655
Pet (tpw).

D2156 Dreame, 1641
Yk.

D2160 Drelincourt, Charles, 1675
Bur.

D2162 Drelincourt, Charles, 1664
Carl.

D2166 Drew, John, 1649
Ex.

D2167 Drewry, H., 1641[2]
Dur.

D2175 Drexel, Jeremy, 1666
Cant.

D2178 Drexel, Jeremy, 1684
Impr. as Wing2.
Yk (2 − 1 imp).

D2187 Dring, Thomas, 1655
Impr. as Wing2.
Carl. Dur. Linc. Wor.

D2188 Drope, Francis, 1672
'guid'
Linc.

D2196 Drummond, William, 1655
Carl. Ex (date cropped?). Lich.

D2197 Drummond, William, [1680]
Cant.

D2204 Drummond, William, 1691
S Pl.

D2208 Dryden, John, 1693
Glo.

D2210 Dryden, John, 1695
Yk (vol. 4 only, tpw).

D2212 Dryden, John, 1681
Ches.

D2216 Dryden, John, 1681
4°.
Ely.

D2222 Dryden, John, 1682
'... Latino carmine ...'
S Pl.

D2230 Dryden, John, 1692
Second ed. not on tp.
Ex.

D2233 Dryden, John, 1691
Second ed. not on tp.
Ex.

D2234 Dryden, John, 1690
Cant.

D2239 Dryden, John, 1668
Carl.

D2240 Dryden, John, 1688
Ex.

D2243 Dryden, John, 1692
Ex.

D2245 Dryden, John, 1676
Ex.

D2248 Dryden, John, 1692
Fourth ed. not on tp.
Ex.

D2253 Dryden, John, 1688 [c.1691]
Ex.

D2256 Dryden, John, 1672
Ex.

D2261 Dryden, John, 1686
Ban. Bur. Liv. Wel.

D2268 Dryden, John, 1681
Ches.

D2270 Dryden, John, 1692
Ex. S Pl.

D2277 Dryden, John, 1693
Nor.

D2278 Dryden, John, 1700
Chelm.

D2281 Dryden, John, 1687
S Pl.

D2285 Dryden, John, 1687
Ex.

D2286 Dryden, John, 1681
Carl.

D2297 Dryden, John, 1680
Ex.

D2304 Dryden, John, 1692
No tp, begins B1.
Ex.

D2309 Dryden, John, 1691
Third ed. not on tp; Bentley.
Ex.

D2311 Dryden, John, 1682
Ex. S Pl.

D2314 Dryden, John, 1684
S Pl.

D2325 Dryden, John, 1692
Ex.

D2328 Dryden, John, 1684
Second ed. not on tp.
S Asa.

D2329 Dryden, John, 1693
S Pl.

D2330 Dryden, John, 1659
Ex.

D2342 Dryden, John, 1682
Ex.

D2345 Dryden, John, 1683
Third ed. not on tp.
Ex.

D2350 Dryden, John, 1682
Wor.

D2366? Dryden, John, 1690
By J. Heptinstall for Jacob Tonson.
Cant.

D2376 Dryden, John, 1690
Fifth ed. not on tp.
Ex.

D2378 Dryden, John, 1695
Seventh ed. not on tp.
S Asa.

D2382 Dryden, John, 1682
Second ed. not on tp.
Nor (tp imp). S Pl.

D2383 Dryden, John, 1685
Cant.

D2384 Dryden, John, 1685
Ex.

D2388 Dryden, John, 1679
Ex (2).

D2398 Dryden, John, 1683
Cant. Nor.

D2405 Du Bartas, Guillaume de
Saluste, 1641
Linc (tpw)*.

D2405+ Du Bartas, Guillaume de
Saluste, 1641
=Wing2 D2405A.
Glo.

D2415 Du Cambout de Pont
Château, Sebastian Joseph, 1670
Carl. Ely.

D2417 Du Chastelet de Luzancy,
Hippolite, 1698
Impr. as Wing2.
S Pl.

D2418 Du Chastelet de Luzancy,
Hippolite, 1677
8°.
S Pl (with tp of D2418+ at end).

D2418+ Du Chastelet de Luzancy,
Hippolite, 1677
=Wing2 D2418A; Printed at the
Theater in Oxford ...; 8°.
Linc. Win.

D2420 Du Chastelet de Luzancy,
Hippolite, 1696
Cant.

D2422 Du Chastelet de Luzancy,
Hippolite, 1675
Nor (imp)*.

D2423 Du Chastelet de Luzancy,
Hippolite, 1676
Pet. Wel (2).

D2423+ Du Chastelet de Luzancy,
Hippolite, 1697
=Wing2 D2423A; 'preach'd'
Cant. Carl.

D2423++ Du Chastelet de
Luzancy, Hippolite, 1678
=Wing2 D2423B.
Dur.

D2424 *See*: G1880

D2427 Duck, Arthur, 1653
Cant. Chelm. Ely. Ex. S Pl.

D2428 Duck, Arthur, 1679
S Asa.

D2429 Duck, Arthur, 1689
Yk.

D2429+ Duck, Arthur, 1689
As D2429, but: 12°.
Sal.

D2430 Duck, Arthur, 1699
Cant (2). Ex. Tru.

D2432? Du Clos, Samuel Cotreau,
Sieur, 1684
12°.
Ex.

D2435? Du Coignet, Pierre, 1689
... Randall Taylor.
Nor. Wel.

D2437 Ducros, Simon, 1693
Dur.

D2439 Dudley, *Sir* Gamaliel,
1644[5]
Yk.

D2440 *See*: T1499

D2441 Due, 1654
Carl (tp imp).

D2456 Du Four de Longuerue,
Louis, 1687
Ban. Carl. Sal. Swel.

D2457 Du Four de Longuerue,
Louis, 1687
Bur. Wel.

D2457+ Du Four de Longuerue,
Louis, 1686
=Wing2 D2456A.
S Pl. Yk.

D2457++ Du Four de Longuerue,
Louis, 1687
=Wing2 D2457.
Ely. Lich. Nor. Wel.

D2458 Du Fresnoy, Charles
Alphonse, 1695
Dur.

D2459 Dugard, Samuel, 1673
Cant (2). Carl.

D2460 Dugard, Samuel, 1695
Dur. Nor.

D2462 Dugard, Thomas, 1641
Bur. Ex.

D2466 Du-Gard, William, 1654
'Graecae grammatices rudimenta';
Typis autoris, veneunt apud Andr.
Crook.
Ely. Wel.

D2473 Dugdale, Richard, 1680
Linc. Win.

D2474 Dugdale, Stephen, 1680
Ely. Linc. Yk (imp).

D2475 Dugdale, Stephen, 1680
Ely. Glo. Linc. Win. Yk.

D2477+ Dugdale, *Sir* William,
1682
Oxford, at the Theater, for Fin.
Gardiner in London; 8°.
Carl.

D2478 Dugdale, *Sir* William, 1682
8°.
Ban. Cant. Nor.

D2479 Dugdale, *Sir* William, 1656
Cant. Carl. Dur. Ex (imp).
Lich (imp). Linc. S Pl. Yk.

D2480 Dugdale, *Sir* William, 1675 –
76
Impr. as Wing2.
Cant. Carl. Chelm (imp). Dur.
Ex. Her. Linc. Wel. Win. Wor.
Yk.

D2480+ Dugdale, *Sir* William,
1645
=Wing2 D2480A; 'passages'; ...
Leonard Lichfield.
Cant. Liv. Win.

D2481 Dugdale, *Sir* William, 1662
Cant. Carl.

D2482 Dugdale, *Sir* William, 1658
Cant. Carl. Linc. S Pl. Wel.
Win.

D2483 Dugdale, *Sir* William, 1673
Ban. Cant. Ches. Dur. Ely.
Glo. Lich. Linc. Pet. S Pl. Sal
(2). Wel. Wor. Yk.

D2483A Dugdale, *Sir* William,
1673
S Pl. Wor.

D2484 Dugdale, *Sir* William, 1655
Typis Richardi Hodgkinsonne.
Cant (3 – 1 imp). Carl. Dur.
Ely. Glo. Lich. Linc. Pet. Rip
(tpw). S Alb. Sal. Win. Wor.
Yk.

D2485 Dugdale, *Sir* William, 1682
Impensis Christopheri Wilkinson,
Thomae Dring & Caroli Harper.
Ches. Roch. S Pl. Sal. Wel.

D2486 Dugdale, *Sir* William, 1661
'Monastici Anglicani ...'
Ban. Cant. Carl. Ches. Dur.
Ely. Glo. Lich. Linc. Pet. Sal
(2). Wel. Win. Yk.

D2486+ Dugdale, *Sir* William,
[1672]
'Monasticon Anglicanum or the
cathedrall ... churches'; [N.pl.],
printed and sould by Iohn Ouerton;
obl. 4°; Plates.
Ex.

D2487 Dugdale, *Sir* William, 1693
Cant. S Alb (2). Wel. Wor.

D2488 Dugdale, *Sir* William, 1666
Cant. Ex.

D2489 Dugdale, *Sir* William, 1671
Dur. Linc. Win. Wor. Yk.

D2490 Dugdale, *Sir* William, 1680
S Asa. Wel.

D2491 Dugdale, *Sir* William, 1685
Dur. Nor. S Pl. Wel.

D2492 Dugdale, *Sir* William, 1681
Anonymous; ... for Moses Pitt.
Cant. Chelm. Dur. Nor. Pet.
S Asa (imp). Wel. Win. Wor.

D2492+ Dugdale, *Sir* William,
1681
As D2492, but: 'By Sir William
Dugdale'
Chi. Glo. Lich. Yk.

D2493 Dugres, Gabriel, 1652
Sal.

D2496 Du Hamel, Jean Baptiste,
1669
Entry as Wing2, but: ... Curteyn.
Ely. Pet. Yk.

D2499 Du Hamel, Jean Baptiste,
1685
Impr. should be in Latin?
S Asa (tpw).

D2500 Duke, Francis, 1660
'principal'; ... Miles Michel ...
Sal.

D2502 Duke, Francis, 1655
Sal (pt 2 only).

D2503 Duke, Francis, 1656
Sal.

D2504 *See*: M2539

D2505- Duke, Richard, [1679?]
=Wing2 D2504.
Ches.

D2505A Duke, Richard, [1680]
'Bedloe'
Ches.

D2521? Du May, Lewis, 1664
... for Richard Royston.
Carl. Sal.

D2522 Du May, Lewis, 1676
Ex.

D2530 Du Moulin, Louis, 1681
Carl. Pet.

D2534 Du Moulin, Louis, 1642
S Pl.

D2541 Du Moulin, Louis, 1671
[N.pl.], juxta exemplar Londinense.
Carl. Dur. Ex. Pet. Wor.

D2542 Du Moulin, Louis, 1680
Pt 2 of L2593A.
Ban. Carl. Lich. Wel (2). Yk.

D2543 Du Moulin, Louis, 1680
Cant.

D2544 Du Moulin, Louis, 1658
Pet.

D2546 Du Moulin, Louis, 1652
... Leon. Lichfield.
Linc.

D2548 Du Moulin, Louis, 1656
4°.
Linc. Sal.

D2549 Du Moulin, Louis, 1672
Entry as Wing2.
Pet. Win.

D2550 Du Moulin, Louis, 1641
Cant. Ex (2). S Pl.

D2552 Du Moulin, Louis, 1659
Dur.

D2553 Du Moulin, Louis, 1680
Cant (imp). Pet. S Pl.

D2555- Du Moulin, Louis, 1641
'... XVIII motions'; Imprint and
format not available.
Yk.

D2555 Du Moulin, Louis, 1641
Pet. Sal.

D2556 Du Moulin, Peter, *the
Younger*, 1677
Cant (2 – 1 imp). Wel.

D2557A Du Moulin, Peter, *the Younger*, 1649
8°.
Linc.

D2558 Du Moulin, Peter, *the Younger*, 1673
Cant.

D2560 Du Moulin, Peter, *the Younger*, 1657
Carl.

D2561 Du Moulin, Peter, *the Younger*, 1670
'... libelli tres'
Cant. Win.

D2562 Du Moulin, Peter, *the Younger*, 1671
Ban. Llan.

D2563 Du Moulin, Peter, *the Younger*, 1671
Ban. Llan.

D2564 Du Moulin, Peter, *the Younger*, 1675
Cant. Win (tp imp).

D2565 Du Moulin, Peter, *the Younger*, 1678
S Asa.

D2567 Du Moulin, Peter, *the Younger*, 1672
Cant. Carl. Linc.

D2569 Du Moulin, Peter, *the Younger*, 1671
Cant. Chelm.

D2570 Du Moulin, Peter, *the Younger*, 1678
Nor. Yk.

D2571 Du Moulin, Peter, *the Younger*, 1664
Cant. Carl. Win. Yk.

D2572 Du Moulin, Peter, *the Younger*, 1667
Second ed. not on tp; For John Crook.
Dur. Linc. Sal.

D2573 Du Moulin, Peter, *the Younger*, 1668
Cant.

D2574 Du Moulin, Peter, *the Younger*, 1679
Ban.

D2574+ Du Moulin, Peter, *the Younger*, 1679
=Wing2 D2574A; The fourth edition.
S Pl.

D2576 Du Moulin, Peter, *the Younger*, 1677
Yk.

D2577 Du Moulin, Peter, *the Younger*, 1679
· Cant (2 − both imp).

D2585 Du Moulin, Pierre, *the Elder*, 1659
Carl. Lich. Nor. Yk (2).

D2586 Du Moulin, Pierre, *the Elder*, 1660
Cant. Yk.

D2589+ Du Moulin, Pierre, *the Elder*, 1641
By Stephen Bulkley; 8°.
Ex.

D2591 Du Moulin, Pierre, *the Elder*, 1641
By Steven Bulkley ...
Cant. Carl.

D2592 Du Moulin, Pierre, *the Elder*, 1671
Carl.

D2593 Du Moulin, Pierre, *the Elder*, 1662
Cant.

D2594 Du Moulin, Pierre, *the Elder*, 1664
Dur. Pet. Sal.

D2595 Du Moulin, Pierre, *the Elder*, 1674
Cant. Ely. Linc. Wel.

D2595+ Du Moulin, Pierre, *the Elder*, 1650
See: CLC43.
Cant (imp).

D2596- Du Moulin, Pierre, *the Elder*, 1680
As D2596, apart from date.
Win.

D2601? Duncon, Eleazar, 1660
16° *or* 8°?
Linc. Yk.

D2602 Duncon, Eleazar, 1661
With an addit. tp with same impr., but title as D2603.
Carl. Chelm.

D2604 Duncon, John, 1653
Sal.

D2605 Duncon, John, 1648
Win.

D2606 Duncon, John, 1649
For R. Royston.
Linc.

D2610 Duncomb, Thomas, 1671
Bur. Cant.

D2619 Dunstervile, Thomas, 1654
Pet.

D2630 Dunton, John, 1692
Liv.

D2635 Dunton, John, 1692
Dur.

D2640 Dupin, Louis Ellies, 1699−1700
Dur. Ex. Linc. Roch. Wel. Yk (2).

D2643 Dupin, Louis Ellies, 1692−99
For Abell Swalle and Tim Childe; In D2643, D2644, D2645, the impr. and ed. statements are for vol. 1 only; Other vols are found in different combinations.
Ches (vol. 1−5). Dur. Ex. Her (vol. 5−6, 8−13). Lich (vol. 1−6, 9−10). Linc (2 − 1 vol. 3−13). Roch. S Pl (vol. 1−2). Wel. Yk (vol. 3−4).

D2644 Dupin, Louis Ellies, 1693−99
For Abel Swalle and Tim Childe.
Glo (vol. 1−6). Liv (vol. 1−2). Llan (2 copies of vol. 6 only). Pet (vol. 1−6). Rip (vol. 1−2). S Asa. Sal (vol. 1−2). Swel. Yk (3 − 1 vol. 1−6; 1 vol. 3−5).

D2645 Dupin, Louis Ellies, 1696−99
For Abel Swalle and Tim Childe; 13v.; 18th cent. vols not recorded.
Cant. Chi (vol. 3−7, 11−13). Ely (2). Her. Rip (vol. 3−4). Wel. Yk.

D2648- Duport, James, 1666
As D2648, but: Greek only; 216p.
Glo.

D2648? Duport, James, 1666
... excudit Joannes Field; Greek & Latin; 431p.
Chi (tpw). Ely. Glo (tpw). Linc. S Asa. S Pl. Sal (tpw). Win.

D2649 Duport, James, 1674
Roch. S Pl.

D2650 Duport, James, 1660
Pet. S Pl.

D2651? Duport, James, 1660
... Johannes Field.
Cant. Ches. Ely. Ex. Linc. Liv. Nor. S Asa. S Pl. Wel. Win.

D2652 Duport, James, 1676
Carl. Ely. Linc (2).

D2653? Duport, James, 1696
... Sam. Buckley.
S Pl.

D2654 Duport, James, 1646
Linc.

D2655 Duport, James, 1676
Her (tp imp). Pet. Sal (imp).

D2657 Duport, James, 1653
Linc.

D2657 *See*: B2800+

D2658 Duppa, Brian, 1648
Linc. Yk.

D2662+ Duppa, Brian, 1675
=Wing2 D2661; 2 pts.
Sal.

D2662++ Duppa, Brian, 1679
=Wing2 D2662; 2 pts.
Pet (tp imp).

D2663 Duppa, Brian, 1683
The fourth edition; For W. Hensman.
Win.

D2665 Duppa, Brian, 1645
... by Leonard Lichfield.
Win.

D2666 Duppa, Brian, 1648
Cant. Sal. Yk.

D2666+ Duppa, Brian, 1648
[N.pl.], for R. Royston; 4°.
Chelm.

D2667 Duppa, Brian, 1644
Linc.

D2672 Durant, John, 1660
... H. Mortlocke.
Chelm.

D2674 Durant, John, 1653
Bur.

D2675 Durant, John, 1658
Cant.

D2677 Durant, John, 1655
Yk.

D2678A Durant, John, 1649
Yk.

D2686+ Du Refuge, Eustache, 1673
=Wing2 D2686A.
Carl.

D2688 Durel, Jean, 1667
... Octavien Pulleyn ...; 8°.
Dur. S Pl.

D2688+ Durel, Jean, 1677
=Wing2 D2688A.
S Pl (tpw).

D2690 Durel, Jean, 1683
Impr. as Wing2.
Liv. Yk.

D2691+ Durel, Jean, 1695
=Wing2 D2691B.
Yk.

D2692 Durel, Jean, 1662
Ban. Bur. Cant. Carl. Ches.
Chi. Dur. Ely. Ex (2). Lich.
Linc. Sal (2). Wel. Win. Wor.
Yk (2).

D2693 Durel, Jean, 1688
Cant. Lich.

D2694 Durel, Jean, 1669
Dur. Ely. Ex. Lich. Linc (2).
Pet. S Pl. Sal. Win. Yk.

D2694+ Durel, Jean, 1661
'Sermon, prononcé en l'eglise
Françoise ...'; Par Guillaume Godbid,
et se vendent chez Iean Martin, Iaques
Alestry & Th. Dicas; 4°; Original of
D2692-3.
Win.

D2695 Durel, Jean, 1662
Ban. Bur. Cant. Carl. Ches.
Chi. Dur. Ely. Ex (2). Lich.
Linc. Sal (2). Wel. Win. Wor.
Yk (2).

D2764 D'Urfey, Thomas, 1681
Ches. Linc.

D2770 D'Urfey, Thomas, 1682
Ex.

D2803 Durham, James, 1669
Second ed. not on tp; By J.W., sold
by ...
Carl.

D2807 Durham, James, 1660
Third ed. not on tp.
Carl.

D2822? Durham, James, 1675
By T.(?) Milbourn ...
Bur.

D2830 Durham, William, 1679
Wor.

D2831 Durham, William, 1660
Carl.

D2832 Durham, William, 1652
Carl.

D2834 Durham, William, 1676
Carl. Her. Wor.

D2835 Dury, John, 1641
Cant (2 — 1 imp). Pet. Yk.

D2836 Dury, John, 1650
Pet. Yk.

D2838 Dury, John, 1656
Yk (2).

D2839 Dury, John, 1642
Sal. Yk.

D2841 Dury, John, 1651
Yk.

D2842 Dury, John, 1649
Ex.

D2844 Dury, John, 1650
Yk.

D2850? Dury, John, 1660
8°.
Yk.

D2851 Dury, John, 1654
Ex. Yk (2).

D2854 Dury, John, 1650
Chelm. Yk.

D2856 Dury, John, 1654
Wodnothe.
Yk (2).

D2857 Dury, John, [1657?]
Carl. Yk (2 eds — 1: last page
blank; 2: last page has 'To the
Christian reader').

D2858 Dury, John, 1659[60]
Win.

D2859 Dury, John, 1644
Pet (2). Yk.

D2864 Dury, John, 1659
Yk.

D2865 Dury, John, 1654
Or D2866.
Dur (tp imp).

D2868A Dury, John, 1650
Dur (tpw). Yk.

D2872 Dury, John, 1641
Linc. Sal. Yk.

D2873 Dury, John, 1647
Pet. Sal. Win. Yk.

D2874 Dury, John, 1642
Yk.

D2876 Dury, John, 1650
Woodnothe; 4°.
Cant. Ex. Yk.

D2878? Dury, John, 1641
'... House of the Commons'
Linc. Sal. Yk.

D2879 Dury, John, 1642
'A petition ...'; Different text from
D2878.
Sal. Yk.

D2886 Dury, John, 1649
Yk.

D2887 Dury, John, 1650
Yk.

D2888 Dury, John, 1657
Carl. Yk.

D2889 Dury, John, 1641
S Pl. Sal. Yk.

D2890 Dury, John, 1654
Yk.

D2891 Dury, John, [1656]
Carl. Yk.

D2893 *See*: Periodicals

D2894 Dury, John, 1650
Win. Yk.

D2908 Dutiful, 1690
Nor.

D2909 Du Trieu, Philippus, 1662
Her.

D2916 Du Vair, Guillaume, 1667
Carl.

D2917 Du Vair, Guillaume, 1671
Pet.

D2920+ Du Val, Pierre, 1678
= Wing2 D2920C.
Win.

D2926? Dyer, *Sir* James, 1672
Excudebant Johannes Streater &
Henricus Twyford, delegati Edwardi &
Richardi Atkyns. Prostant apud J.
Martin, R. Horn, H. Brome, R.
Chiswell, & R. Boulter.
Dur.

D2941+ Dyer, William, 1695
For Jonathan Robinson; 12°.
Cant.

D2959 Dyke, Daniel, 1642
Ex. Sal (2).

D2960- Dyke, Jeremiah, 1652
= Wing2 D2959A?; For Thomas
Pierrepont.
Ex (tp imp).

D2961 Dyke, Jeremiah, 1642
Glo (imp)*.

D2963+ Dyke, Jeremiah, 1657
= Wing2 D2963A.
Carl. Yk.

D2964 Dyke, Jeremiah, 1661
S Asa.

D2972 Dymock, James, 1676
12°.
Yk.

D2974? Dymock, James, 1686
The fifth addition [*sic*]; [N.pl.], for
B.W.
Wel.

D2976 Dymock, Thomas, 1648
Pet. Yk.

D2979 Dyve, *Sir* Lewis, 1650
Linc. Sal.

E13 E., I., 1645
Yk.

E18+ E., N., 1668
= Wing2 E18A; 'Dialogue ...'
Carl.

E27? E., R., 1678
Sold by Enoch Wyer.
Carl. Ely. Pet. Win.

E46? Eachard, John, 1646
'sin'
Pet.

E47 Eachard, John, 1673
Win.

E50 Eachard, John, 1670
Ely. Linc. Liv. S Pl. Sal.

E52? Eachard, John, 1672
By E. Tyler and R. Holt for Nathaniel
Brooke.
Ex.

E53 Eachard, John, 1685
Dur (also has gen. tp, with same
impr., no ed. statement, enabling
E53, E62 & E58 to be sold
together). Glo (as Dur). Nor (2
− 1 as Dur). S Pl (as Dur).

E57 Eachard, John, 1672
Ely. Ex. Nor. Sal.

E57A Eachard, John, 1672
Ex.

E58 Eachard, John, 1685
8°.
Dur. Nor.

E60 Eachard, John, 1671
8°.
Carl. Ely. Linc. Sal.

E61 Eachard, John, 1672
Ex.

E62 Eachard, John, 1685
Dur. Nor.

E64 Eachard, John, 1673
Ban. Carl. Dur. Ely. Ex. Yk
(imp).

E65 Eachard, John, 1672
Clark.
Carl. S Pl. Sal.

E79+ Earle, 1648
= Wing2 E79 *or* E79A.
Pet.

E82 Earle, 1641
Cant.

E86 Earl, 1645
Yk.

E93- Earle, John, 1669
The ninth edition; By Thomas
Ratcliffe and Thomas Daniel for
Philip Chetwind; 12°.
Pet.

E98A? Earnest, 1676
[N.pl.].
Linc.

E107 Easton, Thomas, 1692
Her.

E112- Eaton, John, 1641
By R. Bishop, for William Adderton;
12°.
Carl.

E115 Eaton, John, 1642
Wor (tpw).

E116 Eaton, Nathanael, 1661
Her.

E126? Eaton, Samuel, 1651
'A vindication, ...'; ... Ludowick
Lloyd.
Pet.

E136 *See*: D2557A

E137 Ecclesiasticall, 1642
Lich.

E150 Echard, Laurence, 1697
Yk.

E151 Echard, Laurence, 1695
Ely. Glo.

E154 Echard, Laurence, 1699
By T. Hodgkin ...
Ex. S Pl.

E155 Echard, Laurence, 1698
Ely.

E156 Echard, Laurence, 1699
Ex. S Asa.

E157A Eclectical, 1700
Wel.

E178A Edmonds, Hugh, 1661
For Philemon Stephens the Younger.
Ex.

E183 Edmundson, Henry, 1655
Carl.

E185 Edward VI, 1682
Carl.

E186 Edward VI, 1641
Linc.

E188 Edward, 1642
Yk (2).

E195 Edwards, Charles, [1675]
cap.; 4°.
Yk.

E198 Edwards, John, 1697
Cant. Carl. S Pl.

E201 Edwards, John, 1696
Carl. Ches. Dur. Lich. Nor.
Wel.

E202 Edwards, John, 1693−95
Ex (vol. 2 only). New. Nor. Pet
(lacks vol. 3). S Pl (vol. 2 only).

E204 Edwards, John, 1699
Nor.

E205 Edwards, John, 1700
Impr. as E204.
Ely. S Pl. Win.

E206 Edwards, John, 1692
Carl. Dur. Nor. Pet. Yk.

E208 Edwards, John, 1692
8°.
Dur. Nor. Pet.

E209 Edwards, John, 1665
Pet.

E210 Edwards, John, 1699
Bur. Nor.

E211 Edwards, John, 1698
Bur. Dur. Nor.

E212 Edwards, John, 1697
Cant. Nor.

E214 Edwards, John, 1696
Carl.

E215 Edwards, John, 1695
Bur. Carl. Wel.

E216 Edwards, Jonathan, 1693
Nor. Sal.

E217 Edwards, Jonathan, 1693
Carl.

E218 Edwards, Jonathan, 1698
Ely. Wel. Win. Yk (2).

E219 Edwards, Jonathan, 1694
Carl. Nor. Sal. Wel.

E219+ Edwards, Jonathan, 1698
=Wing2 E219A.
Ely. Win. Yk (2).

E220 Edwards, Jonathan, 1697
Carl. Ely. Nor. Sal. Wel. Yk
(2).

E221 Edwards, Jonathan, 1695
Bris. Carl. Ex. Her. Nor. S Pl.

E222 Edwards, Thomas, 1644
Sal.

E223 Edwards, Thomas, 1644
Win.

E225 Edwards, Thomas, 1647
Cant. Dur. Win.

E227? Edwards, Thomas, 1646
The third edition.
Cant. Ex. S Pl. Win. Yk (2).

E228 Edwards, Thomas, 1646
Her (imp). Win.

E229 Edwards, Thomas, 1646
Bur. Cant (2). Linc (imp). Pet
(2).

E231 Edwards, Thomas, 1699
Bur. Yk.

E233? Edwards, Thomas, 1641
... John Bellamie ...
Pet. Yk.

E234 Edwards, Thomas, 1646
Cant. Ex. Linc (tp imp). S Pl.
Win. Yk (2).

E237 Edwards, Thomas, 1646
Ex. S Pl. Win. Yk.

E239 Edzard, Johann Ezdras, 1696
Heading corrected.
Cant.

E240? Edzard, Sebastian, 1698
Prostant venales apud T. Bennet.
Ex.

E245 Egan, Anthony, 1673
Win. Yk.

E246 Egan, Anthony, 1674
Dur. Ex. Her.

E247 Egan, Anthony, 1678
The second impression.
Her.

E248 Egan, Anthony, 1673
Title as E249.
Dur. Wel.

E250 Egan, Anthony, 1678
Win.

E251 Egan, Anthony, 1674
Cant. Dur. Glo. Linc. Wel (2).

E256? Eglisham, George, 1642
8, [8]p.
Cant. Yk*.

E256+ Eglisham, George, 1642
As E256, but: 23p.
Linc.

E262+ Eight, 1642
=Wing2 E262A?; For G. Lindsey,
Octob. 31.
Dur.

E262++ Eight, 1642
=Wing2 E262B.
Linc.

E265A Eighth, 1689
S Asa. Wel.

E265B Eighth, 1689
Pet. Wel.

E267 Εἴκων 'Αληθίνη, 1649
Chi.

E269? Εἰκὼν Βασιλικὴ, 1648
Second ed. not on tp; 8°.
Ex.

E270 Εἰκὼν Βασιλικὴ, 1648
8°.
Pet. Yk.

E271* Εἰκὼν Βασιλικὴ, 1648
Llan. S Asa.

E273 Εἰκον βασιλικη, 1648
Linc.

E276 Εἰκὼν Βασιλικὴ, 1648
Linc.

E276+ Εἰκὼν Βασιλικὴ, 1648
As E276; 8°.
Ely.

E279 Εἰκὼν Βασιλικὴ, 1648
Sal. Win.

E280 Εἰκὼν Βασιλικὴ, 1648
Ely. Ex.

E283 Εἰκὼν βασιλικὴ, 1648
Sal.

E287- Εἰκὼν Βασιλικὴ, 1648
[London], reprinted in R.M.; 8°;
Almack 22.
Cant. Yk.

E288 Εἰκὼν Βασιλικη, 1648
Nor (imp).

E290 Εἰκὼν Βασιλικη, 1649
Pet (imp).

E304 Εικον βασιλικη, 1649
Cant (imp). Lich.

E304+ Εἰκὼν βασιλικη, 1649
As E304, but: 'Majesty'
Cant. Yk.

E306 Εικον βασιλικη, 1649
Ches (imp)*. Lich. Wel*. Yk*.

E308 Εἰκὼν βασιλικη, 1649
Cant. Sal*.

E311+ Εἰκον βασιλικη, 1649
Imprimées a La Haye [i.e. London, by
Du Gard]; 12°; Almack 57.
Cant.

E311++ Εικων Βασιλικη, 1681
By R. Norton for Richard Royston;
8°.
Ban.

E312 Εικων βασιλικὴ Δεύτερα,
1694
Cant. Nor.

E314 Εικων ἡ πιστη, 1649
Yk (2 − 1 frag.*).

E320 Elborough, Robert, 1666
S Pl.

E321 Elborow, Thomas, 1663
Carl. Dur.

E322+ Elborow, Thomas, 1675
=Wing2 E322A.
Carl.

E323 Elborow, Thomas, 1668
8°.
Ex. Yk.

E324 Elborow, Thomas, 1678
For Richard Chiswell.
Ban. Win.

E325 Elcock, Ephraim, 1651
Ex. Linc.

E327 Elderfield, Christopher, 1650
Sal.

E333 Eleazar bar Isaiah, *pseud.*,
1653
Pet.

E370+ Elegie, 1670
See: CLC44.
Linc.

E396A Elegy, 1677
Linc.

E407 Elegy, [1643]
Linc.

E422 Elegie, 1649
Pet.

E426 Elegie, 1644[5]
Yk.

E458 Elegie, 1679
Linc.

E498 Eleventh, 1689
S Asa. Wel.

E501 Eliot, *Sir* John, 1641
Dur. Linc. Sal.

E510 Eliot, John, 1659
Dur (imp).

E519 Eliot, John, 1643
Carl.

E522? Eliot, John, 1653
Dedication to Cromwell on A2.
Yk.

E522+ Eliot, John, 1653
As E522, but: dedication to Cromwell
on B1.
Yk.

E530+ Elizabeth, *Queen of England*,
1679
London; 2°.
Linc.

E534+ Elizabeth, *Queen of England*,
[1642?]
As E534, but: A of sig. A3, under 'y'
of 'you'
Pet.

E537 Ellesby, James, 1685
Ex. Yk.

E543 Elliot, Adam, 1682
Carl (frag.). Ely (imp). Wel.

E551 Ellis, Clement, 1694
Wor.

E555 Ellis, Clement, 1692
Yk.

E556 Ellis, Clement, 1660
Impr. as Wing2.
Cant. Carl.

E557 Ellis, Clement, 1661
Oxford, by A. and L. Lichfield, for
Edward and John Forrest.
S Asa.

E559 Ellis, Clement, 1668
Pet.

E560+ Ellis, Clement, 1672
The fifth edition; Oxford, by Henry
Hall for John Forrest; 8°.
Linc.

E565 Ellis, Clement, 1687
Ban. Bur. Ex. Roch. Wel. Yk.

E568? Ellis, Clement, 1688
91p.
Ban. Nor. Sal. Wel.

E568+ Ellis, Clement, 1688
As E568, but: 80p.
Dur.

E569 Ellis, Clement, 1688
Ex.

E570 Ellis, Clement, 1688
Ban. Ex. Roch. Swel.

E571 Ellis, Clement, 1691
Cant.

E573 Ellis, Clement, 1661
Carl. Pet. Wor.

E573+ Ellis, Clement, 1661
=Wing2 E573.
Yk.

E575 Ellis, Clement, 1674
Ex. Linc. Pet.

E576 Ellis, Edward, 1649[50]
Chelm.

E580 Ellis, Humphrey, 1647
Cant (2).

E581 Ellis, John, 1694
Bur. Cant. Ely. Lich. Linc.
Pet. S Asa. Yk (2).

E585 Ellis, John, 1668
Ely.

E587 Ellis, John, 1700
'defence'
Dur. Liv. Wel.

E588+ Ellis, John, 1663
Entry as E588, apart from date.
Ex.

E590 Ellis, John, 1662
Ex. Pet. Win. Yk (2).

E592 Ellis, John, 1643
Cant (2).

E592+ Ellis, John, 1643
By John Raworth, for George
Latham; 4°.
Pet (2).

E593 Ellis, John, 1647
Ban. Pet. Win.

E594 Ellis, Philip, 1686
Cant. Carl.

E595 Ellis, Philip, 1686
Cant. Carl. S Asa. Sal (2).

E596 Ellis, Philip, 1686
Cant.

E597 Ellis, Philip, 1686
Cant. Carl. Sal (3).

E598 Ellis, Philip, 1686
By Henry Hills.
Cant. Sal.

E599 Ellis, Philip, 1686
Cant.

E600 Ellis, Philip, 1687
Cant.

E601? Ellis, Philip, 1687
'before'
Cant.

E602 Ellis, Philip, 1686
Cant. Carl.

E603 Ellis, Philip, 1686
Cant. Carl. Sal.

E604 Ellis, Philip, 1686
Cant.

E608 Ellis, Tobias, 1678
Yk.

E610 Ellison, Nathanael, 1700
Carl. Dur. New. S Asa.

E620 Ellwood, Thomas , 1694
8°.
Dur.

E622 Ellwood, Thomas, 1678
Yk.

E623 Ellwood, Thomas , 1694
Dur.

E629 Ellwood, Thomas , 1695
Dur.

E630 Ellwood, Thomas , 1676
Chelm.

E631 Ellyson, John, 1647
Pet.

E633 Ellyson, Thomas, [1647]
cap.
Dur.

E644 Elsynge, Henry, 1663
Second ed. not on tp.
Sal.

E645 Elsynge, Henry, 1660
'... holding of Parliaments'
Cant. Pet (tp imp).

E645A Elsynge, Henry, 1675
... Tho. Dring.
Yk.

E646? Elsynge, Henry, 1679
For Thomas Dring; 12°.
Ex.

E647 Elsynge, Henry, [1648]
Linc.

E648 Elsynge, Henry, 1648
Yk.

E661+ Elys, Edmund, 1699
See: CLC45.
Nor.

E662? Elys, Edmund, [1695]
'... concerning the divinity'
Wel.

E675 Elys, Edmund, 1670
Win.

E675A Elys, Edmund, 1697
cap.
Dur.

E685 Elys, Edmund, 1696
Wel.

E688+ Elys, Edmund, [1698]
=Wing2 E688A.
Dur.

E692+ Elys, Edmund, 1697
=Wing2 E692A?; ... Will. Marshal
and John Marshal.
Dur.

E698 Elys, Edmund, 1699
Dur.

E714 Emmot, George, 1655
Yk.

E716 *See*: C1673-, for an earlier ed.
of this

E728 Enderbie, Percie, 1661
Cant.

E741? England. Army Council,
1647
29p.
Ex. Linc. Yk (4)*.

E741+ England. Army Council,
1647
As E741, but: 28p.
Ex.

E809 England. King in Council,
1674/5
Linc (imp).

E817 England. King in Council,
[1667]
Linc.

E819 England. King in Council,
1666
brs.
Carl.

E820 England. King in Council,
1678/9
'... Whitehall, January the
seventeenth, 1678/9 ... there ...'
Linc.

E846 England. King in Council,
1678/9
Linc.

E873 England. Laws, statutes, 1658
Ban. Cant. Carl. Dur. Ex.
Nor. Sal. Wor. Yk.

E878 England. Laws, statutes, 1646
S Asa (tpw). Win. Yk.

E881 England. Laws, statutes, 1667
Carl.

E883A England. Laws, statutes,
1697
By Charles Bill ... Thomas Newcomb;
12°.
Yk.

E884 England. Laws, statutes, 1670
Bris (tp imp). Dur. Ex. Linc.
Sal.

E887 England. Laws, statutes, 1644
Dur (imp).

E889 England. Laws, statutes, 1651
'Parliament'
Cant.

E890 England. Laws, statutes, 1653
Yk.

E891 England. Laws, statutes, 1657
Liv.

E898 England. Laws, statutes, 1667
Cant. Yk.

E901? England. Laws, statutes,
1699
... assigns of Richard and Edward
Atkins.
S Pl.

E902 England. Laws, statutes
[Hughes], 1663
Entry as Wing2; 8°.
Carl. Yk.

E904 England. Laws, statutes
[Manby], 1674
... Richard Atkins ...
Carl.

E905 England. Laws, statutes
[Wingate], 1655
Bur.

E905+ England. Laws, statutes
[Wingate], 1659
=Wing2 E905A, apart from date.
Carl. Sal. Yk.

E908? England. Laws, statutes,
1675
Fifth ed. not on tp.
Yk.

E909? England. Laws, statutes,
1681
Sixth ed. not on tp; ... Atkins ...
Atkins ...
Dur. Nor.

E911? England. Laws, statutes,
1689
Eighth ed. not on tp.
Wel.

E912? England. Laws, statutes ,
1700
Ninth ed. not on tp; ... R. Atkins ...
Cant.

E914? England. Laws, statutes,
1696
Second ed. not on tp.
Ban. S Pl.

E916 England. Laws, statutes, 1642
Dur. Linc.

E923A+ England. Laws, statutes,
1676
=Wing2 E923E; ... the assigns of
Richard Atkins and Edward Atkins.
Ches (2).

E923A++ England. Laws, statutes,
1681
=Wing2 E923F; ... Newcomb ... the
assigns of Richard Atkins and Edward
Atkins.
Roch. S Pl. Yk (tpw).

E923A+++ England. Laws, statutes,
1684
=Wing2 E923G; By the assigns of
John Bill deceas'd: and by Henry
Hills, Thomas Newcomb, the assigns
of Richard Atkins, and Edward
Atkins.
Ex. Linc. Nor. Wor.

E923A++++ England. Laws,
statutes, 1695
=Wing2 E923H; ... deceas'd, and by
the assigns of Richard Atkins and
Edward Atkins.
Carl. Linc.

E924? England. Laws, statutes,
1673
'... statute-laws of this kingdom now
in force, made against Jesuites'
Win.

E931A *See*: I626A

E958B+ England. Parliament, 1696
=Wing2 E958C; cap.
Cant.

E972 England. Parliament, 1657
Linc.

E976 England. Parliament, 1657
Linc.

E997+ England. Parliament, 1657
As E997, but: By Henry Hills ...
Linc.

E998 England. Parliament, 1657
Linc.

E1016 England. Parliament, 1657
Linc.

E1030 England. Parliament, 1657
Linc.

E1042? England. Parliament, 1657
'indepmnifying [*sic*]'
Linc.

E1046 England. Parliament, 1657
Linc.

E1049 England. Parliament, 1657
cap.
Linc.

E1051 England. Parliament, 1657
Linc.

E1054+ England. Parliament, 1657
As E1054, but: By Hen: Hills ...
Linc.

E1064? England. Parliament, 1657
'... disanulling ... Charles ...'
Linc.

E1087 England. Parliament, 1657
Linc.

E1091 England. Parliament, 1657
Linc.

E1092 England. Parliament, 1657
Linc.

E1094 England. Parliament, 1657
Dur. Linc.

E1097+ England. Parliament, 1650
Printed by John Field; 2°; pp. 903 – 8.
Dur.

E1100 England. Parliament, 1657
Linc.

E1110+ England. Parliament, 1657
By Henry Hills and Iohn Field; 2°.
Linc.

E1113 England. Parliament, 1657
cap.
Linc.

E1119 England. Parliament, 1657
Linc.

E1123? England. Parliament, 1657
Impr. on tp.
Linc.

E1131 England. Parliament, 1657
Linc.

E1134 England. Parliament, 1657
Linc.

E1138 England. Parliament, 1657
cap.
Linc.

E1148A? England. Parliament, 1675
'tonnage & poundage'
Glo.

E1150A England. Parliament, 1649
cap.
Ex.

E1163+ England. Parliament, 1671
=Wing2 E1163A?; 'The acts ...'; In
the Savoy ...; 12°.
Ex. Yk.

E1171 England. Parliament, 1657
Linc.

E1172+ England. Parliament, 1650
By Iohn Field; 2°; pp. 809 – 26.
Dur.

E1176 England. Parliament, 1647
'... dayes of recreation ...'
Pet.

E1177 England. Parliament, 1645
Ex.

E1182 England. Parliament, 1647
'additionall'
Ex.

E1198 England. Parliament, 1647
Yk.

E1202A England. Parliament, 1644
Sal.

E1206? England. Parliament, 1646
For Edw. Husband.
S Asa.

E1208? England. Parliament, 1650
For Edward Husband.
Her.

E1211 England. Parliament, 1646
Cant (2 – 1 imp). Liv (imp). Sal
(imp).

E1213 England. Parliament, 1641[2]
Cant.

E1215 England. Parliament, 1642
Dur (imp). Linc (2).

E1216 England. Parliament, 1642
Pet.

E1217 England. Parliament, 1642
Linc.

E1219 England. Parliament, 1642
Dur. Linc. Yk (4).

E1219A England. Parliament, 1642
Yk.

E1224 England. Parliament, 1646
Linc.

E1228 England. Parliament, 1652
4°.
Ex.

E1229? England. Parliament, 1642
For Theophilus Bonrne [*sic*].
Linc.

E1230 England. Parliament, 1641
Yk.

E1230+ England. Parliament, 1641
=Wing2 E1230A.
Yk.

E1234 England. Parliament, 1642
Dur.

E1235 England. Parliament, 1641
Dur. Linc. Yk.

E1271 England. Parliament, 1654
Linc.

E1273 England. Parliament, [1642]
Linc.

E1274 England. Parliament, 1642
Dur. Yk.

E1279 *See*: E878

E1279A+ England. Parliament,
1652
'A collection of severall proceedings in
Parliament'; For R.I., sold by John
Wright; 2°.
Ex.

E1281 England. Parliament, 1695
Ban.

E1284+ England. Parliament, 1643
=Wing2 E1284; For Edward
Husbands ...
Cant.

E1288 England. Parliament, 1641[2]
Cant.

E1301 England. Parliament, 1643
Linc.

E1302 England. Parliament, 1643
Yk.

E1302+ England. Parliament, 1643
=Wing2 E1302A?; For Iohn Wright
and Iohn Franke.
Pet.

E1307 England. Parliament, 1643
Yk.

E1308 England. Parliament, 1642
Dur.

E1309- England. Parliament, 1642
As E1309, but no date in title or impr.
Dur.

E1309 England. Parliament, 1642
Cant.

E1310 England. Parliament, 1642
Linc.

E1310A+ England. Parliament, 1642
=Wing2 E1310B.
Sal.

E1311 England. Parliament, 1642
Pet.

E1312 England. Parliament, 1642
Cant.

E1313+ England. Parliament, 1642
For E. Husband and Iohn Franke, 15
August; 4°.
Ex.

E1314 England. Parliament, 1642
Linc.

E1315 England. Parliament, 1642
Dur. Linc.

E1317 England. Parliament, 1642
Dur.

E1320 England. Parliament, 1642
Dur.

E1321 England. Parliament, [1642]
Cant (2). Linc.

E1325A England. Parliament, 1642
Yk.

E1326 England. Parliament, 1642
... assignes ...
Dur. Pet. Yk (2).

E1326+ England. Parliament, 1642
=Wing2 E1326A.
Yk (2).

E1326++ England. Parliament,
1642
For F. Cowles, and T. Bates; 4°.
Cant.

E1327? England. Parliament, 1642
.. London, for Iohn Wright.
Dur. Linc. Yk (2).

E1336 England. Parliament, 1652
Linc. Win.

E1341 England. Parliament, 1641[2]
Linc.

E1342 England. Parliament, 1642
Yk.

E1361 England. Parliament, 1642
Linc. Pet.

E1363 England. Parliament, 1642
'... Commons ... Concerning ...'
Linc.

E1365 England. Parliament, 1642
Dur.

E1366 England. Parliament, 1642
Yk.

E1367 England. Parliament, 1642
Linc. Yk.

E1369 England. Parliament, 1644
Pet.

E1370? England. Parliament, 1642
'The declaration ...'
Dur. Yk.

E1371 England. Parliament, 1642
Dur.

E1372 England. Parliament, 1642
Linc. Yk.

E1372A England. Parliament, 1642
Linc. Yk.

E1374 England. Parliament, 1642[3]
Yk.

E1376+ England. Parliament, 1642
'The declaration ... His Maiesties ...';
For I.T.; 4°.
Pet.

E1377 England. Parliament, 1642
Linc.

E1377+ England. Parliament,
[1642]
As E1377, but no date.
Cant.

E1385 England. Parliament, 1643[4]
'... estates, rents, ...'
Linc. Sal. Yk.

E1388 England. Parliament, 1642[3]
Linc.

E1390 England. Parliament, 1642
Cant.

E1391 England. Parliament, 1642
Dur. Linc. Yk (3).

E1392 England. Parliament, 1647[8]
Pet (2). Yk.

E1396 England. Parliament, 1642
Yk.

E1397 England. Parliament, 1642[3]
Cant. Linc (2).

E1398 England. Parliament, 1642
Linc.

E1400 England. Parliament, [1642]
Dur.

E1401 England. Parliament, [1649]
Yk.

E1407 England. Parliament, 1642
Dur (cropped)*.

E1411+ England. Parliament, 1642
'quieting'; For J. Wright, Septemb. 3.;
4°.
Dur. Pet.

E1414+ England. Parliament, 1642
As E1414, but: ... August 25.
Linc. Yk*.

E1416 England. Parliament, 1642
Dur. Linc.

E1419 England. Parliament, 1642
Impr. as Wing2.
Linc. Yk (2).

E1419A England. Parliament, 1642
Impr. as Wing2.
Yk (2).

E1420 England. Parliament, 1642[3]
Pet.

E1422 England. Parliament, 1642
Linc.

E1423+ England. Parliament, 1642
For E. Husbands and I. Franck,
August 9.; 4°.
Dur.

E1424 England. Parliament, 1642
Ex.

E1426 England. Parliament, 1642
For Iohn Wright.
Linc.

E1430 England. Parliament, 1642
Dur.

E1431 England. Parliament, 1642
Linc.

E1434 England. Parliament, 1648
Yk.

E1435 England. Parliament, 1642
'The declaration ...'
Dur. Yk (2).

E1436 England. Parliament, 1642
'The declaration ...'
Yk (2).

E1438 England. Parliament, 1642[3]
Entry as Wing2.
Yk.

E1439 England. Parliament, 1642
Pet.

E1442+ England. Parliament, 1642
=Wing2 E1442A?; 'The declaration
... '; ... and Ioseph Hunscot.
Yk (2).

E1443? England. Parliament, 1642
B2ᵛ line 14: 'Maiesties'
Yk (3).

E1443+ England. Parliament, 1642
As E1443, but: 'Majesties'
Yk.

E1446 England. Parliament, 1642
'Julii 4. 1642. The declaration ...'
Cant (imp). Ex. Linc.

E1449? England. Parliament, 1642
4°.
Ex.

E1449A? England. Parliament, 1642
4°.
Sal.

E1450 England. Parliament, 1642
Chi. Linc. Yk (2).

E1451 England. Parliament, 1642
Yk.

E1452 England. Parliament, 1642
Dur. Sal.

E1454 England. Parliament, 1643
Linc. Yk.

E1455 England. Parliament, 1642[3]
Cant. Chi (2). Linc.

E1459 England. Parliament, 1643
Linc.

E1467 England. Parliament, 1642
Linc. Sal.

E1470 England. Parliament, 1642
Dur.

E1471 England. Parliament, 1642
Cant (2).

E1472 England. Parliament, 1642
Yk (2).

E1473+ England. Parliament,
1643[4]
'... touching a treatie for peace';
[N.pl.], by Leonard Lichfield; 4°;
Madan 1562.
Cant.

E1475 England. Parliament, 1642
32p.
Dur. Linc. Pet. Yk*.

E1477- England. Parliament, 1642
As E1477, but: August 20 in impr.
Dur.

E1477 England. Parliament, 1642
Pet. Yk.

E1478 England. Parliament, 1642
Linc. Pet.

E1484 England. Parliament, 1641
Impr. as Wing2.
Cant.

E1484A England. Parliament, 1641
Sal.

E1484B England. Parliament, 1641
Dur.

E1486- England. Parliament, 1644
=Wing2 E1486.
Ex.

E1486 England. Parliament, 1644
Pet.

E1488 England. Parliament, 1642
Linc.

E1489 England. Parliament, 1689
Wel.

E1491 England. Parliament,
1659[60]
Ex.

E1494 *See*: E1503

E1495 England. Parliament, 1650
Yk.

E1498 England. Parliament, 1649
Wing2 transcribes the tp of pt 2 of
E1505.
Cant. Pet (imp). Yk.

E1503 England. Parliament, 1649
Cant. Her. Pet. Yk.

E1505 England. Parliament, 1650
'Parlament'
Ex (2). Pet (2). Sal.

E1507 England. Parliament, 1645
'Low-Countreys'
Pet. Yk.

E1509 England. Parliament, 1652
Pet.

E1511 England. Parliament, 1652
Ex. Pet.

E1512 England. Parliament, 1648
Pet.

E1513? England. Parliament, 1642
'severall'; No date in impr.
Yk.

E1515 England. Parliament, 1643
Pet.

E1517 England. Parliament, 1642
Ex. Liv. Sal. Yk (4).

E1518? England. Parliament, 1642
'kingdome'
Cant. Linc. Yk.

E1520 England. Parliament, 1642
Cant. Dur (imp). Linc (2 – 1
imp). Yk (2).

E1521 England. Parliament, 1642
Dur (cropped).

E1523 England. Parliament, 1645
For John Wright ...
Linc. Liv.

E1523+ England. Parliament, 1645
As E1523, but: 'advise'
Ex (2).

E1525 England. Parliament, 1645
Cant (2). Sal.

E1527 England. Parliament, 1641
Linc.

E1529 England. Parliament, 1643
For Edw. Husbands.
Linc.

E1531 England. Parliament, 1679
Dur. Linc.

E1532 England. Parliament, 1642
For Edward Husbands ...
Ex. S Asa. Yk (2).

E1533 England. Parliament, 1643
Ely. Liv. Yk.

E1533A England. Parliament, 1660
Dur. S Asa.

E1539 England. Parliament, 1648
Ches. Pet. Yk.

E1542 England. Parliament, 1643
Linc.

E1552 England. Parliament, 1643
Linc.

E1553 England. Parliament, 1642
Linc.

E1553+ England. Parliament, 1642
=Wing2 E1553.
Dur.

E1553++ England. Parliament,
1642
=Wing2 E1553A.
Linc.

E1553A England. Parliament, 1644
For Edw. Husbands ...
Cant. Linc. Yk.

E1553C England. Parliament, 1645
Yk.

E1555 England. Parliament, 1642[3]
Yk.

E1557 England. Parliament, 1642
Same title as E1554; date given in
Wing is that of the order to print.
Cant. Linc.

E1563 England. Parliament, 1642[3]
Yk.

E1565+ England. Parliament,
[1642]
As E1565, but no date.
Dur.

E1566 England. Parliament, 1657
Linc.

E1568 England. Parliament, 1641
Yk (2).

E1569- England. Parliament, 1642
=Wing2 E1568A.
Pet.

E1571 England. Parliament, 1642
London counterfeit.
Linc. Pet.

E1573? England. Parliament, 1642
'17 of June'
Sal. Yk.

E1573A England. Parliament, 1642
Yk (3).

E1574? England. Parliament, 1642
... Iohn Franke ...
Linc. Pet (imp). Yk (2)

E1576 England. Parliament, 1642
Yk (4).

E1577 England. Parliament, 1642
Yk (3).

E1580? England. Parliament, 1642
'Earl'
Linc.

E1580+ England. Parliament, 1642
'The humble petition ... Robert Earle
of Essex'; For Ed. Husbands and
Iohn Francke; 4°.
Linc.

E1581? England. Parliament, 1642
... Septemb. 27.
Cant. Linc (2).

E1582 England. Parliament, 1642
'... Commons in Parliament, ...'; ...
assignes ...
Linc. Yk (2).

E1583 England. Parliament, 1642
Linc. Pet. Yk (2 issues: tp date
in Roman or Arabic).

E1583+ England. Parliament,
[1642]
=Wing2 E1583A.
Yk.

E1583++ England. Parliament,
1642
For Thomas Powell; 4°.
Yk.

E1584 England. Parliament, 1642
Anr ed. of E1585 etc.
Linc. Yk.

E1585A *See*: E1584

E1585B+ England. Parliament,
1642
=Wing2 E1585B.
Yk.

E1586 England. Parliament, 1642
Yk (3).

E1588A England. Parliament, 1643
Linc.

E1590? England. Parliament, 1642
... Richard Best.
Dur.

E1592 England. Parliament, 1657
Linc.

E1598? England. Parliament, 1642
'Die Martis 26. April. 1642. It is
declared ...'; ... assignes ...
Linc.

E1605? England. Parliament, 1642
'Die Martis, 20. Maii. 1642. It is this
day ...'
Linc.

E1607 England. Parliament, 1642
Linc.

E1608 England. Parliament, 1642
Linc.

E1622 England. Parliament, 1642
Yk.

E1624 England. Parliament, 1642
Dur. Linc.

E1625 England. Parliament, 1642
Dur.

E1635? England. Parliament, 1642
'Die Sabbati 9. April 1642. The Lords
...'; ... assignes ...
Linc.

E1639? England. Parliament, 1642
'Die September 29. 1642. The Lords
...'; ... I. Frrnk [*sic*].
Linc.

E1648 England. Parliament, 1641[2]
Dur.

E1649 England. Parliament, 1641[2]
Dur.

E1650 England. Parliament, 1641[2]
Entry as Wing2.
Ex. Yk.

E1651 England. Parliament, 1642
Linc.

E1653 England. Parliament, 1642
Yk.

E1658 England. Parliament, 1642
Cant. Linc (2).

E1660 England. Parliament, 1648
Pet.

E1660A England. Parliament, 1648
Cant. Yk.

E1661 England. Parliament, 1641[2]
'March 1. A message ...'
Dur (cropped). Linc.

E1665 England. Parliament, 1642
Pet.

E1667? England. Parliament, 1642
'June 21. 1642. A new ...'; ... Iohn
Franke.
Dur. Yk (2).

E1668 England. Parliament, [1642]
Linc.

E1669 England. Parliament, 1642
Yk.

E1669+ England. Parliament, 1642
=Wing2 E1669A?; brs.
Linc (on verso of C2164+).

E1670+ England. Parliament, 1642
=Wing2 E1670A, which has wrong
date.
Yk.

E1671 England. Parliament, 1642
Dur. Ex. Yk.

E1673? England. Parliament, 1642
By Roger Daniel.
Sal.

E1674 England. Parliament, 1642
... John Bill.
Yk (2 − 1 imp).

E1675 England. Parliament, 1642
Impr. as Wing2.
Yk.

E1684 England. Parliament, 1641
S Pl.

E1686 England. Parliament, 1641[2]
'Die Sabbati, 29 Januarii, 1641. An
order ...'
Dur (cropped). Linc.

E1687 England. Parliament, 1642
Ex.

E1688 England. Parliament, 1642
... assignes ...
Dur (cropped). Yk.

E1689 England. Parliament, 1642
'Die Martis, 19 Julii, 1642. An order
...'
Linc.

E1696? England. Parliament, 1642
... Novemb. 4.
Dur.

E1697 England. Parliament, 1642
Linc.

E1711 England. Parliament, 1643
'... Commons assembled in
Parliament. For ...'
Linc.

E1717? England. Parliament, 1642
'Die Sabbati 28 Maii, 1642. An order
...'; For Joseph Hunscott.
Linc.

E1720 England. Parliament, 1642
'Die Martis 26. April 1642. Ordered
by ...'
Linc.

E1762+ England. Parliament, 1654
By Will. du-Gard and Hen. Hills; 2°;
pp. 447−51.
Dur.

E1765? England. Parliament, 1642
'authorising'; ... I. Wright.
Linc. Sal.

E1768- England. Parliament, 1642
As E1768, but: 14p.; Madan 1107.
Linc.

E1768 England. Parliament, 1642
6, 8p.
Linc. Pet. Sal. Yk*.

E1769? England. Parliament, 1642
'An ordinance ...'; ... Decemb. 1.
Linc.

E1770 England. Parliament, 1642
Entry as Wing2 E1768.
Cant.

E1772 England. Parliament, 1644
Sal.

E1775? England. Parliament,
1642[3]
'Lord Mayor'
Linc.

E1782 England. Parliament, 1654
'April 6.'
Dur (cropped?).

E1783 England. Parliament, 1654
Dur (cropped).

E1787 England. Parliament, [1642]
... and G.D. ...
Ex.

E1788 England. Parliament, 1642
For Iohn Wright.
Dur. Linc.

E1789 England. Parliament, 1641
Ex (2). Sal.

E1794+ England. Parliament, 1642
'An ordinance of both Houses of
Parliament for the suppressing of
publike stage-playes'; For Iohn
Wright, Septemb. 3; brs.
Dur.

E1795 England. Parliament, 1642
... for Lawrence Blaikelock.
Ex.

E1795A England. Parliament, 1642
Entry as Wing2.
Sal.

E1801 England. Parliament, 1644
Chelm. Ely. Linc.

E1814+ England. Parliament, 1645
=Wing2 E1814A?; Date as given; 4°.
Liv.

E1854 England. Parliament, 1645
Yk.

E1865 England. Parliament, 1647
Yk.

E1890 England. Parliament, [1644]
Linc.

E1894 England. Parliament, 1645
Liv.

E1895 England. Parliament, 1645[6]
Dur. Yk.

E1895A? England. Parliament, 1646
For Edward Husband.
Cant (2). Liv. Sal.

E1906 England. Parliament, 1644[5]
Yk.

E1908 England. Parliament, 1644
Pet.

E1912 England. Parliament, 1647[8]
Yk.

E1935 England. Parliament, 1644
Ex.

E1940 England. Parliament, 1645
Yk (2).

E1943 England. Parliament, 1642
Dur.

E1944 England. Parliament, 1644
Pet.

E1952 England. Parliament, 1643
Impr. as Wing2.
Linc. Pet.

E1977 England. Parliament, 1644
Ex.

E1981 England. Parliament, 1646
Yk.

E1988 England. Parliament, 1643
Yk.

E1990 England. Parliament, 1644
Pet.

E1995 England. Parliament, 1645
... Edw. Husband.
Yk.

E1995+ England. Parliament, 1645
'putting'; [London], by T.W., for
Edw. Husband; 4°.
Ches (2). Dur.

E1996 England. Parliament, 1646
[London], ...
Sal.

E2000 England. Parliament, 1646
Liv. Pet.

E2000+ England. Parliament, 1646
As E2000, but no date in impr.
Cant (2). Sal.

E2003 England. Parliament, 1646
Bris. Cant (2). Liv.

E2003+ England. Parliament, 1646
For John Wright; 4°.
Cant. Sal.

E2020 England. Parliament, 1647
Pet. Yk.

E2020+ England. Parliament, 1647
=Wing2 E2020A.
Yk*.

E2030 England. Parliament, 1642
Linc. Sal.

E2032? England. Parliament,
1647[8]
4°.
Cant. Yk.

E2032+ England. Parliament, 1647
At Kondon [sic] for Iohn Wright; 4°.
Pet. Yk.

E2033 England. Parliament, 1641
Linc.

E2035 England. Parliament, 1642
For Richard Best.
Cant.

E2038 England. Parliament, 1646
Ex. Yk.

E2043 England. Parliament, 1647[8]
Cant. Linc.

E2052 England. Parliament, 1643
Yk.

E2059 England. Parliament, 1645
Ex.

E2060 England. Parliament, 1645
Cant.

E2063 England. Parliament, 1642
Linc.

E2065 England. Parliament, 1644
Ex. Pet.

E2065+ England. Parliament, 1644
=Wing2 E2065A.
Ex.

E2069 England. Parliament, [1643]
Pet.

E2082 England. Parliament, 1643
Pet.

E2098 England. Parliament, 1645
Ex.

E2099? England. Parliament, 1645
For Iohn Wright.
Cant (2). Liv. Sal.

E2106 England. Parliament, 1643
Linc.

E2107 England. Parliament, 1643
Cant.

E2108 England. Parliament, 1644
Yk.

E2109+ England. Parliament, 1643
=Wing2 E2109A.
Linc.

E2110 England. Parliament, [1644?]
Cant. Yk.

E2113 England. Parliament, 1643
Linc.

E2115 England. Parliament, 1642
'... in London and all parts of
England ...'
Dur. Linc.

E2115+ England. Parliament, 1642
As E2115, but: '... within and about
the Citty of London ...'
Linc.

E2117 England. Parliament, 1642
Dur. Linc.

E2117+ England. Parliament, 1651
'Ordinances of the Lords and
Commons ... for the leavying of
moneys'; By Matthew Simmons and
Gartrude Dawson; 2°.
Pet.

E2130 England. Parliament, 1642
Linc.

E2132 England. Parliament, 1642
Dur (tp imp). Linc.

E2135? England. Parliament, 1642
Day and month not in impr.
Yk (3).

E2139 England. Parliament, [1642]
Yk.

E2141 England. Parliament, 1642
Yk.

E2142 England. Parliament, 1642
Yk.

E2143 England. Parliament, 1641[2]
Linc.

E2145+ England. Parliament, 1642
=Wing2 E2145A.
Yk (2).

E2149 England. Parliament, 1642
Ex.

E2153 England. Parliament, 1648
Dur. Yk.

E2156 England. Parliament, 1641
Sal.

E2157 England. Parliament, 1641
Pet.

E2158 England. Parliament, 1641
Linc.

E2158+ England. Parliament, 1641
=Wing2 E2158.
Yk.

E2159 England. Parliament, 1642
Linc.

E2159+ England. Parliament, 1642
=Wing2 E2159A.
Dur. Yk.

E2161 England. Parliament, 1642
Yk.

E2162 England. Parliament, 1642
Yk.

E2164 England. Parliament, 1642
... assignes ...
Linc. Yk (3).

E2165 England. Parliament, 1642
... assignes ...
Yk (3).

E2166? England. Parliament, 1642
... now reprinted [*sic*] ...
Linc.

E2167 England. Parliament, 1642
Yk.

E2168+ England. Parliament, 1642
For Iohn Wright; 4°.
Cant.

E2170 England. Parliament, 1642
Cant (imp). Dur.

E2171 England. Parliament, 1642
Impr. as Wing2.
Dur. Yk.

E2174? England. Parliament, 1642
... assignes ...; 7p.
Linc.

E2174+ England. Parliament, 1642
As E2174, but no pagination.
Linc.

E2174++ England. Parliament,
1642
As E2174, but has 18p.
Pet. Sal.

E2176 England. Parliament, 1642
Yk (2).

E2179 England. Parliament, 1642
... assignes ...
Linc. Yk.

E2180 England. Parliament, 1641
Cant.

E2182 England. Parliament, 1642
'Majesty'
Linc.

E2194 England. Parliament, 1651
Cant.

E2195 England. Parliament, 1648[9]
Yk.

E2196 England. Parliament, 1660
Linc.

E2202 England. Parliament, 1642
Pet.

E2204 England. Parliament, 1642
Linc (2). Pet.

E2209 England. Parliament, 1646
Cant. Linc. Pet. Yk.

E2210 England. Parliament, 1648
Pet.

E2211 England. Parliament, 1641
Linc. Nor (imp). Yk.

E2213 England. Parliament, 1641[2]
Linc.

E2217? England. Parliament, 1642
'August 20. A remonstrance ...';
[London], for George Tomlingson.
Ex.

E2219 England. Parliament, 1642
Linc.

E2220 England. Parliament, 1642
Or E2221.
Cant. Dur. Linc. Pet. Yk (2).

E2221A? England. Parliament, 1641
Hunscutt.
Pet.

E2221B England. Parliament, 1641
Dur. Sal.

E2221C? England. Parliament, 1641
Newly corrected; Hunscutt.
Pet.

E2222? England. Parliament, 1642
'19 of May'
Ex.

E2223 England. Parliament, 1642
Yk.

E2224 England. Parliament, 1643
Entry as Wing2.
Cant.

E2226 England. Parliament, 1642
Linc. Pet. Yk.

E2226A England. Parliament, 1642
Cant. Linc. Yk.

E2227 England. Parliament, 1742
[*i.e.* 1642]
Cant (imp). Yk (2).

E2230 England. Parliament, 1642
Dur. Linc. Yk.

E2237 England. Parliament, 1642
Yk.

E2243+ England. Parliament,
[1646]
[N.pl.]; cap.; 4°.
Cant (2). Sal.

E2270 England. Parliament, 1642
... assignes ...
Linc.

E2279 England. Parliament, 1649
Linc.

E2284 England. Parliament, 1643
4°.
Cant. Yk.

E2286 England. Parliament, 1645
Cant. Sal.

E2287 England. Parliament, 1642[3]
Cant. Ex. Linc. Pet.

E2289 England. Parliament, 1641[2]
Linc.

E2291 England. Parliament, 1646
Pet.

E2293 England. Parliament, 1649
Yk.

E2294? England. Parliament, 1647
Printed for John Wright.
Cant. Yk.

E2296 England. Parliament, 1641[2]
'Parliament'; ... assignes of John Bill.
Sal.

E2300 England. Parliament, 1641[2]
Linc.

E2306 England. Parliament, 1641[2]
Linc.

E2308 England. Parliament, 1642
Linc.

E2309 England. Parliament, 1641
Ban. Carl. Glo. Sal.

E2311? England. Parliament, 1642
For Laurence Blaiklocke.
Sal.

E2312? England. Parliament, 1642
For Laurence Blaiklock.
Ex.

E2314 England. Parliament, 1660
12°.
Yk.

E2316 England. Parliament, 1641
Dur. Ex. Linc.

E2358 England. Parliament, 1642
Sal.

E2360 England. Parliament, 1643
Linc.

E2362 England. Parliament, 1647
Cant.

E2365 England. Parliament, 1644
Linc.

E2378+ England. Parliament,
[1696]
=Wing2 E2379.
Dur.

E2380 England. Parliament, 1642
Dur.

E2382 England. Parliament, 1659
Carl. S Pl.

E2386 England. Parliament, 1643
Pet.

E2387 England. Parliament, 1642
Cant. Yk.

E2389 England. Parliament, 1642
Yk.

E2390 England. Parliament, 1642
Pet.

E2391 England. Parliament, 1642
Pet.

E2393 England. Parliament, 1642
Yk.

E2394 England. Parliament, 1652
Glo.

E2397A England. Parliament, 1642
Linc.

E2406 England. Parliament, 1645
... Decemb. 29.
Yk.

E2407 England. Parliament, 1647
Ex.

E2408 England. Parliament, 1644
Pet.

E2411 England. Parliament, 1646
Ex.

E2416 England. Parliament, 1643
Linc.

E2417 England. Parliament, 1646
Pet.

E2426 England. Parliament, 1645
Ex.

E2429 England. Parliament, 1641[2]
'Febr.'; ... assignes ...
Cant (imp). Dur. Linc. Sal.

E2436 England. Parliament, 1642
Linc.

E2437 England. Parliament, 1642[3]
Cant.

E2438 England. Parliament, 1642
Yk.

E2442 England. Parliament, 1642
Linc.

E2446 England. Parliament, 1642
Linc. Yk (2).

E2448 England. Parliament, 1642
Yk.

E2461+ England. Parliament, 1643
For Edw. Husbands; 4°.
Cant.

E2481 England. Parliament, 1642
Linc.

E2487 England. Parliament, [1642]
Linc.

E2520 England. Parliament. House
of Commons, 1646
Ex (2). Pet. Yk.

E2521 England. Parliament. House
of Commons, 1641
Yk.

E2522 England. Parliament. House
of Commons, 1641
48p.
Ely. Linc. Pet. Yk (2)*.

E2522+ England. Parliament.
House of Commons, 1641
As E2522, but: 31p.
Dur.

E2523 England. Parliament. House
of Commons, 1642
Yk.

E2524A? England. Parliament.
House of Commons, 1642
[London] ...
Ex.

E2525? England. Parliament. House
of Commons, 1641
'... for ... crimes, ... committed ...
when he was Bishop of Norwich'
Dur. Linc. Yk*.

E2525+ England. Parliament.
House of Commons, 1641
As E2525 but: '... Bishop of Norwich.
With Sir Thomas Widdringtons
speech'
Ely.

E2526 England. Parliament. House
of Commons, 1641
'The articles or charge exhibited in
Parliament ...'
Yk.

E2527 England. Parliament. House
of Commons, 1643[4]
'their accusation'
Yk (2).

E2528 England. Parliament. House
of Commons, 1641
Pet (2). Yk.

E2532 England. Parliament. House
of Commons, [1679]
Dur. Linc.

E2533 England. Parliament. House
of Commons, 1641
Yk (2 − 1 tp imp).

E2533+ England. Parliament.
House of Commons, 1641
=Wing2 E2533A.
Cant.

E2537 England. Parliament. House
of Commons, 1648[9]
Cant. Dur. Her. Yk.

E2538 England. Parliament. House
of Commons, 1681
Linc.

E2543+ England. Parliament.
House of Commons, 1641
'A copy of the bill'; Formerly C6206.
Dur (cropped).

E2544 England. Parliament. House
of Commons, 1680
S Pl.

E2548+ England. Parliament.
House of Commons, 1642
For Joseph Hunscott; brs.
Dur.

E2552 England. Parliament. House
of Commons, 1641
Dur. Linc. Yk.

E2553 England. Parliament. House of Commons, 1646[7]
Ex.

E2557 England. Parliament. House of Commons, 1643
Sal.

E2559 England. Parliament. House of Commons, 1647[8]
Cant. Ex. Pet. Sal. Yk.

E2560 England. Parliament. House of Commons, 1648[9]
Ex. Yk.

E2561 England. Parliament. House of Commons, 1642
Dur.

E2562 England. Parliament. House of Commons, 1646
Linc. Yk.

E2564 England. Parliament. House of Commons, 1643
Linc.

E2568 England. Parliament. House of Commons, 1642
'House'
Linc.

E2568+ England. Parliament. House of Commons, 1642
As E2568, but: '... the late breach'
Dur (cropped).

E2569 England. Parliament. House of Commons, 1641[2]
Linc.

E2570 England. Parliament. House of Commons, 1643
Sal.

E2572 England. Parliament. House of Commons, 1640[1]
'Depositions ...'; =STC 25248.3.
Linc. Yk (2 eds)*.

E2573 England. Parliament. House of Commons, 1643
Cant. Linc. Pet (imp).

E2574 England. Parliament. House of Commons, 1689
Cant. Wel. Yk.

E2586 England. Parliament. House of Commons, 1641[2]
Dur (cropped).

E2587+ England. Parliament. House of Commons, 1642
=Wing2 E2587B.
Dur. Yk.

E2587++ England. Parliament. House of Commons, 1642
As E2587+, but: '... L. Strange ...';
For Iohn Wright.
Linc.

E2590 England. Parliament. House of Commons, 1642
Linc (2).

E2592 England. Parliament. House of Commons, 1642
'Die Jovis 2^d. Junii, 1642. It is this day ...'
Linc.

E2611 England. Parliament. House of Commons, 1641
Dur. Linc.

E2613+ England. Parliament. House of Commons, [1641]
=Wing2 E2613A.
Linc.

E2614 England. Parliament. House of Commons, 1641
Yk.

E2617A England. Parliament. House of Commons, 1674
Yk.

E2621 England. Parliament. House of Commons, 1648
Yk.

E2622 England. Parliament. House of Commons, 1660
Lich.

E2625 England. Parliament. House of Commons, 1679
Linc.

E2628 England. Parliament. House of Commons, [1649]
Yk.

E2641 England. Parliament. House of Commons, 1642
Ex. Yk.

E2654? England. Parliament. House of Commons, 1642
'priviledge'; For Joseph Hunscott.
Ex.

E2661+ England. Parliament. House of Commons, [1648?]
'Die Veneris 31. Martij 1648. Ordered by the Commons ... that the petition of the ... Walloon Church in ... Canterbury ...'; [N.pl.]; brs.
Cant.

E2674 England. Parliament. House of Commons, 1641
Dur. Linc.

E2675 England. Parliament. House of Commons, 1641
'priviledges'
Dur. Pet.

E2678 England. Parliament. House of Commons, 1643
Linc.

E2679 England. Parliament. House of Commons, 1641[2]
Dur.

E2683 England. Parliament. House of Commons, 1700
Entry as Wing2.
Wel.

E2685? England. Parliament. House of Commons, 1681
'The proceedings ...'
Win.

E2688? England. Parliament. House of Commons, 1641[2]
... assignes ...
Cant (imp). Linc.

E2692+ England. Parliament. House of Commons, 1642
=Wing2 E2692A?; By R. Badger for Laurence Blaiklock; 4°.
Sal.

E2698 England. Parliament. House of Commons, 1641
Ex.

E2702 England. Parliament. House of Commons, 1642[3]
Linc.

E2703 England. Parliament. House of Commons, 1643
Dur. Yk.

E2704 England. Parliament. House of Commons, 1641
Hunscutt.
S Asa.

E2704A? England. Parliament. House of Commons, 1641
'kingdom'; 26p.
Cant.

E2704A+ England. Parliament. House of Commons, 1641
As E2704A, but: 'kingdome'; 43p.
Linc.

E2704B? England. Parliament. House of Commons, 1641
'Mathew'
Dur. Linc.

E2704B+ England. Parliament. House of Commons, 1641
For Francis Constable; 4°.
Pet.

E2724 England. Parliament. House of Commons, 1642
Linc.

E2725 England. Parliament. House of Commons, 1697
Nor.

E2743 England. Parliament. House of Commons, 1643
Yk.

E2745 England. Parliament. House of Commons, 1641[2]
Dur (cropped).

E2746 England. Parliament. House of Commons, 1680
Linc.

E2747? England. Parliament. House of Commons, 1641
'the honourable'
Dur. Linc.

E2748? England. Parliament. House of Commons, 1680
'A true copy ...'
Yk.

E2752? England. Parliament. House of Commons, 1642[3]
For John Frank ...
Linc.

E2757 England. Parliament. House of Commons, [1673]
Yk.

E2758 England. Parliament. House of Commons, 1662[3]
Linc.

E2760? England. Parliament. House of Commons, [1663]
cap.; 4°.
Carl. Wel. Win.

E2764 *See*: Periodicals

E2765 *See*: Periodicals

E2766A *See*: Periodicals

E2767 England. Parliament. House of Commons, 1648
Cant.

E2768 *See*: Periodicals

E2791+ England. Parliament. House of Lords, 1642
=Wing2 E2791A.
Linc.

E2793 England. Parliament. House of Lords, 1642
Ely.

E2836 England. Parliament. House of Lords, 1646
Yk.

E2842 England. Parliament. House of Lords, 1647
Yk.

E2843 England. Parliament. House of Lords, 1681
Linc. Win.

E2870 England. Parliament. House of Lords, 1642
Dur (cropped).

E2876+ England. Parliament. House of Lords, 1681
=Wing2 E2876A.
Linc. Yk.

E2882? England. Privy Council, 1688
'22. of October'; Impr. as Wing2; 4°.
S Asa.

E2887 England. Privy Council, 1681
Ches.

E2890 England. Privy Council, [1667]
No date in impr.
Linc.

E2897+ England. Privy Council, [1688]
'At the Court at Whitehall. The fourth of May, 1688'; [N.pl.]; brs.
S Pl.

E2898 England. Privy Council, 1688
Pet (frag.).

E2902 *See*: L2852Q

Location of English books 1641–1700
as enumerated in Wing's *Short-Title Catalogue*
Volume Two

E2931A England, 1646
Linc.

E2936 England, 1691
Cant.

E2939 England's, 1679
Linc.

E2940+ Englands, 1691
See: CLC46.
S Pl.

E2945 Englands, 1681
Linc.

E2946 England's, 1660
Ely.

E2952 Englands, [1642]
Dur. Linc.

E2969 Englands, 1641
Yk.

E2988+ England's, 1640[1]
'Englands joy, for the kings ...';
=STC 10009.
Pet.

E2997 Englands, 1644
Pet.

E3013 Englands, 1643
Linc. Pet (2).

E3023 Englands, 1641
Yk.

E3033 Englands, 1645[6]
Yk.

E3045 England's, 1679
Dur. Linc.

E3046 Englands, [1643]
Cant.

E3047 Englands, 1643
Pet (imp).

E3049 England's, [1680]
Linc (2 – 1 imp).

E3095 English, 1657
Ex.

E3096 English, 1681
Wel.

E3097 Englishman, 1670
Yk.

E3099 English-man's, [1691?]
Ban. Dur (cropped).

E3109 English, 1643
Chelm (36p.). Sal (40p.). Yk
(44p.).

E3110 English, 1641
Yk.

E3111 English, 1661
Ches.

E3113A English, 1656
Yk.

E3113B English, 1657
Pet.

E3117 English, 1646
Linc.

E3125 Ἐνιαυτός, 1664
Linc. Sal.

E3126A Ἐνιαυτός, 1674
The second edition.
Carl. Yk.

E3135A Ent, *Sir* George, 1641
Carl.

E3138 Entire, 1691
Her.

E3144? Epictetus, 1655
... ex academiae ...
Bur. Cant (2). Dur.

E3145 Epictetus, 1659
Ches.

E3145A Epictetus, 1659
Win.

E3146? Epictetus, 1670
'... cum Cebetis ... tabula ...'
Ches. Ely. Ex. Rip. S Asa.
Wor.

E3147 Epictetus, 1670
Carl.

E3148 Epictetus, 1680
Yk.

E3149 Epictetus, 1692
Glo.

E3152 Epictetus, 1670
Carl. Ex.

E3153 Epictetus, 1694
Glo. Yk.

E3153+ Epictetus, 1694
For Richard Sare; 8°.
Llan.

E3154 Epictetus, 1700
Dur.

E3156 Epicurus, 1670
Ex.

E3160 Episcopal, 1679
Ex. Wel.

E3162 Episcopius, Simon, 1678
Bris. Bur. S Asa.

E3163 Episcopius, Simon, 1673
Carl (2).

E3164aA Epistle, 1659
Sal (2).

E3168 Epistle, 1654
Carl.

E3173A? Epitaphia, [1657]
No date.
Linc.

E3184 Epulae, 1649
Ex. Linc.

E3185 Equitable, 1642
Yk.

E3187 Erasmus, Desiderius, 1666
Dur. Her.

E3190 Erasmus, Desiderius, 1671
Liv.

E3193 Erasmus, Desiderius, 1666
Cant.

E3197C Erasmus, Desiderius, 1685
Nor.

E3200 Erasmus, Desiderius, 1685
Ban. Cant. Yk.

E3201 Erasmus, Desiderius, 1642
Pt 2 = M1635.
Bris (pt 1 only). Cant. Dur. Ely.
Ex (2 – 1 pt 1 only). Lich (2 – 1
pt 1 only). Linc. Nor. S Pl.
Wor.

E3201A Erasmus, Desiderius, 1642
Pt 2 = M1635A.
Ex (pt 2 only). Lich. Pet. Swel.

E3206 Erasmus, Desiderius, 1633
[*i.e.* 1663]
Nor. S Asa.

E3207 Erasmus, Desiderius, 1668
Ches. Dur. Ely.

E3208 Erasmus, Desiderius, 1668
Ex.

E3210 Erasmus, Desiderius, 1680
Carl. Yk (2).

E3213 Erasmus, Desiderius, 1689
Glo (imp).

E3234+ Erbery, William, 1647
As E3234, but: 'errour'; 26p.; Madan
1954.
Carl. Pet. Yk.

E3236 Erbery, William, 1654
Ex.

E3239 Erbery, William, 1658
Pet.

E3250 Erswicke, John, 1642
'brief'
Chi.

E3254 Espagne, Jean d', 1648
Dur.

E3257 Espagne, Jean d', 1652
Pet.

E3263 Espagne, Jean d', 1647
Cant. Carl.

E3264 Espagne, Jean d', 1649
Linc.

E3267 Espagne, Jean d', 1648
8°.
Cant. Carl. Roch.

E3291A? Essay, 1663
Wing has wrong date? or another ed.?
Linc.

E3299 Essay, 1680
Cant.

E3313 Essex, Robert Devereux, *3rd
Earl of*, 1642
Linc.

E3316A Essex, Robert Devereux,
3rd Earl of, 1646
Yk.

E3317 Essex, Robert Devereux, *3rd
Earl of*, 1643
Linc. Yk.

E3321 Essex, Robert Devereux, *3rd
Earl of*, 1642
Dur.

E3325 Essex, Robert Devereux, *3rd
Earl of*, 1645
Yk.

E3339 Essex, Robert Devereux, *3rd
Earl of*, 1642[3]
Linc.

E3340 Essex, Robert Devereux, *3rd
Earl of*, 1642
Dur. Yk.

E3343 Essex's, [1679]
cap.
Linc.

E3344 Established, 1679
Ban. Cant. Carl. Linc.

E3347 Estienne, Charles, 1670
Her. S Pl. Yk.

E3347A Estienne, Charles, 1670
Cant.

E3348 Estienne, Charles, 1671
Lich. Linc. Wel.

E3348A Estienne, Charles, 1671
Dur. S Dv.

E3349 Estienne, Charles, 1686
Second ed. not on tp.
Dur. Ex. Glo. Nor. Roch.
S Asa (2). S Pl. Swel. Yk.

E3358 Estwick, Nicolas, 1644
Pet. Yk.

E3360 Estwick, Nicolas, 1656
... Nath. Ekins.
Pet.

E3361 Estwick, Nicolas, 1648
Linc. Pet.

E3362 Estwick, Sampson, 1698
Cant. Her. S Pl.

E3365 Eternal, 1681
S Pl.

E3384 Etherington, John, 1641
Ex.

E3385+ Ettmüller, Michael, 1689
Francfurti ad Moenum, sumptibus
Johannis Davidis Zunneri, Londini,
prostant apud Abelem Swalle; 2°.
Wel.

E3385A Ettmüller, Michael, 1699
Dur.

E3389 Euclid, 1677
Linc.

E3391 Euclid, 1666
Yk.

E3392 Euclid, 1678
Sal.

E3392A Euclid, 1655
Should be 2 vols?
Linc. Pet.

E3393 Euclid, 1659
S Pl.

E3394 Euclid, 1678
Cant. Ex. Nor.

E3395A Euclid, 1687
Linc.

E3396 Euclid, 1651
Carl. Ely (imp). Glo.

E3397 Euclid, 1660
Carl.

E3406? Euclid, 1665
24°.
Ex.

E3412 Euer, Samson, 1666
Carl.

E3416 Euripides, 1694
Cant. Ches. Dur. Ely. Ex.
Her. Linc. Pet. S Dv. S Pl.
Wor. Yk.

E3420 Eusebius Pamphili, 1698
Bur.

E3421 Eusebius Pamphili, 1650
Bris. Ely.

E3421A Eusebius Pamphili, 1663
Chi.

E3423 Eusebius Pamphili, 1683
... at London.
Her. Wor. Yk.

E3424 Eusebius Pamphili, 1692
Bur.

E3429A Eustachius, 1658
Ban. Bur. Cant.

E3429B Eustachius, 1666
Nor.

E3430 Eustachius, 1677
Yk (2).

E3430A Eustachius, 1693
S Asa.

E3433 Eustachius, 1649
Dur. Her. Yk.

E3435 Eutropius, 1694
Carl.

E3436 Eutropius, 1696
Ely.

E3437? Eutychius, 1654
Oxoniis, typis Academiae publicis,
excudebat ...
Cant. Win.

E3438 Eutychius, 1656
Cant. Win.

E3439 Eutychius, 1658–59
Ex (vol. 1 only). S Pl. Wel
(both vols 1658).

E3440 Eutychius, 1642
Glo. S Pl (2). Wel.

E3440A Eutychius, 1642
Dur.

E3443 Evance, Daniel, 1646
Pet (4).

E3444 Evank, George, 1663
Pet.

E3445 Evans, John, 1683
Nor. S Pl.

E3447 Evans, John, 1683
Yk.

E3448 Evans, John, 1683
Nor (imp). S Pl.

E3450 Evans, John, 1682
Cant. Wor.

E3470 Evans, Rhys, 1653
Linc (frag.)*.

E3471 Evans, Rhys, 1655
Pet.

E3473 Evans, Rhys, 1655
Pet.

E3479 Evelyn, Sir John, 1641
Dur. Linc.

E3480 Evelyn, John, 1699
Yk.

E3482 Evelyn, John, 1659
Carl*. Win*.

E3495 Evelyn, John, 1673
Yk.

E3504 Evelyn, John, 1674
Carl. Linc.

E3505 Evelyn, John, 1697
Cant. Chi. Dur. Lich. Wel.

E3507 Evelyn, John, 1676
Carl. Ex.

E3508 Evelyn, John, 1664
Yk.

E3510 Evelyn, John, 1667
Carl.

E3511 Evelyn, John, 1667
Cant. Yk.

E3515 Evelyn, John, 1652
Carl*. Sal.

E3516 Evelyn, John, 1664
Yk.

E3517 Evelyn, John, 1670
Sal.

E3518 Evelyn, John, 1679
Lich. Pet. Yk.

E3527 Everard, Edmund, 1679
Carl. Dur. Glo. Linc. Yk.

E3528 Everard, Edmund, 1679
Carl. Dur. Win. Yk (imp).

E3533 Everard, John, 1575?—1650?,
1653
Ex.

E3537? Everard, Robert, 1649
London, for Wil. Larnar.
Cant.

E3555 Evil, 1670
Carl. Win.

E3571 Exact, 1679
4°.
Linc.

E3587 Exact, 1689
Nor.

E3591 Exact, 1688
Cant. S Pl. Yk.

E3606 Exact, 1643
Yk.

E3614 Exact, 1642
Linc.

E3617 Exact, 1642
Dur.

E3621 Exact, 1641
Linc.

E3639A Exact, 1659
Win.

E3641 Exact, 1689
Ex.

E3644 Exact, 1679
Cant. Dur (imp)*. Yk.

E3659 Exact, 1642
Linc (Wing S1303 printed on
verso).

E3668 Exact, 1664
Win.

E3685 Exact, 1679
Linc.

E3690 Exact, 1679
Linc.

E3696 Exact, 1673
Cant.

E3697 Exact, 1644
Yk (2).

E3708 Examen, 1698
Nor.

E3717 Examination, 1681
Linc. Nor. Win.

E3718 Examination, 1642
Dur.

E3724 Examination, 1642
Linc.

E3725 Examination, 1688
Cant. S Pl.

E3727 Examination, 1680
Glo. Linc.

E3731 Examinations, [c.1684]
Yk.

E3734 Examples, 1642
Dur.

E3737? Exceeding, 1642
August.
Linc.

E3743 Exceeding, 1642
Linc.

E3748A? Exceeding, 1642
... Horton [sic?].
Yk.

E3767B Exceeding, 1642
Yk.

E3847 Excommunication, 1680
Rip. Yk.

E3854 Execution, 1661
Linc.

E3863 Exercise, 1690
Glo.

E3865 Exercitation, 1650
Bur. Chelm. Pet.

E3867 Exhortation, 1655
Dur.

E3872 Expedient, 1688
S Asa (imp).

E3872aA Expedient, 1688
Ban. Cant. Wel.

E3875+ Expedient, [1688?]
See: CLC47.
Ex.

E3877 Expedients, 1660
Win.

E3889 Expostulatorie, [c.1655—65]
Possibly should be dated c.1689;
Author may be Christopher Wyville.
Cant.

E3905A Extract, 1642
Yk.

E3907 Extract, 1642
Yk (2).

E3912 Extract, 1642
Yk.

E3937 Eye-salve, 1648
Sal.

E3940 Eyre, Mrs Elizabeth, 1689
Wel.

E3942 Eyre, Robert, 1693
Cant. Ex. S Asa. Yk.

F1A F., 1642
Linc (2 − 1: tp with border; 2: tp without border). Sal (tp with border).

F2 F., A., 1642
Linc. Yk.

F3 F., C., [1680]
Linc.

F7 F., D., 1641
Linc.

F8 F., D., [1657]
Ex (imp).

F9 F., D., 1663
Fictitious imprint.
Ches (imp). Yk.

F10 F., D., 1663
Carl. Linc. Yk (with this tp, and also the Oxford tp of F9).

F14 F., E., 1679
Ches ('country'; imp). Dur ('countrey'). Linc ('country'). Win ('country').

F23 F., H., 1645
Yk.

F34 F., J., 1679
Linc.

F50 F., R., 1649
S Pl.

F76 Fabricius, Johannes Seobaldus, 1676
Cant. Carl. Ely. Yk.

F82 Faerno, Gabrieldo, 1672
Win.

F88 Fagel, Gaspar, 1688
Dur.

F89 Fagel, Gaspar, 1688
Dur.

F93A Failing, 1663
Ex.

F104- Fair, 1662
As F104, apart from date; cf. B1263 & W3548.
Carl.

F104 Fair, 1663
cf. B1263 & W3548.
Cant. Wel. Yk.

F106 Fairclough, Richard, 1663
Carl.

F107 Fairclough, Samuel, 1653
Pet.

F109 Fairclough, Samuel, 1641
Ely. Ex. Pet.

F111 Fairfax, *Sir* Ferdinando, 1642
Cant.

F112 Fairfax, *Sir* Ferdinando, 1644
Yk (2).

F113 Fairfax, *Sir* Ferdinando, 1642
Linc. Yk.

F114 Fairfax, *Sir* Ferdinando, 1642
Yk.

F115 Fairfax, *Sir* Ferdinando, 1642
Yk.

F116 Fairfax, *Sir* Ferdinando, 1642
Dur. Yk (2).

F117 Fairfax, *Sir* Ferdinando, 1642
Yk.

F119 Fairfax, *Sir* Ferdinando, 1643
Yk (2).

F121 Fairfax, *Sir* Ferdinando, 1644
Yk.

F121+ Fairfax, *Sir* Ferdinando, 1644
[London], for Edward Husbands, April 19; 4°.
Pet.

F121B- Fairfax, *Sir* Ferdinando, 1643
As F121B, but: May 27 in impr.; 12p.
Linc. Yk.

F121B Fairfax, *Sir* Ferdinando, 1643
8p.
Yk.

F122 Fairfax, *Sir* Ferdinando, 1642
Yk.

F122A Fairfax, *Sir* Ferdinando, 1642
'The reall ...'
Yk.

F123 Fairfax, *Sir* Ferdinando, 1642
January.
Yk (3).

F124 Fairfax, Henry, 1688
Her. Nor. Yk.

F125 Fairfax, Henry, 1688
Linc.

F127 Fairfax, John, 1679
... in Norwich.
Cant.

F154 Fairfax, *Sir* Thomas, [1660]
Yk (cropped).

F156 Fairfax, *Sir* Thomas, 1647
'June 14. 1647' is on tp.
Yk (2 − 1 has 'iust and fundamentall').

F156A Fairfax, *Sir* Thomas, 1647
Cant. Pet. Yk.

F160 Fairfax, *Sir* Thomas, 1647
Yk.

F163A Fairfax, *Sir* Thomas, 1648[9]
Yk (dated Jan. 22)*.

F164 Fairfax, *Sir* Thomas, 1648
Yk (2 − 1 has Decemb. 6).

F165 Fairfax, *Sir* Thomas, 1647
Pet (2).

F166 Fairfax, *Sir* Thomas, 1647
Yk.

F167 Fairfax, *Sir* Thomas, 1647
Pet. Yk.

F168 Fairfax, *Sir* Thomas, 1647
Yk.

F169+ Fairfax, *Sir* Thomas, 1647
Imprinted at York by Tho: Broad; 4°.
Yk.

F172 Fairfax, *Sir* Thomas, [1647]
Yk.

F174 Fairfax, *Sir* Thomas, 1547 [*i.e.* 1647]
Yk.

F178 Fairfax, *Sir* Thomas, 1647
Yk.

F179 Fairfax, *Sir* Thomas, 1647
Cant. Yk.

F180 Fairfax, *Sir* Thomas, 1648
Dur.

F181 Fairfax, *Sir* Thomas, 1648
Yk.

F195? Fairfax, *Sir* Thomas, 1645[6]
'Lenthall'
Pet.

F206 Fairfax, *Sir* Thomas, 1647
Yk.

F213 Fairfax, *Sir* Thomas, 1649
Cant. Ex.

F227A Fairfax, *Sir* Thomas, 1647
Yk.

F228 Fairfax, *Sir* Thomas, 1647
Yk (3).

F229 Fairfax, *Sir* Thomas, 1648
Her. Linc. Pet (2). Yk (4).

F230 Fairfax, *Sir* Thomas, 1647
Yk.

F234 Fairfax, *Sir* Thomas, 1647
Yk.

F235 Fairfax, *Sir* Thomas, 1699
Yk (3).

F241 Fairfax, *Sir* Thomas, 1647
Pet.

F242 Fairfax, *Sir* Thomas, 1648
Dur.

F243 Fairfax, *Sir* Thomas, 1647
Yk.

F244 Fairfax, *Sir* Thomas, 1647
Yk.

F245 Fairfax, *Sir* Thomas, 1647
Yk.

F253 Fairfax, *Sir* Thomas, 1649
Yk.

F257+ Fairweather, Thomas, 1697
See: CLC48.
Yk.

F258B Faith, 1691
Cant.

F266 Faithful, 1679
Carl. Linc (2).

F268 Faithfull, [1648]
Yk.

F290 Faithful, 1649
Yk.

F291 Faithful, 1660
Cant. Chi. Yk.

F305 Faldo, John, 1698
Chi.

F310 Fale, Thomas, 1652
Cant (imp). Wor.

F317 Falkland, Lucius Cary,
Viscount, 1651
Carl. Ches. Dur. Ex (tpw).
Her. Linc. S Pl. Wel. Yk.

F319 Falkland, Lucius Cary,
Viscount, 1644
Yk.

F320 Falkland, Lucius Cary,
Viscount, 1641
Cant (2 — 1: prtntee [*sic*]; 2:
printed).

F320A Falkland, Lucius Cary,
Viscount, 1642
Pet.

F324 Falkland, Lucius Cary,
Viscount, 1641
Cant ('Faulkeland'). Linc
('Faulkland'). Yk (2 — 1:
'Faulkland'; 2: 'Faulkland').

F325 Falkland, Lucius Cary,
Viscount, 1641
Cant (3). Linc. Yk.

F329 Falkner, William, 1679
Ban. Carl. Ely. Ex. Lich. Nor.
S Pl. Win. Yk.

F331 Falkner, William, 1674
Chelm. Ely. Ex. S Pl (2). Wel.
Yk.

F332 Falkner, William, 1674
Ban. Bur (2). Cant. Carl. Ex.
Llan. Nor. S Asa.

F333 Falkner, William, 1677
Ex. Lich (2). S Pl. Wel. Yk.

F334 Falkner, William, 1683
Yk.

F335 Falkner, William, 1684
Ban. Cant. Carl. Ely. Ex.
S Asa. Win.

F335A Falkner, William, 1684
S Pl. Yk.

F335B Falkner, William, 1684
· Nor.

F336 Falkner, William, 1680
Carl. Ely. Ex (2). Lich (2).
Nor. S Asa. S Pl. Win. Yk (2).

F338 Falle, Philip, 1694
Ely. S Pl.

F339 Falle, Philip, 1695
Cant. Dur. S Pl.

F340 Falle, Philip, 1695
Cant.

F341 Falle, Philip, 1692
Wor.

F342 Falle, Philip, 1700
Cant.

F343 False, 1644
Pet (imp).

F345 False, 1642
Linc.

F346 False, 1642
Dur.

F352F Familiar, 1695
Cant.

F356A Famous, 1642
Linc.

F366 Famous, 1689
Ex.

F384 Famous, 1649
Yk.

F389 Famous, 1643
Pet.

F390A Famous, 1642
Linc.

F390B Famous, 1642
Linc.

F415 Fannant, Thomas, 1641
Yk.

F416 Fannant, Thomas, 1641
Pet.

F422 Farewell, James, 1689
8°.
Ex.

F425 Faria, Francisco de, 1680
Ely. Glo. Linc. Win. Yk.

F426 Faria, Francisco de, 1680
Win. Yk (imp).

F429A Farindon, Anthony, 1672
Cant (3 — 1 imp). Chi. Lich.
Linc. Llan. Nor. S Asa. Wor.

F432 Farindon, Anthony, 1674
Cant (3). Chi. Lich. Linc. Llan.
Nor. S Asa. Sal. Wel. Wor.

F432A Farindon, Anthony, 1663
Cant. Carl. Dur. Wel. Win.

F434 Farindon, Anthony, 1647 [*i.e.*
1657]
Nor. Wel. Yk.

F435 Farindon, Anthony, 1657
Cant. Carl. Dur. Pet.

F438 Farisol, Abraham ben
Mordecai, 1691
Dur. Ex. S Pl.

F444 Farmer, Ralph, 1657
Yk.

F449 Farnaby, Thomas, 1650
Ex. Pet.

F464 Farnaby, Thomas, 1641
Carl. Yk.

F470 Farnworth, Richard, 1655
Yk.

F471 Farnworth, Richard, 1655
Yk.

F479 Farnworth, Richard, 1653
Yk.

F481- Farnworth, Richard, 1653
As F481, apart from date.
Yk.

F482 Farnworth, Richard, 1653
Yk.

F483 Farnworth, Richard, 1653
Yk.

F486 Farnworth, Richard, 1655
Yk.

F489 Farnworth, Richard, 1664
Yk.

F491 Farnworth, Richard, 1665
Yk.

F494 Farnworth, Richard, 1655
Yk.

F499 Farnworth, Richard, 1663
Yk.

F501 Farnworth, Richard, 1655
Yk.

F504 Farnworth, Richard, 1663
Yk.

F505 Farnworth, Richard, 1655
Yk.

F513 Farnworth, Richard, 1655
Yk.

F560 Faustinus, 1678
Carl. Ches. Ex. S Pl (2). Win.

F562 Fawcet, Samuel, 1641
Ex.

F563 Fawket, James, 1681
Dur (imp?).

F568 Feake, Christopher, 1653
Yk.

F569 Feake, Christopher, 1655
Second ed. not on tp.
Her. Yk.

F574A Fear, 1663
Pet.

F578 Featley, Daniel, 1656
Carl.

F580? Featley, Daniel, 1661
'Dr. Daniel Featley ...'
Ex.

F581 Featley, Daniel, 1660
'Featlaei ...'
Ex.

F582 Featley, Daniel, 1644
Cant.

F585 Featley, Daniel, 1645
Cant. Ex.

F586 Featley, Daniel, 1645
Nor.

F587 Featley, Daniel, 1646
Carl. Ely. Yk.

F588 Featley, Daniel, 1647
Yk.

F589 Featley, Daniel, 1651
Pet.

F590 Featley, Daniel, 1660
Win.

F590A Featley, Daniel, 1660
The seventh edition.
Sal. Yk.

F591 Featley, Daniel, 1660
Dur (imp). Ex. Linc. Nor. Pet.

F592 Featley, Daniel, 1644
Cant. Ex. Pet. S Pl. Yk (2).

F593 Featley, Daniel, 1644
Cant (imp).

F595 Featley, Daniel, 1660
Ex. Sal.

F596 Featley, Daniel, 1672
Nor.

F597? Featley, Daniel, 1642
... for Nicholas Bourne ...
Sal.

F602 Felgate, Samuel, 1682
S Pl. Yk.

F607 Fell, John, 1675
Cant. Carl. Her (pasted slip:
Sold by William Leak, London).

F608 Fell, John, 1673
Carl. Yk.

F609 Fell, John, 1675
Ex.

F613 Fell, John, 1659
Carl. Yk.

F617 Fell, John, 1661
'... Dr. H. Hammond ...'
Cant. Carl. Linc. S Pl. Win.

F618 Fell, John, 1662
Cant. Ely. Liv. Sal.

F626 Fell, Margaret, [1668?]
Yk.

F638A Fell, Margaret, [1659]
cap.
Dur.

F644 Fell, Philip, 1676
Bur. Cant. Carl. Chelm. Ex.
Linc. Sal. Wel. Win.

F648 Feltham, Owen, 1652
Pet.

F654A? Feltham, Owen, 1647
'... The second century'; Seventh ed.
not on tp.
S Alb.

F655 Feltham, Owen, 1661
Nor. S Asa.

F656 Feltham, Owen, 1670
Dur. Yk.

F657A Feltham, Owen, 1677
The tenth impression.
Pet.

F658 Feltham, Owen, 1696
S Asa. Win.

F673 Fen, James, 1686
Cant.

F675 Fenelon, François de Salignac
de la Mothe, 1698
Wel. Yk.

F676 Fenn, Humphrey, 1641
Yk.

F679 Fenner, William, 1657
Cant.

F683 Fenner, William, 1650
Chi.

F683A Fenner, William, 1657
Cant.

F691 Fenner, William, 1668
Cant (imp).

F692 Fenner, William, 1652
Yk.

F696 Fenner, William, 1657
S Asa.

F708 Fenner, William, 1650
Chi.

F709 Fenner, William, 1657
Cant.

F710? Fenner, William, 1657
2°.
Cant.

F723? Fenwick, Sir John, [1696/7]
'delivered'
Ely.

F725 Fenwick, William, 1642
Cant.

F733? Ferguson, Robert, 1689
... sold by Richard Baldwin.
Ban (2). S Asa. Wel.

F734 Ferguson, Robert, 1689
Cant. Yk.

F738 Ferguson, Robert, 1689
Wel.

F740 Ferguson, Robert, 1675
Carl. Chelm. Ex.

F743 Ferguson, Robert, 1668
Carl.

F744 Ferguson, Robert, 1682
S Asa.

F747 Ferguson, Robert, 1689
Cant (imp).

F756 Ferguson, Robert, 1681
Cant (3). Carl. Dur.

F757 Ferguson, Robert, 1689
Nor. Pet. S Asa. Wel. Yk.

F759 Ferguson, Robert, 1682
Cant (imp). Carl. Pet.

F760 Ferguson, Robert, 1673
Carl. Chelm. Win.

F762 Ferguson, Robert, 1682
Cant. Ex. Pet (imp). S Pl.

F766 Ferguson, Robert, [1695]
Nor.

F773 Fergusson, James, 1659
Ex.

F786 Ferne, Henry, 1660
Ely. Ex. S Asa. Sal.

F788 Ferne, Henry, 1643
Carl.

F789 Ferne, Henry, 1653
Ches (2). Ex. Pet. Sal. Yk.

F790? Ferne, Henry, 1655
... for R. Royston.
Ban. Carl. Ches. Yk.

F791 Ferne, Henry, 1643
Cant (2). Carl. Ches. Ex. Linc.
Pet (imp). Yk (2).

F793 Ferne, Henry, 1644
Cant. Carl.

F794 Ferne, Henry, 1647
Cant. Carl. Ches (2). Ex. Pet.
S Asa. Yk (2).

F795 Ferne, Henry, 1652
Cant (imp). Ches. Linc. Wel.

F798 Ferne, Henry, 1643
Ches. Yk.

F799 Ferne, Henry, 1643
Ches (2). Pet. Yk.

F800 Ferne, Henry, 1642
Carl (imp). Ches. Linc. Pet.
Sal.

F802 Ferne, Henry, 1642
Carl.

F803 Ferne, Henry, 2642 [*i.e.* 1642]
Yk.

F805 Ferne, Henry, 1644
Cant (Madan 1619, imp). Ches
(Madan 1619). Pet (Madan 1619).
Wel (Madan 1618). Yk.

F806 Ferne, Henry, 1649
Cant. Carl. Linc. Yk.

F812 Ferrarius, Johannes Baptista,
1657
Yk.

F814 Ferrarius, Philippus, 1657
Carl. Ely. Glo. Her. Linc.
S Pl. Wel.

F819 Ferriby, John, 1652
Chelm. Dur (tpw). Ex. Pet. Yk.

F819A Ferriby, John, 1653
The second impression.
Ex.

F821 Festa, 1678
Carl. S Pl.

F823C Festeau, Paul, 1674
Linc.

F823D Festeau, Paul, 1675
Nor.

F828 Festered, 1650
... and are to be sold at Ipswich.
Cant. Yk.

F832B Feversham, George Sondes,
Earl of, 1655
Linc.

F838 Few, 1668
Cant (imp).

F838AB Few, [1679/80]
cap.
Linc.

F840 Few, [1655]
Dur (imp).

F843 Feyens, Thomas, 1657
Dur. Ex.

F845 Fiat, [1679?]
Dur. Linc (2).

F873 Fiennes, Nathaniel, 1642[3]
Linc. Pet.

F875 Fiennes, Nathaniel, 1642
Linc.

F876 Fiennes, Nathaniel, [1643]
Her.

F877 Fiennes, Nathaniel, 1643
Yk.

F878 Fiennes, Nathaniel, 1641
Cant.

F880 Fiennes, Nathaniel, 1641
Cant ('in answer'). Linc ('in
answer'). Sal ('in answer'). Yk
('in answere').

F882 Fiennes, Nathaniel, 1659
Ex (2). S Asa. Sal.

F883 Fiennes, Nathaniel, 1642
Yk.

F889 Fifth, 1688
Pet. S Asa. Wel.

F892 Fifth, 1644
Sal.

F910 Filmer, *Sir* Robert, 1648
Cant. Carl. Linc.

F911 Filmer, *Sir* Robert, 1678
Chelm. Ely. Her.

F912 Filmer, *Sir* Robert, [1648]
Cant.

F914 Filmer, *Sir* Robert, 1679
Ban. Cant (imp). Ely*. Linc.

F915 Filmer, *Sir* Robert, 1680
Win.

F916 Filmer, *Sir* Robert, 1684
Ban (imp). Nor. Yk.

F917 Filmer, *Sir* Robert, 1648
Yk.

F918? Filmer, *Sir* Robert, 1652
50p.
Cant.

F918+ Filmer, *Sir* Robert, 1652
As F918, but: 48, 39p.
Cant (2).

F921 Filmer, *Sir* Robert, 1652
Cant (2).

F922 Filmer, *Sir* Robert, 1680
Ban (2). Cant. Carl. Ex. Linc.
Win (imp).

F923 Filmer, *Sir* Robert, 1680
Yk.

F924? Filmer, *Sir* Robert, 1685
Chiswel.
Ban. S Asa.

F926 Filmer, *Sir* Robert, 1680
Linc. Wel.

F927 Filmer, *Sir* Robert, 1653
Cant. Carl. Chelm. Linc.

F930 Finch, Edward, 1641
Linc.

F931 Finch, *Sir* Henry, 1661
Carl.

F947 Finett, *Sir* John, 1656
Carl.

F948A+ Finger, Gottfried, 1691
By J. Heptinstall, for John Banister,
to be sold at his house, Mr. Carr's
shop, Mr. Playford's; Impr. of pt 2 as
F948A; obl.fol.
Dur.

F958 Firmin, Giles, 1658
Wor.

F961 Firmin, Giles, 1660
Cant (tp imp). Carl. Pet. Win.
Wor.

F962 Firmin, Giles, 1681
Dur. Yk (imp).

F965 Firmin, Giles, 1651
Dur.

F967 Firmin, Giles, 1656
Pet.

F971 Firmin, Thomas, 1678
Win.

F973 First, 1641
Cant (imp). Linc. Pet.

F973A First, 1641
Dur. Nor. Yk.

F987 Fisher, Edward, [1643]
Linc. Pet.

F988 Fisher, Edward, 1644
Yk.

F989 Fisher, Edward, 1650
Dur. Her.

F990 Fisher, Edward, 1652
The fourth edition.
Cant. Carl. Pet.

F991 Fisher, Edward, 1653
Ex.

F994 Fisher, Edward, 1644
Linc.

F997B? Fisher, Edward, 1647
By Robert Ibbitson for Giles Calvert.
Cant.

F1000 Fisher, Edward, 1655
Yk.

F1007 Fisher, James, 1658
Yk (2 − 1 tpw*).

F1010 Fisher, Joseph, 1695
Nor.

F1013+ Fisher, Payne, 1663
See: CLC49.
Win.

F1015 Fisher, Payne, [1675]
8°.
Win. Yk.

F1015B *See*: F1015: apparently,
F1015B is a sub-tp in F1015

F1027 Fisher, Payne, 1652
Yk (tpw).

F1029 Fisher, Payne, 1650
Linc. Yk (2).

F1034 Fisher, Payne, 1656
Ex.

F1037 Fisher, Payne, 1662
Win.

F1041 Fisher, Payne, [1684]
S Pl (imp)*.

F1042 Fisher, Payne, [1684]
S Pl.

F1058 Fisher, Samuel, *d.1665*, 1679
Ches.

F1072 Fitzgerald, David, 1680
Ely. Linc. Yk.

F1074 Fitz-Gerald, John, 1681
Win. Yk.

F1075 Fitzgerald, Maurice, 1680
Linc.

F1102 Fitzherbert, Thomas, 1652
Ban. Carl.

F1106 Fitz-William, John, 1683
Cant.

F1112 Five, 1642
Yk.

F1114 Five, 1641
Dur. Linc. Yk.

F1120 Five, [1642]
Cant. Yk.

F1122 Five, 1642
Yk.

F1124 Five, 1659
'The five ...'
Yk.

F1147 Flatman, Thomas, 1670
Linc.

F1151 Flatman, Thomas, 1674
Linc.

F1159A Flavell, John, 1689
Ex.

F1160 Flavell, John, 1692
Cant.

F1162 Flavell, John, 1673
Ex.

F1164 Flavell, John, 1700
Cant.

F1165 Flavell, John, 1669
Cant.

F1169 Flavell, John, 1681
Ex.

F1175 Flavell, John, 1691
Ex.

F1176 Flavell, John, 1685
Ex.

F1177 Flavell, John, 1698
Linc.

F1191aA+ Flavell, John, 1682
By H.H. sold by Robert Boulter; 8°.
Ex.

F1197 Flavell, John, 1674
Ex.

F1202 Flavell, John, 1698
S Asa.

F1204 Flavell, John, 1682
Cant (imp).

F1205A Flavell, John, 1690
Ex.

F1207 Fléchier, Valentin Esprit,
1693
S Dv.

F1243 Fleetwood, William, *Bp*,
1687
Ban. Bur. Nor. Sal. Swel.

F1247 Fleetwood, William, *Bp*,
1691
Ches. Ex (2). Glo.

F1247aA Fleetwood, William, *Bp*,
1691
Liv. Nor. S Asa. S Pl.

F1247A Fleetwood, William, *Bp*,
1688
Cant.

F1248 Fleetwood, William, *Bp*,
1694
Cant (2 − 1 imp). Dur. Ely.
Her. Nor. Wor.

F1249 Fleetwood, William, *Bp*,
1696
Ban. Bur. Ex. Her. Nor. Wor.

F1251 Fleetwood, William, *Bp*,
1689
Cant. Dur. Nor. Yk (2).

F1252 Fleetwood, William, *Bp*,
1691
Cant. Her. Pet. Wor. Yk.

F1253 Fleetwood, William, *Bp*,
1692
Her. Pet. Wor.

F1254 Fleetwood, William, *Bp*,
1693
Ches (imp). Wor.

F1255 Fleetwood, William, *Bp*,
1693
Ches. Her. S Pl. Wor.

F1256 Fleetwood, William, *Bp*,
1698/9
Ban (2). Bur. Her.

F1257 Fleetwood, William, *Bp*,
1700
Ban. Cant (2 − 1 imp). S Pl.

F1258 Fleetwood, William, *Bp*,
1700
Ban. Dur. Her (2). Wor.

F1263B Fleming, Robert, *the Elder*,
1693
S Pl.

F1290 Fleta, 1647
S Pl.

F1290A? Fleta, 1647
4°.
Sal. Yk.

F1291 Fleta, 1685
Wel.

F1291+ Fleta, 1685
As F1291, but: [N.pl.], ...
Wor.

F1294 Fletcher, Andrew, 1697
Ban. Nor. S Pl.

F1353? Fletcher, John, 1649
Moseley.
Carl.

F1354 Fletcher, John, 1685
Cant.

F1363 Fleury, Claude, 1698
Ex. Liv.

F1368 Florio, Giovanni, 1659
'Vocabolario ...'
Lich.

F1369 Florio, Giovanni, 1688
'Vocabolario ...'; Ed. statement from
tp to English-Italian section.
Dur. Ex.

F1370 Florus, Lucius Annaeus,
1658
Carl.

F1371 Florus, Lucius Annaeus, 1650
Carl.

F1375 Florus, Lucius Annaeus, 1669
Pet. Yk.

F1376 Florus, Lucius Annaeus, 1680
... Ioannes Hayes.
Nor.

F1377 Florus, Lucius Annaeus, 1683
Bur.

F1378 Florus, Lucius Annaeus, 1692
Cant. Ches. Linc. Rip. S Asa.

F1379 Florus, Lucius Annaeus, 1669
Bris.

F1387 Floyer, *Sir* John, 1697
Lich.

F1390 Floyer, *Sir* John, 1698
Lich.

F1393 Foedus, 1644
Dur. Yk.

F1394 Foedus, 1643
... Evanus Tyler.
Dur.

F1400 Foley, Samuel, 1683
Ban. Carl. Chi.

F1405B Fonseca, Christoval de, 1652
Ex.

F1406 Fontaine, Nicolas, 1688
Cant.

F1406B Fontaine, Nicolas, 1697
Dur.

F1407 Fontaine, Nicolas, 1699
Cant. Yk.

F1408 Fontaine, Nicolas, 1690
Cant.

F1439 Forbes, Alexander Forbes, *Baron*, 1644
Win.

F1440 Forbes, Alexander Forbes, *Baron*, 1642
Dur.

F1454 Forbes, William, 1658
Ban. Carl. Ex. Pet. S Asa (2 – 1 imp). Sal. Win. Yk.

F1464 Ford, John, 1657
Carl.

F1469 Ford, Philip, 1642
Linc.

F1475 Ford, Simon, 1650
Carl. Chelm.

F1475+ Ford, Simon, 1650
As F1475, apart from: ... Al. Curteyne.
Pet.

F1476 Ford, Simon, 1692
Sal. Wor.

F1477 Ford, Simon, 1674
Win.

F1479 Ford, Simon, 1667
Ban.

F1484? Ford, Simon, 1678
'judgments'; ... Henry Brome.
Carl. Ches.

F1487 Ford, Simon, 1646
Chelm. Pet (2).

F1487A Ford, Simon, 1646
Carl.

F1488 Ford, Simon, 1667
Ban.

F1489 Ford, Simon, 1668
Ban. S Pl.

F1491 Ford, Simon, 1661
Cant (imp). Ex.

F1492A Ford, Simon, 1660
Carl. Pet.

F1495 Ford, Simon, 1668
Excudebat A.M., pro Sa. Gellibrand.
S Pl.

F1498 Ford, Simon, 1697
Dur.

F1504 Ford, Simon, 1665
Ban. Bur. Pet. Yk (tp cropped).

F1505 Ford, Simon, 1667
Linc.

F1515 Ford, Thomas, 1641
Ex (2).

F1516? Ford, Thomas, 1653
'The singing ...'
Ex.

F1519 Forde, *Sir* Edward, 1641
Dur.

F1530 Forde, Emanuel, [c.1690]
Cant.

F1549 Forde, Thomas, 1660
Pet.

F1551A Fordwich, John Finch, *Baron*, 1641
Cant. Sal.

F1551D Fordwich, John Finch, *Baron*, 1641
Cant.

F1554 Foreness, E., 1683
S Asa.

F1555 Foreness, E., 1684
Carl.

F1564? Form, 1654
'The form ...'; pp. 361 – 2; Pt of collection of statutes?
Dur.

F1565? Form, [1654]
'The form ...'; pp. 359 – 60; See F1564.
Dur.

F1586 Fornace, W., 1647
Dur.

F1612 Fortescue, *Sir* John, 1660
Nor. Sal.

F1613 Fortescue, *Sir* John, 1672
S Pl.

F1619 Fortune, 1678
Linc. Pet.

F1621 Fourtie, [1642]
Linc.

F1639A Foulis, *Sir* Henry, 1642
Yk.

F1640 Foulis, Henry, 1671
Carl. Chi. Dur. Ely. Ex. S Pl. Win. Wor.

F1640B? Foulis, Henry, 1671
... Tho. Dring.
Glo.

F1641 Foulis, Henry, 1681
Lich. S Asa.

F1642 Foulis, Henry, 1662
Cant. Linc. Win.

F1643 Foulis, Henry, 1674
Dur. Glo. Lich. Sal. Wor. Yk (2).

F1644 Foulkes, Robert, 1679
Carl. Dur. Linc. Wel. Yk.

F1658A Foure, 1642
Linc.

F1664 Foure, 1642
Linc.

F1666 Four, 1645
Yk (2).

F1668 Four, 1689
Dur.

F1671 Foure, 1646
Ex. Yk (tpw).

F1672 Foure, 1646
Pet.

F1676 Fourcroy, ? de, *Abbé*, 1695
Carl.

F1680 Fourteen, 1642
Dur (tpw). Sal. Yk.

F1686 Fourth, 1688
Pet. S Asa. Wel.

F1691? Fowler, ?, 1699
… Samuel Ady.
Bris.

F1692 Fowler, Christopher, 1655
Sal. Yk.

F1694 Fowler, Christopher, 1656
Dur.

F1695 Fowler, Edward, 1690
Carl. S Pl.

F1696 Fowler, Edward, 1694
Wel.

F1697 Fowler, Edward, 1684
S Pl.

F1697A Fowler, Edward, 1684
Yk.

F1698? Fowler, Edward, 1671
… Lodowick Loyd.
Bur. Carl. Ely. Her. S Asa.

F1699 Fowler, Edward, 1676
Dur.

F1700 Fowler, Edward, 1699
Glo. Pet.

F1702 Fowler, Edward, 1683
Cant (2 — both imp). Carl. Dur.
Glo (imp). Wor.

F1703 Fowler, Edward, 1695
Ex.

F1706 Fowler, Edward, 1676
Carl. Ely. Ex. Yk.

F1707 Fowler, Edward, 1685
Wor.

F1708 Fowler, Edward, 1685
Cant.

F1709 Fowler, Edward, 1680
Carl. Ely. Her.

F1711 Fowler, Edward, 1670
Ban. Carl. Ely.

F1712 Fowler, Edward, 1671
Lich. Sal.

F1713 Fowler, Edward, 1683
Cant (imp). S Pl. Yk.

F1714 Fowler, Edward, 1683
Yk.

F1715 Fowler, Edward, 1695
Carl.

F1716 Fowler, Edward, 1681
Cant. Glo. Llan.

F1718 Fowler, Edward, 1685
Wor.

F1719 Fowler, Edward, 1688
Cant. Wel. Wor.

F1720 Fowler, Edward, 1690
Glo. Wor.

F1721 Fowler, Edward, 1691
Cant. Wor.

F1722 Fowler, Edward, 1692
Cant.

F1723 Fowler, Edward, 1692
Cant. Wor.

F1724 Fowler, Edward, 1696
Cant. Wor.

F1725 Fowler, Edward, 1699
Nor.

F1727 Fowler, Edward, 1692
Carl.

F1728 Fowler, Edward, 1689
Nor. Wel. Yk.

F1729 Fowler, Edward, 1678
Win.

F1732 Fowler, John, 1656
Carl. Ex.

F1733 Fowler, Matthew, 1682
Cant. Dur.

F1735 Fowler, Matthew, 1662
Carl.

F1748 Fox, George, *the Elder*, 1675
Pet.

F1751 Fox, George, *the Elder*, 1660
Pet (imp). Yk.

F1778 Fox, George, *the Elder*, 1660
Yk.

F1780 *See*: B1900

F1788 Fox, George, *the Elder*,
[1684?]
Dur*.

F1880 Fox, George, *the Elder*, 1660
Yk.

F1884 Fox, George, *the Elder*, 1659
Yk.

F1895 Fox, George, *the Elder*, 1654
Yk.

F1916 Fox, George, *the Elder*, 1660
Linc. Yk.

F1945 Fox, George, *the Elder*, 1660
The fourth edition.
Yk.

F1970 Fox, George, *the Elder*, 1653
Yk.

F1996 Fox, George, *the Younger*,
1662
Cant.

F2007 Fox, George, *the Younger*,
1660
Linc.

F2009 Fox, George, *the Younger*,
1660
Yk.

F2033 Foxcroft, John, 1697
Sal.

F2035 Foxe, John, 1641
Ban. Bris (lacks vol. 3). Cant (2
— 1: lacks vol. 3; 2: vol. 2 only,
imp). Lich. Rip (tpw). Roch (2
— 1 imp). S Asa. S Dv. Wor.

F2036 Foxe, John, 1684
Ban. Cant (2). Ely. Ex. Glo
(imp). Linc. New. Nor. Pet.
Roch. Wel.

F2043 Foxe, John, 1694
S Pl.

F2053A France. Parliament, 1688
Carl. Linc. Pet. S Pl. Wel.

F2066A Franco, Solomon, 1668
Llan. Win.

F2070 François de Sales, *St*, 1675
S Pl.

F2072A François de Sales, *St*, 1669
Cant.

F2073 François, Claude, 1677
Cant (2). Her (2).

F2074A Frank, Mark, 1672
Ex (tpw)*. Her. Yk.

F2074B Frank, Mark, 1672
Dur. S Dv. Yk.

F2077 Frankland, Richard, 1697
S Asa.

F2078 Frankland, Thomas, 1681
Cant. Dur. Swel.

F2083 Franklin, Richard, *fl. 1675*,
1675
Linc. Win.

F2083A Franklin, Richard, *fl. 1675*,
1675
Bris. Carl.

F2084 Franklin, Richard, *d.1632*,
1650
Sal.

F2085 Franklin, Richard, *d.1632*,
1673
Ely. Yk (tpw).

F2102 Frederick III, *of Denmark*,
1657
Ex (2).

F2111 Free, 1689
Ban. Wel.

F2112 Free, 1668
Carl.

F2114 Freeholders, [1679]
Dur. Linc (2).

F2125A Freedom, 1654
Dur.

F2127 Freeman, Francis, 1647
Sal.

F2134 Freeman, John, 1643
Pet.

F2138 Freeman, Samuel, 1683
S Pl (2 − 1 imp).

F2140? Freeman, Samuel, 1684
72p.
Ban. Cant (tpw). Carl. Ches.
Ex (2). S Pl (2). Sal. Wel.

F2140+ Freeman, Samuel, 1684
As F2140, but: 70p.
Bris. Ex. Swel*.

F2141 Freeman, Samuel, 1682
Bris. Carl. Her.

F2142 Freeman, Samuel, 1687
Bur. Ex. S Asa. S Pl. Sal.
Swel. Yk.

F2143 Freeman, Samuel, 1682
Carl. Her.

F2144 Freeman, Samuel, [1682]
Dur. Sal.

F2145 Freeman, Samuel, 1690
Cant.

F2146 Freeman, Samuel, 1690
Cant.

F2147 Freeman, Samuel, 1694
Ban. Cant.

F2148 Freeman, Samuel, 1694
Cant. Her.

F2150 Freeman, Samuel, 1700
Her.

F2154 Freher, Philip, 1646
Win (tp imp).

F2155 Freire de Andrade, Jacinto,
1664
Pet.

F2162 Freke, William, [1691]
Cant.

F2175 French, John, 1652
Yk (2).

F2176? French, John, 1654
8°.
Yk (2).

F2194 French, 1680
Dur.

F2202 Frezer, Augustine, 1685
Her. New.

F2203 Frezer, Augustine, 1685
Nor. Wor.

F2213 Friend, 1681
Linc.

F2235 Froidmont, Libert, 1656
Ches. Ely. Sal.

F2243? Fromman, Andreas, 1669
... Tho. Gilbert; 12°.
Ex. Her.

F2247 Frost, John, 1658
Carl. Chelm.

F2251 Froysell, Thomas, 1678
S Asa.

F2255 Fry, John, 1650
Yk.

F2257 Fryer, John, 1698
Cant. Wor.

F2259 Fugitive, 1683
Carl.

F2303A+ Full, 1696
See: CLC50.
Ely.

F2308A Full, 1680
Carl. Sal.

F2318A Full, 1679
Dur.

F2334 Full, [1679]
Linc.

F2339 Full, 1697
Nor.

F2340 Full, 1645
Yk.

F2341 Full, 1687
Ex.

F2352 Full, 1679
Linc.

F2358 Full, 1642
Linc.

F2358A Full, 1642
Dur. Yk.

F2368A Full, 1647
Cant.

F2369 Full, 1644
Yk.

F2390 Fuller, Ignatius, 1672
Cant. Carl. Yk.

F2391 Fuller, Ignatius, 1672
Cant. Carl. Yk.

F2392 Fuller, Ignatius, 1672
Cant. Carl. Yk.

F2394 Fuller, Nicholas, 1641
Ely. Linc. Sal.

F2395? Fuller, Robert, 1674
8°.
Carl. Win.

F2396 Fuller, Samuel, 1690
Ex. Her.

F2397 Fuller, Samuel, 1679
Linc.

F2398 Fuller, Samuel, 1682
Carl. Linc.

F2399 Fuller, Samuel, 1693
Cant.

F2400 Fuller, Thomas, 1651
Bur. Cant (2). Llan ('redivivus').
Sal.

F2401 Fuller, Thomas, 1652
Wor (pr. tpw).

F2403 Fuller, Thomas, 1646
Bur.

F2410 Fuller, Thomas, 1659
Cant. Carl. Liv. Sal. Win.

F2414 Fuller, Thomas, 1647
Liv.

F2416 Fuller, Thomas, 1655
Ban. Cant (2). Carl. Chi. Dur.
Ely. Ex. Glo. Lich. Linc. Liv.
Nor (2). Pet. S Alb (imp).
S Asa. S Pl. Sal (3 − 1 imp).
Swel. Win. Wor. Yk (3).

F2417 Fuller, Thomas, 1656
Tru.

F2422 Fuller, Thomas, 1654
Ex. Lich. Sal. Wel. Wor.

F2423 Fuller, Thomas, 1642
Cant (imp). Ex (imp). Linc.
Nor. Sal. Win. Yk.

F2424 Fuller, Thomas, 1646
S Pl. Yk.

F2435 Fuller, Thomas, 1680
Liv.

F2438 Fuller, Thomas, 1647
Cant (imp). Carl. Dur
('history'). Ex. Lich (imp). Linc.
Nor. Yk.

F2439 Fuller, Thomas, 1651
Cant.

F2440 Fuller, Thomas, 1662
Cant (2 − 1 imp). Carl. Dur.
Ely. Her. Lich. Liv. Nor. S Pl
Win. Yk (imp).

F2443 Fuller, Thomas, 1642
Cant (imp). Ches. Her. Llan.
S Asa. Sal. Win.

F2444 Fuller, Thomas, 1648
Cant. Dur. Ely. Ex. Lich.
Wor. Yk.

F2445 Fuller, Thomas, 1652
Carl. Linc. Nor. Swel.

F2446 Fuller, Thomas, 1663
Cant (2). Ex. S Dv.

F2447 Fuller, Thomas, 1653
Ex.

F2449 Fuller, Thomas, 1649
Ex.

F2450 Fuller, Thomas, 1655
Ban. Cant. Dur. Yk.

F2455 Fuller, Thomas, 1650
Cant. Ches. Ely. Glo. Lich.
Linc (engr. tpw). Nor. S Pl. Sal.
Win. Wor. Yk.

F2457 Fuller, Thomas, 1662
Cant. Liv. Pet.

F2458 Fuller, Thomas, 1647
Cant (imp).

F2459 Fuller, Thomas, 1648
Ex. Yk.

F2462 Fuller, Thomas, 1643
Cant. Carl. Ex. Pet. Win.

F2465 Fuller, Thomas, 1643
Nor. Win.

F2466 Fuller, Thomas, 1654
Ban. Cant. Dur. Yk.

F2472 Fuller, Thomas, 1654
Ban. Cant. Dur. Yk.

F2474 Fuller, Thomas, 1643
Pet.

F2486B Fuller, William, *Bp*, [1672?]
Linc.

F2491 Fuller, 1645
Yk.

F2491A Fuller, 1643
Yk (3).

F2497 Fullwood, Francis, 1683
Win.

F2498 Fullwood, Francis, 1652
Cant. Chelm.

F2501A Fullwood, Francis, 1672
Win.

F2501A+ Fullwood, Francis, 1672
By S.G. and B.G. for James Collins;
8°.
Bur. Wel.

F2502 Fullwood, Francis, 1681
Ex.

F2504 Fullwood, Francis, 1667
Carl.

F2505 Fullwood, Francis, 1662
Carl. Dur. Pet. Win.

F2506 Fullwood, Francis, 1663
Wel.

F2508 Fullwood, Francis, 1673
Carl. S Pl. Win.

F2509 Fullwood, Francis, 1681
Carl. Sal (imp). Win. Yk.

F2510 Fullwood, Francis, 1672
Carl.

F2511 Fullwood, Francis, 1689
Ban. Dur. Ex. S Asa. Wel.
Yk.

F2513 Fullwood, Francis, 1693
Ex. Wel.

F2514 Fullwood, Francis, 1663
Win.

F2515 Fullwood, Francis, 1679
Carl. Ex. Win.

F2516 Fullwood, Francis, 1693
Ely. Ex. Wel.

F2517A? Fullwood, Francis, 1662
16°.
Carl. Pet.

F2519 Fullwood, Francis, 1672
Nor.

F2523 Fulman, William, 1665
S Asa. Sal.

F2524 Fulman, William, 1675
Ches. Dur. Lich. S Pl. Wel.
Yk.

F2525 Fulman, William, 1684−91
Vols 2−3 = G154.
Ban (lacks vol. 3). Cant (2 − 1
lacks vol. 1). Carl (vol. 1 only).
Ches. Dur. Ely. Ex. Linc. Rip.
S Pl. Wel (lacks vol. 3?). Yk.

F2527 Fulwar, Thomas, 1642
Yk.

F2544 Further, [1679]
Linc.

F2551 Further, [1679]
Linc.

F2568 Fyler, Samuel, 1682
Ban. Nor (tpw).

F2569 Fysh, Thomas, 1685
Her.

G8 G., D., 1679
Dur.

G12 G., E., 1679
Cant.

G18 G., F., 1660
Carl.

G25 G., H., 1662
Carl. Linc.

G33 G., J., 1643
Linc (tp imp).

G40 G., J., 1686
Cant. Carl.

G45 G., L., 1661
Carl.

G53A G., R., [1656]
Ex.

G61 G., T., 1698
Yk (frag.).

G63 G., T., 1642
Yk.

G64 G., T., 1687
Wel.

G71 G., W., 1646
Yk.

G81 Gadbury, John, 1665
S Pl.

G87 Gadbury, John, 1680
Linc.

G105 Gaffarel, Jacques, 1650
Carl. Ex. Pet.

G108 Gage, Thomas, 1651
Yk.

G109 Gage, Thomas, 1648
Dur.

G113 Gage, Thomas, 1655
Bris.

G116 Gage, Thomas, 1642
Pet.

G117 Gailhard, Jean, 1697
Pet.

G118 Gailhard, Jean, 1678
Ex.

G121A Gailhard, Jean, 1699
8°.
S Pl.

G126 Gailhard, Jean, 1669
Cant (imp).

G129 Gailhard, Jean, 1694
Cant.

G134 Gale, Theophilus, 1672
Carl.

G134A Gale, Theophilus, 1672
Chelm.

G136 Gale, Theophilus, 1669
Cant. Ches. Dur. Lich. Wor.
Yk.

G137 Gale, Theophilus, 1672
Ex (2). New. Nor. Wel.

G138 Gale, Theophilus, 1670
Ex (2). New. Nor. Wel.

G139 Gale, Theophilus, 1671
Cant. Ches. Nor. Wor. Yk.

G140 Gale, Theophilus, 1676
Ex. Lich. Wel.

G141 Gale, Theophilus, 1677
Cant. Ches. Ex. Lich. Nor.
Wel. Yk.

G142 Gale, Theophilus, 1677
Cant. Ex. Nor. Wel. Yk.

G143 Gale, Theophilus, 1678
Cant. Ex. Win.

G144 Gale, Theophilus, 1673
Cant. Carl.

G145 Gale, Theophilus, 1673
Linc. Yk.

G146? Gale, Theophilus, 1673
4°.
S Pl.

G149 Gale, Theophilus, 1671
Ex.

G154 Gale, Thomas, 1691
Also entered as vols 2 – 3 of F2525;
Vol. 1: 'Historiae Britannicae
Saxonicae …'; Vol. 2: 'Historiae
Anglicanae …', 1687.
Ban (vol. 2 only). Cant (2).
Ches. Dur. Ely. Ex. Linc. Rip.
Roch (vol. 1 only?). S Pl. Wel
(vol. 1 only?). Yk (2).

G155 Gale, Thomas, 1675
Ches. Ely. Linc. S Pl (2). Yk
(imp).

G156 Gale, Thomas, 1671
Ban. Ches. Linc. Nor. S Asa.
Yk.

G157 Gale, Thomas, 1676
Ches. Ex. S Pl (2). Yk.

G164 Galen, Christopher Bernard
Matthew van, 1665
Wing has wrong date.
Linc.

G167 Galilei, Galileo, 1653
Dur. Ely. New. Pet. Wor. Yk.

G167A Galilei, Galileo, 1653
Cant.

G168 Galilei, Galileo, 1663
Ban. Dur. Pet.

G178? Gallaway, William, 1694
Date correctly printed.
Nor.

G179 Gallaway, William, 1692
Cant.

G180 Gallaway, William, 1697
Her.

G197 Gandy, Henry, 1700
Wel.

G204 Garbrand, John, 1680
Linc.

G207 Garbutt, Richard, 1657
Carl. Yk (3).

G207A Garbutt, Richard, 1669
S Pl.

G208? Garbutt, Richard, [1675?]
12°.
Carl. Yk.

G217 Garcilaso de la Vega, 1688
Wel.

G223 Gardiner, James, 1697
Sal.

G227 Gardiner, James, 1695
Carl. Dur. Her (2). Linc. Pet.
Wor.

G227A Gardiner, James, 1700
'preach'd'
Cant.

G228 Gardiner, James, 1696
Cant (2). Wor.

G228A Gardiner, James, 1697
Cant.

G230 Gardiner, Ralph, 1655
For R. Ibbitson …; 4°.
S Pl.

G231 Gardiner, Richard, 1642
S Asa. S Pl. Yk (2).

G232 Gardiner, Richard, 1659
Win.

G234 Gardiner, Richard, 1662
Win. Yk.

G235 Gardiner, Richard, 1668
Cant. Her.

G236 Gardiner, Richard, 1675
Yk.

G243 Gardiner, Robert, *Royalist*,
1649
Linc. Win.

G245 Gardiner, Samuel, 1660
Bur. Carl. Dur.

G246? Gardiner, Samuel, 1677
Impensis B. Tooke.
Ex. S Asa. S Pl. Win.

G247 Gardiner, Samuel, 1653
Carl. Chelm.

G248 Gardiner, Samuel, 1681
8°.
S Pl. Sal.

G248A Gardiner, Samuel, 1672
Cant.

G250? Gardiner, Thomas, 1643
… John Browne.
Cant.

G256 Garencières, Théophile, 1665
S Asa.

G264 Garnet, Richard, 1649
Pet. Win.

G265 Garnet, Richard, 1689
Yk.

G268 Garret, Walter, 1680
S Pl. Win.

G271C Garret, Walter, [1700?]
Wel.

G273 Garth, *Sir* Samuel, 1699
S Pl (imp).

G279 Garway, *Sir* Henry, [1679]
Linc.

G281 Garway, *Sir* Henry, 1643
Linc.

G286 Gaskarth, John, 1700
Ely. Wor.

G289 Gaskarth, John, 1683
Llan.

G291A Gassendi, Pierre, 1653
Secunda editio.
Dur. Ely. New. Pet. Wor. Yk.

G296? Gassendi, Pierre, 1660
… Rogeri Danielis.
Carl.

G296A Gassendi, Pierre, 1668
Nor.

G300 Gastrell, Francis, 1697
Ban. Ches. Her. Nor. S Pl.
Wel.

G301 Gastrell, Francis, 1699
Ban. Ches (2). Ex. Her. New.

G303 Gastrell, Francis, 1696
Ches. S Asa.

G304 Gastrell, Francis, 1698
Wel.

G305 Gataker, Charles, 1675
Win.

G306 Gataker, Charles, 1673
Bris. Cant. Sal. Win.

G307 Gataker, Charles, 1681
S Pl. Sal.

G308 Gataker, Charles, 1674
Glo. Sal.

G309 Gataker, Thomas, 1659
Cant. Ely. Ex. Llan. S Pl.
Wor.

G311 Gataker, Thomas, 1670
Wel. Win.

G312 Gataker, Thomas, 1652
Carl.

G313 Gataker, Thomas, 1651
Pet. S Pl. Win.

G314 Gataker, Thomas, 1661
Wor.

G318 Gataker, Thomas, 1648
Found with Harperii *or* Harperi in impr.
Ex (Harperii). Lich (Harperii). Linc (Harperii). Pet (2 — 1: Harperi; 2: Harperii). S Asa (Harperii). S Pl (Harperii). Sal (Harperi).

G320 Gataker, Thomas, 1652
S Pl.

G321 Gataker, Thomas, 1645
Ex. Pet.

G323 Gataker, Thomas, 1646
Dur.

G325 Gataker, Thomas, 1654
Sal.

G326 Gataker, Thomas, 1646
Cant. Carl. Linc. Pet (imp).

G330 Gataker, Thomas, 1653
Cant.

G331B Gataker, Thomas, 1653
4°.
Carl.

G333 Gatford, Lionel, 1643
Linc. Wor.

G333B+ Gatford, Lionel, 1643
Cambridge, by Roger Daniel; 4°.
Pet (imp).

G336 Gatford, Lionel, 1655
Pet.

G337 Gatford, Lionel, 1657
Ex.

G338 Gatford, Lionel, [1661]
Linc. Win.

G340 Gauden, John, 1660
Dur (26p.). Pet (2 — both 26p.). Sal (24p.). Win (26p.).

G341 Gauden, John, 1660
Pet.

G343 Gauden, John, 1660
Carl.

G344 Gauden, John, 1653
Cant. Ex (imp). Nor. Pet. Yk.

G344A Gauden, John, 1661
S Asa.

G345 Gauden, John, [1645]
Linc. Yk.

G347 Gauden, John, 1662
Pet.

G348 Gauden, John, 1661
Carl. Liv. Nor. Win. Yk.

G350A Gauden, John, 1661
Sal. Win.

G353 Gauden, John, 1662
Dur.

G355 Gauden, John, 1656
Carl.

G356 Gauden, John, 1658
Cant (imp). Carl. Pet.

G357 Gauden, John, 1653
Ban. Bur. Cant. Ex (engr. tpw). Her. Lich (engr. tpw). Linc. Pet. Yk.

G359 Gauden, John, 1659
Bris. Cant (2). Carl. Ely. Ex. Lich. Pet. S Pl. Wor. Yk.

G360 Gauden, John, 1654
Ex.

G361A Gauden, John, 1660
4°.
Cant. Carl. Ex. Pet (2). S Pl.

G362 Gauden, John, 1641
Her. Linc (2). Wor.

G363 Gauden, John, 1641
Carl. Ex (2). Liv. Pet (2).

G364 Gauden, John, 1660
Carl. Wor.

G366 Gauden, John, 1661
Win.

G367? Gauden, John, 1648[9]
12p.
Cant. Pet. Yk (2).

G367+ Gauden, John, 1648[9]
As G367, but: 13p.
Pet.

G370 Gauden, John, 1660
'... February 28. 1659 ...'
Pet (imp). S Pl. Yk.

G371 Gauden, John, 1660
Carl. Ex (2 — tps vary slightly).

G373 Gauden, John, 1642
Cant. Carl. Ex. Pet.

G377 Gaule, John, 1652
Sal.

G378 Gaule, John, 1657
Carl. Pet.

G379 Gaule, John, 1646
Cant (imp).

G380 Gaule, John, 1649
Carl.

G381A Gaunt, *Mrs* Elizabeth, [1685]
Ban.

G382 Gautruche, Pierre, 1668
Ches. Yk.

G383+ Gautruche, Pierre, 1683
Typis M. Clarke; 8°.
S Pl.

G387A Gautruche, Pierre, 1678
Dur.

G389aA Gautruche, Pierre, 1686
The sixth edition; ... sold by Charles Shortgrave.
Ban.

G389bA Gautruche, Pierre, 1691
The fifth edition.
Cant.

G390 Gavin, Antonio, 1691
Ely.

G392 Gavin, Antonio, 1691
Bur. Carl. Dur. Ely.

G393? Gavin, Antonio, 1691
'journey'
Bur. Ely. S Pl.

G394 Gavin, Antonio, 1693
Bur.

G394A Gavin, Antonio, 1693
Ely. Ex.

G395 Gawen, Nicholas, 1668
Pet.

G396 Gawler, Francis, 1659
Linc (imp).

G403 Gayer, *Sir* John, 1647
Yk.

G413 Gayton, Edmund, [1655]
Ex. Lich.

G416 Gayton, Edmund, 1663
Win.

G420 Gayton, Edmund, 1655
By Tho. Roycroft.
S Pl.

G425 Gazet, Angelin, 1657
Bur. Carl. Lich.

G435B Gearing, William, 1674
Carl. Dur. Ex. Yk.

G435D Gearing, William, 1675
Nor.

G435E Gearing, William, 1688
Cant.

G436C Gearing, William, 1670
Win.

G438A Gearing, William, 1676
Carl. Ex. Glo.

G444 Geddes, Michael, 1696
Cant (3). Ex. Wel.

G445 Geddes, Michael, 1697
S Pl. Wel.

G448 Gee, Edward, *the Elder*, 1658
Ban.

G449 Gee, Edward, *the Elder*, 1650
Bur. Chelm. Dur. Lich. Pet. S Asa.

G450 Gee, Edward, *the Elder*, 1650
Chelm ('non-scribers'). Ches (as
Chelm). Liv (imp). Pet (as
Chelm).

G451 Gee, Edward, *the Elder*, 1653
Ex.

G452 Gee, Edward, *the Elder*,
1650[1]
Chelm.

G453 Gee, Edward, *the Younger*,
1688
Ban. Cant. Ex. Wel.

G454 Gee, Edward, *the Younger*,
1689
Ban (2). Cant. Ex (imp).

G455 Gee, Edward, *the Younger*,
1688
Ban.

G456 Gee, Edward, *the Younger*,
1688
Ex. Wel.

G457 Gee, Edward, *the Younger*,
1688
Ex. Wel (2).

G458 Gee, Edward, *the Younger*,
1692
Cant. Her.

G459 Gee, Edward, *the Younger*,
1688
Ban. Cant (imp). Dur. Ex.
Nor. S Pl. Wel.

G460 Gee, Edward, *the Younger*,
1688
Ban. Ex. Wel.

G461 Gee, Edward, *the Younger*,
1688
Ban. Ex. S Pl. Wel. Yk.

G462 Gee, Edward, *the Younger*,
1687
Ban. Cant. Ex. Nor. Swel.
Wel. Yk.

G463 Gee, Edward, *the Younger*,
1687
Bur. Cant. Chi. Ely. Yk.

G464 Gee, Edward, *the Younger*,
1688
Ban. Ex. Nor. Wel.

G468 Gell, Robert, 1650
Chelm. Pet (imp)*. S Pl. Wor.

G470 Gell, Robert, 1659
Cant. Wor.

G472 Gell, Robert, 1676
Yk.

G473 Gell, Robert, 1649
S Pl. Wor.

G483 Gemitus, 1654
Pet. Yk.

G488 Generall, 1646
Carl.

G488A General, [1687]
Wel.

G491? Generall, [1665]
'generall'
Win.

G506 Generall, [1641]
Dur.

G507 Generall, 1641
Linc.

G509 General, 1642
Dur.

G511B Generall, 1659
Printed by ...
Cant.

G523A Genuine, 1693
Nor. Pet. S Alb. S Pl. Yk.

G536 Georgirenes, Joseph, 1678
Ely.

G540 Gerbier, *Sir* Balthazar, 1662
Colophon: By A.M. to be sold by
Richard Lowns, Thomas Heath, and
Matthew Collins.
Cant.

G551A Gerbier, *Sir* Balthazar, 1665
Linc.

G554 Gerbier, *Sir* Balthazar, 1664
Linc (also has tp of G551).

G580 Gerbier, *Sir* Balthazar,
[1650?]
Ex.

G586 Geree, John, 1646
Ex.

G589 Geree, John, 1646
Cant.

G596 Geree, John, 1648
Cant (imp). S Pl (tp imp).

G597 Geree, John, 1641
Pet. S Asa.

G598 Geree, John, 1649
S Pl. Yk (3).

G599 Geree, John, 1648
S Pl.

G602 Geree, John, 1644
Pet. Win.

G603 Geree, John, 1646
Cant. Chelm. Ex. Her.

G604 Geree, John, 1647
Cant. Chelm.

G605 Geree, John, 1641
Pet.

G606 Geree, Stephen, 1644
Sal (tpw). Yk.

G609D Gerhard, Johann, 1644
Seventh ed. not on tp; 12°.
Yk.

G610 Gerhard, Johann, 1670
Yk.

G611B Gerhard, Johann, 1683
24°.
Cant.

G617 Gery, Thomas, 1656
Pet.

G624 Gesner, Konrad, 1658
Cant (imp).

G632 Getsius, Johann Daniel, 1658
Ex.

G644 Gibbes, Charles, 1677
Yk.

G647 Gibbon, John, [1679]
Linc.

G649A Gibbon, John, [1679]
Linc.

G650? Gibbon, John, 1682
... R. Billingsley ...
Bur. Pet.

G659 Gibbons, John, 1651
Linc.

G671 Gibson, Samuel, 1645
Cant.

G672 Gibson, Thomas, 1682
Ely. Wel.

G672+ Gibson, Thomas, 1682
By M.F. for T. Flesher; 8°.
Dur.

G689 Giffard, Bonaventure, 1688
Cant.

G690 Giffard, Francis, 1681
Her.

G691 Giffard, John, 1642
Linc.

G694 Gifford, George, 1695
Cant.

G702 Gilbert, Claudius, 1657
Dur. Yk.

G703 Gilbert, Claudius, 1658
Ex.

G704 Gilbert, Claudius, 1658
Dur. Ex. Pet. S Asa.

G706 Gilbert, Eleazer, 1645
Yk.

G708 Gilbert, John, 1686
Ban. Ex. Nor. S Pl (2). Sal.
Swel.

G709 Gilbert, John, 1699
Lich.

G710 Gilbert, John, 1699
New.

G711 Gilbert, John, 1699
Lich. Wor (2).

G719 Gilbert, Thomas, 1657
Ex.

G724 Gilbert, Thomas, 1655
Win.

G737A Giles, Mascall, 1643
'A defence of a treatise ...'
Sal (2 – 1 imp).

G739 Giles, William, 1688
Dur. Her. S Pl. Swel. Yk.

G740 Giles, William, 1688
S Asa (tpw). Wel.

G741 Giles, William, 1688
Ex (2).

G743 Gillespie, George, 1646
Yk.

G745 Gillespie, George, 1641
Ban. Pet.

G748 Gillespie, George, 1660
Chelm.

G749 Gillespie, George, 1647
Pet.

G750 Gillespie, George, 1648
Dur.

G754 Gillespie, George, 1646
Win.

G755 Gillespie, George, 1645
Pet. Win.

G756 Gillespie, George, 1644
Ex. Pet. Yk.

G758+ Gillespie, George, 1645
For Robert Bostock; 4°.
Pet. Win.

G765 Gillespie, George, 1645
Cant. Pet. Yk.

G771 Gilpin, John, 1655
Ex. Pet.

G773 Gilpin, Randolph, 1657
Win.

G774 Gilpin, Richard, 1656
Carl. Dur. S Pl. Yk.

G776 Gilpin, Richard, 1700
Cant (imp).

G777 Gilpin, Richard, 1677
Ely. Ex. Linc. S Pl. Win.

G778 Gilpin, Richard, 1658
Carl.

G779 Gipps, George, 1645
Her. Yk.

G779A Gipps, Thomas, [1699]
Carl.

G780 Gipps, Thomas, 1698
Carl (frag.). Ex.

G781 Gipps, Thomas, 1697
Carl. Her. Wor.

G781A Gipps, Thomas, 1696
Carl. Ches.

G782 Gipps, Thomas, 1699
Carl. S Asa.

G783 Gipps, Thomas, 1683
Cant.

G784 Giraffi, Alessandro, 1650
Carl.

G785A Giraffi, Alessandro, 1650
Linc.

G788 Girard, Guillaume, 1670
Carl. Ely. Ex (imp). S Asa
(imp). Wel.

G792 Glance, 1690
Wel.

G793 Glanius, W., 1682
Ex.

G797 Glanvill, *Sir* John, 1641
Pet.

G798 Glanvill, Joseph, 1675
Carl.

G799 Glanvill, Joseph, 1668
Ex.

G800 Glanvill, Joseph, 1668
Linc.

G801 Glanvill, Joseph, 1669
Bur.

G802 Glanvill, Joseph, 1673
Pet.

G804 Glanvill, Joseph, 1677
Carl. Sal.

G808 Glanvill, Joseph, 1678
12°.
Ban. Carl. Ex. Her.

G809 Glanvill, Joseph, 1676
Carl. Ex.

G811 Glanvill, Joseph, 1671
Llan.

G813 Glanvill, Joseph, 1667
Carl.

G814 Glanvill, Joseph, 1662
Carl.

G817 Glanvill, Joseph, 1671
Carl. Wel.

G820 Glanvill, Joseph, 1668
Carl. Ex. Pet.

G821 Glanvill, Joseph, 1671
Carl. Sal. Win.

G822 Glanvill, Joseph, 1681
Carl. Ex.

G823 Glanvill, Joseph, 1682
Nor. Pet. S Asa.

G825? Glanvill, Joseph, 1689
The third edition; ... Anth. Baskerville.
Ely.

G826 Glanvill, Joseph, 1700
The third edition.
Dur.

G827 Glanvill, Joseph, 1665
Carl. Dur. Pet. Wor. Yk.

G828 Glanvill, Joseph, 1665
Carl. Dur. Pet. Wor. Yk.

G829 Glanvill, Joseph, 1678
Ban. Her.

G830 Glanvill, Joseph, 1676
Carl.

G831 Glanvill, Joseph, 1681
Ex. Llan. Nor.

G832 Glanvill, Joseph, 1667
Nor (tpw). S Pl. Yk.

G833 Glanvill, Joseph, 1682
Carl. S Asa. S Pl. Yk.

G835 Glanvill, Joseph, 1670
'The way to ...'
Carl.

G837 Glanvill, Joseph, 1681
Cant. Ex. Wel. Win.

G838 Glanvill, Joseph, 1681
Carl. Dur (imp).

G839 Glanville, Ranulphe de, 1673
S Pl. Wel.

G842 Glascock, John, 1659
Cant (imp).

G846 Glauber, John Rudolph, 1651
Cant. Carl.

G853 Glisson, Francis, 1654
Pet. Wor.

G859 Glisson, Francis, 1677
Ex.

G868 Glorious, 1642
Sal.

G871A Glorious, 1641[2]
Linc.

G885 Gloucester-shire, 1648
Yk.

G889 Glover, Henry, 1664
Pet.

G891 Glyn, *Sir* John, 1641
Cant (imp). Yk.

G891A? Glyn, *Sir* John, 1641
'Glynn'; 19p.
Linc.

G892 Glyn, *Sir* John, 1641
Cant. Carl.

G894 Glyn, *Sir* John, 1642
Cant.

G895 Glyn, *Sir* John, 1641
Cant (2).

G897 Goad, John, 1686
Wor.

G900 Goad, John, 1687
Cant (imp).

G901 Goad, John, 1663
Carl. S Pl.

G902 Goad, John, 1664
Carl. S Pl.

G904 Goad, Thomas, 1661
Yk.

G906 God, 1644[5]
Yk (2).

G911 Godbolt, John, 1652
… Gabriell Bedell.
Pet.

G914 Goddard, Jonathan, 1670
Win.

G917 Goddard, Thomas, 1684
Carl. Ex.

G918 Godden, Thomas, 1672
Carl. Ex. S Pl. Win.

G919 Godden, Thomas, 1677
Ex. Win.

G920 Godden, Thomas, 1686
Dur.

G922 Godden, Thomas, 1688
Cant.

G924 Godefroy, Jacques, 1673
Dur. Linc. S Pl.

G933G Godly, [1670?]
Linc.

G937 Godly, 1680
Llan.

G941 Godman, William, 1660
Cant. Carl. Ely. Pet (2). Wor.

G946 Godolphin, John, 1674
Carl. Sal. Wel.

G947 Godolphin, John, 1677
Linc.

G948 Godolphin, John, 1685
Pet.

G949 Godolphin, John, 1678
Carl. Ely. Lich. Linc. S Pl.
Wel. Wor. Yk.

G949A? Godolphin, John, 1680
… Richard and Edw. Atkins … for
Christopher Wilkinson.
Ex. Pet.

G950 Godolphin, John, 1680
The second edition.
Ban. S Pl.

G951 Godolphin, John, 1687
Chi. Ex. Glo. S Asa. S Pl.

G952 Godolphin, John, 1661
Sal.

G958 Gods, 1641
Linc.

G971 Godwin, Morgan, 1680
Ely. S Pl.

G976 Godwyn, Thomas, 1641
Bur. Her. S Asa. Yk.

G977 Godwyn, Thomas, 1655
S Pl. Swel. Wel. Yk.

G979 Godwyn, Thomas, 1667
Dur. Swel. Yk.

G981 Godwyn, Thomas, 1672
The eighth edition.
Lich.

G982 Godwyn, Thomas, 1672
The twelfth edition.
Cant. Ely. Nor.

G983 Godwyn, Thomas, 1678
Cant.

G984A? Godwyn, Thomas, 1685
The twelfth edition.
Yk.

G986 Godwyn, Thomas, 1648
Bur. Glo. Her. S Asa.

G987 Godwyn, Thomas, 1655
Swel. Yk.

G988 Godwyn, Thomas, 1658
Thirteenth ed. not on tp.
Cant. S Pl. Wel.

G989 Godwyn, Thomas, 1661
Cant. Wor.

G990 Godwyn, Thomas, 1661
Her.

G991 Godwyn, Thomas, 1668
Dur. Swel. Yk.

G994 Godwyn, Thomas, 1674
Ely. Lich. Nor.

G995? Godwyn, Thomas, 1680
By Margaret White …
Cant.

G1003 Goedaert, Johannes, 1682
Yk (2).

G1021 Golius, Theophilus, 1662
Dur.

G1029 Good, Thomas, 1674
Cant (imp). Her.

G1035 Good, 1642
Linc.

G1036A Good, 1643
'Good and true'; For R. Astine, A.
Coe.
Yk.

G1043 Good, 1648
Sal.

G1069+ Good, 1642
'Good newes …'; For Jo. Watson; 4°.
Dur.

G1080 Good, 1687
Dur.

G1093 Goode, William, 1645
Pet.

G1099 Gooden, Peter, 1687
Nor. Wel.

G1100 Goodman, Godfrey, [1650]
Carl (cropped).

G1103 Goodman, Godfrey, 1653
Carl. Glo. Pet.

G1104 Goodman, John, 1648 [*i.e.*
1684]
Ban. Bris. Cant (2). Ex (3).
Nor. S Pl (2). Sal. Swel. Wel.

G1105? Goodman, John, 1684
Second ed. not on tp.
Carl. Ex (tp imp).

G1109 Goodman, John, 1683
Ban. Wor.

G1110 Goodman, John, 1688/9
Carl. S Asa.

G1111 Goodman, John, 1684
Carl.

G1113 Goodman, John, 1693
The second edition.
Yk.

G1114 Goodman, John, 1698
12°.
Ely.

G1115 Goodman, John, 1679
Cant. Carl. Her. Pet. Sal. Wel.

G1116 Goodman, John, 1683
Ban (engr. tpw). Ely. S Pl. Yk.

G1117 Goodman, John, 1689
Bur.

G1118 Goodman, John, 1694
Llan. Yk.

G1119A Goodman, John, 1690
Wel.

G1120 Goodman, John, 1674
Carl. Lich. Nor (engr. tpw).
S Alb.

G1121 Goodman, John, 1675
Cant. Win. Yk (2).

G1122 Goodman, John, 1675
Ely. Sal. Wor.

G1122A Goodman, John, [1684?]
The third edition.
Dur. Ex (3 − 1 imp). Her. Llan.

G1123 Goodman, John, 1677
Cant. Dur. Ex. Yk.

G1124 Goodman, John, 1678
Cant. Her. Sal.

G1125 Goodman, John, 1680
Cant. Nor.

G1126 Goodman, John, 1681
Ban. Ely. Yk.

G1127 Goodman, John, 1685
S Asa.

G1128 Goodman, John, 1697
Her. Nor. Yk.

G1128A Goodman, John, 1697
S Pl.

G1131 Goodman, John, 1684
Carl.

G1132 Goodman, John, 1686
Cant (imp). Ely. Ex. Llan. Yk.

G1138 Goodman, John, 1686
Carl. Ely. Llan.

G1145 Goodwin, John, 1646
Win.

G1146 Goodwin, John, [1642]
Ex. Linc.

G1146A Goodwin, John, 1642
Pet.

G1149 Goodwin, John, 1651
Ban. Bur. Carl. Chelm. Her.
Pet.

G1150 Goodwin, John, 1647
Yk (2).

G1151 Goodwin, John, 1657
Ex. Yk.

G1152 Goodwin, John, 1642
Linc. Pet.

G1161 Goodwin, John, 1646
Win.

G1162 Goodwin, John, 1646
Linc. Win.

G1163 Goodwin, John, 1648
Linc. Sal.

G1165 Goodwin, John, 1671
Wel.

G1166 Goodwin, John, 1653
Ban. Bur. Her. Pet.

G1170? Goodwin, John, 1649
'obstructours'
Carl. Pet. Yk.

G1172 Goodwin, John, 1642
Her.

G1178 Goodwin, John, 1641
Ex.

G1183 Goodwin, John, 1648
Ex (tpw).

G1185 Goodwin, John, 1643
Sal.

G1186 Goodwin, John, 1651
Carl. Chelm.

G1187 Goodwin, John, 1671
Wel.

G1192 Goodwin, John, 1663
Cant.

G1195 Goodwin, John, 1643
Pet.

G1200? Goodwin, John, 1648
… Henery Cripps.
Yk (2 − 1 as Wing).

G1206 Goodwin, John, 1644
Cant.

G1207 Goodwin, John, 1644
Cant (52p.). Carl (50p., imp?).

G1210 Goodwin, John, 1658
Carl. Ex.

G1213 Goodwin, John, 1653
Ex. Win.

G1220 Goodwin, Thomas, 1683
Her.

G1221 Goodwin, Thomas, 1692
Her.

G1223 Goodwin, Thomas, 1643
Cant.

G1224 Goodwin, Thomas, 1650
Carl*. S Pl. Sal. Win. Yk.

G1225 Goodwin, Thomas, 1643
Carl.

G1229 Goodwin, Thomas, 1647
[i.e. 1651]
S Pl. Win.

G1229A Goodwin, Thomas, 1651
Carl. Sal. Yk.

G1230 Goodwin, Thomas, 1643
Cant.

G1231 Goodwin, Thomas, [1647]
Carl. S Pl. Sal. Win. Yk.

G1232 Goodwin, Thomas, 1642
Cant.

G1235 Goodwin, Thomas, 1651
S Pl. Sal. Win.

G1237 Goodwin, Thomas, 1651
S Pl (tpw). Sal.

G1242 Goodwin, Thomas, 1645
Cant.

G1244 Goodwin, Thomas, 1650
S Pl. Sal. Win.

G1245A? Goodwin, Thomas, 1641
'Syons'
Pet. S Asa.

G1246 Goodwin, Thomas, 1646
Ex. Win.

G1254 Goodwin, Thomas, 1643
Cant.

G1255 Goodwin, Thomas, 1651
Carl. S Pl. Sal. Win. Yk.

G1257 Goodwin, Thomas, 1657
Ex. S Pl.

G1259 Goodwin, Thomas, 1688
48p.
Dur. Ex. Lich. Pet. Sal. Wel
(2). Win. Yk*.

G1261 Goodwin, Thomas, 1643
Cant.

G1262 Goodwin, Thomas, 1650
Carl. S Pl. Sal. Win. Yk.

G1264 Goodwin, Thomas, 1643
Cant.

G1265 Goodwin, Thomas, 1650
S Pl. Sal. Win.

G1266 Goodwin, Thomas, 1655
Cant.

G1267 Goodwin, Thomas, 1642
Ex. Win.

G1268 Goodwin, Thomas, 1642
Cant. Pet (2).

G1268A Goodwin, Thomas, of
Pinner, 1695
Ex. Sal.

G1269 Goodwin, Thomas, of Pinner,
1695
Cant. Ches.

G1270 Goodwin, Thomas, of Pinner,
[1699]
8°.
Cant.

G1270B Goodwin, Thomas,
Minister, 1658
Cant.

G1280 Gordon, James, 1680
Win.

G1282 Gordon, James, 1687
Cant. Wel. Yk (2).

G1283 Gordon, James, 1687
Ex.

G1285 Gordon, John, 1689
Cant.

G1288 Gordon, Patrick, 1699
8°.
Nor.

G1298 Gore, Thomas, 1674
S Pl. Sal. Win.

G1299 Gore, Thomas, 1667
S Pl.

G1300 Gorges, *Sir* Ferdinando, 1658
Cant.

G1302 Gorges, *Sir* Ferdinando, 1659
Cant (imp).

G1303B? Goring, George, *Baron*, 1641
'Colonell'
Linc.

G1303C Goring, George, *Baron*, 1641
Cant.

G1303D Goring, George, *Baron*, 1642
Dur.

G1312 Gosnold, Paul, [1644]
Wel.

G1318 Gostelo, Walter, 1655
Pet. Wor.

G1321 Gostwyke, William, 1696
Wor.

G1322 Gostwyke, William, 1692
Cant.

G1323A Gother, John, 1699
Dur.

G1324 Gother, John, 1687
Wel.

G1325? Gother, John, 1686
'accommodation'
Bur. Carl. Dur. Sal. Swel (2).
Wel.

G1326 Gother, John, 1687
Cant. Wel.

G1327 Gother, John, 1687
Bur.

G1328 Gother, John, 1687
Bur. Wel.

G1328A Gother, John, 1687
'Good advice to the pulpits'; ... and sold at his printing-house.
Linc.

G1329 Gother, John, 1687
'Good advice to the pulpits'
Cant. Nor. Wel.

G1329cA Gother, John, 1699
Dur.

G1329hA Gother, John, 1700
Dur.

G1329B Gother, John, 1695
Dur.

G1329E Gother, John, 1698
12°.
Dur.

G1329G Gother, John, 1699
Dur.

G1329G+ Gother, John, 1700
[N.pl.], printed in the year; 12°.
Dur.

G1330 Gother, John, 1687
Wel.

G1332 Gother, John, 1686
Bur. Cant. Wel.

G1333 Gother, John, 1665 [*i.e.* 1685]
Swel (2). Yk.

G1334 Gother, John, 1685
Ban. Carl. Ex (3 — 1 tpw). Nor (tpw). Sal.

G1334A Gother, John, 1685
Cant. Swel.

G1335 Gother, John, 1685
Bur. Ex. Swel. Wel.

G1335A Gother, John, 1685
Nor.

G1337 Gother, John, 1686
16 chapters issued separately in weekly pts, pagination and signing continuous.
Ban (p. 1 — 8). Dur (p. 1 — 88, cropped). Ex (p. 25 — 32). Swel (p. 9 — 16). Wel (p. 1 — 8, 17 — 24, 33 — 40).

G1339 Gother, John, 1687
Nor.

G1340 Gother, John, 1686
Ex. Swel. Wel.

G1341 Gother, John, 1686
Dur. Ex. S Pl. Sal.

G1342 Gother, John, 1687
Bur.

G1343 Gother, John, 1687
Bur. Wel.

G1344 Gother, John, 1688
Wel.

G1346 Gother, John, 1700
Dur.

G1347 Gother, John, 1688
Ban. Wel.

G1348 Gother, John, [1686]
Ban. Bur. Carl. Dur. Ex (2).
Sal. Swel. Wel.

G1349 Gother, John, 1686
'accommodation'
Bur. Nor (imp). Sal. Swel (2).
Wel.

G1350 Gother, John, 1687
Sal. Wel. Yk.

G1353 Gott, Samuel, 1670
Llan. Sal.

G1355 Gott, Samuel, 1648
Linc.

G1359A Gouge, Thomas, 1661
Pet.

G1362 Gouge, Thomas, 1675
Ban.

G1373A Gouge, Thomas, 1675
Ban.

G1374 Gouge, Thomas, 1679
S Asa.

G1381 Gouge, Thomas, 1674
Ban.

G1391 Gouge, William, 1655
Bur (2). Ex. Her. IoM.

G1393 Gouge, William, 1645
Pet. Win.

G1395 Gouge, William, 1641
Pet.

G1397 Gouge, William, 1642
Ex. Pet (3).

G1400? Gouge, William, 1647
4°.
Linc.

G1408 Gough, John, 1661
Ban. Cant. Chi. S Pl. Win.

G1433 Gould, Robert, 1683
Wel.

G1438 Gould, William, 1674
Pet (imp).

G1439 Gould, William, 1672
Cant. Ex.

G1440 Gould, William, 1676
Carl. Dur.

G1441 Gould, William, 1682
Carl. Pet.

G1443 Gouldman, Francis, 1664
Carl. Her. Linc.

G1444 Gouldman, Francis, 1669
Bur. Ely. Her (imp). Sal. Yk.

G1450 Gouldsborough, John, 1653
Cant (imp).

G1456 Government, 1647
Win.

G1457- Government, 1653
'of'; Printed by William du-Gard, and Henry Hills; 2°.
Dur.

G1457? Government, 1654
'The government of ...'
Yk.

G1458 Gower, Humfrey, 1685
Ex. Yk.

G1459? Gower, Humfrey, 1685
'Christmass-day'
Yk.

G1462 Gower, Stanley, 1644
Yk.

G1464 Grabe, Johann Ernst,
1698−9
Ban. Dur (vol. 1 only). Ely. Ex.
Glo. Liv. Nor (vol. 1 only).
S Pl. Wor. Yk (vol. 1 only,
tpw)*.

G1465 Grabe, Johann Ernst, 1700
Ches. Nor (vol. 2 only).

G1467A Graces, 1655
Pet.

G1470 Gracian y Morales, Baltasar,
1681
Carl.

G1472C? Gradus, 1691
... Took ...; 8°.
Pet.

G1477 Graile, John, 1655
Sal (tp imp).

G1478 Graile, John, 1699
Linc.

G1486A Grand, 1650
Yk (2).

G1495+ Grand, 1652
For Thomas Egglesfield; 4°.
Ely. Yk.

G1496 Grand, 1657
Carl.

G1500 Grand, 1681
Ches.

G1504 Grand, 1643
Yk.

G1507 Grand, 1643
Cant.

G1523 Grant, Thomas, 1644
Linc.

G1524 Grant, W., 1652
Sal.

G1527 Grantham, Thomas, *Baptist*,
1663
Pet.

G1528 Grantham, Thomas, *Baptist*,
1678
Win.

G1535 Grantham, Thomas, *Baptist*,
1691
Cant.

G1543 Grantham, Thomas, *Baptist*,
[c.1662]
Linc (2).

G1556 Grantham, Thomas, *M.A.*,
1656
Linc.

G1560+ Grantham, Thomas, *M.A.*,
1646
See: CLC51.
Yk.

G1568 Grascombe, Samuel, [1691]
Ely. Wel.

G1569 Grascombe, Samuel, 1693
Wel.

G1570 Grascombe, Samuel, 1691
'... Humfredum Hody'
Wel.

G1572 Grascombe, Samuel, 1692
Ex.

G1575? Grascombe, Samuel, 1693
cap.
Ely.

G1576 Grascombe, Samuel, 1691
S Pl (2).

G1577 Grascombe, Samuel, [1688]
Yk.

G1577+ Grascombe, Samuel,
[1688?]
[N.pl.]; 8°.
Yk.

G1579 Grascombe, Samuel, 1692
Wel. Yk.

G1581 Gratius, *Faliscus*, 1654
Ex.

G1582 Gratius, *Faliscus*, 1699
Ches. Nor. S Pl.

G1583 Gratius, Ortwinus, 1690
Ban (2 − 1 vol. 1 only). Cant (2).
Ches. Chi. Dur. Glo. Her.
Lich. Linc. Pet. Rip. S Asa.
S Pl. Sal. Wel. Win. Yk.

G1590 Graunt, John, *of
Bucklersbury*, 1649
Ex.

G1593 Graunt, John, *of
Bucklersbury*, [1650]
Ex.

G1593A Graunt, John, *of
Bucklersbury*, 1665
Win.

G1594 Graunt, John, *of
Bucklersbury*, 1652
... and J. Hancock.
Linc.

G1596 Graunt, John, *of
Bucklersbury*, 1651
Ex.

G1599 Graunt, John, *F.R.S.*, 1662
Carl. Nor.

G1600 Graunt, John, *F.R.S.*, 1665
Glo. Linc.

G1601 Graunt, John, *F.R.S.*, 1665
Carl. Sal.

G1602 Graunt, John, *F.R.S.*, 1676
Cant. Pet.

G1603 Graunt, John, *F.R.S.*, 1665
Carl.

G1607F Gray, Andrew, 1680
Edinburgh, by the heirs of Andrew
Anderson.
Yk.

G1611 Gray, Andrew, 1678
Yk.

G1618B Gray, Andrew, 1684
Edinburgh, by the heir of Andrew
Anderson.
Yk.

G1620B Gray, Andrew, 1679
Yk.

G1627 Grayes, Isaac, 1654
Ex.

G1628 Graziani, Antonio Maria,
1687
Ex.

G1660 Great, [1679]
Dur.

G1663 Great, 1689
Pet. S Pl.

G1674 Great, 1681
Dur.

G1675 Great, 1681
Dur.

G1686? Great, 1642
... Decemb. 17.
Linc. Yk.

G1691 Great, 1645
'... inthronization of ... George ...'
Yk.

G1751 Great, [1641?]
Cant. Yk.

G1766 Great, 1651
Glo. Yk.

G1773 Great, 1645
Yk.

G1787 Great, 1642
Linc.

G1789 Greatrakes, Valentine, 1666
S Pl.

G1792 Greaves, *Sir* Edward, 1643
Carl.

G1800 Greaves, John, 1647
Carl. Linc. Pet.

G1804 Greaves, John, 1646
Cant (imp). Lich.

G1805 Greaves, Thomas, 1656
Carl.

G1820 Greene, John, 1647
Yk.

G1822 Greene, John, 1644
Pet.

G1825 Greene, Martin, 1661
Ely.

G1827 Greene, Richard, 1679
Linc.

G1848 Greenhill, William, 1643
Cant (2). Ex (imp).

G1851 Greenhill, William, 1645
IoM.

G1853? Greenhill, William, 1650
The second edition; 4°.
Ex.

G1854 Greenhill, William, 1649
Ex.

G1855 Greenhill, William, 1651
Ex.

G1856 Greenhill, William, 1658
Ex.

G1859 Greenhill, William, 1670
8°.
Ex.

G1869 Greenwood, William, 1657
Dur.

G1870 Greenwood, William, 1659
Dur (tpw).

G1877 Gregg, Hugh, 1691
Wel.

G1880 Gregory XV, *Pope*, 1642
Linc. Pet.

G1885 Gregory, Edmund, 1646
Cant (imp).

G1886 Gregory, Francis, 1675
Carl. Wor.

G1887 Gregory, Francis, 1673
S Asa.

G1888 Gregory, Francis, 1660
Cant. Carl. Wor.

G1889 Gregory, Francis, 1696
S Pl.

G1890 Gregory, Francis, 1695
Ely.

G1892 Gregory, Francis, 1654
Wel.

G1893? Gregory, Francis, 1670
... T. Passinger; 8°.
Nor.

G1894 Gregory, Francis, 1675
Cant (imp). Ex. Her.

G1895 Gregory, Francis, 1673
Bur.

G1897 Gregory, Francis, 1697
Her.

G1897A+ Gregory, Francis, 1651
Editio secunda; By William Du-Gard,
sold by Richard Royston; 8°.
Carl.

G1905 Gregory, Francis, 1660
Cant.

G1906 Gregory, Francis, 1696
Cant. Her.

G1907 Gregory, Francis, 1674
Ex. Glo.

G1909 Gregory, James, 1668
Bris.

G1913- Gregory, John, 1664
As G1913, apart from date.
Llan.

G1913 Gregory, John, 1665
S Pl.

G1914 Gregory, John, 1671
Dur. Ely. Ex. Lich. Linc.
Swel.

G1915 Gregory, John, 1684
Ban. Ches. Wel.

G1919 Gregory, John, 1693
Ban.

G1921 Gregory, John, 1650
Carl. Ches. Dur. Ely. Ex.
S Asa (2). Sal (2). Win. Wor.
Yk.

G1923 Gregory, John, 1671 .
Dur. Ely. Ex. Lich. Linc.
Swel.

G1925 Gregory, John, 1650
Ely. Ex. Sal. Wor.

G1926 Gregory, John, 1649
Win.

G1927 Gregory, John, 1650
Cant. Carl. Ely. Ex. S Asa.
S Pl. Sal (3 — 1 frag.). Wor. Yk.

G1928 Gregory, John, 1664
Llan. S Pl.

G1929 Gregory, John, 1671
Dur. Ely. Ex. Lich. Linc.
Swel.

G1930 Gregory, John, 1683
Ban. Ches. Wel.

G1933 Gregory, Thomas, 1694
Dur. S Pl.

G1934 Grelot, Guillaume Joseph,
1683
Cant.

G1937A Grenfield, Thomas, 1661
Carl. S Asa.

G1938 Grenville, Denis, 1684
Dur (2 – 1 imp). Ex.

G1938aA? Grenville, Denis, 1684
Hutchenson.
Dur.

G1938A Grenville, Denis, 1685
For Robert Clavell.
Ban. Dur. Yk.

G1939+ Grenville, Denis, 1685
See: CLC52.
Carl. Dur.

G1940 Grenville, Denis, 1689
Dur.

G1941 Grenville, Denis, 1686
Dur. Wor.

G1945 Grew, Nehemiah, 1682
Cant. Carl. Ex. Glo. Lich.
Wel.

G1946 Grew, Nehemiah, 1672
Carl.

G1948 Grew, Nehemiah, 1675
Yk.

G1952 Grew, Nehemiah, 1681
Cant (2). Dur. Ely. Glo. Lich.
New. S Pl (tpw). Wel. Wor. Yk
(2).

G1955? Grew, Nehemiah, 1694
For Hugh Newman.
Wel.

G1967 Grew, Obadiah, 1698
S Dv.

G1971 Grey, Thomas, *M.A.*, 1685
Cant (cropped). Wor.

G1975 Grey, William, 1649
'Tine'
Chelm.

G1979 Grievances, 1689
Wel.

G1981B Griffin, Lewis, [1661]
Ches.

G1983 Griffin, Lewis, 1663
Linc.

G1985 Griffin, William, 1642
Linc.

G1988 Griffith, Alexander, 1654
Yk.

G1989 Griffith, Alexander, 1654
Carl. Pet.

G1995 Griffith, Evan, 1677
Her.

G1997 Griffith, George, 1685
8°.
Ban.

G2004 Griffith, John, 1663
Pet.

G2010 Griffith, Matthew, 1661
Pet (tp imp).

G2011 Griffith, Matthew, 1661
S Pl.

G2012 Griffith, Matthew, 1660
Win.

G2013 Griffith, Matthew, [1647]
'... 1641 to ... 1647'
Linc.

G2015 Griffith, Matthew, 1665
Pet. Yk.

G2016 Griffith, Matthew, 1642
'persvvasion'
Cant. Linc. Pet. S Pl. Yk (2 —
1 tpw*).

G2017 Griffith, Matthew, 1643
Cant (imp). Linc. Pet. Yk.

G2020 Griffyth, John, 1693
Ex. Wor.

G2024 Grighor, Abu al-Faraj, 1663
'dynastiarum'
Cant (imp). Dur. Ely (imp?).
Ex (2). S Pl. Sal. Win. Yk.

G2025 Grighor, Abu al-Faraj, 1650
Cant. Carl. Ely. Ex. Sal. Wel.

G2026 Grimalkin, 1681
Ches.

G2028 Grimston, *Sir* Harbottle,
1641
Dur ('orders concerning'). Linc
('orders newly made in Parliament
concerning'). Pet (as Linc).

G2032 Grimston, *Sir* Harbottle,
1642
Linc.

G2033 Grimston, *Sir* Harbottle,
1642
Cant (2).

G2036 Grimston, *Sir* Harbottle,
1642
Cant.

G2037 Grimston, *Sir* Harbottle,
1641
Cant. Linc. Nor. Pet.

G2039 Grimston, *Sir* Harbottle,
1642
Cant. Dur. Ex. Linc. Yk.

G2040 Grimston, *Sir* Harbottle,
1660
Yk.

G2043 Grimston, *Sir* Harbottle,
1660
Yk.

G2045 Grimston, *Sir* Harbottle,
1660
Lich.

G2051 Grimston, *Sir* Harbottle,
1641
Cant. Dur.

G2060 Groeneveldt, Jan, 1698
Ex.

G2062 Groeneveldt, Jan, 1687
Ex.

G2067 Groot, William, 1673
Cantabrigiae ...
Ely. Ex.

G2074 Grosse, Alexander, 1649
For John Bartlet.
Cant (imp?).

G2076 Grosse, Alexander, 1647
Yk.

G2077 Grosse, Alexander, 1632
[*i.e.* 1642]
Yk.

G2079 Grosseteste, Robert, 1658
Linc. S Pl.

G2081 Grotius, Hugo, 1679
Ban. Cant. Chelm. Ches. Chi.
Dur. Ely. Ex. Lich. Pet. Roch.
S Asa. S Pl (2). Swel. Wel (vol.
3 only). Win. Wor. Yk.

G2083 Grotius, Hugo, 1683
Yk.

G2087 Grotius, Hugo, 1650
Cant.

G2091 Grotius, Hugo, 1668
Ches.

G2092 Grotius, Hugo, 1682
S Pl.

G2096 Grotius, Hugo, 1685
Dur. Ex. Yk.

G2102 Grotius, Hugo, 1660
Yk.

G2104 Grotius, Hugo, 1675
Oxoniae ...
Yk.

G2105 Grotius, Hugo, 1700
Yk.

G2110 Grotius, Hugo, 1668
Ches.

G2111 Grotius, Hugo, 1682
S Pl.

G2112 Grotius, Hugo, 1658
The third edition; For W. Lee.
Cant (imp).

G2115 Grotius, Hugo, 1658
Cant (imp).

G2116 Grotius, Hugo, 1694
Cant.

G2117 Grotius, Hugo, 1651
Ban (several corrected proof
sheets only). Glo. Lich. Sal.

G2124 Grotius, Hugo, 1689
Ban. Carl. S Asa. Wel.

G2126 Grotius, Hugo, 1682
Bris. Cant. Ex.

G2128 Grotius, Hugo, 1680
Pet.

G2129 Grotius, Hugo, 1683
Ban. Ex.

G2130 Grotius, Hugo, 1689
Bur (Coddenham Parish Lib.
deposited here). Ely. S Alb.

G2131 Grotius, Hugo, 1694
Glo.

G2131A Grotius, Hugo, 1700
Cant (2). New.

G2132? Grotius, Hugo, 1652
As G2109, but: 'Two discourses'; 16°.
Pet.

G2134 Grounds, 1643
Pet.

G2135 Grounds, 1698
S Asa.

G2145 Grounds, 1679
Cant. Linc. Sal.

G2147 Grove, Robert, 1687
Ban. S Pl.

G2148 Grove, Robert, 1685
Cant.

G2150 Grove, Robert, 1682
Chi.

G2150B Grove, Robert, [1697]
S Pl.

G2152 Grove, Robert, 1682/3
Cant. S Pl.

G2154 Grove, Robert, 1695
Cant. Dur. S Asa.

G2155 Grove, Robert, 1689
Ban. Carl. Nor. Roch.

G2157 Grove, Robert, 1680
Carl. Chi. Dur. Ely. Win
(imp).

G2158 Grove, Robert, 1685
Ban. Cant.

G2159 Grove, Robert, 1690
Cant. Her.

G2160 Grove, Robert, 1681
Cant. Dur. Ely. Nor. Yk.

G2161 Grove, Robert, 1676
Carl (2). Chelm. Yk.

G2162A Groves, Robert, 1651
Cant (imp).

G2164 Grumbletonian, 1689
S Pl.

G2166 Gualdo Priorato, Galeazzo,
1676
Wel.

G2167 Gualdo Priorato, Galeazzo,
1648
Cant (imp). Ex. Pet. Wel. Wor
(tpw).

G2171 Gualdo Priorato, Galeazzo,
1658
Carl.

G2174 Guarini, Giovanni Battista,
1647
Carl.

G2175 Guarini, Giovanni Battista,
1648
Linc.

G2176 Guarini, Giovanni Battista,
1664
Nor.

G2182 Guevara, Antonio de, 1697
Yk.

G2184D Guide, 1682
Cant.

G2191 Guidott, Thomas, 1691
Her.

G2191A Guidott, Thomas, 1691
Wel.

G2204 Guild, William, 1641
Linc. Yk (pt 3 only).

G2206 Guild, William, 1658
Wor.

G2211 Guild, William, 1656
Chelm.

G2212 Guild, William, 1659
Ex.

G2213? Guilelmus Arvernus, 1674
Aureliae, ex typographia F. Hotot. Et
vaeneunt Londini, apud Robertum
Scott.
Win.

G2215 Guilford, Francis North,
Baron, 1680
Ches. Ely. Glo. Linc. Win.
Yk.

G2219 Guillim, John, 1660
Lich. Yk.

G2219A Guillim, John, 1660
The fourth edition.
Bris. Nor. Yk.

G2222 Guillim, John, 1679
The fifth edition.
Ex. Linc. Wel.

G2226 Guise, Henri, *Duc de*, 1669
Carl.

G2230 Gumble, Thomas, 1671
Chelm. Linc. Win. Yk.

G2234 Gunning, Peter, 1658
Carl. Ex. S Pl.

G2236 Gunning, Peter, 1662
Cant. Carl. Ex. Lich. Linc.
S Asa. S Pl. Sal. Wel. Win.
Wor.

G2236A Gunning, Peter, 1681
S Pl.

G2239+ Gunter, Edmund, 1653
The third edition; [N.pl.], for Fr:
Eglesfeild; 4°.
Wor. Yk.

G2241 Gunter, Edmund, 1673
Glo.

G2245 Gunton, Simon, 1657
Ex (2). Pet.

G2246 Gunton, Simon, 1686
Dur. Ely. Pet (3). Wor. Yk.

G2248 Gunton, Simon, 1661
Ex.

G2251 Gurnall, William, 1655
Ex.

G2252 Gurnall, William, 1656
S Asa.

G2252A Gurnall, William, 1658
Nor. S Pl.

G2253 Gurnall, William, 1658
Ex. Nor. S Asa. S Pl. Yk.

G2254 Gurnall, William, 1659
Chelm.

G2255 Gurnall, William, 1662
Nor. S Asa. S Pl.

G2258 Gurnall, William, 1672
Pet.

G2260 Gurnay, Edmund, 1660
12°.
Dur (tpw).

G2261 Gurney, *Sir* Richard, [1642]
Dur. Linc.

H4 H., A., 1642
Linc.

H17 H., C., 1660
Linc (imp).

H18 H., D., [1643]
Yk.

H19- H., E., 1662
See: CLC53.
Win.

H24 H., E., 1646
Yk.

H24A H., E., 1657
Ex.

H26 H., G., [1642]
Linc.

H30? H., G., 1669
For William Birch.
Carl.

H33 H., G., [1642]
Linc.

H39 H., H., 1659
Carl. Dur.

H45A H., I., [1643]
Yk.

H47 H., I., 1642
Linc.

H73A H., J., 1641
Dur. Sal.

H74A H., J., 1611 [*i.e.* 1661]
Cant. Linc.

H77C H., J., 1667
Carl. Sal.

H78 H., J., 1642
Sal (tp imp).

H82B H., J., 1671
S Asa.

H83 H., J., 1663
Pet.

H85? H., J., 1675
'worshippers'
S Asa.

H104 H., P., 1642
Yk.

H106 H., R., 1647
Yk.

H124A H., S., 1643
Yk.

H135 H., T., 1670
S Pl.

H138 H., T., 1642
Ex.

H154 H., W., 1642
Linc.

H157 H., W., 1645
Pet.

H162 Haak, Theodore, 1657
Cant (imp). Carl. Ex. Glo. Rip.

H166 Habington, William, 1641
Cant (imp).

H169 Hacket, John, 1675
Cant. Ches. Chi. Ely. Ex. Her.
Lich. Pet. S Pl. Sal. Swel.
Win. Yk (3 — 1 imp).

H170 Hacket, John, 1648
Linc. Pet.

H171 Hacket, John, 1693
Cant (2 — 1 imp). Carl. Ches.
Chi (2). Dur. Linc. Liv. Pet.
S Asa (imp). Swel. Wel. Yk.

H172 Hacket, John, 1660
Cant. Her (imp). Lich. Pet (2).
Wor.

H173 Hackett, Thomas, 1662
Pet. S Asa. Win.

H175 Hackluyt, John, 1647
Pet.

H176A+ Hacon, Joseph, 1668
Impr. as H176A; 8°.
Ely.

H177 Hacon, Joseph, 1660
Pet.

H178 Hacon, Joseph, 1662
Pet (2).

H188 Haggar, Henry, 1654
Pet.

H202 Haines, Richard, 1678
Linc.

H205 Haines, Richard, 1677
Carl. Win.

H208 Hakewill, George, 1641
Linc. Yk.

H209 Hakewill, George, 1641
Cant.

H210 Hakewill, William, 1641
Liv. Pet. Yk.

H215 Hakewill, William, 1659
Sal.

H216? Hakewill, William, 1660
12°.
Sal.

H217 Hakewill, William, 1671
Chi. Dur (cropped). Ex. S Pl.

H218 Hakewill, William, 1641
Linc.

H225+ Hale, *Sir* Matthew, 1676
By William Godbid, for William
Shrowsbury; 8°.
Carl. Win.

H225A Hale, *Sir* Matthew, 1677
Ban. Linc.

H226 Hale, *Sir* Matthew, 1679
Wel. Yk.

H227A Hale, *Sir* Matthew, 1682
2 pts.
Swar.

H228 Hale, *Sir* Matthew, 1685
Chi. S Asa.

H229 Hale, *Sir* Matthew, 1689
Ely.

H230 Hale, *Sir* Matthew, 1695
Linc. S Dv.

H231 Hale, *Sir* Matthew, 1699
Cant. Lich.

H232 Hale, *Sir* Matthew, 1676
Carl. Yk (2 states).

H232+ Hale, *Sir* Matthew, 1676
Impr. as H225; 8°.
Ban.

H235+ Hale, *Sir* Matthew, 1696
For William Shrowsbury; 8°.
Linc.

H235A Hale, *Sir* Matthew, 1700
Ban.

H238 Hale, *Sir* Matthew, 1674
Carl. Linc.

H240 Hale, *Sir* Matthew, 1688
Linc.

H241 Hale, *Sir* Matthew, 1683
Carl.

H244 Hale, *Sir* Matthew, 1673
Linc. Pet.

H247 Hale, *Sir* Matthew, 1684
Bris. Carl. Lich. Yk.

H250 Hale, *Sir* Matthew, 1695
Chi.

H252 Hale, *Sir* Matthew, 1677
Carl.

H257 Hale, *Sir* Matthew, 1694
Glo. Linc. Yk.

H258 Hale, *Sir* Matthew, 1677
Chi (2). Dur. Ely. Ex. Her.
Lich (2). Linc. Pet. Win.

H267 Hales, *Sir* Edward, 1641
Dur.

H268A Hales, John, 1677
S Asa.

H269 Hales, John, 1659
Bur. Cant (2). Carl. Glo. Linc.
S Asa. Win.

H271 Hales, John, 1673
Bur. Cant (imp). Ches. Dur.
Ely. Her. Lich (engr. tpw). Linc.
Pet. Rip. S Pl.

H272 Hales, John, 1688
Cant (tpw). Ches (2). Chi. Ex.
Nor. Sal (engr. tpw). Yk.

H275 Hales, John, 1673
Carl. Ely. Her. S Asa. Wor.

H276A Hales, John, 1677
Chi. Dur.

H277 Hales, John, 1642
Ex. Linc. Wel.

H278 Hales, John, 1642
Cant. Carl.

H279 Hales, John, 1700
8°.
Ex. Sal.

H280 Hales, John, 1677
Ches. Dur. Nor.

H281 Hales, John, 1641
Cant. Ex. Pet.

H291 Halifax, George Savile,
Marquis of, [1688]
Ban. Cant (cropped). Carl. Ex.

H296 Halifax, George Savile,
Marquis of, 1688
Cant. Wel. Yk.

H297 Halifax, George Savile,
Marquis of, 1689
Ban. Bris.

H298 Halifax, George Savile,
Marquis of, 1689
Cant.

H310 *See*: W122A+

H311 Halifax, George Savile,
Marquis of, [1687]
S Asa.

H313 Halifax, George Savile,
Marquis of, 1687
Cant. S Asa.

H315? Halifax, George Savile,
Marquis of, 1700
Gilliflower.
Ex.

H316 Halifax, George Savile,
Marquis of, 1681
Ches.

H317 Halifax, George Savile,
Marquis of, 1681
Wor.

H320 Halifax, George Savile,
Marquis of, 1681
Dur (18p.). Ex (20p.).

H334 Hall, Francis, 1661
Sal.

H335 Hall, George, 1666
Cant. Ches. Pet. S Asa.

H336? Hall, George, 1655
31p.
Carl. Ches. Ex. Pet. Wor*.
Yk.

H336+ Hall, George, 1655
As H336, but: 28p.
Cant.

H337 Hall, George, 1655
Carl. Ches (2).

H338? Hall, George, 1667
Mortlock.
Ban. Carl. Chelm. Ches. S Asa.
Win.

H339 Hall, George, 1641
Pet.

H340 Hall, Henry, 1644
Cant. Carl. Pet (3).

H343 Hall, John, *Poet*, 1694
Sal.

H346 Hall, John, *Poet*, 1650
Carl.

H349 Hall, John, *Poet*, 1646
Yk.

H350 Hall, John, *Poet*, 1649
Chelm.

H356 Hall, John, *Physician*, 1657
Cant (imp).

H359A? Hall, John, *of Gray's Inn*,
1649
'Mr. William Prynne'
Ex.

H360 Hall, John, *of Richmond*,
1654
Ex. Sal.

H361 Hall, John, *of Richmond*,
1656
Carl. Yk.

H361B Hall, Joseph, 1647
Carl. Dur. Ely. Win.

H362 Hall, Joseph, 1647
Bur. Cant (imp). Lich (imp).
Linc.

H362bA+ Hall, Joseph, 1647
By M. Flesher for Ph. Stephens; 2°.
S Pl.

H373 Hall, Joseph, 1649 [*i.e.* 1659]
Carl.

H375 Hall, Joseph, 1661
Dur. Her. Linc. Nor.

H376 Hall, Joseph, 1679
Cant. Yk.

H378 Hall, Joseph, 1641
Ban (200p.). Cant (frag.). Dur
(200p.). Ex. Her. Win (188p.).

H380 Hall, Joseph, 1650
Ely. Ex.

H381 Hall, Joseph, 1662
Cant (imp). Carl. Chelm. Dur.
Ex. Her. Linc (imp). Nor. S Pl.
Win.

H383 Hall, Joseph, 1652
Cant. Ex. Sal.

H384 Hall, Joseph, 1659
S Asa.

H386A Hall, Joseph, 1654
Pet.

H386A+ Hall, Joseph, 1640[1]
'An humble remonstrance'; =STC
12675.
Ex (3). Yk.

H386A++ Hall, Joseph, 1640[1]
'An humble remonstrance'; =STC
12676.
Carl. Win.

H388 Hall, Joseph, 1643
Yk.

H390 Hall, Joseph, 1642
Ex (2). Yk.

H391 Hall, Joseph, 1642
Pet (imp). S Pl.

H392 Hall, Joseph, 1641
Linc.

H393 Hall, Joseph, 1642
Ex. Linc.

H394 Hall, Joseph, 1644
Cant. Carl.

H401 Hall, Joseph, 1647
Cant.

H403+ Hall, Joseph, 1646
Impr. as H403; 12°.
S Asa.

H407 Hall, Joseph, 1650
Ban. Linc.

H410 Hall, Joseph, 1650
Dur. Pet.

H411 Hall, Joseph, 1674
Linc.

H416 Hall, Joseph, 1660
Bur (2). Cant. Carl. Ely. Nor
(2). Yk.

H417 Hall, Joseph, 1641
Ban. Ex (2). Win.

H418 Hall, Joseph, 1641
Linc. Sal.

H421 Hall, Joseph, 1659
S Asa (tpw, possibly H421A).

H422 Hall, Joseph, 1646
S Asa (frag.).

H423 Hall, Ralph, 1656
Yk.

H432 Hall, Thomas, 1652
Chelm. Ex. S Pl. Win.

H436 Hall, Thomas, 1658
Ex.

H437 Hall, Thomas, 1651
Ex. Liv (tp imp)*. Pet.

H438 Hall, Thomas, 1651
Ely. Ex. Yk.

H443 Hall, Timothy, 1684
Her.

H444 Hall, Timothy, 1689
Ban. Her.

H446 Hall, William, *fl. 1642*, 1642
Ex. Linc. S Asa. Yk.

H447 Hall, William, *Chaplain*, 1686
Carl.

H454 Halley, George, 1689
Dur (imp). Yk (3 − 1 tpw).

H455 Halley, George, 1691
Yk (2).

H455A Halley, George, 1691
Yk.

H455B? Halley, George, 1695
'Novemb.'
Her. Yk.

H456 Halley, George, 1698
London, printed ...
Yk (2).

H459 Hallywell, Henry, 1694
S Pl.

H460 Hallywell, Henry, 1668
Carl. Dur.

H461 Hallywell, Henry, 1671
Ban.

H465 Hallywell, Henry, 1667
Ban.

H482 Hamilton, James, *1st Duke of
Hamilton*, 1649
Pet. Yk (2).

H484 Hamilton, James, *1st Duke of
Hamilton*, 1641
Cant.

H485 Hamilton, James, *1st Duke of
Hamilton*, 1649
Date in colophon.
Linc.

H489 Hamilton, William, *Gent.*,
1660
Carl.

H498 Hammond, Charles, 1664
Win.

H506 Hammond, Henry, 1674
Bur (2). Carl. Dur. Glo. Her.
IoM. Lich (2). S Dv. Sal. Wor.
Yk.

H507 Hammond, Henry, 1684
Ban. Cant. Chi. Dur. Ely. Ex.
Glo. Her. Nor. Pet. S Asa.
S Dv. Sal. Tru. Wel. Wor. Yk.

H508 Hammond, Henry, 1684
Vol. 2 = H509; Vol. 3 = H573A,
H574, H575, H576, H576+, or H577;
Vol. 4 = H507.
Ban. Cant. Chi. Dur. Ely. Ex.
Her. Linc. Llan. Nor. Pet.
S Asa. Sal. Swel. Tru. Wel.

H509 Hammond, Henry, 1684
Ban. Cant. Chi. Dur. Ely. Ex.
Glo. Her. Linc. Llan. Nor. Pet.
S Asa. Sal. Swel. Tru. Wel.
Wor. Yk.

H510 Hammond, Henry, 1655
Carl. Sal. Yk.

H511 Hammond, Henry, 1655
Dur. Glo.

H512A Hammond, Henry, 1660
Yk.

H514 Hammond, Henry, 1654
Carl. Ches. Dur. Glo. Sal (2).
Yk.

H515 Hammond, Henry, 1665
Cant. Yk.

H515A Hammond, Henry, 1655
Dur. Ex. Glo. S Asa. Yk.

H516 Hammond, Henry, 1655
Carl. S Asa. Sal.

H518 Hammond, Henry, 1648
Sal.

H519 Hammond, Henry, 1660
Ban. Dur. S Pl.

H519A Hammond, Henry, 1660
Carl. Yk.

H520 Hammond, Henry, 1649
First ed. not on tp.
Carl. Pet (2). Sal (2).

H521 Hammond, Henry, 1652
Dur. Ely. S Asa. Yk.

H522 Hammond, Henry, 1664
Llan.

H523 Hammond, Henry, 1657
Sal.

H524 Hammond, Henry, 1657
Yk.

H524A Hammond, Henry, 1657
Ches.

H524B Hammond, Henry, 1657
Yk.

H525 Hammond, Henry, 1644[5]
Carl.

H526 Hammond, Henry, 1644[5]
Dur.

H526+ Hammond, Henry, 1644[5]
[N.pl.]; 4°; 13p.; Not in Madan.
Cant. Carl. Liv. Pet. Sal. Yk.

H527 Hammond, Henry, 1646
Cant. Ches. Ely. Liv. Yk.

H528 Hammond, Henry, 1682
Ex.

H529 Hammond, Henry, 1657
Carl. Ches. Glo. Sal. Yk (2).

H530 Hammond, Henry, 1647
Linc. Pet.

H530+ Hammond, Henry, 1647
By R. Cotes for Richard Royston, to
be sold by Edward Martin in
Norwich; 4°.
Sal.

H531 Hammond, Henry, 1650
Dur. Ely. Yk.

H533? Hammond, Henry, 1661
With 2nd tp as H533B.
Carl. Nor. Yk.

H533A Hammond, Henry, [1661?]
Linc. S Pl. Sal. Win. Wor.

H534 Hammond, Henry, 1656
Cant. Carl. Ex. Lich. S Asa.
Yk.

H536 Hammond, Henry, 1656
Dur. Glo. Sal. Yk.

H537+ Hammond, Henry, 1659
For Richard Royston; 4°.
Carl. Dur. Yk.

H538 Hammond, Henry, 1651[2]
Glo. S Pl (2 − 1 imp). Yk (imp).

H539 Hammond, Henry, 1651[2]
Cant. Chi. Dur. Linc. Sal (2).
Yk (imp).

H540 Hammond, Henry, 1656
Glo. Yk (2).

H541 Hammond, Henry, 1657
Glo. Yk (2).

H544 Hammond, Henry, 1646
Chelm. Ely. Lich. Yk.

H545 Hammond, Henry, 1653
Dur. Pet. S Pl. Sal.

H545A Hammond, Henry, 1653
Linc.

H546 Hammond, Henry, 1649
Yk.

H547 Hammond, Henry, 1645
Cant.

H548 Hammond, Henry, 1644[5]
Bur (tpw). Yk.

H549 Hammond, Henry, 1645
Cant.

H550 Hammond, Henry, 1645
Cant. Chelm. Ely. Liv. Yk.

H552 Hammond, Henry, 1650
Dur. S Asa. Yk.

H553 Hammond, Henry, 1647
Chelm. Sal.

H554 Hammond, Henry, 1654
Cant. Carl. Dur. S Pl. Yk.

H555 Hammond, Henry, 1646
Cant (2).

H555A Hammond, Henry, 1646
Cant. Ely*. Liv. Yk.

H556 Hammond, Henry, 1643
Sal.

H557 Hammond, Henry, 1644
Cant. Chelm. Ches. Ely. S Pl
(2 − 1 imp). Yk.

H557A Hammond, Henry, 1644
Cant (2). Liv. Yk.

H559 Hammond, Henry, 1647
Carl. Dur. Linc. Liv. Pet (2).
S Asa. Sal. Yk.

H560 Hammond, Henry, 1644
Cant.

H562A Hammond, Henry, 1653
Sal.

H563 Hammond, Henry, 1654
Dur. Lich. Pet. Yk.

H564 Hammond, Henry, 1645
Cant (2).

H566 Hammond, Henry, 1645
Cant.

H567 Hammond, Henry, 1647
Bur. Carl. Dur. Linc. Pet.
S Pl. Sal. Win.

H569 Hammond, Henry, 1651
Ely. Yk.

H570A Hammond, Henry, 1650
12°.
Cant. Linc. Nor.

H570B Hammond, Henry, 1650
Dur. Ely. S Asa. Yk.

H571 Hammond, Henry, 1644
Cant.

H572 Hammond, Henry, 1656
Cant. Lich. S Pl. Sal.

H573 Hammond, Henry, 1653
Bur. Cant (2). Ches. Lich.
Llan. Pet.

H573A Hammond, Henry, 1659
Ban. Bur (2). Cant. Ches. Dur.
Her (imp)*. Llan. S Dv*. Sal.
Tru. Wor*. Yk.

H573B Hammond, Henry, 1659
The second edition.
Carl. Glo. IoM.

H574 Hammond, Henry, 1671
Linc. S Asa. Win. Yk.

H574A Hammond, Henry, 1671
The third edition.
Her.

H575 Hammond, Henry, 1675
Bur (= Wing's St James' Parish).

H575A Hammond, Henry, 1675
The fourth edition.
S Asa.

H576 Hammond, Henry, 1681
Bur. Dur. Her. Nor. Pet.

H576+ Hammond, Henry, 1681
The fifth edition; By J. Macock and
M. Flesher, for Richard Royston; 2°.
Glo. Wor.

H577 Hammond, Henry, 1689
Chi. Her. IoM. Sal. Swel.
Wel. Yk.

H578A Hammond, Henry, 1659
Cant. Carl. Ches (2). Chi. Glo.
Her. Lich. New. S Pl. Sal.
Win. Yk.

H579 Hammond, Henry, 1659
Her.

H579A Hammond, Henry, 1659
Bur. Dur (imp). Linc.

H580 Hammond, Henry, 1683
Llan. Swel.

H582 Hammond, Henry, 1646
Cant. Chelm. Ely. Yk.

H583 Hammond, Henry, 1646
Cant. Lich. Liv (tp imp).

H583+ Hammond, Henry, [1646?]
Last gathering differs from H583;
208p.
S Asa (tpw).

H583A Hammond, Henry, 1648
S Pl.

H584 Hammond, Henry, 1649
Dur. Sal.

H585 Hammond, Henry, 1652
Dur.

H587 Hammond, Henry, 1662
Ely.

H589 Hammond, Henry, 1668
Ban. S Asa.

H590 Hammond, Henry, 1670
Ban. New. Yk.

H593 Hammond, Henry, 1683
Ely.

H595 Hammond, Henry, 1691
New. S Dv. Yk.

H596 Hammond, Henry, 1700
Chi. Rip.

H597 Hammond, Henry, 1660
Carl.

H598 Hammond, Henry, 1654
Carl. Dur. Glo. S Pl. Sal. Yk.

H599 Hammond, Henry, 1655
Dur. Yk.

H599A Hammond, Henry, 1655
Carl. Ches. Glo. S Pl. Sal (2).

H600 Hammond, Henry, 1664
Carl. Ex. New. Win.

H601 Hammond, Henry, 1675
Her (tpw). Pet. S Asa.

H602 Hammond, Henry, 1664
Ex. New.

H603- Hammond, Henry, 1646
As H603, but only 7 tracts listed on tp.
Cant. Lich. Sal.

H603 Hammond, Henry, 1646
11 tracts listed on tp.
Ely (tpw). Liv (tpw). Yk.

H604 Hammond, Henry, 1656
Dur.

H605 Hammond, Henry, 1657
Ban. Cant. Carl. Ches. Lich.
S Asa. Yk.

H606 Hammond, Henry, 1649
Carl. Dur. Ely. Pet (2). Yk.

H607 Hammond, Henry, 1649
Sal. Wel (imp)*. Yk (2).

H608 Hammond, Henry, 1645
Cant.

H609 Hammond, Henry, 1646
Cant. Carl. Chelm. Ely. Liv.
Pet. S Pl. Sal. Yk.

H610 Hammond, Henry, 1650
Dur. Ely. Pet. Yk.

H611 Hammond, Henry, [1650]
Dur. Ely. Yk.

H612 Hammond, Henry, 1645
Pet (2 - 1 tp imp). Win. Yk.

H613 Hammond, Henry, 1646
Lich. Linc. Win.

H614 Hammond, Henry, 1646
Cant. Chelm. Ches. Dur. Ely.
Liv. S Pl. Yk (3 - 2 imp).

H614B? Hammond, Henry, 1646
The third edition; ... by Henry Hall.
Carl. Liv. Pet (2). S Pl. Sal.
Win. Yk.

H615 Hammond, Henry, 1649
Pet. Sal.

H616 Hammond, Henry, 1650
Carl. Dur. Ely. Yk.

H618 Hammond, Henry, 1654
Carl. Ches. Dur. Ex. Glo.
S Pl (2). Sal (2). Yk.

H625A Hammond, Thomas, 1690
Yk.

H628 Hampden, John, 1641[2]
Cant.

H630 Hampden, John, 1641
Yk.

H634 Hampton, William, 1661
'Lacrymae'
Win.

H635 Hampton, William, 1667
Wor.

H637 Hanbury, Nathaniel, 1683
Ex. Yk.

H638? Hanbury, Nathaniel, 1691
... Edvardum Hall.
Yk.

H642 Hancock, John, 1699
Nor.

H643 Hancock, Robert, 1682
Pet.

H646 Hancocke, Thomas, 1696
Ely.

H648 Hanger, Philip, 1675
Linc.

H652 Hanmer, Jonathan, 1677
Cant. Ches. Ex. S Pl.

H653 Hanmer, Jonathan, 1657
S Pl.

H654 Hanmer, Jonathan, 1658
Ban. Chelm. S Pl. Yk.

H658 Hannes, Edward, 1688
Ex. Wel.

H662 Hansley, John, 1662
S Asa.

H667 Happy, 1641
Linc.

H687 Harby, Thomas, 1673
Win.

H687A Harby, Thomas, 1674
Ely.

H687B Harby, Thomas, 1675
Linc (with a part printed, part
MS list of subscribers: 'The copy
of a list contracted').

H688 Harby, Thomas, 1678
Ches. Her. Yk (imp).

H695 Harcourt, *Sir* Simon, 1641
Dur.

H696 Harcourt, William, [1679]
Linc.

H698 Hardcastle, Peter, 1671
Yk.

H699A Hardcastle, Thomas, 1665
Yk (imp).

H702 Hardres, Peter, 1647
Carl. Yk (2).

H704 Hardwick, Humphrey, 1644
Cant (imp). Pet. Yk.

H709 Hardy, Nathaniel, 1647
Nor. Pet.

H710 Hardy, Nathaniel, 1647
Cant (imp). Ex. Pet.

H711 Hardy, Nathaniel, 1657
Chelm.

H712 Hardy, Nathaniel, 1659
Chelm (2).

H713 Hardy, Nathaniel, 1660
Carl.

H714 Hardy, Nathaniel, 1654
Chelm.

H715 Hardy, Nathaniel, 1649
Her. Pet.

H717 Hardy, Nathaniel, 1660
Chelm. Linc.

H718 Hardy, Nathaniel, 1653
Pet.

H719 Hardy, Nathaniel, 1659
Chelm.

H720 Hardy, Nathaniel, 1655
Chelm. Yk.

H721 Hardy, Nathaniel, 1648
Chelm. Ex. Her. Pet. Wor.

H721A Hardy, Nathaniel, 1658
... Nathanael Webb ...
Chelm.

H722 Hardy, Nathaniel, 1656
Chelm. Sal.

H723 Hardy, Nathaniel, 1659
Chelm. Her. Sal.

H725 Hardy, Nathaniel, 1647
Nor. S Pl.

H726 Hardy, Nathaniel, 1648
Ex.

H727 Hardy, Nathaniel, 1656
Chelm. S Pl.

H728 Hardy, Nathaniel, 1666
Carl. Ex. Pet. S Pl. Win.

H729 Hardy, Nathaniel, 1659
4°.
Chelm.

H730 Hardy, Nathaniel, 1662
Ex. Pet.

H733 Hardy, Nathaniel, 1658
Chelm.

H735 Hardy, Nathaniel, 1659
Chelm (2).

H736 Hardy, Nathaniel, 1653
Chelm.

H737 Hardy, Nathaniel, 1658
Chelm. Pet. S Pl (imp).

H738 Hardy, Nathaniel, 1659
Chelm (2).

H740 Hardy, Nathaniel, 1658
Chelm (2).

H742 Hardy, Nathaniel, 1668
Carl.

H743+ Hardy, Nathaniel, 1658
As H743, but: 4°.
Chelm. New.

H745 Hardy, Nathaniel, 1649
Wor.

H746 Hardy, Nathaniel, 1653
Chelm.

H747 Hardy, Nathaniel, 1656
Chelm. Wor.

H747A Hardy, Nathaniel, 1658
Lich.

H749 Hardy, Nathaniel, 1654
Chelm.

H751 Hardy, Nathaniel, 1653
Chelm.

H752 Hardy, Nathaniel, 1656
4°.
Chelm.

H753 Hardy, Nathaniel, 1656
Chelm.

H760 Hare, Hugh, 1692
Dur.

H761 Hare, Hugh, 1696
Nor.

H768 Harford, Rapha, 1649
Printed (to save transcribing) for R.H.
Yk.

H770 Harington, *Sir* John, 1653
Ex. Linc. Yk.

H776 Harlay-Chanvallon, François
de, 1696
... and Will. Keblewhite.
Yk.

H781 Harmar, John, 1649
Ex.

H784 Harmar, John, 1658
Pet.

H792A Harmar, John, [1660]
'... in honorem Caroli II.'; Date not
on tp.
Win.

H794 Harmar, John, 1654
Linc.

H799 Harmar, Samuel, 1642
Linc.

H800A Harmonious, 1648
Sal.

H803E Harrington, *Sir* James, 1682
Ex.

H805 Harrington, James, *the Elder*,
1659
Pet.

H806 Harrington, James, *the Elder*,
1659
Carl. Pet.

H806A Harrington, James, *the
Elder*, [1680]
Dur.

H809 Harrington, James, *the Elder*,
1656
Ex. Lich. Pet. Wel. Yk.

H813 Harrington, James, *the Elder*,
[1659]
Ex.

H819 Harrington, James, *the Elder*,
1659
Ex.

H820 Harrington, James, *the Elder*,
1658
Ex.

H821 Harrington, James, *the Elder*,
1660
Yk.

H826 Harrington, James, *the
Younger*, 1690
Carl. S Pl. Sal.

H827? Harrington, James, *the
Younger*, 1690
Theater.
Cant.

H830 Harrington, James, *the
Younger*, 1691
Wor (imp).

H834 Harrington, James, *the Younger*, 1688
Ex (2). Lich. Sal. Wel.

H846 Harris, John, 1698
Cant. S Asa. S Pl (2). Wel.

H847 Harris, John, 1698
Dated 1698.
Cant. S Asa. S Pl (2). Wel.

H850 Harris, John, 1698
Cant. Her. S Asa. S Pl (2).
Wel.

H852 Harris, John, 1698
Cant. S Asa. S Pl (2). Wel.

H853 Harris, John, 1698
Cant. S Asa. S Pl (2). Wel.

H854 Harris, John, 1698
Cant. S Asa. S Pl (2). Wel.

H855 Harris, John, 1698
Cant. S Asa. S Pl (2). Wel.

H856 Harris, John, 1697
Cant.

H868 Harris, Robert, 1654
Sal.

H869 Harris, Robert, 1641
Carl. Ex. Pet.

H872 Harris, Robert, 1641
Carl. Ex (2). Pet.

H875 Harris, Robert, 1642
Dur. Ex (2). Pet.

H876 Harris, Robert, 1654
Carl.

H878 Harris, Robert, 1645
Carl. Ex.

H879 Harris, Robert, 1648
Linc.

H880 Harris, Walter, 1689
Ex.

H884 Harris, Walter, 1679
Cant (2). Carl. Nor. S Pl. Wel.

H889 Harrison, Edward, *of Keensworth*, 1649
Pet.

H892 Harrison, Henry, 1692
Sal.

H893A Harrison, Henry, 1681
Ely.

H894 Harrison, John, 1649
Ex.

H895 Harrison, John, 1683
Win.

H896 Harrison, John, 1656
Pet.

H899 Harrison, Joseph, 1698
... in Cirencester.
Dur.

H907 Harrison, Richard, 1644
Not cap.
Sal.

H914 Harrison, Thomas, *of St Dunstan*, 1655
Chelm.

H916 Harrison, Thomas, *of St Dunstan*, 1659
Ex. Yk (tp imp).

H917C Harrison, Thomas, *Publisher*, 1690
Nor.

H923 Harst, ? de, 1656
8°.
Carl.

H951A Hart, John, 1652
Carl.

H953 Hart, John, 1656
The third edition.
New.

H959C+ Hart, John, [c.1686?]
The fifty-ninth edition; By W.O.; 8°.
Yk.

H965 Hartcliffe, John, 1685
Carl. Dur. Ex (3). Nor. Sal.
Swel.

H969 Hartcliffe, John, 1694
Cant.

H970 Hartcliffe, John, 1695
Ban. Cant. Yk.

H971 Hartcliffe, John, 1691
Ches.

H973 Hartley, John, 1699
Carl. Lich. Wor.

H974 Hartley, William, 1650
Cant.

H975 Hartley, William, 1651
Cant.

H979A Hartlib, Samuel, 1651
Cant. Yk.

H986 Hartlib, Samuel, 1643
Linc.

H991 Hartlib, Samuel, 1655
Carl.

H1002 Hartlib, Samuel, 1654
Cant.

H1043 Harvey, Christopher, 1661
Dur.

H1046 Harvey, Christopher, 1657
Wel.

H1048 Harvey, Christopher, 1667
Cant.

H1049 Harvey, Christopher, 1673
Sal.

H1050 Harvey, Christopher, 1679
Dur. Ely.

H1052 Harvey, Edmund, 1642
Cant. Linc.

H1065 Harvey, Gideon, 1678
Cant.

H1089 Harvey, William, 1660
Carl. Dur.

H1091 Harvey, William, 1651
Ex. Linc. Sal (engr. tpw). Win.

H1096 Harwood, *Sir* Edward, 1642
Linc.

H1102aA Harwood, James, 1657
Pet. Win.

H1106 Harwood, Richard, 1644
Wel.

H1107 Harwood, Richard, 1645
Wel. Win (imp).

H1108 Hascard, Gregory, 1683
Nor. S Pl.

H1109 Hascard, Gregory, 1684
Yk (2).

H1110 Hascard, Gregory, 1683
Cant. Carl. S Pl. Swel.

H1111 Hascard, Gregory, 1685
Carl. Chi. Ex (2). Nor. S Pl.
Sal. Wel. Yk.

H1112 Hascard, Gregory, 1668
Linc.

H1113 Hascard, Gregory, 1679
Carl. Her.

H1114 Hascard, Gregory, 1680
Cant. Carl. Wor.

H1115 Hascard, Gregory, 1685
Wor.

H1116 Hascard, Gregory, 1696
Her.

H1117 Hascard, Gregory, 1696
Ban. Cant. Her. Wor.

H1125 Haslerig, *Sir* Arthur, 1653
Sal.

H1125A Haslerig, *Sir* Arthur, 1653
Yk.

H1129 Haslerig, *Sir* Arthur, 1642
Cant.

H1129+ Haslerig, *Sir* Arthur, 1642
For F. Coules and T.B.; 4°.
Yk.

H1130 Haslerig, *Sir* Arthur, 1642
Linc.

H1142 Hatton, *Sir* Christopher, 1677
Linc.

H1150 Haudicquer de Blancourt, Jean, 1699
Yk.

H1157 Hausted, Peter, 1642
Dur.

H1162 Havers, Clopton, 1691
Ex.

H1164 Haward, Lazarus, 1660
Win.

H1171A Hawke, Michael, 1657
Yk.

H1185 Hawles, *Sir* John, 1680
Cant.

H1188 Hawles, *Sir* John, 1689
S Pl (imp).

H1189 Hawles, *Sir* John, 1689
Wel.

H1205 Hay, [1642]
Yk.

H1210 Hayley, William, 1687
Sal.

H1211 Hayley, William, 1696
Her. Nor. S Asa. Wor.

H1214 Hayley, William, 1699
Nor.

H1217 Hayne, Thomas, 1645
Ex.

H1220 Hayne, Thomas, 1642
Ex.

H1225 Hayter, Richard, 1675
Ely. Win.

H1230 Hayward, Edward, 1660
Sal.

H1233 Hayward, *Sir* John, 1683
Pet.

H1235 Hayward, Roger, 1673
Her. Lich.

H1236 Hayward, Roger, 1676
Bur. Her. Wor.

H1238 Haywood, William, 1663
Pet.

H1239 Haywood, William, 1660
Carl. Ex.

H1240 Haywood, William, 1648
Carl.

H1241 Haywood, William, 1642
Ex.

H1256 Head, Richard, 1674
Sal.

H1272? Head, Richard, 1675
... and are to be sold at the Sign of the Ship in St. Mary Axe [T. Drant], and by most booksellers.
Cant.

H1277 Head, Richard, 1674
S Pl.

H1281 Heads, 1647
Dur.

H1282A Heads, 1691
Dur. Linc. Yk.

H1283 Heads, 1642
Yk.

H1289 Heads, 1641
Win (tp only).

H1294 Heads, 1681
Linc.

H1299 Heads, 1647
Pet.

H1307 Hearne, Robert, 1681
Linc.

H1309 Hearne, Thomas, 1698
Glo. Her.

H1317 Heath, James, 1654
Ex. Pet.

H1321 Heath, James, 1676
Chi. Lich. S Asa. Swel. Yk.

H1329 Heath, James, 1663
Carl.

H1335 Heath, James, 1662
Ex.

H1336 Heath, James, [1665?]
Carl. Linc.

H1339 Heath, *Sir* Robert, 1642
Linc.

H1346 Heavens, 1657
Pet.

H1354 Heereboord, Adrian, 1658
Her.

H1357 Heereboord, Adrian, 1658
Bur.

H1358 Heereboord, Adrian, 1663
Her. S Pl. Yk.

H1361 Heereboord, Adrian, 1680
S Asa.

H1362A Heereboord, Adrian, 1665
Wel.

H1365 Heereboord, Adrian, 1676
Her.

H1366 Heereboord, Adrian, 1684
Yk.

H1369 Hegg, Robert, 1647
Dur.

H1370 Hegg, Robert, 1663
Carl. Dur (3 − 2 eds). Linc. S Pl (imp). Yk (2).

H1372 Heinsius, Daniel, 1646
Nor. Sal. Swel.

H1377+ Hell, 1646
'catalogu [*sic*]'; The third impression; Impr. as H1377; 4°.
Linc.

H1380? Hellier, Henry, 1688
... London.
Ex.

H1380+ Hellier, Henry, 1688
Oxford, at the Theater for Richard Chiswell; 4°; Differs from H1380 only in impr.
Ex. Llan (tp imp)*.

H1381 Hellier, Henry, 1697
Yk.

H1396 Helmont, Franciscus Mercurius van, 1684
S Pl.

H1398 Helmont, Jean Baptiste van, 1650
Carl. Pet (2 − 1 imp).

H1401 Helmont, Jean Baptiste van, 1650
Glo. Wor.

H1402 Helmont, Jean Baptiste van, 1650
Carl. Pet.

H1404A Help, 1700
Yk.

H1405 Help, 1681
'help'
Linc

H1411 Helwich, Christopher, 1687
Ely. Ex. Wel.

H1412 Helwich, Christopher, 1651
Carl. Ches. Sal. Swel.

H1413 Helwich, Christopher, 1662
Cant. Ely. Ex. Her. Lich. Nor. Pet. Roch. S Asa. S Pl. Wor. Yk.

H1427 Henchman, Humphrey, 1677
... Robertum Scott.
Dur. Linc.

H1428? Henchman, Richard, 1661
4°.
Chelm.

H1429 Henchman, Richard, 1661
S Pl.

H1433 Henderson, Alexander, 1641
Yk (2).

H1436 Henderson, Alexander, 1644
Pet. Win. Yk (2 eds).

H1438 Henderson, Alexander, 1642
Dur. Linc (2).

H1439 Henderson, Alexander, 1644
Wor.

H1441 Henderson, Alexander, 1644
Carl. Her. Yk.

H1443 Henderson, Alexander, 1645
Carl. Pet.

H1444 Henderson, Alexander, 1641
'unlawfulnes'
Linc. Yk (2).

H1458 Henrietta Maria, [1642]
Cant.

H1463 Henrietta Maria, [1642]
Dur. Linc.

H1465 Henrietta Maria, 1642
Yk.

H1466 Henrietta Maria, 1643
Linc.

H1467 Henrietta Maria, 1641
Yk.

H1468 Henry VIII, *King of England*,
1687
Wel.

H1469 Henry VIII, *King of England*,
1688
12°.
Chi. Sal.

H1473 Henry VIII, *King of England*,
1642
Pet.

H1482 Henshaw, Nathaniel, 1677
Yk.

H1490A Herault, Louis, [1670]
Win.

H1490A+ Herault, Louis, [1670?]
'A speech made to ... William Henry
... November 4th 1670'; [N.pl.]; 4°.
Llan. Win.

H1496 Herbert, *Sir* Edward, *1648−*
1698, 1688
Wel.

H1498 Herbert, Edward, *Lord*
Herbert of Cherbury, 1645
Pars prima.
Glo.

H1500 Herbert, Edward, *Lord*
Herbert of Cherbury, 1656
Carl. Ex.

H1501? Herbert, Edward, *Lord*
Herbert of Cherbury, 1645
Third ed. not on tp.
Win.

H1502 Herbert, Edward, *Lord*
Herbert of Cherbury, 1656
Carl. Ex. Pet.

H1503 Herbert, Edward, *Lord*
Herbert of Cherbury, 1656
Carl. Linc. Sal.

H1504 Herbert, Edward, *Lord*
Herbert of Cherbury, 1649
Ban (imp). Cant (imp). Carl.
Ely. Glo (imp). Llan (imp). Pet
(imp). S Asa (imp). S Pl. Wel.

H1505B Herbert, Edward, *Lord*
Herbert of Cherbury, 1672
Cant. Ex. Linc. Sal (imp). Win.
Wor.

H1506 Herbert, Edward, *Lord*
Herbert of Cherbury, 1682
Chi.

H1507 Herbert, Edward, *Lord*
Herbert of Cherbury, 1683
Glo.

H1507A Herbert, Edward, *Lord*
Herbert of Cherbury, 1683
Lich.

H1507AB Herbert, Edward, *Lord*
Herbert of Cherbury, 1683
Nor.

H1509 Herbert, George, 1651
12°.
Carl. Linc. S Pl. Yk (2).

H1512 Herbert, George, 1652
12°.
Carl. Linc. S Pl. Yk (2).

H1513 Herbert, George, 1671
Sal. Win. Yk.

H1514 Herbert, George, 1675
Cant. Ely. Sal (2).

H1515 Herbert, George, 1652
Carl. Linc. S Pl. Yk (2).

H1519 Herbert, George, 1660
Wel.

H1520 Herbert, George, 1667
Nor.

H1520A Herbert, George, 1667
The ninth edition.
Cant.

H1521 Herbert, George, 1674
Ex. Sal.

H1522 Herbert, George, 1678
Dur.

H1523 Herbert, George, 1679
The eleventh edition.
Ely.

H1531 Herbert, Thomas, 1641
Linc.

H1533A Herbert, *Sir* Thomas, 1664
Yk.

H1534 Herbert, *Sir* Thomas, 1665
The third impression.
Dur. Ex.

H1536 Herbert, *Sir* Thomas, 1677
Cant (engr. tpw). Linc. Roch.
Yk.

H1546B Herdson, Henry, 1652
'The penitent pilgrim'
Ely.

H1550 Herle, Charles, 1644
Pet.

H1551 Herle, Charles, 1644
Ex (2). Yk.

H1552 Herle, Charles, 1643
Cant. Carl. Ex. Linc.

H1553 Herle, Charles, 1642
Linc. Pet. Sal.

H1553+ Herle, Charles, 1642
'Answer to mis-led Doctor Fearne'; 4°.
Cant (cropped).

H1554 Herle, Charles, 1645
Her.

H1555 Herle, Charles, 1646
Yk.

H1556 Herle, Charles, 1643
Cant (2). Carl. Ex. S Asa. Yk.

H1558 Herle, Charles, 1642
Linc (28p.). Pet (24p.). Sal
(28p.).

H1558+ Herle, Charles, 1643
Oxford, by Leonard Lichfield; 4°.
Carl.

H1559 Herle, Charles, 1643
Carl. Pet. Yk.

H1561 Herle, Charles, 1642
Cant. Chelm. S Asa.

H1562 Herle, Charles, 1655
Carl.

H1565 Hermes Trismegistus, 1650
Ban.

H1569 Herne, John, 1663
Sal.

H1571 Herne, John, 1658
Cant.

H1577 Herne, Samuel, 1679
Llan.

H1578 Herne, Samuel, 1677
Cant. Ex. Linc. Nor. S Dv.
Yk.

H1579 Herodian, 1678
Ely. Ex. S Asa.

H1581 Herodian, 1698
Glo.

H1583 Herodian, 1652
'Herodian of ...'
Ex.

H1584 Herodotus, 1679
Ely. Pet. Roch.

H1602 Herring, Francis, 1641
Pet.

H1605 Hesiod, 1659
Yk.

H1606 Hesiod, 1672
Nor.

H1608 Hesketh, Henry, 1683
Carl. S Pl.

H1610 Hesketh, Henry, 1684
Carl.

H1612 Hesketh, Henry, 1683
Llan.

H1613 Hesketh, Henry, 1680
Carl.

H1614 Hesketh, Henry, 1684
Wor.

H1615 Hesketh, Henry, 1678
Ban. Her.

H1616 Hesketh, Henry, 1679
Ex. Wor.

H1617 Hesketh, Henry, 1682
Carl. Dur. Her (imp).

H1618 Hesketh, Henry, 1684
Yk.

H1619 Hesketh, Henry, 1684
Carl.

H1621 Hesketh, Henry, 1699
Wor.

H1623 Heskith, Thomas, 1700
Her.

H1634 Hewitt, John, 1658
Lich. Yk.

H1634A Hewitt, John, [1658]
S Pl. Yk.

H1636 Hewitt, John, 1659
12°.
Linc. S Pl.

H1637 Hewitt, John, 1658
Cant. Carl. Lich. Yk.

H1639A Hewitt, John, [1658?]
S Pl.

H1643 Hewlett, James, 1668
S Pl.

H1649 Hexham, Henry, 1648
Linc.

H1651 Hexham, Henry, 1675
Ex.

H1680 Heylyn, Peter, 1681
Ban. Bris. Cant. Chi. Dur. Ex.
Glo. S Pl (2 − 1 imp). Sal. Yk
(2).

H1681 Heylyn, Peter, 1670
Dur. Ex. Linc. Pet. S Pl. Sal.
Wel. Win. Wor. Yk.

H1681A Heylyn, Peter, 1670
Carl. Chi. Her.

H1682 Heylyn, Peter, 1672
Ches. Her. S Asa. Yk.

H1685 Heylyn, Peter, 1644[5]
Yk (2).

H1687 Heylyn, Peter, 1659
Cant. Carl. Yk.

H1689 Heylyn, Peter, 1652
Cant. Carl. Lich. Yk.

H1690 Heylyn, Peter, 1657
Cant. Lich. S Pl. Wel.

H1691A Heylyn, Peter, 1666
Ely.

H1692A Heylyn, Peter, 1669
Glo. Pet. Swel. Wel.

H1693 Heylyn, Peter, 1670
Dur. Ex.

H1694 Heylyn, Peter, 1674
Bris. Bur. Sal. Yk.

H1695? Heylyn, Peter, 1677
... R. Chiswel ...
Her. Linc. Wor.

H1696 Heylyn, Peter, 1682
Glo. Sal (tpw). Win. Yk.

H1699 Heylyn, Peter, 1668
'... William [Laud] ... Archbishop ...'
Cant (2). Carl. Her. Lich. Linc.
Liv. Nor. Pet (2). Sal (2). Wel.
Yk.

H1700 Heylyn, Peter, 1671
Dur. Her. Linc (tp imp). Liv.
S Asa. S Dv. S Pl. Wel. Win.
Yk.

H1701 Heylyn, Peter, 1661
Cant. Carl. Her. S Asa. Win.
Wor.

H1702 Heylyn, Peter, 1670
Chi. Dur. Linc.

H1703 Heylyn, Peter, 1674
Ex. Pet. S Pl. Sal (2). Wel.
Yk (2).

H1704 Heylyn, Peter, 1657
Carl. Lich. Linc. Pet. S Asa.
Yk (2 − 1 imp).

H1706 Heylyn, Peter, 1659
Carl. Ex. Lich. S Asa. S Pl.

H1707 Heylyn, Peter, 1659
Cant. S Pl. Yk.

H1708? Heylyn, Peter, 1656
8°.
Carl. Linc. Sal. Yk.

H1712 Heylyn, Peter, 1656
See also H1737.
Her (tp imp). Yk.

H1713 Heylyn, Peter, 1641
Cant.

H1714 Heylyn, Peter, 1642
Cant (imp).

H1715 Heylyn, Peter, 1652
Cant (tp & suppl. only).

H1717? Heylyn, Peter, 1670
12°.
Ex. Linc. Win.

H1718 Heylyn, Peter, 1671
Dur. Yk.

H1719 Heylyn, Peter, 1675
Carl.

H1720 Heylyn, Peter, 1680
Ely. Yk.

H1721 Heylyn, Peter, 1660
Bur. Cant. Carl. Nor. Pet. Yk.

H1722 Heylyn, Peter, 1642
Ex. S Pl. Wor. Yk.

H1724 Heylyn, Peter, 1643
Cant. Carl. Linc.

H1724A Heylyn, Peter, 1643
Cant.

H1725A Heylyn, Peter, 1643
Cant*.

H1726 Heylyn, Peter, 1643
Cant. Yk.

H1727 Heylyn, Peter, 1656
Carl. Linc. Yk.

H1729 Heylyn, Peter, 1659
Carl. Chelm.

H1729A? Heylyn, Peter, 1659
Marriot.
Sal. Yk.

H1730 Heylyn, Peter, 1645
36p.
Carl. Linc.

H1730+ Heylyn, Peter, 1645
As H1730, but: 40p.
Yk.

H1731 Heylyn, Peter, 1643
Cant (not Madan 1543; 'familiar'
[etc.]).

H1731A Heylyn, Peter, 1643
Pet*.

H1731B Heylyn, Peter, 1644
Yk.

H1732 Heylyn, Peter, 1658
Cant. Carl. Sal. Yk.

H1734 Heylyn, Peter, 1661
Cant. Linc. Yk.

H1735 Heylyn, Peter, 1658
Linc. Yk.

H1736 Heylyn, Peter, 1658
Ban. Bur. Carl. Lich. Pet.
Roch. Win. Wor.

H1737 Heylyn, Peter, 1656
Anr issue of H1712 with cancel tp.
Carl. Lich (tpw, possibly
H1712)*. S Asa. S Pl.

H1738 Heylyn, Peter, 1654
Carl. Lich. Llan. Nor. Win.

H1739 Heylyn, Peter, 1673
Ely. Her. IoM. Linc. S Asa.
Sal (2). Yk (2).

H1741 Heylyn, Peter, 1648
Nor. Sal. Wor.

H1743 Heylyn, Peter, 1657
Carl.

H1748 Heyrick, Richard, 1646
Carl. Yk.

H1750 Heyrick, Richard, 1661
'A sermon ...'
Carl.

H1753 Heyrick, Thomas, 1691
Dur.

H1760 Heywood, Oliver, 1687
Yk.

H1762 Heywood, Oliver, 1671
Yk.

H1767 Heywood, Oliver, 1667
Yk.

H1767A? Heywood, Oliver, 1697
For Ephraim Johnston in Manchester.
Yk.

H1768 Heywood, Oliver, 1683
Yk.

H1774 Heywood, Oliver, 1695
'A new creature: or, a short discourse'
Yk.

H1776 Heywood, Oliver, 1672
. Yk.

H1786 Heywood, Thomas, 1641
Lich.

H1787 Heywood, Thomas, 1641
Dur.

H1792 Hibbert, Henry, 1661
S Pl.

H1793 Hibbert, Henry, 1662
Yk.

H1795 Hibner, Israel, 1698
... W. Feltham.
Cant.

H1796? Hickeringill, Edmund, 1682
By George Larkin, ...
Carl. S Pl (tp imp). Win.

H1803 Hickeringill, Edmund, 1680
Cant. Carl. Her. Pet (tp imp).
S Asa.

H1804 Hickeringill, Edmund, 1680
Dur (2 − 1 tp imp).

H1806 Hickeringill, Edmund, 1682
S Pl.

H1808 Hickeringill, Edmund, 1673
Carl. Pet. Yk.

H1812 Hickeringill, Edmund, 1681
S Asa.

H1813 Hickeringill, Edmund, 1681
Wor.

H1818 Hickeringill, Edmund, 1695
Ely.

H1821 Hickeringill, Edmund, 1681
Carl. Ely. Linc. S Pl. Win.

H1822 Hickeringill, Edmund, 1681
Win.

H1824 Hickeringill, Edmund, 1680
Carl.

H1825 Hickeringill, Edmund, 1682
S Pl.

H1828 Hickeringill, Edmund, 1683
S Pl.

H1832 Hickeringill, Edmund, 1681
S Pl.

H1836 Hickes, Edward, 1682
Carl.

H1838 Hickes, Gaspar, 1644
Pet (2). Yk.

H1839 Hickes, Gaspar, 1645
Cant.

H1840 Hickes, George, 1687
Ban. Bur. Cant. Carl. Ex (2).
S Pl. Yk (2).

H1842 Hickes, George, 1683
S Pl (2).

H1844 Hickes, George, 1685
Yk.

H1845 Hickes, George, 1682
Cant. Carl. Her. Sal. Wor.
Yk.

H1846 Hickes, George, 1677
Carl. Yk.

H1847 Hickes, George, 1683
Ban. Her.

H1850 Hickes, George, 1684
Carl. Her (imp). Pet. Tru. Wel.

H1851? Hickes, George, 1689
... typis Junianis.
Dur. Glo. Lich. S Asa. Yk.

H1852 Hickes, George, 1683
Carl. Ches. Dur. Ely. Glo.
S Asa. Sal. Wel. Win. Yk.

H1853 Hickes, George, 1683
Yk.

H1853+ Hickes, George, 1683
The second edition; By Sam. Roycroft
for Walter Kettilby; 8°.
Ches. Nor. S Pl.

H1855? Hickes, George, 1674
4°.
Carl.

H1856 Hickes, George, 1689
Wel.

H1857 Hickes, George, 1682
Dur. Her. Llan. Yk (2).

H1858 Hickes, George, 1681
Ban. Carl. Her. Nor. S Asa.
S Pl.

H1860 Hickes, George, 1678
Cant (tp imp). Win. Yk (2).

H1862 Hickes, George, 1682
S Dv. Wor (mutilated).

H1863 Hickes, George, [1689?]
Dur. Wel.

H1864 Hickes, George, 1682
Ban. Cant. Carl. S Asa.

H1865 Hickes, George, 1683
Her.

H1866 Hickes, George, 1684
Cant. Carl. Her. Llan. Sal.

H1867 Hickes, George, 1684
Cant. Carl. Her. Wor.

H1868 Hickes, George, 1695
Carl (imp). Wel. Yk (2).

H1869? Hickes, George, 1686
39p.
Dur. Wel. Yk.

H1869+ Hickes, George, 1686
As H1869, but: 42p.
Ex. Lich. Nor. Swel.

H1870 Hickes, George, 1686
Bur. Sal. Yk (2).

H1871 Hickes, George, 1680
Ban. S Asa. Yk (3).

H1872 Hickes, George, 1681
Carl.

H1873 Hickes, George, 1683
Chi. Her. Linc. Nor. Wor.

H1874 Hickes, George, 1680
Ban. Linc (frag.). Wel. Win.
Wor.

H1875 Hickes, George, 1681
Ban. Carl. Wor. Yk.

H1876 Hickes, George, 1682
Cant.

H1878 Hickes, George, 1692
Yk.

H1879 Hickes, John, 1673
Win.

H1880 Hickes, John, [1685]
Ban.

H1894 Hickman, Charles, 1700
Dur. Ex.

H1895 Hickman, Charles, 1680
Cant (2). Carl. Chi. Ely. Llan.
Wel.

H1896 Hickman, Charles, 1681
Cant. Llan.

H1897 Hickman, Charles, 1687
Cant.

H1898 Hickman, Charles, 1690
Her. S Pl. Wel. Wor. Yk.

H1899 Hickman, Charles, 1690
Her. Pet.

H1900 Hickman, Charles, 1690
Cant. Her. Wor.

H1901 Hickman, Charles, 1692
Cant. Her. Sal. Wor.

H1902 Hickman, Charles, 1693
Ban. Cant (2). Wor.

H1903 Hickman, Charles, 1696
Dur. Ex.

H1904 Hickman, Henry, 1664
Eleutheropolis; 12°.
Carl. Sal.

H1906 Hickman, Henry, 1665
Carl.

H1907 Hickman, Henry, 1700
Glo.

H1908 Hickman, Henry, 1672
Sal.

H1908+ Hickman, Henry, 1672
As H1908, but: 8°.
Carl.

H1909 Hickman, Henry, 1673
Win.

H1910 Hickman, Henry, 1674
Ches. Her.

H1911 Hickman, Henry, 1660
Carl. Yk (2).

H1911A Hickman, Henry, 1659
S Asa.

H1912 Hickman, Henry, 1659
Carl.

H1913 Hickman, Henry, 1661
Dur.

H1915 Hickman, Henry, 1659
Carl.

H1916 Hickman, Henry, 1674
Win.

H1918B Hicks, Henry, 1681
Her.

H1919 Hicks, Thomas, 1673
Pet.

H1922 Hicks, Thomas, 1673
Pet (tpw).

H1923 Hicks, Thomas, 1674
Pet.

H1924 Hicks, Thomas, 1674
32p.
Pet.

H1924+ Hicks, Thomas, 1674
As H1924, but: 33p.
Her.

H1930 Hickson, James, 1682
Yk.

H1933 Hierocles, 1654
Vol. 2 = H1936 or H1936+?
Bur. S Asa. Win.

H1934 Hierocles, 1654
Vol. 2 = H1936 or H1936+?
Carl. Ches. Lich.

H1935 Hierocles, 1673
Ches. Ely. Ex. Nor. S Pl.

H1936+ Hierocles, 1655
Ex officina Rogeri Danielis; 8°.
Bur. Cant. Carl. Ches. Lich.
S Asa. Win.

H1937 Hierocles, 1673
Ex. Nor. S Pl. Wel.

H1939 Hierocles, 1682
'of the Pythagoreans'
Ex.

H1944 Hierro, Augustin de, 1651
Yk.

H1958 Higgons, Thomas, 1660
Ches (frag.).

H1964 High, 1643
Cant (cropped).

H1968 Highmore, Nathaniel, 1660
Sal.

H1971 Hildebrand, Friedrich, 1673
Ely.

H1975 Hildersam, Arthur, 1672
Wel.

H1976 Hildersam, Arthur, 1647
Carl. Ex. S Dv. Yk.

H1977 Hildersam, Arthur, 1656
Carl (imp). S Pl.

H1978 Hildersam, Arthur, 1642
Carl. Dur. Ex. Her. Llan
(imp). Pet. S Pl.

H1983 Hilgard, 1641
Linc.

H1986 Hill, Henry, 1696
Dur. Nor.

H1991C+ Hill, John, *Gent.*, 1691
The fourth edition; For H. Rhodes;
12°.
Cant.

H1995 Hill, John, *of St Mabyn*,
1694
Cant.

H1996 Hill, John, *of St Mabyn*,
1680
Pet.

H1998 Hill, Joseph, 1696
Ex.

H2000 Hill, Joseph, 1673
Carl. Linc.

H2004 Hill, Miles, 1650
Ex.

H2006 Hill, Samuel, 1687
Ban. Bur. Cant. Carl. Chi. Ex.
Sal. Wel.

H2007 Hill, Samuel, 1691
Wel.

H2008 Hill, Samuel, 1696
S Asa.

H2009 Hill, Samuel, 1697
Printed and are to be sold by the
booksellers of London and
Westminster.
Ex. S Pl.

H2012 Hill, Samuel, 1692
Carl. Pet. Wel.

H2013 Hill, Samuel, 1695
S Pl.

H2023 Hill, Thomas, *of Trinity
Coll., Cambridge*, 1644
Ex. Yk.

H2024 Hill, Thomas, *of Trinity
Coll., Cambridge*, 1643
Cant.

H2026 Hill, Thomas, *of Trinity
Coll., Cambridge*, 1645
Pet (2).

H2027 Hill, Thomas, *of Trinity
Coll., Cambridge*, 1644
Pet. Win. Yk.

H2031 Hill, Thomas, *of Trinity Coll., Cambridge,* 1642
Ex. Pet (4).

H2033 Hill, William, 1658
Yk.

H2035AB Hillenius, François, 1664
'Engelschen'; ... by Bastiaan Wagens.
Pet.

H2041A Hilton, Thomas, 1700
Her.

H2046 Hinckley, John, 1680
Win.

H2047 Hinckley, John, 1670
Carl. Win.

H2048 Hinckley, John, 1661
Win.

H2049 Hinckley, John, 1657
Carl. Win.

H2056 Hinde, Samuel, 1663
Carl. Pet.

H2058+ Hinde, Samuel, 1662
For Robert Paulett; 4°.
Cant (imp).

H2062- Hinde, Thomas, [166-?]
'Directions for the use of Thomas Hind's ... cordial elixir'; Sold in London at my house on Snow Hill; brs.
Dur.

H2063 Hinde, William, 1641
Pet. S Asa (imp). Yk.

H2063A Hindmarsh, Thomas, 1680
Pet.

H2067 Hinton, Edward, 1651
Carl.

H2069 *See*: T466

H2091- Histoire, 1700
See: CLC54.
S Pl.

H2094 Historiae, 1652
Cant. Carl. Ches. Dur. Her. Linc. Nor. Pet. Rip. S Pl. Wel. Win. Wor. Yk.

H2094B Historians, 1679
Ex. Yk.

H2094D Historian's, 1690
12°.
S Pl.

H2098A Historical, 1696
Sal. Yk (2).

H2108 Historical, 1688
Ban. Linc. Wel.

H2109 Historical, 1675
Ex.

H2148 History, 1694
Cant (3). Dur. S Pl. Wel.

H2170 History, 1688
8°.
Ex. Pet.

H2173B History, 1671
Lich. Liv.

H2174 History, 1699
S Asa (2). S Pl.

H2178 History, 1691
S Asa.

H2187- History, 1694
As H2187, apart from date.
Cant.

H2193 Hitchcock, John, 1697
Carl.

H2202 Hoard, Samuel, 1658
Ex. S Asa.

H2204 Hoard, Samuel, 1658
Carl. S Asa.

H2206? Hobart, *Sir* Henry, 1650
Second ed. not on tp.
Cant.

H2207 Hobart, *Sir* Henry, 1658
Dur.

H2208 Hobart, *Sir* Henry, 1671
Sal.

H2211 Hobbes, Thomas, 1682
'An answer ...'
Cant.

H2212 Hobbes, Thomas, 1681
Cant (imp). Ex. Yk.

H2213 Hobbes, Thomas, 1679
Pet.

H2215 Hobbes, Thomas, 1682
Cant.

H2218 Hobbes, Thomas, 1680
Ex.

H2219 Hobbes, Thomas, 1650
Carl.

H2221 Hobbes, Thomas, 1652
Cant.

H2222 Hobbes, Thomas, [1666?]
Ban.

H2224 Hobbes, Thomas, 1678
Fourth ed. not on tp.
Win.

H2226 Hobbes, Thomas, 1678
Ex. Yk.

H2230 Hobbes, Thomas, 1655
Carl. Sal.

H2231 Hobbes, Thomas, 1658
Sal.

H2232 Hobbes, Thomas, 1656
Wor.

H2236 Hobbes, Thomas, 1660
Sal.

H2239 Hobbes, Thomas, 1679
Cant.

H2240 Hobbes, Thomas, 1679
Dur.

H2242 Hobbes, Thomas, 1650
Wel.

H2243 Hobbes, Thomas, 1651
Cant.

H2245 Hobbes, Thomas, 1680
Linc.

H2245A Hobbes, Thomas, 1676
Linc. Wel.

H2245B Hobbes, Thomas, 1677
Ely.

H2246 Hobbes, Thomas, 1651
Ban. Bris. Cant. Carl. Ches. Linc. Nor. Wor.

H2247 Hobbes, Thomas, 1651 [*i.e.* 1655?]
[Amsterdam, for Cristoffel Conradus?].
Cant (Macdonald & Hargreaves, no. 43, with bear on tp).

H2252 Hobbes, Thomas, 1654
Carl.

H2252A Hobbes, Thomas, 1668
Ex. Yk.

H2253 Hobbes, Thomas, 1651
Carl. Linc.

H2257 Hobbes, Thomas, 1656
Carl. Linc. S Pl.

H2258 Hobbes, Thomas, 1671
Ex.

H2259 Hobbes, Thomas, 1682
Cant.

H2260 Hobbes, Thomas, [1656]
Wor.

H2262 Hobbes, Thomas, 1675
Dur (lacks pts 2-6).

H2265 Hobbes, Thomas, 1682
Cant. Ex.

H2266 Hobbes, Thomas, 1684
Dur. Ex.

H2267 Hobbes, Thomas, 1679
Cant.

H2268 Hobbes, Thomas, 1681
Carl. Dur (imp). Ex (lacks colophon?). S Pl. Sal. Wel. Yk.

H2296 Hoddesdon, John, 1652
Yk.

H2304 Hodges, Nathaniel, 1671
Win.

H2314 Hodges, Thomas, *of
Kensington*, 1642
Cant.

H2315 Hodges, Thomas, *of
Kensington*, 1647
Chelm. Ex. Pet (3).

H2317 Hodges, Thomas, *of
Kensington*, 1660
Carl.

H2318 Hodges, Thomas, *of
Soulderne*, 1659
Cant. Pet. Wor.

H2320? Hodges, Thomas, *of
Soulderne*, 1652
... Leon Lichfield, for Tho. Robinson.
Pet (2).

H2321 Hodges, Thomas, *of
Soulderne*, 1685
S Asa.

H2325+ Hodges, Thomas, *of
Soulderne*, [1676?]
Does not match BL copy of H2325.
Wor (imp).

H2337 Hody, Humfrey, 1691
S Pl. Wel. Yk.

H2339 Hody, Humfrey, 1693
Carl. Glo. Nor. Yk.

H2340 Hody, Humfrey, 1684
S Pl. Yk.

H2341 Hody, Humfrey, 1685
Pet.

H2342 Hody, Humfrey, 1692
Wel. Yk.

H2344 Hody, Humfrey, 1694
'... of the (same) body ...'
Ban. Ex. S Pl.

H2347 Hoffman, Benjamin, 1683
Her. Llan. Yk.

H2364 Hog, William, [1685]
Roch.

H2374 Holbourne, *Sir* Robert, 1642
Linc.

H2376 Holden, Henry, 1662
Carl.

H2379 Holden, Henry, 1661
Carl. S Asa.

H2380 Holden, Richard, 1680
Carl. Llan. Wor.

H2381A Holden, Samuel, 1662
Carl.

H2385 Holder, William, 1694
Ely (2). S Asa. Swel.

H2386 Holder, William, 1669
Cant. S Asa. Sal. Win.

H2389B Holder, William, 1694
Ely.

H2396 Holdsworth, Richard, 1642
Nor.

H2397 Holdsworth, Richard, 1661
Carl. Dur. Ely. Ex. S Pl. Win.

H2401 Holdsworth, Richard, 1642
Carl. Linc. Pet. Yk.

H2404 Holdsworth, Richard, 1651
Linc (2).

H2409 Hole, Matthew, 1697
Cant.

H2411+ Hole, Matthew, 1700
See: CLC55.
Dur.

H2412 Hole, Matthew, 1689
Yk.

H2413 Hole, Matthew, 1696
Cant.

H2415 Holgate, William, 1686
Yk.

H2416 Holgate, William, 1683
Yk.

H2417 Holland, Guy, 1653
S Asa. Sal.

H2418 Holland, Henry Rich, *Earl
of*, 1641
Yk.

H2420A Holland, Henry Rich, *Earl
of*, 1641
Dur.

H2422 Holland, Henry Rich, *Earl
of*, 1642
Cant.

H2426 Holland, Hezekiah, 1650
Chelm. Ex.

H2429 Holland, *Sir* John, 1641
Cant. Linc.

H2434 Holland, Richard, *Chaplain*,
1700
Wor.

H2435 Holland, Richard, *Chaplain*,
1685
Pet.

H2436A Holland, Richard,
Chaplain, 1700
Pet.

H2442 Holland, Samuel, 1662
Win.

H2446 Hollanders, 1642
Linc.

H2451A Hollar, Wenceslaus, [1666]
Wenceslaus Hollar: delin: et sculp:
1666.
Cant.

H2452 Holles, Denzil Holles, *Baron*,
1675
Cant.

H2453 Holles, Denzil Holles, *Baron*,
1676
Cant.

H2459 Holles, Denzil Holles, *Baron*,
1669
Sal.

H2461 Holles, Denzil Holles, *Baron*,
1679
Yk.

H2461aA Holles, Denzil Holles,
Baron, 1679
Cant. Linc. Sal.

H2461A Holles, Denzil Holles,
Baron, 1679
Win.

H2462 Holles, Denzil Holles, *Baron*,
[1676]
Bris.

H2468 Holles, Denzil Holles, *Baron*,
1641
Yk.

H2468A Holles, Denzil Holles,
Baron, 1641
Cant (2 – both cropped). Nor.

H2469? Holles, Denzil Holles,
Baron, 1642
'... Ianuary, ... 1642'
Cant. Linc.

H2469B? Holles, Denzil Holles,
Baron, 1642
For F.C. and T.B.
Cant.

H2470 Holles, Denzil Holles, *Baron*,
1642
Cant.

H2471 Holles, Denzil Holles, *Baron*,
1641
Cant.

H2472 Holles, Denzil Holles, *Baron*,
1641
Cant (2).

H2472A Holles, Denzil Holles,
Baron, 1641
Linc.

H2474 Holles, Denzil Holles, *Baron*,
1641
Cant ('at the dellvery [sic]').
Linc ('at the delivery').

H2475 Holles, Denzil Holles, *Baron*, 1641
Cant. Dur.

H2476A Holles, Denzil Holles, *Baron*, 1642
Cant. Dur. Ex.

H2477 Holles, Denzil Holles, *Baron*, 1641
Linc.

H2480? Holles, Denzil Holles, *Baron*, 1671
By J. Darby for Richard Chiswel.
Cant.

H2481 Holles, Denzil Holles, *Baron*, 1676
Pet.

H2482 Holles, Denzil Holles, *Baron*, 1641
Cant.

H2485 Hollingworth, Richard, *the Elder*, 1680
Carl.

H2486 Hollingworth, Richard, *the Elder*, 1643
Ex.

H2488 Hollingworth, Richard, *the Elder*, 1646
Sal.

H2500A Hollingworth, Richard, *the Younger*, 1681
Carl. Win. Wor.

H2501 Hollingworth, Richard, *the Younger*, 1693
Cant. Her.

H2503A Hollingworth, Richard, *the Younger*, 1676
Carl.

H2504B Hollingworth, Richard, *the Younger*, 1682
Ban. Her. Llan. Wor.

H2509 Holloway, James, 1684
Ely.

H2523- Holy, 1662
See: CLC56.
Carl.

H2525 Holy, 1677
S Pl.

H2529 Holy, 1676
Linc.

H2530? Holyday, Barten, 1661
... for Sam. Pocock.
Cant. Nor.

H2531 Holyday, Barten, 1657
Linc. Nor.

H2535 Holyoke, Francis, 1677
Ban. Bur. Dur. Nor. S Dv.
Swel. Yk (tpw).

H2536A Home, *Sir* James Home, *Earl of*, 1641
Linc.

H2540 Homer, 1664
Rip.

H2542 Homer, 1676
S Pl.

H2545 Homer, 1689
Cant. Nor. Sal (imp).

H2546 Homer, 1695
Dated in Greek.
Linc. S Pl.

H2548 Homer, 1660
... to be had at the author's [*i.e.* John Ogilby's] house.
Glo (tpw). Linc.

H2549 Homer, 1669
Chelm (tpw).

H2553 Homer, 1664
Ely. Rip.

H2554 Homer, 1665
Linc.

H2555 Homer, 1669
Chelm.

H2556 Homer, 1675
Ex.

H2561 Homes, Nathaniel, 1654
Llan.

H2562 Homes, Nathaniel, 1650
Cant (imp).

H2563 Homes, Nathaniel, 1652
Chelm. Sal (tpw).

H2566+ Homes, Nathaniel, 1647
London, by Matthew Simmons; 4°.
Pet (2).

H2570 Homes, Nathaniel, 1641
Cant. Chelm. Ex. Pet.

H2577 Homes, Nathaniel, 1660
Yk.

H2578 Homes, Nathaniel, 1646
Ex. Win.

H2578A Homes, Nathaniel, 1646
Chelm.

H2604 Honyman, Andrew, 1668
Win.

H2606 Hooke, Richard, 1661
Chelm. S Asa. Yk.

H2607 Hooke, Richard, 1653
S Asa.

H2608 Hooke, Richard, 1682
Carl. Yk (2).

H2610 Hooke, Richard, 1684
Cant. Ex.

H2613 Hooke, Robert, 1674
Wel.

H2617 Hooke, Robert, 1679
Ex.

H2618 Hooke, Robert, 1678
Wel.

H2619 Hooke, Robert, 1678
Wel.

H2620 Hooke, Robert, 1665
Ex.

H2630 Hooker, Richard, 1662
Carl. Liv. Yk.

H2631 Hooker, Richard, 1666
Ex. Glo. Sal. Win.

H2632? Hooker, Richard, 1676
Chiswel.
Ban. Cant. Chelm. Chi. Ex.
Liv*. Nor. Pet. S Pl. Yk.

H2632+ Hooker, Richard, 1676
As H2632, but omitting Robert Boulter from impr.
New.

H2633 Hooker, Richard, 1682
Ban (imp). Cant. Ex (engr. tpw).
Her. Nor. Rip (imp). Roch.
S Alb. S Pl. Sal (imp). Yk.

H2635 Hooker, Richard, 1648
Yk.

H2635B Hooker, Richard, 1648
Pet.

H2637 Hooker, Richard, 1666
Ban. Bur. Cant (imp). Pet.
Swel. Wor.

H2644 Hooker, Thomas, 1649
Pet.

H2645 Hooker, Thomas, 1641
Yk.

H2649 Hooker, Thomas, 1646
Carl.

H2651A Hooker, Thomas, 1646
Cant.

H2698 Hooper, George, 1683
Cant (2 eds: 1. For W. Abington next the Wonder Tavern; 2. ...
Wonder-Tavern). S Pl (2).

H2700 Hooper, George, 1695
Ches. Ely (2). Ex. S Asa. S Dv.
Wel. Wor. Yk (2).

H2701 Hooper, George, 1696
Ches. Lich. Nor.

H2703 Hooper, George, 1689
Cant (imp).

H2705 Hooper, George, 1682
Carl. Her.

H2706 Hooper, George, 1682
Cant (tp has 'THF FIFTH').
Carl. Her.

H2707 Hooper, George, 1691
Her. S Asa. Wor.

H2708 Hooper, George, 1694
Carl. S Asa.

H2709 Hooper, George, 1695
Cant (2 − 1 imp). Ely. S Asa.

H2730 Hopkins, Ezekiel, 1692
Ban. Ely. Ex.

H2732 Hopkins, Ezekiel, 1692
Ely. Llan. Sal.

H2732A Hopkins, Ezekiel, 1692
Ban. Wel.

H2735 Hopkins, Ezekiel, 1693
Ban.

H2738 Hopkins, Ezekiel, 1671
Wor.

H2740? Hopkins, Ezekiel, 1694
... for Nathaniel Ranew.
IoM.

H2743 Hopkins, George, 1655
Carl.

H2750A Hopkins, Marmaduke,
1689
S Pl.

H2754 Hopkins, William, *D.D.*,
1683
Ban. Cant.

H2757 Hopton, Ralph Hopton,
Baron, 1650
Pet.

H2764 Horace, 1699
Dur. Ely. Ex (2). Lich. Linc.
Nor. Pet. Sal. Wel.

H2765 Horace, 1699
Ex. Yk.

H2768 Horace, 1680
Bris. S Asa.

H2774 Horace, 1684
Ex.

H2774B Horace, 1684
Glo.

H2777 Horace, 1660
Linc. Wel (imp)*.

H2780 Horace, 1690
Wel.

H2781 Horace, 1666
Carl.

H2785 Horace, 1678
12°.
Cant.

H2788 Horden, John, 1676
Pet (tpw).

H2788A? Horn, Georg, 1700
Janssons; 2°.
Nor. S Pl.

H2789 Horne, Andrew, 1646
Cant. Sal. Wel.

H2790? Horne, Andrew, 1642
Walbanke.
Cant. S Pl.

H2798 Horne, John, 1654
Ex (tp imp).

H2803 Horne, John, 1668
Pet.

H2810 Horne, John, 1660
S Asa (cropped).

H2812 Horne, Thomas, 1687
8°.
Nor.

H2814 Horne, Thomas, 1685
Bris. Cant. Wor.

H2815 Horneck, Anthony, 1689
Cant. Wel.

H2822 Horneck, Anthony, 1689
Cant.

H2824A Horneck, Anthony, 1684
Carl.

H2827 Horneck, Anthony, 1684
Nor.

H2830 Horneck, Anthony, 1686
Cant.

H2832 Horneck, Anthony, 1682
Carl.

H2833 Horneck, Anthony, 1677
Cant. Carl. Ex.

H2835? Horneck, Anthony, 1682
... Samuel Lowndes.
Ely.

H2838 Horneck, Anthony, 1695
S Asa.

H2839 Horneck, Anthony, 1681
Cant. Nor.

H2840? Horneck, Anthony, 1686
... by Joshuah Phillips ...
Ban. Ex.

H2841 Horneck, Anthony, 1693
Cant (imp). Linc.

H2846 Horneck, Anthony, 1689
Cant. Wel.

H2848 Horneck, Anthony, 1688
Dur.

H2849 Horneck, Anthony, 1677
Her (2).

H2850 Horneck, Anthony, 1689
Ban. Cant. Her. S Asa. Wel.
Wor. Yk.

H2851 Horneck, Anthony, 1698
Bur. S Asa.

H2852 Horneck, Anthony, 1698
Bur.

H2854 Horneck, Philip, 1699
'... death of ... Lady Guilford'
Her.

H2863 Horrid, 1663
Dur. Linc.

H2868 Horrocks, Jeremiah, 1673 −
72
Sal.

H2871 Horsley, Thomas, [1679]
Linc.

H2875? Horton, Thomas, 1675
4°.
Ex. Nor.

H2876? Horton, Thomas, 1674
4°.
Ex. Nor.

H2877 Horton, Thomas, 1679
Ex. S Asa.

H2878 Horton, Thomas, 1655
S Pl.

H2879? Horton, Thomas, 1663
4°; 19p.
Carl. Pet.

H2881 Horton, Thomas, 1672
Bur.

H2882 Horton, Thomas, 1646
Ex. Yk.

H2883 Horton, Thomas, 1661
Pet.

H2884 Horton, Thomas, 1653
Ex.

H2885 Horton, Thomas, 1656
Pet (2). S Pl.

H2889A Hott, 1645
Yk.

H2890 Hotchkis, Thomas, 1675
Carl. Ex. S Pl. Yk.

H2892 Hotchkis, Thomas, 1675
8°.
Carl.

H2893 Hotchkis, Thomas, 1678
Ex. S Pl. Win.

H2895 Hotham, Charles, 1651
Linc. Pet.

H2896 Hotham, Charles, 1650
Yk.

H2897 Hotham, Charles, 1651
Yk.

H2898 Hotham, Charles, 1651
Linc. Pet.

H2900 Hotham, Charles, 1651
Linc. Pet.

H2902B Hotham, *Capt.* John, 1642
Yk.

H2903 Hotham, *Sir* John, 1643
Linc.

H2905 Hotham, *Sir* John, 1642
Dur. Yk.

H2907 Hotham, *Sir* John, 1642
Linc (2). Yk.

H2908 Hotham, *Sir* John, [1642]
Yk (2).

H2911- Hough, Edward, 1700
See: CLC57.
Yk.

H2933 Houghton, Thomas, 1681
12°.
Linc.

H2935 Houghton, Thomas, 1694
12°.
Pet.

H2937 Houghton, Thomas, [1694]
Pet.

H2937A? Houghton, William, 1661
... for Nathanael Webb.
Pet.

H2938 Houghton, William, 1650
New (pt 2 only).

H2938+ Houghton, William, 1651
As H2938, apart from date.
New.

H2956 How, William, 1650
Yk.

H2958 How, 1690
Wel. Yk.

H2965 Howard, Edward, 1669
Ex.

H2983 Howard, John, 1700
S Pl.

H2990 Howard, *Sir* Robert, 1681
Linc.

H2995A Howard, *Sir* Robert, 1697
Dur.

H2997 Howard, *Sir* Robert, 1689
Nor. Pet.

H3001 Howard, *Sir* Robert, 1681
Ban.

H3006 Howard, *Sir* Robert, 1696
Ex.

H3014A Howe, John, 1680
S Pl.

H3015 Howe, John, 1668
'blessednesse'
Ex.

H3016 Howe, John, 1673
Bur. Carl.

H3018 Howe, John, 1694
Cant. Glo.

H3021 Howe, John, 1699
Her.

H3023 Howe, John, 1695
Ches. Her.

H3025 Howe, John, 1699
Cant.

H3027 Howe, John, 1682
Cant.

H3028 Howe, John, 1699
Dur (imp).

H3030A? Howe, John, 1694
By J. Astwood ...
Cant (2). Glo.

H3032 Howe, John, 1675
Chelm. Her.

H3034 Howe, John, 1681
Ex.

H3036 Howe, John, 1677
Carl. Chelm. Ex. Her. S Pl (2).

H3039 Howe, John, 1698
Cant.

H3047? Howe, John, 1695
For Tho. Parkhurst.
Cant (2).

H3049 Howe, Obadiah, 1664
Linc.

H3050 Howe, Obadiah, 1663
Linc.

H3051 Howe, Obadiah, 1655
Win (tpw).

H3053 Howell, Humphrey, 1656
Yk.

H3054 Howell, James, 1653
Lich.

H3056 Howell, James, 1648
Lich.

H3057 Howell, James, 1662
Pet.

H3059 Howell, James, 1644
Cant. Carl. Pet. Sal.

H3060+ Howell, James, [1645?]
Date from tp of 'The pre-eminence';
Possibly Madan's 4th ed. of 1645;
191, 23p.
Cant (imp; neither of Wing's 12°
eds).

H3062 Howell, James, 1650
Carl (2).

H3063? Howell, James, 1664
'discours'; 8°.
Win.

H3066 Howell, James, 1658
Carl.

H3067- Howell, James, 1659
As H3067, but no ed. statement.
Pet.

H3068 Howell, James, 1661
Ex.

H3069 Howell, James, 1647
Yk.

H3071 Howell, James, 1645
Cant.

H3072 Howell, James, 1650
Bur. Cant. Rip.

H3073A Howell, James, 1655
Cant.

H3074 Howell, James, 1673
Cant (2 — 1 addit. engr. tpw).

H3075 Howell, James, 1678
Cant (3 — 1 imp, 1 tp imp).

H3076 Howell, James, 1688
Cant.

H3078 Howell, James, 1655
Lich.

H3079 Howell, James, 1653
Carl. Lich.

H3080 Howell, James, 1649
Lich.

H3081 Howell, James, 1650
Yk.

H3082 Howell, James, 1642
Cant (imp).

H3083 Howell, James, 1648
Dur. Lich. Yk.

H3085 Howell, James, 1647
Lich. Pet.

H3087 Howell, James, 1660
Cant (2).

H3089 Howell, James, [1660]
Date not on tp.
Lich.

H3091 Howell, James, 1657
Cant (imp). Chi. Ex. Lich
(imp). Sal.

H3092 Howell, James, 1646
Lich. Pet.

H3093 Howell, James, 1644
Carl.

H3094 Howell, James, 1644
Pet.

H3095 Howell, James, 1662
Ches.

H3096 Howell, James, 1647
Cant (imp).

H3098 Howell, James, 1659
Cant (2).

H3101 Howell, James, 1658
Pet.

H3102 Howell, James, 1660
Cant.

H3106 Howell, James, 1644
Pet (imp).

H3106A Howell, James, 1645
Cant.

H3108 Howell, James, 1677
Chelm.

H3109 Howell, James, 1664
Nor. Sal.

H3111 Howell, James, 1664
Win.

H3112 Howell, James, 1651
Bris. Lich. Pet.

H3113 Howell, James, 1652
Carl. Linc.

H3116 Howell, James, 1655
Yk.

H3117 Howell, James, 1656
Second ed. not on tp.
Cant. Carl. Linc.

H3119 Howell, James, 1660
'The first tome'
Lich.

H3120 Howell, James, 1649
Lich.

H3122 Howell, James, 1643
'discovereth'
S Pl. Yk.

H3122+ Howell, James, 1643
As H3122, but: 'discovvereth'
Linc. Pet.

H3128A Howell, James, 1642
Lich.

H3129 Howell, James, 1649
Lich.

H3130 Howell, John, 1685
Her.

H3130A? Howell, William, *1656 –
1714*, 1686
8°.
Yk (impr. not confirmed).

H3133F Howell, William, *1656 –
1714*, 1689
Sal.

H3134 Howell, William, *1638? – 1683*,
1671
Ely. Linc. S Pl. Yk.

H3137 Howell, William, *1638? – 1683*,
1662
Carl. Dur. Linc.

H3138 Howell, William, *1638? – 1683*,
1680 – 85
Cant. Dur. Ely. Glo (vol. 1 – 2
only). Nor (vol. 1 – 2 only).
S Asa. Swel. Wel (vol. 1 – 2 only).
Win. Yk.

H3139 Howell, William, *1638? – 1683*,
1685
Cant. Dur. Nor. Swel. Win.
Yk.

H3142 Howell, William, *1638? – 1683*,
1687
Yk.

H3142A+ Howell, William, *1638? –
1683*, 1694
The fourth edition; For Abel Swalle,
sold by James Adamson; 8°.
S Pl.

H3144 Howell, William, *of
Fittleworth*, 1676
Ban.

H3148 Howes, John, 1657
Pet.

H3149 Howes, John, 1660
New. Pet.

H3150 Howes, John, 1670
Yk (tp imp).

H3170 Howgill, Francis, 1656
Yk.

H3188 Howgill, Francis, 1656
Yk.

H3207 Hubbard, Benjamin, 1648
Cant. Pet.

H3230 Hubberthorn, Richard, 1658
Yk.

H3232 *See*: N317

H3246A Hubert, William, 1676
Wel. Win.

H3248 Huddleston, Ferdinando,
[1679]
Linc.

H3256 Hudibras, [1663]
Linc (cropped).

H3257 Hudleston, Richard, 1688
Cant.

H3260 Hudson, John, 1698
8°.
Carl. Ches.

H3261 Hudson, Michael, 1647
Carl. Sal. Yk.

H3262 Hudson, Michael, 1647
Yk.

H3264 Hudson, Samuel, 1689
Her.

H3265 Hudson, Samuel, 1645
S Pl.

H3266 Hudson, Samuel, 1650
Her.

H3282 Hue, [1686]
Linc.

H3296 Hue, 1646
Yk.

H3300B Huet, Pierre Daniel, 1684
Ex.

H3301 Huet, Pierre Daniel, 1672
Carl.

H3302 Huet, Pierre Daniel, 1694
Ely. Wel (imp).

H3305 Hughes, George, 1672
Ex (2).

H3306 Hughes, George, 1670
Ex.

H3307 Hughes, George, 1642
Yk.

H3308 Hughes, George, 1644
Ex.

H3309A Hughes, George, 1668
Carl.

H3310A Hughes, John, *1615 – 1686*,
1670
S Asa.

H3313A Hughes, John, *Minister*,
1683
Llan.

H3314 Hughes, Lewis, 1641
Yk.

H3316 Hughes, Lewis, 1645
Yk.

H3321 Hughes, William, *of Gray's
Inn*, 1656
Ex.

H3322 Hughes, William, *of Gray's
Inn*, 1655
Dur.

H3324? Hughes, William, *of Gray's Inn*, 1660 – 62
Different dates.
Ex. Sal.

H3326 Hughes, William, *of Gray's Inn*, 1641
Ex. Pet.

H3327 Hughes, William, *of Gray's Inn*, 1663
Carl.

H3327B Hughes, William, *of Gray's Inn*, 1673
Cant.

H3328 Hughes, William, *of Gray's Inn*, 1673
The third edition.
Ely. Linc.

H3332 Hughes, William, *Horticulturist*, 1672
Ex.

H3342 Hughes, William, *Hospitaller*, 1652
Chelm.

H3343 Hughes, William, *Hospitaller*, 1677
Ex (2). Pet. Win.

H3348A Hughes, William, *Hospitaller*, 1684
Clark.
Yk.

H3349 Hugo, Hermann, 1677
24°.
Nor.

H3350 Hugo, Hermann, 1686
Tru.

H3351 Hugo, Hermann, 1690
Ex.

H3353 Huise, John, 1659
Wel.

H3362 Hulls, 1644
Yk.

H3363 Hulsius, Anthony, 1660
Pet. S Asa.

H3367 Humble, 1647
'... thousands, young-men'
Yk.

H3375 Humble, [1680]
Linc.

H3377 Humble, [1647]
Yk (2).

H3380B Humble, 1659
Yk.

H3387 Humble, [1695]
Wel (2).

H3388 Humble, 1680
Win.

H3399 Humble, 1648
Yk.

H3400 Humble, 1648
Yk (2).

H3402 Humble, 1669
Carl. Chelm. Win.

H3404 Humble, 1660
Pet. Win.

H3407 - Humble, [N.d.]
See: CLC58.
Yk.

H3407 Humble, 1642
Linc (3).

H3419 Humble, 1657
Ex.

H3421 Humble, 1641
Cant. Linc. Pet.

H3442 Humble, 1642
Yk.

H3443 Humble, 1642
Dur. Linc. Yk.

H3446 Humble, 1642
Cant. Linc (2).

H3447 Humble, 1642
Linc.

H3448? Humble, 1642
'eleventh of this instant December'
Yk.

H3453 Humble, 1642
Ex. Linc. Yk.

H3458 Humble, 1642
Yk (2).

H3462 Humble, 1648
Ex.

H3463A Humble, 1642
Yk.

H3472 Humble, 1647
Yk.

H3474 Humble, 1658[9]
Ex.

H3479? Humble, 1659
For Livewell Chapman.
Ex.

H3498 Humble, 1642
Cant. Carl. Linc.

H3499 Humble, 1648
Ex.

H3502 Humble, 1642
Dur. Linc.

H3503? Humble, 1642
'... York, presented ... April 22. 1642. ...'
Dur. Linc (2). Yk (2).

H3504A Humble, 1642
Yk*.

H3505 Humble, 1642
Linc. Yk (2).

H3508 Humble, 1642
Yk (3).

H3509 Humble, 1642
Linc. Yk.

H3509A Humble, 1642
Pet. Yk (2).

H3525 Humble, 1642
Linc (tp has misprints).

H3526 Humble, 1642
Dur. Linc.

H3530 Humble, 1642
Linc. Pet.

H3533 Humble, 1646
Printing history confused, see NUC.
Pet. Yk.

H3541 Humble, [1648]
Yk.

H3544 Humble, 1648
'... with the answer of the Lords';
H3545 should be 'Commons'
Pet. Yk.

H3551 Humble, 1683
Wel.

H3555A Humble, [1642/3]
Linc.

H3557 Humble, 1643
Linc.

H3562 Humble, 1641
Dur. Pet. Yk (2).

H3563 Humble, 1647
Dur.

H3567 Humble, 1642
Linc.

H3569 Humble, 1642
Ex.

H3573 Humble, 1641
Dur. Linc. Pet.

H3577 Humble, 1680[1]
Glo. Linc. Win.

H3578 Humble, 1642
Linc.

H3581 Humble, [1644?]
Linc.

H3590A Humble, 1641[2]
Linc.

H3596 Humble, 1673/4
Linc.

H3625 Humble, 1647
Pet.

H3641 Humble, 1648
Yk.

H3643 Humble, 1661
Carl. Linc.

H3658 Hume, David, 1644
Dur (imp).

H3659 Hume, David, 1648
Third ed. not on tp.
Ex.

H3662 Hume, John, 1676
Yk.

H3663C Hume, Robert, 1695
'... Hodgson, ... March 11, 1694'
Bris.

H3668 Humfrey, John, 1680
Carl (44p.). S Pl (36p.).

H3669 Humfrey, John, 1672
Carl. Win.

H3676 Humfrey, John, 1668
Win.

H3678 Humfrey, John, 1698
Ely.

H3679 Humfrey, John, 1689
Cant.

H3680 Humfrey, John, 1678
Cant. Carl.

H3683? Humfrey, John, 1653
8°.
Cant.

H3687? Humfrey, John, 1695
For T. Parkhurst.
Ely.

H3691 Humfrey, John, 1672
Win.

H3692A Humfrey, John, 1679
Bris.

H3694 Humfrey, John, 1681
S Pl.

H3695 Humfrey, John, 1678
Linc.

H3696A Humfrey, John, 1695
cap.
Ely.

H3697 Humfrey, John, 1696
Ely.

H3702 Humfrey, John, 1678
Carl.

H3703 Humfrey, John, 1680
Ban.

H3705 Humfrey, John, 1654
Cant (imp). Chelm.

H3708? Humfrey, John, 1697
For T. Parkhurst.
Ely.

H3709 Humfrey, John, 1662
Chelm. Dur. Yk (tpw).

H3710 Humfrey, John, 1656
Wor.

H3715 Humfrey, John, 1698
4°.
Ely.

H3721 Humphreys, Humphrey, 1696
Ban. Cant. Wor.

H3721B Humphreys, John, 1680
Lich.

H3726B Hungarian, 1672
12°.
S Asa (tpw).

H3733 Hunt, James, 1641
[N.pl.].
Dur. Linc. S Pl.

H3749 Hunt, Thomas, *1627?—1688*, 1682
Cant. Dur.

H3749A Hunt, Thomas, *1627?—1688*, 1682
Pet. Yk.

H3750 Hunt, Thomas, *1627?—1688*, [1683]
Pet. S Pl. Win.

H3751 Hunt, Thomas, *1627?—1688*, 1680
Linc. Win (2).

H3752 Hunt, Thomas, *1627?—1688*, 1680
Dur.

H3755 Hunt, Thomas, *1627?—1688*, 1679
Carl (imp). Dur. Linc.

H3758 Hunt, Thomas, *1627?—1688*, 1682
Yk.

H3758+ Hunt, Thomas, *1627?—1688*, 1682
See: CLC59.
Dur.

H3759 Hunt, Thomas, *1627?—1688*, 1680
Bur. Cant. Carl. Sal (2). Win.

H3765B Hunter, Josiah, 1660
Yk (2).

H3766 Hunter, Josiah, 1666
Yk (2).

H3767 Hunter, Josiah, 1661
Yk.

H3768 Hunter, Josiah, 1656
Carl. Yk (imp).

H3775 Huntington, Robert, 1648
Yk (2).

H3780? Huntly, Lewis Gordon, *3rd Marquis of*, 1650
'The declaration & engagement ...'
Linc.

H3781 Hunton, Philip, 1643
Carl. Chelm. S Pl. Yk.

H3783 Hunton, Philip, 1689
Carl. Pet. Wel. Yk.

H3783A Hunton, Philip, 1689
Bur. Cant.

H3784 Hunton, Philip, 1644
Carl. Chelm. Dur. Ex.

H3790 Hurst, Henry, 1659
Sal.

H3792 Hurst, Henry, 1678
Ex. Win.

H3793 Hurst, Henry, 1677
Her.

H3793+ Hurste, Thomas, 1644
See: CLC60.
Carl.

H3804 Husain ibn 'Ali, 1661
Carl. Ex. Llan. Wel (imp?). Yk.

H3807 Husbandmans, 1647
Pet (imp).

H3814 Hussey, Joseph, 1693
Ex.

H3815 Hussey, William, 1646
S Asa.

H3817 Hussey, William, 1646
Pet.

H3819 Hussey, William, 1646
Win.

H3822 Hutcheson, George, 1654
Carl.

H3823 Hutcheson, George, 1655
Carl.

H3825 Hutcheson, George, 1669
Glo.

H3828B Hutchinson, Charles, 1687
Ban. Bur. Cant. Ches (2). Dur. Nor. S Asa. S Pl. Sal. Swel (2).

H3830 Hutchinson, Francis, 1692
Cant.

H3837 Hutchinson, William, 1679
Dur. Linc.

H3838 Hutchinson, William, 1676
Wel.

H3854 Hutton, *Sir* Richard, 1673
Cant.

H3855 Hutton, *Sir* Richard, 1689
Ches.

H3862 Hyde, Edward, *D.D.*, 1658
Win.

H3863? Hyde, Edward, *D.D.*, 1657
… for Rich. Davis in Oxon.
Linc.

H3864 Hyde, Edward, *D.D.*, 1659
Win.

H3868 Hyde, Edward, *D.D.*, 1662
Linc. Pet. Win.

H3871 Hyde, *Sir* Henry, 1650
Yk.

H3876 Hyde, Thomas, 1700
Dur. Ely. Ex (2). Linc. Swel.
Wel. Wor.

H3877 Hyde, Thomas, 1694
Cant. Dur. Ex.

H3882 Hylton, Walter, 1659
Ely. Yk.

H3883 Hymn, [1661]
S Pl.

I10A? I., R., 1661
'… that novel controversie …'
Carl.

I17 I., W., 1681
Win.

I26 Iamblichus, 1678
Cant. Ches. Ex. Glo. Pet (imp).
S Asa. S Pl (2). Win. Wor. Yk.

I28A Ibbitson, Robert, 1647
By Robert Ibbitson.
Pet (tp imp).

I31 Ιχθυοθηρα, 1662
Linc.

I38 Ignatius, *St*, 1647
Ches. Dur (2). Linc (2). S Pl
(2). Sal. Wor.

I39? Ignatius, *St*, 1680
'S. Ignatii martyris: epistolae …'; …
Roberti Sollers.
Ches (3). Ex. Linc. Rip. Roch.
Sal. Wor. Yk.

I41 Ignatius, 1642
Cant. Linc.

I43A Ignoramus, 1661
Sal.

I46 Ignoramus, 1681
Cant.

I61 Impartial, 1679
Dur.

I63 Impartial, 1679
Carl. Linc.

I73 Impartial, 1681
Pet.

I78? Impartial, 1679
'Cornwallis'
Linc.

I78A Impartial, 1691
Cant.

I80 Impartiall, 1648
Dur.

I83 Impartial, 1683
Cant.

I88 Impartial, 1679
Carl. Linc. Win.

I89 Impartial, [1679?]
Dur.

I93 Impeachment, 1641
Yk.

I97 Impeachment, 1641
Dur.

I99 Impeachment, [1679]
Dur. Linc.

I104? Impostor, 1681
For James Vade.
Linc. Pet.

I109 In, 1641
Cant ('In answer … Strafords
…'). Yk ('In answer … Straffords
…').

I109aA In, 1641
Linc (2 − 1: 'answer' & cruciform
orn. on tp; 2: 'answere' & square
orn.).

I119? In, 1667
Oxoniae, excudebat H.H., impensis
Edv. Forrest.
Cant.

I135 Inchiquin, Murrough O'Brien,
Lord, 1649
Sal.

I156? Indulgence, 1673
For Richard Royston.
S Asa.

I162 Infants, 1644
S Asa.

I163A Information, [1680]
Linc.

I175 Ingelo, Nathaniel, 1660
Carl. Yk (imp).

I176 Ingelo, Nathaniel, 1669
Glo. Nor.

I178 Ingelo, Nathaniel, 1682
Ex.

I182A Ingelo, Nathaniel, 1677
Carl. Ex.

I184 Ingelo, Nathaniel, 1659
Carl. Chelm. Pet. S Asa.

I190 Iniquity, 1643[4]
Carl.

I196 Innocency, 1651
Yk.

I199? Innocent XI, *Pope*, 1679
'… Rome, the second …'
Cant. Linc (2).

I201 Innocent XI, *Pope*, 1679
Cant.

I202 Innocent XI, *Pope*, [1680]
Linc.

I203 Innocent XI, *Pope*, 1681
Yk.

I204 Innocent XI, *Pope*, 1681
Carl. Win.

I218 Enquiry, 1693
Ely. Wel.

I220 Enquiry, [1693]
Dur.

I222A? Enquiry, 1685
For Robert Clavel.
Ban. Carl. Win.

I226 Insolence, 1669
Win.

I227 Insolency, 1643
Linc.

I231 Instance, 1687
Wel.

I233A Institutions, 1687
8°.
Ches.

I256 Instrument, 1679
Linc. Win.

I263 Intelligence, 1642
'Yorke'
Yk.

I270 Interest, 1680
Wel.

I270A Interest, 1680
Carl. Dur.

I271 Interest, 1653
Linc.

I275 Intimation, [1680]
Ches.

I279 Intreigues, 1689
Wel.

I292 Invocation, 1659
S Pl.

I323 Ireland, 1642
Dur. Linc.

I381 Ireland, 1660
S Pl (imp).

I414? Ireland, 1641
'... burgesses, in Parliament ... in Ireland'
Linc.

I414A Ireland, 1642
Linc.

I422A Ireland, 1689
Carl. Dur. Pet.

I626A Ireland, 1641
Dur. Sal.

I642B+ Ireland, 1700
See: CLC61.
Ban.

I652 Ireland, 1641
Cant. Pet.

I653A Ireland, 1641
Linc.

I1029 Irenicum, 1700
Wel.

I1037 Irish, 1642
Dur.

I1049 Ironside, Gilbert, 1685
Cant. S Asa. Sal.

I1050 Irvine, Alexander, 1694
Yk.

I1051 Irvine, Christopher, 1682
Yk.

I1053 Irvine, Christopher, 1656
Pet.

I1061C Isacius, Thomas, 1650
'cognoscendi'
Ex (apparently the author's proof copy).

I1064? Isendoorn, Gisbert, 1658
... sumptibus Rob. Blagrave.
Ex. Nor.

I1067D Isham, Zacheus, 1699
Ely.

I1068 Isham, Zacheus, 1695
Her. Wor.

I1069 Isham, Zacheus, 1695
Chelm.

I1070 Isham, Zacheus, 1697
Cant. Ex. Her. S Pl. Wor.

I1071 Isham, Zacheus, 1700
Her.

I1073 Isma'il Ibn' Ali, 1650
Wel.

I1076? Isocrates, 1677
8°.
Win.

I1076A? Isocrates, 1680
Editio tertia; ... Johannis Baker.
Nor.

I1110 Izacke, Richard, 1677
S Pl.

I1111 Izacke, Richard, 1681
Ex.

J9+ J., G., 1649
Anr ed. with title: 'A letter sent to a noble Lord of this kingdome [Duke of Buckingham] ...'; [N.pl.]; 4°; Both eds signed G.I.
Yk.

J23 J., N., [1690]
cap.
Cant.

J25 J., P., 1680
cap.
Linc.

J45A J., T., 1655
Yk.

J52 J., W., 1643
Sal. Yk.

J53? J., W., 1693
'Doctor Wallis'
Cant.

J64 Jackson, Arthur, 1658
Ex.

J65 Jackson, Arthur, 1646
Ex.

J66 Jackson, Arthur, 1682
Ex. Lich.

J67 Jackson, Arthur, 1643
Ex.

J68 Jackson, Christopher, 1685
Yk (2).

J69 Jackson, Henry, [1662]
Yk.

J79 Jackson, John, of Queens Coll., Cambridge, 1668
Ely (2). Her. Roch. Wel.

J79+ Jackson, John, of Queens Coll., Cambridge, [1668]
Cambridge, by John Field, and to be sold by William Fisher and Richard Mount, London; 4°.
Cant.

J87A Jackson, Richard, 1655
Yk.

J88 Jackson, Thomas, 1653
Linc. Wel. Yk.

J89 Jackson, Thomas, 1654
Nor. S Asa. Sal. Wel. Yk.

J90 Jackson, Thomas, 1673
Ban (2). Bris (vol. 2 only). Bur. Cant. Carl. Ches. Chi. Dur. Ely. Ex (2). Glo. Her (lacks vol. 3). Lich. New. Pet (2). S Pl. Win. Wor. Yk.

J91B Jackson, Thomas, 1672
Ex.

J92 Jackson, Thomas, 1657
S Asa. Wel. Yk.

J95 Jackson, William, 1675
Carl.

J109 Jacombe, Samuel, 1657
Chelm. New.

J111? Jacombe, Thomas, 1682
For Brabazon Aylmer.
Cant.

J112 Jacombe, Thomas, 1657
S Pl.

J115 Jacombe, Thomas, 1656
Cant (imp).

J115A Jacombe, Thomas, 1656
Pet (tp and prelims only).

J116? Jacombe, Thomas, 1656
Second ed. not on tp.
Pet.

J118 Jacombe, Thomas, 1668
Ex.

J120 Jacombe, Thomas, 1682
Carl.

J122A Jagel, Abraham, 1679
Yk.

J122B+ Jagel, Abraham, 1679
Typis A. Godbid & J. Playford; 8°.
S Pl.

J128A James I, *King of England*, 1682
Ex.

J136 James I, *King of England*, 1642
cap.
Linc.

J139 James I, *King of England*, 1642
Linc. S Pl.

J141 James I, *King of England*, 1689
Ban.

J153 James II, *King of England*, 1687
Ban.

J183 James II, *King of England*, 1647
Pet.

J190+ James II, *King of England,*
1688
As J190, but: 4p.
S Pl.

J190++ James II, *King of England,*
1688
As J190, but: 6p.
Wel.

J196 James II, *King of England,*
1688/9
S Pl.

J204 James II, *King of England,*
[1692]
Wel.

J208 James II, *King of England,*
[1688/9]
Wel ('Majesties').

J225 James II, *King of England,*
1685
Nor.

J228 James II, *King of England,*
1685
Nor.

J312+ James II, *King of England,*
[N.d.]
See: CLC62.
Carl.

J376 James II, *King of England,*
[1688]
S Pl.

J376B James II, *King of England,*
1689
Ban.

J389 James II, *King of England,*
1685[6]
Cant. Dur. S Asa.

J413 James V, *King of Scotland,*
1663
Linc.

J424 James, Francis, 1647
Pet.

J426 James, Henry, 1674
Ban. Carl. Her. Llan (2).

J427 James, John, *of Latimers,*
1678
Ban. Cant.

J428 James, John, *of Latimers,*
1683
Carl. Her.

J432 James, Marmaduke, 1659
S Pl (pt 2 only).

J434 James, Thomas, 1678
Ches. S Asa. S Pl. Win.

J436 James, Thomas, 1688
Ban. Bur (2 — 1 tpw). Cant.
Ches. Ely. Ex (2). Linc. Liv
(tpw). S Pl.

J451 Jane, Joseph, 1651
Carl. Ex. Linc. Wel. Win. Yk.

J453 Jane, William, [1689]
Wel.

J454 Jane, William, 1678
Carl. Win.

J455 Jane, William, 1675
Cant. Carl. Ex.

J456 Jane, William, 1679
Cant. Carl. Her. Wel.

J457 Jane, William, 1691
Pet.

J458 Jane, William, 1692
Ches. Her. Pet.

J470 Janeway, James, 1673
Pet.

J477A- Janeway, James, 1671
Printed for John Wilkins; 12°.
Cant (imp).

J482 Janson, *Sir* Henry, 1663
Yk (tpw)*.

J484? Janson, *Sir* Henry, 1670
For Will. Cademan.
Linc.

J488? Jarrige, Pierre, 1658
12°.
Ely. Ex. Pet.

J489 Jarrige, Pierre, 1658
S Pl.

J489A? Jarrige, Pierre, 1658
12°.
Carl. Chelm.

J491 Jasz-Berenyi, Pál, 1662
Cant. Carl. Ex. Sal. Win. Yk.

J492 Jasz-Berenyi, Pál, 1664
Pet.

J503 Jeamson, Thomas, 1665
Linc.

J505 Jeanes, Henry, 1661
Carl.

J506 Jeanes, Henry, 1657
Carl.

J507 Jeanes, Henry, 1656
Carl. Her.

J508 Jeanes, Henry, 1660
Sal.

J511 Jeanes, Henry, 1650
Carl. Pet. Sal. Yk.

J512 Jeanes, Henry, 1653
Carl.

J513 Jeanes, Henry, 1649
Carl.

J516 Jeffery, John, 1699
Yk.

J517? Jeffery, John, 1700
8°.
Win.

J520 Jeffery, John, 1693
Cant. Nor.

J521 Jeffery, John, 1696
Cant. Nor (2). S Asa.

J535 Jekyll, Thomas, 1697
Cant. Wor.

J537 Jekyll, Thomas, 1681
Carl.

J559 Jenison, Robert, *1649 — 1688,*
1680
Linc.

J560 Jenison, Robert, *1649 — 1688,*
1680
Yk (imp).

J561 Jenison, Robert, *1649 — 1688,*
1679
Dur. Ely. Linc. Win. Yk (imp).

J562A Jenison, Robert, *1584 — 1652,*
1649
Chelm.

J563 Jenison, Robert, *1584 — 1652,*
1648
Yk.

J568 Jenkin, Robert, 1688
Ban. Cant (imp). Carl. Dur.
Ex. S Pl. Wel (2). Yk.

J569 Jenkin, Robert, 1688
Sal. Swel.

J570 Jenkin, Robert, 1698
Ex. Glo.

J571 Jenkin, Robert, 1700
Roch.

J571A Jenkin, Robert, 1700
Ex.

J572 Jenkin, Robert, 1691
Llan.

J574 Jenkins, David, 1648
Cant.

J574+ Jenkins, David, 1648
'The vvorks ...'; For I. Giles; 12°.
Cant.

J576? Jenkins, David, 1648
192p.
Cant. Carl*. Yk (tp imp)*.

J576+ Jenkins, David, 1648
As J576, but: 198p.
Glo.

J584+ Jenkins, David, [1647] 'indempnity'; [N.pl.]; cap.; 4°.
Dur.

J592A Jenkins, David, 1680
Win.

J595 Jenkins, David, 1648
Cant.

J598 Jenkins, David, 1647[8]
Cant.

J604 Jenkins, David, 1647[8]
Cant.

J613 Jenkins, David, [1647]
Yk.

J618A Jenks, Benjamin, 1690
Cant.

J619 Jenks, Benjamin, 1695
S Asa.

J621 Jenks, Benjamin, 1697
Wor.

J622 Jenks, Benjamin, 1700
Ban. Cant.

J627 Jenks, Francis, [1679]
Linc.

J628 Jenks, Henry, 1683
Carl.

J630D Jenks, Silvester, 1699
Dur.

J630E Jenks, Silvester, 1700
Dur.

J632 Jenkyn, William, 1648
Sal.

J632+ Jenkyn, William, 1648
By A.M. for Christopher Meredith; 4°.
Pet.

J634 Jenkyn, William, 1679
Dur. Yk.

J636 Jenkyn, William, 1659
Pet.

J638 Jenkyn, William, 1675
Her (2).

J639 Jenkyn, William, 1652
Ex (tpw)*.

J641 Jenkyn, William, 1656
IoM. S Asa.

J642 Jenkyn, William, 1654
Ex.

J645? Jenkyn, William, [1648]
Meridith.
Pet.

J647 Jenkyn, William, 1656
Cant.

J650 Jenkyn, William, 1646
Pet.

J654 Jenkyn, William, 1647
Pet (tpw).

J655 Jenkyn, William, 1645
Pet.

J658A Jenner, David, 1680
Llan.

J660 Jenner, David, 1676
Bur.

J667B Jenner, Thomas, 1656
Cant (tpw).

J667B+ Jenner, Thomas, 1650
See: CLC63.
Cant.

J670 Jennings, Samuel, 1694
Dur.

J677A Jephcott, John, 1698
Dur.

J681cA Jerome, Stephen, 1650
Pet.

J694 Jessey, Henry, 1660
Yk.

J701 Jessop, Francis, 1687
Yk.

J704 Jesuite, 1681
Win (date changed in MS to 1682).

J709 Jesuitical, 1679
Bris.

J715 Jesuites, 1680
Linc.

J717 Jesuites, 1669
Cant. Llan. Pet. Sal. Win.

J718 Jesuits, [1679]
Linc.

J728 Jesuits, 1679
Carl.

J733 Jewel, John, 1683
Nor. Yk (2).

J734 Jewel, John, 1692
Sal.

J735? Jewel, John, 1685
... Randal Taylor.
Ex.

J736 Jewel, John, 1685
Cant. Dur. Ely. Ex. Her.
S Asa. Wel.

J737 Jewel, John, 1641
Linc. Yk.

J738 Jewel, John, 1671
S Asa.

J739 Jewel, John, 1641
Carl. Sal. Yk (2 — 1 imp).

J745 Joannes, *Malalas*, 1691
Ches. Ex. Liv. S Pl. Wor.

J745+ Joannes, *Malalas*, 1692
Oxonii, e Theatro Sheldoniano;
veneunt in officina Gualt. Kettilby; 8°.
Dur.

J747 Joannes, *Scotus*, 1681
Cant. Ely. Glo. Lich. Pet.
S Pl. Wor.

J755 Jobert, Louis, 1697
Cant. Dur. Tru.

J757 Joceline, Nathaniel, 1644
Sal. Yk.

J762 John, Theodore, 1693
12°.
Cant. Yk.

J770bA Johnson, Christopher, 1696
Cant.

J771 Johnson, Edward, *1599? – 1672*,
1654[3]
Cant.

J773 Johnson, Francis, *Franciscan*,
[1679]
cap.
Win.

J774 Johnson, Francis, *Franciscan*,
[1679]
cap.
Win.

J775 Johnson, Francis, *Franciscan*,
[1679]
Dur. Linc. Yk.

J777 Johnson, James, 1670
Yk (4).

J778 Johnson, James, 1670
Yk (4).

J783 Johnson, John, *New College
Fellow*, 1680
Cant. Her.

J800? Johnson, Richard, 1696
8°.
Ely.

J813 Johnson, Richard, *of the
Parliamentary Army*, 1642
Linc.

J816 Johnson, Robert, *M.D.*, 1684
Ban.

J818 Johnson, Robert, *Rev.*, 1647
Yk (2).

J819 Johnson, Samuel, 1688
Ban. Cant. Ex. Nor. S Pl. Sal.
Swel. Wel. Yk.

J820+ Johnson, Samuel, 1700
See: CLC64.
Cant.

J821 Johnson, Samuel, 1692
Cant. Dur. S Pl.

J821A Johnson, Samuel, 1692
Wel.

J822 Johnson, Samuel, 1692
Ban.

J824 Johnson, Samuel, 1698
Cant.

J825 Johnson, Samuel, 1698
Ban. Cant. Ely.

J826 Johnson, Samuel, 1693
Yk.

J830 Johnson, Samuel, 1682
Carl. Dur. Pet. S Pl. Wel.
Win.

J832 Johnson, Samuel, 1689
Cant. Glo. Wel.

J835 Johnson, Samuel, 1694
Ban. Carl. Wel.

J836 Johnson, Samuel, 1689
Wel.

J837 Johnson, Samuel, 1688
Ban. Ex. Sal. Wel.

J838 Johnson, Samuel, 1689
Cant. Wel.

J840 Johnson, Samuel, 1690
Wel.

J841 Johnson, Samuel, 1690
Lich. Llan.

J843 Johnson, Samuel, 1689
Cant.

J845+ Johnson, Samuel, [1700?]
See: CLC65.
Cant (imp). Dur.

J850 Johnson, Thomas, *Merchant*,
1646
Win.

J851 Johnson, Thomas, *of
Samburne*, 1642
Sal.

J853B? Johnson, Thomas, *fl. 1718*,
1699
Editio altera.
Nor.

J855 Johnson, William, *Chemist*,
1652
Pet (pt 1 only?).

J859 Johnson, William, *D.D.*, 1664
Pet.

J860 Johnson, William, *D.D.*, 1672
Carl. S Asa.

J863 Johnson, William, *of
Lurgyshall*, 1642
'commonalty'
Linc.

J868 Johnston, Joseph, 1687
Wel.

J869 Johnston, Joseph, 1687
Wel.

J870 Johnston, Joseph, 1687
Pet. Sal. Swel.

J871 Johnston, Joseph, 1686
Pagination varies.
Ban. Bur. Carl. Ex (2). Lich.
Nor. Sal. Swel. Wel.

J872 Johnston, Nathaniel, 1687
Cant. Yk.

J874 Johnston, Nathaniel, [1688]
Yk.

J877 Johnston, Nathaniel, 1686
Ban. Cant. Chi. Swel. Yk.

J879 Johnston, Nathaniel, 1688
S Pl. Yk.

J882 Johnston, Robert, 1642
Linc.

J887 Jole, William, 1671
Carl.

J929 Jones, David, *fl. 1676 − 1720*,
1697
Carl. Linc.

J934 Jones, David, *fl. 1676 − 1720*,
1697
Carl.

J934F Jones, David, *1663 − 1724?*,
1692
Cant. Sal.

J935 Jones, David, *1663 − 1724?*,
1699
Her.

J936 Jones, David, *1663 − 1724?*,
1692
Cant.

J937 Jones, David, *1663 − 1724?*,
1690
Cant.

J939 Jones, David, *1663 − 1724?*,
1699
Bur. Her.

J942B Jones, Henry, 1642
Pet.

J943 Jones, Henry, 1642
Ex. Linc. Sal. Yk.

J947 Jones, Henry, 1679
Cant. Carl. Linc. Yk.

J949 Jones, Henry, 1676
Win.

J950 Jones, Henry, 1679
Sal.

J954 Jones, Inigo, 1655
Ex. Wel. Wor.

J957 Jones, James, 1683
Win.

J961 Jones, John, *Bp*, 1642
Carl. Linc.

J961A Jones, John, *Bp*, 1643
Pet (issued as pt of M2844). Yk.

J961C Jones, John, *Captain*, 1646
Sal.

J968 Jones, John, *Gent.*, 1643
Cant (imp).

J981? Jones, John, *of
Merionethshire*, 1693
... sold by L. Meredith.
Ban.

J988 Jones, Roger, 1663
Sal.

J991? Jones, Thomas, *1618 − 1665*,
1660
12°.
Yk.

J991A? Jones, Thomas, *1618 − 1665*,
1660
12°.
Sal. Win. Yk.

J995 Jones, Thomas, *of Llandyrnog*,
1681
'... preached ... (December ...) at ...';
Hinchman.
Cant.

J996 Jones, Thomas, *of Llandyrnog*,
1678
Wing1 heading correct?
Ex. S Pl. Win.

J1006 Jonson, Ben, 1692
Liv.

J1011 Jonson, Ben, 1641
Cant.

J1046 Jordan, Thomas, 1641
Yk.

J1074 Jorden, Edward, 1669
Dur (imp).

J1076 Josephus, Flavius, 1655 − 56
Yk (2).

J1077 Josephus, Flavius, 1670
Linc (tpw).

J1077A Josephus, Flavius, 1670
Wel.

J1079A Josephus, Flavius, 1683
Ban.

J1080A Josephus, Flavius, 1693
Glo. Win.

J1081 Josephus, Flavius, 1700
'Flavii Josephi ...'
Ban. Cant. Dur. S Pl. Wel.
Yk.

J1082A Josephus, Flavius, 1687
Wor (tpw)*.

J1086 Josippon, 1669
Dur.

J1099 Journal, 1690
Cant.

J1109- Journal, 1663 [*i.e.* 1673]
At the theater in Oxford; 8°; Madan
2977.
Carl. Ex.

J1113 Journall, 1644
Yk.

J1123 Joyce, George, [1647]
Pet.

J1126A Joyful, 1644
Linc.

J1136A Joyfull, 1642
Yk.

J1144A Joyfull, 1642
Linc.

J1168 Judges, 1641
Cant.

J1169 Judges, 1679
Linc.

J1172 Judgment, [1687]
Cant. Wel.

J1176 Judgement, 1660
Bur. Yk.

J1184aA Judgment, [1679]
Linc.

J1189 Julius II, *Pope*, 1669
Linc (imp).

J1196 Jurieu, Pierre, 1687
New.

J1203 Jurieu, Pierre, 1684
Ely. Lich. Llan (tpw).

J1203+ Jurieu, Pierre, 1684
By J. Heptinstall, for Henry Faithorne
and John Kersey, and Edward Evets;
8°.
Wel.

J1204 Jurieu, Pierre, 1689
Wel.

J1207 Jurieu, Pierre, 1688
Nor. Wel.

J1208 Jurieu, Pierre, 1689
Cant. Ely.

J1210 Jurieu, Pierre, 1681
Ely. Linc.

J1212 Jurieu, Pierre, 1689
Ban.

J1213 Jurieu, Pierre, 1689
Wel.

J1215 Jury, 1641
Yk.

J1216 Jus, 1654
Carl. Dur. Her. Sal.

J1217 Jus, 1646
Chelm. Pet.

J1217+ Jus, 1647
As J1217, apart from date.
Lich.

J1218 Jus, 1647
Liv.

J1219 Jus, 1654
Carl.

J1222 Just, 1680
Linc (tp imp).

J1230 Just, 1690
Dur. Wel.

J1232 Just, 1642[3]
Pet (tp imp).

J1235 Just, 1679
Ely. Win. Yk.

J1244 Just, 1674
Linc. Sal.

J1264 Justification, 1689
Ban.

J1265 Justinus, *Martyr*, 1700
Dated in Greek.
Ex. Nor. S Pl. Yk.

J1267 Justinus, Marcus Junianus,
1674
Carl. S Pl. Yk.

J1269 Justinus, Marcus Junianus,
1684
Nor.

J1275 Justinus, Marcus Junianus,
1688
Cant (imp). Nor.

J1276 Juvenal, 1673
Ban. Ex. Rip.

J1280 Juvenal, 1660
Ely. Ex. Pet. S Dv.

J1282 Juvenal, 1648
Wel.

J1284aA? Juvenal, 1677
Ex officinâ Johannis Redmayne.
Nor.

J1285 Juvenal, 1691
Rip.

J1288 Juvenal, 1693
Ex. Glo (tpw). Rip.

J1290 Juvenal, 1697
Third ed. not on tp.
Cant. Yk.

J1291 Juvenal, 1647
Ban. Cant (imp). Lich (imp).

K5 K., C., 1696
Dur (imp).

K8 K., F., [1679]
Linc.

K23 K., T., 1642
Yk.

K23B K., W., 1668
Ex.

K27 K. William, 1689
Ban (9p.). Carl (9p., imp). S Pl
(9p.). Wel (6p., or 9p. imp?).

K28+ Kaerius, Petrus, [1646?]
See: CLC66.
Ban (tpw?).

K29A- Κατηχησις, 1658
Excudebat J.M., sumptibus Henrici
Fletcher apud quem veneunt & Tobi
Jordan, Gloucestriae bibliopolam; 8°.
Ex.

K29A Κατηχησις, 1659
Pet.

K31 Kaye, Stephen, 1686
Dur. Yk (2).

K32 Kaye, William, 1653
Yk.

K36 Kaye, William, 1658
Pet (imp).

K38 Kaye, William, 1654
Yk.

K41 Kaye, William, 1645
Yk.

K42A Kaye, William, 1657
Yk.

K60 Keach, Benjamin, 1689
Cant (imp).

K113A Keble, Joseph, 1683
Wel.

K121B Keble, Samuel, 1691
Liv.

K122 Keck, *Sir* Anthony, 1697
Dur.

K123 Keckermann, Bartholomaeus,
1661
Her. Pet.

K126 Keepe, Henry, 1682
Cant. Carl.

K132 Keill, John, 1698
Ely. Ex.

K137 Keith, George, 1700
Wel.

K142 Keith, George, 1698
Wel.

K161 Keith, George, 1696
S Pl.

K176 Keith, George, 1675
S Pl (tpw).

K193 Keith, George, 1695
Wel.

K207 Keith, George, 1699
S Pl.

K208 Keith, George, 1696
Cant.

K209 Keith, George, 1700
Lich. Wel.

K218 Keith, George, 1698
Wel.

K220 Keith, George, 1695
Wel.

K226 Keith, George, 1700
Wel. Wor.

K235 Keith, George, 1678
S Pl.

K238 Kellett, Edward, 1641
Ex (2). Linc.

K248 Kelsey, Joseph, 1691
Cant. Yk.

K249 Kelsey, Joseph, 1674
Carl. Sal (2).

K251 Kem, Samuel, 1660
Ex.

K252 Kem, Samuel, 1644
Yk.

K253 Kem, Samuel, 1647
Yk.

K258 Kemp, Edward, 1668
Cant.

K259 Kemp, Edward, 1668
Carl. Pet.

K260 Kemp, William, 1665
Carl.

K261 Ken, Thomas, 1685
Lich. Win.

K261+ Ken, Thomas, 1685
For Charles Brome; 8°.
Ches.

K262 Ken, Thomas, 1686
Cant. S Pl. Wel. Yk.

K262+ Ken, Thomas, 1686
For Charles Brome; 8°.
Carl.

K264 Ken, Thomas, 1696
Pet.

K264A Ken, Thomas, 1663
Cant.

K264B Ken, Thomas, 1691
Nor.

K264C Ken, Thomas, 1689
Yk.

K265+ Ken, Thomas, 1695
London; 4°.
Wel.

K273 Ken, Thomas, 1687
Sixth ed. not on tp.
Ely.

K276 Ken, Thomas, 1688
Sig. A2 matches K280A.
Dur. S Asa (tpw). Wel.

K279 Ken, Thomas, 1682
Cant (2). Her. Lich. Win. Wor.
Yk.

K280 Ken, Thomas, 1688
Her.

K280A *See:* K276

K281dA Ken, Thomas, [1686]
'diocess'
Ches (p. 9–24; imp?).

K284 Kendall, George, *D.D.*, 1657
Carl (tp imp). Sal.

K286 Kendall, George, *D.D.*, 1657
Bur.

K287 Kendall, George, *D.D.*, 1653
Bur. Carl. Ex.

K297 Kennet, Basil, 1697
Cant. Wel. Yk.

K298 Kennet, Basil, 1696
S Pl. Wel.

K300 Kennet, White, 1689
Wel (imp).

K302 Kennet, White, 1695
Cant (2). Chi. Ex. Linc. Pet.
Wel. Wor. Yk.

K303 Kennet, White, 1695
Cant. Ches. Ex. Her.

K304 Kennet, White, 1699
Pet.

K320 Kentish, Richard, 1648
Cant. S Pl.

K352 Kersey, John, 1673–4
Includes K353?
Glo.

K358 Kettlewell, John, 1691
Carl. Lich. Nor. S Asa (tpw).
S Pl. Wel.

K363 Kettlewell, John, 1695
Her.

K363+ Kettlewell, John, 1695
Sold by Sam. Keble, Jos. Hindmarsh
and R. Sare; 12°.
Carl.

K364 Kettlewell, John, [1694/5]
Yk.

K365 Kettlewell, John, 1684
Her. Wor.

K366 Kettlewell, John, 1691
Wel.

K367 Kettlewell, John, 1696
Ches. Llan.

K368 Kettlewell, John, 1684
Cant. Carl. Llan. Wel.

K369 Kettlewell, John, 1683
Cant (imp). Carl. Pet. Yk.

K372 Kettlewell, John, 1681
Carl. Ex. Her. Pet.

K373 Kettlewell, John, 1684
Ban. Bur. Ely.

K376 Kettlewell, John, 1700
S Asa.

K377 Kettlewell, John, 1693
Wel. Yk.

K378 Kettlewell, John, 1691
Ely. Wel.

K380 Kettlewell, John, 1688
Ban. Ex.

K380+ Kettlewell, John, 1688
For Robert Kettlewell, sold by R.
Clavel and W. Rogers; 8°.
S Asa.

K380++ Kettlewell, John, 1688
For Robert Kettlewell, sold by the
booksellers of London and
Westminster; 8°.
Cant. Pet.

K380A Kettlewell, John, 1689
Ban. Cant. Ex. Pet. S Asa.

K381 Kettlewell, John, 1686
Carl. Llan. Nor. Yk (2).

K382 Kettlewell, John, 1686
Carl.

K393 Keynes, John, 1674
Linc.

K394 Khrypffs, Nicolaus, 1650
Carl.

K398 Kidder, Richard, 1680
Ban (2). Carl.

K399 Kidder, Richard, 1694
Cant. Dur. Ely. Nor. S Asa.
S Pl (2). Wel. Yk (vol. 1 only).

K400 Kidder, Richard, 1674
Carl.

K402 Kidder, Richard, 1684
Ely. Roch. S Pl.

K403 Kidder, Richard, 1699
Roch. S Pl.

K404 Kidder, Richard, 1700
Roch. S Pl.

K405 Kidder, Richard, 1690
Cant. Pet. Wel.

K406 Kidder, Richard, 1687
Ban. Bur. Her. Roch. Sal.

K407 Kidder, Richard, 1698
Dur. Ex.

K410 Kidder, Richard, 1690
Dur.

K411 Kidder, Richard, 1687
Ban. Cant. Ex. Sal. Wel.

K412 Kidder, Richard, 1682
Llan.

K414 Kidder, Richard, 1692
Cant. Her. Pet. Wor.

K415 Kidder, Richard, 1693
Cant.

K416 Kidder, Richard, 1693
Ban. Cant.

K417 Kidder, Richard, 1694
Cant. S Asa. Wor.

K418 Kidder, Richard, 1697
Ex. Yk.

K419 Kidder, Richard, 1673
Her.

K420? Kidder, Richard, 1671
... for George Calvert and Samuel
Sprint.
Carl.

K422 Kidner, Thomas, 1676/7
Linc.

K428 Kilburne, Richard, 1657
oblong 4°.
Cant.

K433 Kilburne, Richard, 1700
Nor.

K434 Kilburne, Richard, 1659
Cant (3 − 1 imp). S Pl. Wor.

K437 Killcop, Thomas, 1648
Pet (imp).

K446? Killigrew, Henry, 1666
'in Advent'
Carl.

K447 Killigrew, Henry, 1668
Carl. Chelm. Ches.

K449 Killigrew, Henry, 1685
Pet.

K479 Kimberley, Jonathan, 1683
... in Coventry.
Chi.

K486 King, Daniel, *of Chester*,
1672
Dur (imp).

K488 King, Daniel, *of Chester*,
1656
Cant. Lich. Wor.

K492A King, Edward, [1666]
Linc.

K498 King, Henry, 1649
Yk.

K499A King, Henry, 1661
Ex.

K504 King, Henry, 1661
Cant. Ex. Wor.

K505 King, Henry, 1662
Cant (2). Carl. Win.

K506 King, Henry, 1663
Ex (2).

K507 King, Henry, 1665
Cant. Pet.

K508 King, John, *d.1679*, 1680
Carl. Linc.

K509 King, John, *fl. 1661*, 1661
Carl.

K512 King, Josiah, 1698
Yk.

K513 King, Peter, *Baron*, 1691
Her. Yk.

K521 King, William, *Abp*, 1694
Cant. S Pl.

K522A King, William, *Abp*, [1693]
Carl.

K523 King, William, *Abp*, 1687
Ban. Bur. Ex.

K526 King, William, *Abp*, 1694
Carl. Ches. Dur. Ely.

K527 King, William, *Abp*, 1694
Cant. S Pl.

K529A? King, William, *Abp*, 1694
The second edition.
Yk.

K530 King, William, *Abp*, 1696
Cant. Yk.

K534 King, William, *Abp*, 1696
S Pl.

K537? King, William, *Abp*, 1691
4°.
Cant (2).

K538 King, William, *Abp*, 1691
Dur. Glo. Wel.

K539 King, William, *Abp*, 1692
S Pl.

K540 King, William, *Abp*, 1692
Carl. S Asa.

K541 King, William, *Abp*, 1688
Ban.

K542 King, William, *Abp*, 1688
Ban.

K543A King, William, *1663 − 1712*,
1694
Wel.

K545A King, William, *1663 − 1712*,
1698
S Pl.

K571 King, 1650
Ex.

K582 Kingdomes, 1648
Cant.

K583 Kingdomes, 1643
Linc. Pet.

K605 King's, [1688]
Cant. Ex.

K614 Kingston, Richard, 1665
S Pl.

K653 Kirle, R., [1643]
Cant.

K660+ Kitchin, John, 1675
The fifth edition; Printed by T.R. to
be sold by William Crook; 8°.
Cant.

K662A Knaggs, Thomas, 1697
Cant.

K663 Knaggs, Thomas, 1699
Bur. Her.

K663B Knaggs, Thomas, 1689
Dur.

K663C? Knaggs, Thomas, 1691
'... before the ... mayor ...'
Dur.

K663D Knaggs, Thomas, 1693
Ban. Cant. Wor.

K664 Knaggs, Thomas, 1696
'preacht'
Cant.

K668 Knatchbull, *Sir* Norton, 1659
'Testamenti'
Linc. Pet.

K669 Knatchbull, *Sir* Norton, 1672
Chelm. Her. Wel.

K670 Knatchbull, *Sir* Norton, 1676
S Pl.

K671 Knatchbull, *Sir* Norton, 1677
Carl. Ely. Pet.

K672 Knatchbull, *Sir* Norton, 1693
Ches. Dur. Ely. Lich. Nor.

K675 Knave, 1679
Linc. S Asa.

K678 Knell, Paul, 1660[1]
Carl.

K679? Knell, Paul, 1648
19p.
Cant (cropped). Pet (2).

K679+ Knell, Paul, 1648
As K679, but: 20p.
Ex.

K680 Knell, Paul, 1681
Cant (tp imp).

K682 Knell, Paul, 1648
Ex. Pet. Yk.

K683 Knell, Paul, 1648
Pet.

K686 Knight, *Sir* John, [1694]
Ban.

K688 Knight, John, *D.D.*, 1682
Wel.

K702 Knolles, Richard, 1687
Cant. Dur. S Asa. Wor.

K703A Knolles, Richard, 1687
Yk.

K706 Knollys, Hanserd, 1645
Pet.

K717 Knollys, Hanserd, 1645
Ex. Sal. Win.

K730 Knowles, John, 1648
Pet (tpw).

K738 Knox, John, 1644
Linc (lacks pp. 399−400). Pet.
S Asa (as Linc). S Pl. Sal. Swel
(as Linc). Yk.

K742 Knox, Robert, 1681
S Dv.

K744 Knutton, Immanuel, 1645
Pet. Yk.

K746 *Κολλούριον*, 1649
Yk.

K747 Koran, 1649
Cant. Carl.

K747A Koran, 1649
Yk.

K748 Koran, 1688
Glo. Yk.

L1 L., 1642[3]
S Pl.

L4 L., A., 1689
Carl. Wel (2).

L8 L., B., [1679?]
Linc.

L10 L., D., 1642
Dur.

L11 L., D., 1642
Linc (22p.: anr ed. or imp?). Pet
(48p.).

L23 L., I., 1642
Ex.

L28 L., J., 1641
Sal.

L43 L., L., 1681
Linc.

L46 L., N., 1689
Ely. Ex.

L49 L., N., 1685
Yk.

L61 L., S., 1670
Llan. Sal.

L64 *See*: R932+

L75 L., T., 1659
Ex.

L85? L., W., 1642
'... dayes passages'
Linc.

L103 La Brune, Jean de, 1691
Ex.

L104 La Bruyère, Jean de, 1699
Dur. Ely.

L105 La Bruyère, Jean de, 1700
Ex.

L112 La Calprenède, Gaultier de
Coste, *Seigneur de*, 1654
Carl.

L128 La Chambre, Marin Cureau
de, 1665
Cant (imp).

L129 La Chambre, Marin Cureau
de, 1650
Cant (imp). Carl.

L134B Lachrymae, 1681
Linc.

L139? Lactantius, 1684
8°.
Cant. Carl. Chi. Ely. Ex. Linc.
Llan. Nor. S Asa. S Pl (2 − 1
imp). Sal. Wel. Win. Yk (2).

L140 Lactantius, 1685
Ban. Cant. Chi (2). Nor. Pet.
Roch. S Asa.

L141 Lactantius, 1680
Tru. Win.

L142 Lactantius, 1687
Rip. Wel. Yk.

L143 Lacy, John, 1672
Yk.

L149 La Devéze, Abel Rodolphe de,
1688
Ban. Llan.

L165 Lady, 1681
Linc.

L171 La Fayette, Marie Madeleine
de La Vergne, *Comtesse de*, 1666
Ex.

L185 Lake, Arthur, 1641
Cant. S Pl.

L186A Lake, *Sir* Edward, [1665?]
Linc.

L187 Lake, *Sir* Edward, 1642
Ex.

L188 Lake, *Sir* Edward, 1662
Cant (tpw). Carl. Ex. Linc. Sal.

L188A Lake, Edward, 1673
Linc.

L193 Lake, Edward, 1684
Cant. Carl. Yk.

L194 Lake, Edward, 1694
Cant.

L195A Lake, John, [1690]
Her.

L198 Lake, John, 1671
Yk.

L201 La Loubère, Simon de, 1693
Glo.

L203 La Martelière, Pierre de, 1689
Dur.

L210 Lamb, Thomas, 1677
Ely. Pet. S Pl.

L211 Lamb, Thomas, 1672
Bur. Chelm. S Pl.

L212? Lamb, Thomas, 1693
For W. Kettilby.
Roch.

L216+ Lambard, William, 1656
'A perambulation ...'; The third
edition; By R. Hodgkinsonne for D.
Pakeman; 8°.
Cant.

L218 Lambe, John, 1684
Ban.

L219 Lambe, John, 1673
Carl.

L220 Lambe, John, 1680
Carl. Chi. Her.

L221 Lambe, John, 1682
Carl.

L223 Lambe, John, 1691
Wor.

L224 Lambe, John, 1693
Ban. Nor.

L225 Lambe, John, 1693
Cant.

L227 Lambe, John, 1696
Cant.

L237 Lambert, John, 1659[60]
Yk.

L244 Lambert, Thomas, 1670
Dur. Yk.

L246 Lambeth, 1641
S Pl.

L288 Lamentation, 1647
Pet.

L298 Lamothe, Claude Grostête de,
1694
S Pl.

L301? La Mothe le Vayer, François
de, 1678
8°.
Ex.

L303 La Motte, François de, 1675
Cant. Ex. Linc. Nor. Wel (2 –
1 has date altered in MS to 1677).

L304A - Lamplugh, Thomas,
[1690?]
See: CLC67.
Yk.

L304B Lamplugh, Thomas, [167-?]
Ex.

L305 Lamplugh, Thomas, 1678
Ban. Carl. Ex. Her. Linc. Pet
(2). S Asa. Sal (imp). Wor. Yk
(3).

L307A? Lamy, Bernard, 1676
… M. Pitt.
Carl.

L307B? Lamy, Bernard, 1696
12°.
Nor.

L315 Lancaster, William, 1697
Cant. Dur.

L317A Lancton, Thomas, 1641
Linc.

L321A Lander, Thomas, 1681
=Pt 2 of S2767A.
Yk.

L324 Landskip, 1660
Cant (2). Carl. Yk.

L329 Lane, Bartholomew, 1683
Carl.

L331 Lane, Edward, 1681
Wel. Win.

L332 Lane, Edward, 1663
Win.

L333 Lane, Edward, 1680
Win.

L335 Lane, Edward, *Colonel*, 1654
Ex.

L341 Lane, Samuel, 1645
Chelm.

L342 Laney, Benjamin, 1669
Bur. Cant. S Pl.

L345? Laney, Benjamin, 1662
Garthwait.
Carl. Linc. Pet (2). S Asa. Win.

L346 Laney, Benjamin, 1663
Carl. Pet. S Asa.

L347 Laney, Benjamin, 1665
Cant. Carl. Linc. Pet. Wor.

L348 Laney, Benjamin, 1665
Cant. Carl. Pet. S Asa. Yk.

L349 Laney, Benjamin, 1666
Carl. Pet. Wor. Yk.

L350 Laney, Benjamin, 1675
Cant. Carl. Linc. S Asa.

L350+ Laney, Benjamin, 1680
The second edition; For Henry
Brome; 4°; Or 2nd ed. of another
sermon?, subtitle is: 'Against
comprehension'
Wor.

L351 Laney, Benjamin, 1668
Cant. S Pl.

L351B Laney, Benjamin, 1665
Linc.

L352 Laney, Benjamin, 1668
Cant. S Pl.

L363 Langbaine, Gerard, *the Elder*,
1649
Carl.

L364 Langbaine, Gerard, *the Elder*,
1678
Yk.

L366 Langbaine, Gerard, *the Elder*,
1690
Cant. Carl. Yk.

L367 Langbaine, Gerard, *the Elder*,
1641
Ex (2). Pet. S Pl.

L368 Langbaine, Gerard, *the Elder*,
1651
Cant. Lich.

L370 Langbaine, Gerard, *the Elder*,
1651
Cant.

L371 Langbaine, Gerard, *the Elder*,
1644[5]
Carl. Ex. S Asa.

L372 Langbaine, Gerard, *the Elder*,
1661
Dur (3 – 1 tpw). Win.

L373 Langbaine, Gerard, *the
Younger*, 1691
Glo. S Pl.

L378 Langdale, Marmaduke, *Baron*,
1648
'Verclaringe'
Linc.

L382 Langdale, Marmaduke, *Baron*,
1648
Cant.

L386 Langford, Emanuel, 1698
Cant. Dur. Her. Nor.

L392 Langhorne, Daniel, 1679
Carl. S Pl. Win.

L393 Langhorne, Daniel, 1673
Dur. Ex. Linc. Sal. Wel.

L395 Langhorne, Daniel, 1676
Ex. S Pl.

L396 Langhorne, Richard, 1687
Ban.

L397 Langhorne, Richard, 1679
Carl. Wor.

L398 Langhorne, Richard, [1679]
Linc (2). Yk.

L399 Langhorne, Richard, [1679]
Linc (2). Yk.

L401 Langhorne, Rowland, 1648
Ex.

L403 L'Angle, Samuel de, 1660
Yk.

L404 Langley, John, 1644
Her. Yk.

L405 Langley, Samuel, 1658
Chelm.

L408 Langley, William, 1656
Bur. Chelm. Lich. Pet (2). Yk.

L427 La Peyrère, Isaac de, 1656
Ex. Lich.

L429 La Placette, Jean, 1588 [*i.e.*
1688]
Ban. Cant. Ely. Ex. Llan.
Nor. Swel. Wel. Yk.

L430 La Placette, Jean, 1687
Cant. Ex (2). Linc. Llan. Nor.
Sal. Swel. Wel.

L431 La Quintinie, Jean de, 1693
Yk.

L432 La Quintinie, Jean de, 1699
Glo.

L434 - La Ramée, Pierre de, 1655
Sumptibus T. Garthwait; 8°.
Carl.

L434 La Ramée, Pierre de, 1669
'libri duo'; ... veneunt per ...
Pet.

L435 La Ramée, Pierre de, 1672
Ely. Wel. Win.

L439 Large, 1675
Ex. S Pl.

L444 Larkin, Edward, 1659
Pet.

L451A La Rochefoucauld,
François, *Duc de*, 1683
Carl. Wel.

L454 Larroque, Matthieu de, 1684
Ex. Pet. Tru (tpw). Wor.

L455 La Rue, Charles de, 1695
Carl. Llan.

L465 Lassels, Richard, 1670
Linc.

L487+ Last, 1652
See: CLC68.
Cant (imp).

L506 Last, [1679]
Linc.

L526 Last, 1647
Ex.

L536 Last, 1690
Nor.

L537 Latch, John, 1661
Dur.

L539+ Late, 1641
For Ioseph Hunskott; 4°.
Sal.

L547 Late, 1681
S Pl.

L550 Late, 1697
Ban. Carl. Dur. Nor.

L552 Late, 1697
Ban.

L554 Late, 1691
Cant (2).

L557 Late, 1645
Her.

L559 Late, 1647/8
Yk.

L566 Latest, 1642
Dur. Linc. Yk.

L574 Lathom, Paul, 1683
Ex.

L575 Lathom, Paul, 1676
Llan.

L579 Laud, William, 1645
S Pl. Yk.

L581 Laud, William, 1641
Yk.

L584 Laud, William, 1688
The fifth edition.
Cant (imp). Yk.

L586 Laud, William, 1695
Cant (3 − 1 v. imp). Carl. Chi.
Dur. Ely. Ex. Glo. Liv. Llan.
S Asa (imp). Sal (2). Swel. Wel.
Win. Yk.

L590 Laud, William, 1641
Pet.

L594 Laud, William, 1673
Cant. Ches. Nor. S Asa. S Dv.
S Pl. Sal. Wor.

L595 Laud, William, 1686
Ban. Bur. Cant. Chi. Lich.
Wel. Yk (2).

L596 Laud, William, 1700
Carl. Chi. Dur. Ex (2). Liv.
Swel.

L598 Laud, William, 1651
Cant. Lich. Linc. Liv. S Asa.
S Dv. Win. Yk.

L599? Laud, William, 1644[5]
Impr. date 1644.
Cant (tpw). Linc. Yk (2).

L600 Laud, William, 1667
Liv. S Asa. Win. Yk.

L601 Laud, William, 1641
Ex. Pet. Yk.

L602 Laud, William, 1644[5]
Yk (2).

L606 Lauderdale, John Maitland,
Duke of, 1687
Wor.

L610A- Lauderdale, John
Maitland, *Duke of*, [c.1679?]
'A dialogue between Duke
Lauderdale, and the Lord Danby';
[N.pl.]; brs.
Linc.

L621 Launoy, Jean de, 1689
Ches. Dur. Ex. Her. Lich.
Linc. Nor. Pet. S Asa (2). S Pl.
Sal. Wor. Yk.

L623G? La Vallière, Louise
Françoise, *Duchesse de*, 1684
16°.
Ex.

L639 Lawes, Henry, 1658
Dur.

L643 Lawes, Henry, 1669
Dur.

L651 Lawrence, Anthony, 1677
Win.

L662 Lawrence, Henry, 1652
Cant.

L663 Lawrence, Henry, 1646
Dur (tpw).

L665 Lawrence, Henry, 1646
Cant.

L673? Lawrence, Matthew, 1657
Rothwell.
Chelm.

L674 Lawrence, Richard, 1647
Sal.

L682 Lawrence, Richard, 1647
Sal.

L695 Lawes, [1642]
Date should rather be [1645/6]?
Her.

L697 Lawes, 1643
Yk.

L697+ Lawes, 1643
By Tho. Fawcet; 4°.
Ex.

L707 Lawson, George, 1662
Sal.

L707A Lawson, George, 1665
Sal.

L711 Lawson, George, 1689
Ex.

L730 Lawson, William, 1648
Cant. Yk.

L739B Lawton, Charlwood, [1693]
cap.
Dur.

L739C Lawton, Charlwood, 1693
Dur (cropped).

L744 Laxton, Thomas, 1682
Cant.

L756 Layton, Henry, [1695?]
Yk.

L757 Layton, Henry, [1698?]
Yk.

L758 Layton, Henry, [1690?]
Yk.

L759 Layton, Henry, [1700]
Yk.

L781? Leach, William, [1661]
'To the King's most excellent majesty,
... Reasons offered ...'; cap.
Yk.

L791A Lead, Jane, 1700
Wel.

L800 Leather-more, 1668
Linc.

L801 Le Blanc, Vincent, 1660
Bris.

L802 Le Blanc de Beaulieu,
Ludovicus, 1675
Cant. Chelm. Dur. Ely. Ex.
Glo. Her. S Pl. Win.

L803 Le Blanc de Beaulieu,
Ludovicus, 1683
Chi. Ex. Her (tp imp). Lich.
Llan. Nor. S Asa. S Pl (tp imp).
Win. Wor.

L804 Le Bossu, René, 1695
Dur. Ex. Glo. S Dv (tp imp).
Wel.

L806 Le Camus, Etienne, 1687
Wel.

L809 Lechford, Thomas, 1644
Linc.

L810 Lechford, Thomas, 1642
Linc.

L812 Le Clerc, Jean, 1698
Editio altera.
Cant. Ely. S Asa.

L815 Le Clerc, Jean, 1690
Cant. Ely. Nor.

L816 Le Clerc, Jean, 1690
Cant. Carl. Ex. Her.

L818 Le Clerc, Jean, 1695
'The life of the ...'
Ex.

L819 Le Clerc, Jean, 1695
Ex. Wel.

L821 Le Clerc, Jean, 1692
Ex. Nor. S Asa.

L823 Le Clerc, Jean, 1700
Ex. S Pl.

L823A? Le Clerc, Jean, 1696
Swall.
S Asa.

L824 Le Clerc, Jean, 1700
Ely. Wor (imp).

L826 Le Clerc, Jean, 1699
Dur. Ely. Lich (2). Pet. S Dv
(includes another tp with
'English'd by W.P.')*. Sal.

L827 Le Clerc, Jean, 1697
Nor.

L828 Le Clerc, Jean, 1696
Ex.

L831 Le Comte, Louis Daniel, 1697
Nor.

L839 Lee, E., 1653
Linc.

L840 Lee, Francis, 1689
S Pl.

L842 Lee, Francis, 1697
Wel.

L852 Lee, Nathaniel, 1681
Ex.

L885B Lee, Obadiah, 1685
Yk (impr. not confirmed).

L888 Lee, Richard, 1663
Ex. Pet (2 − 1 tp imp). S Asa.
S Pl (2). Win.

L889 Lee, Richard, 1664
Carl.

L903C Lee, Samuel, 1659
Wor.

L905 Leech, Jeremiah, 1644
Ex.

L908A Leedes, Edward, 1677
Wel (imp)*.

L909 Leedes, Edward, 1690
Wel.

L910 Leedes, Edward, 1699
Ely.

L914 Leeds, Daniel, 1697
S Pl.

L918 Leeds, Thomas Osborne,
Duke of, 1682
Win.

L920 Leeds, Thomas Osborne,
Duke of, 1680
Linc. Win.

L922 Leeds, Thomas Osborne,
Duke of, 1682
Carl.

L923 Leeds, Thomas Osborne,
Duke of, 1679
Win.

L923A Leeds, Thomas Osborne,
Duke of, 1689
Bur. Cant. Ely. Wel. Yk.

L929 Lefevre, Raoul, 1663
Cant.

L930+ Lefevre, Raoul, 1670
No ed. statement; By E.T. & R.H. for
Thomas Passenger; 4°.
Yk.

L934 Lefevre, Raoul, 1663
Cant.

L938 Lefevre, Raoul, 1663
Cant.

L943A Le Gendre, *Sieur de*, 1660
Author was R. Arnauld d'Andilly
(BM).
Cant.

L944 Le Gendre, Louis, 1699
Carl.

L949 Le Grand, Antoine, 1676
Carl.

L950? Le Grand, Antoine, 1694
... Mr. Horne ... Mr. Gillyflower ...
Bris. Glo.

L951 Le Grand, Antoine, 1673
Yk.

L954 Le Grand, Antoine, 1672
Cant. Ex.

L958 Le Grand, Antoine, 1675
Carl. Ex.

L960 Le Grand, Joachim, [1690]
Pet.

L960A Le Grosse, Robert, 1667
Linc.

L962? Leibnitz, Gottfried Wilhelm
von, 1671
8°.
Pet.

L965 Leicester, Philip Sidney, *Earl
of*, 1642
Sal.

L967? Leicester, Robert Sidney,
Earl of, 1642
... Sep. 27; Wing has wrong heading.
Linc.

L968 Leycesters, 1641
Carl. Chelm. Linc. Pet (3). Yk.

L969 Leicester's, 1641
Cant (tpw)*. Carl. Yk.

L969aA+ Leycester's, 1661
Printed for William Sheares; 4°.
Dur.

L973 Leycestershires, 1642
Linc.

L975 Leigh, Charles, 1700
Carl. Dur.

L981 Leigh, Dorothy, 1663
Cant (imp).

L985 Leigh, Edward, 1657
Lich (tp imp).

L986 Leigh, Edward, 1650
Chelm. Ely. Ex.

L988 Leigh, Edward, 1641
Wel.

L989 Leigh, Edward, 1642
Rip (imp). Yk.

L990 Leigh, Edward, 1646
Carl. Chelm. Dur. Her. Lich.
Linc. Nor. S Asa. S Dv. Yk.

L991 Leigh, Edward, 1650
Bur. Ely (2 − 1 imp). Her. Nor.
Pet. Roch. S Pl. Sal. Swel.
Wor (2).

L992 Leigh, Edward, 1662
Ches. Ex.

L994 Leigh, Edward, 1659
Nor.

L1001+ Leigh, Edward, 1651
The second edition; By Abraham
Miller for William Lee; 12°.
Ely.

L1003 Leigh, Edward, 1657
Chelm. Ely.

L1005 Leigh, Edward, 1670
Yk.

L1008 Leigh, Edward, 1654
'systeme'
S Asa.

L1009 Leigh, Edward, 1662
'systeme'
Ex. Wel.

L1013 Leigh, Edward, 1656
Cant. Chelm. Ely. Ex. Wor.

L1014 Leigh, Edward, 1641
Ely. Her.

L1015 Leigh, Edward, 1650
S Asa.

L1017A Leigh, John, 1654
Pet. Yk.

L1020 Leigh, Richard, 1673
Carl. Linc. Nor.

L1021 Leigh, Thomas, 1684
S Pl. Yk (2).

L1023 Leighton, Alexander, 1641
Yk.

L1028 Leighton, Robert, 1693
Yk (2).

L1028A Leighton, Robert, 1693
... sold at London by ...
Carl. Yk.

L1029 Leighton, Robert, 1694
Yk.

L1030? Leighton, Robert, 1693
Typis excusae [sic] ...
Yk.

L1031A Leighton, Robert, 1692
Dur.

L1032 Leightonhouse, Walter, 1689
Cant. Her.

L1032A Leightonhouse, Walter,
1695
Cant.

L1033 Leightonhouse, Walter, 1697
Linc. Nor.

L1038 Lemery, Nicolas, 1677
Ex.

L1042 Lemery, Nicolas, 1700
'... pharmacopaeia abridg'd'
Nor.

L1045 Le Moyne, Pierre, 1652
Lich.

L1049 Leng, John, 1698
Ely.

L1050 Leng, John, 1699
Cant. Wor.

L1054B Le Noir, Jean, 1678
8°.
Win.

L1064B Lent, 1675
Linc.

L1069 Lenthall, William, *Speaker*,
1642
Dur.

L1073 Lenthall, William, *Speaker*,
1642
Linc. Yk (2).

L1074 Lenthall, William, *Speaker*,
1641[2]
Dur (imp). Yk (2).

L1079 Lenthall, William, *Speaker*,
1641
Cant (2). Linc. Sal. Yk (2
issues).

L1080 Lenthall, William, *Speaker*,
1641
Cant. Ex.

L1083 Lenthall, William, *Speaker*,
1641
Cant. Dur.

L1084 Lenthall, William, *Speaker*,
1641
Cant.

L1089 Lenthall, William, *Speaker*,
1641
Cant. Ex. Linc. Yk.

L1099A Leon, *of Modena*, 1650
Carl.

L1103 Leonard, William, 1658
Dur.

L1104A Leonard, William, 1659
Dur.

L1105A Leonard, William, 1663
Dur (imp).

L1108 Leopold I, *Emperor of
Germany*, 1688
Carl. S Pl. Wel.

L1113 Leopold I, *Emperor of
Germany*, 1689
Carl.

L1123 Leslie, Charles, 1700
Cant. S Pl. Wel. Yk.

L1124 Leslie, Charles, 1695
Cant. Ely. Yk.

L1126 Leslie, Charles, 1700
Bur (2). Chi. Ely. S Pl. Wel.

L1128 Leslie, Charles, 1697
Bris. Yk.

L1132 Leslie, Charles, 1700
Bur. Ely. Llan. S Pl.

L1133 Leslie, Charles, 1700
Bur. Yk.

L1137 Leslie, Charles, 1700
Wel.

L1140 Leslie, Charles, 1698
Cant. Yk.

L1143 Leslie, Charles, 1695
Yk.

L1145+ Leslie, Charles, 1696
For A. and J. Churchil, and sold by
John Pearce in Exon.; 4°.
Cant.

L1146 Leslie, Charles, 1698
Her.

L1148 Leslie, Charles, 1695
Carl. Lich. Wel. Yk.

L1149A Leslie, Charles, 1697
S Pl.

L1151 Leslie, Charles, 1698
Wel.

L1152 Leslie, Charles, 1698
Dur.

L1154? Leslie, Charles, 1699
... Geo. Strahan.
Sal.

L1154B Leslie, Charles, 1699
The second edition.
Nor.

L1156 Leslie, Charles, 1696
Ely. Pet. Yk.

L1157 Leslie, Charles, 1697
8°.
Chi. S Asa. S Pl.

L1158 Leslie, Charles, 1698
Bris. Bur (2). Carl. Ches (engr.
tpw). Ex (engr. tpw). S Pl. Wel.

L1159 Leslie, Charles, 1697
Wel.

L1160 Leslie, Charles, 1694
Dur. Wel.

L1161 Leslie, Henry, 1644
Carl. Wel.

L1163 Leslie, Henry, 1649
Pet.

L1164 Leslie, Henry, 1649
Yk.

L1165 Leslie, Henry, 1649
Bris. S Pl.

L1166? Leslie, Henry, 1660
Hague.
Chelm.

L1167 Leslie, Henry, 1643
Carl. Pet (imp). Wel. Yk (2).

L1170A Leslie, John, *Bp*, 1677
Linc.

L1178A? Lesly, George, 1678
For Charles Smith.
Win.

L1180 Lessius, Leonard, 1651
S Pl.

L1183? L'Estrange, Hamon, 1659
'... as also the late Scotch
service-book ...'
Cant. Dur. Ex (2). Her. Linc.
Wor. Yk (2 — 1 copy*).

L1183+ L'Estrange, Hamon, 1659
As L1183, but: '... as also the Scotch
service-book ...'
Ban. Carl. Nor. Sal (tp imp).
Win.

L1184 L'Estrange, Hamon, 1690
Cant. Ches. Ely (2). Linc. S Pl.
Wel.

L1185? L'Estrange, Hamon, 1699
For Ch. Brome.
Lich. Nor.

L1186 L'Estrange, Hamon, 1652
Linc.

L1187 L'Estrange, Hamon, 1651
Ex. Win.

L1188 L'Estrange, Hamon, 1641
Bur (imp). Linc. Pet (3).

L1189 L'Estrange, Hamon, 1655
Lich.

L1190 L'Estrange, Hamon, 1656
2°.
Carl. Linc (2 — 1 engr. tpw).

L1192 L'Estrange, *Sir* Roger, 1682
Wel.

L1193 L'Estrange, *Sir* Roger, 1678
4°.
Carl. Dur. Win.

L1194 L'Estrange, *Sir* Roger, 1681
Ex. Wel.

L1195 L'Estrange, *Sir* Roger, 1687
Cant (2). Dur. Ely. Ex. Linc.
Wel. Yk.

L1197 L'Estrange, *Sir* Roger, 1679
Carl. Linc. Win.

L1198 L'Estrange, *Sir* Roger, 1681
Dur. Wel.

L1200 L'Estrange, *Sir* Roger, 1660
Carl (tp imp).

L1202 L'Estrange, *Sir* Roger, 1681
Cant. Carl. Dur. Linc. Wel.
Win. Yk.

L1203 L'Estrange, *Sir* Roger,
1687–88
Ex.

L1203A L'Estrange, *Sir* Roger,
1687
Glo.

L1204 L'Estrange, *Sir* Roger, 1680
Wel.

L1205 L'Estrange, *Sir* Roger, 1680
Cant. Carl. Win.

L1206 L'Estrange, *Sir* Roger, 1679
Linc. Win.

L1207 L'Estrange, *Sir* Roger, 1679
Carl (tpw). Yk.

L1208 L'Estrange, *Sir* Roger, 1680
Dur. S Pl. Wel.

L1209 L'Estrange, *Sir* Roger, 1680
Pet.

L1210 L'Estrange, *Sir* Roger, 1681
Cant. Carl. Dur (2). Her. Wel.
Win. Yk (2).

L1211 L'Estrange, *Sir* Roger, 1661
Linc.

L1213 L'Estrange, *Sir* Roger, 1661
Yk.

L1214 L'Estrange, *Sir* Roger, 1661
Carl. Pet. Win. Yk.

L1215 L'Estrange, *Sir* Roger, 1681
Cant (2). Carl. Wel. Win. Yk
(3).

L1216 L'Estrange, *Sir* Roger, 1680
Linc. Win.

L1218 L'Estrange, *Sir* Roger, 1680
Dur.

L1219 L'Estrange, *Sir* Roger, 1680
Ely. S Pl. Wel.

L1221 L'Estrange, *Sir* Roger, 1680
S Pl.

L1223 L'Estrange, *Sir* Roger, 1680
Wel.

L1225 L'Estrange, *Sir* Roger, 1681
Wel.

L1229 L'Estrange, *Sir* Roger, 1663
Linc. S Pl. Win.

L1230 L'Estrange, *Sir* Roger, 1683
Nor. Win.

L1233 L'Estrange, *Sir* Roger, 1683
Wel.

L1235 L'Estrange, *Sir* Roger, 1689
'... Sir R.L. Knight ...'; For Robert
Waston.
Cant.

L1236 L'Estrange, *Sir* Roger, 1674
Linc. Wel.

L1238 L'Estrange, *Sir* Roger, 1680
Carl. Ex.

L1239 L'Estrange, *Sir* Roger, 1680
Wel.

L1240 L'Estrange, *Sir* Roger, 1681
Win. Yk.

L1241 L'Estrange, *Sir* Roger, 1681
Wel.

L1242 L'Estrange, *Sir* Roger, 1681
Dur (2 — 1 sig E only). Yk.

L1243 L'Estrange, *Sir* Roger, 1683
S Pl.

L1245 L'Estrange, *Sir* Roger, 1681
Yk.

L1246 L'Estrange, *Sir* Roger, 1681
Dur (imp). S Pl.

L1246A L'Estrange, *Sir* Roger,
1660
Linc.

L1247 L'Estrange, *Sir* Roger, 1699
Yk.

L1248 L'Estrange, *Sir* Roger, 1679
Linc. Wel. Win.

L1249 L'Estrange, *Sir* Roger, 1680
Wel (2).

L1251 L'Estrange, *Sir* Roger, 1680
Win.

L1252 L'Estrange, *Sir* Roger, 1680
Cant. Dur. Win. Yk.

L1253 L'Estrange, *Sir* Roger, 1680
Wel.

L1258 L'Estrange, *Sir* Roger, 1679
Linc. Nor.

L1259 L'Estrange, *Sir* Roger, 1680
Second ed. not on tp.
Wel.

L1260 L'Estrange, *Sir* Roger, 1682
Yk.

L1261 L'Estrange, *Sir* Roger, 1661
Carl. Dur. S Pl.

L1262 L'Estrange, *Sir* Roger, 1661
Bris.

L1263 L'Estrange, *Sir* Roger, 1662
Pet. Win. Yk.

L1266 L'Estrange, *Sir* Roger, 1683
Wel.

L1267 L'Estrange, *Sir* Roger, 1681
Wel. Win.

L1270 L'Estrange, *Sir* Roger, 1662
Cant. Carl. Sal. Win. Yk.

L1272 L'Estrange, *Sir* Roger, 1661
Linc (tpw). Yk.

L1273 L'Estrange, *Sir* Roger, 1661
Pet. Win.

L1274 L'Estrange, *Sir* Roger, 1662
Carl.

L1275 L'Estrange, *Sir* Roger, 1680
Dur (tp imp). Win.

L1277 L'Estrange, *Sir* Roger, 1680
S Pl. Wel.

L1279 L'Estrange, *Sir* Roger, 1660
... Brome.
Carl. S Pl.

L1281 L'Estrange, *Sir* Roger, 1681
Dur. Ex (imp). Yk (2).

L1282 L'Estrange, *Sir* Roger, 1681
Carl.

L1283 L'Estrange, *Sir* Roger, 1685
Carl. Wel. Yk.

L1284 L'Estrange, *Sir* Roger, 1679
Carl. Linc.

L1285 L'Estrange, *Sir* Roger, 1660
Yk.

L1287 L'Estrange, *Sir* Roger, 1681
Carl (imp).

L1289 L'Estrange, *Sir* Roger, 1679
Sal. Win.

L1290 L'Estrange, *Sir* Roger, 1679
Carl. Wel (2). Yk.

L1293 L'Estrange, *Sir* Roger, 1641
[*i.e.* 1661]
Cant. S Pl. Yk.

L1294 L'Estrange, *Sir* Roger, 1661
Cant. Pet. Win. Yk.

L1295 L'Estrange, *Sir* Roger, 1681
Carl. Wel. Win.

L1296 L'Estrange, *Sir* Roger, 1682
Carl.

L1298 L'Estrange, *Sir* Roger, 1681
Carl. Dur. Yk.

L1301 L'Estrange, *Sir* Roger, 1680
Cant. Linc. Win (2).

L1303 L'Estrange, *Sir* Roger, 1680
Wel.

L1306 L'Estrange, *Sir* Roger, 1681
Carl.

L1307 L'Estrange, *Sir* Roger, 1680
Cant.

L1307A L'Estrange, *Sir* Roger,
1680
Carl. Wel.

L1308? L'Estrange, *Sir* Roger, 1660
For Henry Brome.
S Pl. Yk.

L1308B L'Estrange, *Sir* Roger,
1690
Pet.

L1309 L'Estrange, *Sir* Roger, 1680
Dur (2 − 1 imp). Linc. Win.

L1310 L'Estrange, *Sir* Roger, 1661
Carl. Yk.

L1311 L'Estrange, *Sir* Roger, 1661
Pet (imp?). Win.

L1315 L'Estrange, *Sir* Roger, 1663
Carl. Chi. Ely. Linc. S Pl.

L1316 L'Estrange, *Sir* Roger, 1670
Bur. Carl (2). Chelm. Ely. S Pl.
Win (2).

L1317 L'Estrange, *Sir* Roger, 1673
Pet.

L1320 L'Estrange, *Sir* Roger, 1662
Carl. Ex.

L1321 L'Estrange, *Sir* Roger, 1678
Wel. Win. Yk.

L1321A L'Estrange, *Sir* Roger,
1678
Carl. S Dv.

L1323 L'Estrange, *Sir* Roger, 1681
The second edition.
Dur.

L1324 L'Estrange, *Sir* Roger, 1649
Linc.

L1325 L'Estrange, *Sir* Roger, 1662
Carl. Linc.

L1326 L'Estrange, *Sir* Roger, 1662
Carl.

L1327 L'Estrange, *Sir* Roger, 1681
Dur. Wel.

L1328 L'Estrange, *Sir* Roger, 1681
Carl (imp).

L1328B L'Estrange, 1681
Linc. Wel. Yk (tp imp).

L1329 Let, 1659
Linc.

L1330 Leti, Gregorio, 1670
Ely. Her.

L1330C Leti, Gregorio, 1671
Cant. Ex (tp imp?: 'Ceremonies
of ...').

L1332 Leti, Gregorio, 1666
Carl.

L1334? Leti, Gregorio, 1667
... R. Littlebury.
Dur. Linc.

L1334C Leti, Gregorio, 1677
Cant (imp).

L1335 Leti, Gregorio, 1669
Ely ('... nephews from the time
...'). Ex ('... nephews; wherein is
related ...'). Pet (as Ex).

L1337 Leti, Gregorio, 1673
Ches.

L1354 Letter, 1645
Sal (tp imp).

L1356? Letter, 1681
'Stephen Colledge'
Ches.

L1364 Letter, 1675
Carl.

L1371 Letter, 1688
Cant.

L1372A Letter, [1679]
Linc (2).

L1387 Letter, 1688
Chi.

L1390 Letter, 1680
Linc.

L1391 Letter, 1680
Linc.

L1396 Letter, 1695
Carl. Yk.

L1399 Letter, 1674
Cant.

L1403 Letter, 1643
Dur.

L1405 Letter, [1680]
Cant. Linc.

L1414B Letter, 1700
S Asa.

L1414B+ Letter, 1700
For T. Leigh and D. Midwinter; 8°.
Ban.

L1432 Letter, 1643
Carl.

L1439 Letter, 1678
Dur.

L1469 Letter, 1692
Dur.

L1489 Letter, 1691
Dur (imp).

L1491 Letter, 1679
Yk.

L1510 Letter, 1679
Yk.

L1515 Letter, 1682
Win.

L1516 Letter, 1659
Yk.

L1536+ Letter, 1650
See: CLC69.
Dur.

L1538 Letter, 1653
Dur.

L1553 Letter, 1687
Dur.

L1557 Letter, 1645
Carl. Linc.

L1558 Letter, 1645
Win.

L1564 Letter, 1659
Linc.

L1567 Letter, 1688
Dur.

L1568+ Letter, [1688?]
Sold by Sam. Keble; 8°.
Cant.

L1569 Letter, 1681
Ches.

L1573A Letter, 1643
Ex.

L1574 Letter, 1675
Win.

L1574A Letter, 1675
Linc.

L1575 Letter, [1688]
Cant (2). S Pl.

L1576A Letter, 1643
Pet.

L1578 Letter, 1645[6]
Carl. Chelm.

L1581 Letter, 1668
Wel.

L1584 Letter, 1679
Win.

L1589 Letter, 1642[3]
Linc.

L1594 Letter, 1642
Carl.

L1605 Letter, 1647
Yk.

L1609 Letter, 1642
Yk (2).

L1609AB Letter, 1642
Yk (2)*.

L1613 Letter, [1642]
Linc.

L1619 Letter, 1642
Ex.

L1632 Letter, 1689
Wel.

L1651 Letter, 1695
Dur.

L1652 Letter, [1680]
Linc.

L1655 Letter, 1679
Linc.

L1658 Letter, 1689
S Pl. Wel.

L1659 Letter, 1677
Carl.

L1662 Letter, 1696
Bris. Dur. Her.

L1678 Letter, 1695
Carl.

L1680 Letter, 1698
Cant. Wel.

L1686B Letter, 1647
Win (tp imp).

L1690 Letter, 1643
Carl. Win.

L1700 Letter, 1680
Win.

L1713B Letter, 1670
Llan. Win.

L1714 Letter, 1691
Llan.

L1718 Letter, [1672]
Dur. Linc.

L1727 Letter, [1688]
Cant. Wel.

L1728 Letter, [1688]
Linc. S Pl.

L1733 Letter, 1648
Linc. Yk.

L1734 Letter, [1680]
Linc.

L1746A Letter, 1693
Bris. Carl.

L1747 Letter, 1679
Wel.

L1751 Letter, 1696
Carl.

L1757 Letter, 1643
Carl.

L1758 Letter, 1689
Ban. Carl. Nor.

L1759 Letter, 1683
Carl. Dur. Ely. Ex. Pet.
S Asa.

L1764 Letter, 1643
Linc.

L1768 Letter, 1643
Linc. Yk.

L1773 Letters, 1672
Lich.

L1790 Leurechon, Jean, 1653
Cant.

L1793A? Leusden, John, 1686
8°.
Ely.

L1794A Levassor, Michel, 1700
Ex.

L1795 Levassor, Michel, 1695
Ban. Nor.

L1799 Leveller, 1659
Ex (tp imp).

L1800A Levellers, [1649]
2 eds?
Cant. Ex.

L1807A Leven, Alexander Leslie,
1st Earl of, 1641
Cant. Linc. Yk.

L1807B Leven, Alexander Leslie,
1st Earl of, 1641
Dur.

L1812 Leven, Alexander Leslie, *1st
Earl of*, 1646
Yk.

L1822B? Levet, John, [1645?]
cap.
Linc. Win.

L1831 Lewgar, John, 1660
Yk.

L1832 Lewgar, John, 1662
Ches.

L1832A Lewgar, John, 1657
Linc.

L1836 Lewis, David, [1679]
Dur.

L1849 Lewis, Mark, [1678]
Linc.

L1851 Lewis, William, 1680
Linc. Yk.

L1854+ Lewthwat, Richard, 1679
By A. Godbid, and J. Playford; 8°.
Pet. Win.

L1860 Lex, 1680
Linc.

L1861 Lex, 1647
Sal.

L1868 Ley, John, 1654
Pet.

L1870 Ley, John, 1646
Pet.

L1871 Ley, John, 1641
Cant. Ches. Wor. Yk.

L1872 Ley, John, 1641
Linc.

L1873 Ley, John, 1656
Pet.

L1874 Ley, John, 1641
Cant. Ches. Wor.· Yk.

L1875 Ley, John, 1641
Pet. Sal. Yk (2).

L1876 Ley, John, 1641
S Pl.

L1877 Ley, John, 1658
Pet.

L1879 Ley, John, 1643
Cant (2).

L1881 Ley, John, 1641
Cant. Ches. Wor. Yk.

L1883 Ley, John, 1646
Pet. Yk.

L1884 Ley, John, 1643
Yk.

L1884A Ley, John, 1643
Yk.

L1886? Ley, John, 1641
Latham.
Her (imp). Wor.

L1907 Leybourn, William, 1653
Yk.

L1911 Leybourn, William, 1690
Bris. Glo.

L1915 Leybourn, William, 1675
Ex.

L1925 Leybourn, William, 1669
Cant (imp).

L1929? Leybourn, William, 1685
... in Bath ...
Cant.

L1931 Leybourn, William, 1694
Glo.

L1943 Leycester, *Sir* Peter, 1673
2°.
Dur. Ex. Lich. Wor.

L1948 Lier, 1648
Sal.

L1960 Liberty, 1661
Cant.

L1963 Liberty, 1648
Carl.

L1965 Liberty, 1681
Carl.

L1980 Life, 1680
Pet.

L2001 Life, 1649
Yk.

L2012? Life, 1669
For Sam. Speed.
Cant. Linc.

L2020B Life, 1651
8°.
Cant.

L2025D Life, 1697
Cant.

L2036 Life, 1695
Carl.

L2045 Light, 1656
Yk.

L2047 Light, 1648
Yk.

L2051 Lightfoot, John, 1684
Ban. Bris. Cant (2). Carl. Ches.
Chi. Dur. Ely. Ex. Glo. Her
(2). Lich. Nor. Roch. S Dv.
Sal. Wel. Yk (2).

L2053 Lightfoot, John, 1643
Cant (2 – 1 imp). Nor. Pet.

L2055 Lightfoot, John, 1643
Dur. Ex. Nor. Yk.

L2057 Lightfoot, John, 1655
Cant. S Alb. S Pl.

L2058 Lightfoot, John, 1644
Ex.

L2061 Lightfoot, John, 1658
Linc. S Pl. Win. Wor.

L2062 Lightfoot, John, 1671
'S. Johannis'
Ely. Pet. S Pl. Sal. Wor.

L2063 Lightfoot, John, 1674
Wor.

L2065 Lightfoot, John, 1663
Win.

L2065A Lightfoot, John, 1663
S Pl*. Wor*.

L2068 Lightfoot, John, 1645
Nor.

L2069 Lightfoot, John, 1647
S Asa.

L2070 Lightfoot, John, 1700
Dur. Ex. Linc. Nor. Wel.

L2071 Lightfoot, John, 1650
Nor. Yk.

L2072 Lightfoot, John, [1649]
Cant. Dur. Yk (2).

L2073 Lightfoot, Peter, 1649
Yk.

L2075 Ligon, Richard, 1657
Pet.

L2076 Ligon, Richard, 1673
Bris. Win.

L2079 Lilburne, John, [1649]
Cant (2 – 1 imp). Ex. Pet. Yk.

L2080 Lilburne, John, [1646]
Yk.

L2085 Lilburne, John, [1653]
Dur (imp).

L2089 Lilburne, John, 1641
Yk.

L2090 Lilburne, John, [1645]
Pet ('friend'). Yk ('freind').

L2092 Lilburne, John, [1645]
Yk.

L2097 Lilburne, John, [1653]
Sal (cropped).

L2101 Lilburne, John, 1650
Yk.

L2103 Lilburne, John, 1645
Pet.

L2106 Lilburne, John, [1649]
Pet. Yk.

L2110 Lilburne, John, 1648
Ex (2).

L2110A Lilburne, John, 1648
[N.pl.].
Linc.

L2111 Lilburne, John, [1646]
Linc.

L2112 Lilburne, John, [1647]
Pet.

L2115 Lilburne, John, 1649
Cant. Yk.

L2118+ Lilburne, John, 1646
London, printed by Thomas Paine; 4°.
Yk.

L2123 Lilburne, John, [1647]
Yk.

L2125 Lilburne, John, [1646]
Cant.

L2138 Lilburne, John, 1641
S Asa.

L2139? Lilburne, John, 1646
[N.pl.], Octob. 1646.
Sal.

L2141 Lilburne, John, 1653
Ex.

L2142 Lilburne, John, 1649
Cant. Ex.

L2150 Lilburne, John, [1647]
Cant.

L2154 Lilburne, John, 1649
Cant. Yk (tpw, or anr ed.
without impr. & date?)*.

L2162 Lilburne, John, [1649]
Cant.

L2168 Lilburne, John, 1645
Yk.

L2171 Lilburne, John, 1647
Dur.

L2174 Lilburne, John, [1647]
Cant.

L2180 Lilburne, John, 1649
Cant*.

L2182 Lilburne, John, 1649
Yk.

L2188 Lilburne, John, [1648]
Linc.

L2193 Lilburne, John, [1647]
Yk.

L2195 Lilburne, John, 1646
Sal. Yk.

L2200 Lilburne, Robert, 1651
Glo. Linc.

L2202 Lilburns, 1659
Ex.

L2227 Lilly, William, 1653
Not a Wing book: the impr. refers to
L2228; BM has [Amsterdam] for this
ed.
Linc.

L2228 Lilly, William, 1651
Linc. Yk (imp).

L2242 Lilly, William, 1642
Linc.

L2258 Lily, William, 1672
Yk.

L2261 Lily, William, 1699
Nor. S Dv.

L2262 Lily, William, 1641
Wel.

L2265D Lily, William, 1680
'Prosodia'
Wel.

L2265E+ Lily, William, 1693
As L2265E, apart from date.
Cant.

L2274 Lily, William, 1689
Her.

L2274C Lily, William, 1694
Cant.

L2275+ Lily, William, 1644
'A shorte ...'; Printed by the printers
of London; 4°.
Yk (imp).

L2279 Lily, William, 1653
Cant.

L2280B Lily, William, 1660
Bur (Wing's location deposited
here).

L2286 Lily, William, 1668
Yk.

L2293 Lily, William, 1673
Yk.

L2296 Lily, William, 1679
Ex.

L2299D Lily, William, 1690
Her.

L2299E Lily, William, 1691
Nor.

L2300A Lily, William, 1693
Cant.

L2303 Lily, William, 1699
Nor. S Dv.

L2305 Limborch, Philipp, 1700
Glo. Llan. Nor. Sal. Yk.

L2308 Linch, Samuel, 1662
8°.
Ex.

L2311 Lindley, Benjamin, 1678
Yk.

L2324 Lindsay, John Lindsay, *Earl
of*, 1641
Cant (imp). Linc.

L2335 Linfield, James, 1679
Linc.

L2345 Ling, Nicholas, 1678
Cant (imp).

L2353 Lingard, Richard, 1668
Dur.

L2358 Lips, Joest, 1663
Wel.

L2361 Lips, Joest, 1688
Ban.

L2362 Lips, Joest, 1692
Ches. Ex. Nor. S Asa. Sal.
Yk.

L2363 Lips, Joest, 1698
Ely.

L2370 Lisola, François Paul, *Baron
de*, 1667
Carl. Pet.

L2371 Lisola, François Paul, *Baron
de*, 1673
Sal.

L2372 Lisola, François Paul, *Baron
de*, 1673
'appeal'; 52p.
Linc*. Pet*.

L2376 List, [1681]
No impr.
Linc (2).

L2395 List, 1672
Linc.

L2402 List, 1663
Win.

L2403 List, [1679]
Dur. Linc (2).

L2413 List, 1642
Linc.

L2415A? List, 1662
'Hampshire'
Pet.

L2442A List, 1642
For Edmund Paxton.
Dur.

L2463 List, 1653
Linc.

L2471 List, 1649
'... for tryall ...'
Yk.

L2473A List, 1679
Linc.

L2497 List, 1651
Glo.

L2498E+ List, 1666
For John Martyn and James Allestry;
brs.
Carl.

L2516 Lister, Martin, 1696
Ex.

L2518 Lister, Martin, 1682
Yk.

L2519 Lister, Martin, 1684
Ex.

L2520 Lister, Martin, 1694
Ex.

L2521 Lister, Martin, 1695
Ex.

L2523 Lister, Martin, 1678
Yk.

L2524 Lister, Martin, 1685−92
Cant.

L2525 Lister, Martin, 1699
Ex.

L2526 Lister, Martin, 1699
Yk.

L2528 Lister, Martin, 1683
Yk.

L2553 Little, 1641[2]
Dur.

L2558B Littlebury, Robert, [1676]
Linc.

L2563 Littleton, Adam, 1678
Ban. Ex. Pet. S Dv. S Pl.
Swel. Win.

L2565 Littleton, Adam, 1693
Cant (imp?). Ches (tpw)*.

L2565+ Littleton, Adam, 1693
Cambridge, for W. Rawlins, T. Dring,
J. Place and the executors of S. Leigh;
4°.
Wel.

L2566 Littleton, Adam, 1658
Dur.

L2567 Littleton, Adam, 1680
Carl.

L2570 Littleton, Adam, 1671
Win.

L2571 Littleton, Adam, 1680
Cant. Chi. Llan. New.

L2572 Littleton, Adam, 1680
Cant. Dur. Ex. Her. S Dv.
Wel. Win.

L2573 Littleton, Adam, 1662
Carl. Ches.

L2577 Littleton, Edward, *fl. 1694*,
1689
Yk.

L2581 Littleton, Edward, *fl. 1694*
1691
Cant.

L2584A Littleton, Edward, *Baron*,
1641[2]
Cant. Dur.

L2589 Liturgia, 1693
Ches. Linc. Sal. Yk.

L2593A Lively, 1680
For Richard Royston; Consists of
D116 & D2542.
Ban. Carl.

L2594A Lively, 1659
Ex. Win.

L2595 Livesey, James, 1674
Carl.

L2612 Livius, Titus, 1679
Bur (imp). S Dv (vol. 2 only).

L2615 Livius, Titus, 1686
Cant (2). Ex. Glo.

L2617 Livro, 1695
Nor. Win.

L2619 Llanvaedonon, William,
1655
Pet.

L2621 Llewellin, Edward, 1650
Yk (2).

L2623 Llewellyn, Martin, 1660
Win.

L2628 Llewellyn, Martin, 1660
Win (imp)*.

L2636 Lloyd, David, *1635 – 1692*,
1664
Ex. Pet (imp).

L2639 Lloyd, David, *1635 – 1692*,
1682
Carl.

L2640 Lloyd, David, *1635 – 1692*,
1660
Cant (2 − 1: As Wing, but
'Charls'; 2: As Win). Win
(anon.; 'pourtraiture … Charls').

L2642 Lloyd, David, *1635 – 1692*,
1668
Cant. Dur. Ex. Liv. S Asa (2).
Wor.

L2646 Lloyd, David, *1635 – 1692*,
1670
Cant. Roch. Win.

L2648 Lloyd, David, *1635 – 1692*,
1665
Nor. Yk.

L2660 Lloyd, Lodowick, 1653
Sal (imp). Yk.

L2673 Lloyd, William, *Bp*, 1688
Dur (30p., cropped). Her (46p.,
imp). Wel (46p., imp).

L2673A *See*: C4081++

L2674 Lloyd, William, *Bp*, 1699
S Asa. Sal.

L2675 Lloyd, William, *Bp*, 1673
Cant. Wel.

L2676 Lloyd, William, *Bp*, 1677
Ban. Ely. Ex. Her. Sal (2).
Wel. Win (imp)*.

L2677 Lloyd, William, *Bp*, 1674
Cant (2). Her. Sal. Wel.

L2678 Lloyd, William, *Bp*, 1674
Ban. Bris. Cant. Ely. Ex. Glo.
Her. Linc. Wel. Win.

L2679 Lloyd, William, *Bp*, 1691
Carl. Her. Pet (imp).

L2681 Lloyd, William, *Bp*, 1684
Cant. Carl. Ches. Dur. Ely.
Ex. Llan. S Pl. Wel.

L2682 Lloyd, William, *Bp*, 1684
Lich. S Asa.

L2683 Lloyd, William, *Bp*, 1667
Cant. Chelm. Ex. Linc. S Pl.
Sal. Wel. Win.

L2685 Lloyd, William, *Bp*, 1675
Ban. Ely. Ex. Her. Sal.

L2686 Lloyd, William, *Bp*, 1691
Llan.

L2687 Lloyd, William, *Bp*, 1691
S Asa (imp).

L2688 Lloyd, William, *Bp*, 1677
Carl. Wel.

L2689 Lloyd, William, *Bp*, 1679
Ex.

L2690 Lloyd, William, *Bp*, 1692
Cant (2). Carl. Dur. Pet.

L2692 Lloyd, William, *Bp*, 1674
Ban. Bris. Cant (3). Ely. Ex
(2). Glo (tp imp). Her. Sal.
Wel. Win (tp imp).

L2692B Lloyd, William, *Bp*, 1688
'Seasonable advice …'
Cant. Nor. Wel.

L2693 Lloyd, William, *Bp*, 1673
Dur.

L2694 Lloyd, William, *Bp*, 1673
Pet. Yk.

L2695 Lloyd, William, *Bp*, 1673
Cant. Wel. Wor.

L2696 Lloyd, William, *Bp*, 1673
Cant. Pet. Wel.

L2697 Lloyd, William, *Bp*, 1673
Ban. Bris. Ely. Ex. Glo. Her
(tpw). Nor. Sal.

L2700? Lloyd, William, *Bp*, 1678
'… Sr Edmund-Berry Godfrey …'
Carl. Her. Linc. Pet. S Dv.
Yk.

L2700+ Lloyd, William, *Bp*, 1678
As L2700, but: '… Sr Edmund-Bury
Godfrey …'
Cant (2 − 1 imp). Dur (2 states).
Her (2 states). Llan. Wor.

L2702 Lloyd, William, *Bp*, 1668
Cant. Carl. Ely. Ex. Wor.

L2703 Lloyd, William, *Bp*, 1672
Carl. Ches (2). Ely. Yk.

L2704 Lloyd, William, *Bp*, 1673
Ban. Bur. Wel.

L2705 Lloyd, William, *Bp*, 1675
Ban. Carl. Ches (2). Ely. Llan.
Pet. Win.

L2705A Lloyd, William, *Bp*, 1678
8°.
Bur (Wing's location deposited
here). Ches. Ex (2). Roch. S Pl.

L2706? Lloyd, William, *Bp*, 1694
8°.
Llan. S Asa.

L2707 Lloyd, William, *Bp*, 1698
Yk*.

L2708 Lloyd, William, *Bp*, 1674
Carl. Ely. Her. Linc. S Asa (tp
imp). Sal (tpw). Wor.

L2709 Lloyd, William, *Bp*, 1679
Ban. Cant. Carl. Ely. Linc.
Wel. Wor (2).

L2711 Lloyd, William, *Bp*, 1679
Ban. Cant. Carl. Ely. Linc.
Sal. Wel.

L2712 Lloyd, William, *Bp*, 1680
Ban. Cant. Carl. Chi. Dur.
Linc. Wor.

L2712+ Lloyd, William, *Bp*, 1680
For Henry Brome; 4°.
S Asa.

L2713 Lloyd, William, *Bp*, 1689
Ban. Cant. Carl. Sal (imp).

L2714 Lloyd, William, *Bp*, 1690
Cant. Carl. Lich. S Asa. Sal.
Wel.

L2715 Lloyd, William, *Bp*, 1691
Cant. S Dv.

L2716 Lloyd, William, *Bp*, 1692
Cant (2). Her. Wor.

L2717 Lloyd, William, *Bp*, 1697
Bur. Cant. Her.

L2720B Lloyd, William, *1674 – 1719*,
1700
Dur.

L2721A Lobb, Stephen, 1698
S Asa.

L2726 Lobb, Stephen, 1682
Yk.

L2729A Lobb, Stephen, 1687
Yk (apparently not cap.).

L2730 Lobb, Stephen, 1685
Nor.

L2733 Lobo, Jeronymo, 1669
Cant (tp imp).

L2736 Locke, John, 1700
Dur. S Asa.

L2737 Locke, John, 1697
Her.

L2740 Locke, John, 1694
Carl. Chelm. Glo. Wel.

L2741 Locke, John, 1695
Bur. Linc. Pet. S Alb. S Asa
(imp). Yk.

L2742? Locke, John, 1700
Churchill.
Chi.

L2746B Locke, John, 1676
Glo. Nor.

L2747 Locke, John, 1689
Bris.

L2748A Locke, John, 1697
Win.

L2749 Locke, John, 1697
Ban. Pet. S Asa.

L2751 Locke, John, 1695
Ban (Churchil). Bur (Churchill).
Cant (as Ban). Ex (as Ban). Wel
(as Ban).

L2753 Locke, John, 1697
Ban.

L2754 Locke, John, 1699
Llan. S Asa.

L2755 Locke, John, 1690
Nor.

L2756 Locke, John, 1697
Cant. Pet.

L2762 Locke, John, 1693
Ely*.

L2767 Locke, John, 1694
Yk.

L2768 Locke, John, 1698
Carl.

L2769 Locke, John, 1695
Dur. Ely.

L2770 Locke, Matthew, 1675
Dur. Yk (imp).

L2771 Locke, Matthew, 1656
Dur.

L2772 Locke, Matthew, 1656
Dur.

L2773 Locke, Matthew, 1656
Dur.

L2774 Locke, Matthew, 1673
Dur.

L2777 Locke, Matthew, 1673
Dur.

L2785 Lockyer, Nicholas, 1646
Ex.

L2788? Lockyer, Nicholas, 1645
The fourth edition; Cambridge, by
Roger Daniel for John Rothwell.
Linc.

L2794 Lockyer, Nicholas, 1646
4°.
Ex.

L2812 Lodington, Thomas, 1674
Pet.

L2812A Lodington, Thomas, 1674
Pet.

L2817 Loe, William, 1645
Her. Wel.

L2834 Logan, John, 1677
2°.
Ex. Linc. Wel.

L2837 Loggan, David, [1690?]
Cant. Wel.

L2838 Loggan, David, 1675
Ex. Glo. Roch. Wel. Win.
Wor.

L2838+ Loggan, David, [1675?]
Oxoniae, e Theatro Sheldoniano.
London. Printed & sold by H:
Overton; 2°.
Cant.

L2841? Λογικη, 1661
'reasonablenesse'
Carl. Pet.

L2848 London, William, 1660
Yk.

L2850 London, William, 1658
Cant. Yk.

L2851N London. Common Council,
1641
Dur.

L2851S London. Common Council,
1647
London is on tp.
Yk (2).

L2852Q London. Common Council,
1660
Yk (2).

L2854 London. Common Council,
1668
Linc.

L2864I? London. Court of
Aldermen, [1665]
No impr.
S Pl.

L2905A London-ministers, 1662
Carl.

L2922 Londons, 1642
Sal.

L2927 London's, 1679
Yk.

L2937 Londons, [1665]
Carl.

L2940 Londons, [1679]
Linc.

L2958 Long, Thomas, 1691
Ex. S Pl.

L2959 Long, Thomas, 1673
Ex (2).

L2960 Long, Thomas, 1673
Ex.

L2961 Long, Thomas, 1689
Ex. Nor.

L2962 Long, Thomas, 1677
Carl. Ex.

L2963 Long, Thomas, 1684
Ex. Pet.

L2964 Long, Thomas, 1682
Carl. Her. S Pl. Win.

L2964A Long, Thomas, 1682
8°.
Dur. Wor.

L2965 Long, Thomas, 1693
Ex (2). Nor.

L2966 Long, Thomas, 1658
Ex (3). Yk.

L2967 Long, Thomas, 1689
Ban. Ex. Nor. Wel.

L2968 Long, Thomas, 1689
Ex (3). Nor.

L2969 Long, Thomas, 1689
Ex (2). Nor (2). Pet. Wel.

L2970 Long, Thomas, 1684
Ex. Nor.

L2971 Long, Thomas, 1677
Cant. Carl. Dur. Ex.

L2972 Long, Thomas, 1683
Ex (2). Nor (tpw).

L2973 Long, Thomas, 1689
Ex. Nor.

L2974 Long, Thomas, 1678
Carl (imp). Ex (imp). Llan. Pet.
Win. Yk.

L2975 Long, Thomas, 1684
Ex. Nor.

L2976 Long, Thomas, 1682
Carl. Ex. S Pl. Sal.

L2977 Long, Thomas, 1680
Ex. Win.

L2978 Long, Thomas, 1684
Dur. Ex. Nor. Yk.

L2979 Long, Thomas, 1689
Carl. Ex. Wel.

L2980 Long, Thomas, 1689
Ban. Carl. Ex. Nor (2). S Pl.

L2981 Long, Thomas, 1697
Ex. S Asa.

L2982 Long, Thomas, 1680
Ex (2).

L2982A Long, Thomas, 1680
Cant.

L2983 Long, Thomas, 1685
Nor.

L2984 Long, Thomas, 1682
Ban. Carl. Ex (3). S Pl. Sal.
Win. Yk.

L2985 Long, Thomas, 1683
Carl. Ex. Win.

L2986 Long, Thomas, 1690
Ex (2). Nor. Yk (2).

L2987 Long, Thomas, 1690
Carl. Ex (2). Yk (2).

L2987A Long, Thomas, 1690
Wel.

L3028 Looking glasse, 1645
Yk.

L3045 Lord, 1654
Her.

L3046 Lord, 1650
Glo.

L3062 Lord's, [1689]
Wel.

L3065 Loredano, Giovanni
Francesco, 1681
Cant. Chi. S Pl. Yk.

L3067 Loredano, Giovanni
Francesco, 1659
Cant.

L3079? Lortie, André, 1677
8°.
Carl. Wel.

L3080B Loss, Friedrich, 1672
Chelm.

L3084 Lotius, Eleasar, 1649
Sal.

L3085 Loudoun, John Campbell,
Earl of, 1641
Cant.

L3086 Loudoun, John Campbell,
Earl of, 1641
Cant.

L3090 Loudoun, John Campbell,
Earl of, 1645
Cant. Pet.

L3097 Louis XIII, *King of France*,
1642
Dur.

L3100 Louis XIV, *King of France*,
1688
S Pl. Wel.

L3109 Louis XIV, *King of France*,
1649
Cant.

L3110 Louis XIV, *King of France*,
1674
Linc.

L3112 Louis XIV, *King of France*,
1666
Linc. Sal.

L3119 Louis XIV, *King of France*,
1686
Ban. Dur.

L3120 Louis XIV, *King of France*,
1686
Carl.

L3129 Louis XIV, *King of France*,
1688
Ban. S Pl. Wel.

L3130 Louis XIV, *King of France*,
1688
S Pl.

L3139 Louis XIV, *King of France*,
1700
Wel.

L3139B Louis XIV, *King of France*,
1660
Carl.

L3140 Louis XIV, *King of France*,
1678
Ex.

L3140A Louis XIV, *King of France*,
[1659]
Cant.

L3143 Love, Christopher, 1651
Pet. Yk.

L3146 Love, Christopher, 1658
Chelm.

L3149 Love, Christopher, 1654
Yk.

L3150 Love, Christopher, 1658
Second ed. not on tp.
Chelm.

L3151 Love, Christopher, 1657
Carl. Chelm.

L3152 Love, Christopher, 1645
Pet (2 − 1 imp). Win. Yk.

L3159+ Love, Christopher, 1657
No ed. statement; For Iohn Rothwell;
4°.
Chelm.

L3161 Love, Christopher, 1653
S Asa.

L3163 Love, Christopher, 1658
Chelm.

L3164 Love, Christopher, 1671
Carl. Yk.

L3167? Love, Christopher, 1649
Wing has wrong date?
Yk.

L3171 Love, Christopher, 1657
Chelm.

L3174 Love, Christopher, 1646
Pet.

L3175 Love, Christopher, 1647
Pet.

L3178 Love, Christopher, 1653
S Asa. Yk.

L3180 Love, Christopher, 1658
Chelm.

L3181 Love, Christopher, [1651]
Cant (imp).

L3187 Love, Christopher, 1657
Chelm.

L3192 Love, Richard, 1660
Ely. Linc. Pet. Win.

L3193 Love, Richard, 1642
Pet. S Asa. Yk.

L3243 Lovell, Robert, 1659
12°.
Cant.

L3244 Lovell, Robert, 1665
Chelm. Wel.

L3246 Lovell, Robert, 1661
Carl. Ex.

L3247 Lovell, William, 1661
8°.
Yk.

L3299 Lowde, James, 1694
S Pl. Yk.

L3301 Lowde, James, 1699
Ex. Yk (2).

L3304 Lowe, Edward, 1664
... Richard Davis.
Win. Yk (Madan 2663).

L3323 Lowndes, William, 1695
Glo.

L3324 Lowth, Simon, 1673
Linc.

L3325 Lowth, Simon, 1674
Yk.

L3328 Lowth, Simon, 1687
Cant.

L3329 Lowth, Simon, 1685
Ex. S Asa. S Pl (2). Sal. Yk.

L3330 Lowth, William, 1692
Ely (2). Ex. Llan. New. Yk.

L3331 Lowth, William, 1699
Ely. Nor. S Asa. Sal.

L3334 Lowthorp, Jonathan, 1690
Her.

L3337 Loyal, 1661
Linc.

L3353A Loyal, [1691?]
Wel (imp).

L3360 Loyal, 1680
Linc.

L3363 Loyall, 1642
Yk (2).

L3364 Loyall, 1648
Linc.

L3391 Lucas, John Lucas, *Baron*,
1673
Dur ('subsidy bill'). Pet
('subsidie bill'). Yk.

L3392 Lucas, John Lucas, *Baron*,
1670[1]
Linc.

L3394 Lucas, Richard, 1692
Cant. Sal.

L3395 Lucas, Richard, 1692
Cant.

L3396 Lucas, Richard, 1685
Cant.

L3398 Lucas, Richard, 1690
Ches. Dur. Ex.

L3399 Lucas, Richard, 1696
Bur. Ely.

L3400 Lucas, Richard, 1700
S Asa.

L3401 Lucas, Richard, 1694
Cant.

L3402 Lucas, Richard, 1685
For George Pawlett and Samuel Smith.
Ex.

L3403 Lucas, Richard, 1692
8°.
Bur. Dur. Ely.

L3405 Lucas, Richard, 1696
Cant. Her.

L3408 Lucas, Richard, 1677
Carl. Ex.

L3410 Lucas, Richard, 1685
Bur.

L3411 Lucas, Richard, 1693
Ely. Lich. New.

L3412? Lucas, Richard, 1700
... H. Bonwick.
Bur. S Asa.

L3413 Lucas, Richard, 1697
Carl. Wor.

L3414 Lucas, Richard, 1696
Bur. Dur. Ely. Ex. Yk.

L3415 Lucas, Richard, 1697
S Pl.

L3416 Lucas, Richard, 1693
Ely ('Bieng the day'). Her (as
Ely). S Dv ('Being the day'). Sal
(as Ely).

L3417 Lucas, Richard, 1686
Llan. Wor.

L3418 Lucas, Richard, 1691
Cant.

L3420 Lucas, Richard, 1699
S Asa.

L3421 Lucas, Richard, 1699
Bur. Dur.

L3422 Lucas, Richard, 1683
Cant. Liv.

L3423 Lucas, *Sir* Thomas, 1641[2]
Linc.

L3426C Lucian, 1684
... authoris.
Rip.

L3427B Lucian, 1664
Bris.

L3427C Lucian, 1667
Ex. Nor.

L3434 Lucian, 1663
Ex.

L3441 Lucilla, 1686
Cant. Sal.

L3444 Lucretius, 1686
Cantabrigiae, ... H. Dickenson.
Ely. Nor. S Dv.

L3445 Lucretius, 1695
... bibliopol. Lond.
Cant. Ches. Ex. Linc. Nor.
S Asa.

L3447 Lucretius, 1682
Ches.

L3449 Lucretius, 1683
... in Oxford.
Ex. Pet.

L3450 Lucretius, 1700
Ex.

L3451 Luctus, 1700
2°.
Sal (imp).

L3453 Lucy, William, 1657
Lich. Sal.

L3454 Lucy, William, 1663
Dur. Ex. Her.

L3454A? Lucy, William, 1673
4°.
Ex. Win (imp).

L3456 Lucy, William, 1670
Ches. Ex. Her. Sal. Win. Yk.

L3460 Ludlow, Edmund, 1698
8°.
Ex. Swel.

L3462 Ludlow, Edmund, 1699
Vevay.
Swel.

L3463 Ludolf, Heinrich Wilhelm,
1696
Wel.

L3465 Ludolf, Hiob, 1661
Cant. Ex. Linc. S Pl. Wel. Yk.

L3466 Ludolf, Hiob, 1661
Cant. Ex. Linc. S Pl. Wel. Yk.

L3467 Ludolf, Hiob, 1661
Cant. Ex. Linc. S Pl. Wel. Yk.

L3468A Ludolf, Hiob, 1682
Wel.

L3470 Ludolf, Hiob, 1684
The second edition.
Ex.

L3474? Lukin, Henry, 1670
… Bassett.
Carl.

L3476 Lukin, Henry, 1669
Liv. Yk.

L3484 Lumsden, Alexander, [1680]
Linc.

L3488 Lunsford, *Sir* Thomas, 1642
Cant.

L3493 Lupton, Donald, 1655
Pet (imp). Yk.

L3510 Luther, Martin, 1652
Nor. Pet. S Asa. S Dv. Swel.

L3515 Luther, Martin, 1666
Yk.

L3517 Luther, Martin, 1649
Pet.

L3521 Lux, 1662
Yk.

L3523 Lycophron, 1697
Cant. Wor. Yk.

L3525 Lydeott, E., 1684
Yk.

L3526 Lydiat, Thomas, 1675
Lich. Wel.

L3531 Lye, Thomas, 1681
Her.

L3533 Lye, Thomas, 1676
Cant.

L3544 Lyford, William, 1652
Cant.

L3545 Lyford, William, 1653
Cant (cropped). Carl. Pet (2).

L3549A Lyford, William, 1654
Cant.

L3550A Lyford, William, 1655
S Pl.

L3558 Lyford, William, 1648
Pet. Yk.

L3562 Lying, [1680]
Linc.

L3564C Lyndwood, William, 1664
Cant. Carl. Ex (2). Lich (tpw).
S Pl (2). Sal.

L3565 Lyndwood, William, 1679
Ban. Cant. Chelm. Ches. Chi.
Dur. Ely. Ex (2). Glo. Her.
Lich. Linc (2). Liv. Nor. Roch.
S Asa. S Pl. Tru. Wel. Win
(2nd tpw). Wor. Yk (3).

L3566 Lynford, Thomas, 1689
Cant. Sal (tpw). Wor.

L3567 Lynford, Thomas, 1691
Cant.

L3568 Lynford, Thomas, 1679
Carl. Wor. Yk.

L3569 Lynford, Thomas, 1698
S Asa. Wor.

L3573 Lytler, Richard, 1662
Ex.

M4A M., A., 1675
Cant.

M4B M., A., 1675
Ely.

M11 M., C., [1642]
Linc.

M13 M., D., [1681]
Ches. Linc (imp).

M17 M., E., 1647
Carl.

M28 M., H., 1659
Ex.

M29 M., H., 1663
Carl. Yk.

M31 M., H., 1642
Linc.

M31A M., I., 1642
8°.
Linc.

M33 M., J., 1672
Carl.

M56 M., M., [1689?]
Wel.

M62 M., N., 1681
Win.

M63 M., N. N., 1657
Ex.

M65 M., P., 1690
Not by P.M.; An answer to M68.
Cant.

M68 M., P., 1690
Cant. Dur. Ex.

M69 M., R., 1641
Ex. Linc.

M71 M., R., 1642
Linc.

M72 M., R., 1648
[London], …
Cant.

M73 M., R., 1693
Yk.

M80 M., T., 1642
Linc.

M81B M., T., 1660
Ban. Cant. Carl. Nor.

M84 M., T., 1644
Yk.

M105A M., W., 1696
The tenth edition.
Carl.

M113 Mabbut, George, 1686
Ex.

M117 MacConnor, Dermond, 1642
Linc.

M118 Maccov, Johannes, 1656
Ex.

M120 Mace, Thomas, 1676
Dur. Swel.

M128A Machiavelli, Niccolo, 1675
Ban. Dur.

M129 Machiavelli, Niccolo, 1680
Ex.

M130 Machiavelli, Niccolo, 1694
Cant.

M131 Machiavelli, Niccolo, 1695
Glo.

M134 Machiavelli, Niccolo, 1663
Nor.

M136 Machiavelli, Niccolo, 1674
Ely.

M141 Machiavelli, Niccolo, 1691
Yk.

M150 Mackenzie, *Sir* George, 1686
Carl. Dur. Sal.

M155 Mackenzie, *Sir* George, 1685
Pet.

M156 Mackenzie, *Sir* George, 1685
Ex. Wel.

M156+ Mackenzie, *Sir* George,
1685
For Ri. Chiswell; 8°.
Carl.

M160 Mackenzie, *Sir* George, 1694
Third ed. not on tp.
S Pl.

M163 Mackenzie, *Sir* George, 1684
Ban. Ex. Wel. Yk.

M169 Mackenzie, *Sir* George, 1689
Dur. Nor. Yk.

M172 Mackenzie, *Sir* George, 1666
Cant.

M177 Mackenzie, *Sir* George, 1669
Carl. Pet.

M187 Mackenzie, *Sir* George, 1675
Carl.

M191 Mackenzie, *Sir* George, 1672
Carl.

M198 Mackenzie, *Sir* George, 1665
Carl*. Pet*.

M213 Mackenzie, *Sir* George, 1691
Linc. Wel.

M216 Mackenzie, John, 1690
Cant.

M221 Macky, John, 1696
Ban.

M224 Macnamara, John, 1680
Nor.

M226 MacQueen, John, 1687
S Pl.

M227 MacQueen, John, 1694
S Pl.

M228 MacQueen, John, 1693
4°.
S Pl.

M229 Macrobius, Ambrosius
Aurelius Theodosius, 1694
Cant. Ely. Glo. Nor.

M247 Magaillans, Gabriel de, 1688
Wel.

M248 Magazine, 1642
Pet.

M251 Magirus, Johann, 1642
4°.
Chelm. Her. Roch. S Asa. Wel.
Yk.

M252 Magistrates, 1682
Cant. Yk.

M253 Magna Carta, 1680
'K. Henry'
Cant.

M253A Magna Carta, 1680
Cant. Ely*.

M255A Magnen, Jean Chrysostome,
1658
Linc. S Pl.

M257 Magnus, Olaus, 1658
Yk.

M280 Maids, 1647
Linc.

M289 Maimbourg, Louis, 1685
Dur. Ex. Wor.

M290 Maimbourg, Louis, 1685
Bur. Linc (tpw).

M292 Maimbourg, Louis, 1684
Carl. Ely. Ex. S Asa. S Pl.

M294 Maimbourg, Louis, 1686
Ban. Bur. Ex. Nor. S Pl (tp
imp). Wel.

M295 Maintenance, 1642
Carl. Linc.

M303 Mainwaring, *Sir* Thomas,
1673
Pet (tpw).

M304 Maisterson, Henry, 1641
Linc. S Asa.

M312 Malbon, Samuel, 1669
Bur (Assington Parish Lib.
deposited here).

M315 Malebranche, Nicolas, 1694
Carl. S Asa.

M316 Malebranche, Nicolas, 1695
S Asa.

M317 Malebranche, Nicolas, 1694
Chi. Glo. S Asa.

M318A Malebranche, Nicolas, 1700
The second edition.
Dur.

M324 Malignants, 1645
Yk.

M345 Malpighi, Marcello, 1675–79
Ex (vol. 1 only).

M349 Malpighi, Marcello, 1669
Sal.

M355 Malvezzi, Virgilio, *Marchese*,
1647
Cant.

M359 Malvezzi, Virgilio, *Marchese*,
1642
Ban. Cant. Llan.

M360 Malvezzi, Virgilio, *Marchese*,
1647
Cant (imp).

M361 Malvezzi, Virgilio, *Marchese*,
1648
Pet.

M362 Malvezzi, Virgilio, *Marchese*,
1651
Carl.

M377 Manasseh Ben Israel, 1652
The second edition.
Chelm.

M380 Manasseh Ben Israel, [1655]
Linc.

M383 Manby, Peter, 1687
Ban. S Pl.

M384 Manby, Peter, 1687
Bur.

M384A Manby, Peter, 1687
Ex.

M387A Manby, Peter, 1687
Linc.

M390 Manchester, Edward
Montagu, *Earl of*, 1642
Linc.

M395 Manchester, Edward
Montagu, *Earl of*, 1641[2]
Cant.

M396 Manchester, Edward
Montagu, *Earl of*, 1642
Cant.

M400A Manchester, Edward
Montagu, *Earl of*, 1643
Linc.

M401 Manchester, Edward
Montagu, *Earl of*, 1642
Cant. Dur. Linc.

M402 Manchester, Edward
Montagu, *Earl of*, 1643
Linc. Pet. Yk.

M407A+ Manchester, Henry
Montagu, *Earl of*, 1666
No ed. statement; By W.G. for
Richard Thrale and James Thrale; 12°.
Cant.

M418 Mandey, Venterus, 1696
Glo.

M428A Manifesto, 1677
Linc.

M430 Manilius, Marcus, 1697
Ex.

M437 Manley, *Sir* Roger, 1686
Sal. Wel.

M439 Manley, *Sir* Roger, 1670
Ex. Linc.

M440 Manley, *Sir* Roger, 1691
S Pl.

M444 Manley, Thomas, 1677
Cant.

M446 Manley, Thomas, 1661
Linc.

M450 Manley, Thomas, 1669
Win.

M453A Manlove, Edward, 1657
Linc.

M454 Manlove, Timothy, 1697
Yk.

M455 Manlove, Timothy, 1698
8°.
Yk.

M468 Manner, 1681
Linc.

M474 Manner, 1642
Dur. Yk.

M492 Manningham, Thomas, 1693
Cant. S Dv.

M493 Manningham, Thomas, 1692
Ban. Cant. S Asa.

M494 Manningham, Thomas, 1694
Ban. Cant. Her.

M497 Manningham, Thomas, 1682
Cant. Carl.

M498 Manningham, Thomas, 1687
Wor. Yk.

M499 Manningham, Thomas, 1692
Cant. Dur. Ely.

M500 Manningham, Thomas, 1694
Cant. Ex. S Asa.

M502 Manningham, Thomas, 1680
Ex. Llan. Nor. Yk.

M504 Manningham, Thomas, 1695
Cant. Carl. Ely. Llan. Nor.
Wor.

M505 Manningham, Thomas, 1695
Ches. S Dv.

M509 Manningham, Thomas, 1686
Chi.

M512 Mansell, John, 1695
Cant.

M513 Mansell, John, 1695
Cant.

M514 Mansell, Roderick, 1680
Ely. Glo. Linc. Nor.

M518 Manton, Thomas, 1656
Pet. Sal.

M519 Manton, Thomas, 1678
Linc.

M520 Manton, Thomas, 1685
Ex.

M521 Manton, Thomas, 1685
Ex.

M523 Manton, Thomas, 1648
S Pl.

M524 Manton, Thomas, 1693
Chi. Glo.

M525 Manton, Thomas, 1647
Cant.

M526 Manton, Thomas, 1681
Glo. Pet. S Dv. Sal.

M527 Manton, Thomas, 1651
Ex. Lich. Win.

M529 Manton, Thomas, 1657
Carl. Chelm.

M530 Manton, Thomas, 1658
Chelm. Ex.

M534 Manton, Thomas, 1684
Win.

M534A Manton, Thomas, 1684
Glo.

M534B Manton, Thomas, 1684
... in Exon.
S Dv.

M535 Manton, Thomas, 1651
Chelm ('St. Laurence Church').
Pet ('Laurence Church').

M537 Manton, Thomas, 1685
Ex.

M539A Manton, Thomas, 1689
Chi. Glo. S Dv.

M541B Manual, 1660
Bur (Wing's location deposited here).

M542A Manual, 1675
18°.
Cant.

M544H Manual, 1662
12°.
Yk.

M545C Manuall, 1642
Carl.

M554 Manwood, John, 1665
Linc.

M558 Manzini, Giovanni Battista, 1655
Lich. Yk.

M559A+ Map, 1672
By John Overton; 4°.
Yk.

M562 Mapletoft, John, 1687
S Pl (2).

M563 Mapletoft, John, 1695
Cant. Dur.

M565F Marbeck, John, 1681
Cant.

M568 Marbury, Edward, 1650
'A commentarie ...'
Cant (tp imp)*.

M569 Marbury, Edward, 1652
Ex.

M575 March, John, *of Gray's Inn*, 1642
Dur. Pet.

M579 March, John, *B.D.*, 1682
Carl. Dur (imp). Her. Yk (2).

M580 March, John, *B.D.*, 1683
Dur. Yk (2).

M581 March, John, *B.D.*, 1677
Cant. New. Wor. Yk.

M581A March, John, *B.D.*, 1684
Yk (2).

M582? March, John, *B.D.*, 1693
... Newcastle.
Yk.

M599 Mariana, Juan de, 1699
Chi. Dur. Nor.

M600 Marianus, 1641
Cant (engr. tpw).

M605 Marius, John, 1670
Second ed. not on tp?
Yk.

M611 Markham, Gervase, 1648
Cant.

M620 Markham, Gervase, 1649
Cant.

M629 Markham, Gervase, 1649
Cant.

M637? Markham, Gervase, 1649
Harison.
Cant.

M648 Markham, Gervase, 1649
Cant.

M675 Markham, Gervase, 1648[9]
Cant.

M685 Markland, Abraham, 1683
Dur.

M686+ Marlborough, James Ley, *Earl of*, 1666
York, by Stephen Bulkley, sold by Francis Mawbarne; 8°.
Carl.

M691A Marloe, John, 1682
Carl.

M695 Marlow, Isaac, 1693/4
Ex.

M696 Marlow, Isaac, 1690
Linc.

M715 Marriott, Robert, 1641
Ex. Nor.

M717 Marriott, Thomas, 1661
Ex.

M718 Marriott, Thomas, 1689
Nor.

M725 Marsden, Thomas, 1688
Cant. Dur. Ex. Nor. Wel.

M738 Marsh, Richard, 1699
Nor. Wor.

M748 Marshall, Stephen, 1641
Ban. Ex. Her. Linc. Win. Yk.

M748A Marshall, Stephen, 1641
Her. Pet.

M748B Marshall, Stephen, 1641
Ex (2).

M749 Marshall, Stephen, 1643
Carl. Linc.

M751 Marshall, Stephen, 1646
Pet (3). Sal. Win.

M752 Marshall, Stephen, 1644
Pet (2).

M756 Marshall, Stephen, 1645
Carl. Pet (2).

M757 Marshall, Stephen, 1648
Carl. Win.

M758 Marshall, Stephen, 1660[1]
Lich. Yk.

M762 Marshall, Stephen, 1641[2]
Chelm (imp). Ex. Pet (3 − 1
imp). S Asa.

M766 Marshall, Stephen, 1641
Carl. Ex. Pet (3).

M769 Marshall, Stephen, 1657
4°.
Cant. Carl.

M770 Marshall, Stephen, 1642
Ex (2 − 54p. & 52p.). Pet (52p.).

M771 Marshall, Stephen, 1647
Carl. Yk.

M772 Marshall, Stephen, 1644
Cant. Carl. Ex (2).

M773 Marshall, Stephen, [1645]
Carl. Ex. Her. Yk.

M774 Marshall, Stephen, 1644
Carl.

M775 Marshall, Stephen, 1645
Chelm.

M776 Marshall, Stephen, 1641
Cant (2 − 1 imp). Carl. Linc.
Pet (tpw)*.

M776A Marshall, Stephen, 1641
Ex (imp, or anr ed.?: 46p.). Nor.
Pet.

M779 Marshall, Stephen, 1647
Ex. Pet.

M781 Marshall, Stephen, 1652
Cant. Carl.

M783 Marshall, Stephen, 1648
Pet.

M785 Marshall, Stephen, 1660
Dur.

M786 Marshall, Stephen, 1660
Pet (tp imp).

M787 Marshall, Stephen, 1661
Chelm.

M789 Marshall, Stephen, 1643
Cant. Carl. Pet.

M790 Marshall, Stephen, 1645
Carl.

M791 Marshall, Stephen, 1648
S Pl.

M793 Marshall, Stephen, 1644
Ex (2).

M797 Marshall, Stephen, 1646
Carl. Pet. Yk.

M798 Marshall, Stephen, 1641
Cant. Her. S Pl. Win. Yk.

M798A Marshall, Stephen, 1641
Ex.

M800 Marshall, Thomas, *1621 −
1685*, 1679
Ely.

M810 Marsham, *Sir* John, 1672
Cant. Ely. Sal. Win.

M810A Marsham, *Sir* John, 1672
Cant (imp). Glo. Roch.

M811 Marsham, *Sir* John, 1649
Dur. Linc. S Pl. Sal. Win. Yk.

M813B Marsin, M., 1700
… John Gwillam's.
Cant.

M814 Marston, Edward, 1699
Yk.

M817 Marston, John, *Minister*,
1642
'… VVestminster, … the sixt …'
Cant (3).

M820? Marten, Henry, 1663
Printed by Edmundus de Speciosâ
Villâ …
Pet.

M822 Marten, Henry, 1648
Sal. Yk (2).

M823 Marten, Henry, 1648
Yk.

M828 Martial, 1677
Yk.

M833 Martial, 1689
First ed. not on tp.
Glo.

M837 Martin, Edward, 1662
'… his opinion concerning 1. The
difference …'
Cant. Carl.

M840 Martin, John, 1674
12°.
Carl. Pet.

M842 Martin, John, 1660
Pet.

M843 Martin, John, 1664
Yk.

M848 Martin, Richard, 1643
Cant.

M850 Martin, T., 1659
Carl.

M852 Martin, Thomas, 1690
Sal. Wel. Win.

M858 Martini, Martino, 1654
Cant (imp).

M860 Marvell, Andrew, 1677
Cant (imp). Yk (2 − 1 imp).

M861 Marvell, Andrew, [1678]
Win. Yk.

M867 Marvell, Andrew, 1665
Linc.

M869B Marvell, Andrew, 1667
Cant (imp; date changed to 1689
in MS).

M871 Marvell, Andrew, 1655
Cant.

M871B Marvell, Andrew, 1677
Cant. Win.

M873 Marvell, Andrew, 1676
Cant.

M873A Marvell, Andrew, 1676
Bur. Carl. S Asa (tp imp). Win
(tpw)*. Yk.

M878 Marvell, Andrew, 1672
Nor.

M878A Marvell, Andrew, 1672
Ex (2).

M879 Marvell, Andrew, 1672
The second impression.
Dur (… sold by N. Ponder). Ely
(as Dur). Linc (… sould by N.
Ponder).

M880 Marvell, Andrew, 1672
Carl.

M882 Marvell, Andrew, 1673
Chelm. Ex. Linc. Nor. Pet.

M883 Marvell, Andrew, 1674
Carl. Ely.

M884 Marvell, Andrew, 1678
'… by one T.D. …'
Carl. Win.

M888 Marvell, Andrew, 1680
Linc. Pet.

M889 Marvell, Andrew, 1687
S Pl.

M904 Mascardi, Agostino, 1693
Nor.

M909 Mason, Charles, 1676
Yk.

M910 Mason, Charles, 1673
Carl.

M911 Mason, Charles, 1663
Carl. Ex (tpw). S Asa.

M939 Mason, Richard Angelus, 1654
... Baltazar Bellers.
Wel.

M1043 Massinello, 1683
Lich (imp).

M1056 Master, Thomas, 1661
Carl. Wel.

M1067 Masters, Samuel, 1689
Ban. Bur. Carl. Lich. Pet.
Wel.

M1068 Masters, Samuel, 1690
Cant.

M1072 Masterson, George, 1651
Chelm.

M1181 Mather, Increase, 1696
Cant.

M1265 Mather, Nathaniel, 1694
Her. Wor.

M1269 Mather, Richard, 1643
Pet.

M1271A Mather, Richard, 1659
Bur.

M1281 Mather, Samuel, *1626 – 1671*, 1695
Dur.

M1283+ Mather, Samuel, *1626 – 1671*, 1652
See: CLC70.
Carl (tpw).

M1287H Mathew, Francis, 1670
Llan (tpw).

M1288A Mathew, John, 1680
Win (2). Wor.

M1289 Mathews, Lemuel, 1667
S Asa.

M1293 Maton, Robert, 1652
Cant (tp imp).

M1303 Matter, 1680
Linc.

M1306 Matters, 1641[2]
Linc (2).

M1319 Matthew, *Sir* Tobie, 1660
Yk (2).

M1322 Matthew, *Sir* Tobie, 1647
Yk.

M1335 Mauger, Claude, 1676
'Claudius Mauger's French ...'
Dur.

M1336 Mauger, Claude, 1656
Carl (tp imp?).

M1338 Mauger, Claude, 1667
Cant.

M1340 Mauger, Claude, 1673
Yk.

M1340aA Mauger, Claude, 1676
Cant.

M1356 Maundrell, Henry, 1696
Wor.

M1357A Maurice, David, 1700
S Asa.

M1358 Maurice, Henry, *1650? – 1699*, 1695
Carl.

M1359 Maurice, Henry, *1648 – 1691*, 1685
Carl. S Pl. Sal.

M1360 Maurice, Henry, *1648 – 1691*, 1691
Ches. Dur. Ely. Ex. Llan.
Nor. S Pl. Sal. Wel.

M1361 Maurice, Henry, *1648 – 1691*, 1700
Ex. Llan. S Asa.

M1362 Maurice, Henry, *1648 – 1691*, 1688
Nor. Sal.

M1364 Maurice, Henry, *1648 – 1691*, 1689
Ban. Carl. Wel (3).

M1365 Maurice, Henry, *1648 – 1691*, 1689
Wel.

M1366 Maurice, Henry, *1648 – 1691*, 1689
Cant. Yk.

M1369 Maurice, Henry, *1648 – 1691*, 1689/90
Cant. Ely. Ex (3). Yk.

M1370 Maurice, Henry, *1648 – 1691*, 1682
Ban. Cant. Chi. Llan (2). Pet.

M1371 Maurice, Henry, *1648 – 1691*, 1682
Carl. Ely. Ex (2). S Asa. S Pl.
Wel. Win. Yk.

M1374 Maximes, [1643]
Linc.

M1375? Maximes, [1643]
cap.
Linc.

M1376 Maximus, *Tyrius*, 1677
Cant. Ches. Liv.

M1377 Maxwell, John, 1644
S Asa. Yk.

M1379 Maxwell, John, 1646
Win. Yk (2).

M1379A Maxwell, John, 1646
S Pl. Yk.

M1381 Maxwell, John, 1663
Carl. Pet. Win.

M1382 Maxwell, John, 1668
Wel.

M1383 Maxwell, John, 1681
Cant.

M1384 Maxwell, John, 1644
Ban. Cant. Pet.

M1385 Maxwell, John, 1680
S Pl.

M1404 May, Thomas, 1642
Cant. Carl.

M1409 May, Thomas, 1651
Linc (2). Wel.

M1410 May, Thomas, 1647
Liv. Pet. Swel. Wor.

M1415 May, Thomas, 1643
Yk.

M1422 Mayer, John, 1652
Ex. Her. Lich.

M1423 Mayer, John, 1653
Ex. Her. Lich.

M1424 Mayer, John, 1653
Her. Rip.

M1424A Mayer, John, 1654
Ches.

M1425 Mayer, John, 1647
Ches. Ex. Her. Lich.

M1454 Maynard, *Sir* John, 1643
Yk.

M1459 Maynard, *Sir* John, 1648
Yk.

M1460? Maynard, *Sir* John, *Judge*, 1678
... Atkins ...
Nor.

M1461 Maynard, *Sir* John, *Judge*, 1642
Linc.

M1462 Maynard, *Sir* John, *Judge*, 1641
Cant (2 – 1 imp). Linc ('M.
Maynards ...'). Pet (as Linc).

M1463 Mayne, Jasper, 1648
Cant.

M1466 Mayne, Jasper, 1653
Carl. Yk.

M1469 Mayne, Jasper, 1662
Carl.

M1471 Mayne, Jasper, 1647
Carl. Dur. Linc. Pet. S Pl.
Win. Yk (2 – 1 imp).

M1472 Mayne, Jasper, 1647
Cant. Carl. Dur. Linc. Yk (2).

M1473 Mayne, Jasper, 1646[7]
Carl. S Asa. Yk.

M1474 Mayne, Jasper, 1647
Carl. Dur. Linc. Wel. Yk.

M1475 Mayne, Jasper, 1652
Cant. Carl (2). Nor. Yk.

M1476 Mayne, Jasper, 1646
Carl. Dur. Pet.

M1477 Mayne, Jasper, 1647
Cant. Carl. Linc. S Pl. Wel.
Yk.

M1478 Mayne, Jasper, 1662
Carl. Ex. Her. Pet (2). S Asa.
Sal.

M1522 Mayo, Richard, 1678
Cant. Carl. Win.

M1523 Mayo, Richard, 1678
Carl. Win.

M1524? Mayo, Richard, 1664
12°.
Linc.

M1528 Mayo, Richard, 1673
Pet.

M1530 Mayo, Richard, 1678
Win.

M1537 Mayow, John, 1674
Ex.

M1542 Mazzella, Scipio, 1654
Lich.

M1558 Mead, Matthew, 1666
Chelm.

M1559 Mead, Matthew, 1660
Pet.

M1562 Mead, Matthew, 1691
Cant.

M1563 Mead, Matthew, 1689
Ex.

M1566 Meadows, *Sir* Philip, 1677
Carl. Ex. Pet.

M1567 Meadows, *Sir* Philip, 1689
Wel (imp).

M1585 Mede, Joseph, 1648
Ban. Ely (frag.). Lich. S Pl.
Yk.

M1586 Mede, Joseph, 1664
Second ed. not on tp.
Ban (tpw). Cant. Chi. Glo.
Nor. S Asa. Sal (tp imp). Wel.
Win. Yk.

M1588 Mede, Joseph, 1672
Bur. Carl. Ches. Chi. Ely. Ex.
Lich. New. Roch (2). S Dv.
Wor. Yk.

M1589 Mede, Joseph, 1677
Ed. statement from half-title.
Bur. Cant. Chelm. Dur. Ex.
Glo. Her. Linc. Llan. Nor. Pet.
S Asa. Sal.

M1590 Mede, Joseph, 1641
Linc.

M1591 Mede, Joseph, 1642
Ex.

M1592 Mede, Joseph, 1644
The second edition.
Carl. Ely. Linc.

M1594 Mede, Joseph, 1649
Hac tertia editione.
Ely. S Pl. Sal.

M1595 Mede, Joseph, 1643
Ely. Linc. Pet. Sal.

M1596 Mede, Joseph, 1642
Cant. Linc.

M1597 Mede, Joseph, 1648
Ches. Linc (pts 2 — 3 only). Sal
(pt 3 only). Yk (pts 2 — 3 only,
imp).

M1598? Mede, Joseph, 1652
4°.
Lich. Linc. Sal.

M1599 Mede, Joseph, 1653
Linc. Llan. Sal.

M1600 Mede, Joseph, 1643
Linc.

M1601 Mede, Joseph, 1650
Bur. Ex.

M1603 Mede, Joseph, 1652
Chelm. Linc.

M1604 Mede, Joseph, 1650
Ban. Ely. Linc. Sal.

M1605 Mede, Joseph, 1642
Linc. Pet.

M1606? Mede, Joseph, 1649
Leybourne.
Ches.

M1615 Meeke, William, 1646
Yk*.

M1618 Meggot, Richard, 1662
Ex.

M1619 Meggot, Richard, 1656
Ex (2).

M1620 Meggot, Richard, 1670
Carl. Ex. Her. S Asa.

M1621 Meggot, Richard, [1674]
Wor.

M1622 Meggot, Richard, 1675
Linc. Nor. Wor.

M1624 Meggot, Richard, 1676
Nor. Wor.

M1626 Meggot, Richard, 1682
Sal. Wor.

M1627 Meggot, Richard, 1683
Cant. Wel. Wor.

M1628 Meggot, Richard, 1689
Cant. Ches. Her. Nor. Wor.

M1629 Meggot, Richard, 1690
Her.

M1630 Meggot, Richard, 1691
Ches.

M1631 Meggot, Richard, 1691
Win.

M1632? Meggot, Richard, 1692
Bennet.
Cant.

M1633 Meggot, Richard, 1696
Ches. Her.

M1635 Melanchthon, Philipp, 1642
Pt 2 of E3201.
Cant. Dur. Ely. Ex. Lich.
Linc. Nor. Pet. S Pl. Wor.

M1635A Melanchthon, Philipp,
1642
Pt 2 of E3201A.
Ex. Lich. Pet. Swel. Win.

M1637 Meldrum, George, 1690
Cant.

M1640 Meldrum, *Sir* John, 1642
Cant. Linc.

M1647A Melius, 1689
Ban. Carl.

M1654 Melville, *Sir* James, 1683
Carl. Chelm. Her. Sal. Wel.
Win.

M1669 Memoirs, [1679]
Linc.

M1669aA? Memoires, 1675
... for T. Dring.
Ex.

M1669A? Memoires, 1671
12°.
Carl.

M1671 Memoires, 1682/3
Wor.

M1677C? Memorable, [1658 — 64]
... Coles, J. Wright, T. Vere ...
Ches (imp).

M1681 Memorandums, 1650
Ex.

M1686 Memorial, [1688]
Wel.

M1691 Memorial, 1689
S Pl.

M1706 Mendes Pinto, Fernando, 1663
Lich (tpw)*.

M1711 Mennes, *Sir* John, 1656
Ex.

M1728aA Mercator, Gerard, 1641
Pet (vol. 2 only).

M1728A Mercator, Nicolaus, 1664
Sal.

M1728B *See*: E3392

M1729? Mercator, Nicolaus, 1676
... sumtibus ...
Ely.

M1730 Mercator, Nicolaus, 1668
Bris.

M1733 Mercer, Richard, 1649
Pet (tpw).

M1748 Mercuries, 1641
Nor. Pet. Yk.

M1753- Mercurius, 1646
By Sir G. Wharton.
Ex. Linc. Liv. Pet. Yk.

M1753 Mercurius, 1685
By Sir G. Wharton.
Cant. Win. Yk.

M1756 Mercurius, 1645
Pet.

M1772 Mercurius, 1650
Linc. Sal.

M1775 Mercurius, 1644
Pet.

M1781 Meredith, Edward, 1687
Bur. Wel.

M1782 Meredith, Edward, 1687
Ban. Bur. Cant.

M1783 Meredith, Edward, 1688
Cant. Wel.

M1784? Meredith, Edward, 1682
For T. Davis.
Carl (imp).

M1786 Merit, 1662
Carl. Dur. S Pl.

M1792 Meriton, George, 1679
Yk.

M1795 Meriton, George, 1674
Carl.

M1796 Meriton, George, 1679
Yk.

M1799? Meriton, George, 1694
... Fr. Hillyard in York.
Yk.

M1803A? Meriton, George, 1668
The second edition; 12°.
Carl.

M1804 Meriton, George, 1669
Yk (tp imp).

M1805? Meriton, George, 1681
For Thomas Basset and John Place.
Yk.

M1806 Meriton, George, 1697
Yk.

M1807 Meriton, George, 1685
Yk.

M1808 Meriton, George, 1681
Carl.

M1809 Meriton, George, 1685
Yk.

M1810 Meriton, George, 1697
Yk.

M1811 Meriton, George, 1668
Carl.

M1812 Meriton, George, 1671
Dur.

M1815 Meriton, Henry, 1696
Cant.

M1817 Meriton, John, *1636−1704*, 1660[1]
Sal.

M1820 Meriton, John, *1636−1704*, 1672
Ex. Pet.

M1821 Meriton, John, *b.1629*, 1677
Pet. S Asa. Yk (imp).

M1821A Meriton, L., 1696
Yk (2).

M1821B? Meriton, L., 1698
Second ed. not on tp.
Yk.

M1826 Merks, Thomas, [1642?]
Cant. Dur.

M1827 Merks, Thomas, 1679
Linc.

M1828 Merlin, 1681
Yk.

M1840A? Merret, Christopher, 1667
Editio secunda; ... prostat apud Sam. Thomson.
Linc.

M1842? Merret, Christopher, 1670
... James Allestry.
Win.

M1843 Merret, Christopher, 1669
Win.

M1877A Merryweather, John, 1681
Ely (imp)*.

M1879 Mervault, Pierre de, 1680
Ely.

M1880A Mervyn, *Sir* Audley, [1642]
Dur (tp imp).

M1887 Mervyn, *Sir* Audley, 1641
Carl.

M1888 Mervyn, *Sir* Audley, 1641
Ely.

M1888A Mervyn, *Sir* Audley, 1641
Cant. Ely.

M1889 Mervyn, *Sir* Audley, 1641
Linc.

M1890 Mervyn, *Sir* Audley, 1661
Win.

M1895 Mervyn, *Sir* Audley, 1663
Dur.

M1915 Mestrezat, Jean, 1654
Carl.

M1919+ Metcalfe, Philip, 1688
See: CLC71.
Carl. Dur.

M1937 Metford, James, 1698
Cant (tp imp). Dur.

M1938 Metford, James, 1682
Carl.

M1950 Mewe, William, 1643
Pet (2 − 1 imp).

M1958 Mézeray, François-Eudes de, 1683
Carl (2). Ex. Sal. Wel. Wor.

M1959 Micanzio, Fulgenzio, 1651
Carl. Pet.

M1978 Middleton, John, 1679
Ex.

M1990 Middleton, Thomas, *Divine*, 1677
Bur. Cant (2). Linc. Yk.

M2007 Miege, Guy, 1691
Carl. Wel.

M2012 Miege, Guy, 1688
Dur (imp). Ex. S Asa. S Pl.

M2016 Miege, Guy, 1677
Ches. Yk.

M2017 Miege, Guy, 1679
Cant. Ex (imp?).

M2018 Miege, Guy, 1678
Ex.

M2025 Miege, Guy, 1669
'... by ... the Earle ...'; 8°.
Ex. Yk.

M2028 Miege, Guy, 1690
Cant.

M2029A Miege, Guy, 1699
Yk.

M2031 Milbourne, Luke, 1698
Bur. Dur. S Pl.

M2032 Milbourne, Luke, 1699
Wor.

M2034 Milbourne, Luke, 1692
S Pl.

M2038 Milbourne, Luke, 1688
Ex. Wel.

M2039 Mild, [1679]
Linc.

M2069? Millet, John, 1652
... Henry Hall.
Cant.

M2072 Mills, John, [1642]
Yk.

M2075 Milner, John, 1700
Ely. Ex. Nor. Wel.

M2076 Milner, John, [1700?]
... Randal Taylor; 4°.
Yk.

M2077 Milner, John, 1688
Ely.

M2078 Milner, John, 1673
Dur. Linc. Yk.

M2080 Milner, John, 1694
Ex. Yk.

M2084 Milner, William, 1698
Ches. Ex.

M2086 Milton, John, 1697
Cant.

M2087 Milton, John, 1698
Ex. Nor. Roch. Sal (vols 1
[imp] & 2 only).

M2088A Milton, John, 1669
Wel.

M2089 Milton, John, 1641
Ex (2 − 1 tpw). Sal (imp). Yk.

M2092 Milton, John, 1644
Carl. S Pl. Sal.

M2096 Milton, John, 1682
Carl.

M2097 Milton, John, 1660
Cant.

M2099 Milton, John, 1645
Carl. S Pl.

M2104 Milton, John, 1692
Yk.

M2106 Milton, John, 1651
Yk.

M2108 Milton, John, 1643
Linc.

M2109 Milton, John, 1644
Carl. Ex.

M2110? Milton, John, 1645
'... doctrine & discipline ...'; 82p.
S Pl.

M2112 Milton, John, 1649
Linc. Nor (tpw)*. Yk.

M2114 Milton, John, 1650
Publish'd now the second time.
Cant.

M2115 Milton, John, 1690
Cant (imp).

M2117 Milton, John, 1674
Dur. Ely. Linc. Liv. Nor. S Pl.

M2119 Milton, John, 1670
Lich.

M2120 Milton, John, 1671
Linc.

M2121 Milton, John, 1677
Second ed. not on tp.
Ely. S Asa.

M2128 Milton, John, 1676
Ches*. Ely*. Linc*. Rip*.
S Pl*.

M2133 Milton, John, 1641
Cant. Pet. Yk.

M2135 Milton, John, 1673
Cant. Linc. Sal.

M2137 Milton, John, 1667
Linc.

M2142 Milton, John, 1669
Ely. Win.

M2144 Milton, John, 1674
Liv. Wel. Yk.

M2145 Milton, John, 1678
Yk.

M2147 Milton, John, 1688
The fourth edition.
Ches.

M2151 Milton, John, 1695
Carl. Glo.

M2154+ Milton, John, 1715 [*i.e.*
1695]
By R.E. to be sold by John Whitlock;
2°.
Glo.

M2156 Milton, John, 1691
Ely.

M2158 Milton, John, 1690
Glo.

M2161 Milton, John, 1673
Second ed. not on tp.
Linc*.

M2164 Milton, John, 1689
Ex. S Asa.

M2165 Milton, John, 1650[1]
Impr. false: Utrecht, Theodorus ab
Ackersdijk et Gisbertus à Zijll
(Madan, *The Library*, 1923−4).
Linc (tpw).

M2166 Milton, John, 1651
Carl. Ely.

M2167 Milton, John, 1651
Ches. S Pl.

M2168C Milton, John, 1651
Impr. false: Elzevir, Amsterdam
(Madan).
Wel.

M2168D Milton, John, 1651
Impr. false: J. Jansson, Amsterdam
(Madan).
Sal.

M2169 Milton, John, 1652
Bris*.

M2171 Milton, John, 1654
Cant (2). Ely. Linc.

M2172 Milton, John, 1655
Cant. Ely.

M2173 Milton, John, 1660
Carl (imp?)*. Yk (2).

M2175 Milton, John, 1641
Carl. Linc.

M2181 Milton, John, 1649
Ex. S Pl.

M2184 Milton, John, 1645
Carl. Linc. S Pl.

M2185 Milton, John, 1659
Carl.

M2195 Minister's, 1688
Dur. Wel.

M2199 Minucius Felix, Marcus,
1662
S Pl.

M2200 Minucius Felix, Marcus,
1678
12°.
Ban. Cant. Linc.

M2201 Minucius Felix, Marcus,
1682
Carl.

M2225 Mirror, 1660
Win.

M2233 Mischief, 1685
Carl. S Asa.

M2238 Mischiefs, 1681
Carl.

M2238A Mis-chiefs, 1684
Ban.

M2248A Misfortunes, [1678]
S Pl.

M2248B Mishnah, 1648
Cant. Chi. Dur. Llan. S Pl.
Wel.

M2250 Mishnah, 1690
Chi. Wel.

M2259 Mr. Cowley's, 1680
Linc.

M2276 Mr. Speaker, [1651]
Linc.

M2302 Mocket, Richard, 1663
Ex. Linc. Pet (2). S Asa. Sal.

M2302A Mocket, Richard, 1663
York, imprinted by special priviledge.
Yk.

M2303 Mocket, Richard, 1683
Ex (2). New. S Pl (3 − 1 imp).
Yk.

M2304 Mockett, Thomas, 1651
Cant. Chelm.

M2307 Mockett, Thomas, 1642
Pet.

M2317A Model, 1679
Linc (on verso of M2318).

M2318 Model, 1677
Impr. from colophon.
Linc (on verso of M2317A).

M2319 Modell, 1642
Linc.

M2320A Moderate, 1642
Yk.

M2321 Moderate, 1643
Linc.

M2324 Moderate, [1680]
Linc.

M2325 Moderate, 1660
Chelm.

M2326 Moderate, 1659
Carl. Ex. Pet.

M2327 Moderate, 1646
Dur.

M2329 Moderate, 1645
Ex.

M2330 Moderate, 1643
Linc.

M2347 Modern, 1692
Carl (imp).

M2349 Modest, 1682
Carl. Nor.

M2358 Modest, 1690
Yk.

M2359 Modest, 1690
Wel.

M2361 Modest, 1660
Wor.

M2363 Modest, 1689
S Asa.

M2365 Modest, 1682
S Pl.

M2367 Modest, 1690
Cant. Carl. Sal.

M2382 Moffet, Thomas, 1655
Carl.

M2382A Molesworth, Robert
Molesworth, *Viscount*, 1694
Carl. Ely. Ex. Nor.

M2383 Molesworth, Robert
Molesworth, *Viscount*, 1694
Wel.

M2387 Molinos, Miguel de, 1688
Wel.

M2389 Molins, William, 1648
Carl.

M2390 Molins, William, 1676
Carl.

M2396 Molloy, Charles, 1677
Glo.

M2406A+ Molyneux, William,
1700
For Phillip Lea; 4°.
Cant.

M2410 Monck, Thomas, 1673
Cant.

M2425 Monmouth, Henry Carey,
Earl of, 1641[2]
Linc.

M2426 Monmouth, Henry Carey,
Earl of, 1641[2]
[London], ...
Cant.

M2435 Monpersan, Louis de, 1688
Lich.

M2437 Monro, Alexander, *d.1715?*,
1693
Wel. Yk.

M2437A? Monro, Alexander,
d.1715?, 1692
'Collection of tracts relating to ...
Scotland'
Wel.

M2439 Monro, Alexander, *d.1715?*,
1696
Carl. Wel.

M2440 Monro, Alexander, *d.1715?*,
1692
Yk.

M2443 Monro, Alexander, *d.1715?*,
1691
S Pl. Yk.

M2444? Monro, Alexander, *d.1715?*,
1693
12°.
Bur (format?). Her.

M2461 Monson, *Sir* John, 1647
Linc. Yk.

M2462 Monson, *Sir* John, 1680
Ban. Linc. Win.

M2463 Monson, *Sir* John, 1678
Win.

M2464 Monson, *Sir* John, 1647
Linc. Yk.

M2468 Montagu, Ralph Montagu,
Duke of, 1679
Carl.

M2469 Montagu, Richard, 1642
Ban. Bur (2). Cant (2). Carl.
Glo. Her. Lich. Linc. Llan.
Nor. Pet. S Pl. Yk.

M2472 Montagu, Walter, 1641
Carl. Chelm (tpw). Pet.

M2473 Montagu, Walter, 1648
Carl. Lich. Sal. Wor (tpw).

M2474 Montagu, Walter, 1654
Cant. Carl. Sal.

M2479 Montaigne, Michel de,
1685 − 6
'... New rendred into English by
Charles Cotton'
Nor.

M2479+ Montaigne, Michel de,
1685 − 86
As M2479, but: 'The essays ... Made
English by Charles Cotton'
Ex.

M2485 Montanus, Arnoldus, 1670
Cant. Ex. Win.

M2504 Montgomery, James, 1692
Wel. Yk.

M2506 Montluc, Blaise de, 1674
Linc.

M2507 Montpensier, Anne Marie
Louise d'Orleans, *Duchesse de*, 1668
Carl.

M2508 Montrose, James Graham,
Marquis of, 1641
Linc.

M2516 Montrose, James Graham,
Marquis, 1649
'... July 9. 1649'
Cant.

M2539 Moore, *Sir* Francis, 1676
Ely. Wor.

M2545 Moore, John, *Bp*, 1684
Cant.

M2546 Moore, John, *Bp*, 1692
Ban. Cant. Sal.

M2547 Moore, John, *Bp*, 1692
Carl.

M2550 Moore, John, *Bp*, 1694
Ban. Cant. Her.

M2551 Moore, John, *Bp*, 1690
Cant. Carl.

M2552 Moore, John, *Bp*, 1682
S Asa.

M2553 Moore, John, *Bp*, 1691
Cant. Her.

M2554 Moore, John, *Bp*, 1696
Cant (2). Llan. Nor (2). S Asa
(tp imp).

M2555 Moore, John, *Bp*, 1697
Her. Nor. S Asa.

M2558 Moore, John, *of Knaptoft*,
1653
Pet.

M2579 Moore, *Sir* Jonas, 1681
Ex.

M2592 Moore, Thomas, *the Elder*,
[1646]
Pet (tpw *or* cap.?).

M2615? Moral, 1687
By Henry Hills jun. ...
Dur.

M2630 More, Cresacre, 1642
Carl (imp)*. Ches. Ely (imp).

M2633 More, Henry, 1679
Ban. Glo. Nor.

M2633A+ More, Henry, 1679
As M2633A, but: Typis J. Macock, ...
Yk.

M2636 More, Henry, 1675
Ban. Glo. Nor. Yk.

M2639 More, Henry, 1653
Carl.

M2641 More, Henry, 1680
By J.M. for ...
Ban. Dur. Ex. Pet. Swel. Win.

M2642? More, Henry, 1673
'An appendix ...'
Carl. Win (2).

M2643 More, Henry, 1686
Ches. Dur. Nor (2). S Pl. Sal.
Wel.

M2644 More, Henry, 1686
Bur. Ex (2). Lich. Sal. Swel.

M2645 More, Henry, 1672
Pet. S Pl. Win.

M2646 More, Henry, 1662
Ban. Carl. Ely. Ex. Nor. Pet.
Swel. Wor.

M2647 More, Henry, 1653
Carl.

M2648 More, Henry, 1646
Carl (with addit. tp: 'A song of
the soul').

M2649 More, Henry, 1692
Cant. Ex.

M2650 More, Henry, 1668
Carl. Dur. Ex. Lich. Swel.

M2651 More, Henry, 1668
Dur. Ex. Lich. Swel.

M2652 More, Henry, 1668
Carl. Lich.

M2653 More, Henry, 1669
Ban. Carl. Dur. Linc. Pet.

M2654 More, Henry, 1671
Dur. Pet.

M2655 More, Henry, 1656
Pet. Sal.

M2656 More, Henry, 1664
Ban. Ex. Sal.

M2658 More, Henry, 1660
Carl. Ely. Ex. Lich. Pet. Swel.
Wor.

M2660 More, Henry, 1669
Carl. Dur. Ex. Pet.

M2663 More, Henry, 1659
Bur. Linc.

M2666 More, Henry, 1664
Ely. Ex. Pet. Sal (frag.). Swel.
Win. Wor.

M2670 More, Henry, 1647
Dur. Pet.

M2673 More, Henry, 1681
Cant. Pet. Swel. Win.

M2674 More, Henry, 1642
Carl. Linc. Pet.

M2675 More, Henry, 1676
Carl. Ex.

M2676 More, Henry, 1679
Ban. Glo. Nor. Yk.

M2677A More, Henry, 1685
Ban.

M2679 More, Henry, 1681
Ex. Nor. Pet. Win.

M2690 More, *Sir* Thomas, 1663
Ely.

M2691 More, *Sir* Thomas, 1684
Cant. Carl. Swel.

M2709 More, 1649
Yk.

M2714 More, 1643
Yk.

M2722 Morer, Thomas, 1690
Cant. Dur. Yk (2).

M2722A Morer, Thomas, 1690
Wel.

M2723 Morer, Thomas, 1699
S Pl. Wor.

M2724 Morer, Thomas, 1699
S Pl.

M2725 Moreri, Louis, 1694
Bur (2). Chi. S Asa. Wel. Yk.

M2738 Morgan, Sylvanus, 1666
Ex.

M2743 Morgan, Sylvanus, 1661
Linc.

M2749 Morgan, *Sir* Thomas, 1645
Her. Yk.

M2762 Morice, *Sir* William, 1657
Chelm. Ex. Lich.

M2763 Morice, *Sir* William, 1660
Ex. Sal. Win.

M2763A+ Morice, *Sir* William,
1660
The second edition; By R. Norton for
Richard Royston, sold by Abisha
Brocas in Exon.; 2°.
Ban.

M2764 Morin, Jean, 1682
Heading corrected.
Carl. Dur. Ex. S Asa. S Pl.

M2766 Morin, Lucas, [1658]
Carl.

M2770? Morison, Robert, 1669
Allestry.
Ex. Wor.

M2771 Morison, Robert, 1680
Cant. Dur. Ex. Wor.

M2772 Morison, Robert, 1699
Cant. Dur.

M2773 Morison, Robert, 1672
Cant. Ex. Sal. Win.

M2778 Morland, *Sir* Samuel, 1679
Carl.

M2779 Morland, *Sir* Samuel, 1658
Carl. Dur. Ex. Rip. Win.

M2784 Morland, *Sir* Samuel, 1672
Linc.

M2785 Morland, *Sir* Samuel, 1695
Dur.

M2788 Morley, Christopher Love,
1680
Ex.

M2789 Morley, George, 1663
Carl. S Asa. Wel.

M2790 Morley, George, 1662
Carl. Linc. Pet. S Asa. Sal.
Wel.

M2793 Morley, George, 1641
Cant. Linc. Pet.

M2794 Morley, George, 1661
Cant (3). Carl. Ex. Linc.
S Asa. Yk (2).

M2796 Morley, George, 1683
Carl. Dur. Ely. Ex. S Pl. Tru.
Wel. Win (2).

M2797 Morley, George, 1683
Bur. Carl. Ches. Ex (with a
2nd tp: For Joanna Brome, 1683).
S Pl. Sal (as Ex). Yk.

M2827 Morton, Nathaniel, 1669
Cant.

M2831 Morton, Richard, 1689
Ex.

M2832 Morton, Richard, 1692
Ex.

M2833 Morton, Richard, 1694
Ex.

M2835 Morton, Thomas, 1644
Ches. Lich. Sal.

M2836 Morton, Thomas, 1662
4°.
Cant.

M2838 Morton, Thomas, 1670
Carl. Ches (imp). Dur. Ex (2 –
1 imp). S Pl. Sal (imp). Yk.

M2839 Morton, Thomas, 1679
Pet (tp imp). Sal. Yk.

M2840 Morton, Thomas, 1653
Ban. Carl. Chelm. Ches. Dur.
Lich. Pet. Sal. Wor. Yk.

M2840A? Morton, Thomas, 1652
Ches (... Minsheu). Lich (...
Minsheu). Yk (... Minshew).

M2843 Morton, Thomas, 1643
Yk*.

M2844 Morton, Thomas, 1643
Includes J961A.
Pet.

M2844+ Morton, Thomas, 1643
[N.pl.], printed in the yeare; 8°.
Wel.

M2845+ Morton, Thomas, 1642
As M2845, but: The second
impression.
Cant (2). Yk.

M2846 Morton, Thomas, 1642
Ches. Dur. Linc. S Asa. S Pl.
Wel.

M2848 Morton, Thomas, 1641
Dur. Yk.

M2852- Moseley, Humphrey,
[1656?]
See: CLC72.
Cant.

M2853? Moses ben Maimon, 1679
... Mosem Pit, Londini.
Ely. Nor. S Pl. Wel. Yk.

M2854 Moses ben Maimon, 1683
... sumtibus ...
Ban. Cant. Chi. Dur. Ely.
Her (2). S Pl. Sal. Wel. Wor.
Yk (2).

M2855 Moses ben Maimon, 1655
Cant. Chelm. Dur. Ely. Ex.
Linc. Rip. S Pl (2). Sal. Swel.
Wel. Win.

M2857 Mosley, Nicholas, 1653
Her.

M2857cA? Moss, Robert, [1696]
'Transubstantiatio ...'
Ely.

M2860 Mossom, Robert, 1660
Cant. Chelm. Pet. S Asa. Sal.
Yk.

M2861 Mossom, Robert, 1660
Carl. Pet. Wor. Yk.

M2862 Mossom, Robert, 1642
Carl. Yk*.

M2862A Mossom, Robert, 1643
Yk*.

M2863 Mossom, Robert, 1643
Yk (2).

M2864 Mossom, Robert, 1665/6
Carl.

M2865 Mossom, Robert, 1660
Win.

M2866 Mossom, Robert, 1657
Carl. Ex. Lich. Llan. Yk.

M2866A Mossom, Robert, 1685
By Edward Jones, for Luke Meredith.
Yk.

M2867 Mossom, Robert, 1651
Cant. Lich. Yk (2).

M2868 Mossom, Robert, 1653
Carl. S Asa. Sal. Yk.

M2890 Most, 1650
Cant.

M2900 Most, 1642
Yk.

M2902 Most, [1642]
Yk.

M2903A? Most, [1680]
Date correct? BM has [1647].
Ches.

M2919A Most, [1680?]
Linc.

M2928 Most, 1643
Linc.

M2931 Most, 1642
Linc (printed catalogue: For I.C.;
CLC slip: For I.E.)*.

M2931B? Most, 1642
'newes'
Ex.

M2940 Motion, 1641
Dur.

M2944 Motte, B., 1700
Dur. Her.

M2994 Mowbray, Laurence, 1680
Ely. Linc. Rip. Win. Yk (2).

M3009 Moxon, Joseph, 1668 [1678]
Ex. Glo.

M3013 Moxon, Joseph, 1677–80
Now identified as a periodical.
Glo.

M3021 Moxon, Joseph, 1659
Pet.

M3025 Moxon, Joseph, 1686
Glo.

M3029 Moyle, Robert, 1658
Dur.

M3030 Moyle, Walter, 1697
Nor.

M3038 Mudie, Alexander, 1682
'Scotiae'
Carl. Yk.

M3040 Muggleton, Lodowick, 1699
Cant.

M3041 Muggleton, Lodowick, 1673
4°.
S Pl (imp).

M3044 Muggleton, Lodowick, 1665
S Pl.

M3046 Muggleton, Lodowick, 1667
S Pl (date altered in MS to 1668).

M3048 Muggleton, Lodowick, 1663
[*i.e.* 1667?]
Cant. S Pl.

M3049? Muggleton, Lodowick,
1665
[N.pl.].
S Pl.

M3050 Muggleton, Lodowick, 1662
Cant. S Pl.

M3051 Muggleton, Lodowick, 1669
S Pl.

M3057 Mullen, Allan, 1682
Ex.

M3063 Mumford, James, 1662
Pet.

M3073 Mun, Thomas, 1664
Pet. Sal.

M3083 Murcot, John, 1657
Ex.

M3087 Murther, 1659
Yk.

M3116 Murray, Robert, 1682
Ban.

M3130? Musaeus, 1655
... autoris.
Ches. Sal.

M3133A Musaeus, 1699
Nor.

M3135 Musarum, 1692
... Lond.
Cant. Ex. Glo. Nor. S Pl.

M3135A Musarum, 1699
S Asa.

M3136 Musarum, 1699
Lich.

M3137 Musarum, 1699
Cant. Lich. Nor. S Asa.

M3143 Musgrave, Christopher,
1688
Wel.

M3152 Musgrave, John, 1651
Pet.

M3156? Musgrave, 1650
'muzled'
Dur.

M3167 Muzled, 1650
Ex (imp). Nor.

M3171A My, 1660
Pet.

M3184 Mystery, 1663
Linc.

M3185 Mistery, [1680]
Linc.

M3186 Mystery, 1689
Pet. Wel.

N3 N., A., 1687
Sal.

N16A N., G., 1654
Ex.

N26 N., N., 1655
Carl.

N30 N., N., 1687
Wel.

N40 N., N., 1693
Ban.

N43 N., N., 1689
Carl (cropped? or anr ed. without
impr. & date?; 8p.)*.

N51 N., N., 1689
Ex.

N53 N., N., 1653
Cant. Carl.

N55 N., N., 1679
Cant. Sal. Wel.

N63 N., N., 1683
Carl. Win.

N77 N., T., 1646
Linc.

N82A? N., W., 1642
'occurrance'
Dur.

N85 Nailour, William, 1675
Carl. Sal.

N91 Nalson, John, 1681
Ches.

N93 Nalson, John, 1678
Dur. Ely. Ex. Yk.

N94 Nalson, John, 1681
Ches.

N96 Nalson, John, 1677
New. S Pl (2 − 1 tpw).

N97 Nalson, John, 1677
Carl (also has tp of N96). Ely
(as Carl). Linc.

N98 Nalson, John, 1678
Dur. New.

N99A Nalson, John, 1684
The fourth impression.
Cant. Ex (2). Lich.

N101 Nalson, John, 1681
Carl.

N102 Nalson, John, 1680
Cant. Dur. Nor. Yk.

N103 Nalson, John, 1681
Ex. Wel. Yk.

N104? Nalson, John, 1682
The second edition; ... sold by the
booksellers of Dublin; 8°.
Lich. Yk.

N105 Nalson, John, 1682
The second edition.
Ely (... Churchill, London). Ex
(2 − 1 as Ely; 1 tpw). Lich (as
Ely). S Pl.

N106 Nalson, John, 1682
Chi. Dur. Ex. Linc. Roch.
S Asa (imp). S Pl. Wel. Wor.
Yk.

N106A Nalson, John, 1682
Cant.

N107 Nalson, John, 1683
Yk.

N107+ Nalson, John, 1683
As N107, but impr. begins: For A.
Mearne, ...
Chi. Ex. Roch. S Pl. Wel.

N107A Nalson, John, 1683
Cant. Dur. Linc. S Asa (imp).
Wor.

N110 Nalson, John, 1679
Cant. Ex.

N111 Nalson, John, 1683
Ban. Carl. Dur (2).

N113 Nalson, John, 1678
Dur. S Pl. Win.

N114 Nalson, John, 1684
Carl.

N115 Nalson, John, 1685
Carl.

N116 Nalson, John, 1684
Cant (2). Chelm. Chi (imp).
Dur. Ex.

N117 Nalson, John, 1677
Carl. S Pl.

N118 Nalson, John, 1678
Dur. Yk.

N119 Nalson, John, 1681
Ches. Linc.

N122 Nalton, James, 1646
Yk.

N126 *See*: B3717

N128 Names, 1642
Linc.

N129 Names, 1642
Linc.

N129B Names, 1674
Linc.

N133 Names, 1650
Pet.

N143 Names, 1642
Dur.

N151 Nani, Giovanni Battista,
1673
Ex. Wor.

N154 Narborough, *Sir* John, 1694
Pet.

N169 Narrative, 1683
Win.

N174+ Narrative, 1647
See: CLC73.
Linc.

N187 Narrative, 1677
Linc.

N188+ Narrative, 1671
See: CLC74.
Llan.

N194+ Narrative, 1658
As N194, apart from date.
Carl.

N194A Narrative, 1670
Yk.

N212 Narrative, 1680
'The narrative ... session-house'; cap.
Linc.

N213 Narrative, [1680]
cap.
Linc.

N213A Narrative, [1662]
Pet.

N225 Narrative, 1673
Linc.

N233B Nathan, Isaac, 1654
... G. & H. Eversden.
Cant. Dur. Ex. Sal.

N241 Natura, 1655
Linc.

N246 Naudé, Gabriel, 1657
Carl.

N249 Naunton, *Sir* Robert, 1641
Carl (3 − 1 tp imp).

N250 Naunton, *Sir* Robert, 1641
Carl. Pet.

N252 Naunton, *Sir* Robert, 1650
Ches.

N257 Nayler, James, [1654?]
Yk.

N266 Nayler, James, 1655
Yk.

N275 Nayler, James, 1655
Yk.

N277 Nayler, James, 1667
Yk.

N295 Nayler, James, 1656
Yk (2).

N297 Nayler, James, 1671
Yk (tp imp).

N299 Nayler, James, 1661
Yk.

N305 Nayler, James, 1656
Yk.

N306 Nayler, James, [1655?]
Yk.

N311A Nayler, James, 1656
Yk.

N312 Nayler, James, 1665
Yk.

N317 Nayler, James, 1660
Yk.

N318 Nayler, James, [1655]
Yk.

N326 Nayler, James, 1656
Yk.

N328 Nayler, James, 1659
Yk.

N331 Nayler, James, 1656
Yk.

N363 Neau, Elie, 1699
4°.
Nor.

N374 Nedham, Marchamont, 1648
Cant.

N376 Nedham, Marchamont,
[1650]
Cant (tp cropped). Chelm. Pet.

N377 Nedham, Marchamont, 1650
Linc.

N378 Nedham, Marchamont, 1647
Linc.

N383A Nedham, Marchamont,
1678
Carl. Linc. Win.

N386 Nedham, Marchamont, 1649
Ex (imp). Yk.

N388 Nedham, Marchamont, 1656
Carl.

N389 Nedham, Marchamont, 1657
Carl.

N392 Nedham, Marchamont, 1659
Yk.

N396 Nedham, Marchamont, 1648
Yk.

N397 Nedham, Marchamont, 1665
Cant. Pet.

N398 Nedham, Marchamont, 1660
Dur. Yk (2).

N398A Nedham, Marchamont,
1660
Cant.

N399 Nedham, Marchamont, 1678
Linc.

N400 Nedham, Marchamont, 1676
Dur. Linc. Yk*.

N401 Nedham, Marchamont, 1676
Win.

N402 Nedham, Marchamont, 1648
Pet.

N403 Nedham, Marchamont, 1677
Carl. Wel.

N405 Nedham, Marchamont,
[1680]
Linc.

N410 Needham, Robert, 1679
Bur. Ely. Nor. Yk.

N411 Needham, Walter, 1667
Ex. Nor. Pet.

N417 Nelson, Robert, 1688
Cant. Ex. Lich. Wel.

N419 Nemesius, 1671
Carl. Ches. Ex. S Asa. S Pl.
Wel. Win.

N425 Nepos, Cornelius, 1691
S Asa.

N425A Nepos, Cornelius, 1691
S Pl.

N426B Nepos, Cornelius, 1697
'Corn. Nepotis Excellentium ...'
Cant. Nor.

N427 Nepos, Cornelius, 1677
Carl. Ex. Yk.

N430 Nepos, Cornelius, 1675
12°.
Win.

N434 *See*: N426B

N438 Neri, Antonio, 1662
Carl.

N439? Nero, 1690
... R. Taylor.
S Pl.

N440 Nesbitt, John, 1700
'... preached at the Merchants
Lecture, ... upon the death ...'
Cant.

N444 Nesse, Christopher, 1678
Yk.

N456 Nesse, Christopher, 1680
Yk (cropped, impr. lost?; has
colophon: Published by L.
Curtiss)*.

N463 Nesse, Christopher, 1681
Yk.

N478 Netherlands, 1675
Linc.

N480 Netherlands, 1652
Carl.

N485 Netherlands, 1673
Lich. Linc. Win.

N488+ Netherlands, 1641[2]
See: CLC75.
Dur.

N489 Netherlands, 1672
Lich.

N500 Neutrality, 1642[3]
Linc.

N502 Neville, Francis de, 1642
Ex.

N505 Neville, Henry, 1668
Linc.

N513 Neville, Henry, 1681[80]
Linc. Sal.

N515 Neville, Henry, 1681
Ban. Carl. Ely. Wel.

N520 Neville, Robert, 1687
Her. Sal (tpw).

N522 Neville, Robert, 1683
Ban. Wor.

N523 Neville, Robert, 1679
Linc.

N525 Neville, Robert, 1679
Llan.

N526? Neville, Robert, 1683
Billingsley.
Wor.

N584A New, 1680
Cant.

N600 New-come, 1644
Yk (2).

N611 New, 1689
Bris. S Pl.

N625 New, 1645
Yk.

N638? New, 1667
Date as Wing 1st ed.
Sal.

N649 New, 1642
Linc.

N650 New, 1644
Yk.

N688 New, [1679]
Linc.

N691 New, 1689
Ex.

N700 New, 1642
Yk*.

N700+ New, 1642
'... of the county of Yorke'; For John
Wright; brs.
Linc.

N701 New, 1642
Yk.

N702 New, 1641
Dur.

N704A New, [1643]
cap.
Pet.

N706 New, 1641
Dur. Linc.

N706A New, 1641
Ex.

N718 New, 1681
Linc.

N728 New, 1648
Ex.

N734 New, 1641
Dur. Linc.

N743 New, 1647
Linc.

N745 New, 1642
Pet.

N781 New, 1687
Dur. S Asa. Wel.

N783 New, 1687
Cant (2). Dur. S Asa. Wel.

N794 New, 1652
Pet.

N798? New-Year's, 1696
Colophon: For John Barnes.
Cant.

N807 New-years-gift, [1679]
Linc (2).

N835C Newark, David Leslie,
Baron, 1642
Yk.

N839 Newark, David Leslie, *Baron*,
1641
Cant (tp cropped).

N843 Newark, David Leslie, *Baron*,
1646
Yk.

N847 Newbury, Nathanael, 1652[3]
Pet.

N848 Newcastle, Margaret
Cavendish, *Duchess of*, 1668
Ex.

N850 Newcastle, Margaret
Cavendish, *Duchess of*, 1668
Yk.

N851 Newcastle, Margaret
Cavendish, *Duchess of*, 1668
Swel.

N853 Newcastle, Margaret
Cavendish, *Duchess of*, 1667
Carl. Ex. Swel. Yk (2).

N858 Newcastle, Margaret
Cavendish, *Duchess of*, 1668
Swel. Yk.

N862 Newcastle, Margaret
Cavendish, *Duchess of*, 1668
The second edition.
Swel. Yk.

N864 Newcastle, Margaret
Cavendish, *Duchess of*, 1663
Swel.

N866 Newcastle, Margaret
Cavendish, *Duchess of*, 1664
Swel.

N867 Newcastle, Margaret
Cavendish, *Duchess of*, 1668
Yk.

N869 Newcastle, Margaret
Cavendish, *Duchess of*, 1653
Lich.

N870 Newcastle, Margaret
Cavendish, *Duchess of*, 1664
Swel.

N871 Newcastle, Margaret
Cavendish, *Duchess of*, 1668
2°.
Yk.

N872 Newcastle, Margaret
Cavendish, *Duchess of*, 1664
Swel.

N874 Newcastle, Margaret
Cavendish, *Duchess of*, 1671
Swel. Yk.

N874A Newcastle, William
Cavendish, *Duke of*, 1643
Dur. Yk.

N875? Newcastle, William
Cavendish, *Duke of*, 1642[3]
Printed at Yorke, ...
Linc. Yk.

N879 Newcastle, William
Cavendish, *Duke of*, 1642
Linc. Yk (2).

N880 Newcastle, William
Cavendish, *Duke of*, 1642
Linc.

N882 Newcastle, William
Cavendish, *Duke of*, 1642[3]
Dur. Yk (3 issues).

N887 Newcastle, William
Cavendish, *Duke of*, 1667
Ex.

N895 Newcome, Henry, *1627–1695*,
1689
Sal.

N901 Newcome, Peter, 1700
Cant. Ely. Glo (vol. 2 only).
Llan (vol. 2 only).

N902 Newcome, Peter, 1686
Ban.

N903 Newcome, Peter, 1696
Cant.

N907 Newcomen, Matthew, 1643
Linc.

N908 Newcomen, Matthew, 1643
Cant.

N908A Newcomen, Matthew, 1643
Ex.

N909 Newcomen, Matthew, 1646
Ex. S Pl.

N911 Newcomen, Matthew, 1643
Cant (34p.). Pet (imp, or anr
ed.?; 32p.).

N913 Newcomen, Matthew, 1644
Her.

N925 Newman, Samuel, 1662
Ban. Lich.

N926 Newman, Samuel, 1672
Ches. Ely. Pet.

N927 Newman, Samuel, 1682
Ban. Her. Nor. Sal.

N927A? Newman, Samuel, 1685
The third edition.
Ex.

N928 Newman, Samuel, 1698
Ban. Bur. Linc (2). Swel. Win.
Yk.

N929 Newman, Samuel, 1643
Cant. Chelm. Chi. Glo. Nor.
S Dv. Wor (imp).

N930 Newman, Samuel, 1650
Carl. Dur. Ely. Swel. Yk.

N931 Newman, Samuel, 1658
Cant. Her. Wel. Yk.

N939A Newport, Maurice, 1669
Dur.

N940 Newport, William, 1644
Pet.

N941 Newrobe, Richard, 1642
Pet.

N954 News, 1681
S Pl.

N955 News, [1667]
Linc.

N976A News, 1677
Linc.

N980 Newes, 1642
Linc.

N989 Newes, 1642
S Pl.

N990 Newes, 1649
S Pl.

N990A Newes, 1645
Yk.

N1010 Nevves, 1641
Yk.

N1028 News, 1642
Dur.

N1029 Newes, 1642[3]
Yk (2).

N1030 Newes, 1642
Linc.

N1040 Newte, John, 1696
Bris.

N1044B Newton, George, 1660
Ex.

N1047 Newton, George, 1672
S Asa.

N1047A Newton, George, 1673
Printed for and sold by ...
Liv.

N1049 Newton, *Sir* Isaac, 1687
Cant.

N1059 Newton, John, 1659
Sal.

N1061 Newton, John, 1654
Sal.

N1066 Newton, John, 1660
By R. and W. Leybourn ...
Cant. Pet.

N1067A Newton, John, 1668
Win.

N1071 Newton, John, 1654
Sal.

N1072? Newton, John, 1658
By R. & W. Leybourn, ... Joshuah
Kirton, ...
Sal.

N1073 Newton, John, *of St.
Martin's*, 1684
Llan.

N1075 Newton, William, [1642]
Dur.

N1076 Nicephorus, 1691
Carl. Wel. Yk.

N1085? Nicholetts, Charles, 1696
... Marshal, and ... Marshal.
Cant (imp). Sal (imp).

N1086 Nicholetts, Charles, 1687
Wel.

N1090 Nicholls, William, 1697/8
Her. S Pl. Wor.

N1091 Nicholls, William, 1691
Ely. Ex. S Asa.

N1092 Nicholls, William, 1696
Ely. Ex.

N1092+ Nicholls, William, 1698
'... In four parts'; Impr. as N1093;
8°; Gen. tp for N1093, N1094,
N1095, N1096.
Ban. Carl. S Asa.

N1093 Nicholls, William, 1698
Pt 1; By T.W. for Francis ...
Ban. Carl. S Asa.

N1094 Nicholls, William, 1697
Ban. Bur. Carl. Ches. Ely. Ex.
Llan. S Asa. S Pl.

N1095 Nicholls, William, 1698
Ban. Bur (2). Carl. Ely. Ex.
S Asa.

N1096 Nicholls, William, 1699
Ban. Bur (2). Carl. Ely. Ex.
S Asa.

N1097 Nicholls, William, 1694
Ches.

N1098 Nicholls, William, 1698
Ban. S Asa.

N1099A? Nichols, Charles, 1655
For Livewell Chapman.
Carl.

N1104 Nicholson, Benjamin, 1653
Yk.

N1106 Nicholson, Benjamin, 1653
Yk.

N1110 Nicholson, William, 1659[8]
Carl. Chelm. Ex (2). Glo.

N1111 Nicholson, William, 1662
Glo. Win.

N1112 Nicholson, William, 1661
Carl. Glo. Nor. Win. Wor.

N1113 Nicholson, William, 1655
Ex.

N1114 Nicholson, William, 1661
Sal.

N1115 Nicholson, William, 1662
S Asa. Yk.

N1116 Nicholson, William, 1663
Ex. Glo. S Asa. S Pl.

N1117 Nicholson, William, 1671
Bur (imp). Carl. Her. Yk.

N1118 Nicholson, William, 1676
Ely. Yk.

N1119 Nicholson, William, 1678
Ban. Dur. Her. Nor.

N1135? Nicole, Pierre, 1699
Quintâ editione; Sumtibus ...
Nor (imp).

N1136 Nicole, Pierre, 1677
Carl.

N1137D Nicole, Pierre, 1678
Ex.

N1139 Nicolls, Ferdinando, 1654[5]
Pet. Yk.

N1144 Nicols, Thomas, 1659
Cant.

N1146 Nicolson, William, 1696
Cant. Carl. Dur. Ex.

N1146A Nicolson, William, [1697?]
S Pl.

N1147 Nicolson, William, 1697
Carl. Dur. Ex. S Pl.

N1148 Nicolson, William, 1699
Carl. Dur. Ex. S Pl.

N1149cA Nieremberg, Juan Eusebio, 1699
The fifth edition.
Ely.

N1150A Nieremberg, Juan Eusebio, 1673
S Pl.

N1151 Nieremberg, Juan Eusebio, 1672
S Pl.

N1152 Nieuhof, Johan, 1669
Ex.

N1158 Nil, 1646
Linc. Sal.

N1162 Nine, 1642
Yk.

N1164 Ninth, 1689
S Asa. Wel.

N1196A Noble, David, 1700
'The visions and ...'
Pet. Yk.

N1224 Non-conformist's, 1674
Sal. Wel. Win.

N1226A None-such, 1651
Yk.

N1230 Norfolk, Henry Howard, *6th Duke of*, 1681
S Pl. Wor.

N1239A Norman, John, 1673
Carl. Chelm.

N1243 Norris, John, 1697
Cant (2). Carl. Dur. Ely. Ex. Sal.

N1245? Norris, John, 1691
12°.
Carl. Dur. Ex. Sal.

N1246 Norris, John, 1690
Ban. Ex.

N1248 Norris, John, 1687
Chi (imp).

N1249 Norris, John, 1692
Carl. Ely. Sal.

N1251 Norris, John, 1685
S Pl.

N1254 Norris, John, 1695
Cant. Ex.

N1256 Norris, John, 1684
Ex. Sal.

N1257 Norris, John, 1691
Cant.

N1261 Norris, John, 1693
Bur.

N1263 Norris, John, 1693
Bur (2). Carl.

N1266 Norris, John, 1693
Carl. Ely. Yk.

N1267 Norris, John, 1690
Nor. Wel.

N1268 Norris, John, 1691
Carl. Yk.

N1269 Norris, John, 1685
Her. S Pl.

N1272 Norris, John, 1688
Yk.

N1273 Norris, John, 1694
Carl.

N1274 Norris, John, 1697
Chi. Sal.

N1276 Norris, John, 1692
Carl.

N1279 Nortcliffe, M., 1653
Carl.

N1285 North, Dudley North, *4th Baron*, 1670
Cant. Linc.

N1286 North, Dudley North, *4th Baron*, 1669
Carl.

N1289 North, John, *Minister*, 1671
Ban. Cant. Lich.

N1290 North, John, *Minister*, 1671
Dur.

N1294- Northern, [1643]
See: CLC76.
Dur.

N1298 Northleigh, John, 1688
Wel.

N1301 Northleigh, John, 1682
Carl. Wel. Wor.

N1313 Norton, John, 1658
New. Yk (3).

N1317 Norton, John, 1653
Pet.

N1320 Norton, John, 1654
Yk.

N1321 Norton, John, 1657
Her. Sal. Yk.

N1322 Norton, John, 1648
Carl. Sal.

N1342 Norwood, Anthony, 1654
Ex.

N1381 Norwood, Robert, 1651
Yk.

N1385 Norwood, Thomas, 1642
Sal.

N1392 Notes, 1688
Ban. Cant (v. imp). Dur. Ex (tpw). Nor. S Asa. Wel (imp).

N1399 Notredame, Michel de, 1672
Cant.

N1399+ Notredame, Michel de, 1672
By Thomas Ratcliffe and Nathaniel Thompson; 2°.
Ex. Wor.

N1402 Nottingham, Heneage Finch, *Earl of*, 1685
Wel.

N1403 Nottingham, Heneage Finch, *Earl of*, 1660
Yk (2).

N1403A Nottingham, Heneage Finch, *Earl of*, 1660
Carl. Linc. Yk.

N1409 Nottingham, Heneage Finch, *Earl of*, 1680
Ches. Linc. Win.

N1413 Nottinghamshires, 1642
Dur.

N1414A Nourse, Peter, [1698]
Ely.

N1417 Nourse, Timothy, 1691
Ely (tpw).

N1436B- Nowell, Alexander, 1641
Per M.F. sumptibus bibliopolarum; 8°.
Ex.

N1436D- Nowell, Alexander, 1661
Excudebat A.H., pro Societate Stationariorum; 8°.
S Alb.

N1438A Nowell, Alexander, 1679
Glo.

N1450 Noye, *Sir* William, 1669
Carl.

N1451 Noye, *Sir* William, 1641
Linc. Yk.

N1457? Noyes, James, 1661
... for Edmund Paxton.
Win.

N1460 Noyes, James, 1647
Win.

N1484 Nye, Philip, 1660
Chelm (tpw).

N1485 Nye, Philip, 1677
Yk.

N1487 Nye, Philip, 1659
Carl. Ex (2).

N1488 Nye, Philip, 1659
Dur.

N1489 Nye, Philip, 1659
Bur. Cant.

N1490? Nye, Philip, 1688
8°.
Ely.

N1494 Nye, Philip, 1644
Cant (imp?).

N1496 Nye, Philip, 1683
Cant.

N1502A Nye, Stephen, 1692
Cant. Carl.

N1504 Nye, Stephen, 1691
Cant. Wel.

N1505A Nye, Stephen, 1691
Cant. Carl.

N1505B Nye, Stephen, 1693
Cant. Carl.

N1505C Nye, Stephen, 1694
Carl. Wel.

N1506 Nye, Stephen, 1696
Cant. Ex. S Pl.

N1506A? Nye, Stephen, [1691]
'answer'd'
Cant. Wel.

N1507 Nye, Stephen, 1700
Ex.

N1507+ Nye, Stephen, 1700
As N1507, but: 4°.
S Pl.

N1507B Nye, Stephen, [1691?]
cap.
Cant.

N1508A Nye, Stephen, 1691
Cant (2). Wel.

N1508B Nye, Stephen, 1693
Cant. Carl.

N1508E Nye, Stephen, 1691
Cant. Carl.

N1509A Nye, Stephen, 1692
Cant. Carl.

O2A? O., I. V. C., 1663
London, ...
Pet.

O6 O., J., 1696
Author = James Owen?
Cant.

O13 O. Cromwell's, [1660]
Pet.

O29? Oates, Titus, [1679/80]
'misdemeanour'
Linc.

O31 Oates, Titus, [1680]
'misdemeanours'
Linc. Win.

O41 Oates, Titus, 1680
Glo. Linc. Win. Yk (imp).

O46 Oates, Titus, 1679
Linc. Win. Yk.

O49 Oates, Titus, 1679
Dur. Linc. Win.

O53 Oates, Titus, 1679
Carl. Dur. Ex. Her.

O58 Oates, Titus, 1696
Bris.

O59 Oates, Titus, 1679
Carl. Dur. Ely. Lich. Linc.
Nor. Win. Yk (imp).

O62 Oates, Titus, 1679
Ely. Win.

O66 Oates's, 1683
Wor.

O73 Oath, [1641]
Linc. Yk.

O75 Oath, 1642
Linc.

O77 Oath, 1642
Ex. Linc.

O92 Observations, 1667
S Pl.

O97 *See*: S4534: O97 is anr ed.?, or
abbreviated entry?

O100 Observations, 1680
Linc.

O104 Observations, 1679
Linc. S Asa.

O104A Observations, [1679]
Yk.

O109 Observations, [1691?]
Dur.

O111 Observations, 1642
Linc.

O115? Observations, [1698]
'... constitution of the company of the
Bank ...'
Cant.

O116 Observations, 1643
Yk.

O123B Observations, [1642]
Linc.

O123D Observations, [1642]
Pet.

O123KA Observator, 1685
4°.
Carl.

O126 Ochino, Bernardino, 1657
Cant (imp).

O129 O'Connor, William, 1641
Pet.

O144B Of, [1692]
'expresly'
Cant.

O157 Officium, 1655
Carl. Wel.

O158 Officium, 1676
Dur.

O159B? Offley, William, 1694
For Robert Clavell.
Carl.

O163 Ogilby, John, 1670
Ex. Wel. Win.

O165 Ogilby, John, 1671
Win.

O166 Ogilby, John, 1673
Glo.

O168 Ogilby, John, 1675
Yk (imp).

O169 Ogilby, John, 1698
Ely (tp imp). Pet.

O171 Ogilby, John, 1662
Dur. Linc.

O181 Ogilby, John, 1661
Ches. Linc. Win.

O184 Ogilby, John, 1699
Chelm.

O186 Ogilvy, Michael, 1660
Carl.

O187 Ogle, Thomas, 1642[3]
Linc.

O191 Okeley, William, 1675
Linc.

O205 Old, 1658
Ex.

O212 Old, 1660
40p.
Cant. Ex.

O212+ Old, 1660
As O212, but: 43p.
Pet.

O213 Old, 1645
Yk.

O233 Oldham, John, 1680
Ches.

O237 Oldham, John, 1683
Cant.

O237+ Oldham, John, 1684
For Joseph Hindmarsh; 8°; Different collection from O237; 134p.
Cant.

O241 Oldham, John, 1687
Cant.

O244 Oldham, John, 1681
Yk.

O246 Oldham, John, 1685
Cant.

O252 Oldisworth, Giles, 1664
Yk.

O269 Olearius, Adam, 1662
Ex.

O270 Olearius, Adam, 1669
Ely. Wel. Wor.

O272 Oliver, Edward, 1698
S Pl. Wor.

O273 Oliver, Edward, 1698
Dur. S Asa.

O275 Oliver, John, 1682
Pet. S Asa.

O280? Oliver, Richard, 1700
'preach'd'
Her.

O28## Olivier, Pierre, 1674
'academicae'
Dur. Ely.

O286 Ollyffe, John, 1699
Nor (imp).

O288 Ollyffe, John, 1689
Llan. Sal.

O291 Omnia, 1679
Linc.

O304 On, 1669
Linc.

O318 On, [1645]
Linc.

O333 One, [1643]
Linc.

O342 O'Neill, *Sir* Phelim, [1642]
Linc.

O344 O'Neill, *Sir* Phelim, 1641[2]
Dur.

O352 Opinion, 1680
Wel.

O366A Orchard, N., 1676
Carl.

O377 Order, 1646
Win.

O384A Order, 1671
Win.

O389 Order, 1557 [*i.e.* 1695?]
Cant.

O391 Orderly, 1644
Yk.

O399 Orders, 1642
Yk.

O416 Ordo, 1686
12°.
S Pl. Yk (2).

O424 Origen, 1658
Cant (2). Ches. Chi. Ely. Her.
Linc. Pet. S Asa. S Pl (3 − 1
imp). Sal. Yk.

O425 Origen, 1677
Dur. Ex. Glo. Her. Lich. Nor.
Roch. Swel. Wor. Yk.

O427 Origen, [1700]
Bris.

O429 Origen, 1686
Ely. Ex. S Pl. Yk.

O437 Orme, William, 1681
Cant. Wor.

O444 Ormonde, James Butler, *Duke of*, 1649
Cant. Pet (imp).

O448 Ormonde, James Butler, *Duke of*, 1682
Wor.

O450 Ormonde, James Butler, *Duke of*, [1642]
Linc.

O452 Ormonde, James Butler, *Duke of*, 1649
Cant.

O453 Ormonde, James Butler, *Duke of*, 1649
Date on tp.
Cant.

O458 Ormonde, James Butler, *Duke of*, 1649
Cant.

O466 Orpen, Richard, 1689
Ex.

O469 Orrery, Charles Boyle, *Earl of*, 1698
Ex. Nor.

O470 Orrery, Charles Boyle, *Earl of*, 1698
Glo. Pet.

O471 Orrery, Charles Boyle, *Earl of*, 1699
Dur. Llan. Yk.

O473 Orrery, Roger Boyle, *Earl of*, 1662
Cant. Win.

O476 Orrery, Roger Boyle, *Earl of*, 1676
Carl.

O485 Orrery, Roger Boyle, *Earl of*, 1662
Win.

O486 Orrery, Roger Boyle, *Earl of*, 1651
Glo.

O490 Orrery, Roger Boyle, *Earl of*, 1676
Linc.

O494 Orrery, Roger Boyle, *Earl of*, 1669
Ex.

O499 Orrery, Roger Boyle, *Earl of*, 1677
Carl.

O506? Osborne, Francis, 1682
… Banks.
Dur. Nor. Yk.

O514 Osborne, Francis, 1658
Cant.

O515? Osborne, Francis, 1658
By James Grismond …
Carl.

O516 Osborne, Francis, 1659
Cant (imp).

O519 Osborne, Francis, 1656
Carl.

O523 Osborne, Francis, 1652
Win.

O525 Osborne, John, 1659
Pet.

O528 Osborne, Richard, 1648
Yk.

O532 Ostervald, Jean Frédéric, 1700
Dur. Ex. S Pl. Yk.

O538? Otway, Thomas, 1692
For R. Bentley.
Ex (tp only).

O567 Otway, Thomas, 1682
Ex.

O572 Oughtred, William, 1660
Cant.

O574 Oughtred, William, 1652
Ches. Roch. Yk.

O582 Oughtred, William, 1647
Linc. Yk.

O583 Oughtred, William, 1694
'Mr. William Oughtred's Key …'
Cant.

O586 Oughtred, William, 1677
Cant.

O589 Oughtred, William, 1657
Sal.

O591 Our, 1695
Dur.

O600 Outram, William, [1681]
[London], distributed gratis by
William Cooper, Richard Chiswel,
Christopher Wilkinson, William Nott,
Robert Horn and William Henshman.
Dur.

O601 Outram, William, 1677
Cant (3). Carl. Ches. Chi. Ely.
Ex (2). Her. Lich. Linc. Nor.
S Asa. S Dv. S Pl. Sal. Win.
Yk.

O603 Outram, William, 1680
Carl. Win.

O604 Outram, William, 1682
Carl. Her.

O605 Outram, William, 1697
Ely.

O606 Ovatio, 1641
Linc.

O607 Overall, John, 1690
Bris. Cant. Carl. Ches. Chi (2).
Dur. Ely. Ex (2). Glo (2). Her.
Linc. Liv. Llan. Nor. S Asa.
S Pl (2). Sal. Wel (2). Win. Yk
(2).

O612? Overbury, *Sir* Thomas, *the
Younger*, 1678
8°.
Pet.

O618 Overton, Richard, 1646
Linc.

O620? Overton, Richard, 1645
... Claw Clergie.
Linc.

O623 Overton, Richard, 1642
S Pl.

O628A Overton, Richard, [1647]
Yk.

O629E Overton, Richard, 1644
Yk.

O630 Overton, Richard, [1645]
Sal.

O632 Overton, Richard, 1646
Pet.

O632B Overton, Richard, 1646
Cant. Linc (imp). Pet.

O637 Overton, Robert, 1659
Ex.

O659 Ovid, 1680
Ely.

O663A Ovid, 1688
The fourth edition.
Cant.

O667 Ovid, 1699
Ely.

O682 Ovid, 1696
Ely. Ex. Pet. S Asa.

O684 Ovid, 1656
Bur (Lawshall Parish Lib.
deposited here).

O684A Ovid, 1656
The fourth edition.
Linc.

O702 Owen, Corbett, 1669
Ban. Bris.

O704 Owen, David, 1642
S Asa. Sal. Yk.

O708 Owen, James, 1694
Ex.

O709 Owen, James, 1697
Carl.

O711 Owen, John, *D.D.*, 1651
Pet (imp).

O711A Owen, John, *D.D.*, 1651
Chelm (imp).

O713 Owen, John, *D.D.*, 1662
Carl. Ex. Linc. Wor.

O714 Owen, John, *D.D.*, 1684
Wor.

O717 Owen, John, *D.D.*, 1690
Ex.

O718 Owen, John, *D.D.*, 1669
Carl.

O721 Owen, John, *D.D.*, 1667
Wel.

O723 Owen, John, *D.D.*, 1680
Carl. Pet.

O724 Owen, John, *D.D.*, 1680
Win.

O725 Owen, John, *D.D.*, 1649
Bur.

O726 Owen, John, *D.D.*, 1679
Linc. Win.

O727 Owen, John, *D.D.*, 1679
Ex. Yk.

O729 Owen, John, *D.D.*, 1680
Cant. Dur.

O732 Owen, John, *D.D.*, 1684
Cant. Dur.

O734 Owen, John, *D.D.*, 1653
Linc. Sal.

O737 Owen, John, *D.D.*, 1662
Yk.

O738 Owen, John, *D.D.*, 1682
Llan.

O739? Owen, John, *D.D.*, 1677
4°.
Llan. S Pl.

O740 Owen, John, *D.D.*, 1654
Cant (2).

O751 Owen, John, *D.D.*, 1671
Llan.

O752 Owen, John, *D.D.*, 1671
Cant.

O753 Owen, John, *D.D.*, 1668
Cant. Dur. Linc. Nor. Rip.

O753B Owen, John, *D.D.*, 1674
Cant.

O754 Owen, John, *D.D.*, 1674
Cant. Dur.

O756 Owen, John, *D.D.*, 1659
Cant.

O757 Owen, John, *D.D.*, 1656
Carl. Pet (imp).

O758 Owen, John, *D.D.*, 1656
Cant. Carl. Pet (imp). Win.

O762 Owen, John, *D.D.*, 1681
Cant (tp imp). Carl. Llan.

O763 Owen, John, *D.D.*, 1667
Win.

O764 Owen, John, *D.D.*, 1681
Bur. Win.

O768? Owen, John, *D.D.*, 1684
By A.M. and R.E. ...
Llan.

O779 Owen, John, *D.D.*, 1700
Llan.

O780 Owen, John, *D.D.*, 1657
Carl. Chelm. Sal.

O782 Owen, John, *D.D.*, 1658
Cant. Llan.

O784 Owen, John, *D.D.*, 1659
Cant. Carl. Llan.

O785 Owen, John, *D.D.*, 1656
Llan.

O786 Owen, John, *D.D.*, 1658
Cant.

O791 Owen, John, *D.D.*, 1667
Carl. Win.

O793 Owen, John, *D.D.*, 1674
Cant. Chelm.

O794 Owen, John, *D.D.*, 1669
Cant. Ex.

O801 Owen, John, *D.D.*, 1677
Llan. S Pl. Win.

O802 Owen, John, *D.D.*, 1656
Cant. Carl.

O803 Owen, John, *D.D.*, 1657
Carl. Chelm (tp imp).

O805A Owen, John, *D.D.*, 1649
Yk.

O806 Owen, John, *D.D.*, 1652
Chi. Pet.

O806A Owen, John, *D.D.*, 1682
Carl.

O809 Owen, John, *D.D.*, 1678
Llan. S Pl.

O810 Owen, John, *D.D.*, 1661
Ex. Pet.

O811 Owen, John, *D.D.*, 1643
Ex.

O815 Owen, John, *D.D.*, 1689
Cant. Ex.

O817 Owen, John, *D.D.*, 1669
Carl. Glo. Linc. Llan. Win.

O819? Owen, John, *D.D.*, [1700? or later?]
No date.
Ely.

O820 Owen, John, *D.D.*, 1659
Yk.

O821? Owen, John, *D.D.*, 1674
For N. Ponder.
S Pl. Win.

O822 Owen, John, *D.D.*, 1664
Carl. Ex. Llan. S Asa. Wor.

O823 Owen, John, *D.D.*, 1655
Bur. Carl. Ex. Her. Nor. Sal
(imp).

O825aA Owen, John, *Chaplain*,
1680
Cant.

O825C Owen, John, *the
Epigrammatist*, 1668
Cant ('Eigrammatum [*sic*]'). Dur.
S Pl.

O827? Owen, Jonathan, 1700
'... sermon ... occasioned by the death
of ... Philip King'
Cant.

O829A Owen, Richard, 1666
Carl.

O830 Owen, Thankfull, 1679
Carl. Ex. Sal.

O832A Owen, Vincent, 1685
... junior, in Ludlow.
Her.

O839 Oxenden, George, [1679]
Ely. Linc.

O841 Oxenden, Henry, 1647
Cant.

O847? Oxford-act, 1613 [*i.e.* 1693]
Wing has wrong date?
Carl.

O858 Oxford, University of, 1690
Sal (tpw).

O863? Oxford, University of, 1660
... excudebat ...
Chelm. Dur. Lich (2). Linc.
Wel.

O863K Oxford, University of, 1682
cap.
Dur.

O864 Oxford, University of, 1674
Cant. Carl. Dur. Ely. Ex. Her.
Linc. Nor. Pet. Sal. Wel. Win.
Wor.

O875 Oxford, University of, 1662
Wel. Yk.

O876 Oxford, University of, 1660
Linc. Wel. Yk.

O878 Oxford, University of, 1661
Linc.

O879? Oxford, University of, 1669
'... in obitum ... Henriettae Mariae'
Win.

O880 Oxford, University of, 1670
Linc. Sal.

O881 Oxford, University of, 1670
Sal.

O882 Oxford, University of, 1671
Sal.

O883 Oxford, University of, 1641
Carl. Pet. Yk.

O885 Oxford, University of, 1700
Linc. Sal (2 − 1 tpw).

O893 Oxford, University of, 1683
Sal (tpw).

O894 Oxford, University of, 1690
2 issues: with engr. device *or* woodcut
on tp.
Cant (engr. device).

O897 Oxford, University of, 1676
Carl. Dur. Ely. Ex. Pet. S Pl.
Sal. Wor. Yk.

O902 Oxford, University of, 1654
Linc.

O929- Oxford, University of, 1670
As O929, apart from date.
S Asa.

O929 Oxford, University of, 1671
'statutorum'
Cant. Sal.

O930 Oxford, University of, 1674
Liv.

O931 Oxford, University of, 1682
Pet.

O936 Oxford, University of, 1685
Bris.

O937 Oxford, University of, 1695
Sal (tpw). Yk.

O941 Oxford, University of, 1641
Linc. Yk.

O966? Oxford, University of, 1661
Lichfieldianis; 12°.
Ely. Win.

O969 Oxford, University of, 1688
Ely. Sal (3 − 1 tpw).

O970 Oxford, University of, 1685
Bris. S Asa.

O974 Oxford, University of, 1677
Carl.

O984 Oxford, University of, 1693
Sal (tpw).

O985 Oxford, University of, 1641
'honourable'
Cant. Ex. Pet. Yk.

O986 Oxford, University of, 1641
Linc. Nor.

O986A? Oxford, University of,
1641
Not in Madan; As O986, but month,
day and year at end.
Nor. Sal.

O986B+ Oxford, University of,
1652
Oxford, by Leonard Lichfield; 4°.
Carl.

O990 Oxford, University of, 1643
'Verses on the death of ...'
Pet. Yk (2).

O992 Oxford, University of, 1689
Bris (imp)*.

O994 Oxfords, 1681
Linc.

Location of English books 1641—1700
as enumerated in Wing's *Short-Title Catalogue*
Volume Three

P7 P., B., 1668
Ex.

P8 P., B., 1694
... sold by Randal Taylor.
Chi.

P10? P., C., 1684
For J. Wickins and Rob. Kettlewell;
12°.
S Pl.

P15 P., D. P., 1644[5]
Yk.

P16 P., D. P., 1644
Pet.

P19 P., E., 1679
Win.

P24 P., G., [1679]
Dur. Linc.

P35 P., H., 1676
Yk.

P37 P., H., 1659
Ex.

P38 P., H., 1641
Cant. Nor. Yk.

P39 P., H., 1641
Pet.

P43 *See*: Periodicals

P55 P., J., [1681]
Dur. Linc (2).

P60+ P., J., [1692?]
'A new guide ...'; By the assigns of
Richard & Edward Atkins; 12°.
Yk.

P77? P., L., 1695
'a letter'
Dur.

P83+ P., M., 1642
'True intelligence'; Formerly M67.
Linc.

P91- P., O., [1660?]
See: CLC77.
Dur.

P97 P., R., 1648
Yk.

P103 P., R., 1642
Dur. Yk.

P104 P., R., 1642[3]
Wing has wrong date.
Linc.

P112? P., T., 1662
'Jerub-baal'
Pet.

P113 P., T., 1663
Dur. Pet.

P125? P., W., 1660
'Charles I'
Pet.

P126 P., W., 1673
Sal.

P128 P., W., [1679]
Dur. Linc.

P135 P., W., 1652
Carl.

P142 Pachymeres, Georgius, 1666
Lich. Linc. Pet.

P155 Pack, 1650
By the Company of Covenant-Keepers.
Chelm. Pet. Yk.

P165+ Pageau, *Abbé*, 1679
'The intrigues ...'; Formerly I278.
Ely.

P166 Paget, John, 1641
Win.

P168A- Paget, Thomas, 1650
As P168A, apart from date and
'faithfull'
Cant.

P169 Paget, Thomas, 1649
Ex.

P169B Paget, Thomas, 1650
Cant.

P170 Paget, William, *Lord*, 1642
'copie'
Dur.

P171 Paget, William, *Lord*, 1642
Linc.

P172 Pagitt, Ephraim, 1646
Ely (tp imp).

P173? Pagitt, Ephraim, 1674
For Robert Clavell.
Ex.

P175 Pagitt, Ephraim, 1645
Ely.

P176 Pagitt, Ephraim, 1646
Cant.

P177 Pagitt, Ephraim, 1647
The third edition.
Carl.

P178 Pagitt, Ephraim, 1647
Both tps dated 1647.
Linc. Pet.

P179 Pagitt, Ephraim, 1648
As P178, but: Letterpress tp dated
1647, engr. tp 1648.
Linc.

P180 Pagitt, Ephraim, 1654
Ex. Pet. Win.

P192 Paine, William, 1682
Wor.

P194? Pair, 1670
'A pair of spectacles, very useful, and
needful, for all those ...'
Yk.

P203? Palafox y Mendoza, Juan de,
1693
For Samuel Smith; 12°.
Ely.

P208 Palladio, Andrea, 1693
Glo (imp).

P209? Palladio, Andrea, 1700
For Thomas Braddyll ...
Nor.

P210 Palladius, 1665
S Pl. Win. Wor.

P212 Pallavicino, Ferrante, 1644
Carl.

P218 Palmer, Anthony, 1654
Wor.

P219 Palmer, Anthony, 1653
Wor.

P224? Palmer, Edward, 1667
... for Fran. Oxlad.
Ban.

P228 Palmer, George, 1649
Cant.

P230 Palmer, Herbert, 1646
'and'
Yk.

P230A - Palmer, Herbert, 1643
The second impression; For Thomas
Underhill; 8°.
Cant (cropped).

P235 Palmer, Herbert, 1644
Yk.

P242 Palmer, Herbert, 1643
Cant. Pet (imp)*.

P243 Palmer, Herbert, 1643
4°.
Ex. Pet.

P244 Palmer, Herbert, 1643
Pet. Yk.

P248 Palmer, John, *of Ecton*, 1658
Cant.

P251 Palmer, Samuel, 1680
Her. Linc. Pet. S Asa. Yk.

P269 Panegyrick, [1679]
Ches.

P272 Panegyricus, 1656
Carl.

P287 Paper, 1643
Linc.

P309 Papin, Denys, 1681
Wel.

P318+ Papists, 1679
Printed for J.C.; 4°.
Linc.

P327 Paradise, John, 1661
'Hadadrimmon'
Cant (imp). Carl. Ex. Wor.

P334A+ Parallel, 1700
'A parallel between the faith';
Formerly L1139.
S Asa.

P334A++ Parallel, 1700
'A parallel between the faith'; For G.
Strahan; 4°.
Wel.

P336 Parallell, 1642
Linc.

P336A Paralell, 1642
Linc.

P339 Paralell, 1647
Yk.

P342+ Paraphrasis, 1655
See: CLC78.
Cant (imp). Linc (tpw).

P349 Paré, Ambroise, 1649
Sal.

P351 Paré, Ambroise, 1678
Cant.

P353 Paré, David, 1644
Wor.

P356 Pargiter, Thomas, 1682
Carl.

P359 Paris, Matthew, 1684
Chi. Ely. Ex. Nor. Pet. Sal.
Wel.

P361 Parival, Jean Nicolas de, 1656
'history'; Davies.
Carl. Lich.

P361+ Parival, Jean Nicolas de,
1659
No. missing in Wing; ... Simon Miller
and Thomas Davies.
Nor.

P362 Park, Henry, 1695
... Edm. Richardson.
Yk.

P376 Parke, James, 1679
S Pl.

P395 Parker, Henry, 1647
Linc.

P396 Parker, Henry, 1647
Yk.

P403 Parker, Henry, 1644
Ex. Sal.

P410 Parker, Henry, 1643
Cant. Ex.

P412? Parker, Henry, [1642]
[N.pl., n.d.]; 47p.
Ex.

P412+ Parker, Henry, [1642]
As P412, but: 32p.
Dur.

P413 Parker, Henry, [1642]
Linc. Pet. Yk.

P415 Parker, Henry, 1642
'Majestie'
Dur.

P416 Parker, Henry, 1643
Linc. Win (imp). Yk.

P417 Parker, Henry, [1643?]
4°.
Yk.

P418 Parker, Henry, 1641
Cant. Linc.

P420 Parker, Henry, 1651
Cant.

P423 Parker, Henry, [1642]
Pet.

P424 Parker, Henry, [1642]
Cant. Dur. Linc. Yk.

P428 Parker, Henry, 1641
Linc. S Pl.

P429 Parker, Henry, 1650
Ex (MS attrib. to John Milton).

P430 Parker, Henry, 1688
S Pl.

P449+ Parker, Peter, *Bookseller*,
[1677?]
See: CLC79.
Cant.

P453 Parker, Samuel, 1683
Cant. Carl. Ely. Ex (2). S Pl.
Wel. Win.

P454 Parker, Samuel, 1666
Chelm. S Pl.

P455 Parker, Samuel, 1681
Bur. Carl. Ely. Ex (2). Nor.
Pet (2). S Pl. Win. Yk (2).

P457 Parker, Samuel, 1671
Carl (2). Ex. Glo. Linc (2). Pet.
S Pl. Sal. Yk.

P458 Parker, Samuel, 1681
4°.
Ban. Carl. Ely. Ex. Her. Pet.
Roch. S Asa. S Pl. Wel. Win.

P459 Parker, Samuel, 1670
Bur. Carl. Chelm. Ches. Dur.
Pet. S Asa. Win.

P460 Parker, Samuel, 1671
Ex. Glo.

P461 Parker, Samuel, 1690
Cant (2 – 1 tp imp). Her. Wel.

P462 Parker, Samuel, 1678
Dur. Ex. Pet. Roch. S Asa.
S Pl.

P463? Parker, Samuel, 1666
... for Richard Davis.
S Pl.

P464 Parker, Samuel, 1667
Ban. Carl. Dur. Ex. Pet. Win.

P467? Parker, Samuel, 1688
131p.
Carl. Dur (imp).

P467+ Parker, Samuel, 1688
As P467, but: 135p.
Wel.

P470 Parker, Samuel, 1684
Carl. Ches. Pet. S Pl. Win.
Yk.

P471 Parker, Samuel, 1685
8°.
Ches. Pet. S Pl.

P473 Parker, Samuel, 1673
Bur. Carl. Ex (2). Nor. Pet.
Win. Yk.

P474 Parker, Samuel, 1665
Typis A.M., venales apud Jo. Sherley
& Sam. Thomson, & Rich. Davis,
Oxon.
Ban. Carl. Her. Lich. Pet. Sal.
Win.

P477 Parker, Thomas, 1657
Sal.

P486 Parker, William, 1651
Ex (imp). Pet.

P492 Parkinson, James, 1689
Cant.

P493 Parkinson, James, 1691
Wel.

P494 Parkinson, James, [1690?]
Carl.

P495 Parkinson, John, 1656
... sold by Richard Thrale.
Carl.

P496 Parkyns, *Sir* William, 1641
Dur. Yk.

P502 Parliament, 1648[9]
Ex.

P509 Parliament, [1648]
Yk.

P510B+ Parliaments, 1642
As P510B, apart from date.
Linc.

P524 Parliaments, 1645[6]
Yk.

P543 Parr, Elnathan, 1651
Carl. Chelm. Ex. Linc.

P544 Parr, Elnathan, 1651
Carl. Chelm. Ex. Linc.

P547 Parr, Richard, 1658
Yk.

P548 Parr, Richard, 1686
Copies vary.
Ban. Cant. Ches (2). Dur. Ex.
Glo. Lich. Liv. S Asa. Tru.
Wel. Yk (2).

P548+ Parr, Richard, 1686
For Nathaniel Ranew; 2°; Copies
vary.
Carl. S Pl. Sal. Swel. Win.
Wor (2).

P549 Parr, Richard, 1672
Her.

P556 Parry, Edward, 1660
Carl.

P556+ Parry, James, 1661
See: CLC80.
Pet.

P558? Parry, John, 1670
... for Ric. Davis.
Carl. Llan.

P559+ Parsons, Bartholomew,
[1700?]
See: CLC81.
Sal.

P565 Parsons, Robert, *Jesuit*, 1673
Chi.

P565+ Parsons, Robert, *Jesuit*,
1687
By Henry Hills, for him and Matt.
Turner; 8°.
S Asa.

P568 Parsons, Robert, *Jesuit*, 1681
Ches. Yk.

P569 Parsons, Robert, *Jesuit*, 1690
Cant. Dur (imp). Ely. Ex (2).
Wel. Win.

P569+ Parsons, Robert, *Jesuit*,
1684
'Llyfr y resolusion'; Formerly B5473A.
S Asa.

P570? Parsons, Robert, *Rector*,
1680
... Richard Davis ...; Wing confuses 2
Robert Parsons.
Ban (tpw). Cant. Carl. Her.
Llan (2). S Pl. Win. Yk.

P571? Parsons, Robert, *Rector*,
1681
... reprinted by Benjamin Took and
John Crook, sold by Mary Crook.
Cant.

P575 Parsons, Robert, *Jesuit*, 1688
S Asa.

P578 Part, 1648
Cant.

P593 Particular, 1680
Linc.

P602 Particular, 1642
Linc.

P636 Paruta, Paulo, 1658
Chi. Lich.

P639 Paruta, Paulo, 1657
Linc. Wel. Yk.

P640 Pascal, Blaise, 1658
Cant. Dur. Ex. Nor. Pet. S Pl.
Win. Yk.

P642 Pascal, Blaise, 1679
Third ed. not on tp.
Ely. Wel.

P643 Pascal, Blaise, 1657
Ches.

P644 Pascal, Blaise, 1658
12°.
Cant. Ex. Nor. Pet. S Pl. Win.

P644+ Pascal, Blaise, 1658
The second edition; For Richard
Royston; 12°.
Dur. Yk.

P645 Pascal, Blaise, 1688
Ex. Llan.

P646 Paske, Thomas, 1642
Cant. Dur. Linc.

P648 Pasor, George, 1644
Carl. Ely. Glo. Wel. Wor. Yk.

P648A Pasor, George, 1649
Dur. Ex. S Pl. Wel.

P649 Pasor, George, 1644
... Jacobus Junius ... Richardi
Whittakeri.
Carl. Ely. Glo. Wel. Wor.

P650 Pasor, George, 1650
... Iosuae Kirton ...
Wel (tpw)*. Yk.

P650+ Pasor, George, 1650
Excudebat Edw. Griffin, sumptibus
J.K. & S.T. & prostant venales apud
Abelem Roper; 8°.
Dur. Ex. S Pl.

P650A Pasor, George, 1644
... Jacobus Junius ... Richardi
Whittakeri.
Carl. Ely. Glo. Wel. Wor. Yk.

P651 Pasor, George, 1650
... Iosuae Kirton ...
Dur. Ex. S Pl (tpw). Wel.

P656 Pasquin, 1674
Cant.

P659 Passes, 1648
Yk.

P663 Passive, 1691
Carl. Wel.

P665 Paston, James, 1688
Cant.

P715 *See*: J667B

P721 Patin, Charles, 1696
Ex. Her.

P727 *See*: G1464

P728 *See*: G1464

P729 Patrick, John, 1688
Ban. Bur. Carl. Lich. Wel.

P732 Patrick, John, 1674
Ban. Cant. Carl. Ex. Linc.
S Asa. S Pl. Yk.

P733 Patrick, John, 1686
Ches. Ex. Lich. Yk.

P734? Patrick, John, 1696
For Richard Cumberland.
Pet.

P735 Patrick, John, 1687
Bur. Ex.

P736 Patrick, John, 1688
Ban. Ex. Nor. S Pl (2). Swel.
Wel.

P738 Patrick, Symon, 1673
Pet. Yk.

P739? Patrick, Symon, 1674
12°.
Carl. Ely.

P744 Patrick, Symon, 1678
Ban. Cant. Carl.

P745 Patrick, Symon, 1692
Ely. Pet.

P746 Patrick, Symon, 1670
Carl. Linc. Pet. S Pl. Win.

P747 Patrick, Symon, 1659
Her.

P749 Patrick, Symon, 1670
S Asa.

P751 Patrick, Symon, 1680
S Dv (frag.)*.

P752 Patrick, Symon, 1692
24°.
Ely.

P754 Patrick, Symon, 1662
Pet. Wel.

P755 Patrick, Symon, 1669
Linc. Pet.

P761 Patrick, Symon, 1672
Carl. Ely.

P770 Patrick, Symon, 1681
Cant. Carl. S Asa.

P771 Patrick, Symon, 1700
IoM. Llan. Rip.

P772 Patrick, Symon, 1695
Ches. Dur. Her. S Pl.

P773 Patrick, Symon, 1698
IoM. Rip.

P774 Patrick, Symon, 1699
IoM. Llan. Rip.

P775 Patrick, Symon, 1697
Ches. Dur. Her. IoM. Llan.
Rip. S Dv.

P776 Patrick, Symon, 1698
Ches. IoM. Rip. S Dv.

P779 Patrick, Symon, 1669
Carl. Chelm (tp imp). Ely. Ex.
Linc. Pet. S Pl. Win.

P780 Patrick, Symon, 1673
Carl.

P781+ Patrick, Symon, 1676
The third edition; Printed for R.
Royston; 12°.
Yk.

P787 Patrick, Symon, 1683
Cant. Carl. Ex. S Pl. Sal.

P788 Patrick, Symon, 1685
Ban. S Pl. Sal. Wel.

P788+ Patrick, Symon, 1685
No ed. statement; For R.H. and
F.G., sold by Abel Swalle; 4°.
Ex.

P789 Patrick, Symon, 1686
Nor.

P789+ Patrick, Symon, 1693
For Luke Meredith, sold by R.
Wilkin; 12°.
Ely.

P790 Patrick, Symon, 1683
S Pl.

P792 Patrick, Symon, 1659
Chelm. New. Yk.

P793 Patrick, Symon, 1660
Second ed. not on tp.
Carl. Ex. S Pl.

P794 Patrick, Symon, 1672
Ex. Liv.

P796 Patrick, Symon, 1676
Cant. Carl. Chelm. Win.

P799- Patrick, Symon, 1669
No ed. statement; For Richard
Royston; 8°.
Carl. Ely. Sal.

P799 Patrick, Symon, 1669
For Richard Royston.
Ely. Nor.

P800 Patrick, Symon, 1669
8°.
Dur. S Pl.

P801 Patrick, Symon, 1669
For R. Royston.
Ely. Ex.

P802 Patrick, Symon, 1669
For R. Royston.
Linc.

P803? Patrick, Symon, 1684
For R. Royston.
Brec. S Asa.

P805 Patrick, Symon, 1670
Carl. Linc. Pet. S Pl. Win.

P807 Patrick, Symon, 1678
Carl. Ely (engr. tpw). Pet. Win.
Yk.

P807+ Patrick, Symon, 1686
The second edition; For Rich.
Royston; 8°.
Ex.

P809 Patrick, Symon, 1660
Carl.

P816 Patrick, Symon, 1677
Ely. S Asa.

P818 Patrick, Symon, 1670
Ban. Carl. Llan. Pet. S Asa.

P820 Patrick, Symon, 1690
Chi. Dur. Her.

P821 Patrick, Symon, 1692
Dur.

P822+ Patrick, Symon, 1667
As P822, apart from date.
S Asa.

P823? Patrick, Symon, 1667
For F. Tyton, sold by Richard
Chiswell.
Carl. Ex. Her.

P824 Patrick, Symon, 1676
Ches. Ex. Rip.

P825 Patrick, Symon, 1684
Ban. Bur. Ely. Her. Pet.
S Asa.

P826 Patrick, Symon, 1665
Ex.

P828 Patrick, Symon, 1668
4°.
Carl. Dur. Lich. Nor. Tru.

P829 Patrick, Symon, 1670
Third ed. not on tp.
Llan. S Asa. Wel.

P830 Patrick, Symon, 1673
Ely.

P832? Patrick, Symon, 1687
For Richard Chiswell.
Ban. Pet. S Dv. Win.

P833 Patrick, Symon, 1687
Ban. Bur. Cant. Carl. Chi. Ex
(2). Nor. Sal. Swel. Wel. Yk.

P835 Patrick, Symon, 1685
Carl. Ely. Nor. S Pl.

P836? Patrick, Symon, 1693
For Luke Meredith, sold by R. Wilkin.
Cant.

P838 Patrick, Symon, 1670
Carl. Her. Pet.

P839 Patrick, Symon, 1676
Bur. Cant. Carl. Sal.

P840 Patrick, Symon, 1678
Linc.

P841 Patrick, Symon, 1678
Cant. Pet. Wor.

P842 Patrick, Symon, 1680
Ban. Carl. Dur. S Asa.

P844 Patrick, Symon, 1686
Ban. Dur (imp). Ex. S Asa (2).

P845 Patrick, Symon, 1687
Ban. Bur. Carl. Dur (2 − 1
imp). Ex. Sal. Wel. Yk.

P846 Patrick, Symon, 1689
Cant. Pet. Sal. Wel. Yk (2).

P847 Patrick, Symon, 1689
Llan (imp). Pet. Wel. Wor. Yk.

P848 Patrick, Symon, 1689
Cant. Pet. Wel. Wor. Yk.

P849 Patrick, Symon, 1690
Pet. S Dv. Wel. Wor.

P850 Patrick, Symon, 1691
Pet. Yk.

P851 Patrick, Symon, 1689
Cant. Wor.

P853 Patrick, Symon, 1692
Wor.

P854 Patrick, Symon, 1696
Cant.

P855 Patrick, Symon, 1696
Cant. Dur. Wor.

P857 Patrick, Symon, 1686
Carl. Ely.

P858? Patrick, Symon, 1700
By W.B. for Luke Meredith.
Pet.

P860 Patrick, Symon, 1685
Ex.

P861 Patrick, Symon, 1688
Ely.

P862 Patrick, Symon, 1696
S Asa.

P863 Patrick, Symon, 1689
Cant.

P864 Patrick, Symon, 1675
Bris. Bur (2). Carl. Dur. Ely.
Ex. Llan. Pet. S Asa. S Pl.
Win.

P866 Patrick, Symon, 1677
'Part II'; Printed by E. Flesher for R.
Royston.
Carl. Dur. Ely. Llan*. Pet.
S Asa.

P867 Patrick, Symon, 1698
Dur. Ely.

P869 Pattenson, Matthew, 1653
Cant. Carl. Linc.

P870? Patern, 1679
For T. Burrel.
S Pl.

P872A? Patterne, 1641
8°.
Yk.

P878 Paule, *Sir* George, 1699
For Ri. Chiswell.
Ches (imp). Dur. Ex.

P880 Pawson, John, 1652
S Pl.

P887 Payne, Henry, 1687
Yk.

P896 Payne, William, 1690
Cant. Ex (2). Wel. Yk (2).

P898 Payne, William, 1685
Ban. Cant (tp imp). Carl. Ex.
Nor. S Pl (2). Sal. Swel. Yk.

P900 Payne, William, 1687
Ban. Bur. Cant. Chi. Ex (3).
Nor. S Pl. Sal. Wel.

P901 Payne, William, 1688
Ban. Her. Sal. Swel. Yk.

P902 Payne, William, 1698
Ex. S Asa.

P903 Payne, William, 1691
Cant. Her.

P904 Payne, William, 1682
Llan.

P905 Payne, William, 1696
S Asa.

P906 Payne, William, 1697
S Pl.

P907+ Payne, William, 1693
Printed for Samuel Smith; 8°.
Carl. Dur. Ex. Roch. Swel.

P908 Payne, William, 1695
Dur.

P909 Payne, William, 1695
Carl. Ches. S Dv.

P911 Payne, William, 1695
Her.

P912 Payne, William, 1683
Her.

P918 Peace, 1643
Ex.

P923+ Peaceable, 1661
See: CLC82.
Win.

P924 Peaceable, 1648
Yk.

P942 Peachum, Henry, 1642
Dur.

P943 Peachum, Henry, 1661
Linc.

P953 Peachum, Henry, 1669
Fourth ed. not on tp.
Llan.

P962 Pead, Deuel, 1695
Ches.

P964 Pead, Deuel, 1696
Llan. Sal.

P968 Pearle, [1646]
Yk.

P989 Pearson, Anthony, 1657
Dur. Ex.

P990 Pearson, Anthony, 1658
Carl. Dur. S Pl.

P993 Pearson, John, 1660
Carl. Ches. Dur. Ex. Pet.

P994A Pearson, John, 1660
9v.
Cant. Chelm (lacks vol. 8).
Ches. Chi. Dur. Ely. Glo (2).
Her. Lich. Linc. New. Rip.
Roch. S Pl. Sal. Wel. Wor. Yk.

P995 Pearson, John, 1659
Ches (3). Chi. Pet. Yk.

P996 Pearson, John, 1662
Ches. Wel. Win.

P997 Pearson, John, 1669
Ban. Bur. Ely. Linc. S Asa.
S Pl. Sal. Wor.

P998 Pearson, John, 1676
Cant. Carl. Ches. Chi. Ely.
Her. Liv. Rip. Roch. S Pl. Yk
(2).

P999 Pearson, John, 1683
Brec. Ches (2 − 1 imp). Glo.
Her. Llan. Nor. Rip. Roch.
Yk.

P1000 Pearson, John, 1692
Bur (2). Chi. Dur (imp). Lich.
S Dv. S Pl. Swel.

P1001 Pearson, John, 1660
Carl. Ches. Dur. Ex. Linc.
S Pl. Yk (2).

P1003 Pearson, John, 1688
Ches (2). Chi. Dur. Ely (2 − 1
imp). Ex (2). Glo. Her. Lich.
Llan. S Asa. S Pl. Win. Wor*.
Yk (2).

P1003+ Pearson, John, 1688
Typis S. Roycroft, impensis R.
Clavell; 4°.
Ban. Cant.

P1004 Pearson, John, 1658
Ex.

P1005 Pearson, John, 1668
Ches.

P1008 Pearson, John, 1671
S Asa.

P1009 Pearson, John, 1673
Wing has wrong date.
Carl. Ches. Pet. Wel. Yk.

P1010 Pearson, John, 1672
Bris. Cant. Ches (3). Chi. Dur.
Ely. Ex. Her. Linc. Liv. Nor.
Pet. S Asa. S Pl. Sal. Win.
Wor. Yk.

P1012 Pearson, Richard, 1664
Cant. Carl. Chelm. Wor.

P1013 Pearson, Richard, 1700
Her.

P1014 Pearson, Richard, 1684
Carl. Dur. Llan. Wor.

P1015 Pearson, Richard, 1684
Cant. Her.

P1016 Pearson, Richard, 1690
Cant. Dur.

P1017 Pearson, Richard, 1684
Dur. S Asa. Wor.

P1028 Pechey, John, 1693
12°.
Ches.

P1031- Peck, Francis, [N.d.]
See: CLC83.
Cant (tpw).

P1037 Peck, Samuel, 1684
Her.

P1043 Pecock, Reginald, 1688
Ban. Dur. Ex. Pet. Roch. S Pl.
Wel.

P1056 Peers, Richard, 1667
Ban.

P1060 Peirce, *Sir* Edmond, 1660
'appeal'; 8°.
Win (2).

P1061 Peirce, *Sir* Edmond, 1660
Win.

P1062 Peirce, *Sir* Edmond, 1660
By Tho. Leach ...
Linc. Win.

P1063 Peirce, *Sir* Edmond, [1660]
Carl.

P1064 Peirce, *Sir* Edmond, 1642
Not by Peirce; Drawn up by Sir E.
Dering & Sir G. Strode.
Linc. Sal.

P1064+ Peirce, *Sir* Edmond, 1642
As P1064, but: 'gentrie'
Pet.

P1065 Peirce, *Sir* Edmond, 1642
Cant.

P1066 Peirce, *Sir* Edmond, 1659
'... verè ... loud ...'
Carl. Yk (tp imp).

P1070 Pell, John, 1664
Carl. Linc. S Asa. Win.

P1071 Pelling, Edward, 1679
Wor.

P1072 Pelling, Edward, 1687
Ban. Bur. Carl. Chi. Ely. Ex.
Sal. Swel. Yk (2).

P1073 Pelling, Edward, 1687
Ban. Bur. Chi. Ely. Ex (2).
S Pl. Swel. Yk.

P1074 Pelling, Edward, 1687
Bur.

P1075 Pelling, Edward, 1682
Dur.

P1077 Pelling, Edward, 1683
Ban.

P1078 Pelling, Edward, 1696
S Asa. S Pl.

P1079 Pelling, Edward, 1685
Ely. Nor. Pet. S Asa.

P1081 Pelling, Edward, 1688
Cant. Ex. Lich. Wel.

P1082 Pelling, Edward, 1680
Ex. Lich. S Asa. Win.

P1086 Pelling, Edward, 1693
Bur.

P1087 Pelling, Edward, 1694
Bur. Ches. S Pl.

P1088+ Pelling, Edward, [1693]
[N.pl.]; 8°.
Dur.

P1090 Pelling, Edward, 1682
Ban. Carl. Dur. Wel. Wor (2).

P1091 Pelling, Edward, 1679
Cant. Pet. Wor (2). Yk (frag.).

P1092 Pelling, Edward, 1679
Cant. Nor.

P1093 Pelling, Edward, 1683
Carl. Llan. Wel. Wor.

P1094 Pelling, Edward, 1683
Win. Yk (2).

P1095 Pelling, Edward, 1683
Ban. Cant. Wor.

P1096 Pelling, Edward, 1684
Hills.
Cant. Llan. S Asa (2). S Dv.

P1098 Pelling, Edward, 1685
Her. Yk.

P1100 Pelling, Edward, 1690
Ban. Wel.

P1101 Pelling, Edward, 1692
Cant.

P1103 Pelling, Edward, 1693
Cant. Wor. Yk.

P1104 Pelling, Edward, 1695
Wor.

P1105 Pelling, Edward, 1687
Ban. Bur. Ex. Wel.

P1110 Pellisson-Fontanier, Paul,
1657
Carl. Pet.

P1111? Pemble, William, 1659
... Henry Hall, for John Adams, Edw.
and John Forrest.
Carl. S Dv.

P1112- Pemble, William, 1669
No ed. statement; Oxford, by William
Hall for Iohn Forrest; 4°.
Bris. Cant.

P1114 Pemble, William, [1650?]
Pet. Sal.

P1115 Pemble, William, 1647
Sal.

P1116+ Pemble, William, 1669
See: CLC84.
Sal.

P1121 Pembroke, Philip Herbert,
Earl of, 1642
'11. day of June'; ... June 14.
Dur.

P1125 Pembroke and Montgomery,
Philip Herbert, *Earl of*, 1642
Cant.

P1141 Pendlebury, Henry, 1687
Carl. Ex. Swel. Yk.

P1144 Penington, Edward, 1696
8°.
Dur.

P1153 Penington, Isaac, *jr*, 1659
Yk.

P1160 Penington, Isaac, *jr*, 1653
Carl.

P1177 Penington, Isaac, *jr*, 1650
Pet.

P1180 Penington, Isaac, *jr*, 1660
Yk.

P1185 Penington, Isaac, *jr*, 1660
Yk.

P1216 Penington, Isaac, *jr*, 1648
Chelm.

P1217 Penington, Isaac, *jr*, 1650
Pet.

P1224 Penington, John, 1695
Dur.

P1227 Penington, John, 1697
'... covering discovered'
Dur.

P1232 Penitent, 1663
Wing puts [sic] after dàte.
Yk.

P1248 Penn, William, 1679
Dur. S Pl.

P1266 Penn, William, 1674
Pt 2 = W1908.
Sal. Win.

P1278 Penn, William, [1679]
Dur. Linc.

P1296 Penn, William, 1687
Wel.

P1298 Penn, William, 1688
'The great ...'
Wel.

P1299 Penn, William, 1670
55p.
Glo. Win.

P1299+ Penn, William, 1670
As P1299, but: 30p.
Win.

P1300 Penn, William, [1679]
Linc.

P1311 Penn, William, 1674
Win.

P1318 Penn, William, 1687
Carl. Wel.

P1318+ Penn, William, [1687]
[N.pl.]; brs.
Dur.

P1333 Penn, William, 1681
Cant.

P1336 Penn, William, 1670
Second ed. not on tp; 'asserted'
Cant. Yk.

P1338A Penn, William, [1686]
Ban. Carl. Dur.

P1352 Penn, William, 1687
Wel.

P1361 Penn, William, 1687
Wel. Yk.

P1381 Penn, William, 1687
Wel.

P1399 Penning, William, 1679
Linc.

P1404 Pennyman, John, 1680
Swel.

P1423 Pennyman, John, 1675
Swel.

P1437 Penton, Stephen, 1688
Ban. Dur. Ely. S Pl. Yk.

P1438 Penton, Stephen, 1682
Ex (tpw).

P1439 Penton, Stephen, 1688
Carl. Ches.

P1444 People, [1693?]
Dur.

P1450 Pepys, Samuel, 1690
Ex. S Asa. Yk.

P1452 Pepys, Samuel, 1677
Carl. Ely.

P1455 Percy, Henry, *Baron*, 1641
Cant. Carl.

P1464 *See*: S4969+

P1465 Pereat, [1681]
Dur.

P1465+ Perefixe, Hardouyn de
Beaumont de, 1672
See: CLC85.
Pet.

P1472 Perfect, 1647
Yk.

P1473 Perfect, 1660[1]
Cant.

P1474 Perfect, [1679]
Linc.

P1479+ Perfect, 1655
By F.L. for Matthew Walbancke, and
are to be sold by Gabriel Bedell and
Thomas Collins; 4°.
Dur.

P1498 Perfect, 1660
Yk.

P1506- Perfect, 1645
See: CLC86.
Yk.

P1509 Perfect, 1643
Linc.

P1510 Perfect, 1641
Yk.

P1531+ Perfecta, 1649
[Trial of Charles I]; Ex officina
Guilielmi Bentley, impensis Guilielmi
Shears; 12°.
Linc.

P1534? Perion, Joachim, 1660
... apud Franc. Oxlad.
Yk.

P1540 Perjury, 1690
Wel.

P1541 Perkin, Richard, 1681
=Pt 3 of S2767A.
Linc. Yk.

P1542B? Perkins, George, 1656
Editio quarta.
Cant.

P1543 Perkins, John, 1642
Ex.

P1577 Perne, Andrew, 1643
Cant (2).

P1582 Perpoynt, William, 1641
Cant. Linc.

P1590 Perrault, Nicholas, 1670
Ely. Sal.

P1590A Perrault, Nicholas, 1679
Wing's date incomplete.
Bur. Cant (dated MDCLXXVX).
Linc. Yk.

P1593B Perrinchief, Richard, 1668
Carl. Chelm. Ex. Pet. S Pl.
Win.

P1594 Perrinchief, Richard, 1668
Carl. Ex. S Pl. Win (2).

P1596 Perrinchief, Richard, 1697
Glo.

P1597 Perrinchief, Richard, 1658
Yk.

P1598 Perrinchief, Richard, 1657
8°.
Pet.

P1599 Perrinchief, Richard, 1659
Pet.

P1601 Perrinchief, Richard, 1676
Carl.

P1604 Perrinchief, Richard, [1664?]
Ex. Linc. Wel.

P1605? Perrinchief, Richard, 1669
8°.
S Pl.

P1606 Perrinchief, Richard, 1666
Cant. Carl. Yk.

P1607 Perrinchief, Richard, 1676
Carl.

P1620 Perrot, John, 1660
Yk.

P1621 Perrot, John, 1660
Yk.

P1624 Perrot, John, 1660
Yk.

P1639 Perrot, John, 1660
Yk.

P1642 Perrot, John, 1660
Yk.

P1645? Perrot, Robert, 1658
For John Hancock; 8°.
Sal.

P1647 Perrot, Robert, 1671
Cant. Pet.

P1651 Persall, John, 1686
Cant. Dur.

P1652 Persall, John, 1686
Yk.

P1654 Perse, William, 1689
Yk.

P1655 Perse, William, 1695
Ches.

P1656 Perse, William, 1696
Cant. Wor. Yk.

P1663 Persius, 1647
'Satirarum'
Cant. Ches. Ely.

P1668 Persons, [1642]
Dur.

P1669 Perswasion, 1645
Ex. Yk.

P1675 Pestel, Thomas, 1659
S Pl.

P1676 Pestel, Thomas, 1660
Ban.

P1677+ Petavius, Dionysius, 1659
By J. Streater, sold by Francis Tyton;
2°.
Lich.

P1677++ Petavius, Dionysius, 1659
By J. Streater, sold by Richard
Tomlins; 2°.
Carl.

P1689 Peter, John, 1684
Carl.

P1704 Peters, Hugh, 1646
Her. S Pl.

P1706 Peters, Hugh, 1651
Linc.

P1707 Peters, Hugh, 1646
Yk.

P1722 Peters, Hugh, 1642
Dur.

P1726 Peters, Hugh, 1647
Yk (2 eds).

P1730 Peterson, William, 1642
Yk.

P1735 Petition, 1641[2]
Dur.

P1738 Petition, 1649
Yk.

P1738A Petition, 1642
Dur.

P1749 Petition, 1641
Ex. Linc. Sal. Yk (2).

P1752 Petition, [1648]
Yk.

P1759 Petition, 1654
Pet.

P1761 Petition, 1647
Yk.

P1765 Petition, 1642
Yk.

P1784 Petition, 1641[2]
Linc.

P1785 Petition, 1641[2]
Linc.

P1786 Petition, 1643
For Thomas Hudson ...
Linc.

P1788 Petition, 1646
Carl.

P1789 Petition, 1642
Linc.

P1793 Petition, [1642]
Linc.

P1796 Petition, 1649
Yk (2).

P1801 Petition, 1642[3]
Linc.

P1802 Petition, 1641
Pet.

P1805+ Petition, 1649
See: CLC87.
Ex.

P1807A Petition, 1642
Yk.

P1809 Petition, 1642
Dur (date not fully printed)*.

P1815 Petition, 1645
Yk.

P1818 Petition, 1641
Pet.

P1824 Petition, 1642
Linc.

P1849 Petition, 1641
Sal (2).

P1850 Petition, 1648
Sal.

P1854 Petition, 1641
Dur. Linc.

P1858 Petition, 1644
Yk.

P1864 Petitioning-comet, 1681
By Nat. Thompson.
Win.

P1872 Petrarca, Francesco, 1697
12°.
Ely. Ex.

P1879 Petrie, Alexander, 1662
Ex. Pet.

P1880 Petronius, 1693
Ches. Sal.

P1882 Pett, *Sir* Peter, 1689
Wel (pt 2 only).

P1883 Pett, *Sir* Peter, 1688
Pet.

P1888 Petter, George, 1661
Ex. IoM.

P1890 Petter, John, 1694
Her.

P1892 Pettit, Edward, 1684
Cant (imp).

P1893 Pettit, Edward, 1686
Ex.

P1894 Pettit, Edward, 1685
Ex.

P1895 Pettit, Edward, 1683
Carl. Ex.

P1896 Petto, Samuel, 1674
Yk.

P1906 Pettus, *Sir* John, 1683
Sal.

P1908 Pettus, *Sir* John, 1670
Ex.

P1914A Petty, *Sir* William, 1648
Cant.

P1915+ Petty, *Sir* William,
[c.1690?]
See: CLC88.
Glo.

P1919 Petty, *Sir* William, 1674
Carl.

P1929 Petty, *Sir* William, 1683
Ex. Win.

P1933 Petty, *Sir* William, 1691
Cant (2). Ely.

P1936 Petty, *Sir* William, 1660
Carl.

P1939 Petty, *Sir* William, 1667
Win.

P1940+ Petty, *Sir* William, 1679
For Robert Harford; 4°.
Carl.

P1945? Petyt, William, 1680
Wing heading incorrect; Basset.
S Asa. Win.

P1951 Peyton, *Sir* Edward, 1642
Ex. Linc.

P1959? Phaedrus, 1688
'Fabularum ...'; Typis Mariae Clark,
impensis Benj. Tooke & Tho. Cockeril.
S Asa.

P1959+ Phaedrus, 1699
'Fabularum ...'; Typis Mariae Clark,
impensis H. Bonwick & T.
Newborough; 8°.
Ex.

P1960 Phalaris, 1695
Dated in Greek.
Dur. Ex.

P1970 Pharisee, 1687
Wel.

P1972- Phelpes, Charles, 1680
See: CLC89.
Pet.

P1976 Phelpes, Charles, 1678
Ex (tp imp).

P1980 Phelpes, Charles, 1669
Pet.

P1983 *See:* D2550

P1987A Philip IV, [1648]
Linc. Sal.

P1988 Philipot, John, 1660
8°.
Cant. Linc. Yk.

P1988A Philipot, John, 1646
Pet.

P1989 Philipot, John, 1659
Cant (4 – 1 tpw; 2 imp). Linc.

P1990 Philipot, Thomas, 1670
Cant. Ex.

P1991 Philipot, Thomas, 1672
S Pl. Yk.

P1997 Philipot, Thomas, 1661
'first'
Linc.

P1998 Philipot, Thomas, 1664
Carl.

P2004 Philipps, Fabian, 1663
Cant.

P2005A Philipps, Fabian, 1663
Llan.

P2008 Philipps, Fabian, 1649
Yk.

P2013+ Philipps, Fabian, 1671
As P2013, apart from date.
Linc.

P2016 Philipps, Fabian, 1671
Linc.

P2017 Philipps, Fabian, 1662
Win.

P2019 Philipps, Fabian, 1660
... Leach, for the author and are to be
sold by Abel Roper.
Cant. Dur.

P2020 Philipps, Fabian, 1660
Cant.

P2025 Philips, Ambrose, 1700
Carl. Ches. Ex. Yk (2).

P2027 Philips, George, *1599 – 1696*,
1689
Wel.

P2027A Philips, George, *1599 – 1696*,
1676
Carl.

P2033 Philips, *Mrs* Katherine, 1667
Second ed. not on tp.
Pet.

P2034 Philips, *Mrs* Katherine, 1669
Glo.

P2035 Philips, *Mrs* Katherine, 1678
Glo.

P2039 Philips, Robert, 1641
Sal.

P2048A+ Phillippes, Henry, 1678
By M. Clark, for W. Fisher, E.
Thomas, R. Boulter, T. Passenger, R.
Smith and R. Northcot; 8°.
Ex.

P2063 Phillips, Daniel, 1700
Dur.

P2072+ Phillips, Edward, 1678
The fourth edition; By W.R. for
Robert Harford; 2°.
Yk.

P2081 Phillips, John, 1681
Carl.

P2083 Phillips, John, 1680
'Oates's'
Win.

P2092+ Phillips, John, 1650
See: CLC90.
Pet.

P2098 Phillips, John, 1652
Linc.

P2098+ Phillips, John, 1652
As P2098, but: 12°; Counterfeit, pr.
by J. Jansson of Amsterdam? (BM).
Ely. S Pl. Sal. Wel.

P2110 Phillips, John, 1682
Carl (imp)*.

P2111 Phillips, John, 1682
Carl.

P2121? Phillpott, Nicholas, 1671
... for Ric. Davis.
Linc.

P2132 Philostratus, 1680
Ex. Linc. Nor. S Pl.

P2136 Photius, 1651
Cant. Carl. Dur. Ely. Ex. Her.
Lich. Linc. S Pl. Sal. Wel.
Win. Wor.

P2143? Physical, 1657
By G. Dawson ...; 2°.
Cant.

P2146 Physician, 1660
S Pl.

P2150 Pickering, Benjamin, 1645
Cant. Her. Yk.

P2152 Pickering, Robert, 1641[2]
Dur.

P2153 Pictet, Bernard, 1694
Yk.

P2160+ Pielat, B., 1679
See: CLC91.
Cant.

P2160++ Pielat, B., 1669
See: CLC92.
Cant.

P2164 Pierce, Thomas, 1658
Bris. Cant. Carl. Dur. Ely.

P2165+ Pierce, Thomas, 1649
For R: Royston; 8°.
Yk.

P2166 Pierce, Thomas, 1658
Bris. Cant. Dur (prelims and pt
5 [=P2164] only). Ely.

P2167 Pierce, Thomas, 1671
Oxford, by W. Hall, for Ric. Royston
[London] and Ric. Davis.
Cant. S Asa. S Pl (frag.)*. Sal.
Win.

P2168 Pierce, Thomas, 1671
Carl. Dur.

P2169 Pierce, Thomas, 1661
Carl. S Asa (2). S Pl.

P2170 Pierce, Thomas, 1655
S Asa. Wel.

P2171 Pierce, Thomas, 1657
Second ed. not on tp.
Carl. Pet. Yk.

P2172 Pierce, Thomas, 1658
Bris. Cant. Ely.

P2173 Pierce, Thomas, 1671
Nor. Sal.

P2174 Pierce, Thomas, 1672
Oxford, re-printed by ...
Carl.

P2176 Pierce, Thomas, 1679
For Richard Davis in Oxford.
Cant. Carl. Pet. Win.

P2177? Pierce, Thomas, 1663
Broun.
Win.

P2178 Pierce, Thomas, 1657
'... defended against ...'
Carl. Dur. Pet. S Pl. Sal. Yk.

P2178+ Pierce, Thomas, 1657
'... defended with ...'; For Richard
Royston; 4°.
Ex.

P2179 Pierce, Thomas, 1658
Bris. Cant. Ely.

P2180 Pierce, Thomas, 1657
Bris. Carl. Ely. Ex*. Pet.
S Asa. Win. Yk.

P2180A Pierce, Thomas, 1659
Cant.

P2181 Pierce, Thomas, 1658
Bris. Cant. Carl. Ely.

P2182 Pierce, Thomas, 1659
Carl. Her (2). Yk.

P2183 Pierce, Thomas, 1660
Cant (imp). Carl. Pet. S Asa.
S Pl. Win.

P2183+ Pierce, Thomas, [1660?]
[N.pl.]; 4°; 40p.
S Pl.

P2184 Pierce, Thomas, 1660
Cant (imp). Carl. Ex. S Asa.
Win. Yk.

P2185 Pierce, Thomas, 1686
Cant. Ex. Her. S Pl.

P2186 Pierce, Thomas, 1659[60]
Carl. Ely. Linc. S Asa. Sal.
Wel. Yk.

P2187 Pierce, Thomas, 1683
Win.

P2188? Pierce, Thomas, 1685
'... accesserunt φροντίδες δεύτεραι'
Cant. Pet.

P2188+ Pierce, Thomas, 1685
As P2188, but: '... accesserunt Πάσης
τῆς φροντίδες Δεύτεραι'
Ban. Ex. S Asa.

P2189 Pierce, Thomas, 1658
Carl. Ex. Her. S Asa. S Pl.
Wor. Yk.

P2190 Pierce, Thomas, 1658
Liv.

P2191 Pierce, Thomas, 1663
Cant (6 − 4 imp). Carl. Linc.
Pet. S Asa. S Pl. Yk (imp).

P2192 Pierce, Thomas, 1663
Cant (imp).

P2194 Pierce, Thomas, 1663
Ban. Wor. Yk (2).

P2195 Pierce, Thomas, 1688
Wel (2).

P2196 Pierce, Thomas, 1679
Cant. Her. Nor. S Asa. Wor.

P2198 Pierce, Thomas, 1661
Cant. Carl. S Asa (2).

P2199 Pierce, Thomas, 1670
Cant. Ex. Yk.

P2201 Pierce, Thomas, 1656
Carl.

P2203 Pierce, Thomas, 1670
Cant. Ex. Yk.

P2207 Pierce, Thomas, 1682
Ex. Sal. Win.

P2211 Pierce, William, 1642
Yk.

P2212 *See*: P1582

P2216 Pierson, Thomas, 1647
Bur.

P2222 Piggot, John, 1643
Cant. Carl. Linc. Pet. Sal.

P2223 Pigges, 1642
Yk.

P2224 Pike, Roger, 1642
Linc.

P2235? Pilkington, *Sir* Thomas,
1683
'The proceedings ...'
S Dv.

P2245 Pindar, 1697
Cant. Ches (2). Dur. Glo. Linc
(imp). Wor.

P2250 Pindar, William, 1679
Ban. Cant. Carl. Her. Llan (2).

P2251 Pindar, William, 1677
Ban. Cant. Llan. Sal. Wor.

P2252+ Pindarique, 1679
'A pindarique ode'; Formerly O236,
with incorrect title.
Linc.

P2265 Pineton de Chambrun,
Jacques, 1689
Cant. S Pl.

P2267 Pinke, Robert, 1642
Dur. Linc.

P2268? Pinke, Robert, 1680
... Leon. Lichfield.
S Pl.

P2269 Pinke, William, 1657[56]
S Asa.

P2272 Pinkney, Miles, 1646
Pt 2 = V81.
Bur. Carl. Linc. Yk (2 − 1 pt 1
only).

P2284? Piscator, Johann, 1641
'quaedam'; Brewstero; 12°.
Win.

P2306 Pitt, Moses, 1680
Bur. Cant. Sal. Win. Yk.

P2306+ Pitt, Moses, 1680
Oxford, at the Theater, for Joh.
Jansonius a Waesberge, and Steven
Swart, Amsterdam; 2°.
Ex. Wor*.

P2306A Pitt, Moses, 1681
Bur. Cant. Ex. Sal. Win. Wor.
Yk.

P2306B Pitt, Moses, 1683
Bur. Cant. Ex. Sal. Win. Wor.
Yk.

P2306C Pitt, Moses, 1682
Bur. Cant. Ex. Sal. Win. Wor.
Yk.

P2307 Pitt, Moses, 1695
Carl.

P2308? Pitt, Moses, [1678]
'The proposals for printing the
English atlas'
Cant.

P2313 Pittis, Thomas, 1683
S Pl. Win.

P2314 Pittis, Thomas, 1683
Win.

P2315 Pittis, Thomas, 1682
Carl. Sal. Wel. Wor.

P2316 Pittis, Thomas, 1670
Carl. Chelm. Ely. Ex. Linc.
Pet.

P2317 Pittis, Thomas, 1677
Cant. Wor.

P2345 Plain, 1690
Cant.

P2346 Plain, 1658[9]
Ex.

P2347 Plaine, 1643
Sal.

P2351 Plain, 1688
Wel.

P2353 Plain, 1681
Linc.

P2356 Plain, 1690
Ex. Wor (tp imp).

P2357 Plain, 1690
Yk.

P2365- Plain, 1670
By J.M. for James Allestry; 12°.
Ely. Pet.

P2365+ Plain, 1677
The fourth edition; For R. White and
J. Martin; 12°.
S Pl.

P2366 Plain, 1644
Win. Yk.

P2372 Plain, 1659
Ex.

P2376? *Πλανης αποκαλυψις*, 1673
For R. C.
S Pl. Sal. Win.

P2398 Platform, 1653
Carl.

P2401 Platforme, 1644
Dur (imp).

P2403 Platina, Bartolomeo, 1685
Ban. Carl. Ches. Chi. Dur.
Ex (2). Glo. Lich. S Asa. Swel.
Wel. Yk.

P2404? Platina, Bartolomeo, 1688
For C. Wilkinson, sold by A.
Churchil.
Bur. Ely.

P2405 Plato, 1675
Carl. Chelm. Pet.

P2406 Plato, 1673
'selecti'
Carl. Ches.

P2407 Plato, 1683
S Pl. Wel.

P2411 Plattes, Gabriel, 1679
Third ed. not on tp.
Glo.

P2414A+ Plautus, 1646
Typis & impensis Jacobi Junii; 8°.
S Asa.

P2415 Plautus, 1694
Nor.

P2419 Playfere, John, 1651
Carl. Ex. S Pl. Wel.

P2420 Playfere, John, 1652
Ely. Liv.

P2420+ Playfere, John, 1653
For Robert Clark; 8°.
Chelm.

P2427+ Playford, Henry, 1700
See: CLC93.
Dur.

P2436 Playford, Henry, 1688
Dur.

P2437 Playford, Henry, 1693
Linc.

P2450 Playford, John, 1662
Yk.

P2466 Playford, John, 1655
Dur.

P2480 Playford, John, 1674
Ely.

P2482 Playford, John, 1683
S Pl.

P2486 Playford, John, 1700
Dur (imp).

P2497 Playford, John, 1682
Dur.

P2498 Playford, John, 1671
Ely.

P2511 Plea, 1660
Pet.

P2512 Plea, 1642
Linc.

P2515 Plea, 1642
Dur. Linc.

P2520 Plea, 1642[3]
Linc.

P2522 Plea, 1642
Dur. Pet.

P2524 Plea, 1642
Ex.

P2525 Plea, [1688]
Wel.

P2526 Plea, [1680]
Dur. Linc (2).

P2528 Pleadings, 1696
'arguments'; ... by S. Keble, D.
Browne and J. Walthoe.
Cant.

P2537 Pleasant, 1681
Linc.

P2564 Pleasant, 1673
Carl.

P2567 Plessington, William, [1679]
Linc.

P2570 Pleydell, Josias, 1681
Cant.

P2571 Pleydell, William, 1641[2]
'Plydell'
Cant (2). Ex. Nor.

P2575? Pliny, 1686
... William Hart ...
Glo. S Dv.

P2576? Pliny, 1660
... per Edward: & Joh: Forrest.
Yk.

P2577 Pliny, 1677
Pet. Yk.

P2581 Pliny, 1662
Ely. S Pl.

P2585 Plot, Robert, [1676]
Dur. Glo. Lich. Wel.

P2586 Plot, Robert, 1677
'By R.P.'
Cant (imp). Ex. Nor. Wel.

P2586+ Plot, Robert, 1677
As P2586, but: 'By Robert Plot'
Win.

P2588 Plot, Robert, 1686
Cant. Dur. Ex. Lich. Nor (tp
imp).

P2601 Plot, [1680]
Linc.

P2603 Plots, 1653
Carl.

P2620 Plukenet, Leonard, 1691 –
1705
7 pt; 4°; Includes P2620 & P2621?
S Dv.

P2632 Plutarch, 1694
Dated in Greek.
Nor (cropped with loss of Latin
text?).

P2633 Plutarch, 1657
Fifth ed. not on tp.
Cant. Yk.

P2635? Plutarch, 1683
For Jacob Tonson.
Ex. Yk (tpw).

P2636 Plutarch, 1684
Ex. Yk.

P2638 Plutarch, 1684
Yk.

P2639 Plutarch, 1685
Ex. Yk.

P2640 Plutarch, 1686
Ex. Yk.

P2642 Plutarch, 1684
Yk.

P2642A Plutarch, 1691
Glo (tpw).

P2643 Plutarch, 1694
Rip.

P2644 Plutarch, 1684
Yk.

P2645 Plutarch, 1691
Glo.

P2646 Plutarch, 1694
Rip.

P2646A? Plutarch, 1685
Gellibrand.
Yk.

P2648 Plutarch, 1691
Glo.

P2649 Plutarch, 1694
Rip.

P2650- Plutarch, 1690
For R. Bently; 8°.
Yk.

P2650 Plutarch, 1691
Glo.

P2651 Plutarch, 1694
Rip (imp).

P2652- Plutarch, 1690
For R. Bently; 8°.
Yk.

P2652 Plutarch, 1691
Glo.

P2653 Plutarch, 1694
Rip.

P2655A Plutarch, 1657
Second ed. not on tp.
IoM. Yk.

P2658 Plutarch, 1665
Yk.

P2660 Pococke, Edward, 1685
Ban. Chi. Dur. Ely. Ex. Her.
Sal. Wel. Win. Wor. Yk.

P2661 Pococke, Edward, 1691
Dur. Ex. Sal (tp imp). Wel.
Win. Wor.

P2662- Pococke, Edward, 1677
Oxford, at the Theater; 2°.
Sal. Win. Yk.

P2662 Pococke, Edward, 1692
Dur. Wel.

P2663 Pococke, Edward, 1677
Ban. Carl. Ex. Sal (tp imp).
Wel. Win. Yk.

P2663A Pococke, Edward, 1692
Dur. Wor.

P2716+ Poem, [c.1680?]
See: CLC94.
Linc.

P2719 Poems, 1697
260, 16p.
Glo.

P2722 Poems, 1698
'Part III'
Glo.

P2729 Poetae, 1652
Ely. Linc (imp). New. Nor
(imp). S Pl. Yk.

P2731 Poetae, 1667
Wel.

P2733 Poetae, 1677
S Dv (2 − 1 tpw).

P2735 Poetae, 1700
Yk.

P2749 Polhill, Edward, 1675
Bur. Carl.

P2753 Polhill, Edward, 1673
Carl.

P2755 Polhill, Edward, 1675
Carl. S Asa.

P2756? Polhill, Edward, 1682
For Tho. Simmons.
Ban. Carl.

P2789 Polycarp, *St*, 1644[5]
Cant. Ches. Chi. Ely. Ex.
Lich. Sal. Yk.

P2789+ Polycarp, *St*, 1644[5]
As P2789, but: ... Licfield [*sic*].
Chelm (imp). Ches. Dur. Linc.
S Pl. Sal. Wor.

P2790? Polycarp, *St*, 1648
Oxoniae, excudebat Hen. Hall,
impensis Hen. Curteyn.
S Asa.

P2804A Ponet, John, 1688
Ban. Ex. Wel.

P2804B Ponet, John, 1642
Linc.

P2806 Pontier, Gideon, 1684
Carl.

P2807 Pontis, Louis de, 1694
Bris. Ely.

P2811 Poole, John, 1650
Cant.

P2814 Poole, Joshua, 1657
Sal.

P2815 Poole, Joshua, 1677
Ex. Lich.

P2820 Poole, Matthew, 1683
Vol.1: By John Richardson, for
Thomas Parkhurst, Dorman Newman,
Jonathan Robinson, Brabazon Ailmer,
Thomas Cockeril, and Benjamin
Alsop.
Ex. Linc. Wor.

P2823 Poole, Matthew, 1685
Ex. Linc. Wor.

P2824A Poole, Matthew, 1700
Cant (imp?).

P2828 Poole, Matthew, 1667
Cant. Carl.

P2828+ Poole, Matthew, 1667
By E. Cotes, and are to be sold by R.
Smith, S. Tomson, F. Titan and H.
Mortlock; 12°.
Ex. Yk.

P2829 Poole, Matthew, 1670
Ban.

P2830 Poole, Matthew, 1672
Pet.

P2836 Poole, Matthew, 1660
Cant (2 − both imp?). Chelm.
Pet. S Pl.

P2837 Poole, Matthew, 1660
For Sa. Thomson.
Pet. S Pl.

P2840 Poole, Matthew, 1659
4°.
Pet.

P2843 Poole, Matthew, 1666
Carl. Ex. Pet. Win.

P2846 Poole, Matthew, 1671
Ex.

P2848 Poole, Matthew, 1679
Yk.

P2851 Poole, Matthew, 1698
S Pl.

P2852 Poole, Matthew, 1673
Cant. Carl. Chelm. Her. Yk
(2).

P2853 Poole, Matthew, 1669−76
'... aliorumque S. Scripturae'; Some
locations on P2853+ may belong to
this no.
Ban. Bur (3 − 1 vol. 1−2, 4
only)*. Cant (3). Carl. Dur.
Linc. Sal. Wel (2 − 1 lacks vol.
1). Yk.

P2853+ Poole, Matthew, 1669−76
As P2853, but: '... Sacrae Scripturae'
Chelm. Ches (4 − 3 imp). Chi
(vol. 1−3 only). Ely. Ex (3 − 1
vol. 1 tpw). Glo (2). Her (imp).
IoM. Lich. Llan. New. Nor (2).
Pet (3). Rip. Roch. S Alb.
S Asa. S Dv. S Pl. Swel. Tru.
Win. Wor.

P2856 Poole, William, 1650
Yk (imp).

P2899 Poortmans, John, 1653
Pet.

P2904 Pope, Mary, 1647
Chelm. Pet.

P2911 Pope, Walter, 1697
Carl. Ches. Dur. Ex. Nor. Sal
(2 − 1 tpw). Yk.

P2912 Pope, Walter, 1670
Cant.

P2915+ Pope, Walter, 1676
See: CLC95.
Linc.

P2920+ Popery, 1679
For C. Harper; 8°.
Bur (impr. & format not
confirmed).

P2921 Popery, 1686
Wel.

P2922 Popery, 1679
Linc.

P2923 Popery, 1689
Wel.

P2936 Pope's, 1681
Linc.

P2939 Popes, 1641
S Pl (2).

P2945 Popish, 1680
Ely. Linc. Wel. Win.

P2949? Popish, [1687?]
Colophon: Dulibn, printedy b [sic] Jo.
Ray.
Dur (2).

P2952 Popish, 1679
By Th. Dawks; 4°.
Dur. Linc.

P2954 Popish, [1680?]
Linc.

P2956 Popish, [1680?]
Linc.

P2958 Popish, 1689
Dur.

P2960 Popish, [1688?]
Wel. Yk.

P2978 Porphyry, 1655
Bur. Cant (2). Dur.

P2979 Porré, Jonas, 1669
Cant. Lich. Yk.

P2980 Porré, Jonas, 1668
8°.
Yk.

P2984A Porter, Edmund, 1659
Ely. S Asa. Wor.

P2987 Porter, Robert, 1691
Dur.

P3018A Possel, Johann, 1667
Yk.

P3021+ Post, 1641
[N.pl.], printed; 4°.
Sal.

P3028 Potter, Francis, 1642
Cant (tpw). Pet.

P3030 Potter, John, 1697
Dur. Glo. Lich.

P3031? Potter, John, 1699
Impr. as P3032.
Nor.

P3032 Potter, John, 1699
Dur. Glo. Lich. Nor.

P3039 Poulton, [1688]
Cant. S Pl.

P3042 Povey, Thomas, 1642[3]
Cant. Carl. Linc. Win. Yk.

P3043 Povey, Thomas, 1643
Pet.

P3063 Powell, Joseph, 1695
Ches. Nor. Wor.

P3064 Powell, Joseph, 1692
Her.

P3067 Powell, Robert, 1642
Pet.

P3071 Powell, Thomas, 1651
Carl. Sal.

P3083 Powell, Vavasor, 1661
Carl.

P3090+ Powell, Vavasor, 1671
For R. Clark and F. Smith; 8°.
Roch.

P3093+ Powell, Vavasor, 1647
The third edition corrected; By M.S.
for Hannah Allen; 8°.
Cant.

P3097 Powell, Walter, 1648
Yk (tpw).

P3098 Powell, Walter, 1645
Nor.

P3099 Power, Henry, 1664
Carl. Dur. Linc.

P3111 Powers, 1643
Yk.

P3114 Powle, Henry, 1689
Wel.

P3119 Poyer, John, 1648
Pet.

P3139? Practick, 1653
By Tho: Roycroft for H. Twyford.
Cant (imp).

P3153 *See*: J630D & J630E

P3156 Practice, 1652
Sal.

P3160 Prade, Roger de, 1689
Bris.

P3165+ Praed, John, 1693
For Abel Roper; 4°.
Pet.

P3166 Praemonitus, 1648
Pet.

P3170 Prance, Miles, 1679
Carl. Glo. Win.

P3171 Prance, Miles, 1680
'Prance's'
Ches.

P3172 Prance, Miles, [1682]
Wor.

P3174 Prance, Miles, 1681
Linc. Win.

P3177 Prance, Miles, 1679
Carl. Dur. Ely. Linc. Win.
Yk.

P3182 Pratt, Samuel, 1697
S Asa. Wor.

P3183 Pratt, Samuel, 1700
Her. S Asa.

P3185 Pratt, Samuel, 1698
Bur. S Asa.

P3192+ Prayer, [1694]
See: CLC96.
Cant.

P3194 Prayer, [1642]
Dur.

P3195 Prayer, [1642]
Linc.

P3195A+ Prayers, [c.1680?]
See: CLC97.
Yk.

P3197 Preacher, 1658
Bur.

P3199+ Preamble, 1641
Lon don [sic]; brs.; Should be under
'England'
Linc.

P3206? Préchac, Jean, *Sieur de*,
1678
'heroine'; For James Mages, Richard
Bentley and Richard Tonson.
Carl.

P3211 Prelacie, 1641
Yk.

P3220 Prerogative, 1645
Ex (tp imp).

P3223 Presbyteriall, 1641
Ex. Her.

P3233 Present, 1682
Cant.

P3234 Present, 1683
Win.

P3237 Present, 1689
Ban. Dur. Nor.

P3258 Present, 1678
Carl.

P3259+ Present, 1691
See: CLC98.
Carl.

P3264 Present, 1684
Carl (tpw)*.

P3265 Present, 1690
Ex.

P3267+ Present, 1673
By M.D., for Chr. Wilkinson and T.
Burrell; 12°.
Nor.

P3274 Present, 1681
Carl.

P3279- Presentment, 1642
York, by Robert Barker and by the
assignes of John Bill; 4°.
Linc. Yk (tp imp).

P3279 Presentment, 1642
Yk (2).

P3297 Pressick, George, 1663
Ex.

P3301A? Preston, John, *Master of Emmanuel Coll.*, 1651
By George Purslow.
Win.

P3302 Preston, John, *Master of Emmanuel Coll.*, 1641
Yk.

P3305 Preston, John, *Master of Emmanuel Coll.*, 1654
Cant.

P3306+ Preston, John, *Master of Emmanuel Coll.*, 1658
By J.T. for Francis Eglesfield; 4°.
Win.

P3308 Preston, John, *Master of Emmanuel Coll.*, 1641
Ex (2 – 1 imp). Yk.

P3314+ Preston, Thomas, *Benedictine monk*, 1688
See: CLC99.
Cant.

P3315 Prestwich, Edmund, 1656
Yk.

P3319- Pretensions, 1697
'The pretensions of the French King';
The second edition; For Henry Rhodes; 4°; 2nd ed. of P3319.
Ban.

P3330 Priaulx, John, 1662
Cant. Carl.

P3334 Price, John, *D.D.*, 1663
Pet.

P3335 Price, John, *D.D.*, 1680
Ban.

P3335A? Price, John, *D.D.*, 1683
... Dan. Brown and J. Waltho.
Pet (date altered in MS to 1688).

P3336 Price, John, *D.D.*, 1660
Cant. Pet. Yk.

P3340 Price, John, *of London*, 1648[9]
Yk.

P3342? Price, John, *of London*, 1660
Excudebat Jacobus Flesher, prostant apud Cornelium Bee.
Ely. Yk.

P3344- Price, John, *of London*, 1646
'A moderate reply'; Formerly M2331.
Pet (2 issues: A2, orn in 2 rows or 3 rows).

P3345 Price, John, *of London*, 1648
Yk.

P3346 Price, John, *of London*, 1648
Nor.

P3347 Price, John, *of London*, [1642]
Linc.

P3351 Price, John, *of London*, [1649]
Cant.

P3352+ Price, John, *of Oxford*, 1661
'Sermons'; [Oxford?], for the author; 8°; Apparently 1st issue of P3352, without the cancels.
Win.

P3401 Price, William, 1646
Pet (2). Yk.

P3402 Price, William, 1642
Ex.

P3413 Prideaux, Humphrey, 1690
Ely. Ex (2 – 1 tpw). Wel.

P3415 Prideaux, Humphrey, 1697
Ban. Ches. Nor.

P3416 Prideaux, Humphrey, 1697
8°.
Ban. Ches. Nor.

P3417 Prideaux, Humphrey, 1697
Bur. Ely. S Pl.

P3419 Prideaux, Humphrey, 1688
Dur. Ex. Wel. Yk.

P3421 Prideaux, John, 1651
Oxoniae, typis & impensis Leonardi Lichfield, veneunt apud Tho. Robinson.
Bur. Ex. S Pl. Yk.

P3422 Prideaux, John, 1661
Ban. Cant. Chi. Her. Lich.

P3425 Prideaux, John, 1656
Wor.

P3428 Prideaux, John, 1649
Chelm. Glo. Linc. Nor. Pet. Sal.

P3429 Prideaux, John, 1652
Bur. Ex. S Pl. Yk.

P3430 Prideaux, John, 1664
Also found with impr.: ... apud Joh. Wilmot & Joh. Crosley.
Ban (impr. as given). Cant (impr. as given). Chi (impr. as Wing). Her (impr. as given). Lich (impr. as Wing).

P3430A Prideaux, John, [1650?]
... Leonar: Lichfield.
Ex. Linc.

P3431? Prideaux, John, 1657
Oxoniae, excudebat Leonardus Lichfield, veneunt apud Tho. Robinson; 8°.
Carl. Dur. Lich. Wor.

P3432? Prideaux, John, 1641
... Lichfield ... & Henry Curteyne.
Carl. Ex (contains 20 sermons). Sal.

P3433 Prideaux, John, 1659
Carl.

P3434 Prideaux, John, 1651
Oxoniae, excudebat impensis suis Leonardus Lichfield.
Bur (2). Carl. Ex. S Pl. Yk.

P3435 Prideaux, John, 1660
'theologiae'
Ban. Cant. Chi. Her. Lich.

P3436 Prideaux, John, 1656
Yk.

P3436A Prideaux, John, 1654
Ban. Cant. Chelm.

P3436A+ Prideaux, John, 1661
Oxford, by A. & L. Lichfield; 4°.
Dur. Pet (2)*. Yk*.

P3436A++ Prideaux, John, 1671
Oxford, by A. and L. Lichfield; 4°.
Carl. Ely.

P3437 Prideaux, John, 1681
Ex (2).

P3438 Prideaux, John, 1648
... Hen. Curteyn ...
Ban. Carl. Ex. Pet. S Pl. Wor.

P3439 Prideaux, Mathias, 1648
Bur. Cant. Nor. Sal. Yk.

P3440 Prideaux, Mathias, 1650
Carl. S Dv.

P3441? Prideaux, Mathias, 1654
... Tho. Robinson.
Ban. Chelm.

P3442? Prideaux, Mathias, 1655
The third edition; Oxford, for Leonard Lichfield, to be sold by Tho: Robinson.
Cant.

P3443 Prideaux, Mathias, 1664
Pet (2 – 1 tpw). Yk.

P3443+ Prideaux, Mathias, 1664
As P3443, but: ... sold by Joh. Crosley & Joh. Wilmot.
Dur.

P3444 Prideaux, Mathias, 1672
Carl. Ely.

P3445 Prideaux, Mathias, 1682
Ex (2 – 1 tpw).

P3455 Primate, Stephen, [1667?]
Sal.

P3461 Primer, 1669
Maurry.
Liv.

P3472 Primitive, 1688
S Pl (2).

P3474 Primrose, *Sir* Archibald, 1644
Pet. Sal.

P3476 Primrose, James, 1651
Yk.

P3486 Prince, 1642
Linc.

P3491 Princely, 1649
Pet. Yk.

P3502 Printed, 1641
Cant.

P3511 Prior, Matthew, 1687
Ban.

P3520 Prisoners, 1654
Pet.

P3527 Pritchard, Thomas, 1693
'September'
Her.

P3530 Private, 1642
Linc.

P3532 Private, 1699
Dur (2).

P3534 Priviledges, 1641
Yk.

P3535 Privileges, 1680
Yk.

P3538 Proast, Jonas, 1690
Carl.

P3539 Proast, Jonas, 1691
Wel.

P3539+ Proavi, (1684)
See: CLC100.
Ely.

P3545 Proceedings, 1698
Dur. Yk.

P3556 Proceedings, [1642]
Dur. Linc.

P3557 Proceedings, 1681
Yk.

P3562A? Proceedings, [1679]
cap.
Linc.

P3564 Proceedings, 1681
Ely. Wel.

P3571 Proceedings, 1643
Cant. Linc. Yk.

P3573 *See*: Periodicals

P3639 Proclamation, 1678
Linc.

P3647 Proffet, Nicholas, 1645
Her. Yk.

P3685 Prophesie, [1679]
Linc.

P3699 Proposal, 1663
4°.
Chelm.

P3721 Proposalls, 1647
Yk.

P3737 Proposals, 1679
Cant.

P3763 Proposals, 1672
S Pl.

P3780 Propositions, [1647]
Linc. Pet.

P3784 Propositions, 1642
Yk.

P3790+ Propositions, 1642
'City'; For Iohn Borroughs and Iohn
Franke; 4°.
Dur. Linc.

P3795 Propositions, 1641[2]
... assignes ...
Dur.

P3796 Propositions, 1642
Linc.

P3801 Propositions, 1647
Cant.

P3803 Pro-quiritatio, 1642
Linc. Pet.

P3813 Προσφωνησις, 1643
Linc.

P3817 Protestancy, 1687
Sal.

P3819 Protestant, [1681]
Dur. Linc.

P3822 Protestant, [1680]
Linc (2).

P3840 Protestant, 1682
Carl.

P3856 Protestation, 1641
Cant. Linc. Yk (2).

P3857 Protestation, 1643
Linc.

P3865 Protestation, 1641
Linc.

P3870? Protestation, 1642
For I.H.
Linc.

P3875 Proteus, 1691
Llan. Wel.

P3879 Prowde, Francis, 1694
Cant. Yk.

P3888 Prynne, William, 1668
Yk.

P3891 Prynne, William, 1641
Lich. S Asa. Yk (2).

P3897 Prynne, William, 1648
Cant.

P3898 Prynne, William, 1668
... Josias Robinson.
Pet. Yk.

P3900 Prynne, William, 1659
S Pl. Sal. Yk.

P3902 Prynne, William, 1662
Yk (2).

P3904? Prynne, William, 1644
... Michaell Sparke, senior.
Cant. Chelm. Ex (tpw). Sal.
Win. Yk.

P3905 Prynne, William, 1669
Sal (tpw).

P3908 Prynne, William, 1647
Pet. Yk.

P3911 Prynne, William, 1649
Yk.

P3912 Prynne, William, 1660[59]
S Pl (imp).

P3913 Prynne, William, 1659
Pet.

P3917 Prynne, William, 1646
Cant. Carl. Ex. Linc (2 − 1
imp). Sal. Win. Yk.

P3918 Prynne, William, [1641?]
Yk.

P3919 Prynne, William, 1648
Cant.

P3925 Prynne, William, 1648
Yk.

P3926 Prynne, William, 1644
Yk.

P3928 Prynne, William, 1659
Dur. Pet. Wel. Yk.

P3929 Prynne, William, 1683
For Edw. Thomas ...
Ex. Yk.

P3930 Prynne, William, 1660
Carl. Ex. Pet (imp).

P3931 Prynne, William, 1660
Carl. Pet.

P3936 Prynne, William, 1654
Pet. Yk (2).

P3938 Prynne, William, 1647
Yk.

P3945 Prynne, William, 1646
Yk.

P3947− Prynne, William, 1643
As P3947, but: 'cowardisze'
Yk.

P3949 Prynne, William, 1647
Pet.

P3950+ Prynne, William, 1660
'An exact catalogue'; As P3950
(second entry), but: Printed for
Michael Sparke, senior, 1643 ...
Carl (tp imp).

P3950++ Prynne, William, 1666
'An exact chronological ...'; As P3950
(first entry), but: For the author, by
Thomas Ratcliffe, to be sold ... Bedell
...
Wel.

P3955 Prynne, William, 1660
Lich.

P3956 Prynne, William, 1659
Yk.

P3961 Prynne, William, 1664
Yk.

P3962 Prynne, William, 1643
Bur. Cant. Pet. Sal. Yk.

P3963 Prynne, William, 1645
'wandring-blasing-stars'
Pet. Yk (2).

P3964 Prynne, William, 1646[45]
Pet.

P3965 Prynne, William, 1660
Carl. S Pl.

P3966 Prynne, William, 1644
Sal.

P3967 Prynne, William, 1644
Yk.

P3968 Prynne, William, 1647
Yk (2).

P3971 Prynne, William, 1653
Cant (imp). Chelm. Yk.

P3972? Prynne, William, 1660
Second ed. not on tp.
Bur. Cant. Sal.

P3972+ Prynne, William, 1678
'The grand designs of the Papists';
Formerly H163.
Linc.

P3973? Prynne, William, 1645
By Thomas Brudenell, for Michael
Sparke, senior.
Cant. Chelm. Ex. Yk.

P3974 Prynne, William, 1659
Yk.

P3980 Prynne, William, 1670
Ex (2). Wel. Wor. Yk.

P3981 Prynne, William, 1641
Linc.

P3982 Prynne, William, 1643
Cant. Yk.

P3983 Prynne, William, 1641
Ely. Linc.

P3986 Prynne, William, 1651
Yk.

P3987 Prynne, William, 1648
Sal.

P3988 Prynne, William, 1654
Yk.

P3992 Prynne, William, 1648[9]
Yk.

P3994+ Prynne, William, 1656
Printed in the year; 4°.
Yk.

P3996 Prynne, William, 1649
Ex. Sal.

P4001 Prynne, William, 1647[8]
Yk.

P4002 Prynne, William, 1645
Pet.

P4003 Prynne, William, 1660
Cant. Yk.

P4005 Prynne, William, 1658
Pet (2 – 1 imp). Yk.

P4008 Prynne, William, 1646
Yk.

P4010 Prynne, William, 1644
Yk.

P4011 Prynne, William, 1662
Bur. Dur.

P4012 *See*: B6325+

P4018 Prynne, William, 1641
Yk (2).

P4022 Prynne, William, 1647
Yk.

P4023 Prynne, William, 1647
Yk.

P4026 Prynne, William, 1643
Spark.
Cant. Yk.

P4032 Prynne, William, 1648
'... House of Peeres'
Sal.

P4032+ Prynne, William, 1648
As P4032, but: '... Peers'
Linc.

P4034 Prynne, William, 1658
Lich.

P4039 Prynne, William, 1643
Spark.
Ex. Pet. Sal. Yk.

P4043 Prynne, William, 1649
Yk.

P4045 Prynne, William, 1655
Carl.

P4046 Prynne, William, 1655
Pet. Yk.

P4052- Prynne, William, 1659
As P4052, but: 'supekious' *for*
'spurious'
Yk.

P4052 Prynne, William, 1659
Carl. Dur. Ex (tp imp). Pet.
Yk.

P4055 Prynne, William, 1643
Bur. Yk.

P4056 Prynne, William, 1644
Yk.

P4062 Prynne, William, 1654
Yk.

P4070 Prynne, William, 1656
Pet.

P4071 Prynne, William, 1660
4°.
Yk.

P4074 Prynne, William, 1641
Yk.

P4078 Prynne, William, 1656
Ex. Yk.

P4079 Prynne, William, 1656
Bur.

P4080 Prynne, William, 1659
Carl.

P4081 Prynne, William, 1661
Carl.

P4082 Prynne, William, 1660
Yk.

P4082+ Prynne, William, 1680
For Edward Thomas; 4°.
Roch.

P4085 Prynne, William, 1658
Yk.

P4086 Prynne, William, 1642
Linc. Pet.

P4087 Prynne, William, 1642
The second impression.
Yk (3 – 1 tpw*).

P4087+ Prynne, William, 1642
As P4087, but: The second addition
[*sic*].
Yk.

P4088 Prynne, William, 1643
Bur. Cant. Pet. Sal. Yk.

P4089? Prynne, William, 1643
'... foure parts. ... with an appendix';
For Michael Sparke senior; Includes
P4109, P4088, P4103, P3962.
Bur. Cant.

P4092 Prynne, William, 1649
Cant. Pet.

P4093 Prynne, William, 1649
Yk.

P4094 Prynne, William, 1656
Ex.

P4096+ Prynne, William, [1661?]
See: CLC101.
Linc.

P4097 Prynne, William, 1646
Yk.

P4098 Prynne, William, 1647
Ex.

P4099 Prynne, William, 1653
Dur.

P4100 Prynne, William, 1659
Bur. Cant. Carl. Pet. Yk.

P4103 Prynne, William, 1643
Bur. Cant. Pet. S Asa (frag.).
Sal. Yk.

P4104 Prynne, William, 1668
Cant (tpw).

P4107 Prynne, William, 1647
Yk.

P4108 Prynne, William, 1643
Pet.

P4109 Prynne, William, 1643
Bur. Cant. Sal. Yk (2).

P4110 Prynne, William, 1648
Cant.

P4113 Prynne, William, 1659
Carl. Yk.

P4115 Prynne, William, 1645
Glo. Pet. Sal.

P4116 Prynne, William, 1644
Linc. Sal.

P4119 Prynne, William, 1660
Carl.

P4120 Prynne, William, 1661
Pet. Yk.

P4124 Prynne, William, 1645
Ex. Pet (2 – both imp). Yk.

P4126 Prynne, William, 1644
Yk.

P4128 Prynne, William, 1649
Cant. Yk.

P4132 Pryor, William, 1659
Ex.

P4133 Przipcovius, Samuel, 1653
Dur (imp).

P4134+ Przipcovius, Samuel, 1684
By J.G., for Thomas Maltus; 4°.
Her. S Pl.

P4136 Przipcovius, Samuel, 1653
S Pl.

P4149 Ptolomaeus, Claudius, 1682
Dur. Ely. Glo (imp). Pet.

P4158 Puccini, Vincentio, 1687
Ban. Ex. Nor. S Pl (imp). Sal.

P4158+ Puccini, Vincentio, 1687
For Samuel Smith, sold by Randal
Taylor; 4°.
Swel.

P4160 Puckle, James, 1696
8°.
Dur.

P4174 Pufendorf, Samuel, 1682
Cant. Dur. Glo. S Asa. Yk.

P4175 Pufendorf, Samuel, 1672
Ely. S Asa.

P4177 Pufendorf, Samuel, 1695
Carl.

P4180 Pufendorf, Samuel, 1698
Ely. Glo. Wel.

P4182 Pufendorf, Samuel, 1691
Ban.

P4183 Pufendorf, Samuel, 1698
Motte.
S Dv.

P4186+ Pugh, Robert, 1664
See: CLC102.
Carl. Linc. S Asa. Win.

P4189 Pujolas, J., 1690
8°.
Yk.

P4197 Puller, Timothy, 1679
Ban (engr. tpw). Carl. Ely. Liv.
Llan. S Pl. Win.

P4197+ Puller, Timothy, 1689
The second edition; For Richard
Chiswell; 8°.
Lich.

P4199 Pulleyn, John, 1699
S Pl.

P4201 Pulleyn, Octavian, 1657
Linc.

P4205 Pulton, Andrew, [1687?]
Wel.

P4207 Pulton, Andrew, 1687
Wel.

P4208 Pulton, Andrew, 1688
Ban. Wel.

P4209? Pulton, Andrew, 1687
'... Dr. Tho. Tenison'
Ex. S Dv (frag.). Wel.

P4209+ Pulton, Andrew, 1687
As P4209, but: '... Dr. Tenison'
Wel.

P4210 *See*: R2400+

P4214- Purcell, Henry, 1699
As P4214, apart from date; obl. 8°.
Dur.

P4215 Purcell, Henry, 1697
Dur.

P4218 Purcell, Henry, 1698
Dur.

P4223 Purcell, Henry, 1691
Dur.

P4230 Purge, 1642
Pet.

P4247 Pury, Thomas, 1641
Glo.

P4248 Pusey, Caleb, 1696
Dur (tp imp).

P4251 Puttock, Roger, 1642
Cant. Linc.

P4256? Pyke, William, 1680
For Nathanael Ranew.
Cant.

P4257 Pym, John, 1641[2]
'Deering'; For Iohn Thomas.
Cant. Dur. Linc.

P4259 Pym, John, 1643
Cant. Linc.

P4260 Pym, John, 1641
Cant. Yk.

P4261 Pym, John, 1641
Yk*.

P4265 Pym, John, 1643
Linc.

P4268 Pym, John, 1641
Anr ed. at P4299+.
Linc. Pet. Yk.

P4270? Pym, John, 1642
... William Larner.
Dur.

P4273+ Pym, John, 161 [*i.e.* 1641]
London, printed; 4°.
Linc.

P4276 Pym, John, [1642?]
'fourteenth of Ianuary'
Linc.

P4278 Pym, John, 1641[2]
Cant. Dur. Sal.

P4280 Pym, John, 1641
Cant.

P4283 Pym, John, 1642
Cant. Dur. Linc.

P4286? Pym, John, 1641
'... to Thomas Lord ...'; ... John
Aston.
Cant.

P4288 Pym, John, 1641[2]
Cant.

P4289 Pym, John, 1641[2]
Linc. Yk.

P4290 Pym, John, 1641
Cant.

P4291 Pym, John, 1641[2]
Cant (2 − 1 (at least) has London
only partly printed). Linc.

P4292 Pym, John, 1641[2]
Cant.

P4293 Pym, John, 1641
Cant. Nor.

P4295 Pym, John, 1641
Cant (2 − both 'John Pymm,
Esquire').

P4296 Pym, John, 1641
Linc. Yk.

P4297 Pym, John, 1641
Yk.

P4299 Pym, John, 1641
Cant.

P4299+ Pym, John, 1641
'Ten heads of a conference ...';
[N.pl.]; 4°; Anr ed. of P4268.
Linc.

P4302 Pym, John, 1641
Linc.

P4304 Pym, John, 1641
Cant (2).

P4311 Pynchon, William, 1650
Ex. Pet.

P4313 Pynchon, William, 1654
4°.
Yk.

P4318 Pyrotechnica, 1667
S Pl (2).

Q12 Quakers, 1674
Her.

Q54 Quarles, Francis, 1657
'Boanerges and Barnabas ...'; For R.
Royston.
Ban.

Q68 Quarles, Francis, 1675
Yk.

Q70? Quarles, Francis, 1642
Fifth ed. not on tp; Addit. engr. tp
dated 1643.
Chi.

Q76 Quarles, Francis, 1680
Yk.

Q85 Quarles, Francis, 1696
Ex (tpw)*.

Q104 Quarles, Francis, 1643
Ex.

Q105 Quarles, Francis, 1644
Carl.

Q106? Quarles, Francis, 1644
For Edward Husbands.
Yk.

Q107 Quarles, Francis, 1644
Pet. Yk (tpw)*.

Q110 Quarles, Francis, 1645
Pet. Yk (2).

Q121 Quarles, Francis, 1644
Cant. Yk (2).

Q148+ Quatermayne, Roger, 1642
By Tho. Paine for Roger
Quartermayne, sold by Samuel
Satterthwaite; 4°.
Yk.

Q152 Queene, 1642
Pet.

Q157+ Queens, 1642
'The Queens Majesties declaration';
Formerly H1457.
Yk.

Q158 Queens, 1643
Yk (2).

Q165 Queres, 1643
Cant. Carl. Yk.

Q166+ Queries, 1673
Printed at Kilkenny, 1648 and
re-printed; 2°.
Ely. S Asa. Wel (2). Win. Yk.

Q179 Question, [1642]
Dur.

Q185+ Questions, 1642
As Q185, apart from date.
Linc.

Q186 Questions, [1642]
Linc.

Q194 Quevedo y Villegas, Francisco
Gomez de, 1675
Carl.

Q197? Quevedo y Villegas,
Francisco Gomez de, 1668
For H. Herringman.
Carl.

Q201 Quevedo y Villegas, Francisco
Gomez de, 1689
Nor.

Q209 Quick, John, 1692
2v.
Bris. Cant. Carl. Ches. Chi.
Dur. Glo (2 − 1 vol. 1 only, tpw).
Lich. Linc. S Asa. Sal (imp).
Wel. Yk.

Q221 Quintilian, Marcus Fabius,
1693
... Henrici Cruttenden.
Carl. Ches. Linc. Nor. S Asa.
Wel. Yk.

Q222 Quintilian, Marcus Fabius,
1675
Theatro.
Yk.

Q223 Quintilian, Marcus Fabius,
1692
Oxonii, e Theatro Sheldoniano,
veneunt in officina Hen. Clements.
Nor. S Asa.

Q225 Quintilian, Marcus Fabius,
1641
Whitakeri.
Roch.

Q228 Quintine, Michael, 1645
'A short discovery of the mystery of
iniquitie'
Yk.

R4 R., B., 1642
Linc.

R6 R., B., 1678
Yk.

R11 R., C. D., 1641
Cant (tp imp). Pet.

R21 R., H., 1643
Linc.

R22A R., I., 1644
Stafford.
Ex.

R30 R., J., 1688
Wel.

R32 R., J., 1659
Ex.

R36 R., J., 1689
Ex. Nor. Wel.

R68 R., S., 1647
Cant (3). Linc. Pet. S Pl. Yk.

R73 R., S., 1680
Bur. Carl.

R83 R., T., 1642
Yk.

R84 R., T., 1642[3]
Carl.

R88 R., T., 1642
Pet.

R107 Rabelais, François, 1694
Carl.

R118 Rabshakeh's, 1658
Yk.

R121 Racovian, 1652
... Amsterledam ...
S Pl. Yk.

R122 Radau, Michaele, 1673
Dur. Yk.

R136 Rahn, Johann Heinrich, 1668
'An introduction ...'
Carl. Glo.

R141 Rainbowe, Edward, 1649
Chelm (imp). S Asa. Yk.

R142 Rainbowe, Edward, 1677
Cant. Carl. Her. Yk (3).

R143- Rainolds, John, 1641
See: CLC103.
Pet.

R144 *See*: R2336+ & R2336++

R149 Raleigh, Carew, 1656
Carl.

R150 Raleigh, George, 1641
Cant.

R151 Raleigh, *Sir* Walter, 1698
S Dv.

R156 Raleigh, *Sir* Walter, 1658
Pet.

R162? Raleigh, *Sir* Walter, 1652
'history'
Wel.

R163 Raleigh, *Sir* Walter, 1652
Her. Sal.

R164+ Raleigh, *Sir* Walter, 1666
For Robert White, John Place, and
George Dawes, sold by Thomas
Rookes; 2°.
Lich.

R167 Raleigh, *Sir* Walter, 1677
Cant. Carl. Chelm. Dur. Roch.

R168 Raleigh, *Sir* Walter, 1687
Ely.

R170 Raleigh, *Sir* Walter, 1650
Carl.

R172 Raleigh, *Sir* Walter, 1650
Pet.

R178A+ Raleigh, *Sir* Walter, 1669
For Margaret Sheares; 12°; Pt of
R183.
Cant.

R179 Raleigh, *Sir* Walter, 1642
Chelm.

R182 Raleigh, *Sir* Walter, 1664
Ely.

R183 Raleigh, *Sir* Walter, 1669
Cant.

R192 Raleigh, Walter, *of Wells*,
1679
'Reliquiae'
Cant. Pet. Wel (2). Win.

R195 Ram, Robert, 1646
Ex. Pet.

R198 Ram, Robert, 1684
Ex. Yk.

R199? Ramazzini, Bernardino, 1697
'Abassinian'
Ely.

R200? Ramesay, William, 1661
Brooks.
Linc.

R201 Ramesay, William, 1653
2°.
Glo (imp). Lich.

R216 Ramsay, William, 1681
Carl.

R218 Ramsay, William, 1680
Wor.

R219 Ramsay, William, 1679
Llan.

R221 Ramsay, William, 1672
Carl. Ex.

R227 Ramsey, John, 1661
S Asa. Win.

R235 Randolph, Bernard, 1686
S Asa.

R236 Randolph, Bernard, 1686
Wel. Yk.

R239A? Randolph, Thomas, 1642
For F. Cowles ...; Author is Thomas
Randall.
Dur.

R240 Randolph, Thomas, 1643
Yk.

R241 Randolph, Thomas, 1643
'Poems with the Muses looking-glasse,
and Amyntas ...'
Yk.

R246? Randolph, Thomas, 1668
The fifth edition; ... John Crossley.
Lich.

R249 Ranson, William, 1644
Yk.

R259 Rapin, René, 1672
Carl.

R260 Rapin, René, 1673
Dur (tp imp).

R263 *See*: S303+

R266+ Rapin, René, 1672
By S.G. and B.G. to be sold by
Dorman Newman, and Jonathan
Edwin; 8°.
Dur.

R267? Rapin, René, [1672?]
... Jonathan Edwin.
Carl. Wel.

R270 Rapin, René, 1674
Lich. Wel. Yk.

R271 Rapin, René, 1694
'Monsieur Rapin's reflections on ...'
Yk.

R272+ Rapin, René, 1678
By R.E. for Will. Cademan; 8°.
Her.

R275 Rapin, René, 1672
8°.
Carl*.

R277 Rapin, René, 1699
Gillyflower.
Wel.

R286 Rastell, John, 1641
Nineteenth ed. not on tp.
Cant.

R289? Rastell, John, 1659
Twenty-first ed. not on tp.
Dur. Lich.

R290 Rastell, John, 1667
Twenty-second ed. not on tp.
Cant. Carl. Her. Yk.

R291 Rastell, John, 1671
Twenty-third ed. not on tp.
Yk.

R298 Rathband, William, 1644
Ex.

R300 Ratio, 1654
Ex.

R305+ Rationall, 1661
See: CLC104.
Carl.

R311 Raue, Christian, 1649
Wel.

R315 Raue, Christian, 1648
Wel.

R332 Ravenscroft, Edward, 1682
For Jos. Hindmarsh.
S Pl.

R352 Rawlet, John, 1685
For Samuel Tidmarsh.
Carl. S Pl.

R353 Rawlet, John, 1686
Ely. Nor. Yk.

R354 Rawlet, John, 1686
Ban. Ches. S Pl.

R355 Rawlet, John, 1691
For Samuel Manship.
Ex.

R357 Rawlet, John, 1679
Carl.

R358 Rawlet, John, 1687
Carl.

R360A Rawlet, John, 1667
Carl.

R361 Rawlet, John, 1674
Carl.

R363 Rawlet, John, 1692
Her.

R381 Ray, John, 1670
Ex. Sal. Wel.

R382 Ray, John, 1677
S Asa. Yk.

R383 Ray, John, 1660
Ban.

R385 Ray, John, 1693
Ely. Glo.

R386 Ray, John, 1670
Ely. Linc.

R387 Ray, John, 1678
Yk.

R389 Ray, John, 1691
Cant.

R391 Ray, John, 1675
Carl.

R394 Ray, John, 1686 [−88]
2v.
Dur. S Dv.

R394+ Ray, John, 1686−88
As R394, but impr. vol. 1: ... &
Joannem Kersey.
Cant.

R395 Ray, John, 1693
Impensis Samuelis Smith ...
Wor. Yk.

R396 Ray, John, 1682
Wel. Yk.

R397 Ray, John, 1692
Ely. Lich. Nor. Yk.

R399 Ray, John, 1673
Bris. Ex.

R399+ Ray, John, 1673
As R399, but: 4°.
Ely.

R401 Ray, John, 1700
Ely. Ex.

R406 Ray, John, 1690
Ex.

R407 Ray, John, 1696
S Asa. S Dv.

R409 Ray, John, 1693
New. Wel (imp).

R411 Ray, John, 1692
Ely. Ex. Pet.

R413 Raymond, George, 1692
Ban. Cant. Nor.

R415 Raymond, John, 1648
Cant. Glo (imp).

R418 Raymund, John, 1667
Ex.

R419+ Raynes, Henry, (1698)
See: CLC105.
Ely.

R447 Reading, John, 1651
Cant. Lich.

R451 Reading, John, 1642
'August'
Cant (imp).

R460 Reason, 1649
Cant.

R460+ Reason, 1694
'Reason and religion'; Formerly
L2750.
Pet.

R462? Rreasonable, 1641
'in behalfe of'
Yk.

R462+ Reasonable, 1641
As R462, but: 'A reasonable ... in the
behalfe ...'
Nor.

R463 Reasonableness, 1688
Wel.

R466 Reasons, 1678
Cant. Linc.

R475 Reasons, 1653
Ex.

R478 Reasons, 1642
Dur.

R486 Reasons, 1678
Cant. Carl. Linc.

R519 Reasons, 1687
Wel.

R577 Reasons, [1680]
Linc. Yk.

R581 Reasons, 1648
Chelm. Pet (2).

R586- Reasons, [c.1680?]
See: CLC106.
Linc.

R586 Reasons, [1661]
Carl. Chelm. Win.

R587 Reasons, 1687
Cant. Wel (imp).

R588 Reasons, 1641
Ex. Linc.

R589 Reasons, 1647
Pet.

R592 Reasons, [1642]
Pet. Yk.

R594 Rebellion, 1642
Linc.

R595 Rebellion, 1648
Yk.

R602? Rebells, 1642
'rebells'
Linc.

R604 Rebels, 1649
Yk.

R646 Recorde, Robert, 1662
Pet.

R652 Recorde, Robert, 1665
Yk.

R671 Reeve, Gabriel, 1670
Llan.

R676 Reeve, John, *M.A.*, 1661
Second ed. not on tp.
Cant. S Pl.

R678 Reeve, John, *M.A.*, [1653]
Cant.

R679 Reeve, John, *M.A.*, 1658
Cant.

R680 Reeve, John, *M.A.*, [1653]
Cant.

R682 Reeve, John, *M.A.*, 1653
Cant.

R683 Reeve, John, *M.A.*, [1652]
48p.
S Pl.

R683+ Reeve, John, *M.A.*, [1652?]
As R683, but: 'spirituall'; 59p.
Cant (imp).

R686 Reeve, Thomas, 1661
Win.

R688 Reeve, Thomas, 1661
Win.

R689 Reeve, Thomas, 1661
Carl.

R691 Reeve, Thomas, 1647
Nor (tp imp).

R692 Reeve, Thomas, 1683
S Pl.

R692+ Reeve, Thomas, 1651
See: CLC107.
Carl.

R694A *See:* B5849+

R696 Reflections, 1681
Linc. S Pl.

R709 Reflections, 1690
Yk.

R712 Reflections, 1699
Ban. S Asa.

R714 Reflections, 1690
Carl.

R716 Reflexions, 1683
Carl.

R716+ Reflections, 1696
'Reflections upon a libel'; Formerly
L1144.
Yk.

R721 Reflections, [1700]
Wel.

R722 Reflections, 1689
Ban. S Asa.

R724 Reflections, 1683
Carl. Ex.

R732 Reflections, 1687
Dur. S Asa.

R733 Reflections, 1689
Carl. Dur. Pet. Wel.

R736 Reformado, 1643
Pet.

R740A Reformation, [1696]
'... worshipping of God ...'
Her.

R742 Reformation, 1641
Pet.

R743 Reformation, 1643
Win.

R744 Reformed, 1684
Ex.

R752 Refutation, [1681]
Linc.

R757 Registrum, 1687
Nor.

R770 Rejoynder, 1679
Linc.

R774 Relation, 1672
Wel.

R778 Relation, 1642
Bartlet.
Linc.

R778+ Relation, 1642
'August,17.1642. A relation from
Belfast, sent to a friend'; For John
Bartlet; 4°.
Linc.

R780 Relation, 1642
Dur.

R807 Relation, 1646
Yk.

R812 Relation, [1680]
Linc.

R814 Relation, 1678
'bloody'
Bris. Cant. Wel. Win.

R816 Relation, [1679]
Linc.

R821? Relation, 1666
For Hen. Herringman.
Carl. Ex.

R856+ Relation, 1666
See: CLC108.
Pet.

R871 Relation, [1680]
Linc.

R872 Relation, 1642
Dur. Linc.

R884 Relation, 1648
Pet.

R893 Relation, 1680
Dur.

R898 Relation, 1641[2]
Dur.

R902A Religion, 1678
Second ed. not on tp.
Pet.

R923 Remarkable, 1642
Linc.

R928 Remarks, 1687
Wel.

R932+ Remarques, 1673
'Remarques on the humours and
conversations of the town'; Formerly
L64.
Carl.

R934 Remarks, 1696
Ban. Dur.

R936 Remarks, 1687
Wel.

R941 Remarks, 1697
S Pl.

R942 Remarks, [1696]
Dur (2).

R950 Remarques, 1682
Wel.

R962 Remonstrance, 1648
Yk.

R964 Remonstrance, 1647
Pet.

R967 Remonstrance, 1641[2]
'The remonstrance ... Huntington'
Dur. Linc.

R970 Remonstrance, 1689
Nor. Wel.

R971+ Remonstrance, 1642
By L.N. and R.C. for F.E., Decemb.
9; 4°.
Yk.

R975 Remonstrance, 1648[7]
Ex.

R976 Remonstrance, 1646
Yk.

R982 Remonstrance, 1641
Yk.

R988 *See*: B1864

R991 Remonstrance, 1642
Ex.

R993 *See*: O632B

R998 Remonstrance, 1650
'assemblie'
Linc. Sal.

R1004 Remonstrance, 1647
Pet.

R1007 Remonstrance, 1647
Cant.

R1008 Remonstrance, 1677
Linc.

R1009+ Remonstrance, 1651
[N.pl.], printed; 4°.
Yk.

R1011 Remonstrance, 1643
Linc. Yk.

R1017 Remonstrance, 1652
Linc. Sal.

R1019 Remonstrance, 1641
Linc.

R1020 Remonstrance, 1648
'Surrey'
Cant.

R1026 Remonstrance, 1643
Linc.

R1032 Remonstrance, 1643
Yk.

R1033A Renaudot, Eusèbe, 1665
Carl.

R1034 Renaudot, Eusèbe, 1664
Carl.

R1035 Rendezvouz, [1659]
Yk.

R1037? Renou, Joannes de, 1657
By Jo. Streater and Ja. Cottrel, and
are to be sold by John Garfield.
Cant.

R1045 Renwick, James, 1688
4°.
Cant (frag.).

R1047 Replication, 1682
S Pl.

R1058 Reply, 1688
4°.
S Pl.

R1066+ Reply, 1686
'A reply to the answer made';
Formerly L1941.
Ban. Bur. Cant. Carl. Liv.
S Asa. S Pl. Wel.

R1067+ Reply, 1642[3]
'A reply to the answer (printed ...)';
Formerly M2176.
Linc. Pet.

R1068 Reply, 1690
Wel.

R1074 Reply, 1699
Printed for, and sold by ...
Ex.

R1077 Reply, 1687
Cant. Nor.

R1078 Reply, 1687
cap.?
S Asa. Wel.

R1080+ Reply, 1693
Printed in the year; 4°.
Yk.

R1083 Reply, 1687
Cant (imp).

R1084A *See*: Periodicals

R1088 Reports, 1679
[Edward III].
Nor.

R1088+ Reports, 1679
[Henry IV, V.] Entry as R1088.
Nor.

R1088++ Reports, 1679
[Henry VI.] Entry as R1088.
Nor.

R1088+++ Reports, 1680
[Edward IV.] Entry as R1088.
Nor.

R1105 Representation, 1692
Pet.

R1108 Representation, 1674
Ban. Linc. Wel. Win. Yk.

R1109 Representation, 1652
Dur.

R1119 Request, 1686
Sal. Wel.

R1126 Resbury, Nathaniel, 1684
S Pl.

R1128 Resbury, Nathaniel, 1693
Cant. Wor.

R1129 Resbury, Nathaniel, 1681
Chi. Her.

R1130 Resbury, Nathaniel, 1681
Llan. Wor.

R1131 Resbury, Nathaniel, 1689
Dur. Her. Wel.

R1133 Resbury, Nathaniel, 1692
S Asa. Wor.

R1134 Resbury, Richard, 1652
Pet.

R1136A Resbury, Richard, 1649
Wing has wrong date.
Cant (imp).

R1148 Resolution, 1689
9p.
Wel.

R1148+ Resolution, 1689
For R. Chiswell; 4°; 7p.
Carl.

R1150 Resolution, 1648
Yk.

R1156 Resolution, 1642
Dur. Ex.

R1157+ Resolution, 1642
'down'; [N.pl.]; 4°.
S Pl.

R1160? Resolution, 1641[2]
For T. Reinor.
S Pl.

R1175 *See*: K121B

R1183 Returne, 1648
Cant (cropped).

R1187 Reuniting, 1673
Carl.

R1190 Revelation, 1641
'A revelation of Mr. Brigtmans [*sic*]
revelation'
Pet.

R1192 Reverend, 1699
For Luke Meredith.
Cant. Carl. Ex. Lich. S Asa.
S Pl. Win.

R1196 Review, 1645
Ex.

R1197 Review, 1691
4°.
Lich. Llan.

R1201 Review, 1687
Wel.

R1202 Revindication, 1643
... Daniel, printer to the Universitie of
Cambridge.
Pet.

R1204 Revision, 1684
Ex.

R1208 Revolution, 1697
Nor.

R1211 Reymes, B., 1647
Sal.

R1216 Reynell, Edward, 1659
Cant.

R1218+ Reynell, Edward, 1662
See: CLC109.
Carl.

R1222 Reyner, Edward, 1646
Cant. Chelm. Yk.

R1226 Reyner, Edward, 1656
Ely.

R1227 Reyner, Edward, 1658
Carl.

R1228A Reyner, Edward, 1668
Ex.

R1230 Reyner, Edward, 1656
Ely.

R1234 Reynolds, Edward, 1658
'works'
Carl (tpw). Chi (2 − 1 imp). Glo.
Her (imp?). IoM. Lich. Nor.

R1235 Reynolds, Edward, 1679
Her. Wor.

R1236 Reynolds, Edward, 1650
Cant. Carl. Liv.

R1239 Reynolds, Edward, 1660
Dur (imp). Ex. Liv. Pet. S Asa.

R1240 Reynolds, Edward, 1659
Pet. S Pl.

R1241 Reynolds, Edward, 1662
Bur. Pet. Wor.

R1248 Reynolds, Edward, 1642
Bostocke.
Carl. Pet.

R1251+ Reynolds, Edward, 1649
The second edition; Impr. as R1251;
4°.
Carl.

R1252 Reynolds, Edward, 1659
Pet.

R1254 Reynolds, Edward, 1650
Chelm. Dur. Yk.

R1255 Reynolds, Edward, 1689
Wel.

R1256 Reynolds, Edward, 1642
'publique'
Carl. Pet (2).

R1256+ Reynolds, Edward, 1642
'publike'; ... Rober [*sic*] Bostock.
Ex.

R1259 Reynolds, Edward, 1649
Pet.

R1261 Reynolds, Edward, 1655
Pet. S Pl.

R1266? Reynolds, Edward, 1677
8°.
Carl. Llan.

R1267 Reynolds, Edward, 1647
Carl.

R1268 Reynolds, Edward, 1659
Pet. S Pl.

R1269 Reynolds, Edward, 1663
Carl. Liv. S Asa.

R1270 Reynolds, Edward, 1657
Liv. Win.

R1272 Reynolds, Edward, 1662
Liv.

R1274 Reynolds, Edward, 1658
Wor.

R1276 Reynolds, Edward, 1660
Cant. Yk.

R1278 Reynolds, Edward, 1646
Yk.

R1281 Reynolds, Edward, 1666
Bur. Carl. Pet. Yk.

R1281+ Reynolds, Edward, 1666
By Tho. Ratcliffe, for John Durham;
4°.
Ex.

R1283 Reynolds, Edward, 1668
Cant (2). Carl. Yk.

R1284 Reynolds, Edward, 1669
Cant. Carl. Ex. Nor. Wor.

R1285 Reynolds, Edward, 1678
Dur.

R1286- Reynolds, Edward, 1638
[*i.e.* c.1650]
For Robert Bostock; 4°; =STC
20931.5.
Carl.

R1287 Reynolds, Edward, 1658
S Pl.

R1289 Reynolds, Edward, 1657
Wor.

R1290 Reynolds, Edward, 1663
Carl. Liv.

R1291 Reynolds, Edward, 1659
Carl. Pet. Sal.

R1292 Reynolds, Edward, 1642
Carl.

R1294 Reynolds, Edward, 1647
Yk.

R1295+ Reynolds, Edward, 1650
By F.N. for Robert Bostock; 4°.
Carl.

R1299 Reynolds, Edward, 1657
Cant. Pet (2). S Pl.

R1301+ Reynolds, Edward, 1663
See: CLC110.
S Asa.

R1301++ Reynolds, Edward, 1663
See: CLC111.
Nor.

R1302 Reynolds, Edward, 1660
Carl. Pet (2). S Pl. Wor.

R1303 Reynolds, John, *of Exeter*,
1661
Pet. Yk.

R1314 Reynolds, John, *of King's
Norton*, 1669
Sal (imp).

R1318 Reynolds, John, *Rev.*, 1678
Cant.

R1323 Reynolds, William, 1658
Her. Pet.

R1323+ Reynolds, William, 1658
'The vanitie of man'; For J. Rothwel;
4°.
Yk.

R1324 Reynor, William, 1644
Ex. Her. Pet. Yk.

R1326 Rhijne, Willem ten, 1683
Ex.

R1330 Rhodes, Simon, 1642
Yk (2).

R1331 Rhodes, William, 1642
Yk.

R1356 Rich, Robert, 1680
Yk.

R1358 Rich, Robert, 1678
Win (lacks colophon?).

R1362 Rich, Robert, 1669
Cant.

R1365 Rich, S., 1685
Cant.

R1371? Richards, Jacob, 1687
[N.pl.], for M. Gilliflower …
Wel. Yk.

R1376 Richardson, 1691
Wel.

R1377 Richardson, 1691
S Asa.

R1384 Richardson, John, 1700
Dur. Pet. Wel.

R1385 Richardson, John, 1655
Ely. Ex.

R1385+ Richardson, John, 1655
For John Stafford; 2°.
Carl.

R1389 Richardson, Joshua, 1682
Dur.

R1403 Richardson, Samuel, 1654
Linc.

R1417? Richelieu, Armand Jean du
Plessis, *Cardinal*, 1562 [*i.e.* 1662]
Error in date.
Dur.

R1422 Richelieu, Armand Jean du
Plessis, *Cardinal*, 1642
Yk.

R1423 Richelieu, Armand Jean du
Plessis, *Cardinal*, 1695
Ex. Nor.

R1424+ Richerius, Edmundus,
1691
See: CLC112.
S Pl.

R1430 Ricraft, Josiah, 1645
Ex. Yk.

R1442A? Rider, John, 1649
By Felix Kingston; Pt 2 has another
tp (which names the 'Dictionary' as pt
2): 'Dictionarium etymologicum'; The
sixth time newly corrected; By Felix
Kingston for Andrew Crooke.
Cant.

R1442A+ Rider, John, 1649
By Felix Kingston, for John
Waterson; 4°.
Yk.

R1447 Rider, 1643
Yk.

R1449 Ridley, Humphrey, 1695
Ex.

R1450 Ridley, John, 1649
Carl. Ex (2). Pet.

R1451 Ridley, Nicholas, 1688
Ban. Ex. Lich. Sal. Wel.

R1452 Ridley, Nicholas, 1688
4°.
Ban. Ely. Ex. Pet. S Dv.

R1453 Ridley, Nicholas, 1688
Her. Yk (tpw).

R1454 Ridley, *Sir* Thomas, 1662
'ecclesiasticall'; … for John Forrest.
Cant. Ely. Pet.

R1455 Ridley, *Sir* Thomas, 1664
The third edition.
S Asa.

R1456 Ridley, *Sir* Thomas, 1675
… for Ric. Davis.
Yk.

R1457 Ridley, *Sir* Thomas, 1676
The fourth edition.
Wel.

R1458 Ridpath, George, 1693
4°.
Cant. Wel. Yk.

R1461 Ridpath, George, 1697
Dur.

R1462 Ridpath, George, 1694
Cant.

R1463 Ridpath, George, 1699
S Pl (2).

R1465 Ridpath, George, 1694
Wel.

R1470 Rigby, Alexander, 1641
Cant (2 states — 1: Tp has
elephant; 2: Tp has Hermes).
Linc.

R1474 Rigby, *Sir* Nathaniel,
1641[2]
Yk.

R1507 Right, 1653
Carl. Yk.

R1516 Rights, 1682
Wor.

R1518 Riland, John, 1663
Cant (imp).

R1525 Riolan, Jean, 1657
Carl.

R1541 Ritor, Andrew, 1642[3]
Ex.

R1542 Ritor, Andrew, 1642
'baptisme'; Wing has wrong date.
Ex. Pet (tpw).

R1543+ Ritschel, George, 1648
Oxoniae, excudebat L. Lichfield, &
prostant venales apud R. Davis & E.
Forrest jun.; 8°.
Sal.

R1544 Ritschel, George, 1661
Dur.

R1545 Rivadeneira, Pedro de, 1669
… Ioachim Carlier.
Cant (imp). S Pl.

R1548 Riveley, Benedict, 1677
Carl.

R1555 Rivière, Lazare, 1658
Carl.

R1559+ Rivière, Lazare, 1661
By Peter Cole and Edward Cole; 2°.
Carl.

R1564 Rivière, Lazare, 1678
Cant. Her.

R1567+ Rivière, Lazare, 1657
For Philip Briggs; 2°.
Yk.

R1568+ Riville, P., 1641
By T.F. for J. Thomas; 4°.
Her.

R1577 Roberts, Edward, 1694
Wor.

R1579? Roberts, Francis, 1655
The second impression.
Ex.

R1580 Roberts, Francis, 1647
Yk.

R1581 Roberts, Francis, 1657
Glo.

R1583 Roberts, Francis, 1648
Roch.

R1584 Roberts, Francis, 1649
Carl. Chelm. Yk.

R1587 Roberts, Francis, 1665
IoM.

R1588 Roberts, Francis, 1675
Ex. Her. Liv. S Dv.

R1590 Roberts, Francis, 1653
Ex.

R1592 Roberts, Francis, 1659
The third edition; By T.R. for George
Calvert.
Ely.

R1594 Roberts, Francis, 1657
Ex. Linc.

R1597A+ Roberts, Hugh, 1660
See: CLC113.
Pet.

R1611 Robertson, William, [1654?]
Nor. S Asa. Yk.

R1613 Robertson, William, 1656
Nor. S Asa. Yk (2).

R1614 Robertson, William, 1683
8°.
Ely. Ex. Linc. S Asa. Yk.

R1617A? Robertson, William, 1693
… Brown, John Lawrence …
S Pl.

R1618 Robertson, William, [1655]
Ex. Nor.

R1619 Robertson, William, 1676
Ely. Nor. Swel.

R1621 Robertson, William, 1680
Cant. Carl. Ex. Lich. Sal.

R1621+ Robertson, William, 1686
Excudebat Samuel Roycroft. Impensis
Thomae Sawbridge; 4°.
Cant.

R1664 Robinson, Henry, 1644
Yk.

R1667 Robinson, Henry, 1644
Cant.

R1671 Robinson, Henry, 1641
Pet.

R1672 Robinson, Henry, 1645
Cant.

R1675+ Robinson, Henry, 1644
[N.pl.]; 4°.
Carl (tp imp).

R1676 Robinson, Henry, 1645
Sal (2).

R1679 Robinson, Henry, 1646
Pet (imp). Yk.

R1680 Robinson, Hugh, 1677
… Eliz. Flesher …
Bur.

R1680+ Robinson, Hugh, 1677
Typis Eliz. Flesher, prostat apud Ric.
Davis, bibliopolam Oxoniensem.
Ban. Cant. Carl. Ex. Glo.
Linc. Pet. Roch. S Pl. Sal (2).
Swel. Wel. Yk.

R1683 Robinson, Hugh, 1661
Cant.

R1688A? Robinson, Hugh, 1681
The tenth edition; Chiswell.
Liv.

R1690 Robinson, John, *Bp*, 1694
Wel.

R1691 Robinson, John, *of Leyden*,
1641
Yk.

R1697 Robinson, John, *of Leyden*,
1646
Pet. Yk.

R1702? Robinson, John, *M.D.*,
1656
8°.
Carl.

R1707 Robinson, Ralph, 1656
Ex.

R1709 Robinson, Ralph, 1658
Yk (tp imp).

R1712 Robinson, Ralph, 1655
S Pl. Yk.

R1716+ Robinson, *Sir* Tancred,
(1679)
See: CLC114.
Linc.

R1719 Robinson, Thomas, *of
Ousby*, 1696
Carl. Ex. Wel.

R1726 *See*: S5874A

R1728 Robotham, Charles, 1694
Pet.

R1729 Robotham, Charles, 1695
Ex.

R1731+ Robotham, John, 1652
By M.S. sold by George Eversden; 4°.
Ex.

R1740 Rochefort, Charles César de,
1666
Ex.

R1761A Rochester, John Wilmot,
Earl of, [1679?]
Linc.

R1763 Rocket, John, 1651
Chelm.

R1764 Rocket, John, 1650
Wing has wrong date.
Nor.

R1770 Roderick, Richard, 1683
Cant. Carl. Chi. Yk (imp).

R1777 Roe, *Sir* Thomas, 1642
Yk.

R1780 Roe, *Sir* Thomas, 1641
Cant.

R1782? Roe, William, 1662
... for Richard Davis.
Carl.

R1812 Rogers, John, 1659
Ex.

R1818 Rogers, John, *Chaplain*,
1681
Dur.

R1822 Rogers, Nehemiah, 1658
Chelm.

R1829? Rogers, Thomas, 1694
12°.
Carl.

R1829+ Rogers, Thomas, 1694
'unmask'd'; Sold by Randal Taylor;
12°.
Carl.

R1833 Rogers, Thomas, 1661
Dur. Sal. Yk.

R1834 Rogers, Thomas, 1668
Bur. Cant. Glo. Her. Linc.
Nor. Yk.

R1835 Rogers, Thomas, 1675
Ely. Ex. Nor.

R1836 Rogers, Thomas, 1681
Her. Tru. Yk.

R1837 Rogers, Thomas, 1691
Cant. Her.

R1837+ Rogers, Thomas, 1641
'Leycester's ghost'; Formerly L970.
Linc. Pet.

R1848 Rogers, Timothy, *M.A.*,
1691
Her.

R1849 Rogers, Timothy, *M.A.*,
1683
Dur.

R1867 Rohan, Henri, *Duc de*, 1660
Ex.

R1868 Rohan, Henri, *Duc de*, 1641
Pet. Win.

R1870? Rohault, Jacques, 1697
Impensis Jacobi Knapton.
Ches.

R1872 Rolle, Henry, 1668
Dur.

R1873 Rolle, Henry, 1676
Dur.

R1875? Rolle, Henry, 1675
... F. Titon, ... T. Basset.
Dur (2).

R1876 Rolle, Samuel, 1667
Dur (tp imp)*.

R1877 Rolle, Samuel, 1667
Dur.

R1879 Rolle, Samuel, 1668
Cant. Ex.

R1880+ Rolle, Samuel, 1678
By Tho. James; 8°.
Win.

R1882 Rolle, Samuel, 1667
Dur.

R1883 Rolle, Samuel, 1669
Carl. Linc. Sal. Win.

R1884 Rolle, Samuel, 1667
Dur.

R1885 Rollock, Robert, 1641
Ex (tp imp). Yk.

R1892A Roman, 1700
Cant.

R1893 Roman, 1680
Win.

R1895 Rome, 1641
Linc. Nor. Yk (2 issues – 1:
Printed in the same; 2: Printed
also in the same).

R1896+ Romes, 1641
'Romes A B C'; Formerly L95.
Yk.

R1907 Romish, 1683
Ex. Yk.

R1917+ Ronsgore, John, 1642
[N.pl.], July 23. for T. Norworth; 4°.
Sal.

R1917++ Rookes, Thomas, [1667?]
See: CLC115.
Pet.

R1929- Roper, Abel, 1700–04
See: CLC116.
Cant (lacks pt 2).

R1930 Roscommon, Wentworth
Dillon, *4th Earl of*, 1684
Cant. Carl.

R1931 Roscommon, Wentworth
Dillon, *4th Earl of*, 1685
Ely. Wel (imp)*.

R1931+ Roscommon, Wentworth
Dillon, *4th Earl of*, [1681]
'A letter from Scotland'; Formerly
L1504.
Ches. Linc. Win.

R1945 Ross, Alexander, 1658
Ban. Glo.

R1946 Ross, Alexander, 1651
Linc.

R1949 Ross, Alexander, 1646
S Asa.

R1956 Ross, Alexander, 1652
Cant. Lich.

R1961 Ross, Alexander, 1645
Cant (imp). Linc.

R1963 Ross, Alexander, 1643
Cant.

R1964 Ross, Alexander, 1647
Cant.

R1965 Ross, Alexander, 1648
Yk.

R1966 Ross, Alexander, 1653
Her.

R1973 Ross, Alexander, 1658
For John Saywell.
Ban. Glo.

R1975 Ross, Alexander, 1672
The fourth edition; Williams.
Yk.

R1975A Ross, Alexander, 1673
London, for John Williams.
Ely.

R1976? Ross, Alexander, 1675
The fifth edition; ... sold by Ben.
Billingsley and Tho. Cockeril.
Nor.

R1978 Ross, Alexander, 1696
Sixth edition.
Glo.

R1979 Ross, Alexander, 1645
Cant.

R1982 Ross, Alexander, 1648
'... Μαθηταῖς. ...'; Larner; Author
was Alexander Rowley.
Cant.

R1983 Ross, Alexander, 1656
S Pl.

R1993? Rossington, James, 1700
... Launceston ...
Ex.

R2000 Rotherham, Thomas
Atwood, 1643
Pet.

R2005 Rothwell, John, 1693
For John Dunton.
S Pl.

R2011 Rous, Francis, *the Elder*,
1645
Yk.

R2015 Rous, Francis, *the Elder*,
[1649]
Cant.

R2020 Rous, Francis, *the Elder*,
1649
Chelm. Pet.

R2023 Rous, Francis, *the Elder*,
1650
Ely. Glo. Yk.

R2025 Rous, Francis, *the Elder*,
1641
Sal.

R2027 Rous, Francis, *the Elder*,
1641
Cant.

R2028 Rous, Francis, *the Elder*,
1641
Yk.

R2029 Rous, Francis, *the Elder*,
1642
Cant. Linc.

R2033? Rous, Francis, *the Younger*,
1649
... Lichfield, for John Addams, and
Ed. Forrest, junior.
Her. S Asa (tpw). Sal. Yk.

R2033+ Rous, Francis, *the Younger*,
1652
The third edition; Oxford, by L.L. for
John Williams; 4°.
Bur.

R2034 Rous, Francis, *the Younger*,
1654
Swel.

R2035 Rous, Francis, *the Younger*,
1658
S Pl. Wel. Yk.

R2036 Rous, Francis, *the Younger*,
1662
Glo.

R2037 Rous, Francis, *the Younger*,
1667
The sixt edition; ... Adams and
Edward Forrest.
Bur. Dur. Swel. Yk.

R2039 Rous, Francis, *the Younger*,
1671
The seventh edition; ... Henry Hall ...
Ches.

R2040 Rous, Francis, *the Younger*,
1675
... Ric: Davis.
Cant. Dur. Ely. Lich. Nor.

R2062? Rowe, Elizabeth Singer,
1696
Dunton.
Dur.

R2105-- Royal College of
Physicians, 1665
See: CLC117.
Carl.

R2105- Royal College of Physicians,
1665
See: CLC118.
Carl.

R2105+ Royal College of
Physicians, 1677
Typis Tho. Newcomb, prostant
venales apud Joh. Martyn, Joh.
Starkey, Tho. Basset, Joh. Wright,
Ric. Chiswel & Rob. Bowlter; 2°.
Linc.

R2108 Royal College of Physicians,
1689
Ex.

R2129+ Royal, [1695]
See: CLC119.
Yk (imp).

R2142 Royal, 1660
Carl.

R2162 Royse, George, 1689
Cant. Sal.

R2163 Royse, George, 1691
Cant.

R2164 Royse, George, 1691
Wor.

R2170+ Rudd, Thomas, 1650
'Practicall ...'; By J.G. for Robert
Boydell; 4°.
Cant.

R2186 Rudyerd, *Sir* Benjamin,
1641
Cant. Linc.

R2190 Rudyerd, *Sir* Benjamin,
1641
Cant. Ex.

R2192 Rudyerd, *Sir* Benjamin,
1641
Linc.

R2194 Rudyerd, *Sir* Benjamin,
1642
... William Sheares.
Linc.

R2195 Rudyerd, *Sir* Benjamin,
1643
Cant.

R2196 Rudyerd, *Sir* Benjamin,
1643
Cant.

R2197? Rudyerd, *Sir* Benjamin,
1641
'... made in answer to the Spanish and
French embassadors ...'
Sal.

R2198 Rudyerd, *Sir* Benjamin,
1641
Cant (cropped). Carl. Dur.

R2200 Rudyerd, *Sir* Benjamin,
1641
Cant (3 – 2 imp). Ex. Yk.

R2201 Rudyerd, *Sir* Benjamin,
1641
Dur (imp). Yk.

R2202 Rudyerd, *Sir* Benjamin,
1641
Linc.

R2204 Rudyerd, *Sir* Benjamin,
1642
Linc.

R2206 Rudyerd, *Sir* Benjamin,
1642
Dur.

R2207 Rudyerd, *Sir* Benjamin,
1642
Cant.

R2208? Rudyerd, *Sir* Benjamin,
1642
'... July the ninth, 1642'; Iulie 18. ...
Lownds.
Linc.

R2214 Ruggle, George, 1659
Glo.

R2215 Ruggle, George, 1668
Liv. Pet. Sal (imp). Yk.

R2220? Rule, Gilbert, 1691
No impr., half-title only.
Cant.

R2223 Rule, Gilbert, 1680
Carl.

R2224 Rule, Gilbert, 1689
Yk.

R2233 Rule, Gilbert, 1691
Cant.

R2250 Rules, 1655
Yk.

R2251 Rules, 1682
Pet. Win.

R2269 Rumbold, Richard, [1685]
Ban.

R2290 Rupert, *Prince*, 1642
Linc.

R2293 Rupert, *Prince*, 1649
Cant.

R2294 Rupert, *Prince*, 1645
Yk.

R2302 Rupert, *Prince*, 1673
Linc.

R2313 Rusden, Moses, 1679
Cant.

R2316 Rushworth, John, 1659
Copies vary.
Carl. Dur. Ely. Ex. Glo. Her.
Lich. Linc (2). Roch. Wel (2).
Win. Wor.

R2317 Rushworth, John, 1682
Cant.

R2318 Rushworth, John, 1680
2v.
Cant. Dur. Ely. Glo. Linc.
Sal. Wel (2). Win. Wor.

R2319 Rushworth, John, 1692
2v.
Cant. Dur. Ely. Ex. Linc (vol.
1 only). Wor.

R2325? Rushworth, John, 1648
For Edward Husband …
Cant.

R2327 Rushworth, John, 1645[6]
Yk.

R2333 *See*: T2232

R2334 *See*: T2232A

R2336+ Rushworth, John, 1645
'A true relation'; [N.pl.], printed in
the year; 4°; Wing wrongly enters
under Rainsborough.
Yk.

R2336++ Rushworth, John, 1645
As R144, but: … Sept. 13.
Yk.

R2338B+ Rushworth, William,
1654
Reprinted at Paris; 12°.
Carl.

R2343 Russell, John, *of Chingford*,
1660
Dur. Ex.

R2351 Russell, William, *Lord*, 1683
Wel. Wor.

R2358 Russell, William, 1674
Dur.

R2361 Rust, George, 1683
Ex.

R2362 Rust, George, 1668
Carl. S Asa.

R2362+ Rust, George, 1668
By E. Tyler for Richard Royston; 2°.
Cant. Sal.

R2365 Rust, George, 1661
Bur. Carl. Lich. Pet (2). S Asa.
S Pl. Yk.

R2366 Rust, George, 1686
Dur.

R2372 Rutherford, James, 1658
Pet.

R2376? Rutherford, Samuel, 1650
… pro Roberto Brouno.
Carl. Pet.

R2379 Rutherford, Samuel, 1649
Pet.

R2382 Rutherford, Samuel, 1671
Win.

R2391 Rutherford, Samuel, 1644
Ex (tpw).

R2393 Rutherford, Samuel, 1645
Pet.

R2400+ Rutton, Thomas, 1658
'Judgement to come'; Wrongly placed
at P4210; By J.H. for J. Rothwell; 4°.
Pet. S Pl.

R2400A Ruvio, Antonio, 1641
4°.
Yk.

R2403 Rycaut, *Sir* Paul, 1682
Ex.

R2404? Rycaut, *Sir* Paul, 1682
The fifth edition .
Yk.

R2406 Rycaut, *Sir* Paul, 1680
2°.
Bur. Carl. Ely. Ex. Glo. Wel.
Win.

R2407 Rycaut, *Sir* Paul, 1687
Cant. Dur. S Asa. Wor.

R2408 Rycaut, *Sir* Paul, 1700
Cant. Carl. Ely. S Asa (imp).
Wel.

R2411 Rycaut, *Sir* Paul, 1679
Cant (2 − 1 imp). Carl. Ches.
Ely. Ex. Her. Linc. S Pl. Wel.
Win. Yk.

R2413? Rycaut, *Sir* Paul, 1668
Second ed. not on tp; … Henry
Brome; 2°; 218p.
Cant. Carl*. Glo. Nor (tp imp).
Win*.

R2413+ Rycaut, *Sir* Paul, 1668
As R2413, but: 216p.
Cant.

R2414? Rycaut, *Sir* Paul, 1670
… Henry Brome, sold by Robert
Boulter.
Bur. Ely. Linc. Wel.

R2414A Rycaut, *Sir* Paul, 1687
Cant. Dur. S Asa. Wor.

R2421 Ryff, Peter, 1665
Oxoniae, typis W.H. impensis Fran:
Oxlad.
Ex.

R2422 Ryley, William, 1661
Dur. Nor. Sal.

R2430 Rymer, Thomas, 1678
Ely. Yk.

R2446 Ryves, Bruno, 1647
Carl.

R2448 Ryves, Bruno, 1646
Ex. Linc. Liv. Pet. Yk.

R2448+ Ryves, Bruno, 1648
'… complaint of the murders …';
[N.pl.]; 8°; Pt of an ed. of R2448,
etc.?
Carl.

R2449 Ryves, Bruno, 1685
Yk.

R2450 Ryves, Bruno, 1685
Cant. Win.

S6A S., A., 1696
Cant.

S10 S., B., 1645
S Pl.

S35 S., I., 1655
Cant.

S40A S., I., 1648
Wing has wrong date.
Dur.

S48 S., J., 1674
S Asa.

S66 S., J., 1686
Cant. Ex. Yk.

S81 S., J., 1642
Linc.

S85 S., J., 1682
Carl.

S87 S., J., 1672
Yk.

S91 S., J., [1643]
Yk.

S100 S., J., 1642
Linc.

S110 S., L., [1681]
brs.
Ches. Linc.

S113 S., M., 1642
Linc.

S116+ S., M., 1644
'M.S. to A.S.'; Formerly G1180.
Win.

S117 S., M., 1695
Ely.

S120A S., N., 1675
Wel.

S122? S., P., 1663
York, by A. Broade, and are to be
sold by R. Lambert.
Yk.

S130 S., R., 1663
Pet.

S133 S., R., [1688?]
4°; 8p.
Cant.

S133+ S., R., [1688?]
As S133, but: 'by news'; 8, 22p.
Ex.

S140+ S., R., 1663
See: CLC120.
Pet.

S149 *See*: S3045

S166 S., T., 1681
Nor (tpw).

S168 S., T., [1642]
Linc.

S176 S., T., [1680]
Linc.

S183 S., T., 1679
Linc. Llan (2).

S186+ S., S., 1700
See: CLC121.
Dur.

S188 S., W., 1671
Carl. Dur. Linc. Nor. S Pl.
Sal.

S194 S., W., 1679
Linc (2).

S205 S., W., 1660
Carl.

S213 Sabino, Angelo, 1688
Cant.

S214 Sabran, Lewis, 1688
Ex. Swel.

S215 Sabran, Lewis, 1688
Wel.

S216 Sabran, Lewis, 1687
Nor. Wel.

S217 Sabran, Lewis, 1688
Sal.

S218 Sabran, Lewis, 1687
Ban. Wel.

S219 Sabran, Lewis, 1688
Wel.

S220 Sabran, Lewis, 1687
Ban. Ex.

S238A? Sad, 1682
'The sad ...'; For Jonas Hyther; 2°.
Win.

S239 Sad, [1654]
Dur.

S263 Sad, 1642
Pet.

S265 Sadler, Anthony, 1654
Dur. Linc. Pet (2). Yk.

S266 Sadler, Anthony, 1660
'loyall'
S Asa.

S268 Sadler, Anthony, 1660
S Asa (tpw).

S276 Sadler, John, 1645
S Pl.

S278A Sadler, John, 1649
Carl.

S279 Sadler, John, 1682
Cant.

S280 Sadler, John, 1646
Pet.

S284 Sage, John, 1693
4°.
Cant. Yk.

S285 Sage, John, 1690
Cant. Ex (imp). Wel. Yk.

S286 Sage, John, 1695
S Pl. Wel.

S288 Sage, John, 1695
Cant (tp imp). Yk.

S289? Sage, John, 1695
For Walter Kettilby; 4°.
S Pl.

S296 St Amour, Louis Gorin de,
1664
Carl. Ely. Ex. Pet. S Pl. Sal.
Win. Wor.

S296+ St Amour, Louis Gorin de,
1664
By T. Ratcliff, for George Thomason;
2°.
Dur. Linc.

S297? St Andrews University, 1689
'addres [*sic*]'
Yk.

S301 Saint-Evremond, Charles
Marguetel de Saint Denis, *Seigneur
de*, 1700
Glo.

S303+ Saint-Evremond, Charles
Marguetel de Saint Denis, *Seigneur
de*, 1672
'Judgment on Alexander ...'; By A.
Maxwell, for Jonathan Edwin; 8°;
Wing wrongly enters at R263.
Dur. Yk*.

S305 Saint-Evremond, Charles
Marguetel de Saint Denis, *Seigneur
de*, 1692
Ex.

S306A Saint-Evremond, Charles
Marguetel de Saint Denis, *Seigneur
de*, 1694
Ex (imp).

S318+ St Germain, *Sir* Christopher,
1687
By the assigns of Rich. and Edw.
Atkins, sold by Charles Harper,
William Crook and Richard Tonson;
8°.
Cant. Liv. Nor.

S322 St John, Oliver, 1641
Cant. Yk.

S323 St John, Oliver, 1641
78p.
Linc. Nor. Yk.

S323+ St John, Oliver, 1641
As S323, but: 38p.
Cant (mixed sheets?).

S326 St John, Oliver, 1641[2]
Sal.

S328 St John, Oliver, 1641[2]
Cant. Dur.

S329 St John, Oliver, 1641
Dur. Linc. Yk.

S331 St John, Oliver, 1640[1]
=STC 21589.
Carl. Ex (2). Pet.

S331+ St John, Oliver, 1640[1]
=STC 21589.3.
Pet.

S331++ St John, Oliver, 1640[1]
=STC 21589.7.
Cant. Sal. Yk.

S333 St John, Oliver, 1641
Yk.

S334 Saint Jure, Jean Baptiste,
1658[7]
Ely.

S335 Saint Jure, Jean Baptiste,
1684
Dur (imp).

S338A St Leger, *Sir* William, 1642
Dur. Ex.

S338A+ St Leger, *Sir* William, 1642
As S338A, but: '... Also, the votes of the Parliament ...'
Linc.

S342? St Lo, George, 1693
For W. Miller.
Cant.

S345 St Nicholas, John, 1678
Win.

S347+ Saint Paul, ? , *d.1684?*, 1682
'The kingdom of Sweden'; Formerly K581?; By M. Flesher for Joanna Brome.
Win.

S350 Saint, 1641
S Pl.

S353 Saint-Real, Caesar Vischard de, 1674
... Hen. Herringman and John Crump.
Carl.

S355? Saint-Real, Caesar Vischard de, 1676
Printed, and sold by William Cademan.
Cant.

S355+ Saint Real, Caesar Vischard de, 1676
The second impression; Sold by William Cademan; 8°.
Carl.

S362- Saints, 1648
Same work as S362?: STC suggests author was A. Fawkner or A. Farindon; The eight edition; Printed by R. Cotes for Richard Royston; 12°.
Cant.

S364+ Saints, 1641
See: CLC122.
Yk.

S371 Sales, *Sir* W., 1655
Lich.

S380 Salgado, James, 1679
Dur.

S386 Salisbury, Robert Cecil, *Earl of*, [1681]
Pt 2 of T1877.
Win.

S391 Sall, Andrew, 1680
... typis L. Lichfield, impensis Ric. Davis.
Carl. Win.

S393 Sall, Andrew, 1675
Carl.

S394+ Sall, Andrew, 1676
Printed at the Theater in Oxford; 12°.
Ban. Ches. Dur. Ely. Ex. S Pl. Win.

S395 Sall, Andrew, 1678
Carl. Dur. Linc. S Pl. Wel.

S402 Sallust, 1697
Swall.
Wor.

S403 Sallust, 1687
Cant.

S406 Sallust, 1679
Nor.

S418 Salmon, Thomas, 1688
Dur.

S422 Salmon, William, 1698
Cant.

S427 Salmon, William, 1688
Cant.

S432? Salmon, William, 1684
For Th. Dawks: also sold by T. Passinger.
Ban. Cant.

S434 Salmon, William, 1692
Cant.

S435 Salmon, William, 1687
Cant.

S438 Salmon, William, 1682
Yk.

S439+ Salmon, William, 1685
The third edition; For Thomas Dawks, Tho. Bassett, and Richard Chiswell; 8°.
Ban. Cant.

S440? Salmon, William, 1691
For T. Bassett ...
Cant.

S442 Salmon, William, 1688
Cant (imp).

S452 Salmon, William, 1693
Cant (2). Glo.

S456 Salmon, William, 1695
Cant.

S468 Salteren, George, 1641
Ex (2). Linc.

S478 Saltmarsh, John, 1646
Ex. Liv (imp).

S479 Saltmarsh, John, 1646
Yk.

S481 Saltmarsh, John, 1643
For Lawrence Blacklock.
Carl.

S489 Saltmarsh, John, 1646
Liv (tpw).

S490 Saltmarsh, John, 1647
Yk.

S493 Saltmarsh, John, 1645
Pet.

S495 Saltmarsh, John, 1646
Yk.

S496 Saltmarsh, John, 1646
Yk.

S502 Saltmarsh, John, 1644
Yk (2).

S507 Saltmarsh, John, 1648
Yk.

S517 Salusbury, Thomas, 1661
By William Leybourne.
Linc. Sal. Win.

S519 Salvianus, *Massiliensis*, 1700
Cant.

S520 Salvin, John, [1642]
Linc.

S535 Sammes, Aylett, 1676
Cant (2). Ely. Ex. Glo. Her. Linc. Nor. Pet. Win.

S537 Sammon, Edward, 1659
Linc.

S538 Sampford, H., 1642
Linc.

S539 Sampson, Latimer, 1642
'diurnall'
Dur. Linc.

S546 Samwaies, Peter, 1652
Carl. Ely. Ex.

S547 Samwaies, Richard, 1653
12°.
Carl. S Pl.

S550 Sancroft, William, [1688]
S Pl.

S553 Sancroft, William, [1666]
Cant. Yk.

S554 Sancroft, William, 1666
Cant (imp). Carl. Pet. S Asa. S Pl (2). Yk.

S555 Sancroft, William, 1652
Carl. Ex.

S558 Sancroft, William, 1654
For Tho. Dring.
Dur. Pet.

S561 Sancroft, William, 1694
Bassett.
Cant (2 − 1 imp). S Pl.

S564 Sancroft, William, 1689
Ban. Ely. S Asa. Wel.

S566 Sancroft, William, 1660
Bur. Cant (3). Carl. Ches. Chi. Ex. Llan. Nor. S Asa (2 − 1 imp). Wel. Yk (2).

S568 Sancroft, William, 1678
Cant. Carl. Her. Linc. Llan (2). Nor. Pet. S Asa. Sal. Wor.

S572 Sanders, Edward, 1642
Yk (2).

S580 Sanderson, Robert, 1670
Carl. Ex.

S581 Sanderson, Robert, 1688
Ely. Nor. Pet.

S582 Sanderson, Robert, 1647
8°.
Carl. Ches. Ely. Linc. Pet.
Swel. Yk (2 eds).

S583 Sanderson, Robert, 1661
Impr. as S582.
S Pl. Sal.

S584 Sanderson, Robert, 1670
Cant. Dur. Ex.

S585 Sanderson, Robert, 1676
Linc. Liv. Win.

S586 Sanderson, Robert, 1683
S Pl (2).

S587 Sanderson, Robert, 1686
Cant. Ches. Ely. Liv. Wel. Yk.

S588 Sanderson, Robert, 1696
Ban. Nor. Pet.

S589 Sanderson, Robert, 1655
Pet.

S590 Sanderson, Robert, 1660
Impr. as S591.
Carl. Linc. Pet. S Asa (imp).
S Pl. Sal. Swel. Yk.

S591 Sanderson, Robert, 1661
Chi. Her. S Pl. Sal.

S592 Sanderson, Robert, 1670
Cant. Dur.

S593? Sanderson, Robert, 1676
Typis J.M. impensis J. Martin.
Ex. Linc. Liv. Win.

S594 Sanderson, Robert, 1682
Ban. S Pl (2). Yk.

S595 Sanderson, Robert, 1686
Cant. Ches. Ely. Liv. Wel. Yk.

S596+ Sanderson, Robert, 1696
Typis M.C., prostant apud S. Smith
& B. Walford; 8°.
Nor.

S597 Sanderson, Robert, 1688
Bris. Ches. Ex. Pet (imp). Wel.
Yk.

S598+ Sanderson, Robert, 1674
For Henry Brome; 8°.
Ex. Liv. S Pl. Yk.

S599 Sanderson, Robert, 1661
Dur. Ely. Linc. Nor. S Asa.
Sal. Win. Yk.

S600 Sanderson, Robert, 1673
Carl. Ely. Ex. Liv. S Pl. Wel.
Yk.

S601 Sanderson, Robert, 1678
Bris.

S602 Sanderson, Robert, 1683
The third edition; ... in Oxford.
Ches.

S603 Sanderson, Robert, 1666
Carl.

S604 Sanderson, Robert, 1667
Addit. engr. tp dated 1666 *or* 1667.
Ely (1666). Linc (1666). Pet
(1667).

S605 Sanderson, Robert, 1657
Chelm. S Pl. Tru (imp)*.

S606? Sanderson, Robert, 1664
'XIV.'; 2°.
Ely.

S607 Sanderson, Robert, 1678
Pt of W667.
Ban. Carl. Dur. Linc (2). S Pl.
Win. Yk (3).

S608 Sanderson, Robert, 1648
Carl. Linc. Win. Yk.

S610 Sanderson, Robert, 1682
Ely. S Pl. Yk.

S611? Sanderson, Robert, 1689
Typis J.L., impensis L. Meredith.
Cant. Pet.

S612? Sanderson, Robert, 1657
... Leonardus Lichfield, impensis Ric.
& Nic. Davis.
Ex.

S613 Sanderson, Robert, 1664
... impensis Ric. & Nic. Davis.
Ches. Yk.

S615 Sanderson, Robert, 1680
Oxoniae, excudebat Leon. Lichfield,
impensis Ric. Davis; 8°.
Wel.

S618 Sanderson, Robert, 1678
Dur. Liv. S Pl (2). Win. Yk.

S619 Sanderson, Robert, 1685
Linc. S Pl. Yk (2).

S621 Sanderson, Robert, 1690
Ches.

S622 *See*: F9 & F10

S623 Sanderson, Robert, 1647
Dur. Linc. S Pl. Wel.

S625 Sanderson, Robert, 1647
Second ed. not on tp.
Carl. S Asa (2 − 1 tp imp).

S625+ Sanderson, Robert, 1647
As S623, but: Not in Madan, matches
Madan 1929, but 'Convocation, I.
Jun. 1647' on one line, and p. 23 has
'Haeretici'
Cant (imp).

S626 Sanderson, Robert, 1660
S Pl. Sal. Yk.

S627A Sanderson, Robert, 1649
Carl.

S628- Sanderson, Robert, 1648
For R. Royston; 8°.
Carl.

S628 Sanderson, Robert, 1653
... Andrew Crook.
Pet. Wor. Yk (2).

S630 Sanderson, Robert, 1660
Chelm. Ches. Ely. Rip.

S632 Sanderson, Robert, 1657
'XXXIIII sermons'
Her (tp imp). Linc.

S633 Sanderson, Robert, 1661
Carl.

S635 Sanderson, Robert, 1671
Ches (2 − 1 tp imp). Glo. Lich
(tpw).

S636 Sanderson, Robert, 1674
Ches. Dur. Ex. Her. Win.
Wor. Yk.

S637 Sanderson, Robert, 1681
Ban (2 − 1 imp). Bur. Ches.
Chi. Rip. S Asa. S Dv. Wel.
Yk.

S638 Sanderson, Robert, 1686
Ches. Her. Linc. Llan. Pet.

S639 Sanderson, Robert, 1689
For Joseph Hindmarsh.
Ban. Ex. Linc (2). S Asa. Swel.
Wel.

S640 Sanderson, Robert, 1656
2°.
Ely. Her. Lich. S Pl.

S641? Sanderson, Robert, 1660
The second impression; 2°.
Chelm.

S641A Sanderson, Robert, 1671
Ches (2). Glo. Lich.

S642 Sanderson, Robert, 1673
Ches*. Dur. Ex*. Her. Win*.
Wor. Yk.

S643 Sanderson, Robert, 1681
Ban (2 − 1 imp). Bur. Ches.
Chi. Rip. S Asa. S Dv. Wel.

S643+ Sanderson, Robert, 1668
See: CLC123.
Ely.

S644 Sanderson, *Sir* William, 1656
Tomlins.
Linc.

S645 Sanderson, *Sir* William, 1650
Yk.

S646 Sanderson, *Sir* William, 1658
Bur. Ely (imp?).

S647 Sanderson, *Sir* William, 1656
Carl. Dur. Linc.

S649 Sanderson, *Sir* William, 1658
4°.
Carl.

S651 Sandford, Francis, 1677
... by Tho. Newcomb for the author.
Cant. Dur. Nor. Win. Wor.
Yk (tp imp).

S651A Sandford, Francis, 1683
Her.

S652 Sandford, Francis, 1687
... by Thomas Newcomb.
Cant. Dur. Sal. Wor. Yk.

S664 Sandoval, Prudencio de, 1652
Pet.

S665 Sandoval, Prudencio de, 1655
Bur.

S666 Sandys, *Sir* Edwin, 1673
Ban. Cant. Dur. Lich. Liv.
Roch.

S667 Sandys, *Sir* Edwin, 1687
Yk.

S668 Sandys, *Col* Edwin, 1642
Dur. Linc.

S672 Sandys, George, 1684
Ely. Ex. S Dv. Yk (imp).

S674 Sandys, George, 1648
Cant (tpw)*. Yk.

S675 Sandys, George, 1676
Fourth ed. not on tp.
Nor. Wel.

S677 Sandys, George, 1652
Yk.

S678 Sandys, George, 1658
Ches.

S679 Sandys, George, 1670
For Rob. Clavel, Tho. Passinger,
Will. Cadman, Will. Whitwood, Tho.
Sawbridge and Will. Birch.
Ex. Her. Sal. Swel.

S680 Sandys, George, 1673
Ban. Cant. Lich.

S685 Sansom, Oliver, 1696
Dur.

S687-- Sanson, Nicolas, 1680
See: CLC124.
Linc.

S687- Sanson, Nicolas, 1696
See: CLC125.
Wor.

S692 *See*: B3779+

S693 Sarpi, Paolo, 1693
Wel.

S694 Sarpi, Paolo, 1693
Carl.

S696 Sarpi, Paolo, 1676
Bris. Bur. Ches (2). Chi. Ely.
Ex. Nor. S Asa. Sal. Tru. Win.
Yk.

S698 Sarpi, Paolo, 1693
Carl. Ely. Linc (2 − 1 imp).
S Asa. S Pl.

S701 Sarpi, Paolo, 1680
2°.
Ex.

S702? Sarson, Laurence, 1645
'1. Timoth. 1.15'
Ex. Linc. Wel.

S704 Sarson, Laurence, 1643
Pet.

S715 Satyr, [1685]
Linc.

S732 Sault, J., 1693
Author should be Richard Sault.
Cant.

S733B+ Sault, Richard, 1693
The fifth edition; For John Dunton;
12°.
Carl (tp imp).

S733C Sault, Richard, 1693
Printed for John Dunton; Wing has
wrong date.
Cant.

S736 Saumaise, Claude de, 1660
Carl. Ches. S Pl.

S742 Saunders, *Sir* Edmund, 1685
Carl.

S745 Saunders, *Sir* Edmund, 1680
Win.

S746 Saunders, Humphrey, 1655
Chelm.

S757? Saunders, Richard, 1682
For George Downes.
Carl.

S759 Savage, Henry, 1668
Ex. Sal. Wor.

S760 Savage, Henry, 1663
Carl. Win.

S761 Savage, Henry, 1653
Carl.

S762 Savage, Henry, 1660
'By H.S.'
Carl. Dur.

S767 Savage, John, 1690
Wel.

S770 Savage, John, 1683
S Pl.

S774 Savile, *Sir* Henry, 1658
Ban. Carl. Yk.

S783 Sawle, William, 1691
Cant. S Pl.

S785 Sawyer, *Sir* Robert, 1682
Carl.

S790 Say and Sele, William
Fiennes, *Viscount*, 1641
For Thomas Vnderhill.
Cant.

S792 Say and Sele, William
Fiennes, *Viscount*, 1642
Cant.

S793 Say and Sele, William
Fiennes, *Viscount*, 1642
Cant.

S795 Say and Sele, William
Fiennes, *Viscount*, 1641
Cant. Ex. Linc.

S796 Say and Sele, William
Fiennes, *Viscount*, 1641
Cant.

S797 Sayer, Joseph, 1673
Carl.

S799 Saywell, Samuel, 1696
Cant. Her. Pet. S Asa.

S800 Saywell, William, 1682
Cant (imp). Carl. Ex. Pet. Win.
Yk.

S800+ Saywell, William, 1682
By T.H. for Robert Scott; 8°.
Ex.

S802 Saywell, William, 1680
Carl. S Asa. Yk.

S803 Saywell, William, 1688
Ely. Ex. Nor. Win.

S805 Saywell, William, 1681
Win.

S811 Scamozzi, Vincenzo, 1687
The third edition.
Ex.

S816 Scandalum, 1682
Ex.

S817 Scandrett, Stephen, 1671
Chelm.

S818+ Scapula, Joannes, 1652
See: CLC126.
Cant. Ches. S Pl.

S820 Scarborough, *Sir* Charles, 1694/5
'Bibliotheca Scarburghiana ... eighth day of February 1694/5'; [London?], sold by Jos. Hindmarsh, James Partridge, and at the place of sale. Mrs Dickenson at Cambridge and Henry Clements at Oxford; 4°.
Cant.

S823 Scargill, Daniel, 1669
Cant. Ely. Linc. Pet. Yk.

S824 Scarisbrike, Edward, 1688
Cant.

S826 Scarlet, [1680]
Linc (imp).

S832 Scarron, Paul, 1677
Carl.

S839 Scattergood, Anthony, 1653
Carl. Linc. Pet. S Pl. Sal. Yk.

S842 Scattergood, Anthony, 1664
Cant. Carl. Pet. S Asa.

S843 Scattergood, Samuel, 1676
Ban. Dur.

S851 Scheffer, Johannes, 1674
... Amos Curtein.
Dur.

S851+ Scheffer, Johannes, 1674
Oxford, at the Theater; 2°.
Ex. Wor.

S852 Scheibler, Christoph, 1653
Forest.
Ely. Pet.

S853+ Scheibler, Christoph, 1665
Oxoniae, excudebat Hen. Hall, impensis Joh: Adams; 4°.
Sal.

S856 Scheibler, Christoph, 1671
... Henricus Hall, impensis Richardi Davis.
Nor.

S858 Scheiner, Christoph, 1652
Dur. Pet. Sal.

S858+ Scheiner, Christoph, 1652
Excudebat J. Flesher, prostant apud Cornelium Bee; 4°.
Bur. Glo.

S878 Schomberg, Ralph, 1683
Ex.

S881 Schonaeus, Cornelius, 1674
Pro Societate Bibliopolarum.
S Pl.

S891 Schott, Frans, 1660
Glo. Yk.

S893? Schrevelius, Cornelius, 1663
Quartâ editione; ... Joannes Field.
Her (imp).

S894 Schrevelius, Cornelius, 1668
Yk.

S895 Schrevelius, Cornelius, 1685
Nor.

S896? Schrevelius, Cornelius, 1699
Impensis A. & J. Churchill.
Linc.

S907A+ Schweitzer, Johann Heinrich, 1694
Typis J. Leake pro Edvardo Hall, apud Cantabrigienses bibliopola; 12°.
Nor.

S908 Scialitti, Moses, 1663
Linc. S Asa.

S910 Sclater, Edward, 1686
Bur. Cant. Ex. Swel. Wel.

S912 Sclater, Edward, 1681
Wor.

S913 Sclater, William, 1650
Pet.

S914 Sclater, William, 1653
Cant. Nor.

S915 Sclater, William, 1653
Ex.

S916 Sclater, William, 1654
'righteousnes'
Ex (2). Her.

S917- Sclater, William, 1651
Impr. as S917; 4°.
Linc.

S917 Sclater, William, 1652
Pet.

S918 Sclater, William, 1650
Chelm. Ex.

S919 Sclater, William, 1642
Ex.

S920 Sclater, William, 1642
Cant.

S921 Sclater, William, 1671
S Asa.

S924 Scobell, Henry, 1670
Chi. Dur. Ex. S Pl.

S925? Scobell, Henry, 1689
8°.
Ex.

S927 Scobell, Henry, 1680
4°.
Linc.

S942 Scot, Philip, 1650
Carl.

S962 Scotch, 1649
Pet.

S963 Scotch, 1647
Dur. Linc. Pet.

S970 Scotland. Commissioners, 1642[3]
'Ianuary the 15'
Linc. Pet.

S976A Scotland. Commissioners, [1641]
Linc.

S978 Scotland. Commissioners, 1641
Cant.

S981 Scotland. Commissioners, 1642
Linc.

S987 Scotland. Commissioners, 1649
Sal.

S991 Scotland. Commissioners, 1642
Dur. Linc.

S997? Scotland. Commissioners, 1643
... by Evan Tyler.
Pet.

S998 *See:* S1304

S1002 Scotland. Commissioners, 1642
Pet.

S1136 Scotland. Estates, 1643
Pet.

S1146 Scotland. Estates, 1650
Dur.

S1154 *See:* C4196B

S1180 Scotland. Estates, 1647
Dur (tp imp). Ex. Pet (2). Yk.

S1184? Scotland. Estates, 1641
'Arguments ... conformitie'
Linc. Yk*.

S1184+ Scotland. Estates, 1641
As S1184, but: 'conformity'
Sal (2).

S1187 Scotland. Estates, 1644
Pet. Sal.

S1208 Scotland. Estates, 1648
Yk.

S1213 Scotland. Estates, 1648
Yk.

S1221 Scotland. Estates, 1647
Yk.

S1225? Scotland. Estates, 1648
... Edenburgh ...
Ex (8p., imp?). Pet (15p.).

S1228 Scotland. Estates, 1648[9]
Dur (imp).

S1232 Scotland. Estates, 1641
Pet (imp)*.

S1233 Scotland. Estates, 1641
Linc.

S1247? Scotland. Estates, 1685
... by John Reid.
Wel.

S1248 Scotland. Estates, 1648
'declarations'
Cant. Pet.

S1252 Scotland. Estates, 1685–1701
10 pts, continuously paged & signed;
12°; Prob. includes other Wing nos.
Wel.

S1266? Scotland. Estates, 1682–83
... Iosua ...; 12°.
Wel.

S1280 *See*: C4231B

S1300? Scotland. Estates, 1646
'kingdome'
Pet (imp).

S1301 Scotland. Estates, 1646
Cant. Win.

S1303 Scotland. Estates, 1642
Linc (Wing E3659 printed on
verso).

S1304? Scotland. Estates, 1649
'kingdome'
Cant. Yk.

S1326 Scotland. Estates, 1648[9]
Yk.

S1328 Scotland. Estates, 1641
Yk.

S1330 Scotland. Estates, 1642
Cant. Linc.

S1343 Scotland. Estates, 1646
42p.
Pet.

S1344 Scotland. Estates, 1646
Second ed. not on tp; 30p.
Pet.

S1345 Scotland. Estates, 1646
48p.
Pet. Sal (imp).

S1346 Scotland. Estates, 1646
Linc (tp imp). S Asa.

S1347 Scotland. Estates, 1650
Cant.

S1347A? Scotland. Estates, [1680?]
'Parliaments'
Linc.

S1491? Scotland. Privy Council,
1643
... 29 Junii.
Sal.

S1595 Scotland. Privy Council,
1679
Reprinted at London according to the
original printed at Edinburgh, sold by
Andrew Forrester, Westminster;
obl.fol.
Linc.

S1615 Scotland. Privy Council,
[1679]
Edenburgh, by the heir of Andrew
Anderson 1679. And now re-printed
at London.
Linc.

S1719 Scotland. Privy Council,
1679
Linc.

S1726 Scotland. Privy Council,
[1681]
... Andrew Anderson ... reprinted at
London ...
Linc.

S1848 Scotland. Privy Council,
1679
Edinburgh, by the heir of Andrew
Anderson and now re-printed at
London.
Linc.

S1997 Scotland. Privy Council,
1643
Linc.

S2000 Scotland. Privy Council,
1642
Cant. Yk.

S2003 Scotland. Privy Council,
1678
Linc. Wel. Win.

S2004 Scotland. Privy Council,
[1642]
Dur (imp).

S2014 Scotlands, 1643
[Edinburgh, by Evan Tyler].
Dur.

S2022 Scots, 1644
Pet. Sal.

S2031 Scots, 1649
Cant.

S2034 Scott, Christopher, 1673
Bris.

S2039 Scott, John, 1683
Ex. Nor. S Pl.

S2041 Scott, John, 1683
No ed. statement; Impr. as S2040.
Nor. S Pl (2 – 1 tpw).

S2043 Scott, John, 1681
Carl. Rip.

S2044 Scott, John, 1683
Ban. Her.

S2045 Scott, John, 1684
Ban. Bur. Pet. Yk.

S2046 Scott, John, 1686
Chelm. Ex.

S2047+ Scott, John, 1690
Pt 1; The fifth edition; By J.M. for
Walter Kettilby; 8°.
Bur. Cant (imp). Wel.

S2049 Scott, John, 1700
8°.
Ches. Llan.

S2050 Scott, John, 1685
Ban. Carl. Pet.

S2051 Scott, John, 1686
Ches.

S2051+ Scott, John, 1690
The third edition; By M.C. for Walter
Kettilby; 8°.
Llan.

S2052- Scott, John, 1690
The third edition; By M.C. for Walter
Kettilby and Thomas Horne; 8°.
Ban. Bur. Cant. Wel.

S2052 Scott, John, 1695
By M.C. for Walter Kettilby and
Thomas Horne; 8°.
S Pl.

S2053- Scott, John, 1686
No ed. statement; For Walter Kettilby
and Thomas Horn; 8°.
Ban. Bur. Carl. Llan.

S2053 Scott, John, 1687
Wel.

S2054 Scott, John, 1692
For Walter Kettilby, and Thomas
Horn; Wing has wrong date.
Bur. Cant.

S2055 Scott, John, 1697
8°.
Ban.

S2055+ Scott, John, 1700
The fifth edition; For Walter Kettilby
and Thomas Horn; 8°.
Ches. Llan. S Pl.

S2056 Scott, John, 1696
Ban (tpw). Bur.

S2057 Scott, John, 1698
'Part III. Vol. IV'
Ban. S Pl.

S2059 Scott, John, 1699
Ban.

S2060+ Scott, John, 1700
The second edition; For S. Manship
and R. Wilkin; 12°.
Ches. S Pl.

S2061 Scott, John, 1697
Bur. Llan.

S2062 Scott, John, 1698
Bur. Llan.

S2065 Scott, John, 1673
Carl. Dur.

S2066 Scott, John, 1680
Ban. Cant. Wor.

S2067 Scott, John, 1684
Cant.

S2068 Scott, John, 1685
Her. Llan.

S2069 Scott, John, 1685
S Asa. S Pl. Wor.

S2070? Scott, John, 1686
'August'
Cant.

S2071 Scott, John, 1686
Ban. Cant.

S2072 Scott, John, 1688
Her.

S2073 Scott, John, 1689
Chelm. Wel. Yk.

S2074 Scott, John, 1689
Cant. Her. Nor. Sal.

S2076 Scott, John, 1692
S Pl. Sal (2).

S2078 Scott, Robert, 1674
Cant. Linc. Pet. S Pl. Wor.

S2080? Scott, Robert, [1688]
'Catalogus librorum Roberti Scott ...
ex variis Europae partibus ... decimo
tertio die Februarii 1687/8. ...';
[London], distributed by William
Nott, Mr. Holford, Mr. Willis, Mr.
Fox [etc.]; 4°.
Dur. Wor.

S2082 Scott, Thomas, 1647
Pet.

S2083 Scott, Thomas, 1659
For John Garfield.
Yk.

S2087 Scott, Thomas, [1642]
Pet.

S2096 Scottish, 1648
Sal.

S2101 Scougal, Henry, 1677
Carl. Pet (tpw)*.

S2102 Scougal, Henry, 1691
Ex. Her. Lich.

S2109 Scrinia, 1663
'... state & government ...'
S Asa. Yk.

S2110 Scrinia, 1654
Carl. Linc. Sal. Wel. Yk.

S2116 Scrivener, Matthew, 1672
Carl. Dur. Ex. Lich. Liv.
S Asa. S Pl (2). Sal. Win. Wor.

S2117 Scrivener, Matthew, 1674
Carl. Ex. Yk.

S2118 Scrivener, Matthew, 1688
Llan.

S2119 Scrivener, Matthew, 1685
Brown.
Ely.

S2122 Scroggs, *Sir* William, 1679
Linc. Win.

S2124 Scroggs, *Sir* William, 1676
Linc. Win (frag.).

S2126 Scroggs, *Sir* William, [1678]
Ches.

S2128 Scrupler's, 1691
Wel.

S2139 Scudder, Henry, 1644
Her. Yk.

S2140? Scudéry, George de, 1654
For Humphrey Moseley.
Cant. Carl. Nor. Wor.

S2144 Scudéry, Madeleine de,
1653 – 55
5v., including S2162.
Lich (vol. 5 tpw).

S2157? Scudéry, Madeleine de, 1683
For H. Rhodes; 12°.
Carl.

S2160 Scudéry, Madeleine de, 1652
Lich.

S2161 Scudéry, Madeleine de, 1674
Ex.

S2162 *See*: S2144

S2166+ Scupoli, Lorenzo, 1652
'The Christian pilgrim'; Formerly
C1218; Includes S2166++ &
S2166+++.
Carl. Yk.

S2166++ Scupoli, Lorenzo, 1652
'The spiritual conflict'; Formerly
C1219?; 12°.
Carl. Ely. Yk.

S2166+++ Scupoli, Lorenzo, 1651
'The spiritual conquest'; Formerly
C1220?; 12°.
Carl. Ely. Yk.

S2173 Seaman, Lazarus, 1676
Linc. S Pl.

S2174 Seaman, Lazarus, 1647
Chelm. Ex. Pet.

S2175 Seaman, Lazarus, 1650
Pet.

S2176 Seaman, Lazarus, 1647
Pet.

S2177 Seaman, Lazarus, 1644
Ex. Her. Pet. Yk.

S2179 Seaman, William, 1670
... Hen: Hall, prostant apud
Edvardum Millington.
Sal. Wor.

S2191 Seamans, 1642
Pet. Yk.

S2208 Seasonable, 1661
Carl.

S2215 Seasonable, 1649
4°.
Dur.

S2227+ Seasonable, 1676
See: CLC127.
Cant. Llan.

S2228 Seasonable, 1688
Wel (2).

S2230 Seasonable, 1659
Carl (tp imp).

S2235 Seasonable, 1647
Cant.

S2236 Seasonable, 1653
Pet.

S2245? Seasonable, 1657
... J. Briscot.
Pet.

S2246 Seasonable, 1678
Dur.

S2248 Seasonable, [1679]
Dur. Linc.

S2251 Seasonable, 1659
Ex.

S2253 Secker, William, 1660
S Asa.

S2257 Second, 1663
Carl.

S2264 Second, 1688
Ban. Ely. Pet. S Asa. Wel.

S2267 Second, [1693]
Cant.

S2273 Second, 1642
Glo. Yk (2).

S2281 Second, 1643
Linc.

S2284 Second, 1647
Yk.

S2286 Second, 1668
Win (imp).

S2287 Second, 1684
Wel.

S2292 Second, 1690
Cant.

S2293? Second, 1665
By W.G. and T.M.
Linc.

S2297 Second, 1694
Nor.

S2312 Second, 1670
Yk.

S2323 Second, 1642
Linc (imp).

S2359 Sedgwick, John, 1643
Ex.

S2362 Sedgwick, Joseph, 1653
Chelm. Pet.

S2364 Sedgwick, Obadiah, 1644
Without the misprint?
Ex. Her. Pet. Wor. Yk.

S2371 Sedgwick, Obadiah, 1654
Cant. Ex.

S2372 Sedgwick, Obadiah, 1642
Ex (2). Pet.

S2373 Sedgwick, Obadiah, 1657
Ex.

S2374 Sedgwick, Obadiah, 1643
Cant (2). Chelm. Ex.

S2375 Sedgwick, Obadiah, 1656[7]
Wor.

S2377 Sedgwick, Obadiah, 1647
Cant. Ex. Pet (2).

S2380 Sedgwick, Obadiah, 1658
Maxwell.
Ex.

S2383 Sedgwick, William, 1656
Ex. Pet (imp).

S2384 Sedgwick, William, 1649
Yk.

S2388 Sedgwick, William, [1643]
Ex.

S2392 Sedgwick, William, 1642
Ex.

S2393 Sedgwick, William, 1643
Ex. Pet.

S2411 Seekers, 1687
Wel.

S2415 Seidel, Caspar, 1653
... apud Andr. Crook.
Ex.

S2416 Seidel, Caspar, 1665
Ex (tpw).

S2417 Seignior, George, 1670
Carl.

S2418 Seignior, George, 1670
Cant. Pet. S Asa. Win.

S2420 Selden, John, 1671
Linc.

S2423 Selden, John, 1644
Dur. Wel. Win.

S2425 Selden, John, 1650
'liber primus'
Lich. S Dv. S Pl. Swel (tpw)*.
Win.

S2425+ Selden, John, 1653
'liber secundus'; Typis Jacobi Flesheri,
prostant apud Cornelium Bee; 4°.
Lich. S Pl.

S2426+ Selden, John, 1655
'liber tertius'; Typis Jacobi Flesheri,
prostant apud Cornelium Bee; 4°.
S Pl.

S2427 Selden, John, 1683
Wing has wrong date.
Cant. Ex (2). S Asa. Wel. Yk.

S2428 Selden, John, 1689
... sold by J. Robinson, R. Bentley,
Jacob Tonson, T. Godwin and T. Fox.
Ex.

S2428+ Selden, John, 1618 [i.e.
1680]
See: CLC128.
Carl. Linc. S Pl. Win.

S2431 Selden, John, 1663
S Asa (imp). Wor.

S2432 Selden, John, 1652
... to bee sold at the sign of the Ship
at the New-Exchange.
Cant. Glo. Lich. Nor (tp imp).
S Asa.

S2433 Selden, John, [1681?]
Linc. Win.

S2436 Selden, John, 1682
Cant. Ex (2). S Asa. Wel. Yk.

S2437 Selden, John, 1689
Wel.

S2439 Selden, John, 1661
Cant. Carl. Ex. Yk.

S2440 Selden, John, 1672
or Thomas Bassett.
Ches (Thomas Bassett). Nor
(John Leigh). Pet (John Leigh).

S2441 Selden, John, 1683
Ex (2 − 1 has some words on tp
pr. in red).

S2441+ Selden, John, 1683
As S2441, but title begins: 'Tracts: 1.
Jani Anglorum ...'
Yk.

S2441A Selden, John, 1683
Cant. Wel.

S2442 Selden, John, 1683
Cant. Ex (2). S Asa. Wel. Yk.

S2443 Selden, John, 1646
Ex. S Dv. Win. Wor. Yk.

S2444 Selden, John, 1653
Ban. Linc.

S2448 Seller, Abednigo, 1696
Wel.

S2449 Seller, Abednigo, 1690
Wel.

S2451 Seller, Abednigo, 1695
Yk.

S2453 Seller, Abednigo, 1689
Nor. Pet. Yk.

S2455 Seller, Abednigo, 1689
S Asa.

S2456 Seller, Abednigo, 1680 [i.e.
1690?]
Ex.

S2458 Seller, Abednigo, 1688
Ban. Ex. Wel.

S2459 Seller, Abednigo, 1689
Cant. Wel.

S2460 Seller, Abednigo, 1680
Ches. Dur. Ely. Ex.

S2461 Seller, Abednigo, 1686
Bur. Ex. Nor. S Pl. Swel. Wel.

S2472? Seller, John, 1671−75
... sold by the author, and by John
Wingfield; 3 pts.
Lich (lacks pt 3).

S2474- Seller, John, 1693
Printed, sold by John Taylor; 2°.
Carl.

S2482 Seller, John, 1672
Yk (table only, with S2482+).

S2482+ Seller, John, 1676
The third edition; 4°.
Yk (impr. not confirmed).

S2489 Selwood, Samuel, 1655
Sal.

S2490 Semmedo, Alvarez, 1655
Lich.

S2491 Semper, 1662
Bur. Linc.

S2499 Senault, Jean François, 1650
S Asa. Wor.

S2500 Senault, Jean François, 1650
Cant. S Asa.

S2501 See: C3684+

S2502 Senault, Jean François, 1648
Cant.

S2504 Senault, Jean François, 1649
Ban. Linc. Yk.

S2508 Seneca, 1648
Cant.

S2513 Seneca, 1648
Cant.

S2514 Seneca, 1678
Carl.

S2515 Seneca, 1682
Second ed. not on tp.
Cant (Lodon [*sic*]). Rip.

S2517+ Seneca, 1688
The fourth edition; By R.E. for R.
Bentley, J. Tonson and J. Hindmarsh;
8°.
Linc.

S2519 Seneca, 1693
Fifth edition.
Bur.

S2521 Seneca, 1699
Dur.

S2524A Seneca, 1675
Yk.

S2550 Sence, [1664]
Carl. Linc.

S2553 Sense, 1693
Dur.

S2559? Seppens, Robert, 1679
London, by M.C. for William Oliver
in Norwich.
Sal.

S2560 Seppens, Robert, 1664
Bur. Carl (pt 1 only). Pet.

S2566 Sergeant, John, 1667
Lovain.
Carl. Win.

S2569 Sergeant, John, 1688
Ex. Wel.

S2572 Sergeant, John, 1681
Linc.

S2573? Sergeant, John, 1679
'Loiola'; For Norman Nelson.
Ely. Linc.

S2573+ Sergeant, John, 1662
'The Jesuite's reasons ...'; Formerly
J725.
Carl.

S2575 Sergeant, John, 1666
Carl. Win.

S2577 Sergeant, John, 1687
4°.
Ban. Bur. Cant.

S2581 Sergeant, John, 1665
Yk.

S2585A Sergeant, John, 1678
S Pl.

S2587 Sergeant, John, 1672
Win.

S2588 *See*: C6901+

S2589 Sergeant, John, 1655
Carl. S Asa. Sal.

S2590 Sergeant, John, 1657
Carl.

S2592 Sergeant, John, 1687
Ban. Wel.

S2594 Sergeant, John, 1697
Ex.

S2595 Sergeant, John, 1665
Carl. Pet (imp). S Asa (imp).
Win.

S2597 Sergeant, John, 1687
Ban.

S2604 Serious, 1649
Cant. Dur. Ex (2). Pet. Yk.

S2607+ Serious, 1685
See: CLC129.
Sal.

S2624 Sermon, Edmund, 1679
Cant.

S2631? Sermon, 1653
By Will. Bentley for Thomas Heath.
S Pl.

S2633 Sermon, 1695
Ches. Wor.

S2638 Sermon, 1696
Cant.

S2646 Service, 1641
Carl. Yk.

S2653 Settle, Elkanah, 1682
Wel.

S2662 Settle, Elkanah, 1682
S Pl.

S2670 Settle, Elkanah, 1681
Ches. Linc.

S2700 Settle, Elkanah, 1683
Carl. Wel.

S2703 Settle, Elkanah, 1692
Yk.

S2711 Settle, Elkanah, 1684
Win.

S2715 Settle, Elkanah, 1683
Ely. Wel. Wor.

S2720 Settle, Elkanah, 1683
Wor (imp).

S2738 Seven, 1689
Pet.

S2743 Seventh, 1689
Pet. Wel.

S2744 Seventh, 1689
Pet. S Asa. Wel.

S2751 Several, 1660
Cant (2). Ches. Pet.

S2753 Several, 1689
Cant.

S2762A? Severall, 1647
'severall'; 4°.
Cant.

S2765 Severall, 1641
Yk.

S2766 Several, 1680
Linc. Nor. Win. Yk (imp).

S2767A Several, 1681
'... Simeon Wright'; Includes L321A
& P1541.
Yk (imp).

S2775 Severall, 1642
Ex. Yk.

S2784 Severall, 1642
Dur. Linc.

S2809 Several, 1659
Linc.

S2814 Severall, 1658
Dur (imp). S Pl. Yk.

S2818+ Sevill, William, 1694
See: CLC130.
Cant. Llan.

S2827 Seymour, Thomas, 1682
Bur. Her.

S2828 Seymour, Thomas, 1683
Ely. Yk.

S2870 Shadwell, Thomas, 1682
S Pl.

S2871 Shadwell, Thomas, 1682
S Pl.

S2873 Shadwell, Thomas, 1683
Carl. Win.

S2888+ Shafte, J., 1673
For the author, sold by Will. Crook;
12°.
Carl.

S2896 Shaftesbury, Anthony Ashley
Cooper, *Earl of*, 1675
Linc.

S2897 Shaftesbury, Anthony Ashley
Cooper, *Earl of*, 1675
Cant (tpw).

S2897A Shaftesbury, Anthony
Ashley Cooper, *Earl of*, [1679]
2°.
Linc.

S2898 Shaftesbury, Anthony Ashley
Cooper, *Earl of*, [1659]
Cant. Carl. Dur. Ex. S Pl
(imp). Wel.

S2900 Shaftesbury, Anthony Ashley
Cooper, *Earl of*, 1672[3]
Lich.

S2902 Shaftesbury, Anthony Ashley
Cooper, *Earl of*, 1681
Ches. Linc.

S2904 Shaftesbury, Anthony Ashley
Cooper, *Earl of*, 1672
Lich. Linc.

S2905 Shaftesbury, Anthony Ashley
Cooper, *Earl of*, 1673
Lich.

S2906 Shaftesbury, Anthony Ashley
Cooper, *Earl of*, 1675
Linc.

S2907 Shaftesbury, Anthony Ashley
Cooper, *Earl of*, 1675
Linc. Yk.

S2915 Shakespeare, William, 1685
Glo.

S2965A? Shannon, Francis Boyle,
Viscount, 1689
... sold by Thomas Salusbury.
Ely.

S2969 Sharp, James, 1657
'A true ...'
Ex.

S2970 Sharp, John, 1684
S Pl. Yk (2).

S2971 Sharp, John, 1684
Her.

S2972 Sharp, John, 1687
Ches. Nor. Yk (2).

S2973 Sharp, John, 1685
Her. S Pl (2). Yk.

S2974 Sharp, John, 1688
Ches. Nor. Yk (2).

S2976 Sharp, John, 1680
Carl. Dur. Llan. Yk (2 – 1 pt 1
only).

S2977 Sharp, John, 1700
Bur. Dur. Ex.

S2977+ Sharp, John, [169–]
See: CLC131.
Dur.

S2977A Sharp, John, [1694]
Yk (imp).

S2977A+ Sharp, John, [after 1700?]
Printed and sold by Hen. Hills; 8°;
Probably 18th cent.
S Asa.

S2979 Sharp, John, 1700
Yk.

S2980 Sharp, John, 1694
Cant.

S2981 Sharp, John, 1694
Ex. Nor. Sal. Yk.

S2982 Sharp, John, 1694
Her. S Pl.

S2983 Sharp, John, 1698
Dur.

S2984 Sharp, John, 1679
Bur (tpw). Cant (2). Carl. Dur.
Ex. Her (tpw). Sal. Wor. Yk
(3).

S2985 Sharp, John, 1680
Carl. Dur. Llan. Yk (2).

S2986 Sharp, John, 1680
Cant. Carl. Dur. Llan. Yk (2).

S2987 Sharp, John, 1680
Cant. Carl. Wor. Yk (2).

S2988 Sharp, John, 1685
Ban. Cant. Nor. S Pl. Yk (2).

S2989 Sharp, John, 1690
Cant. Sal. Yk (2).

S2990 Sharp, John, 1690
Wel. Yk.

S2991 Sharp, John, 1690
Yk (3 – 1 imp).

S2992 Sharp, John, 1691
Cant. Ex. Sal.

S2993 Sharp, John, 1691
Yk.

S2994 Sharp, John, 1691
Ely. Yk.

S2995 Sharp, John, 1691
Cant. Her. Nor. Pet. Wel. Yk.

S2996 Sharp, John, 1692
Cant. Carl. S Pl. Yk.

S2997 Sharp, John, 1692
Cant. S Asa. Yk (2).

S2998 Sharp, John, 1693
... for Walter Kettilby.
Carl. Her. Wel. Wor. Yk (2).

S2999 Sharp, John, 1700
Bris. Cant. Ex. S Asa (2). Wel.
Wor. Yk (2).

S3000 Sharp, John, 1700
S Asa. Yk (3 – 2 imp).

S3001 Sharp, John, 1676
Ban. Carl. Dur. Her. Llan.
Yk (3).

S3002 Sharp, John, 1691
Yk (2).

S3002+ Sharp, John, 1691
See: CLC132.
Yk.

S3003 Sharp, John, 1674
Carl. Yk (2 – both imp).

S3004 Sharp, John, 1691
Yk (2).

S3007 Sharp, Thomas, 1700
Yk (2).

S3009 Sharrock, Robert, 1673
Bur. Ches. Yk.

S3010 Sharrock, Robert, 1660
Carl. Win.

S3013 Sharrock, Robert, 1662
... impensis Thom. Robinson.
Win.

S3014? Sharrock, Robert, 1660
Oxoniae, typis Lichfieldianis, impensis
Tho. Robinson; 8°.
Carl. Sal.

S3015 Sharrock, Robert, 1682
Ex. S Pl.

S3015+ Sharrock, Robert, 1682
Prostant venales apud H. Dickinson,
& S. Simpson, bibliop. Cantab.; 8°.
Ely. Nor.

S3015++ Sharrock, Robert, 1682
As S3015, but: '... de finibus & officiis
secundum naturae jus'.
Sal. Yk.

S3015+++ Sharrock, Robert, 1682
Title as S3015++; Impr. as S3015+;
8°.
Pet. S Asa. Yk.

S3022 Shaw, John, *of Whalton*,
1685
Sal.

S3023+ Shaw, John, *of Whalton*,
1677
For H. Brome; 4°.
Cant. Dur (imp). S Pl. Yk.

S3024-- Shaw, John, *of York*, 1644
As S3024, but no ed. statement.
Yk.

S3024- Shaw, John, *of York*, 1644
The second impression; York, by Tho.
Broad; 4°.
S Pl.

S3025 Shaw, John, *of York*, 1644
The third impression.
Yk.

S3026 Shaw, John, *of York*, 1649
Yk.

S3027 Shaw, John, *of York*, 1643
Yk.

S3028 Shaw, John, *of York*, 1650
Yk.

S3029 Shaw, John, *of York*, 1658
Yk (2).

S3030 Shaw, John, *of York*, 1646
Linc. Yk.

S3031 Shaw, John, *of York*, 1644
Yk (2).

S3032 Shaw, Jonathan, 1659
4°.
Yk.

S3033 Shaw, Jonathan, 1652
Yk.

S3034+ Shaw, Samuel, 1694
See: CLC133.
Cant.

S3036+ Shaw, Samuel, 1679
See: CLC134.
Carl.

S3037 Shaw, Samuel, 1658
Yk.

S3039 Shaw, Samuel, 1669
Carl.

S3045? Shaw, Samuel, 1682
... Samuel Tidmarsh.
Carl.

S3048 Shaw, Samuel, 1668
Carl.

S3057 Sheeres, *Sir* Henry, 1680
Author and date misprinted in Wing;
'Tanger'
Linc.

S3060+ Sheering, R., [N.d.]
See: CLC135.
Yk.

S3066 Sheffield, John, *of Southwark*,
1659
'sinfulnesse'
Chelm.

S3067 Sheldon, Gilbert, 1670
Dur.

S3068 Sheldon, Gilbert, 1660
Cant. Carl.

S3069 Sheldon, Gilbert, 1660
Lich.

S3069A+ Sheldon, Gilbert, [1670?]
See: CLC136.
Linc.

S3098 Shelton, William, 1680
Carl.

S3100 Shelton, William, 1690
Her.

S3114 Shepard, Thomas, 1660
Bris.

S3115+ Shepard, Thomas, [N.d.]
See: CLC137.
Yk.

S3122 Shepard, Thomas, 1648
Cant (tpw).

S3123? Shepard, Thomas, 1650
The fifth edition; By Matthew
Simmons for John Sweeting.
Carl.

S3130 Shepard, Thomas, 1672
Yk.

S3131A+ Shepard, Thomas, [1692?]
Pt 2 has impr. as S3131A, but book
has 198p.; 12°.
Nor (tpw).

S3131A++ Shepard, Thomas,
[N.d.]
See: CLC138.
Yk.

S3134A Shepard, Thomas, 1650
... by Gedeon Lithgow.
Carl.

S3140 Shepard, Thomas, 1671
S Asa.

S3144 Shepard, Thomas, 1649
Lich.

S3145 Shepard, Thomas, 1650
Second ed. not on tp.
Ex.

S3148+ Shepard, Thomas, [N.d.]
See: CLC139.
Yk.

S3162 Sheppard, Samuel, 1646
Pet.

S3163 Sheppard, Samuel, 1646
Pet.

S3172 Sheppard, Samuel, 1646
Yk.

S3173 Sheppard, Simon, 1646
Ex.

S3182+ Sheppard, William, 1653
See: CLC140.
Dur.

S3184 Sheppard, William, 1656
'and' *not* '&'
Carl.

S3188 Sheppard, William, 1675
Cant. Wor. Yk.

S3194 Sheppard, William, 1659
12°.
Yk.

S3205 Sheppard, William, 1654
Cant. S Pl (imp).

S3206+ Sheppard, William, 1671
By J. Streater, one of the assigns of
R. & Edw. Atkyns; 12°.
Linc.

S3207 Sheppard, William, 1652
Chelm.

S3208+ Sheppard, William, 1671
'counsellor'; Printed for A. Crooke, J.
Place, T. Collins and T. Bassett; 2°.
Cant.

S3209C? Sheppard, William, 1654
'faithfull'
Dur.

S3210 Sheppard, William, 1658
Carl.

S3211 Sheppard, William, 1663
Carl.

S3212 Sheppard, William, 1669
Linc.

S3214 Sheppard, William, 1648
'assurances'; 4°.
Glo.

S3215? Sheppard, William, 1651
'common'; Impr. without printer, but
otherwise as S3214.
Cant.

S3215+ Sheppard, William, 1651
'comon' [*sic*]; For W. Lee, D.
Pakeman and Gabriel Bedell; 4°.
Ex.

S3218 Sheppard, William, 1652
Linc.

S3219 Sheppard, William, 1656
Carl.

S3221 Sheppey, Thomas, 1682
Sal.

S3225 Sheridan, Thomas, 1677
Chi.

S3226 Sheridan, Thomas, 1685
Glo.

S3227? Sheridan, Thomas, [1681]
'Decemebr [*sic*]'
Linc.

S3236 Sheringham, Robert, 1670
... Joann. Hayes ...
Dur. Ely. Ex. Linc. Nor. Pet.
Wel. Yk.

S3238 Sheringham, Robert, 1682
S Asa (imp). Yk (2).

S3239 Sheringham, Robert, 1645
Pet.

S3240 Sherley, William, 1662
Ex.

S3244A Sherlock, Richard, *Bp*,
1687
Ely.

S3244B Sherlock, Richard, *Bp*,
1699
Yk.

S3250+ Sherlock, Richard, *Bp*,
1664
The seventh edition; For R. Royston
[colophon:] By J. Flesher for R.
Royston; 8°.
Carl.

S3251 - Sherlock, Richard, *Bp*, 1672
The tenth edition; By E. Tyler and R. Holt, for Rich. Royston; 8°.
Linc.

S3251A + Sherlock, Richard, *Bp*, 1681
The fourteenth edition; For R. Royston; 8°.
Yk.

S3255 Sherlock, Richard, *Bp*, 1656[5]
Carl. Ex. Lich. Yk.

S3256 Sherlock, Richard, *Bp*, 1669
Bur. Carl. S Pl.

S3259 Sherlock, William, 1686
Bur. Ex (3). S Pl. Sal. Swel. Wel (2).

S3260? Sherlock, William, 1688
For John Amery and William Rogers.
Swel.

S3261 Sherlock, William, 1687
Ban. Bur. Ex. Sal. Wel.

S3262 Sherlock, William, 1677
Carl (imp). Linc. Swel. Win.

S3263 Sherlock, William, 1686
'accommodation'
Bur. Ex. Sal. Swel (2). Wel.

S3264 Sherlock, William, 1687
Ban. Bur. Cant. Sal.

S3264 + Sherlock, William, 1687
'An answer to three late pamphlets';
Formerly A3455.
Ex.

S3265 Sherlock, William, 1693
32p.
Wel.

S3265 + Sherlock, William, 1693
As S3265, but: 30p.
Carl.

S3266 Sherlock, William, 1687
Ban. Cant. Dur. Ex (2). Nor (2 − 1 imp). S Asa. Wel. Yk (2).

S3267 Sherlock, William, 1684
Ex. Win.

S3267 + Sherlock, William, 1684
For Finch. Gardiner, sold by Abel Swalle; 8°.
Carl.

S3268 Sherlock, William, 1690
Ches. S Asa.

S3269 Sherlock, William, 1691
Bur. Cant. Dur (imp). Lich. Llan (imp). Nor. Pet (imp). S Asa. Wel.

S3273 Sherlock, William, 1691
Glo. S Pl. Yk.

S3275 Sherlock, William, 1691
Carl.

S3276 Sherlock, William, 1691
Sal.

S3278 Sherlock, William, 1692
Cant. Carl. Ches. Wor.

S3279 Sherlock, William, 1692
Dur.

S3280 Sherlock, William, 1697
Ban. Cant. Ex. Nor. S Pl. Yk.

S3281 + Sherlock, William, 1675
By A.C. for Walter Kettilby; 8°.
Bur. Carl. Ches. Ely. Ex. Her. Wel. Win.

S3282 Sherlock, William, 1694
4°.
Carl (2). Her. S Asa. Wel.

S3283 Sherlock, William, 1694
Carl.

S3284 Sherlock, William, 1681
Carl. Ely. Ex. Her. S Pl. Win. Wor.

S3285? Sherlock, William, 1686
82p.
Carl. Chi. Dur. Ex (5). Nor. S Pl. Sal. Swel. Yk.

S3285 + Sherlock, William, 1686
As S3285, but: 98p.
Ban. Dur. S Asa. Wel.

S3285 + + Sherlock, William, 1686
As S3285, but: 84p.
Bur.

S3286 Sherlock, William, 1694
Ban. Cant. Carl. Ches. Dur. Ely. Her. S Pl.

S3287 Sherlock, William, 1694
Carl. Ex.

S3288 Sherlock, William, 1674
Ely.

S3289 Sherlock, William, 1674
Carl. Ely. Ex. New.

S3290 Sherlock, William, 1678
Bur. Ches.

S3291 Sherlock, William, 1688
Ban. Ex (3). Lich. S Pl. Sal. Wel.

S3292 Sherlock, William, 1685
4°.
Cant. Carl. Ex (3). Nor (2). S Pl. Sal. Swel. Wel.

S3293 Sherlock, William, 1686
Ban. Ex. S Pl.

S3294A + Sherlock, William, [1688]
'A letter from a clergy-man'; Formerly H308.
Bris. Cant. Carl. Dur. Pet (imp). S Pl (2).

S3295 Sherlock, William, 1692
Cant. Dur.

S3298 Sherlock, William, [1688?]
4°.
Yk.

S3300 Sherlock, William, 1683
S Pl.

S3303 Sherlock, William, 1696
Bris. Ex. Her. Wel. Yk.

S3304 Sherlock, William, 1697
Cant. S Pl. Yk.

S3305 Sherlock, William, 1689
Cant.

S3306 Sherlock, William, 1686
Ban. Bur. Cant (imp). Carl. Chi. Dur (imp). Ex (3). S Pl. Sal. Swel. Wel. Yk.

S3307 Sherlock, William, 1692
Ely. Glo. S Asa.

S3308 Sherlock, William, 1692
Ban. Bur.

S3309 Sherlock, William, 1693
Ban. Carl.

S3311 Sherlock, William, 1699
Cant. Dur.

S3314 Sherlock, William, 1690
Ely.

S3315 Sherlock, William, 1690
Dur. Yk.

S3316 Sherlock, William, 1691
Ches.

S3318 Sherlock, William, 1693
Ban.

S3321? Sherlock, William, 1699
For William Rogers.
Cant.

S3322 Sherlock, William, 1681
Ely. Llan. Win.

S3323 Sherlock, William, 1682
Ches.

S3324 Sherlock, William, 1700
Dur. Llan.

S3325 Sherlock, William, 1698
Ches. S Pl.

S3326 Sherlock, William, 1688
Ban. Carl. Dur. Ex (2). Her. Llan. S Asa. S Pl. Sal. Wel.

S3328 Sherlock, William, 1688
Yk.

S3329 Sherlock, William, 1688
Ex (2).

S3330 Sherlock, William, 1688
Carl. Nor. S Dv. Swel.

S3331 Sherlock, William, 1686
Ban. Bur. Ex. Sal. Wel.

S3332 Sherlock, William, 1683
S Pl.

S3333 Sherlock, William, 1685
Swalle.
Cant. Carl (2).

S3334 Sherlock, William, 1686
Dur (tp imp). Ex. Sal. Wel (2).
Yk.

S3334+ Sherlock, William, 1686
As S3334, but: … A. Swalle.
Ban. Chi. Ex (2). S Pl. Swel.

S3336 Sherlock, William, 1682/3
Cant. S Pl.

S3339 Sherlock, William, 1692
Dur. Pet (2).

S3342 Sherlock, William, 1688
Ban. Bris. Dur. Ex (3). Nor.
S Pl. Sal. Wel.

S3343 Sherlock, William, 1688
Carl. Ex. Llan. Nor. S Dv.

S3344? Sherlock, William, 1691
For W. Rogers.
Her. Swel. Yk.

S3345 Sherlock, William, 1685
Ban. Cant. Carl. Dur. S Pl.
Yk (2).

S3347 Sherlock, William, 1686
4°.
Carl. Chelm. Dur (imp). Her.

S3348 Sherlock, William, 1689
Ches. Wel.

S3349 Sherlock, William, 1691
Ches. New. S Asa. Wor.

S3350 Sherlock, William, 1692
Ban. Cant. Ches. S Asa (imp).
Sal. Wor.

S3352 Sherlock, William, 1692
Cant. Ches. Liv. Sal. Yk.

S3353 Sherlock, William, 1692
Cant. Sal. Wor. Yk.

S3354 Sherlock, William, 1692
Ches.

S3355 Sherlock, William, 1693
Cant (2). Carl. Ches. S Pl.

S3356? Sherlock, William, 1694
'preach'd'
Cant. Carl. Llan. Nor.

S3358 Sherlock, William, 1694
Ches. Wel. Wor.

S3359 Sherlock, William, 1694
Ban. Ely. S Asa.

S3360 Sherlock, William, 1694
Ches.

S3361? Sherlock, William, 1695
The fourth edition.
Cant.

S3362 Sherlock, William, 1699
S Asa. S Pl. Yk.

S3363 Sherlock, William, 1699
Cant. Dur. S Asa. S Pl.

S3364? Sherlock, William, 1700
'preach'd'; For William Rogers.
Ely.

S3365 Sherlock, William, 1687
Ban. Bur. Ex (2). Nor. Sal.
Wel. Yk (2).

S3366 Sherlock, William, 1683
Cant. Carl. Chi. Yk.

S3367 Sherlock, William, 1683
Liv. Yk.

S3368+ Sherlock, William, 1691
As S3368, but no bookseller.
S Pl.

S3369 Sherlock, William, 1685
Ban. Cant. S Pl.

S3369+ Sherlock, William, 1685
For J. Amery, and A. Swalle; 4°.
Carl. Yk.

S3370 Sherlock, William, 1688
Ban. Carl. Ex (2). Sal. Swel.
Wel. Yk.

S3371 Sherlock, William, 1697
Cant. Nor. S Pl.

S3372 Sherlock, William, 1688
Ban. Ex (2). Llan. Sal. Wel.
Win (imp).

S3374 Sherlock, William, 1687
Ban. Dur. Ex. Nor. Nor*.
Wel. Yk.

S3375 Sherlock, William, 1691
Bur. Ely. Lich. Linc. Llan.
Nor. S Asa. S Pl.

S3376 Sherlock, William, 1690
4°.
Ban. Cant. Ches. Ely. Ex.
S Alb. S Asa. S Pl. Wel. Yk.

S3378 Sherlock, William, 1694
Carl.

S3379 Sherlock, William, 1685
Carl. Ches. Dur. Ely. Wel.

S3384? Sherman, John, 1661
By W. Godbid for Richard Skelton
and Richard Head.
Pet.

S3385 Sherman, John, 1641
Pet.

S3386 Sherman, John, 1664
Carl. Her. Win.

S3387 Sherman, John, 1654
Carl.

S3391 Sherman, Thomas, 1680
Cant.

S3397? Sherwin, William, 1675
4°.
Yk.

S3398 Sherwin, William, 1672
Her (tp imp). Yk.

S3400 Sherwin, William, 1671
Her. Yk.

S3401 Sherwin, William, 1674
Her. Yk.

S3402 Sherwin, William, 1676
Win*. Yk*.

S3405 Sherwin, William, [1670?]
Her. Yk.

S3406 Sherwin, William, [1670?]
Her. Yk.

S3407 Sherwin, William, 1671
Her. Yk.

S3410 Sherwin, William, 1674
Her. Yk.

S3432 Shields, Alexander, 1692
Yk.

S3433 Shields, Alexander, 1699
Dur.

S3436 Shifts, 1684
Nor.

S3445 Shipton, Ursula, 1641
Cant.

S3470 Shirley, James, 1651
Wel.

S3486 Shirley, James, 1653
Carl.

S3505? Shirley, John, *fl. 1680 – 1702*,
1692
'An epitomy …'; The second edition;
By J. Millet …
Nor.

S3511+ Shirley, John, *fl. 1680 – 1702*,
1671
By A.M. for Edward Brewster; 4°.
Dur.

S3512 Shirley, John, *fl. 1680 – 1702*,
1681
Nor (tpw).

S3525 Shore, John, 1695
Ches. Wor.

S3528 Short, Richard, 1656
Yk.

S3535? Short, 1699
Second ed. not on tp.
Ex.

S3550 Short, 1679
Linc.

S3551 Short, 1667
S Pl.

S3561 Short, 1685
Carl. Wel.

S3565 Short, 1679[80]
Linc. Win.

S3571+ Short, 1676
See: CLC141.
Cant.

S3587 Short, [1642]
Dur.

S3591 Short, [1655]
Ex.

S3599? Short, 1643
The second edition; York, by Stephen
Bulkley.
Yk.

S3607 Short, 1676
Linc.

S3608- Short, [c.1690?]
See: CLC142.
Ex (impr. torn away).

S3610 Short, 1651
Pet (tpw)*.

S3625? Short, 1650
'Edinb. 22. July, 1650. Sess. 17. A
short ...'; 4°.
Ex.

S3626 Short, 1650
Cant. Ely. Ex.

S3635 Short, 1641
Carl. Linc.

S3637A Short, 1697
Nor.

S3650 Shower, *Sir* Bartholomew,
1698
Ex. Wel.

S3651 Shower, *Sir* Bartholomew,
1689
Chi.

S3652 Shower, *Sir* Bartholomew,
1697
Bris. Cant. Ex. Pet. Wel. Yk.

S3656 Shower, *Sir* Bartholomew,
1696
Carl. S Pl (imp).

S3660 Shower, *Sir* Bartholomew,
[1689?]
Dur.

S3663 Shower, John, 1688
Bur. Sal.

S3664? Shower, John, 1681
... Benjamen Alsop.
Cant. Chelm. Sal.

S3681 Shower, John, 1685
Sal.

S3684 Shower, John, 1692
Sal.

S3685 Shower, John, 1692
Sal.

S3690 Shower, John, 1682
Sal.

S3693 Shower, John, 1696
Cant.

S3700 Shrove-Tuesday, 1641[2]
Linc.

S3704 Shute, Christopher, 1662
Carl. Ex. Linc.

S3706 Shute, Giles, 1693
... to be sold by Randal Taylor.
Sal.

S3709 Shute, Giles, 1688
Cant. Wel.

S3711 Shute, Giles, 1688
Cant. Wel.

S3714 Shute, Josiah, 1644
Ex. Sal.

S3716 Shute, Josiah, 1649
Bur. Carl. Dur. Her. Sal.

S3718 Sibbald, James, 1658
Ex.

S3731 Sibbes, Richard, 1648
Sal. Win.

S3735 Sibbes, Richard, 1647
Carl.

S3737 Sibbes, Richard, 1656
Win.

S3738 Sibbes, Richard, 1655
Ex. Her. Sal. Win.

S3740 Sibbes, Richard, 1656
Win.

S3741 Sibbes, Richard, 1641
The second edition.
Ex.

S3742? Sibbes, Richard, 1650
... for John Saywell.
Carl. Sal. Yk.

S3743 Sibbes, Richard, 1658
Nor. Sal.

S3745 Sibbes, Richard, 1651
Cant.

S3756 *See*: C7431+

S3761 Sidney, Algernon, 1698
Cant. Ches. S Dv.

S3762 Sidney, Algernon, 1684
Ex.

S3766 Sidney, Algernon, 1683
'sheriffs'
Wel. Wor.

S3768 Sidney, *Sir* Philip, 1655
Nor.

S3770 Sidney, *Sir* Philip, 1674
Cant.

S3770A Sidway, John, 1681
Pet (2).

S3774 Sighs, 1654
Ex.

S3780 Sikes, George, 1662
Cant (imp).

S3781 Silhon, Jean de, 1658
Carl. Lich. Sal. Wor.

S3783 Silius Italicus, 1661
Ex. Linc. Win.

S3787 Sill, William, 1681
Cant. Carl. Dur.

S3788 Simeon, [1679]
Linc.

S3795 *See*: M2764

S3796 Simon, Richard, 1682
Ex (2).

S3796+ Simon, Richard, 1682
Printed, and sold by Walter Davis; 4°.
Carl. S Asa. Sal. Yk.

S3797 Simon, Richard, 1685
Ban. Ex. S Asa.

S3798 Simon, Richard, 1689
Dur. Ex (2). S Asa. Sal. Win.

S3799 Simon, Richard, 1692
Dur. Sal.

S3800 Simon, Richard, 1684
Bris. Ex. Lich. Linc. S Pl.

S3801 Simon, Richard, 1684
Cant (2). Carl. Pet. S Pl.

S3802 Simon, Richard, 1685
Ches. Dur (imp). Ely. Ex. Pet.
S Pl.

S3803? Simon, Richard, 1685
Edinburgi, typis Joannis Calderwood.
Cant. Ely. Ex. S Pl.

S3805- Simons, Joseph, 1663
As S3805, but: '... Pierce's sermon ...
Feb. 1. 1662'
Chelm. Yk.

S3805 Simons, Joseph, 1663
'... Feb. 1. 1663'
Carl. Nor.

S3809A Simpson, Christopher, 1667
Editio secunda.
Dur.

S3810 Simpson, Christopher, 1667
Second ed. not on tp; ... Henry
Brome.
Dur.

S3811 Simpson, Christopher, 1678
Ely. Glo.

S3820? Simpson, Richard, 1686
8°.
Carl.

S3823 Simpson, Sidrach, 1647
Pet.

S3825 Simpson, Sidrach, 1643
Cant (imp). S Asa.

S3826 Simpson, Sidrach, 1643
Yk.

S3829A? Simpson, Thomas, 1660
'desirable'
Win.

S3832 Simpson, William, *M.D.*,
1679
'Scarbrough-spaw'
Dur. Yk (2).

S3833 Simpson, William, *M.D.*,
1669
Yk (3).

S3834 Simpson, William, *M.D.*,
1670
Yk (3).

S3835 Simpson, William, *M.D.*,
1977 [*i.e.* 1677]
Cant. Dur.

S3840 Simpson, William, *M.D.*,
1675
8°.
Cant. Yk (3).

S3849? Simson, Edward, 1652
Oxoniae, excudebant L.L. & H.H.,
veneunt apud Tho. Robinson.
Cant. Carl. Dur. Ely. Ex. Glo.
Linc. S Asa. Wel. Wor. Yk.

S3850 Sin, 1664
Carl.

S3861 Sine, 1647
Pet.

S3876 Sir, 1682
Glo.

S3876+ Sir, 1682
The second edition; For R. Janeway;
2°.
Wor.

S3877A? Sir, 1659
'Sir Harry Vane's last speech for the
Committee of Safety ...'
Pet.

S3902A Sir, 1680
Linc.

S3914 Sixe, 1642
Linc. Yk.

S3919 Six, [1649]
Yk.

S3927? 1662. The last years
intelligencer, 1663
cap.
Pet.

S3929 Sixth, 1689
Pet. Wel.

S3930 Sixth, 1689
S Asa. Wel.

S3933 Skelton, Bernard, 1692
Cant. Sal.

S3945 Skinner, Robert, 1649
Chelm (date cropped?).

S3946 Skinner, Stephen, 1693
S Alb.

S3947 Skinner, Stephen, 1671
...& T. Sawbridge.
Bur. Cant. Carl. Dur. Ely. Ex.
Linc. S Pl. Swel. Wel. Win.
Wor. Yk.

S3948 Skinner, Thomas, 1676
Cant (imp). Ex. Linc. Pet.
S Asa. S Pl. Wor. Yk.

S3949 Skipp, Edmund, 1655
Pet.

S3964 Slater, Samuel, 1682
Her.

S3979 Slater, Samuel, 1679
Cant. Her.

S3981 Slatholm, William, 1657
Sal.

S3982 Slatius, Henricus, 1651
Carl. Linc. Nor. Sal.

S3983? Slatyer, William, 1643
8°.
Carl. Yk (tp imp).

S3989 Sleidan, John, 1689
Ban. Bris. Bur. Ches. Dur.
Ely. Ex. Her. Lich. Nor. S Pl.
Swel. Wel.

S4001 Smalridge, George, 1687
4°.
Ex (4). Lich. S Pl (2). Sal. Wel.
Yk.

S4003 Smalridge, George, 1687
4°.
Ex (4). Lich. Sal.

S4004+ Smallwood, Allan, 1668
As S4004, apart from date.
Yk (impr. not confirmed).

S4004++ Smallwood, Allan, 1656
See: CLC143.
Yk.

S4005 Smallwood, Allan, 1665
Carl. Yk.

S4006 Smalwood, George, 1661
Pet.

S4007- Smalwood, James, 1694
'A sermon ...'; For Jacob Tonson; 4°.
Nor.

S4007 Smalwood, James, 1695
'A sermon ...'
Cant. Nor.

S4008+ Smalwood, James, 1696
'A sermon preach'd ...'; Printed for
the author and sold by E. Whitlock;
4°.
Cant. Dur (imp).

S4009 Smalwood, James, 1699
Bur. Her. Llan. Wor.

S4013+ Smart, Peter, [1643?]
See: CLC144.
Dur.

S4014 Smart, Peter, [1643]
Dur.

S4017 Smet, Henrich, 1654
Cantabrigiae ...
Wel (imp).

S4019 Smet, Henrich, 1681
Ex.

S4020 Smiglecki, Martin, 1658
Excudebat ...; 4°.
Bur. Cant.

S4020+ Smiglecki, Martin, 1658
As S4020, but: ... H. Cripps ...
Dur. Sal.

S4021A? Smith, Benjamin, 1675
... for Thomas Parkhurst.
Her. Pet (tp imp).

S4023- Smith, Edward, 1689
For Sam. Crouch; 4°.
Wel. Wor.

S4027+ Smith, Francis, 1691
4°.
Wor.

S4031 Smith, Francis, 1672
Cant (imp).

S4035 Smith, George, 1645
Yk.

S4037 Smith, George, 1643
Yk.

S4046 Smith, Henry, 1675
Cant. IoM (tp imp). Sal.

S4048 Smith, Henry, 1673
Cant.

S4049 Smith, Henry, 1688
Cant. Her. Wel.

S4071 Smith, Humphry, *Quaker*,
1660
Yk.

S4079 Smith, Humphry, *Quaker*,
1660
Yk.

S4083 Smith, Humphry, *Quaker*,
1658
S Pl.

S4087 Smith, Humphry, *of
Dartmouth*, 1690
Llan.

S4091+ Smith, John, *of Badgworth*,
1651
See: CLC145.
Sal.

S4092 Smith, John, *Capt.*, 1670
Pet.

S4103 Smith, John, *Clockmaker*,
1695
Dur.

S4109 Smith, John, *of Colchester*,
1675
Chi. S Asa. S Pl. Win. Yk.

S4111? Smith, John, *of Colchester*,
1683
For Richard Chiswell.
Ban. Nor.

S4112 Smith, John, *of Colchester*,
1694
Second ed. not on tp; Johnston.
Ex.

S4113 Smith, John, *Dr*, 1656
Cant.

S4114 Smith, John, *Dr*, 1666
Carl. Linc. Nor.

S4117 Smith, John, *of Queen's
Camb.*, 1660
Cant. Chelm. Ely. Glo. Llan.
Rip. S Asa (2). Swel. Win.

S4118 Smith, John, *of Queen's
Camb.*, 1673
Ban. Carl. Chi. Her. Liv.

S4120 Smith, John, *of Sandwich*,
[1646]
Cant.

S4122 Smith, John, *of Snenton*,
1677
Yk (3).

S4127 Smith, John, *of Walworth*,
1679
Carl. Ely. Glo. Linc. Nor (2).
Win. Yk (imp).

S4128 Smith, John, *of Walworth*,
1681
Yk.

S4128A+ Smith, Lawrence, 1694
See: CLC146.
Carl.

S4132 Smith, Matthew, 1700
Yk.

S4142 Smith, Peter, 1644
Pet (2).

S4144 Smith, Philip, 1641
Cant.

S4145 Smith, Philip, 1641
Linc.

S4146? Smith, Philip, 1641
'A speech made ... in the Lower
House ... 29th. of December. 1641';
For Tho. Bankes.
Cant.

S4151? Smith, Richard, *Bp*, 1682
'... auctio habebitur Londini ... Maii
die 15. 1682. Per Richardum Chiswel.
... catalogues are distributed gratis by
... Ric. Chiswel, Christopher
Wilkinson, William Nott, Sam.
Tidmarsh and William Henshman'
Carl. S Pl.

S4152? Smith, Richard, *Bp*, 1655
12°.
Carl.

S4154 Smith, Richard, *Bp*, 1684
Lich. Pet.

S4157 Smith, Richard, *Bp*, 1645
Carl. Linc. Yk.

S4158- Smith, Richard, *Bp*, 1645
[N.pl.]; 8°.
Carl. Linc. Yk.

S4166 Smith, Samuel, 1658
Cant.

S4168 Smith, Samuel, 1682
S Dv (tp imp).

S4194 Smith, Samuel, *of Magdalen,
Oxford*, 1649
Yk.

S4195 Smith, Samuel, *of Magdalen,
Oxford*, 1656
... impensis Rich. Davis.
Roch. S Pl.

S4195+ Smith, Samuel, *of
Magdalen, Oxford*, 1667
Editio octava; Impr. as S4194; 12°.
Ches (tpw)*. Yk.

S4197 Smith, Samuel, *of Newgate*,
1679
Ely. Linc. Yk (tp imp).

S4201 Smith, Samuel, *of Newgate*,
1680
Wor.

S4207+ Smith, Sebastian, [1700?]
'The religious imposter'; Formerly
L3436.
Yk.

S4225 Smith, Thomas, *Divine*, 1659
'A gagg ...'
Ex (imp?).

S4226 Smith, Thomas, *Divine*, 1688
Ex. Sal. Wel.

S4227 Smith, Thomas, *Divine*, 1659
Pet.

S4230 Smith, Thomas, *Gunner*,
1647
Yk.

S4232 Smith, Thomas, *of Magdalen,
Oxford*, 1680
Ban (2). Carl. Chi. Ely. Ex (3).
Yk.

S4233 Smith, Thomas, *of Magdalen,
Oxford*, 1696
'Bibliothecae'
Cant. Chi (2). Dur. Ex. S Pl.
Wor. Yk.

S4234 Smith, Thomas, *of Magdalen,
Oxford*, 1699
Wel.

S4235 Smith, Thomas, *of Magdalen,
Oxford*, 1676
Oxonii, e Theatro Sheldoniano.
Ely. Linc. S Asa.

S4236 Smith, Thomas, *of Magdalen,
Oxford*, 1678
Cant. Ches. Ex. Liv. S Pl.
Win.

S4237 Smith, Thomas, *of Magdalen,
Oxford*, 1662
S Pl. Win.

S4239 Smith, Thomas, *of Magdalen,
Oxford*, 1675
Carl.

S4241 Smith, Thomas, *of Magdalen,
Oxford*, 1672
... Ric. Davis.
Carl. Sal. Yk.

S4242? Smith, Thomas, *of Magdalen, Oxford*, 1674
... impensis Ric. Davis.
Ches. Ely. Yk (imp).

S4244 Smith, Thomas, *of Magdalen, Oxford*, 1686
'Miscellanea'
Ban. Cant. Ely. Linc.

S4245 Smith, Thomas, *of Magdalen, Oxford*, 1690
'Miscellanea'
Ex. S Pl.

S4246 Smith, Thomas, *of Magdalen, Oxford*, 1678
Carl. Ely. Linc. Win.

S4247 Smith, Thomas, *of Magdalen, Oxford*, 1676
Dur.

S4248 Smith, Thomas, *of Magdalen, Oxford*, 1685
'August the 17th 1679'
Ex. Her.

S4249 Smith, Thomas, *of Magdalen, Oxford*, 1682
Yk.

S4250 Smith, Thomas, *of Magdalen, Oxford*, 1675
Carl. Wor.

S4251 Smith, Thomas, *of Magdalen, Oxford*, 1696
Cant. S Asa.

S4252 Smith, Thomas, *of Magdalen, Oxford*, 1668
S Pl.

S4254 Smith, Thomas, *of Magdalen, Oxford*, 1699
Bur. Cant. Sal.

S4279 Smith, William, *Prebendary*, 1696
Bur. Wor.

S4281 Smith, William, *Prebendary*, 1683
Carl. Nor.

S4282 Smith, William, *Prebendary*, 1680
Cant. Carl. Chi. Llan. Nor. Pet.

S4283? Smith, William, *Prebendary*, 1674
8°.
Carl.

S4284 Smith, William, *Prebendary*, 1677
Carl. Nor.

S4285 Smith, William, *Prebendary*, 1670
Carl. S Asa.

S4317 Smith, William, *Quaker*, 1660
Yk.

S4359 Smyth, Edward, 1698
Her.

S4361 Smyth, Zephaniah, 1648
Pet.

S4363 Smyth, Zephaniah, 1648
Pet.

S4370 Smythies, William, 1684
Wor.

S4372 Smythies, William, 1684
Liv.

S4373 Smythies, William, 1692
Wor.

S4373+ Smythies, William, 1692
The second impression; For J. Southby; 4°.
Sal.

S4374 Smythies, William, 1684
Carl.

S4375 Smythies, William, 1684
'rrplies' [*sic*]; The fourth edition.
Cant (For John Southhy [*sic*]).
S Pl.

S4380 Smythies, William, 1683
Carl (tp imp).

S4382 Snape, Andrew, 1683
Wor.

S4396 Snowden, Samuel, 1693
Nor.

S4400A Sober, 1681
Linc.

S4402 Sober, [1679]
Dur. Linc.

S4406 Sober, 1688
Cant. Wel (2).

S4409A+ Sober, 1680
'A sober discourse'; Formerly O350.
Ex. Wel.

S4410 Sober, [1659/60]
S Pl.

S4411? Sober, 1679
For Jonathan Robinson.
Bris.

S4417A Sober, (1682)
Linc.

S4438 Solemne, 1647
Yk.

S4441+ Solemne, 1643
As S4441; Aldis 1108.5.
Dur (imp).

S4446A? Solemne, 1643
For Edward Husbands ...
Ex.

S4452- Solemn, [1679]
'The solemn ... November ye. 17th. 1679'; Printed, and are to be sold at the Kings-Arms in the Poultrey, and at the Feathers in Lumbard-Street; brs.
Linc.

S4454- Solemn, [1697]
See: CLC147.
Dur.

S4471 Some, 1681
S Pl.

S4477A+ Some, 1683
[N.pl.], printed by N. Thompson for the author; 4°.
Yk.

S4480A Some, [1688]
Cant.

S4482 Some, 1657
Ex.

S4495 Some, [1642]
Linc.

S4496 Some, 1689
For Richard Chiswell.
Ban. Cant (2 − 1 imp).

S4498 Some, 1648[9]
Cant.

S4502A Some, [1679]
Dur. Linc.

S4506 Some, 1699
Wel.

S4506A+ Some, [1641?]
See: CLC148.
Dur.

S4514 Some, 1642
'occurrences'
Linc.

S4517 Some, [1654]
Dur.

S4526? Some, 1691
Printed and sold by the booksellers of London and Westminster.
Cant. Carl. Wel.

S4527 Some, 1642
Yk (2).

S4534? Some, 1689
... Randall Taylor.
Wel.

S4536 Some, 1699
S Pl.

S4537 Some, 1648
Pet.

S4540 Some, 1679
Carl. Linc. Win.

S4542 Some, 1681
Win.

S4546 Some, [1680]
Linc.

S4549? Some, [1680?]
p. 1 catchword: 'ment'
Linc.

S4549+ Some, [1680?]
As S4549, but p.1 catchword: 'VI.
That'
Dur. Linc.

S4551 Some, 1641[2]
Dur (cropped).

S4552 Some, 1642
Linc.

S4553 Some, [1642]
Linc.

S4559 Some, [1688]
Wel.

S4564? Some, [1654]
'quaeries'
Dur.

S4580? Some, 1688
... Richard Janeway.
Wel.

S4598 Some, 1695
Dur.

S4604 Some, 1697
S Pl.

S4610 Some, 1681
Yk.

S4614 Some, 1689
S Asa.

S4616 Some, 1680
For Randal Taylor.
Win.

S4638 Somers, John Somers, *Baron*,
[1680]
Ches. Linc.

S4642 Somers, John Somers, *Baron*,
1697
Nor (2). S Pl.

S4644? Somers, John Somers, *Baron*,
1682
For Benj. Alsop.
Carl.

S4647 Somerset, William Seymour,
Marquess of, 1642
Linc.

S4649 Somerset, William Seymour,
Marquess of, 1642
Dur. Linc.

S4662 Somner, William, 1669
4°.
Win.

S4663? Somner, William, 1659
Oxonii, excudebat Guliel. Hall, pro
authore; prostant Londini, apud
Danielem White.
Cant. Carl. Dur. Ex. Linc.
Nor. Wel. Wor.

S4666 Somner, William, 1694
'Portus'
Cant. Carl. Swel.

S4668 Somner, William, 1660
Carl. Dur.

S4669? Somner, William, 1693
Theater.
Cant (5 − 2 imp). Carl. Pet.
S Pl. Swel.

S4691 Sophocles, 1665
Pet (2nd tpw). S Asa.

S4692 Sophocles, [1668]
S Asa (details not known).

S4693 Sophocles, 1669
Bur.

S4694 Sophocles, 1669
... apud Jonam Hart.
Yk.

S4698 *See*: K545A

S4724 Sousa de Macedo, Antonio
de, 1643
Glo (tp imp).

S4727 Sousa de Macedo, Antonio
de, 1645
Linc. Wor.

S4730 South, Robert, 1693
Carl. S Pl. Wel.

S4731 South, Robert, 1693
Ban. S Asa. Swel. Yk.

S4733 South, Robert, 1660
Oxford, by A. & L. Lichfield, for ...
Cant (imp). Carl. Ex. Pet.
S Asa.

S4734? South, Robert, 1668
... George West.
Cant.

S4735? South, Robert, 1655
Oxonii, typis Leon: Lichfield, impensis
Tho. Robinson.
Carl.

S4736 South, Robert, 1667
Oxonii, typis W.H. ...
Ban.

S4738? South, Robert, 1663
... Tho. Robinson in Oxon.
Carl. Pet. S Pl (2). Win.

S4739 South, Robert, 1666
Carl. Wor.

S4740 South, Robert, 1665
Carl. Ex.

S4742 South, Robert, 1665
Yk.

S4743? South, Robert, 1679
... for Ric. Davis and Will. Nott.
Ban.

S4743+ South, Robert, [1693]
See: CLC149.
Wel.

S4744 South, Robert, 1695
Carl. Dur. S Asa. S Pl. Swel.
Wel.

S4745 South, Robert, 1692
Ban. Carl.

S4748- South, Robert, 1694
No ed. statement; Impr. as S4745; 8°.
Carl. Lich.

S4749 South, Robert, 1698
Carl.

S4752- Southcomb, Lewis, 1682
See: CLC150.
Carl.

S4762+ Southerne, Thomas, 1699
As S4762, but: ... A. Bettesworth.
Cant.

S4772 Southouse, Thomas, 1671
Cant.

S4775 Southworth, John, 1679
Linc.

S4777 Sovereign, 1680
Win.

S4780 Soveraignty, 1642
Linc.

S4782 Spademan, John, 1691
Sal.

S4784 Spademan, John, 1699
Nor.

S4788+ Spagnuoli, Baptista, 1672
Excudebat E.F. pro Societate
Stationariorum; 8°.
Sal.

S4798 Spanheim, Friedrich, 1646
Cant. Ex. Linc (tpw).

S4800 Spanheim, Friedrich, 1695
Yk.

S4801 Spanheim, Friedrich, 1676
Pet.

S4804 Spanish, 1678
Carl. Dur. Ely (tpw). Ex. Sal.
Wel.

S4806- Sparke, Edward, 1678
See: CLC151.
Dur (imp).

S4808 Sparke, Edward, 1660
'... scintilla-altaris. Being ...'
Cant. Her. Nor.

S4809 Sparke, Edward, 1663
Cant. Linc.

S4811 Sparke, Edward, 1673
Cant. Chi. Sal. Yk.

S4813 Sparke, Edward, 1682
Cant. Llan. Yk.

S4814 Sparke, Edward, 1700
Linc.

S4815 Sparke, Michael, 1643
Pet.

S4818C Sparke, Michael, 1692
8°.
Carl.

S4820 Sparke, Thomas, 1691
Wor.

S4822 Sparrow, Anthony, 1669
Ex.

S4823 Sparrow, Anthony, 1661
4°.
Bris. Cant. Ex. Linc. S Dv.
S Pl. Sal. Swar (imp). Wor. Yk.

S4824 Sparrow, Anthony, 1671
Cant. Ches. Ely. Ex (2). Linc.
Llan. Nor. S Asa. S Pl. Yk.

S4824+ Sparrow, Anthony, 1671
The second edition; For Joseph
Clarke; 4°.
Yk.

S4825 Sparrow, Anthony, 1675
Ban. Bris. Ches. Dur (imp).
Ex (imp). Her (2). Lich. Linc.
Pet. S Asa. S Pl (2 — 1 imp). Sal.
Wel.

S4826 Sparrow, Anthony, 1684
Ches. Ex. Glo. Linc. Liv (imp).
Llan. Wel.

S4828 Sparrow, Anthony, 1657
Second ed. not on tp.
Bur. Cant. Carl. Dur. Linc.
Liv. S Asa (imp). S Pl.

S4829 Sparrow, Anthony, 1661
Second ed. not on tp.
Cant. Sal.

S4830 Sparrow, Anthony, 1664
Yk.

S4831 Sparrow, Anthony, 1668
For T. Garthwait.
Chi. S Asa. Tru. Win.

S4832 Sparrow, Anthony, 1672
12°.
Cant. Chi. Ely. S Alb. Yk.

S4833 Sparrow, Anthony, 1676
Ex (tpw). Lich. Nor. Pet. Win.

S4834 Sparrow, Anthony, 1684
Linc. Tru.

S4843 Specimen, [1679]
Ches. Linc.

S4846 Specimen, [1692]
Wel.

S4861 Speech, 1679
Cant (2).

S4862 Speech, 1642
Pet.

S4868 Speech, [1661]
Yk.

S4872 Speech, 1668
Ex.

S4874A Speeches, 1660
Yk.

S4875 Speeches, 1660
Bur.

S4880 Speed, John, *1552?—1629*,
1650
'Britaine'; The third edition.
Pet (imp). S Pl.

S4886 Speed, John, *1552?—1629*,
1676
Dur. Ely. Roch.

S4892 Speed, Robert, 1658
Pet.

S4906 Speed, Thomas, 1691
Yk.

S4914+ Speke, Hugh, [1688?]
See: CLC152.
Ban. Nor.

S4915 Spelman, Clement, 1648
Yk.

S4916 Spelman, Clement, 1647
Dur.

S4917 Spelman, *Sir* Henry, 1646
'apology'
Cant. Carl (2). Ex. Linc. Nor
(tpw). S Pl. Yk.

S4919 Spelman, *Sir* Henry, 1654
Yk.

S4920 Spelman, *Sir* Henry, 1664
Carl. Dur. Ex. IoM. Linc. Liv.
Wel. Win.

S4921 Spelman, *Sir* Henry, 1646
Cant. Carl. Ex. Linc. Nor.
S Asa.

S4923 Spelman, *Sir* Henry, 1676
Cant. Ex. Yk.

S4924 Spelman, *Sir* Henry, 1641
Ex. Linc. Yk.

S4925 Spelman, *Sir* Henry, 1664
Second ed. not on tp.
Ban. Cant. Carl. Chi. Dur.
Ely. Lich. Linc. Nor. S Asa.
S Pl. Wel. Win. Yk.

S4926 Spelman, *Sir* Henry, 1687
Cant. Chi. Ex. Liv. Sal. Swel.
Wor. Yk.

S4927 Spelman, *Sir* Henry, 1698
Dur. Ex. Swel. Yk.

S4928 Spelman, *Sir* Henry, 1647
By M.F. ...
Cant. Carl. Ex (includes tp &
dedication of S4931). Linc. S Pl.
Yk.

S4930 Spelman, *Sir* Henry, 1698
'Spelmannianae'
Chi (2 — 1 with addit. tp with
shorter impr.). Dur. Liv. S Pl
(2). Wel. Yk.

S4931 Spelman, *Sir* Henry, [1646]
Carl. Nor.

S4932 Spelman, *Sir* Henry, 1656
Cant. Linc. S Pl. Sal.

S4933 Spelman, *Sir* Henry, 1678
Nor.

S4933+ Spelman, *Sir* Henry, 1678
As S4933, but: By T.H. for Robert
Pawlett.
Liv. S Pl.

S4934 Spelman, *Sir* John, 1678
Cant. Dur. Glo. Lich. Linc.
Rip. Roch. S Pl. Sal. Swel.
Wel. Wor.

S4935 Spelman, *Sir* John, 1643[4]
Dur. Linc (imp). Yk (imp).

S4936 Spelman, *Sir* John, 1643[4]
Cant. Sal.

S4937 Spelman, *Sir* John, 1642[3]
Carl.

S4938 Spelman, *Sir* John, 1642[3]
Linc. Pet. Yk.

S4939 Spelman, *Sir* John, 1642
Carl. Linc. Pet. S Asa. Yk.

S4941 Spelman, *Sir* John, 1642[3]
London counterfeit (Madan).
Cant. Linc. Pet.

S4943 Spencer, Benjamin, 1642
S Pl.

S4944 Spencer, Benjamin, 1659
Cant.

S4946 Spencer, John, *Dean*, 1685
Bris. Cant. Chelm. Ches. Ex.
Her. Lich. Pet. S Dv. S Pl.
Swel. Wel. Wor. Yk.

S4948 Spencer, John, *Dean*, 1665
... in Cambridge.
Cant. Carl. Ely. Lich. Linc.
Nor. Pet. S Pl. Win.

S4949 Spencer, John, *Dean*, 1665
Cant. Carl. Ely. Lich. Linc.
Nor. Pet. S Pl. Win.

S4950? Spencer, John, *Dean*, 1669
'Thummim'; ... Timoth. Garthwait.
Carl. Win.

S4951 Spencer, John, *Dean*, 1670
Second ed. not on tp.
S Pl.

S4952 Spencer, John, *Dean*, 1660
Nor. Pet.

S4959 Spencer, John, *Librarian*, 1650
'Londinenses'; Leybourni; 4°.
Carl. Linc. S Pl. Sal. Wor.

S4960 Spencer, John, *Librarian*, 1658
Ex. Lich (imp). S Asa.

S4965 Spenser, Edmund, 1679
Lich. Liv. Win. Yk.

S4969+ Spencer, John, 1658
'Schisme unmask't'; Formerly G2237.
Ches. Ely. S Pl.

S4971 Sphinx, 1683
Cant.

S4978 Spinckes, Nathaniel, 1696
Llan. S Pl.

S4982 Spinkes, Richard, 1643
Cant. Ex.

S4983 Spinola, George, 1642
Linc.

S4991A Spirit, 1689
Printed and sold by ...
S Pl.

S5009 Spittlehouse, John, 1653
Linc (tpw).

S5017 Spon, Jacob, 1687
For Bernard White.
Dur. S Asa. Wel.

S5021 Spottiswoode, John, 1677
Bur. Cant (2 − 1 imp). Ely.
Nor. Roch. Wel. Yk.

S5022 Spottiswoode, John, 1655
Carl. Chelm. Ex. Lich. Win.
Wor.

S5024? Spottiswoode, John, 1668
By R. Norton for R. Royston.
Cant. Chi (imp). Dur. Linc.
Pet (imp). S Pl (imp). Swel (imp).

S5026 Sprackling, Robert, 1665
Pet.

S5029 Sprat, Thomas, 1685
Carl. Pet. S Asa. S Pl. Win.
Yk.

S5029+ Sprat, Thomas, 1685
In the Savoy, by Thomas Newcomb;
2°.
Dur. Nor. Wel.

S5031 Sprat, Thomas, 1696
Cant. Dur (2). Her. Roch.

S5032 Sprat, Thomas, 1667
Dur. Ely. Ex. Linc. Pet. S Pl.
Wel. Win.

S5033 Sprat, Thomas, 1688[9]
Cant. Carl. Pet (imp). Roch.
Wel.

S5035 Sprat, Thomas, 1665
... James Allestry.
Carl. Ex. Linc. Wel.

S5041 Sprat, Thomas, 1667
Ban.

S5043 Sprat, Thomas, 1683
8°.
Yk.

S5046 Sprat, Thomas, 1692
Carl. Roch. Wel.

S5047 Sprat, Thomas, 1693
Yk.

S5049 Sprat, Thomas, 1689
Wel.

S5050 Sprat, Thomas, 1689
Roch.

S5051 Sprat, Thomas, 1693
Carl. Roch. Wel.

S5052 Sprat, Thomas, 1677
Carl. Chi (2). S Pl. Wor.

S5053? Sprat, Thomas, 1678
By Tho. Newcomb for ...
Ex.

S5054 Sprat, Thomas, 1678
Ban. Her.

S5055 Sprat, Thomas, 1678
Cant.

S5055+ Sprat, Thomas, 1678
As S5055, but: ... Henry Brome.
Carl. Chi (2 − 1 tpw*). Dur.
Her (2). Wel. Wor. Yk.

S5056 Sprat, Thomas, 1678
Ban. Cant. Carl. Her.

S5057? Sprat, Thomas, 1682
42p.
Ches.

S5057+ Sprat, Thomas, 1682
As S5057, but: 36p.
Llan.

S5058 Sprat, Thomas, 1682
Carl. Nor. S Pl.

S5059 Sprat, Thomas, 1682
Pet. Yk.

S5061 Sprat, Thomas, 1690
Cant (imp?). Carl. Wel.

S5062 Sprat, Thomas, 1693
Ches. Her.

S5063 Sprat, Thomas, 1694
Cant. Ches.

S5064 Sprat, Thomas, 1697
Nor. Pet.

S5066 Sprat, Thomas, 1685
Dur. Nor. Wel.

S5067 Sprat, Thomas, 1685
Carl. Pet. S Asa. S Pl. Win.
Yk.

S5070 Sprigg, Joshua, 1647
Dur. Glo. Yk (imp).

S5072 Sprigg, Joshua, 1649
Cant.

S5085? Sprint, John, 1694
For Jonathan Robinson.
Sal.

S5091 Spurstowe, William, 1662
Her.

S5092 Spurstowe, William, 1656
Yk.

S5093 Spurstowe, William, 1644
Cant. Her. Sal.

S5094 Spurstowe, William, 1643
Carl. Pet (2).

S5095 Spurstowe, William, 1654
S Pl. Yk.

S5099? Spurstowe, William, 1668
By E.T. for Simon Miller.
Carl. Linc. Pet.

S5100+ Spurstowe, William, 1659
The second edition; By E.M. for
Ralph Smith; 8°.
Carl.

S5101 Squire, John, 1641
Linc.

S5101A Squire, William, 1674
Carl. Yk.

S5102 Squire, William, 1670
Carl. S Pl. Yk.

S5111 Stafford, Richard, 1690
Wel.

S5112+ Stafford, Richard, [1694?]
See: CLC153.
Wel.

S5119+ Stafford, Richard, 1700
See: CLC154.
Cant.

S5134 Stafford, Richard, [1690]
Wel.

S5144 Stafford, Richard, 1691
Wel.

S5145 Stafford, Richard, [1692]
Wel.

S5149 Stafford, Richard, 1691
Wel.

S5150 Stafford, Richard, [1692]
Wel.

S5151 Stafford, William, 1645
Ex. Yk.

S5157 Stafford, William Howard,
Viscount, [1680]
Linc.

S5159 - Stafford, William Howard,
Viscount, 1680
'The two ...'; 12°.
Yk.

S5164 Stahl, Daniel, 1651
Carl. Ely. Wel.

S5165 Stahl, Daniel, 1651
Wel.

S5166 Stahl, Daniel, 1658
Dur. Ex. Pet. S Asa.

S5167 Stahl, Daniel, 1663
Oxoniae, impensis J. Webb.
Her. Yk.

S5168 Stahl, Daniel, 1672
Nor.

S5170 Stainforth, William, 1685
Dur. Yk (5).

S5171 Stainforth, William, 1686
Dur. Yk.

S5172 Stainforth, William, 1676
Wor. Yk.

S5173 Stainforth, William, 1689
Wel. Yk (2).

S5194 Stampe, William, 1643
Carl. Wel.

S5196? Stampe, William, 1650
... Samuel Broun.
Linc.

S5197 Stampe, William, [1653]
Carl.

S5204 Standfast, Richard, 1660
Pet.

S5213? Standfast, Richard, 1676
Bristol.
Carl (imp).

S5215 Standish, John, 1676
Her. S Asa.

S5216 Standish, John, 1676
Carl.

S5217 Standish, John, [1683]
Cant. Ex. Wor.

S5218 Standish, John, 1684
Yk (imp).

S5219 Standish, John, 1683
Sal. Wor.

S5222 Stanhope, George, 1698
Cant. Her. Nor. S Asa.

S5223 Stanhope, George, 1699
Cant. Her.

S5225 Stanhope, George, 1695
Cant. Ches. Ely. Her.

S5226 Stanhope, George, 1697
Cant. Carl. Dur (imp). Nor.
S Asa.

S5227 Stanhope, George, 1699
Her. Nor. Wor.

S5228 Stanhope, George, 1695
Ban. Ely.

S5230 Stanhope, George, 1693
S Dv.

S5232 Stanhope, George, 1698
Carl. Dur. Her (2). S Asa.
S Pl. Wor.

S5233 Stanhope, George, 1700
Ely.

S5233 + Stanhope, Thomas, 1670
See: CLC155.
Carl.

S5234 - Stanley, Edward, 1662
See: CLC156.
Win.

S5234? Stanley, Francis, [1655]
8°.
Linc.

S5235 Stanley, Francis, 1696
Ex.

S5237 Stanley, Thomas, 1655
Vol. 1.
Cant.

S5238 Stanley, Thomas, 1656
Vol. 1.
S Pl.

S5238 + Stanley, Thomas, 1656
Vol. 2; As S5238.
Cant. Pet.

S5238A? Stanley, Thomas, 1660
Vol. 3.
Pet. S Pl.

S5239 Stanley, Thomas, 1687
Ely. Ex. S Alb. Wor.

S5240 Stanley, Thomas, 1662
S Pl.

S5244 Stanley, William, 1685
Ban. Carl. Ex (3). Nor. Pet.
S Pl (2). Sal. Swel. Wel.

S5247 Stanley, William, 1688
Bur (tpw)*. Nor. Yk.

S5249 Stanley, William, 1692
Cant.

S5252 Stanwix, Richard, 1652
8°.
Pet.

S5257 Stapleton, *Sir* Philip, 1642
Yk.

S5258 Stapleton, *Sir* Philip, 1641[2]
Cant.

S5260 Stapylton, *Sir* Robert, 1663
Yk.

S5293 Starkey, William, 1675
Carl. Dur. S Pl. Yk.

S5294 Starkey, William, 1668
Pet (2).

S5296 Starling, Samuel, 1671
Linc.

S5301 State, 1688
Ex.

S5324 State, 1642
Yk (misprint corrected).

S5325 State, 1642
Ex.

S5327 State-Proteus, 1690
Dur (imp).

S5329 State, 1689
S Asa. Sal. Wel.

S5330 State, 1693
Ban. Cant. Chi.

S5331 State, 1692
Ban. Cant. Wel.

S5332 State-tracts, 1693
Includes S5330 & S5331.
Cant.

S5336 Statius, 1651
Ban. Dur. Ely. Nor. S Pl. Sal.

S5341 Staunton, Edmund, 1645
Pet.

S5342 Staunton, Edmund, 1644
Yk.

S5345 Staveley, Ambrose, 1655
Pet.

S5346 Staveley, Thomas, 1674
Chi. Yk.

S5353 Staynoe, Thomas, 1700
Bur. Ely. Wel.

S5355 Staynoe, Thomas, 1699
Her.

S5356 Staynoe, Thomas, 1686
Cant. Her.

S5363 Stearne, John, *D.D.*, 1700
Ely. Glo. Yk.

S5366 Stearne, John, *M.D.*, 1658
Carl.

S5372? Stearne, John, *M.D.*, 1672
'posthumum'; ... Joseph. Wilde; 8°.
Ches. Nor.

S5373 Stearne, John, *M.D.*, 1659
Carl.

S5382 Steele, Richard, 1667
Bur.

S5384 Steele, Richard, 1673
Ex.

S5387 Steele, Richard, 1668
S Asa.

S5394 Steele, Richard, 1684
Ban.

S5395 Steele, William, 1649
Cant.

S5396A Steele, William, 1653[4]
Dur.

S5409 Steno, Nicolaus, 1671
Ex.

S5415 Stephens, Edward, 1691
Pet.

S5422 Stephens, Edward, 1691
Carl.

S5425+ Stephens, Edward, [1696?]
See: CLC157.
Ex.

S5427 Stephens, Edward, 1689
Wel.

S5430 Stephens, Edward, 1675
Cant. Linc. Win.

S5434 Stephens, Edward, 1690
Cant.

S5435+ Stephens, Edward, [1695?]
See: CLC158.
Ex.

S5436 Stephens, Edward, 1700
S Asa.

S5437 Stephens, Edward, 1689
Nor.

S5438 Stephens, Edward, 1687
Bris.

S5439 Stephens, Edward, [1700?]
Cant.

S5442 Stephens, Edward, [1689]
Bris.

S5444 Stephens, Edward, 1697
S Pl.

S5445 Stephens, Edward, 1689
Bris.

S5446 Stephens, Jeremiah, 1660
Carl. Ex. Pet (imp; possibly
S5447). Sal.

S5448 Stephens, John, 1661
Carl. Ex. Lich. S Pl. Yk.

S5449 Stephens, John, 1661
Dur. Linc.

S5450? Stephens, Nathaniel, 1656
Keynton.
Sal.

S5451 Stephens, Nathaniel, 1651
Dur.

S5456 Stephens, Thomas, 1661
Ely.

S5459 Stephens, William, 1696
Her. Sal.

S5460- Stephens, William, 1698
'A letter humbly addrest'; Formerly
L1551.
Cant. Wel.

S5461? Stephens, William, 1699
... and sold by A. Baldwin.
Cant.

S5462 Stephens, William, 1694
Cant. Wor.

S5463? Stephens, William, 1700
4°.
Her. Pet.

S5464+ Stephens, William, 1700
Sold by A. Baldwin; 4°.
Wor.

S5465 Stephens, William, 1696
Cant. Llan. Sal. Wor.

S5466 Stephenson, Marmaduke,
1660
Yk.

S5468 Stepney, George, 1695
Sal (tpw).

S5473 Sterne, Richard, 1649
Carl.

S5474 Sterne, Richard, 1685
Dur. Ex. S Asa. Yk.

S5475 Sterry, Peter, 1648
Chelm.

S5476 Sterry, Peter, 1650
'commings'
Pet.

S5477? Sterry, Peter, 1675
For John Starkey.
Her.

S5478 Sterry, Peter, 1652[1]
Chelm. Ex. Yk.

S5491 Steuart, Adam, 1644
Cant. Win.

S5493 Steuart, Adam, 1644
Sal. Win.

S5494 Steuart, Adam, 1645
Cant (imp). Pet. Yk.

S5499 Stevens, Joseph, 1697
Ely.

S5500 Stevenson, Matthew, 1661
Linc.

S5516 Steward, Richard, 1647
Cant. Carl. Linc. Liv. Nor.
S Asa.

S5517 Steward, Richard, 1688
Ex.

S5518 Steward, Richard, 1657
S Pl.

S5518+ Steward, Richard, 1661
'Catholick divinity'; The second
edition; For H.M., sold by Samuel
Speed; 8°.
Pet.

S5520 Steward, Richard, 1659
Pet (2 — both imp). S Asa. Win.

S5521 Steward, Richard, 1687
S Pl (2). Wor.

S5524 Steward, Richard, 1682
Dur (imp). Yk.

S5526 Steward, Richard, 1656
Carl. S Pl. Yk.

S5527 Steward, Richard, 1658
Linc. S Asa. S Pl. Yk.

S5528 Steward, Richard, 1659
S Pl.

S5532 Stewart, *Sir* James, [1672]
Yk.

S5533+ Stewart, *Sir* James, 1688
Printed and sold by Andrew Sowle; 4°.
Carl. S Asa. Wel.

S5538? Stier, Johann, 1647
Cantabrigiae, ex officina Rogeri
Danielis.
Pet.

S5540 Stier, Johann, 1659
Londini, ex officina Rogeri Danielis.
Carl.

S5541 Stier, Johann, 1667
Impr. ends: ... Johan Williams; 4°.
Dur. Ely. Her.

S5542 Stier, Johann, 1671
Her.

S5544 *See*: S5541

S5545 *See*: S5542

S5547 *See*: S5541

S5548 *See*: S5541

S5549 *See*: S5541

S5550 *See*: S5541

S5552 Stileman, John, 1662
Yk.

S5554 Stileman, John, 1662
Carl. Ex. Win. Yk.

S5556 Stillingfleet, Edward, 1675
Carl. Ely. Ex. Linc. S Asa.
Sal. Win.

S5557 Stillingfleet, Edward, 1697
Carl. Ches. Ely. S Asa. Wel.

S5558 Stillingfleet, Edward, 1698
Ban. Ches. Ex. S Asa.

S5559 Stillingfleet, Edward, 1673
Bur (imp). Cant (2). Carl.
Chelm. Ely. Ex. Linc. Nor.
Wel. Win.

S5560? Stillingfleet, Edward, 1674
By R.W. for H. Mortlock.
Her.

S5562 Stillingfleet, Edward, 1686
Ban. Bur. Chi. Ex (4 − 1 imp).
Liv. Nor. S Asa. S Pl (2). Sal.
Wel (2). Yk.

S5565 Stillingfleet, Edward, 1691
Yk.

S5565+ Stillingfleet, Edward, 1691
For Henry Mortlock; 4°.
Ban. Ches. Ex. Her. Nor.
S Pl. Wel.

S5566 Stillingfleet, Edward, 1690
Cant. Ex. Pet.

S5569 Stillingfleet, Edward, 1688
Author's name on half-title.
Ban (with an appendix). Cant.
Ex. Liv. Llan. Pet. Sal. Swel.

S5570 Stillingfleet, Edward, 1688
Author's name on half-title.
Ely. Yk.

S5571 Stillingfleet, Edward, 1676
Bur. Cant (imp). Carl. Ely. Ex.
S Pl. Win.

S5572 Stillingfleet, Edward, 1695
Ches. Nor. Yk.

S5573 *See*: Pt 2 of S5593

S5574 Stillingfleet, Edward, 1696
Ches. Rip.

S5576 Stillingfleet, Edward, 1700
S Pl.

S5577 Stillingfleet, Edward, 1671
Cant (2). Chelm. Linc.

S5578 Stillingfleet, Edward, 1671
Ely. Ex.

S5578+ Stillingfleet, Edward, 1672
The second edition; By Robert White
for Henry Mortlock; 8°.
Carl. New. Rip. S Asa.

S5580 Stillingfleet, Edward, 1676
Ex. Nor.

S5581 Stillingfleet, Edward, 1689
Carl (imp)*. Linc. Wel.

S5582 Stillingfleet, Edward, 1688
Ban. Cant. Carl. Ex (2). Roch.
Wel.

S5584 Stillingfleet, Edward, 1689
'unreasonableness'
Bur. Ex. Nor. Pet. Wel.

S5585 Stillingfleet, Edward, 1697
Carl. Ches. Ely. Ex. S Pl. Wel.

S5586 Stillingfleet, Edward, 1697
S Asa.

S5587 Stillingfleet, Edward, 1687
Ban. Bur. Cant. Ex. Nor.
S Pl. Sal. Wel. Yk.

S5587+ Stillingfleet, Edward, 1688
The second edition; For W. Rogers;
4°.
Ely. Ex.

S5588 Stillingfleet, Edward, 1687
Ban. Bur. Cant. Carl. Ely. Ex
(2 − 1 imp). Nor (2). S Pl. Sal.
Wel. Yk.

S5590 Stillingfleet, Edward, 1686
Cant (imp). Ex. Nor. S Pl (2 −
1 imp). Yk.

S5591 Stillingfleet, Edward, 1686
Swel.

S5592 Stillingfleet, Edward, 1686
Ban. Bur. Chi. Ex. Nor. Sal.
Swel. Wel.

S5593 Stillingfleet, Edward, 1698
... Henry Mortlock.
Cant (2 − 1 pt 1 only, imp).
Ches. Chi. Ely. Ex (2). Glo.
New. S Asa. S Pl. Win. Yk.

S5594 Stillingfleet, Edward, 1680
... Richard Rumball.
Cant. Carl. Ex. Linc. S Pl.
Win. Yk.

S5596 Stillingfleet, Edward, 1661
Lich. S Asa.

S5597- Stillingfleet, Edward, 1662
As S5597, but no ed. statement.
Ches. Ely.

S5597 Stillingfleet, Edward, 1662
Nor. S Pl. Sal. Win.

S5597+ Stillingfleet, Edward, 1662
The second edition; For Henry
Mortlock; 4°.
Llan. Rip.

S5597++ Stillingfleet, Edward, 1662
The second edition; By R.I. for Henry
Mortlock and Iohn Simmes; 4°.
Carl.

S5597+++ Stillingfleet, Edward,
1662
The second edition; Impr. as S5598;
4°.
Ex.

S5599 Stillingfleet, Edward, 1677
Ban. Bur. Chi. Dur (imp).
Linc. Nor. Sal. Wel. Win.

S5600 Stillingfleet, Edward, 1677
Carl. Ely. Ex. Nor. S Pl.

S5602 Stillingfleet, Edward, 1687
Ban. Bur. Carl. Dur. Ex. S Pl.
Wel. Yk.

S5605? Stillingfleet, Edward, 1680
Number missing in Wing; No ed.
statement; For Henry Mortlock; 4°.
Cant (3). Carl. Chi. Pet. Wor
(2).

S5606 Stillingfleet, Edward, 1680
For Henry Mortlock.
Her. Yk (2).

S5607 Stillingfleet, Edward, 1680
For Henry Mortlock.
Pet.

S5608 Stillingfleet, Edward, 1680
For Henry Mortlock.
Ex. Pet.

S5609 Stillingfleet, Edward, 1687
Ches.

S5610 Stillingfleet, Edward, 1691
Cant (2). Ex. Pet.

S5611 Stillingfleet, Edward, 1691
Ely. Pet. S Asa.

S5614 Stillingfleet, Edward, 1682
Ban. Cant. Carl. Chi. Dur.
Her. Wor.

S5615 Stillingfleet, Edward, 1685
Bur. Cant (2 − 1 imp). Carl.
Ches. Chi. Ely. Ex. Her. Lich.
Linc. Llan. Nor. Pet. S Asa.
S Pl. Tru. Wel. Win. Yk.

S5616 Stillingfleet, Edward, 1662
Carl. Ches. Ex. Lich. Llan.
Sal. Win.

S5617 Stillingfleet, Edward, 1663
Second ed. not on tp.
Bur. Chi. Dur. Rip (tpw). Yk.

S5618 Stillingfleet, Edward, 1666
Ban. Ches. Her. Llan. S Asa.
Swel.

S5619 Stillingfleet, Edward, 1675
Her. S Pl. Sal. Wel. Yk.

S5620+ Stillingfleet, Edward, 1680
The fifth edition; By M.W. for Henry
Mortlock; 4°.
Ex.

S5621 Stillingfleet, Edward, 1689
S Asa. Yk.

S5622 Stillingfleet, Edward, 1681
Cant. Carl. Llan. S Asa. Yk.

S5624 Stillingfleet, Edward, 1665
Cant. Carl. Chelm. Ches. Ely.
Ex. Glo. Her. Llan. Nor.
S Asa (2). S Dv. S Pl. Win.

S5625 Stillingfleet, Edward, 1681
Ban. Lich. Pet. Swel.

S5626 Stillingfleet, Edward, 1674
Bur. Cant. Her. S Pl. Wel.

S5627 Stillingfleet, Edward, 1674
Cant. Llan.

S5630? Stillingfleet, Edward, 1666
'A reply ...'; By R.W. for Henry
Mortlock.
Ban. Carl. Ex (2). Win.

S5630+ Stillingfleet, Edward, 1675
By H.C. for Henry Mortlock; 8°.
Ex. Pet. S Pl. Yk.

S5631 Stillingfleet, Edward, 1688
Ches. S Asa.

S5632 Stillingfleet, Edward, 1688
Ban. Dur. Ex. Swel. Wor.

S5633 Stillingfleet, Edward, 1688
Carl. Roch. Sal.

S5634 Stillingfleet, Edward, 1673
Carl. Ely. Ex. Nor. Wel. Win.

S5635 Stillingfleet, Edward, 1687
Ban. Bur. Cant. Ex. Roch.
S Pl. Wel. Yk.

S5636 Stillingfleet, Edward, 1694
Ban (2). Cant. Ely. Her. Nor.

S5637 Stillingfleet, Edward, 1666
Cant.

S5638 Stillingfleet, Edward, 1666
Carl. Yk.

S5639 Stillingfleet, Edward, 1666
S Pl (2). Sal.

S5641 Stillingfleet, Edward, 1667
Cant. Carl. S Pl. Win. Wor.
Yk.

S5642 Stillingfleet, Edward, 1669
Cant. Chelm (imp). S Pl. Win.
Yk.

S5643 Stillingfleet, Edward, 1674
Her. Llan. Pet. Wor.

S5645 Stillingfleet, Edward, 1674
S Pl.

S5646 Stillingfleet, Edward, 1674
Bur. Cant (2). Wel.

S5647 Stillingfleet, Edward, 1675
Bur. Wor.

S5648 Stillingfleet, Edward, 1675
Cant (2). Carl.

S5649 Stillingfleet, Edward, 1678
Llan. Nor. Yk.

S5650 Stillingfleet, Edward, 1678
Ban. Cant. Wor.

S5651 Stillingfleet, Edward, 1678
Cant. Carl. Ely. Her (3). S Dv.
S Pl.

S5653 Stillingfleet, Edward, 1679
Her. Pet (2).

S5654 Stillingfleet, Edward, 1679
Cant (2). Carl. S Pl.

S5655 Stillingfleet, Edward, 1684
Chelm. Wor. Yk.

S5656 Stillingfleet, Edward, 1684
Cant (2).

S5657 Stillingfleet, Edward, 1685
Ban. Cant (2). Dur. Ex (3).
S Asa. S Pl. Wor.

S5658 Stillingfleet, Edward, 1686
Ban. Cant. Carl. Ex. S Pl.

S5660 Stillingfleet, Edward, 1689
Ban. Cant (2). Ex. S Asa. Wor.
Yk.

S5661 Stillingfleet, Edward, 1690
Cant. Ex. Her. S Asa. Yk.

S5662 Stillingfleet, Edward, 1691
'... March the 1st ...'
Ban. Cant. Ex.

S5663 Stillingfleet, Edward, 1692
Ban. Wor.

S5664 Stillingfleet, Edward, 1692
Ban. Cant. Ely.

S5665 Stillingfleet, Edward, 1694
'... Christmass-Day ...'
Cant. Her. Nor.

S5666 Stillingfleet, Edward, 1673
Bris. Ex. Lich. Linc. Nor.
Win.

S5667 Stillingfleet, Edward, 1679
Carl. Ely. Ex (2). S Pl. Sal.

S5669 Stillingfleet, Edward, 1669
Carl. Ely. Llan. S Pl. Win.

S5670 Stillingfleet, Edward, 1697
Carl.

S5675 Stillingfleet, Edward, 1681
Cant. Chi. Ely. Ex. Her. Linc.
Pet. S Pl. Sal. Wel. Win.

S5676 Stillingfleet, Edward, 1681
By T.N. for Henry Mortlock.
Bur (2). Carl. Chelm. Ches.
Lich. S Asa (2). Yk.

S5677 Stillingfleet, Edward, 1682
4°.
Ches. Linc.

S5678 Stillingfleet, Edward, 1687
Ban. Bur. Cant (imp). Chi. Ex
(2). Liv. S Pl. Sal. Wel.

S5679 Stillingfleet, Edward, 1691
Carl. Wel.

S5680? Stillingfleet, John, 1663
'Shecinah'
Carl. Ex. Nor. Pet.

S5690+ Stirry, Thomas, 1641
Printed in the yeare; 8°.
Linc.

S5692 Stock, Richard, 1641
Ex.

S5692+ Stock, Richard, 1641
By T.H. and R.H. for Samuel
Enderbey; 2°.
Carl.

S5692++ Stock, Richard, [1641?]
By T.H. and R.H. for Thomas
Nichols [...?]; 2°.
Linc (tp imp).

S5705+ Stockwood, John, 1682
By Roger Norton; 8°.
Wel.

S5705A+ Stockwood, John, 1693
'The treatise ...'; By Roger Norton;
8°.
Cant (imp).

S5713 Stoddon, Samuel, 1700
Ex.

S5718 Stokes, David, 1646
'Habakkuk'
Pet.

S5719 Stokes, David, 1659
'A paraphrasticall explication of the
twelve minor prophets'
Ches. Ely. Nor (imp). S Asa.
Yk.

S5720 Stokes, David, 1667
Carl. Ex. Win.

S5721? Stokes, David, 1667
By William Hall for Richard Davis.
Carl. Ex. Win.

S5722 Stokes, David, 1667
... Richard Davis.
Carl. Ex. Win.

S5723? Stokes, David, 1668
... by Henry Hall ...
Carl (tp only). Linc.

S5724 Stokes, David, 1668
Carl (2).

S5726 Stokes, Richard, 1685
Latin tp: 'Catalogus librorum
theologicorum ...'
Wor.

S5735 Stone, Samuel, 1661
Carl. Pet. S Pl.

S5740 S'too, 1673
'S'too him Bayes'; Formerly M890.
Carl. Ex. Win.

S5742 Stop, 1648
Yk.

S5744 Stopford, Joshua, 1675
Lich. Yk.

S5744+ Stopford, Joshua, 1675
By A. Maxwell; 8°.
S Pl.

S5745 Stopford, Joshua, 1672
Yk.

S5746 Stopford, Joshua, 1675
Lich. S Pl.

S5749 Story, George Walter, 1693
Carl.

S5752 Story, John, 1660
Yk.

S5757 Stott, *Sir* Richard, [1679?]
Linc.

S5758 Stoughton, John, 1650
Nor.

S5767 Stouppe, Jean Baptiste, 1655
Carl. Ex.

S5769 Stouppe, Jean Baptiste, 1680
Carl. Her.

S5771 Stout, Henry, [1678]
Dur.

S5777- Strada, Famianus, 1672
See: CLC159.
Pet.

S5777 Strada, Famianus, 1650
Pet. Sal. Yk (3 − 2 imp).

S5778 Strada, Famianus, 1662
Cant. Ex. Llan.

S5779 Strada, Famianus, 1667
Ex.

S5782 Stradling, George, 1675
Cant. Chi. Pet (tpw).

S5783 Stradling, George, 1692
Chi.

S5784? Strafford, Thomas
Wentworth, *Earl of*, 1641
'... April'; 6p.
Cant. Linc. Yk (3)*.

S5784+ Strafford, Thomas
Wentworth, *Earl of*, 1641
As S5784, but: '... Aprill'; 5p.
Cant.

S5785+ Strafford, Thomas
Wentworth, *Earl of*, 1641
'The last speeches of ...'; Printed; 4°;
9p.; Anr ed. of S5799, etc.
Cant.

S5786 Strafford, Thomas
Wentworth, *Earl of*, 1641
Yk.

S5787+ Strafford, Thomas
Wentworth, *Earl of*, 1641
'May the 11th. 1641'; [N.pl.], printed
in the yeare; 4°.
Cant.

S5788- Strafford, Thomas
Wentworth, *Earl of*, 1641
'The Earle of Straffords last letter. To
his lady ...'; [N.pl.]; 4°.
Linc.

S5789 Strafford, Thomas
Wentworth, *Earl of*, 1641
Linc. Yk (2 eds).

S5789+ Strafford, Thomas
Wentworth, *Earl of*, 1641
'Maiesty'; [N.pl.]; 4°.
Linc.

S5790 Strafford, Thomas
Wentworth, *Earl of*, 1641
Cant. Yk.

S5791 Strafford, Thomas
Wentworth, *Earl of*, 1680
Linc.

S5795 Strafford, Thomas
Wentworth, *Earl of*, 1641
Yk.

S5795+ Strafford, Thomas
Wentworth, *Earl of*, 1641
4°; 6p.
Carl.

S5795++ Strafford, Thomas
Wentworth, *Earl of*, 1641
4°; 4p.
Cant.

S5797 Strafford, Thomas
Wentworth, *Earl of*, 1641
Cant. Carl. Pet.

S5797+ Strafford, Thomas
Wentworth, *Earl of*, 1641
See: CLC160.
Pet.

S5799 Strafford, Thomas
Wentworth, *Earl of*, 1641
Linc. Yk.

S5799+ Strafford, Thomas
Wentworth, *Earl of*, 1641
'two'; Printed anno Domini; 4°; 6,
3p.
Cant.

S5799++ Strafford, Thomas
Wentworth, *Earl of*, 1641
'The two ... By a revised copy';
Printed anno; 4°; 10p.
Cant.

S5800A Strafford, Thomas
Wentworth, *Earl of*, [1641]
Yk.

S5801 Strafford, Thomas
Wentworth, *Earl of*, 1641
Cant.

S5802 Strafford, Thomas
Wentworth, *Earl of*, 1641
Cant (2 − 1 imp). Linc. Pet. Yk.

S5807 Straight, John, 1643
Sal. Wel.

S5808? Straight, John, [1670?]
[N.d.].
Sal.

S5808A+ Straight, John, 1671
'A sermon preached ... 18th of June
... 1671'; For Edward Thomas; 4°;
Anr ed. of S5806.
Sal.

S5810 Strange, Richard, 1674
Dur. Her.

S5815B Strange, [1680?]
Yk.

S5874A Strange, 1679
Linc.

S5887 Strange, [1679]
Linc.

S5890 Strange, 1678
Linc.

S5891 Strange, 1681
Ches.

S5892+ Strange, 1667
See: CLC161.
Linc.

S5896 Strange, 1647
S Pl.

S5929 Stratford, Nicholas, 1692
Ban. Cant. Ches. Her. Sal
(imp).

S5930 Stratford, Nicholas, 1685
Ches (2). Ex (2). Nor. S Pl (2).
Sal. Swel. Wel.

S5931 Stratford, Nicholas, 1687
Ban. Ex. Nor. S Pl.

S5932 Stratford, Nicholas, 1688
Ban. Ches. Ex. Wel.

S5933 Stratford, Nicholas, 1684
Ban. Carl. Ches.

S5934 Stratford, Nicholas, 1687
Ban. Bur. Ches. Ex (2). Her.
Llan. Roch. S Pl. Sal. Yk.

S5935 Stratford, Nicholas, 1686
Ban. Carl. Ches. Dur. Ex (2).
Nor. S Pl (2). Sal. Swel. Wel.

S5936 Stratford, Nicholas, 1700
Cant. S Asa.

S5937 Stratford, Nicholas, 1694
Cant (2). Ches.

S5938 Stratford, Nicholas, 1687
4°.
Ban. Bur. Cant. Ches (2). Chi.
Ex (2). Nor. Roch. Sal. Wel.

S5939 Stratford, Nicholas, 1681
Ches.

S5940? Stratford, Nicholas, 1683
Chiswell.
Pet.

S5941 Strauch, Aegidius, 1699
Ches. Ex.

S5942 Streat, William, 1654
Ex. Yk.

S5944 Streater, Aaron, 1642
Linc.

S5952 Streete, Thomas, 1664
Sal.

S5953 Streete, Thomas, 1661
'… celestial motions'
Pet.

S5953+ Streete, Thomas, 1661
As S5953, but: '… coelestial motions'
Sal.

S5956 Streete, Thomas, 1667
Sal.

S5961 Strengfellow, William, 1693
Cant. Wor.

S5962 Strength, 1652
Ex.

S5969 Strickland, John, 1644
Pet.

S5970 Strickland, John, 1644
Yk.

S5971 Strickland, John, 1644
Her.

S5972 Strickland, John, 1641[2]
Yk.

S5978A Stripling, Thomas, 1681
Cant. Sal.

S5984 Strode, William, 1644
Wel. Yk.

S5985 Strode, William, 1644
Wel.

S5986 Strode, William, 1660
Bur. Linc. Pet.

S5987 Strode, William,
Parliamentarian, 1642
Cant.

S5995 Strong, Martin, 1692
Her.

S6002 Strong, William, 1678
Her. S Pl.

S6007 Strong, William, 1656
Chelm. Ex.

S6012 Strong, William, 1654
Cant. S Pl.

S6013 Strong, William, 1647
Ex.

S6021 Strype, John, 1696
Bur. Cant.

S6023 Strype, John, 1698
8°.
Cant. Ex. Glo. Liv. Nor. Wor.

S6024 Strype, John, 1694
Ban. Bur. Cant (2). Chi. Dur.
Glo. Her (2). Lich. Linc. Liv.
Nor. Pet. Wel. Win. Wor.

S6025 Strype, John, 1689
Cant. Her.

S6026 Stuart, George, 1686
Dur. Yk.

S6028 Stuart, William, 1657
8°.
Dur.

S6030 Stubbe, Henry, 1670
Win.

S6033 Stubbe, Henry, 1670
Llan (Madan 2866: erased & 'our
author' in MS). Win (Madan
2866**). Yk (as Llan).

S6034+ Stubbe, Henry, 1657
'Clamor, rixa …'; 4°; Wing wrongly
enters under Wallis.
Ban.

S6036? Stubbe, Henry, 1660
For Giles Calvert.
Carl.

S6045 Stubbe, Henry, 1659
Carl. Win. Yk.

S6046 Stubbe, Henry, 1673
Linc. Win.

S6049 Stubbe, Henry, 1662
Linc.

S6050 Stubbe, Henry, 1672
Cant. Linc. Wel.

S6053 Stubbe, Henry, 1670
Win. Yk.

S6054 Stubbe, Henry, 1659
Printed, and are to be sold by T.B.
Carl.

S6056 Stubbe, Henry, 1659
Carl.

S6059 Stubbe, Henry, 1671
Ex. Linc.

S6060 Stubbe, Henry, 1659
Carl. Win. Yk.

S6062 Stubbe, Henry, 1666
Carl. Chelm. Linc.

S6063 Stubbe, Henry, 1670
Win.

S6063A Stubbe, Henry, 1671
Nor.

S6064 Stubbe, Henry, 1672
Yk.

S6065+ Stubbe, Henry, 1658
By J.T. for Andrew Crook; 4°; S6065
with impr. cropped?, see Madan 2371.
Ban.

S6068 Stubbe, Henry, 1659
Carl.

S6070 Stubbs, John, 1670
Linc.

S6074- Stubbs, Philip, *Senior*, 1641
For Iohn Wright; 4°.
Pet.

S6078 Stubbs, Philip, *of St Albans*,
1693
Cant. Her. Wor. Yk.

S6079 Stubbs, Philip, *of St Albans*,
1693
Cant. Her. S Asa.

S6082 Stubbs, Philip, *of St Albans*,
1696
Cant.

S6092 Study, 1680
Dur (2 − 1 imp).

S6096 Sturmy, Samuel, 1669
Roch.

S6103 Suarez, Francisco, 1679
Bris. Ex. Her. Pet. S Asa (2).
Win.

S6104 Subject, 1643
Ex.

S6105- Subjects, 1641
See: CLC162.
Dur (cropped). Pet.

S6120 Suckling, *Sir* John, 1696
Yk.

S6123 Suckling, *Sir* John, 1641
Ex. Linc. Yk.

S6124 *See*: C6176+

S6130 Suckling, *Sir* John, 1659
Lich.

S6132 Suckling, *Sir* John, [1679]
Linc.

S6136 Sudbury, John, 1660
Ban. Carl. Dur. Ex. Pet (2).
S Asa. Win.

S6137 Sudbury, John, 1675
Dur. Linc. Nor.

S6138 Sudbury, John, 1676
Linc. Liv.

S6138+ Sudbury, John, 1676
In the Savoy, printed by Tho:
Newcomb; 4°.
Dur.

S6139 Sudbury, John, 1677
Carl. Dur. Wel. Yk.

S6140 Sudden, [1647]
Yk.

S6144 Suetonius Tranquillus, Caius, 1661
Wel.

S6146 Suetonius Tranquillus, Caius, 1690
Cant. Llan. S Asa. Sal.

S6148 Suetonius Tranquillus, Caius, 1677
S Dv.

S6149+ Suetonius Tranquillus, Caius, 1688
By Tho. Hodgkin, sold by John Walthoe; 8°.
Glo. Rip.

S6164 Suffolks, 1653
Pet.

S6180 *See*: H3775

S6190 Supplication, 1642
Linc.

S6195 Sur-rejoinder, 1682
S Pl.

S6215 Swadlin, Thomas, 1653
S Pl.

S6218 Swadlin, Thomas, 1647
Pet (imp). Win.

S6219? Swadlin, Thomas, 1661
Clowes.
Cant. Ex.

S6220A Swadlin, Thomas, 1645[6]
6p.
Linc.

S6221? Swadlin, Thomas, 1647
'Loyall'
Pet.

S6223 Swadlin, Thomas, 1643
4°.
S Asa.

S6227 Swadlin, Thomas, 1643
Pet. Yk.

S6228 Swadlin, Thomas, 1659
4°.
Sal.

S6235 Swan, John, 1653
'mensurans'
Sal.

S6237 Swan, John, 1652
28p.
Sal.

S6237+ Swan, John, 1652
As S6237, but: 24p.
S Pl.

S6240 Swan, John, 1670
Bur.

S6255 Swift, Daniel, 1643
Dur (imp).

S6260 Swinburne, Henry, 1686
Dur. Ex. Yk.

S6261 Swinburne, Henry, 1677
Cant.

S6264 Swinnock, George, 1665
S Asa.

S6265 Swinnock, George, 1662
Bur.

S6266? Swinnock, George, 1662
For T.P., sold by Dorman Newman.
S Asa.

S6270 Swinnock, George, 1663
S Asa.

S6279A Swinnock, George, 1663
Nor.

S6289+ Swynfen, John, 1695
See: CLC163.
Dur.

S6294? Sydenham, Cuthbert, 1651
64p.
Cant. Dur (imp). Yk*.

S6294+ Sydenham, Cuthbert, 1651
As S6294, but: 55p.
Pet.

S6296 Sydenham, Cuthbert, 1654
Yk.

S6300 Sydenham, Cuthbert, 1654
Yk (2).

S6309 Sydenham, Thomas, 1682
Cant.

S6310 Sydenham, Thomas, 1680
Cant. Ely. Sal.

S6311 Sydenham, Thomas, 1685
Nor.

S6313 Sydenham, Thomas, 1668
Sal.

S6314 Sydenham, Thomas, 1676
... Gualteri Kettilby.
Cant (imp). Ely (imp). Ex (2).

S6314A? Sydenham, Thomas, 1685
... Gualteri Kettilby.
Nor.

S6315 Sydenham, Thomas, 1695
Cant.

S6318 Sydenham, Thomas, 1686
Cant.

S6319 Sydenham, Thomas, 1688
Nor.

S6325 Sylburg, Fredrich, 1648
Sal (tp imp).

S6326 *See*: CLC Foreign books

S6330 Sylvester, Matthew, 1696
Cant. Linc (2).

S6332A Sylvester, Matthew, 1683
Her.

S6338? Sylvius, Franciscus de le Boe, 1675
For Brabazon Aylmer; 8°.
Cant.

S6343 Symmons, Edward, 1642
Pet (3rd sermon only).

S6346 Symmons, Edward, 1644
Her*.

S6348 Symmons, Edward, 1644[5]
Win.

S6350 Symmons, Edward, 1648[7]
Cant (2 eds). Carl (imp). Ex (imp). Glo (imp). Nor. S Pl. Sal (imp). Win. Yk.

S6352 Symmons, Edward, 1693
Ex.

S6358 Symonds, Joseph, 1641
Ex. Linc. Pet (2).

S6360A? Symons, Henry, 1657
By J.H. & are to be sold by H. Crips.
Cant.

S6360B+ Symonson, Philip, [c.1650?]
See: CLC164.
Cant.

S6367 Symson, Andrew, 1658
Ban. Ex. Lich (tpw).

S6368? Symson, Andrew, 1658
For I. Clark, G. Sawbridge, T. Williams and T. Johnson.
Lich.

S6379 Synge, Edward, 1697
Ely.

S6380? Synge, Edward, 1698
Second ed. not on tp; ... R. Sare; 12°.
Ely.

S6383 Synodus, 1672
Ely.

T4 T., D., 1672
8°.
Carl. S Pl.

T9 T., G., 1642
Linc.

T19 T., J., 1647
Sal.

T25 T., L., 1681
Linc.

T42 T., R., 1654
Carl.

T46 T., R., 1652
Pet.

T50 T., R., 1670
Carl.

T61+ T., T., 1696
See: CLC165.
Yk.

T64 T., U., 1656
Ex (tp imp).

T93 Tabor, John, 1667
S Pl.

T95 Tabula, 1672
Sal.

T96? Tachard, Gui, 1688
8°.
Wel.

T101 Tacitus, Cornelius, 1698
Rip.

T102 Tacitus, Cornelius, 1698
Glo. Rip.

T103 Tacitus, Cornelius, 1698
Glo. Rip.

T105? Tacitus, Cornelius, 1687
By H. Clark for John Taylor; 12°.
Dur.

T117? Talbot, Peter, 1659
Printhed [*sic*] ...; 8°.
Linc.

T117+ Talbot, Peter, 1658
'The polititians cathechisme';
Formerly F2181.
Sal.

T121 Talbot, William, 1695
Cant. Carl. Nor. S Asa.

T123 Talbot, William, 1692
Cant.

T124 Talbot, William, 1696
Cant. Dur. Her.

T125 Talbot, William, 1700
Her (tpw).

T126 Talbot, William, 1699
Yk.

T127 Talbot, William, 1694
Cant. S Asa.

T130 Tallents, Francis, [1695]
Printed and sold by Awnsham and
John Churchil; cap.; 1° (8 engr.
tables).
Dur.

T132+ Talon, Nicolas, 1653
For Iohn Crook & Iohn Baker; 4°.
Carl. Ely (date cropped).

T140 Tanner, Thomas, 1657
Carl. Ex.

T144 Tanner, Thomas, 1695
Ex (2). Wel.

T145 Tanner, Thomas, 1683
Carl. Dur. Ex (2 − 1 imp).

T146 Tanner, Thomas, 1677
Cant.

T148 Tanner, Thomas, [1677]
Dur (imp)*.

T148+ Tanner, Thomas, [1677?]
[London], for Thomas Passinger; 4°.
S Asa.

T156 Tany, Thomas, 1653
Pet.

T174 Tasso, Torquato, 1687
Yk.

T174B+ Taste, 1652
See: CLC166.
Pet.

T186 Tate, Nahum, 1695
'... God, his grace, John ...'
Nor.

T190 Tate, Nahum, 1682
Ex.

T193+ Tate, Nahum, 1681
As T193, apart from date.
Ex.

T210 Tate, Nahum, 1685
Yk.

T236+ Tatian, 1700
... impensis Joannis Oweni; 8°.
Ches. Chi. Ely. Nor. S Pl.
Wel. Yk.

T250 Tavernier, Jean Baptiste, 1680
Cant (2). Dur. Wor.

T253 Tavernier, Jean Baptiste, 1684
Nor.

T254 Tavernier, Jean Baptiste, 1684
Nor.

T256+ Tavernier, Jean Baptiste,
1678
For R.L. and M.P. and are to be sold
by John Starkey, and Moses Pitt; 2°.
Cant. Dur.

T256++ Tavernier, Jean Baptiste,
1678
Printed and sold by Robert Littlebury
and Moses Pitt; 2°.
Win.

T258 Taxes, 1690
Wel.

T258+ Tayler, Robert, 1680
See: CLC167.
Dur.

T271 Taylor, Francis, 1651
... ex typographiâ Tho: Roycroft ...
Cant. Chelm.

T272 Taylor, Francis, 1646
Yk.

T273 Taylor, Francis, 1655
Ex.

T274 Taylor, Francis, 1657
Ex.

T276 Taylor, Francis, 1641
Cant.

T278 Taylor, Francis, 1645
Ex (2). Pet.

T281 *See*: B2775+

T283 Taylor, James, 1687
Bur. Dur. S Pl.

T284 Taylor, James, 1689
Ex.

T285 Taylor, James, 1687
16p.
Bur. Ex. Swel.

T286 Taylor, Jeremy, 1656
Ex.

T287 Taylor, Jeremy, 1675
Glo. Linc. Nor. S Pl. Sal.
Win.

T287A Taylor, Jeremy, 1678
... for R. Royston.
Chelm. Wor.

T288 Taylor, Jeremy, 1684
Brec. Dur. S Asa. S Dv. Swel.
Win.

T288+ Taylor, Jeremy, 1694
The eighth edition; By R.N. for Luke
Meredith; 2°.
Chi. Her. S Alb. S Asa.

T289 Taylor, Jeremy, 1649
Ches. Linc. S Asa. S Pl. Wel.
Yk.

T290 Taylor, Jeremy, [1664]
Carl (pt 2 only). Ex.

T294 Taylor, Jeremy, 1664
Ex. S Asa. S Pl.

T296 Taylor, Jeremy, 1651
Carl. Dur. Ely. Ex. Her. Lich.
Nor. Pet. S Asa. Tru. Yk (2).

T297 Taylor, Jeremy, 1655
Cant. Ely. Ex. Her. Pet.

T298 Taylor, Jeremy, 1668
Cant. Sal.

T299 Taylor, Jeremy, 1672
Ban. Chelm. Her. Pet (2).

T300 Taylor, Jeremy, 1658
Carl. Dur (2 − 1 v. imp). Ely.
S Asa.

T301 Taylor, Jeremy, 1690
12°.
Yk.

T306? Taylor, Jeremy, 1687
12°.
Ex.

T308 Taylor, Jeremy, 1667
Cant. Nor. Sal.

T309 Taylor, Jeremy, 1673
Ban. Chelm. Her. Pet (2).

T312 Taylor, Jeremy, 1646
Ex. S Asa. Win.

T313 Taylor, Jeremy, 1647
Cant (tpw). Chelm. Yk.

T315 Taylor, Jeremy, 1652
Cant. Carl. S Asa (2 − 1 imp).
S Pl.

T319- Taylor, Jeremy, 1664
Dublin, by John Crooke, sold by
Samuel Dancer; 4°.
Win.

T319 Taylor, Jeremy, 1664
Cant.

T320 Taylor, Jeremy, 1664
Linc.

T321 Taylor, Jeremy, 1664
Liv. S Asa. Yk.

T322 Taylor, Jeremy, 1668
Bur. Carl.

T324 Taylor, Jeremy, 1660
Ban. Cant (2). Carl. Dur. Ely.
Ex. Glo (imp). Her. IoM. Pet.
Rip. S Asa (vol. 1 only). S Pl
(imp). Sal. Swel. Tru (tpw).
Wel (2 − 1 v. imp*). Win.

T325 Taylor, Jeremy, 1671
Cant. Liv. Nor. Wor. Yk.

T326 Taylor, Jeremy, 1676
By R. Norton for R. Royston.
Bris. Glo. Lich. Linc. Sal (2 −
1 imp). Yk.

T327 Taylor, Jeremy, 1696
Chi. Ex (imp). Her (2). Linc.
Liv. Roch.

T328 Taylor, Jeremy, 1663
Consists of T359, T392−3, T416, T396
& T389, with gen. tp.
Carl. Pet.

T328+ Taylor, Jeremy, 1664
As T328, apart from date.
Ex.

T329 Taylor, Jeremy, 1653
Consists of T408, T405, & T296, with
gen. tp.
S Asa. Yk.

T330 Taylor, Jeremy, 1655
Consists of T408 or T409, T406, &
T297, with gen. tp.
Cant. Ely. Ex. Her. Pet.

T331 Taylor, Jeremy, 1668
Consists of T410, T412, T298, T308,
& R2362+, with gen. tp.
Cant. Sal.

T332 Taylor, Jeremy, 1673
Consists of T411, T413, T309, &
T299, with gen. tp.
Ban. Chelm. Her. Pet.

T333 Taylor, Jeremy, 1678
Ex. Her. IoM. Roch. Sal (2 −
1 imp). Win. Yk.

T335+ Taylor, Jeremy, 1656
See: CLC168.
Pet.

T336 Taylor, Jeremy, 1655
Her.

T342 Taylor, Jeremy, 1649
Her. Lich. Wel.

T343 Taylor, Jeremy, 1653
Second ed. not on tp.
Bur. Dur. Ely. Lich. Linc.
Wor. Yk.

T344 Taylor, Jeremy, 1657
Ban (engr. tpw). Cant. Carl.
Ches. Ex (2 − 1 imp). Liv. Nor
(imp). Sal.

T345 Taylor, Jeremy, 1667
Cant. Her. Rip.

T345+ Taylor, Jeremy, 1675
The fifth edition; Impr. not known (pt
of T287); 2°.
Glo. Linc. Nor. S Pl. Sal.
Win.

T345++ Taylor, Jeremy, 1678
The sixth edition; By E. Flesher for
R. Royston; 2°.
Chelm. Wor.

T346 Taylor, Jeremy, 1684
Brec. Dur. S Asa. S Dv. Swel.
Win.

T346+ Taylor, Jeremy, 1693
For Luke Meredith; 2°; Details not
confirmed, pt of T288+, poss. not
separate.
Chi. Her. S Alb. S Asa.

T350 Taylor, Jeremy, 1657
Cant.

T353 Taylor, Jeremy, 1642
Ches. Ex (imp). S Asa. Win.

T354 Taylor, Jeremy, 1647
For Richard Royston.
Lich. Linc. S Pl.

T358 Taylor, Jeremy, 1654
Cant. S Asa. S Dv.

T359 Taylor, Jeremy, 1663
Carl. Ex. Pet.

T362 Taylor, Jeremy, 1652
For R. Royston.
Carl.

T363 Taylor, Jeremy, 1655
... by James Flesher for ...
Ex. Yk.

T364 Taylor, Jeremy, 1658
By James Flesher for R. Royston.
S Pl.

T364A Taylor, Jeremy, 1663
Llan.

T365 Taylor, Jeremy, 1668
Ely.

T367 Taylor, Jeremy, 1676
Yk.

T369+ Taylor, Jeremy, 1686
The fourteenth edition; By M. Flesher
for Richard Royston; 8°.
Cant. Liv. Llan.

T369A Taylor, Jeremy, 1690
S Asa.

T369A+ Taylor, Jeremy, 1693
The sixteenth edition; By J.L. for
Luke Meredith; 8°.
Sal.

T370 Taylor, Jeremy, 1695
Liv.

T373 Taylor, Jeremy, 1654
For Richard Royston; 12°.
Ex.

T374 Taylor, Jeremy, 1656
For Richard Royston.
Cant (tpw). S Pl.

T375 Taylor, Jeremy, 1663
By James Flesher for Richard
Royston.
Llan.

T376 Taylor, Jeremy, 1668
... Richard Royston.
Ely.

T379 Taylor, Jeremy, 1676
... Richard Royston.
Yk.

T382? Taylor, Jeremy, 1686
By M. Flesher ... .
Cant. Liv. Llan.

T383 Taylor, Jeremy, 1690
... Luke Meredith.
S Asa.

T383A Taylor, Jeremy, 1693
Sal.

T384 Taylor, Jeremy, 1695
Liv.

T389 Taylor, Jeremy, 1663
Carl. Ex (2). Pet.

T390 Taylor, Jeremy, 1667
4°.
Bur. Carl. Pet. S Asa. Win.
Yk.

T391 Taylor, Jeremy, 1661
Ex. Yk.

T392 Taylor, Jeremy, 1663
Carl. Ex. Pet.

T392+ Taylor, Jeremy, 1658
See: CLC169.
Carl. Her.

T393 Taylor, Jeremy, 1661
'... preached at the opening of the
Parliament of Ireland, May ...'
Carl. Ex. Pet.

T394 Taylor, Jeremy, 1663
... sold by Samuel Dancer.
Yk.

T395 Taylor, Jeremy, 1663
'Christ-Church'; No date in title;
Same sermon as T394.
Carl. Linc.

T396 Taylor, Jeremy, 1663
Carl. Ex. Linc. Pet.

T397 Taylor, Jeremy, 1652
... [colophon:] for Richard Royston,
sold by William Ballard in Bristol.
Carl.

T398 Taylor, Jeremy, 1657
Carl. Dur. Ely. Ex (imp). Her
(imp). Linc. Rip (imp). Sal (tp
imp). Wor.

T399 Taylor, Jeremy, 1674
'Συμβολον θεολογικον ...'
Ban. Cant. Chi. Dur. Ex.
Linc. New. Nor. S Pl. Wel (2).
Yk.

T400 Taylor, Jeremy, 1647
Bur. Cant. Chelm. Linc. Rip
(engr. tpw). S Asa. S Pl. Win.

T401 Taylor, Jeremy, [1687]
Wing's location not dated.
Wel (*or* T402 with impr.
cropped?).

T405 Taylor, Jeremy, 1651
Carl. Dur. Lich. Nor. Pet.
S Asa. Yk (2).

T406 Taylor, Jeremy, 1654
Cant. Ely. Ex. Her. Pet.
S Asa. Tru (tpw).

T408 Taylor, Jeremy, 1653
Ban. Cant. Carl. Dur. Ely*.
Ex*. Her*. Nor. Pet*. S Asa.
Yk (2).

T410 Taylor, Jeremy, 1668
Cant. Sal.

T411 Taylor, Jeremy, 1673
Ban. Chelm. Her. Pet.

T412 Taylor, Jeremy, 1668
Cant. Sal.

T413 Taylor, Jeremy, 1673
Ban. Chelm. Her. Pet.

T414 Taylor, Jeremy, 1653
Cant (pt 2 tpw).

T415 Taylor, Jeremy, 1655
Carl. Ely. Ex. Nor (imp). Pet.
S Asa.

T416 Taylor, Jeremy, 1662
Cant (imp). Carl. Ex. Pet (2).
Yk.

T417 Taylor, Jeremy, 1660
Lich. Pet. S Dv. Yk.

T417A Taylor, Jeremy, 1661
Carl.

T420 Taylor, Jeremy, 1674
New (2 − 1 engr. tpw).

T420+ Taylor, Jeremy, 1678
By T.N. for John Martyn; 8°.
Cant. Liv. Nor.

T421 Taylor, Jeremy, 1683
Ex.

T422 Taylor, Jeremy, 1686
Pet. Sal.

T427 Taylor, John, 1642
Linc.

T428 Taylor, John, 1641[2]
Linc.

T430 Taylor, John, 1642
Linc.

T452 Taylor, John, 1641
Linc.

T454 Taylor, John, 1642
Linc.

T461 Taylor, John, 1642
Pet.

T466 Taylor, John, 1648
'Ἱππ-ανθρωπος ...'
Cant.

T473B Taylor, John, 1641
Linc.

T475 Taylor, John, 1641
Pet.

T481 Taylor, John, 1644
Pet (imp).

T507 Taylor, John, 1642
'Saint'
Pet.

T508 Taylor, John, 1642
'St.'
Linc.

T516 Taylor, John, 1642
Second ed. not on tp.
Pet.

T530 Taylor, John, 1642
Linc.

T534 Taylor, John, *Mathematician*,
1687
Yk.

T553? Taylor, Silas, 1663
For John Starkey.
Cant (2).

T553+ Taylor, Silas, 1654
'Impostor Magnus ...'; Formerly I105.
Ex.

T558 Taylor, Thomas, *of
Cambridge*, 1697
Her.

T559 Taylor, Thomas, *of
Cambridge*, 1693
Yk.

T560 Taylor, Thomas, *Divine*, 1653
Cant (tp imp). Ex.

T563A? Taylor, Thomas, *Divine*,
1658
... William Gilbertson.
Ex.

T564 Taylor, Thomas, *Divine*, 1676
Carl.

T565 Taylor, Thomas, *Divine*, 1659
Ex.

T567 Taylor, Thomas, *Divine*, 1653
S Asa.

T570 Taylor, Thomas, *Divine*, 1642
Yk.

T576 Taylor, Thomas, *Quaker*, 1662
Yk.

T592 Taylor, Thomas, *Quaker*, [1667]
Yk.

T595? Taylor, Zachary, 1696
For E. Whitlock.
Cant.

T616? Teate, Faithful, 1658
By J.H. for T. Underhill.
Pet.

T623B Tell-Truth's, [1680]
Linc.

T627 Temple, *Sir* John, 1646
Chi. Dur. Wel. Win.

T633 Temple, *Sir* Richard, 1696
Ban.

T634 Temple, Thomas, 1642
Cant. Win.

T635 Temple, *Sir* William, 1693
Dur (imp).

T638 Temple, *Sir* William, 1695
Ely.

T640 Temple, *Sir* William, 1699
Ex. Yk.

T641 Temple, *Sir* William, 1700
Ely. Ex.

T642 Temple, *Sir* William, 1692
Ely.

T643 Temple, *Sir* William, 1692
Wel.

T645 Temple, *Sir* William, 1700
Pet.

T646 Temple, *Sir* William, 1680
'Miscellanea. I. A survey ...'; ... for
Edward Gellibrand.
Carl.

T648 Temple, *Sir* William, 1691
For Jacob Tonson ...
Ely.

T651 Temple, *Sir* William, 1697
The fifth edition.
S Asa.

T653 Temple, *Sir* William, 1690
By J.R., for ...
Ely.

T655 Temple, *Sir* William, 1696
S Asa.

T656 Temple, *Sir* William, 1673
Carl. Linc. Win.

T658 Temple, *Sir* William, 1676
Ex.

T664 Templer, John, 1673
... Cantabr.
Ex. S Asa. Win.

T665 Templer, John, 1676
Ban. Cant. Nor. S Asa.

T666 Templer, John, 1659
S Pl.

T667 Templer, John, 1694
Ban.

T670- Ten, 1656
See: CLC170.
Yk.

T677? Tena, Luis de, 1661
Typis R. Hodgkinson, prostant apud
Rob. Scott; Vol. 3 of Pearson's
'Critici sacri'
Carl. Chi. Ely (imp). Glo.
Linc. Pet (imp). S Pl. Win. Yk.

T677+ Tena, Luis de, 1661
'Tractatum biblicorum volumen
tertium ...'; Excudebat R.
Hodgkinson, prostant apud Robertum
Scott; 2°; Vol. 3 of Pearson's 'Critici
sacri'
Ches. S Pl.

T678 Tende, Gaspard de, 1698
Carl.

T684 Tenison, Richard, 1691
Her.

T687 Tenison, Thomas, 1688
Ban. Ex. Llan.

T688 Tenison, Thomas, 1683
S Pl.

T689? Tenison, Thomas, [1695?]
'February the 16th'
Glo. Llan.

T691 Tenison, Thomas, 1670
Ban. Dur. Ely. Yk.

T692 Tenison, Thomas, 1671
Carl. Ex. Sal. Win.

T693 Tenison, Thomas, [1688]
Ex.

T694 Tenison, Thomas, 1687
Ban. Bur. Cant. Ex. Roch.
Sal.

T695 Tenison, Thomas, 1683
Cant. Carl. Ex. Linc. Nor.
S Pl. Sal. Wel.

T696 Tenison, Thomas, 1687
Ban. Ex. Linc. S Pl (2). Swel.

T697 Tenison, Thomas, 1689
Cant. Ex. Llan. Pet. Wel.

T698 Tenison, Thomas, 1688
Wel.

T700+ Tenison, Thomas, 1699
'... Bishops of his province. To the ...
Bishop of Coventry and Lichfield';
Colophon (including date) as T699;
cap.; 4°.
Dur.

T703 Tenison, Thomas, 1687
Ban. Ex. Llan. Wel. Yk.

T704 Tenison, Thomas, 1678
Ches. Ely. Ex. Llan. Nor. Pet.
S Pl. Win. Yk.

T706 Tenison, Thomas, 1688
Ex.

T707 Tenison, Thomas, 1688
Should be under title.
Ban. Cant (frag.). Ex (3 – 1
frag.). Her. Lich (frag.). Nor.
Pet. S Pl. Sal. Swel. Wel (imp;
2 copies of some sections). Wor.
Yk.

T708 Tenison, Thomas, 1689
S Asa. Sal. Wel. Wor.

T709 Tenison, Thomas, 1681
Cant. Her. Llan.

T710 Tenison, Thomas, 1688
12°.
Ely.

T711 Tenison, Thomas, 1690
Her. Wel. Wor.

T712 Tenison, Thomas, 1695
Ban (2). Llan. S Asa. Yk.

T713? Tenison, Thomas, 1694
'coelestial ... April 8'
Ban. Cant. Nor (2).

T715 Tenison, Thomas, 1691
Cant. Yk.

T718 Tenison, Thomas, 1691
Cant.

T720 Tenison, Thomas, 1695
Cant (2 – 1 imp). Chelm. Ches.
Her (4 – 1 tpw). Llan. S Asa.
S Dv. S Pl. Wel.

T723 Tenison, Thomas, 1687
Ban. Ex. Llan. Nor. Pet.
S Dv. Wel. Yk.

T725 Tenison, Thomas, 1687
Llan.

T727 Tenth, 1689
S Asa. Wel.

T742 Terentius Afer, Publius, 1676
Yk.

T744 Terentius Afer, Publius, 1688
Yk.

T745 Terentius Afer, Publius, 1692
... Joannis Hayes.
Liv.

T749 Terentius Afer, Publius, 1694
Dur.

T751 Terentius Afer, Publius, 1641
Yk (2).

T753 Teresa, *St*, 1642
Cant. Carl. Yk.

T756? Terms, 1661
'accommodation'
Cant (2). Wor.

T767 Terrible, 1642
Dur.

T773 Terrible, 1642
Yk.

T781 Terry, Edward, 1646
S Pl. Win.

T784 Tertullian, 1686
Yk (2).

T785 Tertullian, 1655
New.

T786+ Tertullian, 1689
See: CLC171.
Linc.

T790 Tesauro, Emmanuele, *Conte*,
1651
Carl. Chelm.

T791 Tesauro, Emmanuele, *Conte*,
1657
Cant. Ex.

T792 Tesdale, Christopher, 1644
Cant. Her. Yk.

T795B+ Testament, 1671
By Andrew Clark, for the Company
of Stationers; 8°.
Linc.

T798? Testament, 1681
By M. Clark for the Company of
Stationers.
Sal.

T800 Testament, 1686
Linc (tp imp).

T806 Testimony, [1680]
Linc.

T815 Testimony, [1686]
cap.
Yk.

T817 Testimony, 1648
Yk.

T823 Testimony, 1648
Dur (2 eds: catchword p. 37
'Nicol.' *or* 'Nicolas'). Yk.

T826 *See*: T707

T826A *See*: T707

T832? Thaddeus, John, 1662
Second ed. not on tp; For Simon
Miller.
Roch.

T838A? Tharpe, Edward, 1655
4°.
Carl.

T839 That, 1642
Sal.

T848+ Themylthorpe, Nicholas,
[c.1700?]
York, by John White; 8°; Possibly
18th cent.
Yk.

T850 Theocritus, 1676
Dated in Greek.
Nor. Pet.

T852 Theocritus, 1699
Cant. Ches.

T854 Theocritus, 1684
Ex.

T855 Theocritus, 1684
Nor. S Asa.

T857A Theodosius, 1675
Yk.

T859 Theophilus, 1684
Ex. Pet (tp imp). S Asa. S Pl.
Win. Yk.

T861 There, [1653]
Yk.

T887 Thévenot, Jean de, 1687
Ex. Pet. Yk.

T889 Theyer, John, 1643
Her (2).

T900 Third, 1688
Pet. S Asa. Wel.

T918 Thirty, 1688
Wel.

T945 Thomas, à Kempis, 1697
'The Christian pattern paraphras'd'
Sal.

T946 Thomas, à Kempis, 1698
S Alb.

T949 Thomas, à Kempis, 1685
Cant. Chi. Dur.

T950? Thomas, à Kempis, 1688
... Joan Hayes. Impensis Guil. Graves.
Cant. Nor.

T957+ Thomas, à Kempis, 1653
See: CLC172.
Cant.

T958 Thomas, à Kempis, 1653
Cant.

T967 Thomas, John, 1679
Linc.

T969 Thomas, Michael, 1655
New.

T970A Thomas, Richard, [1677]
Dur.

T971? Thomas, Samuel, 1683
For Richard Chiswell; 4°.
Dur.

T972 Thomas, Samuel, 1680
Carl. Wel.

T973 Thomas, Samuel, 1676
Carl. Pet (2).

T974 Thomas, Samuel, 1683
Ex. Wel. Win.

T975 Thomas, William, *Bp*, 1679
Dur. Her. S Pl. Yk.

T980 Thomas, William, *Bp*, 1689
Cant. Her. Wor.

T982 Thomas, William, *Bp*, 1678
Carl. Her. Llan. Wor.

T984 Thomas, William, *M.P.*,
1641[2]
Sal.

T985 Thomas, William, *M.P.*, 1641
Ex.

T988+ Thomas, William, *of Ubley*,
1662
For Edward Thomaas [*sic*]; 4°.
Pet.

T989 Thomas, William, *of Ubley*,
1656
By T.M. for Edward Thomas.
Pet.

T996 Thomason, William, 1641
Linc. Pet. Yk.

T1000 Thompson, *Sir* John, 1694
Cant.

T1007 Thompson, Richard, 1685
Wor.

T1017 Thompson, William, [1649]
Sal.

T1027 Thomson, George, 1666
'the pest'
Carl. Linc.

T1035A+ Thomson, Samuel, 1692
'Exercitations and meditations in
scripture phrases ...'; For Edward
Brewster; 8°; Anr ed., or a different
work?
Cant.

T1036+ Thomson, William, 1683
See: CLC173.
Dur (imp). Wor.

T1041 Thorius, Raphael, 1651
Carl.

T1042A Thornborough, John, 1641
... for Charles Duncomb.
Cant (2). Linc.

T1043 Thorndike, Herbert, 1670
Ban. Bur. Cant. Carl (2). Ely.
Ex. Linc. S Pl. Win. Yk.

T1044 Thorndike, Herbert, 1670
Carl. Dur. Ely. Ex. Nor. S Pl.
Wel. Win. Yk (2).

T1045 Thorndike, Herbert, 1649
Carl. Dur. Ely. Ex. Linc. Nor.
S Pl.

T1046? Thorndike, Herbert, 1670
For John Lutton.
Yk.

T1050 Thorndike, Herbert, 1659
Cant. Carl. Chelm. Chi. Dur.
Ely. Ex. Linc. Pet. S Asa. S Pl.
Win. Wor. Yk (3).

T1051 Thorndike, Herbert, 1662
Carl. Ex (tp imp). Pet. Wel.
Win. Yk.

T1052 Thorndike, Herbert, 1680
Ches. Ely. Ex. S Pl. Yk.

T1053 Thorndike, Herbert, [1656]
Dur (imp). Linc (imp). S Asa.

T1054 Thorndike, Herbert, 1642
Carl. Ches. Dur. Her. Linc.
Nor. S Pl. Yk (2).

T1055 Thorndike, Herbert, 1641
Carl. Ex. Linc. S Pl. Yk.

T1056 Thorndike, Herbert, 1674
Ely. Lich. Swel.

T1056+ Thorndike, Herbert, 1677
See: CLC174.
Dur.

T1057 Thorndike, Herbert, 1650
Ely. Ex. S Pl (imp).

T1057A- Thorne, Edmond, 1684
See: CLC175.
Chi. Llan.

T1057A+ Thorne, J., 1672
See: CLC176.
Ex.

T1061 Thornton, Stephen, 1691
Cant.

T1063 Thoroton, Robert, 1677
Dur. Linc. S Pl. Swel. Wor.
Yk.

T1067 Thorowgood, Thomas, 1650
S Asa.

T1069 Thorowgood, Thomas, 1645
Her. Yk.

T1070 Thorpe, Francis, 1649
Carl. Ex. Yk (2 − 1 tpw).

T1071 Thorpe, Francis, 1649
Yk.

T1072 Thorpe, George, 1677
'A sermon preached before the ...
Lord Mayor'; Clark.
Carl. Llan. Wel.

T1073 Thou, Jacques Auguste de,
1671
Carl.

T1077 Thou, Jacques Auguste de,
1674
For John Leigh.
Ex.

T1087? Three, 1688
Printed, and are to be sold by Randal
Taylor.
Cant.

T1088+ Three, 1688
See: CLC177.
Pet.

T1097 Three, 1660
Linc.

T1099 Three, [1689]
Cant (2). Wel.

T1102 Three, 1643
Cant.

T1104 Three, 1643
S Pl.

T1107 Three, 1642
Linc (3).

T1114 Three, [1688]
S Pl.

T1119 Three, [1643]
Cant.

T1120 Three, 1644[5]
Cant. Yk (2).

T1121 Three, 1645
Linc. Yk.

T1125A? Three, 1642
'... particulars. 1 A letter ...'
Cant (cropped).

T1132 Thruston, Malachi, 1670
... Johannem Martyn.
Ex.

T1133 Thucydides, 1696
Cant (2). Ches. Dur. Ely. Ex.
Her. Linc. Pet. S Pl (2).

T1134? Thucydides, 1676
By Andrew Clark, for Charles Harper.
Carl. Ex. S Dv.

T1138 Thurlin, Thomas, 1686
Her.

T1148 Tichborn, Robert, 1469 [*i.e.*
1649]
Cant.

T1151 Tichborn, Robert, 1649
Cant.

T1157 Tickell, John, 1665
cap.
Carl (date imp.).

T1160 Tydings, 1667
Yk.

T1185 Tillotson, John, 1696
Pet.

T1186 Tillotson, John, 1699
Chi. Nor. S Dv.

T1190 Tillotson, John, 1684
Dur. Ex (3). Lich. Nor. S Pl.

T1191 Tillotson, John, 1684
Cant (imp).

T1192? Tillotson, John, 1685
Impr. as T1190.
Carl. Dur.

T1193 Tillotson, John, 1685
Cant. Ex (4). S Pl. Sal. Wel.
Yk.

T1195 Tillotson, John, 1687
Cant. Dur (2 states).

T1196 Tillotson, John, 1687
Cant.

T1200 Tillotson, John, 1681
Carl. Llan (2). Pet.

T1204? Tillotson, John, 1695
For Ri. Chiswell.
Bris. Ex. Pet. Yk.

T1206 Tillotson, John, 1683
Nor (tpw). Pet.

T1207 Tillotson, John, 1684
Second ed. not on tp.
S Pl.

T1208 Tillotson, John, 1685
Cant.

T1210+ Tillotson, John, 1688
The sixth edition; For B. Aylmer and
W. Rogers; 8°.
Yk.

T1214 Tillotson, John, 1680
Carl. Ex (imp). Llan. Pet (2 − 1
imp). Yk (2).

T1217 Tillotson, John, 1666
Ban. Carl. Ex (2). Win.

T1218 Tillotson, John, 1676
Ex. Pet. S Pl. Yk.

T1219 Tillotson, John, 1688
Ches. S Asa.

T1221 Tillotson, John, 1697
Ban. Cant. Ely. S Asa. S Pl.
Yk.

T1222 Tillotson, John, 1693
Carl. Dur. Wel.

T1223 Tillotson, John, 1673
Cant. Carl. S Pl.

T1227 Tillotson, John, 1675
Cant (imp). Carl. Chi. Llan.
S Asa.

T1228 Tillotson, John, 1675
Carl. Her. Llan. Wor.

T1229 Tillotson, John, 1676
Carl. Her. Llan. Nor. S Asa.
Wel. Yk.

T1230 Tillotson, John, 1678
'preached'
S Asa. Wel. Yk.

T1230+ Tillotson, John, 1678
'preached'; By J.D. for Brabazon
Aylmer, and William Rogers; 4°.
Ban. Ex. Her. Llan. Nor (imp).
Pet. Wor (tp imp). Yk.

T1231 Tillotson, John, 1678
... for Brabazon Aylmer ...
Chi. Yk.

T1232 Tillotson, John, 1679
Carl. Dur (imp). Her. Pet. Wel.
Wor. Yk (4).

T1233 Tillotson, John, 1679
Carl. Ex. Llan.

T1234 Tillotson, John, 1682
Cant. Carl. Yk.

T1235 Tillotson, John, 1683
Cant. Chi. Llan (2). S Asa.
S Dv (imp). Yk.

T1236 Tillotson, John, 1689
Cant (2). S Asa. Wel. Wor.
Yk (2).

T1237 Tillotson, John, 1689
Ban. Ches. Wor. Yk.

T1238 Tillotson, John, 1689
Ban. Ches. S Asa. Sal. Wel.

T1240 Tillotson, John, 1690
Her. Wel. Yk.

T1241 Tillotson, John, 1690
Cant. Ches. Her. Sal. Wel.
Wor.

T1242? Tillotson, John, 1690
... and J. Tillotson.
Carl. Ches. Linc. S Asa. Wor.

T1243 Tillotson, John, 1691
Ches. Pet. S Asa.

T1244 Tillotson, John, 1691
Pet. S Asa. Wor.

T1245 Tillotson, John, 1692
Ches. S Asa.

T1246 Tillotson, John, 1692
Ches. Dur (imp). S Pl. Wor.
Yk (2).

T1248 Tillotson, John, 1693
Carl. Ches. Dur. Her. S Pl.
Wel. Wor.

T1249 Tillotson, John, 1694
Cant. Carl. Ches. Ex. S Asa
(2). Wel. Yk.

T1250 Tillotson, John, 1694
Her. S Asa.

T1252? Tillotson, John, 1686
'The third volume'; For B. Aylmer
and W. Rogers.
Carl. Her.

T1255 Tillotson, John, 1693
Carl. Dur. Llan. Pet. S Pl (2).
Wel. Yk.

T1256 Tillotson, John, 1671
Ex. Her. Win.

T1257? Tillotson, John, 1673
By A.M. for Sa. Gellibrand.
Bur. Yk.

T1258+ Tillotson, John, 1678
'The first volume'; The third edition;
For Ed. Gellibrand; 8°.
S Pl.

T1258++ Tillotson, John, 1680
'The first volume'; The fourth edition;
For E. Gellibrand; 8°.
Bur (details not confirmed).

T1258+++ Tillotson, John, 1681
'The first volume'; The fifth edition;
For Ed. Gellibrand; 8°.
Cant.

T1258++++ Tillotson, John, 1686
'The first volume'; The sixth edition;
For B. Aylmer, sold by S. Eddowes;
8°.
Her (impr. not confirmed).

T1260? Tillotson, John, 1694
'The first volume'; For Brabazon
Aylmer and William Rogers.
Cant.

T1260A----- Tillotson, John, 1678
'The second volume'; For Ed.
Gellibrand; 8°.
Pet. S Pl. Win.

T1260A---- Tillotson, John, 1678
'The second volume'; For Edw.
Gellibrand, sold by Henry Bonwicke;
8°.
Carl.

T1260A--- Tillotson, John, 1680
'The second volume'; The second
edition; For E. Gellibrand; 8°.
Bur (details not confirmed).

T1260A-- Tillotson, John, 1681
'The second volume'; The third
edition; For Ed. Gellibrand; 8°.
Cant. Ex.

T1260A- Tillotson, John, 1685
'The second volume'; The fourth
edition; For B. Aylmer, sold by S.
Eddowes; 8°.
Her (impr. not confirmed).

T1260A+ Tillotson, John, 1694
'The second volume'; The sixth
edition; Printed by J.H. for B. Aylmer
and W. Rogers; 8°.
Cant.

T1260B? Tillotson, John, 1694
'The fourth volume'; For B. Aylmer
and W. Rogers.
Ex. Yk.

T1261- Tillotson, John, 1697
No ed. statement; For Ri. Chiswell;
8°.
Dur. Ex. Pet. Yk.

T1263- Tillotson, John, 1698
No ed. statement; For Ri. Chiswell;
8°; Date may be wrong.
Ex. Pet.

T1264 Tillotson, John, 1699
Ex. Pet.

T1266 Tillotson, John, 1700
Should this be T1216-?
Ex. Pet.

T1267 Tillotson, John, 1700
Ches. Ex.

T1268 Tillotson, John, 1694
Ban (imp). Cant. Dur. Ex.
S Pl. Yk.

T1269- Tillotson, John, 1696
No ed. statement; For Ri. Chiswell;
8°.
Dur. Ex. Yk.

T1270? Tillotson, John, 1696
For Ri. Chiswell.
Dur. Ex. Her. Pet. Yk.

T1271+ Tillotson, John, 1698[9]
For Walter Kettilby, Brabazon
Aylmer and William Rogers; 8°.
Dur.

T1272 Tillotson, John, 1664
S Pl.

T1286 Times, 1643
Yk.

T1289 Times, 1642
Linc.

T1292 Timothy, [1679]
Linc.

T1294 Timson, John, 1654
Yk.

T1296 Timson, John, 1655
... Leicestershire.
Chelm. Yk.

T1299 Tindal, Matthew, 1694
Nor (imp). Wel.

T1300 Tindal, Matthew, 1694
Wel.

T1303 Tindal, Matthew, 1694
Bris.

T1310 Titus, Silas, [1657]
S Pl.

T1311 Titus, Silas, 1659
Cant (2 − 1 imp). Dur (imp).

T1312 Titus, Silas, 1689
Ex. Wel.

T1312+ Titus, Silas, 1689
London; 4°.
Yk.

T1317A- Tixier, Jean, 1647
Londini, excusae sumptibus Societatis
Stationariorum; 8°.
Pet.

T1317E- Tixier, Jean, 1642
Ex officina typographica Societatis
Stationariorum; 12°.
Yk.

T1367 To, 1659
S Pl.

T1382 To, 1675
Linc (date altered in MS to 1676).

T1383 To, 1647
Dur.

T1397 To, [1642]
Dur. Linc.

T1411? To, 1642
… T. Howell.
Linc.

T1416 To, [1641]
Dur. Linc.

T1420 To, 1641[2]
'… of the lords knights and gentlemen
of … Ireland'
Linc.

T1432 To, [1644]
Linc.

T1437 To, 1642
Dur.

T1439 To, 1642
Linc.

T1439+ To, 1642
See: CLC178.
Linc.

T1443 To, 1642
Dur. Linc.

T1445 To, 1646
Includes T1664; Printing history
confused, see NUC.
Cant. Pet (imp). Yk (2 - both
imp).

T1447 To, 1646
Cant. Pet.

T1451 To, 1641[2]
'… petition of the Lay-Catholikes of
England'
Pet.

T1451A+ To, [1700?]
See: CLC179.
Dur.

T1453? To, 1641
Dated 1641.
Linc.

T1455 To, 1641[2]
Linc.

T1461 To, 1641[2]
Dur.

T1465 To, 1642
Dur.

T1472 To, 1641[2]
Linc.

T1475 See: T1420

T1477 To, 1641
Linc.

T1496A+ To, 1642
See: CLC180.
Linc.

T1499? To, 1661
'… liturgy'; Some locations may be
T1499+.
Bur. Cant (2 − 1 imp). Carl.
Ches. Linc. Pet. S Pl. Win.

T1499+ To, 1661
As T1499, but: '… lyturgy'
Cant (2).

T1519? To, 1642
For M.Y.
Dur.

T1520 To, 1680
Ches.

T1523+ To, 1642
'majestie'; For E. Husbands and J.
Franck, Novem. 15; 4°.
Linc.

T1527+ To, [1641]
As T1527 but with impr.: For Henry
Overton.
Linc.

T1530 To, 1642
Linc.

T1531 To, 1642
Yk.

T1533 To, 1642
Linc.

T1541 To, [1642]
Linc.

T1543 To, 1642
Linc.

T1554 To, 1641[2]
Yk.

T1562 To, 1648
S Pl.

T1565 To, 1642[3]
Linc.

T1569 To, [1679]
Linc.

T1574 To, [1642]
Linc.

T1575 To, [1641/2]
Linc.

T1576 To, 1642
Dur. Linc.

T1583 To, 1654
Linc.

T1601 To, [1690]
Ex. Yk (2).

T1617 To, [1647]
Pet (tpw or cap.).*

T1624+ To, 1641[2]
For S.N.; brs.
Linc.

T1628 To, 1641[2]
'Peeres'
Dur (cropped).

T1633? To, 1641[2]
For Joseph Hunscott.
Ex. Linc.

T1651+ To, [1659?]
'… Lord Fleetwood'; [N.pl.]; brs.
Yk.

T1663 To, 1641[2]
Linc.

T1664 To, 1646
Pt of T1445; Printing history
confused, see NUC.
Cant. Yk (imp).

T1670 To, 1642
Dur.

T1671 To, 1642
Linc.

T1680 To, [1642]
Linc.

T1684 To, 1642
Linc.

T1695+ To, [1642?]
See: CLC181.
Linc.

T1707 To, 1641[2]
Linc.

T1717 To, [1689]
Wel. Yk.

T1762 Toland, John, 1696
Cant (2). Nor.

T1763 Toland, John, 1696
Dur.

T1771 Toleration, 1670
By J.C. for Robert Pawlet.
Win.

T1778 Tolson, John, 1643
Linc.

T1793 Tombeau, 1673
Win.

T1795? Tombes, John, 1676
'Bulli'; ... Tho: Bowman.
Win. Yk.

T1798 Tombes, John, 1652
Win.

T1799 Tombes, John, 1654
Win.

T1800 Tombes, John, 1657
Win.

T1801 Tombes, John, 1646
Chelm.

T1803 Tombes, John, 1669
Win.

T1816 Tombes, John, 1664
Win.

T1817? Tombes, John, 1662
By John Twyn for Andrew Crook.
Carl. Win.

T1818? Tombes, John, [1660]
34p.
Pet.

T1818+ Tombes, John, [1660]
As T1818, but: 27p.
Win.

T1822 Tombes, John, 1667
Sal. Win. Yk.

T1825 Tombes, John, 1645
Ex. Win.

T1826 Tombes, John, 1646
Second ed. not on tp.
Chelm. Win.

T1827 Tombes, John, 1641
12°.
Carl. Sal.

T1835 Tomkins, Thomas, 1667
'inconveniencies'
Carl. Ex. Yk.

T1836 Tomkins, Thomas, 1675
Carl. S Pl.

T1837 Tomkins, Thomas, 1668
Glo (Medius (tpw), Tenor (2)).
Nor (Pars organica, Medius (2),
Contratenor (2), Tenor (2),
Bassus (3)). Wor (Pars organica,
Contratenor (2), Tenor, Bassus
(3)).

T1837+ Tomkins, Thomas, 1680
See: CLC182.
Carl. Pet.

T1838 Tomkins, Thomas, 1660
Win. Yk.

T1839 Tomkins, Thomas, 1661
Carl. Yk.

T1840 Tomkinson, Thomas, 1695
Yk.

T1855 Tomlinson, William, 1653
Yk.

T1859 Tomlyns, Samuel, 1680
Her.

T1865 Tompkins, Nathaniel, [1643]
Cant (2).

T1874 Tong, William, 1693
Yk.

T1877 Tonge, Ezerel, 1680
Pt 2 = S386.
Win.

T1878 Tonge, Ezerel, 1679
Win.

T1879 Tonge, Ezerel, 1680
Win.

T1886 Tonge, Thomas, 1654
Typis T.M. pro Andraeo Crook.
Yk.

T1888 Tonstall, George, 1672
Dur. Yk.

T1889 Tonstall, George, 1670
'Scarbrough'
Dur. Yk (3).

T1907 Topham, George, 1690
Cant.

T1908 Topham, George, 1682
Pet (2).

T1919? Torriano, Giovanni, 1657
For J. Martin and J. Allestrye.
Cant. Lich.

T1921+ Torriano, Giovanni, 1673
By T.R. for J. Martyn; 8°.
Ches.

T1936 Torshell, Samuel, 1647
Bur. Carl.

T1937 Torshell, Samuel, 1644
Bur. Chelm.

T1938 Torshell, Samuel, 1644
Bur. Carl. Ex. Pet.

T1939 See: S5692

T1940 Torshell, Samuel, 1646
Bur. Carl.

T1943? Tortello, Arcangelo, 1680
Cleve.
Ex.

T1946 Tory, 1682
Cant.

T1956 Touching, 1643
Liv.

T1958 Towers, John, 1660
Carl.

T1959 Towers, William, 1654
Carl.

T1963 Towers, William, 1663
Linc. Pet. S Asa.

T1964 Towers, William, 1660
Pet.

T1966 Towerson, Gabriel, 1678
'Part I'
Ban. Cant. Dur. Ex. Glo. Her.
Linc. S Pl. Yk (imp).

T1967? Towerson, Gabriel, 1685
Second ed. not on tp; By J. Playford,
...
Chi. Ely. Ex. Nor. Roch. Sal.

T1968- Towerson, Gabriel, 1680
'Part III'; By J. Macock for John
Martyn; 2°.
Ban. Cant. Chi. Dur. Glo.
Nor. S Pl. Yk.

T1968? Towerson, Gabriel, 1685
The second edition; ... Ric. Chiswell
...
Bur. Ely. Roch. Sal.

T1969 Towerson, Gabriel, 1688
Ban. Bur. Glo. Roch. S Pl.
Sal.

T1970 Towerson, Gabriel, 1676
Bur. Cant. Carl. Ely (2). Glo.
Yk.

T1971- Towerson, Gabriel, 1681
No ed. statement; By J. Macock, for
Robert Littlebury, Robert Scott and
George Wells; 2°.
Ban. Dur. Nor.

T1971 Towerson, Gabriel, 1685
The third edition.
Bur. Chi. Ex. Lich. Roch. Sal.

T1973 Towerson, Gabriel, 1686
8°.
Ely. Ex.

T1974 Towerson, Gabriel, 1696
Cant.

T1975? Towgood, Richard, 1676
'The Almighty his gracious token of love'; By H.C. for H. Brome, sold by Humphrey Dixon in Bristol.
Carl.

T1982 Townesend, George, 1685
Cant.

T2020 Traherne, Thomas, 1675
Dur. Glo.

T2021 Traherne, Thomas, 1673
Ban. Her (imp?)*. Liv. Pet. S Pl. Sal. Wel. Wor.

T2025 Traytors, 1650
Linc. Win.

T2026+ Traytors, 1662
See: CLC183.
Pet.

T2028 Transactions, 1648
Yk.

T2029 Trap, 1670
S Pl.

T2036 Trapp, John, 1662
Chelm. Ex (tpw). Lich.

T2038 Trapp, John, 1650
Chelm. Glo. Rip.

T2039? Trapp, John, 1656
The second edition.
Chelm. Ex. Nor.

T2040 Trapp, John, 1647
Glo. Rip (tpw).

T2041 Trapp, John, 1657
Chelm. Ex.

T2042 Trapp, John, 1647
Pet. Rip.

T2043 Trapp, John, 1654
Chelm. Ex. Rip. Win.

T2044? Trapp, John, 1660
Second ed. not on tp; ... Simmons in Kederminster ...
Ches. Ex. Rip. Win.

T2046 Trapp, John, 1650
Sal.

T2073 Treason, 1660
Carl.

T2076 Treason, 1641
Linc.

T2095 Treatise, [166-]
Sal (imp).

T2100 Treatie, 1642
Linc.

T2102 Treby, *Sir* George, 1681
Ban. Ely. Linc. Win.

T2104 Treby, *Sir* George, 1681
Ban. Linc. Win.

T2107 Treby, *Sir* George, 1681
Pet. Win.

T2108 Trelawny, *Sir* John, 1642
Linc.

T2110 Trenchard, John, 1697
Ban. Dur (2). Nor. Pet. S Pl. Sal.

T2111 Trenchard, John, 1698
Cant.

T2113 Trenchard, John, 1697
Nor. S Pl.

T2114 Trenchard, John, 1694
'29th. of May'
Cant. Her.

T2116 Trenchard, John, 1698
Ban. Cant. S Pl.

T2117 Trenchard, John, 1698
Cant.

T2124+ Trent, *Council of*, 1687
See: CLC184.
S Asa.

T2126 Trescot, Thomas, 1642[3]
Carl.

T2134 Trevor, *Sir* John, 1680
... John Gain.
Yk (imp).

T2140 Tryal, 1681
Glo (imp). Linc. Nor. S Pl (tpw). Wor.

T2149 Tryal, 1681
Linc.

T2152 Tryal, 1696
Ely.

T2160 Tryal, 1684
Ely.

T2161? Tryal, 1679/80
Pawlett.
Ely. Linc. Yk.

T2164 Tryal, 1684
Ely.

T2165 Tryal, 1680
Linc. Win.

T2168 Triall, 1649
Pet.

T2171 Tryal, 1680
Ely. Linc. Nor.

T2176 Trial, 1679
Linc. Win. Yk.

T2177 Tryal, 1680
Linc (2 – 1 imp).

T2185 Tryal, 1678
Carl. Ely. Linc. Nor. S Pl (imp). Win.

T2187 Triall, 1680
Wor.

T2189 Tryal, 1686
Ely.

T2190 Trial, 1681
Wor.

T2192 Tryal, 1681
Nor.

T2196 Tryal, 1684
Ely. S Dv.

T2203+ Triall, 1661
See: CLC185.
Linc.

T2205 Tryal, 1679
Ely. Linc. Nor.

T2207 Tryal, 1682
Glo.

T2209 Tryal, 1679
Linc. Win.

T2212 Tryall, 1679
Carl. Ely. Linc. Nor. Win. Yk.

T2214 Tryal, 1681
Linc. Wor (imp).

T2216 Tryal, 1662
Cant. Dur (imp). Pet (imp).

T2217 Tryal, 1681
Nor.

T2219? Tryal, 1680
Basset.
Win.

T2226 Triall, 1643
'A triall ...'
Cant. Pet.

T2231 Tryal, 1683
S Dv.

T2232 Tryal, 1680
Dur. Glo. Linc. Wel (2 – 1 imp*). Win. Wor.

T2232A? Tryal, 1700
For Ri. Chiswell, M. Wotton, and G. Conyers.
Cant (2). Her.

T2237 Tryal, 1678
Carl. Linc. Nor. Wel. Win.

T2238 Tryal, 1680/1
Ely. Glo. Linc. Nor. Wor. Yk.

T2240 Tryal, 1682
8°.
Ex.

T2243 Tryals, 1680
Ely. Linc. Win.

T2247? Tryals, 1679
95p.
Carl. Ely*. Linc. Wel. Win*.
Yk*.

T2247+ Tryals, 1679
As T2247, but: 99p.
Nor. S Pl (tpw).

T2249? Tryals, 1685
'... convictions & sentence ...'; ...
Randal Taylor.
Ely.

T2250 Tryals, 1685
Printed and sold by ...
Ely.

T2254 Tryals, 1693
Cant.

T2255+ Tryals, 1696
For Samuel Heyrick; 2°.
Ely.

T2256? Tryals, 1679
Pawlet.
Carl. Ely. Linc. Nor. S Pl
(imp). Wel. Win.

T2259 Tryals, 1679
Carl. Ely. Linc. Nor. S Pl.
Win. Yk.

T2261 Tryals, 1658
Pet.

T2265 Tryals, 1683
Ely. S Dv.

T2268 Tryals, 1678
Carl. Ely. Linc. Nor. Wel.
Win.

T2280 Trimnell, Charles, 1697
Dur.

T2281 Trimnell, Charles, 1697
Nor.

T2283 Trinder, Charles, 1687/8
Printed and to be sold by ...
Wel.

T2286A Tripla, 1677
Dur.

T2287 Triple, 1641
Pet (tp imp).

T2297 Triumphs, 1681
Linc.

T2302 Troia, 1674
Linc.

T2307 Trotti de la Chétardie, J.,
1683
'nobleman' *not* 'man'
Carl.

T2312 Troughton, John, 1681
Lich. Yk.

T2314 Troughton, John, 1677–78
Pet (pt 1 only).

T2321 Trowbridge, Francis
Seymour, *Baron*, 1641
Dur.

T2373 True, 1692
Ely.

T2396 True, 1677
Linc.

T2399 True, 1679
Linc.

T2409 True, [1679]
Linc.

T2415 True, 1681
Linc (2).

T2416 True, 1660
Yk.

T2417 True, 1642
Dur. Linc.

T2423A True, 1685
Nor.

T2427 True, 1642
Yk.

T2439 True, 1642
Yk.

T2440 True, 1643
Linc. Yk (2).

T2449 True, 1642
Linc.

T2452 True, 1642
Linc.

T2470? True, 1667
35p.
Cant. S Pl (2)*. Yk*.

T2475A? True, [1642]
'faithfull'
Linc.

T2476 True, 1656[7]
Ex.

T2488? True, 1663[4]
By William Godbid, for Nath. Brook
& Henry Marsh.
Sal. Yk.

T2497 True, 1690
S Pl.

T2498+ True, [1672]
As T2498, but no date on tp.
Bris.

T2501 True, 1654
Pet.

T2505 True, 1642
Linc.

T2506 True, 1643
Wing has wrong date.
Yk.

T2528 True, 1690
Cant.

T2529+ True, 1660
See: CLC186.
Linc.

T2533 True, 1678
Linc.

T2535 True, [1681]
Linc.

T2537 True, [1679–80]
Linc.

T2540 True, 1642
Linc.

T2547 True, 1642
Yk*.

T2551 True, 1642
'cruell'
Dur. Linc.

T2552 True, [1642]
Linc.

T2560 True, 1656
Ex.

T2561+ True, 1650
See: CLC187.
Linc.

T2572? True, 1679
'plaine'; For William Crook ...
Win.

T2578 True, 1642
Linc.

T2584 True, 1681
Ches.

T2592 True, 1642
Dur.

T2598A True, [168-?]
Cant.

T2600 True, 1641
Sal. Yk.

T2609+ True, 1644
See: CLC188.
Yk.

T2611+ True, 1660
See: CLC189.
Llan.

T2621 True, 1642[3]
Linc.

T2627 True, 1659
Ex.

T2632 True, 1648
Yk.

T2633 True, 1642
Dur (imp).

T2637 True, 1649
Yk.

T2644? True, 1695[6]
Colophon: [N.pl.], printed for John
Everingham and sold by E. Whitlock;
Pt of E2378+.
Dur.

T2650 True, 1641[2]
Cant. Dur.

T2651+ True, [1672?]
See: CLC190.
Linc.

T2656 True, 1641[2]
Dur.

T2657 True, 1642
Linc.

T2662 True, 1641[2]
Dur (impr. cropped; '... to the ...
Peeres ... March 18. 1641')*.

T2663 True, 1642
Linc.

T2665 True, 1641
Cant. Linc. Pet (2). Sal. Yk.

T2672 True, 1666
Lich. Linc.

T2673 True, 1642
'... plot intended ... by the Lord
Digby ... at Sherborne ...'
Linc.

T2679 True, 1641
'William'
Yk.

T2693 True, 1680
Linc.

T2696? True, 1681
For William Crooke.
Ex (imp). Wel. Win. Yk.

T2697 True, 1680
Carl. Win.

T2703 True, 1683
Bris. Carl.

T2709 True, 1642
Linc.

T2711+ True, [N.d.]
See: CLC191.
Yk.

T2733A True, [1680]
'appointed'
Linc.

T2758 True, 1659
Yk.

T2758+ True, 1646
'The true mannor [*sic*] and forme ...
funerall of ... Robert Earle of Essex';
Formerly G5.
Pet.

T2774 True, 1689
Ex.

T2777 True, 1653
London, printed in the year.
Dur.

T2787 True, 1666
Linc.

T2804 True, 1690
S Asa.

T2809 True, 1681
'A true ...'
Linc.

T2827A True, [1680]
'The true narrative of the proceedings
...'
Linc.

T2843 True, 1641
Linc.

T2845+ True, 1647
See: CLC192.
Pet.

T2847 True, 1642
Yk.

T2850 True, 1690
Nor.

T2850+ True, 1673
See: CLC193.
Carl. Linc. Win.

T2860 True, 1642
Linc (3). Yk.

T2863 True, [1680]
Linc.

T2883A True, 1643
Linc.

T2885 True, 1681
Linc.

T2893 True, 1681
Linc.

T2898+ True, [N.d.]
See: CLC194.
Yk.

T2904 True, 1642
Dur.

T2906 True, 1642
Ex. Linc.

T2907 True, 1642
Dur. Linc.

T2909 True, 1647
Yk.

T2911 True, 1642
Yk.

T2922 True, 1642
Linc.

T2931? True, 1642
'Caveleers'
Linc.

T2942 True, 1643
Linc.

T2953 True, 1642
Yk.

T2954 True, 1648
Yk.

T2956 True, 1643
Chi. Linc.

T2957 True, 1641
Yk.

T2971 True, 1679
Linc.

T2975 True, 1642[3]
Yk.

T2979 True, 1643
Cant.

T2980 True, 1644
Yk.

T2982 True, 1643
Pet.

T2986 True, [1685]
Wel.

T2998+ True, [1657?]
Different ed. from BL copy of T2998.
Yk (tpw).

T3002? True, 1689
Printed and sold by Richard Baldwin.
Dur. S Asa. Wel.

T3002A+ True, 1641
'Strafford'; [N.pl.]; 4°.
Pet.

T3014 True, 1643
Yk.

T3015 True, 1642
Dur.

T3022 True, 1643
Linc.

T3029 True, 1642
For B.W. ...
Linc. Yk.

T3031 True, 1643
Yk.

T3032? True, 1643
Printed at Yorke ...
Linc.

T3033 True, 1658
Pet. Sal.

T3033+ True, 1660
See: CLC195.
Pet.

T3039 True, 1654
Yk.

T3060 True, [1642]
Linc.

T3060+ True, 1642
As T3060, apart from date.
Dur.

T3065 True, 1651
Carl.

T3077 True, 1643
Pet.

T3082? True, 1666
'... whole procedure between the
Corporation of Canterbury, and Mr.
John Somner'
Cant.

T3082+ True, 1643
See: CLC196.
Linc.

T3099? True, 1679
For T. Hills ... T. Cockeril ...
Carl. Ely. Linc. Yk (2 — 1 tp
imp).

T3101 True, 1688
S Pl.

T3114 True, 1654
Ex (tp imp).

T3126 True, 1690
Wel.

T3138 Truman, Joseph, 1671
Carl. Chelm.

T3140 Truman, Joseph, 1671
By T.M. for Robert Clavel.
Carl. S Asa.

T3141 Truman, Joseph, 1669
By A. Maxwell, for H. Brome and R.
Clavell.
Carl. Chelm.

T3142? Truman, Joseph, 1672
By A. Maxwell, for R. Clavell; 8°.
S Asa.

T3146 Trussel, John, 1685
S Asa.

T3149 Truth, 1679
Nor.

T3150 Truth, 1642
Sal.

T3153 Truth, 1693
Cant.

T3154+ Truth, 1685
See: CLC197.
Yk.

T3168 Truths, [1646]
Linc. Sal. Yk.

T3171 Truths, 1642
Linc.

T3175+ Tryon, Thomas, 1691
'The art of brewing beer'; The second
edition; For Tho. Salusbury; 12°.
Carl.

T3209 Tucker, Fr., 1661
Ex.

T3211 Tuckney, Anthony, 1654
Carl.

T3215 Tuckney, Anthony, 1676
Bur. Ely.

T3216 Tuckney, Anthony, 1656
Carl.

T3216+ Tuckney, Anthony, 1656
By J.F. for I. Rothwell; 12°.
S Pl.

T3217 Tuckney, Anthony, 1654
Carl.

T3218 Tuckney, Anthony, 1654
Rothwel.
Carl.

T3218+ Tuckney, Anthony, 1654
For J. Rothwell and S. Gellebrand; 8°.
Pet.

T3224? Tuke, Edward, 1642
'Jehovah'
Ex.

T3228 Tuke, Richard, 1672
Nor.

T3232 Tuke, *Sir* Samuel, 1660
Pet (imp). Win.

T3235 Tully, George, 1688
Ex (4 — 1 imp). Nor. Sal. Yk.

T3236 Tully, George, 1687
4°.
Dur. Ex. Wel. Yk.

T3237 Tully, George, 1689
Ban. Cant. Ex. Her. Yk.

T3238 Tully, George, 1694
Carl. Yk.

T3240 Tully, George, 1699
Dur.

T3241 Tully, George, 1689
Cant. Carl. Her. New. Sal.
Wor. Yk.

T3242 Tully, George, 1691
Wor. Yk (4).

T3244 Tully, Thomas, 1674
Carl. Chelm. Her. Pet. Win.

T3245 Tully, Thomas, 1675
Carl (with sigs F—G, see Madan).
Win.

T3247- Tully, Thomas, 1665
Typis Tho. Ratcliff, impensis Humphr.
Robinson; 8°.
Her.

T3247 Tully, Thomas, 1668
Editio altera.
Ex. Win. Yk.

T3248 Tully, Thomas, 1673
Typis Guil. Downing ...
Carl. Lich. Win.

T3249 Tully, Thomas, 1683
Ban. Her. Wel.

T3250 Tully, Thomas, 1700
Dur. Nor. Yk.

T3251A Turbervill, Edward, 1681
Linc. Yk.

T3252 Turbervill, Edward, 1680
Ely. Glo. Linc. Win. Yk.

T3256+ Turbervill, Henry, 1695
Printed in the year; 12°.
Yk.

T3257 Turbervill, Henry, 1654
'manuel'
Carl. Sal.

T3263 Turmiger, Bevill, 1653
Carl.

T3269 Turner, Bryan, 1691
Wel.

T3270 Turner, Bryan, 1678
Carl. Linc. Wor.

T3271 Turner, Bryan, 1681
Carl. Nor.

T3274 Turner, Francis, 1676
Bur. Cant. Chelm. Win.

T3275 Turner, Francis, 1676
Bur. Carl. Ely. Linc. Pet. Sal.

T3280 Turner, Francis, 1681
Cant. Carl. Wel. Wor.

T3281 Turner, Francis, 1682
Carl. S Asa (imp). Wel. Wor.

T3282 Turner, Francis, 1683
Carl. Win.

T3283 Turner, Francis, 1684
Carl. Wel. Yk.

T3284 Turner, Francis, 1684
Carl. Wel.

T3285 Turner, Francis, 1685
Cant (2). Wel.

T3286 Turner, Francis, 1685
Cant (2). Wel.

T3287 Turner, Francis, 1685
Cant. Wel.

T3288 Turner, Francis, 1685
Cant (2 — 1 imp). Carl. Dur (2).
Ex (tpw)*. Llan (tpw?)*. Nor.
Wor. Yk (4).

T3292 Turner, *Sir* James, 1683
... for Richard Chiswell.
Carl. Wel.

T3296 Turner, John, *of Christs Coll., Cambridge*, 1684
For Walter Kettilby; pp. 191–9, 316–41; 199–211, 248–312; Prob. pt of a work by John Turner, *Hospitaller*.
S Pl.

T3299 Turner, John, *Hospitaller*, 1679
Bur. Cant. Llan. Wor.

T3303 Turner, John, *Hospitaller*, 1685
Ex.

T3304 Turner, John, *Hospitaller*, 1686
Wel.

T3306 Turner, John, *Hospitaller*, 1685
S Pl. Yk.

T3307 Turner, John, *Hospitaller*, 1683
Sal.

T3310 Turner, John, *Hospitaller*, 1682
Cant. Ely.

T3311 Turner, John, *Hospitaller*, 1690
Cant.

T3312A - Turner, John, *Hospitaller*, 1683
'... The second part'; London, printed for Samuel Sympson in Cambridge; 8°.
Dur (tp imp). S Pl.

T3312A Turner, John, *Hospitaller*, 1684
Ex.

T3315 Turner, John, *Hospitaller*, 1684
Cant.

T3317 Turner, John, *Hospitaller*, 1683
Bur. Carl. Wor.

T3318A Turner, John, *Hospitaller*, 1683
Carl.

T3319 Turner, John, *Hospitaller*, 1682
Cant.

T3321? Turner, John, *Hospitaller*, 1699
Wyat.
Lich.

T3333+ Turner, Roger, 1661
See: CLC198.
S Asa. Wor.

T3337 Turner, Thomas, 1675
Linc.

T3338 Turner, Thomas, 1675
Carl.

T3339 Turner, Thomas, 1677
Carl.

T3340 Turner, Thomas, 1685
Cant.

T3344 Turner, William, [1696]
Ely.

T3345 Turner, William, *of Walberton*, 1697
Lich.

T3347 Turner, William, *of Walberton*, 1695
Cant.

T3349 Turnor, *Sir* Edward, 1661
Win.

T3352? Turnor, *Sir* Edward, 1661
'thirtieth day of July'; Twyford.
Lich (2). Linc.

T3352A Turnor, *Sir* Edward, 1661
Linc.

T3354? Turnor, *Sir* Edward, 1662
'nineteenth day of May'; ... for Henry Twyford.
Lich. Linc.

T3355? Turnor, *Sir* Edward, [1663]
... for Robert Pawlet.
Lich. Linc.

T3356 Turnor, *Sir* Edward, 1664[5]
Linc.

T3357 Turnor, *Sir* Edward, 1664
Ches. Lich. Linc.

T3358 Turnor, *Sir* Edward, 1665
Lich.

T3360 Turnor, *Sir* Edward, 1666[7]
Lich. Linc.

T3361 Turnor, *Sir* Edward, 1666[7]
Linc.

T3362 Turnor, *Sir* Edward, 1670
Lich.

T3365 Turnor, *Sir* Edward, 1661
pp. 31–49 of C3071.
Lich. Linc.

T3371 - Tutchin, John, 1689
'The bloody assizes'; Formerly B1905.
S Pl.

T3380 Tutchin, John, 1693
Wor.

T3384? Tutchin, John, 1691
4°.
Sal.

T3387+ Tuthill, Henry, 1645
See: CLC199.
Linc.

T3387++ Tuthill, Henry, 1645
See: CLC200.
Linc.

T3392 Twelfth, 1689
S Asa. Wel.

T3409 XXV, 1659
Ex.

T3411? Twenty four, 1680
For Benjamin Harris.
Linc.

T3416A Twisse, Robert, 1665
Chelm.

T3420 Twisse, William, [1650/1]
=STC 24403; Not a Wing book, date = [1631?].
Chelm. Yk (imp).

T3422 Twisse, William, 1641
Chelm.

T3423 Twisse, William, 1653
Carl. Ex.

T3428 Two, 1681
Ches. Wel.

T3443 Two, 1642
Linc.

T3456+ Two, 1652
See: CLC201.
Ex.

T3481? Two, 1659[60]
'... to ... Gen. Monck'; By J. Macock.
Ex.

T3482 Two, 1692
Yk.

T3483 Two, [1692]
4°.
Cant.

T3498A Two , 1641
Linc (2).

T3499 Two, [1643]
Linc. Pet. Yk.

T3504 Two, [1642]
Dur.

T3505 Two , [1642]
Linc.

T3505A Two, 1644
Carl.

T3507 Two, 1642
Yk (3).

T3507A Two, 1642
Linc. Yk.

T3512 Two, 1641[2]
Linc.

T3516 Two, 1647
Carl. Pet. Yk.

T3516+ Two, 1647
Oxford, by H.H.; 4°.
Carl.

T3521 Two, 1642
Linc.

T3526 Two, 1648
Pet.

T3540 *See*: Periodicals

T3552 Twysden, *Sir* Roger, 1657
'historicall'; ... for Daniel Pakeman.
Carl. Dur. Lich. Linc. Sal.
Win. Yk.

T3554 Twysden, *Sir* Roger, 1675
Dur. Ely. Ex. Her. Llan. S Pl
(2). Sal. Wel. Yk.

T3555 *See*: F927

T3560 Tyler, John, 1694
'March xxiii'
Ban. Cant. Carl. Her.

T3581 Tyrrell, James, 1691/2
Ely (includes tp of T3582).

T3582? Tyrrell, James, 1694
'... enquiry ... in thirteen dialogues'
Bris (dialogue 2 only). Carl
(dialogue 12 only). S Asa.

T3583 Tyrrell, James, 1692
Carl. Pet. Yk.

T3585 Tyrrell, James, 1696
Glo.

T3588 Tyrrell, James, 1700
Pet.

T3589 Tyrrell, James, 1700
Glo. Pet.

T3591 Tyrrell, James, 1681
'monarcha'
Win.

T3598 Tyson, Edward, 1699
... to be had of Mr. Hunt.
Bris.

U1 U., O., 1683
S Pl.

U4 Udall, Ephraim, 1642
Cant.

U5+ Udall, Ephraim, 1660
As U5, apart from date.
Yk.

U8 Udall, Ephraim, 1642
Carl.

U9 Udall, Ephraim, 1642
Cant. Pet. S Pl.

U11 Udall, Ephraim, 1642
S Asa. Yk.

U12 Udall, Ephraim, 1642
Carl. Ex. Pet.

U14 Udall, John, 1643
Dur. Yk.

U17? Udall, O., 1663
'uzza'
Pet.

U23 Ulugh Beg, *ibn Shahrukh*, 1665
... venales prostant apud ...
Sal. Wor.

U24 Ulugh Beg, *ibn Shahrukh*, 1650
Ex. Sal. Wel.

U26 Umfreville, William, 1646
Sal.

U28 Unanimous, 1649
Yk.

U41 Un-deceiver, 1643
Cant. Pet.

U43 Underhill, Thomas, 1660
Pet.

U68 Unhappy, 1659
Pet.

U74? Universal, 1680
For Tho. Parkhurst.
Carl.

U84 Unlimited, [1642]
Cant. Linc.

U91 Unparalleld, 1656
Carl.

U94 Unreasonableness, 1692
Cant.

U103 Untrussing, 1642
Cant.

U104A+ Upon, 1665
See: CLC202.
Linc.

U109 Upon, 1664
Linc.

U124 Upton, Nicholas, 1654
'Nicolai Vptoni de studio militari'
Yk.

U127+ Urban VIII, 1642
By E.G. for M. Sparkes junior; 4°.
Linc.

U128 Urban VIII, 1643
Pet.

U129 Urban VIII, 1641
Dur.

U140 Urquhart, *Sir* Thomas, 1645
Sal.

U142 Ursin, Zacharias, 1645
Carl. Yk.

U144 Use, 1687
By Nathaniel Thompson.
Ban. Wel.

U147 Ussher, James, 1650
Ban. Cant. Ex. S Asa. S Pl.

U147A Ussher, James, 1650
Ches. Ely. Lich. Linc. Wel.
Wor.

U147B Ussher, James, 1650
Dur. Her. Rip. Win. Yk.

U148 Ussher, James, 1654
'Jacobi Usserii Armachani annalium
...'
Ban. Ches (tpw?). Dur. Ely.
Ex. Glo (imp). Rip. S Asa.
S Pl. Win. Wor. Yk.

U148+ Ussher, James, 1654
As U148, but: 'Jacobi Vsserii ...
Annales. In quibus, ...'; Some
locations on U148 may belong to this
no.
Cant. Wel.

U149 Ussher, James, 1658
Cant. Ex. Glo. Her (imp).
S Dv.

U150 Ussher, James, 1686
S Pl.

U151 Ussher, James, 1645
Cant (tpw). Ely. Her. Llan.

U152 Ussher, James, 1647
Ban. Chi. Ex. Sal.

U153 Ussher, James, 1648
Chelm. Her. Swel. Wor. Yk.

U154 Ussher, James, 1649
... sold by Thomas Dring.
Carl. Dur. Linc (2 — 1 imp).

U155 Ussher, James, 1653
Chelm.

U155+ Ussher, James, 1653
The fourth edition; By T. Dawes for
W. Hunt, T. Downs and G. Badger;
2°.
Bur (details not confirmed).

U156? Ussher, James, 1658
... and Francis Eglesfield.
Bris.

U157? Ussher, James, 1670
For Nath. Ranew and J. Robinson.
Nor. S Dv.

U158 Ussher, James, 1677
Carl. Win.

U159 Ussher, James, 1687
S Pl.

U160 Ussher, James, 1687
Cant. Ches. Chi. Ely. Ex (2).
Glo (2). Linc. Pet. S Asa. S Pl.
Wel (2). Wor. Yk.

U161 Ussher, James, 1659
Carl. Her. Win.

U162 Ussher, James, 1660
Bur. Carl. Ely. Ex. Linc. Nor.
S Asa. Sal. Win. Wor.

U162+ Ussher, James, 1660
Oxoniae, excudebat W. Hall, impensis
Joh: Forrest; 4°.
S Pl.

U163 *See*: P548 & P548+

U165 Ussher, James, 1655
Carl. Ches. Ely. Ex. Lich.
S Pl. Wor.

U166 Ussher, James, 1648
Ches. Win. Yk.

U167 Ussher, James, 1647
Dur. Linc. S Pl. Yk.

U168 Ussher, James, 1660
Bur. Ely. Ex. Linc. Nor.
S Asa. S Pl. Sal. Win. Wor.
Yk.

U169 Ussher, James, 1652
... impensis J. Crook ...
Linc. Yk.

U170 Ussher, James, 1687
S Pl.

U174 Ussher, James, 1660
Lich (tpw)*.

U175 Ussher, James, 1679
Linc.

U179 Ussher, James, 1689
Glo. S Asa.

U179A Ussher, James, 1690
Ban. Dur. Ely. Linc. Pet.
S Asa. S Pl (2). Swel. Wel. Win.
Wor. Yk.

U181 Ussher, James, 1645
Cant. Ely. Ex. Her. Llan.

U181+ Ussher, James, 1647
Impr. as U182; 2°.
Ban. Chi. Ex. Sal.

U182 Ussher, James, 1649
Carl. Chelm. Dur. Linc (2).
Swel. Wor. Yk*.

U183 Ussher, James, 1653
Bur*. Chelm*.

U184 Ussher, James, 1658
Bris.

U184A Ussher, James, 1670
Nor. S Dv.

U185 Ussher, James, 1644
Cant. Chelm. Ches (2). Chi.
Dur. Ely. Ex. Lich. Linc.
S Asa. S Pl. Sal (2). Wor. Yk.

U186 Ussher, James, 1641
Cant (2). Dur (2). Ex. Her.
Linc. Pet. Win. Yk (2).

U186A Ussher, James, 1641
Cant. Carl. Linc. Nor. Pet.
Yk.

U187 Ussher, James, 1657
'judgement'
Carl. Pet.

U188 Ussher, James, 1658
'judgement'
Bur. Cant (imp). Ely. Win.

U189 Ussher, James, 1659
'judgement'
Ely.

U192 Ussher, James, 1657
Llan. S Asa.

U193? Ussher, James, 1687
Impensis Samuelis Smith.
Wel.

U194 Ussher, James, 1688
S Pl.

U196 Ussher, James, 1661
Bur. Carl. Ches. Ex. S Pl.

U197 Ussher, James, 1683
Ban. Ches. Linc.

U198? Ussher, James, 1688
For Charles Harper.
S Asa.

U207 Ussher, James, 1678
Pet.

U207+ Ussher, James, 1678
No ed. statement; For Nathaniel
Ranew; 2°.
Yk.

U217 Ussher, James, 1656
Cant. Carl. Ex. Linc. Win.
Yk.

U218 *See*: U188

U220 Ussher, James, 1689
Cant.

U221 Ussher, James, 1648
Wor. Yk.

U222 Ussher, James, 1681
Her.

U224 Ussher, James, 1644
Cant.

U227? Ussher, James, 1678
For Nathanael Ranew.
Yk.

U228 Ussher, James, 1642
Pet. S Pl.

U231 Utrum, 1691
Dur.

V5 V., G. L., 1643
Linc. Sal (2).

V14 V., V. N., [1641]
Yk.

V22 Valdés, Juan de, 1646
Carl. Win. Yk.

V24- Valentine, Henry, 1671
See: CLC203.
Cant.

V24 Valentine, Thomas, 1647
Pet.

V25 Valentine, Thomas, 1647
Pet.

V26 Valentine, Thomas, 1643
Cant. Pet.

V46 Valla, Lorenzo, 1688
Ely. Ex. Glo (tpw). Nor.
S Asa. Wel. Yk.

V48 Valle, Pietro della, 1665
By J. Macock, for John Martin, and
James Allestry.
Wel.

V50 Valor, 1695
'beneficiorum'; ... W. Freeman and G.
Sawbridge.
Chi. Lich. S Asa. Swel.

V50+ Valor, 1695
As V50, but: 12°.
Wel. Win. Yk.

V72 Vane, *Sir* Henry, [1660]
Ex.

V75A Vane, *Sir* Henry, 1655
Yk.

V75A+ Vane, *Sir* Henry, 1698
Sold by Ed. Bell; 4°.
Ban.

V76 Vane, *Sir* Henry, 1641
Cant. Linc (imp). Yk.

V78 Vane, *Sir* Henry, 1643
Cant (2). Sal.

V80 Vane, *Sir* Henry, 1662
Cant.

V81 Vane, Thomas, 1646
8°; Pt 2 of P2272.
Bur. Carl. Linc. Yk.

V82? Vane, Thomas, 1645
8°.
Linc.

V84 Vane, Thomas, 1648
Sal.

V86 Vane, Thomas, 1649
Carl. Yk.

V104 Varen, Bernhard, 1693
Sal. Wel.

V105 Varen, Bernhard, 1673
Ches. S Asa.

V106? Varen, Bernhard, 1672
... ex officina Joann. Hayes ...
Carl. Ely. Ex. Wor.

V107 Varen, Bernhard, 1681
... sumptibus Henrici Dickinson.
Cant. Dur. Glo. Nor. S Asa.

V110? Varet, Alexandre Louis, 1676
'fryers'
Carl.

V112 Varillas, Antoine, 1686
Ex.

V113 Varillas, Antoine, 1687
Carl.

V114 Varillas, Antoine, 1688
Cant (imp).

V121 Vaughan, Henry, 1654
Carl.

V125 Vaughan, Henry, 1650
Brec.

V128 Vaughan, Henry, *M.A.*, 1644
Madan 1590.
Cant. Carl. Pet. Wel (tp imp).
Yk.

V128+ Vaughan, Henry, *M.A.*, 1644
Entry as V128; Madan 1591 (London counterfeit).
Chelm.

V130 Vaughan, *Sir* John, 1677
Carl. Wel. Win.

V136 Vaughan, Rice, 1672
S Asa.

V138? Vaughan, Richard, 1684
'The speech of ... of Carmarthen ... entrance into the said town'; cap.; 2°.
Win.

V142 Vaughan, Thomas, 1650
Cant. Carl.

V143 Vaughan, Thomas, 1650
Cant. Carl.

V163 Vauts, Moses à, 1650
Pet.

V168 Vedel, Nicolaus, 1647
Pet.

V170 Veil, Charles Marie de, 1684
Typis T. Snowden, impensis T. Malthus.
Ban. Ex. S Pl.

V171? Veil, Charles Marie de, 1681
'Ecclesiastae explicatio literalis';
Excudebat Nathaniel Thompson, prostant venales apud Richardum Butt.
Win. Yk.

V173 Veil, Charles Marie de, 1679
Ex.

V174+ Veil, Charles Marie de, 1678
'litteralis'; Excudebat Sam. Roycroft & prostant venales apud Robertum Littlebury; 8°.
Ex. Yk.

V175 Veil, Charles Marie de, 1680
Typis Tho. James, impensis Abelis Swalle.
Ex. Yk.

V178+ Veil, Charles Marie de, 1685
For Tho. Malthus; 8°.
Rip (imp).

V179 Veil, Charles Marie de, 1685
Llan.

V181 Velleius Paterculus, 1693
Oxoniae, e Theatro Sheldoniano ... Joh. Howel; 8°.
Carl. Ches. Lich. Nor.

V182 *See*: D1802A

V193 Venn, 1679
Carl. Linc. Win. Yk.

V195 Venner, Tobias, 1650
Third ed. not on tp.
S Asa.

V196 Venner, Tobias, 1660
Linc.

V200A Venning, Ralph, 1658
Cant.

V204 Venning, Ralph, 1657
Pet. S Pl.

V204+ Venning, Ralph, 1657
Printed for J. Rothwell; 8°.
Cant (imp).

V212 Venning, Ralph, 1657
Cant.

V216 Venning, Ralph, 1657
Cant.

V222 Venning, Ralph, 1657
Cant.

V224 Venning, Ralph, 1657
8°.
Cant.

V231 Venning, Ralph, 1657
Cant.

V232 Venning, Ralph, 1655
Yk.

V237 Verbum, 1685
Carl. Pet.

V240 Vere, *Sir* Francis, 1657
Carl. Dur. Lich. Linc. Pet.

V242 Verneuil, John, 1642
12°.
Cant. S Asa.

V243 Verney, Robert, 1682
Ban.

V244 Vernon, Christopher, 1642
Pet.

V245 Vernon, Francis, 1667
Ban. Bris.

V246 Vernon, George, 1677
Carl.

V247 Vernon, George, 1670
Cant. Her. Linc. Win.

V248? Vernon, George, 1682
'Heylin'
Ex. Pet.

V248+ Vernon, George, 1682
For C.H. and sold by Edward Vize; 8°.
Carl. Ches. Ex. Linc. S Asa.
Yk.

V252 Vernon, John, 1648
Yk.

V256? Veron, François, 1660
By John Billaine.
Carl. Wel.

V271 Verstegan, Richard, 1673
Heading corrected.
Ex. Sal. Wel.

V272? Vertot, René Aubert de, 1700
For Mat. Gilliflower, Tim. Goodwin, Mat. Wotton, Rich. Parker and Benj. Tooke.
Ely.

V273? Vertot, René Aubert de, 1696
For Abel Swalle and Tim. Childe.
Dur.

V274 Vertue, Henry, 1659
Ely. Nor.

V281? Vesey, John, 1683
... for Sam. Helsham.
Cant.

V282 Vesey, John, 1684
Carl.

V282+ Vesey, John, 1684
For Robert Clavel, sold by Samuel Helsham in Dublin; 4°.
Llan.

V283 Vesey, John, 1689
Nor. Wor.

V290 Via, 1643
brs.
Yk.

V293 Vicars, John, 1644
Yk.

V298 Vicars, John, 1660
Yk.

V301 Vicars, John, 1643
Pet.

V306 Vicars, John, 1656
S Pl.

V309 Vicars, John, 1646
Yk.

V313 Vicars, John, 1644
Yk.

V318 Vicars, John, 1645
Yk.

V320 Vicars, John, 1643
Cant. Pet.

V326 Vicars, John, 1646
Cant. Pet.

V332? Vicars, John, 1645
Rothwell.
Chelm (2). Pet.

V334 Vicary, Thomas, 1641
Yk.

V344 *See*: W543

V366 View, 1642
Dur. Linc.

V374 Viger, François, 1647
Bur. Ches. Ely.

V375? Viger, François, 1647
Undecima editio; Excudebat J.
Dawsonus, impensis Guilielmi
Addertoni.
Pet. Yk.

V376 Viger, François, 1678
Ches. Glo.

V377 Viger, François, 1695
Cant. Ches.

V379 Vigne, 1688
Wel (tpw)*. Yk.

V379+ Vigne, 1688
As V379, but: 2°.
Ban. Chi. Ex. S Dv. Swel.
Wel.

V384 Villanova, Arnaldus de, 1649
Linc.

V392? Villiers, Jacob, 1680
By J.D. for Jonathan Robinson and
George Wells.
Yk.

V407 Vincent, Nathanael, 1679
Her.

V410 Vincent, Nathanael, 1677
Ex. Her.

V414 Vincent, Nathanael, 1675
Bris. Ex (2 − 1 tp imp). Llan.
S Asa. Win (imp).

V419 Vincent, Nathanael, 1685
Llan. Wor.

V420 Vincent, Nathanael, 1674
Cant.

V429 Vincent, Thomas, 1667
Win.

V435+ Vincent, Thomas, 1690
For Thomas Parkhurst, D. Newman
and Samuel Sprint; 12°.
Llan.

V440 Vincent, Thomas, 1667
Llan.

V441? Vincent, Thomas, 1667
For George Calvert.
Win. Yk (impr. not confirmed).

V442 Vincent, Thomas, 1668
Yk.

V446+ Vincent, Thomas, 1670
See: CLC204.
Yk (imp?).

V453? Vincentius, *St*, 1687
Cantabrigiae, ex officinâ Joh. Hayes,
impensis Guiliel. Graves.
Ban. Chi. Ely. Nor. Yk.

V454? Vincentius, *St*, 1689
Impr. as V453.
Dur. Yk (impr. not confirmed).

V465 Vindication, 1646
Pet.

V466 Vindication, 1688
... in Oxford.
Ban. Ex. Nor. Wel.

V469 Vindication, 1681
Ches.

V477 Vindication, 1644
Ban. Cant (2). Ex.

V478A Vindication, 1681
Linc.

V480 Vindication, 1646
Pet.

V483 Vindication, 1677
Cant. Linc. Win.

V502 Vindication, [1691]
Ely.

V509 Vindication, 1642
Linc.

V510 Vindication, 1647
Yk.

V521 Vindication, 1642
Linc.

V523? Vindication, 1650
175p.
Ban. Chelm. Pet. Sal*.

V523+ Vindication, 1650
As V523, but: 152p.
Dur.

V524 Vindication, 1688
S Pl. Wel.

V526 Vindication, 1689
Wel.

V531 *See*: D2167

V532 Vindication, 1698
Dur.

V533 Vindication, 1690
Cant.

V535 Vindication, 1689
Wel.

V536 Vindication, 1646
Pet.

V544 Vindiciae, 1648
Yk.

V545 Vines, Richard, 1647
Carl. Ex. Pet. Swel.

V546 Vines, Richard, 1642
Cant. Pet.

V547? Vines, Richard, 1646
Roper.
Swel.

V549 Vines, Richard, [1655]
Carl. S Pl.

V550 Vines, Richard, 1662
Carl.

V551 Vines, Richard, 1645
Cant. Carl. Her. Pet. Swel.
Win.

V553 Vines, Richard, 1646
Carl. Swel. Win.

V554? Vines, Richard, 1646
Second ed. not on tp.
Cant. Pet. Yk.

V556 Vines, Richard, 1660
Cant. Yk.

V557 Vines, Richard, 1644
Swel.

V559 Vines, Richard, 1644
Yk (2 eds).

V560 Vines, Richard, 1646
Second ed. not on tp.
Carl. Swel. Yk (2).

V562 Vines, Richard, 1659
S Pl.

V563 Vines, Richard, 1644
Carl. Her. Swel. Yk.

V565 Vines, Richard, 1646
Chelm. Pet (3). Win. Yk.

V566 Vines, Richard, 1646
Second ed. not on tp.
Carl. Ex (imp). Pet (imp). Swel.

V569 Vines, Richard, 1656
Pet.

V572 Vines, Richard, 1657
Ban. Carl (possibly V575)*.
Chelm. Ex (possibly V575)*.
Nor. S Asa.

V575 Vines, Richard, 1657
See also V572.
Pet. Swel.

V585 Violet, Thomas, 1656
Lich.

V600 Virgil, 1658
Lich.

V604 Virgil, 1687
Impensis T. Dring, G. Wells & A.
Swalle.
Pet. S Asa.

V606 Virgil, 1695
Nor. Rip.

V607? Virgil, 1696
Impensis A. Swalle & T. Childe.
Ely.

V610 Virgil, 1654
Lich (2 — 1 imp). Linc.

V612? Virgil, 1665
12°.
Bris.

V613 Virgil, 1668
Glo.

V614? Virgil, 1675
Printed by the author, for Peter
Parker and Thomas Guy.
Cant.

V615 Virgil, 1684
Third ed. not on tp; … Tho: Guy.
Cant (date erased). Glo.

V616 Virgil, 1697
Dur. Ex. Yk.

V617 Virgil, 1698
The second edition .
Cant (2 — 1 imp).

V621 Virgil, 1661
Pet.

V624 Virgil, 1656
Llan.

V633 Virgil, 1658
Dur.

V650 Vertue's, 1688
Wel.

V668 Vives, Juan Luis, 1674
Ex.

V669? Vivianus, Joannes, 1662
Ex officina Joannis Field, prostant
venales apud Robertum Nicholson.
Ban. Her.

V670? Vivianus, Joannes, 1664
… prostant venales apud Octavian.
Pulleyn.
Linc.

V675 Voet, Gisbert, 1678
… distributed gratis by Moses Pitt,
William Nott, William Leake, Edward
Millington [London], John Hall,
Oxford, and Jacob Hooke, Cambridge.
Linc.

V676 Voice, 1664
Cant.

V682 Voiture, Vincent, 1700
Glo.

V683 Voiture, Vincent de, 1657
Carl (imp).

V689- Voss, Gerard Johann, 1668
See: CLC205.
Cant (imp).

V691+ Voss, Gerard Johann, 1690
'Gerardi Joan. …'; Typis R.R. &
M.C., impensis Adielis Mill; 2°.
Ches. Dur. Ex. S Pl. Wor.

V692? Voss, Gerard Johann, 1693
Prostant apud Sam. Smith & Benj.
Walford.
Lich.

V693 Voss, Gerard Johann, 1662
Carl.

V698? Voss, Gerard Johann, 1672
H.H. *not* H. Hall.
Dur. Wel.

V699 Voss, Isaac, 1673
… Rob. Scot, bibliop.; 8°.
Ches. Dur. Ely. Ex. Linc.
S Pl. Yk.

V700 Voss, Isaac, 1679
Ex. Lich. S Asa.

V701 Voss, Isaac, 1680
… venales prostant apud Mosem Pitt,
Londini; 8°.
Ches. S Pl.

V704 Voss, Isaac, 1686
'… ad Pomp. Melam …'
Ex. Linc.

V707 Voss, Isaac, 1685
Ban. Dur. S Pl. Sal. Wel.

V710 Vowell, Peter, 1654
Pet.

V712 Vox, 1641
Pet. Yk.

V715 Vox, 1688
Wel.

V722 Vox, 1646
Yk*.

V726 Vox, 1646
Pet.

V729 Vox, 1681
Yk.

V731 Vox, 1642
Sal.

V739 Vox, 1679
Wel.

V741 Vox, 1650
Linc.

V746 Voyages, 1698
Yk.

V750 Vulgar, 1643
Carl.

W3 W., B., 1680
Linc.

W7 W., C., 1645
Her.

W8? W., C., 1649
14th line on tp ends: 'learned speech
of'
Cant. Dur.

W9 *See:* Periodicals

W24 W., F., 1691
Cant.

W25 W., F., 1692
Carl.

W28 W., F. N., 1684
S Dv. Wor.

W30 W., G., 1642
Dur. Linc. Yk.

W35? W., H., 1668
Crooks.
Win.

W39 W., I., 1641
Cant. Sal. Yk.

W40 W., I., 1641
Sal.

W41? W., I., 1641
'discovery'
Yk.

W59A W., J., 1671
Cant (imp).

W62 W., J., 1642
Linc. Pet. Sal (2).

W68 W., J., 1645
'royall'
Pet.

W69 W., J., 1682
Cant.

W73 W., J., 1642
Dur.

W81 W., L., 1679
Ban (tp imp). Cant.

W85 W., N., 1650
Ex.

W94 W., R., 1689
Wel.

W95 W., R., [1699/1700]
Wel.

W110 W., S., 1642
Pet.

W112 W., T., 1641
Yk.

W122A W., T., [1679]
Linc.

W122A+ W., T., 1647
'A letter of friendly admonition';
[London], printed; 4°; Wing wrongly
places at H310.
Cant.

W127A+ W., T., [1687]
'Remarkes upon a pamphlet'; [N.pl.];
4°; Formerly H318.
Cant.

W157+ Wadding, Luke, 1684
'Small garland of pious and godly
songs'; Printed in Gant; 8°; Formerly
N35.
S Pl.

W160 Wade, Christopher, 1659
Pet.

W177 Wade, John, *of Hammersmith*,
1697
S Pl.

W178 Wade, John, *of Hammersmith*,
1683
Cant (imp). Her.

W179 Wade, John, *of Hammersmith*,
1692
S Pl.

W183 Wadsworth, James, 1679
Wel. Yk.

W185 Wadsworth, Thomas, 1670
Chelm.

W186 Wadsworth, Thomas, 1670
Chelm.

W192 Waersegger, Abraham, 1642
Linc.

W195 *See*: C499+

W196 Wagstaffe, John, 1660
Dur.

W196+ Wagstaffe, John, 1660
Oxford, by Hen: Hall for Ric. Davis;
4°.
S Pl.

W197+ Wagstaffe, John, 1684
By Thomas Snowden, sold by Henry
Mortlock.
S Asa.

W202 Wagstaffe, Thomas, 1690
Cant. Llan.

W203 Wagstaffe, Thomas, 1690
Dur. S Asa.

W204 Wagstaffe, Thomas, 1692
Dur. Llan. Wel.

W205 Wagstaffe, Thomas, 1692
Dur. Llan. Wel.

W206 Wagstaffe, Thomas, 1699
Cant. S Asa. Wel.

W207? Wagstaffe, Thomas, [1692]
Speech made Nov. 4th 1692; 4°.
Dur.

W209 Wagstaffe, Thomas, 1694
Ely.

W210 Wagstaffe, Thomas, [1694]
Dur.

W211 Wagstaffe, Thomas, [1690]
Wel. Yk.

W216 Wagstaffe, Thomas, 1690
Llan (tp imp). Wel (imp).

W218 Wagstaffe, Thomas, 1693
Dur.

W219 Wagstaffe, Thomas, 1697
S Asa.

W221 Wails, Isabel, 1685
Yk (imp).

W223 Waite, Joseph, 1668
By E.T. for R. Royston.
Pet.

W224 Waite, Mary, [1679]
Yk (2).

W224+ Waite, John, 1650
See: CLC206.
Yk.

W227 Wake, *Sir* Isaac, 1663
... G. West.
S Alb. Sal.

W228 Wake, *Sir* Isaac, 1655
Carl.

W229 Wake, William, 1698
Ely. Ex (2). Glo. S Pl.

W230 Wake, William, 1697
Cant (2). Carl. Dur. Ex. Liv.
S Pl. Wel (2). Yk.

W233 Wake, William, 1700
For Richard Sare.
Dur. Ex.

W234 Wake, William, 1688
Ban. Ex (2). Wel. Yk (2).

W235 Wake, William, 1688
Sal. Wel.

W236 Wake, William, 1686
Ban. Bur. Cant (imp). Carl.
Ex. Lich. S Pl. Sal. Swel. Wel.
Wor.

W236+ Wake, William, 1688
The second edition; For Richard
Chiswell; 4°.
Ex (3). Lich. Nor. Wel.

W238 Wake, William, 1689
Ban. Wel (tp only).

W239 Wake, William, 1688
Ban. Bris. Ex. Nor (2). Pet.
S Pl. Sal. Wel (2). Yk.

W240 Wake, William, 1687
Ban. Bur. Carl. Dur (imp). Ex
(imp). Lich. Nor. Sal. Swel.
Wel. Wor. Yk.

W241 Wake, William, 1688
Ex. Wel.

W242 Wake, William, 1689
Cant.

W243 Wake, William, 1686
Ban. Cant (imp). Carl. Chi.
Dur (2). Ex. Her. Lich. S Pl.
Sal. Wel. Wor. Yk.

W244 Wake, William, 1687
Bur. Dur. Ex. Swel.

W245 Wake, William, 1688
Ex (2). Wel.

W246 Wake, William, 1700
Ban. S Pl.

W246A Wake, William, 1688
4°.
Ban. Cant. Nor. Wel.

W247 Wake, William, 1695
Carl. Ely. Her. S Asa.

W248 Wake, William, 1695
Llan.

W249 Wake, William, 1695
Sal. Yk.

W250 Wake, William, 1695
Cant (2). Chelm. Ches.

W251 Wake, William, 1695
Her.

W252 Wake, William, 1696
Ches.

W258 Wake, William, 1699
Ex. Yk.

W259 Wake, William, 1700
Glo. S Pl. Yk (2).

W260 Wake, William, 1687
Ban. Cant. Ex. Lich. Nor. Pet.
S Pl. Sal. Swel. Wel (2). Wor.
Yk.

W261 Wake, William, 1688
Ban. Cant. Carl. Ex (2). Lich.
Nor (tpw). Pet. S Pl. Sal. Swel.
Wel (2). Wor.

W263 Wake, William, 1689
Carl. Her. Llan. S Asa. Wor.

W264 Wake, William, 1690
Ban. Cant. S Asa.

W265 Wake, William, 1690
Cant. Her. Wor.

W266 Wake, William, 1690
Sal.

W267 Wake, William, 1690
Her.

W268 Wake, William, 1691
Her. New.

W269 Wake, William, 1691
Her.

W270 Wake, William, 1696
Her. Llan. Wor.

W271 Wake, William, 1690
Ban. Ely. Her.

W272 Wake, William, 1687
Ban. Bur. Cant. Ex (2). Sal.
Swel. Wel (2). Yk (2).

W273? Wakely, Andrew, 1665
'mariners-compasse'
Sal.

W275 Wakeman, Edward, 1664
S Pl.

W276 Wakeman, *Sir* George, 1681
Linc (2).

W277 *See*: S4540

W280 Waker, Nathaniel, 1664
Cant. Carl. Ex. Her. Pet.
S Asa.

W294 Wales, Elkanah, 1659
Yk (2).

W296 Wales, Samuel, 1681
Yk (3).

W301 Walker, Anthony, 1678
Cant.

W305 Walker, Anthony, 1690
Yk.

W305+ Walker, Anthony, 1690
By John Leake, for the author; 8°.
Pet.

W306 Walker, Anthony, 1673
'Leez'
Carl. Llan.

W309 Walker, Anthony, 1682
Linc.

W310? Walker, Anthony, 1692
'... Εασιλικὴ [*sic*]'
Cant. Chi.

W310+ Walker, Anthony, 1692
As W310, but: '... βασιλικὴ ...
sufferings: proved ...'
Ex. Yk*.

W310++ Walker, Anthony, 1692
As W310+, but: '... sufferings. With
...'
S Pl.

W311 Walker, Anthony, 1691
Her. Wor.

W316 Walker, Clement, 1649
Glo. Her (tpw)*.

W317 Walker, Clement, 1649
Cant*. Linc*. S Pl*.

W318 Walker, Clement, 1649 [repr.
1660?]
Bur*. Linc*.

W318+ Walker, Clement, 1661
Printed for R. Royston; 4°.
Ban. Cant. Nor.

W319 Walker, Clement, 1648
Yk.

W320 Walker, Clement, 1643
Yk.

W321 Walker, Clement, 1648
18p.
Bur. Glo. Linc. S Pl.

W321+ Walker, Clement, 1648
[N.pl.]; 20p.; 4°.
Carl.

W324 Walker, Clement, 1661
Ban. Cant. Nor.

W325 Walker, Clement, 1651
Glo. Linc. S Pl. Win. Yk.

W326 Walker, Clement, 1651 [repr.
1660?]
Bur*.

W326+ Walker, Clement, 1660
Printed for R. Royston; 4°.
Ban. Cant. Nor.

W329 Walker, Clement, 1648
Yk (tpw)*.

W330 Walker, Clement, 1648[9]
Carl. Liv. Sal. Yk.

W332 Walker, Clement, 1647
Cant. Yk (imp).

W332+ Walker, Clement, 1647
As W332, but: 'mystery'
Sal. Yk.

W334 Walker, Clement, 1648
'... Iuntoes ...'
Glo. Linc. S Pl.

W334+ Walker, Clement, 1650
[London], printed; 4°.
Linc. Win.

W335 Walker, Clement, 1648 [repr.
1660?]
'... Junto's ...'
Bur.

W336 Walker, Clement, 1643
Linc. Pet.

W338 Walker, Clement, [1649]
Cant. Ely. Yk.

W349 Walker, George, *of
Londonderry*, 1689
Ex. Wel.

W350 Walker, George, *of
Londonderry*, 1689
Glo (imp)*. S Asa. Wel.

W354 Walker, George, *of
Londonderry*, 1689
Wel.

W362 Walker, George, *of Watling
Street*, 1646
Pet.

W369 Walker, Henry, 1641
Pet.

W372? Walker, Henry, 1641
'expressions'
Pet.

W374 Walker, Henry, 1649
Pet.

W375+ Walker, Henry, 1642
'Five lookes ...'; Formerly F1109.
Linc.

W380 Walker, Henry, 1649
Yk.

W385 Walker, Henry, 1649
Pet.

W389 Walker, Henry, 1641
Yk.

W396 Walker, Obadiah, 1673
Carl.

W397 Walker, Obadiah, 1692
Cant. Dur. Yk.

W398- Walker, Obadiah, 1667
[N.pl.]; 4°.
S Pl.

W400 Walker, Obadiah, 1673
Carl. Ex.

W402? Walker, Obadiah, 1683
Impr. as W403.
Ches.

W403 Walker, Obadiah, 1687
S Asa.

W404 Walker, Obadiah, 1699
Nor. S Asa.

W404A Walker, Obadiah, 1699
The sixth edition.
Ban. Yk (2).

W404B Walker, Obadiah, 1688
S Pl.

W405 Walker, Obadiah, 1680
Carl. Ches. Nor.

W406+ Walker, Obadiah, 1684
At the Theater in Oxford; 8°.
Bur. Ches. Ely. Ex. Win.

W407 Walker, Obadiah, 1675
'... upon the epistles ...'; 8°.
Bur. Carl. Ely. Ex. Rip. Yk.

W415 Walker, Thomas, 1691
Ely. Pet. S Pl.

W416 Walker, Thomas, 1693
Pet.

W417 Walker, William, 1678
Linc.

W418 Walker, William, 1672
Ely.

W424? Walker, William, 1670
... impensis Josephi Clark.
Carl. Linc.

W427 Walker, William, 1685
Pet.

W428 Walker, William, 1690
Yk.

W430 Walker, William, 1677
Ban. Ely.

W433 Walker, William, 1670
Chelm.

W436 Walker, William, 1669
Linc.

W441? Walker, William, 1655
By R. & W.L. for T. Garthwait.
Ely. Nor.

W445 Walker, William, 1673
Cant.

W448 Walker, William, 1683
Her. Yk.

W452? Walker, William, 1668
Excudebat J. Winter.
Ely.

W460 Walkley, Thomas, 1642
Carl (imp)*.

W462+ Walkley, Thomas, 1652
For Tho. Walkley; 8°.
Carl.

W462A Walkley, Thomas, 1661
'catalogue'
Linc.

W462A+ Walkley, Thomas, 1662
'... of nobility ...'; For Robert
Pawley; 8°.
Cant.

W464 Walkley, Thomas, 1652
Carl.

W465 Walkley, Thomas, 1658
Ex. Yk.

W468? Wall, John, 1662
... Ri: Davis.
Win.

W472? Wall, John, 1653
Oxoniae, excudebat Leon. Lichfield,
impensis Rich. Davis.
Chi. Sal.

W475 Wall, Thomas, 1682
Win.

W480 Wall, Thomas, 1661
Impr. as W479.
Linc. Sal (imp)*. Wor.

W483 Wall, Thomas, 1658
Linc. Sal. Wor*.

W490+ Wall, William, 1687
'A sermon preach'd'; Formerly M108
(also M739 & M2424).
Cant.

W498 Waller, Edmund, 1641
'honorable'
Cant.

W505 Waller, Edmund, 1659
Linc.

W517 Waller, Edmund, 1686
Linc.

W519 Waller, Edmund, 1694
The sixth edition.
Nor.

W521 Waller, Edmund, 1690
8°.
Linc.

W522 Waller, Edmund, 1641
Cant. Linc. Yk.

W523 Waller, Edmund, 1643
Cant (2).

W524 Waller, Edmund, 1641
Ex*. Linc.

W530 Waller, Edmund, 1642
Linc. Pet.

W543 Waller, *Sir* William, *the Elder*,
1643
Linc. Pet.

W544 Waller, *Sir* William, *the
Younger*, 1680
Liv.

W545? Waller, *Sir* William, *the
Younger*, 1678
For R.G.
Ex.

W548? Waller, *Sir* William, *the
Younger*, 1679
For Nathanael Ponder.
Linc. Win.

W556 Wallis, John, 1696
Bris. Wel.

W557 Wallis, John, 1696
Ex.

W563 *See*: S6034+

W566 Wallis, John, 1693
'Johannis Wallis ... de algebra ...';
Vol. 2 of his 'Opera mathematica'
Cant. Dur. Yk.

W568 Wallis, John, 1697
Nor.

W569+ Wallis, John, 1692
Oxford, by Leonard Lichfield; 4°.
Ex. Wel.

W570 Wallis, John, 1693
Dur. Wel.

W570+ Wallis, John, 1693
The second edition; Oxford, by
Leonard Lichfield; 4°.
Carl*. Nor.

W571 Wallis, John, 1694
Nor.

W572 Wallis, John, 1694
Dur.

W573 Wallis, John, 1678
Carl.

W575 Wallis, John, 1690
Bris. Cant. Dur. Ely. S Pl.
Wel.

W576+ Wallis, John, 1656
'... for Mr. Hobbes'; Oxford, by
Leonard Lichfield; 8°.
Carl.

W576++ Wallis, John, 1655
See: CLC207.
Sal.

W578 Wallis, John, 1692
Cant. Dur*. Ely*. Wel.

W579 Wallis, John, 1655
Carl. Pet. Sal.

W581 Wallis, John, 1691
Cant. S Pl. Wel.

W582 Wallis, John, 1691
Cant. Dur. Ely. S Pl. Wel.

W583 Wallis, John, 1691
Cant. Dur. Ely. S Pl. Wel.

W584 Wallis, John, 1653
Pet. Sal.

W586 Wallis, John, 1674
Ely. Ex.

W589 Wallis, John, 1662
Carl. Ex. Win.

W590 Wallis, John, 1687
Glo.

W591 *See*: N1506A

W592 Wallis, John, 1684
Cant.

W593 Wallis, John, 1670
Cant. Roch.

W594 Wallis, John, 1657
Carl. Her.

W595 Wallis, John, 1682
Carl. Ex.

W596 Wallis, John, 1695
'Johannis Wallis ... Opera
mathematica. Volumen primum'; Vol.
2 = W566; Vol. 3 = W599+.
Dur. Yk.

W597 Wallis, John, 1699
Vol. 2 = W566; Vol. 3 = W599+.
Cant.

W599+ Wallis, John, 1699
'Johannis Wallis ... operum
mathematicorum volumen tertium';
Oxoniae, e Theatro Sheldoniano; 2°.
Cant. Dur. Yk.

W602 Wallis, John, 1679
Llan.

W603 Wallis, John, 1691
Cant. Dur. Ely. S Pl. Wel.

W604 Wallis, John, 1691
Cant. Dur. Ely. S Pl. Wel.

W605 Wallis, John, 1691
Cant. Dur. Ely. S Pl. Wel.

W606 Wallis, John, 1692
Consists of W575, W603, W608,
W583, W582, W605, W604, W578 &
W611 with gen. tp.
Dur. Ely.

W607 Wallis, John, 1692
Cant. Dur.

W608 Wallis, John, 1691
Dur. Ely.

W609 Wallis, John, 1669
Llan.

W611 Wallis, John, 1691
Cant. Dur. Ely. Her. Wel.

W613 Wallis, John, 1685
Ex.

W615 Wallis, John, 1643
Linc.

W616 Wallis, Ralph, 1666
Glo. Yk (tp imp).

W623 Walls, George, 1681
Llan.

W625 Walsall, Francis, 1661
Pet.

W626 Walsh, Peter, [1672]
cap.
Win.

W628 Walsh, Peter, 1678
Ban. Bur. S Pl. Sal. Win.

W629 Walsh, Peter, 1684
'epistolis'; ... Joannam Brome.
Ely. Sal. Wel. Win.

W630 Walsh, Peter, 1673
'... The first two letters'
Cant. S Pl (tpw). Wel.

W632 Walsh, Peter, 1674
'... The first two letters'; The second
edition; For Henry Brome, and
Benjamin Toke [*sic*].
Cant. Pet. S Pl.

W632+ Walsh, Peter, 1674
'The eleventh and twelfth of the
Controversial letters'; As W630.
Cant. Pet. S Pl. Wel.

W632++ Walsh, Peter, 1679
'The fifteenth and sixteenth of the
Controversial letters'; As W630.
Pet. Wel. Win.

W632+++ Walsh, Peter, 1673
'The fifth and sixth of the
Controversial letters'; As W630.
Cant (2). Pet. S Pl (2). Wel.

W633 Walsh, Peter, 1686
Carl. Sal. Wor.

W634 Walsh, Peter, 1674
'... & vindication ...'
Ely. S Asa. Sal (dedication
only). Wel (2). Win (2 − 1
dedication only). Yk.

W636 Walsh, Peter, [1662]
Win.

W638 Walsh, Peter, 1674
Linc. Wel.

W639+ Walsh, Peter, 1674
'The ninth and tenth of the
Controversial letters'; As W630.
Cant (2). Pet. S Pl. Wel.

W640 Walsh, Peter, 1682
Win.

W640+ Walsh, Peter, 1664
See: CLC208.
Carl (tp imp).

W640++ Walsh, Peter, 1673
'The seventh and eighth of the
Controversial letters'; As W630.
Cant (2). Pet. S Pl. Wel.

W641 Walsh, Peter, 1661
Linc.

W642 Walsh, Peter, 1674
For Hen. Brome and Benj. Tooke.
Win.

W643 Walsh, Peter, 1677
Wel.

W643+ Walsh, Peter, 1673
'The third and fourth of the
Controversial letters'; As W630.
Cant (2). Pet. S Pl (2). Wel.

W643++ Walsh, Peter, 1675
'The thirteenth and fourteenth of the
Controversial letters'; As W630.
Cant. Carl. Pet. Wel.

W644 Walsh, *Sir* Robert, 1679
Linc.

W646 Walsh, William, 1695
Nor.

W653? Walton, Brian, 1641
27 lines of errata at end.
Cant. Win.

W653+ Walton, Brian, 1641
As W653, but: 11 lines of errata.
Win.

W654 Walton, Brian, 1662
S Asa.

W657 Walton, Brian, 1659
Ban. Carl. Ches (2). Ely. Ex.

W658 Walton, Brian, 1655
... habentur ...
Ches. Yk.

W659 Walton, Brian, 1655
12°.
Carl. Ches (2). Ely. S Pl.

W667 Walton, Izaak, 1678
Includes S607.
Ban (imp). Carl. Dur (imp).
Linc (2). S Pl. Win. Yk (3).

W667+ Walton, Izaak, 1681
The second impression; For Benjamin
Tooke and Thomas Sawbridge; 2°.
Nor.

W667++ Walton, Izaak, 1686
The third impression; For B. Tooke,
T. Passenger and T. Sawbridge, sold
by Thomas Hodgkin; 2°.
S Dv.

W668 Walton, Izaak, 1658
Yk.

W669 Walton, Izaak, 1670
Carl (tpw). Sal.

W670 Walton, Izaak, 1665
Cant. Ely. Wel.

W671 Walton, Izaak, 1670
Ely (frag.)*. Lich. Linc. S Pl.
Wor.

W672 Walton, Izaak, 1675
Cant.

W673 Walton, Izaak, 1680
Carl. Wel.

W683 Walwyn, William, 1660
Carl.

W686 Walwyn, William, 1646
Sal.

W691 Walwyn, William, 1646
Yk.

W709 Wanley, Nathaniel, 1678
Cant. Dur. Lich. Nor (tpw).

W710 Wansleben, Johann Michael,
1679
Yk.

W724+ Waple, Edward, 1693
See: CLC209.
Wel.

W726 War, 1689
Wel.

W733+ Ward, Edward, 1698
As W733, but: 8°.
S Pl.

W768 Ward, Hamnet, 1674
Carl. Her. Sal.

W774 Ward, John, of Ipswich, 1645
Cant. Her.

W779 Ward, Nathaniel, 1650
'Discolliminium'
Chelm. Ex. Pet.

W782 Ward, Nathaniel, 1647
Yk.

W784 Ward, Nathaniel, 1647
Cant. S Asa. Yk.

W786 Ward, Nathaniel, 1647
Win.

W791 Ward, Nathaniel, 1648
Pet. Sal.

W794+ Ward, Sir Patience, 1680
Colophon: For Ben Harris; cap.; 2°.
Win.

W798 Ward, Richard, 1643
Dur.

W799 Ward, Richard, 1643
Ex (2 − 1 tp imp).

W809 Ward, Samuel, of Ipswich,
1652
Cant. Chelm.

W809+ Ward, Samuel, of Ipswich,
1653
Excudebat Rogerus Daniel, prostat
autem venale apud Joan. Martin &
Jacob. Alestrye; 8°.
Linc (retains tp of W809).

W811 Ward, Samuel, of Cambridge,
1658
Chi. Ex. S Pl. Win.

W811+ Ward, Samuel, of
Cambridge, 1658
Apud Sam. Gellibrand & Sam.
Tomson; 2°.
Dur.

W812 Ward, Seth, 1661
Cant. Carl. Win.

W813 Ward, Seth, 1670
Pt of W827.
Yk.

W814 Ward, Seth, 1673
Cant (cropped). Carl. Ely. Her.
Linc (tp imp). S Asa. Wor (2).

W815 Ward, Seth, 1674
Dur. Ex. S Dv. Sal.

W816 Ward, Seth, 1656
Pet.

W817 Ward, Seth, 1674
Carl. Wor.

W818 Ward, Seth, 1670
Cant (3 − 1 imp). Carl. Ely.
Her (2). Linc. Pet. S Dv. Yk (2
− 1 tp imp).

W819 Ward, Seth, 1670
Pt of W827.
Yk.

W820 Ward, Seth, 1653
S Pl. Sal.

W821 Ward, Seth, 1654
S Pl. Sal.

W822 Ward, Seth, 1656
Carl. Dur. Ex. Nor. Pet.

W823 Ward, Seth, 1652
'philosophicall'
Dur. Ex.

W825 Ward, Seth, 1667
... sold by John Crosley ...
Ely. Ex.

W826 Ward, Seth, 1677
Sal.

W827 Ward, Seth, 1670
=W813 & W819, with added gen. tp.
Yk.

W828 Ward, Seth, 1666
Cant (2 − 1 imp). Carl. Pet.
Wor.

W830 Ward, Seth, 1674
Dur. Ex. S Dv (frag.). Sal
(imp).

W831 Ward, Seth, 1672
Ban. Carl. Chelm. Ely. Sal.
Win.

W831+ Ward, Seth, 1672
For James Collins, sold by John
Gurney; 8°.
Yk.

W832 Ward, Seth, 1654
Carl. Pet. Yk.

W836 Ward, Thomas, 1687
Bur.

W843 Ware, Sir James, 1654
... impensis Jo. Crook & Thomae
Heath.
Cant. Sal (2). Win. Yk.

W844 Ware, Sir James, 1658
... impensis Jo. Crook.
S Pl.

W845? Ware, Sir James, 1665
... Johannis Crook, vaeneunt apud
Sam. Dancer.
Yk.

W847 Ware, Sir James, 1664
Dublinii, typis Johannis Crook &
impensis Sam. Dancer & sociorum.
Dur (imp). Yk.

W847B Ware, Robert, 1689
8°.
Dur. Ex. Lich. S Asa.

W848 Ware, Robert, 1681
Sal.

W849 Ware, Robert, 1683
Carl. Ex. Lich.

W859 Waring, Robert, 1648
Win.

W868 Waring, Robert, 1646
Pet.

W876? Warly, John, 1676
Printed, and are to be sold by Thomas
Basset.
Cant. Carl.

W877 Warly, John, 1677
Cant. Carl.

W880 Warmstrey, Thomas, 1658
Carl. Dur. Ely. Win.

W882 Warmstrey, Thomas, 1641
Cant (3). Ex. Linc.

W886 Warmstrey, Thomas, 1641
Pet.

W888 Warmstrey, Thomas, 1642
Pet.

W891 Warmstrey, Thomas, 1648
'Suspiria Ecclesiae'
Lich.

W893 Warmstrey, Thomas, 1648
Cant.

W894 Warner, James, 1688
Wor.

W900 Warner, John, *Bp*, 1648
Cant. Lich. Pet. S Asa.

W902 Warner, John, *Bp*, 1648
45p.
Pet. Yk.

W902+ Warner, John, *Bp*, 1648
As W902, but: 42p.
Cant.

W925 Warning, 1648
Cant (cropped).

W950 Warren, Albertus, 1680
Carl.

W954 Warren, Albertus, 1650
Dur.

W955 Warren, Edmund, 1659
Nor.

W957 Warren, Edward, 1667
Pet. S Asa. Yk.

W962 Warren, Erasmus, 1687
Wor.

W965 Warren, Erasmus, 1684
Carl.

W966+ Warren, Erasmus, 1690
By R. Chiswell; 4°.
Ex.

W967 Warren, Erasmus, 1698
Ex.

W973 Warren, John, *of Cambridge*, 1696
Ely.

W974 Warren, John, *of Hatfield*, 1657
Pet.

W982 Warriston, Archibald Johnston, *Lord*, 1653
Dur (tpw).

W987 Warton, Anthony, 1657
Yk.

W988? Warwell, James, 1660
'thanksgiving'; Franckling.
Pet.

W991 Warwick, *Sir* Philip, 1694
Pet. S Asa. S Pl.

W992? Warwick, *Sir* Philip, 1646
'... Lenthall shewing ...'
Carl.

W999? Warwick, Robert Rich, *Earl of*, 1642
Franck.
Linc.

W1004 Warwick, Robert Rich, *Earl of*, 1642
Linc.

W1013? Warwickshire, 1648
4°.
Dur.

W1023 Wase, Christopher, 1687
Ches. Linc. Sal (tpw).

W1027? Washbourne, Thomas, 1661
Leake.
Pet.

W1029 Washington, Robert, 1689
Cant. Ex.

W1031 Wastall, L., 1679
Win.

W1043 Waterhouse, David, 1700
Llan (imp).

W1044 Waterhouse, Edward, 1660
Yk.

W1046 Waterhouse, Edward, 1663
Dur. Win.

W1047 Waterhouse, Edward, 1665
8°.
Win.

W1049 Waterhouse, Edward, 1655
Pet. Yk.

W1050? Waterhouse, Edward, 1667
... and James Thrale.
Ex.

W1057 Waters, James, 1682
Her.

W1062 Watkins, *Sir* David, 1642
Linc.

W1073 Watkins, Richard, 1651
S Pl.

W1079 Watkinson, Peter, 1674
Cant. Yk.

W1084 Watson, Richard, 1651
Linc. Sal.

W1086 Watson, Richard, 1665
Liv.

W1087 *See*: C2302

W1088? Watson, Richard, 1661
Impensis Elisae Wallis.
Linc. Sal.

W1093 Watson, Richard, 1649
Linc. Sal.

W1094 Watson, Richard, 1684
Sal. Yk.

W1095 Watson, Richard, 1642
Cant. Pet. S Asa. Sal. Wel.
Yk.

W1098 Watson, Samuel, 1683
Yk.

W1107 Watson, Thomas, 1660
Carl. Ex.

W1121 Watson, Thomas, 1663
Llan. S Pl.

W1123 Watson, Thomas, 1678
Her.

W1125 Watson, Thomas, 1649
Wor.

W1129 Watson, Thomas, [1668]
Bur.

W1134 Watson, Thomas, 1656
S Pl.

W1143? Watson, Thomas, 1676
4°.
Her.

W1156 Watts, Thomas, 1688
Ex. Nor. Swel. Wel.

W1156+ Watts, Thomas, 1688
'Dialogues between a lover of peace, and a lover of truth ... Part I'; As W1156.
S Pl.

W1158 Watts, Thomas, 1689
Wel.

W1159 Watts, Thomas, 1697
Wor.

W1161+ Way, [1653?]
See: CLC210.
Yk.

W1162 Way, 1680
Wel. Win.

W1163 Way, [1643]
Pet.

W1164 Way, 1653
S Asa.

W1173B Way, 1642
Cant.

W1173B+ Way, 1642
By Robert Young; 8°.
S Pl.

W1184 *See*: Pt 2 of S4649

W1203 Webb, John, 1665
'Stone-Heng'
Ex. Wel.

W1209 Webster, John, *Chaplain*, 1654
Carl. Yk.

W1212 Webster, John, *Chaplain*, 1653
Yk.

W1213 Webster, John, *Chaplain*, 1654
Second ed. not on tp.
Yk.

W1230 Webster, John, *Metallist*, 1677
'witchcraft'
Yk.

W1258+ Weighty, 1642
By E. Griffin; 4°.
Linc.

W1262 Welde, Thomas, 1644
Yk (frag.)*.

W1266 Welde, Thomas, 1653
Yk.

W1268A- Welde, Thomas, 1653
'... Pharisee'; Gateside, printed by S.B. and sould by Will: London in Newcastle; 4°.
Carl. Dur.

W1268A Welde, Thomas, 1654
For Richard Tomlins.
Yk.

W1269 Welde, Thomas, 1644
Third ed. not on tp.
Carl. Ex.

W1273 Weldon, *Sir* Anthony, 1650
At least 2 eds with this impr. & date: C of sig. C1 under 'is' of 'this' *or* under space between 'this' & 'saying' Cant (tpw; C under space). Carl. Pet (tp imp). Yk.

W1280 Weldon, Robert, 1648
Ex. Lich. Pet.

W1281 Weldon, Robert, 1651
Lich.

W1286 Wells, Edward, 1698
Dur.

W1288+ Wells, Edward, 1700
Oxford, at the Theater; 2°.
Ely (maps only).

W1292 Wells, John, 1658
Carl. Pet. S Pl. Wor.

W1298 Wellwood, James, 1689
Carl. Pet.

W1302 Wellwood, James, 1693
Ban. Carl. Ely. Pet. Sal. Wel.

W1306 Wellwood, James, 1700
8°.
Ex. Nor.

W1309 Wellwood, James, 1689
Carl.

W1310 Wellwood, James, 1689
Carl.

W1320 Welshman, Edward, 1691
Wel. Yk.

W1321? Welshman, Edward, 1693
Second ed. not on tp.
Carl.

W1322 Welshman, Edward, 1698
Nor.

W1327 Welchmans, 1642
Linc.

W1347 Wemys, Thomas, 1674
Carl. Ex. Yk.

W1348 Wendelin, Marcus Frederick, 1648
[Cantabrigiae], ex officina Rogeri Danielis.
Dur. Sal.

W1349? Wendelin, Marcus Frederick, 1648
... Danielis, Almae Academiae Cantabrigiensis typographi; 4°.
Pet. Sal. Wor.

W1350 Wenlock, John, 1662
Win.

W1353? Wensley, Robert, 1679
For Benjamin Tooke; 12°.
S Pl.

W1354 Wensley, Robert, 1682
Ban.

W1357 Wentworth, *Sir* Peter, 1641
Carl.

W1358? Wentworth, Thomas, 1641
4°.
Cant.

W1366 Werge, Richard, 1683
Carl.

W1366+ Werge, Richard, 1683
See: CLC211.
Yk.

W1371 Wesley, Samuel, 1693
Glo. S Asa.

W1373A Wesley, Samuel, 1697
The second edition.
Pet.

W1376 Wesley, Samuel, 1700
Yk.

W1380? West, Richard, 1671
For R. Royston.
Cant. Sal. Wor.

W1381 West, Richard, 1700
Cant.

W1394 West, William, 1647, 1641
'The first part of ...'; 'The second part of ...'
Yk.

W1415? Westfield, Thomas, 1656
4°.
Carl.

W1416+ Westfield, Thomas, 1646
By James Young, for Charles Greene; 4°.
Cant.

W1419 Westfield, Thomas, 1641
Carl. Ex. Pet. S Pl.

W1420 Westfield, Thomas, 1660
Pet. Yk.

W1423 Westminster Assembly of Divines, 1645
Ex.

W1425 Westminster Assembly of Divines, 1648
Ely. Yk.

W1429 Westminster Assembly of Divines, [1647]
Pet. Sal.

W1430 Westminster Assembly of Divines, 1647
Bur. Cant. Pet. Yk.

W1431 Westminster Assembly of Divines, 1648
Linc.

W1437A Westminster Assembly of Divines, 1647
Printed at London, and re-printed ...
Bur. Cant. Pet. Sal. Yk.

W1438+ Westminster Assembly of Divines, 1648
For Robert Bostock; 4°.
Linc.

W1440+ Westminster Assembly of Divines, 1648
'catechism'; For Robert Bostock; 8°.
Linc.

W1440++ Westminster Assembly of Divines, [1648?]
At Rotterdam, by Henry Goddaeus; 8°.
Cant.

W1442? Westminster Assembly of Divines, [1646]
4°.
Ex.

W1443 Westminster Assembly of Divines, 1644
Dur. Pet. Sal.

W1444 Westminster Assembly of Divines, 1644
Dur. S Pl. Yk.

W1444A Westminster Assembly of Divines, [1647]
Pet. Sal.

W1446 Westminster Assembly of
Divines, 1647
Linc. Pet. Win (2 eds − 1: B, B −
E⁴; 2: A − C, E − F⁴). Yk.

W1469 *See*: Periodicals

W1487 Wetenhall, Edward, 1693
Bris. Carl.

W1488 Wetenhall, Edward, 1694
Carl.

W1490 Wetenhall, Edward, 1691
S Pl.

W1491 Wetenhall, Edward, 1678
Yk.

W1494 Wetenhall, Edward, 1691
Nath.
Carl.

W1495+ Wetenhall, Edward, 1666
Printed for John Martyn, and are to
be sold at Will. Faithornes; 12°.
Yk.

W1496? Wetenhall, Edward, 1668
This second edition.
Carl.

W1498 Wetenhall, Edward, 1672
Cant.

W1499 Wetenhall, Edward, 1676
Carl. Ely.

W1500+ Wetenhall, Edward, 1684
The fifth edition; For R. Bentley; 12°.
Cant.

W1500++ Wetenhall, Edward,
1684
As W1500+, but: For T. Sawbridge.
Chi.

W1501- Wetenhall, Edward, 1688
'Free thoughts ...'; Formerly F2123.
Ex.

W1501? Wetenhall, Edward, 1686
... for William Norman, Samuel
Helsham and Eliphal Dobson.
Ban.

W1505 Wetenhall, Edward, 1668
Carl.

W1507 Wetenhall, Edward, 1679
Second ed. not on tp.
Carl. Dur. Her. S Pl.

W1512+ Wetenhall, Edward, 1683
'A practical and ...'; Dublin, by J.
Ray, for J. North, J. Howes, S.
Helsham and W. Winter; 8°.
Ex.

W1513 Wetenhall, Edward, 1682
Cant. Carl. Her. Win.

W1514 Wetenhall, Edward, 1686
Nor.

W1515 Wetenhall, Edward, 1686
Ban. Carl. Ely. Ex.

W1516 Wetenhall, Edward, 1663
Carl.

W1521? Wetenhall, Edward, 1695
For William Whitwood.
Carl.

W1522? Wetenhall, Edward, 1671
By J.M. for ...
Cant. Carl. Chelm. Ely.

W1523 Wetherall, John, 1652
Linc. Sal.

W1525+ Weyer, Florence, 1681
For T. Baldwin; 2°.
Linc.

W1527? Whalley, Edward, 1647
'Joyful news ... arrivall ...'
Cant.

W1530 Whalley, Edward, 1647
Yk.

W1532? Whalley, Nathaniel, 1695
Everingham.
Nor.

W1534? Whalley, Peniston, 1661
... younger.
Carl.

W1535 Whalley, Peniston, 1674
Linc. Sal. Win.

W1543 Wharton, *Sir* George, 1647
Sal. Yk.

W1550 Wharton, *Sir* George, 1644
Yk.

W1551 Wharton, *Sir* George,
[1643/4]
Yk.

W1556 Wharton, *Sir* George, 1658
Yk (2).

W1560 Wharton, Henry, 1691
2v.
Ban. Cant (2). Chi. Dur. Ely.
Ex. Glo. Her. Lich. Linc. Liv.
Nor. Pet. Roch. S Asa. S Pl (2).
Sal (2 − 1 lacks vol. 2). Swel.
Wel. Win. Wor. Yk.

W1561 Wharton, Henry, 1692
Dur. Llan. S Pl. Yk.

W1562 Wharton, Henry, 1688
Ban. Cant. Dur (imp). Ex.
Llan. Nor. S Pl. Swel. Wel.

W1563 Wharton, Henry, 1697
For Ri. Chiswell.
Carl. Dur. Nor.

W1565 Wharton, Henry, 1695
Carl. Dur. Ely. Ex (2). Lich.
Liv. S Pl. Wel. Wor. Yk.

W1566A? Wharton, Henry, 1700
For Ri. Chiswell.
Dur.

W1568 Wharton, Henry, 1688
Ban. Dur. Ex.

W1569 Wharton, Henry, 1693
Cant. Carl. Dur. Ely. Lich.
Linc. Liv. Nor. S Asa. S Pl (2).
Sal. Wel. Yk.

W1570 Wharton, Henry, 1688
Ban. Cant. Ex (2). Nor. Sal.
Wel. Yk.

W1574 Wharton, Philip, *Baron*,
1642
Her.

W1576 Wharton, Thomas, 1656
Ex.

W1581 What, 1687
Wel.

W1592? Whear, Degory, 1685
By M. Flesher for Charles Brome.
Bur (2). Cant. Wel.

W1593 Whear, Degory, 1694
Glo.

W1595? Whear, Degory, 1662
... Ed. & Joh. Forrest.
Ex.

W1596? Whear, Degory, 1684
Fifth ed. not on tp; ... H. Dickinson
& R. Green.
Ely. Nor. S Pl. Yk.

W1606 Wheler, *Sir* George, 1689
Cant (2). Carl. Dur. Ex. Lich.
Nor (tpw). S Pl. Yk (2).

W1607? Wheler, *Sir* George, 1682
For William Cademan, Robert
Kettlewell, and Awnsham Churchill.
Carl. Dur. Ex. Liv. Nor. Sal.
Wel. Win.

W1608 Wheler, *Sir* George, 1698
Yk.

W1639 Whetcombe, Tristram, 1642
Linc. Pet. Sal.

W1642 Whichcote, Benjamin, 1698
Chi. Nor.

W1662 Whincop, John, 1645
Ex. S Asa.

W1664 Whincop, John, 1645
Ex. Pet.

W1665- Whincop, Thomas, (1679)
See: CLC212.
Linc.

W1665 Whincop, Thomas, 1696
Cant. Lich.

W1675 Whirligigge, 1647
Yk.

W1678 Whistler, Henry, 1653
Yk.

W1679 Whiston, Edward, 1671
Pet.

W1696 Whiston, William, 1696
Ely. Ex. Pet.

W1699 Whitaker, Edward, 1682
Cant.

W1707 Whitaker, Edward, 1681
Linc.

W1709 Whitaker, Jeremiah, 1645
Pet. Yk.

W1710 Whitaker, Jeremiah, 1645
Ex. Pet (2). Yk.

W1711 Whitaker, Jeremiah, 1646
Pet. Yk.

W1712 Whitaker, Jeremiah, 1642
Cant. Ex. Pet. Yk.

W1713? Whitaker, Thomas, 1693
8°.
Yk.

W1714? Whitaker, Tobias, 1654
Second ed. not on tp; 12°.
Linc.

W1715 Whitaker, Tobias, 1661
Linc.

W1719 Whitby, Daniel, 1679
Carl. Ex. S Pl.

W1720 Whitby, Daniel, 1689
Cant. Wel.

W1721 Whitby, Daniel, 1688
Ban. Nor.

W1721+ Whitby, Daniel, 1688
By J. Leake, for Awnsham Churchill;
4°.
Ex. Sal. Wel.

W1722 Whitby, Daniel, 1674
Bur (2). Ex. S Asa.

W1723 Whitby, Daniel, 1691
Ely. Sal.

W1724 Whitby, Daniel, 1697
Ex. Wel.

W1725 Whitby, Daniel, 1666
Carl. Sal. Win.

W1727+ Whitby, Daniel, 1676
See: CLC213.
Ex (tp imp).

W1728 Whitby, Daniel, 1687
Ban. Wel.

W1728+ Whitby, Daniel, 1687
By J.D. for Awnsham Churchill; 4°.
Ches.

W1730 Whitby, Daniel, 1689
Ban. Ely. S Asa. Yk.

W1731 Whitby, Daniel, 1671
Ban. Cant. Carl. Chi. Ex.
Lich. Nor.

W1732 Whitby, Daniel, 1700
Dur. Linc. Pet. Yk (2).

W1733 Whitby, Daniel, 1683
Carl. Dur. Ely. Linc. Win.

W1735 Whitby, Daniel, 1683
Ex.

W1736 Whitby, Daniel, 1664
Cant. Carl. Dur. Ex. Rip. Sal.
Win.

W1737 Whitby, Daniel, 1685
Llan.

W1738 Whitby, Daniel, 1691
Ely. S Pl.

W1738+ Whitby, Daniel, 1691
Oxoniae, typis L. Lichfield, sumptibus
Awnsham Churchil, bibliop. London.;
4°.
Sal.

W1739 Whitby, Daniel, 1687
Ban. Bur. Ex (2). Nor (2). Sal.
Swel. Wel. Yk.

W1740 Whitby, Daniel, 1688
Ban. Dur. Ex.

W1741 Whitby, Daniel, 1688
Cant (imp). Sal.

W1742 Whitby, Daniel, 1689
Ban. Ex. Pet. Sal. Wel.

W1764A White, Francis, 1647
Yk.

W1765 White, Francis, 1652
Carl.

W1772 White, John, *Counsellor*,
[1641]
Cant. Linc.

W1773 White, John, *Counsellor*,
1641
Possibly 2 eds or issues, with or
without 'Printed by his own copie ...'
on tp.
Cant. Dur. Ex. Linc. Yk (tpw).

W1774 White, John, *Counsellor*,
1641
Cant. Yk.

W1775 White, John, *of Dorchester*,
1656
Carl.

W1777 White, John, *of Dorchester*,
1643
Author is, in fact, John White,
Counsellor.
Cant. Linc. Yk.

W1784 White, John, *of Dorchester*,
1646
Rothwell.
Pet.

W1797 White, Matthew, 1641
Pet (tp imp).

W1798? White, Nathaniel, 1645
Printed by Matth. Simmons.
Yk.

W1799 White, Nathaniel, [1645]
Ex (tp imp).

W1806 White, Thomas, *of
Aldersgate*, 1654
Ely.

W1809 White, Thomas, *Catholic*,
1654
Carl. S Pl.

W1816 White, Thomas, *Catholic*,
1659
Carl. S Pl.

W1821 White, Thomas, *Catholic*,
1658
12°.
Sal.

W1822 White, Thomas, *Catholic*,
1657
Carl. Linc. Pet. Sal.

W1825 White, Thomas, *Catholic*,
1658
Sal.

W1826 White, Thomas, *Catholic*,
1662
Carl. S Pl.

W1827A White, Thomas, *Catholic*,
1655
Carl.

W1829? White, Thomas, *Catholic*,
1652
'Institutionum sacrarum peripateticis
in aedificatarum ... Tomus primus';
12°.
Wel (vol. 1 only).

W1830 White, Thomas, *Catholic*,
1660
Carl.

W1832+ White, Thomas, *Catholic*,
1659
[Douai?]; 12°.
Carl.

W1836 White, Thomas, *Catholic*,
1659
Carl. Ely.

W1846- White, Thomas, *Catholic*,
1654
As W1846, apart from date.
Carl.

W1846 White, Thomas, *Catholic*, 1655
Win.

W1850+ White, Thomas, *of Carmarthen*, [c.1655?]
See: CLC214.
Ex.

W1853 White, Thomas, *of Wisbeach*, 1653
Cant.

W1863 Whitefoot, John, 1656
Cant (imp).

W1864 Whitefoot, John, 1657
Nor (imp). Pet.

W1865 Whitehall, John, 1680
Win.

W1872? Whitehall, Robert, 1677
'... Ιερον ...'; ... Leonard Lichfield; 2°.
Win.

W1884+ Whitehead, Anne, 1670
[N.pl.]; 4°; 19p.
Linc.

W1885 Whitehead, Anne, 1686
Cant.

W1905 Whitehead, George, 1693
Dur.

W1908 Whitehead, George, 1673
Pt 1 = P1266.
Sal. Win.

W1925 Whitehead, George, 1669
Sal.

W1933 Whitehead, George, 1660
Yk.

W1947 Whitehead, George, 1672
Dur.

W1968 Whitehead, George, 1660
Yk.

W1980 Whitehead, John, 1656
Yk.

W1986 Whitelock, *Sir* Bulstrode, 1682
Cant. Ely. Ex. Linc. Nor. Pet. S Asa. S Pl. Swel. Wel. Win. Yk.

W1988 Whitelock, *Sir* Bulstrode, 1660
Carl. Ex. Yk (Chetwin).

W1992 Whitelock, *Sir* Bulstrode, 1642
Cant. Dur.

W1995 Whitelocke, *Sir* James, 1641
Cant. Yk.

W1995B? Whitelocke, *Sir* James, 1641
By Richard Bishop for Thomas Slater.
Linc.

W1997 Whitfield, Edmund, 1688
Ex. Sal.

W1999 Whitfield, Henry, 1651
Ex.

W2005 Whitfield, Thomas, 1649
Dur.

W2007 Whitfield, Thomas, 1651
Pet (imp)*.

W2009 Whitfield, Thomas, 1646
Cant.

W2011+ Whitfield, Thomas, 1657
See: CLC215.
Pet.

W2017 Whiting, Charles, 1692
Cant.

W2025 Whiting, William, 1653
Ex.

W2025+ Whiting, William, 1653
Impensis autoris; 8°.
Pet.

W2030 Whitlock, Richard, 1654
Ex.

W2042 Whittel, John, 1692
Wor.

W2044 Whittie, John, 1689
Carl. Pet (2).

W2045 Whittingham, William, 1642
Ches. Yk.

W2049 Whitton, Joshua, 1644
Yk.

W2055- Whole, 1683
See: CLC216.
Dur.

W2064 Whole, [1678]
Ban.

W2068 Whore, 1679/80
Linc. Yk (imp).

W2070 Whorwood, Thomas, 1679
Yk.

W2070+ Why, [1679?]
'Why are you not a Roman-Catholic?'; [N.pl.]; 8°; Anr ed. formerly C6903.
Dur.

W2075+ Whyte, Humphrey, 1694
'preach'd'; For Tho. Hodgkin, sold by Randal Taylor; 4°.
Her.

W2081 Wickens, Robert, 1655
Cant (imp). Yk.

W2084 Wickins, William, 1660
Cant.

W2085 Wickins, William, 1650
Chelm.

W2086 Wickins, William, 1660
Cant. Pet.

W2086+ Wickins, William, 1660
As W2086, but: The second edition.
Chelm. Ches.

W2087 Widdrington, Roger, 1679
For Jonathan Robinson.
Linc.

W2088 Widdrington, *Sir* Thomas, 1641
Yk (2).

W2089 Widdrington, *Sir* William, 1643
Yk.

W2090? Widenfeldt, Adam, 1687
Tayler.
Ban. Bur. Cant. Ex (2). Sal. Swel. Wel. Yk.

W2094 Wife, 1679
Linc.

W2098 Wigan, William, 1697
Her. Wor.

W2099 Wigan, William, 1693
S Asa.

W2107- Wight, Thomas, [1698?]
See: CLC217.
Wor.

W2112 Wilbee, Amon, 1647
Linc.

W2117 Wilcock, James, 1641
Linc. Pet. Sal.

W2119 Wilcock, James, 1642
Cant. Pet.

W2125 Wild, Robert, 1660
Yk*.

W2131 Wild, Robert, 1660
Yk.

W2132 Wild, Robert, 1660
Chelm. Linc. Pet (2 − 1 tp imp).

W2134? Wild, Robert, 1661
Second ed. not on tp; 8°.
Pet.

W2138 Wild, Robert, 1671
Linc.

W2150+ Wild, Robert, 1660
For Francis Egglesfield; 4°.
Pet.

W2160 Wilde, George, 1643
Carl. Pet. Wel. Yk.

W2163 Wilde, John, 1642
Linc.

W2165 Wilde, Robert, 1656
Pet.

W2166+ Wildgos, John, 1658
See: CLC218.
Yk.

W2167 Wildman, John, 1647
Yk.

W2168 Wildman, John, 1647
Yk (2).

W2169+ Wildman, John, 1648
'The lawes subversion'; Formerly
H3193.
Yk (2).

W2173 Wildman, John, 1647
Pet.

W2176 Wilkins, John, 1668
2°.
Bris. Cant (2). Carl. Ches (2).
Dur. Ely. Glo. Rip. Sal. Win.
Yk.

W2180 Wilkins, John, 1653
Carl.

W2181? Wilkins, John, 1655
By T.M. for ...
Cant. Ches (2). Ex. S Pl. Sal.

W2182 Wilkins, John, 1667
Bur. Ches. S Dv.

W2182A Wilkins, John, 1674
Her. Linc.

W2183 Wilkins, John, 1678
Her.

W2185 Wilkins, John, 1695
Seventh ed. not on tp.
Liv.

W2187? Wilkins, John, 1684
8°.
Linc.

W2188 Wilkins, John, 1646
Ches.

W2189 Wilkins, John, 1647
The second edition .
Chelm. Ches.

W2190 Wilkins, John, 1651
Ches.

W2191 Wilkins, John, 1653
Carl.

W2192? Wilkins, John, 1656
By T.R. and E.M. for ...
Cant. Ches. Ex. S Pl.

W2192+ Wilkins, John, 1659
No ed. statement; For Samuel
Gellibrand; 8°.
Ches. Dur. Sal.

W2193 Wilkins, John, 1669
The fifth impression .
Ban. Bur. Ely. S Dv. Win.

W2193A Wilkins, John, 1675
Her*. Linc.

W2194 Wilkins, John, 1679
The sixth impression .
Ches. Her.

W2195 Wilkins, John, 1693
Ban. Liv.

W2196 Wilkins, John, 1668
Bris. Cant (2). Carl. Ches (2).
Dur. Ely. Glo. Rip. Sal. Win.
Yk.

W2198 Wilkins, John, 1648
Same as W2199?
Carl. Ches. Rip.

W2200 Wilkins, John, 1680
Third ed. not on tp.
Ches.

W2201 Wilkins, John, 1691
Ches (2 — 1 imp).

W2202 Wilkins, John, 1641
Cant (imp). Ches.

W2203 Wilkins, John, 1694
Ches.

W2204 Wilkins, John, 1675
Ban. Carl. Ches (2 — 1 imp).
Ely. Llan. Pet. Win.

W2205? Wilkins, John, 1678
For T. Basset, H. Brome and R.
Chiswel.
Bur. Ches. Ex (2). Roch. S Pl.

W2206 Wilkins, John, 1683
Ban. Bur. Wel.

W2207 Wilkins, John, 1693
Third ed. not on tp.
Llan. S Asa.

W2208? Wilkins, John, 1699
For R. Chiswell, W. Battersby, and
C. Brome.
Yk.

W2209 Wilkins, John, 1669
Cant. Carl. Ches (3). Yk.

W2210 Wilkins, John, 1670
Cant (2). Carl. Ches. Nor.
S Asa. Yk.

W2211 Wilkins, John, 1671
Cant (2). Carl. Ches (2). S Asa.
Wor.

W2213 Wilkins, John, 1677
Ches. Ex.

W2214 Wilkins, John, 1680
S Pl (2).

W2215 Wilkins, John, 1682
Ban (imp). Carl. Ches. Dur.
Ely. Ex. Nor. Yk (tp imp).

W2218 Wilkinson, Henry, *Capt.*,
1681
Yk.

W2220 Wilkinson, Henry, *of
Christchurch*, 1643
Chelm.

W2222 Wilkinson, Henry, *of
Christchurch*, 1644
Cant. Pet. S Pl.

W2225 Wilkinson, Henry, *of
Christchurch*, 1641
'lukewarmeness'
Pet.

W2230 Wilkinson, Henry, *of
Magdalen*, 1660
Dur. Linc.

W2231 Wilkinson, Henry, *of
Magdalen*, 1659
Win.

W2232 Wilkinson, Henry, *of
Magdalen*, 1658
Ex. Sal.

W2236 Wilkinson, Henry, *of
Magdalen*, 1658
Chelm.

W2238 Wilkinson, Henry, *of
Magdalen*, 1660
4°.
Ex.

W2239 Wilkinson, Henry, *of
Magdalen*, 1660
Pet.

W2240 Wilkinson, Henry, *of
Magdalen*, 1681
Ex.

W2249 Wilkinson, Robert, 1682
Carl. Sal (imp).

W2261+ Willan, Edward, 1651
For R. Royston; 4°.
S Pl.

W2302 Willes, John, 1695
Carl. Her.

W2303 Willes, John, 1690
Cant. Her. Pet. Sal.

W2304 Willes, John, 1696
Cant.

W2305 Willes, Samuel, 1679
Her. Wor.

W2306? Willes, Samuel, 1660
'kigns' [*sic*].
Pet.

W2331 William III, 1688
Cant (tp imp). Nor. S Asa.

W2331A William III, [1688]
Ban.

W2340 William III, 1694
Dur.

W2343 William III, [1674]
Linc.

W2355 William III, 1689[90]
Bris.

W2356 William III, 1689
Dur. Wel.

W2358 William III, 1689
Wel.

W2367 William III, 1678
Linc.

W2379 William III, 1689
Wel.

W2442? William III, 1697
'seventeenth day of November'
Cant.

W2498+ William and Mary, 1692
See: CLC219.
S Pl.

W2519 *See*: W2379

W2648 Williams, Daniel, 1697
Carl.

W2649 Williams, Daniel, 1692
Nor.

W2652 Williams, Daniel, 1688
Cant. Dur.

W2655 Williams, Daniel, 1698
Nor.

W2663 Williams, Griffith, 1663
Win.

W2664? Williams, Griffith, 1663
By Tho. Roycroft for Philemon
Stephens.
Win.

W2665 Williams, Griffith, 1643
Pet. Yk.

W2667 Williams, Griffith, 1644
Win.

W2668 Williams, Griffith, 1667
Carl.

W2669 Williams, Griffith, 1644
Cant. Pet (imp).

W2671 Williams, Griffith, 1644
Wel (imp). Yk.

W2673A Williams, Griffith, 1663
Win.

W2675 Williams, Griffith, 1643
Cant. Pet.

W2676 Williams, John, *Abp*, 1641
Dur. Ex. Sal.

W2677 Williams, John, *Abp*, 1641
Yk.

W2678 Williams, John, *Bp*, 1686
Bur. Cant. Ex. Yk.

W2680? Williams, John, *Bp*, 1688
31p.
Ban. Nor. S Pl. Wel.

W2680+ Williams, John, *Bp*, 1688
As W2680, but: 29p.
Ely.

W2681 Williams, John, *Bp*, 1688
Cant. Ex. S Pl. Sal.

W2683 Williams, John, *Bp*, 1694
For Ri. Chiswell.
Cant.

W2684 Williams, John, *Bp*, 1696
For Ri. Chiswell.
Cant.

W2687 Williams, John, *Bp*, 1693
Dur.

W2689 Williams, John, *Bp*, 1682/3
Cant. Nor. S Pl (2).

W2690 Williams, John, *Bp*, 1683
Yk (2).

W2691 Williams, John, *Bp*, 1683
Dur. Nor.

W2692 Williams, John, *Bp*, 1684
Pet (imp). S Pl.

W2693+ Williams, John, *Bp*, 1687
As W2693, apart from date.
S Pl.

W2694 Williams, John, *Bp*, 1687
Dur. Ex. Yk.

W2695 Williams, John, *Bp*, 1695
Cant.

W2696 Williams, John, *Bp*, 1695
Cant.

W2698 Williams, John, *Bp*, 1679
Cant. Carl. Dur. Ex. Nor.
Wel.

W2699 Williams, John, *Bp*, 1696
Carl. Pet (2 − 1 tp imp). Yk (2).

W2700 Williams, John, *Bp*, 1695
Her (2). S Dv.

W2701 Williams, John, *Bp*, 1687
Her. Nor. S Dv. Wel.

W2701A Williams, John, *Bp*, 1687
Ban. Ex. Sal.

W2702 Williams, John, *Bp*, 1685
Ban. Cant. Ex (3). Nor. S Pl
(2). Sal. Swel (2). Wel. Yk.

W2703 Williams, John, *Bp*, 1695
Cant. Nor.

W2704 Williams, John, *Bp*, 1696
Cant. Nor.

W2705 Williams, John, *Bp*, 1678
Bris. Dur (2).

W2709 Williams, John, *Bp*, 1679
Linc*. Yk*.

W2711 Williams, John, *Bp*, 1672
Carl. Yk.

W2711+ Williams, John, *Bp*, 1672
For W. Garret, sold by Edward
Thomas & Jos. Clark; 8°.
Win. Yk.

W2712 Williams, John, *Bp*, 1696
Cant. Ex. Nor.

W2713 Williams, John, *Bp*, 1687
Ban. Bur. Dur. Ex (2). S Pl.
Swel.

W2714 Williams, John, *Bp*, 1687
Bur. Dur. Ex (2). S Pl.

W2715 Williams, John, *Bp*, 1687
Bur. Dur. Ex.

W2716 Williams, John, *Bp*, 1696
Cant. Nor.

W2717 Williams, John, *Bp*, 1696
Cant. Ex. Nor.

W2718 Williams, John, *Bp*, 1695
Cant. Carl.

W2720 Williams, John, *Bp*, 1688
Ex. Lich.

W2721 Williams, John, *Bp*, 1688
… Randall Taylor.
Ban. Ex. Nor. Sal. Wel.

W2722 Williams, John, *Bp*, 1696
Cant. Ex. Nor.

W2723 Williams, John, *Bp*, 1678
Ban. Bur. Wor.

W2724 Williams, John, *Bp*, 1679
Cant. S Pl. Wor.

W2725 Williams, John, *Bp*, 1684
Carl. Dur. Yk (imp).

W2727 Williams, John, *Bp*, 1695
Cant. Wor.

W2728 Williams, John, *Bp*, 1695
Yk.

W2729 Williams, John, *Bp*, 1697
Cant. Ex. Yk.

W2730 Williams, John, *Bp*, 1697
… and Ralph Smith.
Bur (as Cant?). Cant (2nd
bookseller deleted in MS). Wor
(as Cant).

W2731 Williams, John, *Bp*, 1698
Cant.

W2732 Williams, John, *Bp*, 1697
Cant. Ex. S Asa.

W2733 Williams, John, *Bp*, 1696
Cant. Nor.

W2734 Williams, John, *Bp*, 1687
Bur. Ex. S Pl. Wel.

W2735 Williams, John, *Bp*, 1694
Yk (2).

W2736 Williams, John, *Bp*, 1695
Cant. Nor. Wor.

W2737 Williams, John, *Bp*, 1696
Cant. Ex. Yk (imp).

W2738 Williams, John, *Bp*, 1691
Wel.

W2739 Williams, John, *Bp*, 1688
Ban. Cant. Ex. Nor. Wel.

W2740 Williams, John, *Bp*, 1684
Gardner.
S Pl.

W2741 Williams, John, *Bp*, 1681
Dur.

W2742 Williams, John, *Bp*, 1695
Carl.

W2750+ Williams, Peter, 1665
By E.M. for Nathanael Webb; 8°.
Yk.

W2758 Williams, Roger, 1644
Lich.

W2767 Williams, Roger, 1644
Lich.

W2768 Williams, Roger, 1644
Yk*.

W2770 Williams, Roger, 1644
Lich.

W2773A? Williams, Walter, 1683
... sold by Walter Davis.
Wel.

W2780 Williams, *Sir* William, 1680
Linc.

W2781? Williams, *Sir* William,
1681
For Gabriel Kunholt; Same speech as
W2780.
Win.

W2784+ Williams, William,
Astrologer, 1660
By Tho. Leach, for H. Marsh and W.
Palmer; 8°.
Ex.

W2787 Williams, William, *of
Haverford*, 1682
Lich. Wor.

W2791 Williams, William, *Minister*,
1696
Cant.

W2796 Williamson, David, 1690
Cant.

W2800 *See*: C2300

W2801 Willington, George, 1670
Carl.

W2807 Willis, John, *Divine*, 1690
Ches. Lich. Nor. S Asa. Wor.

W2808 Willis, John, *Divine*, 1700
4°.
Pet.

W2815 Willis, Richard, 1700
For Mat. Wotton; 12°.
S Asa. Wel.

W2816 Willis, Richard, 1696
Dur. Her. Nor. Wel.

W2817 Willis, Thomas, *D.D.*, 1676
Carl.

W2818 Willis, Thomas, *D.D.*, 1683
Yk (imp?).

W2823 Willis, Thomas, *M.D.*, 1664
Carl.

W2824? Willis, Thomas, *M.D.*,
1664
... Jo. Martin ...
Win. Wor.

W2825 Willis, Thomas, *M.D.*, 1672
... Ric. Davis.
Ches. Dur (imp). Linc. Win.

W2826? Willis, Thomas, *M.D.*,
1672
Londini, typis E.F., impensis Ric.
Davis, Oxon.
Pet.

W2834 Willis, Thomas, *M.D.*, 1662
Carl. Pet. Win.

W2836A? Willis, Thomas, *M.D.*,
1684
... J. Leigh and C. Harper.
Cant.

W2840+ Willis, Thomas, *M.D.*,
1684
Printed by H. Clark, for T. Dring, C.
Harper, and J. Leigh; 2°.
Cant.

W2841 Willis, Thomas, *M.D.*, 1667
Win. Wor.

W2842? Willis, Thomas, *M.D.*,
1668
12°.
Yk.

W2843? Willis, Thomas, *M.D.*,
1678
Typis S. Roycroft, impensis Jo.
Martyn.
Ches.

W2844 Willis, Thomas, *M.D.*, 1674
Wor.

W2845 Willis, Thomas, *M.D.*, 1674
... Londinensem; 12°.
Cant. Pet.

W2846 Willis, Thomas, *M.D.*, 1675
Second ed. not on tp; E Theatro
Sheldoniano.
Wor.

W2846+ Willis, Thomas, *M.D.*,
1675
No ed. statement; Oxoniae, e Theatro
Sheldoniano; 12°.
Ely.

W2847? Willis, Thomas, *M.D.*,
1679
Impr. as Wing, but: ... prostant apud
Ric. Davis.
Ex.

W2848 Willis, Thomas, *M.D.*, 1679
Linc.

W2849 Willis, Thomas, *M.D.*, 1684
Cant (imp).

W2850 Willis, Thomas, *M.D.*, 1679
Linc.

W2851 Willis, Thomas, *M.D.*, 1684
Cant (imp).

W2852 Willis, Thomas, *M.D.*, 1691
[12], 74p.
Cant.

W2854 Willis, Thomas, *M.D.*, 1684
Cant (imp).

W2856 Willis, Thomas, *M.D.*, 1683
Cant (imp).

W2857A? Willis, Thomas, *of St
Helen's, London*, 1696
'... 16th day of April ...'; For John
Gwillim.
Wor.

W2858A Willoughby, *of Parham*,
Francis, *Lord*, [1649]
Ex.

W2860+ Willoughby *of Parham*,
Francis, *Lord*, [1642]
[N.pl.]; cap.; 4°; Possibly pt of
another work.
Dur (closely cropped).

W2867 Wills, Obed, 1674
Her.

W2875+ Willsford, Thomas, 1665
For N. Brooke; 8°.
Carl.

W2877 Willughby, Francis, 1686
With addit. engr. tp; ... sumptibus
Societatis Regalis Londinensis.
Cant.

W2879 Willughby, Francis, 1676
Wor.

W2880 Willughby, Francis, 1678
Cant (2). Dur. Glo.

W2885 Wilmot, Henry, *Earl of Rochester*, 1642
Dur. Linc.

W2887 Wilson, Arthur, 1643
Linc. Yk.

W2888 - Wilson, Arthur, 1652
For Richard Lownds; 2°.
Bris.

W2888 Wilson, Arthur, 1653
Carl. S Asa. Sal (imp). Win.
Yk.

W2891 Wilson, Edward, 1675
Carl.

W2891+ Wilson, Edward, 1675
By W.G. and are to be sold by
William Shrowsbury; 8°.
Yk.

W2891A Wilson, Elias, 1673
Yk.

W2893 Wilson, George, 1700
Ex.

W2895A *See*: P2979

W2903 Wilson, John, *of St Catherine's, Cambridge*, 1678
Carl. Dur.

W2906 Wilson, John, *of St Catherine's, Cambridge*, 1668
Ex.

W2907 Wilson, John, *of Lincoln's Inn*, 1688
4°.
Ban. Wel.

W2907+ Wilson, John, *of Lincoln's Inn*, 1692
'Vindiciae Carolinae'; Formerly
H2505.
Ex. Wel.

W2909 Wilson, John, *Musician*, 1659
Dur.

W2921 Wilson, John, *Recorder*, 1684
Win.

W2927 Wilson, Joseph, 1668
Ely.

W2929 Wilson, Matthew, 1652
Carl. Her. Linc (imp). Sal.

W2930 Wilson, Matthias, 1654
Nor.

W2932 Wilson, Samuel, 1682
Bris. Dur.

W2936 Wilson, Thomas, *of Arrow*, 1679
Cant. Dur.

W2940+ Wilson, Thomas, *of Canterbury*, 1648
The fifth edition; By Richard Cotes,
sold by William Hope; 2°.
Glo.

W2944 Wilson, Thomas, *of Canterbury*, 1661
Chelm. Ches. Sal.

W2945 Wilson, Thomas, *of Canterbury*, 1678
Chelm. Ely. Ex. Her.

W2947 Wilson, Thomas, *of Kent*, 1641
Chelm. Pet (2).

W2948 Wilson, Thomas, *of Kent*, 1643
Cant.

W2950 Wilson, Timothy, 1691
Nor.

W2951 Wilson, Timothy, 1690
Cant.

W2954 Wilson, William, 1694
S Pl.

W2957 Wilson, William, 1689
Nor.

W2961 Wiltshires, 1642
Linc. S Asa. Sal.

W2967 Winchelsea, Heneage Finch,
Earl of, 1669
Bris. Linc. Yk.

W2977 Windet, James, 1663
Carl. S Pl. Yk.

W2978 Windet, James, 1664
Ex. Lich. S Pl.

W2979 Windet, James, 1677
Carl. Wel.

W2992+ Wing, Vincent, 1700
By J. Matthews for Awnsham and
John Churchill; 2°.
Glo.

W2993 Wing, Vincent, 1651
Ex.

W2995 Wing, Vincent, 1652
Cant.

W2997 Wingate, Edmund, 1650
... Phil. Stephens.
Wor.

W2998 Wingate, Edmund, 1652
... Phil. Stephens; 8°.
Wor.

W3000 Wingate, Edmund, 1673
Yk.

W3001 Wingate, Edmund, 1678
Ely. S Pl.

W3004+ Wingate, Edmund, 1696
The ninth edition; For J. Philips and
J. Knapton; 8°.
Ex.

W3026? Wingate, Edmund, 1658
By J.B. for Philemon Stephens.
Pet.

W3033 Winnell, Thomas, 1657
Chelm.

W3044 Winstanley, Gerrard, 1650
Pet.

W3059 Winstanley, William, 1684
Cant.

W3066 Winstanley, William, 1665
'martyrology'
Cant.

W3081 Winter, *Sir* John, [1662?]
Wing inserts this & next into works of
another John Winter.
Win.

W3082 Winter, *Sir* John, 1679
Linc. Pet. Win (2).

W3083A Winter, John, *Curate of East Dereham*, 1662
... in Norwich.
Bur.

W3107 Wiseman, Richard, 1676
'Severall'
Linc. Wel. Wor.

W3109? Wiseman, Richard, 1692
The second edition; Printed, and are
to be sold by Samuel Clement.
Cant.

W3113 Wiseman, *Sir* Robert, 1657
Ex. Linc. Sal. Wel.

W3113A? Wiseman, *Sir* Robert, 1664
For R. Royston; 4°.
Cant.

W3114+ Wiseman, *Sir* Robert, 1686
For R. Royston, sold by Richard
Green in Cambridge; 8°.
Ely.

W3120 Wishart, George, [1647]
Linc.

W3121 Wishart, George, 1648
Yk.

W3124 Wishart, George, 1652
Carl.

W3141 Wither, George, 1647
Pet.

W3148 Wither, George, 1649
Ex.

W3160 Wither, George, 1645
Linc.

W3172A Wither, George, 1654
Carl.

W3206 Wither, George, [1649]
Yk.

W3212 Wither, George, 1646
Pet.

W3213 Withers, Robert, 1650
Pet.

W3215+ Witnesses, [N.d.]
See: CLC220.
Yk.

W3224 Witte, Petrus de, [1664]
Yk.

W3225 Wittewrong, John, 1643
Linc.

W3227 Witty, Robert, 1678
Yk (3).

W3229+ Witty, Robert, 1681
By J.M. for the author, to be sold by
R. Clavell and J. Robinson, and R.
Boulter; 8°.
Yk.

W3230 Witty, Robert, 1669
Dur. Yk (2).

W3231 Witty, Robert, 1660
'Scarbrough'; ... in York.
Ely. Yk (3).

W3232 Witty, Robert, 1667
'Scarbrough'; Second ed. not on tp.
Yk (3).

W3237 Witty, 1669
Carl.

W3242 Wodenote, Theophilus,
1649
Cant (engr. tpw). Linc. Pet.

W3249 Wolfall, Thomas, 1641
Yk.

W3250A? Wolfall, Thomas, 1653
Gateside, by Ste: Bulkley, to be sold
at his house.
Chelm.

W3254 Wolleb, John, 1650
Bur.

W3257 Wolleb, John, 1642
Her. Yk.

W3258 Wolleb, John, 1647
S Asa.

W3259 Wolleb, John, 1648
Her.

W3259A? Wolleb, John, 1654
12°.
Ely. Pet. S Pl. Wel.

W3261 Wolleb, John, 1657
... Rob: Blagrave & Joh: Forrest.
Bur.

W3262+ Wolleb, John, 1661
Oxoniae, excudebat H. Hall, impensis
Edw. Forrest & Rob. Blagrave; 12°.
Wel.

W3266 Wolley, Edward, 1662
Pet.

W3307 Wolseley, *Sir* Charles, 1673
Linc. Yk.

W3308 Wolseley, *Sir* Charles, 1677
Ban. Carl. Chelm. Ely. Win.

W3309 Wolseley, *Sir* Charles, 1668
Cant. Win.

W3310 Wolseley, *Sir* Charles, 1668
Cant (imp?).

W3313 Wolseley, *Sir* Charles, 1672
'reasonableness'
Ex. Swel.

W3314 Wolseley, *Sir* Charles, 1669
For Nathanael Ponder.
Ban. Her.

W3315 Wolseley, *Sir* Charles, 1669
Cant. Ex. Nor.

W3316 Wolseley, *Sir* Charles, 1675
For Nathaniel Ponder.
Swel.

W3333 Womock, Laurence, 1680
Linc. Win.

W3336 Womock, Laurence, 1659
Bur. Carl. Ely. Pet. Sal.

W3336+ Womock, Laurence, 1663
Anr issue of W3335, with tp
beginning: 'Aron-bimnucha: or an
antidote'; As W3335.
Carl. Ex. Win. Yk.

W3338 Womock, Laurence, 1641
Linc. Pet (2 − 1 imp). S Pl (imp).
Sal. Yk (imp).

W3340 Womock, Laurence, 1682
Cant. Dur. Win.

W3341 Womock, Laurence, 1664
Win.

W3342 Womock, Laurence, [1660]
Carl.

W3343 Womock, Laurence, 1658
Ban. Ex. Lich. Linc. Pet. S Pl
Wor. Yk.

W3344 Womock, Laurence, 1679
Carl. Her. Wel. Yk.

W3345 Womock, Laurence, 1679
Carl. Linc.

W3346 Womock, Laurence, 1675
Carl. Her.

W3347 Womock, Laurence, 1662
Bur. Carl. Pet. S Asa. Sal. Yk
(2).

W3349 Womock, Laurence, [1678]
Carl (imp). Wel.

W3350 Womock, Laurence, 1661
Carl. S Pl. Win. Yk.

W3351 Womock, Laurence, 1683
Carl. Dur. Win. Yk.

W3352 Womock, Laurence, 1643
Cant. Linc. Yk.

W3354 Womock, Laurence, 1683
Sal. Win.

W3355 Womock, Laurence, 1680
Linc. Win.

W3356 Womock, Laurence, 1681
Yk.

W3382 Wood, Anthony à, 1691
Carl. Ches. Ely. Ex. Glo. Her.
Lich. S Pl. Sal. Wel. Wor. Yk.

W3383A Wood, Anthony à, 1692
For Tho. Bennet.
Carl. Ches. Ely. Ex. Glo.
Lich. S Pl. Wor. Yk.

W3385 Wood, Anthony à , 1674
Carl (2). Dur. Ex. Glo. Her.
Nor. Roch. S Pl. Swel. Wel.
Win. Wor.

W3387 Wood, Edward, 1656
Sal. Yk.

W3404+ Wood, Owen, 1656
See: CLC221.
Cant (imp).

W3406 Wood, Seth, 1651
Yk.

W3407 Wood, Thomas, 1697
Cant.

W3408 Wood, Thomas, 1682
Ban. Cant (imp). Carl.

W3412 Wood, Thomas, 1693
Carl. Dur. Wel.

W3419 Woodall, Frederick, 1659
Nor.

W3424 Woodbridge, Benjamin,
1652
Cant.

W3425 Woodbridge, Benjamin,
1653
Pet.

W3426 Woodbridge, Benjamin,
1656
Carl. Ex. Her. Sal.

W3429 Woodcock, Francis, 1644
Her. Yk.

W3430 Woodcock, Francis, 1646
Her.

W3433 Woodcock, Francis, 1643
Ex. S Asa.

W3436- Woodhead, Abraham,
[1689]
See: CLC222.
S Pl (imp). Wel.

W3436 Woodhead, Abraham, 1662
Ban. Carl. Nor. Wel. Yk.

W3437 Woodhead, Abraham, 1685
Ely. Ex. Wel. Yk.

W3439 Woodhead, Abraham, 1687
Carl.

W3440 Woodhead, Abraham, 1687
Carl. Ex (2). S Pl.

W3440A Woodhead, Abraham,
1688
Ban. Nor. Sal. Swel. Wel.

W3442 Woodhead, Abraham, 1671
Glo. S Pl.

W3444 Woodhead, Abraham, 1687
For William Cademan.
Wor.

W3446 Woodhead, Abraham, 1675
Glo. Roch. Wor.

W3448 Woodhead, Abraham, 1685
4°.
Ban. Carl. Yk.

W3449 Woodhead, Abraham, 1688
Carl. S Pl.

W3450 *See*: A3033

W3451 Woodhead, Abraham, 1686
Bur. Carl. Sal.

W3453 Woodhead, Abraham, 1673
Glo. Roch. S Pl. Wor.

W3454 Woodhead, Abraham, 1672
Ex. Glo. Linc. Win.

W3455 Woodhead, Abraham, 1672
Glo. Linc. Win.

W3456 Woodhead, Abraham, 1679
Wor.

W3457 Woodhead, Abraham, 1688
S Pl.

W3459? Woodhead, Abraham,
1687
2 pts: 32, 38p.
Carl. Ex. Nor. S Pl.

W3459+ Woodhead, Abraham,
1687
As W3459, but: 33, 38p.
Carl. Ex. Sal. Wel.

W3460 Woodhead, Abraham, 1687
Ex. S Pl. Sal.

W3461 *See*: W3440A

W3466 Woodroffe, Benjamin, 1700
S Pl.

W3468 Woodroffe, Benjamin, 1679
Carl.

W3469 Woodroffe, Benjamin, 1685
Her.

W3471 Woodroffe, Benjamin, 1673
Win.

W3475 Woodstock Grammar
School, 1660
Carl.

W3482 Woodward, Hezekiah, 1656
Cant.

W3502 Woodward, Hezekiah, 1644
Pet (tpw). Win.

W3505 Woodward, Hezekiah, 1643
Ex.

W3510 Woodward, John, 1695
Wel.

W3511 Woodward, Josiah, 1698
'... of the rise and progress of the
religious societies'; 12°.
Ely.

W3512 Woodward, Josiah, 1699
'An account of the societies for
reformation of manners'; ... sold by
the booksellers of London and
Westminster.
Carl. Chi. Ex. S Pl. Yk.

W3515 Woodward, Josiah, 1698
Bur.

W3517 Woodward, Josiah, 1700
Dur.

W3518 Woodward, Josiah, 1694
Wor.

W3519 Woodward, Josiah, 1692
Chelm. Wor.

W3520 Woodward, Josiah, 1695
Wor.

W3521 Woodward, Josiah, 1697
Bur. Wor.

W3526 Woolner, Henry, 1641
Cant.

W3533 Worcester, Edward
Somerset, *Earl of*, 1645[6]
Yk.

W3546 Word, 1680
Win.

W3548? Word, 1663
With a 2nd tp: 'Fair warning. First
and second part', London, for
S.T.V.T., 1663; cf. B1263 & F104.
Carl. Yk.

W3548+ Word, 1663
For Honest Meanewell; 4°.
Pet (imp).

W3550 Word, [1688]
Wel (2).

W3554 Word, [1651]
Yk (2).

W3565 Word, 1647
Cant.

W3567 Word, 1659
Yk.

W3570 Word, 1679[80]
Linc.

W3576 Word, [1679?]
Linc.

W3580 Worden, Thomas, [1670]
Ex.

W3582 Worke, 1641
Linc. Pet. Win.

W3585 Works, 1647
Yk (2).

W3592- World's, [N.d.]
See: CLC223.
Yk.

W3599+ Worlidge, John, 1675
No ed. statement; By J.C. for T.
Dring, sold by Charles Smith and
Tho. Burrell; 2°.
Bris.

W3600 Worlidge, John, 1681
S Dv. S Pl.

W3601? Worlidge, John, 1687
Fourth ed. not on tp.
Ex.

W3602? Worlidge, John, 1697
The fourth edition; Sold by Nath.
Rolls.
Yk.

W3606 Worlidge, John, 1688
Ex.

W3611 Worse, 1643
Yk.

W3612 Worsley, Benjamin, 1678
Tp in Latin: 'Catalogus librorum ...
Maii 13. 1678. Per Joan. Dunmore &
Ric. Chiswell'
Carl. Pet.

W3614 Worsley, Edward, 1676
S Pl.

W3616 Worsley, Edward, 1668
Pet. Win.

W3617 Worsley, Edward, 1672
Nor.

W3618 Worsley, Edward, 1665
Sal.

W3623 Worthington, John, 1675
Carl.

W3624 Worthington, John, 1689
Cant. Llan.

W3625 Worthington, John, 1673
Linc.

W3634 Wortley, *Sir* Francis, 1646
Pet.

W3635 Wortley, *Sir* Francis, 1642
Dur. Pet. Yk (2).

W3636 Wortley, *Sir* Francis, 1641
Yk.

W3637 Wortley, *Sir* Francis, 1641
Cant. Linc. Yk.

W3643 Wotton, Anthony, 1641
Sal. Yk.

W3644- Wotton, *Sir* Henry, 1686
See: CLC224.
Ex.

W3644 Wotton, *Sir* Henry, 1661
Cant. Linc.

W3647 Wotton, *Sir* Henry, 1641
'A parallell ... Earle ...'
Carl. Chelm. Pet.

W3648 Wotton, *Sir* Henry, 1651
Cant (imp). Carl.

W3650 Wotton, *Sir* Henry, 1672
Ely. Ex. Linc. Nor. Pet.

W3651 Wotton, *Sir* Henry, 1685
Ban. Yk.

W3652+ Wotton, *Sir* Henry, 1642
As W3652, apart from date.
Linc.

W3653 Wotton, *Sir* Henry, 1642
'Villers'
Pet.

W3654 Wotton, *Sir* Henry, 1657
Lich. Liv. S Dv.

W3658 Wotton, William, 1694
Carl. Dur. Wel.

W3659 Wotton, William, 1697
Ches. Ely. Ex. Glo. Llan. Nor.
S Pl.

W3664 Wounds, 1651
Linc.

W3667 Wray, *Sir* John, 1641
'occasionall'
Cant (2). Linc. Sal.

W3669 Wray, *Sir* John, 1641
Cant. Dur.

W3670? Wray, *Sir* John, 1641
'... made by ...'
Cant.

W3672 Wray, William, 1683
Dur. Pet.

W3673 Wray, William, 1682
Ban. Cant. Carl. Nor. Sal
(tpw).

W3674 Wren, Matthew, 1662
Carl. Linc. S Asa. S Pl. Sal.
Win.

W3675 Wren, Matthew, 1657
Carl. Ex.

W3676 Wren, Matthew, 1660
Ely (2). Linc.

W3677 Wren, Matthew, 1659
8°.
Carl.

W3677+ Wren, Matthew, 1659
... sold by J. Martin, J. Allestree, T.
Dicas [London]; 8°.
Ex.

W3678 Wren, Matthew, 1660
Win.

W3679+ Wrench, Jonathan, 1700
See: CLC225.
Ban. S Asa.

W3680 Wrens, 1641
Pet.

W3685 Wright, Abraham, 1656
Carl. Lich (tp imp).

W3687 Wright, Abraham, 1661
Pet.

W3691? Wright, James, 1687
Colophon: For the author by Edw.
Jones.
Dur.

W3692 Wright, James, 1685
Ex.

W3696 Wright, James, 1684
Cant (2). Dur. Wor.

W3697 Wright, James, 1668
Ban.

W3707 Wright, Robert, 1641[2]
Linc. Yk.

W3712 Wright, Timothy, 1692
Pet.

W3715 Wright, William, 1697
Dur. Ex.

W3722 Writer, Clement, [1658]
Carl.

W3723 Writer, Clement, 1657
'true'
Carl.

W3725 Writer, Clement, 1655
Carl.

W3728 Wroe, Richard, 1694
Chelm. Ches. Her.

W3729 Wroe, Richard, 1691
Cant. Chelm. Ches. Her.

W3731 Wroth, *Sir* Thomas, 1642
Linc.

W3735 Wyatt, William, 1679
S Pl.

W3745? Wycherley, William, 1693
Second ed. not on tp.
Cant.

W3746 Wycherley, William, 1669
Ex.

W3748 Wycherley, William, 1694
Cant.

W3755 Wycherley, William, 1694
Cant (tpw).

W3757 Wyeth, Joseph, 1699
S Pl. Wel.

W3764? Wykes, R., 1698
For Tho. Parkhurst.
Wor.

W3778 Wynell, Thomas, 1642
Yk.

W3779 Wynne, Robert, 1689
Ban. Bur. Wel.

W3780+ Wynne, Robert, 1690
Sold by Randal Taylor; 4°.
Carl.

W3783 Wyvill, Christopher, *Dean
of Ripon*, 1686
Dur. Yk.

W3784 Wyvill, *Sir* Christopher,
1647
Wing inserts this & W3787 into works
of another Christopher Wyvill.
Yk (2).

W3784+ Wyvill, *Sir* Christopher,
1679
See: CLC226.
Yk.

W3785 Wyvill, Christopher, *Dean
of Ripon*, 1694
Cant. Yk.

W3786 Wyvill, Christopher, *Dean
of Ripon*, 1686
Yk (2).

W3786+ Wyvill, Christopher, *Dean
of Ripon*, 1697
See: CLC227.
Cant. Yk.

W3787 Wyvill, *Sir* Christopher,
1672
See W3784.
Chelm. Yk.

W3788 Wyvill, Christopher, *Dean
of Ripon*, 1695
Yk (3).

X2 *Το ξειφος των μαρτυρων*, 1651
4°.
Ex.

X7- Xenophon, 1674
As X7, apart from date; '... *Κυρου Παιδειας* ...'
Ex. Nor.

X11 Xenophon, 1696
'*Ξενοφωντος* ...'; *Εκ Θεατρου* ...
Dur. Ex.

X12 Xenophon, 1691
Dated in Greek; Contains *Agesilaus*, etc.
Dur. S Pl.

X13 Xenophon, 1693
Impr. & contents not known.
Dur*.

X14 Xenophon, 1693
Dated in Greek; Contains *De re equestri*, etc.
Dur*.

X15 Xenophon, 1694
Contains *Memorabilia*, etc.
Dur.

X16 Xenophon, 1700
Dated in Greek; Contains *Hellenica*, etc.
Dur.

X17 Xenophon, 1654
Lich.

X18 Xenophon, 1697
Glo.

X19 Xenophon, 1685
Ex.

Y1 *See*: M2919A

Y10 Yarranton, Andrew, [1679?]
Linc.

Y13 Yarranton, Andrew, 1677
... and N. Simmons.
Cant (imp). Carl. Glo. Pet.

Y15 Yarranton, Andrew, 1681
Yk.

Y25? Yelverton, *Sir* Henry, 1661
'Les reports de Sr Henry Yelverton ... de divers speciall cases ...'; ... for Edward Powell.
Dur.

Y29 Yelverton, *Sir* Henry, 1662
Carl.

Y30 Yelverton, *Sir* Henry, 1662
Carl. Linc. Pet.

Y59 Young, Edward, 1686
S Pl (2).

Y60 Young, Edward, 1694
Ban. Ely. Her (2). S Asa. Wor.

Y62 Young, Edward, 1695
Cant (2). Ex. Her. Pet. S Asa. Wel.

Y63 Young, Edward, 1693
Cant. Carl. Ches. Ex. S Asa.

Y64 Young, Edward, 1688
Cant. Ches. Dur. Wor. Yk.

Y65 Young, Edward, 1678
33p.
Ely. Llan. Wel.

Y65+ Young, Edward, 1678
As Y65, but: 'February 17th'; 32p.
Ban. Cant. S Pl.

Y66 Young, Edward, 1679
Her.

Y67 Young, Edward, 1683
Her. Wel. Win.

Y68 Young, Edward, 1685
Ban. Wel (2).

Y69 Young, Edward, 1693
Cant. Ches. Ex. Her. S Asa. Wel.

Y70 Young, Edward, 1695
Cant (2). Her (2). S Asa. Wel.

Y71 Young, Edward, 1700
59p.
Ex. Her (2). Wor.

Y71+ Young, Edward, 1700
As Y71, but: 61p.
Wel.

Y72 Young, Edward, 1700
Ex. Her. S Pl. Wel.

Y92 Young, Thomas, 1644
Yk.

Y132+ Yong, 1645
By Joh. Raworth, for Joseph Hunscott; 4°.
Pet.

Y144 Younge, Richard, 1655
Pet (frag., pt 3 of Y190).

Y190 Younge, Richard, 1654
Pet (pt 3 only).

Y211? Youths, 1672
Impr. as Y210.
Carl.

Y218 Y-Worth, William, 1692
Cant.

Z7 Zanchius, Hieronymus, 1659
Nor.

Z15 Zosimus, 1679
Ches. Ely. Lich. S Asa. S Pl. Yk.

Z19? Zouche, Richard, 1657
... excudebat Hen. Hall, impensis Th. Robinson; 16°.
Carl. Ex.

Z20 Zouche, Richard, 1650
Carl. S Pl.

Z22? Zouche, Richard, 1663
For Francis Tyton and Thomas Dring.
Cant (tp imp). Carl.

Z24 Zouche, Richard, 1660
Sal.

Z25? Zouche, Richard, 1682
Excudebat Milo Flesher, pro Gulielmo Robinson ...
S Asa.

Z26 Zouche, Richard, 1657
... excudebat Hen: Hall ...
Cant. Carl. Ely. Sal.

Z27? Zouche, Richard, 1653
... Leon. Lichfield, impensis Thomae Robinson.
Ban. Pet.

English books to 1640 not in Pollard and Redgrave's
Short-Title Catalogue

The following items were reported when the main STC material had already been typeset. It has not therefore been possible to incorporate references for them in the main STC sequence.

CLCa   England. *Public documents. Miscellaneous*
Carolus Dei gratia Angliae ... rex ... &c. Omnibus, ad quos praesentes literae pervenerint, ...
[N.pl., 1636?], cap., 8°; 8p.
[Letter ordering publication of the Laudian statutes of Oxford University, 1636.]
Cant.

CLCb   England, Church of. *Orders for penance*
An order for penance, prescribed by ... Iohn, Lord Bishop of Chester, ... for such as have committed adulterie or fornication.
London, by William Stansby, 1634, s.sh.fol.
Yk.

CLCc   F., T.
The first relation: concerning the warres now being betweene the pope and the Duke of Ferrara.
London, by Iohn Windet, to bee solde by Edmund Mats, 1598, 4°.
Yk.

CLCd   Godlie admonition
[A godlie admonition for the time present.]
[N.pl., c.1582?], 4°.
[Title from running title.]
Sal (sigs C−F⁴).

CLCe   Hermann V, *Abp of Cologne*
Of a Christian reformation till a general council be appointed.
London, J. D[aye], 1547.
Bur.

CLCf   Saxo-Bosco, D. de
The rare vertue of a most excellent pil, beeing an antidotum against the plague. Newly inuented and composed, by ... D. Saxo-bosco. ... translated out of the high Almain.
Imprinted at Antwerp according to the copy imprinted at Coolen, by H.VV., 1603, [1603?], s.sh.fol.
Cant.

CLCg   Themata
Themata com[...]. Positions to be comm[...] or, assertions to be disputed ... Against the pope.
[N.pl.], 1598, 8°; [8]ff.
[Printed abroad?]
Yk.

The following items were not reported in time to be included in the main STC sequence.

1608.7+   Bayly, Lewis, 1629
The 24. edition; 12°; f. R. Allott; A−Mm¹², pp. 814; A6ʳ line 5: '23. time'.
Win (imp).

4152+   Burton, Henry, [1631?]
[Variant?] J.N. f. Timothy Clardue.
Yk.

18626a.1+   Norden, John, 1597
The thirde time corrected and augmented; 12°; I.W. f. Iohn Oxenbridge.
Win.

18617.5+   Norden, John, 1597
12°; Printed by Robert Robinson.
Win.

CLC1 ABSTRACT
The abstract of some letters written out of Spaine concerning the death of Mr. Ascham, agent there, for the rebells of England. Together with the figure of a plate found on his left side next his skinne.
Hagae, by Samuell Broun, 1650, brs.
Linc.

ADVICE to a friend
See: H., E.

CLC2 AFBEELDINGEN
Afbeeldingen der voornaamste historien, soo van het Oude als Nieuwe Testament, ... Zynde tot verklaringe van ieder afbeeldinge daar by gevoegt, sinryke rymen, in de Latynse, Franse, Engelse, Hoog- en Nederduitse talen: ... [Addit. engr. tp:] Historiae sacrae tam Veteris quam Novi Testamenti ... iconibus expressae. De heylige historien ... Die heylige historien ... The sacred histories ... Histoires sacrées ...
Tot Amsteldam, uitgegeven door Nicolaus Visscher, [1700?], 4°.
[Texts in Dutch, English, French and German. Ed. by N. Visscher?]
Nor (imp).

CLC3 ALEXANDER, Benjamin
The last advice of Mr. Ben. Alexander (late minister of West-Markham, in the county of Nottingham) to his children.
London, for Nath. Ekins, 1659, 8°; 75p.
Pet.

CLC4 ANIMADVERSIONS
Animadversions on Christ's ministery [*sic*] & ministers. Wherein is shewed by Scripture what the ministery ... is; and who are his ministers. By one ... waiting for the restoration of the creation.
[London?], printed in the year 1654, 4°; 30p.
Cant.

CLC5 AUTHORS
The authors letter to an anti-episcopall minister concerning the government of the church.
London, for Philemon Stephens, the younger, 1661, 4°; 48p.
[In prose and verse. Prose part signed Christianus Philalethes.]
Ex.

CLC6 AYLOFFE, James
Filio mortuo ante secutum matrimonium nepotes ex eo legitimantur per matrimonium avi postea contractum. — In testamento personæ vel rei falsa designatio dispositionem non vitiat.
[Tripos verses:] Jul. 7. 1696. Resp. in die Comit. Jac. Ayloffe, LL. Bac. Aul. Trin. Soc.
[N.pl.], (1696), brs.
Ely.

CLC7 B., E.
A letter from a minister in his excellence his army, to a brother of his in London, by way of prevention to Mercurius Aulicus and his complices. Dated ... before Reading. April 18. 1643.
London, printed for J. Rothwell, and S. Gellibrand, 1643, 4°; 7p.
[Signed E.B.]
Cant.

B., J.
See: BARTON, John

CLC8 B., Thomas
Ratihabitio matrimonii per procuratorem contracti, cujus mandatum eo ignorante revocatum fuit, est nullius momenti. In omnibus obligationibus facie[...] si id non fiat quod promissum condemnatio fit solum in id q[...] interest.
[Carmina Comitalia:] In die Com., Jul. 1. resp. Tho. B[...] Aul. Trin. Soc. L. Bac.
[Cambridge?, 1679?], brs.
Linc (imp).

CLC9 BARTON, John, *Master of the Free School of Birmingham*
The Latine grammar composed in the English tongue; ... By J.B.
London, printed by A. Miller, for Tho. Vnderhill, 1652, 8°; 66p.
[Preface signed by author.]
Cant.

CLC10 BAYNES, Paul
A commentary upon the second chapter of the Epistle of St. Paul, written to the Ephesians.
At London, 1641, fol.
Ex.

CLC11 BELCHER, William
Inflammatio sanguinis non requiritur ad vitam. — In
febribus intermittentibus semper vitiatur haematosis.
[Tripos verses:] Jul. 6. 1680. In die Comit. resp. Gulielmo
Belcher, Coll. D. Joan. pro gradu M.B.
[Cambridge?], (1680), brs.
Ely.

CLC12 BERIDGE, John
No king in Israel. In a sermon preached the 29th day
of May, 1662.
London, 1662, 4°; 47p.
Pet.

BIBLIOTHECA Annua
See: ROPER, Abel

CLC13 BLAGRAVE, Obadiah
Books printed for Obadiah Blagrave at the Black Bear
in St. Paul's Churchyard.
[London, 1677?], cap., 8°; [20]p.
[Date from Blagrave's address and contents of list.]
Cant.

The BOOK of the Revelation
See: WAPLE, Edward

CLC14 BOWLES, Edward
A plain and short catechisme.
The third impression
At York, by T. Broad, sold by Nathaniel Brookes,
London, 1647, 8°; 18p.
[By E. Bowles.]
Carl.

CLC15 BOWLES, Edward
A plain and short catechism.
The sixt impression, with some additions by the
author.
London: printed in the year, 1659, 8°; 9p.
Cant.

CLC16 BOYS, John, *of Hode Court*
A panegyrick to His Sacred Majesty upon the ...
marriage between the ... crowns of England and
Portugal.
London, printed for Henry Broome, 1662, 4°; 14p.
Cant.

CLC17 BRABOURNE, Theophilus
Of the changing of Church-discipline. The opinion of
Theophylus Brabourn.
London, printed by William Bentley, for Richard
Tomlins, 1653, 12°; 79 [*i.e.* 81]p.
Cant.

CLC18 BREREWOOD, Edward
Tractatus duo quorum primus est De meteoris.
Secundus De oculo. Quos scripsit ... Eduardus
Brierwoodus: restituit tandem, ab erroribus mendisque
vindicavit, ... T.S.
Oxoniae, excudebat Hen: Hall, 1659, 8°; 104, 26p.
[Pt of Wing B4380, but with separate signatures.]
Cant.

CLC19 BROUGHTON, William
Sacra Scriptura continet omnia quae ad salutem sunt
necessaria. — Leges Ecclesiasticæ circa adiaphora latæ
obligant.
[Tripos verses:] Jul. 1. 1678. In vesp. Comit. resp. Guil.
Broughton, pro gradu S.T.D. T.C.
[Cambridge?], (1678), brs.
Ely.

CLC20 BROWNE, Humphry
An alarm to all impenitent sinners.
London, for Edw. Blackmore, 1650, 8°; 79p.
Pet.

CLC21 BURNET, Gilbert
Dr. Burnet's sermon, before ... the Prince of Orange.
At the cathedral of Exon, on reading his declaration.
London, printed for W. Coldham, 1689, 4°; 12p.
Cant. Yk.

CLC22 BY COMMISSION
By commission under the Great Seal of England,
directed to all arch. bishops, dukes, ... and gentlemen
within England and Wales, ... That whereas ... the
Kings Heralds and Pursuivants of Armes by their
humble petition ...
[London?, 1672?], brs.
[Concerning the rebuilding of the College of Arms after the
Great Fire.]
Linc.

CLC23 C., T.
'Ειρηνωδία nuperas Europae aerumnas, necnon ejusdem
res prosperas sub auspicio felicissimo augustissimi
Monarchae Gulielmi III ...
Londini, impensis Thomae Parkhurst, 1698, 4°; 28p.
[Dedication signed T.C.]
Sal.

CAEDMON
See: PARAPHRASIS

CLC24 CARY, Thomas
A sermon preached in the parish-church of St Nicholas, in ... Bristol, August the 27th, 1691. being the
anniversary festival of the natives of that city.
London, for Thomas Wall, bookseller in Bristol, 1691,
4°.
Wor.

CLC25 CASE
The case stated, with some observations concerning Sir
Richard Onslow, Major James Pitson, Capt. Thomas
Moore esq; and Richard Forbench gentleman.
[N.pl., c.1660?], cap., 4°; 8p.
[Title from p. 1.]
Ex.

CLC26 CATECHISME
Le catechisme pour l'examen de la jeunesse qui se
prepare pour participer au sacrament de la Cene ... en
l'Eglise Walonne de Canterbury.
Imprimé a Londres, 1664, 8°; 36p.
Cant.

CATECHISMUS
See: TRENT, Council of

CLC27 CHARLES II
Charles R. Charles .by the grace of God being ...
Whereas we are informed, that Edmund Castel ... hath
... undertaken to compile an Heptaglot Lexicon ... We
have ... thought fit to recommend the said work to the
consideration, and bountie of all persons of honour,
and favourers of learning, that ... doctour Castel may
be enabled to go through with his worthy intention.
[White-Hall. Dec. 20. 1660.]
[London, 1660], brs.
Linc.

CLC28 CHARLES II
Charles Rex. Most reverend, and right-reverend
Fathers in God ... Whereas a very fair English Bible
... hath been (lately) published, and adorn'd by John
Ogilby ... with chorographical sculptures ... we have
been moved at his humble sute; and do ... recommend
this ... impression of the said Bible to your care, and
consideration.
[White-Hall, Oct. 24. 1660.]
[London?, 1660], brs.
Linc.

CLC29 CHISWELL, Richard
An advertisement of books printed for Richard
Chiswell.
[London?, 1686], 4°; [2]p.
[Date from known date of final work which is 'in the press'.]
Cant.

CHOICE and profitable secrets
See: WOOD, Owen

CLC30 CHURCHWARDENS
The churchwardens of our Diocess having been
generally very remiss in making due presentments.
[March 10. 1682/83. Issued by Henry Compton, Bp of
London.]
[London?, 1683], brs.
Yk.

COLE, Abdiah
See: RATIONALL

COLLECTION
See: PLAYFORD, Henry

COLLEGE of Arms
See: BY COMMISSION

CLC31 COLLINS, John
Collin's arithmetick, in whole numbers and fractions,
both vulgar and decimal. With tables for the fore-
bearance and rebate of money, the summing up of
annuities, and the purchase of leases at compound
interest.
London, printed for Benjamin Crayle, 1688, 12°; 140p.
Dur.

CLC32 COLOM, Jacob Aertsz
Atlas or Fyrie Colom wherein are lively portraijed all
the knowne coasts of the whole ocean. By Jacob
Colom.
Printed by himselfe dwellinge on the Corne-market in
the Fyrie Colom in Amsterdam, 1668, fol.
[Tp engr. Plates.]
Pet.

COMPTON, Henry
See: CHURCHWARDENS

COMPTON, Henry
See: PRAYER

CLC33 CONFESSIONS
The confessions and execution of the two Jesuites,
drawn, hang'd, and quartered at Tyburn, on ... the
24th of January, 1678/9, for high treason. Viz. William
Ireland, and John Grove.
London, for R.G., 1678/9, 4°; 8p.
Ex.

CLC34 COULT, Nicholas
The history of Thomas Dydimus his incredulitie:
plainely opened and applied for the instruction and
comfort of the godly.
London, by R.B., for Thomas Man, [1645], 8°; [44]ff.
[Author's name at end of dedication.]
Yk.

COUNTRY minister's
See: HOUGH, Edward

CRANMERIAN liturgy
See: STEPHENS, Edward

CLC35 CROMWELL, Oliver
A declaration of the lord generall and his councel of
officers; shewing the grounds and reasons for the
dissolution of the late Parliament.
London, by Hen. Hills and Tho. Brewster, 1653, 4°;
11p.
Pet.

CLC36 CROOK, Samuel
A briefe direction to true happinesse. Abridged out of
the larger treatise.
London, by M. Flesher, 1643, 8°.
Pet.

CLC37 CROSSE, William
Ecclesia Romana est idololatrica. — Satisfactio
Christi & gratuita peccatorum remisso [*sic*?] non
sunt ἀσίστατα.
[Tripos verses:] Jul. 2. 1678. In die Comit. respond. Guil.
Crosse, S. T. B. Sid. Coll. Soc.
[Cambridge?], (1678), brs.
Ely.

CLC38 CROUCH, John
'Αι δρυαδες. A poem or fancy upon the English oke, in
particular the Royal Oke.
[London], for S. Gape, 1662, 4°; 8p.
Linc.

CLC39 CROUCH, Nathaniel
A catalogue of books printed for Nath. Crouch at the
Bell in the Poultry near Cheapside.
[London, 1689], 12°; [12]p.
[Date from books listed.]
Cant.

D., T.
See: DOOLITTLE, Thomas

CLC40 DAVENPORT, Thomas
The word of the Lord to all rulers, governors, and
magistrates of England, to try themselves by what
spirit and power they rule by.
[N.pl., 1675?], 4°; 11p.
Dur.

DECLARATION
See: CROMWELL, Oliver

DECLARATIONS in the Upper Bench
See: SHEPPARD, William

CLC41 DENISON, Stephen
The white wolfe or, a sermon preached at Pauls
Crosse, Feb. 11 ... 1627 ... whereunto is added, a
briefe answer to Etheringtons late Defence.
London, by George Miller, 1641, 4°; 91p.
S Pl.

CLC42 DOOLITTLE, Thomas
The protestants answer to that question, where was
your Church before Luther? Wherein popery is proved
a novelty ... By T.D. To which is prefixed an epistle of
Mr. Richard Baxter's.
London, for Tho. Parkhurst, 1679, 4°; 165–260p.
[Anr issue of pp. 165–260 of Wing V414 with tp and preface
added.]
Llan.

CLC43 DU MOULIN, Pierre, *the Elder*
The second part of the Christian combate, in two
books. Written in French ... Translated ... by John
Bulteel.
London, printed by W. Hunt, 1650, 12°; 324p.
Cant (imp).

DURY, John
See: WAY

EIRENODIA
See: C., T.

CLC44 ELEGIE
An elegie on the death of George Monck, general of
his majesty's forces, Duke of Albermarle, &c. Appear-
ing about the same time an extraordinary starr.
London, by and for Thomas Ratcliffe and Thomas
Daniel, 1670, brs.
[In verse. Signed Thorn. Fr.]
Linc.

CLC45 ELYS, Edmund
Animadversiones in sententiam Crellianam de
satisfactione Christi.
Londini, typis J.M., impensis R. Wilkin, 1699, 8°; 16p.
Nor.

ENGLAND. Court of King's Bench
See: SHEPPARD, William

ENGLAND. Royal College of Arms
See: BY COMMISSION

CLC46 ENGLANDS
Englands alarm: or, the French-King's cruelties
exposed. Containing a true account of what usage
these three nations may expect, if ever they ... become
a prey to that most cruel ... tyrant.
London, for L.C., 1691, 8°; 42p.
S Pl.

CLC47 EXPEDIENT
An expedient to extricate one's self out of the guilt of
schism, and enter effectually into a virtual catholick
communion ... In a letter to a friend.
[N.pl., 1688?], cap., 4°; 4p.
[Title from p. 1.]
Ex.

CLC48 FAIRWEATHER, Thomas
Two sermons preached in the Trinity-church in
Kingston upon Hull, on Sunday, January 3d. 1696/7.
London, for Charles Brome, 1697, 4°; 40p.
Yk.

FALLIBILITY
See: WHITBY, Daniel

CLC49 FISHER, Payne
Carmen anniversarium vel pro valetudine recuperata
felicissimi Britanniarum restauratoris ... Georgii Ducis
de Albemarle &c. pæan panegyricus per P.P. bis
ebuccinnatus, et nunc ... revocatus ... Gulielmi Morrice.
Londini, typis Rogeri Danielis, 1663, fol.
[P.P. = P. Piscator (Fisher).]
Win.

CLC50 FULL
A full and true account of the dying behaviour of Sir
John Fenwick, baronet. Who was beheaded ... the
28th of January, 1696/7. for High-Treason.
London, for C. Wilcox, 1696, brs.
Ely.

CLC51 GRANTHAM, Thomas, *M.A.*
Upon the conversion of many school-masters ...
(certain quæries and propositions presented to all the
schooles in and about the city of London;) with a brief
syntaxis.
London, sold at Mr Dunkoms, 1646, 4°; 6p.
Yk.

GREENHILL, William
See: MATHER, Samuel

CLC52 GRENVILLE, Denis
A letter of advice, to the clergy of the Arch-deaconry
of Durham.
London, printed for Robert Clavell, 1685, 4°; 31p.
[Signed D.G. *i.e.* Denis Grenville. Another issue of pt 2 of
Wing G1938.]
Carl. Dur.

CLC53 H., E.
Advice to a friend, in a letter, written in answer to this quære: What do you think of the Act for Uniformity?
London, for John Williams, 1662, 4°; 8p.
[Signed E: H.]
Win.

H., J.
See: S., S.

H., M.
See: HOLE, Matthew

HARRISON, Thomas
See: LETTER

HEREFORD
See: PETITION

CLC54 HISTOIRE
Histoire des premiers tems, contenant, celle de la religion, des patriarches, & des anciens Israëlites.
A Londres, chez D. Du Chemin, 1700, 12°; 2 vols.
S Pl.

HISTORIAE sacrae
See: AFBEELDINGEN

HISTORY of Henry IV
See: PEREFIXE, Hardouyn de Beaumont de

CLC55 HOLE, Matthew
A practical exposition of the first part of the church-catechism: containing the preliminary questions, and the baptismal covenant. By a divine of the Church of England.
Exon, printed by Samuel Farley, and S. Darker, for Charles Yeo, 1700, 8°; 281 [*i.e.* 271]p.
[Dedication signed M.H.]
Dur.

CLC56 HOLY
Holy anthems, usually sung in his majesties Chappell Royall, and in the Cathedral and Collegiate quires of the Church of England.
York, by Stephen Bulkley, 1662, 8°.
Carl.

CLC57 HOUGH, Edward
A country minister's serious advice to his parishioners.
[London?], for Nevil Simmons, in Sheffield, 1700, 8°.
[By E. Hough]
Yk.

CLC58 HUMBLE
The humble declaration, cordial congratulation, and lowly supplication of divers ministers of the Gospel, in the western part of Yorkshire ... known by the name of Craven.
London, printed by W. Godbid, 1660, 4°; 8p.
Yk.

CLC59 HUNT, Thomas, *1627?—1688*
The postscript to Mr, Hunt's Argument, for the bishops right of judging in capital causes in Parliament, which he calls, a letter to a friend for vindicating the clergy.
London, printed for T. Davis, 1682, 12°; 166p.
Dur.

CLC60 HURSTE, Thomas
A sermon lately preached at Newarke.
At York, by Stephen Bulkley, 1644, 4°; 21p.
Carl.

CLC61 IRELAND
The report made to the honourable House of Commons, Decemb. 15. 1699. by the Commissioners appointed to enquire into the Forfeited Estates in Ireland.
London, 1700, 4°; 52p.
[Followed by: A letter to a friend: with a copy of the Report.]
Ban.

CLC62 JAMES II, *King of England*
King James his Proclamation and Order against all such as held a man should not flye from the Plague.
[N.pl., n.d.], brs.
[Official document?]
Carl.

CLC63 JENNER, Thomas
Wonderful and strange punishments inflicted on the breakers of the Ten Commandments instanced both out of divine and humane history.
London, printed by James Moxon for Thomas Jenner, 1650, 4°; 10ff.
[Author from DNB.]
Cant.

CLC64 JOHNSON, Samuel
An answer to the History of passive obedience, just now reprinted under the title of A defence of Dr Sacheverel.
[Colophon:] London, printed by John Darby, 1700, cap., 8°; 8p.
Cant.

CLC65 JOHNSON, Samuel
Several reasons for the establishment of a standing army, and dissolving the militia.
[London?, 1700?], brs.
[Single leaf, printed on one side only. A satire.]
Cant (imp). Dur.

JOSEPHUS redivivus
See: ROBERTS, Hugh

CLC66 KAERIUS, Petrus
A new and accurat map of the world. Drawne according to yᵉ truest descriptions latest discoveries.
[London?, 1646?], obl. 8°.
[Engr.: excluded by Wing. Signed 'Pe. Kærius Cælavit 1646'.]
Ban (tpw?).

CLC67 LAMPLUGH, Thomas
Certain injunctions given, amongst others, by ...
Thomas ... Arch-bishop of York, in His Grace's
visitation, 1690.
[York, 1690?], brs.
[Incorporating the injunctions of Abp Edwin Sandys, 1578.
Relates to visitations of York Minster.]
Yk.

CLC68 LAST
The last houers, of ... Andrew Rivet, ... Faithfully
collected[.] Translated by G.L.
Hagh, printed by Samuel Broun, 1652, 8°; 92p.
Cant (imp).

LETTER from a minister
See: B., E.

CLC69 LETTER
A letter from the officers of the army at the head-
quarters in the south. To the Lord Generall Cromwell,
and the army in the north. Vpon their expedition into
Scotland.
Newcastle, printed by S. B[ulkley], 1650, 4°; 8p.
[Signed by Thomas Harrison and 6 others.]
Dur.

LINDLEY, Isaac
See: TRUTH

M., S.
See: TWO LETTERS

CLC70 MATHER, Samuel, *1626 – 1671*
[A wholesome caveat for a time of liberty.]
[N.pl.], 1652, 8°.
[Title from running title. 'To the Reader' signed William
Greenhill, Samuel Mather. DNB cites Mather as author.
Imprint not known.]
Carl (tpw).

CLC71 METCALFE, Philip
A sermon preached before the ... Mayor of ...
Newcastle Upon Tyne, on the 29th. of January,
1687/8. being the day of thanksgiving at the Catholic
chappel.
London, printed by Henry Hills, 1688, 4°; 40p.
Carl. Dur.

CLC72 MOSELEY, Humphrey
Courteous reader, these books following are printed
for Humphrey Moseley, at the Princes Armes in St.
Paul's Church-yard.
[London, for Humphrey Moseley, 1656?], 8°; [20]p.
[Date from contents of list.]
Cant.

CLC73 NARRATIVE
A narrative of the affares of the west, since the defeate
of the Earle of Essex, at Listithiell in Cornwall; anno
1644.
[N.pl.], 1647, 4°; 24p.
Linc.

CLC74 NARRATIVE
A narrative of the greatest victory known in the
memory of man: being the total overthrow of ...
Stepan Radzin, with his army of one hundred
thousand men, by the Grand Czar of Russia, and his
renowned general Dolerucko. Written by an English
factor, from the port of Moscow.
London, by J.C., for Nath. Crouch, 1671, 4°; 5p.
Llan.

CLC75 NETHERLANDS
An ordinance or proclamation by the Prince of Orange
and States of Holland, in her Majesties behalf, and at
her request wherein is expresly commanded, that no
fugitive or delinquent fled from the Parliament in
England, shall presume to come within ten miles of her
Maiesties court ... Whereuuto [*sic*] is added the maner
of scituation [*sic*] ... of her Majesties Court at the
Hage.
[Concerning Henrietta Maria.]
London, printed for Andrew C. and Marmaduke B.,
1641[2], 4°; [8]p.
Dur.

The NEW distemper
See: TOMKINS, Thomas

CLC76 NORTHERN
Northern intelligence. A true relation of the principall
passages and proceedings of his Majesties army under
the command of ... the Earle of Newcastle. From the
20. of June 1643. untill the eight of July following.
With his great victory and ... overthrow of the
Yorkshire and Lancashire rebels under the command
of the Lord Fairefax, at Atherton, neer Bradford.
[London?, 1643], cap., 4°; 8p.
Dur.

ONSLOW, *Sir* Richard
See: CASE

CLC77 P., O.
A true character of the deportment for these 18. years
last past, of the principal gentry within the counties of
Carmarthen, Pembrocke, and Cardigan ...
[N.pl., 1660?], 4°; 8p.
[Signed O. P. Maridunensis. Internal evidence suggests it was
written in 1660, by a royalist sympathiser, shortly after the
Restoration.]
Dur.

CLC78 PARAPHRASIS
Caedmonis monachi paraphrasis poetica Genesios ac
praecipuarum sacrae paginae historiarum, ... Anglo-
Saxonice conscripta, & nunc primum edita à Francisco
Junio.
Amstelodami, apud Christophorum Cunradi, typis &
sumptibus editoris. Prostant Hagae-Comitum apud
Adrianum Vlacq, 1655, 4°; 106p.
Cant (imp). Linc (tpw).

CLC79 PARKER, Peter, *Bookseller*
Books printed for and sould by Peter Parker, at the
Leg and Star, right against the Royal Exchange in
Cornhill.
[London, for Peter Parker, 1677?], 8°; [20]p.
[Date from contents of list.]
Cant.

CLC80 PARRY, James
Two horrid murthers, one, committed upon the person
of Henry the Fourth of France. The other upon his
son in law, Charles the First of England.
London, for Henry Broom, 1661, 4°; 12p.
Pet.

CLC81 PARSONS, Bartholomew
The first fruits of the Gentiles. In three sermons,
preached in the Cathedral Church at Salisbury.
London, by H. Hills, [1700?], 8°.
Sal.

CLC82 PEACEABLE
A peaceable enquiry into that novel controversie about
reordination. With certain close ... animadversions
upon an ingenious tract for the lawfulness of
reordination; written by ... J. Humfrey.
London, printed, 1661, 8°.
Win.

CLC83 PECK, Francis
[The great danger of little sins.]
12°; 116p.
[Title from running title. Dedication signed by Francis Peck;
preface signed by William Greenhill.]
Cant (tpw).

CLC84 PEMBLE, William
Tractatus tres. 1. De formarum origine. 2. De sensibus
internis. 3. De creatione, & providentia Dei. Editio
posthuma.
Oxoniae, typis W.H. impensis Ed. & Jo. Forrest, 1669,
12°; 3 pts.
Sal.

CLC85 PEREFIXE, Hardouyn de Beaumont de
The history of Henry IV. surnamed the Great, King of
France and Navarre. Written ... by the Bishop of
Rodez ... and made English by J.D.
London, for John Martyn and Henry Herringman,
1672, 8°.
Pet.

CLC86 PERFECT
A perfect relation of all the proceedings betwixt his
excellency Sir Thomas Fairfax, and his Highnesse
Prince Rupert. ... Read in the House of Peeres, on
Friday the 12th of September 1645.
London, printed for John Wright ... Sept. 13, 1645, 4°.
Yk.

CLC87 PETITION
A petition of the justices of peace, grand jury men,
and other gentlemen, at the quarter sessions holden at
Hereford for the same county. Presented to the ...
House of Commons ... With a joyful acclamation from
the wel-affected in ... Worcester.
London, for Giles Calvert, 1649, 4°; 8p.
Ex.

CLC88 PETTY, *Sir* William
[An atlas of Ireland containing a general map of
Ireland, and maps of the provinces of Ulster, Leinster,
Connought and Munster.]
London, published by William Berry, [c.1690?].
[Engr. maps: excluded by Wing.]
Glo.

CLC89 PHELPES, Charles
An antidote against desperation and presumption.
London, by T.J., for Tho. Parkhurst, 1680, 8°.
Pet.

PHILALETHES, Christianus, *pseud.*
See: AUTHORS

CLC90 PHILLIPS, John
Mercurius Pædaneus: or a short and sure way,
towards attaining of the Latine tongue.
London, by James Flesher, for Richard Royston, sold
by Edward Martin, 1650, 8°.
Pet.

PHILOLOGUS, *pseud.*
See: SEASONABLE

CLC91 PIELAT, B.
Sermon de consolation contre la mort, prononcê ...
apres le decês ... [du] Comte de Dhona.
[London], imprimé pour Jaques Magnes en Russel
Street, 1679, 8°; 24p.
[Author signs dedication.]
Cant.

CLC92 PIELAT, B.
Sermon presente au Roy Charles Second, contenant les
solides consolations contre la mort, et le souverain
remede contre les afflictions de tous les ... Chrestiens;
... le 30me de Ianvier, jour anniversaire ... de Charles
Premier.
Londres, imprimé par permission, 1669, 8°; 38p.
[Author signs dedication.]
Cant.

A PLAIN and short catechism
See: BOWLES, Edward

CLC93 PLAYFORD, Henry
A collection of original Scotch-tunes.
London, by William Pearson, for Henry Playford,
1700, obl. 8°.
Dur.

CLC94 POEM
A poem upon the right of succession to the Crown of England.
[Begins: That precious gem call'd loyalty grows scarce.]
[N.pl., c.1680?], brs.
Linc.

CLC95 POPE, Walter
The Salisbury-ballad, with the learned commentaries of a friend to the authors memory.
London, for Henry Brome, 1676, brs.
[By W. Pope.]
Linc.

PRACTICAL exposition
See: HOLE, Matthew

CLC96 PRAYER
A prayer for the Right Honourable East-India Company.
[London, 1694], fol.; 1 leaf.
[Signed H. London = Bp Henry Compton; pt of a larger work?]
Cant.

CLC97 PRAYERS
Prayers in time of persecution.
[N.pl., c.1680?], cap., 12°; [12]p.
[Bound between 2 items of related subject matter, dated 1680.]
Yk.

CLC98 PRESENT
The present state of Christendom consider'd, in nine dialogues ... Done out of French.
London, for R. Baldwin, 1691, 8°.
Carl.

CLC99 PRESTON, Thomas, *Benedictine monk*
Δεῖπνον, καὶ ἐπίδειπνον, coena dominica cum micis aliquot epidorpidum. Anthore [*sic*] R. Widdrington.
Cantabrigiae, ex officina Joan. Hayes. Impensis W. Graves, 1688, 12°; 35p.
[Part of Thomas à Kempis, *De Christo imitando*, 1688. Author from BM.]
Cant.

PRIVATE devotions
See: VALENTINE, Henry

CLC100 PROAVI
Proavi nostri Plautinos laudavere sales. — Vivitur ingenio.
[Carmina Comitalia:] In Comitiis posterioribus, Martii 13. 1683/4.
[Cambridge?], (1684), brs.
Ely.

CLC101 PRYNNE, William
Summary reasons, humbly tendered to the most honourable House of Peers by some citizens and members of London, and other cities, boroughs, corporations, and ports, against the new intended bill for governing and reforming corporations.
[London?, 1661?] brs.
Linc.

PUBLIKE devotions
See: REEVE, Thomas

CLC102 PUGH, Robert
Elenchus elenchi: sive animadversiones in Georgii Batei, Cromwelli parricidae aliquando protomedici, Elenchum motuum nuperorum in Angliâ. Post alteram & tertiam ejusdem editionem. Autore R.P. Regio milite veterano.
Parisiis [*i.e.* London], 1664, 8°; 61p.
[R.P. = Robert Pugh.]
Carl. Linc. S Asa. Win.

CLC103 RAINOLDS, John
Dr. Reignolds his letter to that worthy councellor, Sir Francis Knolles, concerning some passages in Dr. Bancrofts sermon at Paules Crosse, Feb. 9. 1588. in the Parliament time. Also a question resolved by a learned doctor.
London, by W.I., 1641, 4°.
Pet.

CLC104 RATIONALL
The rationall physician's library ... Partly collected out of the best authors ... partly from Dr. Reason ... and Experience ... published ... by Abdiah Cole ... and Nich. Culpeper.
London, by Peter Cole and Edward Cole, 1661, fol.
Carl.

CLC105 RAYNES, Henry
Qui damnum infert, ad id resarciendum tenetur, nisi se inculpabilem esse probaverit. — Dolus dans causam contractui bonae Fidei cum reddit ipso jure nullum.
[Tripos verses:] Jul. 5. 1698. Resp. in die Comit. Hen. Raynes pro gradu Bacc. in Jur. Civili Aul. Trin.
[Cambridge?], (1698), brs.
Ely.

CLC106 REASONS
Reasons why bishops ought not to have votes in Parliament.
[London, c.1680?], brs.
[Dated 1641? in Lincoln catalogue.]
Linc.

CLC107 REEVE, Thomas
Publike devotions: or a collection of prayers used at sundry times, by divers ... divines.
London, by T.R. & E.M., for G.B., 1651, 16°.
['To the reader' signed Tho. Reeve.]
Carl.

REIGNOLDS, John
See: RAINOLDS, John

CLC108 RELATION
A relation of the passages in the battel at sea, between the fleet of England and the United Neitherlands; collected according to the charge & order of the Lords States General: dated June 24/14 1666 ... Translated ... out of the Dutch copy.
[N.pl.], 1666, 4°.
Pet.

REPORT
See: IRELAND

CLC109 REYNELL, Edward
Eternity weigh'd with the temporal and fading things
of this life.
London, by T.R., for Abel Roper, 1662, 8°.
Carl.

CLC110 REYNOLDS, Edward
Twenty five sermons preached upon several occasions.
The first volume.
London, by Tho. Ratcliffe, for George Thomason,
1663, (1659 – 63), 4°.
S Asa.

CLC111 REYNOLDS, Edward
Twenty five sermons preached upon several occasions.
The second volume.
London, by Tho. Ratcliffe, for George Thomason,
1663, (1659 – 63), 4°.
['The second volume' pr. on paste-on strip.]
Nor.

CLC112 RICHERIUS, Edmundus
De potestate Ecclesiae in rebus temporalibus libri IV.
Coloniae, apud Bernardum Hestingh; Londini,
prostant in Coemeterio D. Pauli, 1691, 4°.
S Pl.

CLC113 ROBERTS, Hugh
Josephus redivivus: or, innocencie violated and
vindicated. In a sermon preached ... in Wandsworth in
Surrey; by the vicar there. On ... May the 24th, 1660.
London, by James Cottrel, for Humphrey Robinson,
1660, 4°; 16p.
Pet.

ROBINSON, ?
See: STRANGE

CLC114 ROBINSON, *Sir* Tancred
Scorbutus fundatur in salinâ, vel rancidâ sanguinis
dyscrasiâ. — Pestes epidemicae oriuntur à depravatâ
aeris diathesi.
[Carmina Comitialia:] In die Comit. Julii 1. 1679. Resp. pro
Gradu Baccalaurei in Medicina, Tankredo Robinson, Coll.
Div. Johan.
[Cambridge?], (1679), brs.
Linc.

CLC115 ROOKES, Thomas
The late conflagration consumed my own, together
with the stock ... of the Company of Stationers,
London ... wherefore to let all men know notwith-
standing ... that there are books yet to be had ... I
publish this ensuing Catalogue.
[London?, 1667?], cap., 4°.
[Catalogue of books for sale. Introductory paragraph signed
(in MS) Tho. Rookes.]
Pet.

CLC116 ROPER, Abel
Bibliotheca annua: or, the annual catalogue for ...
1699 [– 1703]. ... of all English and Latin books,
printed in England ... French books imported ... by A.
Roper and W. Turner.
[London], sold by J. Nutt near Stationers-Hall, 1700
[– 1704], 4°; 4pts.
Cant (lacks pt 2).

CLC117 ROYAL COLLEGE OF PHYSICIANS
The choicest and approved antidotes against the
plague. Formerly used ... by the Colledge of Physitians, and now humbly presented to the Lord Mayor
and Sheriffes of London.
York, by A. Broad, 1665, brs.
Carl.

CLC118 ROYAL COLLEGE OF PHYSICIANS
Having received from an excellent person a receipt of
a soveraign water for the plague ... it is looked upon
as a work of piety to expose it to the publique. As
also, certain necessary directions ... By the Colledge of
Physitians. 1665.
York, by Stephen Bulkley, 1665, brs.
Carl.

CLC119 ROYAL FUNERAL
The royal funeral: o[r t]he mourning sta[te] and
solemnity of [t]he fun[e]ral o[f] Mary, queen of
England, &c. who was intered at Westmins[ter] the
fifth of March, 1695. Licens'd March the 6th 1694[/5].
[In verse.]
[London, 1695], brs.
Yk (imp).

CLC120 S., R.
A word to Dr. Womocke. Or, a short reply to his
pretended Resolution of Mr. Croftons Position ... By
R.S. the publisher of Reformation not separation.
London, 1663, 4°; 29p.
Pet.

CLC121 S., S.
Tunes to the Psalmes of David in four parts.
London, by William Pearson, for Henry Playford, sold
by John Richardson in Leeds, 1700, obl. 8°.
[By S.S. and J.H.]
Dur.

S., W.
See: SHEPPARD, William

CLC122 SAINTS
The saints refuge. A sermon preached by a reverend
divine and now published by a wellwiller.
Rotterdam, printed by Iames Moxon or Thomas
Lappadg, 1641, 8°; 57p.
[By Thomas Shepard?]
Yk.

SALISBURY-ballad
See: POPE, Walter

CLC123 SANDERSON, Robert
Two cases of conscience.
London, by E.C., for C. Wilkinson, 1668, 12°.
Ely.

CLC124 SANSON, Nicolas
A mapp of all the world. In two hemispheres in which
are exactly described all the parts of the earth and
seas. Described by Sanson, corrected and amended by
William Berry.
London, sold by William Berry, 1680, fol.
[Engr. plates: excluded by Wing.]
Linc.

CLC125 SANSON, Nicolas
Nouvelle introduction à la geographie pour l'usage de
monseigneur le Dauphin ... Presenté à monseigneur le
Dauphin par ... Hubert Jaillot.
À Paris, chez Hubert Jaillot, 1696, large fol.
[Engr. tp:] Atlas nouveau, contenant toutes les parties du
monde ... Par le Sr. Sanson. Presenté ... par Hubert Jaillot.
[Impr. pasted on over 'Amsterdam ... Mortier ...':]
London, sold by David Mortier ... at the Seing [*sic*] of
Erasmus' Head, [n.d.]
[Engr. plates: excluded by Wing.]
Wor.

CLC126 SCAPULA, Joannes
Lexicon Graeco-Latinum, è probatis auctoribus
locupletatum, cum indicibus ... Additum auctarium
dialectorum ... Accedunt lexicon etymologicum ... et
Ioan. Meursii glossarium contractum. Editio nova
accurata.
Londini, impensis Iosuae Kirton & Samuelis
Thomson, 1652, fol.
[A 2nd copy at Cant has variant imprint 'Amstelaedami,
apud Ioannem Blaeuw, & Ludovicum Elzevirium'.]
Cant. Ches. S Pl.

CLC127 SEASONABLE
A seasonable dis-course of the right use and abuse of
reason in matters of religion. By Philologus.
London, for Thomas Passinger, 1676, 8°; 223p.
Cant. Llan.

CLC128 SELDEN, John
The history of tythes.
[London], 1618 [*i.e.* 1680], 4°; 491p.
[STC 22173.]
Carl. Linc. S Pl. Win.

CLC129 SERIOUS
A serious apology for the laws established in the
exercise of religion.
London, for Charles Brome, 1685, 8°.
Sal.

SEVERAL reasons
See: JOHNSON, Samuel

CLC130 SEVILL, William
A sermon design'd for the funeral of Ed. Wiseman
Esq. late of East-Lockinge in ... Berks. W ho was
buried at Stevinton near Abingdon November the
ninth, 1694.
For John Wilmot and John Howell booksellers in
Oxford, 1694, 4°; 28p.
Cant. Llan.

CLC131 SHARP, John
Good brother, all good men are sensible how much
vice and prophaneness and irreligion have of late
prevailed.
[N.pl., 169–], half sheet.
[A letter on the duties of the clergy signed Jo: Ebor, *i.e.* John
Sharp, and addressed to the Archdeacon of the North
Riding.]
Dur.

CLC132 SHARP, John
Ten sermons formerly preach'd on several occasions,
with two discourses of conscience.
The second edition.
London, for Walter Kettilby, 1691, 4°.
Yk.

CLC133 SHAW, Samuel
Επινικιον, or a sermon preacht at the funeral of ...
Richard Chantrye.
London, printed for Tho. Parkhurst, 1694, 8°; 40p.
Cant.

CLC134 SHAW, Samuel
The great commandment. A discourse upon Psal. 73.
25.
London, by R.W., for H. Mortlock, 1679, 12°.
[By S. Shaw.]
Carl.

CLC135 SHEERING, R.
The hearts happinesse: a treatise, discovering the
difference betwixt true and feigned happinesse.
London, printed for George Whittington, 1650, 12°;
167p.
Yk.

CLC136 SHELDON, Gilbert
To the right reverend Father in God, my very good
lord and brother, the lord bishop of Lincoln.
[London?, 1670?], fol.; [2]ff.
[A letter dated: Lambeth house May the 7. 1670.]
Linc.

CLC137 SHEPARD, Thomas
The saints iewell, shevving hovv to apply the promise.
In a sermon ...
[Netherlands?], printed in the yeere, 1642, 12°; 24p.
Yk.

SHEPARD, Thomas
See: SAINTS

CLC138 SHEPARD, Thomas
The sovles invitation vnto Iesvs Christ. ... a sermon ...
[Netherlands?], printed in the yeee [*sic*], 1641, 12°; 24p.
Yk.

CLC139 SHEPARD, Thomas
A trial of regeneration, or a discovery of bastard births ... a sermon ... .
[Netherlands?], printed in the yeere, 1641, 12°; 45p.
Yk.

SHEPHEARD, Thomas
See: SHEPARD, Thomas

CLC140 SHEPPARD, William
Declarations in the Vpper Bench. With pleas, replications, rejoynders, demurrers, assignement of errours: and the entries of judgments thereupon affirmed. Collected by W.S. ... translated into English.
London, printed by T.W. and T.R. for John Place, 1653, 4°; 3 pts.
Dur.

CLC141 SHORT CATECHISME
A short catechisme: for their help, that desire to be admitted to ... the Lord's Supper. ... also for the instruction of youth.
The second edition, somewhat enlarged and amended.
Printed at Dort: by Nicolas de Vries: for R.P., 1676, 8°; [16]p.
Cant.

CLC142 SHORT NARRATIVE
A short narrative concerning the government of the Church in Scotland, from the Reformation down to the Revolution.
[N.pl., c.1690?], 8°; 69p.
Ex (imprint torn away).

A SHORT view
See: WRENCH, Jonathan

CLC143 SMALLWOOD, Allan
A sermon preached the twentieth day of October, 1655. at the funeral ... of James Pennyman.
London, by T.W. for John Place, 1656, 8°; 39p.
Yk.

CLC144 SMART, Peter
Septuagenarii senis itinerantis cantus epithalamicus.
[London?, 1643?], cap., 4°; 48p.
Dur.

CLC145 SMITH, John, *of Badgworth*
A true and exact narrative for substance of a conference had betweene Mr John Smith ... and Thomas Collier ... March 6. 1650.
London, to be sold by Thomas Thomas in Bristoll, 1651, 8°.
Sal.

CLC146 SMITH, Lawrence
Conversation in Heaven ... Being devotions; consisting of meditations and prayers.
The second edition.
London, for Thomas Speed [pt. 2: by T.H. for Thomas Speed,] 1694, 12°.
Carl.

CLC147 SOLEMN
A solemn protestation against George Keith's advertisment, arbitrary summons and proceedings against certain persons, and a meeting of the people called Quakers.
[London?, 1697], cap., 4°; 4p.
Dur.

CLC148 SOME
Some fruits of reformation, or, an old popish priest iustly rewarded. Being a ... narration of the life and death of Father Ward, alias Walker, alias Waller: who for seducing the Kings leige people ... was at the last, drawne, hang'd, and quarter'd at Tiburne, on ... Iuly the 26th 1641. With his confession at the time of his execution.
[N.pl., 1641?], 4°; 5p.
Dur.

CLC149 SOUTH, Robert
A table of the additions and alterations made in the second edition of the Animadversions upon Dr. Sherlock's book of the Trinity.
[London, 1693], 4°; [16p].
Wel.

CLC150 SOUTHCOMB, Lewis
The penitent Christian, fitted with meditations and prayers.
London, for R. Royston, 1682, 12°.
Carl.

CLC151 SPARKE, Edward
An appendix, or supplement to Scintilla altaris. Being some account of the three grand solemnities last added to the liturgy of the Church of England.
London, printed by T. Hodgkin for H. Brome, 1678, 8°; 441 [*i.e.* 645]p.
Dur (imp).

CLC152 SPEKE, Hugh
The prince of Orange his third declaration.
[London?, 1688?], 4°; 4p.
[Dated at Sherburn Castle, Nov. 28, 1688. Countersigned C. Huygens. Spurious; by Speke, acc. BM.]
Ban. Nor.

CLC153 STAFFORD, Richard
A copy of a letter sent to some of the members, of a certain congregation in Gloucestershire ...
[London, 1694?], cap., 4°; 4p.
[Signed 'Richard Stafford', and dated May 9. 1694.]
Wel.

CLC154 STAFFORD, Richard
The great, useful and blessed duty of a contentment, ... and desire to die.
Printed and are to be sold by the booksellers of London and Westminster, 1700, 8°; 4 pts.
Cant.

CLC155 STANHOPE, Thomas
Four sermons preached upon solemne occasions.
London, for Henry Brome, 1670, 8°.
Carl.

CLC156 STANLEY, Edward
Three sermons preached in the cathedral church of
Winchester.
London, by J.G., for John Clark, 1662, 12°.
Win.

CLC157 STEPHENS, Edward
The Cranmerian liturgy, or, the subtilty of the serpent,
in corrupting the true English liturgy, by Cranmer and
a faction of Calvinists.
[N.pl., 1696?], cap., 4°.
[By E. Stephens.]
Ex.

CLC158 STEPHENS, Edward
Positions concerning the differences between the true
English liturgy, and the reformed disordered
Cranmerian changeling, by which it was supplanted.
[N.pl., 1695?], 4°; 4p.
[Title from p. 1.]
Ex.

CLC159 STRADA, Famianus
An account of the famous siege of Antwerp by
Alexander prince of Parma, in ... 1584 ... Englished by
T.L. gent.
London, for Peter Parker, 1672, 8°.
Pet.

CLC160 STRAFFORD, Thomas Wentworth, *Earl of*
The true copies of two letters: written by the late earle
of Strafford. The one to his sacred majesty. The other
to a lady of great note.
[N.pl.], 1641, 4°; 12p.
Pet.

CLC161 STRANGE
Strange news from Ireland: or, a true and perfect
relation of a famous fish taken at Kingsale. The
manner of its taking, and description of its horrible
shapes; as it was certified in a letter from one Mr.
Robinson, living in Kingsale.
London, for C.N., 1667, 4°; 8p.
Linc.

CLC162 SUBJECTS
The subjects happinesse, and the citizens joy. For the
Kings Majesties happy and safe returne from Scotland.
Expressed in the sumptuous and magnificent entertain-
ment of his ... Majestie, by the ... Lord Major, with
the aldermen and the rest of the companies of this
famous city of London, on Thursday, Novemb. 25.
1641.
London, printed for Iohn Thomas, 1641, 4°; [8]p.
Dur (cropped). Pet.

CLC163 SWYNFEN, John
A sermon preached at St. Paul's Covent-Garden
upon Sunday the second of December, 1694, being the
day appointed by their Majesties for a publick
thanksgiving for the preservation of his Majesty from
the dangers to which his royal person was exposed
during his late expedition; and for his safe return to
his people, and for the success of his forces by sea and
land.
[On Ezekiel xx. 44.]
London, printed for Sam. Crouch, 1695, 4°; 28p.
Dur.

CLC164 SYMONSON, Philip
A new description of Kent ... By the travayle of Phil.
Symonson ... 1596.
[London?], printed and sould by P. Stent, [c.1650?],
folio plates.
[Engr. plates: excluded by Wing; inserted in P1989. An issue
with views of Rye and Dover, earlier than that of 1659.]
Cant.

T., J.
See: TAYLOR, Jeremy

CLC165 T., T.
A loyal protestant's answer to a Roman Catholique's
question, viz. When may we expect good days,
prosperous and flourishing years, here in England,
considering our present circumstances. With some
serious observations, intermixed, upon the doctrine of
the holy trinity, transubstantiation, and our saviour's
satisfaction ... By a person of quality, but a true friend
to old English liberty and property, and the present
government.
London, for the author, 1696, 4°; 41p.
Yk.

CLC166 TASTE
A taste of the doctrine of the newly erected exercise at
Thomas-Apostles London ... By a lover of verity &
unity.
London, by A.M., for Nathaniel Webb and William
Grantham, 1652, 4°; 10p.
Pet.

CLC167 TAYLER, Robert
A sermon preach'd at the anniversary meeting of the
Warwick-shire men. At the Church of St. Laurence,
Novemb. 25. 1680.
[On I John iv. 21.]
London, printed for T. Basset, 1680, 4°; 4, 19p.
Dur.

CLC168 TAYLOR, Jeremy
A further explication of the doctrine of originall sin.
London, by James Flesher, for R. Royston, 1656, 8°;
Hh–Ll⁸; 449–404p. (pagination irregular).
[Gathorne-Hardy and Williams, *A bibliography of Jeremy
Taylor*, no. 24A.]
Pet.

CLC169 TAYLOR, Jeremy
A sermon preached at the funerall of that worthy knight Sr. George Dalston ... September 28. 1657. By J.T.
London, for John Martin, James Allestrye and Thomas Dicas, 1658, 4°; 36p.
[Gathorne-Hardy and Williams, *Bibliography of Jeremy Taylor*, no. 31A.]
Carl. Her.

CLC170 TEN
The Ten commandments, Exodus XX.
Printed in York by Tho: Broad, 1656, brs.
Yk.

CLC171 TERTULLIAN
Opera ad vetustissimorum exemplarium fidem sedulo emendata, diligentia Nic. Rigaltii. ... Accedunt Novatiani tractatus, de trinitate, & Cibis Judaicis.
Lutetiae Parisiorum, apud Petrum le Petit & socios. Londini, prostant apud Abelem Swalle, & Sam. Smith, 1689, fol.; 735p.
Linc.

THEIR Majesties
See: WILLIAM and MARY

CLC172 THOMAS, *à Kempis*
Thomas of Kempis ... his sermons of the incarnation and passion of Christ. Translated out of Latine &c. by Thomas Carre.
Printed at Paris, by Mrs. Blageart, 1653, 12°; 196, 214p.
Cant.

CLC173 THOMSON, William
The treasures of the sea. A sermon to the mariners upon Deut. XXXIII. xviii, xix.
London, for Robert Kettlewell, 1683, 4°.
[By W. Thomson.]
Dur (imp). Wor.

CLC174 THORNDIKE, Herbert
Restauratio ecclesiae: sive accuratissima demonstratio, qua ratione ac modo ecclesia ab erroribus legitime repurgari, & ob controversias ... in unum redigi corpus possit ac debeat.
Londini, typis T. Roycroft, prostant apud Rob. Scott, 1677, fol.; 701p.
Dur.

CLC175 THORNE, Edmond
A funeral sermon upon the much lamented death of Col. Edward Cook; who died in London ... and was buried ... at Highnam near Gloucester, on February the 2d 1683/4.
London, by T.B., for Walter Davies, 1684, 4°; 39p.
Chi. Llan.

CLC175a THORNE, George
The saints great duty in time of the dangerous afflictions, ... a farewel-sermon ...
London, printed in the year, 1664, 8°.
Win.

CLC176 THORNE, J.
A serious warning of imminent danger. Being a sermon preached with reference to the sins of the nation.
London, 1672, 4°; 28p.
Ex.

CLC177 THREE
The three grand corruptions of the Eucharist in the Church of Rome.
London, for Brabazon Aylmer, 1688, 4°; 3 pts.
Pet.

CLC178 TO THE HONOURABLE
To the honourable, the House of Commons now assembled in Parliament, the humble petition of the distressed and oppressed prisoners of the Prison of Kings Bench.
At London, for Francis Couls and Thomas Banks, 1642, brs.
Linc.

CLC179 TO THE HONOURABLE
To the honourable, the knights, citizens, and burgesses of the House of Commons. The ensuing abstract of the Acts for annuities, with observations thereon, are humbly presented.
[N.pl., 1700?], cap., 4°; 7p.
Dur.

CLC180 TO THE KINGS
To the kings most excellent majesty, and the lords and peeres now assembled in Parliament. The humble petition and protestation of all the bishops and prelates now called ... to attend the Parliament, and present about London and Westminster for that service.
London, for Joseph Hunscutt [*sic*], 1642, brs.
[Probably formerly Wing H3434.]
Linc.

CLC181 TO THE RIGHT HONOURABLE
To the right honourable the Lords and Commons now assembled in the high and honourable court of Parliament. The humble petition of the well affected youngmen, apprentices, and others of the City of London, and liberties thereof.
[London?, 1642?], brs.
Linc.

CLC182 TOMKINS, Thomas
The new distemper. Or the dissenters usual pleas for comprehension, toleration, and the renouncing the Covenant, consider'd and discuss'd.
London, for R. Royston, 1680, 8°.
[By T. Tomkins.]
Carl. Pet.

CLC183 TRAYTORS

The traytors pilgrimage from the Tower to Tyeburn: being a true relation of the drawing of William Lord Munson, Sir Henry Mildmay, and Esquire Wallop, upon three ... sledges ... With ... their declaratory speeches.
London, by J. Johnson, 1662, 4°; 7p.
Pet.

TREASURES
See: THOMSON, William

CLC184 TRENT, Council of

Catechismus ad parochos ex decreto Concilii Tridentini editus. Et Pii V. pont. max. jussu promulgatus. Sincerus & intiger, mendísque iterùm repurgatus opera P.D.L.H.P.
Londini, apud Nathanaelem Thompson, 1687, 8°; 522p.
S Asa.

CLC185 TRIALL

The triall of Mr. Mordaunt, second son to John Earl of Peterburgh, at the pretended high court of justice in Westminster-Hall, the first and second of June, 1658.
London, by James Flesher, 1661, fol.; 42p.
[Published by Tho. Weston.]
Linc.

CLC186 TRUE AND PERFECT LIST

A true and perfect list of the names of the Commissioners ordered by both Houses of Lords and Commons to attend his sacred majesty: together with the names of the aldermen and Common Councill men approved by both Houses.
London, for Henry Marsh, 1660, brs.
Linc.

CLC187 TRUE AND PERFECT RELATION

A true and perfect relation, of the most remarkable passages and speeches at, and before the death of ... Iames marques of Montrose ... Faithfully colected [*sic*] by an eye witnes; in Edenburgh as they happened upon the 18. 20. and the 21. of May 1650.
[N.pl.], 1650, 4°; [5]ff.
Linc.

CLC188 TRUE COPIES

True copies of two letters ... The first from Sir William Armin ...
1644, 4°.
[Full details not available.]
Yk.

CLC189 TRUE COPY

The true copy of a letter directed to the provost and preachers of the city of Edenburgh, delivered by an unknown hand at the Cross, on June 19. 1660. In the time of ... the proclaiming of ... Charles the II. Fully discovering the horrid treacheries of the Lord Marquess of Arguile, and his accomplices ...
Published by a worthy hand.
London, by T.J., 1660, 4°; 8p.
Llan.

CLC190 TRUE COPY

A true copy of the opinions of his majesties counsel learned in the law, concerning the duty of six pence for appearances in inferiour courts.
[London? 1672?], fol.; [2]ff.
[Signed H. Finch, Fra. North, W. Jones, Fra. Winington, 1672.]
Linc.

CLC191 TRUE INTELLIGENCE

True intelligence from Yorksheire, as it was sent to the House of Parliament, November the 7th. Being a trve relation of the proceedings of the Cavaleirs at Yorke, Leeds, and Bradford.
London, printed for Thomas Hanson, 1642, 4°; [8]p.
Yk.

CLC192 TRUE NEWES

True newes from Scotland, in a letter, communicated from Edenborough, to a friend in London, touching the state of things there, March 14. 1647.
[N.pl.], 1647, 4°; 7p.
Pet.

CLC193 TRUE NOTION

A true notion of the worship of God: or a vindication of the service of the Church of England.
London, by T.R. and N.T. for Richard Thrale, 1673, 8°; 67p.
Carl. Linc. Win.

CLC194 TRUE RELATION

A true relation of all the passages in York, Beverle [*sic*], Hull and Burton. Since the first of August to the ninth.
London, printed for Thomas Wright, 1642, 4°; 8p.
Yk.

CLC195 TRUE RELATION

A true relation of the reception of his majestie and conducting him through the city of London ... on ... the 29 of this instant May.
London, for Iohn Clarke, 1660, 4°; 8p.
Pet.

CLC196 TRUE RELATION

A true relation, or, catalogue of the gentry, and persons of estate in the county of Essex that are malignants, and have not contributed towards the publike charge of the kingdome ... As it was presented to the ... House of Commons on the 15. of May. 1643.
London, for Ph. Smith, 1643, 4°; [4]ff.
Linc.

CLC197 TRUTH

Truth exalted, and the peaceable fellowship ... thereof vindicated. ... In answer to a printed paper subscribed, Edward Nightingale, ... called An account of their offers in the quarterly meetings at York ...
[York? *or* London?], 1685, 4°; 28p.
[Preface signed by I. Lindley and others (BM).]
Yk.

CLC198 TURNER, Roger
God save the king. A sermon preached at
Southstoneham: nere Southampton. The xxiii of April
1661. Being the day of the ... inauguration of ...
Charles the II.
London, by J.C., for T. Garthwait, 1661, 4°; 22p.
S Asa. Wor.

CLC199 TUTHILL, Henry
The mysterious kingdome discovered. Wherein is layd
open, how all the supreame magistrates of Christen-
dome have beene abused by their state-clergie, in all
their severall dominions (where but one sort of religion
is tollerated) for many ages last past.
At Rotterdam, by Henry Tuthill, 1645, 4°; 63p.
Linc.

CLC200 TUTHILL, Henry
Paul and Timothies visitation of the Christian
churches of Europe. Wherein is layd open so much
weaknes in every sort of Christian, as ... may well
trouble every Christians spirit, when he shall entertaine
any thoughts in his heart, to persecute another, for not
serving of God just after his fashion.
At Rotterdam, by Henry Tuthill, 1645, 4°; 63p.
Linc.

CLC201 TWO LETTERS
Two letters containing a relation of a bloudy fight at
sea: between Sir George Ascue and the Hollanders.
London, for L.R., 1652, 4°; 8p.
[The first letter signed T.W.; the second, S.M.]
Ex.

CLC202 UPON
Upon his majesties navall preparations.
[In verse, begins: Rise lazy muse, and narrow springs forsake,
Thy Helicon the boundless ocean make.]
Oxford, printed March 28, 1665, brs.
Linc.

CLC203 VALENTINE, Henry
Private devotions, digested into six litanies.
The eighteenth edition.
London, printed by E.O. for R.C., 1671, 24°; 377p.
[By H. Valentine.]
Cant.

CLC204 VINCENT, Thomas
A sermon preached at the funeral of Mr. Abraham
Janeway.
London, 1670, 8°.
Yk (imp?).

CLC205 VOSS, Gerard Johann
Gerardi Ioannis Vossii de theologia Gentili, et
physiologia Christiana; sive de origine ac progressu
idololatriae; ... editio nova, ...
Amsterdami: apud Ioannem Blaeu. Prostant etiam
Londini apud Cornelium Bee, 1668, fol.; 2 vols.
Cant (imp).

W., P.
See: WALSH, Peter

W., T.
See: TWO LETTERS

CLC206 WAITE, John
Of the creatures liberation from the bondage of
corruption.
York, by Tho. Broad, and are to be sold at his shop,
1650, 4°.
Yk.

CLC207 WALLIS, John
Eclipsis solaris Oxonii visae anno ... 1654. 2° die
mensis Augusti, stilo veteri, observatio. Observatore
Johanne Wallisio.
Oxonii, typis L. Lichfield, 1655, fol. plate.
Sal.

CLC208 WALSH, Peter
P.W.'s reply, to the person of quality's answer.
Paris, 1664, 8°.
Carl (tp imp).

CLC209 WAPLE, Edward
The book of the Revelation paraphrased; with
annotations on each chapter ...
London, 1693, 4°.
[By E. Waple.]
Wel.

CLC210 WAY
The way how a religious correspondencie may be
procured and maintained amongst the churches.
[London, 1653?], cap., 4°; 4p.
[By J. Dury?]
Yk.

CLC211 WERGE, Richard
A sermon preached in St. Maries church at Gates-
head, ... upon Hosea V. 12.
London, for Joseph Hall, Newcastle upon Tyne, and
Robert Clavell at [London], 1683, 4°.
[Different text from Wing W1366.]
Yk.

CLC212 WHINCOP, Thomas
Indulgentiae pontificiae nullum habent in S. Scripturâ
fundamentum. — Religio Christiana non est vi &
armis propaganda.
[Carmina Comitialia:] Jul. 1.1679. In die Comit. Resp. Tho.
Whincop, S.T.B. Coll. Corp. Christ. Soc.
[Cambridge?], (1679), brs.
Linc.

CLC213 WHITBY, Daniel
The fallibility & falsehood of the Church of Rome,
briefly detected and made manifest, both in several
instances thereof, and in the Scripture assertion
thereabout.
London, for Benjamin Southwood, 1676, 4°; 74p.
[By D. Whitby.]
Ex (tp imp).

CLC214 WHITE, Thomas, *of Carmarthen*
To his highness the Lord Protector. The humble remonstrance of Thomas White, late of the County of Carmarthen, gent.
[N.pl., c.1655?], 4°; 8p.
[Author possibly to be identified with one of Wing's Thomas Whites.]
Ex.

CLC215 WHITFIELD, Thomas
A vindication of the doctrine of Gods absolute decree, and of Christ's absolute ... redemption. In way of answer to ... Tho: Pierce.
London, by Henry Hills and John Field, 1657, 4°.
Pet.

CLC216 WHOLE
The whole duty of man. Part II. Teaching a Christian ... How to grow in grace ... How to demean himself in his sickness ... How to prepare himself for a happy death. Together with advice ... and some general considerations, that may induce his relations and friends, to take his death patiently.
London, printed by Francis Clark for John Kidgell, 1683, 8°; 371p.
[A supplement to *The whole duty of man* (normally ascribed to R. Allestree), by a different anonymous author.]
Dur.

WIDDRINGTON, Roger, *pseud.*
See: PRESTON, Thomas, *Benedictine monk*

CLC217 WIGHT, Thomas
A devout man described, and his death lamented: in a sermon preach'd at the funeral of ... Mr. Joshua Brumley, who departed this life the 15th day of November, 1698.
London, for the author, sold by Will. Marshal, [1698?], 4°.
Wor.

CLC218 WILDGOS, John
Mr Crofton answered, or a reply to the slanderous untruths.
London, by Edward Cole, 1658, 4°.
Yk.

WILLIAM III
See: SPEKE, Hugh

CLC219 WILLIAM and MARY
Their majesties commission for the rebuilding of the cathedral church of S. Paul in London.
London, by Benj. Motte, 1692, fol.
S Pl.

CLC220 WITNESSES
Witnesses produced against Mr. John Shaw of Hull, attesting the publike charge against him, and much more.
Printed at London, 1653, 4°; 14p.
Yk.

WONDERFUL and strange
See: JENNER, Thomas

CLC221 WOOD, Owen
Choice and profitable secrets both physical, and chirurgical: formerly concealed by the ... Dutchesse of Lenox, ... now published for the use ... of such as live farr from physicians.
London, printed for John Stafford, 1656, 12°; 317 [*i.e.* 308], 94, 7p.
[Same text as Wood's *Alphabetical book of physicall secrets*, 1639. Wood signs preface.]
Cant (imp).

CLC222 WOODHEAD, Abraham
The Apocalyps paraphrased.
[Oxford, 1689], 4°; 117p.
[Begins with sig. B; issued in this incomplete form (DNB). Includes 'An extract out of Bishop Mountague's Appeal'.]
S Pl (imp). Wel.

CLC223 WORLD'S
The world's wonder: being a true relation of the strange and dreadful apparitions seen in the air, ... at New-Market-Heath, and in the western parts: ... also, the ... ringing of the bells by four white spirits ... at Ferry-Briggs in York-shire.
London, printed for George Horton, 1659, 4°; 8p.
Yk.

CLC224 WOTTON, *Sir* Henry
The ground-rules of architecture, collected from the best authors and examples.
London, printed in the year, 1686, 4°; 22p., plates.
Ex.

CLC225 WRENCH, Jonathan
A short view of the principal duties of the Christian religion.
London, for J. Knapton, 1700, 12°.
[By J. Wrench.]
Ban. S Asa.

CLC226 WYVILL, *Sir* Christopher
A discourse, prepared for the ears of some Romanists.
York, by Stephen Bulkley, and are to be sold by Richard Lambert, 1679, 4°.
Yk.

CLC227 WYVILL, Christopher, *Dean of Ripon*
Of Christian magistracy. A sermon preach'd ... in York, at the Assizes ... July the 26th, 1697.
London, printed for B. Aylmer and F. Hildyard, 1697, 4°; 25p.
Cant. Yk.

Locations of periodicals published 1641 – 1700

The reference numbers and details of publication given in this section are taken from the forthcoming *Short-Title Catalogue of British Serials, 1641 – 1700*, by kind permission of its compilers

7 Account of the proceedings of the meeting of the Estates in Scotland / Continuation of the proceedings (Mar 1689 – Oct 1690)
Wel (pp. 12, 57 – 62 [No. 22]).

Address humbly presented (Nov 1680)
See: Votes (1680)

Address of the Commons (Nov 1680)
See: Votes (1680)

Advice from Parnassus (Feb 1680)
See: News from Parnassus

Armies scout (Apr – Jun 1653)
See: Faithful scout

Articles of impeachment (Nov 1680, Dec 1680)
See: Votes (1680)

Bibliotheca politica (1692 – 1694)
Entered at Wing T3581 and T3582.

27 Briefe relation of some affairs (Oct 1649 – Oct 1650)
Glo (Nos 2 – 24, 26 – 28, 30, 32 – 46, 50, 52, 54 – 57).

Catalogue of books continued (Trinity 1671 – Michaelmas 1700+)
See: Catalogue of books printed

30 Catalogue of books printed / Catalogue of books continued (Easter 1670 – Michaelmas 1700+)
Linc (Nos 10, 23 – 24 [1677, 1680]; 1 – 2 [1680]). Pet (Nos 1 – 2 [1680]). S Pl (Nos 1 – 24 [1674 – 80]; 1 – 13 [1680 – 83]). Sal (Nos 1 – 10 [1674 – 77]). Yk (Nos 1 – 9 [1681 – 2]).

35 Catholick intelligence (Mar 1680)
Linc (Nos 4 – 5).

36 Certaine informations (Jan 1643 – Feb 1644)
Linc (Nos 7, 16, 19 – 21).

Certaine speciall and remarkable passages (Aug 1642)
See: True relation

City mercury: from the office (Oct 1680 – Jun 1681)
See: City mercury: or advertisements

43 City mercury: or advertisements concerning trade / Mercury: or advertisements / City mercury: from the office at the Royal Exchange (Nov 1675 – Jun 1681)
Linc (Nos 108, 132, 147).

Continuation of a journall of passages (Nov 1646)
See: Papers sent from the Scotts quarters

Continuation of certaine speciall and remarkable passages (Aug 1642 – Oct 1643; by Samuel Pecke)
See: True relation of certaine … passages (pub. F. Coles)

54 Continuation of certaine speciall and remarkable passages (Oct 1642 – Jun 1643; pub. R. Wood)
Linc (Nos 21, 52).

55 Continuation of certaine speciall and remarkable passages (Oct 1642; pub. M. Walbanke)
Linc (No. 1).

Continuation of papers (Oct 1646)
See: Papers sent from the Scotts quarters

Continuation of the diurnal occurrences (Feb 1642; pub. by J. Thomas)
See: Heads of several proceedings

Continuation of the narrative (Jan 1649)
See: Perfect narrative of the whole proceedings

Continuation of the proceedings of the army (Jul 1645)
See: Proceedings of the army

Continuation of the proceedings of the Convention (Mar 1689 – Oct 1690)
See: Account of the proceedings of the meeting

67 Continuation of the true diurnall occurrences in Parliament (Feb – Mar 1642)
Linc (No. 8).

68 Continuation of the true diurnall of all the passages in Parliament (Feb – Mar 1642)
Linc (No. 8).

Continuation of the true diurnall of passages in Parliament (Jan – Mar 1642; pub. H. Blunden)
See: True diurnall of the last weeks passages

69 Continuation of the true diurnall of passages in Parliament (Jan 1642; 'sold by stationers')
Linc (No. 2).

Continuation of true intelligence (Jun – Aug 1644; by S. Ash and W. Goode
See: Particular relation

77 Coranto from beyond sea (Jun 1643)
Linc (No. 1).

83 Currant intelligence: or an impartial account / Smith's currant intelligence (Feb–May 1680)
Linc (Nos 9, 13, 15–17, 22–24).

85 Currant intelligence (Apr–Dec 1681)
Ches (No. 31).

90 Declaration, collected out of the journalls / Heads of a diarie (Nov 1648 – Jan 1649)
Yk (Nos 3, 5).

91 Democritus ridens (Mar–Apr 1681)
Linc (Nos 4 [2 copies], 5–6).

95 Dilucidator: or, reflections upon modern transactions (Jan 1689)
Wel (No. 1).

Diurnall and particula [sic] of the last weekes daily occurrents (Jul 1642)
See: Diurnall out of the North

97 Diurnall occurrences in Parliament (Dec 1641 – Jan 1642; pub. W. Cook)
Dur (Nos [1–2]). Linc (Nos [1, 37]).

99 Diurnall occurrances in Parliament (Jan–Feb 1642; pub. F. Coles and T. Banks)
Linc (No. 4).

100 Diurnall occurrences in Parliament (May–Jun 1642)
Linc (May 30 – Jun 6, Jun 6 – Jun 13, Jun 20 – Jun 25).

101 Divrnal occvrrences, or, proceedings in Parliament / True diurnall or the passages in Parliament / True diurnall of the passages in Parliament (Jan–Mar 1642; pub. H. Tuckey)
Dur (Nos [1], 2).

102 Divrnal occvrrences, or proceedings in the Parliament / True diurnall occurrences: or proceedings (Jan 1642)
Dur (No. 3).

103 Diurnall occvrrances: or, the heads of proceedings (Dec 1641; pub. T. Bates and F. Coles)
Dur (No. [1]).

Diurnall occurrences: or the heads of severall proceedings (Dec 1641 – Feb 1642; pub. J. Thomas)
See: Heads of severall proceedings

104 Diurnal occvrrences; or, the heads of the proceedings / True diurnal of the last weeks passage (Jan–Feb 1642; pub. J. Greensmith)
Dur (No. 6).

109 Diurnall: or the heads of all the proceedings (Dec 1641)
Dur (No. [1] 6–13 Dec 1641). Linc (No. [2] 13–20 Dec 1641).

110 Diurnall out of the North (Jul 1642)
Linc (18 and 26 Jul).

112 Domestick intelligence: or news / Protestant (domestick) intelligence (Jul 1679 – Apr 1681; pub. B. Harris)
Linc (Nos 1–25, 27–84, 91–98). Yk (No. 35).

113 Domestick intelligence: or news / True domestick intelligence (Aug 1679 – May 1680; pub. N. Thompson)
Linc (Nos 16, 18, 20–89).

England's memorable accidents (Sep 1642 – Jan 1643)
See: Quotidian occurrences

132 English intelligencer (Jul–Aug 1679)
Linc (Nos 3–4, 6–8).

English post (1641)
See: Wing E3110

Exact and perfect relation (Jul 1645)
See: Proceedings of the army

143 Exact and true divrnall (Aug–Sep 1642)
Linc (15–22 Aug, 22–29 Aug, 29 Aug – 5 Sep).

Extract of letters (Apr 1644)
See: True relation of the late proceedings

148 Faithful post (Mar–Aug 1653; pub. G. Horton Mar–May, R. Eels and T.L. thereafter)
Glo (5–11 Aug, No. 1).

Faithfull post (Mar–Jun 1660)
See: Weekly post

Faithfull relation ... Scottish army (Feb 1644; by Edward Bowles)
See: True relation of the late proceedings

150 Faithful scout / Armies scout (Dec 1651 – Sep 1655)
Glo (No. 194).

153 Five matters of note (May 1642)
Ex (16–23 May). Yk (16–23 May).

161 French occurrences (May 1652 – Jan 1653)
Pet (No. 3).

General history of Europe (1690–1700+)
Title-page for: Present state of Europe

Grand politique post (Jan–Apr 1654)
See: Politique post

Heads of a diarie (Dec 1648)
See: Declaration collected

181 Heads of severall proceedings / Divrnall occvrrences / Continuation of the diurnall occurrences (Nov 1641 – Feb 1642; pub. John Thomas *et al.*)
Dur (Nos [2, 4–7]; another ed. of [5]). Linc (Nos [1–2, 7]).

183 Heraclitus ridens (Feb 1681 – Aug 1682)
Glo (Nos 1–82). Linc (Nos 1–2, 8–9).

His Majesties message (Nov 1680)
See: Votes (1680)

Humble address of the Commons (Nov 1680)
See: Votes (1680)

Humble address of the House (Dec 1680)
See: Votes (1680)

Impartial London intelligence (Apr 1681)
See: Protestant Oxford intelligence

Intelligence from the Scottish army (Apr 1644; by Edward Bowles)
See: True relation of the late proceedings

Intelligence from the south borders (May 1644; by Edward Bowles)
See: True relation of the late proceedings

201 Intelligencer (Aug 1663 — Jan 1666; ed. R. L'Estrange)
Carl (24 Aug 1663 — 20 Nov 1665). Yk (No. 11 [9 Nov 1663]).

Irelands trve divrnall (Feb 1642)
See: Wing B3106

211 Kingdomes intelligencer. Faithfully communicating (May—Jul 1660)
Carl (various numbers).

Kingdomes intelligencer of the affairs (Jan 1661 — Aug 1663)
See: Parliamentary intelligencer

214 Kingdomes vveekly intelligencer (Dec 1642 — Oct 1649)
Linc (Nos 2—5, 8, 11—12, 15—23).

217 Kingdomes weekly post, with his packet of letters (Nov 1643 — Jan 1644)
Linc (28 Nov — 6 Dec 1643).

Latest remarkable truths (1642)
See: Wing L566

Letter of the King sent to the Parliament of Paris (Jan 1650)
See: Briefe relation

London gazette (Feb 1666 — Dec 1700+)
See: Oxford gazette

Matters of great note (Mar 1642)
See: Wing M1306

Mechanick exercises [now identified as a periodical]
See: Wing M3013

256 Memoirs of the present state of Europe (Jan 1692 — Dec 1693)
Carl (Jan 1692 — Dec 1693). Cant (May 1692).

264 Mercurius Anglicus, communicating moderate intelligence (Sep—Oct 1650)
Glo (No. 1).

266 Mercurius Anglicus: or, the weekly occurrences / True news (Nov 1679 — May 1680)
Linc (Nos 6, 12—13, 33, 37, 39—43, 45, 47, 51).

Mercurius aulicus, a diurnall.
Title-page for: Mercurius avlicvs, communicating the intelligence

275 Mercurius aulicvs, communicating the intelligence (Oxford, Jan 1643 — Sep 1645; by Sir John Berkenhead and Peter Heylyn; including counterfeit and London reprints)
Linc (Weeks 2—3, 7—8, 17—22). Yk (complete?). Pet (Weeks 8, 12—13, 20).

279 Mercurius bellicvs (Nov 1647 — Jul 1648)
Pet (No. 8).

281 Mercurius bifrons (Feb—Mar 1681)
Linc (Nos 2—3).

286 Mercurius Britanicus: communicating the affaires of great Britaine (Aug 1643 — May 1646)
Linc (No. 18). Pet (No. 94).

298 Mercurius civicus, Londons intelligencer (May 1643 — Dec 1646)
Linc (Nos 2—6, 36).

299 Mercurius civicus: or, a true account / Mercurius civicus: or the city mercury (Mar—Jun 1680)
Linc (Nos 3, 7, 10 [1st title], 242 [2nd title]).

300 Mercurius civicus, or the cities intelligencer (Mar—Jul 1660)
Carl (Nos 4, 5 [+?]).

312 Mercurius elencticus. Communicating the unparallel'd proceedings (Nov 1647 — Jan 1649)
Pet (Nos 6, 8, 13, 17, 22-23, 25, 27—31, 34—51, 53).

335 Mercurius insanus, insanissimus (Mar—May 1648)
Linc (No. 7).

344 Mercurius melancholicus: or, news from Westminster (Sep 1647 — Nov 1648; by John Hackluyt; including counterfeits)
Pet (Nos 2, 6, 12, 25, 29).

Mercurius politicus, communicating (May—Jul 1660)
See: Mercurius politicus, from the Office of Intelligence

361 Mercurius politicus. Comprising the summ (Jun 1650 — Apr 1660)
Glo (Nos 1—4, 6, 13, 15—17, 19—25, 27—55, 57—63, 65—142, 146—192, 196—200, 202—215, 217, 220—222, 224—226, 229—232, 234—240, 242—245, 250—257, 259—265, 267, 270—275, 277—298, 301—333, 374—387, 390—391, 393—396, 398—404, 406, 408—411, 414). Carl (No. 10). Pet (Nos 14—15, 55, 108, 115, 134, 149—150, 153, 156, 191). Linc (No. 369). Yk (Nos 416—420, 546, 602, 611).

363 Mercurius politicus, from the Office of Intelligence / Publick intelligencer / Mercurius politicus, communicating (Apr—Jul 1660)
Carl (8 and 17 May).

369 Mercurius pragmaticvs. Communicating intelligence from all parts (Sep 1647 — May 1649)
Pet (Nos 5—10, 13—15 [1647], 16—25, 27—28 [1648]; 1—3, 5—18, 20—33, 35—37, 39 [1648], 43 [1649]).

370 Mercurius pragmaticus, (for King Charles II.) (Apr 1649 — May 1650)
Pet (2 Pars. nos 4, 6—8 [1649]).

378 Mercurius publicus: comprising the sum (Dec 1659 — Sep 1663)
Yk (Nos 14, 18, 51). Carl (various numbers, 1661—2).

384 Mercvrius rusticvs, or the covntries complaint (Oxford, May 1643 — March 1644)
Linc (weeks II and III).

Mercury: or advertisements (Feb—Sep 1678)
See: City mercury

419 Moderate intelligencer: impartially communicating (Feb 1645 — Oct 1649)
Yk (No. 191).

445 News from Parnassus / Advice from Parnassus (Jan—Feb 1681)
Linc (Nos 2—3, = pt of 1—4 Feb 1680/1).

Newes, published for satisfaction and information of the people (Sep—Dec 1663; ed. Sir Roger L'Estrange)
For later numbers, see: Intelligencer

458 Observator. In question and answer / Observator, in dialogue / Observator (Apr 1681 — Mar 1687)
Linc (No. 34 [= pt of Vol. 1]). Glo (Vols 1—3, 1684—87). Ely (No. 8 [= pt of Vol. 3]). Win (Vol. 1, 1684).

462 Occasional paper (1697—1698)
Ely (Nos I, IV, VI—VIII, X). Bris (Nos I—IV, VI—X). Nor (Nos I—II, V—X).

465 Occurrences of certain speciall and remarkable passages / Perfect occurrences of Parliament / Perfect occurrences of both Houses / Perfect occurrences of every dayes journall (Jan 1644 — Oct 1649)
Cant ('sixteenth week, ending 17 Apr 1646'). Linc (No. 6 [2 Feb 1644]; 'fiftieth week, ending 12 Dec 1646'). Glo (No. 145 [5—12 Oct 1649]).

471 Oxford gazette / London gazette (Nov 1665 — Dec 1700+)
Linc (Nos 1324, 1329). Dur (No. 2221).

480 Packets of letters (Mar—Nov 1648)
Yk (Nos 4, 8).

477 Pacquet of advice from Rome / Weekly pacquet of advice from Rome / New anti-Roman pacquet / Anti-Roman pacquet / Weekly pacquet of advice from Rome restored / Weekly pacquet of advice from Rome (Dec 1678 — Jul 1683)
Ex (5v.) . Pet (vol. 3—4).

482 Papers sent from the Scots quarters / Continuation of papers / Continvation of a iournall of passages (Oct—Nov 1646)
Yk (No. 3).

485 Parliament scout (Jun 1643 — Jan 1645)
Linc (No. 32). Yk (No. 33).

486 Parliamentary intelligencer / Kingdomes intelligencer (Dec 1659 — Aug 1663)
Carl (1660: 30 Apr — 4 Jun, 3 Sep — 10 Sep, 29 Oct — 5 Nov, 12 Nov — 19 Nov, 3 Dec — 31 Dec; 1661: various numbers; 1662: nos 18—25, 27—52; 1663: nos 1—16, 18—24, 26—34).

492 Particular relation of the severall removes / Continuation of true intelligence / Particular relation of the most remarkable occurrences / Continuation of true intelligence (May—Aug 1644)
Cant (No. 1). Pet (No. 1). Yk (Nos 2, 3 [2 copies], 5).

501 Perfect diurnal of every dayes proceedings / Perfect diurnal: or the dayly proceedings / Perfect diurnal of the dayly proceedings (Feb—Mar 1660)
Yk (21 Feb — 16 Mar).

502 Perfect diurnall of passages in Parliament (Jul 1649)
Glo (No. 2). Yk (No. 2).

503 Perfect diurnall of some passages and proceedings of and in relation to the armies (Dec 1649 — Sep 1655)
Glo (Nos 1—11, 13—14, 16—31, 34, 36—40, 42—44, 46—98, 100—109, 111, 113—139, 141—149, 151—169, 172—181, 183—186, 188, 191—200, 202, 206, 208—213, 217, 223—228, 230—233, 235—236, 239—241, 243—245, 249—251, 253, 256, 258—259, 263—265, 267, 271, 274—278, 281 [numbered 286], 282—293, 295—298, 301). Yk (Nos 18, 226).

504 Perfect diurnall of some passages in Parliament (Jul 1643 —Nov 1649)
Dur (Nos 1—5). Glo (Nos 103—208, 211-216, 218—243, 245—308, 310—311, 313—321). Yk (Nos 173, 187, 217, 221, 223, 226).

505 Perfect diurnall of some passages in Parliament, and intelligence from the armies (Jul 1650)
Glo (Nos 324—325).

508 Perfect diurnall of the passages in Parliament (pub. T.P.; Feb—Mar 1642)
Linc (28 Feb — 7 Mar).

509 Perfect diurnall of the passages in Parliament (pub. W. Cooke, with imitations and counterfeits; Jun—Aug 1642)
Linc (various issues). Dur (various issues).

510 Perfect diurnall of the passages in Parliament (pub. T. Cook; Jul—Aug 1642)
Linc (No. 8). Dur (various issues).

512 Perfect diurnall of the passages in Parliament (pub. Will. Cooke; Aug—Oct 1642)
Linc (various issues). Dur (various issues).

518 Perfect narrative of the whole proceedings of the High Court of Justice / Continvation of the narrative (Jan 1649)
Ex (Nos 2, 3 [imp]). Her (Nos 1—3). Pet (Nos 1—3). Dur (Nos 1—3). Yk (No. 1).

Perfect occurrences of both Houses (Mar 1646 — Jan 1647)
See: Occurrences of certain speciall and remarkable passages

Perfect occurrences of every dayes journall (Jan 1647 — Oct 1649)
See: Occurrences of certain speciall and remarkable passages

Perfect occurrences of Parliament (May 1644 — Mar 1646)
See: Occurrences of certain speciall and remarkable passages

521 Perfect occurrences of the most remarkable passages (May 1659 — May 1660)
Pet (No. 5).

Perfect proceedings of state affaires (Mar—Sep 1655)
See: Severall proceedings in Parliament

Perfect weekly account, Containing (May—Dec 1647)
See: Weekly account

537 Philosophical collections (1679 — Apr 1682)
Wel (No. 1).

539 Philosophical transactions (London, Oxford; Mar 1665 — Dec 1700+)
Carl (Vols I—VIII [= nos 1—111], X, XI). Wel (Vols I—III [= nos 1—44], nos 137—142). Bris (No. 16 [imp?]). Pet (No. 59).

544 Politique post / Grand politique post / Weekly post (Jan 1654 — Sep 1655)
Glo (No. 200).

548 Poor Robin's intelligence (Mar 1676 — Nov 1677)
Linc (No. 0oo, 22 May 1677).

557 Present state of Europe, or the historical and political mercury (Jul 1690 — Dec 1700+)
Carl (1690—1700; vol. with title 'The general history of Europe', 1692). Pet (Jul 1690 — Dec 1692, some pts are 2nd ed.)

565 Proceedings of the army / Exact and perfect relation / Continvation of the proceedings (Jul—Aug 1645)
Yk (9 Jul; no. 6).

Protestant (domestick) intelligence (Jan 1680 — Apr 1681)
See: Domestick intelligence (pub. B. Harris)

571 Protestant Oxford intelligence / Impartial London intelligence (Mar—Apr 1681)
Linc (Nos 1, 3—5, 7 [of first title]; no. 1 [of second title]).

575 Publick intelligencer. Communicating the chief occurrences (Oct 1655 — Apr 1660)
Glo (Nos 1, 3—20, 22, 27—34, 36—48, 50—55, 93—103, 105—114, 116, 121—126).

Publick intelligencer: communicating the chief transactions (Apr—Jun 1660)
See: Mercurius politicus, from the office

579 Quotidian occurrences in and about London / England's memorable accidents (Sep 1642 — Jan 1643)
Linc (12—19 Sep, 26 Sep — 3 Oct, 10—17 Oct, 31 Oct — 7 Nov, 14—21 Nov, 12—19 Dec, 26 Dec — 2 Jan).

Report from [of] the committee (Dec 1680)
See: Votes (1680)

Resolutions of the House (Dec 1680)
See: Votes (1680)

594 Scotish dove sent out, and returning / Scotish dove sent out the last time (Oct 1643 — Dec 1646)
Linc (No. 16). Dur (Nos 80, 138).

599 Severall proceedings in Parliament / Severall proceedings of state affaires / Severall proceedings of Parliament / Perfect proceedings of state affaires (Sep 1649 — Sep 1655)
Glo (Nos 3—7, 9—29, 31—37, 39—42, 46—53, 55—57, 59—65, 67—91, 93—99, 101—156, 158—180, 182—198, 203—211, 216, 219—224, 229—239, 242, 244—247, 249—254, 260—265, 270—276, 278, 282, 286—288, 294—303, 305—312).

Severall proceedings of Parliament (Oct 1654 — Jan 1655)
See: Severall proceedings in Parliament

Severall proceedings of state affaires (Apr 1653 — Sep 1654)
See: Severall proceedings in Parliament

Smith's currant intelligence (Mar—May 1680)
See: Currant intelligence (pub. J. Smith)

602 Smith's, Protestant intelligence (Feb—Apr 1681)
Linc (Nos 1—7).

605 Some speciall and considerable passages / Speciall passages from divers parts / Some speciall passages from divers parts / Speciall passages and certain informations (Aug 1642 — Jun 1643)
Yk (No. 11).

Some speciall passages from divers parts (Aug 1642)
See: Some speciall and considerable passages

606 Some speciall passages from London (May—Aug 1642)
Dur (Nos 6—7 [28 Jun — 12 Jul], 9 [18—26 Jul]). Yk (Nos 1, 3, 6—7 [as Dur]). Linc (Nos 6—7, 9 [as Dur], 10, 7 [3—10 Jul], 9 [9—16 Aug]).

Speciall passages and certain informations (Aug 1642 — Jun 1643)
See: Some speciall and considerable passages

Speciall passages from divers parts (Aug 1642)
See: Some speciall and considerable passages

611 Theosophical transactions by the Philadelphian society (Mar—Nov 1697)
Wel (Nos I—V).

Tricks of state: or more Westminster projects (Apr 1648)
See: Westminster projects

615 True and perfect diurnall of all the chiefe passages in Lancashire (Jul 1642)
Linc (No. 1).

616 True and perfect diurnall of the passages in Parliament (Aug—Sep 1642)
Linc (No. 11).

True diurnall of the last weeks passage (Jan 1642)
See: Divrnal occvrrences; or, the heads of the proceedings

623 Trve diurnall of the last weeks passages / Continuation of the true diurnall of passages (Jan—Mar 1642; pub H. Blunden)
Linc (Nos 1—2, 4, 8—10). Dur (Nos 3—5, 7, 9).

True diurnall or the passages in Parliament (Jan 1642; pub. H. Tuckey)
See: Diurnall occurrences (pub. H. Tuckey)

True domestick intelligence (Sep 1679 — May 1680)
See: Domestick intelligence (pub. N. Thompson)

True news: or Mercurius Anglicus (Dec 1679 — May 1680)
See: Mercurius Anglicus

634 True Protestant (domestick) intelligence (Apr — May 1680)
Linc (Nos 1 — 7).

636 True Protestant mercury: or, occurrences foreign and domestick (Dec 1680 — Oct 1682; pub. L. Curtis)
Linc (Nos 7 — 15).   Yk (No. 177).

638 Trve relation of certaine speciall and remarkable passages / Certaine speciall and remarkable passages / Continvation of certaine speciall and remarkable passages (Aug 1642 — Oct 1643)
Linc (Nos 4, 6, 8, 10 — 11, 15, 46 — 48).

639 True relation of the late proceedings of the Scottish army / Faithfull relation ... Scottish army / Late proceedings of the Scottish army / True relation of the proceedings / Intelligence from the Scottish army / Extract of letters / Intelligence from the south borders (Feb — Apr 1644)
Yk (No. 7).

642 Two treatises concerning the matter of the engagement (Nov 1650)
Yk (No. 3 [lacks A2]).   Pet (No. 3 [imp]).

Very full and particular relation (Oct 1649)
See: Briefe relation

647 Votes of the House of Commons (Oct 1680 — Mar 1681)
Linc (Nos 1 — 58).   Win (Nos 1 — 3, 28, 51).   Ches (Nos 28, 47, 49).

648 Votes of the House of Commons, at Oxford (Mar 1681)
Linc (Nos 1 — 5).

657 Votes of the House of Commons (Nov 1693 — Apr 1694)
Yk (complete: nos 1 — 138).

Votes of the House, or the dayly proceedings
Title-page for: Perfect diurnal of every dayes proceedings (1660)

671 Weekly account / Perfect weekly account (Sep 1643 — Jan 1648)
Linc (No. 14).

680 Weekly discoverer strip'd naked (Feb — Mar 1681)
Linc (Nos 2 — 3, 6).

681 Wcckly discovery of the mystery of iniquity ... 1641 (Feb — Aug 1681)
Linc (No. 1).

688 Weekly intelligencer of the commonwealth (Dec 1650 — Sep 1655)
Glo (Nos 9, 12 [or 126?]).

693 VVeekly memorials for the ingenious (Jan 1682 — Jan 1683; pub. H. Faithorne and J. Kersey)
Ex (Nos 1 — 50).   Wel (Nos 1 — 42 [2 copies of 1 — 7]).

694 Weekly memorials for the ingenious (Mar — Sep 1682; pub. R. Chiswel [etc.])
Wel (Nos 1 — 29).

701 Weekly pacquet of advice from Germany (Sep 1679 — Feb 1680)
Linc (No. 12).

Weekly pacquet of advice from Rome (Dec 1678 — Jul 1683)
See: Pacquet of advice from Rome

Weekly post, faithfully communicating (Apr 1654 — Sep 1655)
See: Politique post

704 Weekly post: truly communicating / Faithfull post (May 1659 — Jun 1660)
Yk (No. 45 [6 — 13 Mar 1660]).

710 Westminster proiects / Tricks of state / Windsor projects (Mar — Jun 1648)
Pet (Mar 1648).

Windsor projects and Westminster practices (May 1648)
See: Westminster projects

This section is set out in alphabetical order of title, except that the entries starting 'Anno regni ...' are arranged chronologically by regnal year.

CLC228 An act for repealing an ordinance and act of Parliament ...
London, by Edward Husband and Iohn Field, 1650, fol.; 897 – 899p.
Yk.

CLC229 An act of general pardon and oblivion.
London, 1651, fol.; [1551] – 1564p.
Linc (cropped).

CLC230 An act of general pardon and oblivion.
London, by John Field, 1651, fol.; [14]ff.
Cant.

CLC231 An act of the Commons of England ... for the abolishing of deans, deans and chapters, ...
London, by Richard Cotes, 1649, 4°.; sigs I – N⁴ O² (63 – 105p.).
SPl. Yk.

CLC232 An additional ordinance for the excise. [May 1654].
London, by William du-Gard, and Henry Hills, 1654, cap., fol.; 315 – 318p.
[Impr. from colophon.]
Dur.

CLC233 Anno regni Caroli II. ... duodecimo.
London, by John Bill and Christopher Barker, 1660, fol.
Lich (21p.). Linc (5, 150, 90p.; 93 – 96, 27, 9, 17, 20, 9, 35 – 82, 9, 8, 20 [17 – 19]p.). Win (21 – 36p.).

CLC234 Anno regni Caroli II. ... decimo tertio.
London, by John Bill and Christopher Barker, 1661, fol.
Dur (9 – 126p.). Lich (87p.). Linc (126p.; 87p.).

CLC235 Anno regni Caroli II. ... decimo tertio.
London, by John Bill and Christopher Barker, 1662 – 63, fol.
[Colophon dated 1663.]
Dur (87p.).

CLC236 Anno regni Caroli II. ... decimo tertio & quarto.
London, by John Bill and Christopher Barker, 1662, fol.
Linc (64p.).

CLC237 Anno regni Caroli II. ... decimo quarto.
London, by John Bill and Christopher Barker, 1662 – 64, fol.
[Colophons dated 1663, 1664.]
Dur (95 – 444p.). Linc (67 – 242, 331 – 400p.; 265 – 270, 297 – 301p.; 285 – 327, 403 – 444p.). Win (67 – 95p.).

CLC238 Anno regni Caroli II. ... decimo quinto.
London, by John Bill and Christopher Barker, 1663 – 64, fol.
Dur (53 – 370p.). Linc (312p.). Win (55 – 64p.).

CLC239 Anno regni Caroli II. ... decimo quinto.
In the Savoy, by the assigns of John Bill and Christopher Barker, 1669, fol.
Lich (10p.?).

CLC240 Anno regni Caroli II. ... decimo sexto.
London, by John Bill and Christopher Barker, 1664, fol.
Dur (11 – 66p.). Lich (45 – 57p.). Linc (66p.). Win (25 – 41p.).

CLC241 Anno regni Caroli II. ... decimo sexto & decimo septimo.
London, by John Bill and Christopher Barker, 1664, fol.
Linc (218p.).

CLC242 Anno regni Caroli II. ... decimo septimo.
London, by John Bill and Christopher Barker, 1665, fol.
[Colophon: Oxford, by Leonard Lichfield, for Iohn Bill and Christopher Barker.]
Linc (239 – 296p.). Win (261 – 276p.).

CLC243 Anno regni Caroli II. ... decimo octavo.
London, by the assigns of John Bill and Christopher Barker, 1666, fol.
Linc (68p.).

CLC244 Anno regni Caroli II. ... decimo nono.
London, by the assigns of John Bill and Christopher Barker, 1666, fol.
Linc (71 – 167p.).

CLC245 Anno regni Caroli II. ... decimo nono.
In the Savoy, by the assigns of John Bill and Christopher Barker, 1667, fol.
Lich (36p.).

CLC246 Anno regni Caroli II. ... vicesimo.
In the Savoy, by the assigns of John Bill and Christopher Barker, 1668, fol.
Linc (63p.).

CLC247 Anno regni Caroli II. ... vicesimo secundo.
In the Savoy, by the assigns of John Bill and Christopher Barker, 1670, fol.
Lich (179—184p.).   Linc (182p.).

CLC248 Anno regni Caroli II. ... vicesimo secundo & vicesimo tertio.
In the Savoy, by the assigns of John Bill and Christopher Barker, 1670/71, fol.
Linc (104p.; 109—292p.).

CLC249 Anno regni Caroli II. ... vicesimo secundo & vicesimo tertio.
London, by the assigns of John Bill and Christopher Barker, 1674, fol.
Lich (153—173, 249—272 [*i.e.* 292]p.).

CLC250 Anno regni Caroli II. ... vicesimo secundo & vicesimo tertio.
London, by Charles Bill and Thomas Newcomb, 1690, fol.; 12p.
Cant. Dur (2).

CLC251 Anno regni Caroli II. ... vicesimo quinto.
London, by the assigns of John Bill and Christopher Barker, 1673, fol.
Lich (181—202p.).   Linc (211p.).

CLC252 Anno regni Caroli II. ... vicesimo nono.
London, by the assigns of John Bill and Christopher Barker, 1677, fol.
Linc (171p.; 175—242p.).   Sal (155p.).

CLC253 Anno regni Caroli II. ... vicesimo nono.
London, by Charles Bill, Henry Hills, and Thomas Newcomb, 1687—88, fol.
[One of sep. tps to Acts dated 1687.]
Dur ([157]—242p.).

CLC254 Anno regni Caroli II. ... vicesimo nono & tricesimo.
London, by John Bill, Christopher Barker, Thomas Newcomb and Henry Hills, 1677/78, fol.
Linc (47p. [2 copies]; 51—54p.).

CLC255 Anno regni Caroli II. ... vicesimo nono & tricesimo.
London, by Charles Bill, Henry Hills and Thomas Newcomb, 1687, fol.
Dur (51—54p.).

CLC256 Anno regni Caroli II. ... tricesimo.
London, by John Bill, Christopher Barker, Thomas Newcomb and Henry Hills, 1678, fol.
Linc (14p.; 131p.).   Dur (14p.).

CLC257 Anno regni Caroli II. ... tricesimo.
London, by John Bill, Thomas Newcomb, and Henry Hills, 1679, fol.
Dur ([113]—131p.).

CLC258 Anno regni Caroli II. ... tricesimo.
London, by Charles Bill, Henry Hills, and Thomas Newcomb, 1687—91, fol.
[Sep. tp to one of the acts has impr.: Reprinted by Charles Bill and the executrix of Thomas Newcomb, 1691.]
Dur ([73]—[96]p.).

CLC259 Anno regni Caroli II. ... tricesimo primo.
London, by John Bill, Thomas Newcomb and Henry Hills, 1679, fol.
Linc (173—197p.).

CLC260 Anno regni Caroli II. ... tricesimo primo.
London, by Charles Bill and Thomas Newcomb, 1687—91, fol.
[Sep. tp to one of the acts has impr.: Printed by Charles Bill, Henry Hills, and Thomas Newcomb, 1687.]
Dur ([171]—197p.).

CLC261 Anno regni Caroli II. ... tricesimo secundo.
London, by the assigns of John Bill, Thomas Newcomb and Henry Hills, 1680/81, fol.
Dur (11p.).   Linc (11p.).

CLC262 Anno regni Jacobi II. ... primo.
London, by the assigns of John Bill deceas'd, and by Henry Hills and Thomas Newcomb, 1685, fol.
Nor. Wel (138, 839 [*i.e.* 139?], 131—151, [1]—31p.).
Cant (137, 126—151p.).

CLC263 Anno regni Jacobi II. ... primo.
London, by Charles Bill and the executrix of Thomas Newcomb, 1685—91, fol.
[Sep. tps to acts variously dated 1685—1691; Printers vary.]
Cant (31p.).   Dur (139, 131—151, 31p.).   Wor (151, 31p.).

CLC264 Anno regni Gulielmi et Mariae ... primo.
London, by Charles Bill and Thomas Newcomb, 1688—91, fol.
[Sep. tps to acts variously dated 1688—91; One tp has impr.: Printed by Charles Bill, and the executrix of Thomas Newcomb.]
Cant (499p.).   Dur (150—499p.).   Nor. Wor.

CLC265 Anno regni Gulielmi et Mariae ... primo.
London, by Charles Bill and Thomas Newcomb, 1689, fol.
Cant (182—282p.).   Dur (as Cant).   Nor. Wor.

CLC266 Anno regni Gulielmi et Mariae ... secundo.
London, by Charles Bill and Thomas Newcomb, 1690, fol.
Ban. Cant (42—158p.; 178—378p.).   Dur (as Cant).
Nor. Wor. Yk.

CLC267 Anno regni Gulielmi et Mariae ... tertio [— tertio & quarto].
London, by Charles Bill and the executrix of Thomas Newcomb, 1691, fol.
Cant (338p.).   Dur (18—290 [i.e. 288], 257—338p.).
Nor. Wor. Yk.

CLC268 Anno regni Gulielmi et Mariae ... quarto.
London, by Charles Bill and the executrix of Thomas Newcomb, 1692, fol.
Nor. Yk.

CLC269 Anno regni Gulielmi et Mariae ... quinto [—quinto & sexto].
London, by Charles Bill and the executrix of Thomas Newcomb, 1693 (—1694), fol.
Dur (454p.). Nor. Yk.

CLC270 Anno regni Gulielmi et Mariae ... sexto [—sexto & septimo].
London, by Charles Bill and the executrix of Thomas Newcomb, 1694 (—1695), fol.
Dur (12, [233]—515p.; 15—232p.; 263—326p.). Nor. Yk. Bris (263—427p.).

CLC271 Anno regni Gulielmi III ... septimo [—septimo & octavo].
London, by Charles Bill and the executrix of Thomas Newcomb, 1695 (—1696), fol.
Bris (723—739p.). Cant (759p.). Dur ([1]—[52], [281]—759p.). Nor. Wor. Yk.

CLC272 Anno regni Gulielmi III ... octavo [—octavo & nono].
London, by Charles Bill and the executrix of Thomas Newcomb, 1696 (—1697), fol.
Nor. Wor. Yk.

CLC273 Anno regni Gulielmi III ... nono [—nono & decimo].
London, by Charles Bill and the executrix of Thomas Newcomb, 1697 (—1698), fol.
Cant (803p.). Dur (619—652p.). Nor. Wor. Yk.

CLC274 Anno regni Gulielmi III ... decimo [—decimo & undecimo].
London, by Charles Bill and the executrix of Thomas Newcomb, 1699, fol.
Dur (99—223p.). Nor. Wor. Yk.

CLC275 Anno regni Gulielmi III ... undecimo [—undecimo & duodecimo].
London, by Charles Bill and the executrix of Thomas Newcomb, 1699 (—1701), fol.
Dur (7—420p.). Nor. Wor. Yk.

CLC276 Anno regni Gulielmi III ... XII. & XIII.
London, printed by Charles Bill and the executrix of Thomas Newcomb, 1700 (—1701), fol.
Cant (430p.). Wor. Yk.

CLC277 An exact abridgment of all the publick acts of Parliament ... in the 15th year of the reign of King Charles II.
London, by John Bill and Christopher Barker, 1664, 8°.; 249—340p.
Carl.

CLC278 The form of an indenture between the sheriff and the electors of persons to serve in Parliament ... [London, William du-Gard and Henry Hills?, 1654?], cap., fol.; 359—362p.
[Imprimatur dated 8 June 1654.]
Dur.

CLC279 An ordinance appointing a committee for the army, and treasurers at war ... [January 1654].
London, by William du-Gard and Henry Hills, 1653[4], fol.; 69—101 [i.e. 81]p.
Dur.

CLC280 An ordinance appointing commissioners for the better ordering and bringing in the duty of excize, ... [December 1653].
London, by Will. du-Gard and Hen. Hills, 1653, cap., fol.; 47—50p.
[Impr. from colophon.]
Dur.

CLC281 An ordinance declaring that the offences herein mentioned, ... shall be adjudged high treason ... [January 1654].
London, by William du-Gard and Henry Hills, 1653[4], fol.; 59—66p.
Dur.

CLC282 An ordinance declaring that the proceedings in case of murther in Ireland, shall bee as formerly ... [March 1654].
London, by William du-Gard, and Henry Hills, 1653[4], fol.; 149—150p.
Dur.

CLC283 An ordinance for alteration of several names ... used in courts, writs, grants, ... [December 1653].
London, by Henry Hills, 1653, cap., fol.; 9—15p.
[Impr. from colophon.]
Dur.

CLC284 An ordinance for an assessment for six moneths, ... for maintenance of the armies and navies of this Common-wealth, ... [June 1654].
London, by William du-Gard and Henry Hills, 1654, fol.; 365—377p.
Dur.

CLC285 An ordinance for better amending and keeping in repair the common highwaies within this nation ... [March 1654].
London, by William du-Gard and Henry Hills, 1654, fol.; 201—217p.
Dur.

CLC286 An ordinance for continuation of an act intituled, An act for laying an imposition upon coles ... [March 1654].
London, by William du-Gard, and Henry Hills, 1653[4], fol.; 141 [i.e. 1]p.
Dur.

CLC287 An ordinance for continuation of one act of Parliament, entituled, an act for redemption of captives ... [December 1653].
London, by Hen. Hills, 1653, fol.; 7—8p.
Dur.

CLC288 An ordinance for continuing an act for impressing of sea-men ... [March 1654].
London, by William du-Gard, and Henry Hills, 1653[4], fol.; 163—164p.
Dur.

CLC289 An ordinance for continuing an ordinance, entitled, An ordinance for further suspending the proceedings of the judges named in an act ... for relief of creditors & poor prisoners. ... [May 1654].
London, by William du-Gard and Henry Hills, 1654, fol.; 333–334p.
Dur.

CLC290 An ordinance for continuing one act of Parlament, entitled, An act for probate of wills ... [April 1654].
London, by William du-Gard and Henry Hills, 1654, fol.; 197–198p.
Dur.

CLC291 An ordinance for continuing the excise. [December 1653].
London, by Henry Hills, 1653, cap., fol.; 3p.
[Impr. from colophon.]
Dur.

CLC292 An ordinance for continuing the powers of commissioners for compounding, &c. ... [December 1653].
London, by William du-Gard and Henry Hills, 1653, fol.; 51–52p.
Dur.

CLC293 An ordinance for enabling the iudge, or iudges of the northern circuit, to hold assizes and gaol-deliveries at Durham. [June 1654].
[London, William du-Gard and Henry Hills?, 1654?], cap., fol.; 379–386p.
Dur.

CLC294 An ordinance for erecting courts baron in Scotland ... [April 1654].
London, by William du-Gard and Henry Hills, 1654, fol.; 265–266p.
Dur.

CLC295 An ordinance for establishing an high court of iustice ... [June 1654].
London, by William du-Gard and Henry Hills, 1654, fol.; 385–189 [i.e. 389]p.
Dur.

CLC296 An ordinance for further doubling upon and finishing the sale of deans, deans & chapters lands, and of mannors of rectories, ... [May 1654].
London, by William du-Gard and Henry Hills, 1654, fol.; 319–330 [i.e. 332]p.
Dur.

CLC297 An ordinance for further suspending the proceedings of the judges named in ... an act for the relief of creditors and poor prisoners ... [April 1654].
London, by William du-Gard, and Henry Hills, 1654, fol.; 283–284p.
Dur.

CLC298 An ordinance for holding the countie-court for the countie of Chester at the town of Northwich, during the ... plague in Chester ... [May 1654].
London, by William du-Gard, and Henry Hills, 1654, fol.; 335–336p.
Dur.

CLC299 An ordinance for passing custodies of idiots and lunaticks ... [March 1654].
London, by William du-Gard, and Henry Hills, 1653[4], fol.; 145–146p.
Dur.

CLC300 An ordinance for relief of creditors and poor prisoners ... [June 1654].
London, by William du-Gard and Henry Hills, 1654, fol.; 373–382p.
Dur.

CLC301 An ordinance for relief of debtors in Scotland in som cases of extremity ... [May 1654].
London, by William du-Gard, and Henry Hills, 1654, fol.; 339–340p.
Dur.

CLC302 An ordinance for relief of persons that have acted in the service of the Parlament. [March 1654].
London, by William du-Gard and Henry Hills, 1654, cap., fol.; 183–186p.
[Impr. from colophon.]
Dur.

CLC303 An ordinance for repealing of several acts ... touching the subscribing or taking the engagement. [January 1654].
London, by William Du-Gard and Henry Hills, 1653[4], cap., fol.; 53–55p.
[Impr. from colophon.]
Dur.

CLC304 An ordinance for reviving the jurisdiction of the County Palatine of Lancaster, ... [February 1654].
London, by William du-Gard and Henry Hills, 1653[4], fol.; 101–102p.
Dur.

CLC305 An ordinance for settling and confirming of the mannors of Framlingham & Saxtead ... and the lands ... devised by Sir Robert Hitcham, ... [March 1654].
London, by Henry Hills and William du-Gard 1654, fol.; 157–180p.
Dur.

CLC306 An ordinance for settling of the estates of several excepted persons in Scotland ... [April 1654].
London, by William du-Gard and Henry Hills, 1654, fol.; 265–277p.
Dur.

CLC307 An ordinance for suspending the proceedings of the judges named in the ... act for the relief of creditors and poor prisoners. [March 1654].
London, by William du-Gard, and Henry Hills, 1654, cap., fol.; 189–191p.
[Impr. from colophon.]
Dur.

CLC308 An ordinance for the better ordering and disposing the estates under sequestration ... [February 1654].
London, by William du-Gard and Henry Hills, 1653[4], fol.; 85–90p.
Dur.

CLC309 An ordinance for the better regulating and limiting the jurisdiction of the high court of chancery ... [August 1654].
London, by William du-Gard and Henry Hills, 1654, fol.; 495—531p.
Dur.

CLC310 An ordinance for the ejecting of scandalous, ignorant and insufficient ministers and school-masters ... [August 1654].
London, by William du-Gard and Henry Hills, 1654, fol.; 595—633 [i.e. 639]p.
Dur.

CLC311 An ordinance for the preservation of the works of the great level of the fenns ... [May 1654].
London, by William du-Gard and Henry Hills, 1654, fol.; 349—354p.
Dur.

CLC312 An ordinance for the reviving of ... an act for probate of wills, ... [December 1653].
London, by Hen. Hills, 1653, fol.; 19—20p.
Dur.

CLC313 An ordinance for uniting Scotland into one common-wealth with England ... [April 1654].
London, by William du-Gard and Henry Hills, 1654, fol.; 253—260p.
Dur.

CLC314 An ordinance impowring commissioners to put in execution an act ... prohibiting the planting of tobacco in England ... [April 1654].
London, by William du-Gard, and Henry Hills, 1653[4], fol.; 221—222p.
Dur.

CLC315 An ordinance of explanation of a former ordinance ... for better amending and keeping in repair the common high-waies ... [May 1654].
[London, William du-Gard and Henry Hills?, 1654], cap., fol.; 334 [i.e. 339]—341p.
Dur.

CLC316 An ordinance of explanation touching the jurisdiction of the Court of Admiralty ... [June 1654].
London, by William du-Gard, and Henry Hills, 1654, fol.; 357—358p.
Dur.

CLC317 An ordinance of pardon and grace to the people of Scotland ... [April 1654].
London, by William Du-Gard, and Henry Hills, 1654, fol.; 231—244, 249—250p.
Dur.

CLC318 An ordinance of the Lords and Commons assembled in Parliament, for the maintaining of the forces of the seven ... counties under the command of Edward Earl of Manchester. By a weekly payment upon the said ... counties. [September 1644].
London, printed for Edward Husbands, [1644], 4º.; 6p.
Cant.

CLC319 An ordinance touching surveyors of the high-waies for this present year, 1654 ... [April 1654].
London, by William du-Gard and Henry Hills, 1654, fol.; 225—226p.
Dur.

CLC320 An ordinance prohibiting cock-matches ... [March 1654].
London, by William du-Gard and Henry Hills, 1654, fol.; 193—194p.
Dur.

CLC321 An ordinance touching the assessing, levying, and collecting of the latter three months assesment ... [February 1654].
London, by William du-Gard and Henry Hills, 1653[4], fol.; 93—97p.
Dur.

—

CLC322 [A collection of acts dated from 1 Feb. 1649[50] to October 1652 (pagination 685—1753), interspersed with broadsides folded and bound with it.]
London, [1650—1652], fol.
[Entry as noted by Miss Hands.]
Ex.

CLC323 [Collection of Statutes]
London, by John Field, for Edward Husband, 1649, fol.
[Imprint on final page (p.642). Contains 'A Table of the several Acts of Parliament from the 16 of January 1648 to the [21st of December] following.]
Roch (tpw).

CLC324 [Collection of Statutes]
London, by John Field, for Edward Husband, 1650, fol.
[Pp. 553 [i.e. 653]—1268 + a brs. The Table is for Acts of 27 December 1649 to 18 December 1650.]
Roch (tpw).